SOCIOLOGY
Your Compass for a New World

Fourth Canadian Edition

SOCIOLOGY
Your Compass for a New World

Fourth Canadian Edition

Robert J. Brym
University of Toronto

Lance W. Roberts
University of Manitoba

John Lie
University of California, Berkeley

Steven Rytina
McGill University

NELSON / EDUCATION

NELSON / EDUCATION

Sociology: Your Compass for a New World, Fourth Canadian Edition

by Robert J. Brym, Lance W. Roberts, John Lie, and Steven Rytina

Vice President, Editorial Higher Education:
Anne Williams

Acquisitions Editor:
Maya Castle

Marketing Manager:
Terry Fedorkiw

Developmental Editor:
Toni Chahley

Photo Researcher:
Cindy Howard

Permissions Coordinator:
Cindy Howard

Content Production Manager:
Jennifer Hare

Copy Editor:
Lisa Berland

Proofreader:
Dawn Hunter

Indexer:
Jin Tan

Production Coordinator:
Ferial Suleman

Design Director:
Ken Phipps

Managing Designer:
Franca Amore

Interior Design:
Peter Papayanakis

Cover Design:
Peter Papayanakis

Cover Image:
Courtesy of Sam Javanrouh

Compositor:
MPS Limited, a Macmillan Company

Printer:
RR Donnelley

Library and Archives Canada Cataloguing in Publication Data

Sociology: your compass for a new world/Robert J. Brym ... [et al.].—4th Canadian ed.

Second-3rd Canadian eds. by: Robert J. Brym, John Lie, Steven Rytina.
Includes bibliographical references and index.
ISBN 978-0-17-650386-4

1. Sociology—Textbooks.
I. Brym, Robert J., 1951–

HM586.S65 2012   301
C2011-907848-1

ISBN-13: 978-0-17-650386-4
ISBN-10: 0-17-650386-2

Dedication

Many authors seem to be afflicted with stoic family members who gladly allow them to spend endless hours buried in their work. I suffer no such misfortune. The members of my family have demanded that I focus on what really matters in life. I think that focus has made this a better book. I am deeply grateful to Rhonda Lenton, Shira Brym, Talia Lenton-Brym, and Ariella Lenton-Brym. I dedicate this book to them with thanks and love.

Robert J. Brym

To my students who challenge my thinking and to Laverne, Megan, and Jason who provided love and support for my actions.

Lance W. Roberts

For Charis Thompson, Thomas Cussins, Jessica Cussins, and Charlotte Lie, with thanks and love.

John Lie

For Lucia Benaquisto, with love and gratitude.

Steven Rytina

About the Authors

Robert J. Brym (pronounced "brim") was born in Saint John, New Brunswick, studied sociology in Canada and Israel, and received his Ph.D. from the University of Toronto, where he is now on faculty. Bob's research focuses on the social bases of politics and social movements in Canada, Russia, and the Middle East. His most recent book is *Sociology as a Life or Death Issue*, Second Canadian Edition (Toronto: Nelson Education, 2011). He is now completing a book on collective and state violence in Israel and Palestine and conducting research on the democracy movement in the Middle East and North Africa. Bob is a Fellow of the Royal Society of Canada and has won several awards for his research and teaching, including the Northrop Frye Award and the University of Toronto's highest teaching honour, the President's Teaching Award. *Sociology: Your Compass for a New World* has been published in Canadian, Québécois, American, Brazilian, and Australian editions.

Lance W. Roberts was born in Calgary, Alberta, grew up in Edmonton, and received his Ph.D. from the University of Alberta. He is a Fellow of St. John's College and Professor of Sociology at the University of Manitoba, where he teaches Introductory Sociology as well as research methods and statistics courses. In the last decade he has received several teaching awards, including the University of Manitoba 2011 Faculty of Arts Excellence in Teaching Award. His current research interests cover the comparative charting of social change, educational concerns, and mental health issues. In addition to publishing in research journals, Lance recently coauthored *The Methods Coach* and *The Statistics Coach* (Oxford University Press), which aim to help students master fundamental research techniques. He enjoys teaching Introductory Sociology and is currently developing a variety of tools to enlarge his students' sociological imaginations.

John Lie (pronounced "lee") was born in South Korea, grew up in Japan and Hawaii, and received his A.B., A.M., and Ph.D. degrees from Harvard University. His main interests are in social theory and political economy. Currently he is the C. K. Cho Professor of Sociology at the University of California, Berkeley, where he previously served as the Dean of International and Area Studies. His recent publications include *Zainichi (Koreans in Japan)* (Berkeley: University of California Press, 2008) and *Modern Peoplehood: On Race, Racism, Nationalism, Ethnicity, and Identity*, paperback ed. (Berkeley: University of California Press, 2011).

Steven Rytina (pronounced "rye-TEEN-a") was born in Pennsylvania, mostly grew up in Michigan, and completed his Ph.D. at the University of Michigan. From there, he took up positions at the State University of New York at Albany and at Harvard University, where he and John Lie enjoyed many stimulating conversations and Friday night volleyball games. In 1989, he joined the sociology department at McGill University, where he teaches today. His research interests are injustice and stratification, informed by a taste for formal models of scale and complexity. Representative publications include *Encounters with Unjust Authority*, with William Gamson and Bruce Fireman (Homewood, IL: Dorsey Press, 1982); "Scaling in Intergenerational Continuity of Occupation: Is Occupational Inheritance Ascriptive After All?" *American Journal of Sociology* (97, 6: 1992), pp. 1658–88; and "Is Occupational Mobility Declining in the United States?" *American Journal of Sociology* (78, 4: 2000), pp. 1227–76. He began teaching Introductory Sociology as a teaching assistant at Michigan. He found he enjoyed it so much that he continues it to this day.

Brief Contents

Contents

PART III
Inequality, 157

Preface

A Compass for a New World

It was the best of times, it was the worst of times, it was the age of wisdom, it was the age of foolishness, it was the epoch of belief, it was the epoch of incredulity, it was the season of Light, it was the season of Darkness, it was the spring of hope, it was the winter of despair, we had everything before us, we had nothing before us, we were all going direct to Heaven, we were all going direct the other way—in short, the period was so far like the present period, that some of its noisiest authorities insisted on its being received, for good or for evil, in the superlative degree of comparison only.

— Charles Dickens, *A Tale of Two Cities* (2002 [1859])

Dickens refers to the end of the eighteenth century, yet he offers a prophetic description of the times in which we live. We, too, set sail at the dawn of an age of superlatives, an age of uncertainty.

Over the past couple of decades, we have torn old countries apart and created a host of new ones. We proclaimed a new era of medical breakthroughs with the sequencing of the human genome yet learned that the plague is still with us in the form of AIDS, expected to kill 85 million people by 2020. After some economists proclaimed that recessions were a thing of the past, we experienced two devastating economic crises that bankrupted many high-flying companies and individuals; we are still living through the aftermath of the second one. We saw the world's mood and its political and economic outlook buoyant one day, anxious the next, as terrorist attacks and wars led us further into an era of uncertainty.

The world is an unpredictable place. It is especially disorienting for students just entering adulthood. We wrote this book to show undergraduates that sociology can help them make sense of their lives, however uncertain they may appear to be. We hope it will serve as their sociological compass in the new world they are entering as young adults. Moreover, we show that sociology can be a liberating practical activity, not just an abstract intellectual exercise. By revealing the opportunities and constraints we face, sociology can help us navigate our lives, teaching us who we are and what we can become in this particular social and historical context. We cannot know what the future will bring, but we can at least know the choices we confront and the likely consequences of our actions. From this point of view, sociology can help us create the best possible future. That has always been sociology's principal justification, and so it should be today.

Unique Features

We have tried to keep sociology's main purpose and relevance front and centre in this book. As a result, Sociology: *Your Compass for a New World,* Fourth Canadian Edition, differs from other major introductory sociology textbooks in four ways:

1. ***Drawing connections between one's self and the social world.*** To varying degrees, all introductory sociology textbooks try to show students how their personal experiences connect to the larger social world. However, we employ two devices to make these connections clearer than in other textbooks. First, we illustrate key sociological ideas by using examples from popular culture that resonate deeply with student interests and experiences. For example, in Chapter 1 we illustrate the main sociological perspectives (functionalism, conflict theory, symbolic interactionism, and feminism) by analyzing changing fashions from Britney Spears to Avril Lavigne. We analyze Canadian hockey to highlight central features of Durkheim's theory of religion in Chapter 3. In Chapter 21,

we discuss the role of Facebook and Twitter in helping to mobilize the democratic movement in North Africa and the Middle East. We think these and many other examples speak directly to today's students about important sociological ideas in terms they understand, thus making the connection between self and society clear.

Second, we developed several unique pedagogical features to draw the connection between students' experiences and the larger social world. "Sociology at the Movies" takes a universal and popular element of contemporary culture and renders it sociologically relevant. We provide brief reviews of movies, most of them recent releases, and highlight the sociological issues they raise and the sociological insights they embody. In each chapter, we repeatedly challenge students to consider how and why their own lives conform to, or deviate from, various patterns of social relations and actions. For instance, in Chapter 18, we argue that popular music apparently helps to shorten the attention span of today's youth and ask readers to observe this phenomenon in their own lives. Many chapters feature an "It's Your Choice" box that sets out alternative approaches to a range of social problems and asks students to use logic and evidence to devise a course of action. Here we teach students that sociology can be a matter of the most urgent practical importance. Students also learn they can have a say in solving social problems.

2. ***What to think versus how to think.*** All textbooks teach students both *what* to think about a subject and *how* to think about it from a particular disciplinary perspective. In our judgment, however, introductory sociology textbooks usually place too much stress on the "what" and not enough on the "how." The result: They sometimes read more like encyclopedias than enticements to look at the world in a new way. We have tipped the balance in the other direction. Of course, *Sociology: Your Compass for a New World* contains definitions and literature reviews. It features standard pedagogical aids, such as

"Sociology at the Movies" offers sociological insights gleaned from current films and demonstrates sociology's vitality and relevance to students' lives. This feature also encourages students to think critically about the films they watch.

"It's Your Choice" teaches students that sociology can have urgent, practical importance—and that they can have a say in the development of public policy.

a list of **Chapter Aims** at the beginning of each chapter, a new **Summing Up** feature at the end of each major section in each chapter, a detailed **Summary** at the end of each chapter, and definitions of key terms in the margins of the text. However, we devote more space than other authors to showing how sociologists think. The "Social Policy: What Do You Think" feature asks students to think critically and form an opinion about social policy issues by bringing logic and evidence to bear on them. We often relate an anecdote to highlight an issue's importance, present contending interpretations of the issue, and then adduce data to judge the merits of the various interpretations. We do not just refer to tables and graphs, we analyze them. When evidence warrants, we reject theories and endorse others. Thus, many sections of the book read more like a simplified journal article than an encyclopedia. If all this sounds just like what sociologists do professionally, then we have achieved our aim: to present a less antiseptic, more realistic, and therefore intrinsically exciting account of how sociologists practise their craft. Said differently, one of the strengths of this book is that it does not present sociology as a set of immutable truths carved in stone tablets. Instead, it shows how sociologists actually go about the business of solving sociological puzzles.

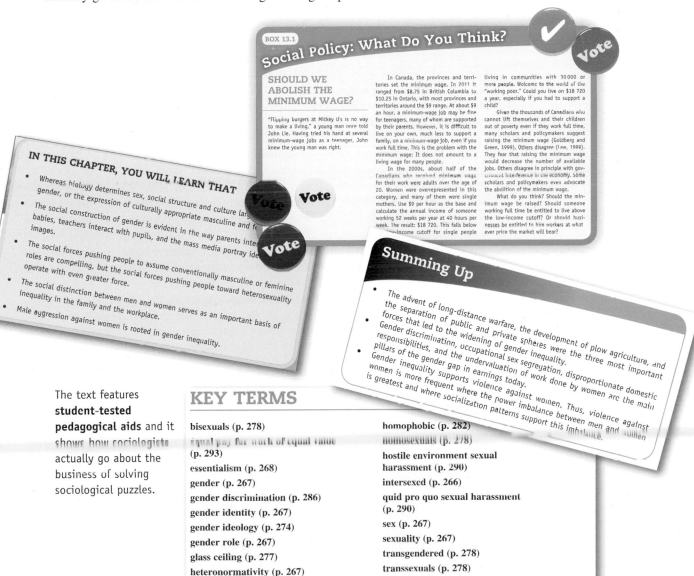

BOX 13.1

Social Policy: What Do You Think?

SHOULD WE ABOLISH THE MINIMUM WAGE?

"Flipping burgers at Mickey D's is no way to make a living," a young man once told John Lie. Having tried his hand at several minimum-wage jobs as a teenager, John knew the young man was right.

In Canada, the provinces and territories set the minimum wage. In 2011 it ranged from $8.75 in British Columbia to $10.25 in Ontario, with most provinces and territories around the $9 range. At about $9 an hour, a minimum-wage job may be fine for teenagers, many of whom are supported by their parents. However, it is difficult to live on your own, much less to support a family, on a minimum-wage job, even if you work full time. This is the problem with the minimum wage: It does not amount to a living wage for many people.

In the 2000s, about half of the Canadians who received minimum wage for their work were adults over the age of 20. Women were overrepresented in this category, and many of them were single mothers. Use $9 per hour as the base and calculate the annual income of someone working 52 weeks per year at 40 hours per week. The result: $18 720. This falls below the low-income cutoff for single people

living in communities with 30 000 or more people. Welcome to the world of the "working poor." Could you live on $18 720 a year, especially if you had to support a child?

Given the thousands of Canadians who cannot lift themselves and their children out of poverty even if they work full time, many scholars and policymakers suggest raising the minimum wage (Goldberg and Green, 1999). Others disagree (Law, 1999). They fear that raising the minimum wage would decrease the number of available jobs. Others disagree in principle with government interference in the economy. Some scholars and policymakers even advocate the abolition of the minimum wage.

What do you think? Should the minimum wage be raised? Should someone working full time be entitled to live above the low-income cutoff? Or should businesses be entitled to hire workers at whatever price the market will bear?

IN THIS CHAPTER, YOU WILL LEARN THAT

- Whereas biology determines sex, social structure and culture largely determine gender, or the expression of culturally appropriate masculine and feminine roles.
- The social construction of gender is evident in the way parents interact with babies, teachers interact with pupils, and the mass media portray ideal images.
- The social forces pushing people to assume conventionally masculine or feminine roles are compelling, but the social forces pushing people toward heterosexuality operate with even greater force.
- The social distinction between men and women serves as an important basis of inequality in the family and the workplace.
- Male aggression against women is rooted in gender inequality.

Summing Up

- The advent of long-distance warfare, the development of plow agriculture, and the separation of public and private spheres were the three most important forces that led to the widening of gender inequality.
- Gender discrimination, occupational sex segregation, disproportionate domestic responsibilities, and the undervaluation of work done by women are the main pillars of the gender gap in earnings today.
- Gender inequality supports violence against women. Thus, violence against women is more frequent where the power imbalance between men and women is greatest and where socialization patterns support this imbalance.

The text features **student-tested pedagogical aids** and it shows how sociologists actually go about the business of solving sociological puzzles.

KEY TERMS

bisexuals (p. 278)

equal pay for work of equal value (p. 293)

essentialism (p. 268)

gender (p. 267)

gender discrimination (p. 286)

gender identity (p. 267)

gender ideology (p. 274)

gender role (p. 267)

glass ceiling (p. 277)

heteronormativity (p. 267)

heterosexuality (p. 268)

homophobic (p. 282)

homosexuals (p. 278)

hostile environment sexual harassment (p. 290)

intersexed (p. 266)

quid pro quo sexual harassment (p. 290)

sex (p. 267)

sexuality (p. 267)

transgendered (p. 278)

transsexuals (p. 278)

3. ***Objectivity versus subjectivity.*** Sociologists since Max Weber have understood that sociologists—indeed, all scientists—are members of society whose thinking and research are influenced by the social and historical context in which they work. Yet most introductory sociology textbooks present a stylized and unsociological view of the research process. Textbooks tend to emphasize sociology's objectivity and the hypothetico-deductive method of reasoning, for the most part ignoring the more subjective factors that go into the research mix. We think this emphasis is a pedagogical error. In our teaching, we have found that drawing the connection between objectivity and subjectivity in sociological research makes the discipline more appealing to students. It shows how research issues are connected to the lives of real flesh-and-blood women and men, and how sociology is related to students' existential concerns. Therefore, in most chapters of *Sociology: Your Compass for a New World* we include a personal anecdote that explains how certain sociological issues first arose in our own minds. We often adopt a narrative style because stories let students understand ideas on an emotional as well as an intellectual level, and when we form an emotional attachment to ideas, they stay with us more effectively than if our attachment is solely intellectual. We place the ideas of important sociological figures in social and historical context. We show how sociological methodologies serve as a reality check, but we also make it clear that socially grounded personal concerns often lead sociologists to decide which aspects of reality are worth checking on in the first place. We believe *Sociology: Your Compass for a New World* is unique in presenting a realistic and balanced account of the role of objectivity and subjectivity in the research process.

4. ***Diversity and a global perspective.*** It is gratifying to see how much less parochial introductory sociology textbooks are today than they were just a couple of decades ago. Contemporary textbooks highlight gender and race issues. They broaden the student's understanding of the world by comparing Canada with other societies. They show how global processes affect local issues and how local issues affect global processes. *Sociology: Your Compass for a New World* makes diversity and globalization prominent themes too. We employ cross-national comparisons between Canada and countries as diverse as India and Sweden. We incorporate maps that illustrate the distribution of sociological variables globally and regionally, and the relationship among variables across time and space. We remain sensitive to gender and race issues throughout. This has been easy for us because we are members of racial and ethnic minority groups. We are multilingual. We have lived in other countries for extended periods. And we have published widely on countries other than Canada, including the United States, Russia, Israel, Palestine, South Korea, and Japan. As you will see in the following pages, our backgrounds have enabled us to bring greater depth to issues of diversity and globalization than other textbooks bring.

New in the Fourth Canadian Edition

We have been gratified and moved by the positive response to earlier editions of this book. At the same time, we benefited from the constructive criticisms generously offered by numerous readers and reviewers. *Sociology: Your Compass for a New World*, Fourth Canadian Edition, is a response to many of their suggestions. The main innovations in this edition include the following:

- Throughout, we added new research findings and incorporated data from the most recent Canadian census to keep the book as up-to-date as possible. The new edition contains more than 50 new figures and tables.
- We streamlined the book, reducing the page count by 13 percent.
- We freshened up the book's interior design to give it a more modern and engaging feel.

- **Sociology at the Movies** was one of the most popular features of earlier editions among both faculty members and students. Building on this popularity, we wrote new movie reviews of *Slumdog Millionaire, Avatar, Harry Potter and the Deathly Hallows: Parts I and II, Inside Job, Never Let Me Go, Redacted, District 9, The Social Network,* and *Food, Inc.*

- In collaboration with Reza Nakhaie, University of Windsor, and Darlene Balandin, University of Western Ontario, we undertook two student surveys with more than 300 students. In response to the feedback from these surveys, we established a new feature called "Summing Up" to help students study. After each major section in each chapter, we include a summary of the major points. This new feature encourages students to pause and reflect on what they have just read before proceeding to the next section.

- We strengthened the discussion of the four main sociological perspectives (functionalism, conflict theory, symbolic interactionism, and feminism) in each chapter, and expanded the coverage of theory to introduce postmodernism, post-structuralism, and queer theory.

Ancillaries

A full range of high-quality ancillaries has been prepared to help instructors and students get the most out of *Sociology: Your Compass for a New World,* Fourth Canadian Edition.

Supplements for Instructors

The **Nelson Education Teaching Advantage (NETA)** program delivers research-based instructor resources that promote student engagement and higher-order thinking to enable the success of Canadian students and educators.

Instructors today face many challenges. Resources are limited, time is scarce, and a new kind of student has emerged, one who is juggling school with work, has gaps in his or her basic knowledge, and is immersed in technology in a way that has led to a completely new style of learning. In response, Nelson Education has gathered a group of dedicated instructors to advise us on the creation of richer and more flexible ancillaries that respond to the needs of today's teaching environments.

The members of our editorial advisory board have experience across a variety of disciplines and are recognized for their commitment to teaching. They include

Norman Althouse, Haskayne School of Business, University of Calgary
Brenda Chant-Smith, Department of Psychology, Trent University
Scott Follows, Manning School of Business Administration, Acadia University
Jon Houseman, Department of Biology, University of Ottawa
Glen Loppnow, Department of Chemistry, University of Alberta
Tanya Noel, Department of Biology, York University
Gary Poole, Director, Centre for Teaching and Academic Growth and School of Population and Public Health, University of British Columbia
Dan Pratt, Department of Educational Studies, University of British Columbia
Mercedes Rowinsky-Geurts, Department of Languages and Literatures, Wilfrid Laurier University
David DiBattista, Department of Psychology, Brock University
Roger Fisher, PhD

In consultation with the editorial advisory board, Nelson Education has completely rethought the structure, approaches, and formats of our key textbook ancillaries. We've also increased our investment in editorial support for our ancillary authors. The result is the Nelson Education Teaching Advantage and its key components: *NETA Engagement, NETA Assessment,* and *NETA Presentation.* Each component includes one or more ancillaries prepared according to our best practices, and a document explaining the theory behind the practices.

NETA Engagement presents materials that help instructors deliver engaging content and activities to their classes. Instead of Instructor's Manuals that regurgitate chapter outlines and key terms from the text, NETA Enriched Instructor's Manuals (EIMs) provide genuine assistance to teachers. The EIMs answer questions like *What should students learn? Why should students care?* and *What are some common student misconceptions and stumbling blocks?* EIMs not only identify the topics that cause students the most difficulty, but also describe techniques and resources to help students master these concepts. Dr. Roger Fisher's *Instructor's Guide to Classroom Engagement (IGCE)* accompanies every Enriched Instructor's Manual. (Information about the NETA Enriched Instructor's Manual prepared for *Sociology: Your Compass for a New World* is included in the description of the Instructor's Resource CD below.)

NETA Assessment relates to testing materials: not just Nelson's Test Banks and Computerized Test Banks, but also in-text self-tests, Study Guides and web quizzes, and homework programs like CourseMate. Under *NETA Assessment*, Nelson's authors create multiple-choice questions that reflect research-based best practices for constructing effective questions and testing not just recall but also higher-order thinking. Our guidelines were developed by David DiBattista, a 3M National Teaching Fellow whose recent research as a professor of psychology at Brock University has focused on multiple-choice testing. All Test Bank authors receive training at workshops conducted by Prof. DiBattista, as do the copyeditors assigned to each Test Bank. A copy of *Multiple Choice Tests: Getting Beyond Remembering,* Prof. DiBattista's guide to writing effective tests, is included with every Nelson Test Bank/Computerized Test Bank package. (Information about the NETA Test Bank prepared for *Sociology: Your Compass for a New World* is included in the description of the Instructor's Resource CD below.)

NETA Presentation has been developed to help instructors make the best use of PowerPoint® in their classrooms. With a clean and uncluttered design developed by Maureen Stone of StoneSoup Consulting, NETA Presentation features slides with improved readability, more multi-media and graphic materials, activities to use in class, and tips for instructors on the Notes page. A copy of *NETA Guidelines for Classroom Presentations* by Maureen Stone is included with each set of PowerPoint slides. (Information about the NETA PowerPoint prepared for *Sociology: Your Compass for a New World* is included in the description of the Instructor's Resource CD below.)

Instructor's Resource CD

Key instructor ancillaries are provided on the *Instructor's Resource CD* (ISBN: 0-17-662771-5), giving instructors the ultimate tool for customizing lectures and presentations. (Downloadable web versions are also available at www.compass4e.nelson.com. The IRCD includes

- **NETA Engagement:** The Enriched Instructor's Manual was written by Darlene Balandin of the University of Western Ontario. It is organized according to the textbook chapters and addresses eight key educational concerns, such as typical stumbling blocks student face and how to address them.
- **NETA Assessment:** The brand new Test Bank was written by Vicki Nygaard of the University of Victoria. It includes over 2200 multiple-choice questions written according to NETA guidelines for effective construction and development of higher-order questions. Also included are true/false, short answer, and essay questions. Test Bank files are provided in Word format for easy editing and in PDF format for convenient printing whatever your system.

   The Computerized Test Bank by ExamView® includes all the questions from the Test Bank. The easy-to-use ExamView software is compatible with Microsoft Windows and MacOS. Create tests by selecting questions from the question bank, modifying these questions as desired, and adding new questions you write yourself. You can administer quizzes online and export tests to WebCT, Blackboard, and other formats.

- **NETA Presentation:** Microsoft PowerPoint lecture slides for every chapter have been created by Tamy Superle of Carleton University. There are on average 25 slides per chapter, many featuring key figures, tables, and photographs from *Sociology: Your Compass for a New World*. NETA principles of clear design and engaging content have been incorporated throughout.
- **Image Library:** This resource consists of digital copies of figures, short tables, and photographs used in the book. Instructors may use these jpegs to create their own PowerPoint presentations.
- **Day One:** Day One—Prof InClass is a PowerPoint presentation that you can customize to orient your students to the class and their text at the beginning of the course.

CourseMate

Nelson Education's Sociology CourseMate brings course concepts to life with interactive learning and exam preparation tools that integrate with the printed textbook. CourseMate provides an opportunity for students to activate their learning through quizzes, games, and flashcards, among many other tools.

The Nelson Sociology CourseMate for *Sociology: Your Compass for a New World,* Fourth Canadian Edition, was created by Lance Roberts and provides immediate feedback that enables students to connect results to the work they have just produced, increasing their learning effectiveness. It also encourages contact between students and faculty: You can select to monitor your students' level of engagement with CourseMate, correlating their efforts to their outcomes. You can even use CourseMate's quizzes to practise "Just in Time" teaching by tracking results in the Engagement Tracker and customizing your lesson plans to address their learning needs.

Watch student comprehension and engagement soar as your class engages with CourseMate. Ask your Nelson representative for a demo today.

DVD Resources

Enhance your classroom experience with the exciting and relevant videos of ***Think Outside the Book: The Nelson Sociology DVD Collection*** prepared to accompany *Sociology: Your Compass for a New World*, Fourth Canadian Edition. Designed to enrich and support chapter concepts, this set of seven 30-minute video segments was created by Robert Brym to stimulate discussion of topics raised in sociology. Produced in conjunction with Face to Face Media (Vancouver), the Jesuit Communication Project (Toronto), and the National Film Board of Canada, the selections have been edited to optimize their impact in the classroom. Many of the selections are taken from films that have won national and international awards.

Student Ancillaries

Sociology: Your Compass for a New World, Fourth Canadian Edition, includes Sociology CourseMate, which helps you make the grade.

Sociology CourseMate includes an interactive eBook, with highlighting, note taking and search capabilities, interactive learning tools including

- quizzes
- flashcards
- videos clips with critical thinking questions
- Internet activities
- and more!

Go to login.NelsonBrain.com to find resources related to your text in Sociology CourseMate.

The following readers can be purchased at NelsonBrain.com in eBook or print-copy format:

- ***Sociology as a Life or Death Issue***, Second Canadian Edition, was written by Robert J. Brym. In a series of beautifully written essays on hip-hop culture, the social bases of cancer, suicide bombers, and the plight of hurricane victims in the Caribbean region and on the coast of the Gulf of Mexico, Robert Brym introduces sociology by analyzing the social causes of death. In doing so, he reveals the powerful social forces that help to determine who lives and who dies, and demonstrates the promise of a well-informed sociological understanding of the world. This brief and inexpensive volume is an eye-opener, an inspiration, and a guide for students of sociology and for anyone with an inquiring mind and hopes for a better world for future generations.

- *Controversies in Canadian Sociology*, First Edition, by Reza Nakhaie, includes a range of classic and contemporary readings, employing the point-counterpoint method to challenge students to evaluate arguments on their merits and to develop their critical imaginations.

- *Society in Question*, Sixth Edition, by Robert J. Brym, provides balanced coverage of the approaches and methods in current sociology as well as unique and surprising perspectives on many major sociological topics. All readings have been chosen for their ability to speak directly to contemporary Canadian students about how sociology can enable them to make sense of their lives in a rapidly changing world.

- *Images of Society: Readings that Inspire and Inform Society*, Second Edition, by Jerry P. White and Michael Carroll, is an exciting collection of readings designed for use in introductory sociology classes. The contents range from classic works in sociology to pieces illustrating recent sociological principles. Academic and journalistic readings have been selected by the authors to convey the distinctive way sociologists think. All readings are excerpts from longer pieces and are introduced with short prologues written by the editors.

- *InfoTrac® College Edition*. Ignite discussions or augment your lectures with the latest developments in sociology and societal change. Create your own course reader by selecting articles or by using the search keywords provided at the end of each chapter. *InfoTrac® College Edition* (available with this text) gives you and your students four months of free access to an easy-to-use online database of reliable, full-length articles (not abstracts) from hundreds of top academic journals and popular sources. Among the journals available 24 hours a day, seven days a week are the *Canadian Review of Sociology and Anthropology,* the *Canadian Journal of Sociology, Canadian Ethnic Studies, Public Policy,* the *American Journal of Sociology, Social Forces, Social Research,* and *Sociology*. Contact your Nelson representative for more information. *InfoTrac® College Edition* is available only to North American college and university students. Journals are subject to change.

Acknowledgments

Anyone who has gone sailing knows that when you embark on a long voyage you need more than a compass. Among other things, you need a helm operator blessed with a strong sense of direction and an intimate knowledge of likely dangers. You need crew members who know all the ropes and can use them to keep things intact and in their proper place. And you need sturdy hands to raise and lower the sails. On the voyage to complete the fourth Canadian edition of this book, the crew demonstrated all these skills. We are especially grateful to our acquisitions editor, **Maya Castle**, who saw this book's promise from the outset, understood clearly the direction we had to take to develop its potential, and on several occasions steered us clear of threatening shoals. We are also deeply indebted to the following crew members:

> **Toni Chahley**, developmental editor
> **Jennifer Hare**, content production manager
> **Terry Fedorkiw**, marketing manager
> **Lisa Berland**, copy editor
> **Dawn Hunter**, proofreader
> **Cindy Howard**, permissions coordinator and photo researcher
> **Tim Melnyk,** research assistant.

We thank the following reviewers for their critical comments on chapter drafts:

Darlene Balandin	University of Western Ontario
Sonia Bookman	University of Manitoba
Christian Caron	Carleton University
Erling Christensen	Kwantlen Polytechnic University
Jim Cosgrave	Trent University
Slobodan Drakulic	Ryerson University
Kimberley A. Ducey	University of Winnipeg
Tara Fidler	University of Western Ontario and University of Toronto
Jean Golden	Ryerson University
Tom Groulx	St. Clair College
Jake Muller	Northwest Community College
Tamy Superle	Carleton University

We are grateful to Reza Nakhaie, University of Windsor, and Darlene Balandin, University of Western Ontario, for facilitating student surveys with over 300 introductory sociology students. We extend our sincere gratitude to the students who provided their feedback, which has significantly informed the fourth edition of the text.

We would also like to acknowledge the assistance of reviewers whose feedback helped shape the third Canadian edition:

Ron McGivern	Thompson Rivers University
Laurie Forbes	Lakehead University
Daniel Popowich	Mohawk College
Juergen Dankwort	Kwantlen Polytechnic University

Robert Brym

Lance Roberts

John Lie

Steven Rytina

Foundations

Ingram Publishing/Jupiter Images

CHAPTER

1

A Sociological Compass

IN THIS CHAPTER, YOU WILL LEARN THAT

- The causes of human behaviour lie partly in the patterns of social relations that surround and permeate us.

- Sociology is the systematic study of human behaviour in social context.

- Sociologists examine the connection between social relations and personal troubles.

- Sociologists are often motivated to do research by the desire to improve people's lives. They use scientific methods to test their ideas.

- Sociology originated during the Industrial Revolution. The founders of sociology diagnosed the massive social transformations of their day and suggested ways of overcoming the social problems created by the Industrial Revolution.

- Today, we are similarly challenged. Sociology clarifies the scope, direction, and significance of social change and suggests ways of dealing with pressing social problems.

- At the personal level, sociology can help to clarify the opportunities and constraints we all face. It suggests what each of us can become in today's social and historical context.

Courtesy of Sam Javanrouh

INTRODUCTION

Why You Need a Compass for a New World

"When I was a child growing up in New Brunswick in the 1950s, it was common for Aboriginal women to be hired to clean homes. Even low- to middle-class families, such as mine, looked to Aboriginal women for domestic help," recalls Robert Brym. So a cleaning lady came to our house twice a month. Her name was Lena White. I was fond of Lena because she possessed two apparently magical powers. First, she could let the ash at the end of her cigarette grow five centimetres before it fell off. This seemed truly magical to me. I sometimes used to play where Lena was working just to see how long she could scrub, vacuum, climb the stepladder, and chatter before the ash made its inevitable descent to the floor. Second, Lena could tell stories. My mother would serve us lunch at the kitchen table. During dessert, as we sipped tea with milk, Lena would spin tales about Gluskap, the Creator of the world.

Lisa M. Ripperton. Yesterday's Classics

"I liked Gluskap because he was mischievous and enormously powerful. He fought giants, drove away monsters, taught people how to hunt and farm, and named the stars. But he also got into trouble and learned from his mistakes. For example, one day the wind was blowing so hard Gluskap couldn't paddle his canoe into the bay to hunt ducks. So he found the source of the wind: the flapping wings of the Wind Eagle. He then tricked the Wind Eagle into getting stuck in a crevice where he could flap no more. Now Gluskap could go hunting. However, the air soon grew so hot he found it difficult to breathe. The water became dirty and began to smell bad, and there was so much foam on it he found it hard to paddle. When he complained to his grandmother, she explained that the wind was needed to cool the air, wash the earth, and move the waters to keep them clean. And so Gluskap freed the Wind Eagle and the winds returned to the earth. Gluskap decided it was better to wait for good weather and then go duck hunting, rather than to conquer the winds.

"Like the tale of the Wind Eagle, many of the Gluskap stories Lena told me were about the need for harmony among humans and between humans and nature. You can imagine my surprise, therefore, when I got to school and learned about the European exploration of what was called the New World. My teachers taught me all about the glories of the *conquest* of nature—and of other people. I learned that in the New World, a Native population perhaps a hundredth as large as Europe's occupied a territory more than four times larger. I was taught that the New World was unimaginably rich in resources. European rulers saw that by controlling it they could increase their power and importance. Christians recognized new possibilities for spreading their religion. Explorers discerned fresh opportunities for rewarding adventures. A wave of excitement swelled as word spread of the New World's vast potential and challenges. I, too, became excited as I heard stories of conquest quite unlike the tales of Gluskap. Of course, I learned little about the violence required to conquer the New World."

In the 1950s, I was caught between thrilling stories of conquest and reflective stories that questioned the wisdom of conquest. Today, I think many people are in a similar position. On the one hand, we feel like the European explorers because we, too, have reached the frontiers of a New World. Like them, we are full of anticipation. Our New World is one of instant long-distance communication, global economies and cultures, weakening nation-states, and technological advances that often make the daily news seem like reports from a distant planet. In a fundamental way, the world is not the same place it was just 50 years ago. On the other hand, we understand that not all is hope and bright horizons. Our anticipation is mixed with dread. Gluskap stories make more sense than ever. Scientific breakthroughs are announced almost daily, but the global environment has never been in worse shape and AIDS is now the leading cause of death in Africa. Marriages and nations unexpectedly break up and then reconstitute themselves in new and unanticipated forms. We celebrate the advances made by women and minority groups only to find that some people oppose their progress, sometimes violently. Waves of people migrate between continents, establishing cooperation but also conflict between previously separated groups. New technologies make work more interesting and creative for some, offering unprecedented opportunities to become rich and famous. They also make jobs more onerous and routine for others. The standard of living goes up for many people but stagnates or deteriorates for many more.

Amid all this contradictory news, good and bad, uncertainty about the future prevails. That is why my colleagues and I wrote this book. We set out to show undergraduates that sociology can help them make sense of their lives, however uncertain they may appear to be. Five hundred years ago, the early European explorers of North and South America set themselves the task of mapping the contours of the New World. We set ourselves a similar task here. Their frontiers were physical; ours are social. Their maps were geographical; ours are sociological. But in terms of functionality, our maps are much like theirs. All maps allow us to find our place in the world and see ourselves in the context of larger forces. *Sociological* maps, as the famous American sociologist C. Wright Mills wrote, allow us to "grasp the interplay of [people] and society, of biography and history" (Mills, 1959: 4). This book, then, shows you how to draw sociological maps so you can see your place in the world, figure out how to navigate through it, and perhaps discover how to improve it. It is your sociological compass.

We emphasize that sociology can be a liberating practical activity, not just an abstract intellectual exercise. By revealing the opportunities and constraints you face, sociology can help teach you who you are and what you can become in today's social and historical context. We cannot know what the future will bring, but we can at least know the choices we confront and the likely consequences of our actions. From this point of view, sociology can help us create the best possible future. That has always been sociology's principal justification, and so it must be today.

The Goals of This Chapter

This chapter has three goals:

1. The first goal is to illustrate the power of sociology to dispel foggy assumptions and help us see the operation of the social world more clearly. To that end, we examine a phenomenon that at first glance appears to be solely the outcome of breakdowns in *individual* functioning: suicide. We show that, in fact, *social* relations powerfully influence suicide rates. This exercise introduces you to what is unique about the sociological perspective.
2. The chapter's second goal is to show that, from its origins, sociological research has been motivated by a desire to improve the social world. Thus, sociology is not just a dry, academic exercise but also a means of charting a better course for society. At the same time, sociologists use scientific methods to test their ideas, thus increasing the validity of the results. We illustrate these points by briefly analyzing the work of the founders of the discipline.
3. The chapter's third goal is to suggest that sociology can help you come to grips with your century, just as it helped the founders of sociology deal with theirs. Today we are witnessing massive and disorienting social changes. As was the case a hundred years ago, sociologists now try to understand social phenomena and suggest credible ways of improving society. By promising to make sociology relevant to you, this chapter is an invitation to participate in sociology's challenge.

Before showing how sociology can help you understand and improve your world, we briefly examine the problem of suicide. This examination will help illustrate how the sociological perspective can clarify and sometimes overturn commonsense beliefs.

THE SOCIOLOGICAL PERSPECTIVE

Analyzing suicide sociologically tests the claim that sociology takes a unique, surprising, and enlightening perspective on social events. After all, suicide appears to be a supremely antisocial and non-social act. First, it is condemned by nearly everyone in society. Second, it is typically committed in private, far from the public's intrusive glare. Third, it is comparatively rare: In 2006, there were 10.8 suicides for every 100 000 people in Canada (compared with the world average of about 16 suicides per 100 000 people; see Figure 1.1). And, finally, when you think about why people commit such acts, you are likely to focus on their individual states of mind rather than on the state of society—we are usually interested in the events that caused individuals to become depressed or angry enough to do something as awful as killing themselves. We do not usually think about the patterns of social relations that might encourage or inhibit such actions. If sociology can reveal the hidden social causes of such an apparently non-social and antisocial phenomenon, there must be something to it!

Courtesy of A.C. Fine Art, Nova Scotia. Photographer: James Chambers

Alex Colville's *Pacific* (1967)

The Sociological Explanation of Suicide

At the end of the nineteenth century, Émile Durkheim (1951 [1897]) demonstrated that suicide is more than just an individual act of desperation that results from a psychological disorder, as was commonly believed at the time. Social forces, he showed, strongly influence suicide rates.

Durkheim made his case by examining the association between rates of suicide and rates of psychological disorder for different groups. The idea that psychological disorder causes suicide is supported, he reasoned, only if suicide rates tend to be high where rates of psychological disorder are high, and low where rates of psychological disorder are low. However, his analysis of European government statistics, hospital records, and other sources revealed nothing of the kind. For example, he discovered that there were slightly more women than men in insane asylums, but there were four male suicides for every female suicide. Jews had the

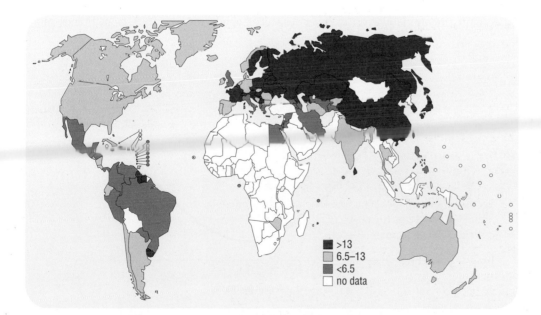

> **>13**
> **6.5–13**
> **<6.5**
> **no data**

FIGURE 1.1

Map of Suicide Rates (per 100 000; most recent year available as of 2009)

Source: World Health Organization. 2010. "Suicide Prevention (SUPRE)." http://www.who.int/mental_health/prevention/suicide/suicideprevent/en/ (accessed 4 October 2010).

Social solidarity refers to (1) the degree to which group members share beliefs and values, and (2) the intensity and frequency of their interaction.

highest rate of psychological disorder among the major religious groups in France, but they also had the lowest suicide rate. Psychological disorders occurred most frequently when a person reached adulthood, but suicide rates increased steadily with age.

Clearly, suicide rates and rates of psychological disorder did not vary directly. In fact, they often appeared to vary inversely. Why? Durkheim held that suicide rates varied because of differences in the degree of **social solidarity** in different categories of the population. According to Durkheim, the greater the degree to which group members share beliefs and values, and the more frequently and intensely they interact, the more social solidarity the group exhibits. In turn, the more social solidarity a group exhibits, the more firmly anchored individuals are to the social world and the less likely they are to take their own life if adversity strikes. In other words, Durkheim expected high-solidarity groups to have lower suicide rates than low-solidarity groups did—at least up to a point (see Figure 1.2).

To support his argument, Durkheim showed that married adults are half as likely as unmarried adults are to commit suicide. That is because marriage creates social ties and a kind of moral cement that bind the individual to society. Similarly, he argued that women are less likely to commit suicide than men are because women are more involved in the intimate social relations of family life. Jews, Durkheim wrote, are less likely to commit suicide than Christians are because centuries of persecution have turned them into a group that is more defensive and tightly knit. Older adults are more prone than the young and the middle-aged are to take their own lives in the face of misfortune because they are most likely to live alone, to have lost a spouse or partner, and to lack a job and a wide network of friends. In general, Durkheim wrote, "suicide varies with the degree of integration of the social groups of which the individual forms a part" (Durkheim, 1951 [1897]: 209). Note that his generalization tells us nothing about why a particular *individual* may take his or her life. That explanation is the province of psychology. But it does tell us that a person's likelihood of committing suicide decreases with the degree to which he or she is anchored in society. And it says something surprising and uniquely sociological about how and why the suicide rate varies across groups.

Suicide in Canada Today

Durkheim's theory is not just a historical curiosity; it sheds light on the factors that account for variations in suicide rates today. Consider Figure 1.3, which shows suicide rates by age and sex in Canada. Comparing rates for men and women, we immediately see that, as in Durkheim's France, men are almost four times as likely as women are to commit suicide. However, in other respects Canada today differs from France more

FIGURE 1.2

Durkheim's Theory of Suicide

Durkheim argued that the suicide rate declines and then rises as social solidarity increases.

Durkheim called suicide in high-solidarity settings *altruistic*. Soldiers who knowingly give up their lives to protect comrades commit altruistic suicide. Suicide in low-solidarity settings is *egoistic* or *anomic*. *Egoistic suicide* results from the poor integration of people into society because of weak social ties to others. All else the same, someone who is unemployed is more likely to commit suicide than someone who is employed because the unemployed person has weaker social ties. *Anomic suicide* occurs when vague norms govern behaviour. The rate of anomic suicide is likely to be high among people living in a society lacking a widely shared code of morality.

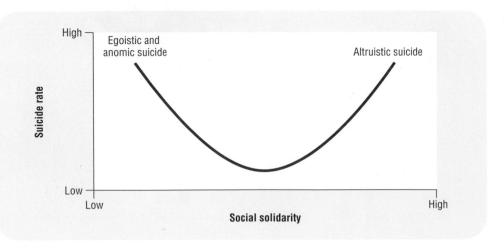

than a century ago. For example, when Durkheim wrote, suicide was rare among youth. In Canada today, it is more common, having increased substantially since the 1960s.

Although the rate of youth suicide was low in Durkheim's France, his theory of social solidarity helps us understand why it has risen in Canada. In brief, shared moral principles and strong social ties have eroded since the early 1960s, especially for Canada's youth. Consider the following facts:

Strong social bonds decrease the probability that a person will commit suicide if adversity strikes.

- Church, synagogue, mosque, and temple attendance is down, particularly among young people. Well over half of Canadians attended religious services weekly in the 1960s. Today the figure is below one-third and is only 15 percent for people born after 1960.
- Unemployment is up, again especially for youth. The unemployment rate was around 3 percent for most of the 1960s. It rose steadily to about 10 percent for most of the 1990s and reached 13.4 percent in 1994. Since then, the unemployment rate has declined, but it remains more than twice as high for Canadians under the age of 25 as it is for Canadians above the age of 24 (in August 2010, 16.8 percent compared with 8.1 percent).
- The rate of divorce has increased sixfold since the early 1960s. Births outside of marriage are also much more common than they used to be. As a result, children are more often brought up in single-parent families now than in the past. This suggests that they enjoy less frequent and intimate social interaction with parents and less adult supervision.

In sum, the figures cited above suggest that the level of social solidarity is now lower than it was just a few decades ago, especially for young people. Less firmly rooted in society, and less likely to share moral standards, young people in Canada today are more likely than they were half a century ago to take their own lives if they happen to find themselves in a deep personal crisis (see also Box 1.1 on page 8).

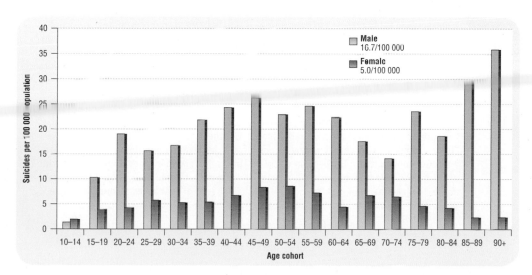

FIGURE 1.3

Suicide Rates by Age and Sex, Canada, 2006

Source: Adapted from Statistics Canada Website, Summary Tables Module, "Suicide and suicide rate, by sex and age group." Retrieved October 4, 2010 (http://www40 .statcan.ca/l01/cst01/hlth66a-eng .htm).

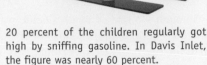

It's Your Choice

SUICIDE AND THE INNU OF LABRADOR

The Canadians with the highest suicide rate are Aboriginal peoples. Among them, the Innu of Labrador have the highest suicide rate. They are, in fact, the most suicide-prone people in the world. Among the Innu, the suicide rate is nearly 13 times the rate for all Canadians (Rogan, 2001; Samson, Wilson, and Mazower, 1999).

Durkheim's theory of suicide helps explain the Innu people's tragic propensity to commit suicide. Over the past six decades, the Innu's traditional norms and values have been destroyed. Moreover, the Innu were prevented from participating in stable and meaningful patterns of social interaction. In other words, social solidarity among the Innu has been cut to an abysmally low level.

How did this happen? Historically, the Innu were a nomadic people who relied on hunting and trapping for their livelihood. In the mid-1950s, however, shortly after Newfoundland and Labrador became part of Canada, the provincial and federal governments were eager to gain more control of traditional Innu land to encourage economic development. Government officials reasoned that if new roads, mines, lumbering operations, hydroelectric projects, and low-level flight-

CP Picture Archive/Ryan Remiorz

training facilities for NATO air forces were to be built, the Innu would have to be concentrated in settlements. Furthermore, government officials believed that, to function in these new settlements, the Innu would have to learn practical and cultural skills associated with a modern industrial society. As a result, governments put tremendous pressure on the Innu to give up their traditional way of life and settle in Davis Inlet and Sheshatshui.

In the new communities, Canadian laws, schools, and churches strongly discouraged the Innu from hunting, practising their religion, and raising their children in the traditional way. For example, Canadian hunting regulations limited Innu access to their age-old livelihood. Priests are known to have beaten children who missed church or school to go hunting, thus introducing interpersonal violence into a culture that formerly knew none. Teachers transmitted North American and European skills and culture, often denigrating Innu practices. At the same time, few alternative jobs existed in the new communities. Most Innu wound up living in despair and on welfare. In the absence of work, and lacking the stabilizing influence of their traditional culture, a people long known for nonviolence and their cooperative spirit became victims of widespread family breakdown, sexual abuse, drunkenness, and alcohol-related illness. In Sheshatshui in 2001, at least

20 percent of the children regularly got high by sniffing gasoline. In Davis Inlet, the figure was nearly 60 percent.

In 2002, the federal and provincial governments decided to move the people of Davis Inlet and create a safer community for them in Natuashish, 15 kilometres away. The new community voted to abolish alcohol in 2008, but it is still smuggled into town. (A 40-ounce bottle of rye sold for $350 in 2010.) Some local mothers openly denounce people who supply alcohol and drugs, but substance abuse is still widespread and anti-abolitionists may still be found in the local government (Moore, 2010).

What is to be done about the tragedy of the Innu? A 1984 study showed that a movement among the Innu to return to the land and traditional hunting practices for up to seven months a year led to a dramatic improvement in health. They lived a vigorous outdoor life. Alcohol abuse stopped. Diet improved. Their emotional and social environments stabilized and became meaningful. Suicide was unknown (Samson, Wilson, and Mazower, 1999: 25).

Unfortunately, a big political obstacle stands in the way of the Innu returning to their traditional lifestyle on a wide scale. The governments of Canada and Newfoundland and Labrador will not allow it. A widespread Innu return to the land conflicts with government and private economic development plans. For instance, the Lower Churchill Falls hydroelectric project (the second-biggest hydroelectric project in the world) and the Voisey's Bay nickel mine (the world's biggest deposit of nickel) are located in the middle of traditional Innu hunting and burial grounds. The Innu are vigorously attempting to regain control of their land. They also want to be able to decide *on their own* when and how to use Canadian health services, training facilities, and the like. Whether some compromise can be worked out between government and private plans for economic development and the continuity of the Innu people is unclear. What is clear is that, as a Canadian citizen, the outcome is partly your choice.

From Personal Troubles to Social Structures

You have known for a long time that you live in a society. Until now, you may not have fully appreciated that society also lives in you. That is, patterns of social relations affect your innermost thoughts and feelings, influence your actions, and thus help shape who you are. As we have seen, one such pattern of social relations is the level of social solidarity characteristic of the various groups to which you belong.

Sociologists call relatively stable patterns of social relations **social structures**. One of the sociologist's main tasks is to identify and explain the connection between people's personal troubles and the social structures in which people are embedded. This is harder work than it may seem at first. In everyday life, we usually see things mainly from our own point of view. Our experiences seem unique to each of us. If we think about them at all, social structures may appear remote and impersonal. To see how social structures influence us, we require sociological training.

An important step in broadening our sociological awareness involves recognizing that three levels of social structure surround and permeate us. Think of these structures as concentric circles radiating out from you:

1. **Microstructures** are patterns of intimate social relations. They are formed during face-to-face interaction. Families, friendship circles, and work associations are all examples of microstructures.

   Understanding the operation of microstructures can be useful. Let's say you are looking for a job. You might think you would do best to ask as many close friends and relatives as possible for leads and contacts. However, sociological research shows that people you know well are likely to know many of the same people. After asking a couple of close connections for help landing a job, you would therefore do best to ask more remote acquaintances for leads and contacts. People to whom you are *weakly* connected (and who are weakly connected among themselves) are more likely to know *different* groups of people. Therefore, they will give you more information about job possibilities and ensure that word about your job search spreads farther. You are more likely to find a job faster if you understand "the strength of weak ties" in microstructural settings (Granovetter, 1973).

2. **Macrostructures** are patterns of social relations that lie outside and above your circle of intimates and acquaintances.[1] Macrostructures include class relations, bureaucracies, and **patriarchy**, the traditional system of economic and political inequality between women and men in most societies (see Chapter 11, Sexualities and Gender Stratification).

   Understanding the operation of macrostructures can also be useful. Consider, for example, one aspect of patriarchy. In our society, most married women who work full-time in the paid labour force are responsible for more housework, child care, and care for seniors than their husbands are. Governments and businesses support this arrangement insofar as they provide little assistance to families in the form of affordable and accessible daycare facilities, after-school programs for children, and the like. Yet an aspect of patriarchy— the unequal division of work in the household—is a major source of dissatisfaction in marriages, especially in families that cannot afford to buy these services privately. Thus, sociological research shows that when spouses share domestic responsibilities equally, they are happier with their marriages and less likely to divorce (Hochschild with Machung, 1989). When a marriage is in danger of dissolving, it is common for partners to blame themselves and each other for their troubles. However, it should now be clear that forces other than incompatible personalities often put stress on families. Understanding how the macrostructure of patriarchy crops up in everyday life, and doing something to change that structure, can thus help people lead happier lives.

3. The third level of society that surrounds and permeates us comprises **global structures**. International organizations, patterns of worldwide travel and communication, and economic relations between countries are examples of global structures. Global structures are increasingly important as inexpensive travel and communication allow all parts of the world to become interconnected culturally, economically, and politically.

Social structures are relatively stable patterns of social relations.

Microstructures are the patterns of relatively intimate social relations formed during face-to-face interaction. Families, friendship circles, and work associations are all examples of microstructures.

Macrostructures are overarching patterns of social relations that lie outside and above your circle of intimates and acquaintances. Macrostructures include classes, bureaucracies, and power systems, such as patriarchy.

Patriarchy is the traditional system of economic and political inequality between women and men.

Global structures are patterns of social relations that lie outside and above the national level. They include international organizations, patterns of worldwide travel and communication, and the economic relations between countries.

Understanding the operation of global structures can be useful, too. For instance, many people are concerned about the world's poor. They donate money to charities to help with famine and disaster relief. They support their government giving aid to poor countries. However, many of them don't see that charity and foreign aid alone can't end world poverty. That is because charity and foreign aid are unable to overcome the structure of social relations among countries that have created and now sustain global inequality.

Let us linger on this point a moment. As we will see in Chapter 9 (Globalization, Inequality, and Development), Britain, France, and other imperial powers locked some countries into poverty when they colonized them between the seventeenth and nineteenth centuries. In the twentieth century, the poor (or "developing") countries borrowed money from these same rich countries and Western banks to pay for airports, roads, harbours, sanitation systems, basic health care, and so on. Today, poor countries pay about seven times as much in interest on those loans as they receive in aid (United Nations, 2004: 201). Thus, it seems that relying exclusively on foreign aid and charity can do little to help solve the problem of world poverty. Understanding how the global structure of international relations created and helps maintain global inequality suggests new policy priorities for helping the world's poor. One such priority might

Sociology at the Movies

SHAKE HANDS WITH THE DEVIL

Over a period of 100 days in 1994, the Hutus of Rwanda massacred 800 000 Tutsis—more than a tenth of Rwanda's population—with guns, machetes, hammers, and spears. Bodies were scattered everywhere, and the streets literally flowed with blood. The French trained and armed the Hutus in full knowledge of what would transpire. The Belgians knew too, and their 2000 troops could have done much to prevent it, but they withdrew their "peacekeepers" just before the massacre began. Canadian General Roméo Dallaire, who led a contingent of United Nations troops in Rwanda, reported to his bosses at the UN that he knew where the Hutu arms caches were located and requested permission to destroy them. Permission was denied. Most

North Americans were busy watching the O. J. Simpson trial on TV and so barely noticed the genocide.

If Rwanda in 1994 was the site of unspeakable cruelty, it was also a place where compassion and bravery shone through. Dallaire and his small contingent of 450 soldiers from Canada, Ghana, Tunisia, and Bangladesh risked their lives to save an estimated 30 000 Rwandans in one of the twentieth century's great heroic acts. Like the Swedish World War II hero Raoul Wallenberg in Hungary, and Japanese consular official Chiune Sugihara in Lithuania, both of whom risked their lives to save thousands of Jews from the Nazis, Dallaire swam against the stream of world apathy. *Shake Hands with the Devil*, which won the 2007 Emmy for best documentary, details Dallaire's actions, the heavy toll they took on his mental health, and his recovery from the trauma of 1994.

By highlighting both the cruelty and the bravery surrounding the events in Rwanda, *Shake*

Hands with the Devil performs a valuable documentary service. However, it falls short precisely where sociology can contribute most—in uncovering the social context that explains *why* cruelty and bravery occur in the first place.

Begin with the cruelty. Hutus and Tutsis had existed as somewhat distinct ethnic groups for centuries before 1994. The Hutus were mainly farmers and the Tutsis mainly cattle herders. The Tutsis were the ruling minority yet they spoke the same language as the Hutus, shared the same religious beliefs, lived side by side, and often intermarried. The two groups never came into serious conflict.

Then the Belgians colonized Rwanda in 1916. They made ethnic divisions far more rigid. Now a person *had* to be a Tutsi to serve in an official capacity, and the Belgians started distinguishing Tutsis from Hutus by measuring the width of their noses; Tutsi noses, they arbitrarily proclaimed, were thinner. It was a preposterous policy, not least because half the population of Rwanda is of mixed Hutu-Tutsi ancestry, and it sharply increased animosity between the two involve campaigning for the cancellation of foreign debt in compensation for past injustices.

As these examples illustrate, personal problems are connected to social structures at the micro-, macro-, and global levels. Whether the personal problem involves finding a job, keeping a marriage intact, or figuring out a way to end world poverty, social-structural considerations broaden our understanding of the problem and suggest appropriate courses of action.

The Sociological Imagination

More than half a century ago, C. Wright Mills (1959) called the ability to see the connection between personal troubles and social structures the **sociological imagination**. He emphasized the difficulty of developing this quality of mind (see Box 1.2). His language is sexist by today's standards but his argument is as true and inspiring today as it was in the 1950s:

> When a society becomes industrialized, a peasant becomes a worker; a feudal lord is liquidated or becomes a businessman. When classes rise or fall, a man is employed or unemployed; when the rate of investment goes up or down, a man takes new heart or goes broke.

The **sociological imagination** is the quality of mind that enables a person to see the connection between personal troubles and social structures.

General Roméo Dallaire

CP PHOTO/Ryan Remiorz

ethnic groups (Organization of African Unity, 2000: 10).

Before the Belgians decolonized Rwanda in 1962, they encouraged power sharing between the Tutsis and the Hutus but by then the damage had been done. The Tutsis objected to any loss of power, and civil war broke out. Tutsi rebels fled to Uganda, and when Rwanda proclaimed independence, the Hutu majority took power. Then, in the early 1990s, descendants of the Tutsi rebels, backed by the United States and Britain, tried to overthrow the Hutu government, backed by France and Belgium. (Western interest and rivalry in the region is high because it is rich in minerals; see Rose, 2001). The 1994 genocide erupted when the plane of the Hutu president was shot down, killing the president. Ethnic cruelty, we may conclude, is not an "inevitable" by-product of "human nature." It is carefully nurtured in social contexts marked by intense competition for scarce resources.

And the heroism? Heroes are typically raised in an atmosphere of high moral principle and ethical standards of conduct that encourages them to demonstrate independence of character and willingness to defy authority and convention long before they commit any heroic acts. Thus, while heroism sometimes requires a split-second decision, it is usually preceded by

years of socialization that predisposes the future hero to act compassionately even if doing so involves refusing to follow the herd (Franco and Zimbardo, 2006–7). We thus see how the sociological perspective helps to illuminate otherwise inexplicable actions.

Understanding the social constraints and possibilities for freedom that envelop us requires an active sociological imagination. The sociological imagination urges us to connect our biography with history and social structure—to make sense of our lives against a larger historical and social background and to act in light of our understanding. Have you ever tried to put events in your own life in the context of history and social structure? Did the exercise help you make sense of your life? Did it in any way lead to a life more worth living? Is the sociological imagination a worthy goal?

Although movies are just entertainment to many people, they often achieve by different means what the sociological imagination aims for. Therefore, in each chapter of this book, we review a movie to shed light on topics of sociological importance.

When war happens, an insurance salesman becomes a rocket launcher; a store clerk, a radar man; a wife lives alone; a child grows up without a father. Neither the life of an individual nor the history of a society can be understood without understanding both.

Yet men do not usually define the troubles they endure in terms of historical change.... The well-being they enjoy, they do not usually impute to the big ups and downs of the society in which they live. Seldom aware of the intricate connection between the patterns of their own lives and the course of world history, ordinary men do not usually know what this connection means for the kind of men they are becoming and for the kind of history-making in which they might take part. They do not possess the quality of mind essential to grasp the interplay of men and society, of biography and history, of self and world. They cannot cope with their personal troubles in such a way as to control the structural transformations that usually lie behind them.

What they need ... is a quality of mind that will help them to [see] ... what is going on in the world and ... what may be happening within themselves. It is this quality ... that ... may be called the sociological imagination. (Mills, 1959: 3–4)

The sociological imagination is a recent addition to the human repertoire. True, in ancient and medieval times, some philosophers wrote about society. However, their thinking was not sociological. They believed God and nature controlled society. They spent much of their time sketching blueprints for the ideal society and urging people to follow those blueprints. They relied on speculation rather than on evidence to reach conclusions about how society works (see Figure 1.4).

Origins of the Sociological Imagination

The sociological imagination was born when three modern revolutions pushed people to think about society in an entirely new way:

The **Scientific Revolution** began about 1550. It encouraged the view that sound conclusions about the workings of society must be based on solid evidence, not just on speculation.

The **Democratic Revolution** began about 1750. It suggested that people are responsible for organizing society and that human intervention can therefore solve social problems.

The **Industrial Revolution,** often regarded as the most important event in world history since the development of agriculture and cities, refers to the rapid economic transformation that began in Britain in the 1780s. It involved the large-scale application of science and technology to industrial processes, the creation of factories, and the formation of a working class.

1. The **Scientific Revolution** began about 1550. It encouraged the view that we must base conclusions about the workings of society on solid evidence, not just on speculation. People often link the Scientific Revolution to specific ideas, such as Newton's laws of motion and Copernicus's theory that the earth revolves around the sun. However, science is less a collection of ideas than a method of inquiry. For instance, in 1609 Galileo pointed his newly invented telescope at the heavens, made some careful observations, and showed that his observations fit Copernicus's theory. This is the core of the scientific method: using evidence to make a case for a particular point of view. By the mid-seventeenth century, some philosophers, such as Descartes in France and Hobbes in England, were calling for a science of society. When sociology emerged as a distinct discipline in the nineteenth century, commitment to the scientific method was one firm pillar of the sociological imagination.
2. The **Democratic Revolution** began about 1750. It suggested that people are responsible for organizing society and that human intervention can therefore solve social problems. Four hundred years ago, most Europeans thought otherwise. For them, God ordained the social order. The American Revolution (1775–83) and the French Revolution (1789–99) helped to undermine that idea. These democratic upheavals showed that society could experience massive change in a short period and that *people* control society. The implications for social thought were profound. For if people could change society, then a science of society could help them improve it. Much of the justification for sociology as a science arose out of the democratic revolutions that shook Europe and North America.
3. The **Industrial Revolution** began about 1780. It created a host of new social problems that attracted the attention of social thinkers. As a result of the growth of industry, masses of people moved from countryside to city, worked agonizingly long hours in crowded and dangerous mines and factories, lost faith in their religions, confronted faceless bureaucracies, and reacted to the filth and poverty of their existence with of strikes, crime, revolutions, and wars. Scholars had never seen a sociological laboratory like this. The Scientific Revolution suggested that a science of society was possible.

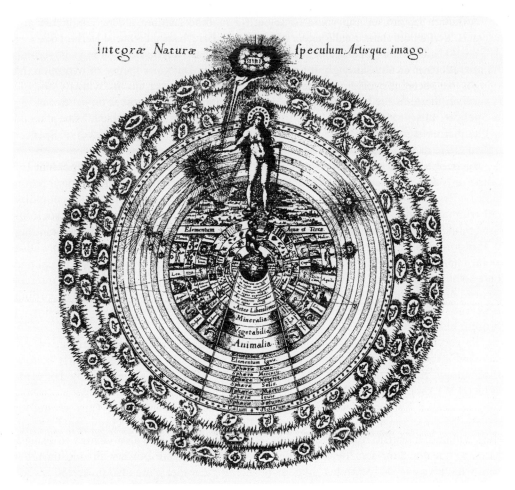

Source: Robert Fludd, *Ultriusque Cosmi Maioris Scilicet et Minoris Metaphysica, Physica Atqve Technica Historia*. 1617–19. (Oppenheim, Germany. Johan-Thedori de Bry.) By permission of Houghton Library, Harvard University.

FIGURE 1.4

The European View of the World, about 1600

In Shakespeare's time, most educated Europeans pictured a universe in which God ultimately determines everything. Thus, in this early-seventeenth-century engraving, a chain extends from God's hand to the hand of a woman representing Nature; she in turn holds a chain extending to the "ape of Nature," representing humankind. The engraving thus suggests that God and his intermediary, Nature, shape all human actions. Notice also that the engraving arranges all the elements of the universe—angels, heavenly objects, humans, animals, vegetables, minerals—in a hierarchy. It suggests that higher elements, such as the stars and the planets, influence lower elements, such as the fate of humans.

The Democratic Revolution suggested that people could intervene to improve society. The Industrial Revolution presented social thinkers with a host of pressing social problems crying out for a solution. They responded by giving birth to the sociological imagination.

THEORY, RESEARCH, AND VALUES

French social thinker Auguste Comte (1798–1857) coined the term *sociology* in 1838 (Thompson, 1975). Comte tried to place the study of society on scientific foundations. He said he wanted to understand the social world as it was, not as he or anyone else imagined it should be. Yet there was a tension in his work: although Comte was eager to adopt the scientific method in studying society, he was a conservative thinker, motivated by strong opposition to rapid change in French society. This inclination was evident in his writings. When he moved from his small, conservative hometown to Paris, Comte witnessed the democratic forces unleashed by the French Revolution, the early industrialization of society, and the rapid growth of cities. What he saw shocked and saddened him. Rapid social change was destroying much of what he valued, especially respect for traditional authority. He therefore urged slow change and the preservation of all that was traditional in social life. Thus, scientific methods of research *and* a vision of the ideal society were evident in sociology at its origins.

Paul Almasy/Corbis

The Scientific Revolution began in Europe around 1550. Scientists proposed new theories about the structure of the universe and developed new methods to collect evidence so they could test those theories. Shown here is an astrolabe used by Copernicus to solve problems relating to the position of the sun, the planets, and the stars.

Although he praised the value of scientific methods, Comte never conducted any research. Neither did the second founder of sociology, British social theorist Herbert Spencer (1820–1903). However, Spencer believed that he had discovered scientific laws governing the operation of society. Strongly influenced by Charles Darwin's theory of evolution, he thought that societies evolve in the same way as biological species do. Individuals struggle to survive, the unfit die before they can bear offspring, and the fittest survive. According to Spencer, this process allows "barbaric" societies to become "civilized." Deep social inequalities exist in society, but that is just as it should be if societies are to evolve, Spencer argued (1975 [1897–1906]).

Spencer's ideas, which came to be known as "social Darwinism," were popular for a time in North America and Great Britain. Wealthy industrialists, such as the oil baron John D. Rockefeller, found much to admire in a doctrine that justified social inequality and trumpeted the superiority of the wealthy and the powerful. Today, few sociologists think that societies are like biological systems. We have a better understanding of the complex economic, political, military, religious, and other forces that cause social change. We know that people can take things into their own hands and change their social environment in ways that no other species can. Spencer remains of interest because he was among the first social thinkers to assert that society operates according to scientific laws—and because his vision of the ideal society nonetheless showed through his writings.

To varying degrees, we see the same tension between belief in the importance of science and a vision of the ideal society in the work of the three giants in the early history of sociology: Karl Marx (1818–83), Émile Durkheim (1858–1917), and Max Weber (pronounced VAY-ber; 1864–1920). The lives of these three men spanned just over a century. They witnessed Europe's wrenching transition to industrial capitalism. They wanted to explain the great transformation of Europe and suggest ways of improving people's lives. They adopted scientific research methods in their work but they also wanted to chart a better course for their societies. The ideas they developed are not just diagnostic tools from which we can still learn but, like many sociological ideas, are also prescriptions for combating social ills.

Eugene Delacroix's *Liberty Leading the People, July 28, 1830*. The democratic forces unleashed by the French Revolution suggested that people are responsible for organizing society and that human intervention can therefore solve social problems. As such, democracy was a foundation stone of sociology.

Musee du Louvre, Paris/Giraudon, Paris/SuperStock

Diego Rivera's *Detroit Industry, North Wall* (1932–33). Fresco (detail). Copyright 1997. The Detroit Institute of Arts. The first Industrial Revolution began in the late eighteenth century. The so-called Second Industrial Revolution began in the early twentieth century. Wealthy entrepreneurs formed large companies. Steel became a basic industrial material. Oil and electricity fuelled much industrial production. At the same time, Henry Ford's assembly lines and other mass-production technologies transformed the workplace.

The tension between analysis and ideal, diagnosis and prescription, is evident throughout sociology. This becomes clear if we distinguish three important terms: theories, research, and values.

Theory

Sociological ideas are usually expressed in the form of theories. **Theories** are tentative explanations of some aspect of social life. They state how and why certain facts are related. For example, in his theory of suicide, Durkheim related facts about suicide rates to facts about social solidarity. This enabled him to explain suicide as a function of social solidarity. In our broad definition, even a hunch qualifies as a theory if it suggests how and why certain facts are related (Einstein, 1954: 270).

Theories are tentative explanations of some aspect of social life that state how and why certain facts are related.

Research

After sociologists formulate theories, they can conduct research. **Research** is the process of systematically observing social reality, often to test a theory or assess its validity. For example, Durkheim collected suicide statistics from various government agencies to see whether the data supported or contradicted his theory. Because research can call a theory's validity into question, theories are only *tentative* explanations. We discuss the research process in detail in Chapter 2, How Sociologists Do Research.

Research is the process of systematically observing reality to assess the validity of a theory.

Values

Before sociologists can formulate a theory, they must make certain judgments. For example, they must decide which problems are worth studying. They must make certain assumptions about how the parts of society fit together. If they are going to recommend ways of improving the operation of some aspect of society, they must even have an opinion about what the ideal society should look like. Sociologists' values shape these issues.

Values are ideas about what is good and bad, right and wrong.

Values are ideas about what is good and bad, right and wrong. Inevitably, values help sociologists formulate and favour certain theories over others (Edel, 1965; Kuhn, 1970 [1962]). As such, sociological theories may be modified and even rejected because of research, but they are often motivated by sociologists' values.

Durkheim, Marx, and Weber stood close to the origins of the major theoretical traditions in sociology: functionalism, conflict theory, and symbolic interactionism. A fourth theoretical tradition, feminism, has arisen in recent decades to correct some deficiencies in the three long-established traditions. It will become clear as you read this book that many more theories exist in addition to these four. However, because these four traditions have been especially influential in the development of sociology, we present a thumbnail sketch of each one.

Summing Up

- The sociological study of suicide shows that a distinctively *social* realm influences all human behaviour, even if the behaviour seems to non-social or anti-social.
- The sociological perspective analyzes the connection between personal troubles and microstructures, macrostructures, and global structures.
- The rise of sociology was stimulated by the Scientific, Industrial, and Democratic Revolutions.
- Theories (tentative explanations of aspects of social life) are typically motivated by values (ideas about what is good and bad, right and wrong) and tested by research (systematically observing social reality).

SOCIOLOGICAL THEORY AND THEORISTS

Functionalism

Durkheim

Functionalism stresses that human behaviour is governed by relatively stable social structures. It underlines how social structures maintain or undermine social stability. It emphasizes that social structures are based mainly on shared values or preferences. And it suggests that re-establishing equilibrium can best solve most social problems.

Durkheim's theory of suicide is an early example of what sociologists now call **functionalism**. Functionalist theories incorporate these four features:

1. They stress that relatively stable patterns of social relations, or social structures, govern human relations. For example, Durkheim emphasized how patterns of social solidarity influence suicide rates. Usually the social structures analyzed by functionalists are macrostructures.
2. Functionalist theories show how social structures maintain or undermine social stability. For example, Durkheim analyzed how the growth of industries and cities in nineteenth-century Europe lowered the level of social solidarity and contributed to social instability, one result of which was a higher suicide rate.
3. Functionalist theories emphasize that social structures are based mainly on shared values or preferences. Thus, when Durkheim wrote about social solidarity, he sometimes meant the frequency and intensity of social interaction, but more often he thought of social solidarity as a sort of moral cement that binds people together.
4. Functionalism suggests that re-establishing equilibrium can best solve most social problems. Thus, Durkheim said that social stability could be restored in late-nineteenth-century Europe by creating new associations of employers and workers that would lower workers' expectations about what they could get out of life. If, said Durkheim, more people could agree on wanting less, social solidarity would rise and there would be fewer strikes, fewer suicides, and so on. Functionalism, then, was a conservative response to widespread social unrest in late-nineteenth-century France. A more liberal

or radical response would have been to argue that if people are expressing discontent because they are getting less out of life than they expect, discontent can be lowered by figuring out ways for them to get more out of life.

Functionalism in North America

Although functionalist thinking influenced North American sociology at the end of the nineteenth century, it was only during the continent's greatest economic crisis ever, the Great Depression of 1929–39, that functionalism took deep root here (Russell, 1966). With a quarter of the paid labour force unemployed and labour unrest rising, it is not surprising that sociologists with a conservative frame of mind were attracted to a theory that focused on how social equilibrium could be restored. Functionalist theory remained popular for about 30 years. It experienced a minor revival in the early 1990s but never regained the dominance it enjoyed from the 1930s to the early 1960s.

Harvard sociologist Talcott Parsons was the foremost North American proponent of functionalism. Parsons is best known for identifying how various institutions must work to ensure the smooth operation of society as a whole. He argued that society is well integrated and in equilibrium when the family successfully raises new generations, the military successfully defends society against external threats, schools are able to teach students the skills and values they need to function as productive adults, and religions create a shared moral code among the people (Parsons, 1951).

Parsons was criticized for exaggerating the degree to which members of society share common values and social institutions contribute to social harmony. This led North America's other leading functionalist, Robert Merton, to propose that social structures may have different consequences for different groups of people. Merton noted that some consequences may be disruptive or **dysfunctional** (Merton, 1968 [1949]). Moreover, said Merton, although some functions are **manifest** (visible and intended), others are **latent** (unintended and less obvious). For instance, a manifest function of schools is to transmit skills from one generation to the next. A latent function of schools is to encourage the development of a separate youth culture that often conflicts with parents' values (Coleman, 1961; Hersch, 1998).

Dysfunctional consequences are effects of social structures that create social instability.

Manifest functions are visible and intended effects of social structures.

Latent functions are invisible and unintended effects of social structures.

Conflict Theory

The second major theoretical tradition in sociology emphasizes the centrality of conflict in social life. **Conflict theory** incorporates these features:

- It generally focuses on large macrolevel structures, such as "class relations" or patterns of domination, submission, and struggle between people of high and low standing.
- Conflict theory shows how major patterns of inequality in society produce social stability in some circumstances and social change in others.
- Conflict theory stresses how members of privileged groups try to maintain their advantages while subordinate groups struggle to increase theirs. From this point of view, social conditions at a given time are the expression of an ongoing power struggle between privileged and subordinate groups.
- Conflict theory typically leads to the suggestion that eliminating privilege will lower the level of conflict and increase human welfare.

Conflict theory generally focuses on large macrolevel structures and shows how major patterns of inequality in society produce social stability in some circumstances and social change in others.

Marx

Conflict theory originated in the work of German social thinker Karl Marx. A generation before Durkheim, Marx observed the destitution and discontent produced by the Industrial Revolution and proposed a sweeping argument about the way societies develop (Marx, 1904 [1859]; Marx and Engels, 1972 [1848]). Marx's theory was radically different from Durkheim's. **Class conflict**, the struggle between classes to resist and overcome the opposition of other classes, lies at the centre of his ideas.

Class conflict is the struggle between classes to resist and overcome the opposition of other classes.

Marx argued that owners of industry are eager to improve the way work is organized and to adopt new tools, machines, and production methods. These innovations allow them to produce more efficiently, earn higher profits, and drive inefficient competitors out of business. However, the drive for profits also causes capitalists to concentrate workers in larger and larger establishments, keep wages as low as possible, and invest as little as possible in improving working conditions. Thus, said Marx, a large and growing class of poor workers opposes a small and shrinking class of wealthy owners.

Marx believed that workers would ultimately become aware of belonging to the same exploited class. He called this awareness "class consciousness." He believed working-class consciousness would encourage the growth of trade unions and labour parties. According to Marx, these organizations would eventually seek to end private ownership of property, replacing it with a "communist" society in which there is no private property and everyone shares wealth according to their needs.

Weber

Although some of Marx's ideas have been usefully adapted to the study of contemporary society, scholars have questioned his predictions about the inevitable collapse of capitalism. Max Weber, a German sociologist who wrote his major works a generation after Marx, was among the first to find flaws in Marx's argument (Weber, 1946). Weber noted the rapid growth of the service sector of the economy, with its many non-manual workers and professionals. He argued that many members of these occupational groups stabilize society because they enjoy higher status and income than do manual workers employed in manufacturing. In addition, Weber showed that class conflict is not the only driving force of history. In his view, politics and religion are also important sources of historical change (see below). Other writers pointed out that Marx did not understand how investing in technology would make it possible for workers to toil fewer hours under less oppressive conditions. Nor did he foresee that higher wages, better working conditions, and welfare state benefits would help to pacify manual workers.

Conflict Theory in North America

Conflict theory had some advocates in North America before the 1960s. Most noteworthy is C. Wright Mills, who laid the foundations for modern conflict theory in the 1950s. Mills conducted pioneering research on American politics and class structure. One of his most important books is *The Power Elite*, a study of the several hundred men who occupied the "command posts" of the American economy, military, and government. He argued that power is highly concentrated in American society, which is therefore less of a democracy than we are often led to believe (Mills, 1956).

Exceptions like Mills notwithstanding, conflict theory did not really take hold in North America until the 1960s, a decade rocked by growing labour unrest, Quebec separatism, anti-Vietnam War protests, the rise of the black power movement, and the revival of feminism, which had fallen dormant after its first stirrings in the late nineteenth and early twentieth centuries. Strikes, demonstrations, and riots were almost daily occurrences in the 1960s and early 1970s, and therefore many sociologists of that era thought conflict among classes, nations, races, and generations was the very essence of society. Many of today's leading sociologists attended graduate school in the 1960s and 1970s, and the spirit of the times strongly influenced them. As you will see throughout this book, they have made important contributions to conflict theory during their professional careers.

Symbolic Interactionism

Weber, Mead, and Goffman

We noted above that Weber criticized Marx's interpretation of the development of capitalism. Among other things, Weber argued that early capitalist development was caused not just by favourable economic circumstances but that certain *religious* beliefs also facilitated robust capitalist growth (Weber 1958 [1904–5]). In particular, sixteenth- and seventeenth-century Protestants believed their religious doubts could be reduced and a state of grace ensured if they worked diligently and lived modestly. Weber called this belief the **Protestant ethic**. He believed it had an unintended effect: People who adhered to the Protestant ethic saved and invested more money than others did. Thus, capitalism developed most vigorously where the Protestant ethic took hold. In much of his research, Weber emphasized the importance of empathically understanding people's motives and the meanings they attach to things to gain a clear sense of the significance of their actions. He called this aspect of his approach to sociological research the method of *Verstehen* ("understanding" in German).

The idea that any complete sociological analysis requires the analysis of subjective meanings and motives was only one of Weber's contributions to early sociological theory. Weber was also an important conflict theorist, as you will learn in later chapters. However, it is enough to note here that his emphasis on subjective meanings found rich soil in the United States in the late nineteenth and early twentieth centuries because his ideas resonated deeply with the individualism of American culture. A century ago, people widely believed that talent and initiative could allow anyone to achieve just about anything. Small wonder, then, that much of early American sociology focused on the individual or, more precisely, on the connection between the individual and the larger society. This was certainly a focus of sociologists at the University of Chicago, the most influential department of sociology in the country before World War II. For example, the University of Chicago's George Herbert Mead (1863–1931) was the driving force behind the study of how the individual's sense of self is formed in the course of interaction with other people. We discuss Mead's contribution in Chapter 4, Socialization. Here, we note only that the work of Mead and his colleagues gave birth to symbolic interactionism, a distinctively American theoretical tradition that continues to be a major force in sociology today.

Functionalist and conflict theories assume that people's group memberships—whether they are rich or poor, male or female, black or white—influence their behaviour. This approach can sometimes make people seem like balls on a pool table: They get knocked around and cannot choose their own destinies. However, we know from our everyday experience that people are not like that. We often make choices, sometimes difficult ones. We sometimes change our minds. Moreover, two people with similar group memberships may react differently to similar social circumstances because they interpret those circumstances differently.

Recognizing these issues, some sociologists focus on the subjective side of social life. They work in the symbolic interactionist tradition. **Symbolic interactionism** incorporates these features:

- Symbolic interactionism's focus on interpersonal communication in microlevel social settings distinguishes it from both functionalist and conflict theories.
- Symbolic interactionism emphasizes that social life is possible only because people attach meanings to things. It follows that an adequate explanation of social behaviour requires understanding the subjective meanings people associate with their social circumstances.
- Symbolic interactionism stresses that people help to create their social circumstances and do not merely react to them. For example, Canadian-born sociologist Erving Goffman (1922–82), one of the most influential symbolic interactionists, analyzed the many ways people present themselves to others in everyday life so as to appear in the best possible light. Goffman compared social interaction to a carefully staged play, complete with front stage, backstage, defined roles, and a wide range of props. In this play, a person's age, gender, race, and other characteristics may help to shape his or her actions, but there is much room for individual creativity as well (Goffman, 1959).
- By focusing on the subjective meanings people create in small social settings, symbolic interactionists sometimes validate unpopular and unofficial viewpoints. This increases our understanding and tolerance of people who may be different from us.

To understand symbolic interactionism better, let us briefly return to the problem of suicide. If a police officer discovers a dead person at the wheel of a car that has run into a tree, it may be difficult to establish whether the death was an accident or suicide. Interviewing friends

The **Protestant ethic** is the belief that religious doubts can be reduced, and a state of grace ensured, if people work diligently and live ascetically. According to Weber, the Protestant work ethic had the unintended effect of increasing savings and investment and thus stimulating capitalist growth.

Symbolic interactionism focuses on interaction in microlevel social settings and emphasizes that an adequate explanation of social behaviour requires understanding the subjective meanings people attach to their social circumstances.

and relatives to discover the driver's state of mind just before the crash may help rule out the possibility of suicide. As this example illustrates, understanding the intention or motive of the actor is critical to understanding the meaning of a social action and explaining it. A state of mind must be interpreted, usually by a coroner, before a dead body becomes a suicide statistic (Douglas, 1967).

For surviving family and friends, suicide is always painful and sometimes embarrassing. Insurance policies often deny payments to beneficiaries in the case of suicide. As a result, coroners are inclined to classify deaths as accidental whenever such an interpretation is plausible. Being human, they want to minimize a family's suffering after such a horrible event. Sociologists therefore believe that official suicide rates are about one-third lower than actual suicide rates.

Social Constructionism and Queer Theory

Social constructionism is a variant of symbolic interactionism that has become popular in recent years. Social constructionists argue that when people interact, they typically assume things are naturally or innately what they seem to be, but in reality, apparently natural or innate features of life are sustained by *social* processes that vary historically and culturally (Hannigan, 1995b).

For example, many people assume that differences in the way women and men behave are the result of their different biological makeup. In contrast, social constructionists show that many of the presumably natural differences between women and men depend on the way power is distributed between them and the degree to which certain ideas about women and men are shared (see Chapter 11, Sexualities and Gender Stratification; Berger and Luckmann, 1966; West and Zimmerman, 1987). Since power distributions and ideas about gender vary over time and place, social constructionists are able to show how changing social conditions produce changes in the way people act out their gender identity. They conclude that gender is more a performance shaped by social conditions than part of a person's essence. People usually do such a good job of building natural-seeming identities in their everyday interactions—not just gender, but also ethnicity, race, nationality, religion, and so on—that they do not notice the materials used in the construction process. Social constructionists identify those materials and analyze how people piece them together.

Queer theory takes the social constructionist argument a step further by denying the very existence of stable identities (Green, 2007). From the queer theorist's point of view, when we apply labels like "male," "female," "gay," and "lesbian" to ourselves or others we are adopting official or at least socially accepted labels that fail to capture the fluidity and variability of people's actual identities and performances. Such labels impose social conventions on people, thus acting as forms of control and domination and drawing attention away from the uniqueness of each individual.

In sum, the study of the subjective side of social life helps us get beyond the official picture, deepening our understanding of how society works and supplementing the insights gained from macrolevel analysis. By stressing the importance and validity of subjective meanings, symbolic interactionists increase tolerance for minority and deviant viewpoints. By stressing how subjective meanings vary historically and culturally, social constructionists and queer theorists show that many seemingly natural features of social life actually require painstaking acts of social creation.

Feminist Theory

Few women figured prominently in the early history of sociology. The strict demands placed on them by the nineteenth-century family and the lack of opportunity in the larger society prevented most women from earning a higher education and making major contributions to the discipline. Women who made their mark on sociology in its early years tended to have unusual biographies. Some of these exceptional people introduced gender issues that were largely ignored by Marx, Durkheim, Weber, Mead, and other early sociologists. Appreciation for the sociological contribution of these pioneering women has grown in recent years because concern with gender issues has come to form a substantial part of the modern sociological enterprise.

Social constructionism argues that apparently natural or innate features of life are often sustained by social processes that vary historically and culturally.

Queer theory argues that people's sexual identities and performances are so variable that conventional labels like "male," female," "gay," and "lesbian" fail to capture the sexual instability that characterizes the lives of many people.

Martineau and Addams

Harriet Martineau (1802–76) is often called the first female sociologist. Born in England to a prosperous family, she never married. She was able to support herself comfortably from her journalistic writings. Martineau translated Comte into English, and she wrote one of the first books on research methods. She undertook critical studies of slavery, factory laws, and gender inequality. She was a leading advocate of voting rights for women, higher education for women, and gender equality in the family. As such, Martineau was one of the first feminists (Yates, 1985).

In the United States in the early twentieth century, a few women from wealthy families attended university, received training as sociologists, and wanted to become professors of sociology, but they were denied faculty appointments. Typically, they turned to social activism and social work instead. A case in point is Jane Addams (1860–1935). Addams was co-founder of Hull House, a shelter for the destitute in Chicago's slums, and she spent a lifetime fighting for social reform. She also provided a research platform for sociologists from the University of Chicago, who often visited Hull House to interview its clients. In recognition of her efforts, Addams received the 1931 Nobel Peace Prize.

Modern Feminism

Despite its early stirrings, feminist thinking had little impact on sociology until the mid-1960s, when the rise of the modern women's movement drew attention to the many remaining inequalities between women and men. Because of feminist theory's major influence on sociology, we regard it as sociology's fourth major theoretical tradition. Modern feminism has several variants (see Chapter 11, Sexualities and Gender Stratification). However, the various strands of **feminist theory** share the following features:

- Feminist theory focuses on various aspects of patriarchy, the system of male domination in society. Most feminists contend that patriarchy is as important as class inequality, if not more so, in determining a person's opportunities in life.
- Feminist theory holds that male domination and female subordination are determined not by biological necessity but by structures of power and social convention. From their point of view, women are subordinate to men only because men enjoy more legal, economic, political, and cultural rights.
- Feminist theory examines the operation of patriarchy in both microlevel and macrolevel settings.
- Feminist theory contends that existing patterns of gender inequality can and should be changed for the benefit of all members of society. The main sources of gender inequality include differences in the way boys and girls are reared; barriers to equal opportunity in education, paid work, and politics; the unequal division of domestic responsibilities between women and men; and (for Marxist feminists) the existing class structure.

For the most part, **feminist theory** claims that patriarchy is at least as important as class inequality in determining a person's opportunities in life. It holds that male domination and female subordination are determined not by biological necessity but by structures of power and social convention. It examines the operation of patriarchy in both micro and macro settings. And it contends that existing patterns of gender inequality can and should be changed for the benefit of all members of society.

Summing Up

- We summarize sociology's four main theoretical traditions in Table 1.1 on page 23 (see also Figure 1.5 on page 23). As you will see in the following pages, sociologists have applied them to all of the discipline's branches. They have elaborated and refined each of them. Some sociologists work exclusively within one tradition. Others conduct research that borrows from more than one tradition. However, all sociologists are deeply indebted to the founders of the discipline.

THE FOUR MAIN THEORETICAL TRADITIONS IN CANADA

Photo Courtesy of Ed Clark

S. D. Clark (1910–2003) received his Ph.D. from the University of Toronto. He became the first chair of the Department of Sociology at that institution. Born in Lloydminster, Alberta, he became known for his studies of Canadian social development as a process of disorganization and reorganization on a series of economic frontiers (Clark, 1968). The influence of functionalism on his work is apparent in his emphasis on the way society re-establishes equilibrium after experiencing disruptions caused by economic change.

Carleton University Archives

John Porter (1921–79) was Canada's premier sociologist in the 1960s and 1970s. Born in Vancouver, he received his Ph.D. from the London School of Economics. He spent his academic career at Carleton University in Ottawa. His major work, *The Vertical Mosaic* (1965), is a study of class and power in Canada. Firmly rooted in conflict theory, the book influenced a generation of Canadian sociologists in their studies on social inequality, elite groups, French–English relations, and Canadian–American relations.

American Sociological Association

Erving Goffman (1922–82) was born in Mannville, Alberta. He studied sociology and anthropology at the University of Toronto. He completed his Ph.D. at the University of Chicago and pursued his academic career at the University of California, Berkeley, and the University of Pennsylvania. Goffman developed an international reputation for his "drama-turgical" approach to symbolic inter-actionism.

Margrit Eichler

Margrit Eichler (1942–) was born in Berlin, Germany. She took her Ph.D. at Duke University in the United States before beginning her academic career at the Ontario Institute for Studies in Education and the University of Toronto. She is internationally known for her work on feminist methodology (Eichler, 1987). Her work on family policy in Canada has strongly influenced students, professional sociologists, and policymakers (Eichler, 1988a).

TABLE 1.1

The Main Theoretical
Traditions in Sociology

Theoretical Tradition	Main Level of Analysis	Main Focus	Main Question	Image of Ideal Society
Functionalism	Macro	Values	How do the institutions of society contribute to social stability?	A state of equilibrium
Conflict theory	Macro	Class inequality	How do privileged groups seek to maintain their advantages and subordinate groups seek to increase theirs, often causing social change in the process?	The elimination of privilege, especially class privilege
Symbolic interactionism	Micro	Meaning	How do individuals communicate so as to make their social settings meaningful?	Respect for the validity of minority views
Feminist theory	Micro and macro	Patriarchy	Which social structures and interaction processes maintain male dominance and female subordination?	The elimination of gender inequality

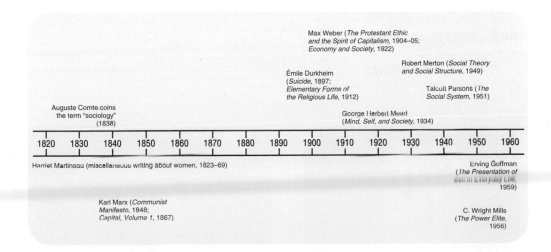

FIGURE 1.5

A Sociological Timeline of Some Major Figures in the Development of Sociological Theory, 1820–1960

To illustrate how much farther we are able to see by using theory as our guide, we now consider how the four traditions outlined above improve our understanding of an aspect of social life familiar to everyone: the world of fashion.

APPLYING THE FOUR THEORETICAL PERSPECTIVES: THE PROBLEM OF FASHION

> "Oh. Two weeks ago I saw Cameron Diaz at Fred Segal and I talked her out of buying this truly heinous angora sweater. Whoever said orange is the new pink is seriously disturbed."
>
> — Elle Woods (Reese Witherspoon) in *Legally Blonde* (2001)

From 1998 to 2002, one of the main fashion trends among white, middle-class, preteen and young teenage girls was the Britney Spears look: bare midriffs, highlighted hair, wide belts, glitter purses, big wedge shoes, and Skechers "energy" sneakers. However, in 2002 a new pop star, Avril Lavigne, was rising in the pop charts. Nominated for a 2003 Grammy Award in the Best New Artist category, the 17-year-old skater-punk from Napanee in eastern Ontario affected a shaggy, unkempt look. She sported worn-out T-shirts, 1970s-style plaid Western shirts with snaps, low-rise blue jeans, baggy pants, undershirts, ties, backpacks, chain wallets, and, for shoes, Converse Chuck Taylors. The style was similar to the Grunge look of the early 1990s, when Nirvana and Pearl Jam were the big stars on MTV and Kurt Cobain was king of the music world. The *Wall Street Journal* announced that Grunge might be back (Tkacik, 2002).

Why in late 2002 were the glamorous trends of the pop era giving way in one market segment to "neo-Grunge"? Why, in general, do fashion shifts take place? Sociological theory has interesting things to say on this subject (Davis, 1992).

Until the 1960s, the standard sociological approach to explaining the ebb and flow of fashion trends was *functionalist*. In the functionalist view, fashion trends worked like this: Every season, exclusive fashion houses in Paris, Milan, New York, and London, would show new styles. Some would catch on among the exclusive clientele of Chanel, Dior, Givenchy, and other big-name designers. The main appeal of wearing expensive, new fashions was that wealthy clients could distinguish themselves from people who were less well off. Thus, fashion performed an important social function. By allowing people of high rank to distinguish themselves from others, fashion helped to preserve the ordered layering of society into classes. ("It is an interesting question," wrote nineteenth-century American writer Henry David Thoreau in *Walden*, "how far [people] would retain their relative rank if they were divested of their clothes.") By the twentieth century, thanks to technological advances in clothes manufacturing, it didn't take long for inexpensive knockoffs to reach the market and trickle down to the lower classes. New styles then had to be introduced frequently so that fashion could continue to perform its function of helping to maintain an orderly class system. Hence the ebb and flow of fashion.

Britney Spears versus
Avril Lavigne

Reuters NewMedia Inc./Corbis

David Bergman/Corbis

The functionalist theory was an accurate account of the way fashion trends worked until the 1960s. Then, fashion became more democratic. Paris, Milan, New York, and London are still important fashion centres today. However, lower classes, minority groups, and people who spurn high fashion altogether increasingly initiate new fashion trends. After all, Napanee is pretty far from Paris, and today big-name designers are more likely to be influenced by the inner-city styles of hip hop than vice versa. As a result, the functionalist theory no longer provides a satisfying explanation of fashion cycles.

Some sociologists have turned to conflict theory as an alternative view of the fashion world. Conflict theorists typically view fashion cycles as a means by which industry owners make big profits. Owners introduce new styles and render old styles unfashionable because they make more money when many people are encouraged to buy new clothes often. At the same time, conflict theorists think fashion keeps people distracted from the many social, economic, and political problems that might otherwise incite them to express dissatisfaction with the existing social order and even rebel against it. Conflict theorists, like functionalists, thus believe that fashion helps to maintain social stability. Unlike functionalists, however, they argue that social stability bestows advantages on industrial owners at the expense of non-owners.

Conflict theorists have a point. Fashion *is* a big and profitable business. Owners *do* introduce new styles to make more money. They have, for example, created the Color Marketing Group (known to insiders as the "Color Mafia"), a committee that meets regularly to help change the international palette of colour preferences for consumer products. According to one committee member, the Color Mafia makes sure that "the mass media, . . . fashion magazines and catalogs, home shopping shows, and big clothing chains all present the same options" (Mundell, 1993).

Yet the Color Mafia and other influential elements of the fashion industry are not all-powerful. Remember what Elle Woods said after she convinced Cameron Diaz not to buy that heinous angora sweater: "Whoever said orange is the new pink is seriously disturbed." Like many consumers, Elle Woods *rejected* the advice of the fashion industry. And, in fact, some of the fashion trends initiated by industry owners flop, one of the biggest being the introduction of the midi-dress (with a hemline midway between knee and ankle) in the mid-1970s. Despite a huge ad campaign, most women simply would not buy it.

And so we arrive at one of the main problems with the conflict interpretation: It incorrectly makes it seem as if fashion decisions are all dictated from above. Reality is more complicated. Consumers make fashion decisions too. This idea can best be understood by thinking of clothing as a form of *symbolic interaction*, a sort of wordless "language" that allows us to tell others who we are and to learn who they are.

If clothes speak, sociologist Fred Davis has perhaps done the most in recent years to help us see how we can decipher what they say (Davis, 1992). According to Davis, a person's identity is always a work in progress. True, we develop a sense of self as we mature. We come to think of ourselves as members of one or more families, occupations, communities, classes, ethnic and racial groups, and countries. We develop patterns of behaviour and belief associated with each of these social categories. Nonetheless, social categories change over time, and so do we as we move through them and as we age. As a result, our identities are in flux, so we may become anxious or insecure about who we are. Clothes help us express our shifting identities. For example, clothes can convey whether you are "straight," sexually available, athletic, conservative, and much else, thus telling others how you want them to see you and the kinds of people with whom you want to associate. At some point, you may become less conservative, sexually available, and so on. Your clothing style is likely to change accordingly. (Of course, the messages you try to send are subject to interpretation and may be misunderstood.) For its part, the fashion industry feeds on the ambiguities within us, investing much effort in trying to discern which new styles might capture current needs for self-expression.

For example, capitalizing on the need for young girls' self-expression in the late 1990s, Britney Spears hit a chord. Feminist interpretations of the meaning and significance of

Britney Spears are especially interesting in this respect because they focus on the gender aspects of fashion.

Traditionally, feminists thought of fashion as a form of patriarchy, a means by which male dominance is maintained. They argued that fashion is mainly a female preoccupation. It takes a lot of time and money to choose, buy, and clean clothes. Fashionable clothing is often impractical and uncomfortable, and some of it is even unhealthy. Modern fashion's focus on youth, slenderness, and eroticism diminishes women by turning them into sexual objects, say some feminists. Britney Spears is of interest to traditional feminists because she supposedly helped to lower the age at which girls fall under male domination.

In recent years, this traditional feminist view has given way to a feminist interpretation that is more compatible with symbolic interactionism ("Why Britney Spears Matters," 2001). Some feminists now applaud the "girl power" movement that crystallized in 1996 with the release of the Spice Girls' hit single "Wannabe." These feminists regard Britney Spears as part of that movement. In their judgment, Spears's music, dance routines, and dress style expressed a self-assuredness and assertiveness that resonated with the less submissive and more independent role that girls are now carving out for themselves. With her kicks, shadow boxing, and songs like the 2000 single "Stronger," Spears spoke for the *empowerment* of young women. Apart from her musical and dancing talent, then, some feminists think many young girls went wild over Britney Spears because she helped them express their own social and sexual power.

Of course, not all young girls agreed. Some, like Avril Lavigne, found Spears "phony" and too much of a "showgirl." They sought "more authentic" ways of asserting their identity through fashion (Pascual, 2002). Still, the symbolic interactionist and feminist interpretations of fashion help us see more clearly the ambiguities of identity that underlie the rise of new fashion trends.

Our analysis of fashion shows that each of the four theoretical perspectives—functionalism, conflict theory, symbolic interactionism, and feminist theory—can clarify different aspects of a sociological problem. This does not mean that each perspective always has equal validity. Often, the interpretations that derive from different theoretical perspectives are incompatible. They offer *competing* interpretations of the same social reality. It is then necessary to do research to determine which perspective works best for the case at hand. Nonetheless, all four theoretical perspectives usefully illuminate some aspects of the social world. We therefore refer to them often in this textbook.

A SOCIOLOGICAL COMPASS

Our summary of the major theoretical perspectives in sociology suggests that the founders of the discipline developed their ideas in an attempt to solve the great sociological puzzle of their time—the causes and consequences of the Industrial Revolution. This raises two interesting questions. What are the great sociological puzzles of *our* time? How are today's sociologists responding to the challenges presented by the social settings in which *we* live? We devote the rest of this book to answering these questions in depth. In the remainder of this chapter, we outline what you can expect to learn from this book.

It would be wrong to suggest that a few key issues animate the research of tens of thousands of sociologists around the world. Viewed up close, sociology today is a heterogeneous enterprise enlivened by hundreds of theoretical debates, some focused on small issues relevant to particular fields and geographical areas, others focused on big issues that seek to characterize the entire historical era for humanity as a whole.

Among the big issues, two stand out. Perhaps the greatest sociological puzzles of our time are the causes and consequences of the **Postindustrial Revolution** and globalization. The Postindustrial Revolution is the technology-driven shift from manufacturing to service industries—the shift from employment in factories to employment in offices—and the consequences of that shift for nearly all human activities (Bell, 1973; Toffler, 1990).

The **Postindustrial Revolution** refers to the technology-driven shift from manufacturing to service industries and the consequences of that shift for virtually all human activities.

For example, because of the Postindustrial Revolution, non-manual occupations now outnumber manual occupations, and women have been drawn into the system of higher education and the paid labour force in large numbers. The shift to service industries has transformed the way we work and study, our standard of living, the way we form families, and much else.

Globalization is the process by which formerly separate economies, states, and cultures become tied together and people become increasingly aware of their growing interdependence (Giddens, 1990: 64; Guillén, 2001). Especially in recent decades, rapid increases in the volume of international trade, travel, and communication have broken down the isolation and independence of most countries and people. Also contributing to globalization is the growth of many institutions that bind corporations, companies, and cultures together. These processes have caused people to depend more than ever on people in other countries for products, services, ideas, and even a sense of identity.

Sociologists agree that globalization and postindustrialism promise many exciting opportunities to enhance the quality of life and increase human freedom. However, they also see many social-structural barriers to the realization of that promise. We can summarize both the promise and the barriers by drawing a compass—a sociological compass (see Figure 1.6). Each axis of the compass contrasts a promise with the barriers to its realization. The vertical axis contrasts the promise of equality of opportunity with the barrier of inequality of opportunity. The horizontal axis contrasts the promise of individual freedom with the barrier of constraint on that freedom. Let us consider these axes in more detail because much of our discussion in the following chapters turns on them.

> **Globalization** is the process by which formerly separate economies, states, and cultures become tied together and people become increasingly aware of their growing interdependence.

Equality versus Inequality of Opportunity

Optimists forecast that postindustrialism will provide more opportunities for people to find creative, interesting, challenging, and rewarding work. In addition, they say, the postindustrial era will generate more "equality of opportunity," that is, better chances for *all* people to get an education, influence government policy, and find good jobs.

You will find evidence to support these claims in this book. For example, we show that the average standard of living and the number of good jobs have increased in the postindustrial era. Women have made rapid strides in the economy, the education system,

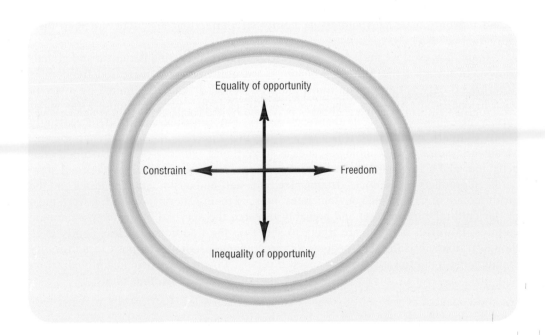

FIGURE 1.6
A Sociological Compass

and other institutions. Postindustrial societies like Canada are characterized by a decline in discrimination against members of minority groups, while democracy is spreading throughout the world. Desperately poor people form a declining percentage of the world's population.

Yet, as you read this book, it will also become clear that all these seemingly happy stories have a dark underside. For example, it turns out that the number of routine jobs with low pay and few benefits is growing faster than the number of creative, high-paying jobs. An enormous opportunity gulf still separates women from men. Racism and discrimination are still a big part of our world. Our health care system is in crisis just as our population is aging rapidly and most in need of health care. Many of the world's new democracies are only superficially democratic, while Canadians and citizens of other postindustrial societies are increasingly cynical about the ability of their political systems to respond to their needs. Many people are looking for alternative forms of political expression. The *absolute* number of desperately poor people in the world continues to grow, as does the gap between rich and poor nations. Some people attribute the world's most serious problems to globalization. They have formed organizations and movements—some of them violent—to oppose it. In short, equality of opportunity is an undeniably attractive ideal, but it is unclear whether it is the inevitable outcome of a globalized, postindustrial society.

Freedom versus Constraint

Growing freedom is also evident—but within limits. In an earlier era, most people retained their religious, ethnic, racial, and sexual identities for a lifetime, even if they were not particularly comfortable with them. They often remained in social relationships, even if they made them unhappy. One of the major themes of this book is that many people are now freer to construct their identities and form social relationships in ways that suit them. More than ever, you can *choose* who you want to be, with whom you want to associate, and how you want to associate with them. The postindustrial and global era frees people from traditional constraints by encouraging virtually instant global communication, international migration, greater acceptance of sexual diversity and a variety of family forms, the growth of ethnically and racially diverse cities, and so on. For instance, in the past people often stayed in marriages even if they were dissatisfied with them. Families often involved a father working in the paid labour force and a mother keeping house and raising children without pay. Today, people are freer to end unhappy marriages and create family structures that are more suited to their individual needs.

Again, however, we must face the less rosy aspects of postindustrialism and globalization. In many of the following chapters, we point out how increased freedom is experienced only within certain limits and how social diversity is limited by a strong push to conformity in some spheres of life. For example, we can choose a far wider variety of consumer products than ever before, but consumerism itself increasingly seems compulsory, although it is a way of life that threatens the natural environment. Meanwhile, some new technologies, such as surveillance cameras, cause us to modify our behaviour and act in more conformist ways. Large, impersonal bureaucracies and standardized products and services dehumanize both staff and customers. The tastes and the profit motive of vast media conglomerates, most of them American-owned, govern most of our cultural consumption and arguably threaten the survival of distinctive national cultures. Powerful interests are trying to shore up the traditional nuclear family even though it does not suit some people. As these examples show, the push to uniformity counters the trend toward growing social diversity. Postindustrialism and globalization may make us freer in some ways, but they also place new constraints on us.

Why Sociology?

Our overview of themes in *Sociology: Your Compass for a New World* drives home a point made by Anthony Giddens, renowned British sociologist and adviser to former British prime minister Tony Blair. According to Giddens, we live in an era "suspended between extraordinary opportunity ... and global catastrophe" (Giddens, 1990: 166). A whole range of environmental issues; profound inequalities in the wealth of nations and of classes; religious, racial, and ethnic violence; and unsolved problems in the relations between women and men continue to affect the quality of our everyday lives profoundly. Despair and apathy are possible responses to these complex issues, but they are not responses that humans favour. If it were our nature to give up hope, we would still be sitting around half-naked in the mud outside a cave. People are more inclined to look for ways of improving their lives, and this period of human history is full of opportunities to do so. For example, we have advanced to the point where, for the first time, we have the means to feed and educate everyone in the world. Similarly, it now seems possible to erode some of the inequalities that have always been the major source of human conflict.

Careers in Sociology

Sociology offers useful advice on how to achieve the goals of equality and freedom because it is more than just an intellectual exercise. Sociology is an applied science with practical, everyday uses in the realms of teaching and public policy, and in the creation of laws and regulations by organizations and governments (see Box 1.3 on page 30). That is because sociologists are trained not just to see what is but also to see what is possible.

Students often ask: "Can I get a good job with a sociology degree?" "Exactly what kind of work could I do with a major in sociology?" "Aren't all the good jobs these days in technical areas and the natural sciences?" To answer these questions—and to help you decide whether it makes sense for you to major in sociology or another social science— consider the following data on the employment of Canadians with degrees in sociology and related fields.

A study based on 1988 data found that a higher percentage of Canadian sociology graduates were employed full-time than were graduates in the other social sciences (Guppy and Hedley, 1993). A study based mainly on 1996 data (Allen, 1999) showed that, in Canada,

- the unemployment rate among social science graduates was lower than among graduates in math, physics, engineering, agriculture, and biology.
- between 1991 and 1996, there were more new jobs for people with social science degrees than for people with degrees in other fields.
- although women earned less than men in all fields in 1996, the discrepancy between men's and women's income was smallest among social science graduates.

Based on these findings, it seems that sociology degrees promise more employment security for both men and women, and less income discrimination against women, than do other degrees. It also seems that the postindustrial economy requires more new employees with a social science background than new employees with a background in some technical and scientific fields.

Tens of thousands of Canadians have a B.A. in sociology. A sociology B.A. improves a person's understanding of the diverse social conditions affecting men and women; people with different sexual orientations; and people from different countries, regions, classes, races, and ethnic groups. Therefore, people with a B.A. in sociology tend to be attracted to jobs requiring good "people skills" and jobs involved in managing and promoting social change (see Table 1.2 on page 31).

Social Policy: What Do You Think?

ARE CORPORATE SCANDALS A PROBLEM OF INDIVIDUAL ETHICS OR SOCIAL POLICY?

The Sloan School of Management at MIT conducted a survey of 600 graduates as part of its 50th anniversary observance. Sixty percent of respondents said that honesty, integrity, and ethics are the main characteristics of a good corporate leader. Most alumni felt that living a moral professional life is more important than pulling in large paycheques and generous perquisites.

Unfortunately, the behaviour of North American executives sometimes fails to reflect high ethical standards. In 2002, for example, investigators uncovered the biggest corporate scandals ever to rock the United States. Things got so bad that Andy Grove, a founder of Intel, said he was "embarrassed and ashamed" to be a corporate executive (quoted in Hochberg, 2002), and the Wall Street investment firm of Charles Schwab ran a defensive television ad claiming to be "almost the opposite of a Wall Street firm." What brought about such astonishing statements was that several corporate giants, including Enron, WorldCom, Tyco, Global

Crossings, and Adelphia Communications, were shown to have engaged in accounting fraud to make their earnings appear higher than they actually were. This practice kept their stock prices artificially high—until investigators made public what was going on, at which time their stock prices took a nosedive. Ordinary stockholders lost hundreds of billions of dollars. Many company employees lost their pensions (because they had been encouraged or compelled to place their retirement funds in company stock) and their jobs (because their companies soon filed for bankruptcy). In contrast, accounting fraud greatly benefited senior executives. They had received stock options as part of their compensation package. If you own stock options, you can buy company stock whenever you want at a fixed low price, even if the market price for the stock is much higher. Senior executives typically exercised their stock options *before* the stocks crashed, netting them billions of dollars in profit.

Canada has not been immune to unethical behaviour in the highest corporate ranks. For example, thousands of ordinary Canadians lost billions of dollars, including substantial pension savings, when senior executives of telecommunications giant Nortel grossly overstated the company's profitability and prospects, earned huge bonuses based on false accounting, and then watched the stock slide from a high of $124.50 in July 2000 to 64 cents in October 2002. Several senior executives lost their jobs, but they were not prosecuted and they all kept their ill-gotten gains. In 2004, a group of Canadian investors launched a class-action lawsuit against newspaper baron Conrad Black and other executives of Hollinger International for $4 billion in damages. The suit claimed market losses may have been caused by

controversies involving Black's management and allegations that he and associates quietly pocketed $400 million to which they were not entitled. (Black was eventually found guilty in an American court of fraud and obstruction of justice and was sentenced to a 6½-year jail term.)

Can we rely on individual morality or ethics to show senior executives how to behave responsibly, that is, in the long-term interest of their companies and society as a whole? Ethics courses have been taught at all business schools for years but, as the dean of one business school noted, these courses can't "turn sinners into saints. . . . If a company does a lot of crazy stuff but its share price continues to rise, a lot of people will look the other way and not really care whether senior management is behaving ethically or not" (quoted in Goll, 2002).

Because individual ethics often seem weak in the face of greed, some observers have suggested that new public policies, that is, laws and regulations passed by organizations and governments, are required to regulate executive compensation. For example, some people think the practice of granting stock options to senior executives should be outlawed, stiff jail terms should be imposed on anyone who engages in accounting fraud, and strong legal protection should be offered to anyone who "blows the whistle" on executive wrongdoing.

Sociology helps us see what may appear to be personal issues in the larger context of public policy. Even our tendency to act ethically or unethically is shaped in part by public policy—or the lack of it. Therefore, we review a public policy debate in each chapter of this book. It is good exercise for the sociological imagination, and it will help you gain more control over the forces that shape your life.

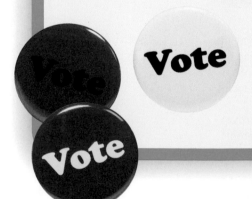

Government
Community affairs officer
Urban/regional planner
Legislative aide
Affirmative action/
  employment equity worker
Foreign service officer
Human rights officer
Personnel coordinator

Research
Social research specialist
Consumer researcher
Data analyst
Market researcher
Survey researcher
Census officer/analyst
Demographer/population
  analyst
Systems analyst

Community Affairs
Occupational/career
  counsellor
Homeless/housing
  worker
Public health/hospital
  administrator

Child development
  technician
Public administration
  assistant
Social assistance
  advocate
Resident planning aide
Group home worker
Rehabilitation program
  worker
Rural health outreach
  worker
Housing coordinator
Fundraising director/
  assistant
Caseworker/aide
Community organizer
Youth outreach worker

Corrections
Corrections officer
Criminology assistant
Police officer
Rehabilitation counsellor
Criminal investigator
Juvenile court worker
Parole officer

Teaching
College/university
  placement worker
Public health educator
Teacher
Admissions counsellor

Business
Market analyst
Project manager
Sales representative
Real estate agent
Journalist
Public relations officer
Actuary
Insurance agent
Human resources manager
Production manager
Labour relations officer
Administrative assistant
Quality control manager
Merchandiser/purchaser
Computer analyst
Data entry manager
Publishing officer
Advertising officer
Sales manager

TABLE 1.2

Jobs Commonly Held by Canadians with Degrees in Sociology

Source: Neil Guppy & R. Alan Hedley. 1993. *Opportunities in Sociology* (Montreal: Canadian Sociology and Anthropology Association). Reprinted with permission of the Canadian Sociological Association.

Note: While more recent data have not been compiled, we have little reason to believe that the job picture has changed significantly since this table was first created.

People with a B.A. in sociology often go on to take graduate and professional degrees in other fields, including law, urban planning, industrial relations, social work, and public policy. Most people with a graduate degree in sociology teach and conduct research in universities, with research being a more important component of the job in larger and more prestigious institutions. Other sociologists conduct research and give policy advice in a wide range of settings outside the system of higher education—in government agencies, trade unions, non-governmental organizations, and professional and public interest associations. In the private sector, you can find sociologists practising their craft in firms specializing in public opinion polling, management consulting, market research, standardized testing, and evaluation research, which assesses the impact of particular policies and programs.

One way to see the benefits of a sociological education is to compile a list of some of the famous practical idealists who studied sociology in university. That list includes several former heads of state, among them Fernando Cardoso, former president of Brazil; Tomas Masaryk, former president of Czechoslovakia; Edward Seaga, former prime minister of Jamaica; and Ronald Reagan, former president of the United States. The former vice-president of the Liberal Party of Canada and former president and vice-chancellor of York University in Toronto, Lorna Marsden, is a sociologist. Anthony Giddens, former director of the London School of Economics and adviser to former British prime minister Tony Blair, also holds a doctorate in sociology. So do Martin Goldfarb, chairman, president, and CEO of Goldfarb Consultants International, and Donna Dasko, senior vice-president of Environics; they head two of Canada's leading public opinion firms with offices and affiliates around the world. Alex Himelfarb, former clerk of the Privy Council and secretary to the cabinet in Ottawa, holds a sociology Ph.D. too. British Columbia native Steve Nash of the Phoenix Suns is widely considered the best team player in professional basketball today, and his agent claims he is "the most color-blind person I've ever known" (Robbins, 2005). Arguably, Nash's sociology degree contributes to his team-building ability and his performance on the court by helping him to better understand the importance of groups and diverse social conditions in shaping human behaviour.

In sum, although sociology does not offer easy solutions to the question of how the goal of improving society may be accomplished, it does provide a useful way of understanding our current predicament and seeing possible ways of dealing with it, of leading us a little farther away from the mud outside the cave. You sampled sociology's ability to tie personal troubles to social-structural issues when we discussed suicide. You reviewed the major theoretical perspectives that enable sociologists to connect the personal with the social-structural. When we outlined the half-fulfilled promises of postindustrialism and globalization, you saw sociology's ability to provide an understanding of where we are and where we can go.

We frankly admit that the questions we raise in this book are tough to answer. Sharp controversy surrounds them all. However, we are sure that if you try to grapple with them, you will enhance your understanding of your society's, and your own, possibilities. In brief, sociology can help you figure out where you fit into society and how you can make society fit you.

Summing Up

- The tensions between equality and inequality of opportunity, and between freedom and constraint, are among the chief interests of sociology today.
- These tensions are growing in the context of the Postindustrial Revolution (the technology-driven shift from manufacturing to service industries) and globalization (the process by which formerly separate economies, states, and cultures become tied together and people become increasingly aware of their growing interdependence).

NOTE

1. Some sociologists also distinguish *mesostructures*, social relations that link microstructures and macrostructures. See Chapter 6, Networks, Groups, Bureaucracies, and Societies.

SUMMARY

1. What does the sociological study of suicide tell us about society and about sociology?
   Durkheim noted that suicide is an apparently non-social and antisocial action that people often, but unsuccessfully, try to explain psychologically. He showed that suicide rates are influenced by the level of social solidarity of the groups to which people belong. This theory suggests that a distinctively *social* realm influences all human behaviour.

2. What is the sociological perspective?
   The sociological perspective analyzes the connection between personal troubles and three levels of social structure: microstructures, macrostructures, and global structures.

3. How are values, theories, and research related?

   Values are ideas about what is good and bad, right and wrong. Values often motivate sociologists to define which problems are worth studying and to make initial assumptions about how to explain sociological phenomena. A theory is a tentative explanation of some aspect of social life. It states how and why specific facts are connected. Research is the process of carefully observing social reality to test the validity of a theory. Sociological theories may be modified and even rejected through research, and those theories are often motivated by sociologists' values.

4. What are the major theoretical traditions in sociology?

   Sociology has four major theoretical traditions. Functionalism analyzes how social order is supported by macrostructures. The conflict approach analyzes how social inequality is maintained and challenged. Symbolic interactionism analyzes how meaning is created when people communicate in microlevel settings. Feminist theories focus on the social sources of patriarchy in both macrolevel and microlevel settings.

5. What were the main influences on the rise of sociology?

   The rise of sociology was stimulated by the Scientific, Industrial, and Democratic Revolutions. The Scientific Revolution encouraged the view that sound conclusions about the workings of society must be based on solid evidence, not just on speculation. The Democratic Revolution suggested that people are responsible for organizing society and that human intervention can therefore solve social problems. The Industrial Revolution created a host of new and serious social problems that attracted the attention of many social thinkers.

6. What are the main influences on sociology today and what are the main interests of sociology?

   The Postindustrial Revolution is the technology-driven shift from manufacturing to service industries. Globalization is the process by which formerly separate economies, states, and cultures become tied together and people become increasingly aware of their growing interdependence. The causes and consequences of postindustrialism and globalization form the great sociological puzzles of our time. The tensions between equality and inequality of opportunity, and between freedom and constraint, are among the chief interests of sociology today.

KEY TERMS

class conflict (p. 17)

conflict theory (p. 17)

Democratic Revolution (p. 12)

dysfunctional consequences (p. 17)

feminist theory (p. 21)

functionalism (p. 16)

global structures (p. 9)

globalization (p. 27)

Industrial Revolution (p. 12)

latent functions (p. 17)

macrostructures (p. 9)

manifest functions (p. 17)

microstructures (p. 9)

patriarchy (p. 9)

Postindustrial Revolution (p. 26)

Protestant ethic (p. 19)

queer theory (p. 20)

research (p. 15)

Scientific Revolution (p. 12)

social constructionism (p. 20)

social solidarity (p. 6)

social structures (p. 9)

sociological imagination (p. 11)

symbolic interactionism (p. 19)

theories (p. 15)

values (p. 16)

WEB RESOURCES

Companion Website for This Book

http://www.compass4e.nelson.com

Begin by clicking on the Student Resources section of the website. Next, select the chapter you are studying from the pull-down menu. From the Student Resources page you have easy access to additional Weblinks and other resources. The website also has many useful tips to aid you in your study of sociology, including practice tests for each chapter.

InfoTrac® Search Terms

These search terms are provided to assist you in beginning to conduct research on this topic by visiting http://www.infotrac-college.com:

conflict theory
feminism
functionalism
social structure
suicide
symbolic interactionism

2

How Sociologists Do Research

IN THIS CHAPTER, YOU WILL LEARN THAT

- Scientific ideas differ from common sense and other forms of knowledge. Scientific ideas are assessed in the clear light of systematically collected evidence and public scrutiny.

- Sociological research depends not just on the rigorous testing of ideas but also on creative insight. Thus, the objective and subjective phases of inquiry are both important in good research.

- The main methods of collecting sociological data include experiments, surveys, systematic observations of natural social settings, and the analysis of existing documents and official statistics.

- Each data collection method has characteristic strengths and weaknesses. Each method is appropriate for different kinds of research problems.

John Kuczala

SCIENCE AND EXPERIENCE

OTTFFSSENT

"Okay, Mr. Smarty Pants, see if you can figure this one out." That's how Robert Brym's 11-year-old daughter, Talia, greeted him one day when she came home from school. "I wrote some letters of the alphabet on this sheet of paper. They form a pattern. Take a look at the letters and tell me the pattern."

Robert took the sheet of paper from Talia and smiled confidently. "Like most North Americans, I'd had a lot of experience with this sort of puzzle," says Robert. "For example, most IQ and SAT tests ask you to find patterns in sequences of letters, and you learn certain ways of solving these problems. One of the most common methods is to see if the 'distance' between adjoining letters stays the same or varies predictably. For example, in the sequence ADGJ, there are two missing letters between each adjoining pair. Insert the missing letters and you get the first 10 letters of the alphabet: A(BC)D(EF)G(HI)J.

"This time, however, I was stumped. On the sheet of paper Talia had written the letters OTTFFSSENT. I tried to use the distance method to solve the problem. Nothing worked. After 10 minutes of head scratching, I gave up."

"The answer's easy," Talia said, clearly pleased at her father's failure. "Spell out the numbers 1 to 10. The first letter of each word—one, two, three, and so on—spells OTTFFSSENT. Looks like you're not as smart as you thought. See ya." And with that she bounced off to her room.

"Later that day, it dawned on me that Talia had taught me more than just a puzzle. She had shown me that experience sometimes prevents people from seeing things. My experience with solving letter puzzles by using certain set methods kept me from solving the unusual problem of OTTFFSSENT."

Said differently, reality (in this case, a pattern of letters) is not just a thing "out there" we can learn to perceive "objectively." As social scientists have appreciated for more than a century, *experience* helps determine how we perceive reality, including what patterns we see and whether we can see patterns at all (Hughes, 1967: 16).

To understand how sociologists use science to conduct research, it is helpful to distinguish two levels of experience.

Levels of Experience

To understand our experience, it is useful to distinguish concrete and abstract levels. Each level has unique characteristics.

Let's begin with the concrete level. You obtain **concrete experience** by seeing, touching, tasting, smelling, and hearing. The parts of concrete experience are **percepts**, which form **patterns** when aggregated. For example, a single dot on a page is a percept, while a collection of dots constitutes a pattern. Likewise, when you hear the loud initial "beep" of a garbage truck reversing, you experience a percept; when you hear "beep, beep, beep," you distinguish a pattern (see Figure 2.1).

Two characteristics of concrete experience are worth noting. First, this is the level of experience you share with all other living creatures. Your pet parakeet experiences life at the concrete level, as does a dog walking down the street. Second, the concrete level of experience is meaningless by itself. If life were experienced exclusively at the concrete level, it would be full of sensations but devoid of meaning. The experience of a newborn infant approximates this condition. What must it be like to leave the warm, muffled world of

Concrete experience is obtained by seeing, touching, tasting, smelling, or hearing.

Percepts are the smallest bits of concrete experience.

Patterns are collections of related percepts.

Level of Experience	Components	Aggregates
Abstract (meaningful experience; occurs in the mind)	Concepts ("bits" of ideas)	Propositions (related concepts)
		Research methods link the concrete to the abstract
Concrete (meaningless experience; occurs through the senses)	Percepts ("bits" of perception)	Patterns (related percepts)

FIGURE 2.1
Levels of Experience
Source: Lance W. Roberts

the womb and be thrust into a barrage of electric light, strange smells, and odd sensations? William James described this uncontaminated concrete experience as "one great blooming, buzzing confusion" (James, 1890, p. 462). Figure 2.2 on page 38 captures this state of affairs regarding American military strategy in Afghanistan.

Fortunately, you do not live exclusively at the concrete level; your experience is not confined to meaninglessness. The abstract level of experience saves you from a state of confusion. **Abstract experience** occurs in your mind. It is the world of imagination, of fantasy. The abstract level is composed of **concepts** that, when linked together, form propositions. Concepts are abstract terms for organizing sense experience. Place six pens in front of you. Examine the pens. You will likely experience each one differently—as objects of different length, diameter, and colour. Some may contain teeth marks, while others are unflawed. Notice, however, that you refer to each of these concretely different objects by the same abstract concept. Each of them, to your mind, is a "pen." Through this naming process, called *conceptualization*, you organize concrete experience by placing the different objects into a single, meaningful category.

Your mind is full of concepts. They let you organize and give meaning to concrete experience. Your mind also relates concepts to one another and, in doing so, forms **propositions**. Propositions are abstract statements that express the relationship between two or more concepts. Imagine someone says, "Watch, table, education, income." After hearing this list of concepts, it is doubtful that you will say, "Now that's a good idea!" Concept lists are not propositions. Propositions emerge when your mind connects concepts in a meaningful way. "The watch is on the table" and "More educated people receive more income" are propositions.

Everybody expresses propositions. If someone approaches you in the bar next Saturday evening and says, "I think I love you," you are being "propositioned." Similarly, a proposition is evident when a political commentator says, "This provincial government is the most corrupt in Canada."

Social issues, such as poverty, deviance, and educational attainment (and all the others that fill this textbook), are often on people's minds, as is evident by browsing through newspapers or blogs. Citizens use concepts to characterize these issues and express propositions about how concepts are related. In the marketplace of ideas, propositions about almost any topic span the whole range of possibilities. Sociologists add their voices to the chorus.

Ideas about social life are like all propositions: they reside in the abstract world of people's minds; they are fantasies. The distinguishing feature of *sociological* ideas is that sociologists connect their abstract concepts and propositions to concrete percepts and patterns. In other words, sociology is interested in sorting out which ideas on a topic best describe experience. In doing so, sociologists endeavour to distinguish groundless speculation from reality.

Abstract experience is the imaginary world of the mind.

Concepts are abstract terms used to organize concrete experience.

Propositions are ideas that result from finding the relationship between concepts.

FIGURE 2.2

"One Great Blooming Buzzing Confusion"

This PowerPoint slide, meant to portray American military strategy in Afghanistan, was shown to Stanley McChrystal, head of U.S. and NATO forces in Afghanistan, in the summer of 2009. "When we understand that slide," said McChrystal, "we'll have won the war." We would say that the slide is meaningless because it focuses too much on concrete experiences rather than abstractions, or propositions that link concepts.

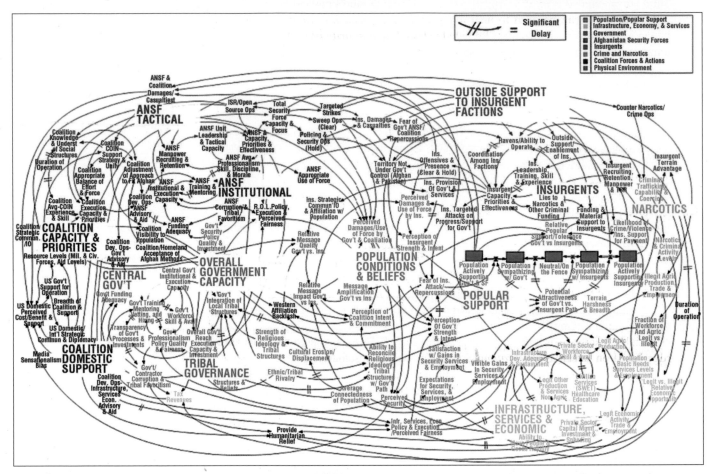

Source: Bumiller, Elisabeth. 2010. "We Have Met the Enemy and He Is PowerPoint." *New York Times* 26 April. www.nytimes.com (accessed 23 October 2010).

The methods of social science research are the principles, protocols, and tools sociologists use to link the abstract and concrete levels of experience. This chapter introduces common methodological procedures used by sociological practitioners to formulate propositions that are sustained by evidence. We begin our review by contrasting scientific and unscientific thinking.

Scientific versus Unscientific Thinking

In science, seeing is believing. In everyday life, believing is seeing. In other words, in everyday life our biases easily influence our observations. This circumstance often leads us to draw incorrect conclusions about what we see. In contrast, scientists, including sociologists, develop ways of collecting, observing, and thinking about evidence that minimize their chance of drawing biased conclusions.

On what basis do you decide statements are true in everyday life? Below we describe 10 types of unscientific thinking (Babbie, 2000). As you read about each one, ask yourself how frequently you think unscientifically. If you often think unscientifically, this chapter will help you develop more objective ways of thinking.

1. "Chicken soup helps get rid of a cold. *It worked for my grandparents, and it works for me.*" This statement represents knowledge based on *tradition*. Although some traditional knowledge is valid (sugar will rot your teeth), some is not (masturbation will not blind you). Science is required to separate valid from invalid knowledge.

2. "Weak magnets can be used to heal many illnesses. *I read all about it in the newspaper.*" This statement represents knowledge based on *authority*. We often think something is true because we read it in an authoritative source or hear it from an expert. However, authoritative sources and experts can be wrong. Scientists should always question authority to arrive at more valid knowledge.

3. "The car that hit the cyclist was dark brown. *I was going for a walk last night when I saw the accident.*" This statement represents knowledge based on *casual observation*. Unfortunately, we are usually pretty careless observers. In general, uncertainty can be reduced by observing in a conscious and deliberate manner and by recording observations. That is just what scientists do.

4. "If you work hard, you can get ahead. *I know because several of my parents' friends started off poor but are now comfortably middle class.*" This statement represents knowledge based on *overgeneralization*. For instance, if you know a few people who started off poor, worked hard, and became rich you may think any poor person can become rich if he or she works hard enough. You may not know about the more numerous poor people who work hard and remain poor or about the rich people who never worked hard. Scientists, however, **sample** cases that are representative of entire **populations**. Sampling enables them to avoid overgeneralization. They also avoid overgeneralization by repeating research, which ensures that they do not draw conclusions from an unusual set of research findings.

5. "I'm right because *I can't think of any contrary cases.*" This statement represents knowledge based on *selective observation*. Sometimes we unconsciously ignore evidence that challenges our firmly held beliefs. Thus, you may actually know some people who work hard but remain poor. However, to maintain your belief that hard work results in wealth, you may keep them out of mind. The scientific requirement that evidence be drawn from representative samples of the population minimizes bias arising from selective observation.

6. "Mr. Smith is poor even though he works hard, but that's because he has a disability. People with disabilities are the only *exception to the rule* that if you work hard you can get ahead." This statement represents knowledge based on *qualification*. Qualifications or "exceptions to the rule" are often made in everyday life, and they are in science, too. The difference is that in everyday life, qualifications are easily accepted as valid, while in scientific inquiry they are treated as statements that must be carefully examined in the light of evidence.

7. "The Toronto Blue Jays won 50 percent of their baseball games over the last three months but 65 percent of the games they played on Thursdays. *Because it happened so often before, I bet they'll win next Thursday.*" This statement represents knowledge based on *illogical reasoning*. In everyday life, we may expect the recurrence of events without reasonable cause, ignoring the fact that rare sequences of events sometimes occur just by chance. For example, it is possible for you to flip a coin 10 times and have it come up heads each time. On average, this will happen once every 1024 times you flip a coin 10 times. In the absence of any apparent reason for this happening, it is merely coincidental. It is illogical to believe otherwise. Scientists refrain from illogical reasoning. They also use statistical techniques to distinguish between events that are probably due to chance and those that are not.

8. "*I just can't be wrong.*" This statement represents knowledge based on *ego-defence*. Even scientists may be passionately committed to the conclusions they reach in their research because they have invested much time, energy, and money in them. It is other

A **sample** is the part of the population of research interest that is selected for analysis.

A **population** is the entire group about which the researcher wants to generalize.

Blood letting, from 'Tractatus de Pestilencia' (vellum), Albik, M. (15th century. / Private Collection, Archives Charmet / The Bridgeman Art Library

The first major advance in modern medicine took place when doctors stopped using unproven interventions in their treatment of patients and started relying on research to assess the value of their interventions. One such intervention involved bleeding patients, shown here in a medieval drawing.

Corbis/Bettman

Even Albert Einstein, often hailed as the most intelligent person of the twentieth century, sometimes ignored evidence in favour of pet theories. However, the social institution of science, which makes ideas public and subjects them to careful scrutiny, often overcomes such bias.

scientists—more accurately, the whole institution of science, with its commitment to publishing research results and critically scrutinizing findings—that put strict limits on ego-defence in scientific understanding.

9. *"The matter is settled once and for all."* This statement represents knowledge based on the *premature closure of inquiry*. This way of thinking involves deciding that all the relevant evidence has been gathered on a particular subject. Science, however, is committed to the idea that all theories are only temporarily true. Matters are never settled.

10. *"There must be supernatural forces at work here."* This statement represents knowledge based on *mystification*. When we can find no rational explanation for a phenomenon, we may attribute it to forces that cannot be observed or fully understood. Although such forces may exist, scientists remain skeptical. They are committed to discovering observable causes of observable effects.

Summing Up

- Sociological methods link the abstract and concrete levels of experience.
- Ten common errors are regularly found in unscientific thinking. Scientific thinking seeks to avoid these types of errors.

RESEARCH PRELIMINARIES

The Research Cycle

Sociological research seeks to overcome the kind of unscientific thinking described above. It is a cyclical process that involves six steps (Figure 2.3).

First, the sociologist must *formulate a research question*. A research question must be stated so it can be answered by systematically collecting and analyzing sociological data. Sociological research cannot determine whether God exists or what the best political system is. Answers to

FIGURE 2.3
The Research Cycle

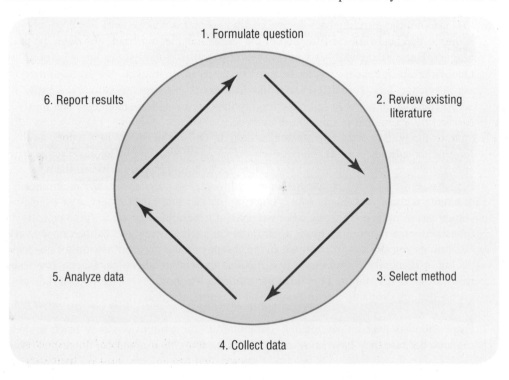

1. Formulate question

6. Report results

2. Review existing literature

5. Analyze data

3. Select method

4. Collect data

Courtesy of Carol Wainio

Carol Wainio's *We Can Be Certain* (1982). Research involves taking the plunge from speculation to testing ideas against evidence.

such questions require faith more than evidence. Sociological research can determine why some people are more religious than others are and which political systems create more opportunities for higher education. Answers to such questions require evidence more than faith.

Second, the sociologist must *review the existing research literature.* Researchers must elaborate their research questions in light of what other sociologists have already debated and discovered. Why? Because reading the relevant sociological literature stimulates researchers' sociological imagination, allows them to refine their initial questions, and prevents duplication of effort.

Selecting a research method is the third step in the research cycle. As we will see in detail later, each data collection method has strengths and weaknesses. Each method is therefore best suited to studying a different kind of problem. When choosing a method, we must keep these strengths and weaknesses in mind. (In the ideal but, unfortunately, infrequent case, several methods are used simultaneously to study the same problem. This can overcome the drawbacks of any single method and increase confidence in the findings.)

The fourth stage of the research cycle involves *collecting data* by observing subjects, interviewing them, reading documents produced by or about them, and so on. Many researchers think this is the most exciting stage of the research cycle because it brings them face to face with the puzzling sociological reality that so fascinates them.

Other researchers find the fifth step of the research cycle, *analyzing the data*, the most challenging. During data analysis you can learn things that nobody ever knew before. It is the time when data confirm some of your expectations and confound others, requiring you to think creatively about familiar issues, reconsider the relevant theoretical and research literature, and abandon pet ideas.

Of course, research is not much use to the sociological community, the subjects of the research, or the wider society if researchers do not *publish the results* in a report, a scientific journal, or a book. That is the research cycle's sixth step. Publication serves another important function, too. It allows other sociologists to scrutinize and criticize the research. On that basis, errors can be corrected and new and more sophisticated research questions can be formulated for the next round of research. In this sense, the practice of science is a social activity governed by rules defined and enforced by the scientific community.

It would be wrong to think that the research cycle always begins at the first stage and then proceeds to stage two, then to stage three, and so on. The research cycle is a useful way of thinking about the stages of research, but the exact starting point and progression of research varies from one project to the next.

Ethical Considerations

Throughout the research cycle, researchers must be mindful of the need to *respect their subjects' rights*, which means, in the first instance, that researchers must do their subjects no harm. This is the right to safety. People must have the right to decide whether they can be studied and, if so, in what way. Second, research subjects must have the right to decide whether their attitudes and behaviours may be revealed to the public and, if so, in what way. This is the right to privacy. Third, researchers cannot use data in a way that allows them to be traced to a particular subject. This is the subject's right to confidentiality. Fourth, subjects must be told how the information they supply will be used. They must also be allowed to judge the degree of personal risk involved in answering questions. This is the right to informed consent.

Ethical issues arise not only in the treatment of subjects but also in the treatment of research results. For example, plagiarism is a concern in academic life, especially among students, who write research papers and submit them for evaluation. Recent studies estimate that 31 percent of students plagiarize (Dee and Jacob, 2010; Walker, 2010). Increased plagiarism is a consequence of the spread of the Web and the growing view that everything on it is public and therefore does not have to be cited. That view is wrong. The Code of Ethics of the American Sociological Association states that we must "explicitly identify, credit, and reference the author" when we make any use of another person's written work, "whether it is published, unpublished, or electronically available" (American Sociological Association, 1999: 16).

Measuring Variables

Earlier we introduced the idea of concrete and abstract levels of experience. We noted that sociologists are interested in determining which abstract propositions about the social world best match observable patterns. For example, someone may propose that people with more education earn higher incomes. This abstract proposition states how the concepts "education" and "income" are related (see Figure 2.4, arrow 1). Because the proposition is abstract, sociologists immediately encounter a problem testing it. Has anyone ever seen, touched, heard, tasted, or smelled "education"? How about "income?" The reason we haven't is that concepts are mental images; they do not have concrete properties.

To overcome this problem, sociologists need to translate abstract propositions into testable forms. They do this through **operationalization**. Operationalization is the process by which a concept is translated into a variable (see Figure 2.4, arrows 2). A **variable** is a measure of a concept that has more than one value or score. Take the abstract concept "education." Operationalization asks us to consider what variable(s) would indicate whether one person is more or less educated than another. One operationalization might be "years of schooling." How about the concept of "income"? What variable(s) might be used to measure it? "Individual gross taxable annual income" might qualify.

Operationalization is the process of translating concepts into variables and propositions into hypotheses.

A **variable** is a measure of a concept that has more than one value or score.

FIGURE 2.4

Translating Propositions into Hypotheses

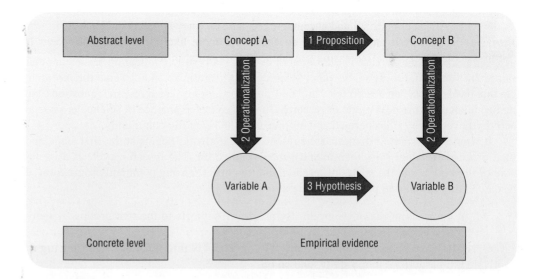

After operationalization, the original idea (proposition), which expressed a relationship between concepts, can be translated into a relationship between variables. The result of this translation is a **hypothesis**, the testable form of a proposition (see Figure 2.4, arrow 3). In our example, the hypothesis is "People with more years of schooling have higher gross taxable annual income." A hypothesis is the testable form of a proposition because you can imagine being able to experience (measure) different levels of the variables in concrete form.

Most students understand that a hypothesis is an educated guess. Figure 2.4 shows what this statement actually means. The "educated" part of an "educated guess" refers to the fact that a hypothesis is informed by an idea. It is a thoughtful guess, not a wild or arbitrary one. A hypothesis remains a guess, though, insofar as we don't know how well it fits observable patterns. We conduct research to collect evidence that will allow us to test hypotheses. Accordingly, we now outline each of sociology's major methods of gathering evidence: experiments, surveys, field research, and the analysis of existing documents and official statistics.

A **hypothesis** is the testable form of a proposition.

Summing Up

- The six basic research steps include formulating a question, reviewing the existing literature, selecting a data collection method, gathering the evidence, analyzing the data, and reporting the results.
- Sociological research is governed by ethical standards that protect subjects' right to safety, privacy, confidentiality, and informed consent.
- Before conducting research, sociologists must convert their propositions into testable hypotheses by turning the concepts that interest them into variables.

THE MAIN METHODS OF SOCIOLOGICAL RESEARCH

Experiments

In the mid-1960s, the first generation of North American children exposed to high levels of TV violence virtually from birth reached their mid-teens. At the same time, the rate of violent crime began to increase. Some commentators said that TV violence made violence in the real world seem normal and acceptable. As a result, they concluded, North American teenagers in the 1960s and subsequent decades were more likely than pre-1960s teens to commit violent acts. The increasing prevalence of violence in movies, video games, and popular music seemed to add weight to their conclusion.

Social scientists soon started investigating the connection between media and real-world violence by using experimental methods. An **experiment** is a carefully controlled artificial situation that allows researchers to isolate presumed causes and measure their effects precisely (Campbell and Stanley, 1963).

Experiments use a procedure called **randomization** to create two similar groups. Randomization involves assigning individuals to two groups by chance processes. For example, researchers may ask 50 children to draw a number from 1 to 50 from a covered box. The researchers assign children who draw odd numbers to one group and those who draw even numbers to the other group. By assigning subjects to the two groups by using a chance process and repeating the experiment many times, researchers ensure that each group has the same proportion of boys and girls, members of different races, children highly motivated to participate in the study, and so on.

Aggressive behaviour among children is common, from siblings fighting to bullying in the school-yard. Since the inception of home TV in the 1950s, social scientists have sought to develop research designs capable of examining the causal effects, if any, of viewing violence on television.

An **experiment** is a carefully controlled artificial situation that allows researchers to isolate hypothesized causes and measure their effects precisely.

Randomization in an experiment involves assigning each individual by chance processes to the group that will be exposed to the presumed cause or to the group that will not be exposed to the presumed cause.

A **dependent variable** is the presumed effect in a cause-and-effect relationship.

An **independent variable** is the presumed cause in a cause-and-effect relationship.

Reliability is the degree to which a measurement procedure yields consistent results.

Validity is the degree to which a measure actually measures what it is intended to measure.

In a **survey**, sociologists ask respondents questions about their knowledge, attitudes, or behaviour, either in a face-to-face or telephone interview or in a paper-and-pencil format.

After randomly assigning subjects to the two groups, the researchers put the groups in separate rooms and give them toys to play with. They observe the children through one-way mirrors, rating each child in terms of the aggressiveness of his or her play. This is the child's initial score on the **dependent variable**, aggressive behaviour. The dependent variable is the effect in any cause-and-effect relationship.

Then the researchers introduce the supposed (or "hypothesized") cause to one group—now called the experimental group. They may show children in the experimental group an hour-long TV program in which many violent acts take place. They do not show the program to children in the other group, now called the control group. In this case, the violent TV show is the **independent variable**. The independent variable is the presumed cause in any cause-and-effect relationship.

Immediately after the children see the TV show, the researchers again observe the children in both groups at play. Each child's play is given a second aggressiveness score. By comparing the aggressiveness scores of the two groups before and after only one of the groups has been exposed to the presumed cause, an experiment can determine whether the presumed cause (watching violent TV) has the predicted effect (increasing violent behaviour; Table 2.1).

Many experiments show that exposure to media violence has a short-term effect on violent behaviour in young children, especially boys. However, the results of experiments are mixed when it comes to assessing longer-term effects, especially on older children and teenagers (Anderson and Bushman, 2002; Browne and Hamilton-Giachritsis, 2005; Freedman, 2002).

Experiments allow researchers to isolate the single cause of theoretical interest and measure its effect with high **reliability**, that is, consistently from one experiment to the next. Yet many sociologists argue that experiments are highly artificial situations. They believe that removing people from their natural social settings lowers the **validity** of experimental results, that is, the degree to which they measure what they are actually supposed to measure.

Why do experiments on the effects of media violence lack validity? First, in the real world, violent behaviour usually means attempting to harm another person physically. Shouting or kicking a toy is not the same thing. In fact, such acts may enable children to relieve frustrations in a fantasy world, lowering their chance of acting violently in the real world. Second, aggressive behaviour is not controlled in the laboratory setting as it is in the real world. If a boy watching a violent TV show stands up and delivers a karate kick to his brother, a parent or other caregiver is likely to take action to prevent a recurrence. In the lab, lack of disciplinary control may facilitate unrealistically high levels of aggression (Felson, 1996). Because of such validity problems, experiments have not convincingly demonstrated that TV violence generally encourages violent behaviour.

Surveys

Surveys are the most widely used sociological research method. In a **survey**, sociologists ask people about their knowledge, attitudes, or behaviour. All survey researchers aim to study part of a group—a sample—to learn about the whole group of interest—the population. To generalize reliably about the population based on findings from a sample, researchers

TABLE 2.1

Steps in a Simple Experiment

Source: Created by Bob Brym

	Time 1	Time 2	Time 3	Time 4
Control group	Randomize assignment of subjects to group	Measure dependent variable	*Do not introduce independent variable*	Measure dependent variable again
Experimental group	Randomize assignment of subjects to group	Measure dependent variable	*Introduce independent variable*	Measure dependent variable again

must be sure that the characteristics of the people in the sample match those of the population. To draw a sample from which they can safely generalize, researchers must choose respondents (people who answer the survey questions) at random, and an individual's chance of being chosen must be known and greater than zero.

When sociologists conduct a survey, they may mail a form containing questions to respondents. Respondents then mail the completed questionnaire back to the researcher. Alternatively, sociologists may conduct face-to-face interviews in which questions are presented to the respondent by the interviewer during a meeting. Sociologists may also conduct surveys by means of telephone interviews.

Researchers collect information using surveys by asking people in a representative sample a set of identical questions. People interviewed on a downtown street corner do *not* constitute a representative sample of Canadian adults: the sample does not include people who live outside the urban core, it underestimates the number of seniors and people with disabilities, it does not take into account regional diversity, and so on.

Questionnaires may contain two types of questions. A closed-ended question provides the respondent with a list of permitted answers. Each answer is given a numerical code so the data can later be easily input into a computer for statistical analysis. An open-ended question allows respondents to answer in their own words. Open-ended questions are particularly useful when researchers don't have enough knowledge to create a meaningful and complete list of possible answers.

Because survey researchers can ask the same questions in subsequent surveys, their measures are often consistent or reliable. They can also make sure that survey questions elicit valid responses by guarding against four dangers:

1. the exclusion of part of the population from the sampling frame;
2. the refusal of some people to participate in the survey;
3. the unwillingness of some respondents to answer questions frankly;
4. the asking of confusing, leading, or inflammatory questions or questions referring to several, unimportant, or non-current events.

Much of the art and science of survey research involves overcoming these threats to validity, and experienced survey researchers are usually quite successful in achieving that aim (Converse and Presser, 1986; Ornstein, 1998). That may be why, in measuring the effects of media violence on behaviour, surveys show a weaker relationship between exposure to violent mass media and violent behaviour than experiments do, and some surveys show no relationship at all between these two variables (Anderson and Bushman, 2002; Huesmann et al., 2003; Johnson et al., 2002).

A **contingency table** is a cross-classification of cases by at least two variables that allows you to see how, if at all, the variables are associated.

Reading Tables

One of the most useful tools for analyzing survey data is the **contingency table**, a cross-classification of cases by at least two variables that allows you to see how, if at all, the variables are associated. To understand this definition, consider Table 2.2, which is based on a national survey. The survey asked respondents how many hours of TV they watched every day on average. It also asked them if they would ever approve of a man punching another adult male. Table 2.2 shows the results for these two questions—the percentage of people who ever approve of a man punching an adult male by the average amount of TV they watch daily.

Note that TV viewing, the independent variable (the presumed cause), is arrayed across the top horizontal row of the table. Attitude toward a man ever punching an adult male, the dependent variable (the presumed effect), is arrayed along the left vertical column of the table. This format is standard. The table consists of four core cells, shaded in grey. One is defined by the cross-classification of approval of punching and watching zero to two hours of TV a day on average, another by the cross-classification of approval of punching and watching three or more hours of TV a day on average, the third by the cross-classification of disapproval of punching and watching zero to two hours of TV per day on average, and the fourth by the cross-classification of disapproval of punching and watching three or more hours of TV per day on average.

To interpret tables, you must pay careful attention to what adds up to 100 percent. Table 2.2 says that 69 percent *of people who watched TV 0–2 hours a day* approved of a man punching an adult male. It does *not* say that 69 percent of all people who approved of a man punching an adult male watched TV zero to two hours a day. We know this because each category of the "TV viewing" variable equals 100 percent.

How many respondents are represented by this 69 percent? You can figure this out once you realize that the bottom row, labelled "*n*" (for number of respondents) tells us that 5188 respondents watched an average of zero to two hours of TV per day and 5022 watched an average of three or more hours of TV per day. The *69* represents 69 percent of 5188, or 3580 respondents.

A **relationship** between two variables exists if the value of one variable changes with the value of the other.

A **relationship** exists between two variables if the value of one variable changes with the value of the other. For example, if the percentage of people who approve of a man punching an adult male is *higher* among those who watch three or more hours of TV a day, a *positive* relationship exists between the two variables. If the percentage of people who approve of a man punching an adult male is *lower* among those who watch three or more hours of TV a day, a *negative* relationship exists between the two variables. The greater the percentage difference between frequent and infrequent TV viewers, the stronger the relationship. This table shows that 69 percent of respondents who watched TV zero to two hours a day approved punching compared with 65 percent of respondents who watched TV three or more hours. Is this a positive or a negative relationship? What does this finding say about the hypothesis that watching more TV causes people to become more violent?

Determining Causes

The meaning of "relationship" in research is the same as in everyday life. Relationships exist when a change in two things are systematically connected. If a change in your life systematically changes someone else's life, the two of you are related in some way. If the

TABLE 2.2

Watching TV and Approval of Violence (in percent)

Source: National Opinion Research Center. 2007. "General Social Survey." http://www.norc.org/ GSS+Website/Data+Analysis/ (accessed 24 July 2011).

	TV Viewing		
Punching Approval	**0–2 hrs/day**	**3+ hrs/day**	**Row Total**
Yes	69	65	67
No	31	35	33
Column total	100	100	100
n	5188	5022	10 210

relationship weakens, what you do in your life makes less of a difference to the other person. If the relationship disintegrates, a change in your life makes no systematic difference to that of the other person. Life goes on, but the connection is lost. In research, the same holds true, except that the components are not people but variables.

Ultimately, researchers are interested in establishing *causal* relationships. Does change in education cause change in income? Does more foreign aid improve the standard of living in receiving nations? Does increasing age at marriage reduce the divorce rate? To establish whether an independent variable causes change in a dependent variable, researchers must satisfy three criteria. We will review these criteria and illustrate them by examining the question, Do storks cause babies to appear?

The first causal criterion requires the researcher to demonstrate that the variables systematically change together. This is the *relationship* test, which establishes that the variables are in fact associated. In our example, the researcher would have to demonstrate that regions with higher numbers of storks also have higher birth rates. In fact, this is the case. Regions in Europe with fewer storks have lower birth rates (number of babies per 100 000 women), while those with more storks have higher birth rates. As a second causal criterion, researchers must establish *sequencing*, showing that the independent variable changes before changes in the dependent variable occur. If the hypothesis is that storks cause babies to appear, the researcher has to demonstrate that the storks arrived prior to the babies (and not vice versa). The first two causal criteria are straightforward; the third one, *non-spuriousness*, requires more elaboration.

Relationships between people do not exist in isolation, and neither do relationships between independent and dependent variables. Instead, connections between variables and people always exist in a context. In research, a **control variable** (or several control variables) specifies the context of a relationship. For example, a young man may declare his undying love for his date on a Saturday night, but the wise date will understand that this declaration may be influenced by the context: "What will he say when he's sober on Sunday morning?" Similarly, the relationship between family income and years of schooling a person attains in various countries may depend on whether the national postsecondary system is funded privately or by the state. High-quality state-funded schools will mute the effect of family income on years of education attained. Contexts affect relationships. In our example, the contextual issue is whether other variables are influencing the observed relationship between stork sightings and babies appearing.

Control variables identify the context for the relationship between independent and dependent variables.

The existence of control variables has an important implication for the interpretation of relationships: The appearance of a relationship between two variables does not always signify that the relationship is real. Appearances and reality do not always coincide. Just ask any broken-hearted former sweetheart.

In research, an important reason for the imperfect alignment between the appearance and the reality of relationships is the operation of control variables. Control variables may affect the nature of any apparent relationship between two variables. Since researchers are interested in identifying real relationships, before they are willing to declare that a relationship between two variables is authentic, they must investigate the influences of potentially contaminating control variables. They do this to avoid being fooled by appearances.

A relationship between an independent variable and a dependent variable may be authentic (real) or phony. Authenticity is the third criterion researchers use to determine causality. Researchers call phony relationships **spurious**. *Spuriousness occurs when change in a control variable causes change in both the independent and dependent variables.* To understand why an inauthentic relationship between two variables may appear real, you need to recall that variables exert effects when they change. This is true of all variables, including the control variables that form the context for an independent–dependent variable relationship.

A spurious relationship exists between an independent and a dependent variable when a control variable causes change in both the independent and dependent variables.

Figure 2.5 on page 48 illustrates a spurious relationship. Note that no line connects the independent and dependent variables, suggesting that the two variables are not really connected. Follow the arrows and you will see how spuriousness operates. Variation in the third variable causes changes in both the independent and dependent variables. Consequently, if you examined only the independent and dependent variables—if you ignored the context—you would

FIGURE 2.5

How Spurious Relationships Occur

Source: Lance W. Roberts

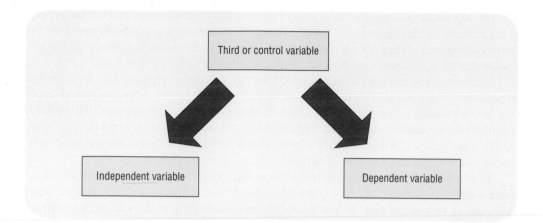

see the independent and dependent variables changing together systematically. Under spurious circumstances, you would see that independent and dependent variables are related when, in fact, they are not. You would be fooled by phony appearances.

Consider the following illustrations of spurious relationships. Earlier we introduced the relationship between the number of storks in a region (the independent variable) and the number of births in the region (the dependent variable). This apparent relationship is, in fact, spurious. In this case, the relevant third variable is whether the region is rural or urban. Rural regions have more stork sightings and higher birth rates than urban regions do. In other words, the apparent connection between stork sightings and babies appearing is not authentic; changes in both are due to regional differences. Take another example: consider the connection between the number of fire trucks at the scene of a fire (independent variable) and the amount of fire damage (dependent variable). An examination of the evidence shows an apparent relationship; as more fire trucks show up, the amount of fire damage increases. However, this is also a spurious relationship because the number of fire trucks and the amount of fire damage are due to a third variable, severity of a fire. More severe fires bring more engines to the scene and cause more damage.

Nobody likes to be fooled, least of all researchers. Therefore, researchers test for potential spuriousness in independent–dependent variable relationships. The easiest way to understand the test for spuriousness is to contrast Figure 2.5 with Figure 2.6, which illustrates what a genuine relationship looks like. In Figure 2.6, the independent and dependent variables are *actually* related, as evidenced by the double-headed arrow connecting them. Moreover, in this diagram, the third variable is *unconnected* to either the independent or dependent variable.

Comparing the spurious and genuine diagrams, we see that the operation of the third variable has either nothing to do with the independent–dependent variable connection (the authentic case, Figure 2.6), or everything to do with the appearance of such a connection (the spurious case, Figure 2.5). Based on this crucial difference between the authentic and inauthentic models, researchers have devised a test for determining the existence of spuriousness. The key idea of the test involves examining the independent–dependent variable

FIGURE 2.6

How Authentic Relationships Occur

Source: Lance W. Roberts

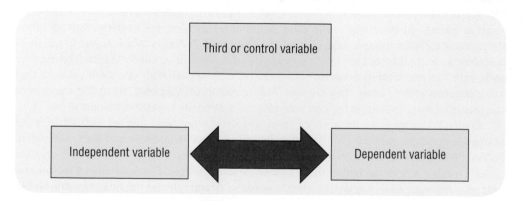

relationship under two conditions—first, when the third variable is allowed to *change* and, second, when the third variable is *held constant*. Using these comparisons, here is how the test for spuriousness works. If the independent–dependent variable relationship is authentic, then the original independent–dependent variable relationship is evident under both conditions, that is, when the third variable is allowed to vary and when it is held constant. By contrast, if the original relationship is spurious, the independent–dependent variable connection is evident only when the third variable is changing (the first condition) and disappears when the third variable is held constant (the second condition).

We can appreciate this logic by returning to our examples. If the connection between storks and babies were authentic (real), then it would be unaffected by the third variable, region. Here is how the test would occur. Under the first condition, the researcher would examine the connection between stork sightings and babies appearing for all regions (i.e., both rural and urban). In this condition, the third variable (region) is being allowed to change. As reported previously, the relationship between stork sightings and babies appearing is evident under this condition. Next, under the second condition, the researcher would examine the storks–babies connection *only for rural regions* and then *only for urban regions*. In doing so, the researcher would be examining the independent–dependent variable connection with the third variable being held constant. This second test would reveal no connection between stork sightings and babies appearing. The researcher would then conclude the storks–babies relationship is spurious because the relationship is evident in the first condition but disappeared in the second condition.

In summary form, here is how the test applies to the fire trucks–fire damage relationship. Condition 1: Examine this independent–dependent variable relationship for all kinds of fires. The evidence will indicate an apparent connection. Condition 2: Examine the fire trucks–fire damage connection *only for small fires* and then *only for large fires*. The evidence will show no connection between the independent and dependent variables. The inability to replicate the relationship under the two conditions leads to the conclusion that the apparent relationship is spurious.

This understanding of the test for spuriousness parallels the situation in everyday life. Imagine you meet someone in a bar this weekend and, after a night of partying, you declare love for each other. Three variables are operating in this situation: your feelings, the other person's feelings, and alcohol. How can you test if your declaration is authentic or spurious? If the declaration is authentic, it will remain the same when the third variable is removed (when you sober up). If the declaration is spurious it will disappear when the third variable is no longer operating.

To summarize, researchers conclude there is a causal connection between two variables when they successfully demonstrate that

1. the variables systematically change together (the relationship criterion);
2. the independent variable changed before observed changes in the dependent variable (the sequencing criterion); and
3. the observed relationship is an authentic one (the non-spuriousness criterion).

Sampling

Demonstrating causal connections is the ultimate goal of both experiments and surveys, but the two methods accomplish this goal in different ways. Experimenters randomly allocate subjects to experimental and control groups, and by repeating an experiment many times, they gain confidence that the only difference between the two groups is that just one of them is exposed to the independent variable. If they observe differences between experimental and control groups after the experimental group is exposed to the independent variable, they know the differences result from the fact that the experimental group alone was exposed to the independent variable. In contrast, survey researchers seek to demonstrate causality by drawing representative samples of the population, asking questions that measure variables of interest, examining relationships between independent and dependent variables, and seeing how the introduction of control variables affects those relationships.

How can survey researchers draw a representative sample? They can't just recruit volunteers or people who are easy to reach because people chosen in this way are almost

In a **probability sample**, the units have a known and nonzero chance of being selected.

certainly unrepresentative of the population. Instead, they have to choose respondents at random, and the chance of choosing an individual must be known and greater than zero. We call a sample with these characteristics a **probability sample**.

To draw a probability sample, you first need a *sampling frame*. This is a list of all the people in the population of interest. You also need a randomizing method. This is a way of ensuring every person in the sampling frame has a known and nonzero chance of being selected.

Up-to-date membership lists of organizations are useful sampling frames if you want to survey members of organizations, but if you want to investigate, say, the religious beliefs of Canadians, then the membership lists of places of worship are inadequate because many Canadians do not belong to such institutions. In such cases, you might turn to another frequently used sampling frame, the telephone directory. The telephone directory for the entire country is now available on DVD, but even it lacks the names and addresses of some poor and homeless people (who do not have phones) and some rich people (who have unlisted phone numbers). Computer programs are available that dial residential phone numbers at random, including unlisted numbers. However, even these random-digit dialling techniques exclude from their sampling frame Canadian households who do not have a telephone (about 1.3 percent of households).

As the example of the telephone directory shows, few sampling frames are perfect. Even the largest and most expensive survey in Canada, the census, misses an estimated 2 percent of the population. Researchers believe that much of the undercounted population is composed of specific groups, such as homeless people, Aboriginal Canadians, and illegal immigrants, thus introducing sampling bias. Nevertheless, researchers maximize the accuracy of their generalizations by using the least-biased sampling frames available and adjusting their analyses and conclusions to take account of known sampling bias.

Once you choose or create a sampling frame, you must select respondents by a chance process. One way to do this is by picking, say, the 10th person in the sampling frame and then every 20th (or 30th or 100th) person after that, depending on how many people you need in the sample. A second method is to assign the number 1 to the first person in the sampling frame, the number 2 to the next person, and so on. Then you create a separate list of random numbers by using a computer or consulting a table of random numbers, which you can find at the back of almost any elementary statistics book or online. Your list of random numbers should have the same number of entries as the number of people you want in your sample. The individuals whose assigned numbers correspond to the list of random numbers are the people in your sample.

CP Picture Archive/Ken Frayer

Homelessness is increasingly a focus of public policy. But public support may not be adequate if the homeless are not counted properly in the census. Statistics Canada first included a count of the homeless in the 2001 census. However, because the count is based on information about the use of shelters and soup kitchens, combined with an attempt at street counts, these numbers are only estimates.

Sample Size and Statistical Significance

How many respondents do you need in a sample? That depends on how much inaccuracy you are willing to tolerate. Large samples give more precise results than small samples do. For most sociological purposes, however, a random sample of 1500 people will give acceptably accurate results, even if the population of interest is the entire adult population of Canada. More precisely, if you draw 20 random samples of 1500 individuals each, 19 of them will provide estimates that will be accurate within 2.5 percent of actual population values. This level of accuracy is called the *margin of error*. Imagine, for instance, that 50 percent of the people in a random sample of 1500 respondents say they support the New Democratic Party (NDP). We can be reasonably confident that only 1 in 20 random samples of that size will *not* yield results between 47.5 percent and 52.5 percent. This confidence comes from adding and subtracting the margin of error (2.5 percent) to the original estimate. When we read that a finding is statistically significant, it usually means we can expect similar findings in 19 out of 20 samples of the same size. Said differently, researchers in the social sciences are generally prepared to tolerate a 5 percent chance that the characteristics of a population are different from the characteristics of their sample (1/20 = 5 percent). If the survey showed that 52 percent of the respondents support the NDP and 48 percent support the Conservatives, the appropriate conclusion is *not* that the NDP are in the lead. Instead, you should conclude that there is no detectable difference in support for the two parties given the 2.5 percent margin of error in the survey (see Figure 2.7).

In short, probability sampling enables us to conduct surveys that permit us to generalize from a sample to the population within known margins of error.

Field Research

Field research is the third major method in sociology. It involves systematically observing people wherever they happen to associate naturally.

When researchers go into the field, they come prepared with strategies to ensure their observations are accurate. One such strategy is **detached observation,** which involves classifying and counting the behaviour of interest according to a predetermined scheme. Although useful for some purposes, two main problems confound direct observation. First, the presence of the researcher may cause **reactivity**; the observed people may conceal certain things or act artificially to impress the researcher (Webb et al., 1966). Second, the meaning of the observed behaviour may remain obscure to the researcher. A wink may be an involuntary muscle contraction, an indication of a secret being kept, a sexual come-on, and so on. We can't know what a wink means just by observing it.

To avoid reactivity and understand the meaning of behaviour, we must be able to see it in its social context and from the point of view of the people we are observing. To do that, researchers must immerse themselves in their subjects' world by learning their language and their culture in depth. When sociologists observe a social setting systematically *and* take part in the activities of the people they are studying, they are engaging in **participant observation** research (Lofland and Lofland, 1995 [1971]).

For example, participant observation research helps us better understand how media violence may influence youth violence. Sociologists have spent time in schools where shooting rampages have taken place; lived in the neighbourhoods where they occur; interviewed students, teachers, neighbours, and shooters' family members; and studied police and psychological reports, and the shooters' own writings (Harding, Fox, and Mehta, 2002; Sullivan, 2002). Based on their observations, they have concluded that only a small number of young people who are weakly connected to family, school, community, and peers are at risk of translating media violence into violent behaviour. Lack of social support allows them to magnify their personal problems, and if guns are available, they are prone to using violent media messages as models for their own behaviour. In contrast, for the great majority of young people, violence in the mass media is just a source of entertainment and a fantasy outlet for emotional issues (Anderson, 2003).

Like other research methods, participant observation has strengths and weaknesses. On the plus side, it allows researchers to develop a deep and sympathetic understanding of the way people see the world. It is especially useful in the "exploratory" stage of research,

Field research is research based on the observation of people in their natural settings.

Detached observation involves classifying and counting the behaviour of interest according to a predetermined scheme.

Reactivity occurs when the presence of a researcher causes the observed people to conceal certain things or act artificially to impress the researcher.

Participant observation involves carefully observing people's face-to-face interactions and participating in their lives over a long period of time, thus achieving a deep and sympathetic understanding of what motivates them to act in the way they do.

FIGURE 2.7

The Margin of Error in a Sample

In a sample of 1500 people, 48 percent of the respondents support the Conservatives and 50 percent support the New Democrats. However, because the 2.5 percent margins of error overlap, we cannot be sure whether support for the two parties differs in the population. To conclude that support for the two parties differs in the population, the margins of error must not overlap.

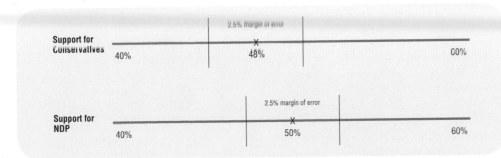

when investigators have only a vague sense of what they are looking for and little sense of what they will discover, and where theory is weakly developed. On the minus side, because participant observation research usually involves just one researcher in one social setting, it is difficult to know if other researchers would measure things in the same way (the reliability problem). Moreover, there is often no way to check whether the researcher is actually measuring what he or she thinks is being measured (the validity problem) and it is difficult to know how broadly findings may be generalized to other settings (the generalizability problem). Experiments and surveys allow for greater reliability, validity, and generalizability than participant observation does (see Figure 2.8).

Analysis of Existing Documents and Official Statistics

The fourth important sociological research method involves analysis of **existing documents and official statistics** that are created by people other than the researcher for purposes other than sociological research.

The types of existing documents that sociologists have mined most widely are diaries, newspapers, and published historical works. For example, one of the early classics of American sociology, a study of Polish immigrants, was based on a close reading of immigrants' diaries and letters (Thomas and Znaniecki, 1958 [1918–20]). More recently, sociologists have made outstanding contributions to the study of political protest by systematically classifying nineteenth- and early-twentieth-century French, Italian, and British newspaper accounts of strikes and demonstrations (Tilly, Tilly, and Tilly, 1975).

Sociologists have also tried to discover the conditions that led some countries to dictatorship and others to democracy, some to economic development and others to underdevelopment, some to becoming thoroughly globalized and others to remaining less tied to global social processes. In trying to answer such broad questions, they have relied on published histories as their main source of data. No other method would allow the breadth of coverage and depth of analysis required for such comparative and historical work. For example, Barrington Moore (1967) spent a decade reading the histories of Britain, France, Russia, Germany, China, India, and other countries to figure out the social origins of dictatorship and democracy in the modern world. Immanuel Wallerstein (1974–89) canvassed the history of virtually the entire world to make sense of why some countries became industrialized while others remain less developed. What distinguishes this type of research from purely historical work is the kind of questions posed by the researchers. Moore and Wallerstein asked the same kind of big, theoretical questions (and used the same kinds of

Existing documents and official statistics are created by people other than the researcher for purposes other than sociological research.

FIGURE 2.8

Measurement as Target Practice: Validity, Reliability, and Generalizability Compared

We can illustrate the meaning of validity, reliability, and generalizability by drawing an analogy between measuring a variable and firing at a bull's-eye. In case 1, shots (measures) are far apart (not reliable) and far from the bull's-eye (not valid). In case 2, shots are close to each other (reliable) but far from the bull's-eye (not valid). In case 3, shots are close to the bull's-eye (valid) and close to each other (reliable). In case 4, we use a second target. Our shots are again close to each other (reliable) and close to the bull's-eye (valid). Because our measures were valid and reliable for both the targets in cases 3 and 4, we conclude our results are generalizable.

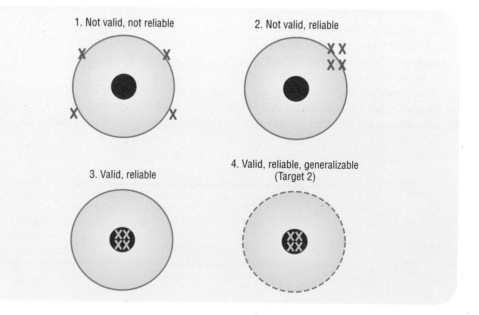

research methods) as Marx and Weber did. They have inspired a generation of younger sociologists to adopt a similar approach. Comparative-historical research is therefore one of the growth areas of the discipline.

Census data, police crime reports, and records of key life events are perhaps the most frequently used sources of official statistics. Canadian censuses have been conducted regularly since 1871. The modern census tallies the number of Canadian residents and classifies them by place of residence, race, ethnic origin, occupation, age, and hundreds of other variables (see Box 2.1). Statistics Canada publishes an annual Uniform Crime Reporting (UCR)

BOX 2.1

It's Your Choice

PRIVACY, COERCION, AND THE CANADIAN CENSUS

Statistics Canada conducts a census every five years. Academics, businesses, government agencies, and non-governmental organizations rely on the breadth, depth, and accuracy of the census to develop strategic plans. Because of its importance in economic and social planning, the law has until recently required all adults to complete the census questionnaire. Penalties for refusing include fines and imprisonment.

In recent decades, Statistics Canada has issued two types of census questionnaires, a "short" and a "long" form. The short form consists of about eight basic socio-demographic questions. The long form consists of

about 60 questions on topics such as home life, work, and ethnicity. Statistics Canada distributes the short form to all households. Until recently, it distributed the long form to 20 percent of households.

In 2010, the federal Conservative government announced that, beginning in 2011, it would replace the mandatory long-form census with a *voluntary* National Household Survey (NHS) distributed to 33 percent of households. The Conservatives gave three reasons for the decision. They claimed that mandatory collection intrudes on people's privacy rights; that threatening non-respondents with fines or imprisonment is unjustifiably coercive; and that the voluntary NHS will in any case provide information that is just as accurate as that provided by the mandatory long-form census.

Scrapping the long-form census produced a groundswell of opposition from a wide range of interest groups in the private, public, and not-for-profit sectors that rely on the detailed information in the long-form census. Their opposition centred on the following points:

- The voluntary NHS will not provide information equivalent to that gained from the mandatory long-form census. The threat of sanctions influences the participation rate, so the NHS results will be less representative, less accurate, and therefore less useful.
- While the mandatory census threatens sanctions for non-compliance, these are not coercive. There are few instances of fines for non-responders, and no instances of imprisonment.

- The broad, collective interests of the many groups that rely on long-form census information outweigh the narrow, individual interests underlying the government's opposition.
- Without the detailed, accurate information provided by the long-form census, many important possibilities for analysis will be lost. For instance, Canadians will no longer be able to evaluate the representativeness of other surveys by comparing them to census standards, examine long-term trends in Canadian society based on comparable data, and conduct detailed analysis of sub-group populations, such as ethnic and racial groups.
- The government's decision to scrap the compulsory long-form census appears motivated more by ideological considerations than by evidence. The resignation of Munir Sheikh, the widely respected chief statistician and head of Statistics Canada, in opposition to the government's move, indicates that political interests are overruling technical expertise.

Given the importance of the mandatory long-form census in shaping our understanding of Canadian society, do you agree with the government's decision? Is requiring citizens to share information about their personal, home, and work life too intrusive? Is the long-form census a case where the collective good should prevail over individual interests? As a citizen who is influenced by policy decisions that are based in part on the accuracy of census data, it's your choice.

Survey that reports the number of crimes in Canada and classifies them by location and type of crime, age and sex of offenders and victims, and other variables. Provincial governments publish annual vital statistics reports of births, deaths, marriages, and divorces by sex, age, and so on.

Existing documents and official statistics have several advantages over other types of data. They can save the researcher time and money because they are usually available at no cost in libraries or on the World Wide Web. Official statistics usually cover entire populations and are collected by using rigorous and uniform methods, thus yielding high-quality data. The analysis of data from existing documents and official statistics is the only sociological method that does not require live subjects, so it is especially useful for historical analysis. Finally, since the method does not require live subjects, reactivity is not a problem; the researcher's presence does not influence the subjects' behaviour.

However, existing documents and official statistics share one big disadvantage. These data sources are not created with the researchers' needs in mind. They often contain biases that reflect the interests of the individuals and organizations that created them. Therefore, they may be less than ideal for research purposes and must always be treated cautiously.

Still, such sources can be extremely useful. For instance, census and crime data put the limited effect of media violence on violent behaviour into perspective. Researchers have discovered big differences in violent behaviour when they compare the United States and Canada. The homicide rate (the number of murders per 100 000 people) has historically been about three to four times higher in the United States. Yet TV programming, movies, and video games are nearly identical in the two countries, so exposure to media violence can't account for the difference. Many researchers instead attribute the difference in homicide rates to the higher level of economic and social inequality and the wider availability of handguns in the United States (Government of Canada, 2002; Lenton, 1989; National Rifle Association, 2005; Sternheimer, 2007).

The preceding discussion should give you a pretty good idea of the basic methodological issues that confront any sociological research project. You should also know the strengths and weaknesses of some of the most widely used data collection techniques (summarized in Table 2.3).

TABLE 2.3
Strengths and Weaknesses of Four Research Methods

Method	Strengths	Weaknesses
Experiments	High reliability; excellent for establishing cause-and-effect relationships	Low validity for many sociology problems
Surveys	High reliability; useful for establishing cause-and-effect relationships; good generalizability if based on representative samples	Potential problems with validity unless researchers take stringent precautions
Participant observation	Allows researchers to get "inside" the minds of their subjects and discover their worldview; especially useful for exploratory research where theory is weakly developed	Low reliability; low validity; low generalizability; not very useful for establishing cause-and-effect relationships
Analysis of existing documents and official statistics	Often inexpensive and easy to obtain, provides good coverage; useful for historical analysis; non-reactive	Can contain biases reflecting the interests of their creators and not the interests of the researcher

Summing Up

- Experiments, surveys, participant observation, and the analysis of existing documents and official statistics are the major methods by which sociologists empirically test their ideas.
- Identifying causes requires researchers to demonstrate a substantial connection, sequence, and non-spuriousness of the relationship between the independent and dependent variable.
- Different methods have different strengths and weaknesses and are useful for different research purposes.

THE IMPORTANCE OF BEING SUBJECTIVE

By now you should have a pretty good idea of the basic methodological issues that confront any sociological research project. You should also understand the strengths and weaknesses of some of the most widely used data collection techniques.

Our synopsis of sociology's tools for checking the reality status of ideas should not obscure the fact that sociological research questions often spring from real-life experiences and the pressing concerns of the day. However, before sociological analysis, we rarely see things as they are. We see them as *we* are. Then, a sort of waltz begins. Subjectivity leads; objectivity follows. When the dance is finished, we see things more accurately (see Box 2.2).

Feminism provides a prime example of this process. Here is a *political* movement of people and ideas that, since the 1960s, has helped shape the sociological *research* agenda. The division of labour in the household, violence against women, the effects of child-rearing responsibilities on women's careers, the social barriers to women's participation in politics and the armed forces, and many other related concerns were sociological "non-issues" before the rise of the modern feminist movement. Sociologists did not study these problems. Effectively, they did not exist for the sociological community (although they did, of course, exist for women). However, subjectivity led. Feminism as a political movement brought these and many other concerns to the attention of the Canadian public. Objectivity followed. Large parts of the sociological community began doing rigorous research on feminist-inspired issues and greatly refined our knowledge of them.

The entire sociological perspective began to shift as a growing number of scholars abandoned gender-biased research (Eichler, 1988b; Tavris, 1992). Thus, approaching sociological problems from an exclusively male perspective is now less common than it used to be. For instance, it is less likely in 2012 than in 1962 that a sociologist would study work but ignore unpaid housework as one type of labour. Similarly, sociologists now frown on using data on one gender to draw conclusions about all people. As these advances in sociological thinking show, and as has often been the case in the history of the discipline, objective sociological knowledge has been enhanced as a result of subjective experiences. And so the waltz continues. As in *Alice in Wonderland*, the question now is, "Will you, won't you, will you, won't you, will you join the dance?"

Summing Up

- Sociological research is a process that relies on the interplay between subjective assessments and objective confirmation of experience.
- For instance, the ideas of the feminist movement have widened the scope of both the formulation of sociological research questions and the interpretation of evidence.

Sociology at the Movies

KINSEY

In early-twentieth-century New Jersey, Alfred Kinsey's father sermonized that the telephone and the automobile were the devil's work, promoting impure thoughts, petting, and all manner of sexual perversions. The adolescent Alfred rejected his father's Puritanism and petty tyranny. He escaped to Harvard to study biology and zoology. He devoted 20 years to collecting and analyzing 100 000 specimens of the gall wasp, but underneath his mania for counting, classifying, and marvelling at natural diversity, his rebellion against sexual repression and imposed sexual uniformity never ended.

In the 1930s, Kinsey began to investigate human sexual behaviour with the same fervour he had formerly invested in the gall wasp.

He and his associates conducted more than 18 000 interviews that formed the basis of two best-selling volumes on human sexual behaviour. In an era when masturbation, contraception, and premarital sex were widely considered sins, Kinsey's work sparked a revolution in attitudes toward sex. For many North Americans, his findings were liberating. For others, they were filthy lies that threatened to undermine the nation's moral fibre. Both reactions, and the life of the man who caused them, are portrayed in *Kinsey*, starring Liam Neeson.

Equipped with the information in this chapter, you can appreciate that Kinsey's methods were primitive and biased by modern sociological standards. We single out four main problems:

1. *Sampling*. Kinsey relied on a "convenience sample" of respondents. He and his colleagues interviewed accessible volunteers rather than a randomized and representative sample of the American population. About one-third of Kinsey's respondents were prostitutes, homosexuals, patients in psychiatric hospitals, residents of homes for unwed mothers, and the like. Two-thirds of these people were convicted felons. Five percent were male prostitutes. It is difficult to generalize from Kinsey's work because his sample is unrepresentative.

2. *Questionnaire design*. Kinsey required that his interviewers memorize long questionnaires including 350 or more questions. He encouraged them to adapt the wording and ordering of the questions to suit the "level" of the respondent. Research now shows that even subtle changes in question wording and ordering can produce sharply different results. Moreover, long surveys typically produce invalid results because they induce respondent fatigue.

3. *Interviewing*. People are generally reluctant to discuss sex with strangers. To gain cooperation, Kinsey and his colleagues did not remain

SUMMARY

1. **What is the aim of science and how is it achieved?**
   The aim of science is to arrive at knowledge that is less subjective than other ways of knowing. A degree of objectivity is achieved by testing ideas against systematically collected data and leaving research open to public scrutiny.

2. **Does science have a subjective side?**
   It does. The subjective side of the research enterprise is no less important than the objective side. Creativity and the motivation to study new problems from new perspectives arise from individual passions and interests.

3. **What methodological issues must be addressed in any research project?**
   To maximize the scientific value of a research project, researchers must address issues of reliability (consistency in measurement), validity (precision in measurement),

Liam Neeson as Alfred Kinsey

Ken Regan/TWENTIETH CENTURY FOX/Bureau L.A.Collections/Corbis

neutral. Instead, they expressed empathy with the pains and frustrations many respondents expressed, often reassuring them that their sexual histories were normal and decent. Today, researchers frown on any departure from neutrality in the interview situation because it may influence respondents to answer questions in a less than truthful way.

4. *Data analysis*. It is unclear how Kinsey decided whether the effect of one variable on another was significant. He rarely used statistical tests for this purpose. He never introduced control variables to see if observed associations between variables were spurious. Moreover, he saw no problem in lumping together data collected over decades, even when sexual attitudes and behaviour dramatically changed during the period.

Since Kinsey, researchers have conducted many hundreds of surveys of the sexual behaviour of North Americans. Today, using modern research methods, we are able to describe and explain sexual behaviour more accurately and insightfully than did Kinsey and his colleagues. We know that many of the details of Kinsey's writings are suspect. However, we also know that despite the serious methodological problems summarized above, his basic finding is accurate. The sexual behaviour of North Americans is highly diverse.

generalizability (the applicability of findings beyond the case studied), and causality (cause-and-effect relations among variables).

4. **What is an experiment?**
An experiment is a carefully controlled artificial situation that allows researchers to isolate hypothesized causes and measure their effects by randomizing the allocation of subjects to experimental and control groups and exposing only the experimental group to an independent variable. Experiments get high marks for reliability and analysis of causality, but validity issues make them less than ideal for many sociological research purposes.

5. **What is a survey?**
In a survey, people are asked questions about their knowledge, attitudes, or behaviour, either in a face-to-face interview, telephone interview, or paper-and-pencil format. Surveys rank high on reliability and validity as long as researchers train interviewers well, phrase questions carefully, and take special measures to ensure high response rates. Generalizability is achieved through probability sampling, statistical control, and the analysis of causality by means of data manipulation.

6. What is participant observation?

Participant observation is one of the main sociological methods. It involves carefully observing people's face-to-face interactions and participating in their lives over a long period. Participant observation is particularly useful for doing exploratory research. Issues of validity, reliability, generalizability, and causality make participant observation less useful for other research purposes.

7. What are the advantages and disadvantages of using existing documents and official statistics as sources of sociological data?

Existing documents and official statistics are inexpensive and convenient sources of high-quality data. However, they must be used cautiously because they often reflect the biases of the individuals or organizations that created them.

KEY TERMS

abstract experience (p. 37)	pattern (p. 36)
concept (p. 37)	percept (p. 36)
concrete experience (p. 36)	population (p. 39)
contingency table (p. 46)	probability sample (p. 50)
control variable (p. 47)	proposition (p. 37)
dependent variable (p. 44)	randomization (p. 43)
detached observation (p. 51)	reactivity (p. 51)
existing documents and official statistics (p. 52)	relationship (p. 46)
	reliability (p. 44)
experiment (p. 43)	sample (p. 39)
field research (p. 51)	spurious relationship (p. 47)
hypothesis (p. 43)	survey (p. 44)
independent variable (p. 44)	validity (p. 44)
operationalization (p. 42)	variable (p. 42)
participant observation (p. 51)	

WEB RESOURCES

Companion Website for This Book

http://www.compass4e.nelson.com

Begin by clicking on the Student Resources section of the website. Next, select the chapter you are studying from the pull-down menu. From the Student Resources page you have easy access to additional Weblinks and other resources. The website also has many useful tips to aid you in your study of sociology, including practice tests for each chapter.

InfoTrac® Search Terms

These search terms are provided to assist you in beginning to conduct research on this topic by visiting http://www.infotrac-college.com:

census
historical sociology
participant observation
sociological survey
sociology experiment

Basic Social Processes

CHAPTER

3

Culture

IN THIS CHAPTER, YOU WILL LEARN THAT

- Culture is a shared set of symbols and their definitions.

- Humans thrive in their environments because of their unique ability to generate and use culture. Crucial aspects of culture include the ability to think abstractly, cooperate, and make tools and other artefacts.

- Although sociologists recognize that biology sets broad human limits and potentials, most sociologists do not believe that specific human behaviours and social arrangements are biologically determined.

- In some respects, the development of culture makes people freer. As cultures become more diversified and consensus declines, people have more choice in how they live.

- In other respects, the development of culture puts limits on who we can become.

© Robert Churchill/iStockphoto.com

CULTURE AS PROBLEM SOLVING

If you follow sports, you probably know that many athletes perform little rituals before each game. Canadian hockey legend Sidney Crosby is a prime example. On game day he enters the home arena through a circuitous route to ensure he doesn't pass the visitors' locker room, tapes his sticks a specific way, eats a peanut butter and jam sandwich at precisely 5 p.m., performs a sequenced series of stretches, suits up in a programmed manner, and performs a unique pre-game handshake before stepping on the ice.

The superstitious practices of athletes make some people chuckle. However, such rituals put athletes at ease. Many students have rituals that serve the same function when they are under exam stress. Some wear a lucky piece of jewellery or item of clothing. Others say special words or a quick prayer. Still others cross themselves. Others engage in more elaborate rituals. One study reports on a student who felt she would do well only if she ate a sausage and two eggs sunny-side up on the morning of each exam. She always placed the sausage vertically on the left side of her plate and the eggs to the right of the sausage—so they formed the "100" percent she was aiming for (Albas and Albas, 1989). Of course, the ritual had a more direct influence on her cholesterol level than on her grades. Yet indirectly it may have had the desired effect. To the degree it helped relieve her anxiety and help her relax, she may have done better on her exams.

Like all elements of culture, superstitions help people to solve the challenges of life. Whether the challenge involves winning a hockey game, performing well on exams, building a house, or facing death, humans turn to their culture for solutions. At the root of culture is solving the problem of meaning.

CULTURE AS MEANING GENERATOR

Chapter 2 introduced a distinction between concrete and abstract levels of experience. The concrete level is composed of your empirical sensations of touch, taste, smell, sound, and sight. Viewing the squiggles in Figure 3.1 will give you several examples of concrete experience. Examine them carefully. What do the squiggles on each line mean to you?

For most readers of this book, the squiggles will be meaningless. This result does not occur because your eyesight is poor. It occurs because concrete, physical sensations, by themselves, are meaningless.

Now read the following sentence: *Were it otherwise, you would understand the marks on this page without learning to read English.* The squiggles in the preceding sentence are meaningful, English words. Culture gives concrete experience meaning.

By the way, the first line in Figure 3.1 is gobbledygook. The remaining three lines are not. They are translations of the italicized sentence in the previous paragraph, expressed in Chinese, Romanian, and German. If you are appropriately connected to Chinese, Romanian, or German culture, the respective lines in Figure 3.1 would be just as meaningful to you as their English counterpart.

FIGURE 3.1
Four Concrete Texts

在相反的情况下，你可以不必学习汉语就能明白此页中的标记。

În caz contrar, ar trebui să înțeleagă notele de pe această pagină, fără a învăța să citească în limba română.

Wäre es anders, könnten Sie die Noten auf dieser Seite verstehen ohne das Sie auf Deutsch lesen lernten.

The power of culture is that it makes our sensory experiences meaningful. Once your cultural experience conditions you to interpret concrete experiences a certain way, this becomes your reality. As evidence, notice that you cannot interpret the squiggles on this page as anything but English words. Similar, readers of Chinese cannot see the second line in Figure 3.1 as anything but Chinese, and readers of Germans cannot see the final line as anything but German.

Culture Defined

In everyday speech, "culture" often refers to **high culture** (opera, ballet, etc.) or **popular culture** (movies, pop music, etc.). For sociologists, however, the definition of culture is much broader. Sociologically speaking, **culture** consists of the shared symbols and their definitions that people create to solve real-life problems. To understand this definition, we need to elaborate its components. Let's start with the term "symbol."

Symbols are concrete things or abstract terms that represent something else. The gold ring on my finger is an object that represents my marital status. The term "Big Mac" is an abstract term that represents a particular type of hamburger supplied by a fast-food establishment. Symbols fill human experience.

The meaning of a symbol is not in the symbol; the meaning resides in what it refers to. For this reason, symbols always have an abstract dimension. This abstract feature of symbols is what the "and their definitions" aspect of culture refers to. A symbol's "definition" informs us what a symbol represents.

Our definition of culture says that symbols are *shared*. Idiosyncratic symbols are not part of culture. A psychotic person who believes that rain clouds represent happiness is using a symbol that is not part of culture. So too are the special terms and signs of endearment that lovers create between themselves. Culture is composed of symbols whose meanings are shared among a substantial number of people. The definition of a pencil as an instrument for writing is part of your culture. So is the idea that obtaining a university degree will improve your life. Members of a community who acquire a set of shared, meaningful symbols participate in a common culture.

Culture is the primary driver of what people do because individuals respond to the meaning of events, and the meaning of events is defined by our culture. Culture intervenes between concrete experience and our responses by assigning significance. As a child, you looked at the night sky and only saw a pattern of twinkling lights. Over time, your culture provided you with concepts like "star" and "Big Dipper." Now, when you look up at night you can distinguish stars, planets, comets, and constellations. The same holds for all your experiences. First you "look" (the concrete behaviour part), then you "name" (the cultural part), and then you "see" (the abstract understanding part).

The Origins of Culture

Culture is the primary means by which humans adapt to their environments; that is why our definition of culture emphasizes that we create culture to solve real-life problems. You can appreciate the importance of culture for human survival by considering the predicament of early humans about 100 000 years ago. They lived in harsh natural environments. They had poor physical endowments, being slower runners and weaker fighters than many other animals. Yet, despite these disadvantages, they survived. They prospered largely because they were the smartest creatures around. Their sophisticated brains enabled them to create cultural "survival kits" of enormous complexity and flexibility. These cultural survival kits contained three main tools. Each tool was a uniquely human talent. Each gave rise to a different element of culture.

The first tool in the cultural survival kit is **abstraction**, the ability to create general concepts that organize sensory experience in meaningful ways. You learned about this process in Chapter 2, which discussed the conceptualization process. The concepts that result from abstraction are the most pervasive type of symbols in human cultures. This is why language is so important to the preservation of any culture.

High culture is culture consumed mainly by upper classes (opera, ballet, etc.).

Popular culture (or mass culture) is culture consumed by all classes.

Culture consists of the shared symbols and their definitions that people create to solve real-life problems.

Symbols are concrete things or abstract terms that represent something else.

Abstraction is the ability to create general concepts that meaningfully organize concrete, sensory experience.

Concepts allow humans to organize, classify, interpret, and generalize their experiences. For instance, we recognize that we can sit on many objects but that only some of them have four legs, a back, and space for one person. We distinguish the latter from other objects by giving them a name: chairs. By the time most babies reach the end of their first year, they have heard the word "chair" often and understand that it refers to a certain class of objects.

Cooperation is the second tool in the human cultural survival kit. It is the capacity to create a complex social life by establishing **norms**, or generally accepted ways of doing things, and **values**, or ideas that identify desirable states (conditions that are true, good, or beautiful). For example, family members cooperate to raise children, and in the process, they develop and apply norms and values about which child-rearing practices are appropriate and desirable. Note, however, that different times and places give rise to different norms and values. Contemporary parents might ground children for swearing, but in pioneer times, parents would typically "beat the devil out of them." As this example suggests, by analyzing how people cooperate and produce norms and values, we can learn much about what distinguishes one culture from another.

Production is the third main tool in the human cultural survival kit. It involves making and using tools and techniques that improve our ability to take what we want from nature. We call such tools and techniques **material culture** because they are tangible, whereas symbols, norms, values, and other elements of **non-material culture** are intangible. All animals take from nature to subsist, and apes may sometimes use rocks to break other objects, or walking sticks to steady themselves as they cross fast-flowing streams. However, only humans are intelligent and agile enough to manufacture tools and use them to produce everything from food to satellites. In this sense, production is a uniquely human activity.

Table 3.1 lists each of the human capacities we have discussed and illustrates their cultural offshoots in the field of medicine. As in medicine, so in all fields of human activity: abstraction, cooperation, and production give rise to specific kinds of ideas, norms, and elements of material culture that help us deal with real-life problems.

Index Stock/Frank Chmura

By cooperating, people are able to accomplish things that no person could possibly do alone.

Cooperation is the capacity to create a complex social life by establishing generally accepted ways of doing things and ideas about what is right and wrong.

Norms are generally accepted ways of doing things.

Values are ideas that identify desirable states (conditions that are true, good, or beautiful.)

Production is the human capacity to make and use tools. It improves our ability to take what we want from nature.

Material culture comprises the tools and techniques that enable people to get tasks accomplished.

Non-material culture is composed of symbols, norms, and other intangible elements.

The human capacity for... Gives rise to these elements of culture	Abstraction ↓ Ideas	Cooperation ↓ Norms and values	Production ↓ Material culture
In medicine, for example...	*Theories* are developed about how a certain drug might cure a disease.	*Experiments* are conducted to test whether the drug works as expected.	*Treatments* are developed on the basis of the experimental results.

TABLE 3.1
The Building Blocks of Culture

Source: Adapted from Bierstedt (1963).

Three Types of Norms: Folkways, Mores, and Taboos

Folkways are the least important norms and they evoke the least severe punishment.

Mores (pronounced MOR-ays) are core norms that most people believe are essential for the survival of their group or their society.

Taboos are among the strongest norms. When someone violates a taboo, it causes revulsion in the community and punishment is severe.

If a man walks down a busy street wearing nothing on the top half of his body, he is violating a **folkway**. If he walks down the street wearing nothing on the bottom half of his body, he is violating a **more** (the Latin word for "custom," pronounced MOR-ay). Folkways are norms that specify social *preferences*. Mores are norms that specify social *requirements*. People are usually punished when they violate norms, but the punishment is usually minor if the norm is a folkway. Some onlookers will raise their eyebrows at the shirtless man. Others will shake their head in disapproval. In contrast, the punishment for walking down the street without pants is bound to be moderately harsh. Someone is bound to call the police, probably sooner than later (Sumner, 1940 [1907]). The strongest and most central norms, however, are **taboos**. When someone violates a taboo, it causes revulsion in the community, and punishment is severe. Incest is one of the most widespread taboos.

Summing Up

- Culture consists of the shared symbols and their definitions that people create to solve real-life problems and that give human life meaning.
- Culture supports human adaption to the environment by means of abstraction, coordination, and production.

CULTURE AND BIOLOGY

"Nature, Mr. Allnut, is what we are put in this world to rise above."
— Rose Sayer (Katharine Hepburn) in *The African Queen* (1951)

The Evolution of Human Behaviour

We have seen how the human capacity for abstraction, cooperation, and production enables us to create culture and makes us distinctively human. This capacity is built on a solid biological foundation. Biology, as every sociologist recognizes, sets broad human limits and potentials, including the potential to create culture.

Some biologically trained students of human behaviour go a step further. For example, evolutionary psychologists claim that genes—chemical units that carry traits from parents to children—account not just for physical characteristics but also for specific behaviours and social practices (Pinker, 2002; Tooby and Cosmides, 1992; Wilson, 1975). They deny the significance of culture. Such thinking is growing in popularity, and it undermines the sociological perspective. As the following example illustrates, it is also misguided.

Male Promiscuity, Female Fidelity, and Other Myths

Evolutionary psychologists employ a three-step argument for their biological explanation of human behaviour and social arrangements. First, they identify a supposedly universal human behavioural trait. Next, they offer an explanation for why this behaviour increases survival chances through reproduction. Finally, they conclude that the behaviour in question cannot easily be changed. For example, they explain alleged male promiscuity and female fidelity as follows.

1. *Universal claim*: Men are more likely than women are to want many sexual partners.
2. *Survival-value argument*: Every time a man ejaculates, he produces hundreds of millions of sperm, while fertile women typically release only one egg per month. Based on these sex differences, men and women develop different strategies to increase the chances of reproducing their genes. Because a woman produces few eggs, she improves her chance of reproducing her genes if she has a mate who stays around to help and protect her while she is pregnant, giving birth, and nursing a small infant. By contrast, because a man's sperm is plentiful, he improves his chance of reproducing his genes if he tries to impregnate as many women as possible.
3. *Conclusion*: These biologically based reproductive strategies are encoded or "hardwired" in our genes. Therefore, male promiscuity and female fidelity are necessary.

Let's apply the table-reading and causal analysis skills you learned in Chapter 2 to illustrate the problems with this argument.

Table 3.2 contains data from a survey of a representative sample of the American population. It shows that a minority of adult American men (21 percent) claimed having more than one sex partner in the previous year. The figure for adult American women was significantly lower (10 percent). However, if we control for marital status, as in Table 3.3, the figures fall to 5 percent for men and 1 percent for women, a much smaller difference. These differences indicate that certain *social arrangements*, such as the institution of marriage, account in substantial measure for variation in male promiscuity. There is no *universal* propensity to male promiscuity.

Still, the data in Table 3.2 indicate that 11 percent more men than women said they had more than one sex partner in the preceding year. Among unmarried people, the male–female difference was 14 percent. Sociologists attribute these gender differences to two main factors (McConaghy, 1999: 311–14). First, men are more likely than women are to have same-sex sexual relations, and gay men are more likely to have many sex partners than lesbians are. This finding contradicts the evolutionary psychologists' argument that male promiscuity reflects an adaptive reproductive strategy because, clearly, gay men do not have sex with other men to make babies. Second, in-depth interviews suggest that men

Number of Sex Partners	Respondent's Sex	
	Male	Female
0 or 1	79	90
More than 1	21	10
Total	100	100
n (number of respondents)	1004	1233

TABLE 3.2

Number of Sex Partners by Respondent's Sex, United States (in percent)

Source: From National Opinion Research Center, 2004, *General Social Survey, 1972–2002* (Chicago: University of Chicago), machine-readable file. Reprinted with permission.

Number of Sex Partners	Respondent's Sex	
	Male	Female
0 or 1	95	99
More than 1	5	1
Total	100	100
n (number of respondents)	499	534

TABLE 3.3

Number of Sex Partners by Respondent's Sex, United States, Married Respondents Only (in percent)

Source: From National Opinion Research Center, 2004, *General Social Survey, 1972–2002* (Chicago: University of Chicago), machine-readable file. Reprinted with permission.

tend to exaggerate how many sexual partners they have because our *culture* puts a premium on male sexual performance. Genes and reproductive strategies play no role in this regard. We conclude that the evolutionary psychologists' claims about male promiscuity and female fidelity are false. So are many of their other claims about so-called behavioural universals.

An additional problem with the evolutionary psychologists' argument is that little evidence links specific behaviours and social arrangements to specific genes. Finally, even if researchers discover an association between particular genes and particular behaviours, it would be wrong to conclude that variations among people are due only to their genes. Genes *never* develop without environmental influence (see Figure 3.2).

In sum, your genes do not hardwire your behaviour patterns. Changes in social environment produce physical and, to an even greater degree, behavioural change. To determine the effects of the social environment on human behaviour, we have to abandon the premises of evolutionary psychology and use sociological skills to analyze the effects of social structure and culture.

Language and the Sapir-Whorf Thesis

Language is one of the most important parts of any culture. A language is a system of symbols strung together to communicate thought. Equipped with language, we can share understandings, pass experience and knowledge from one generation to the next, and make plans for the future. In short, language allows culture to develop. Consequently, sociologists commonly think of language as a cultural invention that distinguishes humans from other animals.

In the 1930s, Edward Sapir and Benjamin Lee Whorf proposed an influential argument about the connection between experience, thought, and language. It is now known as the **Sapir-Whorf thesis** (Whorf, 1956). It holds that we experience important things in our environment and form concepts about those things (path 1 to 2 in Figure 3.3). Then, we develop language to express our concepts (path 2 to 3). Finally, language itself influences how we see the world (path 3 to 1).

The **Sapir-Whorf thesis** holds that we experience certain things in our environment and form concepts about those things. We then develop language to express our concepts. Finally, language itself influences how we see the world.

FIGURE 3.2

A Genetic Misconception

When scientists announced they had finished sequencing the human genome on June 26, 2000, some people thought all human characteristics could be read from the human genetic "map." They cannot. The functions of most genes are still unknown. Moreover, because genes mutate randomly and interact with environmental (including social) conditions, the correspondence between genetic function and behavioural outcome is highly uncertain.

Source: *The National Post*, Toronto, Canada, 2000. Gary Clement.

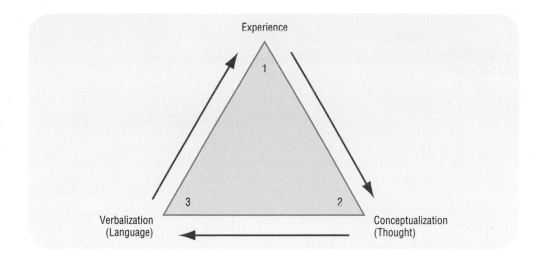

FIGURE 3.3
The Sapir-Whorf Thesis

For example, different types of camel are important in the environment of nomadic Arabs, and different types of snow are important in the lives of Inuit in Canada's far north (path 1 to 2). Consequently, nomadic Arabs have developed many words for different types of camel and Inuit have developed many words for different types of snow (path 2 to 3). Distinctions that these people see elude us because types of camel and snow are less important in our environment.

In turn, language obliges people to think in certain ways (path 3 to 1). If you're walking in a park, you will know whether a certain tree is in front of you, behind you, to the left, or to the right. When asked where the tree is, you will use such directions to describe its position. We think "egocentrically," locating objects relative to ourselves. However, egocentric directions have no meaning for speakers of Tzeltal in southern Mexico or of Guugu Yimithirr in Queensland, Australia. They lack concepts and words for "left," "right," and so on. They think geographically, and will say that the tree is to the "north," "south, "east" or "west." Trained from infancy to attend to geographic direction, Tzeltal speakers are obliged to think in those terms. If a tree to the north is located behind them and they are asked where the tree is, they will point to themselves, as if they don't exist. Reportedly, a Tzeltal speaker can be blindfolded, put in a dark room, and spun around 20 times until he's dizzy yet still point without hesitation to the north, south, east, and west (Boroditsky, 2010; Deutscher, 2010). Or to take an example closer to home, income and power inequality between women and men encourages some men to use terms like *fox, babe, bitch, ho,* and *doll* to refer to women. However, the use of such words in itself influences men to think of women simply as sexual objects. If they are ever going to think of women as equals, gender inequality will have to be reduced, but the language such men use to refer to women will also have to change.

CULTURE AS FREEDOM AND CONSTRAINT

A Functionalist Analysis of Culture:
Culture and Ethnocentrism

Despite its central importance in human life, culture is often invisible. People tend to take their culture for granted. It usually seems so sensible and natural they rarely think about it. In contrast, people are often startled when confronted by cultures other than their own. The ideas, norms, and techniques of other cultures frequently seem odd, irrational, and even inferior.

Judging another culture exclusively by the standards of our own is known as **ethnocentrism** (Box 3.1 on page 68). Ethnocentrism impairs sociological analysis. We can illustrate this point by discussing a practice that seems bizarre to many Westerners: cow worship among Hindu peasants in India.

Ethnocentrism is the tendency for a person to judge other cultures exclusively by the standards of his or her own.

Sociology at the Movies

BORAT: CULTURAL LEARNINGS OF AMERICA FOR MAKE BENEFIT GLORIOUS NATION OF KAZAKHSTAN

Borat (played by Sacha Baron Cohen) is a journalist from Kazakhstan who visits the United States so he can learn about American culture and return home with useful lessons. The movie's humour turns on the apparent differences between Borat's culture, on the one hand, and that of his audience and the people he meets, on the other. His values, beliefs, and norms deeply offend the Americans he encounters. Since Borat is capable of seeing the world only from his own cultural viewpoint, the movie at one level is a story of ethnocentrism gone mad.

Borat is anti-Semitic, racist, homophobic, and sexist, but he directs many of our biggest laughs against Americans. At one point, he secures the agreement of a rodeo organizer to let him sing the national anthem before the show begins. Borat first makes a speech: "My name Borat, I come from Kazakhstan. Can I say first, we support your war of terror. (The audience applauds.) May we show our support to our boys in Iraq. (The audience cheers.) May U.S. and A kill every single terrorist! (The audience roars.) May George Bush drink the blood of every single man, woman and child of Iraq! May you destroy their country so that for the next thousand years not even a single lizard will survive in their desert!" (The audience goes wild.) After thus demonstrating the inhumanity of his audience, Borat sings the Kazakh national anthem in English to the tune of the United States national anthem:

Kazakhstan is the greatest country in the world.
All other countries are run by little girls.
Kazakhstan is number one exporter of potassium.
Other Central Asian countries have inferior potassium.
Kazakhstan is the greatest country in the world.
All other countries is the home of the gays.

To the suggestion that another country exceeds the United States in glory, the audience responds with jeers and boos that grow so loud, one fears for Borat's life. In this and other scenes, the movie forces us to conclude that American culture is as biased in its own way as Kazakh culture allegedly is.

Hindu peasants refuse to slaughter cattle and eat beef because, for them, the cow is a religious symbol of life. Pinup calendars throughout rural India portray beautiful women with the bodies of fat, white cows, milk jetting out of each teat. Cows are permitted to wander the streets, defecate on the sidewalks, and stop to chew their cud in busy intersections and on railroad tracks, causing traffic to come to a complete halt. In Madras, police stations maintain fields where stray cows that have fallen ill can graze and be nursed back to health. The government even runs old-age homes for cows where dry and decrepit cattle are kept free of charge. All this seems utterly inscrutable to most Westerners, for it takes place amid poverty and hunger that could presumably be alleviated if only the peasants would slaughter their "useless" cattle for food instead of squandering scarce resources to feed and protect these animals.

According to anthropologist Marvin Harris, however, ethnocentrism misleads many Western observers (Harris, 1974: 3–32). Cow worship, it turns out, is an economically rational practice in rural India. For one thing, Indian peasants cannot afford tractors, so cows are needed to give birth to oxen, which are in high demand for plowing. For another, the cows produce hundreds of millions of kilograms of recoverable manure, about half of which is used as fertilizer and half as a cooking fuel. With oil, coal, and wood in short supply, and

Borat Sagdiyev (Sacha Baron Cohen) and Azamat Bagatov (Ken Davitian) in *Borat*

Is *Borat* just a rant against Americans, Jews, blacks, gays, women, and so on? Some people think so. However, that opinion is not credible for two reasons. First, it is inconsistent with who Sacha Baron Cohen is: a well-educated liberal who completed a degree in history at Cambridge and wrote his thesis on the civil rights movement in the United States, and a Jew who strongly identifies with his ethnic heritage. (One of the movie's biggest jokes is that Borat often speaks Hebrew to his sidekick, Azamat Bagatov [Ken Davitian].)

Borat certainly is a long and funny rant, but the real objects of its satire are the world's racists, sexists, anti-Semites, and homophobes, regardless of their race, creed, or national origin. The deeper message of Borat is anything but ethnocentric: respect for human dignity is a value that rises above all cultures, and people who think otherwise deserve to be laughed at.

Does *Borat* help you see the prejudices of other people more clearly? Does *Borat* help you see your own prejudices more clearly? Borat talks and acts like a bigot from the opening title to the closing credits. Do you think that the expression of bigotry is inherently offensive and should always be avoided? Or do you believe that the satirical expression of bigotry can usefully reveal hidden prejudices?

with the peasants unable to afford chemical fertilizers, cow dung is, well, a godsend. What is more, cows in India don't cost much to maintain since they eat mostly food that is not fit for human consumption. And they represent an important source of protein and a livelihood for members of low-ranking castes, who have the right to dispose of the bodies of dead cattle. These "untouchables" eat beef and form the workforce of India's large leather-craft industry. The protection of cows by means of cow worship is thus a perfectly sensible and highly efficient economic practice. It only seems irrational when judged by the standards of Western agribusiness.

Harris's analysis of cow worship in rural India is interesting for two reasons. First, it illustrates how functionalist theory can illuminate otherwise mysterious social practices. Harris uncovers a range of latent functions performed by cow worship, thus showing how a particular social practice has unintended and unobvious consequences that make social order possible. Second, we can draw an important lesson about ethnocentrism from Harris's analysis. If you refrain from taking your own culture for granted and judging other cultures by the standards of your own, you take an important first step toward developing a sociological understanding of culture.

Many Westerners find the Indian practice of cow worship bizarre. However, cow worship performs a number of useful economic functions and is in that sense entirely rational. By viewing cow worship exclusively as an outsider (or, for that matter, exclusively as an insider), we fail to see its rational core.

Rob Elliott/AFP/Getty Images

Summing Up

- Biology sets broad parameters to behaviour, not specific lines of human conduct.
- Language is a primary carrier of culture.
- Ethnocentrism—thinking that the beliefs, norms, and values of one's culture are superior to the beliefs, norms and values of other cultures—can hinder sociological analysis.

CULTURE AS FREEDOM

Culture has two faces. First, culture provides us with an opportunity to exercise our *freedom*. We use and elaborate elements of culture in our everyday life to solve practical problems and express our needs, hopes, joys, and fears.

However, creatively utilizing culture is just like any other act of construction in that we need raw materials to get the job done. The raw materials for the culture we create consist of cultural elements that either existed before we were born or are created by other people after our birth. We may put these elements together in ways that produce something genuinely new. However, there is no other well to drink from, so existing culture puts limits on what we can think and do. In that sense, culture *constrains* us. This is culture's second face. In the rest of this chapter, we take a close look at both faces of culture.

Symbolic Interactionism and Cultural Production

Until the 1960s, most sociologists argued that culture is a "reflection" of society. Using a term introduced in Chapter 2, we can say that they regarded culture as a dependent variable.

Harris's analysis of rural Indians certainly fits that mould. In Harris's view, the social necessity of protecting cows caused the cultural belief that cows are holy.

In recent decades, the symbolic interactionist tradition we discussed in Chapter 1 has influenced many sociologists of culture. Symbolic interactionists are inclined to regard culture as an *independent* variable. In their view, people do not accept culture passively. We are not empty vessels into which society pours a defined assortment of beliefs, symbols, and values. Instead, we actively produce and interpret culture, creatively fashioning it and attaching meaning to it in accordance with our diverse needs.

The idea that people actively produce and interpret culture implies that, to a degree, we are at liberty to choose how culture influences us.

Cultural Diversity

Part of the reason we are increasingly able to choose how culture influences us is that Canadian society has diversified. Like many societies in the world, Canada is undergoing rapid cultural diversification because of a rising number of immigrants and change in their countries of origin. Immigrants made up 19.8 percent of Canada's population in 2006, the highest proportion since 1931 (Statistics Canada, 2007c). Moreover, since the 1960s, traditional, European sources of immigrants have become far less important than Caribbean and especially Asian sources. Statistics Canada therefore projects that nearly a third of Canada's population will be members of "visible minorities" by 2031 (Statistics Canada, 2010h).

Multiculturalism

At the political level, cultural diversity has become a source of conflict. The conflict is most evident in the debates that have surfaced in recent years concerning curricula in the Canadian educational system.

Although each provincial and territorial government in Canada has jurisdiction over education, it was common until recent decades for schools across Canada to stress the common elements of our culture, history, and society. Students learned the historical importance of the "charter groups"—the English and the French. School curricula

Canada continues to diversify culturally.

CP PHOTO/Toronto Star - Ron Bull

typically neglected the contributions of non-whites and non-French or non-English to Canada's development. Moreover, students learned little about the less savoury aspects of Canadian history, including immigration policies that sought to preserve Canada's "English stock" by restricting or denying entry to certain groups (Chapter 10, Race and Ethnicity). In general, history books were written from the perspective of the victors, not the vanquished.

For the past few decades, multiculturalists have argued that school, college, and university curricula should present a more balanced view of Canadian history, society, and culture. Curricula that reflect the country's ethnic and racial diversity will presumably allow minority groups "to gain respect, dignity and power" and bring the educational system into line with Canada's status as the first officially multicultural society (Gaskell, McLaren, and Novogrodsky, 1995: 105). In 1971, the Canadian government declared that Canada, while officially bilingual, had no "official" culture—that is, none of the distinguishable cultures in Canada takes precedence over the others. With the passage of the Canadian Multiculturalism Act in 1988, the federal government confirmed its commitment to the recognition of all Canadians "as full and equal participants in Canadian society." Multiculturalists conclude that to the extent that existing curricula are biased, they are failing to provide students with the type of education a country truly devoted to multiculturalism demands.

Most critics of multiculturalism in education do not argue against teaching cultural diversity. What they fear is that multicultural education is being taken too far (Bissoondath, 2002; Fekete, 1994; Glazer, 1997; Schlesinger, 1991; Stotsky, 1999). Specifically, they say multiculturalism has three negative consequences:

1. Critics believe that multicultural education hurts students who are members of minority groups by forcing them to spend too much time on non-core subjects. To get ahead in the world, they say, students need to be skilled in English, French, math, and science. By taking time away from these subjects, multicultural education impedes the success of minority group members in the work world. Multiculturalists counter that minority group students develop self-esteem from a curriculum that stresses cultural diversity, helping them get ahead in the work world.

2. Critics also believe that multicultural education causes political disunity and results in more interethnic and interracial conflict. Therefore, they want curricula to stress the common elements of the national experience and highlight Europe's contribution to Canadian culture. Multiculturalists reply that political unity and interethnic and interracial harmony maintain inequality in Canadian society. Conflict, they say, while unfortunate, is often necessary to achieve equality between majority and minority groups.

Cultural relativism is the belief that all cultures have equal value.

3. Finally, critics complain that multiculturalism encourages the growth of **cultural relativism**. Cultural relativism is the opposite of ethnocentrism. It is the belief that all cultures and all cultural practices have equal value. The trouble with this view is that some cultures oppose the most deeply held values of most Canadians. Critics argue that, to the degree that it promotes cultural relativism, a truly multicultural system of education might encourage respect for practices that are abhorrent to most Canadians (Box 3.2). Multiculturalists reply that we don't have to take cultural relativism to such an extreme. *Moderate* cultural relativism encourages tolerance, and we should promote it.

Clearly, multiculturalism in education is a complex and emotional issue. Globally, cultures are becoming more heterogeneous. This trend has important social and political consequences that are best faced through informed debate.

A Conflict Analysis of Culture: The Rights Revolution

What are the social roots of cultural diversity and multiculturalism? Conflict theory suggests where to look for an answer. Recall from Chapter 1 the central argument of conflict theory: Social life is an ongoing struggle between more and less advantaged groups. Privileged groups try to maintain their advantages while subordinate groups struggle to increase theirs.

And sure enough, if we probe beneath cultural diversification and multiculturalism, we find what has been called the **rights revolution**, the process by which socially excluded groups have struggled to win equal rights under the law and in practice.

After the outburst of nationalism, racism, and genocidal behaviour among the combatants in World War II, the United Nations proclaimed the Universal Declaration of Human Rights in 1948. It recognized the "inherent dignity" and "equal and inalienable rights of all members of the human family" and held that "every organ of society" should "strive by teaching and education to promote respect for these rights and freedoms and by progressive measures, national and international, to secure their universal and effective recognition and observance" (United Nations, 1998a). Fanned by such sentiment, the rights revolution was in full swing by the 1960s. Today, women's rights, minority rights, gay and lesbian rights, the rights of people with special needs, constitutional rights, and language rights are key parts of our political discourse. Because of the rights revolution, democracy has been widened and deepened (Chapter 14, Politics). The rights revolution is by no means finished. Many categories of people are still discriminated against socially, politically, and

The **rights revolution** is the process by which socially excluded groups struggled to win equal rights under the law and in practice beginning in the second half of the twentieth century.

BOX 3.2

It's Your Choice

FEMALE GENITAL MUTILATION: CULTURAL RELATIVISM OR ETHNOCENTRISM?

The World Health Organization (WHO) defines female genital mutilation (FGM) as "procedures that intentionally alter or injure female genital organs for non-medical reasons" (World Health Organization, 2010a). It has no medical benefits. It typically results in pain,

humiliation, psychological trauma, and loss of sexual pleasure. It often causes shock, injury to neighbouring organs, severe bleeding, infertility, chronic infections in the urinary tract and reproductive system, and increased hepatitis B and HIV/AIDS infection. Between 100 million and 140 million girls and women worldwide have undergone FGM, the great majority of them in a handful of African countries (World Health Organization, 2001).

Some people think FGM enhances fertility and that women are "unclean" and "masculine" if they have a clitoris. From this point of view, women who have not experienced genital mutilation are more likely to demonstrate "masculine" levels of sexual interest and activity. They are less likely to remain virgins before marriage and faithful within marriage.

One reaction to FGM takes a "human rights perspective." In this view, the practice is an aspect of gender-based oppression that women experience to varying degrees in societies worldwide. Adopting this perspective, the United Nations defines FGM as a form of violence against women. Many international, regional, and national agreements commit governments to preventing FGM, assisting women at risk of undergoing it, and punishing people who commit it.

In the United States, the penalty for conducting FGM is up to five years in prison.

Cultural relativists regard the human rights perspective as ethnocentric. They view interference with the practice as little more than neo-imperialist attacks on African cultures. From their point of view, talk of "universal human rights" denies cultural rights to less powerful peoples. Moreover, opposition to FGM undermines tolerance and multiculturalism while reinforcing racist attitudes. Cultural relativists therefore argue that we should affirm the right of other cultures to practise FGM even if we regard it as destructive, senseless, oppressive, and abhorrent. We should respect the fact that other cultures regard FGM as meaningful and as serving useful functions.

Which of these perspectives do you find more compelling? Do you believe that certain principles of human decency transcend the particulars of any culture? If so, what are those principles? If you do not believe in the existence of any universal principles of human decency, then does anything go? Would you agree that, say, genocide is acceptable if most people in a society favour it? Or are there limits to your cultural relativism? In a world where supposedly universal principles often clash with the principles of particular cultures, where do you draw the line?

economically. However, in much of the world all categories of people now participate more fully than ever before in the life of their societies (Ignatieff, 2000).

The rights revolution raises some difficult issues. For example, some members of groups that have suffered extraordinarily high levels of discrimination historically, such as Aboriginal Canadians, Chinese Canadians, and others, have demanded reparations in the form of money, symbolic gestures, land, and political autonomy (Chapter 10, Race and Ethnicity). Much controversy surrounds the extent of the obligation of current citizens to compensate for past injustices.

Such problems notwithstanding, the rights revolution is here to stay and it affects our culture profoundly. Specifically, the rights revolution fragments Canadian culture by (1) legitimizing the grievances of groups that were formerly excluded from full social participation and (2) renewing their pride in their identity and heritage. Our history books, our literature, our music, our use of languages, our very sense of what it means to be Canadian have diversified culturally. White, male, heterosexual property owners of north European origin are still disproportionately influential in Canada, but our culture is no longer dominated by them in the way that it was just a half century ago.

From Diversity to Globalization

The cultural diversification we witness today is not evident in preliterate or tribal societies. In such societies, cultural beliefs and practices are virtually the same for all group members. For example, many tribal societies organize **rites of passage**. These cultural ceremonies mark the transition from one stage of life to another (e.g., from childhood to adulthood) or from life to death (funerals). They involve elaborate procedures, such as body painting, and carefully orchestrated chants and movements. They are often conducted in public, and no variation from prescribed practice is allowed. Culture is homogeneous (Durkheim, 1976 [1915]).

In contrast, preindustrial Western Europe and North America were rocked by artistic, religious, scientific, and political forces that fragmented culture. The Renaissance, the Protestant Reformation, the Scientific Revolution, the French and American revolutions—between the fourteenth and eighteenth centuries, all these movements involved people questioning old ways of seeing and doing things. Science placed skepticism about established authority at the very heart of its method. Political revolution proved there was nothing ordained about who should rule and how they should do so. Religious dissent ensured that the Catholic Church would no longer be the supreme interpreter of God's will in the eyes of all Christians. Authority and truth became divided as never before.

Cultural fragmentation picked up steam during industrialization as the variety of occupational roles grew and new political and intellectual movements crystallized. Its pace is quickening again today in the postindustrial era as a result of globalization. Globalization is the process by which formerly separate economies, states, and cultures are tied together and people become aware of their growing interdependence.

One of the most important roots of globalization is the expansion of international trade and investment. Even the most patriotic of Canadians has probably dined at least once at McDonald's—and even a business as "American" as McDonald's has 56 percent of its stores in 120 countries outside of the United States, generating 60 percent of its profits (Tschoegl, 2007: 3). At the same time, members of different ethnic and racial groups are migrating and coming into sustained contact with one another. Influential transnational organizations, such as the International Monetary Fund, the World Bank, the European Union, Greenpeace, and Amnesty International, are multiplying. Relatively inexpensive international travel and communication make contacts among people from diverse cultures routine. The mass media make Ryan Gosling and *The Vampire Diaries* nearly as well known in Warsaw as in Winnipeg. MTV brings rock music to the world via stations in Canada, Brazil, Japan, India, China, Australia, Korea, Russia, and so on. Globalization, in short, destroys political, economic, and cultural isolation, bringing people together in what Canadian media analyst Marshall McLuhan (1964) called a "global village." Because of

Rites of passage are cultural ceremonies that mark the transition from one stage of life to another (e.g., baptisms, confirmations, weddings) or from life to death (funerals).

Courtesy of Kelloggs

The idea of globalization first gained prominence in marketing strategies in the 1970s. In the 1980s, such companies as Coca-Cola and McDonald's expanded into non-Western countries to find new markets. Today, Kellogg's markets products in more than 160 countries. Basmati Flakes cereal was first produced by the Kellogg's plant in Tajola, India, in 1992.

globalization, people are less obliged to accept the culture into which they are born and freer to combine elements of culture from a wide variety of historical periods and geographical settings. Globalization is a school boy in New Delhi, India, listening to Rihanna on his MP3 player as he rushes to slip into his Levis, wolf down a bowl of Kellogg's Basmati Flakes, and say goodbye to his parents in Hindi because he's late for his English-language school.

The Globalization of English

A good indicator of the influence and extent of globalization is the spread of English. In 1600, English was the mother tongue of between four million and seven million people. Not even all people in England spoke it. Today, more than a billion people speak English worldwide, more than half as a second language. With the exception of the many varieties of Chinese, English is the most widespread language on earth (Figure 3.4). English is dominant because Britain and the United States were the world's most powerful and influential countries—economically, militarily, and culturally—for more than 200 years. In recent

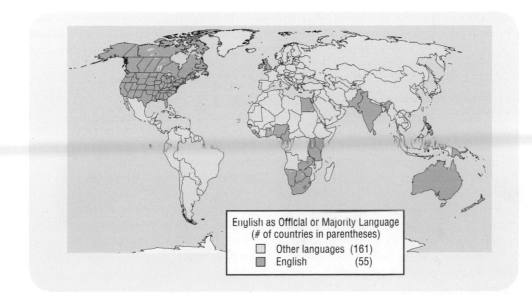

FIGURE 3.4

English as Official or Majority Language

Sources: United Nations Educational, Scientific, and Cultural Organization, 2001; Central Intelligence Agency, 2002.

decades, the global spread of capitalism, the popularity of Hollywood movies and American TV shows, and the widespread access to instant communication via telephone and the Internet have increased the reach of the English language.

Because of the rise of English (as well as the influence of French, Spanish, and the languages of a few other colonizing nations), several thousand languages around the world are being eliminated. These endangered languages are spoken by the tribes of Papua New Guinea; the native peoples of the Americas; the national and tribal minorities of Asia, Africa, and Oceania; and marginalized European peoples, such as the Irish and the Basques. Experts estimate that the 5000 to 6000 languages spoken in the world today will be reduced to between 1000 and 3000 in a century. Since much of culture is encoded in language, the loss of languages amounts to the displacement of local traditions and identity by the traditions and identity of the colonial power. Television and the Internet play an important role in the transformation (Woodbury, 2003).

Still, major languages other than English are holding their own and even pushing back the English onslaught in some areas. Consider the pie charts in Figure 3.5, which show how language use on the Internet changed from June 2001 to June 2010. In this period, English usage dropped nearly 18 percent, while Chinese usage jumped more than 14 percent. These figures suggest that globalization does not necessarily involve the homogenization of culture—an important theme that we will take up again in Chapter 9 (Globalization, Inequality, and Development).

Aspects of Postmodernism

Some sociologists think so much cultural fragmentation and reconfiguration has taken place in the last few decades that a new term is needed to characterize the culture of our times: **postmodernism**. Scholars often characterize the last half of the nineteenth century and the first half of the twentieth century as the era of modernity. During this hundred-year period, belief in the inevitability of progress, respect for authority, and consensus around core values characterized much of Western culture. In contrast, postmodern culture involves an eclectic mix of elements from different times and places, the erosion of authority, and the decline of consensus around core values. Let us consider each of these aspects of postmodernism in turn.

An eclectic mix of elements from different times and places. In the postmodern era, it is easier to create personalized belief systems and practices by blending facets of different cultures and historical periods. Consider religion. The great majority of Canadians say they believe in God and identify as Christians. However, if current trends persist, in the next two decades this proportion will decline from 75 to 65 percent. During the same period, those saying they have no religion will rise from 17 to 21 percent, while those with a non-Christian religion will grow from 8 to 14 percent (Statistics Canada, 2010h). Canadians are

Postmodernism is characterized by an eclectic mix of cultural elements and the erosion of consensus.

FIGURE 3.5

Internet Usage by Language Group, June 2001 and June 2010

Sources: Global Reach, 2001, 2004; Internet World Stats, 2007; Internet World Statistics, 2010, "Internet World Users by Language." Retrieved December 17, 2010 (http://www.internetworldstats.com/stats7.htm).

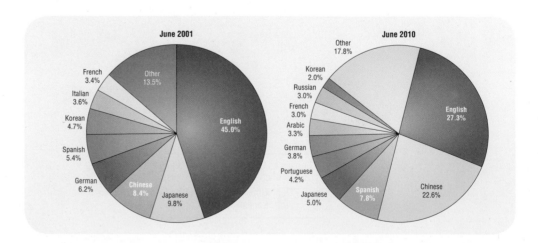

increasingly willing to feast off of a religious buffet that combines a conventional menu with a wide assortment of less conventional beliefs and practices, including astrology, tarot, New Age mysticism, psychic phenomena, and communication with the dead (Bibby, 1987: 233; Bibby, 2001: 195). Many people now draw on religions much like consumers shop in a mall. Meanwhile, churches, mosques, temples, synagogues, and other religious institutions have diversified their services to appeal to the spiritual, leisure, and social needs of religious consumers and retain their loyalties in the competitive market for congregants and parishioners (Finke and Stark, 1992).

The mix-and-match approach we see when it comes to religion is evident in virtually all spheres of culture. Although purists may scoff at such cultural blending, it has an important social consequence. People who engage in cultural blending are likely to be more tolerant and appreciative of ethnic, racial, and religious groups other than their own.

The erosion of authority. Half a century ago, Canadians were more likely than they are today to defer to authority in the family, schools, politics, medicine, and so forth. As the social bases of authority and truth have multiplied, however, we are more likely to challenge authority. Authorities once widely respected, including parents, physicians, and politicians, have come to be held in lower regard by many people. In the 1950s, Robert Young played the firm, wise, and always-present father in the TV hit series *Father Knows Best.* Six decades later, the typical TV father is more like Homer Simpson: a fool. Compared with their counterparts in the twenty-first century, Canadian teenagers in the 1980s were more likely to express confidence in our police, politicians, court system, and religious organizations (Bibby, 2001: 193). Today, both young and old Canadians are likely to be critical of social institutions, including those, such as religious organizations, that previously enjoyed special veneration. The rise of Homer Simpson and the decline of confidence in government both reflect the erosion of traditional authority (Nevitte, 1996).

The decline of consensus around core values. Half a century ago, people's values remained quite stable over the course of their adult lives and many values were widely accepted. Today, value shifts are more rapid and consensus has broken down on many issues. For example, in the middle of the twentieth century, the great majority of adults remained loyal to one political party from one election to the next. However, specific issues and personalities have increasingly eclipsed party loyalty as the driving forces of Canadian politics (Clarke, Jenson, LeDuc, and Pammett, 1996). Today, people are more likely to vote for different political parties in succeeding elections than they were in 1950.

A hallmark of postmodernism is the combining of cultural elements from different times and places. For example, the "Michael Lee-Chin crystal" that was added to the Royal Ontario Museum created a postmodern nightmare in the eyes of some critics.

© Oleksiy Maksymenko / Alamy

We may also illustrate the decline of consensus by considering the fate of big historical projects. For most of the past 200 years, consensus throughout the world was built around big historical projects. Various political and social movements convinced people they could take history into their own hands and create a glorious future just by signing up. German Nazism was a big historical project. Its followers expected the Reich to enjoy a thousand years of power. Communism was an even bigger big historical project, mobilizing hundreds of millions of people for a future that promised to end inequality and injustice for all time. However, the biggest and most successful big historical project was not so much a social movement as a powerful idea—the belief that progress is inevitable, that life will always improve, mainly because of the spread of democracy and scientific innovation.

The twentieth century was unkind to big historical projects. Russian communism lasted 74 years. German Nazism endured a mere 12. The idea of progress fell on hard times as 100 million soldiers and civilians died in wars; the forward march of democracy took wrong turns into fascism, communism, and regimes based on religious fanaticism; and pollution from urbanization and industrialization threatened the planet. In the postmodern era, more and more people recognize that apparent progress, including scientific advances, often has negative consequences (Scott, 1998). As the poet E. E. Cummings once wrote, "nothing recedes like progress."

Postmodernism has many parents, teachers, politicians, religious leaders, and professors worried. Given the eclectic mixing of cultural elements from different times and places, the erosion of authority, and the decline of consensus around core values, how can we make binding decisions? How can we govern? How can we teach children and adolescents the difference between right and wrong? How can we transmit accepted literary tastes and artistic standards from one generation to the next? These are the kinds of issues that plague people in positions of authority today.

Although their concerns are legitimate, many authorities seem not to have considered the other side of the coin. The postmodern condition empowers ordinary people and makes them more responsible for their own fate. It frees people to adopt religious, ethnic, and other identities they are comfortable with, rather than accepting identities imposed on them by others. It makes them more tolerant of difference. That is no small matter in a world torn by group conflict. The postmodern attitude also encourages healthy scepticism about rosy and naive scientific and political promises.

Canada: The First Postmodern Culture?

Until the mid-1960s, the image of Canadians among most sociologists was that of a stodgy people: peaceful, conservative, respectful of authority, and therefore quite unlike our American cousins.

According to conventional wisdom, the United States was born in open rebellion against the British motherland. Its Western frontier was lawless. Vast opportunities for striking it rich bred a spirit of individualism. Thus, American culture became an anti-authoritarian culture.

Canada developed differently according to the conventional view. It became an independent country not through a revolutionary upheaval but in a gradual, evolutionary manner. The North-West Mounted Police and two hierarchical churches (Roman Catholic and Anglican) established themselves on the Western frontier *before* the era of mass settlement, allowing for the creation of an orderly society rather than an American-style Wild West. Beginning with the Hudson's Bay Company, large corporations quickly came to dominate the Canadian economy, hampering individualism and the entrepreneurial spirit. Thus, Canadian culture became a culture of deference to authority. That, at least, was the common view until the 1960s (Lipset, 1963).

Although the contrast between deferential Canadian culture and anti-authoritarian American culture may have had some validity half a century ago, it is an inaccurate characterization today (Adams, 1997: 62–95). As we have seen, the questioning of authority spread throughout the Western world beginning in the 1960s. Nowhere did it spread as quickly and thoroughly as in Canada. Canadians used to express more confidence in big business than Americans did, but surveys now show the opposite. Canadians used to be more religious than Americans were, but that is no longer the case. Fewer Canadians (in percentage terms) say they believe in God and fewer attend weekly religious services. Confidence in government has eroded more quickly in Canada than in the United States. Americans are more patriotic than Canadians are, according more respect to the state. Finally, Americans are more likely than Canadians are to regard the traditional nuclear family as the ideal family form and to think of deviations from tradition—same-sex couples, single-parent families, cohabitation without marriage—as the source of a whole range of social problems. Thus, whether sociologists examine attitudes toward the family, the state, the government, religion, or big business, they now find that Americans are more deferential to traditional institutional authority than Canadians are.

Because Canadians are less deferential to traditional institutional authority than Americans are, some commentators say that Canadians lack a distinct culture. For example, American patriotism sparks awareness of great national accomplishments in art, war, sports, and science. Anthems, rituals, myths, and celebrations commemorate these accomplishments and give Americans a keen sense of who they are and how they differ from non-Americans. Not surprisingly, therefore, a larger percentage of Americans than Canadians think of themselves in unhyphenated terms—as "Americans" plain and simple rather than, say, Italian-Americans. In Canada, a larger percentage of the population thinks of itself in hyphenated terms; compared with the Americans, our identity is qualified, even tentative.

Does this mean that Canadians lack a distinct national culture? Hardly. It means that, while American culture is characterized by a relatively high degree of deference to dominant institutions, Canadian culture is characterized by a relatively high degree of tolerance and respect for diversity. We are more likely than Americans are to favour gender equality, accept gay and lesbian relationships, encourage bilingualism and multiculturalism, and accept the right of Aboriginals to political autonomy. Characteristically, a large international survey by a condom manufacturer found that Americans have sex more often than Canadians do, but Canadians are more likely to say that the pleasure of their partner is very important. As public opinion pollster Michael Adams writes:

> Canadians feel *strongly* about their *weak* attachments to Canada, its political institutions and their fellow citizens. In other words, they feel strongly about the right to live in a society that allows its citizens to be detached from ideology and critical of organizations, and not to feel obliged to be jingoistic or sentimentally patriotic. Canadians' *lack* of nationalism is, in many ways, a distinguishing feature of the country. (Adams, 1997: 171)

In short, Canadian culture *is* distinctive, and its chief distinction may be that it qualifies us as the first thoroughly postmodern society.

Summing Up

- Culture provides the tools for creating novel ideas and solutions to practical issues.
- Canada is a leader in the global trend toward multiculturalism, including the expansion of human rights.
- Globalization tends to reduce cultural diversity.
- Postmodernism challenges the integrity of traditional cultural forms and encourages individual autonomy.

CULTURE AS CONSTRAINT

We noted previously that culture has two faces. One we labelled freedom, the other constraint. On the one hand, diversity, globalization, the rights revolution, and postmodernism are aspects of the new freedoms that culture encourages today. On the other hand, as you will now learn, rationalization and consumerism act as constraining forces on our lives.

Rationalization and Time Use

Rationalization is the application of the most efficient means to achieve given goals and the unintended, negative consequences of doing so.

Max Weber coined the term **rationalization** to describe the application of the most efficient means to achieve given goals and the unintended, negative consequences of doing so. He claimed that rationalization has crept into all spheres of life. In Weber's view, rationalization is one of the most constraining aspects of contemporary culture, making life akin to living inside an "iron cage."

The constraining effects of rationalization are evident, for example, in the way we measure and use time. People did not always let the clock determine the pace of daily life. The first mechanical clocks were installed in public squares in Germany 700 years ago to signal the beginning of the workday, the timing of meals, and quitting time. Workers were accustomed to enjoying a flexible and vague work schedule regulated only approximately by the seasons and the rising and setting of the sun. The strict regime imposed by the work clocks made their lives harder. They staged uprisings to silence the clocks, but to no avail. City officials sided with employers and imposed fines for ignoring the work clocks (Thompson, 1967).

© David Murray

BlackBerries and iPhones allow people to stay in touch with friends and work every waking moment. Many people have mixed feelings about these devices. Sometimes they seem pleasurable and efficient. At other times, they prevent relaxation and intimacy. As such, they typify the two faces of culture.

Today, few people rebel against the work clock. This is especially true of urban North American couples who are employed full-time in the paid labour force and have young children. For them, life often seems an endless round of waking up at 6:30 a.m.; getting everyone washed and dressed; preparing the kids' lunches; getting them out the door in time for the school bus or the car pool; driving to work through rush-hour traffic; facing the speedup at work resulting from the recent downsizing; driving back home through rush-hour traffic; preparing dinner; taking the kids to their soccer game; returning home to clean up the dishes and help with homework; getting the kids washed, their teeth brushed, and then into bed; and (if they have not brought some office work home) grabbing an hour of TV before collapsing, exhausted, for 6½ hours' sleep before the story repeats itself. Life is less hectic for residents of small towns, unmarried people, couples without young children, retirees, and the unemployed. But the lives of others are typically so packed with activities that they must carefully regulate time and parcel out each moment so they may tick off one item after another from an ever-growing list of tasks that need to be completed on time (Schor, 1992). After 700 years of conditioning, allowing clocks to precisely regulate our activities seems the most natural thing in the world, although there is of course nothing natural about it.

The regulation of time ensures efficiency. It maximizes how much work you get done in a day. It enables trains to run on schedule, university classes to begin punctually, and business meetings to start on time. However, many people complain that life has become too hectic to enjoy. A popular restaurant in Japan has even installed a punch-clock for its customers. The restaurant offers all you can eat for 35 yen per minute. As a result, "the diners rush in, punch the clock, load their trays from the buffet table, and concentrate intensely on efficient chewing and swallowing, trying not to waste time talking to their companions before rushing back to punch out" (Gleick, 2000 [1999]: 244). Some upscale restaurants in New York and Los Angeles have gotten in on the act. An increasingly large number of business clients are so pressed for time, they pack in two half-hour lunches with successive guests. The restaurants oblige, making the resetting of tables "resemble the

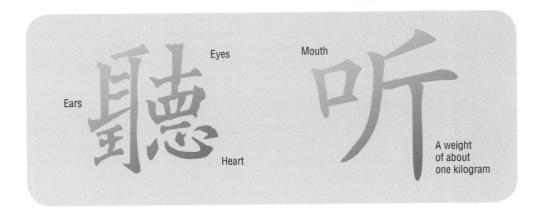

Ears 聽 Eyes Mouth 听

Heart

A weight
of about
one kilogram

Reprinted here are the Chinese characters for "listening" *(t'ing)* in traditional Chinese script (left) and simplified, modern script (right). Each character comprises several word-symbols. In classical script, listening is depicted as a process involving the eyes, the ears, and the heart. It implies that listening demands the utmost empathy and involves the whole person. In contrast, modern script depicts listening as something that merely involves one person speaking and the other "weighing" speech. Modern Chinese script has been rationalized. Has empathy been lost in the process?

pit-stop activity at the Indianapolis 500" (Gleick, 2000 [1999]. 155). As these examples illustrate, a *rational means* (the use of the work clock) has been applied to a *given goal* (maximizing work) but has led to an *irrational end* (a too-hectic life).

Consumerism

The second constraining aspect of culture we examine is **consumerism**, the tendency to define ourselves in terms of the goods and services we purchase. As artist Barbara Kruger put it, "I shop, therefore I am."

Recent innovations in advertising take full advantage of our tendency to define ourselves in terms of the goods we purchase. For example, when VCRs enabled TV viewers to skip ads that cost millions of dollars to produce, advertisers had to think up new ways of drawing products to the attention of consumers. One idea they hit on was paying to place their products in TV shows and movies. Product-placement advertising helps consumers associate the product with characters they identify with. The product becomes part of who we are or who we want to be, and, as a result, sales often soar. For example, in the 2009 movie *Up in the Air*, several travel scenes focused on George Clooney's Travelpro luggage. Sales of the luggage spiked after the film's release.

The effectiveness of advertising encourages businesses to produce more of it. As advertising becomes more pervasive, it becomes accepted as a normal part of daily life. In fact, people often *become* ads. They proudly display consumer labels as marks of status and identity. Advertisers teach us to associate the words "Gucci" and "Nike" with different kinds of people, and when people display these labels on their clothes they are telling us something about the kind of people they are. Advertising becomes us.

The rationalization process, when applied to the production of goods and services, enables us to produce more efficiently, to have more of just about everything than previous generations did. However, it is consumerism that ensures we will buy most of the goods that are produced. Of course, we have lots of choice. We can select from dozens of styles of running shoes, cars, toothpaste, and all the rest. We can also choose to buy items that help define us as members of a particular **subculture**, adherents of a set of distinctive values, norms, and practices within a larger culture. But individual tastes aside, we all have one thing in common. We tend to be good consumers. We are motivated by advertising, which is based on the accurate insight that people will tend to be considered cultural outcasts if they fail to conform to stylish trends. By creating those trends, advertisers push us to buy, even if doing so requires that we work more and incur large debts (Schor, 1999). That is why the "shop-till-you-drop" lifestyle of many North Americans prompted French

Consumerism is the tendency to define ourselves in terms of the goods we purchase.

© INTERFOTO Pressebildagentur/Alamy

Have we come to depend too heavily on the work clock? Harold Lloyd in *Safety Last* (1923).

A **subculture** is a set of distinctive values, norms, and practices within a larger culture.

Consumerism ties identities to purchases.

Countercultures are subversive subcultures.

sociologist Jean Baudrillard to remark pointedly that even what is best in North America is compulsory (Baudrillard, 1988). And it is why many sociologists say that consumerism, like rationalization, acts as a powerful constraint on our lives.

From Counterculture to Subculture

In concluding our discussion of culture as a constraining force, we note that consumerism is remarkably effective at taming countercultures. **Countercultures** are subversive subcultures. They oppose dominant values and seek to replace them. The hippies of the 1960s formed a counterculture and so do environmentalists today. Countercultures rarely pose a serious threat to social stability. Most often, the system of social control, of rewards and punishments, keeps countercultures at bay. In our society, consumerism acts as a social control mechanism that normally prevents countercultures from disrupting the social order. It does that by transforming deviations from mainstream culture into means of making money and by enticing rebels to become entrepreneurs (Frank and Weiland, 1997). The development of hip hop helps to illustrate the point (Brym, 2009: 11–32).

Hip hop originated in the American inner city in the 1970s. At the time, manufacturing industries were leaving the inner city for foreign locales, where land values were lower and labour was less expensive. Unemployment among African American youth rose to more than 40 percent. At the same time, many middle-class blacks left the inner city for the suburbs. Their migration robbed the remaining young people of successful role models. It also eroded the taxing capacity of municipal governments, leading to a decline in public services. Meanwhile, the American public elected conservative governments at the state and federal levels. They cut school and welfare budgets, thus deepening the destitution of ghetto life (Piven and Cloward, 1977: 264–361, 1993; Wilson, 1987).

With few legitimate prospects for advancement, poor African American youth in the inner city turned increasingly to crime and, in particular, the drug trade. In the late 1970s, cocaine was expensive and demand for the drug was flat. Consequently, in the early 1980s, Colombia's Medellin drug cartel introduced a less expensive form of cocaine called crack. Crack was inexpensive, it offered a quick and intense high, and it was highly addictive. It offered many people a temporary escape from hopelessness and soon became wildly popular in the inner city. Turf wars spread as gangs tried to outgun each other for control of the local traffic. The sale and use of crack became so widespread it corroded much of what was left of the inner-city African American community (Davis, 1990).

What is being sold here: the clothes or the attitude?

The shocking conditions described above gave rise to a shocking musical form: hip hop. Stridently at odds with the values and tastes of both whites and middle-class African Americans, hip hop described and glorified the mean streets of the inner city while holding the police, the mass media, and other pillars of society in utter contempt. Furthermore, hip hop tried to offend middle-class sensibilities, black and white, by using highly offensive language.

In 1988, more than a decade after its first stirrings, hip hop reached its political high point with the release of the album *It Takes a Nation to Hold Us Back* by Chuck D and Public Enemy. In "Don't Believe the Hype," Chuck D accused the mass media of maliciously distributing lies. In "Black Steel in the Hour of Chaos," he charged the FBI and the CIA with assassinating the two great leaders of the African American community in the 1960s, Martin Luther King and Malcolm X. In "Party for Your Right to Fight," he blamed the federal government for organizing the fall of the Black Panthers, the radical black nationalist party of the 1960s. Here, it seemed, was an angry expression of subcultural revolt that could not be tamed.

However, the seduction of big money did much to mute the political force of hip hop. As early as 1982, with the release of Grandmaster Flash and the Furious Five's "The Message," hip hop began to win acclaim from mainstream rock music critics. With the success of Run-D.M.C. and Public Enemy in the late 1980s, it became clear there was a big audience for hip hop. Significantly, much of that audience was composed of white youths. As one music critic wrote, they "relished . . . the subversive 'otherness' that the music and its purveyors represented" (Neal, 1999: 144). Sensing the opportunity for profit, major media corporations, such as Time/Warner, Sony, CBS/Columbia, and BMG Entertainment, signed distribution deals with the small independent recording labels that had formerly been the exclusive distributors of hip hop CDs. In 1988, *Yo! MTV Raps* debuted on MTV. The program brought hip hop to middle America.

Most hip hop recording artists proved they were eager to forgo political relevancy for commerce. For instance, Wu-Tang Clan started a line of clothing called Wu Wear, and, with the help of major hip hop recording artists, companies as diverse as Tommy Hilfiger, Timberland, Starter, and Versace began to market clothing influenced by ghetto styles. Independent labels, such as Phat Farm and Fubu, also prospered. Puff Daddy reminded his audience in his 1999 CD, *Forever*: "N—— get money, that's simply the plan." According

Hip hop counterculture is commodified.

to *Forbes* magazine, he became one of the country's 40 richest men under 40. By 2005, having renamed himself Diddy, he had his own line of popular clothing. The members of Run-D.M.C. once said that they "don't want nobody's name on my behind," but those days were long past by the early 1990s. Hip hop was no longer just a musical form but a commodity with spin-offs. Rebellion had been turned into mass consumption. Hip hop's radicalism had given way to the lure of commerce. A counterculture had become a subculture.

Radical political currents in hip hop still exist, but mainly outside North America. In Senegal, the playing of hip hop that was highly critical of the government was widely believed to have helped topple the ruling party in the 2000 election. In France, North African youth living in impoverished and segregated slums use hip hop to express their political discontent, and some analysts say the genre helped to mobilize youth for anti-government rioting in 2005 (Akwagyiram, 2009). "*Rais Lebled* [Mr. President]," a song by a Tunisian rapper, became the anthem of young people participating in the democratic uprisings in Tunisia, Egypt, and Bahrain in 2011: "Mr. President, your people are dying / People are eating rubbish / Look at what is happening / Miseries everywhere, Mr. President / I talk with no fear / Although I know I will get only trouble / I see injustice everywhere" (Ghosh, 2011). However, in North America, hip hop has become, for the most part, an apolitical commodity that increasingly appeals to a racially heterogeneous, middle-class audience. As one of hip hop's leading analysts and academic sympathizers writes, "the discourse of ghetto reality or 'hood authenticity remains largely devoid of political insight or progressive intent" (Forman, 2001: 121). The fate of hip hop is testimony to the capacity of consumerism to change countercultures into mere subcultures, thus constraining dissent and rebellion.

Summing Up

- Rationalization works to limit individual choice and freedom.
- Consumerism is a pervasive feature of contemporary cultures that restricts opportunities for the creation of unique identities and countercultures.

SUMMARY

1. What are the main components of culture and what is culture's main function?
   Culture comprises various types of ideas (including symbols, language, values, and beliefs), norms of behaviour, and material objects. The ability to create symbols, cooperate, and make tools has enabled humans to thrive in their environments.

2. What role does biology play in shaping specific human behaviours and social arrangements?
   Biology sets broad limits and potentials on human behaviour and social arrangements. However, most of the variation in human behaviour and social arrangements is due to social forces.

3. What is the ideal vantage point for analyzing a culture?
   We can see the contours of culture most sharply if we are neither too deeply immersed in it nor too much removed from it. Understanding culture requires refraining from taking your own culture for granted and judging other cultures exclusively by the standards of your own.

4. **What does it mean to say that culture has "two faces"?**
   First, culture provides us with increasing opportunities to exercise our freedom in some respects. The rights revolution, multiculturalism, globalization, and postmodernism reflect this tendency. Second, culture constrains us in other respects, putting limits on what we can become. The growth of rationalization and the spread of consumerism reflect this tendency.

5. **What is the multiculturalism debate?**
   Advocates of multiculturalism want school and postsecondary curricula to reflect the country's growing ethnic and racial diversity. They also want school and postsecondary curricula to stress that all cultures have equal value. They believe that multicultural education will promote self-esteem and economic success among members of racial minorities. Critics fear that multiculturalism results in declining educational standards. They believe that multicultural education causes political disunity and interethnic and interracial conflict. They argue that it promotes an extreme form of cultural relativism.

6. **What is the "rights revolution"?**
   The rights revolution is the process by which socially excluded groups have struggled to win equal rights under the law and in practice. In full swing by the 1960s, the rights revolution involves the promotion of women's rights, the rights of members of minority ethnic and racial groups, gay and lesbian rights, the rights of people with special needs, constitutional rights, and language rights. The rights revolution fragments culture by legitimizing the grievances of groups that were formerly excluded from full social participation and renewing their pride in their identity and heritage.

7. **What does the "globalization" of culture involve?**
   The globalization of culture has resulted from the growth of international trade and investment, ethnic and racial migration, influential transnational organizations, and inexpensive travel and communication.

8. **What is postmodernism?**
   Postmodernism involves an eclectic mixing of elements from different times and places, the decline of authority, and the erosion of consensus around core values.

9. **What is rationalization?**
   Rationalization involves the application of the most efficient means to achieve given goals and the unintended, negative consequences of doing so. Rationalization is evident in the increasingly regulated use of time and in many other areas of social life.

10. **What is consumerism?**
    Consumerism is the tendency to define ourselves in terms of the goods we purchase. Excessive consumption puts limits on who we can become, constrains our capacity to dissent from mainstream culture, and degrades the natural environment.

KEY TERMS

abstraction (p. 62)

consumerism (p. 81)

cooperation (p. 63)

countercultures (p. 82)

cultural relativism (p. 72)

culture (p. 62)

ethnocentrism (p. 67)

folkways (p. 64)

high culture (p. 62)

material culture (p. 63)

mores (p. 64)

non-material culture (p. 63)

norms (p. 63)

popular culture (p. 62)

postmodernism (p. 76)   Sapir-Whorf thesis (p. 66)

production (p. 63)   subculture (p. 81)

rationalization (p. 80)   symbols (p. 62)

rights revolution (p. 73)   taboos (p. 64)

rites of passage (p. 74)   values (p. 63)

WEB RESOURCES

Companion Website for This Book

http://www.compass4e.nelson.com

Begin by clicking on the Student Resources section of the website. Next, select the chapter you are studying from the pull-down menu. From the Student Resources page you have easy access to additional Weblinks and other resources. The website also has many useful tips to aid you in your study of sociology, including practice tests for each chapter.

InfoTrac® Search Terms

These search terms are provided to assist you in beginning to conduct research on this topic by visiting http://www.infotrac-college.com:

consumerism

culture

globalization

multiculturalism

postmodernism

rationalization

CHAPTER

4

Socialization

Brand X Pictures/Getty Images

IN THIS CHAPTER, YOU WILL LEARN THAT

- Children raised in isolation do not develop normal language and other social skills, suggesting that social interaction unleashes human abilities.

- The socializing influence of the family decreased in the twentieth century, while the influence of schools, peer groups, and the mass media increased.

- People's identities change faster, more often, and more completely than they did just a couple of decades ago; the self has become more plastic.

- The main socializing institutions often teach children and adolescents contradictory lessons, making socialization a more confusing and stressful process than it used to be.

- Declining parental supervision and guidance, increasing assumption of adult responsibilities by youth, and declining participation in extracurricular activities are transforming the character of childhood and adolescence.

SOCIAL ISOLATION AND THE CRYSTALLIZATION OF SELF-IDENTITY

One day in 1800, a 10- or 11-year-old boy walked out of the woods in southern France. He was filthy, naked, unable to speak, and had not been toilet trained. After being taken by the police to a local orphanage, he repeatedly tried to escape and refused to wear clothes. No parent ever claimed him. He became known as "the wild boy of Aveyron." A thorough medical examination found no major physical or mental abnormalities. Why, then, did the boy seem more animal than human? Because, until he walked out of the woods, he had been raised in isolation from other human beings (Shattuck, 1980).

Similar horrifying reports lead to the same conclusion. Occasionally a child is found locked in an attic or a cellar, where he or she saw another person for only short periods each day to receive food. Like the wild boy of Aveyron, such children rarely develop normally. Typically, they remain disinterested in games. They cannot form intimate social relationships with other people. They develop only the most basic language skills.

Some of these children may suffer from congenitally subnormal intelligence. It is uncertain how much and what type of social contact they had before they were discovered. Some may have been abused. Therefore, their condition may not be due only to social isolation. However, these examples do at least suggest that the ability to learn culture and become human is only a potential. To be actualized, **socialization** must unleash this human potential. Socialization is the process by which people learn their culture. They do so by (1) entering and disengaging from a succession of roles and (2) becoming aware of themselves as they interact with others. A **role** is the behaviour expected of a person occupying a particular position in society.

Convincing evidence of the importance of socialization in unleashing human potential comes from a study conducted by René Spitz (1945, 1962). Spitz compared babies raised in an orphanage with babies who were being raised in a prison nursing home. Both institutions were hygienic and provided good food and medical care. However, while their mothers cared for the babies in the nursing home, just 6 nurses cared for the 45 orphans. The orphans, therefore, had much less contact with other people. Moreover, from their cribs, the nursing home infants could taste a slice of society. They saw other babies playing and receiving care. They saw mothers, doctors, and nurses talking, cleaning, serving food, and providing medical treatment. In contrast, it was established practice in the orphanage to hang sheets from the cribs to prevent the infants from seeing the activities of the institution. Depriving the infants of social stimuli for most of the day apparently made them less demanding.

Social deprivation had other effects too. Because of the different patterns of child care in the two institutions, by the age of 9 to 12 months the orphans were more susceptible to infections and had a higher death rate than the babies in the nursing home had. By the time they were two to three years old, all the children from the nursing home were walking and talking, compared with fewer than 8 percent of the orphans. Normal children begin to play with their own genitals by the end of their first year. Spitz found that the orphans began this sort of play only in their fourth year. He took this as a sign that they might have an impaired sexual life when they reached maturity. This had happened to rhesus monkeys raised in isolation. Spitz's natural experiment thus amounts to quite compelling evidence for the importance of childhood socialization in making us fully human. Without childhood socialization, most of our human potential remains undeveloped.

The formation of a sense of self continues in adolescence, a particularly turbulent period of rapid self-development. Many people can remember experiences from their youth that helped crystallize their self-identity. Do you? Robert Brym clearly recalls one such defining moment.

Socialization is the process by which people learn their culture—including norms, values, and roles—and become aware of themselves as they interact with others.

A **role** is the behaviour expected of a person occupying a particular position in society.

Mary Evans Picture Library

Corbis/Magma

In the 1960s, researchers Harry and Margaret Harlow placed baby rhesus monkeys in various conditions of isolation to witness and study the animals' reactions. Among other things, they discovered that baby monkeys raised with an artificial mother made of wire mesh, a wooden head, and the nipple of a feeding tube for a breast were later unable to interact normally with other monkeys. However, when the artificial mother was covered with a soft terry cloth, the infant monkeys clung to it in comfort and later exhibited less emotional distress. Infant monkeys preferred the cloth mother even when it had less milk than the wire mother did. The Harlows concluded that emotional development requires affectionate cradling.

"I can date precisely the pivot of my adolescence," says Robert. "I was in grade 10. It was December 16. At 4 p.m. I was a nobody and knew it. Half an hour later, I was walking home from school, delighting in the slight sting of snowflakes melting on my upturned face, knowing I had been swept up in a sea change.

"About 200 students had sat impatiently in the auditorium that last day of school before the winter vacation. We were waiting for Mr. Garrod, the English teacher who headed the school's drama program, to announce the cast of *West Side Story*. I was hoping for a small speaking part and was not surprised when Mr. Garrod failed to read my name as a chorus member. However, as the list of remaining characters grew shorter, I became despondent. Soon only the leads remained. I knew that an unknown kid in grade 10 couldn't possibly be asked to play Tony, the male lead. Leads were almost always reserved for more experienced grade 12 students.

"Then came the thunderclap. 'Tony,' said Mr. Garrod, 'will be played by Robert Brym.'

"'Who's Robert Brym?' whispered a girl two rows ahead of me. Her friend merely shrugged in reply. If she had asked *me* that question, I might have responded similarly. Like nearly all 15-year-olds, I was deeply involved in the process of figuring out exactly who I was. I had little idea of what I was good at. I was insecure about my social status. I wasn't sure what I believed in. In short, I was a typical teenager. I had only a vaguely defined sense of self.

"A sociologist once wrote that 'the central growth process in adolescence is to define the self through the clarification of experience and to establish self-esteem' (Friedenberg, 1959: 190). From this point of view, playing Tony in *West Side Story* turned out to be the first section of a bridge that led me from adolescence to adulthood. Playing Tony raised my social status in the eyes of my classmates, made me more self-confident, taught me I could be good at something, helped me to begin discovering parts of myself I hadn't known before, and showed me that I could act rather than merely be acted upon. In short, it was through my involvement in the play (and, subsequently, in many other plays throughout high school) that I began to develop a clear sense of who I am."

The crystallization of self-identity during adolescence is just one episode in a lifelong process of socialization. To paint a picture of the socialization process in its entirety, we must first review the main theories of how a sense of self develops during early childhood. We then discuss the operation and relative influence of society's main socializing institutions or "agents of socialization": families, schools, peer groups, and the mass media. In these settings, we learn, among other things, how to control our impulses, think of ourselves as members of different groups, value certain ideals, and perform various roles. You will see that these institutions do not always work hand in hand to produce happy, well-adjusted adults. They often give mixed messages and are often at odds with one another. That is, they teach children and adolescents different and even contradictory lessons. You will also see that although recent developments give us more freedom to decide who we are, they can make socialization more disorienting than ever before. In the concluding section of this chapter, we examine how decreasing supervision and guidance by adult family members, increasing assumption of adult responsibilities by youth, and declining participation in extracurricular activities are changing the nature of childhood and adolescence today. Some analysts even say that childhood and adolescence are vanishing before our eyes. Thus, the main theme of this chapter is that the development of self-identity is often a difficult and stressful process—and it is becoming more so.

It is during childhood that the contours of the self are first formed. We therefore begin by discussing the most important social-scientific theories of how the self originates in the first years of life.

Summing Up

- Biology sets the broad limits of human potential.
- Socialization determines the extent to which human potential is realized.

THEORIES OF CHILDHOOD SOCIALIZATION

Socialization begins soon after birth. Infants cry out, driven by elemental needs, and are gratified by food, comfort, and affection. Because their needs are usually satisfied immediately, they do not at first seem able to distinguish themselves from their main caregivers, usually their mothers. However, social interaction soon enables infants to begin developing a self-image or sense of **self**—a set of ideas and attitudes about who they are as independent beings.

The **self** consists of your ideas and attitudes about who you are.

Freud

Austrian psychoanalyst Sigmund Freud proposed the first social-scientific interpretation of the process by which the self emerges (Freud, 1962 [1930], 1973 [1915–17]). He noted that infants demand immediate gratification but begin to form a self-image when their demands are denied—when, for example, parents decide not to feed and comfort them every time they wake up in the middle of the night. The parents' refusal at first incites howls of protest. However, infants soon learn to eat more before going to bed, sleep for longer periods, and go back to sleep if they wake up. Equally important, the infant begins to sense that its needs differ from those of its parents, it has an existence independent of others, and it must somehow balance its needs with the realities of life. Because of many such lessons in self-control, the child eventually develops a sense of what constitutes appropriate behaviour and a moral sense of right and wrong. Soon a personal conscience crystallizes. It is a storehouse of cultural standards. In addition, a psychological mechanism develops that normally balances the pleasure-seeking and restraining components of the self. Earlier thinkers believed that the self emerges naturally, the way a seed germinates. In a revolutionary departure from previous thinking on the subject, Freud argued that only social interaction allows the self to emerge.

Cooley's Symbolic Interactionism

American scholars took ideas about the emergence of the self in a still more sociological direction. Notably, Charles Horton Cooley introduced the idea of the "looking-glass self," making him a founder of the symbolic interactionist tradition and an early contributor to the sociological study of socialization.

Cooley observed that when we interact with others, they gesture and react to us. This allows us to imagine how we appear to them. We then judge how others evaluate us. Finally, from these judgments we develop a self concept or a set of feelings and ideas about who we are. In other words, our feelings about who we are depend largely on how we see ourselves evaluated by others. Just as we see our physical body reflected in a mirror, so we see our social selves reflected in people's gestures and reactions to us (Cooley, 1902).

For instance, when teachers evaluate students negatively, students may develop a negative self-concept that causes them to do poorly in school. Poor performance may have as much to do with teachers' negative evaluations as with students' innate abilities (Sanchez and Roda, 2003). Here, succinctly put, we have the hallmarks of what came to be known as symbolic interactionism—the idea that in the course of face-to-face communication, people engage in a creative process of attaching meaning to things.

Mead

George Herbert Mead (1934) developed the idea of the looking-glass self. Like Freud, Mead noted that a subjective and impulsive aspect of the self is present from birth. Mead called it simply the **I**. Again, like Freud, Mead argued that a repository of culturally approved standards emerges as part of the self during social interaction. Mead called this objective, social component of the self the **me**. However, while Freud focused on the denial of the impulsive side of the self as the mechanism that generates the self's objective side, Mead drew attention to the unique human capacity to "take the role of the other" as the source of the me (Box 4.1 on page 92).

> The **I**, according to Mead, is the subjective and impulsive aspect of the self that is present from birth.

> The **me**, according to Mead, is the objective component of the self that emerges as people communicate symbolically and learn to take the role of the other.

Mead's Four Stages of Development: Role Taking

Mead saw the self as developing in four stages of role taking:

1. At first, children learn to use language and other symbols by imitating important people in their lives, such as their mother and father. Mead called such people **significant others**.
2. Next, children pretend to be other people. That is, they use their imaginations to role-play in games such as "house," "school," and "doctor."
3. Then, about the time they reach the age of seven, children learn to play complex games that require them to simultaneously take the role of several other people. In baseball, for example, the infielders have to be aware of the expectations of everyone in the infield. A shortstop may catch a line drive. If she wants to make a double play, she must almost instantly be aware that a runner is trying to reach second base and that the person playing second base expects her to throw there. If she hesitates, she probably cannot execute the double play.
4. Once a child can think in this complex way, she can begin the fourth stage in the development of the self, which involves taking the role of what Mead called the **generalized other**. Years of experience may teach an individual that other people, employing the cultural standards of their society, usually regard her as funny, temperamental, or intelligent. A person's image of these cultural standards and how they are applied to her is what Mead meant by the generalized other.

> **Significant others** are people who play important roles in the early socialization experiences of children.

> The **generalized other**, according to Mead, is a person's image of cultural standards and how they apply to him or her.

BOX 4.1

Sociology at the Movies

AVATAR

Avatar can be interpreted as a riff on George Herbert Mead in which Canadian filmmaker James Cameron teaches us that we can know ourselves and our world only by taking the role of—and thus truly seeing—the other.

The movie strikes the keynote with its opening frame: the eyes of ex-marine Jake (Sam Worthington) shoot open as he awakes from a deep sleep. He has been in suspended animation aboard a spacecraft for a year, but now he is about to land on Pandora, a moon rich in "unobtanium," the most precious mineral known to humans. His job is to help a giant, greedy Earth corporation mine it, even if that means destroying the moon's ecology and its inhabitants.

Because of a war accident, Jake is a paraplegic, but on Pandora he will inhabit an avatar—the body of a Na'vi, the intelligent, three-metre tall humanoid creatures that inhabit the moon. The Na'vi enjoy the grace (and the directional ears) of a cat and the strength of a lion. Fabulously, they are able to communicate directly with other creatures and with Pandora itself by connecting the tendrils at the end of their tails to matching tendrils on the animals and vegetation of the planet. When Jake inhabits the body of a

THE CANADIAN PRESS/AP-20th Century Fox

Scene from *Avatar*

Na'vi, he is thus freed from a life of immobility. He is also able to see in an entirely new way, understanding and living in complete harmony with his natural environment, just as the Na'vi do.

Events do not unfold as the corporation planned. Jake is assigned to learn the language and the beliefs of the Na'vi but he soon falls in love with Neytiri, a Na'vi princess (Zoe Saldana). They express their devotion to one another not by saying "I love you," as humans do, but in the Na'vi fashion, by proclaiming "I see you." What Jake sees is the world from Neytiri's point of view. He takes the role of the other and soon begins to empathize fully with the Na'vi's harmonious relationship to Pandora—and to understand the poverty of the mining company's plan to destroy the Na'vi and their way of life by exploiting the moon's unobtainium. And so in the movie's climax, Jake goes native. He helps to organize the Na'vi in an effort to save Pandora and its inhabitants from the humans.

The medium is part of *Avatar*'s message. Shot in spectacular 3-D, *Avatar* uses the latest animation technology to help the audience see in a new way. The message is as captivating as the shimmering jellyfish-like animals that float out to entrance the audience: Only if you see the world from the point of view of other people and understand how *they* see things can you learn who you truly are. Such empathy can even save a world.

Since Mead, some psychologists interested in the problem of childhood socialization have analyzed how the style, complexity, and abstractness of thinking (or "cognitive skills") develop in distinct stages from infancy to the late teenage years (Piaget and Inhelder, 1969). Other psychologists have analyzed how the ability to think in abstract moral terms develops in stages (Kohlberg, 1981). However, from a sociological point of view, it is important to recognize that the development of cognitive and moral skills is more than just the unfolding of a person's innate characteristics. As you will now see, the structure of a person's society and his or her place in it also influences socialization.

Gender Differences

One of the best-known examples of how social position affects socialization comes from the research of Carol Gilligan. She showed how sociological factors help explain differences in the sense of self that boys and girls usually develop. Parents and teachers tend to pass on different cultural standards to boys and girls. Such adult authorities usually define the ideal woman as eager to please and therefore non-assertive. Most girls learn this lesson as they mature. The fact that girls usually encounter more male and fewer female teachers and other authority figures as they grow up reinforces the lesson. Consequently, much research shows that girls tend to develop lower self-esteem than boys do, although it seems doubtful that teenage girls in general experience the decline in self-esteem that Gilligan detected in her early work (Brown and Gilligan, 1992; Kling et al., 1999).

Cultural Differences

In a like manner, sociological factors help explain the development of different ways of thinking or cognitive styles of different cultures (Cole, 1995; Vygotsky, 1987).

Consider, for example, the contrast between ancient China and ancient Greece. In part because of complex irrigation needs, the rice agriculture of ancient southern China required substantial cooperation among neighbours. It had to be centrally organized in an elaborate hierarchy within a large state. Harmony and social order were therefore central to ancient Chinese life. Ancient Chinese thinking, in turn, tended to stress the importance of mutual social obligation and consensus rather than debate. Ancient Chinese philosophy focused on the way whole systems, not analytical categories, cause processes and events.

In contrast, the hills and seashores of ancient Greece were suited to small-scale herding and fishing. Ancient Greece was less socially complex than ancient China was. It was more politically decentralized. It gave its citizens more personal freedom. Consequently, philosophies tended to be analytical, which means, among other things, that processes and events were viewed as the result of discrete categories rather than whole systems. Markedly different cultures grew up on these different cognitive foundations. Different ways of thinking depended less on people's innate characteristics than on the structure of society (Nisbett, Peng, Choi, and Norenzayan, 2001).

Clearly, society plays a major role in shaping the way we think and the way we think of ourselves. Freud and the early symbolic interactionists discovered the fundamental process by which the self develops, and later researchers emphasized the gender, civilization, and other social bases of diverse socialization patterns.

Fiotr Sikora/Photonica/Getty Images

Much socialization takes place informally, with the participants unaware they are being socialized. These girls are learning gender roles as they shop at the mall.

Summing Up

- Through socialization, the self develops.
- Cooley's "looking glass self" is composed of our reactions to how we imagine others view us.
- For Mead, the self develops through a broadening ability to emphasize with significant and generalized others.
- Socialization often produces important gender and cultural differences.

HOW SOCIALIZATION WORKS

The social world is composed of a wide range of characters. Some people are passive, others aggressive. Some are gentle, others brutal. Some are selfish, others altruistic. Our species contains the broadest possible variation, from the saintly to the devilish.

Since socialization forms such a wide range of individual characters, it is instructive to ask how this variation occurs. A detailed answer to this question is complicated, but the basic principles are not. Humans are continuously surrounded and influenced by real or imagined others, who constitute a person's **social environment**. To satisfy individual needs and interests, every person needs to adapt to his or her environment. **Adaptation** involves arranging one's actions to maximize the degree to which an environment satisfies one's needs and interests.

The challenge of learning to ride a bicycle illustrates these concepts. If a girl wants to ride a bicycle, she cannot act any way she likes. To be successful, she must adjust her behaviour to satisfy the characteristics of the physical environment. In this case, the dominant environmental characteristic is gravity. On her first attempt, the novice cyclist will do her best, but her adaptive behaviour will likely be imperfect. As a result, the environment provides feedback in the form of skinned knees, scrapped hands, and bruised legs. These are all signals that the environment is not cooperating. To gain cooperation, and satisfy her bike-riding interests, the girl must act differently. She does, and eventually learns the role of cyclist.

The same process occurs in social environments, each of which has distinctive requirements. Different types of families make different kinds of demands on their children. Different kinds of schools have distinctive expectations of students. Neighbourhood environments differ, and so do friendship groups and every other form of community. Each of these environments shapes its participants through socialization. In an abusive family, the adaptive strategies children learn, and the kind of persons they become, are very different from what they learn and become in a warm, supportive family.

As these examples make clear, socialization is fundamentally an evolutionary process. Simply stated, the steps in the process are as follows: (1) In any environment, a person acts on the basis of his or her existing personal characteristics and interests. (2) The environment responds to the person's actions cooperatively or not. (3) The environmental response shapes the individual's conduct by either reinforcing existing patterns (cooperation) or encouraging change (resistance). In short, individual character leads to actions to which environments respond selectively. When environments respond cooperatively—when they satisfy individual needs—the rewards reinforce existing individual characteristics. When environments frustrate individual needs, change (learning) is encouraged.

The **social environment** is composed of the real or imagined others to whom individuals must adapt to satisfy their own needs and interests.

Adaptation is the process of changing one's actions to maximize the degree to which an environment satisfies one's needs and interests.

When this socialization process occurs in infants and children, the results are profound because the social environment (the family) is so demanding and powerful relative to the child's resources. As children grow older and become more fully socialized, they have a wider range of adaptive options at their disposal. This means their characters are more stable, since they are more skilled at getting environments to cooperate. Still, at all stages of life, dramatic resocialization is possible if the social environment is sufficiently imposing. Cults can change recruits into people who are unrecognizable to their former friends and family members by employing the same socialization principles that transform *Biggest Loser* participants.

Summing Up

- Socialization is an evolutionary process through which groups shape the character and conduct of individuals.

THEORIES AND AGENTS OF SOCIALIZATION

Functionalists emphasize how socialization helps to maintain orderly social relations. They also play down the freedom of choice individuals enjoy in the socialization process.

Conflict and feminist theorists typically stress the discord based on class, gender, and other divisions that is inherent in socialization and that sometimes causes social change.

Symbolic interactionists highlight the creativity of individuals in attaching meaning to their social surroundings. They focus on the many ways in which we often step outside of, and modify, the values and roles that authorities try to teach us.

Whether it maintains order or engenders conflict, shapes us or allow us to shape it, socialization processes operate through a variety of social institutions, including families, schools, peer groups, and, in modern times, the mass media. We now consider how these various "agents of socialization" work. As we do so, please take careful note of the functionalist, conflict, symbolic interactionist, and feminist interpretations embedded in our discussion.

Families

The family is the most important agent of **primary socialization**, the process of mastering the basic skills required to function in society during childhood. The family is well suited to providing the kind of careful, intimate attention required for primary socialization. It is a small group, its members are in frequent face-to-face contact, and most parents love their children and are highly motivated to care for them. These characteristics make most families ideal for teaching small children everything from language to their place in the world.

The family into which you are born also exerts an *enduring* influence over the course of your life. Consider the long-term effect of the family's religious atmosphere. Research shows that the main way religious groups grow is by recruiting and retaining children whose parents already belong to the group (Bibby, 2001: 115). Parents are the key source of their children's religious identification throughout life. Even Canadians who say they have abandoned the religious faith of their parents—or claim to have no religious identification—typically readopt the religious identities of their parents when they participate in rites of passage, such as marriage and baptism (Bibby, 2001: 200). Clearly, the religious atmosphere of a child's family exerts a strong influence on his or her religious practice as an adult.

Primary socialization is the process of acquiring the basic skills needed to function in society during childhood. Primary socialization usually takes place in a family.

The family is still an important agent of socialization, although its importance has declined since the early twentieth century.

Note, however, that the socialization function of the family was more pronounced a century ago, partly because adult family members were more readily available for child care than they are today. As industry grew, families left farming for city work in factories and offices. Especially after the 1950s, many women had to work outside the home for a wage to maintain an adequate standard of living for their families. Fathers partially compensated by spending more time with their children. However, because divorce rates have increased and many fathers have less contact with their children after divorce, children probably see less of their fathers on average now than they did a century ago. Because of these developments, child care—and therefore child socialization—became a big social problem.

Schools: Functions and Conflicts

Secondary socialization is socialization outside the family after childhood.

For children over the age of five, the child-care problem was partly resolved by the growth of the public school system, which was increasingly responsible for **secondary socialization**, or socialization outside the family after childhood. Industry needed better-trained and educated employees. In response, provinces passed laws prescribing school attendance by the early twentieth century. By the time of the 2006 census, nearly 85 percent of adult Canadians had completed high school, and 54 percent had postsecondary qualifications (Statistics Canada, 2009g). Canadians are among the most highly educated people in the world.

The **hidden curriculum** in school involves teaching obedience to authority and conformity to cultural norms.

Instructing students in academic and vocational subjects is just one part of the school's job. In addition, a **hidden curriculum** teaches students what will be expected of them in the larger society once they graduate; more generally, it teaches them how to be conventionally "good citizens." Most parents approve of this instruction. According to one survey conducted in several highly industrialized countries, the capacity of schools to socialize students is more important to the public than all academic subjects except mathematics (Galper, 1998).

What is the content of the hidden curriculum? In the family, children tend to be evaluated on the basis of personal and emotional criteria. As students, however, they are led to believe that they are evaluated solely on the basis of their performance on impersonal tests. They are told that similar criteria will be used to evaluate them in the work world. The lesson is, of course, only partly true. As you will see in Chapters 8 (Social Stratification), 10 (Race and Ethnicity), 11 (Sexualities and Gender Stratification), and 17 (Education), it is not just performance but also class, gender, sexual orientation, and racial criteria that help determine success in school and in the work world. But the accuracy of the lesson is not the issue here. The important point is that the hidden curriculum has done its job if it convinces students that they are judged on the basis of performance alone. Similarly, a successful hidden curriculum teaches students punctuality, respect for authority, the importance of competition in leading to excellent performance, and other conformist behaviours and beliefs that are expected of good citizens, conventionally defined.

The idea of the hidden curriculum was first proposed by conflict theorists who see an ongoing struggle between privileged and disadvantaged groups whenever they probe beneath the surface of social life (Willis, 1984 [1977]). Their research highlights that many students from disadvantaged backgrounds struggle with the hidden curriculum. While conflict theorists acknowledge that some students from poor and racial-minority families can accept the hidden curriculum, disproportionate numbers reject it because it is poorly aligned with what their earlier socialization taught them. Consequently, they often do poorly in school and eventually enter the work world near the bottom of the socioeconomic hierarchy. Paradoxically, the resistance of underprivileged students to the hidden curriculum helps sustain the overall structure of society, with its privileges and disadvantages.

Photos.com

Learning disciplined work habits is an important part of the socialization that takes place in schools.

Symbolic Interactionism and the Self-Fulfilling Prophecy

Early in the twentieth century, symbolic interactionists proposed the **Thomas theorem**, which holds that "situations we define as real become real in their consequences" (Thomas, 1966 [1931]: 301). They also developed the closely related idea of the **self-fulfilling prophecy**, an expectation that helps to cause what it predicts. Our analysis of the hidden curriculum suggests that the expectations of working-class and racial-minority students often act as self-fulfilling prophecies. Expecting to achieve little if they play by the rules, they reject the rules and so achieve little.

Self-fulfilling prophecies can affect teachers as well. In one famous study, two researchers informed teachers in a primary school that they were going to administer a special test to the pupils to predict intellectual "blooming." In fact, the test was just a standard IQ test. After the test, they told teachers which students they could expect to become high achievers and which they could expect to become low achievers. In fact, the researchers randomly assigned pupils to the two groups. At the end of the year, the researchers repeated the IQ test. They found that the students singled out as high achievers scored significantly higher than those singled out as low achievers. Since the only difference between the two groups of students was that teachers expected one group to do well and the other to do poorly, the researchers concluded that teachers' expectations alone influenced students' performance (Rosenthal and Jacobson, 1968). The clear implication of this research is that if a teacher believes that poor children or children from minority groups are likely to do poorly in school, chances are they will.

Peer Groups

Like schools, **peer groups** are agents of socialization whose importance grew in the twentieth century. Peer groups consist of individuals who are not necessarily friends but who are about the same age and of similar status. (**Status** refers to a recognized social position an individual can occupy.) Peer groups help children and adolescents separate from their families and develop independent sources of identity. They are especially influential over such lifestyle issues as appearance, social activities, and dating. In fact, from middle childhood through adolescence, the peer group is often the dominant socializing agent.

The **Thomas theorem** states, "Situations we define as real become real in their consequences."

A **self-fulfilling prophecy** is an expectation that helps bring about what it predicts.

A person's **peer group** comprises people who are about the same age and of similar status as the individual. The peer group acts as an agent of socialization.

Status refers to a recognized social position an individual can occupy.

As you have probably learned from experience, conflict often erupts between the values promoted by the family and those promoted by the adolescent peer group. Adolescent peer groups are controlled by youth, and through them young people begin to develop their own identities. They do this by rejecting some parental values, experimenting with new elements of culture, and engaging in various forms of rebellious behaviour. In contrast, families are controlled by parents. They represent the values of childhood. Under these circumstances, such issues as hair and dress styles; music; curfews; tobacco, drug, and alcohol use; and political views are likely to become points of conflict between the generations.

We should not, however, overstate the significance of adolescent–parent conflict. First, the conflict is usually temporary. Once adolescents mature, the family exerts a more enduring influence on many important issues. Research shows that families have more influence than peer groups do on the educational aspirations and the political, social, and religious preferences of adolescents and university students (Bibby, 2001: 55; Simons-Morton and Chen, 2009).

A second reason not to exaggerate the extent of adolescent–parent discord is that peer groups are not just sources of conflict. They also help *integrate* young people into the larger society. A study of preadolescent children in a small North American city illustrates the point. Over eight years, sociologists Patricia and Peter Adler conducted in-depth interviews with school children between the ages of 8 and 11. They lived in a well-to-do community comprising about 80 000 whites and 10 000 racial minority group members (Adler and Adler, 1998). In each school they visited, they found a system of cliques arranged in a strict hierarchy, much like the arrangement of classes and racial groups in adult society. In schools with a substantial number of visible minority students, cliques were divided by race. Visible minority cliques were usually less popular than white cliques were. In all schools, the most popular boys were highly successful in competitive and aggressive achievement-oriented activities, especially athletics. The most popular girls came from well-to-do and permissive families. One of the main bases of their popularity was that they had the means and the opportunity to participate in the most interesting social activities, ranging from skiing to late-night parties. Physical attractiveness was also an important basis of girls' popularity. Thus, elementary-school peer groups prepared these youngsters for the class and racial inequalities of the adult world and the gender-specific criteria that would often be used to evaluate them as adults, such as competitiveness in the case of boys and physical attractiveness in the case of girls. (For more on gender socialization, see the discussion of the mass media below and Chapter 11, Sexualities and Gender Stratification.) What we learn from this research is that peer groups function not only to help adolescents form an independent identity by separating them from their families but also to teach them how to adapt to the ways of the larger society.

Adaptation to social environments can produce generational effects. If families, schools, peer groups, mass media, and other socialization agents change over time, the consequences will be observable between generations. Box 4.2 introduces one example.

The Mass Media

Like the school and the peer group, the mass media have become increasingly important socializing agents in the twenty-first century. The mass media include television, radio, movies, videos, CDs, audiotapes, the Internet, newspapers, magazines, and books.

The fastest-growing mass medium is the Internet. Worldwide, the number of Internet users jumped to almost 2 billion in 2010 from just 36 million in 1996 (Figure 4.1 on page 100). Still, TV viewing consumes more of the average Canadian's free time than any other mass medium. Ninety-nine percent of Canadians own at least one colour television (Statistics Canada, 2001b). In 2007, 29.2 percent of Canadians watched television 15 more hours per week (see Table 4.1 on page 100). Low-income Canadians watch more TV than high-income earners do, men watch more than women do, people over age 54 watch more than younger Canadians do, and those living in the North watch more than those in other regions do.

Social Policy: What Do You Think?

IS "GENERATION ME" SELF-CENTRED?

People are independent agents; we act based on our perceived best interests. People are also interdependent; to some extent, our fate is in the hands of others. The simultaneous conditions of independence and interdependence make social life complicated. Much of everyday social life seeks solutions to the question, how do we coordinate our actions in spite of our autonomy? Socialization plays an important role in solving this puzzle. Specifically, the problems of coordination are greatly assisted if people are socialized to be empathic.

Empathy is the ability to understand and be sensitive to the needs of others. Empathy is learned, and some people have more empathy than others do because they are socialized differently. Likewise, generational differences in levels of empathy may exist. Evidence suggests that the generation now in postsecondary studies may be deficient in empathy.

Seventy-two studies of university undergraduates conducted over the past three decades measured empathic concern about the misfortunes of others, the ability to imagine other people's viewpoints, and the level of anguish over others' misfortunes. Here is how recent undergraduates compare with earlier generations (Konrath, 2010):

- A significant decline has occurred in empathic concern (48 percent) and perspective-taking (34 percent).
- Post-2000 undergraduates are far less likely than pre-2000 undergraduates to agree with statements like "I often have tender, concerned feelings for people less fortunate than me" and "I sometimes try to understand my friends better by imagining how things look from their perspective."
- The largest decline in empathy scores occurred after 2000, when social networks like Facebook and MySpace began to flourish.
- Decline in empathy is related to a rise in narcissism, self-absorption that sees other people as means to ends.

Self-centredness and decreased levels of kindness and helpfulness have led this generation to be labelled "Generation Me." Slogans such as "Believe in yourself," "Be yourself," and "You must love yourself before you can love someone else" define the generational style (Twenge, 2006).

Why is Generation Me relatively self-centred? Many members of the generation come from single-child families where they are the centre of attention. Many come from dual-income families where parents had less time to model and reinforce empathy. Many went to schools with "no fail" and other policies that provided little corrective feedback to self-centred conduct. Many are surrounded by digital technologies that make it possible to be connected to others without caring much about them. Many find themselves in educational and employment situations where individualism and competition are the only paths to success.

Whatever the causes, the generational shift we have described is bound to have important social consequences. Low empathy is correlated with criminal conduct, violence, sexual aggression, and related anti-social behaviour. How will workplaces organized around role conformity have to change to accommodate Generation Me? What consequences will reduced empathy have on the future stability of marriage partnerships and childrearing? How will this generation treat their parents as they become progressively disabled?

How well do the characteristics of Generation Me describe you and your friends? What signs do you see in everyday experiences that indicate a lack of empathy? Do you think your generation is more self-centred than your parents' generation? In what ways does reduced empathy make cooperation more difficult? What strategies could be used to increase empathy in the next generation?

FIGURE 4.1

Number of Internet Users
Worldwide, in Millions,
1996–2010

Source: "Face of the Web," 2000;
and Internet Usage Statistics,
2008, "World Internet Usage and
Population Statistics." Retrieved
December 26, 2010 (http://www.
internetworldstats.com/stats.htm).

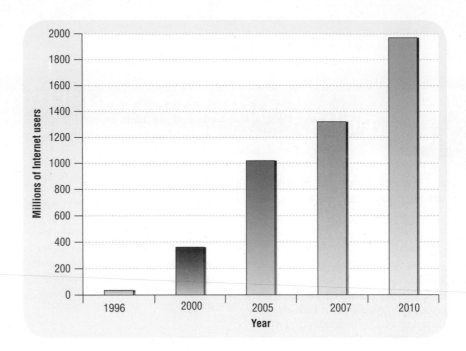

TABLE 4.1

Percentage Viewing
Television 15 or More Hours
per Week, Canada, 2007.

Source: Adapted from Statistics
Canada publication *Overview of
the Time Use of Canadians*, 2005,
Catalogue 12F0080XIE2006001.
Retrieved December 28, 2010
(http://www.statcan.ca/
english/freepub/12F0080XIE/
12F0080XIE2006001.pdf).

	Percentage
Age Cohort	
20–24	20.0
25–34	22.4
35–44	21.5
45–54	26.1
55–64	36.1
65–74	46.9
75+	52.1
Gender	
Male	29.5
Female	28.9
Province or Territory	
Newfoundland and Labrador	31.6
Prince Edward Island	29.0
Nova Scotia	31.3
New Brunswick	32.4
Quebec	31.1
Ontario	29.1
Manitoba	30.7
Saskatchewan	29.8
Alberta	25.7
British Columbia	26.7
Yukon	35.4
Northwest Territories	33.2
Nunavut	43.8
Canada	29.2

The Mass Media and the Feminist Approach to Socialization

The mass media expose individuals to influences that shape their ideas, attitudes, expectations, values, and behaviour. This is especially true for children and adolescents. Although people are to some extent free to choose socialization influences from the mass media, they choose some influences more often than others. Specifically, they tend to choose influences that are more pervasive, fit existing cultural standards, and are made especially appealing by those who control the mass media. We can illustrate this fact by considering how feminist sociologists analyze gender roles. **Gender roles** are widely shared expectations about how males and females are supposed to act. They are of special interest to feminist sociologists, who claim that people are not born knowing how to express masculinity and femininity in conventional ways. Instead, say feminist sociologists, people *learn* gender roles, partly through the mass media.

The learning of gender roles through the mass media begins when small children see that only a kiss from Prince Charming will save Snow White from eternal sleep. Here is an early lesson about who can expect to be passive and who potent. The lesson continues in magazines, romance novels, television, advertisements, music, and the Internet. For example, a central theme in Harlequin romance novels (the world's top sellers in this genre, based in Toronto), is the transformation of women's bodies into objects for men's pleasure. In the typical Harlequin romance, men are expected to be the sexual aggressors. They are typically more experienced and promiscuous than the women are. These themes are well reflected in some of the titles on Harlequin's bestseller list for the third week of February 2010: *In Bed with the Wrangler*; *Greek Tycoon, Inexperienced Mistress*; *Seduction and the CEO*; and *Executive's Pregnancy Ultimatum*. The women who are portrayed in the novels are expected to desire love before intimacy. They are assumed to be sexually passive, giving only subtle cues to indicate their interest in male overtures. Supposedly lacking the urgent sex drive that preoccupies men, women are often held accountable for moral standards and contraception. Readers are assured that adopting this submissive posture ensures that things turn out for the best. As the eHarlequin.com website says, "Happily ever after is always guaranteed with our books" ("About Harlequin," 2010; Grescoe, 1996; Jensen, 1984).

People do not passively accept messages about appropriate gender roles. They often interpret them in unique ways and sometimes resist them. For the most part, however, people try to develop skills that will help them perform gender roles in a conventional way

A **gender role** is the set of behaviours associated with widely shared expectations about how males and females are supposed to act.

Harlequin romance books

© Ted Foxx / Alamy

(Eagley and Wood, 1999: 412–13). Of course, conventions change. It is important to note in this regard that what children learn about femininity and masculinity today is less sexist than what they learned just a few generations ago. For example, comparing *Cinderella* and *Snow White* with *Mulan*, we see immediately that children going to Disney movies today are sometimes presented with more assertive and heroic female role models than the passive heroines of the 1930s and 1940s. However, the amount of change in gender socialization should not be exaggerated. *Cinderella* and *Snow White* are still popular movies. Moreover, for every *Mulan* there is a *Little Mermaid*, a movie that simply modernizes old themes about female passivity and male conquest.

As the learning of gender roles through the mass media suggests, not all media influences are created equal. We may be free to choose which media messages influence us, but most people are inclined to choose the messages that are most widespread, most closely aligned with existing cultural standards, and made most enticing by the mass media. In the case of gender roles, these messages usually support conventional expectations about how males and females are supposed to act.

Resocialization and Total Institutions

Resocialization occurs when powerful socializing agents deliberately cause rapid change in a person's values, roles, and self-conception, sometimes against a person's will.

An **initiation rite** is a ritual that signifies a person's transition from one group to another and ensures his or her loyalty to the new group.

Total institutions are settings in which people are isolated from the larger society and under the strict control and constant supervision of a specialized staff.

In concluding our discussion of socialization agents, we must underline the importance of **resocialization** in contributing to the lifelong process of social learning. Resocialization takes place when powerful socializing agents deliberately cause rapid change in people's values, roles, and self-conception, sometimes against their will.

You can see resocialization at work in the ceremonies that are staged when someone joins a fraternity, a sorority, a sports team, or a religious order. Such a ceremony, or **initiation rite**, signifies the transition of the individual from one group to another and ensures his or her loyalty to the new group. Initiation rites require new recruits to abandon old self-perceptions and assume new identities. Typically, they comprise a three-stage ceremony involving (1) separation from the old status and identity (ritual rejection); (2) degradation, disorientation, and stress (ritual death); and (3) acceptance of the new group culture and status (ritual rebirth).

Much resocialization takes place in what Erving Goffman (1961) called **total institutions**. Total institutions are settings in which people are isolated from the larger society and under the strict control and constant supervision of a specialized staff. Asylums and prisons are examples of total institutions. Because of the "pressure cooker" atmosphere in such institutions, resocialization in total institutions is often rapid and thorough, even in the absence of initiation rites.

A famous failed experiment illustrates the immense resocializing capacity of total institutions (Haney, Banks, and Zimbardo, 1973; Zimbardo, 1972). In the early 1970s, a group of researchers created their own mock prison in the Stanford prison experiment (Zimbardo, 2008). They paid about two dozen male volunteers to act as guards and inmates. The volunteers were mature, emotionally stable, intelligent university students from middle-class homes in the United States and Canada. None had a criminal record. By the flip of a coin, half the volunteers were designated prisoners, the other half guards. The guards made up their own rules for maintaining law and order in the mock prison. The prisoners were picked up by city police officers in a squad car, searched, handcuffed, fingerprinted, booked at the police station, and taken blindfolded to the mock prison. At the mock prison, each prisoner was stripped, deloused, put into a uniform, given a number, and placed in a cell with two other inmates.

To better understand what it means to be a prisoner or a prison guard, the researchers wanted to observe and record social interaction in the mock prison for two weeks. However, they were forced to end the experiment abruptly after only six days because what they witnessed frightened them. In less than a week, the prisoners and prison guards could no longer tell the difference between the roles they were playing and their "real" selves. Much of the socialization these young men had undergone over a period of about 20 years was quickly suspended.

About a third of the guards began to treat the prisoners like despicable animals, taking pleasure in cruelty. Even the guards who were regarded by the prisoners as tough but fair stopped short of interfering in the tyrannical and arbitrary use of power by the most sadistic guards.

All the prisoners became servile and dehumanized, thinking only about survival, escape, and their growing hatred of the guards. Had they been thinking as university students, they could have walked out of the experiment at any time. Some of the prisoners did, in fact, beg for parole. However, by the fifth day of the experiment they were so programmed to think of themselves as prisoners that they returned docilely to their cells when their request for parole was denied.

The Stanford prison experiment suggests that your sense of self and the roles you play are not as fixed as you may think. Radically alter your social setting and, like the university students in the experiment, your self-conception and patterned behaviour are also likely to change. Such change is most evident among people undergoing resocialization in total institutions. However, the sociological eye is able to observe the flexibility of the self in all social settings, including those that greet the individual in adult life.

Summing Up

- Families are agents of primary socialization, while schools are principally responsible for secondary socialization.
- Mastery of the hidden curriculum in schools is an important determinant of success.
- Self-fulfilling prophecies generate expectations that influence performance.
- The mass media often promote and reinforce stereotypical gender roles.
- Total institutions provide comprehensive conditions for resocialization.

SOCIALIZATION ACROSS THE LIFE COURSE

Adult Socialization and the Flexible Self

The development of the self is a lifelong process. When young adults enter a profession or get married, they must learn new occupational and family roles. Retirement and old age present an entirely new set of challenges. Giving up a job, seeing children leave home and start their own families, and losing a spouse and close friends—all these changes later in life require that people think of themselves in new ways and to redefine who they are. Many new roles are predictable. To help us learn them we often engage in **anticipatory socialization**, which involves beginning to take on the norms and behaviours of the roles to which we aspire. (Think of 15-year-old fans of *Gossip Girl* learning from the TV show what it might mean to be a young adult.) Other new roles are unpredictable. You might unexpectedly fall in love and marry someone from a different ethnic, racial, or religious group. You might experience a sudden and difficult transition from peace to war. If so, you will have to learn new roles and adopt new cultural values or at least modify old ones. Even in adulthood, then, the self remains flexible.

Today, people's identities change faster, more often, and more completely than they did just a few decades ago. One factor contributing to the growing flexibility of the self is globalization. As we saw in Chapter 3 (Culture), people are now less obliged to accept the culture into which they are born. Because of globalization, they are freer to combine elements of culture from a wide variety of historical periods and geographical settings.

CP Picture Archive/Tony Gutierrez

American Private Lynndie England became infamous when photographs were made public showing her and other American soldiers abusing Iraqi prisoners in obvious contravention of international law. "She's never been in trouble. She's not the person that the photographs point her out to be," said her childhood friend Destiny Gloin (quoted in "Woman Soldier," 2004). Ms. Gloin was undoubtedly right. Private England at Abu Ghraib prison was not the Lynndie England from high school. As in the Stanford prison experiment, she was transformed by a structure of power and a culture of intimidation that made the prisoners seem subhuman.

Anticipatory socialization involves taking on the norms and behaviours of the role to which we aspire.

A second factor increasing our freedom to design our selves is our growing ability to fashion new bodies from old. People have always defined themselves partly in terms of their bodies; your self-conception is influenced by whether you're a man or a woman, tall or short, healthy or ill, conventionally attractive or plain. However, our bodies used to be fixed by nature. People could do nothing to change the fact that they were born with certain features and grew older at a certain rate.

Now, however, you can change your body, and therefore your self-conception, radically and virtually at will—if, that is, you can afford it. Bodybuilding, aerobic exercise, and weight reduction regimens are more popular than ever. Plastic surgery allows people to buy new breasts, noses, lips, eyelids, and hair—and to remove unwanted fat, skin, and hair from various parts of their bodies. In 2009, about 1.5 million North Americans underwent cosmetic surgery, down a little from the previous year because of the recession, but five times as many as in 1992. Nearly 11 million North Americans underwent collagen, Botox, and other "minimally invasive" procedures in 2009, 160 times as many as in 1992. Other body-altering procedures include sex-change operations and organ transplants. At any given time, more than 50 000 North Americans are waiting for a replacement organ. Brisk, illegal international trade in human hearts, lungs, kidneys, livers, and eyes enables well-to-do people to enhance and extend their lives (Rothman, 1998). Modern bionics makes it possible to wire realistic prosthetic limbs into brain circuitry that, with practice, can function almost like the original limbs. Technologies are also being developed that can restore vision and hearing using cameras, microphones, and microscopic electrodes. As these examples illustrate, many exciting opportunities for changing our bodies, and therefore our self-conception, have been introduced in recent decades.

Self-Identity and the Internet

Further complicating the process of identity formation today is the growth of the Internet. In the 1980s and early 1990s most observers believed that social interaction by means of computer would involve only the exchange of information between individuals. They were wrong. Computer-assisted social interaction can profoundly affect how people think of themselves (Brym and Lenton, 2001; Haythornthwaite and Wellman, 2002).

Internet users interact socially by exchanging text, images, and sound via email, instant messaging, Internet phone, Facebook, Twitter, videoconferencing, computer-assisted work groups, online dating services, and so on. In the process, they often form **virtual communities**. Virtual communities are associations of people, scattered across the country or the planet, who communicate via computer about subjects of common interest.

Because virtual communities allow interaction using concealed identities, people are free to assume new identities and encouraged to discover parts of themselves they were formerly unaware of. In virtual communities, shy people can become bold, normally assertive people can become voyeurs, old people can become young, straight people can become gay, and women can become men (Turkle, 1995). Experience on the Internet thus reinforces our main point: in recent decades, the self has become increasingly flexible, and people are freer than ever to shape their selves as they choose.

However, this freedom comes at a cost, particularly for young people. In concluding this chapter, we consider some of the socialization challenges Canadian youth face today. To set the stage for this discussion, we first examine the emergence of "childhood" and "adolescence" as categories of social thought and experience some 400 years ago.

A **virtual community** is an association of people, scattered across the country, continent, or planet, who communicate via computer about a subject of common interest.

Summing Up

- Globalization, various medical advances, and the pervasiveness of the Internet encourage the development of more fluid, flexible selves.

DILEMMAS OF CHILDHOOD AND ADOLESCENT SOCIALIZATION

In preindustrial societies, children were considered small adults. From a young age, they were expected to conform as much as possible to the norms of the adult world. They were put to work as soon as they could contribute to the welfare of their families. This often meant doing chores by the age of 5 and working full-time by the age of 10 or 12. Marriage, and thus the achievement of full adulthood, was common by the age of 15 or 16.

Children in Europe and North America fit this pattern until the late seventeenth century, when the idea of childhood as a distinct stage of life emerged. At that time, the feeling grew among well-to-do Europeans and North Americans that boys should be permitted to play games and receive an education that would allow them to develop the emotional, physical, and intellectual skills they would need as adults. Girls continued to be treated as "little women" (the title of Louisa May Alcott's 1869 novel) until the nineteenth century. Most working-class boys did not enjoy much of a childhood until the twentieth century. Thus, it is only in the last century that the idea of childhood as a distinct and prolonged period of life became universal in the West (Ariès, 1962).

The Emergence of Childhood and Adolescence

The idea of childhood emerged when and where it did because of social necessity and social possibility. Prolonged childhood was necessary in societies that required better-educated adults to do increasingly complex work, because childhood gave young people a chance to prepare for adult life. Prolonged childhood was possible in societies where improved hygiene and nutrition allowed most people to live more than 35 years, the average lifespan in Europe in the early seventeenth century. In other words, before the late seventeenth century, most people did not live long enough to permit the luxury of childhood. Moreover, young people had no social need for a period of extended training and development before the comparatively simple demands of adulthood were thrust upon them.

In general, wealthier and more complex societies whose populations enjoy a long average life expectancy stretch out the pre-adult period of life. For example, we saw that in seventeenth-century Europe, most people reached mature adulthood by the age of about 16. In contrast, in Canada and other postmodern countries, most people are considered to reach mature adulthood only around the age of 30, by which time they have completed their formal education, married, and "settled down." Once teenagers were relieved of adult responsibilities, people had to coin a new term to describe the teenage years: *adolescence*. Subsequently, the term *young adulthood* entered popular usage as an increasingly large number of people in their late teens, 20s, and early 30s delayed marriage to attend university.

Although these new terms describing the stages of life were firmly entrenched in North America by the middle of the twentieth century, some of the categories of the population they were meant to describe soon began to change dramatically. Some analysts even began to write about the "disappearance" of childhood and adolescence altogether (Friedenberg, 1959; Postman, 1982). Although undoubtedly overstating their case, these social scientists identified some of the social forces responsible for the changing character of childhood and adolescence in recent decades. We examine these social forces in the concluding section of this chapter.

Problems of Childhood and Adolescent Socialization Today

When you were between the ages of 10 and 17, how often were you at home or with friends but without adult supervision? How often did you have to prepare your own meals or take care of a younger sibling while your parent or parents were at work? How many hours a week did you spend cleaning house? How many hours a week did you have to work at a part-time job to earn spending money and save for university? How many hours a week did you spend on extracurricular activities associated with your school? On TV viewing and other mass media use? If you were like most Canadian preteens and teenagers from working- and middle-class families, many of your waking hours outside of school were spent without adult supervision or assuming substantial adult responsibilities, such as those listed above. You are unlikely to have spent much time on extracurricular activities associated with your school but quite a lot of time viewing TV and using other mass media.

Declining adult supervision and guidance, increasing mass media and peer group influence, and the increasing assumption of substantial adult responsibilities to the neglect of extracurricular activities have done much to change the socialization patterns of Canadian youth over the past 40 years or so. Let us consider each of these developments in turn.

Declining Adult Supervision and Guidance

In her study of adolescence, Patricia Hersch wrote that "in all societies since the beginning of time, adolescents have learned to become adults by observing, imitating and interacting with grown-ups around them" (Hersch, 1998: 20). However, in contemporary North America, adults are increasingly absent from the lives of adolescents. Why? According to Hersch, "society has left its children behind as the cost of progress in the workplace" (Hersch, 1998: 19). What she means is that more adults are working longer hours and have less time to spend with their children than they used to. We examine some reasons for the increasing demands of paid work in Chapter 13 (Work and the Economy). One major consequence of reduced support and supervision is that young people, especially those from working- and middle-class families, are increasingly left alone to socialize themselves and build their own community.

This community sometimes revolves around high-risk behaviour. It is therefore not coincidental that the peak hours for juvenile crime are between 3 p.m. and 6 p.m. on weekdays (Hersch, 1998). This research finding suggests that many of the teenage behaviours commonly regarded as problematic result from declining adult guidance and supervision.

Increasing Media Influence

Declining adult supervision and guidance also leaves North American youth more susceptible to the influence of the mass media and peer groups. As one parent put it, "When they hit the teen years, it is as if they can't be children anymore. The outside world has invaded the school environment" (quoted in Hersch, 1998: 111). In an earlier era, family, school, church, and community usually taught young people more or less consistent beliefs and values. Now, however, the mass media and peer groups often pull young people in different directions from the school and the family, leaving them uncertain about what constitutes appropriate behaviour and making the job of growing up more stressful than it used to be (Arnett, 1995).

Declining Extracurricular Activities and Increasing Adult Responsibilities

As the opening anecdote about Robert Brym's involvement in high-school drama illustrates, extracurricular activities are important for adolescent personality development. These activities provide opportunities for students to develop concrete skills and thereby make sense of the world and their place in it. In schools today, academic subjects are too often presented as disconnected bits of knowledge that lack relevance to the student's life. Drama, music, and athletics programs are often better at giving students a framework within which they can develop a strong sense of self, because they are concrete activities with clearly defined rules. By training and playing hard on a hockey team, mastering a string or a band instrument, or acting in plays, you can learn something about your physical, emotional, and social capabilities and limitations, about what you are made of, and about what you can and cannot do. These are just the sorts of activities adolescents require for healthy self-development.

However, if you're like most young Canadians today, you spent fewer hours per week on extracurricular activities associated with school than your parents did when they went to school. Educators estimate that only about a quarter of today's high-school students take part in sports, drama, music, and so forth (Hersch, 1998). Many of them are simply too busy with homework, household chores, child-care responsibilities, and part-time jobs to enjoy the benefits of school activities outside the classroom. Half of Canadian teenagers work at jobs an average of 15 hours a week (Bibby, 2001: 35).

"The Vanishing Adolescent"

Some analysts wonder whether the assumption of so many adult responsibilities, the lack of extracurricular activities, declining adult supervision and guidance, and increasing mass media and peer group influence are causing childhood and adolescence to disappear. As early as 1959, one sociologist spoke of "the vanishing adolescent" in North American society (Friedenberg, 1959). More recently, another commentator remarked, "I think that we who were small in the early sixties were perhaps the last generation ... who actually had a childhood, in the ... sense of ... a space distinct in roles and customs from the world of adults, oriented around children's own needs and culture rather than around the needs and culture of adults" (Wolf, 1997: 13). Childhood and adolescence became universal categories of social thought and experience in the twentieth century. Under the impact of the social forces discussed above, however, the experience and meaning of childhood and adolescence now seem to be changing radically.

Summing Up

- In highly developed societies, the transition period between childhood and adulthood has increased by about 15 years since 1600.
- Reduced adult supervision, increasing media influence, and declining extra-curricular engagement are changing the socialization process for children and adolescents.
- Less-structured social environments provide more freedom to children and adolescents and, in doing so, make socialization outcomes less predictable.

SUMMARY

1. **Why is social interaction necessary?**
   Studies show that children raised in isolation do not develop normally. This finding supports the view that social interaction unleashes human potential.

2. **What is Freud's theory of childhood socialization?**
   Freud argued that a self-image begins to emerge when a baby's impulsive demands are denied. Because of many lessons in self-control, a child eventually develops a sense of what constitutes appropriate behaviour, a moral sense of right and wrong, and a personal conscience. Ongoing social interaction is thus necessary for the self to emerge.

3. **What is Mead's theory of childhood socialization?**
   Like Freud, Mead noted that an impulsive aspect of the self (the "I") is present from birth. Developing Cooley's idea of the "looking-glass self," Mead also argued that a repository of culturally approved standards emerges as part of the self during social interaction. Mead drew attention to the unique human capacity to take the role of the other as the source of the "me." People develop, he wrote, by first imitating and pretending to be their significant others, then learning to play complex games that require understanding several roles simultaneously, and finally developing a sense of cultural standards and how they apply.

4. What are the central principles of socialization?

Socialization is the process through which groups shape the character and conduct of individuals. Shaping occurs because people seek to adapt to their social environment in a way that satisfies their needs and interests. Socialization is thus a form of evolution: character guides conduct, which is in turn "selected" by the social environment as either acceptable or unacceptable for need satisfaction.

5. How has the influence of various social agents changed over the past century?

Over the past century, the increasing socializing influence of schools, peer groups, and the mass media was matched by the decreasing socializing influence of the family.

6. In what sense is the self more flexible than it used to be?

People's self-conceptions are subject to more flux now than they were even a few decades ago. Cultural globalization, medical advances, and computer-assisted communication are among the factors that have made the self more plastic.

7. What social forces are causing change in the character and experience of childhood and adolescence?

Childhood as a distinct stage of life emerged for well-to-do boys in the late seventeenth century when life expectancy started to increase and boys had to be trained for more complex work tasks. Girls were treated as "little women" until the nineteenth century, and most working-class boys first experienced childhood only in the twentieth century. Once teenagers were relieved of adult responsibilities, the term "adolescence" was coined to describe the teenage years. Subsequently, the term "young adulthood" entered popular usage as an increasingly large number of people in their late teens and 20s delayed marriage to attend postsecondary schools.

Today, decreasing parental supervision and guidance, the increasing assumption of substantial adult responsibilities by children and adolescents, declining participation in extracurricular activities, and increased mass media and peer group influence are causing changes in the character and experience of childhood and adolescence. According to some analysts, childhood and adolescence as they were known in the first half of the twentieth century are disappearing.

KEY TERMS

adaptation (p. 94)

anticipatory socialization (p. 103)

gender role (p. 101)

generalized other (p. 91)

hidden curriculum (p. 96)

I (p. 91)

initiation rite (p. 102)

me (p. 91)

peer group (p. 97)

primary socialization (p. 95)

resocialization (p. 102)

role (p. 88)

secondary socialization (p. 96)

self (p. 90)

self-fulfilling prophecy (p. 97)

significant others (p. 91)

social environment (p. 94)

socialization (p. 88)

status (p. 97)

Thomas theorem (p. 97)

total institutions (p. 102)

virtual community (p. 104)

WEB RESOURCES

Companion Website for This Book

http://www.compass4e.nelson.com

Begin by clicking on the Student Resources section of the website. Next, select the chapter you are studying from the pull-down menu. From the Student Resources page you have easy access to additional Weblinks and other resources. The website also has many useful tips to aid you in your study of sociology, including practice tests for each chapter.

InfoTrac® Search Terms

These search terms are provided to assist you in beginning to conduct research on this topic by visiting http://www.infotrac-college.com:

hidden curriculum
initiation rite
peer group
primary socialization
secondary socialization

CHAPTER

5

Social Interaction

IN THIS CHAPTER, YOU WILL LEARN THAT

- Social interaction involves people communicating face to face, acting and reacting in relation to each other. The character of every social interaction depends on people's distinct positions in the interaction (statuses), their standards of conduct (norms), and their sets of expected behaviours (roles).

- Humour, fear, anger, grief, disgust, love, jealousy, and other emotions colour social interactions. However, emotions are not as natural, spontaneous, authentic, and uncontrollable as we commonly believe. Various aspects of social structure influence the texture of our emotional life.

- Nonverbal means of communication, including facial expressions, gestures, body language, and status cues, are as important as language is in social interaction.

- Feminists emphasize how status differences between women and men influence social interaction; conflict theorists focus on how the competitive exchange of valued resources affects social interaction; and symbolic interactionists stress how people interpret, negotiate, and modify norms, roles, and statuses in the course of social interaction.

FEMINIST THEORY, EMOTIONS, AND THE BUILDING BLOCKS OF SOCIAL INTERACTION

A few years ago, a researcher and his assistants eavesdropped on 1200 conversations of people laughing in public places, such as shopping malls (Provine, 2000). When they heard someone laughing, they recorded who laughed (the speaker, the listener, or both) and the gender of the speaker and the listener. To simplify things, they eavesdropped only on two-person groups.

They found that women laugh more than men do in everyday conversations. The biggest discrepancy in laughing occurs when the speaker is a woman and the listener is a man. In such cases, women laugh more than twice as often as men do. However, even when a man speaks and a woman listens, the woman is more likely to laugh than the man is.

Research also shows that men are more likely than women are to engage in long monologues and interrupt when others are talking (Tannen, 1994a, 1994b). Men are less likely to ask for help or directions because doing so would imply a reduction in their authority. Much male–female conflict results from these differences. A stereotypical case is the lost male driver and the helpful female passenger. The female passenger, seeing that the male driver is lost, suggests that they stop and ask for directions. The male driver does not want to ask for directions because he thinks that would make him look incompetent. If both parties remain firm in their positions, an argument is bound to result (see Box 5.1 on page 112).

Social interaction involves communication among people acting and reacting to one another, either face to face or via computer. Feminist sociologists are especially sensitive to gender differences in social interaction like those just described. They see that gender often structures interaction patterns.

Consider laughter. If we define **status** as a recognized social position, it is generally true that people with higher status (in this case, men) get more laughs, while people with lower status (in this case, women) laugh more. That is perhaps why class clowns are nearly always boys. Laughter in everyday life, it turns out, is not as spontaneous as you may think. It is often a signal of who has higher or lower status. Social structure influences who laughs more.

Social statuses are just one of three building blocks that structure all social interactions. The others are roles and norms. A **role** is a set of expected behaviours. Whereas people occupy a status, they perform a role. Students may learn to expect that when things get dull, the class clown will brighten their day. The class clown will rise to the occasion, knowing that his fellow students expect him to do so. A **norm** is a generally accepted way of doing things. Classroom norms are imposed by instructors, who routinely punish class clowns for distracting their classmates from the task at hand (see Figure 5.1 on page 112 and Figure 5.2 on page 113).

Social interaction involves people communicating face to face or via computer and acting and reacting in relation to other people. It is structured around norms, roles, and statuses.

Status refers to a recognized social position an individual can occupy.

Roles are sets of expected behaviours.

Norms are generally accepted ways of doing things.

Emotion Management

Some scholars think that laughter and other emotions are like the common cold. In both cases, an external disturbance causes a reaction that people presumably experience involuntarily. For example, the external disturbance could be a grizzly bear attack that causes us to experience fear, or exposure to a virus that causes us to catch cold. In either case, we can't control our body's patterned response. Emotions, like colds, just happen to us (Thoits, 1989: 319).

It is not surprising that feminists were among the first sociologists to note the flaw in the view that emotional responses are typically involuntary (Hochschild, 1979, 1983). Seeing

Social Policy: What Do You Think?

BOX 5.1

ALLOCATING TIME FAIRLY IN CLASS DISCUSSIONS

When John Lie was chair of the Department of Sociology at the University of Illinois (Urbana-Champaign), he often heard student complaints. Sometimes they were reasonable. Sometimes they were not. A particularly puzzling complaint came from a self-proclaimed feminist taking a women's studies class. She said, "The professor lets the male students talk in class. They don't seem to have done much of the reading, but the professor insists on letting them say something even when they don't really have anything to say." John later talked to the professor, who claimed she was only trying to let different opinions come out in class.

Policy debates often deal with important issues at the provincial or territorial, national, and international levels. However, they may revolve around everyday social interaction. For instance, gender differences in conversational styles influence gender inequality, and many professors use class participation to evaluate students. Your grade may depend in part on how often you speak up and whether you have something interesting to say. However, Tannen's study suggests that men tend to speak up more often and more forcefully than women do. Men are more likely to dominate classroom discussions. Therefore, does the evaluation of class participation in assigning grades unfairly penalize female students? If so, what policies can you recommend that might overcome the problem?

One possibility is to eliminate class participation as a criterion for student evaluation. However, most professors would object to this approach on the grounds that good discussions can demonstrate students' familiarity with course material, sharpen students' ability to reason logically, and enrich everyone's educational experience. A college or university lacking energetic discussion and debate would not be much of an educational institution.

A second option is to systematically encourage women to participate in classroom discussion. A third option is to allot equal time for women and men or to allot each student equal time. Criticisms of such an approach come readily to mind. Shouldn't time be allocated only to people who have done the reading and have something interesting to say? The woman who complained to John Lie made that point. Encouraging everyone to speak or forcing each student to speak for a certain number of minutes, even if they do not have something interesting to contribute, would probably be boring or frustrating for better-prepared students.

As you can see, the question of how time should be allocated in class discussions has no obvious solution. In general, the realm of interpersonal interaction and conversation is an extremely difficult area in which to impose rules and policies. So what should your professor do to ensure that class discussion time is allocated fairly?

FIGURE 5.1

Role Set and Status Set

A person occupies several recognized positions or statuses at the same time—for example, mother, wife, and flight attendant. All of these statuses together form a status set. Each status is composed of several sets of expected behaviours or roles—for example, a wife is expected to act as an intimate companion to her husband and to assume certain legal responsibilities as co-owner of a house. In Figure 5.1, dashed lines separate roles and solid lines separate statuses.

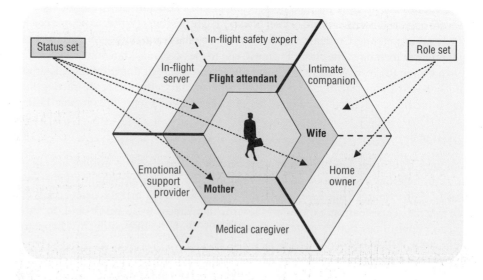

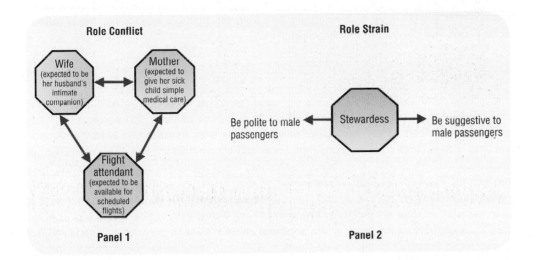

Panel 1

Panel 2

FIGURE 5.2
Role Conflict and Role Strain

(Panel 1): Role conflict takes place when different role demands are placed on a person by two or more statuses held at the same time. How might a flight attendant experience role conflict because of the contradictory demands of the statuses diagrammed in the figure?

(Panel 2): Role strain occurs when incompatible role demands are placed on a person in a single status. Why was the status of stewardess in the 1960s and 1970s high in role strain?

how often women, as status subordinates, must *control* their emotions, they generalized the idea. Emotions don't just happen to us, they argued. We manage them. If a grizzly bear attacks you in the woods, you can run as fast as possible or calm yourself, lie down, play dead, and silently pray for the best. You are more likely to survive the grizzly bear attack if you control your emotions and follow the second strategy. You will also temper your fear with a new emotion: hope (see Figure 5.3).

When people manage their emotions, they usually follow certain cultural "scripts," like the culturally transmitted knowledge that lying down and playing dead gives you a better chance of surviving a grizzly bear attack. That is, individuals usually know the culturally designated emotional response to a particular external stimulus and try to respond appropriately. If they don't succeed in achieving the culturally appropriate emotional response, they are likely to feel guilt, disappointment, or (as in the case of the grizzly bear attack) something much worse.

Sociologist Arlie Russell Hochschild is a leading figure in the study of **emotion management**. In fact, she coined the term. She argues that emotion management involves people obeying "feeling rules" and responding appropriately to the situations in which they find themselves (Hochschild, 1979, 1983). So, for example, people talk about the "right" to feel angry and they acknowledge that they "should" have mourned a relative's death more deeply. People have conventional expectations not only about what they should feel but also about how much they should feel, how long they should feel it, and with whom they should share those feelings. For example, we are expected to mourn the end of a love relationship. Canadians today regard shedding tears as completely natural, though if you shot yourself—a fad among some European Romantics in the early nineteenth century—then the average Canadian would consider you deranged. If you go on a date

Emotion management involves people obeying "feeling rules" and responding appropriately to the situations in which they find themselves.

FIGURE 5.3
How We Get Emotional

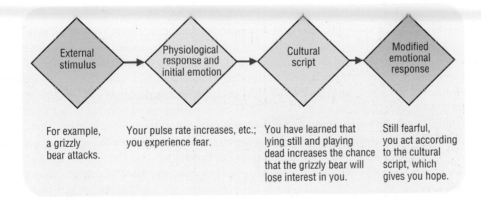

For example, a grizzly bear attacks.

Your pulse rate increases, etc.; you experience fear.

You have learned that lying still and playing dead increases the chance that the grizzly bear will lose interest in you.

Still fearful, you act according to the cultural script, which gives you hope.

minutes after you break up with your long-time love, most people will regard you as callous. Norms and rules govern our emotional life.

Emotion Labour

Emotion labour is emotion management that many people do as part of their job and for which they are paid.

Hochschild distinguishes emotion management (which everyone does in their everyday life) from **emotion labour** (which many people do as part of their job and for which they are paid). We've all seen teachers discipline students who routinely hand in assignments late, pass notes, chatter during class, talk back, and act as class clowns. Those teachers do emotion labour. Similarly, sales clerks, nurses, and flight attendants must be experts in emotion labour. They spend a considerable part of their workday dealing with other people's misbehaviour, anger, rudeness, and unreasonable demands. They spend another part of their workday in what is essentially promotional and public relations work on behalf of the organizations that employ them. ("We hope you enjoyed your flight on Air Canada and that we can serve you again the next time your travel.") In all these tasks, they carefully manage their own emotions while trying to render their clientele happy and orderly. Hochschild estimates that in the United States, nearly half the jobs women do and one-fifth of the jobs men do involve substantial amounts of emotion labour. More women than men do emotion labour because they are typically better socialized to undertake caring and nurturing roles.

Note too that as the focus of the economy shifts from the production of goods to the production of services, the market for emotion labour grows. More and more people are selected, trained, and paid for their skill in emotion labour. Consequently, business organizations increasingly govern the expression of feelings at work, which becomes less spontaneous and authentic over time. This process affects women more than it does men because women do more emotion labour than men do.

Emotions in Historical Perspective

Social structure impinges on emotional experiences in many ways. As we have seen, status hierarchies influence patterns of laughter. Cultural scripts and the expectations of others influence the way we manage our emotions in our personal lives. The growth of the economy's service sector requires more emotion labour, turns it into a commodity, and decreases the ability of people to experience emotions spontaneously and authentically. In these and other ways, the commonsense view of emotions as unique, spontaneous, uncontrollable, authentic, natural, and perhaps even rooted exclusively in our biological makeup proves to be misguided.

We can glean additional evidence of the impact of society on our emotional life from socio-historical studies. It turns out that feeling rules take different forms under different social conditions, which vary historically. Three examples from the social history of emotions help illustrate the point:

•   *Grief.* Among other factors, the crude death rate (the annual number of deaths per 1000 people in a population) helps determine our experience of grief (Lofland, 1985). In Europe as late as 1600, life expectancy was only 35 years. Many infants died at birth or in their first year of life. Infectious diseases decimated populations. The medical profession was in its infancy. The risk of losing family members, especially babies, was thus much greater than it is today. One result of this situation was that people invested less emotionally in their children than we typically do. Their grief response to the death of children was shorter and less intense than ours is; the mourning period was briefer and people became less distraught. As health conditions improved and the infant mortality rate fell over the years, emotional investment in children increased. It intensified especially in the nineteenth century when women starting having fewer babies on average as a result of industrialization (see Chapter 20, Population and Urbanization). As emotional investment in children increased, grief response to children's deaths intensified and lasted longer.

- *Anger.* Industrialization and the growth of competitive markets in nineteenth-century North America and Europe turned the family into an emotional haven from a world increasingly perceived as heartless (see Chapter 15, Families). In keeping with the enhanced emotional function of the family, anger control, particularly by women, became increasingly important for the establishment of a harmonious household. The early twentieth century witnessed mounting labour unrest and the growth of the service sector. Avoiding anger thus became an important labour relations goal. This trend influenced family life too. Child-rearing advice manuals increasingly stressed the importance of teaching children how to control their anger (Stearns and Stearns, 1985, 1986).

- *Disgust.* Manners in Europe in the Middle Ages were disgusting by our standards. Even the most refined aristocrats spat in public and belched shamelessly during banquets. Members of high society did not think twice about scratching themselves in places we regard as private and passing gas at the dinner table, where they ate with their hands and speared food with knives. What was acceptable then causes revulsion now because feeling rules have changed. Specifically, manners began to change with the emergence of the modern political state, especially after 1700. The modern political state raised armies and collected taxes, imposed languages and required loyalty. All this coordination of effort necessitated more self-control on the part of the citizenry. Changes in standards of public conduct—signalled by the introduction of the fork, the nightdress, the handkerchief, the spittoon, and the chamber pot—accompanied the rise of the modern state. Good manners also served to define who had power and who lacked it. For example, there is nothing inherently well-mannered about a father sitting at the head of the table carving the turkey and children waiting to speak until they are spoken to. These rules about the difference between good manners and improper behaviour were created to signify the distribution of power in the family by age and gender (Elias, 1994 [1939]; Scott, 1998).

We thus see that although emotions form an important part of all social interactions, they are neither universal nor constant. They have histories and deep sociological underpinnings in statuses, roles, and norms. This observation flies in the face of common sense. We typically think of our interactions as outcomes of our emotional states. We commonly believe that we interact differently with people depending on whether they love us, make us angry, or make us laugh. We usually think our emotions are evoked involuntarily and result in uncontrollable action. However, emotions are not as unique, involuntary, and uncontrollable as people often believe. Underlying the turbulence of emotional life is a measure of order and predictability governed by sociological principles that vary historically.

Manners in Europe during the Middle Ages were disgusting by our standards today.

Just as building blocks need cement to hold them together, so norms, roles, and statuses require a sort of "social cement" to prevent them from falling apart and to turn them into a durable social structure. What is the nature of the cement that holds the building blocks of social life together? Asked differently, exactly how is social interaction maintained? This is the most fundamental sociological question one can ask, for it is really a question about how social structures, and society as a whole, are possible. It is the subject of the next two sections of this chapter.

Summing Up

- Social interaction is norm-based communication between people occupying statuses and playing roles.
- Emotions are an important component of social interaction. Social position shapes the expression of emotion.
- Forms of emotional management and emotional labour vary across social contexts and historically.

CONFLICT THEORIES OF SOCIAL INTERACTION

Competing for Attention

Have you ever been in a conversation where you couldn't get a word in edgewise? If you are like most people, this situation is bound to happen occasionally. The longer this kind of one-sided conversation persists, the more neglected you feel. You may make increasingly forceful attempts to turn the conversation your way. However, if you fail, you may decide to end the interaction altogether. If this experience repeats itself—if the person you are talking to persistently monopolizes conversations—you are likely to want to avoid getting into conversations with him or her in the future. Maintaining interaction (and maintaining a relationship) requires that both parties' need for attention is met.

Most people do not consistently try to monopolize conversations. If they did, there wouldn't be much talk in the world. In fact, turn-taking is one of the basic norms that govern conversations; people take turns talking to make conversation possible. Nonetheless, a remarkably large part of all conversations involves a subtle competition for attention. Consider the following snippet of dinner conversation:

John: "I'm feeling really starved."
Mary: "Oh, I just ate."
John: "Well, I'm feeling really starved."
Mary: "When was the last time you ate?"

Charles Derber recorded this conversation (Derber, 1979: 24). John starts by saying how hungry he is. The attention is on him. Mary replies that she is not hungry, and the attention shifts to her. John insists he is hungry, shifting attention back to him. Mary finally allows the conversation to focus on John by asking him when he last ate. John thus "wins" the competition for attention.

Derber recorded 1500 conversations in family homes, workplaces, restaurants, classrooms, dormitories, and therapy groups. He concluded that North Americans usually try to turn conversations toward themselves. They usually do so in ways that go unnoticed. Nonetheless, says Derber, the typical conversation is a covert competition for attention. In Derber's words, there exists

a set of extremely common conversational practices which show an unresponsiveness to others' topics and involve turning them into one's own. Because of norms prohibiting blatantly egocentric behaviour, these practices are often exquisitely subtle.... Although conversationalists are free to introduce topics about themselves, they are expected to maintain an appearance of genuine interest in [topics] about others in a conversation. A delicate face-saving system requires that people refrain from openly disregarding others' concerns and keep expressions of disinterest from becoming visible. (1979: 23)

You can observe the competition for attention yourself. Record a couple of minutes of conversation in your dorm, home, or workplace. Then play back the recording. Evaluate each statement in the conversation. Does the statement try to change who is the subject of the conversation? Or does it say something about the *other* conversationalists or ask them about what they said? How does not responding or merely saying "uh-huh" in response operate to shift attention? Are other conversational techniques especially effective in shifting attention? Who "wins" the conversation? What is the winner's gender, race, and class position? Is the winner popular or unpopular? Do you think a connection exists between the person's status in the group and his or her ability to win? You might even want to record yourself in conversation. Where do you fit in?

Derber's analysis is influenced by conflict theory, which holds that social interaction involves competition over valued resources. Such resources include attention, approval, prestige, information, money, and so on (Blau, 1964; Coleman, 1990; Hechter, 1987; Homans, 1961). According to conflict theorists, competitive interaction involves people seeking to gain the most—socially, emotionally, and economically—while paying the least.

Variants of the Conflict Theory of Interaction

The idea that social interaction involves trade in attention and other valued resources is the central insight of **exchange theory**, one variant of the conflict theory of interaction (Blau, 1964; Homans, 1961). Exchange theorists argue that all social relationships involve a literal give and take. From this point of view, when people interact, they exchange valued resources (including attention, pleasure, approval, prestige, information, and money) or punishments. With payoffs, relationships endure and can give rise to various organizational forms. Without payoffs, relationships end. Paradoxically, relationships can also endure because *punishments* are exchanged. The classic case involves "tit-for-tat" violence, where one party to a conflict engages in violence, another party retaliates, the first party seeks revenge, and so on.

A second variant of this approach is **rational choice theory** (Coleman, 1990; Hechter, 1987). Rational choice theory focuses less on the resources exchanged than on the way interacting people weigh the benefits and costs of interaction. According to rational choice theory, interacting people always try to maximize benefits and minimize costs. Businesspeople want to keep their expenses to a minimum so they can keep their profits as high as possible. Similarly, everyone wants to gain the most from their interactions—socially, emotionally, and economically—while paying the least.

From this point of view, the chance of a relationship enduring increases if it provides the interacting parties with payoffs. Ultimately, then, payoffs make social order possible. On the other hand, unequal payoffs mean trouble. The greater the inequality of payoffs to interacting parties, the greater the chance that conflict will erupt and lead to a breakdown in the interaction. Thus, conflict never lies far below the surface of competitive social interactions marked by substantial inequality (Bourdieu, 1977 [1972]; Collins, 1982).

Power and Social Interaction

Many conflict theorists of social interaction emphasize that when people interact, their statuses are often arranged in a hierarchy. People on top enjoy more **power** than those on the bottom—that is, they are "in a position to carry out [their] own will despite resistance"

Exchange theory holds that social interaction involves trade in valued resources.

Rational choice theory focuses on the way interacting people weigh the benefits and costs of interaction. According to rational choice theory, interacting people always try to maximize benefits and minimize costs.

Power is the capacity to carry out one's own will despite resistance.

(Weber, 1947: 152). In face-to-face communication, the degree of inequality strongly affects the character of social interaction between the interacting parties (Bourdieu, 1977 [1972]; Collins, 1982; Kemper, 1978, 1987; Molm, 1997).

To get a better grasp on the role of power in social interaction, consider two extreme cases and the case that lies at the midpoint between the extremes (Table 5.1). **Domination** represents one extreme type of interaction. In social interaction based on domination, nearly all power is concentrated in the hands of people of high status, whereas people of low status enjoy almost no power. Guards versus inmates in a concentration camp, and landowners versus slaves on plantations in the American South before the Civil War were engaged in social interaction based on domination. In extreme cases of domination, subordinates live in a state of near-constant fear.

The other extreme involves interaction based on **cooperation**. Here, power is more or less equally distributed between people of different status. Cooperative interaction is based on feelings of trust. As we will see in Chapter 15, Families, marriages are happier when spouses share housework and child care equitably. Perceived inequity breeds resentment and dissatisfaction. It harms intimacy. It increases the chance that people will have extramarital affairs and will divorce. In contrast, a high level of trust between spouses is associated with marital stability and enduring love (Wood, 1999).

Between the two extremes of interaction based on domination and interaction based on cooperation is interaction based on **competition**. In this mode of interaction, power is unequally distributed but the degree of inequality is less than in systems of domination. If trust is the prototypical emotion of relationships based on cooperation, and fear is the characteristic emotion of subordinates involved in relationships based on domination, envy is an important emotion in competitive interaction.

Significantly, the mode of interaction in an organization strongly influences its efficiency or productivity, that is, its ability to achieve its goals at the least possible cost. Thus, African-American slaves on plantations in the pre-Civil War South, and Jews in Nazi concentration camps, were usually regarded as slow and inept workers by their masters (Collins, 1982: 66–69). This characterization was not just a matter of prejudice. Slavery *is* inefficient because, in the final analysis, fear of coercion is the only motivation for slaves to work. Yet as psychologists have known for more than half a century, punishment is a far less effective motivator than is reward (Skinner, 1953). Slaves hate the tedious and often back-breaking labour, they get little in exchange for it, and therefore they typically work with less than maximum effort.

In a competitive mode of interaction, subordinates receive more benefits, including prestige and money. Prestige and money are stronger motivators than the threat of coercion is. Thus, if bosses pay workers reasonably well and treat them with respect, they will work more efficiently than slaves will, even if they do not particularly enjoy their work or identify with the goals of the company. Knowing they can make more money by working harder and that their efforts are appreciated, workers will often put in extra effort (Collins, 1982: 63–65).

As sociologist Randall Collins and others have shown, however, the most efficient workers are those who enjoy their work and identify with their employer (Collins, 1982: 60–85; Lowe, 2000). Giving workers a bigger say in decision making, encouraging worker creativity, and ensuring that salaries and perks are not too highly skewed in favour of those on top all help to create high worker morale and foster a more cooperative work environment. Company picnics, baseball games, and, in Japan, the singing of company songs before

Domination is a mode of interaction in which nearly all power is concentrated in the hands of people of high status. Fear is the dominant emotion in systems of interaction based on domination.

Cooperation is a basis for social interaction in which power is more or less equally distributed between people of different status. The dominant emotion in cooperative interaction is trust.

Competition is a mode of interaction in which power is unequally distributed but the degree of inequality is less than in systems of domination. Envy is an important emotion in competitive interactions.

TABLE 5.1
Main Modes of Interaction

| | Mode of Cooperation | | |
Mode of Interaction	Domination	Competition	Cooperation
Level of inequality	High	Medium	Low
Characteristic emotion	Fear	Envy	Trust
Efficiency	Low	Medium	High

the workday begins, all help workers feel they are in harmony with their employer and are playing on the same team. Similarly, although sales meetings and other conferences have an instrumental purpose (the discussion of sales strategies, new products, and so on), they also offer opportunities for friendly social interaction that increases workers' identification with their employer. When workers identify strongly with their employers, they will be willing to undergo self-sacrifice, take initiative, and give their best creative effort, even without the prospect of increased material gain.

Summing Up

- When people interact, they exchange valued resources or punishments. With payoffs, relationships endure and can give rise to various organizational forms. Without payoffs, relationships end. Interacting people generally try to maximize benefits and minimize costs. These are the main insights of the conflict theory of social interaction.
- Domination, competition, and cooperation are the main modes of interaction. Each mode is characterized by different levels of inequality (high, medium, and low), characteristic emotions (respectively, fear, envy, and trust), and different degrees of efficiency (respectively, low, medium, and high).

SYMBOLIC INTERACTION

Is social interaction *always* a competitive and conflict-prone struggle over valued resources, as conflict theorists suggest? A moment's reflection suggests otherwise. People frequently act in ways they consider fair or just, even if that does not maximize their personal gain (Gamson, Fireman, and Rytina, 1982). Some people even engage in altruistic or heroic acts from which they gain nothing and risk much. The plain fact is that social life is richer than conflict theorists would have us believe. Selfishness and conflict are not the only bases of social interaction.

When people behave fairly or altruistically, they are interacting with others based on norms they have learned. These norms say they should act justly and help people in need, even if it costs a lot to do so. How then do people learn norms (as well as roles and statuses)? The first step involves what George Herbert Mead called "taking the role of the other," that is, seeing yourself from the point of view of the people with whom you interact (see Chapter 4, Socialization, and Box 5.2 on page 120). According to Mead, we interpret other people's words and nonverbal signals to understand how they see us, and we adjust our behaviour to fit their expectations about how we ought to behave. During such symbolic interaction, we learn norms and adopt roles and statuses.

Such social learning is different from studying a user manual or a textbook. It involves constantly negotiating and modifying the norms, roles, and statuses that we meet as we interact with others, shaping them to suit our preferences. People learn norms, roles, and statuses actively and creatively, not passively and mechanically (Berger and Luckmann, 1966; Blumer, 1969; Strauss, 1993). Let us explore this theme by considering the ingenious ways in which people manage the impressions they give to others during social interaction.

Goffman's Dramaturgical Analysis

One of the most popular variants of symbolic interactionism is **dramaturgical analysis**. As first developed by Erving Goffman (1959), and briefly discussed in Chapter 1, A

Dramaturgical analysis views social interaction as a sort of play in which people present themselves so that they appear in the best possible light.

Sociology at the Movies

CATCH ME IF YOU CAN

Between 1964 and 1967, Frank Abagnale (Leonardo DiCaprio) worked as an airline pilot with Pan Am Airways and flew all around the world. During that time he also served as the chief resident pediatrician at a hospital in Georgia and as an assistant attorney general for the state of Louisiana. To top it all off, he made almost $4 million during that short period. So what's the catch? Frank Abagnale never trained to be a pilot, nor did he go to medical or law school, and much of his income was "earned" by cashing fraudulent cheques. In reality, Frank started his career as a 17-year-old with a keen sense of observation and an uncanny talent in manipulating the perceptions of others.

To maintain his lifestyle over those adventurous four years, Frank Abagnale had to portray different characters, such as co-pilot Frank Taylor or Harvard graduate Frank Conners, all the while avoiding capture from persistent FBI agent Carl Hanratty (Tom Hanks). Whether dealing with bank tellers, airline pilots, lawyers, doctors, girlfriends, or the FBI, Frank's success depended on others' accepting that he was who he claimed to be. Eventually, he just couldn't hold together his intricate web of lies and decided to turn himself in.

Frank Abagnale was an expert at what Erving Goffman (1959) called

© DreamWorks/courtesy Everett Collection

Frank Abagnale (Leonardo DiCaprio) impersonating a pilot in *Catch Me If You Can*.

dramaturgy in everyday life. He could rely on people reacting to his uniform, props, and demeanour. In one memorable scene, Frank walks down a crowded sidewalk wearing his pilot's uniform for the first time, turning the head of every woman he passes. When he reaches his bank, he is offered a loan that he was denied when he was out of uniform. Similarly, when Frank takes on the role of head pediatrician, he uses a host of props—a white coat, a framed "Harvard" diploma, shelves of medical books, a door sign reading "Frank Conners, M.D."—to convince others of his authenticity. However, when a young boy comes into the emergency room

with a badly injured leg, Frank promptly excuses himself to go vomit in the janitor's closet. He retreats backstage to avoid giving away his character.

Early in their careers, doctors, lawyers, and other professionals sometimes feel like impostors because their professional socialization is incomplete. They are relieved when time and experience allow their role discomfort to fade. In contrast, Frank Abagnale experienced little discomfort playing professional roles for which he was untrained because he abandoned the idea that he had a true self. Like Goffman and other proponents of dramaturgical analysis, he saw life merely as a play and people as little more than actors. Perhaps that made it easier for him to pull off one of his scams in particular. At one point in his career, he stole a Columbia University diploma and spent a semester teaching sociology at Brigham Young University in Utah.

Sociological Compass, dramaturgical analysis takes literally Shakespeare's line from *As You Like It:* "All the world's a stage, and all the men and women merely players."

From Goffman's point of view, people constantly engage in role-playing. This fact is most evident when we are "front stage" in public settings. Just as being front stage in a play requires the use of props, set gestures, and memorized lines, so does acting in public space. A server in a restaurant, for example, must dress in a uniform, smile, and recite fixed lines ("How are you? My name is Sam and I'm your server today. May I get you a drink before you order your meal?"). When the server goes "backstage," he or she can relax from the front-stage performance and discuss it with fellow actors ("Those kids at table six are driving me nuts!"). Thus, we often distinguish between our public roles and our "true" selves. Note, however, that even backstage we engage in role-playing and impression management; it's just that we are less likely to be aware of it. For instance, in the kitchen, a server may try to present herself in the best possible light to impress another server so that she can eventually ask him out for a date. Thus, the implication of dramaturgical analysis is that there is no single self, just the ensemble of roles we play in various social contexts. Servers in restaurants play many roles off the job. They play on basketball teams, sing in church choirs, and hang out with friends at shopping malls. Each role is governed by norms about what kinds of clothes to wear, what kind of conversation to engage in, and so on. Everyone plays on many front stages in everyday life.

They do not always do so enthusiastically. If a role is stressful, people may engage in role distancing. **Role distancing** involves giving the impression of just "going through the motions" but lacking serious commitment to a role. Thus, when people think a role they are playing is embarrassing or beneath them, they typically want to give their peers the impression that the role is not their "true" self. My parents force me to sing in the church choir; I'm working at McDonald's just to earn a few extra dollars, but I'm going back to college next semester; this old car I'm driving is just a loaner. These are the kinds of rationalizations individuals offer when distancing themselves from a role.

Onstage, people typically try to place themselves in the best possible light; they engage in "impression management." For example, when students enter medical school they quickly adopt a new medical vocabulary and wear a white lab coat to set themselves apart from patients. They try to model their behaviour after the doctors who have authority over them. When dealing with patients, they may hide their ignorance under medical jargon to maintain their authority. They may ask questions they know the answer to so that they can impress their teachers. According to one third-year student, "The best way of impressing [advisers] with your competence is asking questions you know the answer to. Because if they ever put it back on you, 'Well what do you think?' then you can tell them what you think and you'd give a very intelligent answer because you knew it. You didn't ask it to find out information. You ask it to impress people." Medical students don't take a course in how to act like a doctor, but they learn their new role in the course of impression management (Haas and Shaffir, 1987).

Let us now inquire briefly into the way people use words and nonverbal signals to communicate in face-to-face interaction. Having a conversation is actually a wonder of intricate complexity; even today's most advanced super-computer cannot conduct a natural-sounding conversation with a person (Kurzweil, 1999: 61, 91).

Ethnomethodology

Goffman's view of social interaction seems cynical. He portrays people as inauthentic, or constantly playing roles but never really being themselves. His mindset is not much different from that of Holden Caulfield, the antihero of J. D. Salinger's *The Catcher in the Rye*. To Holden Caulfield, all adults seem "phony," "hypocritical," and "fake," constantly pretending to be people they are not.

However discomforting Goffman's cynicism may be, we should not overlook his valuable sociological point: The stability of social life depends on our adherence to norms, roles, and statuses. If that adherence broke down, social life would become chaotic. Take something as simple as walking down a busy street. Hordes of pedestrians rush toward you

Role distancing involves giving the impression that we are just "going through the motions" but actually lack serious commitment to a role.

yet rarely collide with you. Collision is avoided because of a norm that nobody actually teaches and few people are aware of but almost everyone follows. If someone blocks your way, you move to the right. When you move to the right and the person walking toward you moves to the right (which is your left), you avoid bumping into each other. Similarly, consider the norm of "civil inattention." When we pass people in public, we may establish momentary eye contact out of friendliness but we usually look away quickly. According to Goffman, such a gesture is a "ritual" of respect, a patterned and expected action that affirms our respect for strangers. Just imagine what would happen if you fixed your stare at a stranger for a few seconds longer than the norm. Rather than being seen as respectful, your intention might be viewed as rude, intrusive, or hostile. Thus, we would not even be able to walk down a street in peace were it not for the existence of certain unstated norms. These and many other norms, some explicit and some not, make an orderly social life possible (Goffman, 1963, 1971).

By emphasizing how we construct social reality in the course of interaction, symbolic interactionists downplay the importance of norms and understandings that *precede* any given interaction. **Ethnomethodology** tries to correct this shortcoming. Ethnomethodology is the study of the methods ordinary people use, often unconsciously, to make sense of what others do and say. Ethnomethodologists stress that everyday interactions could not take place without *preexisting* shared norms and understandings. The norm of moving to the right to avoid bumping into an oncoming pedestrian and the norm of civil inattention are both examples of preexisting shared norms and understandings.

To illustrate the importance of preexisting shared norms and understandings, Harold Garfinkel conducted a series of experiments. In one such experiment he asked one of his students to interpret a casual greeting in an unexpected way (Garfinkel, 1967: 44):

> Acquaintance: [waving cheerily] How are you?
> Student: How am I in regard to what? My health, my finances, my schoolwork, my peace of mind, my …?
> Acquaintance: [red in the face and suddenly out of control] Look! I was just trying to be polite. Frankly, I don't give a damn how you are.

As this example shows, social interaction requires tacit agreement between the actors about what is normal and expected. Without shared norms and understandings, no sustained interaction can occur. People are likely to get upset and end an interaction when someone violates the assumptions underlying the stability and meaning of daily life.

Assuming the existence of shared norms and understandings, let us now inquire briefly into the way people communicate in face-to-face interaction. This issue may seem trivial. However, as you will soon see, having a conversation is actually a wonder of intricate complexity.

Verbal and Nonverbal Communication

In the 1950s, an article appeared in the British newspaper *News Chronicle*, trumpeting the invention of an electronic translating device at the University of London. According to the article, "[a]s fast as [a user] could type the words in, say, French, the equivalent in Hungarian or Russian would issue forth on the tape" (quoted in Silberman, 2000: 225). The report was an exaggeration, to put it mildly. It soon became a standing joke that if you ask a computer to translate "The spirit is willing, but the flesh is weak" into Russian, the output would read, "The vodka is good, but the steak is lousy." Today, we are closer to high-quality machine translation than we were in the 1950s. However, a practical Universal Translator exists only on *Star Trek*.

The Social Context of Language

Why can people translate better than computers can? Because computer programs find it difficult to make sense of the social and cultural context in which language is used. The same words can mean different things in different settings, so computers, lacking contextual cues, routinely botch translations. That is why machine translation works best when applications are restricted to a single social context—say, weather forecasting or oil exploration. In such

Ethnomethodology is the study of how people make sense of what others do and say by adhering to preexisting norms.

cases, specialized vocabularies and meanings specific to the context of interest are built into the program. Ambiguity is reduced and computers can "understand" the meaning of words well enough to translate them with reasonable accuracy. Similarly, humans must be able to reduce ambiguity and make sense of words to become good translators. They do so by learning the nuances of meaning in different cultural and social contexts over an extended time. Nonverbal cues assist them in this task.

Facial Expressions, Gestures, and Body Language

A few years ago, *Cosmopolitan* magazine featured an article advising female readers on "how to reduce otherwise evolved men to drooling, panting fools." Basing his analysis on the work of several psychologists, the author of the article first urges readers to "delete the old-school seductress image (smoky eyes, red lips, brazen stare) from your consciousness." Then, he writes, you must "upload a new inner temptress who's equal parts good girl and wild child." The article recommends invading a man's personal space and entering his "intimate zone" by finding an excuse to touch him. Picking a piece of lint off his jacket ought to do the trick. Then you can tell him how much you like his cologne (Willardt, 2000). If things progress, another article in the same issue of *Cosmopolitan* explains how you can read his body language to tell whether he's lying (Dutton, 2000).

Whatever we may think of the soundness of *Cosmopolitan*'s advice or the images of women and men it tries to reinforce, this example drives home the point that social interaction typically involves a complex mix of verbal and nonverbal messages. The face alone is capable of more than a thousand distinct expressions, reflecting the whole range of human emotion. Arm movements, hand gestures, posture, and other aspects of body language send many more messages to a person's audience (Wood, 1999; see Figure 5.4).

FIGURE 5.4
Body Language

Among other things, body language communicates the degree to which people conform to gender roles, or widely shared expectations about how males or females are supposed to act. In these photos, which postures suggest power and aggressiveness? Which suggest pleasant compliance? Which are "appropriate" to the gender of the person?

Source: Courtesy of Robert J. Brym.

Despite the wide variety of facial expressions in the human repertoire, most researchers believed until recently that the facial expressions of six emotions are similar across cultures. These six emotions are happiness, sadness, anger, disgust, fear, and surprise (Ekman, 1978). However, since the mid-1990s, some researchers have questioned whether a universally recognized set of facial expressions reflects basic human emotions. Among other things, critics have argued that "facial expressions are not the readout of emotions but displays that serve social motives and are mostly determined by the presence of an audience" (Fernandez-Dols, Sanchez, Carrera, and Ruiz-Belda, 1997: 163). From this point of view, a smile will reflect pleasure if it serves a person's interest to present a smiling face to his or her audience. Conversely, a person may be motivated to conceal anxiety by smiling or to conceal pleasure by suppressing a smile.

At times, different cultural expectations can lead to colossal misunderstanding. Until recently, it was considered rude among educated Japanese to say no. Disagreement was instead conveyed by discreetly changing the subject and smiling politely. Consequently, it was common for visiting North Americans to think that their Japanese hosts were saying yes because of the politeness, the smile, and the absence of a no, when in fact they were saying no.

Like many hand gestures, the "fig" means different things in different times and places. We probably know it as a sign that adults make when they play with children and pretend "I've got your nose." But in ancient Rome, the fig was meant to convey good luck; in India it represents a threat; and in Russia, Turkey, and South Korea it means "screw you." It means "T" in the American Sign Language alphabet, but it had to be modified in the International Sign Language alphabet to avoid giving offence.

Similarly, no gestures or body postures mean the same thing in all societies and all cultures. In our society, people point with an outstretched hand and an extended finger. However, people raised in other cultures tip their head or use their chin or eyes to point out something. We nod our heads yes and shake no, but others nod no and shake yes.

Finally, we must note that in all societies people communicate by manipulating the space that separates them from others (Hall, 1959, 1966). This point is well illustrated in our *Cosmopolitan* example. Sociologists commonly distinguish four zones that surround us. The size of these zones varies from one society to the next. In North America, an intimate zone extends about 0.5 metres from the body. It is restricted to people with whom we want sustained, intimate physical contact. A personal zone extends from about 0.5 metres to 1.5 metres away. It is reserved for friends and acquaintances. We tolerate only a little physical intimacy from such people. The social zone is situated in the area roughly 1.5 metres to 3.5 metres away from us. Apart from a handshake, no physical contact is permitted from people we restrict to that zone. The public zone starts around 3.5 metres from our bodies. It is used to distinguish a performer or a speaker from an audience.

Dreamstime

Status Cues

Aside from facial expressions, gestures, and body language, nonverbal communication takes place by means of **status cues**, or visual indicators of other people's social position. Goffman (1959) observed that when individuals come into contact, they typically try to acquire information that will help them define the situation and make interaction easier. That goal is accomplished in part by attending to status cues.

Status cues are visual indicators of a person's social position.

Although status cues can be useful in helping people define the situation and thus greasing the wheels of social interaction, they also pose a social danger; status cues can quickly degenerate into **stereotypes**, or rigid views of how members of various groups act, regardless of whether individual group members really behave that way. Stereotypes create social barriers that impair interaction or prevent it altogether. For instance, police officers in some places routinely stop young black male drivers without cause to check for proper

Stereotypes are rigid views of how members of various groups act, regardless of whether individual group members really behave that way.

Theory	Focus
Feminist	Status differences between women and men structure social interaction.
Conflict	The competitive exchange of valued resources structures social interaction.
Symbolic interactionist	Social interaction involves the interpretation, negotiation, and modification of norms, roles, and statuses.

TABLE 5.2

Theories of Social Interaction

licensing, possession of illegal goods, and other similar violations. In this case, a social cue has become a stereotype that guides police policy. Young black males, the great majority of whom never commit an illegal act, view this police practice as harassment. Racial stereo-typing therefore helps perpetuate the sometimes poor relations between young black men and law enforcement officials.

As these examples show, face-to-face interaction may at first glance appear to be straightforward and unproblematic. Most of the time, it is. However, underlying the surface of human communication is a wide range of cultural assumptions, unconscious understandings, and nonverbal cues that make interaction possible (see Table 5.2 above).

Summing Up

- Rather than being just an ongoing competition over valued resources, social interaction also involves learning norms, roles, and statuses, some of which require altruistic action.
- The first step in such learning involves "taking the role of the other" (seeing yourself from the point of view of the people with whom you interact) and then shaping norms, adopting roles, and assuming statuses to suit your preferences.
- Social interaction includes verbal and nonverbal elements that are strongly influenced by the prevailing culture.

FROM SMALL PROCESSES TO BIG STRUCTURES

In this chapter, we referred to norms, roles, and statuses as the "building blocks" of social life. These building blocks form the microstructures within which face-to-face interaction takes place. In concluding, we add that sustained micro-level interaction often gives rise to higher-level structures—mesostructures, such as networks, groups, and organizations. In the next chapter, we examine these intermediate-level structures. Then, in Part 4 of this book, we show how these intermediate-level structures can form macrolevel structures known as *institutions*.

Society, it will emerge, fits together like a set of nested Russian dolls, with face-to-face interaction constituting the smallest doll in the set. Big structures set limits to the behaviour of small structures. However, it is within small structures that people interpret, negotiate, and modify their immediate social settings, thus giving big structures their dynamism and their life.

Society fits together like a set of nested Russian dolls, with face-to-face interaction constituting the smallest doll in the set.

SUMMARY

1. **What is social interaction?**

   Social interaction involves verbal and nonverbal communication between people acting and reacting to each other. Norms, roles, and statuses structure social interaction.

2. **Don't emotions govern all social interaction? Aren't emotions natural, spontaneous, and largely uncontrollable?**

   Emotions form an important part of all social interactions. However, they are less spontaneous and uncontrollable than we commonly believe. For example, your status in an interaction and in the larger society affects how much you laugh and what you laugh at. Similarly, people manage their emotions in personal life and at work according to "feeling rules" that reflect historically changing cultural standards and the demands of organizations.

3. **In what sense is social interaction based on competition?**

   When we interact socially, we exchange valued resources—everything from attention and pleasure to prestige and money. However, because people typically try to maximize their rewards and minimize their losses, social interaction may be seen as a competition for scarce resources.

4. **Are women and men equals in the competition for attention and the exercise of emotion management and emotion labour?**

   Usually not. Because men are generally status superiors, they are at an advantage in the competition for attention. Because of the roles that women typically play in families and in the occupational world, they are more often involved in emotion management and emotion labour.

5. **Is competition the only basis of social interaction?**

   No, it is not. People may interact cooperatively and altruistically because they have been socialized to do so. They may also maintain interaction based on domination. Thus, the three major modes of interaction—domination, competition, and cooperation—are based, respectively, on fear, envy, and trust.

6. **How do symbolic interactionists analyze social interaction?**

   Symbolic interactionists focus on how people create meaning in the course of social interaction and on how they negotiate and modify roles, statuses, and norms. Symbolic interactionism has several variants. For example, dramaturgical analysis is based on the idea that people play roles in their daily lives in much the same way as actors on stage play roles. When we are front stage, we act publicly, sometimes from ready-made scripts. Backstage, we relax from our public performances and allow what we regard as our "true" selves to emerge (even though we engage in role performances backstage, too). We may distance ourselves from our roles when they embarrass us, but role-playing nonetheless pervades social interaction. Together with various norms of interaction, role-playing enables society to function. Ethnomethodology is another symbolic interactionist approach to social interaction. It analyzes the methods people use to make sense of what others do and say. It insists on the importance of preexisting shared norms and understandings in making everyday interaction possible.

7. **Is all social interaction based on language?**

   No, it is not. Nonverbal communication, including socially defined facial expressions, gestures, body language, and status cues, is as important as verbal communication in conveying meaning.

8. Is domination the most efficient basis of social interaction?

Not usually. We might expect slaves to be highly efficient because they must do what their masters dictate. However, slaves typically expend minimal effort because they are rewarded poorly. Efficiency increases in competitive environments where rewards are linked to effort. It increases further in cooperative settings where status differences are low and people enjoy their work and identify with their organization.

KEY TERMS

competition (p. 118)

cooperation (p. 118)

domination (p. 118)

dramaturgical analysis (p. 119)

emotion labour (p. 114)

emotion management (p. 113)

ethnomethodology (p. 122)

exchange theory (p. 117)

norms (p. 111)

power (p. 117)

rational choice theory (p. 117)

role distancing (p. 121)

roles (p. 111)

social interaction (p. 111)

status (p. 111)

status cues (p. 124)

stereotypes (p. 124)

WEB RESOURCES

Companion Website for This Book

http://www.compass4e.nelson.com

Begin by clicking on the Student Resources section of the website. Next, select the chapter you are studying from the pull-down menu. From the Student Resources page you have easy access to additional Weblinks and other resources. The website also has many useful tips to aid you in your study of sociology, including practice tests for each chapter.

InfoTrac® Search Terms

These search terms are provided to assist you in beginning to conduct research on this topic by visiting http://www.infotrac-college.com:

dramaturgical analysis

exchange theory

rational choice theory

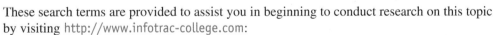

http://www.compass4e.nelson.com

CHAPTER

6

Networks, Groups, Bureaucracies, and Societies

IN THIS CHAPTER, YOU WILL LEARN THAT

- We commonly explain the way people act in terms of their interests and emotions. However, sometimes people act against their interests and suppress their emotions because various social collectives (groups, networks, bureaucracies, and societies) exert a powerful influence on what people do.

- We live in a surprisingly small world. Only a few social ties separate us from complete strangers.

- The patterns of social ties through which emotional and material resources flow form social networks. Information and other resources spread through social networks.

- People who are bound together by interaction and a common identity form social groups. Groups impose conformity on members and draw boundary lines between those who belong and those who do not.

- Bureaucracies are large, impersonal organizations that operate with varying degrees of efficiency.

- Societies are collectives of interacting people who share a culture and a territory. As societies evolve, the relationship of humans to nature changes, with consequences for population size, the permanence of settlements, the specialization of work tasks, labour productivity, and social inequality.

- Although various social collectives constrain our freedom, we can also use them to increase our freedom. Networks, groups, organizations, and entire societies can be mobilized for good or evil.

Jan Halaska/Photolibrary/Getty Images

BEYOND INDIVIDUAL MOTIVES

The Holocaust

In 1941, the large stone and glass train station was one of the proudest structures in Smolensk, a provincial capital of about 100 000 people on Russia's western border. Always bustling, it was especially busy on the morning of June 28. Besides the usual passengers and well-wishers, hundreds of Soviet Red Army soldiers were nervously talking, smoking, writing hurried letters to their loved ones, and sleeping fitfully on the station floor waiting for their train. Nazi troops had invaded the nearby city of Minsk in Belarus a couple of days before. The Soviet soldiers were being positioned to defend Russia against the inevitable German onslaught.

Robert Brym's father, then in his 20s, had been standing in line for nearly two hours to buy food when he noticed flares arching over the station. Within seconds, Stuka bombers, the pride of the German air force, swept down, releasing their bombs just before pulling out of their dive. Inside the station, shards of glass, blocks of stone, and mounds of earth fell indiscriminately on sleeping soldiers and nursing mothers alike. Everyone panicked. People trampled on one another to get out. In minutes, the train station was rubble.

Nearly two years earlier, Robert's father had managed to escape Poland when the Nazis invaded his hometown near Warsaw. Now, he was on the run again. By the time the Nazis occupied Smolensk a few weeks after their dive-bombers had destroyed its train station, Robert's father was deep in the Russian interior serving in a workers' battalion attached to the Soviet Red Army.

"My father was one of 300 000 Polish Jews who fled eastward into Russia before the Nazi genocide machine could reach them," says Robert. "The remaining three million Polish Jews were killed in various ways. Some died in battle. Many more, like my father's mother and younger siblings, were rounded up like diseased cattle and shot. However, most of Poland's Jews wound up in the concentration camps. Those deemed unfit were shipped to the gas chambers. Those declared able to work were turned into slaves until they could work no more. Then they, too, met their fate. A mere 9 percent of Poland's 3.3 million Jews survived World War II. The Nazi regime was responsible for the death of six million Jews in Europe (Burleigh, 2000).

AFP/Getty Images

"One question that always perplexed my father about the war was this: How was it possible for many thousands of ordinary Germans—products of what he regarded as the most advanced civilization on earth—to systematically murder millions of defenceless and innocent Jews, Roma ('Gypsies'), homosexuals, and people with mental disabilities in the death camps? To answer this question adequately, we must borrow ideas from the sociological study of networks, groups, and bureaucracies."

How Social Groups Shape Our Actions

How could ordinary German citizens commit the crime of the century? The conventional, non-sociological answer is that many Nazis were evil, sadistic, or deluded enough to think that Jews and other undesirables threatened the existence of the German people. Therefore, in the Nazi mind, the innocents had to be killed. This answer is given in the 1993 movie *Schindler's List* and in many other accounts.

German industrialist Oskar Schindler (Liam Neeson, centre) searches for his plant manager, Itzhak Stern, among a trainload of Polish Jews about to be deported to Auschwitz-Birkenau in *Schindler's List*. The movie turns the history of Nazism into a morality play, a struggle between good and evil forces. It does not probe into the sociological roots of good and evil.

The Everett Collection/CP Picture Archive

Yet it is far from the whole story. Sociologists emphasize three other factors:

1. *Norms of solidarity demand conformity.* When we form relationships with friends, lovers, spouses, teammates, and comrades-in-arms, we develop shared ideas or "norms of solidarity" about how we should behave toward them to sustain the relationships. Because these relationships are emotionally important to us, we sometimes pay more attention to norms of solidarity than to the morality of our actions. For example, a study of Nazis who roamed the Polish countryside to shoot and kill Jews and other "enemies" of Nazi Germany found that the soldiers often did not hate the people they systematically slaughtered, nor did they have many qualms about their actions (Browning, 1992). They simply developed deep loyalty to one another. They felt they had to get their assigned job done or face letting down their comrades. Thus, they committed atrocities partly because they just wanted to maintain group morale, solidarity, and loyalty. They committed evil deeds not because they were extraordinarily bad but because they were quite ordinary in the sense that they acted to sustain their friendship ties and to serve their group, just like most people.

   The case of the Nazi regime may seem extreme, but other instances of going along with criminal behaviour uncover a similar dynamic at work. Why do people rarely report crimes committed by corporations? Employees may worry about being reprimanded or fired if they become whistleblowers, but they also worry about letting down their co-workers. Why do gang members engage in criminal acts? They may seek financial gain, but they also regard crime as a way of maintaining a close social bond with their fellow gang members (see Box 6.1).

   A study of the small number of Polish Christians who helped save Jews during World War II helps clarify why some people violate group norms (Tec, 1986). The heroism of these Polish Christians was not correlated with their educational attainment, political orientation, religious background, or even attitudes toward Jews. In fact, some Polish Christians who helped save Jews were anti-Semitic. Instead, these Christian heroes were, for one reason or another, estranged or cut off from mainstream norms. Because they were poorly socialized into the norms of their society,

BOX 6.1

Social Policy: What Do You Think?

GROUP LOYALTY OR BETRAYAL?

Glen Ridge, New Jersey, is an affluent suburb of about 8000 people. It was the site of a terrible rape case in 1989. A group of 13 teenage boys lured a sweet-natured young woman with an IQ of 49 into a basement. There, four of them raped her while three others looked on; six left when they realized what was going to happen. The rapists used a baseball bat and a broomstick. The boys were the most popular students in the local high school. The young woman was not a stranger to them. Some of them had known her since she was five years old, when they had convinced her to lick the point of a ballpoint pen that had been coated in dog feces.

Weeks passed before anyone reported the rape to the police. Years later, at trial, many members of the community rallied behind the boys, blaming and ostracizing the victim. The courts eventually found three of the four young men guilty of first-degree rape, but they were allowed to go free for eight years while their cases were appealed and they finally received only light sentences in 1997. One was released from jail in 1998, two others in 1999. Why did members of the community refuse to believe the clear-cut evidence? What made

them defend the rapists? Why were the boys let off so easily?

Bernard Lefkowitz interviewed 250 key players and observers in the Glen Ridge Rape case. Ultimately, he indicted the *community* for the rape. He concluded that "[the rapists] adhered to a code of behaviour that mimicked, distorted, and exaggerated the values of the adult world around them," while "the citizens supported the boys because they didn't want to taint the town they treasured" (Lefkowitz, 1997a: 493). What were some of the community values the elders upheld and the boys aped?

- *The subordination of women*. All the boys grew up in families where men were the dominant personalities. Only one of them had a sister. Not a single woman occupied a position of authority in Glen Ridge High School. The boys classified their female classmates either as "little mothers" who fawned over them or as "bad girls" who were simply sexual objects.
- *Lack of compassion for the weak*. According to the minister of Glen Ridge Congregational Church, "[a]chievement was honored and respected almost to the point of pathology, whether it was the achievements of high school athletes or the achievements of corporate world conquerors." Adds Lefkowitz: "Compassion for the weak wasn't part of the curriculum" (Lefkowitz, 1997a: 130).
- *Tolerance of male misconduct*. The boys routinely engaged in delinquent acts, including one spectacular trashing of a house. However, their parents always paid damages, covered up the misdeeds, and rationalized them with phrases like "boys will be boys."

Especially because they were town football heroes, many people felt they could do no wrong.

- *Intense group loyalty*. "The guys prized their intimacy with each other far above what could be achieved with a girl," writes Lefkowitz (1997a: 146). The boys formed a tight clique, and team sports reinforced group solidarity. Under such circumstances, the probability of someone "ratting" on his friends was very low.

In the end, there was a "rat." His name was Charles Figueroa. He did not participate in the rape but he was an athlete, part of the jock clique, and therefore aware of what had happened. Significantly, he was one of the few black boys in the school, tolerated because of his athletic ability but never trusted because of his race and often called an—— by his teammates behind his back. This young man's family was highly intelligent and morally sensitive. He was the only one to have the courage to betray the group (Lefkowitz, 1997a, 1997b).

The Glen Ridge rape case raises the important question of where we ought to draw the line between group loyalty and group betrayal. Considering your own group loyalties, are there times when you regret not having spoken up? Are there times when you regret not having been more loyal? What is the difference between these two types of situations? Can you specify criteria for deciding when loyalty is required and when betrayal is the right thing to do? You may have to choose between group loyalty and betrayal on more than one occasion, so thinking about these criteria—and clearly understanding the values for which your group stands—will help you make a more informed choice.

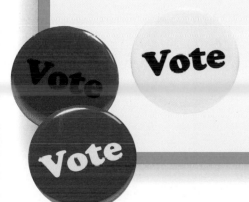

they were freer not to conform and instead to act in ways they believed were right. We could tell a roughly similar story about corporate whistleblowers or people who turn in their fellow gang members. They are disloyal from an insider's point of view but heroic from an outsider's viewpoint, often because they have been poorly socialized into the group's norms.

2. *Structures of authority tend to render people obedient.* Most people find it difficult to disobey authorities because they fear ridicule, ostracism, and punishment. This fact was strikingly demonstrated in an experiment conducted by social psychologist Stanley Milgram (1974). Milgram informed his experimental subjects they were taking part in a study on punishment and learning. He brought each subject to a room where a man was strapped to a chair. An electrode was attached to the man's wrist. The experimental subject sat in front of a console. It contained 30 switches with labels ranging from "15 volts" to "450 volts" in 15-volt increments. Labels ranging from "slight shock" to "danger: severe shock" were pasted below the switches. The experimental subjects were told to administer a 15-volt shock for the man's first wrong answer and then increase the voltage each time he made an error. The man strapped in the chair was, in fact, an actor. He did not actually receive a shock. As the experimental subject increased the current, however, the actor began to writhe, shouting for mercy and begging to be released. If the experimental subjects grew reluctant to administer more current, Milgram assured them the man strapped in the chair would be fine and insisted that the success of the experiment depended on the subject's obedience. The subjects were, however, free to abort the experiment at any time. Remarkably, 71 percent of experimental subjects were prepared to administer shocks of 285 volts or more even though the switches at starting that level were labelled "intense shock," "extreme intensity shock," and "danger: severe shock" and despite the fact that the actor appeared to be in great distress at this level of current (see Figure 6.1).

Milgram's experiment teaches us that as soon as we are introduced to a structure of authority, we are inclined to obey those in power. This is the case even if the authority structure is new and highly artificial, even if we are free to walk away from it with no penalty, and even if we think that by remaining in its grip we are inflicting terrible pain on another human being. In this context, the actions and inactions of German citizens in World War II become more understandable if no more forgivable.

FIGURE 6.1

Social Distance Increases Obedience to Authority

Milgram's experiment supports the view that separating people from the negative effects of their actions increases the likelihood of compliance. When the subject and actor were in the same room and the subject was told to force the actor's hand onto the electrode, 30 percent of subjects administered the maximum 450-volt shock. When the subject and actor were merely in the same room, 40 percent of subjects administered the maximum shock. When the subject and actor were in different rooms but the subject could see and hear the actor, 62.5 percent of subjects administered the maximum shock. When subject and actor were in different rooms and the actor could be seen but not heard, 65 percent of subjects administered the maximum shock.

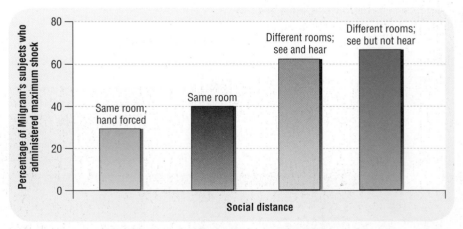

Source: Based on Milgram, 1974: 36. Bar graph based on information in Chapter 4, "Closeness of the Victim," from *Obedience to Authority* by Stanley Milgram. Copyright © 1974 by Stanley Milgram. Reprinted by permission of HarperCollins Publishers, Inc.

3. *Bureaucracies are highly effective structures of authority.* The Nazi genocide machine was effective because it was bureaucratically organized. As Max Weber (1978) defined the term, a **bureaucracy** is a large, impersonal organization comprising many clearly defined positions arranged in a hierarchy. A bureaucracy has a permanent, salaried staff of qualified experts and written goals, rules, and procedures. Staff members usually try to find ways of running their organization more efficiently. *Efficiency* means achieving the bureaucracy's goals at the least cost. The goal of the Nazi genocide machine was to kill Jews and other undesirables. To achieve that goal with maximum efficiency, the job was broken into many small tasks. Most officials performed only one function, such as checking train schedules, organizing entertainment for camp guards, maintaining supplies of Zyklon B gas, and removing ashes from the crematoria. The full horror of what was happening eluded many officials or at least could be conveniently ignored as they concentrated on their jobs, most of them far removed from the gas chambers and death camps in occupied Poland. Many factors account for variations in Jewish victimization rates across Europe during World War II. One factor was bureaucratic organization. Not coincidentally, the proportion of Jews killed was highest not in the Nazi-controlled countries where the hatred of Jews was most intense (e.g., Romania), but in countries where the Nazi bureaucracy was best organized (e.g., Holland; Bauman, 1991; Sofsky, 1997 [1993]).

In short, the sociological reply to the question posed by Robert's father is that it was not just blind hatred but the nature of groups and bureaucracies that made it possible for the Nazis to kill innocent people so ruthlessly.

People commonly think *individual* motives prompt our actions, and for good reason. As we saw in Chapter 5, Social Interaction, we often make rational calculations to maximize gains and minimize losses. In addition, deeply held emotions partly govern our behaviour. However, this chapter asks you to make a conceptual leap beyond the individual motives that prompt us to act in certain ways. We ask you to consider the way four kinds of social *collectivities* shape our actions: networks, groups, bureaucratic organizations, and whole societies. The limitations of an analysis based exclusively on individual motives should be clear from our discussion of the social roots of evil. The advantages of considering how social collectivities affect us should become clear below. We begin by considering the nature and effects of social networks.

A **bureaucracy** is a large, impersonal organization comprising many clearly defined positions arranged in a hierarchy. A bureaucracy has a permanent, salaried staff of qualified experts and written goals, rules, and procedures. Ideally, staff members always try to find ways of running the bureaucracy more efficiently.

Getty Images

Dr. Jeffrey Wigand was one of the most famous whistleblowers of the 1990s. Vice-president of research and development at Brown and Williams Tobacco Corp., Wigand was fired after he discovered that the company was adding ammonia and other chemicals to cigarettes to enhance nicotine absorption and speed up addiction. Despite threats and harassment, Wigand told all on the CBS public affairs program *60 Minutes*, ultimately leading to a US$368 billion suit against big tobacco for health-related damages. The story is the subject of the 1999 movie *The Insider*, starring Russell Crowe.

Summing Up

- Norms of solidarity tend to render people obedient. People often act against their better judgment because they place group loyalty above moral considerations.
- Authority structures enable the implied or actual use of ridicule, ostracism, and punishment to ensure conformity.
- Bureaucracies tend to be especially efficient means of ensuring conformity.

SOCIAL NETWORKS

It's a Small World

Suppose someone asked you to deliver a letter to a complete stranger on the other side of the country by using only acquaintances as intermediaries. You give the letter to an acquaintance, who can give the letter to one of his or her acquaintances, and so on. Research shows that, on average, it would take no more than six acquaintances to get the letter to the stranger. This fact suggests that we live in a small world; just a few social ties separate us from everyone else (Travers and Milgram, 1969).

Our world is small because we are enmeshed in overlapping sets of social relations, or social networks. Although any particular individual may know a small number of people, his or her family members, friends, co-workers, and others know many more people who extend far beyond that individual's personal network. So, for example, the authors of this textbook are likely to be complete strangers to you. Yet your professor may know one of us or at least know someone who knows one of us. Probably no more than three links separate us from you. Put differently, although our personal networks are small, they lead quickly to much larger networks. We live in a small world because our social networks connect us to the larger world (see Box 6.2).

> A **social network** is a bounded set of individuals who are linked by the exchange of material or emotional resources. The patterns of exchange determine the boundaries of the network. Members exchange resources more frequently with one another than with non-members. They also think of themselves as network members. Social networks may be formal (defined in writing), but they are more often informal (defined only in practice).

Sociologists define a **social network** as a bounded set of individuals linked by the exchange of material or emotional resources, everything from money to friendship. The patterns of exchange determine the boundaries of the network. Members exchange resources more frequently with one another than with non-members. They also think of themselves as network members. Social networks may be formal (defined in writing) or informal (defined only in practice). The people you know personally form the boundaries of your personal network. However, each of your network members is linked to other people. This is what connects you to people you have never met, creating a small world that extends far beyond your personal network.

The Value of Network Analysis

The study of social networks is not restricted to ties among individuals (Berkowitz, 1982; Wasserman and Faust, 1994; Wellman and Berkowitz, 1997). The units of analysis or *nodes* in a network can be individuals, groups, organizations, and even countries. Thus, social network analysts have examined everything from intimate relationships between lovers to diplomatic relations among nations.

Unlike organizations, most networks lack names and offices. There is a Boy Scouts of Canada but no North American Trading Bloc. In a sense, networks lie beneath the more visible collectivities of social life, but that makes them no less real or important. Some analysts claim we can gain only a partial sense of why certain things happen in the social world by focusing on highly visible collectivities. From their point of view, the whole story requires probing below the surface and examining the network level. The study of social networks clarifies a wide range of social phenomena, including how people find jobs and how they form communities.

Finding a Job

Many people learn about important events, ideas, and opportunities from their social networks. Friends and acquaintances often introduce you to everything from an interesting college or university course or a great restaurant to a satisfying occupation or a future spouse. Of course, social networks are not the only source of information, but they are highly significant.

Consider how people find jobs. Do you look in the "Help Wanted" section of your local newspaper, scan the Internet, or walk around town looking for "Employee Wanted" signs? Although these strategies are common, people often learn about employment opportunities from other people. But what kind of people? According to Mark Granovetter (1973), you

BOX 6.2

Sociology at the Movies

THE SOCIAL NETWORK

Facebook is one of the world's most popular websites, with more than half a billion users. Its main source of revenue is selling information about its users to advertisers. Mark Zuckerberg, its 26-year-old founder and principal shareholder, is the world's youngest self-made billionaire, with a net worth of $1.5 billion in 2010. *The Social Network* is the remarkable story of how Zuckerberg hatched Facebook in a Harvard dorm room in 2004 and cooked up a corporate omelet valued at $15 billion just six years later—necessarily breaking a few eggs in the process.

Sociologists have mined Facebook for data to test theories about relationships, identity, self-esteem, popularity, collective action, race, and political engagement (Rosenbloom, 2007). However, the movie pays no attention to this research. Instead, it asks whether Zuckerberg's success was due more to his genius, cunning, or greed. Aaron Sorkin, who wrote the crisp, witty, exhilarating screenplay, seems to think it was a little of all three.

If Sorkin had read more sociology, he might have concluded that social networks were also partly responsible for Facebook's stunning ascent. Think of the way Zuckerberg's personal network made the resources needed to create Facebook available to him. Zuckerberg was an undergraduate at Harvard,

Merrick Morton/© Columbia Pictures/Courtesy Everett Collection

which regularly published a hard-copy *Facebook* containing photos and brief bios of Harvard students. Moreover, anyone even fleetingly familiar with the Internet in 2004—let alone a programming nerd like Zuckerberg—knew of the existence of popular dating and social networking sites operating on principles similar to those that Facebook would later adopt (Brym and Lenton, 2001).

Strong and weak ties led Zuckerberg to more specifically useful resources. Harvard upperclassmen Cameron and Tyler Winklevoss hired Zuckerberg to write code for a Harvard-based social-networking site. Zuckerberg liked their idea so much that, while he was ostensibly working for them, he developed Facebook on his own. (The Winklevosses later sued Zuckerberg, settling for $65 million.) For Facebook's startup costs, Zuckerberg borrowed

$15 000 from his roommate, Eduardo Saverin, whom he later defrauded for his share in Facebook. (Saverin also successfully sued.) According to Zuckerberg, he even got the idea of extending Facebook beyond Harvard from Dustin Moskovitz, another roommate. It may have taken a genius to see the enormous potential of a general Web-based social networking site and a combination of cunning and greed to "borrow" useful ideas and money from people in his personal network, but the raw materials for Facebook were in the air for anyone in Zuckerberg's position, and Zuckerberg's personal ties led him to them ("Bloomberg Game Changers," 2010; Wright, 2010).

The irony at the centre of *The Social Network* is that Zuckerberg, who invents the world's most powerful friendship machine, can't keep a friend. In the opening scene, his girlfriend dumps him, and myriad other failed relationships litter the movie. The irony of the irony is that Zuckerberg had just enough of the right kind of friends—or at least access to useful nodes in his personal network—to make him what he is.

Sources: "Bloomberg Game Changers: Mark Zuckerberg." 2010. http://www.bloomberg.com/video/63583008/ (accessed 9 October 2010). Brym, Robert J. and Rhonda Lenton. 2001. *Love Online: A Report on Digital Dating in Canada* (Toronto: MSN.CA). http://projects.chass.utoronto.ca/brym/loveonline.pdf (accessed 9 October 2010). "Company Timeline." 2010. http://www.facebook.com/press/info.php?timeline (accessed 9 October 2010). McKeon, Matt. 2010. "The Evolution of Privacy on Facebook," http://mattmckeon.com/facebook-privacy/ (accessed 9 October 2010). Rosenbloom, Stephanie. 2007. "On Facebook, Scholars Link up with Data." New York Times 17 December. www.nytimes.com (accessed 9 October 2010). Wright, Robert. 2010. "Zuckerberg: Non-Evil Non-Genius," *New York Times* 5 October. www.nytimes.com (accessed 9 October 2010).

Parents can help their graduating children find jobs by getting them plugged into the right social networks. Here, in the 1968 movie *The Graduate*, a friend of the family advises Dustin Hoffman that the future lies in the plastics industry.

The Everett Collection/CP Picture Archive

may have strong or weak ties to another person. You have strong ties to people who are close to you, such as family members and friends. You have weak ties to acquaintances, such as people you meet at parties and friends of friends. In his research, Granovetter found that weak ties are more important than strong ties in finding a job, which is contrary to common sense. You might reasonably assume that an acquaintance would not do much to help you find a job whereas a close friend or relative would make a lot more effort in that regard. However, by focusing on the flow of information in personal networks, Granovetter found something different. Acquaintances are more likely to provide useful information about employment opportunities than friends or family members are because people who are close to you typically share overlapping networks. Therefore, the information they can provide about job opportunities is often redundant. In contrast, acquaintances are likely to be connected to *diverse* networks. They can therefore provide information about many different job openings and introduce you to many different potential employers. Moreover, because people typically have more weak ties than strong ties, the sum of weak ties holds more information about job opportunities than the sum of strong ties. These features of personal networks allow Granovetter to conclude that the "strength of weak ties" lies in their diversity and abundance.

Urban Networks

We rely on social networks for a lot more than job information. Consider everyday life in the big city. We often think of big cities as cold and alienating places where few people know one another. In this view, urban acquaintanceships tend to be few and functionally specific; we know someone fleetingly as a bank teller or a server in a restaurant but not as a whole person. Even dating often involves a long series of brief encounters. In contrast, people often think of small towns as friendly, comfortable places where everyone knows everyone else (and everyone else's business). Some of the founders of sociology emphasized just this distinction. Notably, German sociologist Ferdinand Tönnies (1988 [1887]) contrasted "community" with "society." According to Tönnies, a community is marked by intimate and emotionally intense social ties, whereas a society is marked by impersonal relationships held together largely by self-interest. A big city is a prime example of a society in Tönnies's judgment.

Tönnies's view prevailed until network analysts started studying big city life in the 1970s. Where Tönnies saw only sparse, functionally specific ties, network analysts found elaborate social networks, some functionally specific and some not. For example, Barry Wellman and his colleagues studied personal networks in Toronto (Wellman, Carrington, and Hall, 1997). They found that each Torontonian has an average of about 400 social ties, including immediate and extended kin, neighbours, friends, and co-workers. These ties provide everything from emotional aid (e.g., visits after a personal tragedy) and financial support (e.g., small loans) to minor services (e.g., fixing a car) and information of the kind Granovetter studied. Strong ties that last a long time are typically restricted to immediate family members, a few close relatives and friends, and a close co-worker or two. Beyond that, however, people rely on a wide array of ties for different purposes at different times. Downtown residents sitting on their front porch on a summer evening, sipping soft drinks and chatting with neighbours as the kids play road hockey, may be less common than they were 50 years ago. However, the automobile, public transportation, the telephone, and the Internet help people stay in close touch with a wide range of contacts for a variety of purposes (Haythornthwaite and Wellman, 2002). Far from living in an impersonal and alienating world, Torontonians' lives are network-rich. Research conducted elsewhere in North America reveals much the same pattern of urban life.

The Building Blocks of Social Networks

Researchers often use mathematical models and computer programs to analyze social networks. However, no matter how sophisticated the mathematics or the software, network analysts begin from an understanding of the basic building blocks of social networks.

The most elementary network form is the **dyad**, a social relationship between two nodes or social units (e.g., people, firms, organizations, countries). A **triad** is a social relationship among three nodes. The difference between a dyad and a triad may seem small. However, the social dynamics of these two elementary network forms are fundamentally different, as sociologist Georg Simmel showed early in the twentieth century (Simmel, 1950; see Figure 6.2).

In a dyadic relationship, such as a marriage, both partners tend to be intensely and intimately involved. Moreover, the dyad needs both partners to live—but to "die" it needs only one to opt out. A marriage, for example, can endure only if both partners are intensely involved; if one partner ceases active participation, the marriage is over in practice if not in law. The need for intense involvement on the part of both partners is also why a dyad can have no "free riders," or partners who benefit from the relationship without contributing to it. Finally, in a dyadic relationship, the partners must assume full responsibility for all that transpires. Neither partner can shift responsibility to some larger collectivity because no larger collectivity exists beyond the relationship between the two partners.

A **dyad** is a social relationship between two nodes or social units (e.g., people, firms, organizations, countries).

A **triad** is a social relationship among three nodes or social units (e.g., people, firms, organizations, countries).

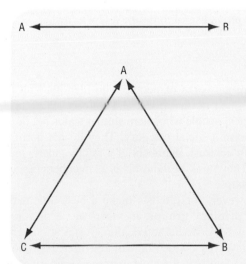

Characteristics of the dyad:
1. Both partners are intensely absorbed in the relationship.
2. The dyad needs both partners to live but only one to die.
3. No "free riders" are possible.
4. Neither partner can deny responsibility by shifting it to a larger collectivity.

Characteristics of the triad:
1. Intensity and intimacy are reduced.
2. The triad restricts individuality by allowing a partner to be constrained for the collective good. A partner may be out-voted by a majority, for example.
3. Coalitions are possible.
4. Third-party mediation of conflict between two partners is possible.
5. Third-party exploitation of rivalry between two partners is possible.
6. A third-party divide-and-conquer strategy is possible.
7. "Free riders" are possible.
8. It is possible to shift responsibility to the larger collectivity.

FIGURE 6.2
Dyad and Triad

In contrast, when a third person enters the picture, thereby creating a triad, relationships tend to be less intimate and intense. Equally significantly, the triad restricts individuality by allowing one partner to be constrained for the collective good. This situation occurs when a majority outvotes one partner. The existence of a triad also allows coalitions or factions to form. Furthermore, it allows one partner to mediate conflict between the other two, exploit rivalry between the other two, or encourage rivalry between the other two to achieve dominance. Thus, the introduction of a third partner makes possible a completely new set of social dynamics that are structurally impossible in a dyadic relationship.

Summing Up

- Because personal networks are linked to other personal networks, surprisingly few social links connect any two strangers.
- The study of social networks reveals many surprises, such as the fact that weak ties can yield strong results in searching for a job, and the fact that seemingly cold and alienating big cities are actually composed of many tightly knit networks.
- Change in the scale of networks, even from two to three units (from dyads to triads), results in many new possibilities for social interaction.

IS GROUP LOYALTY ALWAYS FUNCTIONAL?

Love and Group Loyalty

Intensity and intimacy characterize many dyadic relationships. However, outside forces can destroy them. For instance, the star-crossed lovers in *Romeo and Juliet* are torn between their love for each other and their loyalty to the feuding Montague and Capulet families. In the end, Romeo and Juliet die, victims of the feud.

Love thwarted by conflicting group loyalty is the stuff of many tragic plays, novels, and movies. Most audiences have no problem grasping the fact that group loyalty is often more powerful than romantic love is. However, why group loyalty holds such power over us is unclear. Also unclear is whether the power of group loyalty is always beneficial, as functionalalists are inclined to argue. Before delving into the insights that the sociological study of groups offers on these issues, it will prove useful to define a few terms.

Primary and Secondary Groups

Social groups are composed of one or more networks of people who identify with one another, routinely interact, and adhere to defined norms, roles, and statuses. We usually distinguish social groups from **social categories**, people who share similar status but do not identify with one another. Coffee drinkers form a social category. They do not normally share norms and identify with one another. In contrast, members of a family, sports team, or college are aware of shared membership. They think of themselves as members of a collectivity and routinely interact. They form groups.

Many kinds of social groups exist. However, sociologists make a basic distinction between primary and secondary groups. In **primary groups**, members agree on norms, roles, and statuses but do not define them in writing. Social interaction creates strong emotional ties. It extends over a long period and involves a wide range of activities. It results in group members knowing one another well. The family is the most important primary group.

A **social group** comprises one or more networks of people who identify with one another and adhere to defined norms, roles, and statuses.

A **social category** comprises people who share a similar status but do not identify with one another.

In **primary groups**, norms, roles, and statuses are agreed on but are not put in writing. Social interaction leads to strong emotional ties. It extends over a long period, and involves a wide range of activities. It results in group members knowing one another well.

Secondary groups are larger and more impersonal than primary groups are. Compared with primary groups, social interaction in secondary groups creates weaker emotional ties. It extends over a shorter period and involves a narrow range of activities. It results in most group members having at most a passing acquaintance with one another. Your sociology class is an example of a secondary group.

Bearing these distinctions in mind, we can begin to explore the power of groups to ensure conformity.

Benefits of Group Conformity

Television's first reality TV show was *Candid Camera*. On an early episode, an unsuspecting man waited for an elevator. When the elevator door opened, he found four people, all confederates of the show, facing the elevator's back wall. Seeing the four people with their backs to him, the man at first hesitated. He then tentatively entered the elevator. However, rather than turning around so he would face the door, he remained facing the back wall, just like the others. The scene was repeated several times. Men and women, black and white, all behaved the same way. Confronting unanimously bizarre behaviour, they chose conformity over common sense.

Conformity is an integral part of group life, and primary groups generate more pressure to conform than do secondary groups. Strong social ties create emotional intimacy. They also ensure that primary group members share similar attitudes, beliefs, and information. Beyond the family, friendship groups (or cliques) and gangs demonstrate these features. Group members tend to dress and act alike, speak the same "lingo," share the same likes and dislikes, and demand loyalty, especially in the face of external threat. Conformity ensures group cohesion.

A classic study of soldiers in World War II demonstrates the power of conformity to get people to face extreme danger. Samuel Stouffer and his colleagues (1949) showed that primary group cohesion was the main factor motivating soldiers to engage in combat. Rather than belief in a cause, such as upholding liberty or fighting the evils of Nazism, the feeling of camaraderie, loyalty, and solidarity with fellow soldiers supplied the principal motivation to face danger. Brigadier General S. L. A. Marshall (1947: 160–61) famously wrote: "A man fights to help the man next to him. ... Men do not fight for a cause but because they do not want to let their comrades down." Or as one soldier says in the 2001 movie *Black Hawk Down*: "When I go home people will ask me, 'Hey, Hoot, why do you do it, man? Why? Are you some kinda war junkie?' I won't say a goddamn word. Why? They won't understand. They won't understand why we do it. They won't understand it's about the men next to you. And that's it. That's all it is." As such, if you want to create a great military force, you need to promote group solidarity and identity. Hence the importance of wearing uniforms, singing anthems, displaying insignia, hoisting flags, conducting drills, training under duress, and instilling hatred of the enemy.

The Asch Experiment

A famous experiment conducted by social psychologist Solomon Asch also demonstrates how group pressure creates conformity (Asch, 1955). Asch assembled a group of seven men. One of them was the experimental subject; the other six were Asch's confederates. Asch showed the seven men a card with a line drawn on it. He then showed them a second card with three lines of varying length drawn on it (see Figure 6.3 on page 140). One by one, he asked the confederates to judge which line on card 2 was the same length as the line on card 1. The answer was obvious. One line on card 2 was much shorter than the line on card 1.

Brian Leng/Corbis

The main primary group is the family, which is an enduring, multifunctional social unit characterized by unwritten consensus concerning norms, roles and statuses, emotional intensity, and intimacy.

FIGURE 6.3
The Asch Experiment

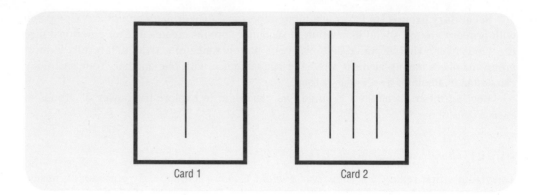

Card 1   Card 2

One line was much longer. One was exactly the same length. Yet, as instructed by Asch, all six confederates said that either the shorter or the longer line was the same length as the line on card 1. When it came time for the experimental subject to make his judgment, he typically overruled his own perception and agreed with the majority. Only 25 percent of Asch's experimental subjects consistently gave the right answer. Asch thus demonstrated how easily group pressure can overturn individual conviction and result in conformity.

Asch's work and subsequent research show that several factors affect the likelihood of conformity (Sternberg, 1998: 499–500). First, the likelihood of conformity increases as *group size* increases to three or four members. For groups larger than four, the likelihood of conformity generally does not increase. Second, as *group cohesiveness* increases, so does the likelihood of conformity. Where greater intimacy and sharing of values occur, group members are less likely to express dissent. Third, *social status* affects the likelihood of conformity. People with low status in a group (e.g., because of their gender or race) are less likely to dissent than are people with high status. Fourth, *culture* matters. People in individualistic societies, like Canada, tend to conform less than do people in collectivist societies, like China. Fifth, the *appearance of unanimity* affects the likelihood of conformity. Even one dissenting voice greatly increases the chance that others will dissent.

Disadvantages of Group Conformity

Groupthink

The power of groups to ensure conformity is often a valuable asset. Armies could not operate without willingness to undergo personal sacrifice for the good of the group, nor could sports teams excel. However, being a good team player can have a downside because the consensus of a group can sometimes be misguided or dangerous. Dissent might save the group from making mistakes, but the pressure to conform despite individual misgivings—sometimes called **groupthink**—can lead to disaster (Janis, 1972).

The dangers of groupthink are greatest in high-stress situations. For example, groupthink was at work in high-level meetings preceding the space shuttle *Columbia* disaster in 2003. Transcripts of those meetings show that the NASA official who ran shuttle management meetings, a non-engineer, believed from the outset that foam insulation debris could not damage the spacecraft. She dismissed the issue and cut off discussion when an engineer expressed his concerns. The others present quickly fell into line with the manager running the meeting (Wald and Schwartz, 2003). A few days later, damage caused by foam insulation debris caused *Columbia* to break apart on re-entry into Earth's atmosphere, killing everyone on board.

A famous example of how the lack of a single dissenting voice can result in tragedy comes from a homicide case that grabbed the world's attention in 1993. Near Liverpool, England, two 10-year-old boys abducted 2-year-old James Bulger from a shopping mall and killed him. They took him on a long, aimless walk, torturing him along the way—dropping

Groupthink is group pressure to conform despite individual misgivings.

him on his head and kicking him in the ribs. Motorists and pedestrians saw the toddler crying, noticed his wounds, and even witnessed some of the violence. "A persuading kick" was the way one motorist later described the blow to the ribs (Scott, 2003). Nobody called the police. This case illustrates "bystander apathy." As the number of bystanders increases, the likelihood of any one bystander helping another decreases because the greater the number of bystanders, the less responsibility any one individual feels. This behaviour shows that people usually take their cues for action from others and again demonstrates the power of groups over individuals.

Group Conformity, Group Conflict, and Group Inequality

We have seen that functionalists, who emphasize the benefits of group conformity, are inclined to overlook the ways in which conflict within groups can avert disaster. We may now add that by emphasizing the benefits of group conformity, functionalists are also inclined to ignore the ways in which group conformity encourages conflict and reinforces inequality.

If a group exists, it follows that some people must not belong to it. Accordingly, sociologists distinguish **in-group** members (those who belong) from **out-group** members (those who do not). Members of an in-group typically draw a boundary separating themselves from members of the out-group, and they try to keep out-group members from crossing the line. Anyone who has gone to high school knows all about in-groups and out-groups. They have seen first-hand how race, class, athletic ability, academic talent, and physical attractiveness act as boundaries separating groups.

In-group members are people who belong to a group.

Out-group members are people who are excluded from an in-group.

Group Boundaries: Competition and Self-Esteem

Why do group boundaries crystallize? One theory is that group boundaries emerge when people compete for scarce resources. For example, old immigrants may greet new immigrants with hostility if the latter are seen as competitors for scarce jobs (Levine and Campbell, 1972). Another theory is that group boundaries emerge when people are motivated to protect their self-esteem. From this point of view, drawing group boundaries allows people to increase their self-esteem by believing that out-groups have low status (Tajfel, 1981).

The classic experiment on prejudice, *The Robber's Cave Study* (Sherif, Harvey, White, Hood, and Sherif, 1988 [1961]), supports both theories. Researchers brought two groups of 11-year-old boys to a summer camp at Robber's Cave State Park in Oklahoma in 1954. The boys were strangers to one another and for about a week the two groups were kept apart. They swam, camped, and hiked. Each group chose a name for itself and the boys printed their group's name on their caps and T-shirts. Then the two groups met. A series of athletic competitions was set up between them. Soon, each group became highly antagonistic toward the other. Each group came to hold the other in low esteem. The boys ransacked cabins, started food fights, and stole various items from members of the other group. Thus, under competitive conditions, the boys drew group boundaries starkly and quickly.

CP PHOTO/Adrian Wyld

Natural or artificial boundaries—rivers, mountains, highways, railway tracks—typically separate groups or communities.

The investigators next stopped the athletic competitions and created several apparent emergencies whose solution required cooperation between the two groups. One such emergency involved a leak in the pipe supplying water to the camp. The researchers assigned the boys to teams of members from *both* groups. Their job was to inspect the pipe and fix the leak. After engaging in several such cooperative ventures, the boys started playing together without fighting. Once cooperation replaced competition and the groups ceased to hold each other in low esteem, group boundaries melted away as quickly as they had formed.

Significantly, the two groups were of equal status—the boys were all white, middle class, and 11 years old—and their contact involved face-to-face interaction in a setting where norms established by the investigators promoted a reduction of group prejudice. Social scientists today recognize that all these conditions must be in place before the boundaries between an in-group and an out-group fade (Sternberg, 1998: 512).

Dominant Groups

The boundaries separating groups often seem unchangeable and even "natural." In general, however, dominant groups construct group boundaries in particular circumstances to further their goals (Barth, 1969; Tajfel, 1981). Consider Germans and Jews. By the early twentieth century, Jews were well integrated into German society. They were economically successful, culturally innovative, and politically influential, and many of them considered themselves more German than Jewish. In 1933, the year Hitler seized power, 44 percent of marriages involving at least one German Jew were marriages to a non-Jew. In addition, some German Jews converted before marrying non-Jewish Germans (Gordon, 1984). Yet, although the boundary separating Germans from Jews was quite weak, the Nazis chose to redraw and reinforce it. Defining a Jew as anyone who had at least one Jewish grandparent, the Nazis passed a series of anti-Jewish laws and, in the end, systematically slaughtered the Jews of Europe. The division between Germans and Jews was not "natural." It came into existence because of its perceived usefulness to a dominant group.

We conclude that both the functionalist and conflict perspectives contribute much to our appreciation of how social groups operate. By emphasizing the benefits of group conformity, functionalists increase our understanding of the means by which individuals are mobilized to achieve group goals. In contrast, conflict theorists caution us to recognize that too much conformity can be dangerous: failure to dissent can have disastrous consequences and high levels of group conformity often reinforce group inequality.

A **reference group** comprises people against whom an individual evaluates his or her situation or conduct.

Groups and Social Imagination

In concluding this section, we note that group interaction is not always face to face. Often, people interact with other group members in their imagination.

Consider **reference groups**, which are composed of people against whom an individual evaluates his or her situation or conduct. Members of a reference group function as role models. Reference groups may influence us even though they represent a largely imaginary ideal. For instance, the advertising industry promotes certain body ideals that many people try to emulate, although we know that hardly anyone can look like a runway model.

We have to exercise our imaginations vigorously to participate in the group life of a society like ours because much social life in a complex society involves belonging to secondary groups without knowing or interacting with most group members. For an individual to interact with any more than a small fraction of the more than 34 million people living in this country is impossible. Nonetheless, most Canadians feel a strong emotional bond to their fellow citizens. Similarly, think about the employees and students at your college or university. They know they belong to the same secondary group and many of them are probably loyal to it. Yet how many people at your school have you met? Probably no more than a small fraction of the total. One way to make sense

JPL/NASA

Is it possible to imagine everyone in the world as a community? Why or why not? Under what conditions might it be possible?

of the paradox of intimacy despite distance is to think of your postsecondary institution or Canada as "imagined communities." They are imagined because you cannot possibly meet most members of the group and can only speculate about what they must be like. They are, nonetheless, communities because people believe strongly in their existence and importance (Anderson, 1991).

Many secondary groups are **formal organizations**, secondary groups designed to achieve explicit objectives. In complex societies like ours, the most common and influential formal organizations are bureaucracies. We now turn to an examination of these often frustrating but necessary organizational forms.

> **Formal organizations** are secondary groups designed to achieve explicit objectives.

Summing Up

- Conformity to group norms is often functional in the sense that it enables individuals to be mobilized to achieve group goals.
- Conformity to group norms (or lack of conflict within groups) can be dangerous insofar as the inability to "think outside the box" and act accordingly may prevent a group from averting disaster.
- Conformity to group norms can also be problematic insofar as it increases or reinforces social inequality.

BUREAUCRACIES

Bureaucratic Inefficiency

Earlier, we noted that Weber regarded bureaucracies as the most efficient type of secondary group. This runs against the grain of common knowledge. In everyday speech, when someone says *bureaucracy*, people commonly think of bored clerks sitting in small cubicles spinning out endless trails of "red tape" that create needless waste and frustrate the goals of clients. The idea that bureaucracies are efficient may seem odd.

How can we square the reality of bureaucratic inefficiencies with Weber's view that bureaucracies are the most efficient type of secondary group? The answer is twofold. First, we must recognize that when Weber wrote about the efficiency of bureaucracy, he was comparing it with older organizational forms. These operated on the basis of either traditional practice ("We do it this way because we've always done it this way") or the charisma of their leaders ("We do it this way because our chief inspires us to do it this way"). Compared with such "traditional" and "charismatic" organizations, bureaucracies *are* generally more efficient. Second, we must recognize that Weber thought bureaucracies could operate efficiently only in the ideal case. He wrote extensively about some of bureaucracy's less admirable aspects in the real world. In other words, he understood that reality is often messier than the ideal case. So should we. In reality, bureaucracies vary in efficiency. Therefore, rather than proclaiming bureaucracy efficient or inefficient, we should find out what makes bureaucracies work well or poorly.

Traditionally, sociologists have lodged four main criticisms against bureaucracies. First is the problem of **dehumanization**. Rather than treating clients and personnel as people with unique needs, bureaucracies sometimes treat clients as standard cases and personnel as cogs in a giant machine. This treatment frustrates clients and lowers worker morale. Second is the problem of **bureaucratic ritualism** (Merton, 1968 [1949]). Bureaucrats sometimes get so preoccupied with rules and regulations they make it difficult for the organization to fulfill

> **Dehumanization** occurs when bureaucracies treat clients as standard cases and personnel as cogs in a giant machine. This treatment frustrates clients and lowers worker morale.

> **Bureaucratic ritualism** involves bureaucrats becoming so preoccupied with rules and regulations that they make it difficult for the organization to fulfill its goals.

Oligarchy means "rule of the few." All bureaucracies have a supposed tendency for power to become increasingly concentrated in the hands of a few people at the top of the organizational pyramid.

Bureaucratic inertia refers to the tendency of large, rigid bureaucracies to continue their policies even when their clients' needs change.

its goals. Third is the problem of **oligarchy**, or "rule of the few" (Michels, 1949 [1911]). Some sociologists have argued that in all bureaucracies power tends to become increasingly concentrated in the hands of a few people at the top of the organizational pyramid. This tendency is particularly problematic in political organizations because it hinders democracy and renders leaders unaccountable to the public. Fourth is the problem of **bureaucratic inertia**. Bureaucracies are sometimes so large and rigid that they lose touch with reality and continue their policies even when their clients' needs change.

Two main factors underlie bureaucratic inefficiency: size and social structure. Consider size first. The larger the bureaucracy, the more difficult it is for functionaries to communicate. Moreover, bigger bureaucracies make it easier for rivalries and coalitions to form. As Figure 6.4 shows, only one dyadic relationship can exist between two people, whereas three dyadic relationships can exist among three people and six dyadic relationships among four people. The number of potential dyadic relationships increases exponentially with the number of people. Hence, 300 dyadic relationships are possible among 25 people and 1225 dyadic relationships are possible among 50 people. The possibility of clique formation, rivalries, conflict, and miscommunication rises as quickly as the number of possible dyadic social relationships in an organization.

The second factor underlying bureaucratic inefficiency is social structure. Figure 6.5 shows a typical bureaucratic structure: a hierarchy. The bureaucracy has a head. Below the head are three divisions. Below the divisions are six departments. As you move up the hierarchy, the power of the staff increases. Note also the lines of communication that join the various bureaucratic units. Departments report only to their divisions. Divisions report only to the head.

FIGURE 6.4

Number of Possible Dyadic Relationships by Number of People in Group

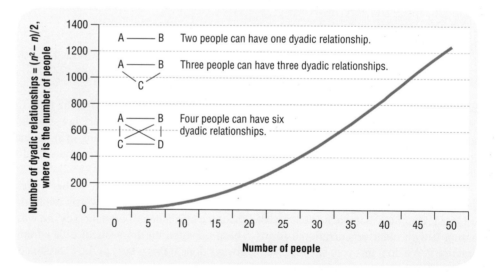

FIGURE 6.5

Bureaucratic Structure

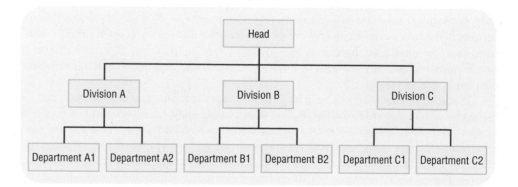

Usually, the more levels in a bureaucratic structure, the more difficult communication becomes, because people have to communicate indirectly, through department and division heads, rather than directly with each other. Information may be lost, blocked, reinterpreted, or distorted as it moves up the hierarchy, or an excess of information may cause top levels to become engulfed in a paperwork blizzard that prevents them from clearly seeing the needs of the organization and its clients. Bureaucratic heads may have only a vague and imprecise idea of what is happening "on the ground" (Wilensky, 1967).

Consider also what happens when the lines of communication directly joining departments or divisions are weak or nonexistent. As the lines joining units in Figure 6.5 suggest, department A1 may have information that could help department B1 do its job better but may have to communicate that information indirectly through the division level. At the division level, the information may be lost, blocked, reinterpreted, or distorted. Thus, just as people who have authority may lack information, people who have information may lack the authority to act on it directly (Crozier, 1964 [1963]).

Below we consider some ways of overcoming bureaucratic inefficiency. As you will see, these typically involve establishing patterns of social relations that flatten the bureaucratic hierarchy and cut across the sort of bureaucratic rigidities illustrated in Figure 6.5. As a useful prelude to this discussion, we first note some shortcomings of Weber's analysis of bureaucracy. Weber tended to ignore both bureaucracy's informal side and the role of leadership in influencing bureaucratic performance. Yet, as you will learn, it is precisely by paying attention to such issues that we can make bureaucracies more efficient.

Bureaucracy's Informal Side

Weber was concerned mainly with the formal structure or chain of command in a bureaucracy. He paid little attention to the social networks that underlie the chain of command.

Evidence for the existence of social networks and their importance in the operation of bureaucracies goes back to the 1930s. Officials at the Hawthorne plant of the Western Electric Company near Chicago wanted to see how various aspects of the work environment affected productivity. They sent social scientists in to investigate. Among other things, researchers found that workers in one section of the plant had established a norm for daily output. Workers who failed to meet the norm were helped by co-workers until their output increased. Workers who exceeded the norm were chided by co-workers until their productivity fell. Company officials and researchers previously had regarded employees merely as individuals who worked as hard or as little as they could in response to wage levels and work conditions. However, the Hawthorne study showed that employees are members of social networks that regulate output (Roethlisberger and Dickson, 1939).

In the 1970s, Rosabeth Moss Kanter conducted another landmark study of informal social relations in bureaucracies (Kanter, 1977). Kanter studied a corporation in which most women were sales agents. They were locked out of managerial positions. However, she did not find that the corporation discriminated against women as a matter of policy. She did find a male-only social network whose members shared gossip, went drinking, and told sexist jokes. The cost of being excluded from the network was high: To get good raises and promotions, a person had to be accepted as "one of the boys" and be sponsored by a male executive, which was impossible for women. Thus, despite a company policy that did not discriminate against women, an informal network of social relations ensured that the company discriminated against women in practice.

Informal interaction is common even in highly bureaucratic organizations. A water cooler, for example, can be a place for exchanging information and gossip, and even a place for decision making.

© Photod'sc/SuperStock

Despite their overt commitment to impersonality and written rules, bureaucracies rely profoundly on informal interaction to get the job done (Barnard, 1938; Blau, 1963). This fact is true even at the highest levels. For example, executives usually decide important matters in face-to-face meetings, not in writing or via the phone. That is because people feel more comfortable in intimate settings, where they can get to know "the whole person." Meeting face to face, people can use their verbal and nonverbal interaction skills to gauge other people's trustworthiness. Socializing—talking over dinner, for example—is an important part of any business because the establishment of trust lies at the heart of all social interactions that require cooperation (Gambetta, 1988).

Leadership

Apart from overlooking the role of informal relations in the operation of bureaucracies, Weber also paid insufficient attention to the issue of leadership. Weber thought the formal structure of a bureaucracy largely determines how it operates. However, sociologists now realize that leadership style also has a big bearing on bureaucratic performance (Barnard, 1938; Ridgeway, 1983).

Research shows that the least effective leader is the one who allows subordinates to work things out largely on their own, with almost no direction from above. This is known as **laissez-faire leadership**, from the French expression "let them do." Note, however, that laissez-faire leadership can be effective under some circumstances. It works best when group members are highly experienced, trained, motivated, and educated, and when trust and confidence in group members are high. In such conditions, a strong leader is not really needed for the group to accomplish its goals. At the other extreme is **authoritarian leadership**. Authoritarian leaders demand strict compliance from subordinates. They are most effective in a crisis, such as a war or the emergency room of a hospital. They may earn grudging respect from subordinates for achieving the group's goals in the face of difficult circumstances, but they rarely win popularity contests. **Democratic leadership** offers more guidance than the laissez-faire variety but less control than the authoritarian type. Democratic leaders try to include all group members in the decision-making process, taking the best ideas from the group and moulding them into a strategy that all can identify with. Except for crisis situations, democratic leadership is usually the most effective leadership style.

In sum, contemporary researchers have modified Weber's characterization of bureaucracy in two main ways. First, they have stressed the importance of informal social networks in shaping bureaucratic operations. Second, they have shown that democratic leaders are most effective in non-crisis situations because they tend to distribute decision-making authority and rewards widely. As you will now see, these lessons are important when it comes to thinking about how to make bureaucracies more efficient.

Overcoming Bureaucratic Inefficiency

In the business world, large bureaucratic organizations sometimes find themselves unable to compete against smaller, innovative firms, particularly in industries that are changing quickly (Burns and Stalker, 1961). This situation occurs partly because innovative firms tend to have flatter and more democratic organizational structures, such as the network illustrated in Figure 6.6. Compare the flat network structure in Figure 6.6 with the traditional bureaucratic structure in Figure 6.5. Note that the network structure has fewer levels than the traditional bureaucratic structure does. Moreover, in the network structure, lines of communication link all units. In the traditional bureaucratic structure, information flows only upward.

Much evidence suggests that flatter bureaucracies with decentralized decision making and multiple lines of communication produce more satisfied workers, happier clients, and bigger profits (Kanter, 1989). Some of this evidence comes from Sweden and Japan. Beginning in the early 1970s, such corporations as Volvo and Toyota were at the forefront of bureaucratic innovation in those countries. They began eliminating middle-management

Laissez-faire leadership allows subordinates to work things out largely on their own, with almost no direction from above. It is the least effective type of leadership.

Authoritarian leadership demands strict compliance from subordinates. Authoritarian leaders are most effective in a crisis, such as a war or the emergency room of a hospital.

Democratic leadership offers more guidance than the laissez-faire variety but less control than the authoritarian type. Democratic leaders try to include all group members in the decision-making process, taking the best ideas from the group and moulding them into a strategy with which all can identify. Outside crisis situations, democratic leadership is usually the most effective leadership style.

FIGURE 6.6
Network Structure

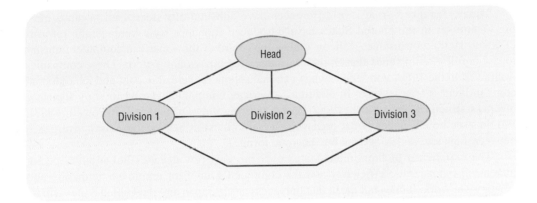

positions. They allowed worker participation in a variety of tasks related to their main functions. They delegated authority to autonomous teams of a dozen or so workers who were allowed to make many decisions themselves. They formed "quality circles" of workers to monitor and correct defects in products and services. As a result, product quality, worker morale, and profitability improved. Today, these ideas have spread well beyond the Swedish and Japanese automobile industry and are evident in such companies as General Motors, Ford, Boeing, and Caterpillar. In the 1980s and 1990s, companies outside the manufacturing sector introduced similar bureaucratic reforms, again with positive results.

Organizational Environments

If flatter organizations are more efficient, why aren't all bureaucracies flatter? Mainly, say sociologists, because of the environment in which they operate. An **organizational environment** comprises a host of economic, political, and cultural factors that lie outside an organization and affect the way it works (Aldrich, 1979; Meyer and Scott, 1983). Some organizational environments are conducive to the formation of flatter, network-like bureaucracies. Others are not. We can illustrate the effects of organizational environments by discussing two cases that have attracted much attention in recent years: the United States and Japan.

In the 1970s, American business bureaucracies tended to be more hierarchical than their Japanese counterparts were. This was one reason that worker dissatisfaction was high and labour productivity was low in the United States. In Japan, where corporate decision making was more decentralized, worker morale and productivity were high (Dore, 1983). Several aspects of the organizational environment help to explain Japanese–American differences in the 1970s:

- *Japanese workers were in a position to demand and achieve more decision-making authority than American workers were.* After World War II, the proportion of Japanese workers in unions increased whereas the proportion of American workers in unions declined. Unions gave Japanese workers more clout than their American counterparts enjoyed.
- *International competition encouraged bureaucratic efficiency in Japan.* Many big Japanese corporations matured in the highly competitive post–World War II international environment. Many big American corporations originated earlier, in an international environment with few competitors. Thus, Japanese corporations had a bigger incentive to develop more efficient organizational structures (Harrison, 1994).
- *The availability of external suppliers allowed Japanese firms to remain lean.* Many large American companies matured when external sources of supply were scarce. For example, when IBM entered the computer market in the 1950s, it had to produce all components internally because nobody else was making them. This situation led IBM to develop a large, hierarchical bureaucracy. In contrast, Japanese computer manufacturers could rely on many external suppliers in the 1970s. Therefore, they could develop flatter organizational structures (Podolny and Page, 1998).

An **organizational environment** comprises a host of economic, political, and cultural forces that lie outside an organization and affect the way it works.

Today, Japanese–American differences have substantially decreased because most big businesses in the United States have introduced Japanese-style bureaucratic reforms (Tsutsui, 1998). For instance, Silicon Valley, the centre of the American computer industry today, is full of companies that fit the "Japanese" organizational pattern. These companies originated in the 1980s and 1990s, when external suppliers were abundant and international competitiveness was intense. In addition, American companies started to copy Japanese business structures because they saw them as successful (DiMaggio and Powell, 1983). We thus see how changes in the organizational environment help account for convergence between Japanese and American bureaucratic forms.

The experience of the United States over the past few decades holds out hope for increasing bureaucratic efficiency and the continued growth of employee autonomy and creativity at work. It does not mean that bureaucracies in Japan and the United States will be alike in all respects in 20 or 50 or 100 years. The organizational environment is unpredictable, and sociologists are just beginning to understand its operation. It is therefore anyone's guess how far convergence will continue.

Summing Up

- Bureaucracies are efficient organizations compared with organizations run on the basis of tradition and charisma.
- Large bureaucracies that suffer from blocked internal communication are less efficient than more open, less hierarchical bureaucracies.

SOCIETIES

Societies are collectivities of interacting people who share a culture and a territory.

Networks, groups, and bureaucracies are embedded in **societies**, collectivities of interacting people who share a culture and a territory.[1] Like smaller collectivities, societies help shape human action. They influence the kind of work we do and how productively we work. They mould patterns of class, gender, racial, and ethnic inequality. They impinge on the way religious, family, and other institutions operate. They affect the way we govern and the way we think of ourselves.

Despite the pervasiveness of these influences, most people are blind to them. We tend to believe that we are free to do what we want. Yet the plain fact is that societies affect even our most personal and intimate choices. For example, deciding how many children to have is one of the most intensely private and emotional issues a woman must face. So why is it that tens of millions of women have decided in the space of just a few decades to have an average of two babies instead of six, or eight babies instead of four? Why do so many individuals make almost exactly the same private decision at almost precisely the same historical moment? The answer is that certain identifiable social conditions prompt them to reach the same conclusion, in this case to have fewer or more babies. And so it is with most decisions. Identifiable social conditions increase the chance that we will choose one course of action over another.

The relationship between people and nature is the most basic determinant of how societies are structured and therefore how people's choices are constrained. Accordingly, researchers have identified six stages of human evolution, each characterized by a shift in the relationship between people and nature. As we review each of these stages, note what happens to the human–nature relationship: With each successive stage, people are less at the mercy of nature and transform it more radically. The changing relationship between people and nature has huge implications for all aspects of social life. Let us identify these implications as we sketch the evolution of human society in bold strokes.

Foraging Societies

Until about 10 000 years ago, all people lived in **foraging societies**. They sustained themselves by searching for wild plants and hunting wild animals (Lenski, Nolan, and Lenski, 1995; O'Neil, 2004; Sahlins, 1972). They depended on nature passively, taking whatever it made available and transforming it only slightly to meet their needs. They built simple tools, such as baskets, bows and arrows, spears, and digging sticks. They sometimes burned grasslands to encourage the growth of new vegetation and attract game, but they neither planted crops nor domesticated many animals.

Most foragers lived in temporary encampments, and when food was scarce they migrated to more bountiful regions. Harsh environments could support 3 people per 25 to 130 square kilometres (1 person per 10 to 50 square miles). Rich environments could support 25 to 80 people per square kilometre (10 to 30 people per square mile). Foraging communities or bands averaged about 25 to 30 people but could be as large as 100 people. *Aquatic foragers*, such as those on the western coast of North America, concentrated on fishing and hunting marine mammals. *Equestrian foragers*, such as the Great Plains Aboriginal peoples of North America, hunted large mammals from horseback. *Pedestrian foragers* engaged in diversified hunting and gathering on foot and could be found on all continents.

Until the middle of the twentieth century, most social scientists thought that foragers lived brief, grim lives. In their view, foragers were engaged in a desperate struggle for existence that was typically cut short by disease, starvation, pestilence, or some other force of nature. We now know that this characterization says more about the biases of early anthropologists than about the lives foragers actually lived. Consider the !Kung of the Kalahari Desert in southern Africa, who maintained their traditional way of life until the 1960s (Lee, 1979). Young !Kung did not fully join the workforce until they reached the age of 20. Adults worked only about 15 hours a week. Mainly because of disease, children faced a much smaller chance of surviving childhood than is the case in contemporary society, but about 10 percent of the !Kung were older than 60, the same percentage as Canadians in the early 1970s. It thus seems that the !Kung who survived childhood lived relatively long, secure, leisurely, healthy, and happy lives. They were not unique. The tall totem poles, ornate wood carvings, colourful masks, and elaborate clothing of the Kwakiutl on Vancouver Island serve as beautiful reminders that many foragers had the leisure time to invest considerable energy in ornamentation.

Equestrian foragers were hierarchical, male-dominated, and warlike, especially after they acquired rifles in the nineteenth century. However, the social structure of pedestrian foragers—the great majority of all foragers—was remarkably non-hierarchical. They shared what little wealth they had, and women and men enjoyed approximately equal status.

Pastoral and Horticultural Societies

Substantial social inequality became widespread about 10 000 years ago, when some bands began to domesticate various wild plants and animals, especially cattle, camels, pigs, goats, sheep, horses, and reindeer (Lenski, Nolan, and Lenski, 1995; O'Neil, 2004). By using hand tools to garden in highly fertile areas (**horticultural societies**) and herding animals in

Foraging societies are societies in which people live by searching for wild plants and hunting wild animals. Such societies predominated until about 10 000 years ago. Inequality, the division of labour, productivity, and settlement size are very low in such societies.

Aquatic foragers had much leisure time to invest in ornamentation, suggesting that their lives were by no means a constant struggle for survival.

Horticultural societies are societies in which people domesticate plants and use simple hand tools to garden. Such societies first emerged about 10 000 years ago.

Pastoral societies are societies in which people domesticate cattle, camels, pigs, goats, sheep, horses, and reindeer. Such societies first emerged about 10 000 years ago.

Agricultural societies are societies in which plows and animal power are used to substantially increase food supply and dependability as compared with horticultural and pastoral societies. Agricultural societies first emerged about 5000 years ago.

more arid areas (**pastoral societies**), people increased the food supply and made it more dependable. Nature could now support more people. Moreover, pastoral and horticultural societies enabled fewer people to specialize in producing food and more people to specialize in constructing tools and weapons, making clothing and jewellery, and trading valuable objects with other bands. Some families and bands accumulated more domesticated animals, cropland, and valued objects than others did. As a result, pastoral and horticultural societies developed a higher level of social inequality than was evident in most foraging societies.

As wealth accumulated, feuding and warfare grew, particularly among pastoralists. Men who controlled large herds of animals and conducted successful predatory raids acquired much prestige and power and came to be recognized as chiefs. Some chiefs formed large, fierce, mobile armies. The Mongols and the Zulus were horse pastoralists who conquered large parts of Asia and Africa, respectively.

Most pastoralists were nomadic, with migration patterns dictated by their animals' needs for food and water. Some pastoralists migrated regularly from the same cool highlands in the summer to the same warm lowland valleys in the winter and were able to establish villages in both locations. Horticulturalists often established permanent settlements beside their croplands. These settlements might include several hundred people. However, the development of large permanent settlements, including the first cities, took place only with the development of intensive agriculture.

Agricultural Societies

Especially in the fertile river valleys of the Middle East, India, China, and South America, human populations flourished—so much so that, about 5000 years ago, they could no longer be sustained by pastoral and horticulture techniques. It was then that **agricultural societies** originated. The plow was invented to harness animal power for more intensive and efficient agricultural production. The plow allowed farmers to plant crops over much larger areas and dig below the topsoil, bringing nutrients to the surface and thus increasing yield (Lenski, Nolan, and Lenski, 1995; O'Neil, 2004).

Because the source of food was immobile, many people now built permanent settlements, and because people were now able to produce considerably more food than was necessary for their own subsistence, surpluses were sold in village markets. Some of these centres became towns and then cities, home to rulers, religious figures, soldiers, craft workers, and government officials. The population of some agricultural societies numbered in the millions.

The crystallization of the idea of private property was one of the most significant developments of the era. Among pedestrian foragers, there was no private ownership of land or water. Among horticulturalists, particular families might be recognized as having rights to some property, but only while they were using it. If the property was not in use, they were obliged to share it or give

A medieval painting showing peasants harvesting outside the walls of their lord and master's castle. Why is it significant that the church is situated inside the walls?

it to a family that needed it. In contrast, in societies that practised intensive agriculture, powerful individuals succeeded in having the idea of individual property rights legally recognized. It was now possible for people to buy land and water, to call them their own, and to transmit ownership to their offspring. People could now become rich and, through inheritance, make their children rich.

Ancient civilizations thus became rigidly divided into classes. Royalty surrounded itself with loyal landowners, protected itself with professional soldiers, and justified its rule with the help of priests, part of whose job was to convince ordinary peasants that the existing social order was God's will. Government officials collected taxes and religious officials collected tithes, thus enriching the upper classes with the peasantry's surplus production. In this era, inequality between women and men also reached its historical high point (Boulding, 1976).

Industrial Societies

Stimulated by international exploration, trade, and commerce, the Industrial Revolution began in Britain in the 1780s. A century later, it had spread to all of Western Europe, North America, Japan, and Russia. It involved the use of fuel—at first, waterpower and steam—to drive machines and thereby greatly increase productivity, the quantity of things that could be produced with a given amount of effort.

If you have ever read a Charles Dickens novel, such as *Oliver Twist*, you know that hellish working conditions and deep social inequalities characterized early **industrial societies**. Work in factories and mines became so productive that owners amassed previously unimaginable fortunes, but ordinary labourers worked 16-hour days in dangerous conditions and earned barely enough to survive. They struggled for the right to form and join unions and expand the vote to all adult citizens, hoping to use union power and political influence to win improvements in the conditions of their existence. At the same time, new technologies and ways of organizing work made it possible to produce ever more goods at a lower cost per unit. This made it possible to meet many of the workers' demands and raise living standards for the entire population.

Increasingly, businesses required a literate, numerate, and highly trained workforce. To raise profits, they were eager to identify and hire the most talented people. They encouraged everyone to develop their talents and rewarded them for doing so by paying higher salaries. Even inequality between women and men began to decrease because of the demand for talent and women's struggles to enter the paid workforce on an equal footing with men. Why hire an incompetent man over a competent woman when you can profit more from the services of a capable employee? Put in this way, women's demands for equality made good business sense. For all these reasons, class and gender inequality declined as industrial societies matured.

Industrial societies are societies that use machines and fuel to greatly increase the supply and dependability of food and finished goods. The first such societies emerged in Great Britain in the last decades of the eighteenth century.

Postindustrial Societies

In the early 1970s, sociologist Daniel Bell (1973) argued that industrial society was rapidly becoming a thing of the past. According to Bell, just as agriculture gave way to manufacturing as the driving force of the economy in the nineteenth century, so did manufacturing give way to service industries by the mid-twentieth century, resulting in the birth of **postindustrial societies**.

Even in pre-agricultural societies, a few individuals specialized in providing services rather than in producing goods. For example, a person considered adept at tending to the ill, forecasting the weather, or predicting the movement of animals might be relieved of hunting responsibilities to focus on these services. However, such jobs were rare because productivity was low. Nearly everyone had to do physical work for the tribe to survive. Even in early agricultural societies, it took 80 to 100 farmers to support one non-farmer (Hodson and Sullivan, 1995: 10). Only at the beginning of the nineteenth century in industrialized countries did productivity increase to the point where a quarter of the labour force could be employed in services. Today, about three-quarters of Canadian workers are in the service sector.

In postindustrial societies, women have been recruited to the service sector in disproportionately large numbers, and that has helped to ensure a gradual increase in equality

Postindustrial societies are societies in which most workers are employed in the service sector and computers spur substantial increases in the division of labour and productivity. Shortly after World War II, the United States became the first postindustrial society.

between women and men in terms of education, income, and other indicators of rank (see Chapter 11, Sexualities and Gender Stratification). The picture with respect to inequality between classes is more complex. Most postindustrial societies, and especially the United States, have experienced large increases in class inequality. Other postindustrial societies, such as Canada, have not. A few postindustrial societies, such as France, had less inequality in 2000 than in 1977, bucking the broader trend (Smeeding, 2004). We discuss the reasons for these different patterns in Chapter 8, Social Stratification.

Rapid change in the composition of the labour force during the final decades of the twentieth century was made possible by the computer. The computer automated many manufacturing and office procedures. It created jobs in the service sector as quickly as it eliminated them in manufacturing. The computer is to the service sector what the steam engine was to manufacturing, the plow was to intensive agriculture, domestication was to horticulture and pastoralism, and simple hand tools were to foraging.

Postnatural Societies

On February 28, 1953, two men walked into a pub in Cambridge, England, and offered drinks all around. "We have discovered the secret of life!" proclaimed one of the men. He was James Watson. With his colleague, Francis Crick, he had found the structure of deoxyribonucleic acid, or DNA, the chemical that makes up genes. During cell division, a single DNA molecule uncoils into two strands. New, identical molecules are formed from each strand. In this way, growth takes place and traits are passed from one generation to the next. It was one of the most important scientific discoveries ever (Watson, 1968).

By the early 1970s, scientists were beginning to develop techniques for manipulating DNA (so-called **recombinant DNA**). Soon they could cut a segment out of a DNA strand and join the remaining sections together, or they could take a DNA strand and connect it to segments of DNA from another living thing. This meant that scientists could create new life forms, a capability that had until then been restricted in the popular imagination to God. Enthusiasts proclaimed a "second genesis" as they began to speculate about the potential of the new technology to rid the world of hereditary disease; feed the hungry with higher-yield, disease-resistant farm products; and even create more intelligent, beautiful, and athletic children. For many millions of years, nature had selected the "fittest" living things for survival. Now it seemed possible for humans to speed up natural selection, thus escaping the whims of nature and creating a more perfect society under their control. The invention of recombinant DNA marked the onset of a new social era—what we prefer to call the era of **postnatural society** (Dyson, 1999; Watson, 2000).

We consider some of the perils of postnatural society in detail in this book's online chapter, Chapter 22, Technology and the Global Environment. Here we want only to emphasize that genetic engineering could easily result in increased social inequality. For example, the technology for creating more perfect babies will undoubtedly be expensive, so rich countries and rich people are more likely to benefit from it. Princeton University biologist Lee Silver and Nobel Prize–winning physicist Freeman Dyson go so far as to speculate that the ultimate result of genetic engineering will be several distinct human species. People who are in a position to take full advantage of genetic engineering will be better looking, more intelligent, less likely to suffer from disease, and more athletic. People who are not so fortunate will have to face nature's caprice in handing out talents and disadvantages, just as our foraging ancestors did (Brave, 2003). The main, and perhaps only, safeguard against such an outcome is true democracy, which would allow ordinary people to decide which risks are worth taking and how the benefits of genetic engineering should be distributed within and across populations (Häyry and Lehto, 1998).

Recombinant DNA involves removing a segment of DNA from a gene or splicing together segments of DNA from different living things, thus effectively creating a new life form.

Postnatural societies are societies in which genetic engineering enables people to create new life forms.

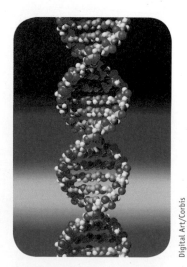

Digital Art/Corbis

The DNA molecule

Summing Up

- As society has evolved, human dependence on nature has decreased.
- Class inequality and gender inequality are low in foraging societies, moderate in pastoral and horticultural societies, and high in agricultural and early industrial societies. Both of these inequalities moderate in industrial societies. However, class inequalities increase in many postindustrial societies and they may increase even more in postnatural societies.

FREEDOM AND CONSTRAINT IN SOCIAL LIFE

Throughout this chapter, we emphasized the capacity of networks, groups, bureaucracies, and societies to constrain human behaviour. As we have seen, such social collectivities can even encourage dangerously high levels of conformity, compel people to act against their better judgment, dominate people in a vice of organizational rigidities, and affect the level of social inequality in society.

We stressed the constraining aspect of social collectives because we wanted to counter the commonsense view that motives alone determine the way people act. Now, however, in conclusion, it would serve us well to remind you that people often have two options other than bowing to the will of their social collectivities: "exit" and "voice" (Hirschman, 1970). In some circumstances, they can leave the social collectivities to which they belong (exit). In other circumstances, they can struggle against the constraints their social collectivities seek to impose on them (voice). As French philosopher Jean-Paul Sartre once remarked, it is always possible to say no, even to the worst tyrant. Less dramatically but no less importantly, knowledge, including sociological knowledge, can increase the ability of people to resist the constraints imposed on them. Recall the Milgram experiment we discussed at the beginning of this chapter, in which subjects administered what they thought were painful shocks to people just because the experimenters told them to. When the experiment was replicated years later, many of the subjects refused to go along with the demands of the experimenters. Some invoked the example of the Nazis to justify their refusal to comply. Others mentioned Milgram's original experiment. Their knowledge, some of it perhaps gained in sociology courses, enabled them to resist unreasonable demands (Gamson, Fireman, and Rytina, 1982).

Paradoxically, to succeed in challenging social collectivities, people must sometimes form a new social collectivity themselves. More than half a century ago, sociologists Seymour Martin Lipset, Martin A. Trow, and James S. Coleman (1956) conducted a classic study that made just this point. They investigated the International Typographical Union (ITU) because it was an exception to the tendency of trade union bureaucracies to turn into oligarchies, or organizations run by the few. The ITU remained democratic because the nature of printing as an occupation and an industry made the resources for democratic politics more widely available than is typical in trade unions. Strong local unions that valued their autonomy founded the international union. The local and regional markets typical of the printing industry at the time strengthened their autonomy. At the same time, strong factions in the union prevented any one faction from becoming dominant. Finally, robust social networks on the shop floor enabled ordinary printers to fight for their rights and resist the slide into oligarchy. This case illustrates how people can form social collectivities to counteract other social collectives. Embedded in social relations, we can use them for good or evil.

NOTE

1. For "virtual societies" on the Internet, however, a shared territory is unnecessary.

SUMMARY

1. Do people act the way they do only because of their interests and emotions?
   People's motives are important determinants of their actions, but social collectivities also influence the way they behave. Because of the power of social collectivities, people sometimes act against their interests, values, and emotions.

2. Is it a small world?
   It is a small world. Most people interact repeatedly with a small circle of family members, friends, and co-workers. However, our personal networks overlap with other social networks, which is why only a few links separate us from complete strangers.

3. What is network analysis?
   Network analysis is the study of the concrete social relations linking people. By focusing on concrete ties, network analysts often come up with surprising results. For example, network analysis has demonstrated the strength of weak ties in job searches and has demonstrated that a rich web of social affiliations underlies urban life.

4. What are groups?
   Groups are clusters of people who identity with one another. Primary groups involve intense, intimate, enduring relations; secondary groups involve less personal and intense ties; and reference groups are groups against which people measure their situation or conduct. Groups impose conformity on members and seek to exclude non-members.

5. Is bureaucracy just "red tape"? Is it possible to overcome bureaucratic inefficiency?
   Although bureaucracies often suffer from various forms of inefficiency, they are generally efficient compared with other organizational forms. Bureaucratic inefficiency increases with size and degree of hierarchy. By flattening bureaucratic structures, decentralizing decision-making authority, and opening lines of communication between bureaucratic units, efficiency can often be improved.

6. How accurate is Weber's analysis of bureaucracy?
   Social networks underlie the chain of command in all bureaucracies and affect their operation. Weber ignored this aspect of bureaucracy. He also downplayed the importance of leadership in the functioning of bureaucracy. Research shows that democratic leadership improves the efficiency of bureaucratic operations in non-crisis situations, authoritarian leadership works best in crises, and laissez-faire leadership is the least effective form of leadership in all situations.

7. What impact does the organizational environment have on bureaucracy?
   The organizational environment influences the degree to which bureaucratic efficiency can be achieved. For example, bureaucracies are less hierarchical where workers are more powerful, competition with other bureaucracies is high, and external sources of supply are available.

8. How have societies evolved over the past 100 000 years?
   Over the past 100 000 years, growing human domination of nature has increased the supply and dependability of food and finished goods, productivity, the division of labour, and the size and permanence of human settlements. Class and gender inequality increased until the nineteenth century and then began to decline. Class inequality began to increase in some societies in the last decades of the twentieth century and may continue to increase in the future.

9. What does the sociological analysis of networks, groups, bureaucracies, and societies tell us about the possibility of human freedom?

Networks, groups, bureaucracies, and societies influence and constrain everyone. However, people can also use these social collectivities to increase their freedom. In this sense, social collectivities are a source of both constraint and freedom.

KEY TERMS

agricultural societies (p. 150)

authoritarian leadership (p. 146)

bureaucracy (p. 133)

bureaucratic inertia (p. 144)

bureaucratic ritualism (p. 143)

dehumanization (p. 143)

democratic leadership (p. 146)

dyad (p. 137)

foraging societies (p. 149)

formal organizations (p. 143)

groupthink (p. 140)

horticultural societies (p. 149)

industrial societies (p. 151)

in-group (p. 141)

laissez-faire leadership (p. 146)

oligarchy (p. 144)

organizational environment (p. 147)

out-group (p. 141)

pastoral societies (p. 150)

postindustrial societies (p. 151)

postnatural societies (p. 152)

primary groups (p. 138)

recombinant DNA (p. 152)

reference group (p. 142)

secondary groups (p. 139)

social category (p. 138)

social group (p. 138)

social network (p. 134)

societies (p. 148)

triad (p. 137)

WEB RESOURCES

Companion Website for This Book

http://www.compass4e.nelson.com

Begin by clicking on the Student Resources section of the website. Next, select the chapter you are studying from the pull-down menu. From the Student Resources page you have easy access to additional Weblinks and other resources. The website also has many useful tips to aid you in your study of sociology, including practice tests for each chapter.

InfoTrac® Search Terms

These search terms are provided to assist you in beginning to conduct research on this topic by visiting http://www.infotrac-college.com:

bureaucracy

rational choice theory

social network

Inequality

Occupy Poster http://www.occupytogether.org/posters/OccupyTogether_poster05.pdf

Deviance and Crime

IN THIS CHAPTER, YOU WILL LEARN THAT

- Deviance and crime, and conceptions of appropriate punishment, vary from one social context to another.

- Deviance and crime are socially defined and constructed, not inherent in certain actions or characteristics of individuals.

- Following dramatic increases during the 1960s and 1970s, Canadian crime rates peaked in the early 1990s and have been falling steadily since then. The decline is due mainly to more effective policing, the declining number of young people in the population, and a booming economy throughout most of this period.

- A disproportionately large number of Aboriginal and black people are arrested, convicted, and imprisoned because of the low social and economic standing of Aboriginals and blacks, the tendency of people with low social and economic standing to commit offences that are likely to be prosecuted, and racial discrimination in the criminal justice system.

- Imprisonment is one of the main forms of punishment in industrial societies.

- Fear of crime may be subject to manipulation by business and political groups that benefit from it.

- Cost-effective and workable alternatives to currently predominant regimes of punishment exist.

THE SOCIAL DEFINITION OF DEVIANCE AND CRIME

If you happen to come across members of the Tukano tribe in northern Brazil, don't be surprised if they greet you with a cheery "Have you bathed today?" You would probably find the question insulting, but think how you would feel if you were greeted by the Yanomamö people in Brazil's central highlands. A French anthropologist reports that when he first encountered the Yanomamö, they rubbed mucus and tobacco juice into their palms, then inspected him by running their filthy hands over his body (Chagnon, 1992). He must have been relieved to return to urban Brazil and be greeted with a simple kiss on the cheek.

Rules for greeting people vary widely from one country to the next and among different cultural groups within one country. That is why a marketing company created an animated website showing business travellers how to greet their hosts in the 15 countries where the firm does business ("The Business of Touch," 2006). After all, violating local norms can cause great offence and result in the loss of a contract, a fact that one visitor to South Korea found out too late. He beckoned his host with an index finger, after which the host grew quiet. He discovered after he lost the deal that Koreans beckon only cats and dogs with an index finger. If you want to beckon someone politely in South Korea, you should do so with all four fingers facing down, much like Canadians wave goodbye.

Because norms vary widely, deviance is relative. What some people consider normal, others consider deviant, and vice versa. No act is deviant in and of itself. People commit deviant acts only when they break a norm and cause others to react negatively. From a sociological point of view, *everyone* is a deviant in one social context or another.

The Difference Between Deviance and Crime

Deviance involves breaking a norm and evoking a negative reaction from others. Societies establish some norms as laws. **Crime** is deviance that breaks a **law**, which is a norm stipulated and enforced by government bodies.

Just as deviance is relative, so is crime. Consider that a list of famous people who have been labelled criminals would include Socrates, Jesus, Martin Luther, Louis Riel, Mahatma Gandhi, Martin Luther King Jr., and Nelson Mandela. For many people today, these figures are heroes. In contrast, people who planned and participated in the extermination of Jews, Roma (Gypsies), and homosexuals in Nazi Germany were acting in a way that was defined in Germany as law-abiding. You would probably consider the actions taken by the Nazis in Germany, rather than the actions of Jesus or Martin Luther, to be deviant or criminal. That is because norms and laws have changed dramatically. Today, anyone who advocates or promotes genocide commits a crime under Canadian law. We conclude that what is considered a crime in some times and places is considered perfectly normal in other times and places (see Box 7.1 on page 160)

Sanctions

People don't notice many deviant acts or they consider them too trivial to warrant punishment. More serious acts of deviance, if noticed, are typically punished, either informally or formally. **Informal punishment** is mild. It may involve raised eyebrows, gossip, ostracism, shaming, or stigmatization (Braithwaite, 1989). When people are **stigmatized**, they are negatively evaluated because of a marker that distinguishes them from others (Goffman, 1963). One of this book's authors, John Lie, was stigmatized as a young child and often bullied by elementary-school classmates because he was a Korean in a Japanese school. "I was normal in other ways," says John. "I played the same sports and games; watched the same television shows; and looked, dressed, and acted like other Japanese students. However, my one deviation was enough to stigmatize me. It gave licence to some of my classmates to beat me up from time to time. I wondered at the time why no rules banned bullying and

Deviance occurs when someone departs from a norm and evokes a negative reaction from others.

Crime is deviance that is against the law.

A **law** is a norm stipulated and enforced by government bodies.

CP Picture Archive/Frank Gunn

Nelson Mandela spent decades imprisoned in South Africa for activities designed to end apartheid. Today Mandela is hailed as a hero. He was awarded the Nobel Peace Prize in 1993 and served as the first democratically elected president of South Africa from 1994 to 1999.

Informal punishment involves a mild sanction that is imposed during face-to-face interaction, not by the judicial system.

People who are **stigmatized** are negatively evaluated because of a marker that distinguishes them from others and that is labelled as socially unacceptable.

Sociology at the Movies

PARADISE NOW

Of all the social types who populate today's world, perhaps none is more difficult to understand than the suicide attacker. Many people in the West wonder who in their right mind would fly a plane into a building. What kind of person do you have to be to blow yourself up in a bus full of ordinary people or a mosque full of worshippers? Somehow, the terms *deviant* and *criminal* seem inadequate to describe such people; they are widely seen by people in the West as crazy fanatics who lack all conscience and humanity.

Paradise Now, nominated for an Oscar as best foreign-language film, demonstrates that the common Western view is ethnocentric. It sketches the social circumstances that shaped the lives of two suicide bombers, showing that they are a lot like us, and that if we found ourselves in similar circumstances we might

turn out to be a lot like them. The film is critical of suicide bombing, but it helps us understand what makes suicide bombers tick, thereby enlightening us sociologically and politically.

Said (Kais Nashef) and Khaled (Ali Suliman) are ordinary 20-something garage mechanics and best friends. They live in the Palestinian city of Nablus, which, like the rest of the West Bank has been under Israeli military occupation their whole lives. As a result of the occupation, Said and Khaled have never been able to travel outside of the West Bank, they enjoy limited economic opportunities, they are bored stiff, and most importantly, they have been robbed of their dignity. Like all Palestinians, they want the Israelis out so they can establish an independent country of their own. But their demonstrations, their rock throwing, and their armed attacks have had no effect on the powerful Israeli military. Consequently, some time before the film begins, Said and Khaled volunteered to

serve as weapons of last resort: suicide bombers.

A study of all 462 suicide bombers who attacked targets worldwide between 1980 and 2003 found not a single case of depression, psychosis, past suicide attempts, or other such mental problems among them. The bombers were rarely poor, came most often from working- or middle-class families, and were better educated than the populations from which they were recruited. Many of them were religious, but most of them, like Said and Khaled, were not. Many of them wanted to liberate territory from what they regarded as foreign occupation or control (Pape, 2005). Said and Khaled are, then, quite typical suicide bombers: They are convinced by their powerlessness and their experience that they have no weapon other than suicide bombing that might help them achieve their aim of national liberation.

As *Paradise Now* opens, the two friends are informed that they have been selected for a suicide attack in 48 hours. Their mundane preparations are peppered with humour, errors, and everyday trivia that make Said and Khaled seem like very ordinary people. For example, in the middle of recording his "martyrdom tape" for TV broadcast, Khaled incongruously

---

why no law existed against what I now call racial discrimination. If such a law did exist, my classmates would have been subject to formal punishment, which is more severe than informal punishment."

Formal punishment takes place when the judicial system penalizes someone for breaking a law.

Formal punishment results from people breaking laws. For example, criminals may be formally punished by having to serve time in prison or perform community service.

Types of deviance and crime vary in terms of the *severity of the social response*, which varies from mild disapproval to capital punishment (Hagan, 1994). Types of deviance and crime also vary in terms of *perceived harmfulness*. Note that actual harmfulness is not the only issue here—*perceived* harmfulness is too. Coca-Cola got its name because, in the early part of the twentieth century, it contained a derivative of cocaine. Now cocaine is an illegal

Ali Suliman and Kais Nashef in *Paradise Now*

remembers to tell his mother, whom he knows will watch the tape, that he saw a bargain on water filters at a local merchant's store. But underlying such humanizing events is a tension that gives the movie its force. Said and Khaled are ambivalent about their mission, not just because they have misgivings about dying but because they feel guilty about its inhumanity to civilians and are unsure of its ultimate political utility.

In the end, only Said manages to go through with the attack, but not before we get the full story about his ambivalence. Suha (Lubna Azabal), the woman he loves, is the daughter of a famous martyr for the Palestinian cause, but she strongly opposes suicide bombing. Said listens intently when she argues that suicide bombing is contrary to the spirit of Islam, it kills innocent victims, and it accomplishes nothing because it invites retaliation in a never-ending cycle of violence. However, the forces compelling Said to carry out the attack are more persuasive than Suha's argument. Thousands of Palestinians are paid, threatened, and blackmailed to serve as informants for the Israelis. Said's father was one of them. When he was caught, he was executed by Palestinian militants. Said has been deeply ashamed of his father's actions his whole life and angry with the Israelis for forcing his father to serve as a collaborator. His ultimate motivation for becoming a suicide bomber is retaliation against Israel for turning his father into an informant. Like most suicide bombers in the country, he is driven by the desire for revenge (Brym, 2007; Brym and Araj, 2006).

From whose point of view are suicide bombers deviant and criminal? From whose point of view are suicide bombers normal? Must you agree with the actions of suicide bombers to understand them? What would you do if you were in Said's position?

drug because people's perceptions of its harmfulness changed. Finally, deviance and crime vary in terms of the *degree of public agreement* about whether an act should be considered deviant or criminal. Even the social definition of murder varies over time and across cultures and societies. Thus, in the nineteenth century, Inuit communities sometimes allowed newborns to freeze to death. Life in the far north was precarious. Killing newborns was not considered a punishable offence if community members agreed that investing scarce resources in keeping the newborn alive could endanger everyone's well-being. Similarly, whether we classify the death of a miner as accidental or a case of manslaughter depends on the kind of worker safety legislation in existence. Some societies have more stringent worker safety rules than others, and deaths considered accidental in some societies are

One of the determinants of the seriousness of a deviant act is its perceived harmfulness. Perceptions vary historically. For instance, until the early part of the twentieth century, cocaine was considered a medicine. It was an ingredient in Coca-Cola and toothache drops and in these forms was commonly given to children.

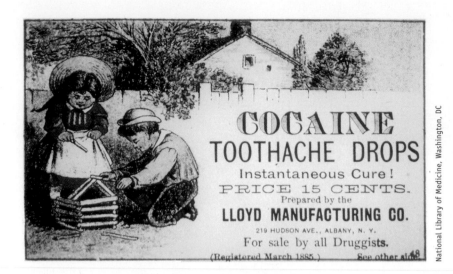

Social diversions are minor acts of deviance that are generally perceived as relatively harmless and that evoke, at most, a mild societal reaction, such as amusement or disdain.

Social deviations are non-criminal departures from norms that are nonetheless subject to official control. Some members of the public regard them as somewhat harmful while other members of the public do not.

classified as criminal offences in others (McCormick, 1999). So we see that, even when it comes to serious crimes, social definitions vary (see Box 7.2).

Figure 7.1 allows us to classify four types of deviance and crime:

1. **Social diversions** are minor acts of deviance, such as participating in fads and fashions like dyeing your hair purple. People usually perceive such acts as harmless. They evoke, at most, a mild societal reaction, such as amusement or disdain, because many people are apathetic or unclear about whether social diversions are, in fact, deviant.
2. **Social deviations** are more serious acts. Large numbers of people agree these acts are deviant and somewhat harmful, and they are usually subject to institutional sanction. For example, John Lie's high school in Hawaii had a rule making long hair on boys a fairly serious deviation punishable by a humiliating public haircut.

FIGURE 7.1

Types of Deviance and Crime

Source: From *Crime and Disrepute* by John Hagan. Copyright © 1994 Pine Forge Press. Reprinted by permission of Sage Publications.

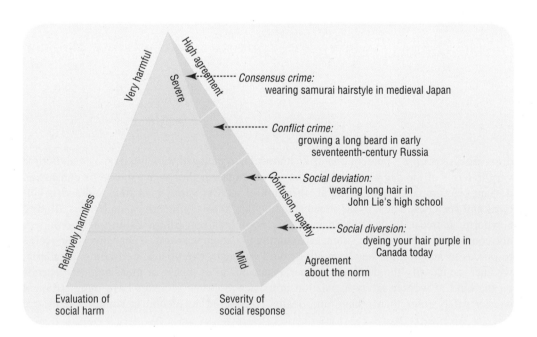

Was Todd Bertuzzi's penalty adequate for his assault on Steve Moore?

BOX 7.2

It's Your Choice

VIOLENCE AND HOCKEY: DEVIANT, CRIMINAL, OR NORMATIVE?

On March 8, 2004, the NHL suspended Todd Bertuzzi of the Vancouver Canucks indefinitely for an on-ice assault whose repercussions echoed across the hockey world. His victim was Steve Moore of the Colorado Avalanche.

Although fighting is not rare in the NHL, this was hardly a fight. The incident occurred in the third period with the Avalanche coasting atop an 8–2 lead. No collision was involved—afterward many described Bertuzzi's action as stalking. In the seconds leading up to the attack, Bertuzzi pursued Moore from one end of the rink to the other. When Moore tried to avoid Bertuzzi by turning his back and skating away, Bertuzzi grabbed the back of Moore's jersey. He then delivered a sucker punch and followed through by using

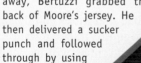

his 110-kilogram (245-pound) body to drive Moore face first into the ice.

As the crowd grew silent with awareness of what had happened, Moore lay in a pool of his own blood for several minutes until a stretcher arrived to carry him off.

There was near-total silence from defenders of the NHL's custom of employing revenge and deterrence to try to maintain order on the ice. Even commentators like Don Cherry were critical of Bertuzzi's blind-side assault against someone trying to avoid a confrontation. Bertuzzi himself expressed remorse in the strongest terms at a tear-filled press conference two days later. "I just want to apologize for what happened out there and I feel awful for what transpired," he said. "I'm relieved to hear that Steve's going to have a full recovery."

Unfortunately, Bertuzzi's prognosis proved overly optimistic. Moore's career in the NHL was over. Bertuzzi was arrested on assault charges. Eventually, he pleaded guilty to a charge of assault causing bodily harm, paid a fine of $500, and was sentenced to 80 hours of community service. The plea left him without a criminal record. The NHL suspended him for 17 months.

Do you think that Bertuzzi's penalty was adequate? Do you believe that athletes involved in contact sports should be treated differently under laws forbidding assault? If so, does this apply even in cases involving severe injury or death? Is this part of the risk that comes along with such sports and best left to sports administrators? Or should there be a crackdown on sports violence? Should more athletes be charged? Should coaches if they encourage such deeds? It's your choice.

Conflict crimes are illegal acts that many people consider harmful to society. However, other people think they are not very harmful. They are punishable by the state.

Consensus crimes are illegal acts that nearly all people agree are bad in themselves and harm society greatly. The state inflicts severe punishment for consensus crimes.

3. **Conflict crimes** are deviant acts that the state defines as illegal but whose definition is controversial in the wider society. For instance, Tsar Peter the Great of Russia wanted to Westernize and modernize his empire, and he viewed long beards as a sign of backwardness. On September 1, 1698, he imposed a tax on beards to discourage men from growing them. Many Russians disagreed with his policy. Others agreed that growing long beards harmed Russia because it symbolized Russia's past rather than its future. Because of disagreement about the harmfulness of the practice, wearing a long beard in late-seventeenth-century Russia can be classified as a conflict crime.

4. Finally, **consensus crimes** are widely recognized to be bad in themselves. There is little controversy over their seriousness. The great majority of people agree that such crimes should be met with severe punishment. For instance, in medieval Japan, hairstyle was an important expression of people's status. If you were a peasant and sported the hairstyle of the samurai (warrior caste), you could be arrested and even killed because you were seen to be calling the entire social order into question.

As these examples show, people's conceptions of deviance and crime vary substantially over time and between societies. Under some circumstances, an issue that seems quite trivial to us, such as hairstyle, can be a matter of life and death.

Measuring Crime

Some crimes are more common than others are, and rates of crime vary over place and time and among different social groups. We now describe some of these variations. Then we review the main sociological explanations of crime and deviance.

First, a word about crime statistics. Information on crime collected by the police is the main source of crime statistics. Since 1962, Canada has used the Uniform Crime Reporting (UCR) Survey to collect data from more than 400 municipal police departments across Canada on 91 detailed categories of crime. Annually, the government publishes data on types of offences and characteristics of offenders.

Victimless crimes involve violations of the law in which no victim steps forward and is identified.

These statistics have two main shortcomings. First, much crime is not reported to the police. This is particularly true for so-called **victimless crimes**, or violations of the law in which no victim steps forward and is identified. Communicating for the purposes of prostitution, illegal gambling, and the use of illegal drugs are all victimless crimes. In addition, many common assaults go unreported because the assailant is a friend or relative of the victim, while many victims of sexual assault are reluctant to report the crime because they are afraid they will be humiliated, not believed, or stigmatized.

The second main shortcoming of official statistics is that authorities and the wider public decide which criminal acts to report and which to ignore. If, for instance, the authorities decide to crack down on drugs, more drug-related crimes will be counted, not necessarily because there are more drug-related crimes but because more drug criminals are apprehended. Changes in legislation, which either create new offences or amend existing offences, also influence the number of recorded offences. Recognizing these difficulties, students of crime often supplement official crime statistics with other sources of information.

In **self-report surveys**, respondents are asked to report their involvement in criminal activities, either as perpetrators or as victims.

Self-report surveys are especially useful. In such surveys, respondents are asked to report their involvement in criminal activities, either as perpetrators or as victims. Self-report surveys compensate for many of the problems associated with official statistics. In general, self-report surveys report approximately the same rate of serious crime as official statistics do but find two or three times the rate of less serious crimes. Consequently, *indirect measures* of crime are sometimes used as well. For instance, sales of syringes are a good index of the use of illegal intravenous drugs. Indirect measures are unavailable for many types of crime, however.

Self-report surveys are also useful because they tell us that a majority of Canadians have engaged in some type of criminal activity and that about a quarter of the population in any given year believe they have been the victim of crime. These large proportions remind us that committing an act in violation of the law does not automatically result in being offi-cially labelled a criminal. To be so identified, an individual's law-violating behaviour must first be observed and felt to justify action. The behaviour must be reported to the police who, in turn, must respond to the incident, decide that it warrants further investigation, file a report, and make an arrest. Next, the accused person must appear at a preliminary hearing, an arraignment, and a trial. If the person does not plead guilty, the possibility always exists that he or she will not be convicted because guilt has not been proven beyond a reasonable doubt.

In **victimization surveys**, people are asked whether they have been victims of crime. Although these types of surveys date back to the mid-1960s in the United States, no national victimization survey was done in Canada until 1988 (Fattah, 1991). The International Crime Victim Survey (ICVS) collected victimization data using the same questionnaire simultane-ously in many countries, including Canada, in 1989, 1992, 1996–97, and 2000 (Besserer, 2002). It examines householders' experiences with crime, policing, crime prevention, and feelings of being unsafe. The survey found that, on average, 55 percent of victimization inci-dents are reported to police, with property crimes more likely to be reported than are crimes against persons. In part, this fact reflects the requirement by insurance companies that indi-viduals file a police report if they want compensation for property stolen or damaged as the result of a criminal act. Although victimization surveys provide detailed information about crime victims, they provide less reliable data about offenders.

Bearing these caveats in mind, what does the official record show? Most Canadians would be understandably alarmed to hear that, in 2009, more than 2.3 million Criminal Code incidents were reported to police agencies. They might assume that these incidents were reflected in the dramatic crimes reported each day in newspaper headlines and on the nightly news. However, that is not the case. In 2009, just 19.2 percent of Criminal Code incidents involved violence (Figure 7.2). True, the 2009 crime rate was almost twice as high as it was 50 years earlier. However, the long crime wave that began its upswing in the early 1960s peaked and fell in the 1990s, and continued to decline in the 2000s. The homicide rate has been falling since the mid-1970s. How do we explain the fall?

Explanations for Declining Crime Rates

Four explanations exist for the decline in Canadian crime rates. First, the "war against crime" is increasingly being fought by a substantially enlarged corps of better trained and equipped law enforcement and correctional officers (Mohr and Spencer, 1999: 588). Recent

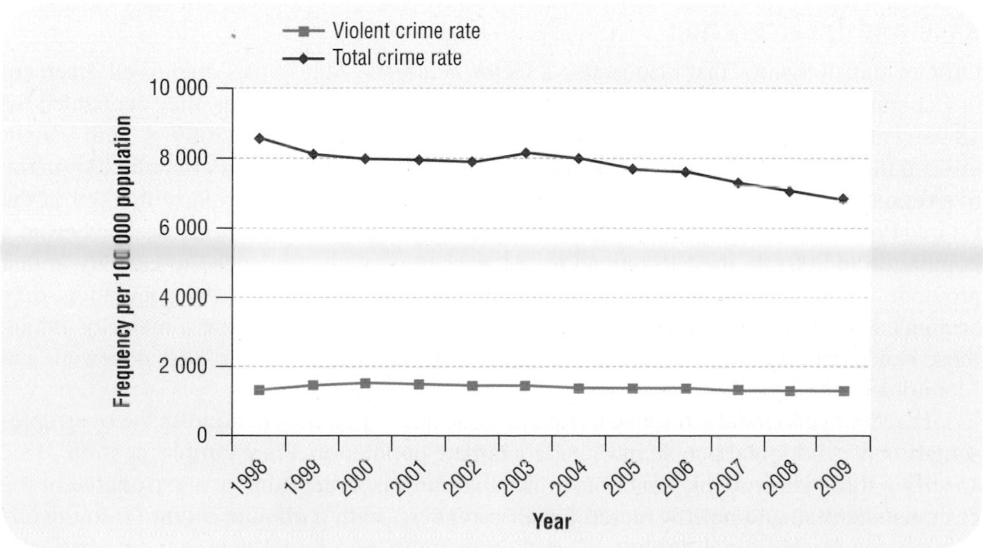

Victimization surveys are surveys in which people are asked whether they have been victims of crime.

FIGURE 7.2

Total and Violent Crime Rate, Canada, 1998–2009

Source: Adapted from Statistics Canada CANSIM Database http://www5.statcan.gc.ca/cansim/home-accueil?lang=eng, Table 252-0051 (retrieved 10 November 2010).

declines in Canada's crime rate may reflect the introduction of new community policing initiatives, enforcement efforts that target specific types of crime and attempt to reduce their incidence, the refinement of case-management methods, improvements in the field of forensics, and efforts directed toward crime prevention (Logan, 2001: 3).

Second, young men are most prone to crime, but Canada is aging and the number of young people in the population has declined. Specifically, the 15–24 age cohort decreased in size by 6 percent between 1980 and 2010 (Logan, 2001: 3; Statistics Canada, 2010b). Unlike the 1980s, when the "baby boomers" born between 1947 and 1966 entered their years of highest risk for crime, the 1990s saw a "baby bust." Birth rates plummeted between 1967 and 1979, so since the 1990s, the pool of people at high risk of criminal behaviour has shrunk.

Third, the variable most strongly correlated with the crime rate is the male unemployment rate (John Howard Society, 1999: 3). Significantly, poor economic conditions in the 1980s made it hard to find a job and contributed to the high crime rate in that decade (Ouimet, 2002). Conversely, following a steep recession in 1990–91, the economy grew in 208 of the 226 months between January 1992 and October 2010 (Trading Economics, 2010). Economic conditions favoured a decrease in crime.

Finally, and more controversially, some researchers argue that declining crime rates may be linked to the legalization of abortion (Donahue and Levitt, 2001). They observe that the crime rate started to decline 19 years after abortion was legalized in the United States. They suggest that this drop occurred because, beginning in the early 1970s with the legalization of abortion, there were proportionately fewer unwanted children in the population. Unwanted children, they argue, are more prone to criminal behaviour than wanted children are because they tend to receive less parental supervision and guidance.

Criminal Profiles

Of the 2008–9 Canadian criminal court cases in which the sex of the accused was reported, 82 percent involved a male accused and 18 percent, a female accused (Thomas, 2010). This pattern reappears for cases processed in youth courts. In 2008–9 youth cases in which the sex of the accussed was reported, males accounted for 77 percent of cases and women, for 23 percent (Milligan, 2010).

People who have not reached middle age commit most crime. The 15- to 24-year-old age cohort is the most prone to criminal behaviour. Although 15- to 24-year-olds represented just 13 percent of the Canadian population in 2006, they accounted for 77 percent of cases in youth court and 31 percent of cases in adult court in 2007–8 (Marth, 2009; Statistics Canada, 2010b; Thomas, 2009).

Race and Incarceration

Official statistics show that race is also a factor in arrests. Aboriginals composed 3 percent of Canadians over the age of 17 according to the 2006 census. However, they accounted for 18 percent of admissions to provincial/territorial and federal prisons in 2007–8, with a slight upward trend over time in both types of institution (Johnson, 2004: 16; Perreault, 2009). The overrepresentation of Aboriginal people in Canada's prisons is particularly marked in the Prairie Provinces. Although Aboriginal people represented 11 percent of Saskatchewan's population in 2007–8, they accounted for 81 percent of adults sentenced to custody in that province. In Alberta, where Aboriginal people make up 5 percent of the population, they accounted for 35 percent of custodial sentences. Aboriginal people were a majority among those sentenced to custody in Nunavut, Northwest Territories, Yukon, Saskatchewan, and Manitoba (see Figure 7.3).

In recent years, changes to the Criminal Code have attempted to address the overrepresentation of Aboriginal people in Canada's inmate population. For example, section 718.2 specifies that "all available sanctions other than imprisonment that are reasonable in the circumstances should be considered for all offenders, with particular attention to the circumstances of aboriginal offenders." Although being Aboriginal does not automatically

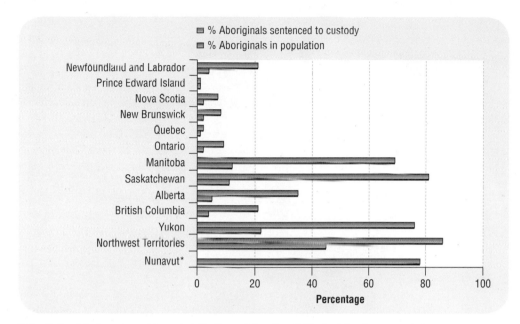

FIGURE 7.3

Aboriginal Canadians Sentenced to Custody, by Jurisdiction, 2007–8

Source: Adapted from Statistics Canada publication *Juristat*, Table 4: Aboriginal people as a proportion of admissions to remand, provincial and territorial sentenced custody, probation and conditional sentence, by jurisdiction, 2007/2008, Catalogue 85-002XWE2009003, http://www.statcan.gc.ca/pub/ 85-002-x/2009003/article/10903/ tbl/t4-eng.htm (accessed 10 November 2010).

* The % Aboriginals sentenced to custody in Nunavut is not available for this reference period.

result in a lesser sentence, the Supreme Court of Canada has urged judges sentencing an Aboriginal offender to recognize the "broad systemic and background factors affecting Aboriginal people" (Lonmo, 2001: 8). Nevertheless, Aboriginal Canadians—particularly Aboriginal women—continue to be overrepresented in the prison population (La Prairie, 1996).

The literature offers four explanations for the overrepresentation of Aboriginal people in Canada's prisons (Hartnagel, 2000). First, a disproportionately large number of Aboriginal people are poor. Although the great majority of poor people are law-abiding, poverty and its handicaps are associated with elevated crime rates. Second, Aboriginal people tend to commit so-called **street crimes**—breaking and entering, robbery, assault, and the like—that are more detectable than **white-collar crimes** such as embezzlement, fraud, copyright infringement, false advertising, and so on. Third, the police, the courts, and other institutions may discriminate against Aboriginal people. As a result, Aboriginal people may be more likely to be apprehended, prosecuted, and convicted. Fourth, contact with Western culture has disrupted social life in many Aboriginal communities (see Chapter 10, Race and Ethnicity). This disruption has led to a weakening of social control over community members. Some people think that certain "races" are *inherently* more law abiding than others, but they are able to hold such an opinion only by ignoring the powerful *social* forces that cause so many Aboriginal people to be incarcerated in Canada (Roberts and Gabor, 1990).

Most of the factors listed above also account for the above-average incarceration rate among black Canadians. Occupying a relatively low class position, engaging mainly in street crime as opposed to white-collar crime, and facing a discriminatory criminal justice system, black people are more likely than are whites to be motivated to commit criminal acts, to be detected and apprehended engaging in criminal acts, and to be prosecuted, convicted, and jailed. The claim that the criminal justice system engages in discriminatory practices based on race may be difficult for some Canadians to accept, but research suggests that the claim is credible. For example, a Toronto survey showed that older and better-educated whites and Asians with no criminal record are significantly less likely to be stopped for police searches than are younger and less well-educated whites and Asians with a criminal record. In contrast, age, education, and lack of a criminal record do not insulate blacks from searches. In fact, better-educated and well-to-do blacks are *more* likely

Street crimes includes arson, break and enter, assault, and other illegal acts disproportionately committed by people from lower classes.

White-collar crime refers to an illegal act committed by a respectable, high-status person in the course of work.

In the 1957 classic movie *12 Angry Men*, the character played by Henry Fonda (third from left) convinces the members of a jury to overcome their prejudices, examine the facts dispassionately, and allow a disadvantaged minority youth accused of murdering his father to go free. Does the problem of ethnic and racial bias still plague the criminal justice system?

The Everett Collection/CP Picture Archive

to be stopped and searched by police than are less well-educated and poorer blacks. These findings suggest that Toronto police keep a closer eye on blacks than they do on whites and Asians, and are particularly suspicious of blacks with education and money (Wortley and Tanner, 2011).

Summing Up

- Deviance and crime vary from one social context to another along three dimensions: severity of the social response, perceived harmfulness, and degree of public agreement about whether an act should be considered deviant or criminal.
- Official crime statistics do not report all crime and they are subject to public and official definitions of what constitutes crime. Therefore, self-report and vicitimization surveys are commonly used to supplement official statistics.
- Official statistics show that crime in Canada increased substantially from the 1960s to the 1980s. The crime rate then started to fall because of larger and better-trained police forces, improving economic conditions, a declining proportion of young men in the population, and perhaps also a decline in the number of unwanted (and therefore relatively unsupervised) children in the population.
- Men between the ages of 15 and 24 are the most crime-prone age–sex cohort. Aboriginal and black Canadians have a higher crime rate than expected given their representation in the population because they are relatively young, experience comparatively widespread poverty and unemployment, and face discrimination in the criminal justice system.

EXPLAINING DEVIANCE AND CRIME

Lep: "I remember your li'l ass used to ride dirt bikes and skateboards, actin' crazy an' shit. Now you want to be a gangster, huh? You wanna hang with real muthaf—and tear shit up, huh? Stand up, get your li'l ass up. How old is you now anyway?"

Kody: "Eleven, but I'll be twelve in November."

—Sanyika Shakur
(*Monster: The autobiography of an L.A. Gang Member*. New York: Penguin, 1993)

"Monster" Kody Scott eagerly joined the notorious gang the Crips in South Central Los Angeles in 1975 when he was in grade 6. He was released from Folsom Prison on parole in 1988, at the age of 24. Until about three years before his release, he was one of the most ruthless gang leaders in Los Angeles and the California prison system. In 1985, however, he decided to reform. He adopted the name Sanyika Shakur, became a black nationalist, and began a crusade against gangs. Few people in his position have chosen that path. In Scott's heyday, about 30 000 gang members roamed Los Angeles County. Today there are more than 150 000.

What makes engaging in crime an attractive prospect to so many people? In general, why do deviance and crime occur at all? Sociologists rely on symbolic interactionism, functionalism, conflict theories, and feminist theories for explanations.

Symbolic Interactionist Approaches to Deviance and Crime

People may learn deviant and criminal behaviour when they interact with others. Identifying the social circumstances that promote the learning of deviant and criminal roles is a traditional focus of symbolic interactionists.

Learning Deviance

The idea that becoming a habitual deviant or criminal is a learning process that occurs in a social context was firmly established by Howard S. Becker's classic study of marijuana users (Becker, 1963: 41–58). In the 1940s, Becker financed his Ph.D. studies by playing piano in Chicago jazz bands. He used the opportunity to carefully observe 50 fellow musicians, informally interview them in depth, and write up detailed field notes after performances.

Scene from *Breaking Bad*

Lewis Jacobs / © AMC / Courtesy Everett Collection

Becker found that his fellow musicians had to pass through a three-stage learning process before becoming regular marijuana users. Failure to pass a stage meant failure to learn the deviant role and become a regular user. These are the three stages:

1. *Learning to smoke the drug in a way that produces real effects.* First-time marijuana smokers do not ordinarily get high. To do so, they must learn how to smoke the drug in a way that ensures a sufficient dosage to produce intoxicating effects (taking deep drags and holding their breath for a long time). This process takes practice, and some first-time users give up, typically claiming that marijuana has no effect on them or that people who claim otherwise are just fooling themselves. Others are more strongly encouraged by their peers to keep trying. If they persist, they are ready to move on to stage two.

2. *Learning to recognize the effects and connect them with drug use.* Those who learn the proper smoking technique may not recognize that they are high or they may not connect the symptoms of being high with smoking the drug. They may get hungry, laugh uncontrollably, play the same song for hours on end, and yet still fail to realize that these are symptoms of intoxication. If so, they will stop using the drug. Becker found, however, that his fellow musicians typically asked experienced users how they knew whether they were high. Experienced users identified the symptoms of marijuana use and helped novices make the connection between what they were experiencing and smoking the drug. Once they made that connection, novices were ready to advance to stage three.

3. *Learning to enjoy the perceived sensations.* Smoking marijuana is not inherently pleasurable. Some users experience a frightening loss of self-control (paranoia). Others feel dizzy, uncomfortably thirsty, itchy, forgetful, or dangerously impaired in their ability to judge time and distance. If these negative sensations persist, marijuana use will cease. However, Becker found that experienced users typically helped novices redefine negative sensations as pleasurable. They taught novices to laugh at their impaired judgment, take special pleasure in quenching their deep thirst, and find deeper meaning in familiar music. If and only if novices learned to define the effects of smoking as pleasurable did they become habitual marijuana smokers.

Learning *any* deviant or criminal role requires a social context in which experienced deviants or criminals teach novices the "tricks of the trade." It follows that more exposure to experienced deviants and criminals increases the chance that an individual will come to value a deviant or criminal lifestyle and consider it normal (Sutherland, 1939, 1949).

Siegfried Kuttig/PhotoLibrary

Moreover, the type of deviant or criminal that predominates in one's social environment has a bearing on the type of deviant or criminal that a novice will become. For example, depending on the availability of different types of deviants and criminals in their neighbourhoods, delinquent youths will turn to different types of crime. In some areas, delinquent youths are recruited by organized crime, such as the Mafia. In areas that lack organized crime networks, delinquent youths are more likely to create violent gangs. Thus, the relative availability of different types of deviants and criminals influences the type of deviant or criminal role a delinquent youth learns (Cloward and Ohlin, 1960).

Labelling

One night in Saskatchewan, after a night of heavy drinking, two 20-year-old university students, Alex Ternowetsky and Steven Kummerfield, both white and middle class, picked up Pamela George, an Aboriginal single mother who occasionally worked as a prostitute, in downtown Regina. They drove the 28-year-old woman outside the city limits, had her perform oral sex without pay, and then savagely beat her to death. Although originally charged with first-degree murder, a jury later found them guilty of the lesser charge of manslaughter. Justice Ted Malone of the Saskatchewan Court of Queen's Bench instructed the jurors to consider that the two men had been drinking and that George was "indeed a prostitute." Members of the victim's family were appalled, Native leaders outraged. Tone Cote of the Yorkton Tribal Council said the sentence would send the message that "it's all right for little white boys to go out on the streets, get drunk and use that for an excuse to start hunting down our people."

A variant of symbolic interactionism known as **labelling theory** holds that deviance results not just from the actions of the deviant but also from the responses of others, who define some actions as deviant and other actions as normal. As the above example suggests, terms like *deviant* or *criminal* are not applied automatically when a person engages in rule-violating behaviour. Some individuals escape being labelled as deviants despite having engaged in deviant behaviour. Others, like Ternowetsky and Kummerfield, are labelled deviant but found to be guilty of a lesser charge than would typically be the case. Still others, such as Pamela George, who do not engage in deviant acts at all or are the victims of such acts, may find themselves labelled as deviant (Matsueda, 1988, 1992).

That labelling plays an important part in who is caught and charged with crime was demonstrated by Aaron Cicourel (1968). Cicourel examined the tendency to label rule-breaking adolescents as juvenile delinquents if they came from families in which the parents were divorced. He found that police officers tended to use their discretionary powers to arrest adolescents from divorced families more often than adolescents from intact families who committed similar delinquent acts. Judges, in turn, tended to give more severe sentences to adolescents from divorced families than to adolescents from intact families who were charged with similar delinquent acts. Sociologists and criminologists then collected data on the social characteristics of adolescents who were charged as juvenile delinquents, "proving" that children from divorced families were more likely to become juvenile delinquents. Their finding reinforced the beliefs of police officers and judges. Thus, the labelling process acted as a self-fulfilling prophecy.

> **Labelling theory** holds that deviance results not so much from the actions of the deviant as from the response of others, who label the rule breaker a deviant.

Functionalist Explanations

While symbolic interactionists focus on the learning and labelling of deviant and criminal roles, functionalists direct their attention to the social dysfunctions that lead to deviant and criminal behaviour.

Durkheim

Functionalist thinking on deviance and crime originated with Durkheim (1938), who made the controversial claim that deviance and crime are beneficial for society. For one thing, he wrote, when someone breaks a rule, it provides others with a chance to condemn and punish the transgression, remind them of their common values, clarify the moral boundaries of the group to which they belong, and thus reinforce social solidarity. For another, deviance and crime help societies adapt to social change. Martin Luther King Jr. was arrested in Alabama in February 1965 for taking part in a demonstration supporting the idea that blacks should be allowed to vote, but later that year the passage of the Voting Rights Acts made it a crime to *prevent* blacks from voting in the United States. King's crime (and similar crimes by other civil rights activists) brought about positive social change, demonstrating the validity of Durkheim's point about the positive functions of deviance and crime.

Merton

Robert Merton (1938) further developed Durkheim's theory by emphasizing the *dysfunctions* of deviance and crime. Merton argued that cultures often teach people to value material success. Just as often, however, societies do not provide enough legitimate opportunities for everyone to succeed. In Merton's view, such a discrepancy between cultural ideals and structural realities is dysfunctional, producing what he called **strain**.

> **Strain theory** holds that people may turn to deviance when they experience strain. Strain results when a culture teaches people the value of material success and society fails to provide enough legitimate opportunities for everyone to succeed.

Most people who experience strain will force themselves to adhere to social norms despite the strain, Merton wrote. The rest adapt by engaging in one of four types of action: (1) They may drop out of conventional society. (2) They may reject the goals of conventional society but continue to follow its rules. (3) They may protest against convention and support alternative values. (4) They may find alternative and illegitimate means of achieving their society's goals—that is, they may become criminals (see Table 7.1). The value of material success starkly contradicts the lack of opportunity available to poor youths, Merton argued. As a result, poor youths sometimes engage in illegal means of attaining socially approved goals.

Criminal Subcultures

It is not only individuals who adapt to the strain caused by social dysfunction. In addition, social groups adapt by forming criminal gangs. Gang members feel the legitimate world has rejected them. They return the favour by rejecting the legitimate world. In the process, they develop distinct norms and values—a criminal **subculture** (Cohen, 1955).

> A **subculture** is a set of distinctive values, norms, and practices within a larger culture

An important part of any gang subculture consists of the justifications its members spin for their criminal activities. These justifications make illegal activities appear morally acceptable and normal, at least to the gang members. Typically, criminals deny personal responsibility for their actions ("It wasn't my fault!") or deny the wrongfulness of the act ("I was just borrowing it."). They condemn those who pass judgment on them ("The cops are bigger crooks than anyone!"). They claim their victims get what they deserve ("She had it coming to her."). And they appeal to higher loyalties, particularly to friends and family ("I had to do it because he dissed my gang."). Such rationalizations enable criminals to clear their consciences and get on with the job (Sykes and Matza, 1957).

Although deviants may depart from mainstream culture in many ways, they are strict conformists when it comes to the norms of their own subculture. They tend to share the same beliefs, dress alike, eat similar food, and adopt the same mannerisms and speech patterns. Although most members of the larger society consider gang subcultures deviant, gang members strongly discourage deviance *within* the subculture.

TABLE 7.1

Merton's Strain Theory of Deviance

Source: Adapted from Merton, 1938.

		Institutionalized Means		
		Accept	*Reject*	*Create New*
Cultural Goals	*Accept*	Conformity	Innovation	—
	Reject	Ritualism	Retreatism	—
	Create New	—	—	Rebellion

© Viviane Moos/CORBIS

Functionalism and the Relationship Between Crime and Class

One of the main problems with functionalist accounts is that they exaggerate the connection between crime and class. Many self-report surveys find, at most, a weak tendency for criminals to come disproportionately from lower classes. Some self-report surveys report no such tendency at all, especially among young people and for less serious types of crime (Weis, 1987). A stronger correlation exists between *serious street crimes* and class. Armed robbery and assault, for instance, are more common among people from lower classes. A stronger correlation also exists between *white-collar* crime and class. Middle- and upper-class people are most likely to commit fraud and embezzlement, for example. Thus, generalizations about the relationship between class and crime must be qualified by taking into account the severity and type of crime (Braithwaite, 1981). Note also that official statistics usually exaggerate class differences because they are more accurate barometers of street crime than suite crime; more police surveillance occurs in lower-class neighbourhoods than in upper-class boardrooms, and widely cited police statistics do not record some white-collar crimes because they are handled by agencies other than the police. As we will now see, conflict theories help to overcome functionalism's inadequate explanation of the relationship between crime and class.

Conflict Theories

Conflict theorists maintain that rich and powerful members of society impose deviant and criminal labels on others, particularly those who challenge the existing social order. Meanwhile, the rich and powerful are usually able to use their money and influence to escape punishment for their own misdeeds.

Steven Spitzer (1980) summarizes this school of thought. He notes that capitalist societies are based on private ownership of property. Moreover, their smooth functioning depends on the availability of productive labour and respect for authority. When thieves steal, they challenge private property. Theft is therefore a crime. When so-called bag ladies and drug addicts drop out of conventional society, they are defined as deviant because their refusal to engage in productive labour undermines a pillar of capitalism. When young, politically volatile students demonstrate and militant trade unionists strike, they, too, represent a threat to the social order. Authorities may therefore define them as deviant or criminal.

Of course, Spitzer notes, the rich and the powerful engage in deviant and criminal acts too. However, they are less likely to be reported, convicted, and prosecuted for criminal acts than other people are (Blumberg, 1989; Clinard and Yeager, 1980; Hagan, 1989; Sherrill, 1997; Snider, 1999; Sutherland, 1949). *Reporting* is less frequent because much white-collar crime takes place in private and is therefore difficult to detect. For instance, corporations may decide to fix prices and divide markets—both crimes—but executives may make such decisions in boardrooms, private clubs, and homes that are not generally subject to police surveillance. *Conviction* and *prosecution* are less frequent partly because wealthy white-collar criminals can afford legal experts, public relations firms, and advertising agencies that advise their clients on how to bend laws, build up their corporate image in the public mind, and influence lawmakers to pass laws "without teeth." In addition, the law is more lenient in meting out punishment for white-collar crime than for street crime. Compare the crime of break and enter with that of fraud. Fraud almost certainly costs society more than break and enter, but breaking and entering is a street crime committed mainly by lower-class people, while fraud is a white-collar crime committed mainly by middle- and upper-class people. Not surprisingly, prison sentences are nearly twice as likely in break and enter convictions than in fraud convictions (Thomas, 2002: 9).

Social Control

Conflict theorists argue that the rich and the powerful exercise disproportionate control over the criminal justice system and are therefore able to engage in deviance and crime with relative impunity. One variant of conflict theory, known as **control theory**, generalizes this argument. According to control theorists, nearly everyone would like to have the fun, pleasure, excitement, and profit that deviance and crime promise. Moreover, they say, if we could get away with it, most of us would commit deviant and criminal acts to acquire more of these rewards. For control theorists, the reason most of us do not engage in deviance and crime is that we are prevented from doing so. In contrast, deviants and criminals break norms and laws because social controls imposed by various authorities are too weak to ensure conformity.

Travis Hirschi developed the control theory of crime (Hirschi, 1969; Gottfredson and Hirschi, 1990). He argued that adolescents are more prone to deviance and crime than adults are because they are incompletely socialized and therefore lack self-control. Adults and adolescents may both experience the impulse to break norms and laws, but adolescents are less likely to control that impulse. Hirschi went on to show that the adolescents who are most prone to delinquency are likely to lack four types of social control. They tend to have few social *attachments* to parents, teachers, and other respectable role models; few legitimate *opportunities* for education and a good job; few *involvements* in conventional institutions; and weak *beliefs* in traditional values and morality. Because of the lack of control stemming from these sources, these adolescents are relatively free to act on their deviant impulses. For similar reasons, boys are more likely to engage in juvenile delinquency than girls are, and people who experience job and marital instability are more likely than others are to engage in crime (Hagan et al., 1987; Peters, 1994; Sampson and Laub, 1993). Tighter social control by authorities in all spheres of life decreases the frequency of deviant and criminal acts.

Feminist Contributions

Although conflict theory shows how the distribution of power in society influences the definition, detection, and prosecution of deviance and criminality, it neglects the consequences of something you will learn about in detail in Chapter 11, Sexualities and Gender Stratification: on average, women are less powerful than men are in all social institutions. Feminist sociologists hold that gender-based power differences influence the framing of laws and therefore the definition and detection of crime and the prosecution of criminals.

To support their claim, feminists note that, until recently, many types of crime against women were largely ignored in Canada and most other parts of the world. This was true even when the crime involved non-consensual sexual intercourse, an act that was defined under Canadian criminal law as *rape* before 1983 and is now considered a form of *sexual assault*. Admittedly, the authorities sometimes severely punished rapes involving strangers. However, date and acquaintance rape were rarely prosecuted, while Canadian law viewed marital rape as a contradiction in terms, as if it were logically impossible for a woman to be

Control theory holds that the rewards of deviance and crime are ample. Therefore, nearly everyone would engage in deviance and crime if they could get away with it. The degree to which people are prevented from violating norms and laws accounts for variations in the level of deviance and crime.

raped by her husband. Law professors, judges, police officers, rapists, and even victims did not think date rape was "real rape" (Estrich, 1987). Similarly, judges, lawyers, and social scientists rarely discussed physical violence against women and sexual harassment until the 1970s. Governments did not collect data on the topic, and few social scientists showed any interest in the subject. Relative powerlessness allowed many women to be victimized while the violence against them went unnoticed by the larger society and their assailants went free.

It follows from the feminist argument that a shift in the distribution of power between women and men would alter this state of affairs. And in fact, that is precisely what happened after about 1970. A series of changes to Canadian criminal law since 1970 have emphasized that non-consensual sexual acts are sexual assaults. The new laws have helped raise people's awareness of date, acquaintance, and marital rape. Sexual assault is more often prosecuted now than it used to be. The same is true for other types of violence against women and for sexual harassment. These changes occurred because women's position in the economy, the family, and other social institutions has improved since 1970. Women now have more autonomy in the family, earn more, and enjoy more political influence. They also created a movement for women's rights that heightened concern about crimes disproportionately affecting them (MacKinnon, 1979). Social definitions of crimes against women changed as women became more powerful in Canadian society.

In the 1970s, some feminists expected that growing gender equality would also change the historical tendency for women to be far less crime-prone than men are. They reasoned that control over the activities of girls and women would weaken, thus allowing them to behave more like men. Widely publicized cases of violent crime by teenage girls add weight to such claims, and official data support them to some degree. As Figure 7.4 shows, the ratio of women to men convicted of homicide shows no clear trend for the period from 1994 to 2006. However, the ratio of women to men convicted of all crimes rose by 2 percent, and the ratio of women to men convicted of youth crime rose by 6 percent. It seems that, with the exception of the most violent crimes, the ratio of female to male criminals is slowly increasing, and the tendency is most pronounced among youth offenders.

Our overview shows that many theories contribute to understanding the social causes of deviance and crime. Each focuses on a different aspect of the phenomenon, so familiarity with all of them allows us to develop a fully rounded appreciation of the complex processes surrounding the sociology of deviance and crime.

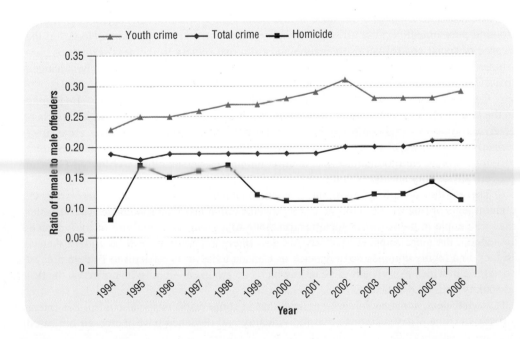

FIGURE 7.4

The Ratio of Female to Male Offenders, Canada, 1994–2006

Source: Statistics Canada. 2010. Adapted from Statistics Canada CANSIM Database. Retrieved March 7, 2010 (http://www5 .statcan.gcw.ca/cansim/ homeaccueil?lang=eng).

Summing Up

- According to *symbolic interactionists*, deviant and criminal roles must be learned in the course of social interaction if they are to become habitual activities. Moreover, deviance results not just from the actions of the deviant but also from the responses of others, who define some actions as deviant and other actions as normal.
- *Functionalists* hold that deviance and crime have positive functions for society insofar as they provide opportunities to clarify societal values, define moral boundaries, increase social solidarity, and allow useful social change. They also have dysfunctions. In particular, if societies do not provide enough legitimate opportunities for everyone to succeed, strain results, one reaction to which is to find alternatives and illegitimate means of achieving one's goals.
- In the view of *conflict theorists*, the rich and the powerful are most likely to impose deviant and criminal labels on others, particularly those who challenge the existing social order. Meanwhile, the rich and powerful are usually able to use their money and influence to escape punishment for their own misdeeds. Most people do not engage in deviance and crime because they are prevented from doing so by authorities. Deviants and criminals break norms and laws because social controls imposed by various authorities are too weak to ensure their conformity.
- *Feminists* maintain that change over time in the distribution of power between women and men influences the degree to which crimes against women are identified and prosecuted, and the degree to which women become criminals.

SOCIAL CONTROL AND PUNISHMENT

Trends in Social Control

No discussion of crime and deviance would be complete without considering social control and punishment because all societies impose sanctions on rule breakers. However, the *degree* of social control varies over time and from one society to the next. *Forms* of punishment also vary. Below we focus on how social control and punishment have changed historically.

Consider first the difference between preindustrial and industrial societies. Beginning in the late nineteenth century, many sociologists argued that preindustrial societies are characterized by strict social control and high conformity, while industrial societies are characterized by less stringent social control and low conformity (Tönnies, 1988 [1887]). Similar differences were said to characterize small communities versus cities. As an old German proverb says, "City air makes you free."

There is much truth in this point of view. Whether they are fans of opera or reggae, connoisseurs of fine wine or marijuana, city dwellers in industrialized societies find it easier than do people in preindustrial societies to belong to a group or subculture of their choice. In general, the more complex a society, the less likely many norms will be widely shared. In fact, in a highly complex society, such as Canada today, it is difficult to find an area of social life in which everyone is alike or in which one group can impose its norms on the rest of society without resistance.

Nonetheless, some sociologists believe that in some respects social control has intensified over time. They recognize that individuality and deviance have increased but insist this has happened only within strict limits, beyond which it is now *more* difficult to move. In their view, many crucial aspects of life have become more regimented, not less.

Much of the regimentation of modern life is tied to the growth of capitalism and the state. Factories require strict labour regimes, with workers arriving and leaving at a fixed time and, in the interim, performing routine tasks at a set pace. Workers initially rebelled against this regimentation since they were used to enjoying many holidays and a flexible and vague work schedule regulated only approximately by the seasons and the rising and setting of the sun. But they had little alternative as wage labour in industry overtook feudal arrangements in agriculture (Thompson, 1967). Meanwhile, institutions linked to the growth of the modern state—armies, police forces, public schools, health care systems, and other bureaucracies—also demanded strict work regimes, curricula, and procedures. These institutions existed on a much smaller scale in preindustrial times or did not exist at all. Today they penetrate our lives and sustain strong norms of belief and conduct (Foucault, 1977).

In preindustrial societies, criminals who committed serious crimes were put to death, often in ways that seem cruel by today's standards. One method involved hanging the criminal with starving dogs.

Electronic technology makes it possible for authorities to exercise more effective social control than ever before. With millions of cameras mounted in public places and workplaces, some sociologists say we now live in a "surveillance society" (Lyon and Zureik, 1996). Cameras enable observers to see deviance and crime that would otherwise go undetected and take quick action to apprehend rule breakers. Moreover, when people are aware of the presence of cameras, they tend to alter their behaviour. For example, attentive shoplifters migrate to stores that lack electronic surveillance. On factory floors and in offices, workers display more conformity to management-imposed work norms. On campuses, students are inhibited from engaging in organized protests (Boal, 1998).

Thanks to computers and satellites, intelligence services in Canada and other Western countries now monitor all international telecommunications traffic, always on the lookout for threats. As easily as you can find the word *anomie* in your sociology essay by using the search function of your word processor, national security agencies can scan digitized telephone and email traffic in many languages for key words and word patterns that suggest unfriendly activity (Omega Foundation, 1998). However, the system is also used to target sensitive business and economic secrets from foreign countries, and some people have expressed the fear that it could be used on ordinary citizens, robbing them of their privacy. Meanwhile, credit

When the Vancouver Canucks lost Game 7 of the Stanley Cup playoffs to the Boston Bruins in 2011, rioting broke out in Vancouver. Surveillance cameras caught much of the action, and police reviewed more than 5000 hours of digital imagery, leading to hundreds of arrests. Some experts believe that once the public better appreciates the capacity of surveillance cameras to help identify rioters and demonstrators, many people will be inhibited from participating not just in hockey riots but also in political demonstrations.

information on 95 percent of North American consumers is available for purchase, the better to tempt you with credit cards, marketing ploys, and junk mail. When you browse the Web, information about your browsing patterns is collected in the background by many of the sites you visit, again largely for marketing purposes. Most large companies monitor and record their employees' phone conversations and email messages. These are all efforts to regulate behaviour, enforce conformity, and prevent deviance and crime more effectively by using the latest technologies (Garfinkel, 2000).

The Prison

In October 2001, a 63-year-old man suffering from Parkinson's disease and addicted to cocaine was arrested in Ottawa. A passerby had noticed that he had a 32-gauge shotgun in his gym bag and notified the police. The man, who was charged with possession of a weapon, did not resist arrest, perhaps because he knew well what awaited him. Roger Caron, dubbed Mad Dog Caron by the press, had first been sentenced to prison at the age of 16 for breaking and entering. He had spent most of his adult life as an inept robber, using the gates of Eastern Canada's major prisons like revolving doors: Guelph, Kingston, Collins Bay, Millhaven, Stoney Mountain, St. Vincent de Paul, Dorchester, and Penetanguishene.

While incarcerated in the 1970s and after having already spent almost 20 years in prison, Caron wrote a chilling account of his life behind bars. He was still in prison when *Go-Boy!* was published in 1978. The book describes in harrowing detail the harshness of the prison experience—the violence, the festering hatreds, the hard labour, the horrors of solitary confinement, the twisted, manipulative friendships, and the brutal use of corporal punishment. He describes the use of the "paddle"—"three leather straps with wooden handles so thick and coarse as to barely sag. Each one was perforated with hundreds of tiny holes designed to trap and rip the flesh from the buttocks." When he was first paddled in 1955,

"[w]hite searing pain exploded throughout my being and blood gushed from my lips as I struggled to stifle a scream. It was brutal and it was horrible" (Caron, 1979: 59; see also Farrell, n.d.).

Go-Boy! was honoured in 1978 with the Governor General's Award for literature and, in the years that followed, Caron wrote other books. However, he was unable to leave his past life totally. Following imprisonment for another botched robbery attempt, Caron was released from prison in 1998 and was still on parole at the time of his 2001 arrest. Regardless of the initial factors that caused Caron to turn to crime, it was his experiences in prison that turned him into a career criminal (CyberPress, 2001).

Caron's experience follows a pattern long known to sociologists. Prisons are agents of socialization, and new inmates often become more serious offenders as they adapt to the culture of the most hardened, long-term prisoners (Wheeler, 1961). Because prison often turns criminals into worse criminals, it is worth pondering the institution's origins, development, and current dilemmas.

As societies industrialized, imprisonment became one of the most important forms of punishment for criminal behaviour (Garland, 1990; Morris and Rothman, 1995). In preindustrial societies, criminals were publicly humiliated, tortured, or put to death, depending on the severity of their transgressions. In the industrial era, depriving criminals of their freedom by putting them in prison seemed less harsh, more "civilized" (Durkheim, 1973 [1899–1900]).

Roger Caron, who was 16 years old when he was first sentenced to prison for breaking and entering, has spent much of his life behind bars. His prison experiences turned him into a career criminal.

CP Picture Archive/Fred Chartrand

Rationales for Incarceration

Some people still take a benign view of prisons, even seeing them as opportunities for *rehabilitation*. They believe that prisoners, while serving time, can be taught how to be productive citizens on release. In Canada, this rehabilitative ethos predominated from the

1950s to the early 1970s, when many prisons sought to reform criminals by offering them psychological counselling, drug therapy, skills training, education, and other programs that would help at least the less violent offenders reintegrate into society (McMahon, 1992: xvii).

Today, however, many Canadians scoff at the idea that prisons can rehabilitate criminals. We have adopted a tougher line. Politicians routinely campaign on promises of a get-tough approach to crime and to criminals. Some people see prison as a means of *deterrence*. In this view, people will be less inclined to commit crimes if they know they are likely to get caught and serve long and unpleasant prison terms. Others think of prisons as institutions of *revenge*. They believe that depriving criminals of their freedom and forcing them to live in poor conditions is fair retribution for their illegal acts. Still others see prisons as institutions of *incapacitation*. From this viewpoint, the chief function of the prison is to keep criminals out of society as long as possible to ensure they can do no more harm (Feeley and Simon, 1992; Simon, 1993; Zimring and Hawkins, 1995).

No matter which of these views predominates, one thing is clear. Since the 1960s, the Canadian public has demanded that more criminals be arrested and imprisoned, and it has got what it wanted. In 2008–9, nearly 260 000 Canadian adults and 20 000 youths between the ages of 12 and 17 were in custody (Calverley, 2010; Calverley, Cotter, and Halla, 2010). Although Canada's incarceration rate is higher than that of most West European countries, it is much lower than that of the United States (Figure 7.5). The United States currently has about 2.3 million people behind bars, second only to China's 2.4 million, although China's population is almost 4.4 times as big as that of the United States.

Moral Panic

What accounts for our increased enthusiasm for get-tough policies? One answer is that the way in which the media has reported crime since the early 1990s may inflame public fears. An analysis of nightly American network newscasts from 1990 through 1996 revealed that although coverage of crime ranked sixth in prominence from 1990 to 1992, it skyrocketed to first place after that. About 5 percent of American network news stories over that period was about a murder, suggesting an unprecedented crime wave (Kurtz, 1997). Similarly, an examination of 98 Canadian supper-hour TV newscasts in 1997 showed that "chaos news"—reports on crime, accidents, and natural disasters—accounted for 22 percent of Canadian TV news items. Canadian newscasts were more likely than American newscasts to feature news about government and "soft news" (general human-interest stories and stories about entertainment, the arts, and culture). American stations were also much more likely

FIGURE 7.5

World Prison Population, 2008

Source: Roy Walsley, Director World Prison Population List. Publisher International Centre for Prison Studies.

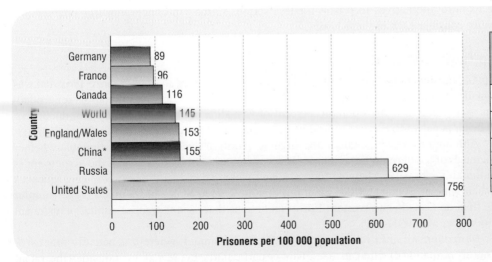

Share of Prisoners per Country

Country	Percentage of World's Prisoners	Percentage of World's Prisoners/ Percentage of World's Population
China*	24.7	1.1
USA	23.4	5.2
Russia	9.1	4.3
France	0.6	0.7
Germany	0.7	0.6
Canada	0.4	0.8
Other	41.1	0.6
Total	100.0	

*Includes 850 000 people in "administrative detention."

to lead or begin their newscasts with a report on crime, accidents, disasters, or other forms of chaos (National Media Archive, 1998). Nevertheless, to the extent we believe that the crimes that draw headlines are typical of crime in Canada, we may believe that the battle to win the "war against crime" requires the most punitive measures.

In short, media presentations of the crime problem may serve to promote a **moral panic**. That is, in response to lurid headlines that direct attention to the most notorious—and atypical—crimes and criminals, the public may conclude that most crime is violent and predatory, that all criminals are dangerous, and that our crime rate signals a grave threat to our society's well-being (Cohen, 1972; Goode and Ben-Yehuda, 1994). Are you part of the moral panic? Have you and your family taken special precautions to protect yourself from the "growing wave" of criminality? Even if you're not part of the moral panic, chances are you know someone who is. Therefore, to put things in perspective, you will need to recall an important fact from our discussion of recent trends in crime rates: According to official statistics, the moral panic is taking place during a period when major crime indexes are *falling*.

Why, then, the moral panic? Does anyone benefit from it? There may be several interested parties. First, the mass media benefit from moral panic because it allows them to rake in hefty profits. They publicize every major crime because crime draws big audiences, and big audiences mean more revenue from advertisers. After all, a front-page photograph of Karla Homolka or Paul Bernardo still generates newspaper sales nearly two decades after their convictions—even if the story that accompanies it is abbreviated or banal. Fictional crime programs also draw millions of viewers to their TVs. Second, the criminal justice system is a huge bureaucracy with thousands of employees. They benefit from moral panic because increased spending on crime prevention, control, and punishment secures their jobs and expands their turf. Third, and probably most importantly, the moral panic is useful politically. Since the early 1970s, many politicians have based entire careers on get-tough policies. At election time, they make combating crime a focal point of their campaign promises. The current Conservative government of Canada is proposing to expand the Canadian prison system and put more Canadians behind bars, despite warnings from criminologists, sociologists, and other experts that this approach to punishment will cost a lot of taxpayer money and serve only to create a larger class of hardened criminals. Law enforcement officials in Texas, who enacted this policy over several decades, have warned the Conservatives of its pitfalls, but as of this writing, their warnings have fallen on deaf ears.

Alternative Forms of Punishment

Two of the most contentious issues concerning the punishment of criminals are these: (1) Should we reintroduce the death penalty to punish the most violent criminals? (2) Should we explore alternatives to prison for less serious crime? In concluding this chapter, we briefly consider each of these issues.

Capital Punishment

Capital punishment (the death penalty) has not been employed in Canada since 1962 and was formally abolished in 1976. However, polls show that many Canadians favour its reintroduction. According to a 2010 poll, 40 percent of Canadian adults favour the reintroduction of the death penalty, 46 percent oppose it, and 14 percent are undecided (CBC News, 2010a).

Although the death penalty ranks high as a form of revenge, it is questionable whether it is much of a deterrent. First, murder is often committed in a rage, when the perpetrator is not thinking rationally. Many murderers are unlikely to consider the costs and consequences of their actions. Second, critics point out that the United States has a much higher murder rate than do Canada and Western European nations that do not practise capital punishment (Mooney et al., 2001: 131).

Moreover, we must remember that capital punishment, where it is actually practised, is hardly a matter of blind justice. This is particularly evident if we consider the racial distribution of people who are sentenced to death and executed in the United States.

A **moral panic** occurs when many people fervently believe that some form of deviance or crime poses a profound threat to society's well-being.

CP PHOTO/Frank Gunn

Intensive media coverage of the most notorious and violent crimes and criminals may lead to a heightened fear of crime and demands for tougher penalties. Karla Homolka, who with her husband, Paul Bernardo, was responsible for the sexual assault and brutal murder of Tammy Homolka, Leslie Mahaffy, and Kristen French in the early 1990s, is still the subject of media attention.

Murdering a white person in the United States is much more likely to result in a death sentence than is murdering a black person. For example, in Florida in the 1970s, an African American who killed a white person was 40 times as likely to receive the death penalty as an African American who killed another African American. Moreover, a white person who murders a black person is rarely sentenced to death, but a black person who murders a white person has the greatest chance of getting the death penalty. Thus, of the 80 white people who murdered African Americans in Florida in the 1970s, not one was charged with a capital crime. In Texas, one was—out of 143 cases (Black, 1989; Haines, 1996; Tonry, 1995). Given this patent racial bias, we cannot view the death penalty as a justly administered punishment.

Sometimes people favour capital punishment because it saves money. They argue that killing someone outright costs less than keeping the person alive in prison for the rest of his or her life. However, after trials and appeals, a typical execution costs the taxpayer several times more than a 40-year stay in a maximum-security prison (Haines, 1996).

Finally, in assessing capital punishment, we must remember that mistakes are common. Nearly 40 percent of death sentences in the United States since 1977 have been overturned because of new evidence or mistrial (Haines, 1996). In Canada, the wrongful convictions of Donald Marshall, Guy Paul Morin, David Milgaard—and many others in recent times—for murders they did not commit should be sufficient to remind us that the wheels of justice do not always turn smoothly.

Alternative Strategies

In recent years, analysts have suggested two main reforms to our current prison regime. First, some analysts have argued that we should reconsider our stance on rehabilitation. Advocates of rehabilitation suggest that **recidivism rates**, or the rate at which convicted offenders commit another crime, can be reduced through such programs as educational and job training, individual and group therapy, substance abuse counselling, and behaviour modification. Second, they have argued that, whenever possible, we should attempt to reduce rather than increase the number of incarcerated offenders. Drawing on labelling theory, they suggest we pursue a policy of "radical non-intervention," diverting offenders from formal processing in the criminal justice system. Proponents of this idea say that at least part of the increase in crime we have witnessed since the 1960s is attributable to the introduction of new and broadened definitions of criminal conduct. They believe that charging and imprisoning more and more Canadians, especially youth, is unlikely to help these individuals develop prosocial behaviour. Accordingly, they advise us to seek alternative methods that divert adults and juveniles from formal criminal justice system processing.

Although alternative procedures vary across provinces and territories, their use generally arises after the police or Crown prosecutor recommends that an offender be considered suitable for "diversion." One example of an alternative measure is a victim–offender reconciliation program (VORP), in which victim and offender meet under controlled circumstances. The victim has an opportunity to describe the impact of the criminal event on himself or herself and the offender might, for example, be required to apologize and agree to compensate the victim financially (Tufts, 2000). Cases dealt with in this way are more likely to involve male than female offenders. Young offenders selected for inclusion in these programs are usually over 15 years of age, and they generally complete the provisions of the agreements they make. Most cases referred for diversion involve theft under $5000. This is not surprising, since to be recommended for diversion, the offence must be minor. As well, to be considered candidates for diversion, offenders must first acknowledge that they are guilty of the act they have been accused of committing.

In like fashion, proponents of *decarceration* recommend that such options as fines (the most commonly used penal sanction in Canada), probation, and community service become more widely used as alternatives to imprisonment. However, not everyone favours this strategy. Some argue that the increased use of community programs does not reduce the numbers of individuals subject to formal social control. Rather, such strategies may

Recidivism rates indicate the proportion of people re-arrested after an initial arrest.

simply widen the net through the creation of more intensive, intrusive, and prolonged control mechanisms. These efforts might more accurately be labelled *transcarceration* than decarceration (Lowman, Menzies, and Palys, 1987). Noting such objections, some analysts suggest that we go further still and lobby for legislative reform that would decriminalize certain categories of conduct currently prohibited under Canadian criminal law, such as marijuana possession. This last suggestion serves to remind us, yet again, that crime and deviance are social constructs.

Summing Up

- The degree of social control and forms of punishment exercised in response to crime vary from one social context to the next.
- In the nineteenth century, imprisonment came to be viewed as the most humane form of punishment and it is now variously justified as a means of rehabilitation, deterrence, revenge, and incapacitation.
- The rate of incarceration in Canada is higher than in Western Europe, lower than the world average, and much lower than in the United States, which has by far the world's highest incarceration rate.
- Government and public enthusiasm for get-tough-on-crime policies is encouraged by media sensationalism, industries that profit from such policies, and politicians who mobilize supporters by creating moral panic.
- Although 4 out of 10 Canadian favour the reintroduction of the death penalty, it is questionable whether it acts as a deterrent. Moreover, capital punishment is often applied unjustly and costs as much as or more than life imprisonment.
- Decarceration and decriminalization have recently been proposed as viable alternatives for less serious crimes.

SUMMARY

1. What is deviance and how does it compare with crime?
   Deviance involves breaking a norm. Crime involves breaking a law. Both crime and deviance evoke societal reactions that help define the seriousness of the rule-breaking incident.

2. What determines the perceived seriousness of deviant and criminal acts?
   The seriousness of deviant and criminal acts depends on the severity of the societal response to them, their perceived harmfulness, and the degree of public agreement about whether they should be considered deviant or criminal.

3. What four broad classes of acts are ranked from lowest to highest on the three dimensions that determine seriousness?
   Acts that rank lowest on these three dimensions are called social diversions. Next come social deviations, and then come conflict crimes. Consensus crimes rank highest.

4. Are the definitions of crime and deviance fixed or variable?
   Definitions of deviance and crime are historically and culturally variable. They are socially defined and constructed. They are not inherent in the actions or characteristics of individuals.

5. What enables some groups to define deviance and crime to best suit their interests?
   Power is a key element in defining deviance and crime. Powerful groups are generally able to create norms and laws that suit their interests. Less powerful groups are usually unable to do so.

6. What is an example of a change in the law brought about by the increasing power of a group and an example of relative immunity brought on by established power?
   The increasing power of women has led to greater recognition of crimes committed against them. However, no similar recognition has occurred in the prosecution of white-collar criminals because the distribution of power between classes has not changed much in recent decades.

7. What are the sources of statistics on how much crime occurs?
   Crime statistics come from official sources, self-report surveys, and indirect measures. Each source has its strengths and weaknesses.

8. What trends in crime have occurred over the last several decades? What helps explain these trends?
   The long crime wave that began its upswing in the early 1960s peaked and started falling in the 1990s because of increased policing, a smaller proportion of young men in the population, and a booming economy.

9. How does race figure in crime and punishment?
   Aboriginal and black people experience disproportionately high arrest, conviction, and incarceration rates because of their relatively low class position on average and institutional bias.

10. What are some major theories of deviance and crime?
    Symbolic interactionist, functionalist, conflict, and feminist theories of deviance and crime illuminate different aspects of the process by which people are motivated to break rules and become defined as rule breakers.

11. What is social control?
    Social control is the effort exerted by all societies to ensure that their members obey norms and laws by imposing sanctions on rule breakers. The degree and form of social control vary historically and culturally.

12. Has social control weakened with the advent of industrialism?
    Although some sociologists say that social control is weaker and deviance is greater in industrial societies than in preindustrial societies, other sociologists note that in some respects social control is greater in industrial societies.

13. What kind of societies use prisons for punishment? How has the rationale for using prisons for punishment shifted?
    Modern industrial societies rely on prisons as an important form of punishment. Prisons now focus less on rehabilitation than on isolating and incapacitating inmates.

14. What is moral panic and where does it come from?
    Moral panic occurs when many people fervently believe that some form of deviance or crime poses a profound threat to society's well-being. It may be set off when people are convinced that crime is rising and tougher measures against criminals are called for. However, such responses to crime may arise, in part, because of media presentations that focus attention on the most violent—and least representative—types of crime committed. A variety of commercial and political groups benefit from the moral panic over crime and therefore encourage it.

15. Does the death penalty effectively deter crime or serve justice?
    Although the death penalty ranks high as a form of revenge, it is doubtful whether it acts as a serious deterrent. Moreover, where it exists, the death penalty is administered in a racially biased manner, does not save money, and sometimes results in tragic mistakes.

16. How should society respond to crime?
    The question of how we should respond to crime results in many different suggestions. These range from the reintroduction of capital punishment to the suggestion that we decriminalize various types of conduct currently prohibited under Canadian law.

KEY TERMS

conflict crimes (p. 164)

consensus crimes (p. 164)

control theory (p. 174)

crime (p. 159)

deviance (p. 159)

formal punishment (p. 160)

informal punishment (p. 159)

labelling theory (p. 171)

law (p. 159)

moral panic (p. 180)

recidivism rate (p. 181)

self-report surveys (p. 164)

social deviation (p. 162)

social diversion (p. 162)

stigmatized (p. 159)

strain theory (p. 172)

street crimes (p. 167)

subculture (p. 172)

victimization surveys (p. 165)

victimless crimes (p. 164)

white-collar crime (p. 167)

WEB RESOURCES

Companion Website for This Book

http://www.compass4e.nelson.com

Begin by clicking on the Student Resources section of the website. Next, select the chapter you are studying from the pull-down menu. From the Student Resources page you have easy access to additional Weblinks and other resources. The website also has many useful tips to aid you in your study of sociology, including practice tests for each chapter.

InfoTrac® Search Terms

These search terms are provided to assist you in beginning to conduct research on this topic by visiting http://www.infotrac-college.com:

moral panic

prison

stigma

street crime

white-collar crime

CHAPTER

8

Social Stratification

IN THIS CHAPTER, YOU WILL LEARN THAT

- Income is unequally distributed in Canada. Government plays a small but important role in redistributing money to children and families who are poor.

- Income inequality is lower in Canada than in the United States but higher than in many Western European countries.

- Most theories of social inequality focus on its economic roots.

- Power is an important non-economic source of inequality.

- Although some sociologists used to think that talent and hard work alone determine a person's position in the socioeconomic hierarchy, it is now clear that being a member of certain groups limits opportunities for success. In this sense, social structure shapes the distribution of inequality.

JN~/Shutterstock.com

PATTERNS OF SOCIAL INEQUALITY

Shipwrecks and Inequality

Writers and filmmakers sometimes tell stories about shipwrecks and their survivors to make a point about **social stratification**, the organization of society in layers or strata. They use the shipwreck as a literary device. It allows them to sweep away all traces of privilege and social convention. What remains are human beings stripped to their essentials, guinea pigs in an imaginary laboratory for the study of wealth and poverty, power and powerlessness, esteem and disrespect.

The tradition began with Daniel Defoe's *Robinson Crusoe*, first published in 1719. Defoe tells the story of an Englishman marooned on a desert island. His strong will, hard work, and inventiveness turn the poor island into a thriving colony. Defoe was one of the first writers to portray capitalism favourably. He believed that people get rich if they possess the virtues of good businesspeople—and stay poor if they don't.

The 1975 Italian movie *Swept Away* tells almost exactly the opposite story. In the movie, a beautiful woman, one of the idle rich, boards her yacht for a cruise in the Mediterranean. She treats the hardworking deckhands in a condescending and abrupt way. The deckhands do their jobs but seethe with resentment. Then comes the storm. The yacht is shipwrecked. Only the beautiful woman and one handsome deckhand remain alive, marooned on a desert island. Now equals, the two survivors soon have passionate sex and fall in love. All is well until the day of their rescue. As soon as they return to the mainland, the woman resumes her haughty ways. She turns her back on the deckhand, who is reduced again to the role of a common labourer. Thus, the movie sends the audience three harsh messages. First, it is possible to be rich without working hard, because a person can inherit wealth. Second, people can work hard without becoming rich. Third, something about the structure of society causes inequality, for inequality disappears only on the desert island, without society as we know it.

Titanic is a more recent movie on the shipwreck-and-inequality theme. At one level, the movie shows that class differences are important. For example, in first class, living conditions are luxurious, whereas in third class they are cramped. Indeed, on the *Titanic*, class differences spell the difference between life and death. After the *Titanic* strikes the iceberg off the coast of Newfoundland and Labrador, the ship's crew prevents second- and third-class passengers from entering the few available lifeboats. They give priority to rescuing first-class passengers. Consequently, 75 percent of third-class passengers perished, compared with 39 percent of first-class passengers. As the tragedy of the *Titanic* unfolds, however, another contradictory theme emerges. Under some circumstances, we learn, class differences can be insignificant. In the movie, the sinking of the *Titanic* is the backdrop to a fictional love story about a wealthy young woman in first class and a working-class youth in the decks below. The sinking of the *Titanic* and the collapse of its elaborate class structure give the young lovers an opportunity to cross class lines and profess their devotion to each other. At one level, then, the movie *Titanic* is an optimistic tale that holds out hope for a society in which class differences matter little.

Robinson Crusoe, Swept Away, and *Titanic* raise many of the issues we address in this chapter. What are the sources of social inequality? Do determination, industry, and ingenuity shape the distribution of advantages and disadvantages in society, as the tale of *Robinson Crusoe* portrays? Or is *Swept Away* more accurate? Do certain patterns of social relations underlie and shape that distribution? Is *Titanic's* first message of social class differences still valid? Does social inequality still have big consequences for the way we live? What about *Titanic's* second message? Can people overcome or reduce inequality in society? If so, how?

Social stratification refers to the way in which society is organized in layers or strata.

Christie's Images/Corbis

To answer these questions, we first sketch patterns of social inequality in Canada, paying special attention to change over time. We then assess major theories of social inequality in the light of logic and evidence.

Economic Inequality in Canada

Canada is one of the world's most prosperous countries. As Figure 8.1 shows, in 2008 Canadian families earned almost $79 000 on average, which, adjusting for inflation, is more than two-and-a-half times what they earned in the early 1950s. Increases in family income adjusted for inflation were most rapid from the end of World War II until the economic downturn that began in 1973. Average family income then remained quite stable for more than two decades, after which it returned to an upward trend.

The purchasing power of families rose for two main reasons. First, economic productivity increased as workers' skills and technologies improved. Second, large numbers of women entered the paid labour force starting in the early 1960s. In the 1950s, most families had only one earner. Today, dual-earner families are the norm.

Figure 8.1 simplifies reality because it is based on averages. In reality, people don't share prosperity equally. Some people are poor, some are rich, and most are in between (see Figure 8.2 on page 188). How then do we measure inequality, the gap between rich and poor? And is economic inequality growing or shrinking?

Social scientists have come up with a simple yet powerful way to display patterns of inequality. Here is the method, by way of analogy:

Step one: Among your classmates, think of how much money each person might have earned in the past three months. A few people with full-time, well-paying, steady jobs may have earned more than $5000. Put those people at the front of a line, the highest earner first. Others will have struggled to find consistent work or may have opted not to work. Put them at the back of the line, with the lowest earner at the very end of the line.

Step two: Add up how much everyone in the line has earned. Imagine you have 100 students in your line and altogether they earned $300 000.

Step three: Divide the line into five equal groups, with 20 percent of your classmates in each group—technically, these groups are known as "quintiles."

Step four: Add up how much the members of each of quintiles earned. The group at the head of the line will have earned the most given how we constructed the line. Imagine that

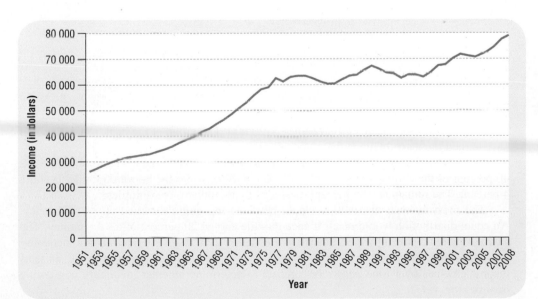

FIGURE 8.1

Average Income of Canadian Families, 1951 to 2008 (in 2007 dollars)

Source: Adapted from various documents from Statistics Canada and from the Canadian Council on Social Development

It's a Long Way to the Top: Canadian Income Inequality

Let the top of the CN Tower represent the average annual income of the top 5 percent of Canadians. Then the average annual income of the bottom 5 percent of Canadians would be represented by a tree 6.2 metres high. The average annual income of all Canadians would be represented by a worker 27.5 percent of the way up the CN tower.

Note: Drawn to scale.

Source: Data from Brian Murphy, Paul Roberts, and Michael Wolfson, 2007, *A Profile of High-Income Canadians, 1982–2004*, Statistics Canada. Retrieved January 15, 2011 (http://www.statcan.ca/english/research/75F0002MIE/75F0002MIE2007006.pdf).

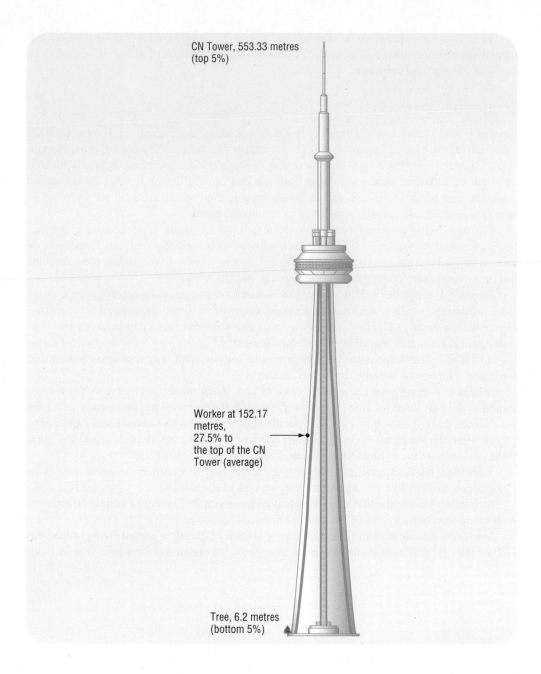

CN Tower, 553.33 metres (top 5%)

Worker at 152.17 metres, 27.5% to the top of the CN Tower (average)

Tree, 6.2 metres (bottom 5%)

together the members of this group earned $120 000. The group at the back of the line will have earned the least. Imagine that they collectively earned $12 000.

Final step: Calculate the percentage of money each group earned. The top quintile has 40 percent of the earnings ($120 000/$300 000 × 100), while the bottom quintile has only 4 percent. The remainder (56 percent) is shared by the other three quintiles.

The most unequal distribution would be if the top quintile earned all of the money. An equal distribution would result if each quintile earned 20 percent of all the money. The share of income earned by each quintile is frequently used to investigate income inequality in Canada and elsewhere. It is an easy idea to visualize, and looking at how the share of income changes over time allows researchers to determine whether inequality is growing or shrinking.

CP Picture Archive/Tibor Kolley

The Thomsons, Canada's wealthiest family, ranked 20th on the *Forbes Magazine* list of the world's richest people in 2010. Their assets totalled $23.36 billion. Sir Kenneth Thomson, who died in June 2006, handed over the reins of the Thomson electronic media, publishing, and information services empire to his son, David. The Thomsons are an example of success through both hard work and family connections.

Figure 8.3 shows that for 2008, the most recent year for which data are available, the lowest quintile of families received 6.1 percent of market income (that is, income before taxes and government transfers), while the top quintile received 43.4 percent. Almost half of all income was earned by 20 percent of families.

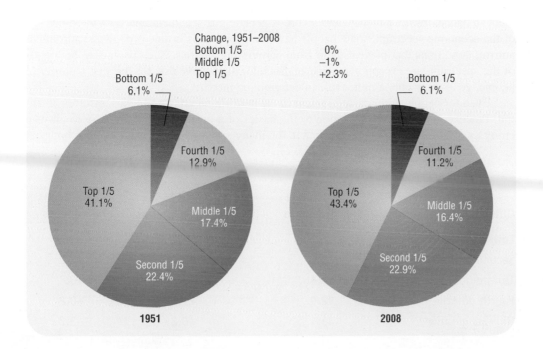

FIGURE 8.3

The Distribution of Total Market Income among Families, Canada, 1951 and 2008

Source: Dominion Bureau of Statistics, Statistics Canada Cat. 13-159, 2008. CANSIM Table 202-0701. Retrieved January 17, 2011 (http:www.statcan.gc.ca/pub/75-202-x/2007000/l195 eng.htm)

This level of inequality can be put into perspective in two ways. First, how does income inequality in Canada compare with income inequality in other countries? Among rich countries, income inequality is lowest in Denmark and highest in the United States. Canada stands between these two extremes.

We can also ask how income inequality has changed within Canada over time. Figure 8.3 shows that the distribution has changed little between 1951 and 2008. In 1951 and 2008, the bottom quintile received 6.1 percent of total income (before income tax). At the top end, the richest quintile increased its share of total income slightly, from 41.1 percent to 43.4 percent. In the past few decades, income inequality has widened in most rich countries, but not by much in Canada (Förster and Pellizzari, 2000).

The incomes reported above and in Figure 8.3 are incomes Canadians receive before paying taxes. Given frequent reference to Canada as a "welfare state," you might imagine that after-tax income is distributed differently. The concept of a welfare state implies the image of Robin Hood, taking from the rich and giving to the poor. To what degree does the Canadian state act like Robin Hood?

As Table 8.1 illustrates, in 2008 the government redirected some income from the top quintile to the other quintiles. Compared with their pre-tax share of total income, the richest quintile of earners saw their income share decline by 3.2 percent. The after-tax income of other quintiles rose modestly. Furthermore, since 1988 the redistributive effort of governments declined in Canada.

Explanations of Income Inequality

Why do some people fall into the highest quintile and others into the lowest quintile? What explains the distribution of income? The job a person holds plays a large role. Bank presidents earn more than branch managers, who in turn earn more than bank tellers do. Other jobs not only pay less well but also involve restricted hours of work or periods of unemployment. Thus, much about income inequality traces back to what kinds of work a person is able to obtain (see Table 8.2).

We know that some individuals earn high salaries because their natural talent allows them to take jobs that pay a lot. Jarome Iginla (hockey), Steve Nash (basketball), Karen Kain (ballet), Measha Brueggergosman (opera), Jim Carrey (acting), Shania Twain (popular music), and Mike Weir (golf) are Canadians whose success on the world stage has provided them with substantial earnings. The principal reason for their excellence is a natural endowment in dance, music, athletics, and so on. A genetic gift sets them apart. At the other end of the economic spectrum, some people have the genetic misfortune of Down syndrome or autism, conditions that prevent them from earning big salaries. Such people, at both ends of the spectrum, are exceptions, however. Sociologists believe that for the vast majority of people, genes play only a minor role in determining income.

Even for people with a natural talent in the performing arts or athletics, effort is essential. Practice and years of dedication to the basics of a profession are common to all who enjoy success. Effort is also significant for many Canadians who spend long hours at

---

TABLE 8.1

Percentage Share of Pre-tax and After-Tax Income by Quintile for Families, 2008

Source: Adapted from Statistics Canada, CANSIM database, http://dc.chass.utoronto.ca.proxy2/lib.umanitoba.ca/cgi-bin/cansimdim/c2_getArray.pl

Quintile	Total Pre-tax Income Share	Total After-Tax Income Share	Gain/Loss
Lowest quintile	6.1	7.1	+1.0
Second quintile	11.2	12.4	+1.2
Third quintile	16.4	17.2	+0.8
Fourth quintile	22.9	23.1	+0.2
Highest quintile	43.4	40.2	−3.2

Occupation	Median Annual Income
Judges, lawyers, and Quebec notaries	99 305
Senior management occupations	80 027
Professional occupations in health	77 515
Specialist managers	69 673
Professional occupations in natural and applied sciences	65 601
Mechanics	45 942
Construction trades	35 639
Clerical occupations	35 028
Secretaries	32 505
Labourers in processing, manufacturing, and utilities	31 538
Retail salespersons and sales clerks	27 225
Child care and home support workers	21 980
Cashiers	17 758
Occupations in food and beverage service	16 654

TABLE 8.2

Median Annual Income, Full-Time Workers, Selected Occupations, Canada, 2005

Sources: Statistics Canada, 2008, "Median Earnings and Employment for Full-Year, Full-Time Earners, All Occupations, Both Sexes, for Canada, Provinces and Territories —20% Sample Data." Retrieved January 20, 2011 (http://www12. statcan.ca/english/census06/data/ highlights/earnings/Table801.cfm? Lang=E&T=801&GH=4&SC=1&SO= 99&O=A); Statistics Canada, 2008, "Earnings and Incomes of Canadian over the Past Quarter Century, 2006 Census." Retrieved January 20, 2011 (http://www12.statcan.ca/english/ census06/analysis/income/pdf/ 97-563-XIE2006001.pdf)

work—whether amassing billable hours in a law practice, doing the endless chores required by a small business, or working overtime on a construction site. However, although diligence and perseverance might be necessary conditions for rewards, they are not sufficient. Effort alone does not result in high income (see Figure 8.4).

Raw talent needs to be sharpened. Training, coaching, schooling—these are crucial ways in which skills are developed and nurtured. Natural talents and our efforts are important ingredients in this process, to be sure, but education matters. Indeed, the importance of education as a determinant of occupation and income continues to increase (Baer, 1999; Statistics Canada, 2003d: 9). As the Canadian occupational structure moves further away from its traditional resource-based foundation to a more mature knowledge-driven economy, the importance of education will continue to grow.

If physical capital is investment in industrial plants and equipment, **human capital** is investment in education and training. Just as productivity increases by upgrading manufacturing plants and introducing new technology, productivity gains can also result from investment in the skills and abilities of people. Jobs requiring advanced skills are increasingly numerous in Canada. Better-educated workers are more skilled and productive in these jobs because they have invested in acquiring the skills and knowledge essential to our economy (Betcherman and Lowe, 1997).

Much evidence supports a human capital interpretation of the link between schooling and incomes (Baer, 1999). However, this is not a complete explanation for why people earn what they earn. For example, in the legal profession, almost everyone makes the same human capital investment. Every lawyer acquires a law degree. Yet economic rewards vary even for people with the same experience and type of legal practice (Kay and Hagan, 1998).

Human capital is the sum of useful skills and knowledge that an individual possesses.

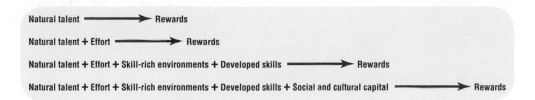

FIGURE 8.4

Explanations for Income Inequality

Social capital refers to the networks or connections that individuals possess.

Cultural capital is the stock of knowledge, tastes, and habits that legitimate the maintenance of status and power.

Part of the reason that people with the same amount of human capital may receive different economic rewards is that they possess different amounts of social capital. **Social capital** refers to people's networks or connections. Individuals are more likely to succeed if they have strong bonds of trust, cooperation, mutual respect, and obligation with well-positioned individuals or families. Knowing the right people, and having strong links to them, helps in finding opportunities and taking advantage of them (Coleman, 1988).

A related version of this argument is captured in the notion of **cultural capital** (Bourdieu and Passeron, 1990). Cultural capital comprises the set of social skills people have: their ability to impress others, to use tasteful language and images effectively, and thus to influence and persuade people. Although the notion of social capital stresses your networks and connections with others, the idea of cultural capital emphasizes your impression management skills, your ability to influence others. In different ways, both concepts emphasize being part of the right "social club."

What the concepts of social and cultural capital also have in common is the idea that families higher in the social hierarchy enjoy more capital of all types. Connections and culture help you find a good job. The hiring of new recruits, then, depends on the talent, effort, and skills that people bring to the interview, but it also depends on the connections and culture that people have. Indeed, culture and connections often influence who gets an interview.

In summary, natural talent and effort are important, and for a few occupations very significant. For most Canadians, level of education (or developed skill) is a critical factor in finding continuous, well-paying employment. In addition, social and cultural capital are consequential for many people in finding economic success. Explaining an individual's position in the income hierarchy depends on several factors, but the four themes outlined in Figure 8.4 are crucial.

Income versus Wealth

How long would it take you to spend a million dollars? If you spent $1000 a day, it would take you nearly three years. How long would it take you to spend a *billion* dollars? If you spent $2500 a day, you couldn't spend the entire sum in a lifetime—at that rate of spending, a billion dollars would last for more than 1000 years. (This scenario assumes you don't invest the money; if you invested it sensibly, you could never exhaust a billion dollars by spending $10 000 a day.) Thus, a billion dollars is an almost unimaginably large sum of money. Yet between 2004 and 2010, the estimated fortune of Canada's richest person, David Thomson, increased 7.8 percent, from $21.67 billion to $23.36 billion. In contrast, the annual income of a full-time worker earning the Ontario minimum wage in 2005 was $15 596. Just the *increase* in Thomson's wealth between 2004 and 2007 was equal to the total annual income of 108 361 minimum-wage earners! We list the 10 richest Canadians in Table 8.3.

What are the sources of the fortunes listed in Table 8.3? For some names on the list (Thomson, Irving, Weston), inheritance is a critical factor. These are family dynasties. Other people on the top-10 list had merely well-to-do or solid middle-class parents. None rose from rags to riches. On the whole, Table 8.3 suggests a mix of family fortune, business acumen, and opportunism as key determinants of wealth.

Only a very few families acquire the great wealth of major business enterprises. However, most families own some assets, and these add up to greater or lesser family wealth. For most adults, assets include a car (minus the car loan) and some appliances, furniture, and savings (minus the credit card balance). Somewhat wealthier families also have equity in a house (the market value minus the mortgage). More fortunate families are able to accumulate other assets, such as stocks and bonds, retirement savings, and vacation homes. Figure 8.5 shows the distribution of wealth among Canadian families in 1984, 1999, and 2005. The families are divided into quintiles. Notice that the bottom 40 percent of families own almost no assets. In fact, the bottom 20 percent owe more than they own. Notice also

Individual or Family	Estimated Wealth	Assets
1. Thomson Family	$23.36B	Media, information distribution; Thomson Reuters, Woodbridge Co. Ltd.
2. Galen Weston	$8.5B	Food, groceries, retail, real estate; George Weston Ltd., Loblaw Cos. Ltd, Holt Renfrew
3. Irving family	$7.46B	Oil, forestry products, gas stations, media, transportation, real estate; Irving Oil Ltd., J.D. Irving Ltd.
4. Rogers family	$6.02B	Cable TV, communications, media, pro sports; Rogers Communication Inc.
5. James Pattison	$5.53B	Auto sales, food, media, forestry products, entertainment, export services; Jim Pattison Group
6. Paul Desmarais Sr.	$4.28B	Financial services, media; Power Corp. of Canada
7. Bernard Sherman	$3.94B	Pharmaceuticals; Apotex Group of Companies
8. Jeff Skoll	$3.56B	Internet, media; eBay Inc., Participant Media
9. Saputo family	$3.52B	Food, real estate, transportation; Saputo Inc.
10. Fred and Ron Mannix	$3.18B	Mining, energy, real estate; Mancal Group

TABLE 8.3

Ten Wealthiest Canadians, 2009

Source: http://list. canadianbusiness.com/rankings/ rich100/2010/ranking/Default. aspx?sp2=1&d1=a&sc1=0

that the assets owned by the bottom 40 percent of families shrank in the 21 years covered by the graph. The assets owned by the top 60 percent of families grew, and by far the biggest increase in wealth was experienced by the top quintile, whose median net worth grew by almost two-thirds between 1984 and 2005.

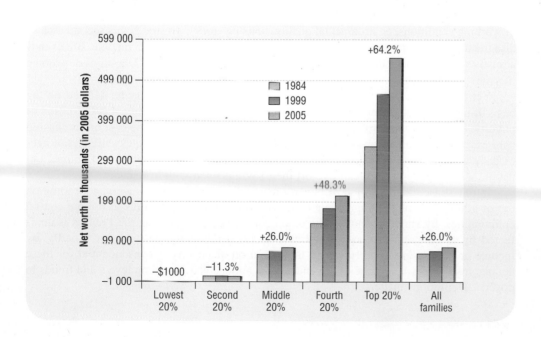

FIGURE 8.5

Median Net Worth of Canadian Families, 1984, 1999, and 2005

Note: To make the three surveys comparable, the following items are not included: employer-sponsored pension plans, contents of the home, collectibles and valuables, annuities, and registered retirement income funds. If it were possible to include these items, wealth inequalities would be greater than shown. Net worth for the lowest quintile in 1984 was 0. Calculating the percentage decline for this quintile would require dividing by zero, which of course is not possible. Accordingly, for the lowest quintile, we show the decline in net worth in dollars rather than as a percentage.

Source: René Morisette and Xuelin Zhang, 2006, "Revisiting Wealth Inequality," *Perspectives* (Statistics Canada). Retrieved May 1, 2008 (http://www.statcan.ca/english/ freepub/75-001-XIE/11206/ art-1.pdf).

Wealth inequality is thus increasing rapidly in Canada—but not as much as in the United States, where 62 percent of the increase in national wealth in the 1990s went to the richest 1 percent of Americans and fully 99 percent of the increase went to the richest 20 percent. The United States surpasses all other highly industrialized countries in wealth inequality. Between 50 percent and 80 percent of the net worth of American families derives from transfers and bequests, usually from parents (Hacker, 1997; Keister, 2000; Keister and Moller, 2000; Levy, 1998; Spilerman, 2000; Wolff, 1996).

Note that only a modest correlation exists between income and wealth. Some wealthy people have low annual incomes and some people with high annual incomes have little accumulated wealth. As such, annual income may not be the best measure of a person's well-being. Policies that seek to redistribute income from the wealthy to the poor, such as income-tax laws, may not get at the root of economic inequality because income redistribution has little effect on the distribution of wealth (Conley, 1999; Oliver and Shapiro, 1995).

Income and Poverty

At the bottom of the income distribution are the homeless. In recent decades, the number of people with "no fixed address" has increased considerably. We do not know how many Canadians are homeless. In cities across the country, people sleep under bridges, in back alleys, behind dumpsters, and in thickets in public parks. They do so night after night, month after month.

Homelessness is one manifestation of poverty. Exactly how many Canadians are poor is a matter of intense debate. Poverty lacks an agreed definition. A first disagreement occurs around whether poverty should be defined in absolute or relative terms. An absolute definition of poverty focuses on bare essentials, suggesting that poor families have resources inadequate for acquiring the basic necessities of life (food, shelter, clothing). Agreement on "bare essentials" depends on values and judgments (Sarlo, 2001). What is essential varies from time to time, place to place, and group to group. Many of our ancestors lived without indoor plumbing, and some Canadians still do, but most people would define indoor plumbing as essential. A family could survive on a steady diet of cod and potatoes, but most would define such a family as poor.

A relative poverty line also has drawbacks. Two questions are central: Relative to what? How relative? Whether poverty ought to be defined narrowly, in terms of economic measures (e.g., income), or more broadly, with respect to community standards (e.g., safety of working conditions, environmental quality, housing stock), illustrates this second area of disagreement. Most definitions tend to be narrow, focusing primarily on income. But even if a relative poverty line is defined narrowly, how relative ought it to be? One-third of average income? one-half? some other fraction?

Yet another disagreement plagues any definition. Should poverty be defined on the basis of income or consumption? Since "bare essentials" is a core idea in any definition of poverty, it makes good sense to ask about, and measure, poverty as the cost of purchasing bare essentials. Deprivation occurs when a family cannot acquire the essentials, not necessarily when income is too low. Income and consumption are correlated, of course, but people with high net wealth can live off their savings even with low income.

In one sense, the definition of poverty means little to a homeless woman sleeping on top of a hot air vent. The immediate experience of poverty by families in remote coastal communities, by single parents in the urban core, and by farmers on the Prairies is unaffected by whether poverty is defined absolutely or relatively, narrowly or broadly, by income or by consumption. However, the definition of poverty is consequential for these people, insofar as social policies are enacted, or not enacted, based on levels and trends in poverty. Definitions matter.

Social policy has a profound impact on the distribution of opportunities and rewards in Canada. Politics can reshape the distribution of income and the system of inequality by changing the laws governing people's right to own property, entitling people to various welfare benefits, and redistributing income through tax policies. When politicians de-emphasize poverty, legislative efforts to maintain or expand welfare benefits and redistribute income are less likely. A definition of poverty showing fewer poor Canadians implies little need for government action. Conversely, for politicians and political parties supporting the poor, a definition of poverty showing a growing proportion of poor people is beneficial to their cause.

Unlike some other countries, such as the United States, Canada does not have an official definition of poverty. Statistics Canada argues that there is no internationally accepted definition of poverty and that any definition is arbitrary. Therefore, it does not attempt to estimate the number of Canadians who are poor. Instead, it reports what it calls a **low-income cutoff**. The low-income cutoff "represents an income threshold where a family is likely to spend [at least] 20% more of its income on food, shelter, and clothing than the average family" (Statistics Canada, 1999). The threshold is reported for seven different family sizes and for five sizes of community. Most advocates for the poor interpret these thresholds, shown for 2006 in Table 8.4, as poverty lines. For example, in Canada's cities with a population of half a million or more, a family of four with an income of $33 221 or less after government transfer payments, such as GST credits and the Canada Child Tax Benefit, would be considered poor.

In recent decades, the prevalence of low income among Canadians peaked at 15.7 percent in 1996, declined to 11.6 percent in 2002, and rose to 15.3 percent in 2005. One difficulty in interpreting such rates is that the risk of low income is different for different types of families. As Figure 8.6 on page 196 indicates, families without any earners are at especially high risk, especially if they are female lone-parent families, more than 81 percent of which are in the low-income category.

The rates reported in Table 8.4 are for the proportion of families living in low income at a given time. However, many families move into poverty because of unemployment, reduced work hours, or episodes of poor health—and then out of poverty because of an improving economy or recovery from illness. As Figure 8.7 on page 196 indicates, many families and individuals go through one or more spells of low income over a period of

Low-income cutoff is Statistic Canada's term for the income threshold below which a family devotes at least 20 percent more of its income to the necessities of food, shelter, and clothing than an average family would, likely resulting in straitened circumstances.

Family Size	Population of Community of Residence				
	500 000+	100 000–499 999	30 000–99 999	Fewer than 30 000*	Rural
1	$18 373	$15 538	$15 344	$13 754	$12 019
2	$22 361	$18 911	$18 676	$16 741	$14 628
3	$27 844	$23 548	$23 255	$20 845	$18 215
4	$34 738	$29 378	$29 013	$26 007	$22 724
5	$39 556	$33 453	$33 037	$29 614	$25 876
6	$43 869	$37 100	$36 640	$32 843	$28 698
7+	$48 181	$40 747	$40 241	$36 072	$31 519

TABLE 8.4

Low-Income Cutoffs after Taxes and Including Government Transfers, 2008

Source: Statistics Canada CANSIM Database. Retrieved April 25, 2011 (http://www5.statcan.gc.ca/cansim/homeaccueil?lang=eng, Table 202-0001).

*Includes cities with a population between 15 000 and 30 000 and small urban areas (fewer than 15 000)

FIGURE 8.6

Low-Income Rates for
Different Family Types,
Canada, 2005

Source: Statistics Canada, 2008,
"Earnings and Incomes of Canadians
over the Past Quarter Century, 2006
Census." Retrieved January 20, 2011
(http://www12.statcan.ca/english/
census06/analysis/income/pdf/
97-563-XIE2006001.pdf).

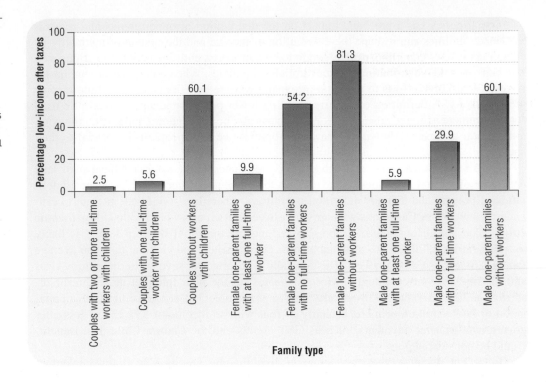

FIGURE 8.7

Persons Experiencing Low
Income at Least One Year
between 2002 and 2007

Source: Based on Statistics Canada.
Persistence of low income, by
selected characteristics, every
3 years (CANSIM Table 202-0807).
Ottawa: Statistics Canada, 2009.
Retrieved January 20, 2011 (http://
www4.hrsdc.gc.ca/.3ndic.1t
.4r@-eng.jsp?iid=83#M_1).

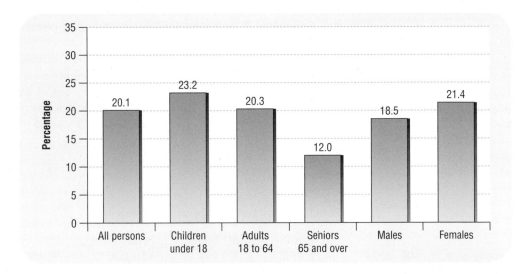

several years. For example, almost 25 percent of Canadian children lived in a low-income family for at least part of the time during the five years summarized by Figure 8.7.

Myths about the Poor

Research conducted in the past few decades shows that popular conceptions of the poor are often inaccurate. In particular, research explodes three myths:

Myth 1: People are poor because they don't want to work. This myth ignores the fact that many of Canada's poor cannot work because of disability or because inadequate child-care services leave them no alternative but to take care of their young children. Moreover, many poor people work full time and many more work part time. Working, however, does not guarantee escape from poverty. Consider the situation of a single person living in a large Canadian city. This person must earn more than $18 373 to be above the low-income cutoff measure (see Table 8.4). To meet this goal, the person must work 40 hours per week for 50 weeks at a wage of at least $9.18. Yet in 2011, Canadian minimum wages varied between $8.75 (British Columbia) and $10.25 (Ontario), with a provincial average of $9.55 (Statistics Canada, 2011a). The number of minimum wage workers continues to grow, currently composing about 6 percent of all employees. Low minimum wages ensure widespread low income and poverty.

Myth 2: Most poor people are immigrants. Individuals and family heads who are immigrants and who arrived in Canada before 1980 generally experience poverty at *lower* rates than native-born Canadians do (National Council of Welfare, 2004: 57). Higher poverty rates are evident among more recent immigrants who are less well established, but recent immigrants represent a fraction of all poor people, and their economic standing tends to improve the longer they stay in the country.

Myth 3: Most poor people are trapped in poverty. In fact, more than 92 percent of people with low income in any given year escape poverty in less than two years, 80 percent in less than a year. Of the 20.1 percent of Canadians who experienced one or more years of low income over a five-year period, only slightly more than 5 percent lived in poverty between four and six years. On average, those who experienced low income for at least one year spent 2.8 years or about one-half the total period in poverty (Statistics Canada, 2004b: 124). Thus, poverty for many is a result of unstable family finances; they slip into and out of difficult circumstances.

Explaining Poverty

Why are some people poor and others not? Answers to this question vary from individual-level to structural explanations.

Individual-level explanations focus on the attributes of poor people, asking how they differ from people who are not poor. This type of explanation focuses on causes that lie "within the person." On this logic, someone is poor because of a personal characteristic, such as low intelligence or a behaviour abnormality.

Some evidence suggests that individual attributes explain a small amount of poverty. For example, we know that people with a disability have a higher risk of living in poverty than others do. However, not all people with a disability live in poverty, and the vast majority of people living in poverty have no disability. On balance, this type of evidence teaches us that poverty is, for the most part, not a consequence of individual attributes, even though these are important in some cases.

A related explanation focuses on people's attitudes. From this point of view, poor families adopt child-rearing practices that encourage low self-esteem, weak motivation to achieve, an inability to delay gratification, lack of self-discipline, a poor work ethic, and other characteristics that cause poverty to persist. Some analysts say that the crystallization and transmission of such attitudes from one generation to the next amounts to the perpetuation of a "culture of poverty."

Many sociologists dismiss this type of reasoning because it is inaccurate and confuses cause and effect. The plain fact is that many poor people work hard, strive to get ahead, and teach their children to value education. Claiming that all poor people are stuck in a culture of poverty is simply false. Moreover, even if some poor people do live in a culture of poverty, analysts must be careful not to confuse cause and effect. Some poor people undoubtedly display "bad attitudes," but they result from poverty and are not the cause of it. Confusing cause and effect blames the victim for his or her plight.

A form of explanation with greater currency in sociology stresses the social organization of society as the cause of poverty. For instance, capitalist economies feature cyclical booms and busts, periods of low unemployment and high profits followed by periods of high unemployment and low profits. When unemployment rates rise, so does the number of families forced to live on reduced earnings, which for many means living in poverty. The right of employers to refuse to renew work contracts is an accepted part of our economic system. The reduction in income that results can hardly be attributed to changes in individual motivation.

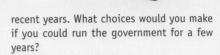

It's Your Choice

INCOME REDISTRIBUTION AND TAXATION

The idea of "rugged individualism" implies that our personal fortunes ought to rest on our own shoulders. People who work hard, persevere, and make wise decisions supposedly deserve big rewards. By implication, those who are lazy and unwise deserve less.

In contrast, the idea of

"collective responsibility" implies that as members of a community, we ought to look out for one another. Those who have should share. The interests of the many should come before the riches of a few.

Few Canadians support either of these extremes, but examples of each principle are easy to find. The unequal distribution of income in Canada and the high salaries of the presidents of large corporations are consistent with rugged individualism. Government support for postsecondary education and health care illustrates collective responsibility.

How much tax revenue should governments collect, and should they redistribute that revenue in ways that benefit lower income groups? Should governments exercise more collective responsibility by giving more support to hospitals and schools with tax dollars, or should people act more as rugged individualists and pay for medical care and education themselves? These are questions of social policy.

Here are some of the arguments for and against income redistribution, arguments that are fundamental to some of the major political debates in many countries in recent years. What choices would you make if you could run the government for a few years?

Against Redistribution

1. Taking from the rich and giving to the poor decreases the motivation for people in both groups to work hard.
2. The cost of redistribution is high. Taking from one group and giving to another requires a government agency to collect money and then to allocate it.
3. Some individuals and families cheat. They hide or misrepresent their earnings, either to pay less in tax or to receive more through welfare. Redistribution promotes tax cheats and welfare frauds.

For Redistribution

1. A society with a low level of inequality is a better place to live than is a society with a high level of inequality.
2. An extra dollar to a poor family is more helpful than an extra dollar to a rich family.
3. Improving the material well-being of a poor family enhances the well-being of a rich family because it encourages less crime and political discord.

Low-wage jobs are also a feature of the economy. Some people in low-skill, nonunionized, seasonal, or part-time jobs do not earn enough to escape poverty. From this point of view, poverty is caused by a lack of well-paying jobs, not by a weak work ethic (Krahn and Lowe, 1998: 405).

Other analysts stress social policy as a factor affecting the poverty level. People earning the minimum hourly wage while working full time all year are still poor, especially if they have to support children. Minimum-wage legislation is thus a social policy that creates the working poor. Of course, if minimum wages were to rise, so too might the level of unemployment because some employers might not be able to afford to pay higher wages. Debate over these issues continues, but the point is that social policies affect people's well-being.

The tax system is another policy that affects poverty. In a progressive tax system, a higher proportion of income is paid in tax as incomes rise. For instance, people earning $100 000 a year pay a larger percentage of their income in tax than do people who earn $50 000 a year. The Canadian income tax system is progressive. However, the overall tax system is not; most Canadian families pay about the same percentage of their total income in tax.

Two factors undermine the "Robin Hood" effect of progressive income tax. First, other taxes, such as the HST and fuel taxes, are "regressive," that is, they are not based on the income of the taxpayer. Since lower-income families typically spend a higher proportion of their income on consumption, such taxes hurt them more than they hurt upper-income families. Second, high-income earners shelter much of their income from taxation. If you are wealthy enough to be able to invest in a registered retirement savings plan, your investment is tax-deductible and earnings in the plan are not taxed. Earnings in registered education saving plans and tax-free savings accounts are also untaxed. In addition, dividend earnings from stock in Canadian corporations and earnings from selling stock or property at a higher price than you paid are taxed at a substantially lower rate than earnings from employment. Of course, low-income Canadians have no dividend earnings or capital gains, nor can they afford registered retirements savings plans, registered education savings plans, and tax-free savings accounts. Consequently, the tax system as a whole does little to redistribute income and diminish poverty (see Box 8.1).

A final structural explanation for poverty stresses ways of thinking, or ideological perspectives. Widespread negative images of some groups, such as Aboriginal Canadians and people with disabilities, results in discrimination. In turn, discrimination may lead to employment in unsteady and low-paying jobs or intermittent or chronic unemployment.

Is poverty an inevitable feature of society? It may be, although it is within our power to substantially reduce the extent of poverty if we chose to follow the example of Western European countries, most of which have poverty rates half that of Canada. Many Western European governments have accomplished this feat by establishing job-training and child-care programs that allow poor people to take jobs with livable wages and benefits. At present, we lack the political will to follow suit.

These, then, are the basic patterns and trends in social stratification in Canada. Bearing them in mind, we now examine how major sociologists have explained social stratification. We begin with Karl Marx, who formulated the first major sociological theory of stratification in the middle of the nineteenth century (Marx and Engels, 1972 [1848]; Marx, 1904 [1859]).

Summing Up

- While the average income of Canadians has grown in the last half century, extensive income inequality endures.
- Differences in human, social, and cultural capital contribute to existing inequalities.
- Levels of poverty are better explained by structural factors than by individual factors.

THEORIES OF STRATIFICATION

Conflict Perspectives

Marx

In medieval Western Europe, peasants worked small plots of land owned by landlords. Peasants were legally obliged to give their landlords a set part of the harvest and to continue working for them under any circumstance. In turn, landlords were required to protect peasants from marauders. They were also obliged to open their storehouses and feed the peasants if crops failed. This arrangement was known as **feudalism**.

According to Marx, by the late fifteenth century, several forces were beginning to undermine feudalism. Most important was the growth of exploration and trade, which increased the demand for many goods and services in commerce, navigation, and industry. By the seventeenth and eighteenth centuries, some urban craftsmen and merchants had opened small manufacturing enterprises and saved enough capital to expand production. However, they faced a big problem: To increase profits they needed more workers. Yet the biggest potential source of workers—the peasantry—was legally bound to the land. Thus, feudalism had to wither if agricultural peasants were to become industrial workers. In Scotland, for example,

Feudalism was a legal arrangement in preindustrial Europe that bound peasants to the land and obliged them to give their landlords a set part of the harvest. In exchange, landlords were required to protect peasants from marauders and open their storehouses to feed the peasants if crops failed.

enterprising landowners recognized they could make more money raising sheep and selling wool than by having their peasants till the soil. Consequently, they turned their cropland into pastures, forcing peasants off the land and into the cities. The former peasants had no choice but to take jobs as urban workers.

In Marx's view, relations between workers and industrialists first encouraged rapid technological change and economic growth. After all, industrial owners wanted to adopt new tools, machines, and production methods so they could produce more efficiently and earn higher profits. But such innovation had unforeseen consequences. In the first place, some owners, driven out of business by more efficient competitors, were forced to become members of the working class. Together with former peasants pouring into the cities from the countryside, this caused the working class to grow. Second, the drive for profits motivated owners to concentrate workers in larger and larger factories, keep wages as low as possible, and invest as little as possible in improving working conditions. Thus, as the ownership class grew richer and smaller, the working class grew larger and more impoverished.

Marx felt that workers would ultimately become aware of their exploitation. Their sense of **class consciousness** would, he wrote, encourage the growth of unions and workers' political parties. These organizations would eventually try to create a communist system in which there would be no private wealth. Instead, under communism, everyone would share wealth, said Marx.

Note several points about Marx's theory. First, according to Marx, a person's **class** is determined by the source of his or her income, or, to use Marx's term, by a person's "relationship to the means of production." For example, members of the capitalist class (or **bourgeoisie**) own the means of production, including factories, tools, and land. They do not do any physical labour. They are thus in a position to earn profits. In contrast, members of the working class (or **proletariat**) do physical labour. They do not own means of production. They are thus in a position to earn wages. It is the source of income, not the amount, that distinguishes classes in Marx's view.

A second noteworthy point about Marx's theory is that it recognizes more than two classes in any society. In particular, the **petite bourgeoisie** is a class of small-scale capitalists who own means of production but employ only a few workers or none at all. Their situation forces them to do physical work themselves. In Marx's view, members of the petite bourgeoisie are bound to disappear as capitalism develops because they are economically inefficient. Just two great classes characterize every economic era, said Marx: landlords and serfs during feudalism, bourgeoisie and proletariat during capitalism.

Critique of Marx

Marx's ideas strongly influenced the development of conflict theory (see Chapter 1, A Sociological Compass). Today, however, it is generally agreed that Marx did not accurately foresee some aspects of capitalist development:

- Industrial societies did not polarize into two opposed classes engaged in bitter conflict. Instead, a large and heterogeneous middle class of "white-collar" workers emerged. Some of them are non-manual employees. Others are professionals. Many of them enjoy higher income and status than manual workers do. With a bigger stake in capitalism than propertyless manual workers have, non-manual employees and professionals generally act as a stabilizing force in society. To take account of these changes, some neo-Marxists recognize *two* main divisions in the social relations of work—between owners and non-owners, and between supervisors/managers and non-supervisors/managers. The class of supervisors and managers is sometimes called the "new middle class." Members of the new middle class take direction from owners and are responsible for coordinating the work of other employees (Clement and Myles, 1994).
- Marx correctly argued that investment in technology makes it possible for capitalists to earn high profits. However, he did not expect investment in technology to make it possible for workers to earn higher wages and toil fewer hours under less oppressive conditions. Yet that is just what happened. Improved living standard tended to pacify workers, as did the availability of various welfare state benefits, such as employment insurance.

Class consciousness refers to being aware of membership in a class.

Class, in Marx's sense of the term, is determined by a person's relationship to the means of production. In Weber's usage, class is determined by a person's "market situation."

The **bourgeoisie** in Marx's usage are owners of the means of production, including factories, tools, and land. They do not do any physical labour. Their income derives from profits.

The **proletariat**, in Marx's usage, is the working class. Members of the proletariat do physical labour but do not own means of production. They are thus in a position to earn wages.

The **petite bourgeoisie**, in Marx's usage, is the class of small-scale capitalists who own means of production but employ only a few workers or none at all, forcing them to do physical work themselves.

- Communism took root not where industry was most highly developed, as Marx predicted, but in semi-industrialized countries, such as Russia in 1917 and China in 1949. Moreover, instead of evolving into classless societies, new forms of privilege emerged under communism, where elite communist party members could enjoy scarce Western goods at nominal prices, luxurious country homes, free trips abroad, and so on. According to a Russian quip from the 1970s, "Under capitalism, one class exploits the other, but under communism it's the other way around."

Weber

Writing in the early twentieth century, Max Weber foretold most of the developments outlined above. He did not think communism would create classlessness. He understood the significance of the growth of the middle class. Consequently, Weber developed an approach to social stratification much different from Marx's.

Weber, like Marx, saw classes as economic categories (Weber, 1946: 180–95). However, he did not think a single criterion—ownership versus non-ownership of property—determines class position. Class position, wrote Weber, is determined by a person's "market situation," including the possession of goods, opportunities for income, level of education, and degree of technical skill. There are four main classes according to Weber: large property owners, small property owners, propertyless but relatively highly educated and well-paid employees, and propertyless manual workers. Thus, white-collar employees and professionals emerge as a large class in Weber's scheme.

If Weber broadened Marx's idea of class, he also recognized that two types of groups other than class have a bearing on the way a society is stratified: status groups and parties.

Status groups differ from one another in the prestige or social honour they enjoy and in their style of life. Consider members of a particular minority ethnic community who have recently immigrated. They may earn relatively high income but endure relatively low prestige. The longer-established members of the majority ethnic community may look down on them as vulgar "new rich." If their cultural practices differ from those of the majority ethnic group, their style of life may also become a subject of scorn. Thus, the position of the minority ethnic group in the social hierarchy does not derive just from its economic position but also from the esteem in which it is held.

In Weber's usage, **parties** are not just political groups but, more generally, organizations that seek to impose their will on others. Control over parties, especially large bureaucratic organizations, does not depend just on wealth or some other class criterion. One can head a military, scientific, or other bureaucracy without being rich, just as one can be rich and still have to endure low prestige.

Weber argued that to draw an accurate picture of a society's stratification system, we must analyze classes, status groups, and parties as somewhat independent bases of social inequality. But to what degree are they independent of one another? Weber said that the importance of status groups as a basis of stratification is greatest in pre-capitalist societies. Under capitalism, classes and parties (especially bureaucracies) become the main bases of stratification.

Although sociologists dissect inequalities into abstract schemes, the underlying differences exist quite apart from abstractions that theorists propose. For many people, the most tangible reality of class is how it sorts people into different neighbourhoods. There is no exact rule involved, and various ranking criteria blend into a complex synthesis. Because the rule is inexact, people act on it without even agreeing on what, if anything, to call it.

Functionalism

Marx and Weber were Germans who wrote their major works between the 1840s and the 1910s. Inevitably, their theories bear the stamp of the age in which they wrote. The next major developments in the field occurred in the United States in the mid-twentieth century. Just as inevitably, these innovations were coloured by the optimism, dynamism, and prejudices of that time and place.

The **functional theory of stratification** was proposed by Kingsley Davis and Wilbert Moore at the end of World War II (Davis and Moore, 1944). Davis and Moore observed that jobs differ in importance. A judge's work, for example, contributes more to society than the

Status groups differ from one another in terms of the prestige or social honour they enjoy and also in terms of their style of life.

Parties, in Weber's usage, are organizations that seek to impose their will on others.

The **functional theory of stratification** argues that (1) some jobs are more important than others are, (2) people must make sacrifices to train for important jobs, and (3) inequality is required to motivate people to undergo these sacrifices.

work of a janitor. This presents a problem: How can people be motivated to undergo the long training they need to serve as judges, physicians, engineers, and so on? Higher education is expensive. You earn little money while training. Long and hard study rather than pleasure seeking is essential. Clearly, an incentive is needed to motivate the most talented people to train for the most important jobs. The incentives, said Davis and Moore, are money and prestige. Thus, social stratification is necessary (or "functional") because the prospect of high rewards motivates people to undergo the sacrifices needed to get a higher education. Without substantial inequality, they conclude, the most talented people would have no incentive to become judges, physicians, and so on.

Although the functional theory of stratification may at first seem plausible, we can conduct what Max Weber called a "thought experiment" to uncover one of its chief flaws. Imagine a society with just two classes of people—physicians and farmers. The farmers grow food. The physicians tend the ill. Then, one day, a rare and deadly virus strikes. The virus has the odd property of attacking only physicians. Within weeks, there are no more doctors in our imaginary society. As a result, the farmers are much worse off. Cures and treatments for their ailments are no long available. Soon the average farmer lives fewer years than his or her predecessors did. The society is less well off, though it survives.

Now imagine the reverse. Again we have a society comprising only physicians and farmers. Again a rare and lethal virus strikes. This time, however, the virus has the odd property of attacking only farmers. Within weeks, the physicians' stores of food are depleted. After a few more weeks, the physicians start dying of starvation. The physicians who try to become farmers catch the new virus and expire. Within months, there is no more society. Who, then, does the more important work, physicians or farmers? Our thought experiment suggests that farmers do, for without them society cannot exist.

From a historical point of view, we can say that *none* of the jobs regarded by Davis and Moore as "important" would exist without the physical labour done by people in "unimportant" jobs. To sustain the witch doctor in a tribal society, hunters and gatherers had to produce enough for their own subsistence plus a surplus to feed, clothe, and house the witch doctor. To sustain the royal court in an agrarian society, serfs had to produce enough for their own subsistence plus a surplus to support the royal family. By using taxes, tithes, and force, government and religious authorities have taken surpluses from ordinary working people for thousands of years. Among other things, these surpluses were used to establish the first institutions of higher learning in the thirteenth century. Out of these, modern universities developed.

The question of which occupations are most important is thus unclear. To be sure, most physicians earn a lot more money than most farmers do today and they also enjoy a lot more prestige. But that is not because their work is more important in any objective sense of the word. (On the question of why physicians and other professionals earn more than non-professionals do, see Chapter 17, Education).

According to the functional theory of stratification, "important" jobs require more training than "less important" jobs. The promise of big salaries motivates people to undergo that training. Therefore, the functionalists conclude, social stratification is necessary. As the text makes clear, however, one of the problems with the functional theory of stratification is that it is difficult to establish which jobs are important, especially when we take a historical perspective.

Agriculture and Agri-Food Canada

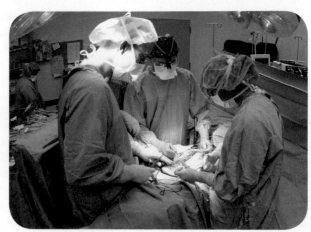

Photos.com

A second problem with the functional theory of stratification is that it stresses how inequality helps society discover talent but ignores the pool of talent lying undiscovered because of inequality (Tumin, 1953). Bright and energetic adolescents may be forced to drop out of high school to help support themselves and their families. Capable and industrious high-school graduates may be forced to forgo a postsecondary education because they can't afford it. Inequality may encourage the discovery of talent but only among those who can afford to take advantage of the opportunities available to them. For the rest, inequality prevents talent from being discovered.

Third, the functional theory of stratification fails to examine how advantages are passed from generation to generation. Like Robinson Crusoe, the functional theory correctly emphasizes that talent and hard work often result in high material rewards. However, it is also true that inheritance allows parents to transfer wealth to children regardless of their talent. For example, glancing back at Table 8.3, we see that many of the largest personal fortunes in Canada were inherited. Even rich people who do not inherit large fortunes often start near the top of the stratification system. Bill Gates, for example, is one of the richest people in the world. He did not inherit his fortune. However, his father was a partner in one of the most successful law firms in Seattle. Gates himself went to the most exclusive and expensive private schools in the city, followed by a stint at Harvard. In the late 1960s, his high school was one of the first in the world to boast a computer terminal connected to a nearby university mainframe. Gates's early fascination with computers dates from this period. Gates is without doubt a highly talented man, but surely the social advantages he was born with, and not just his talents, helped to elevate him to his present lofty status (Wallace and Erickson, 1992). An adequate theory of stratification must take inheritance into account, while recognizing how inequality prevents the discovery of talent.

Many of the ideas reviewed above emphasize the economic sources of inequality. However, as Weber correctly pointed out, inequality is not based on money alone. It is also based on prestige and power.

Power

Tom and Sharon Brown moved from Calgary to tiny Parrsboro, Nova Scotia, in 2010, with their teenage daughter, Courtney. In the local high school and on Facebook, Courtney was mercilessly bullied. She started skipping classes and opened another Facebook account, but to no avail. Things got so bad that on March 30, 2011, Courtney committed suicide. It was the second teen suicide in Nova Scotia caused by bullying in just over two months (Paperny, 2011). When 14-year-old Dawn-Marie Lesley of Mission, B.C., hanged herself in her bedroom with a dog leash almost 11 years earlier, she left a suicide note that spoke for the predicament of many such young people: "If I try to get help it will get worse. They are always looking for a new person to beat up and they are the toughest girls. If I ratted they would get suspended and there would be no stopping them. I love you all so much" (quoted in O'Malley and Ali, 2001).

Bullying was probably part of your upbringing, too. Recall your years in the schoolyard. Remember how some people had the power to "name," while others were forced to "wear" those names? "Four eyes," "fatty," and "spaz" were common names in many schools. If you had the misfortune of needing glasses, having a visible birthmark, or even having an unusual name, you might have been the victim of verbal abuse.

Why are so many children publicly shamed and humiliated? Because it makes those with the power to name feel superior and proud. The peer group is a place to "earn points" and win friends. To become one of the in-crowd, a child must disparage outsiders. If a person is part of the out-crowd, he or she must disparage members of the in-crowd as a defence aimed at maintaining self-esteem. Often it is cliques who do the mocking. Social class, ethnicity, grade level, and neighbourhood often define cliques.

Bullying is one form of power in action. Max Weber defined **power** as the ability of individuals or groups to get their own way, even in the face of resistance from others (Weber, 1947: 152). It would, however, be a mistake to think that power is an attribute that

Power is ability to impose one's will on others despite resistance.

you either have or don't. That is because less powerful groups may organize and resist; and organization and resistance are themselves bases of power. Accordingly, less powerful groups may become more powerful when power holders seek to impose their will. Sometimes, less powerful groups may even prevent power holders from achieving their aims. Power is therefore not an all-or-nothing attribute but a *social relationship*, the exercise of which may cause less powerful people to become more powerful. A movement has grown quickly in Nova Scotia to combat bullying in schools, and it got the provincial government to agree to set up a task force to deal with the problem in April 2011.

Authority is legitimate, institutionalized power.

Sociologists distinguish power from authority. **Authority** rests on moral consent— I comply with your demands not because you force me to but because I believe they are legitimate. In this case, compliance occurs not because sanctions are or could be used, but because I agree your demands are valid. We agree that bringing a gun to school is inappropriate and that halting at stop signs is essential for safety. Most people obey these rules not out of fear of sanctions, but because they agree that they are sensible, legitimate practices.

The use of power is often invisible. Powerful people often don't have to do anything to get their way because others understand it would be futile to resist. Extremely powerful individuals or groups are even able to set agendas, frame issues, and shape ideas—to decide the topics that will be debated and how they will be debated. This enables them to exclude potentially contentious issues from debate. They may then win battles without having to fight them because others haven't even conceived of the need to raise certain issues or at least raise them in certain ways. The invisible use of power is less risky than allowing contentious issues to be put on an agenda, having less powerful individuals and groups organize and resist, and perhaps even having to use force to win an issue. The use of force is a sign of relative weakness.

Summing Up

- Marx's theory of stratification distinguishes the class that owns the means of production (the bourgeoisie) from the class that works the means of production (the proletariat). According to Marx, class conflict eventually produces a communist system.
- In Weber's view, stratification is organized around classes, status groups, and parties. Different combinations of rankings on these dimensions produce varied stratification outcomes.
- Functionalists regard unequal rewards as necessary insofar as they motivate people to make sacrifices and obtain credentials required by more valuable and high-paying jobs.
- The exercise of power—the imposition of an individual's or a group's will on others—does not always require force and is often invisible. Legitimate power, or authority, evokes compliance without force because people view it as valid.

SOCIAL MOBILITY

Mordecai Richler's *The Apprenticeship of Duddy Kravitz* (Richler, 1959) is one of the classics of modern Canadian literature. Made into a 1974 film starring Richard Dreyfuss as Duddy, it is the story of a poor 18-year-old Jewish Montrealer in the mid-1940s desperately seeking to establish himself in the world. To that end, he waits on tables, smuggles drugs, drives a taxi, produces wedding and bar mitzvah films, and rents out pinball machines. He is an obnoxious charmer with relentless drive, a young man so fixed on making it that he is even willing to sacrifice his girlfriend and his only co-worker to achieve his goals. We cannot help but admire Duddy for his ambition and his artfulness even while being shocked by his guile and his single-mindedness.

Part of what makes *The Apprenticeship of Duddy Kravitz* universally appealing is that it could be a story about anyone on the make. It is not just some immigrants and their children who may start out as pushy little guys engaged in shady practices and unethical behaviour. As Richler reminds us repeatedly, some of the wealthiest establishment families in Canada and elsewhere started out in just this way. Duddy, then, is a universal symbol of "upward mobility"—and the compromises a person must sometimes make to achieve it.

Much of our discussion to this point has focused on how we describe inequality and how we explain its persistence. Now we take up a different, although related, set of questions. Is our position in the system of inequality fixed? To what extent, if at all, are we trapped in a disadvantaged social position or assured of maintaining an advantaged position? At birth, do all people have the same freedom to gain wealth and fame? Are opportunities equally accessible to everyone?

Sociologists use the term *social mobility* to refer to the dynamics of the system of inequality and, in particular, to movement up and down the stratification system. If we think about inequality as either a hierarchy of more or less privileged positions or a set of higher and lower social classes, an important question is how much opportunity people have to change positions. Typically, change has been measured using one of two benchmarks: your first position in the hierarchy (your first full-time job) or the position of your parents in the hierarchy. Comparing your first job to your current job is an examination of occupational or **intragenerational mobility**. Comparing the occupation(s) of parents to their children's current occupation is an examination of the inheritance of social position or **intergenerational mobility**.

Whichever benchmark is used, social mobility analysts are interested in the openness or fluidity of society. In open or fluid societies, there is greater equality of access to all positions in the hierarchy of inequality. Regardless of your social origins, in more open societies you are more likely to rise or fall to a position that reflects your capabilities. In contrast, in closed or rigid societies, your social origins determine where you are located in the hierarchy of inequality. In such societies, poverty begets poverty, wealth begets wealth; being born into a particular position is a life sentence. Laws ensured that peasants remained peasants and lords remained lords in medieval Europe. Religion ensured that that Brahmins remained Brahmins and untouchables remained untouchables in the Indian caste system (Box 8.2 on page 206).

More recently, societies have become more open in that social origin does not completely determine one's fate. Think about the changes in Canadian society over the last century. A mainly agrarian, resource-based economy has transformed into an advanced, postindustrial country. We have experienced substantial growth in well-paying occupations in finance, marketing, management, and the professions. To what extent have people from all walks of life, from all economic backgrounds, been able to benefit from this transformation? This question introduces a second, related theme to discussions of mobility—equality of opportunity.

As you can imagine from our earlier discussion, in the 1950s and 1960s proponents of the functional theory of stratification and human capital theory thought that equality of opportunity would become the rule. They argued that as more and more skilled jobs are created in the new economy, the best and the brightest must rise to the top to take those jobs and perform them diligently. We would then move from a society based on *ascription* to one based on *achievement*. In a system of inequality based on ascription, your family's station in life determines your own fortunes. In a system based on achievement, your own talents and hard work determine your lot in life. If you achieve good grades in school, your chance of acquiring a professional or managerial job increases.

Other sociologists cautioned that this scenario of high individual social mobility might not follow from the transformation of the economy. They focused on the reproduction of inequality, emphasizing how advantaged families have long attempted to ensure that their

Intragenerational mobility is social mobility that occurs within a single generation.

Intergenerational mobility is social mobility that occurs between generations.

BOX 8.2

Sociology at the Movies

DISTRICT 9

In 1982, a massive spacecraft descended on Johannesburg, South Africa. It contained more than a million malnourished and disoriented aliens. Pressured by international political forces, the South African government established an aid organization to relocate these extraterrestrial refugees from their home ship to a temporary zone just outside Johannesburg. It was called District 9.

At first, the South African government supported and protected District 9 residents. However, as the years passed, the area degenerated into a militarized slum. Popular opinion turned against the aliens because of the costs associated with feeding and policing them. Facing the threat of civil unrest, the government hired Multi-National United, a private weapons manufacturing and security corporation, to evict the aliens from District 9 and move them to a reservation 320 kilometres away.

Although a work of science fiction, the dynamic between humans and aliens in District 9 is

Scene from *District 9*

a reality that has been played out between human races many times. It is fitting that South Africa was selected as the setting for this alien encounter, since that country's policy of apartheid forced its disempowered black population to "resettle" away from the major cities in designated townships, more appropriately called slums, beginning in 1948. Under apartheid, the white minority enjoyed the best jobs and other privileges, and they consigned the large black majority to menial jobs. Apartheid also prevented marriage between blacks and whites and erected separate public facilities for members of the two races. Asians and people of "mixed race" enjoyed privileges between these two extremes. Although outlawed in 1992, the legacy of apartheid continues in racial divisions and tensions that pervade South Africa. The historical record shows that, in South Africa and elsewhere, we have created systems of social stratification that treat our fellow humans little better than the aliens are treated in *District 9*.

offspring inherit their advantages (Collins, 1979). On the world stage, Blossfeld and Shavit (1993) demonstrated that in 11 of 13 advanced industrial countries, little evidence supports the view that there is greater equality of opportunity in societies with expanding education systems (Sweden and the Netherlands are the two exceptions). In short, the openness or fluidity of the system of inequality did not increase over the last half of the twentieth century.

Richard Wanner (1999) tested these ideas using Canadian data. He set himself the task of examining whether the growth of education—more high schools, colleges, and universities—benefited people from all social backgrounds equally. He reasoned that if ascription is weaker now than in previous decades, then parents' **socioeconomic status (SES)**—an index combining income, education, and occupational prestige data—should now have less effect on a child's education than it used to have. If in earlier decades the chances of children from poor families going to university were small, these chances should have increased in more recent decades if ascription weakened. As measures of socioeconomic background, Wanner used mother's and father's education and father's occupation. He tested his central question by using detailed information from a sample of 31 500 Canadians.

Wanner found that class-based ascription still operates strongly. Despite the fact that more Canadians are acquiring more years of schooling and more degrees than ever before, the long arm of family socioeconomic background continues to exert a strong hold on educational attainment. The link between family advantage and children's educational achievement has not weakened.

Explanations for how and why this link remains strong remain a matter of controversy (Davies, 1999). The school system has become increasingly differentiated. Students from lower socioeconomic backgrounds tend to predominate in high school vocational programs and college diploma programs. Students from higher socioeconomic backgrounds typically attend university. Also, new high school programs have proliferated. These include storefront schools for "at-risk" students in poorer neighbourhoods, language-immersion streams, private schools, and enriched learning tracks. These types of schools tend to enrol students from different socioeconomic backgrounds. In other words, educational opportunities are now more numerous for everyone, but they are highly stratified and they therefore perpetuate inequalities rather than erasing them.

Evidence also shows that children from different socioeconomic backgrounds tend to have different levels of preparedness for school (Ross, Roberts, and Scott, 2000). Children from households with incomes below $20 000 are 4.5 times as likely as children from families earning $50 000 a year or more to experience delayed vocabulary development. Moreover, because low-income families tend to live in the same neighbourhoods, such students often have poorly prepared classmates (Hertzman, 2000). On the somewhat brighter side, the effect of family socioeconomic status on literacy is less pronounced in Canada than in most other rich countries (OECD, 2001).

Sociologists distinguish "equality of opportunity" from "equality of condition" to emphasize this last point. Equality of opportunity focuses on the chances of participation, while equality of condition focuses on the chances of succeeding. Although everyone might have the opportunity to attend school and perform well, not everyone is able to take advantage of the opportunity. Coming to kindergarten hungry or not enjoying high-quality child care before the age of five affects how well children perform in the first years of formal education. By way of analogy, we may all be able to enter the race, but if you come with track shoes and good coaching and I come with boots and no coaching, your chances of winning are higher, assuming that we have equal athletic skills.

Socioeconomic status (SES) combines income, education, and occupational prestige data in a single index of a person's position in the socioeconomic hierarchy.

Summing Up

- Socioeconomic status (SES) is a conventional measure of social ranking, based on a combination of information about income, education, and occupational prestige.
- Social rankings change both within and between generations, but less upward mobility takes place than is commonly believed.

PERCEPTION OF CLASS INEQUALITY

We expect you have had some strong reactions to our review of sociological theories and research on social stratification. You may therefore find it worthwhile to reflect more systematically on your own attitudes to social inequality. To start with, do you consider the family in which you grew up to have been lower class, working class, middle class, or upper class? Do you think the gaps between classes in Canadian society are big, moderate, or small? How strongly do you agree or disagree with the view that big gaps between classes are needed to motivate people to work hard and maintain national prosperity? How strongly do you agree or disagree with the view that inequality persists because it benefits the rich and the powerful? How strongly do you agree or disagree with the view that inequality persists because ordinary people don't join together to get rid of it? Answering these questions will help you clarify the way you perceive and evaluate the Canadian class structure and your place in it. If you take note of your answers, you can compare them with the responses of representative samples of Canadians, which we review below.

Surveys show that few Canadians have trouble placing themselves in the class structure when asked to do so. Most Canadians consider themselves to be middle class or working class. They also think that the gaps between classes are relatively large. But do Canadians think that these big gaps are needed to motivate people to work hard, thus increasing their own wealth and the wealth of the nation? Some Canadians think so, but most do not. A survey conducted in 18 countries, including Canada, asked more than 22 000 respondents if large differences in income are necessary for national prosperity. Canadians were among the most likely to disagree with that view (Pammett, 1997: 77).

So, Canadians know that they live in a class-divided society. They also tend to think that deep class divisions are not necessary for national prosperity. Why then do Canadians think inequality persists? The 18-nation survey cited above sheds light on this issue. One of the survey questions asked respondents how strongly they agree or disagree with the view that "inequality continues because it benefits the rich and powerful." Most Canadians agreed with that statement. Only about a quarter of them disagreed with it in any way. Another question asked respondents how strongly they agree or disagree with the view that "inequality continues because ordinary people don't join together to get rid of it." Again, most Canadians agreed, with less than a third disagreeing in any way (Pammett, 1997: 77–78).

Despite widespread awareness of inequality and considerable dissatisfaction with it, most Canadians are opposed to the government playing an active role in reducing inequality. Most do not want government to provide citizens with a basic income. They tend to oppose government job-creation programs. They even resist the idea that government should reduce income differences through taxation (Pammett, 1997: 81). Most Canadians remain individualistic and self-reliant. On the whole, they persist in the belief that opportunities for mobility are abundant and that it is up to the individual to make something of those opportunities by means of talent and effort.

Significantly, however, all the attitudes summarized above vary by class position. For example, discontent with the level of inequality in Canadian society is stronger at the bottom of the stratification system than at the top. The belief that Canadian society is full of opportunities for upward mobility is stronger at the top of the class hierarchy than at the bottom. Considerably less opposition to the idea that government should reduce inequality exists as we move down the stratification system. This permits us to conclude that, if Canadians allow inequality to persist, it is because the balance of attitudes—and of power—favours continuity over change. We take up this important theme again in Chapter 14 (Politics), where we discuss the social roots of politics.

Summing Up

- Canadians are aware that considerable social inequality exists and they are dissatisfied with it. However, most Canadians do not favour more government intervention to curb it.

SUMMARY

1. What is the difference between wealth and income? How are they distributed in Canada?
   Wealth is assets minus liabilities. Income is the amount of money earned in a given period. Substantial inequality of both wealth and income exists in Canada, but inequality of wealth is greater. Both types of inequality have increased over the past quarter of a century. Canada is less unequal than the United States is in both regards, but Canada is more unequal in income than are many Western European countries.

2. What are the main differences between Marx's and Weber's theories of stratification?
   Marx's theory of stratification distinguishes classes on the basis of their role in the productive process. It predicts inevitable conflict between bourgeoisie and proletariat and the birth of a communist system. Weber distinguished between classes based on their "market relations." His model of stratification included four main classes. He argued that class consciousness may develop under some circumstances but is by no means inevitable. Weber also emphasized prestige and power as important non-economic sources of inequality.

3. What is the functional theory of stratification?
   Davis and Moore's functional theory of stratification argues that (1) some jobs are more important than others, (2) people have to make sacrifices to train for important jobs, and (3) inequality is required to motivate people to undergo these sacrifices. In this sense, stratification is "functional."

4. Is stratification based only on economic criteria?
   No. Politics often influences the shape of stratification systems by changing the distribution of income, welfare entitlements, and property rights. Prestige is also an important basis of stratification.

5. How do Canadians view the class system?
   Most Canadians are aware of the existence of the class system and their place in it. They believe that large inequalities are not necessary to achieve national prosperity. Most Canadians also believe that inequality persists because it serves the interests of the most advantaged members of society and because the disadvantaged do not join together to change things. However, most Canadians disapprove of government intervention to lower the level of inequality.

KEY TERMS

authority (p. 204)

bourgeoisie (p. 200)

class (p. 200)

class consciousness (p. 200)

cultural capital (p. 192)

feudalism (p. 199)

functional theory of stratification
 (p. 201)

human capital (p. 191)

intergenerational mobility (p. 205)

intragenerational mobility (p. 205)

low-income cutoff (p. 195)

parties (p. 201)

petite bourgeoisie (p. 200)

power (p. 203)

proletariat (p. 200)

social capital (p. 192)

social stratification (p. 186)

socioeconomic status (SES) (p. 207)

status groups (p. 201)

WEB RESOURCES

Companion Website for This Book

http://www.compass4e.nelson.com

Begin by clicking on the Student Resources section of the website. Next, select the chapter you are studying from the pull-down menu. From the Student Resources page you have easy access to additional Weblinks and other resources. The website also has many useful tips to aid you in your study of sociology, including practice tests for each chapter.

InfoTrac® Search Terms

These search terms are provided to assist you in beginning to conduct research on this topic by visiting http://www.infotrac-college.com:

class

poverty

class consciousness

social mobility

global inequality

CHAPTER

9

Globalization, Inequality, and Development

IN THIS CHAPTER, YOU WILL LEARN THAT

- People and institutions across the planet are becoming increasingly aware of, and dependent on, one another. Sociologists call this tendency *globalization*.

- Globalization creates a world that is more homogeneous in some ways and more localized in others. Globalization also generates its own opposition.

- Globalization is a process that became highly significant along with the development of capitalism and world exploration about 500 years ago.

- Global inequality has increased tremendously since industrialization and is still increasing in some respects today.

- Global inequality has two competing explanations. One stresses how the deficiencies of some societies contribute to their own lack of economic growth. The other stresses how the history of social relations among countries enriched some nations at the expense of others.

- For identifiable reasons, some non-Western countries have successfully industrialized.

- Globalization has both benefits and disadvantages. Various reforms—especially more democratic participation in economic decision making—can increase the benefits.

Painting: Deigo Rivera. Photo by Enrique Gomez/Dreamstime.com

THE CREATION OF A GLOBAL VILLAGE

Jeremy Horne/Getty Images

Suppose you want to travel to Europe. You might check the Internet to buy an inexpensive plane ticket. You would then get your passport and perhaps download a guidebook. Depending on the kind of person you are, you might spend a lot of time planning and preparing for the trip or you might just pack the basics—the passport, the ticket, a knapsack full of clothes, your credit card—and embark on an adventure.

How different things were just 30 years ago. Then, you probably would have gone to see a travel agent first, as most people did when they wanted airline tickets. Next, you would have had to make sure you had not only a valid passport but also visas for quite a few countries. Obtaining a visa was a tedious process. You had to travel to an embassy or a consulate or mail in your passport. Then you had to wait days or weeks to receive the visa. Today, fewer countries require visas.

The next step in organizing the European trip would involve withdrawing money from your bank account. ATMs were rare, so you had to stand in line at the bank before getting to a teller. Next, you had to take the withdrawn money to the office of a company that sold traveller's cheques because banks did not sell them. When you arrived in Europe, you needed to have local currency, which you could buy only from large banks and money-changers. Few students had credit cards 30 years ago. Even if you were one of the lucky few, you could use it only in large stores and restaurants in big cities. If you ran out of cash and traveller's cheques, you were in big trouble. You could look for another Canadian tourist and try to convince him or her to take your personal cheque. Alternatively, you could go to a special telephone for international calls, phone home, and have money wired to a major bank for you. That was time consuming and expensive. Today, most people have credit and ATM cards. Even in small European towns, you can charge most of your shopping and restaurant bills on your credit card without using local currency. If you need local currency,

Currency conversion, then and now

Chuck Savage/ Corbis

Ariel Skelley/ Corbis

you go to an ATM and withdraw money from your home bank account or charge it to your credit card; the ATM automatically converts your dollars to local currency.

Most European cities and towns today have many North American–style supermarkets. Speakers of English are numerous, so social interaction with Europeans is easier. You would have to try hard to get very far from a McDonald's. It is also easy to receive news and entertainment from back home though the Internet. In contrast, each country you visited 30 years ago would have featured a distinct shopping experience. English speakers were rarer. North American fast-food outlets were practically nonexistent. Apart from the *International Herald-Tribune*, which was available only in larger towns and cities, North American news was hard to come by. TV featured mostly local programming. You might see an American show now and then, but it would not be in English.

Clearly, the world seems a much smaller place today than it did 30 years ago. Some people go so far as to say that we have created a "global village." But what exactly does that mean? Is the creation of a global village uniformly beneficial? Or does it have a downside too?

The Triumphs and Tragedies of Globalization

As suggested by our two imaginary trips to Europe, separated by a mere 30 years, people throughout the world are now linked together as never before (Table 9.1, and Figure 9.1 on page 214).

Consider these facts:

- International telecommunication has become easy and inexpensive. In 1930, a three-minute New York–London phone call cost more than $250[1] in today's dollars and only a minority of North Americans had telephones in their homes. In 2011, you could talk free on Skype for as long as you want to anywhere with an Internet connection.
- Between 1982 and 2008, when the world's population increased by 47 percent, the number of international tourists increased by 233 percent.
- International trade and investment have increased rapidly. For example, from 1982 to 2008, worldwide investment across national borders ("foreign direct investment") increased by a remarkable 2583 percent.
- Many more international organizations and agreements now span the globe. In 1981, about 14 000 international organizations existed. By 2009, there were four-and-a-half times as many. Individual nation-states give up some of their independence when they join international organizations or sign international agreements. For example, when Canada, the United States, and Mexico entered the North American Free Trade Agreement (NAFTA) in 1994, they agreed that trade disputes would be settled by a three-country tribunal. The autonomy of nation-states has eroded somewhat with the creation of many such "transnational" bodies and treaties.

	1981/2	2007/9
International tourist arrivals	277 million	924 million
Foreign direct investment (billions of dollars)	59	1 538
Internet hosts	213	681 million
Number of international organizations	14 273	63 912

TABLE 9.1

Indicators of Globalization, 1981/2–2007/9

Sources: "Foreign direct investment..." (2008); "International tourism..." (2009); Internet Systems Consortium (2010); Union of International Associations (2001, 2010); United Nations Conference on Trade and Development (2007: xv); United Nations World Tourism Organization (2007a).

FIGURE 9.1

Foreign Visitors 2007,
Top 50 Destinations

International tourism leads
to the sense that the world
forms one society. However,
exposure to international tourism
is higher in some countries than
in others. This map shows the
number of foreign visitors who
travelled to each country. Which
countries are most exposed to
international tourism? Which
countries are least exposed?
What consequences might
differential exposure have for
people's self-identity?

Source: UNWTO World Tourism
Barometer. 2008. 6, 2
(http://www.tourismroi.com/
Content_Attachments/27670/
File_633513750035785076.pdf).

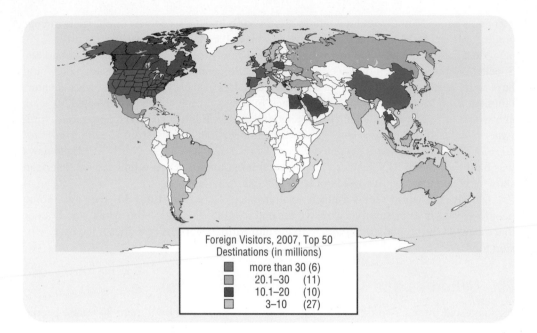

Foreign Visitors, 2007, Top 50
Destinations (in millions)

- more than 30 (6)
- 20.1–30 (11)
- 10.1–20 (10)
- 3–10 (27)

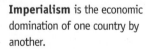

Imperialism is the economic
domination of one country by
another.

• The number of Internet hosts increased from a mere 213 to 681 million between 1981
and 2009, connecting nearly two billion people from around the world through instant
messaging, email, file transfers, websites, and videoconferencing.

The benefits of the rapid movement of capital, commodities, culture, and people across
national boundaries should be clear from comparing our imaginary trips to Europe today
and 30 years ago. What was a struggle for a North American traveller three decades ago is
easy today. In this and many other ways, globalization has transformed and improved the
way we live.

Yet not everyone is happy with globalization. Inequality between rich and poor countries remains staggering. In some respects, it is increasing. Arguably, rather than spreading
the wealth, globalized industries and technologies may be turning the world into a more
unequal place. Many people also oppose globalization because it may be hurting local
cultures and the natural environment. Some anti-globalization activists even suggest that
globalization is a form of **imperialism**, the economic domination of one country by another.
From their point of view, globalization puts the entire world under the control of powerful
commercial interests. Moreover, it contributes to the homogenization of the world, the cultural domination of less powerful by more powerful countries. It is one thing, they say, for
Indonesians and Italians to have closer ties to North Americans, but is it desirable that they
become *like* North Americans?

In the next section, we first explore what globalization is and how it affects our everyday lives. To make the impact of globalization concrete, we trace the global movement of
a commodity familiar to everyone: athletic shoes. This exercise illuminates the many ways
in which far-flung individuals are bound together. Next, we consider the causes of globalization, emphasizing the importance of political, economic, and technological factors. We then
analyze whether globalization is forcing different parts of the world to become alike. We also
explore how the very process of globalization generates its own opposition. Finally, we take
a longer view and examine the roots of globalization historically.

The second task we set ourselves is to examine the nature and causes of global
inequality. We note that the gap between rich and poor countries is wide and that by
some measures it is getting wider. We then discuss the major theories that seek to explain
global inequality and conclude that poor countries are not doomed to remain poor. We
close by considering what people can do to alleviate global inequality and poverty.

Summing Up

- Globalization involves the rapidly increased movement of people, information, commodities, culture, and capital across national borders.
- While globalization has transformed and improved many aspects of life, it is also generating opposition based on fear of growing inequality and the erosion of local cultures.

THE SOURCES AND CONTOURS OF GLOBALIZATION

Globalization in Everyday Life

When we buy a commodity, we often tap into a **global commodity chain**, a worldwide "network of labour and production processes, whose end result is a finished commodity" (Hopkins and Wallerstein, 1986: 159).

We can better understand the web of global social relations by tracing the way one commodity—athletic shoes—binds consumers and producers in a global commodity chain. Until the 1970s, most sports shoes were manufactured in the United States. Today, such corporations as Nike produce all their shoes abroad. Manufacturing plants moved because governments eliminated many of the laws, regulations, and taxes that acted as barriers to foreign investment and trade. Consequently, Nike and other manufacturers started setting up overseas plants, where they could take advantage of low labour costs. The result was a new international division of labour. High-wage management, finance, design, and marketing services were concentrated in the United States and other advanced industrial countries, low-wage manufacturing in the less developed, industrializing countries (Fröbel, Heinrichs, and Kreye, 1980; see Chapter 13, Work and the Economy). Not just Nike but General Motors, General Electric, and many other large corporations closed some or all their plants in the United States and Canada (high-wage countries) and established factories in Mexico, Indonesia, and other developing economies.

In Vietnam, Nike workers make 20 cents an hour. At that rate, the labor cost for a $100 pair of Nikes is 37 cents ("Campaign for Labour Rights," 2004). Many Indonesian workers must work as much as six hours a day overtime. Reports of beatings and sexual harassment by managers are common. When the Indonesian workers tried to form a union, organizers were fired and the military was brought in to restore order (LaFeber, 1999: 142). When Michael Jordan became Nike's poster boy in 1976, his $20 million endorsement fee was bigger than the combined yearly wages of all 25 000 Indonesian workers who made the shoes (LaFeber, 1999: 107). Kobe Bryant's endorsement fee, negotiated in 2005, was $45 million ("Kobe Bryant," 2005).

When people buy a pair of Nike athletic shoes, they insert themselves in a global commodity chain. Of course, the buyers do not create the social relations that exploit Indonesian labour and enrich Kobe Bryant. Still, it would be difficult to deny the buyers' part, however small, in helping those social relations persist.

Sociology makes us aware of the complex web of social relations and interactions in which we are embedded. The sociological imagination allows us to link our biography with history and social structure. Globalization extends the range of that linkage, connecting our biography with global history and global social structure.

A **global commodity chain** is a worldwide network of labour and production processes whose end result is a finished commodity.

The Sources of Globalization

Few people doubt the significance of globalization. Although social scientists disagree on its exact causes, most of them stress the importance of technology, politics, and economics.

Technology

Technological progress has made it possible to move things and information over long distances quickly and inexpensively. The introduction of commercial jets radically shortened the time necessary for international travel, and its cost dropped dramatically after the 1950s. Similarly, various means of communication, such as telephone, fax, and email, allow us to reach people around the globe inexpensively and almost instantly. Whether we think of international trade or international travel, technological progress is an important part of the globalization story. Without modern technology, it is hard to imagine how globalization would be possible.

Politics

Globalization could not occur without advanced technology, but advanced technology by itself could never bring globalization about. Think of the contrast between North Korea and South Korea. Both countries are about the same distance from North America. You have probably heard of major South Korean companies, like Hyundai and Samsung, and may have met people from South Korea or Korean Canadians. Yet unless you are an expert on North Korea, you probably will have had no contact with North Korea and its people. We have the same technological means to reach the two Koreas. Yet although we enjoy strong relations and intense interaction with South Korea, Canada did not extend diplomatic recognition to North Korea until 2001. As of 2011 Canada had not yet opened an embassy there. The reason is political. The South Korean government has been an ally of Canada since the Korean War in the early 1950s and has sought greater political, economic, and cultural integration with the outside world. North Korea, in an effort to preserve its authoritarian political system and communist economic system, has remained isolated from the rest of the world. As this example shows, politics is important in determining the level of globalization.

Economics

Finally, economics is an important source of globalization. As we saw in our discussion of global commodity chains and the new international division of labour, industrial capitalism is always seeking new markets, higher profits, and lower labour costs. Put differently, capitalist competition has been a major spur to international integration (Gilpin, 2001; Stopford and Strange, 1991).

Transnational corporations—also called multinational or international corporations—are the most important agents of globalization in the world today. They are different from traditional corporations in five ways (Gilpin, 2001; LaFeber, 1999):

1. Traditional corporations rely on domestic labour and domestic production. Transnational corporations depend increasingly on foreign labour and foreign production.
2. Traditional corporations extract natural resources or manufacture industrial goods. Transnational corporations increasingly emphasize skills and advances in design, technology, and management.
3. Traditional corporations sell to domestic markets. Transnational corporations depend increasingly on world markets.
4. Traditional corporations rely on established marketing and sales outlets. Transnational corporations depend increasingly on massive advertising campaigns.
5. Traditional corporations work with or under national governments. Transnational corporations are increasingly autonomous from national governments.

Technological, political, and economic factors do not work independently in leading to globalization. For example, governments often promote economic competition to help transnational corporations win global markets. Consider Philip Morris, the company that makes Marlboro cigarettes (Barnet and Cavanagh, 1994). Philip Morris introduced the

Transnational corporations are large businesses that rely increasingly on foreign labour and foreign production; skills and advances in design, technology, and management; world markets; and massive advertising campaigns. They are increasingly autonomous from national governments.

Marlboro brand in 1954. It soon became the best-selling cigarette in the United States, partly because of the success of an advertising campaign featuring the Marlboro Man. The Marlboro Man symbolized the rugged individualism of the American frontier, and he became one of the most widely recognized icons in American advertising. Philip Morris was the smallest of the country's six largest tobacco companies in 1954, but it rode on the popularity of the Marlboro Man to become the country's biggest tobacco company by the 1970s.

John Van Hasselt/Corbis Sygma

In the 1970s, the anti-smoking campaign began to have an impact, leading to slumping domestic sales. Philip Morris and other tobacco companies decided to pursue globalization as a way out of the doldrums. Economic competition and slick advertising alone did not win global markets for American cigarette makers, however. The tobacco companies needed political influence to make cigarettes one of the country's biggest and most profitable exports. To that end, the U.S. trade representative in the Reagan administration, Clayton Yeutter, worked energetically to dismantle trade barriers in Japan, Taiwan, South Korea, and other countries. He threatened legal action for breaking international trade law and said the United States would restrict Asian exports unless these countries allowed the sale of American cigarettes. Such actions were critically important in globalizing world trade in cigarettes. In 1986, the commercial counsellor of the U.S. Embassy in Seoul, South Korea, wrote to the public affairs manager of Philip Morris Asia as follows: "I want to emphasize that the embassy and the various U.S. government agencies in Washington will keep the interests of Philip Morris and the other American cigarette manufacturers in the forefront of our daily concerns" (quoted in Frankel, 1996). As the case of Philip Morris illustrates, economics and politics typically work hand in hand to globalize the world.

"I want to emphasize that the embassy and the various U.S. government agencies in Washington will keep the interests of Philip Morris and the other American cigarette manufacturers in the forefront of our daily concerns."

A World Like the United States?

We have seen that globalization links people around the world, often in ways that are not obvious. We have also seen that the sources of globalization lie in closely connected technological, economic, and political forces. Now let us consider one of the consequences of globalization, the degree to which globalization is homogenizing the world and, in particular, making the whole world look like the United States (see Figure 9.2).

FIGURE 9.2

The Size and Influence of the American Economy

This map will help you gauge the enormous importance of the United States in globalization because it emphasizes just how large the American economy is. The economy of each American state is as big as that of a whole country. Specifically, this map shows how the GDP of various countries compares with that of each state. For example, the GDP of California is equal to that of France, the GDP of New Jersey is equal to that of Russia, and the GDP of Texas is equal to that of Canada.

Source: From *The Globe and Mail*, March 8, 2003, p. F1. Reprinted with permission from *The Globe and Mail*.

Social Policy: What Do You Think?

SHOULD THE WEST PROMOTE WORLD DEMOCRACY?

"In starting and waging a war, it is not right that matters, but victory," said Adolf Hitler (quoted in "A Survey," 1998: 10). The same mindset rationalizes state brutality today, as we recently saw in Libya and Syria. Cherished ideals, such as political democracy and human rights, are trampled on daily by dictatorships and military governments.

Opinions differ as to what Western governments should do about this situation. One influential argument is that of Samuel Huntington. He argues that Western nations should not be ethnocentric and impose Western values on people in other countries. If there are violations of democratic principles and human rights in these countries, they express in some way the indigenous values of those people. The West should not intervene to stop non-democratic forces and human rights abuses abroad.

Critics of Huntington argue that the ideals of democracy and human rights can be found in non-Western cultures, too. If we explore Asian or African traditions, for instance, we find "respect for the sacredness of life and for human dignity, tolerance of differences, and a desire for liberty, order, fairness and stability" (quoted in "A Survey," 1998: 10). Although Asian and African despots champion supposedly traditional values, people in Asia, Africa, and elsewhere struggle for democracy and human rights. For example, in 2011, the citizens of Tunisia, Egypt, and Libya fought valiantly for democracy and overthrew dictators in what came to be called the "Arab Spring."

What do you think the role of the West should be? Should Western governments promote democracy and human rights? Or should they avoid what Huntington regards as ethnocentrism? Because foreign aid to authoritarian regimes may help non-democratic forces and thereby stifle human rights, should Western countries give foreign aid to such regimes?

Much impressionistic evidence supports the view that globalization homogenizes societies. Many economic and financial institutions around the world now operate in roughly the same way. For instance, transnational organizations, such as the World Bank and the International Monetary Fund, have imposed economic guidelines for developing countries that are similar to those governing advanced industrial countries. In the realm of politics, the United Nations (UN) engages in global governance, whereas Western ideas of democracy, representative government, and human rights have become international ideals (see Box 9.1). In the domain of culture, American icons circle the planet: supermarkets, basketball, Hollywood movies, Disney characters, Coca-Cola, MTV, CNN, McDonald's, and so on.

McDonaldization is a form of rationalization. It refers to the spread of the principles of fast-food restaurants—efficiency, predictability, and calculability—to all spheres of life.

Indeed, one common shorthand expression for the homogenizing effects of globalization is **McDonaldization**. George Ritzer (1996: 1) defines McDonaldization as "the process by which the principles of the fast-food restaurant are coming to dominate more and more sectors of American society as well as of the rest of the world." The idea of McDonaldization extends Weber's concept of rationalization, the application of the most efficient means to achieve given ends (see Chapter 3, Culture). Because of McDonaldization, says Ritzer, the values of efficiency, calculability, and predictability have spread from North America to the entire planet and from fast-food restaurants to virtually all spheres of life. As Ritzer shows, McDonald's leaves nothing to chance. McDonald's is even field-testing self-service kiosks in which an automated machine cooks and bags French fries while a vertical grill takes patties from the freezer and grills them to your liking (Carpenter, 2003). Significantly, McDonald's now does most of its business outside the United States. You can find McDonald's restaurants in nearly every country in the world. McDonaldization has come to stand for the global spread of values associated with the United States and its business culture.

However, anyone familiar with symbolic interactionism should be immediately suspicious of sweeping claims about the homogenizing effects of globalization. After all, it is a central principle of symbolic interactionism that people create their social circumstances and do not merely react to them, that they negotiate their identities and do not easily settle for identities imposed on them by others. Accordingly, some analysts find fault with the view that globalization is making the world a more homogeneous place based on North American values. They argue that people always interpret globalizing forces in terms of local conditions and traditions. Globalization, they say, may in fact sharpen some local differences. They have invented the term **glocalization** to describe the simultaneous homogenization of some aspects of life and the strengthening of some local differences under the impact of globalization (Shaw, 2000).

They note, for example, that McDonald's serves different foods in different countries (Watson, 1997). A burger at a Taiwanese McDonald's may be eaten with betel nuts. Vegetarian burgers are available at Indian McDonald's and kosher burgers are the norm at Israeli McDonald's. Dutch McDonald's serves the popular McKrocket, made of 100 percent beef ragout fried in batter. In Hawaii, McDonald's routinely serve Japanese ramen noodles with their burgers. McDonald's began serving poutine in Quebec, and the practice has spread across Canada to consumers undeterred by McDonald's nutrition guide, which lists a large serving as providing 130 percent of the recommended daily allowance for saturated fat (McDonald's, 2005). Although the Golden Arches may suggest that the world is becoming the same everywhere, once we go through them and sample the fare, we find much that is unique.

Those who see globalization merely as homogenization also ignore the **regionalization** of the world, the division of the world into different and often competing economic, political, and cultural areas. The argument here is that the institutional and cultural integration of countries often falls far short of covering the whole world. Figure 9.3 illustrates one aspect of regionalization. World trade is unevenly distributed across the planet and it is not dominated by just one country. Three main trade blocs exist—an Asian bloc dominated by Japan and China, a North American bloc dominated by the United States, and a European bloc dominated by Germany. These three trade blocs contain just over a fifth of the world's countries but account for more than three-quarters of world economic activity as measured by gross domestic product.[2] Most world trade takes place *within* each of these blocs. Each bloc competes against the others for a larger share of world trade. Politically, we can see regionalization in the growth of the European Union. Most Western European–bloc countries now share the same currency, the euro, and they coordinate economic, political, military, social, and cultural policies.

We conclude that globalization does not have a simple, one-way, and inevitable consequence. In fact, as you will now learn, its impact is often messy. Globalization has generated much criticism and opposition, unleashing a growing anti-globalization movement.

Glocalization is the simultaneous homogenization of some aspects of life and the strengthening of some local differences under the impact of globalization.

Regionalization is the division of the world into different and often competing economic, political, and cultural areas.

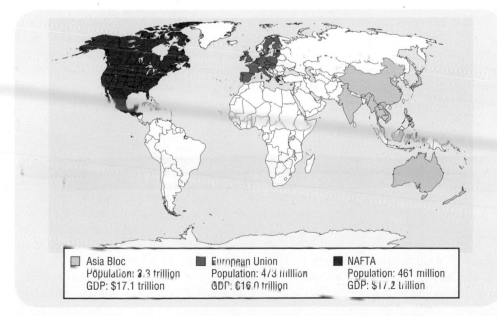

FIGURE 9.3

The Regionalization of World Trade

Source: Geoffrey York. Asian Trade Bloc Would Rival NAFTA, EU. *Globe and Mail*. August 24, 2006. Pg. B1.

Asia Bloc	European Union	NAFTA
Population: 2.3 trillion	Population: 473 million	Population: 461 million
GDP: $17.1 trillion	GDP: €16.0 trillion	GDP: $17.2 trillion

Globalization and Its Discontents: Anti-globalization and Anti-Americanism

In 1996 political scientist Benjamin Barber published an important book titled *Jihad vs. McWorld*. Barber argued that globalization (the making of what he called "McWorld") was generating an anti-globalization reaction, which he called *jihad*. *Jihad* means "striving" or "struggle" in Arabic. Traditionally, Muslims use the term to mean perseverance in achieving a high moral standard. The term can also suggest the idea of a holy war against those who harm Muslims. In the latter sense, it represents an Islamic fundamentalist reaction to globalization. The most spectacular and devastating manifestations of fundamentalist Islamic *jihad* were the September 11, 2001, jet hijackings that led to the crash of an airliner in Pennsylvania and the destruction of the World Trade Center and part of the Pentagon. About 3000 people, 24 of them Canadians, lost their lives as a result of these attacks. The operatives of the al-Qaeda network sought to roll back the forces of globalization by attacking what they thought symbolized the global reach of godless American capitalism.

Islamic fundamentalism is the most far-reaching and violent of many reactions against globalization throughout the world. A less violent and less widespread reaction involved Mexican peasants in the southern state of Chiapas, who staged an armed rebellion against the Mexican government in the 1990s. The government provoked the peasants by turning over land, which was long regarded as communally owned, to commercial farmers so that they could increase their exports to the United States and Canada under the terms of NAFTA. The uprising involved violence and lasted several years.

Finally, we should mention the anti-globalization movement in the advanced industrial countries (Klein, 2000). In 1994 the governments of 134 countries set up the World Trade Organization (WTO) to encourage and referee global commerce. When the WTO met in Seattle in December 1999, some 40000 union activists, environmentalists, supporters of worker and peasant movements in developing countries, and other opponents of transnational corporations staged protests that caused property damage and threatened to disrupt the proceedings. The police and the National Guard replied with concussion grenades, tear gas, rubber bullets, and mass arrests.

Subsequent meetings of the WTO and allied organizations in other countries met with the same sort of protest on the part of anti-globalization forces. These protests were, for the most part, nonviolent, often using street drama to make their point. For example, in spring 2001, 34 heads of government from North, Central, and South America and the Caribbean gathered in Quebec City to discuss the economic integration of the Americas and related matters. Among other tactics, protesters built large wooden catapults that sent volleys of miniature teddy bears at the riot police.

These examples illustrate that although globalization is far from universally welcome, the anti-globalization movement has many currents. Some are extremely violent, some nonviolent. Some reject only what they regard as the excesses of globalization, others reject globalization in its entirety. This complexity supports our view that globalization is not a simple process with predictable consequences. It is a multifaceted phenomenon, the outcome of which is unclear.

The History of Globalization

The extent of globalization since about 1980 is unprecedented in world history. Sociologist Martin Albrow therefore argues that the "global age" is only a few decades old (Albrow, 1997). He dates it from the spread of global awareness and skepticism about the benefits of modernization. However, Albrow and others are inclined to exaggerate the extent of globalization (Gilpin, 2001; Hirst and Thompson, 1999). The nation-state is still a major centre of power in the world. National borders remain important. Most companies concentrate their business in a single country. Most foreign trade occurs between advanced industrial countries and, as we have seen, within distinct regional groups of advanced industrial countries. Many developing countries are poorly integrated in the global economy. Most people in the world have little or no access to the advanced technologies that exemplify globalization, such as email. Cultural differences remain substantial across the planet.

Furthermore, globalization is not as recent as Albrow would have us believe. Anthony Giddens (1990) argues that globalization is the result of industrialization and modernization, which picked up pace in the late nineteenth century. And, in fact, a strong case can be made that the world was highly globalized 100 or more years ago. In the late nineteenth century, people could move across national borders without passports. The extent of international trade and capital flow in the late twentieth century only restored the level achieved before World War I (1914–18; Hirst and Thompson, 1999).

World War I and the Great Depression (1929–39) undermined the globalization of the late nineteenth and early twentieth centuries. They incited racism, protectionism, and military build-up and led to Nazi and communist dictatorships that culminated in World War II (1939–45; Hobsbawm, 1994; James, 2001). International trade and investment plummeted between 1914 and 1945, and governments erected many new barriers to the free movement of people and ideas. A longer view of globalization suggests that globalization is not an inevitable and linear process. Periods of accelerated globalization—including our own—can end.

An even longer historical view leads to additional insight. Some sociologists, such as Roland Robertson (1992), note that globalization is as old as civilization itself and is in fact the *cause* of modernization rather than the other way around. Archaeological remains show that long-distance trade began 5000 years ago. People have been migrating across continents and even oceans for thousands of years. Alexander the Great conquered vast stretches of Europe, western Asia, and northern Africa, while Christianity and Islam spread far beyond their birthplace in the Middle East. All these forces contributed to globalization in Robertson's view.

So is globalization 30, 125, or 5000 years old, as Albrow, Giddens, and Robertson, respectively, suggest? The question has no correct answer. The answer depends on what we want globalization to mean. A short historical view—whether 125 or 30 years—misses the long-term developments that have brought the world's people closer to one another. Yet if we think of globalization as a 5000-year-old phenomenon, the definition and value of the term are diluted.

We prefer to take an intermediate position and think of globalization as a roughly 500-year-old phenomenon. We regard the establishment of colonies and the growth of capitalism as the main forces underlying globalization, and both **colonialism** and capitalism began about 500 years ago, symbolized by Columbus's voyage to the Americas. Colonialism is the direct political control of one country by another. As you will now see, the main advantage of thinking of globalization in this way is that it tells us much about the causes of development or industrialization and the growing gap between rich and poor countries and people. These topics will now be the focus of our attention.

Colonialism involves the control of developing societies by more developed, powerful societies.

Summing Up

- Globalization has been made possible by technological innovations, political efforts, and the unceasing search for new sources of profit.
- Globalization does not necessarily homogenize; local and regional cultural adaptations and trade relationships, and anti-globalization movements, have emerged in reaction to homogenizing forces.
- While international trade and travel took place thousands of years ago, and the pace of globalization since 1980 has been unprecedented, globalization on a wide scale really began 500 years ago in the era of discovery and colonization that preceded the growth of capitalism.

DEVELOPMENT AND UNDERDEVELOPMENT

John Lie decided to study sociology because he was concerned about the poverty and dictatorships he had read about in books and observed during his travels in Asia and Latin America. "Initially," says John, "I thought I would major in economics. In my economics classes, I learned about the importance of birth-control programs to cap population growth, efforts to prevent the runaway growth of cities, and measures to spread Western knowledge, technology, and markets to people in less economically developed countries. My textbooks and professors assumed that if only the less-developed countries would become more like the West, their populations, cities, economies, and societies would experience stable growth. Otherwise, the developing countries were doomed to suffer the triple catastrophe of overpopulation, rapid urbanization, and economic underdevelopment.

"Equipped with this knowledge, I spent a summer in the Philippines working for an organization that offered farmers advice on how to promote economic growth. I assumed that, as in North America, farmers who owned large plots of land and used high technology would be more efficient and better off. Yet I found the most productive villages were those in which most farmers owned *small* plots of land. In such villages, there was little economic inequality. The women in these villages enjoyed low birth rates and the inhabitants were usually happier than were the inhabitants of villages in which there was more inequality.

"As I talked with the villagers, I came to realize that farmers who owned at least some of their own land had an incentive to work hard. The harder they worked, the more they earned. With a higher standard of living, they didn't need as many children to help them on the farm. In contrast, in villages with greater inequality, many farmers owned no land but leased it or worked as farm hands for wealthy landowners. They didn't earn more for working harder, so their productivity and their standard of living were low. They wanted to have more children to increase household income.

"Few Filipino farms could match the productivity of high-tech North American farms, because even large plots were small by North American standards. Much high-tech agricultural equipment would have been useless there. Imagine trying to use a harvesting machine in a plot not much larger than some suburban backyards.

"Thus, my Western assumptions turned out to be wrong. The Filipino farmers I met were knowledgeable and thoughtful about their needs and desires. When I started listening to them, I started understanding the real world of economic development. It was one of the most important sociological lessons I ever learned."

Let us begin our sociological discussion of economic development by examining trends in levels of global inequality. We then discuss two theories of development and underdevelopment, both of which seek to uncover the sources of inequality among nations. Next, we analyze some cases of successful development. Finally, we consider what we can do to alleviate global inequality in light of what we learn from these successful cases.

Levels and Trends in Global Inequality

We learned in Chapter 8 (Social Stratification) that Canada is a highly stratified society. If we shift our attention from the national to the global level, we find an even more dramatic gap between rich and poor. In a Manhattan restaurant, pet owners can treat their cats to $100-a-plate birthday parties. In Cairo (Egypt) and Manila (the Philippines), garbage dumps are home to entire families who sustain themselves by picking through the refuse. People who travel outside the 20 or so highly industrialized countries of North America, Western Europe, Japan, and Australia often encounter scenes of unforgettable poverty and misery. The UN calls the level of inequality worldwide "grotesque" (United Nations, 2002: 19). The term is justified when you consider that that the citizens of the 20 richest countries spend more on cosmetics or alcohol or ice cream or pet food than it would take to provide basic education, or water and sanitation, or basic health and nutrition for everyone in the world (Table 9.2).

Photo by Miro Cernetig, *Globe & Mail*, Toronto, Canada

A half-hour's drive from the centre of Manila, the capital of the Philippines, an estimated 70 000 Filipinos live on a 22-hectare (55-acre) mountain of rotting garbage, 45 metres (150 feet) high. It is infested with flies, rats, dogs, and disease. On a lucky day, residents can earn up to $5 retrieving scraps of metal and other valuables. On a rainy day, the mountain of garbage is especially treacherous. In July 2000 an avalanche buried 300 people alive. People who live on the mountain of garbage call it "The Promised Land."

Has global inequality increased or decreased over time? That depends on how you measure it. If you define inequality as the difference between the average income of rich and poor countries, you find that income inequality was very high in 1950 and rose to an even higher level by 2005 (see the bottom line in Figure 9.4 on page 224). However, this procedure gives equal weight to each country, whether it is a behemoth like China or a tiny city-state like Monaco.

It makes sense to count populous countries more heavily in our calculations. Doing so reveals that income inequality between countries was extremely high in 1950 but declined thereafter, mainly because China started to prosper in the 1980s and India and Brazil

Good or Service	Annual Cost (in US$ billions)
Basic education for everyone in the world	6
Cosmetics in the United States	8
Water and sanitation for everyone in the world	9
Ice cream in Europe	11
Reproductive health for all women in the world	12
Perfumes in Europe and the United States	12
Basic health and nutrition for everyone in the world	13
Pet foods in Europe and the United States	17
Business entertainment in Japan	35
Cigarettes in Europe	50
Alcoholic drinks in Europe	105
Narcotic drugs in the world	400
Military spending in the world	780

TABLE 9.2

Global Priorities: Annual Cost of Various Goods and Services (in US$ billion)

Note: Items in italics represent estimates of what they would cost to achieve. Other items represent estimated actual cost. These figures are for 1998. More recent data are not available for many of the items listed here, but our guess is that more than a decade later the figures were very roughly twice as large.

Source: From United Nations, *Human Development Report 1998*, (Oxford University Press, NY: 1998), p. 37.

FIGURE 9.4

Three Concepts of World Inequality

A Gini index of 0 indicates that every income recipient receives exactly the same amount of income. A Gini index of 1.0 indicates that a single income recipient receives all of the income. To put things in perspective, note that the Gini index of inequality for individuals worldwide is about 0.70, while the Gini index for individuals in Brazil, which has one of the highest levels of inequality of any country, is about 0.52.

Source: Milanovic, Branko. 2010. "The Consequences of Inequality and Wealth Distribution." Accessed February 16, 2010 (http://ineteconomics.org/people/participants/branko-milanovic).

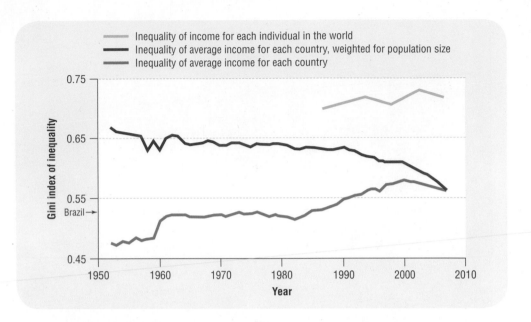

followed suit a little later (see the middle line in Figure 9.4). The emergence of large, new middle classes in these populous countries caused the level of income inequality among countries weighted for population size to fall. Nevertheless, economic conditions in some parts of the world, notably sub-Saharan Africa, deteriorated (see Figure 9.5).

A problem remains. Comparing country averages ignores the fact that poor people live in rich countries and rich people live in poor countries. Country averages fail to capture the extent of inequality between the richest of the rich and the poorest of the poor. That is why it makes most sense to examine income inequality among *individuals* rather than countries. Doing so, we discover that income inequality was astoundingly steep in 1985 and rose even higher over the next 20 years (see the top line in Figure 9.4). Today, the richest 1 percent of the world's population (about 70 million people) earn as much as the bottom 66 percent (about 4.6 billion people) (Milovic, 2010). Of the world's 7 billion people, 1 billion live on less than $1 a day, and more than 2.6 billion on less than $2 a day (see Figure 9.6). Most desperately poor people are women. On the slightly brighter side, the absolute number of people in the world living on less than $1 a day peaked in 1950 and then started declining.

FIGURE 9.5

Gross Domestic Product per Person, Sub-Saharan Africa and High-Income Countries, 1975–2010

Note: Gross domestic product is the dollar value of goods and services produced in a country in a year. The 1975 data are in 2005 dollars adjusted for purchasing power, while the 2010 data are in 2008 dollars adjusted for purchasing power.

Source: United Nations. 2010. "Human development statistical tables." *Human Development Report 2010*. http://hdr.undp.org/en/media/HDR_2010_EN_Tables.pdf (accessed 16 November 2010).

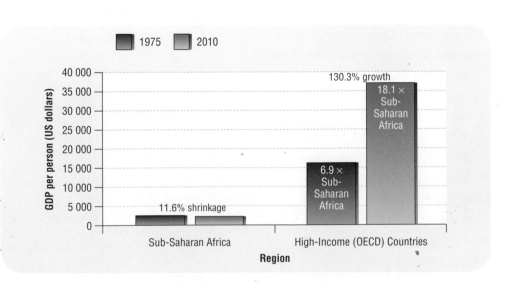

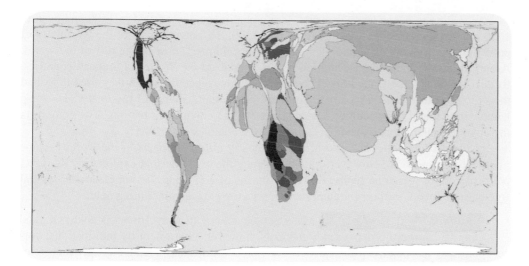

FIGURE 9.6

World Poverty

Note: The size of each country is proportional to the percentage of people in that country living on US$2 a day or less in purchasing power.

Source: University of Sheffield. 2006. "Absolute Poverty." © Copyright SASI Group (University of Sheffield).

In percentage terms, the proportion of people living on less than $1 a day fell from about 84 percent in 1820 to less than 20 percent today (United Nations, 2007: 24).

Statistics never speak for themselves. We need theories to explain them. Let us now outline and critically assess the two main theories that seek to explain the origins and persistence of global inequality.

Modernization Theory: A Functionalist Approach

Two main sociological theories claim to explain global inequality. The first, **modernization theory**, is a variant of functionalism. According to modernization theory, global inequality results from various dysfunctional characteristics of poor societies themselves. Specifically, modernization theorists say the citizens of poor societies lack sufficient *capital* to invest in Western-style agriculture and industry. They lack rational, Western-style *business techniques* of marketing, accounting, sales, and finance. As a result, their productivity and profitability remain low. They lack stable, Western-style *governments* that could provide a secure framework for investment. Finally, they lack a Western *mentality*: values that stress the need for savings, investment, innovation, education, high achievement, and self-control in having children (Inkeles and Smith, 1976; Rostow, 1960). Societies characterized by these dysfunctions are poor. It follows that people living in rich countries can best help their poor cousins by transferring Western culture and capital to them and eliminating the dysfunctions. Only then will the poor countries be able to cap population growth, stimulate democracy, and invigorate agricultural and industrial production. Government-to-government foreign aid can accomplish some of this. Much work also needs to be done to encourage Western businesses to invest directly in poor countries and to increase trade between rich and poor countries.

Modernization theory holds that economic underdevelopment results from poor countries lacking Western attributes. These attributes include Western values, business practices, levels of investment capital, and stable governments.

Dependency Theory: A Conflict Approach

Proponents of **dependency theory**, a variant of conflict theory, have been quick to point out the chief flaw in modernization theory (Baran, 1957; Cardoso and Faletto, 1979; Wallerstein, 1974–89). For the past 500 years, the most powerful countries in the world deliberately impoverished the less powerful countries. Focusing on internal characteristics blames the victim rather than the perpetrator of the crime. It follows that an adequate theory of global inequality should not focus on the internal characteristics of poor countries themselves. Instead, it ought to follow the principles of conflict theory and focus on patterns of domination and submission—specifically, in this case, on the *relationship* between rich and poor countries.

Dependency theory views economic underdevelopment as the result of exploitative relations between rich and poor countries.

According to dependency theorists, less global inequality existed in 1500 and even in 1750 than today. However, beginning around 1500, the armed forces of the world's most powerful countries subdued and then annexed or colonized most of the rest of the world. Around 1780 the Industrial Revolution began. It enabled the Western European countries, Russia, Japan, and the United States to amass enormous wealth, which they used to extend their global reach. They forced their colonies to become a source of raw materials, cheap labour, investment opportunities, and markets for the conquering nations. The colonizers thereby prevented industrialization and locked the colonies into poverty.

In the decades following World War II, nearly all the colonies in the world became politically independent. However, the dependency theorists say that exploitation by direct political control was soon replaced by new means of achieving the same end: substantial foreign investment, support for authoritarian governments, and mounting debt.

- *Substantial foreign investment.* Many people assume that investment is always a good thing. According to dependency theorists, however, investment by multinational corporations has positive consequences for rich countries and negative consequences for poor countries. That is because investment in poor countries is typically used only to extract raw materials, create low-wage jobs, and siphon off wealth in the form of profits. The raw materials are used to create high-wage design, research, manufacturing, and administrative jobs back in the rich countries where multinational corporations have their head offices. Some of the manufactured goods are then sold back to the poor, unindustrialized countries for additional profit. Dependency theorists conclude that, for poor countries, the disadvantages of foreign investment far outweigh the advantages.

- *Support for authoritarian governments.* According to dependency theorists, multi-national corporations and rich countries continued their exploitation of the poor countries in the postcolonial period by giving economic and military support to local authoritarian governments. These governments managed to keep their populations subdued most of the time. When that was not possible, Western governments sent in troops and military advisers, engaging in what became known as "gunboat diplomacy." The term was coined in colonial times. In 1839 the Chinese rebelled against the British importation of opium into China, and the British responded by sending a gunboat up the Yangtze River, starting the Opium War. The war resulted in Britain winning control of Hong Kong and access to five Chinese ports; what started as gunboat diplomacy ended as a rich feast for British traders. In the postcolonial period, the United States has been particularly active in using gunboat diplomacy in Central America. A classic case is Guatemala in the 1950s (LaFeber, 1993). In 1952 the democratic government of Guatemala began to redistribute land to impoverished peasants. Some of the land was owned by the United Fruit Company, a United States multinational corporation and the biggest landowner in Guatemala. Two years later, the CIA backed a right-wing coup in Guatemala, preventing land reform and allowing the United Fruit Company to continue its highly profitable business as usual.

- *Mounting debt.* The governments of the poor countries struggled to create transportation infrastructures (airports, roads, harbours, etc.), build their education systems, and deliver safe water and at least the most basic health care to their people. To accomplish these tasks, they had to borrow money from Western banks and governments. Some rulers also squandered money on luxuries. So it came about that debt—and the interest payments that inevitably accompany debt—grew every year. By 2008, the total debt of poor countries amounted to $3.7 trillion. Interest payments were $1.6 billion a day. Government foreign aid helps, but not much. It amounts to less than 10 percent of interest payments (Jubilee Debt Campaign, 2010: 6; OECD, 2008: 6).

Effects of Foreign Investment

Almost all sociologists agree that the dependency theorists are correct on one score. Since about 1500, Spain, Portugal, Holland, Britain, France, Italy, the United States, Japan, and Russia treated the world's poor with brutality to enrich themselves. They rationalized their actions by claiming they were bringing "civilization" to the "savages" and inventing other such stories, such as the notion of the Dutch colonizers in early-seventeenth-century Brazil that "there is no sin south of the equator." Colonialism did have a devastating economic and human impact on the poor countries of the world. In the postcolonial era, the debt burden has crippled the development efforts of many poor countries.

That said, a big question remains that research has not yet fully answered. Do foreign investment and liberalized trade policies have positive or negative effects today? Much hinges on the answer to this question. Modernization theorists want more foreign investment in poor countries and freer trade because they think that will promote economic growth and general well-being. They want trade and investment barriers to be dropped so free markets can bring prosperity to everyone. Dependency theorists oppose this strategy. They think foreign investment drains wealth out of poor countries. Therefore, they want the poor countries to revolt against the rich countries, throw up barriers to free trade and investment, and find their own paths to economic well-being.

Over the past couple of decades, researchers have carefully examined the effects of free trade and foreign investment. The results of their analyses depend partly on which variables they include, which time periods they analyze, which countries they consider, and which statistical techniques they use (Bornschier and Chase-Dunn, 1985; Centre for Economic Policy Research, 2002; DeSoya and Oneal, 1999; Firebaugh and Beck, 1994; Weisbrot, Baker, Kraev, and Chen, 2001; Weisbrot and Baker, 2002). Not surprisingly, if you throw different countries, variables, time periods, and statistical techniques into the mix, you bake entirely different cakes. Yet a recent summary of research in this area cautiously reaches two conclusions (Centre for Economic Policy Research, 2002). First, in the 1980s and 1990s, but not in the 1960s and 1970s, openness to international trade and foreign investment generally seemed to have stimulated economic growth. Second, in most but not all well-documented cases, openness to international trade and foreign investment also increased inequality. Few benefits of economic growth went to the neediest.

These findings suggest that lumping all periods of history and all countries together when considering the effects of openness on economic growth and inequality is a mistake. After all, countries have different histories and different social structures. They may adopt a variety of economic policies that influence the effects of international trade and foreign direct investment in different ways. Consequently, international trade and foreign direct investment may have different effects in different times and places. Historical, social-structural, and policy factors matter greatly in determining how a particular country responds to international trade and foreign direct investment.

Core, Periphery, and Semiperiphery

Immanuel Wallerstein (1974–89) proposes a variation on this theme. He argues that capitalist development has resulted in the creation of an integrated "world system" comprising three tiers. First are the **core capitalist countries** (the United States, Japan, and Germany), which are major sources of capital and technology. Second are the **peripheral capitalist countries** (the former colonies, such as Guatemala and Angola), which are major sources of raw materials and cheap labour. Third are the **semiperipheral capitalist countries** (such as South Korea, Taiwan, and Israel), consisting of former colonies that are making considerable headway in their attempts to become prosperous. To give just one dramatic illustration of this progress, South Korea and Ghana were among the poorest nations in the world in 1960. Ghana still is. But South Korea, the recipient of enormous foreign investment and aid, was more than 16 times as wealthy as Ghana in 2010 (as measured by gross national product per capita; World Bank, 2011). Comparing the unsuccessful peripheral countries with the more successful semiperipheral countries presents

Weidenfeld and Nicolson Archives

In 1893, leaders of the British mission pose before taking over what became Rhodesia and is now Zimbabwe. To raise a volunteer army, every British trooper was offered about 23 square kilometres (9 square miles) of native land and 20 gold claims. The Matabele and Mashona peoples were subdued in a three-month war. Nine hundred farms and 10 000 gold claims were granted to the troopers and about 100 000 cattle were looted, leaving the native survivors without a livelihood. Forced labour was subsequently introduced by the British so that the natives could pay a £2 a year tax.

Core capitalist countries are rich countries, such as the United States, Japan, and Germany, that are the major sources of capital and technology in the world.

The **peripheral capitalist countries** are former colonies that are poor and are major sources of raw materials and cheap labour.

The **semiperipheral capitalist countries,** such as South Korea, Taiwan, and Israel, consist of former colonies that are making considerable headway in their attempts to industrialize.

us with a useful natural experiment. The comparison suggests the circumstances that help some poor countries overcome the worst effects of colonialism. The semiperipheral countries differ from the peripheral countries in four main ways (Kennedy, 1993: 193–227; Lie, 1998), which we outline below.

Type of Colonialism

Around the turn of the twentieth century, Taiwan and Korea became colonies of Japan. They remained so until 1945. However, in contrast to the European colonizers of Africa, Latin America, and other parts of Asia, the Japanese built up the economies of their colonies. They established transportation networks and communication systems. They built steel, chemical, and hydroelectric power plants. After Japanese colonialism ended, Taiwan and South Korea were thus at an advantage compared with Ghana, for example, at the time Britain gave up control of that country. South Korea and Taiwan could use the Japanese-built infrastructure and Japanese-trained personnel as springboards to development.

Geopolitical Position

Although the United States was the leading economic and military power in the world by the end of World War II, it began to feel its supremacy threatened in the late 1940s by the Soviet Union and China. Fearing that South Korea and Taiwan might fall to the communists, the United States poured unprecedented aid into both countries in the 1960s. It also gave them large, low-interest loans and opened its domestic market to Taiwanese and South Korean products. Because the United States saw Israel as a crucially important ally in the Middle East, it also received special economic assistance. Other countries with less strategic importance to the United States received less help in their drive to industrialize.

State Policy

A third factor that accounts for the relative success of some countries in their efforts to industrialize and become prosperous concerns state policies. As a legacy of colonialism, the Taiwanese and South Korean states were developed on the Japanese model. They kept workers' wages low, restricted trade union growth, and maintained quasi-military discipline in factories. Moreover, by placing high taxes on consumer goods, limiting the import of foreign goods, and preventing their citizens from investing abroad, they encouraged their citizens to put much of their money in the bank. These policies created a large pool of capital for industrial expansion. The South Korean and Taiwanese states also gave subsidies, training grants, and tariff protection to export-based industries from the 1960s onward. (Tariffs are taxes on foreign goods.) These policies did much to stimulate industrial growth. Finally, the Taiwanese and South Korean states invested heavily in basic education, health care, roads, and other public goods. A healthy and well-educated labour force combined with good transportation and communication systems laid solid foundations for economic growth.

Social Structure

Taiwan and South Korea are socially cohesive countries, which makes it easy for them to generate consensus around development policies. It also allows them to get their citizens to work hard, save a lot of money, and devote their energies to scientific education.

Social solidarity in Taiwan and South Korea is based partly on the sweeping land reform they conducted in the late 1940s and early 1950s. By redistributing land to small farmers, both countries eliminated the class of large landowners, who usually oppose industrialization. Land redistribution got rid of a major potential source of social conflict. In contrast, many countries in Latin America and Africa have not undergone land reform. The United States often intervened militarily in Latin America to prevent land reform because U.S. commercial interests profited handsomely from the existence of large plantations (LaFeber, 1993).

Another factor underlying social solidarity in Taiwan and South Korea is that both countries did not suffer from internal conflicts like those that wrack Africa south of the Sahara desert. British, French, and other Western European colonizers often drew the borders of African countries to keep antagonistic tribes living side by side in the same jurisdiction and

Brand X Pictures/Jupiter Images

Seoul, the capital of South Korea, is one of the semiperipheral countries that is making considerable headway in its attempts to become prosperous.

often sought to foment tribal conflict. Keeping tribal tensions alive made it possible to play one tribe off against another. That made it easier for imperial powers to rule. This policy led to much social and political conflict in postcolonial Africa. Today, the region suffers from frequent civil wars, coups, and uprisings. It is the most conflict-ridden area of the world. For example, the civil war in the Democratic Republic of Congo from 1998 to 2003 resulted in millions of deaths, and renewed conflict beginning in 2008 killed many more Congolese. This high level of internal conflict acts as a barrier to economic development in sub-Saharan Africa.

In sum, certain conditions seem to permit foreign investment to have positive economic effects. Postcolonial countries that enjoy a solid industrial infrastructure, strategic geopolitical importance, strong states with strong development policies, and socially cohesive populations are in the best position to join the ranks of the rich countries in the coming decades. We may expect countries that have *some* of these characteristics to experience some economic growth and increase in the well-being of their populations in the near future. Such countries include China, India, Chile, Thailand, Indonesia, Mexico, and Brazil (see Box 9.2). In contrast, African countries south of the Sahara are in the worst position of all. They have inherited the most damaging consequences of colonialism, and they enjoy few of the conditions that could help them escape the history that has been imposed on them.

Canada as a Semiperipheral Country

Many analysts regard Canada as a semiperipheral country that has managed to achieve prosperity despite its colonial past (Brym with Fox, 1989: 34–56; Laxer, 1989):

- The *type of colonialism* that Canada experienced is sometimes called "white settler colonialism." Like Australia, New Zealand, and the United States, Canada was settled by large numbers of Europeans who soon overwhelmed the Aboriginal population. They were determined to reproduce or improve the standard of living they enjoyed in the old country. Much of the wealth they produced was therefore reinvested locally. In contrast, when the European powers colonized Africa, they set up only small enclaves of white settlers. Their main aim was to exploit local resources and populations, sending nearly all of the wealth back to Europe.[3]

BOX 9.2

Sociology at the Movies

SLUMDOG MILLIONAIRE

A shift of world-historic proportions is taking place in the global economy. The rich countries' share of world gross domestic product is slowly shrinking while the share produced by some less developed countries, notably China and India, is rapidly increasing (see Table 9.3). In China and India, most rural residents of non-coastal areas remain poor. However, as peasants move to cities and governments and real estate developers tear down slums and build high-rises in their place, the conditions of existence for hundreds of millions of people are being transformed. "Transformed" does not, of course, mean "improved beyond recognition," despite the theme of the winner of the 2008 best-picture Oscar, *Slumdog Millionaire*.

Slumdog Millionaire is the improbable story of Jamal K. Malik (Dev Patel), a young slum dweller who becomes a contestant on the Indian version of *Who Wants to Be a Millionaire*. He answers every question correctly by drawing on his harrowing experiences growing up in a Mumbai slum, and wins not only the grand prize but also the affection of the beautiful Latika (Freida Pinto), the girlfriend of the dangerous criminal kingpin, Javed Khan (Mahesh Manjrekar). All this takes place amid boisterous Bollywood dance num-

bers and India's frenzied economic growth.

"That ... used to be our slum. Can you believe that, huh?" asks Salim, Jamal's brother, pointing to a high-rise development. "We used to live right there, man. Now, it's all business. India is at the centre of the world now, bhai [brother]. And I, I am at the centre of the centre. This is all Javed bhai's."

Jamal: "Javed Khan, the gangster from our slum? You work for him? What do you do for him?"

Salim: "Anything he asks."

Slumdog Millionaire grossed more than $250 million, including DVD sales, but a scandal erupted when it was learned that the actors who had major roles playing Jamal and Latika as children received a pittance for their efforts (Nelson and Henderson, 2009). According to the children's parents, Rubina Ali and Azaharuddin Ismail, both plucked from a Mumbai slum, received, respectively, £500 and £1700 for a year's work. The exploitation of Ali and Ismail caused widespread outrage, hardly softened by the statement of a spokesperson for Fox Searchlight, the film's

© Fox Searchlight/Courtesy Everett Collection

Scene from *Slumdog Millionaire*

American distributor, that (1) these payments equal three times the adult yearly salary in the slum, (2) the children are also receiving £20 a month each for books and food, and (3) a fund has been established which the children will receive when they turn 18 if they remain in school. (The spokesperson declined to disclose the size of the fund when asked.)

This is not an isolated case involving exploitation of child actors from less developed countries. The poor Afghan child stars of *The Kite Runner* embarrassed their Hollywood producers two years earlier when they disclosed that they had been paid just £9000 for their efforts. As noted earlier, "transformed" does not mean "improved beyond recognition."

	1980	2010	Percent Change
United States	22.4	19.6	−12.5
Canada	2.2	1.8	−18.2
Japan	8.3	6.0	−28.8
Germany	6.1	4.0	−34.4
India	2.2	5.1	131.8
China	2.0	12.7	535.0

TABLE 9.3

Share of World Gross Domestic Product by Selected Countries, 1980 and 2010 (in percent)

Note: Figures are based on purchasing power and therefore control for inflation. Data for 2010 are estimated.

Source: International Monetary Fund, 2009.

- Canada's *geopolitical position* has always been highly favourable to economic development. That is because it has served as a major supplier of raw materials and other goods to France, Great Britain, and the United States, and has fallen under the protective wing of each of these countries, all of which have viewed Canada as a staunch ally. For example, Canada played a disproportionately large role in World War II as a training ground, source of raw materials, and supplier of arms and soldiers to the Allies.

- Canada's *state policy* has sometimes acted to protect and stimulate the growth of Canadian industry, although not as consistently as the state policy of, say, South Korea. For example, the 1879 National Policy established a duty on imported manufactured goods. It sheltered the growth of Canadian industry, then in its infancy, by making foreign-made manufactured goods more expensive. Similarly, the 1965 Auto Pact required that foreign automobile companies wanting to sell cars in Canada duty-free manufacture cars in Canada and use a certain proportion of Canadian-made components. It stimulated the growth of an industry that, directly or indirectly, is responsible for the employment of one-sixth of Ontario's labour force.

- Canada's *social structure* has arguably had fewer positive effects on economic development than is the case in such countries as South Korea and Taiwan. In Canada, the French-English conflict has drawn attention away from development policy. And although strong farmers' and workers' movements have pushed governments in other countries to attend closely to development issues, these movements have been relatively weak in Canada (Brym, 1992; Laxer, 1989). Canada is not a world centre of capital. Our manufacturing sector is proportionately smaller than those of Germany, the United States, and Japan. An unusually large percentage of our industry is foreign-owned. Still, Canada is one of the wealthiest countries in the world. Our semiperipheral status is clear.

Summing Up

- Although the percentage of desperately poor people is falling worldwide, global income inequality for individuals is astoundingly high and increasing.
- Modernization theory holds that global inequality results from various dysfunctional characteristics of poor societies themselves.
- Dependency theory holds that global inequality results from exploitative relations between colonial and colonized countries.
- Some previously poor countries have developed rapidly in recent decades because they enjoyed a relatively well-developed economic infrastructure as a legacy of Japanese colonialism, received abundant aid as important allies of the United States, fostered the growth of export-driven industries as a matter of state policy, and/or have socially cohesive populations, in some cases partly because they underwent land reform before industrialization.

NEOLIBERAL VERSUS DEMOCRATIC GLOBALIZATION

Globalization and Neoliberalism

Neoliberal globalization is a policy that promotes private control of industry; minimal government interference in the running of the economy; the removal of taxes, tariffs, and restrictive regulations that discourage the international buying and selling of goods and services; and the encouragement of foreign investment.

For some political and economic leaders, the road sign that marks the path to prosperity reads "**neoliberal globalization**." Neoliberal globalization is a policy that promotes private control of industry; minimal government interference in the running of the economy; the removal of taxes, tariffs, and restrictive regulations that discourage the international buying and selling of goods and services; and the encouragement of foreign investment. Advocates of neoliberal globalization resemble the modernization theorists of a generation ago. They believe that if only the poor countries would emulate the successful habits of the rich countries, they would prosper as well.

Many social scientists are skeptical of this prescription. For example, Joseph E. Stiglitz (2002), the Nobel Prize–winning economist and former chief economist of the World Bank, argues that the World Bank and other international economic organizations often impose outdated policies on developing countries, putting them at a disadvantage in comparison with developed countries. In the African country of Mozambique, for example, foreign debt was 4.5 times the GNP in the mid-1990s. This means that the amount of money Mozambique owed to foreigners was four-and-a-half times more than the value of goods and services produced by all the people of Mozambique in a year. Facing an economic crisis, Mozambique sought relief from the World Bank and the International Monetary Fund (IMF). The response of the IMF was that Mozambique's government-imposed minimum wage of less than $1 a day is "excessive." The IMF also recommended that Mozambique spend twice as much as its education budget and four times as much as its health budget on interest payments to service its foreign debt (Mittelman, 2000: 104). How such crippling policies might help the people of Mozambique is unclear.

Does historical precedent lead us to believe that neoliberalism works? To the contrary, with the exception of Great Britain, neoliberalism was *never* a successful development strategy in the early stages of industrialization. Germany, the United States, Japan, Sweden, and other rich countries became highly developed economically between the second half of the nineteenth century and the early twentieth century. South Korea, Taiwan, Singapore, and other semiperipheral countries became highly developed economically in the second half of the twentieth century. Today, China and India are industrializing quickly. These countries did not pursue privatization, minimal government intervention in the economy, free trade, and foreign investment in the early stages of industrialization. Rather, the governments of these countries typically intervened to encourage industrialization. They protected infant industries behind tariff walls, invested public money heavily to promote national industries, and so on. Today, China and India maintain among the highest barriers to international trade in the world (Chang, 2002; Gerschenkron, 1962; Laxer, 1989). Typically, it is only after industrial development is well under way and national industries can compete on the global market that countries begin to advocate neoliberal globalization to varying degrees. As one political economist writes, "The sensible ones liberalise in line with the growth of domestic capacities—they try to expose domestic producers to enough competition to make them more efficient, but not enough to kill them" (Wade in Wade and Wolf, 2002: 19). The exception that proves the rule is Great Britain, which needed less government involvement to industrialize because it was the first industrializer and had no international competitors. Even the United States, one of the most vocal advocates of neoliberal globalization today, invested a great deal of public money subsidizing industries and building infrastructure (roads, schools, ports, airports, electricity grids, etc.) in the late nineteenth and early twentieth centuries. It was an extremely protectionist country until the end of World War II. As late as 1930 the Smoot-Hawley Tariff Act raised tariffs on foreign goods 60 percent. Today, the United States still subsidizes large corporations in a variety of ways and maintains substantial tariffs on a whole range of foreign products, including agricultural goods, softwood lumber, and textiles. In this, the United States is little different from Japan, France, and other rich countries.

In sum, there is good reason to be skeptical about the benefits of neoliberal globalization for poor countries (Bourdieu, 1998a; Brennan, 2003). Yet, as you will now see, globalization can be reformed so that its economic and technological benefits are distributed more uniformly throughout the world.

Foreign Aid, Debt Cancellation, and Tariff Reduction

In the film *About Schmidt* (2002), Jack Nicholson plays Warren Schmidt, a former insurance executive. Retirement leaves Schmidt with little purpose in life. His wife dies. His adult daughter has little time or respect for him. He feels his existence lacks meaning. Then, while watching TV one night, Schmidt is moved to support a poor child in a developing country. He decides to send a monthly $27 cheque to sponsor a Tanzanian boy named Ndugu. He writes Ndugu long letters about his life. While Schmidt's world falls apart before our eyes, his sole meaningful human bond is with Ndugu. At the end of the movie, Schmidt cries as he looks at a picture Ndugu drew for him: an adult holding a child's hand.

It does not take a Warren Schmidt to find meaning in helping the desperately poor. Many people contribute to charities that help developing countries in a variety of ways. Many more people contribute development aid indirectly through the taxes they pay to the federal government. Many Canadians think our contributions are generous. Do you? A 2002 survey found that while 71 percent of Canadians thought foreign aid important, only 51 percent favoured the government's announced plan of gradually increasing the total (Asia Pacific Foundation of Canada, 2002).

Was foreign aid by Canada already at a high level? The UN urges the world's 22 richest countries to contribute 0.7 percent of their GDP to development aid. (This goal was set at the urging of then Canadian prime minister Lester Pearson in 1969.) In 2006, only 5 countries reached that goal: Sweden, Luxembourg, Norway, the Netherlands, and Denmark. Canada ranked sixteenth among the 22 rich nations at 0.29 percent. The United States ranked twenty-first at 0.18 percent, less than a fifth of Sweden's 1.02 percent. Only Greece, at 0.17 percent, performed worse than the United States (Organisation for Economic Co-operation and Development, 2007). In 2002, a World Bank official compared (1) the subsidies rich countries gave to farms and businesses within their borders with (2) the amount of development aid they gave developing countries. He concluded that "[t]he average cow [in a rich country] is supported by three times the level of income of a poor person in Africa" (quoted in Schuettler, 2002).

Since the United States is by far the world's richest country, it is the American contribution to foreign aid that potentially makes the greatest difference. But even if the United States quadrupled its foreign aid budget to meet UN guidelines, some foreign aid as presently delivered is not an effective way of helping the developing world. Foreign aid is often accompanied by high administrative and overhead costs. It is often given on condition that it is used to buy goods from donor countries that are not necessarily high-priority items for recipient countries. Food aid often has detrimental effects on poor countries. One expert writes: "As well as creating expensive [dependence on] nonindigenous cereals, and discouraging export-production of items like corn and rice in which the U.S.A. is expanding its own trade, [U.S. food aid] has frequently served as a major disincentive to the efforts of local farmers to grow food even for domestic consumption" (Hancock, 1989: 169). Some foreign aid organizations, such as Oxfam and Caritas Internationalis, waste little money on administration and overhead expenses because they are driven by high principles, pay their staffs low salaries, build partnerships with reputable local organizations, work with their partners to identify the most pressing needs of poor countries, and focus their efforts on meeting those needs (Ron, 2007). The efforts of such organizations remind us that foreign aid can be beneficial and that strict oversight is required to ensure that foreign aid is not wasted and that it is directed to truly helpful projects, such as improving irrigation and sanitation systems and helping people acquire better farming techniques. Increasing the amount of foreign aid and redesigning its delivery can thus help mitigate some of the excesses of neoliberal globalization.

So can debt cancellation. Many analysts argue that the world's rich countries and banks should simply write off the debt owed to them by the developing countries in recognition of historical injustices. They reason that the debt burden of the developing countries is so onerous that it prevents them from focusing on building up economic infrastructure, improving the health and education of their populations, and developing economic policies that can help them emerge from poverty. This proposal for blunting the worst effects of neoliberal globalization may be growing in popularity among politicians in the developed countries. For example, former Canadian prime minister Paul Martin, former British prime minister Tony Blair, and former U.S. president Bill Clinton, among others, support the idea. Former U.S. president George W. Bush and Prime Minister Stephen Harper support limited versions of this proposal.

A third reform proposed in recent years involves the elimination or at least lowering of tariffs by the *rich* countries. Many of these tariffs prevent developing countries from exporting goods that could earn them money for investment in agriculture, industry, and infrastructure. Eliminating or lowering tariffs would require training some farmers in rich countries for new kinds of work, but it would stimulate economic growth in the developing countries. To date, however, there is little room for optimism in this regard. In 2002 a less developed country, like Mexico, gave its farmers an average subsidy of $1000 a year, while the United States gave its farmers an average subsidy of $16 000 a year. The comparable figures for Western Europe and Japan were $17 000 and $27 000, respectively. Talks to lower government subsidies to Western farmers broke down in 2003.

Democratic Globalization

The final reform we consider involves efforts to help spread democracy throughout the developing world. A large body of research shows that democracy lowers inequality and promotes economic growth (Pettersson, 2003; Sylwester, 2002; United Nations, 2002). Democracies have these effects for several reasons. They make it more difficult for elite groups to misuse their power and enhance their wealth and income at the expense of the less well-to-do. They increase political stability, thereby providing a better investment climate. Finally, because they encourage broad political participation, democracies tend to enact policies that are more responsive to people's needs and benefit a wide range of people from all social classes. For example, democratic governments are more inclined to take steps to avoid famines, protect the environment, build infrastructure, and ensure basic needs, such as education and health. These measures help to create a population better suited to pursue economic growth.

Although democracy has spread in recent years, by 2009, only 89 countries with 46 percent of the world's population were fully democratic (Freedom House, 2010; see Chapter 14, Politics). For its part, the United States has supported as many anti-democratic as democratic regimes in the developing world. Especially between the end of World War II in 1945 and the collapse of the Soviet Union in 1991, the U.S. government gave military and financial aid to many anti-democratic regimes, often in the name of halting the spread of Soviet influence. These actions often generated unexpected and undesirable consequences, or what the Central Intelligence Agency (CIA) came to call "blowback" (Johnson, 2000). For example, in the 1980s the U.S. government supported Saddam Hussein when it considered Iraq's enemy, Iran, the greater threat to U.S. security interests. The United States also funded Osama bin Laden when he was fighting the Soviet Union in Afghanistan. Only a decade later, these so-called allies turned into the United States' worst enemies (Chomsky, 1991; Johnson, 2000; Kolko, 2002).

In sum, we have outlined four reforms that could change the nature of neoliberal globalization and turn it into what we would like to call democratic globalization. These reforms include offering stronger support for democracy in the developing world, contributing more and better foreign aid, forgiving the debt owed by developing countries to the rich countries, and eliminating many of the tariffs that restrict exports from developing countries. These kinds of policies could plausibly help the developing world overcome the legacy of colonialism and join the ranks of the well-to-do. They would do much to ensure that the complex process we call globalization would benefit humanity as a whole.

Summing Up

- Neoliberal globalization promotes private control of industry; minimal government interference in the running of the economy; the removal of taxes, tariffs, and restrictive regulations that discourage the international buying and selling of goods and services; and the encouragement of foreign investment. Overall, it has not led to more global equality.
- More and improved foreign aid to poor countries; cancellation of debt owed by poor countries; reduction of tariffs on agricultural goods and textiles produced by poor countries; and the spread of democracy to poor countries would lower the level of global inequality.

NOTES

1. All dollar references are to U.S. currency unless otherwise indicated.

2. Gross national product (GNP) is the total dollar value of goods and services produced in a country in a year. It allocates goods and services based on the nationality of the owners. GDP is a similar measure, but it allocates goods and services based on the location of the owners. So, for example, goods and services produced overseas by foreign subsidiaries would be included in GNP but not in GDP.

3. From this point of view, South Africa and, to a lesser degree, Zimbabwe (formerly Rhodesia) represent intermediate cases between the rest of Africa on the one hand, and Canada, the United States, Australia, and New Zealand on the other.

SUMMARY

1. What is globalization and why is it taking place?
   Globalization is the growing interdependence and mutual awareness of individuals and economic, political, and social institutions around the world. It is a response to many forces, some technological (e.g., the development of inexpensive means of rapid international communication), others economic (e.g., burgeoning international trade and investment), and still others political (e.g., the creation of transnational organizations that limit the sovereign powers of nation states).

2. What are the consequences of globalization?
   Globalization has complex consequences, some of which are captured by the idea of "glocalization," which denotes the homogenization of some aspects of life and the simultaneous sharpening of some local differences. In addition, globalization evokes an anti-globalization reaction.

3. How long is the history of globalization?
   Globalization has a long history. Its origins can be traced to the beginning of long-distance migration and trade. However, it was the beginning of European exploration and capitalism about 500 years ago that really spurred globalization.

4. What are the main trends in global inequality and poverty?
   Global inequality and poverty are staggering and in some respects getting worse. The income gap between rich and poor countries weighted for population size has declined since 1950, but the gap between rich and poor individuals has grown worldwide.

5. What are the main sociological theories of economic development?
   Modernization theory argues that global inequality occurs as a result of some countries lacking sufficient capital, Western values, rational business practices, and stable governments. Dependency theory counters with the claim that global inequality results from the exploitative relationship between rich and poor countries. An important test of the two theories concerns the effect of foreign investment on economic growth, but research on this subject is equivocal. Apparently, historical, social-structural, and policy factors matter greatly in determining how a particular country responds to international trade and foreign direct investment.

6. What are the characteristics of formerly poor countries that emerged from poverty?
   The poor countries best able to emerge from poverty have a colonial past that left them with industrial infrastructures. They also enjoy a favourable geopolitical position. They implement strong, growth-oriented economic policies, and they have socially cohesive populations.

7. Can neoliberal globalization be reformed?
   Neoliberal globalization can be reformed so that the benefits of globalization are more evenly distributed throughout the world. Possible reforms include offering stronger support for democracy in the developing world, contributing more and better foreign aid, forgiving the debt owed by developing countries to the rich countries, and eliminating tariffs that restrict exports from developing countries.

KEY TERMS

colonialism (p. 221)

core capitalist countries (p. 227)

dependency theory (p. 225)

global commodity chain (p. 215)

glocalization (p. 219)

imperialism (p. 214)

McDonaldization (p. 218)

modernization theory (p. 225)

neoliberal globalization (p. 232)

peripheral capitalist countries (p. 227)

regionalization (p. 219)

semiperipheral capitalist countries (p. 227)

transnational corporations (p. 216)

WEB RESOURCES

Companion Website for This Book

http://www.compass4e.nelson.com

Begin by clicking on the Student Resources section of the website. Next, select the chapter you are studying from the pull-down menu. From the Student Resources page you have easy access to additional Weblinks and other resources. The website also has many useful tips to aid you in your study of sociology, including practice tests for each chapter.

InfoTrac® Search Terms

These search terms are provided to assist you in beginning to conduct research on this topic by visiting http://www.infotrac-college.com:

dependency theory

modernization theory

globalization

Race and Ethnicity

IN THIS CHAPTER, YOU WILL LEARN THAT

- Race and ethnicity are socially constructed labels. We use them to distinguish people based on perceived physical or cultural differences, with profound consequences for their lives.

- Racial and ethnic labels and identities change over time and place. Relations among racial and ethnic groups help to shape these labels and identities.

- In Canada, some ethnic racial groups are blending over time. However, this tendency is weaker among members of highly disadvantaged groups, especially Aboriginal peoples and recent immigrants who are members of visible minority groups.

- Identifying with a racial or an ethnic group can be economically, politically, and emotionally advantageous for some people.

- Racial and ethnic inequality is likely to persist in Canada.

dedoma/Shutterstock

DEFINING RACE AND ETHNICITY

The Great Brain Robbery

About 150 years ago, Dr. Samuel George Morton of Philadelphia was the most distinguished scientist in North America. Among other things, Morton collected and measured human skulls. The skulls came from various times and places. Their original occupants were members of different races. Morton believed he could show that the bigger your brain, the smarter you were. To prove his point he packed BB-sized shot into a skull until it was full. Next he poured the shot from the skull into a graduated cylinder. He then recorded the volume of shot in the cylinder. Finally, he noted the race of the person from whom each skull came. This, he thought, allowed him to draw conclusions about the average brain size of different races.

CP Picture Archive/Frank Gunn

As he expected, Morton found that the races ranking highest in the social hierarchy had the biggest brains, while those ranking lowest had the smallest brains. He claimed that the people with the biggest brains were whites of European origin. Next were Asians. Then came Native North Americans. The people at the bottom of the social hierarchy—and those with the smallest brains—were blacks.

Morton's research had profound sociological implications, for he claimed to show that the system of social inequality in North America and throughout the world had natural, biological roots. If, on average, members of some racial groups are rich and others poor, some highly educated and others illiterate, some powerful and others powerless, that was, said Morton, due to differences in brain size and mental capacity. Moreover, because he used science to show that Native North Americans and blacks *naturally* rested at the bottom of the social hierarchy, his ideas were used to justify two of the most oppressive forms of domination and injustice: colonization and slavery.

Despite claims of scientific objectivity, not a shred of evidence supported Morton's ideas. For example, in one of his three main studies, Morton measured the capacity of skulls robbed from Egyptian tombs. He found that the average volume of black people's skulls was 65.5 millilitres (4 cubic inches) smaller than the average volume of white people's skulls. This fact seemed to prove his case. Today, however, we know that three main issues compromise his findings:

1. Morton claimed to be able to distinguish the skulls of white and black people by the shapes of the skulls. Since this is not possible, Morton's sorting of skulls is invalid.
2. Morton's skulls formed a small, unrepresentative sample of 72 skulls.
3. Morton's racial samples were incomparable with respect to gender. Females comprised 71 percent of the "Negroid" group and only 48 percent of the "Caucasian." Given that women's bodies are on average smaller than men's, these group comparisons are unfair. The findings are biased in favour of larger, white, male skulls.

Scientifically speaking, Morton's findings are meaningless. Yet they were influential for a long time. Some people still believe them. For example, in 1963 the author of an article about race in the *Encyclopedia Britannica*, the world's most authoritative general reference source, wrote that blacks have "a rather small brain in relation to their size" (Buxton, 1963: 864A). That claim was repeated in a controversial book written by a Canadian psychologist in the mid-1990s (Rushton, 1995). Yet there is no more evidence today than there was in 1850 that whites have bigger brains than blacks do.[1]

Race, Biology, and Society

Biological arguments about racial differences have grown more sophisticated over time. However, the scientific basis of these arguments is just as shaky now as it always was.

In medieval Europe, some aristocrats saw blue veins underneath their pale skin but could not see blue veins underneath the peasants' suntanned skin. They concluded that the two groups must be racially distinct. The aristocrats called themselves "blue bloods." They ignored the fact that the colour of blood from an aristocrat's wound was just as red as the blood from a peasant's wound.

About 80 years ago, some scholars expressed the belief that racial differences in average IQ scores were genetically based. Typically, in 1927, Canadian professor Peter Sandiford argued that Canada must institute selective immigration to ensure that only the best and the brightest arrived on our shores and that we kept out "misfits" and "defectives." He encouraged the recruitment of people of British, German, and Danish stock, and discouraged the recruitment of Polish people, Italians, and Greeks. Sandiford provided IQ test results supporting his selective immigration policy. He argued that his data showed the mental superiority of Northern Europeans compared with Eastern and Southern Europeans. However, his testing results also provided what he regarded as "profoundly disturbing" evidence. People of Japanese and Chinese ancestry had the highest intelligence scores—something he had not predicted. He dismissed this finding by asserting that a few clever Asians had apparently entered Canada. They were exceptions, he wrote, and should not detract from the "need" to keep Asians out of Canada too (McLaren, 1990).

Similarly, in the United States, Jews scored below non-Jews on IQ tests in the 1920s. This was used as an argument against Jewish immigration. More recently, African Americans have on average scored below European Americans on IQ tests. Some people say this justifies slashing budgets for schools in the inner city, where many African Americans live. Why invest good money in inner-city schooling, such people ask, if low IQ scores are rooted in biology and therefore fixed (Herrnstein and Murray, 1994)? However, the people who argued against Jewish immigration and better education for inner-city African Americans ignored two facts. First, Jewish IQ scores rose as Jews moved up the class hierarchy and could afford better education. Second, enriched educational facilities have routinely boosted the IQ scores of inner-city African-American children (Campbell and Ramey, 1994; Frank Porter Graham Child Development Center, 1999; Hancock, 1994; Steinberg, 1989). Much evidence shows that the social setting in which a person is raised and educated has a big impact on IQ. The claim that racial differences in IQ scores are biologically based is about as strong as evidence that aristocrats have blue blood (Cancio, Evans, and Maume, 1996; Fischer, Hout, Jankowski, Lucas, Swidler, and Voss, 1996; see Chapter 17, Education).[2]

If we cannot reasonably maintain that racial differences in average IQ scores are based in biology, what about differences in athletic prowess or other abilities? For example, some people insist that, for genetic reasons, black people are better than whites at singing and sports, and are more prone to crime. Is there any evidence to support these beliefs?

At first glance, the supporting evidence might seem strong. Consider sports. Aren't 65 percent of NBA players and 67 percent of NFL players black? Don't blacks of West African descent hold the 200 fastest 100-metre-dash times, all under 10 seconds? Don't North and East Africans regularly win 40 percent of the top international distance-running honours yet represent only a fraction of 1 percent of the world's population (Entine, 2000)? Although these facts are undeniable, the argument for the genetic basis of black athletic

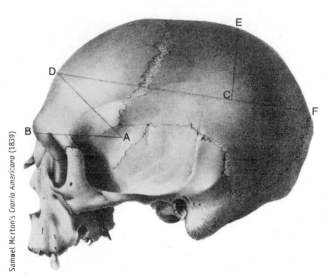

Samuel Merton's *Crania Americana* (1839)

In the nineteenth century, brain size was falsely held to be one of the main indicators of intellectual capacity. Average brain size was incorrectly said to vary by race. Researchers who were eager to prove the existence of such correlations are now widely regarded as practitioners of a racist quasi-science.

Athletic heroes, such as Donovan Bailey, are often held up as role models for black youth even though the chance of making it as an athlete is much less than the chance of getting a postsecondary education and succeeding as a professional. Racial stereotypes about black athletic prowess and intellectual inferiority are often reinforced through the idolization of sports heroes.

CP Picture Archive/Andrew Vaughan

superiority begins to falter once we consider two additional points. First, no gene linked to general athletic superiority has yet been identified. Second, athletes of African descent do not perform unusually well in many sports, such as swimming, hockey, cycling, tennis, gymnastics, and soccer. The idea that people of African descent are in general superior athletes is simply untrue.

Sociologists have identified certain *social* conditions that lead to high levels of participation in sports (as well as entertainment and crime). These operate on all groups of people, whatever their race. Specifically, people who face widespread prejudice and discrimination often enter sports, entertainment, and crime in disproportionately large numbers for lack of other ways to improve their social and economic position. For these people, other avenues of upward mobility are often blocked because of prejudice and discrimination.

Prejudice is an attitude that judges a person on his or her group's real or imagined characteristics.

Discrimination is unfair treatment of people because of their group membership.

Prejudice is an attitude that judges a person on his or her group's real or imagined characteristics. **Discrimination** is unfair treatment of people because of their group membership (see Box 10.1). For example, it was not until the 1950s that prejudice and discrimination against North American Jews began to decline appreciably. Until then, Jews played a prominent role in some professional sports. Thus, when the New York Knicks played their first game on November 1, 1946, beating the Toronto Huskies 68–66, the starting lineup for New York consisted of Ossie Schechtman, Stan Stutz, Jake Weber, Ralph Kaplowitz, and Leo "Ace" Gottlieb—an all-Jewish squad (National Basketball Association, 2000). Similarly, Koreans in Japan today are subject to much prejudice and discrimination. They often pursue careers in sports and entertainment. In contrast, Koreans in Canada face less prejudice and discrimination. Few of them become athletes and entertainers. Instead, they are often said to excel in engineering and science. As these examples suggest, then, social circumstances have a big impact on athletic and other forms of behaviour.

The idea that people of African descent are genetically superior to whites in athletic ability is the complement of the idea that they are genetically inferior to whites in intellectual ability. Both ideas reinforce black–white inequality.[3] For although there are just a few thousand professional athletes in North America, there are millions of pharmacists, graphic designers, lawyers, systems analysts, police officers, nurses, and people in other interesting occupations that offer steady employment and good pay. By promoting only the Jarome Iginlas and Kobe Bryants of the world as suitable role models for youth, the idea of "natural" black athletic superiority and intellectual inferiority in effect asks blacks to bet on a high-risk proposition—that they will make it in professional sports. At the same time, it deflects attention from a much safer bet—that they can achieve upward mobility through academic excellence (Doberman, 1997; Guppy and Davies, 1998).

An additional problem undermines the argument that genes determine the behaviour of racial groups. It is impossible to neatly distinguish races based on genetic differences. Relatively consistent differences are observed only when people from distant locales, such as Norway versus Eastern Asia, are compared. Within continental landmasses, genetic

BOX 10.1

Sociology at the Movies

CRASH

Winner of three Oscars, including best picture, *Crash* is a story about Los Angelenos colliding with one another because of their racist assumptions and then, in some cases, learning that people who differ from them are as human as they are.

The movie mirrors the ethnic and racial complexities of Los Angeles by presenting many intersecting plot lines. Neighbours think an Iranian-American shopkeeper (Shaun Toub) is an Arab so they apparently feel little remorse when they loot his store. The shopkeeper thinks a Chicano locksmith (Michael Peña) is a gang member who will bring his homies in to rob him blind once he finishes the repair job. The locksmith is in fact a hardworking family man and an exemplary father. A black police officer (Don Cheadle) has an affair with his Latina partner (Jennifer Esposito) but keeps on insulting her by not remembering what country she was born in and stopping just one step short of saying "You people all look the same to

Christine (Thandie Newton; left) and Officer John Ryan (Matt Dillon) in *Crash*

© Lions Gate/Courtesy Everett Collection;
CP Picture Archive

me." Ryan, a white police officer (played by Matt Dillon), arbitrarily stops what he at first thinks is a white woman and a black man in an expensive car. He conducts a humiliating, overly thorough body search of the woman (who, he discovers, is actually a light-skinned African American) while her enraged husband looks on, unable to do anything because the police officer makes it clear what would happen if he tried. Later, we learn that Ryan is a compassionate man who is angry about his inability to help his dying father. Perversely, he expresses anger over his impotence by insulting blacks and making them feel powerless. Yet he partly redeems himself when he risks his life to rescue a woman from a horrible car accident—realizing partway through the rescue that the victim is the same black woman he had earlier body-searched.

Some critics have complained that *Crash* exaggerates the extent of racism in the United States. After all, we don't often hear explicit racist comments in public. These critics miss the point of the movie. The apparent intention of *Crash*—and in this it succeeds admirably—is to strip away all political correctness and tell us what people are thinking to themselves or saying to members of their own ethnic or racial group about members of other groups. In that sense it may be more realistic than what we hear in public. At the same time, *Crash* offers a measure of hope that things can be better. Ryan risks his life to save the woman even after realizing that she is black. He helps us appreciate that underlying our prejudices lies a deeper humanity.

contrasts are negligible for adjacent populations because migration and conquest bring about genetic mixing. Such mixing prevails whenever supposedly distinct groups have been in contact for more than a few generations. In North America, for instance, it was not uncommon for white male slave owners to rape black female slaves, who then gave birth to children of mixed race. Many Europeans had children with Aboriginal peoples in the eighteenth and nineteenth centuries. This fact undermines attempts to sort populations into distinct racial types. Many of today's supposed racial schemas, including the well-known "colour code" contrasting red, yellow, brown, and white, are contrasts that derive from European seafarers' early encounters with groups then unfamiliar to them.

We know from the census that ethnic and racial intermarriage has been increasing in Canada at least since 1871. In the 2006 census, more than 41 percent of Canadians reported multiple ethnic or racial identities (Statistics Canada, 2008e). Usually, people who report multiple ethnic or racial identities have parents of different ethnic or racial origins (Kalbach and Kalbach, 1998). A growing number of North Americans are similar to Tiger Woods. Woods claims he is of "Cablinasian" ancestry—part Caucasian, part black, part Native American Indian, and part Asian. As these examples illustrate, the difference among black, white, Asian, and so forth, is often anything but clear-cut. In fact, some respected scholars believe we all belong to one human race, which originated in Africa (Cavalli-Sforza, Menozzi, and Piazza, 1994).

In modern times, humanity has experienced so much intermixing that race as a biological category has lost nearly all meaning. Some biologists and social scientists therefore suggest we drop the term "race" from the vocabulary of science. Most sociologists, however, continue to use the term "race." They do so because *perceptions* of race continue to affect the lives of most people profoundly. Everything from your wealth to your health is influenced by whether others see you as black, white, brown, or something else. Race as a *sociological* concept is thus an invaluable analytical tool. It refers to the existence of classification schemes that are widely understood and widely taken to be relevant. It is invaluable, however, only to the degree that people who use the term remember that it refers to *social significance* that is widely attached to physical differences (e.g., skin colour) rather than to biological differences that shape behaviour patterns.

Said differently, perceptions of racial difference are socially constructed and often arbitrary. The Irish and the Jews were regarded as "blacks" by some people a hundred years ago, and today some northern Italians still think of southern Italians from Sicily and Calabria as "blacks" (Gilman, 1991; Ignatiev, 1995; Roediger, 1991). During World War II, some people made arbitrary physical distinctions between Chinese allies and Japanese enemies that helped justify the Canadian policy of placing Japanese Canadians in internment camps. These examples show that racial distinctions are social constructs, not biological givens.

Finally, then, we can define **race** as a social construct used to distinguish people in terms of one or more physical markers. However, this definition raises an interesting question. If race is merely a social construct and not a useful biological term, why are perceptions of physical difference used to distinguish groups of people in the first place? Why, in other words, does race matter? Most sociologists believe that race matters because it allows social inequality to be created and perpetuated. The English who colonized Ireland, the Americans who went to Africa looking for slaves, and the Germans who used the Jews as a scapegoat to explain their deep economic and political troubles after World War I all created systems of racial domination. (A **scapegoat** is a disadvantaged person or category of people whom others blame for their own problems.) Once colonialism, slavery, and concentration camps were established, behavioural differences developed between subordinates and superordinates. For example, North American slaves and Jewish concentration camp inmates, with little motivating them to work hard except the ultimate threat of the master's whip, tended to do only the minimum work necessary to survive. Their masters noticed this tendency and characterized their subordinates as inherently slow and unreliable workers (Collins, 1982: 66–9). In this way, racial stereotypes are born. The stereotypes then embed themselves in literature, popular lore, journalism, and political debate, which reinforces racial inequalities (see Figure 10.1). We thus see that race matters to the degree that it helps to create and maintain systems of social inequality.

Ethnicity, Culture, and Social Structure

Race is to biology as ethnicity is to culture. A race is a socially defined category of people whose perceived *physical* markers are deemed significant. An **ethnic group** comprises people whose perceived *cultural* markers are deemed significant. Ethnic groups differ from one another in terms of language, religion, customs, values, ancestors, and the

Race is a social construct used to distinguish people in terms of one or more physical markers, usually with profound effects on their lives.

A **scapegoat** is a disadvantaged person or category of people whom others blame for their own problems.

An **ethnic group** comprises people whose perceived cultural markers are deemed socially significant. Ethnic groups differ from one another in terms of language, religion, customs, values, ancestors, and the like.

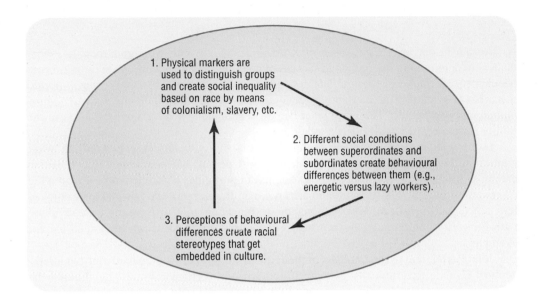

FIGURE 10.1
The Vicious Circle of Racism

like. However, just as physical distinctions don't *cause* differences in the behaviour of various races, so cultural distinctions are often not by themselves the major source of differences in the behaviour of various ethnic groups. In other words, ethnic values and other elements of ethnic culture have less of an effect on the way people behave than we commonly believe. That is because *social structural* differences frequently underlie cultural differences.

An example will help drive home the point. People often praise Jews, Koreans, and other economically successful groups for their cultural values, including an emphasis on education, family, and hard work. People less commonly notice, however, that Canadian immigration policy has been highly selective. For the most part, the Jews and Koreans who arrived in Canada were literate, urbanized, and skilled. Some even came with financial assets (Brym, Shaffir, and Weinfeld, 1993; Li, 1995; Wong and Ng, 1998). They certainly confronted prejudice and discrimination, but far less than that reserved for blacks and members of Canada's Aboriginal peoples. These *social-structural* conditions facilitated Jewish and Korean success. They gave members of these groups a firm basis on which to build and maintain a culture emphasizing education, family, and other middle-class virtues. In contrast, in the first decades of the twentieth century, black descendants of slaves and Aboriginal people were typically illiterate and unskilled, and they experienced more prejudice and discrimination than do other ethnic or racial groups in Canada. These social-structural disadvantages—not their culture—made them less economically successful than Jews and Koreans are on average.

In general, much Canadian research supports the argument that culture, in and of itself, is unimportant in determining the economic success of racial or ethnic groups. There *are* substantial differences in average annual income between some racial groups. For example, the average annual income of Aboriginal peoples is substantially below that of white Canadians. So is the average annual income of non-white immigrants. The point, however, is that these differences are due largely to such factors as how many years of education the average Aboriginal Canadian has and how many years the non-white immigrant has been in the country. There is little income difference between white Canadians and the Canadian-born children of non-white immigrants. A professor of law who happens to be an Aboriginal Canadian earns as much as a professor of law who happens to be white. The problem is that there are so few Aboriginal professors of law. Note, however, that the annual income of some categories of non-white immigrants, such as black men, remains below average even into the second generation because of persistent discrimination. We discuss this issue below.

Ethnic and Racial Stratification in Canada

As we saw in our brief comparison of Koreans and Jews with Aboriginal peoples, what matters in determining the economic success of an ethnic or a racial group are the *resources* people possess, such as education, literacy, urbanity, and financial assets. We may now add that what also matters in determining economic success are the kinds of economic *opportunities* open to people. The latter point can be seen clearly if we compare Canada in the mid-twentieth century with Canada today.

In the middle of the twentieth century, Canada was a society sharply stratified along ethnic and racial lines. The people with the most power and privilege were of British origin. WASPs (white Anglo-Saxon Protestants) in particular controlled almost all the big corporations in the country and dominated politics. Immigrants who arrived later enjoyed less power and privilege. Even among them, big economic differences were evident, with European immigrants enjoying higher status than immigrants of Asian ancestry, for example.

John Porter, one of the founders of modern Canadian sociology, called mid-twentieth-century Canada an ethnically and racially stratified "vertical mosaic." He thought the retention of ethnic and racial culture was a big problem in Canada because it hampered the upward mobility of immigrants. In his view, the "Canadian value system" encouraged the retention of ethnic culture, making Canada a low-mobility society (Porter, 1965, 1979: 91).

By the 1970s, however, many Canadian sociologists, including Porter himself, had to qualify their view that ethnic and racial culture determines economic success or failure. Events upset their earlier assumptions. The Canadian economy grew quickly in the decades after World War II. Many members of ethnic and racial minority groups were economically successful despite ethnic and racial prejudice and discrimination. Economic differences among ethnic groups and, to a lesser degree, among racial groups diminished. Ethnic and racial diversity increased among the wealthy, politicians at all levels of government, and professional groups. Visible minority status, whether Asian, Caribbean, or Hispanic, had little bearing on educational, occupational, and income attainment in Canada, at least among the Canadian-born (Boyd, Goyder, Jones, McRoberts, Pineo, and Porter, 1985; Brym with Fox, 1989: 103–13; Guppy and Davies, 1998; Lian and Matthews, 1998; Nakhaie, 1997; Ogmundson and McLaughlin, 1992; Pendakur and Pendakur, 1998; Pineo and Porter, 1985; Reitz and Breton, 1994). The children of visible minority immigrants considered as a whole actually had above-average success in obtaining education (Boyd, 2002; see Table 10.1). Apparently, then, for the great majority of Canadians after World War II, ethnic and racial culture mattered less than the structure of mobility opportunities in determining economic success.

TABLE 10.1

Percentage with Below-Average Canadian Income by Ethnic Identity and Place of Birth

Note: Data are for a random sample of 31 100 Canadian residents who gave a single ethnic origin in the 2001 census. Average individual annual income was $27 141. The income data were truncated at $200 000.

Source: Adapted from Statistics Canada, 2001 Census, Public-Use Microdata File, using http://dc1.chass.utoronto.ca.myaccess.library.utoronto.ca/census/mainmicro.html (distributor). Computations and interpretation by Robert Brym.

	Born Abroad	Born in Canada
British	53	51
French	51	52
Other European	59	45
African	65	20
Arab	67	35
Other Asian	64	27
Caribbean	67	20
Other Latin, Central, and South American	55	34
Aboriginal	77	54
Canadian	62	50

Beginning in the 1990s, recent immigrants who were members of visible minority groups were less successful economically than one would expect given their educational and other resources (Kazemipur and Halli, 2001; Li, 2000). However, cultural values had little to do with this tendency. Canada experienced an unusually high rate of unemployment in the 1990s, hovering near 10 percent until late in the decade. This level of employment made it more difficult than in previous decades for recently arrived immigrants of visible minority groups to succeed economically, especially those who faced discrimination in the job market. In the early years of the twenty-first century, sociologists began focusing attention on how government policy could be restructured to better use the skills that immigrants from visible minority groups could bring to Canada (Reitz, 2007). This policy shift reinforces the idea that, in addition to the resources a person possesses, the structure of opportunities for economic advancement determines annual income and occupational and educational attainment. Ethnic or racial culture has little to do with it.

Canadian–American Differences

Immigrants face barriers to upward mobility, some more than others. In general, however, as one generation succeeds another, offspring diffuse more widely across the class structure. Sociologists have asked whether this pattern reflects Canada's official policy of **multiculturalism**, which emphasizes tolerance of ethnic and racial differences. Canada's multicultural policy is often seen as distinct from the United States' **melting pot** ideology, which values the disappearance of ethnic and racial difference.

Canadian and American immigration policies, while showing some differences, have shared many similarities since the 1970s. One major difference is that the United States receives a far higher percentage of immigrants from Latin America (especially Mexico), while Canada receives a higher proportion from Asian countries. In addition, Canadian immigration policies tend to focus on economic issues (preferring immigrants with capital to invest), while American policy is more influenced by foreign policy considerations (Fong and Chan, 2008).

Despite these differences, Reitz and Breton's (1994) review found that immigration similarities often contradicted claims about how Canada and the United States differ. For example, surveys show that Canadians are somewhat less likely than Americans are to favour the retention of distinct immigrant cultures but somewhat more likely to accept people of different ethnicity as neighbours or co-workers. Canadians and Americans in roughly equal proportions disdain certain ethnic and racial groups in certain social settings. In both Canada and the United States, fluency in non-official languages falls rapidly with succeeding generations in the receiving country. In both countries, ethnic intermarriage rates are high. In both countries, foreign-born and first-generation immigrants remain relatively separated from the majority group and often face significant barriers to upward mobility, but their offspring face greatly diminished barriers. Thus, differences in ideology and official policy between the two countries appear to have little effect on creating different patterns in the retention of immigrant culture. In both countries, substantial cultural blending takes place between immigrants and natives within one or two generations after immigrants arrive.

In sum, we see that racial and ethnic inequality is more deeply rooted in social structure than in biology and culture. The biological and cultural aspects of race and ethnicity are secondary to their sociological character when it comes to explaining inequality. Moreover, the distinction between race and ethnicity is not as simple as the difference between biology and culture. As noted above for the Irish and the Jews, groups once socially defined as races may be later redefined as ethnicities, even though they do not change biologically. Social definitions, not biology and not culture, determine whether a group is viewed as a race or an ethnic group. The interesting question from a sociological point of view is why social definitions of race and ethnicity change. We now consider that issue.

Canada's **multiculturalism** policy emphasizes tolerance of ethnic and racial differences.

The **melting pot** ideology of the United States values the disappearance of ethnic and racial differences.

Summing Up

- Race is important as a social, rather than biological, classification system. Perceptions of race affect how people are viewed (prejudice) and how they are treated (discrimination). These perceptions, in turn, have important consequences for health, wealth, and other outcomes.
- The social structural underpinnings of ethnic group differences account for most ethnic differences, including stratification.

RACE AND ETHNIC RELATIONS: THE SYMBOLIC INTERACTIONIST APPROACH

Labels and Identity

John Lie moved with his family from South Korea to Japan when he was a baby. He moved from Japan to Hawaii when he was 10 years old, and again from Hawaii to the American mainland when he started university. The move to Hawaii and the move to the U.S. mainland changed the way John thought of himself in ethnic terms.

In Japan, Koreans form a minority group. Before 1945, when Korea was a colony of Japan, some Koreans were brought to Japan to work as miners and unskilled labourers. The Japanese thought the Koreans who lived there were beneath and outside Japanese society (Lie, 2001). Not surprisingly, then, Korean children in Japan, including John, were often teased and occasionally beaten by their Japanese schoolmates. "The beatings hurt," says John, "but the psychological trauma resulting from being socially excluded by my classmates hurt more. In fact, although I initially thought I was Japanese like my classmates, my Korean identity was literally beaten into me.

"When my family immigrated to Hawaii, I was sure things would get worse. I expected Americans to be even meaner than the Japanese were. (By Americans, I thought only of white European Americans.) Was I surprised when I discovered that most of my schoolmates were not white European Americans, but people of Asian and mixed ancestry! Suddenly I was a member of a numerical majority. I was no longer teased or bullied. In fact, I found that students of Asian and non-European origin often singled out white European Americans (called *haole* in Hawaiian) for abuse. We even had a 'beat up *haole* day' in school. Given my own experiences in Japan, I empathized somewhat with the white Americans. But I have to admit that I also felt a great sense of relief and an easing of the psychological trauma associated with being Korean in Japan.

"As the years passed, I finished public school in Hawaii. I then went to college in Massachusetts and got a job as a professor in Illinois. I associated with, and befriended, people from various racial and ethnic groups. My Korean origin became a less and less important factor in the way people treated me. There was simply less prejudice and discrimination against Koreans during my adulthood in the United States than in my early years in Japan. I now think of myself less as Japanese or Korean than as American. When I lived in Illinois, I sometimes thought of myself as a Midwesterner. Now that I have changed jobs and moved to California, my self-conception may shift again; my identity as an Asian American may strengthen given the large number of Asians who live in California. Clearly, my ethnic identity has changed over time in response to the significance others have attached to my Korean origin. I now understand what the French philosopher Jean-Paul Sartre meant when he wrote that "the anti-Semite creates the Jew" (Sartre, 1965 [1948]: 43).

The Formation of Racial and Ethnic Identities

The details of John Lie's life are unique. But experiencing a shift in racial or ethnic identity is common. Social contexts, and in particular the nature of the relations with members of other racial and ethnic groups, shape and continuously reshape a person's racial and ethnic identity. Change your social context and your racial and ethnic self-conception eventually changes too (Miles, 1989; Omi and Winant, 1986).

Consider Italian Canadians. Around 1900, Italian immigrants thought of themselves as people who came from a particular town or perhaps a particular province, such as Sicily or Calabria. They did not usually think of themselves as Italians. Italy had become a unified country only in 1861. A mere 40 years later, many Italian citizens still did not identify with their new Italian nationality. In both Canada and the United States, however, government officials and other residents identified the newcomers as Italians. The designation at first seemed odd to many of the new immigrants. Over time, however, it stuck. Immigrants from Italy started thinking of themselves as Italian Canadians because others defined them that way. A new ethnic identity was born (Yancey, Ericksen, and Leon, 1979).

As symbolic interactionists emphasize, the development of racial and ethnic labels, and ethnic and racial identities, is typically a process of negotiation. For example, members of a group may have a racial or an ethnic identity, but outsiders may impose a new label on them. Group members then reject, accept, or modify the label. The negotiation between outsiders and insiders eventually results in the crystallization of a new, more or less stable ethnic identity. If the social context changes again, the negotiation process begins anew.

One such case involves the labelling of the indigenous peoples of North America by European settlers. When Christopher Columbus landed in North America in 1492, he assumed he had reached India. He called the indigenous peoples *Indians* and the misnomer stuck—not only among European settlers but also among many indigenous peoples themselves. Indigenous peoples still identified themselves in tribal terms—as Mi'kmaq or Mohawk or Haida—but they typically thought of themselves collectively and *in opposition to European settlers* as Indians. A new identity was thus grafted onto tribal identities because indigenous peoples confronted a group that had the power to impose a name on them.

In time, however, an increasingly large number of indigenous people began to reject the term *Indian*. White settlers and their governments took land from the indigenous peoples and forced them onto reserves, causing resentment, anger, and solidarity to grow. Especially since the 1960s, indigenous North Americans have begun to fight back culturally and politically, asserting pride in their languages, art, and customs, and making legal claims to the land that had been taken from them. One aspect of their resistance involved questioning the use of the term *Indian*. In Canada, many of them preferred instead to be called Native Canadians, Indigenous Peoples, Aboriginal Canadians, or First Nations. These new terms, especially the last one, were all assertions of new-found pride. Today, many North Americans of European origin accept these new terms out of respect for indigenous North Americans and in recognition of their neglected rights. New, more or less stable ethnic identities have thus been negotiated as the power struggle between indigenous peoples and more recent settlers continues. As the social context changed, the negotiation of ethnic identities proceeded apace.

Ethnic and Racial Labels: Imposition versus Choice

The idea that race and ethnicity are socially constructed does not mean that everyone can always choose their racial or ethnic identity freely. There are wide variations over time and from one society to the next in the degree to which people can exercise such freedom of choice. Moreover, in a given society at a given time, different categories of people are more or less free to choose.

In Canada, the people with the most freedom to choose are white European Canadians whose ancestors arrived more than two generations ago. For example, identifying yourself as an Irish Canadian no longer has negative implications, as it did in, say, 1900. Then, in

Many white Canadians lived in poor urban ghettos in the nineteenth and early twentieth centuries. However, a larger proportion of them experienced upward mobility than was the case for African Canadians in the late twentieth century. This photo shows a Manitoba tenement in 1912.

National Archives of Canada/C-030939

a city like Toronto, where a substantial number of Irish immigrants were concentrated, the English Protestant majority typically regarded working-class Irish Catholics as often drunk, inherently lazy, and born superstitious. This strong anti-Irish sentiment, which often erupted into conflict, meant the Irish found it difficult to escape their ethnic identity even if they wanted to. Since then, however, Irish Canadians have followed the path taken by many other white European groups. They have achieved upward mobility and blended with the majority.

As a result, Irish Canadians no longer find their identity imposed on them. Instead, they may *choose* whether to march in a St. Patrick's Day parade, enjoy the remarkable contributions of Irish authors to English-language literature and drama, and take pride in the atheticism and precision of Riverdance. For them, ethnicity is largely a *symbolic* matter, as it is for the other white European groups that have undergone similar social processes. Herbert Gans defines **symbolic ethnicity** as "a nostalgic allegiance to the culture of the immigrant generation, or that of the old country; a love for and a pride in a tradition that can be felt without having to be incorporated in everyday behavior" (Gans, 1991: 436).

In contrast, most African Canadians lack the freedom to enjoy symbolic ethnicity. They may well take pride in their cultural heritage and participate in such cultural festivals as Caribana. However, their identity as people of African descent is not an option because a considerable number of non-blacks are racists and impose the identity on them. **Racism** is the belief that a visible characteristic of a group, such as skin colour, indicates group inferiority and justifies discrimination. Recent surveys show that somewhere between 30 percent and 55 percent of Canadians (depending on the wording of the question) hold racist views of varying intensity (Henry et al., 2001: 147–51).

As the contrast between Irish Canadians and African Canadians suggests, then, relations among racial and ethnic groups can take different forms. We now turn to conflict theories, which seek to explain why racial and ethnic relations take different forms in different times and places.

Symbolic ethnicity is a nostalgic allegiance to the culture of the immigrant generation, or that of the old country, that is not usually incorporated in everyday behaviour.

Racism is the belief that a visible characteristic of a group, such as skin colour, indicates group inferiority and justifies discrimination.

CONFLICT THEORIES OF RACE AND ETHNICITY

Many whites of European origin have assimilated in Canadian society. Their families have been here for generations, and they have stopped thinking of themselves as Italian Canadian or Irish Canadian or German Canadian. Today, they think of themselves just as Canadians (Boyd, 1999; Boyd and Norris, 2001), because, over time, they achieved rough equality with members of the majority group. In the process, they began to blend in with them.

In contrast, assimilation is less widespread among Aboriginal peoples, Québécois, African Canadians, and Asian Canadians. Conflict theories explain why.

Internal Colonialism

One conflict theory is the theory of **internal colonialism** (Blauner, 1972; Hechter, 1974). *Colonialism* involves people from one country invading another country. In the process, the invaders change or destroy the native culture. They gain virtually complete control over the native population. They develop the racist belief that the native inhabitants are inherently inferior. And they confine natives to work considered demeaning. *Internal colonialism* involves much the same processes but within the boundaries of a single country. Internal colonialism prevents assimilation by segregating the colonized in terms of jobs, housing, and social contacts ranging from friendship to marriage. To varying degrees, Canada, the United States, Great Britain, Australia, France, Italy, Spain, Russia, and China have engaged in internal colonialism. In Canada, the main victims of internal colonialism are Aboriginal peoples, the Québécois, and people of African descent.

Internal colonialism involves one race or ethnic group subjugating another in the same country. It prevents assimilation by segregating the subordinate group in terms of jobs, housing, and social contacts.

Canada's Aboriginal Peoples

The single word that best describes the treatment of Canada's Aboriginal peoples by European immigrants in the nineteenth century is *expulsion*. **Expulsion** is the forcible removal of a population from a territory claimed by another population.

Expulsion is dramatically illustrated by the plight of the Beothuk (pronounced bee-**aw**-thik), an Aboriginal people from what is today Newfoundland and Labrador. The Beothuk were Algonkian-speaking people who probably numbered fewer than a thousand people at the time of European contact. In the sixteenth century, Europeans used Newfoundland and Labrador as a fishing port, returning to Europe each year after the fishing season. In the seventeenth century, year-round European settlement began. This caused a revolution in the life of the Beothuk because the Europeans viewed them as a nuisance. They offered incentives to the Mi'kmaq from Nova Scotia to kill off the Beothuk. The Beothuk population declined and gradually withdrew from European contact.

Expulsion is the forcible removal of a population from a territory claimed by another population.

As European settlement grew in the eighteenth century, the Beothuk were squeezed into the interior. There they competed for scarce resources with fur traders. Eventually the Beothuk were reduced to a small refugee population along the Exploits River system, living off the meagre resources of the Newfoundland and Labrador interior. The expulsion of the Beothuk from their traditional territories through European colonization led to the tribe's eventual extinction. Today, about all that remains of the Beothuk, aside from their tragic history and a few artifacts, is a statue outside the Newfoundland and Labrador provincial legislature.

The story of the Beothuk is an extreme case. However, *all* Aboriginal tribes had broadly similar experiences. In the eighteenth and nineteenth centuries, as the European settlers' fur trade gave way to the harvesting of timber, minerals, oil, and gas, Aboriginal peoples were shunted aside so the Canadian economy could grow. At the time, Europeans thought they were "assimilating" the Aboriginal peoples. The Indian Act spoke of the need to transform a hunting-gathering people into an agricultural labour force (Menzies, 1999). Sir John A. Macdonald, Canada's first prime minister, spoke of the need "to do away with the tribal system and assimilate the Indian people in all respects with the inhabitants of the Dominion, as speedily as they are fit to change" (quoted in Montgomery, 1965: 13). In contrast, many Aboriginal peoples understood the settlers' actions—the passage of the Indian Act, the establishment of the reserve system, the creation of residential schools, and so forth—less as an attempt to assimilate them than as an attempt to obliterate their heritage. It is in this sense that the government of Canada has been accused by some Aboriginal peoples of perpetuating cultural genocide (Cardinal, 1977). **Genocide** is the intentional extermination of an entire population defined as a "race" or a "people."

Genocide is the intentional extermination of an entire population defined as a "race" or a "people."

Adding insult to injury, early historical writing about Canada depicted Aboriginal peoples as either irrelevant or evil. Typically, in *The History of the Dominion of Canada*, a book widely used in Canadian schools at the turn of the twentieth century, only five pages

The Canadian policy of assimilation: In its annual report of 1904, the Department of Indian Affairs published the photographs of Thomas Moore of the Regina Industrial School "before and after tuition." These images are "a cogent expression of what federal policy had been since Confederation and what it would remain for many decades. It was a policy of assimilation, a policy designed to move Aboriginal communities from their 'savage' state to that of 'civilization' and thus to make in Canada but one community—a non-Aboriginal one" (Milloy, 1999).

Saskatchewan Archives Board, R-82239[1] and R-82239[2]

were devoted to Aboriginal peoples (Clement, 1897). They are described as "cruel," "rude," "false," "crafty," "savages," and "ferocious villains" who plotted against the Europeans with "fiendish ingenuity" (Francis, 1992; Richardson, 1832; Roberts, 1915). Canadian schoolbooks continued to portray Aboriginal peoples in pretty much this way until the mid-twentieth century.

So we see that, throughout North America, the confrontation with European culture undermined the way of life of the Aboriginal peoples. Because of internal colonialism and, in particular, expulsion from their traditional lands, Canada's Aboriginal peoples were prevented from practising their traditional ways and assimilating into the larger society. Most of them languished on reservations and, in more recent times, in urban slums. There they experienced high rates of unemployment, poverty, ill health, and violence. The history of Canada's Aboriginal peoples raises in the most distressing way possible the issue of whether and in what form white society should take responsibility for past injustices, a subject to which we return later.

The Québécois

Conquest is the forcible capture of land and the economic and political domination of its inhabitants.

A second form of internal colonialism involves not expulsion but **conquest**, the forcible capture of land and the economic and political domination of its inhabitants. For example, as part of their centuries-long struggle to control North America, the English conquered New France and its 60 000 settlers in 1759. The English thereby created a system of ethnic stratification that remained in place for more than 200 years and that turned out to be a major source of political conflict (McRoberts, 1988).

The British recognized that any attempt to impose their language, religion, laws, and institutions in the former French colony could result in unacceptably high levels of resistance and conflict. Therefore, they tried to accommodate farmers and the Catholic clergy by reinforcing their rights and privileges. The British believed this would win the allegiance of these two groups, who would in turn help build loyalty to Britain among the population as a whole. In contrast, the British undermined the rights and privileges of merchants engaged mainly in the fur trade. So while agriculture, religion, and politics remained the province of the French, the British took over virtually all large-scale commerce.

As noted, this pattern of ethnic stratification remained intact for two centuries. True, by 1950 most farmers had been transformed into urban, industrial workers. A contingent of Québécois had become physicians, lawyers, and members of the "new middle class" of administrators, technicians, scientists, and intellectuals. However, the upper reaches of the stratification system remained overwhelmingly populated by people of British origin. Social separation reinforced economic segregation. The French and the British tended to speak different languages, live in different towns and neighbourhoods, interact occasionally, befriend one another infrequently, and intermarry rarely. Characteristically, the novel that became emblematic of the social relations between French and English in Quebec is entitled *Two Solitudes* (MacLennan, 1945).

Apart from its rigid system of ethnic stratification, Quebec in the middle of the twentieth century was remarkable because of its undeveloped government services. Health, education, and welfare were largely controlled by the Catholic Church. Government intervention in economic matters was almost unknown. Because of this political backwardness, members of Quebec's new middle class, together with blue-collar workers, began campaigning to modernize the provincial political system in the late 1940s. They pressed for more liberal labour laws that would recognize the right of all workers to form unions and strike. They wanted state control over education and a new curriculum that stressed the natural and social sciences rather than classical languages and catechism. They desired a government that would supply a wide range of social services to the population. They demanded that the state provide better infrastructure for economic development and help francophone entrepreneurs expand their businesses. The partial realization of these aims in the 1960s came to be known as the Quiet Revolution.

However, the modernization of the Quebec state failed to resolve four issues:

1. *The potential demographic decline of the Québécois.* By 1981, Québécois women were giving birth to fewer children on average than were women in any other province. In fact, they were having fewer than the 2.1 children that women must bear on average to ensure that the size of the population does not decline (Romaniuc, 1984: 14–18). Noticing this trend in the 1970s, many Québécois felt they were becoming an endangered species.

2. *The assimilation of immigrants into English culture.* Fears of demographic decline were reinforced by the preference of most new immigrants to have their children educated in English-language schools. Together with the falling birth rate, this development threatened to diminish the size—and therefore, potentially, the power—of Quebec's francophone population.

3. *Persistent ethnic stratification.* The Quiet Revolution helped to create many thousands of jobs for highly educated francophones—but almost exclusively in the government bureaucracy, the educational system, and in new Crown corporations, such as Hydro-Québec. It became apparent in the 1970s that management positions in the private sector remained the preserve of English-origin Canadians.

4. *The continued use of English as the language of private industry.* English remained the language of choice in the private sector because the largest and technologically most advanced businesses were controlled by English Canadians and Americans. This situation was felt particularly keenly when the expansion of the state sector, and therefore the upward mobility of the francophone new middle class, slowed in the 1970s.

Because of the issues just listed, many Québécois felt that the survival and prosperity of their community required vigorous state intervention in non-francophone institutions. For example, many Québécois came to believe that most shares of banks, trust companies, and insurance firms should be held in Quebec and that these financial institutions should be obliged to reinvest their profits in the province. They argued that the state should increase its role as economic planner and initiator of development and should forbid foreign ownership of cultural enterprises. Finally, the Québécois increasingly demanded compulsory French-language education for the children of most immigrants, obligatory use of French among private-sector managers, and French-only signs in public places. Most Québécois regarded these proposals as the only means by which their community could survive and attain equality with the English. Moreover, since the Quebec state did not have the legal authority to enact some of the proposed changes, they felt that the province ought to negotiate broader constitutional powers with the federal government. A large minority of Québécois went a step further. They became convinced that Quebec ought to become a politically sovereign nation, albeit a nation economically associated with Canada.

The pro-independence Parti Québécois won the provincial election in 1976. In 1980, it held a referendum to see whether Quebecers favoured "sovereignty-association." Nearly 60 percent voted no. A second referendum was held in 1995. This time, the forces opposed to sovereignty-association won by the narrowest of margins—about 1 percent. The Parti Québécois promises to hold additional referenda until it gets the result it wants. Thus, in the early twenty-first century, the economic, social, and cultural segregation of the Québécois from English Canada—a legacy of the conquest—meant Canada's future was still uncertain.

African Canadians

Slavery is the ownership and control of people.

We have seen that internal colonialism, whether it is accomplished by means of expulsion or conquest, creates big barriers to assimilation that can endure for centuries. A third form of internal colonialism—slavery—creates similar barriers. **Slavery** is the ownership and control of people.

By 1800, 24 million Africans had been captured and placed on slave ships headed to North, Central, and South America. Because of violence, disease, and shipwreck, fewer than half survived the passage. Black slaves were bought and sold in Canada at least until the 1820s. Only in 1833, when the British government banned slavery throughout the British Empire, did the practice become illegal in Canada. Slavery was abolished in the United States 30 years later.

It is true that the extent of slavery in Canada paled in comparison with its widespread use in the United States, where tobacco and cotton production depended entirely on the work of dirt-cheap black labour. It is also true that for decades Canada served as the terminus of the "underground railway," a network of assistance that smuggled escaped slaves out of the United States to freedom in Canada. However, after the American Civil War (1861–65) the practice of encouraging black settlement in Canada was reversed. Government policy required the rejection of most immigration applications by black people. This policy reflected a deeply felt prejudice on the part of the Canadian population that persisted throughout the twentieth century (Goldstein, 1978; Sissing, 1996). Moreover, social relations between Canadians of African descent and the white European majority were anything but intimate and based on equality. Until the middle of the twentieth century, African Canadians tended to do unskilled labour and be residentially and socially segregated—for example, in the Halifax community

Black Slave for Sale: Many distinguished persons were slave owners, including Peter Russell, who held positions in the executive and legislative councils and became administrator of Upper Canada.

TO BE SOLD,

A BLACK WOMAN, named PEGGY, aged about forty years ; and a Black boy her son, named JUPITER, aged about fifteen years, both of them the property of the Subscriber.

The Woman is a tolerable Cook and washer woman and perfectly understands making Soap and Candles.

The Boy is tall and strong of his age, and has been employed in Country business, but brought up principally as a House Servant—They are each of them Servants for life.   The Price for the Woman is one hundred and fifty Dollars—for the Boy two hundred Dollars, payable in three years with Interest from the day of Sale and to be properly secured by Bond &c.— But one fourth less will be taken in ready Money.

PETER RUSSELL.

York, Feb. 10th 1806.

Upper Canada Gazette, February 10, 1806

of Africville, established around 1850 by runaway American slaves (Clairmont and Magill, 1999).

Canadian immigration policy was liberalized in the 1960s. Racial and ethnic restrictions were removed. Immigrants were now admitted on the basis of their potential economic contribution to Canadian society (about 57 percent of all immigrants in 2004), their close family ties with Canadians (about 26 percent of the total), or their refugee status (about 14 percent of the total; Citizenship and Immigration Canada, 2004). As a result, Canada became a much more racially and ethnically diverse society (see Figure 10.2). Some 783 795 people living in Canada in 2006 were black (2.5 percent of the population, Statistics Canada, 2008k). Many new immigrants had completed postsecondary education abroad. Others attended colleges and universities in Canada. The social standing of Canada's black community thus improved significantly. Nonetheless, Canadians of African descent still tend to interact little with white Canadians of European descent, especially in their intimate relations, and they still tend to live in different neighbourhoods. Like the aftermath of expulsion and conquest, the aftermath of slavery—prejudice, discrimination, disadvantage, and segregation—continues to act as a barrier to assimilation.

You can easily judge for yourself the strength of social barriers between Canadians of different ethnic and racial backgrounds. You can also determine how this barrier has changed over time. Draw up a list of your five closest friends and note the ethnic or racial background of each one. Now ask one of your parents to do the same for *their* five closest friends. Finally, ask one of your grandparents to draw up a similar list. How racially and ethnically diverse is your friendship network? How do you explain its racial and ethnic diversity or lack of diversity? How racially and ethnically diverse is your friendship network compared with the friendship network of your parent and grandparent? How do you explain differences between generations? Now, instead of focusing on friends, perform the same exercise for your cousins and the cousins of your parent and grandparent. How racially and ethnically diverse is your kinship network? How diverse it is compared with the kinship network of your parent and grandparent? How do you explain differences among generations? Finally, compare the racial and ethnic diversity of friendship and kinship networks. For each generation (yours, your parent's, and your grandparent's), is the kinship or the friendship network more racially and ethnically diverse? Why? Where do you and your family fit into the web of racial and ethnic diversity that comprises Canadian society?

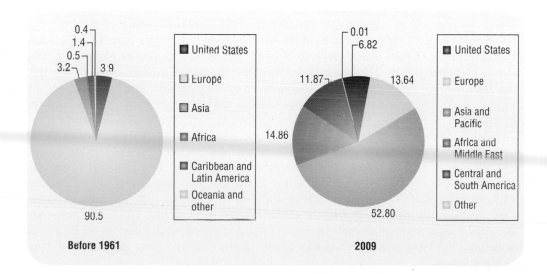

FIGURE 10.2

Immigrants by Place of Birth and Period of Immigration, Canada, before 1961 and 2009 (in percent)

Sources: Adapted from Statistics Canada, 2003, "Canada's Ethnocultural Portrait: The Changing Mosaic, 2001 Census (Analysis series)," Catalogue 96F0030, January. Retrieved April 13, 2007 (http://www.statcan.ca/english/IPS/Data/96F003XIE2001008.htm); Citizenship and Immigration Canada, 2009, "Canada Facts and Figures: Immigrant Overview Permanent and Temporary Residents." Retrieved April 25, 2011 (http://www.cic.gc.ca/english/resources/statistics/menu-fact.asp)

According to the 2006 census, the top 10 ethnic groups in Canada, other than British, French, and Canadian, include (in order of size) Canadians of German, Italian, Chinese, Aboriginal, Ukrainian, Dutch, Polish, East Indian, Russian, and Filipino origins.

© Eyewire/Getty Images

The Theory of the Split Labour Market and the Case of Asian Canadians

The theory of the **split labour market** holds that where low-wage workers of one race and high-wage workers of another race compete for the same jobs, high-wage workers are likely to resent the presence of low-wage competitors and conflict is bound to result. Consequently, racist attitudes develop or are reinforced.

We have seen how the theory of internal colonialism explains the persistence of inequality and segregation between racial and ethnic groups. A second theory that focuses on the social-structural barriers to assimilation is the theory of the **split labour market**, first proposed by sociologist Edna Bonacich (1972). Bonacich's theory explains why racial identities are reinforced by certain labour market conditions. In brief, she argues that where low-wage workers of one race and high-wage workers of another race compete for the same jobs, high-wage workers are likely to resent the presence of low-wage competitors and conflict is bound to result. Consequently, racist attitudes develop or are reinforced.

This is certainly what happened during the early years of Asian immigration in Canada. Chinese, then Japanese, and later Sikhs were allowed into Canada from about the 1850s to the early 1920s for one reason: to provide scarce services and cheap labour in the booming West. Chinese-owned restaurants, grocery stores, laundries, and import businesses dotted the West and especially British Columbia by the early twentieth century (Li, 1998; Whitaker, 1987). Numerically more important, however, were the Asian labourers who worked in lumbering, mining, and railway construction. For example, 15 000 Chinese men were allowed into Canada to complete construction of the final and most difficult section of the Canadian Pacific Railway (CPR), which involved blasting tunnels and laying rail along dangerous Rocky Mountain passes. The Chinese were paid half the wages of white workers. It is said that they "worked like horses." It is also said that they "dropped like flies" due to exposure, disease, malnutrition, and explosions. Four Chinese workers died for every 1.5 kilometres of track laid.

Asian immigration in general was widely viewed as a threat to cherished British values and institutions, an evil to be endured only as long as absolutely necessary. Therefore, once the CPR was completed in 1885, the Chinese were no longer welcome in British Columbia. A prohibitively expensive "head tax" equal to two months' wages was placed on each Chinese immigrant. The tax was increased tenfold in 1903. In 1923, Chinese immigration was banned altogether. During the Great Depression, more than 28 000 Chinese were deported because of high unemployment, and Asian immigration did not resume on a large scale until the 1960s, when racial criteria were finally removed from Canadian immigration regulations.

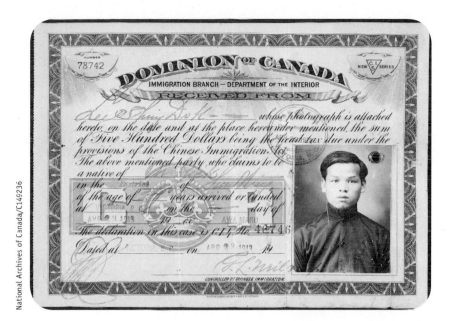

National Archives of Canada/C149236

Head tax certificate: Immigrants from China were required by law to pay a "head tax" to enter Canada between 1885 and 1923. The tax began as a fee of $50 and rose as high as $500.

Underlying European Canadian animosity against Asian immigration was a split labour market. The fact that Asian immigrants were willing to work for much lower wages than were European Canadians fuelled deep resentment among European Canadians, especially when the labour market was flooded with too many job seekers. European Canadians formed "exclusion leagues" to pressure the government to restrict Asian immigration, and on occasion they even staged anti-Asian riots. Such actions solidified racial identities among both the throwers and the victims of the bricks and made assimilation impossible (on the 1907 anti-Asian riots in Vancouver, see Chapter 21, Collective Action and Social Movements).

In sum, the theory of split labour markets, like the theory of internal colonialism, emphasizes the social-structural roots of race and ethnicity. The groups that have had the most trouble assimilating into the British values and institutions that dominate Canadian society are those that were subjected to expulsion from their native lands, conquest, slavery, and split labour markets. These circumstances left a legacy of racism that created social-structural impediments to assimilation—impediments such as forced segregation in low-status jobs and low-income neighbourhoods.

Courtesy of the Pier 21 Society

Pier 21 is located at 1055 Marginal Road, Halifax. Many immigrants entered Canada at Pier 21. It opened its doors in 1928. As the era of ocean travel was coming to an end in March 1971, the Immigration Service left Pier 21. It is now Canada's Immigration Museum.

Some Advantages of Ethnicity

The theories of internal colonialism and split labour markets emphasize how social forces outside a racial or an ethnic group force its members together, preventing their assimilation into the dominant values and institutions of society. It focuses on the disadvantages of race and ethnicity. Moreover, it deals only with the most disadvantaged minorities. The theory has less to say about the internal conditions that promote group cohesion and in particular about the value of group membership. Nor does it help us to understand why some European Canadians, such as those of Greek or Polish or German origin, continue to participate in the life of their ethnic communities, even if their families have been in the country more than two or three generations.

A review of the sociological literature suggests that three main factors enhance the value of ethnic group membership for some white European Canadians who have lived in the country for many generations:

1. *Ethnic group membership can have economic advantages.* The economic advantages of ethnicity are most apparent for immigrants, who composed nearly 20 percent of the Canadian population in 2006 (see Figure 10.3). Immigrants often lack extensive social contacts and fluency in English or French. Therefore, they commonly rely on members of their ethnic group to help them find jobs and housing. In this way, immigrant communities become tightly knit. However, some economic advantages extend into the second generation and beyond. For example, community solidarity is an important resource for "ethnic entrepreneurs." These are businesspeople who operate largely within their ethnic community. They draw on their community for customers, suppliers, employees, and credit, and they may be linked economically to the homeland as importers and exporters. They often pass on their businesses to their children, who in turn can pass the businesses on to the next generation. In this way, strong economic incentives encourage some people to remain ethnic group members, even beyond the immigrant generation (Bonacich, 1973; Light, 1991; Portes and Manning, 1991).

2. *Ethnic group membership can be politically useful.* Consider, for instance, the way some Canadians reacted to the rise of separatism in Quebec in the 1960s. To bridge the growing divide between francophone Quebec and the rest of the country, the federal government under Pierre Trudeau's Liberals promoted a policy of bilingualism. French and English were made official languages. This meant that federal government services would be made available in both languages, and instruction in French, including total

FIGURE 10.3

Foreign-Born as a Percentage of Canada's Population, 1901–2006

Sources: Adapted from Statistics Canada, "2001 Census: Analysis Series, Canada's Ethnocultural Portrait: The Changing Mosaic," Catalogue 96F0030XIE2001008. Retrieved January 21, 2011 (http://www12.statcan.ca/ english/census01/products/analytic/ companion/etoimm/canada.ctm); Statistics Canada, 2007, "Population by Immigrant Status and Period of Immigration, 2006 Counts, for Canada, Provinces and Territories —20% Sample Data." Retrieved January 21, 2011 (http://www12.statcan .ca/english/census06/data/ highlights/Immigration/Table403. cfm?Lang=E&T=403&GH=4&SC= 1&S=99&O=A).

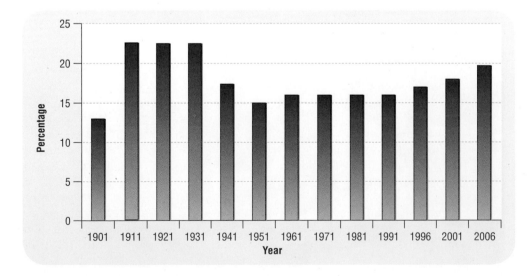

immersion instruction, would be encouraged in English schools. Members of some ethnic groups, such as people of Ukrainian origin in Western Canada, felt neglected and alienated by this turn of events. They saw no reason for the French to be accorded special status and wanted a share of the resources available for promoting ethnic languages and cultures. As a result, the Trudeau government proclaimed a new policy of multiculturalism in 1971. Now federal funds became available for the promotion of Ukrainian and all other ethnic cultures in Canada. This entire episode of Canadian ethnic history bolstered Western support for the Liberal Party for nearly a decade and softened Western opposition to bilingualism. Moreover, it helped to stimulate ethnic culture and ethnic identification throughout the country. We thus see that ethnicity can be a political tool for achieving increased access to resources. This is part of the reason for the persistence of ethnic identification for some white European Canadians whose families have lived in the country for many generations.

3. *Ethnic group membership tends to persist because of the emotional support it provides.* Like economic benefits, the emotional advantages of ethnicity are most apparent in immigrant communities. Speaking the ethnic language and sharing other elements of native culture are valuable sources of comfort in an alien environment. Even beyond the second generation, however, ethnic group membership can perform significant emotional functions. For example, some ethnic groups have experienced unusually high levels of prejudice and discrimination involving expulsion or attempted genocide. For people who belong to such groups, the resulting trauma is so severe it can be transmitted for several generations. In such cases, ethnic group membership offers security in a world still seen as hostile long after the threat of territorial loss or annihilation has disappeared (Bar-On, 1999). Another way in which ethnic group membership offers emotional support beyond the second generation is by providing a sense of rootedness. Especially in a highly mobile, urbanized, technological, and bureaucratic society, such as ours, ties to an ethnic community can be an important source of stability and security (Isajiw, 1978).

Canacian Pacific Airline/National Archives of Canada/C-45080

With the introduction of the point system in 1967, nationality and race were removed as selection criteria from the Immigration Act. Of the more than 250 000 people who came to Canada in 2005, more than 50 percent came from 10 source countries: China, India, Pakistan, the Philippines, Korea, the United States, Iran, Romania, Sri Lanka, and Britain.

The three factors listed above make ethnic group membership useful to some Canadians whose families have been in the country for many generations. In fact, retaining ethnic ties beyond the second generation has never been easier. Inexpensive international communication and travel allow ethnic group members to maintain strong ties to their ancestral homeland in a way that was never possible in earlier times. Immigration used to involve cutting all or most ties to a person's country of origin. Travel by sea and air was expensive, long distance telephone rates were prohibitive, and the occasional letter was about the only communication most immigrants had with relatives in the old country. Lack of communication encouraged assimilation in the newly adopted countries. Today, however, ties to the ancestral communities are often maintained in ways that sustain ethnic culture. For example, about 25 000 Jews have emigrated from the former Soviet Union to Canada since the early 1970s, settling mainly in Toronto. They frequently visit relatives in the former Soviet Union and Israel, speak with them on the phone, and use the Internet to exchange email with them. They also receive Russian-language radio and TV broadcasts, act as conduits for foreign investment, and send money to relatives abroad (Brym, 2001; Brym with Ryvkina, 1994; Markowitz, 1993). This sort of intimate and ongoing connection with the motherland is typical of most recent immigrant communities in North America. Thanks to inexpensive international travel and communication, some ethnic groups have become **transnational communities** whose boundaries extend among countries.

Transnational communities are communities whose boundaries extend between or among countries.

In sum, ethnicity remains a vibrant force in Canadian society for a variety of reasons. Even some white Canadians whose families settled in this country more than two generations ago have reason to identify with their ethnic group. Bearing this in mind, what is the likely future of race and ethnic relations in Canada? We conclude by offering some tentative answers to that question.

Summing Up

- Theories of internal colonialism help explain the historical processes through which Aboriginal peoples have been decimated (through expulsion), the Québécois have been threatened (through conquest), and African Canadians been exploited (through slavery).
- Split labour market theory help explains how powerful groups exploit ethnic differences to perpetuate dominance.
- Connections to an ethnic community can be useful for economic and political advancement, as well as emotional support.

THE FUTURE OF RACE AND ETHNICITY IN CANADA

The world comprises nearly 200 countries and more than 5000 ethnic and racial groups. As a result, no country is ethnically and racially homogeneous, and in many countries, including Canada, the largest ethnic group forms less than half the population (see Table 10.2 and Figure 10.4 on page 260). Of course, Canada's British roots remain important. Our parliamentary democracy is based on the British model. The Queen's representative, the governor general, is our titular head of state. We still celebrate May 24, Queen Victoria's birthday. And English is the country's predominant language, with more than 60 percent of Canadians claiming it as their mother tongue. Nonetheless, Canada is a racially and ethnically heterogeneous society.

As racial and ethnic diversity has increased, Canadian ethnic and race relations have changed radically. Two hundred years ago, Canada was a society based on expulsion, conquest, slavery, and segregation. Today, we are a society based on segregation, pluralism, and assimilation, with **pluralism** being understood as the retention of racial and ethnic culture combined with equal access to basic social resources. Thus, on a scale of tolerance, Canada has come a long way in the past 200 years (see Figure 10.5 on page 260).

In comparison with most other countries, too, Canada is a relatively tolerant land. In the late twentieth and early twenty-first centuries, racial and ethnic tensions in some parts of the world erupted into wars of secession and attempted genocide. Comparing Canada with such countries may seem to stack the deck in favour of concluding that Canada is a relatively tolerant society. However, even when we compare Canada with other rich, stable, postindustrial countries, our society seems relatively tolerant by most measures (see Figure 10.6 on page 262).

Because of such factors as intermarriage and immigration, the growth of tolerance in Canada is taking place in the context of increasing ethnic and racial diversity. Given

Pluralism is the retention of racial and ethnic culture combined with equal access to basic social resources.

Ethnic Groups with Population 200 000+ (single and multiple responses*)	Percentage of Population	Number (millions)
Canadian	32.2	10.07
English	21.0	6.57
French	15.8	4.94
Scottish	15.1	4.72
Irish	13.9	4.35
German	10.2	3.18
Italian	4.6	1.45
Chinese	4.3	1.35
North American Indian	4.0	1.25
Ukrainian	3.9	1.21
Dutch	3.3	1.04
Polish	3.2	0.98
East Indian	3.1	0.96
Russian	1.6	0.50
Welsh	1.4	0.44
Filipino	1.4	0.44
Norwegian	1.4	0.43
Portuguese	1.3	0.41
Métis	1.3	0.41
Other British Isles	1.3	0.40
Swedish	1.1	0.33
Spanish	1.0	0.33
American	1.0	0.32
Hungarian	1.0	0.32
Jewish	1.0	0.32
Greek	0.7	0.24
Jamaican	0.7	0.23
Danish	0.6	0.20

Visible Minorities	Percentage of Population	Number (millions)
South Asian**	4.0	1.26
Chinese	3.9	1.22
Black	2.5	0.78
Filipino	1.3	0.41
Latin American	1.0	0.30
Southeast Asian***	0.8	0.24
Other****	2.7	0.89

TABLE 10.2

Ethnic and Visible Minority Status of Canadians, 2006

Notes:

*In reply to the ethnicity question on the census, people may specify one or more ethnicities. As a result, the number of ethnic responses is much larger than the number of Canadians.

**East Indian, Pakistani, Sri Lankan, etc.

***Vietnamese, etc.

****Arab, etc.

Sources: Statistics Canada, 2008d, 2008f.

FIGURE 10.4

Percentage of Population Accounted for by Largest Ethnic Group

No country is ethnically homogeneous, and in many countries the largest ethnic group forms less than half the population. Ethnic diversity has increased in recent years because of international migration. This map illustrates the world's ethnic diversity by showing the percentage of each country's population that is accounted for by the country's largest ethnic group. Which countries are most diverse? Which are least diverse? How might a country's level of ethnic diversity affect its population's self-identity? How ethnically diverse is Canada compared with other countries?

Sources: "Ethnic Groups," 2001; Central Intelligence Agency, 2001.

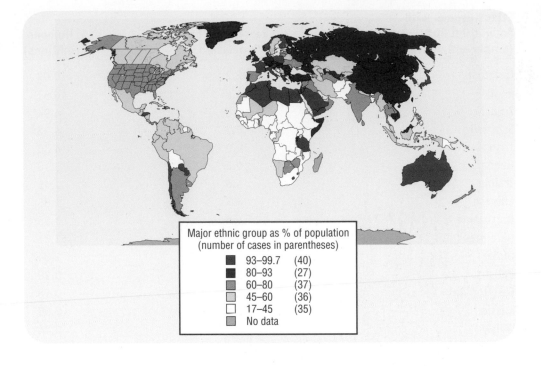

Major ethnic group as % of population (number of cases in parentheses)

- 93–99.7 (40)
- 80–93 (27)
- 60–80 (37)
- 45–60 (36)
- 17–45 (35)
- No data

Affirmative action or employment equity is a policy that gives preference to members of minority groups if equally qualified people are available for a position.

continuing migration in the coming decades, Canada will become even more of a racial and ethnic mosaic than it is now (Pendakur, 2000). However, if present trends continue, the racial and ethnic mosaic will continue to be vertical. That is, some groups, especially Aboriginal peoples, will be disproportionately clustered at the bottom of the socioeconomic hierarchy. Unless dramatic changes occur, they will continue to enjoy less wealth, income, education, good housing, health care, and other social rewards than other Canadians do.

Political initiatives could decrease the verticality of the Canadian mosaic, speeding up the movement from segregation to pluralism and assimilation for the country's most disadvantaged groups. Such political initiatives include compensation for historical injustices (see Box 10.2), **affirmative action or employment equity** programs that encourage the hiring of qualified members of disadvantaged minority groups, government-subsidized job training and child care, improvements in public education, the creation of training courses

FIGURE 10.5

Six Degrees of Separation: Types of Ethnic and Racial Group Relations

Source: From *KORNBLUM. *ACP SOCIOLOGY IN A CHANGING WORLD, 4E. © 1997 Wadsworth, a part of Cengage Learning, Inc. Reproduced by permission. www.cengage.com/permissions.

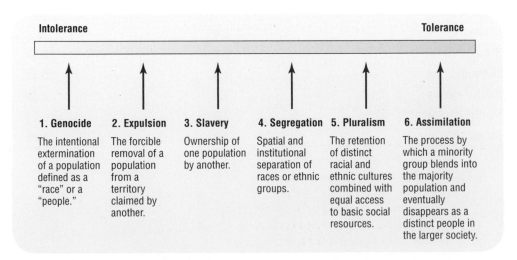

Intolerance   Tolerance

1. Genocide
The intentional extermination of a population defined as a "race" or a "people."

2. Expulsion
The forcible removal of a population from a territory claimed by another.

3. Slavery
Ownership of one population by another.

4. Segregation
Spatial and institutional separation of races or ethnic groups.

5. Pluralism
The retention of distinct racial and ethnic cultures combined with equal access to basic social resources.

6. Assimilation
The process by which a minority group blends into the majority population and eventually disappears as a distinct people in the larger society.

Social Policy: What Do You Think?

SHOULD WE PAY THE PRICE OF PAST WRONGS?

July 28, 2001, was a hot, muggy day in Toronto, and Randall Robinson added to the heat with his fiery oration to the African Canadian Legal Clinic (ACLC). "We're owed at least $11 trillion," he exhorted. "America must pay for slavery." The Harvard-educated Robinson was championing the cause of reparations for the descendants of American slaves—monetary compensation for past injustices. Americans of African descent, he argued, have been "bottom-stuck" since they were slaves. Their disadvantaged position today, he argued, is the legacy of slavery.

Although slavery was abolished in Canada in 1833, Robinson's arguments were endorsed by the ACLC and other Canadian groups that are not of African descent. Japanese, Chinese, Aboriginal, and Jewish Canadians all had representatives and gave advice at the meeting of the ACLC in July 2001.

- *Japanese Canadians.* In 1942, three months after Japan attacked Pearl Harbor, the Canadian government invoked the War Measures Act. All people of Japanese origin residing within 160 kilometres (100 miles) of the Pacific Coast were removed from their homes. With about 24 hours' notice, almost 21 000 Japanese

Canadians, 75 percent of them Canadian citizens, were moved to prisoner of war camps, work camps, and internment camps. Japanese Canadians sought and eventually received reparations for this historical injustice.

- *Chinese Canadians.* As noted earlier, the descendants of many Chinese Canadians were forced to pay a highly discriminatory head tax between 1885 and 1903. Chinese Canadians received compensation for this mistreatment only in 2006.
- *Aboriginal peoples.* Many Aboriginal children were taken from their parents and placed in residential schools in the twentieth century. Many of them were physically and sexually abused in these schools. Aboriginal peoples also claim that much land was illegally taken from them. They, too, have sought and received a redress of grievances.
- *Jewish Canadians.* The Nazis enslaved and slaughtered European Jews by the millions during World War II. Jews were the first group to seek reparations (from the German government) for the historical injustices they suffered. Jewish Canadians have sought compensation from the Canadian government for refusing to allow a boatload of Jews fleeing Nazi Germany to land in Canada in 1939.

Other aggrieved groups who were apparently not represented at the meeting include Ukrainian and Croatian Canadians (some of whom were placed in internment camps during World War I), Italian and German Canadians (some of whom were placed in internment camps during World War II), and Sikh Canadians (a boatload of whom were refused entry in Vancouver in 1914).

In the past, what was past was past. The vanquished were vanquished and the powerful wrote the history books, taking no

responsibility for what their ancestors had done. Today, things are different. Aggrieved groups in Canada and around the world are demanding reparations (Torpey, 2001). The recognition of fundamental human rights, signified first by the Human Rights Declaration of the United Nations in 1948, and the widespread delegitimization of racial and ethnic discrimination have provided fertile terrain for this historical turn. The mobilization of shame has triggered a revolutionary change in how some people and governments view past injustices.

What do you think about the reparations issue? Should *you* compensate African Canadians for slavery, Chinese Canadians for the head tax, Japanese Canadians for the internment camps, and Aboriginal peoples for residential schools and land? How responsible should *you* be for events that took place 50 or 200 years ago? In 1988 the Canadian government condemned the internment of Japanese Canadians during World War II, offered individual and community compensation to Japanese Canadians, and provided a $24 million endowment for the Canadian Race Relations Foundation. In 2005, $50 million in compensation was promised to Canadians of Chinese, Italian, Ukrainian, Croatian, German, Jewish, and Sikh origin. Also in 2005, an Agreement in Principle was reached to compensate former students of Aboriginal residential schools with $10 000 for the first year they spent in residence and $3000 for each additional year. Does this seem fair to you? What about the far larger demands of Aboriginal peoples for self-government and land rights given that they were pushed onto reserves to make way for exploration and resource development? Should Canada recognize its guilt and compensate those who have suffered? If not, why not? If so, what limits, if any, should be placed on reparations?

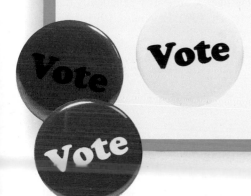

designed to upgrade the credentials of foreign-trained professionals, and the shoring up of Canada's public health system. All these initiatives would most benefit disadvantaged Canadians, a disproportionately large number of whom are visible minority group immigrants and Aboriginal peoples.

FIGURE 10.6

Percentage Not Wanting Neighbour of a Different Race, Selected Countries, 2005

Source: *World Values Survey*. 2005. Machine readable data set. Ann Arbor MI: Inter-University Consortium for Political and Social Research. Reprinted with permission.

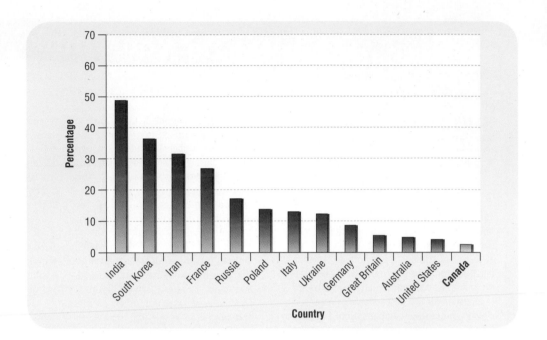

NOTES

1. Controversy surrounds the terminology used throughout this chapter. Some scholars prefer to emphasize common descent and culture by using such terms as *African Canadian* and *European Canadian* rather than *black* and *white*. However, terms that emphasize descent and culture can be ethnocentric. For example, there are millions of black immigrants from former British and French colonies in Europe. Therefore, *European Canadian* does not accurately signify the white majority in Canada. Because there is no perfect set of terms to denote racial or ethnic communities, we use *white* and *European Canadian*, as well as *black*, *African Canadian*, and *African American*.

2. Although sociologists commonly dispute a genetic basis of mean intelligence for races, evidence suggests that *individual* differences in intelligence are partly genetically transmitted (Bouchard, Lykken, McGue, Segal, and Tellegen, 1990; Lewontin, 1991: 19–37; Scarr and Weinberg, 1978; Schiff and Lewontin, 1986).

3. The genetic argument also belittles the athletic activity itself by denying the role of training in developing athletic skills.

SUMMARY

1. Is "race" a meaningful term?
   Some biologists suggest that race is not a meaningful or useful term because the biological differences that distinguish races do not predict differences in social behaviour. However, sociologists retain the term because *perceptions* of racial difference have important consequences for people's lives. Whether a person is seen as belonging to one race or another affects that person's health, wealth, and many others aspects of life.

2. **What is the difference between race and ethnicity?**

   A race is a category of people whose perceived *physical* markers are deemed socially significant. An ethnic group is a category of people whose perceived *cultural* markers are deemed socially significant. Just as physical distinctions do not cause differences in the behaviour of races, cultural distinctions are often not by themselves the major source of differences in the behaviour of various ethnic groups. *Social-structural* differences are typically the most important sources of differences in social behaviour.

3. **What do symbolic interactionist theories of race and ethnicity argue?**

   Symbolic interactionists argue that race and ethnicity are not fixed and they are not inherent in people's biological makeup or cultural heritage. Rather, the way race and ethnicity are perceived and expressed depends on the history and character of race and ethnic relations in particular social contexts. These social contexts shape the way people formulate (or "construct") their perceptions and expressions of race and ethnicity. Thus, racial and ethnic labels and identities are variables. They change over time and place. For example, cordial group relations hasten the blending of labels and identities while ethnic and racial animosity hardens them.

4. **What do conflict theories of ethnicity and race argue?**

   The theory of internal colonialism highlights the way invaders change or destroy native culture, gaining virtually complete control over the native population, developing the racist belief that natives are inherently inferior, and confining natives to work they consider demeaning. Internal colonialism prevents assimilation by segregating the colonized in terms of jobs, housing, and social contacts ranging from friendship to marriage. The theory of the split labour market highlights the way low-wage workers of one race and high-wage workers of another race may compete for the same jobs. In such circumstances, high-wage workers are likely to resent the presence of low-wage competitors. Conflict is bound to result and racist attitudes are likely to develop or get reinforced.

5. **Are racial and ethnic distinctions fading? Which groups are most resistant to change?**

   Some ethnic groups are blending over time as members of society become more tolerant. However, this tendency is weak among members of highly disadvantaged groups, especially racial minorities. That is because such groups remain highly segregated in jobs, housing, and social contacts. To a considerable degree, this is a historical legacy of internal colonialism and split labour markets.

6. **Aside from the historical legacy of internal colonialism and split labour markets, do other reasons exist for the persistence of racial and ethnic identity, even among some white Canadians of European origin whose ancestors came to this country generations ago?**

   Identifying with a racial or an ethnic group can have economic, political, and emotional benefits. These benefits account for the persistence of ethnic identity in some white Canadian families of European origin, even after they have been in Canada for more than two generations. In addition, high levels of immigration renew racial and ethnic communities by providing them with new members who are familiar with ancestral languages, customs, and so on.

7. **What is the future of race and ethnicity in Canada?**

   Racial and ethnic identities and inequalities are likely to persist in the near future. Affirmative action programs, more job training, improvements in public education, the creation of training courses designed to upgrade the credentials of foreign-trained professionals, and state-subsidized health care and child care would promote racial and ethnic equality.

KEY TERMS

affirmative action or employment equity (p. 260)

conquest (p. 250)

discrimination (p. 240)

ethnic group (p. 242)

expulsion (p. 249)

genocide (p. 249)

internal colonialism (p. 249)

melting pot (p. 245)

multiculturalism (p. 245)

pluralism (p. 258)

prejudice (p. 240)

race (p. 242)

racism (p. 248)

scapegoat (p. 242)

slavery (p. 252)

split labour market (p. 254)

symbolic ethnicity (p. 248)

transnational communities (p. 257)

WEB RESOURCES

Companion Website for This Book

http://www.compass4e.nelson.com

Begin by clicking on the Student Resources section of the website. Next, select the chapter you are studying from the pull-down menu. From the Student Resources page you have easy access to additional Weblinks and other resources. The website also has many useful tips to aid you in your study of sociology, including practice tests for each chapter.

InfoTrac® Search Terms

These search terms are provided to assist you in beginning to conduct research on this topic by visiting http://www.infotrac-college.com:

affirmative action

racism

assimilation

transnational community

discrimination

CHAPTER

11

Sexualities and Gender Stratification

IN THIS CHAPTER, YOU WILL LEARN THAT

- Whereas biology determines sex, social structure and culture largely determine gender, or the expression of culturally appropriate masculine and feminine roles.

- The social construction of gender is evident in the way parents interact with babies, teachers interact with pupils, and the mass media portray ideal body images.

- The social forces pushing people to assume conventionally masculine or feminine roles are compelling, but the social forces pushing people toward heterosexuality operate with even greater force.

- The social distinction between men and women serves as an important basis of inequality in the family and the workplace.

- Male aggression against women is rooted in gender inequality.

Mosaic Hair Group, Hairstylist—Peter Salituro, Colourist—Laura Brookes, Photographer—Babak

SEX VERSUS GENDER

Is It a Boy or a Girl?

On April 27, 1966, eight-month-old identical twin boys were brought to a hospital in Winnipeg to be circumcised. Doctors used an electrical cauterizing needle—a device that seals blood vessels as it cuts—for the procedure. However, because of equipment malfunction or doctor error, the needle entirely burned off one baby's penis. The parents desperately sought medical advice. No matter whom they consulted, they received the same prognosis. As one psychiatrist summed up the baby's future, "He will be unable to consummate marriage or have normal heterosexual relations; he will have to recognize that he is incomplete, physically defective, and that he must live apart" (quoted in Colapinto, 1997: 58).

One evening, more than half a year after the accident, the parents, now deeply depressed, were watching TV. They heard Dr. John Money, a psychologist from Johns Hopkins Hospital in Baltimore, say that he could *assign* babies a male or female identity. Money had been the driving force behind the creation of the world's first sex change clinic at Johns Hopkins. He was well known for his research on **intersexed** infants, babies born with ambiguous genitals because of a hormone imbalance in the womb or some other cause. It was Money's opinion that infants with ambiguous genitals should be assigned a sex by surgery and hormone treatments, and reared in accordance with their newly assigned sex. According to Money, these strategies would lead to the child developing a self-identity consistent with its assigned sex.

The Winnipeg couple wrote to Dr. Money, who urged them to bring their child to Baltimore immediately. After consulting various physicians, including Money, the parents agreed to have their son's sex reassigned. In anticipation of what would follow, the boy's parents stopped cutting his hair, dressed him in feminine clothes, and changed his name from Bruce to Brenda. Doctors performed surgical castration when the child was 22 months old.

Early reports of the child's progress indicated success. In contrast to her biologically identical brother, Brenda was said to disdain cars, gas pumps, and tools. She was supposedly fascinated by dolls, a dollhouse, and a doll carriage. Brenda's mother reported that, at the age of four and a half, Brenda took pleasure in her feminine clothing: "[S]he is so feminine. I've never seen a little girl so neat and tidy . . . and yet my son is quite different. I can't wash his face for anything. . . . She is very proud of herself, when she puts on a new dress, or I set her hair" (quoted in Money and Ehrhardt, 1972: 11).

The case generated worldwide attention. Textbooks in medicine and the social sciences were rewritten to incorporate Money's reports of the child's progress (Robertson, 1987: 316). But then, in March 1997, two researchers dropped a bombshell. A biologist from the University of Hawaii and a psychiatrist from the Canadian Ministry of Health unleashed a scientific scandal when they published an article showing that Bruce/Brenda had, in fact, struggled against his/her imposed girlhood from the start (Diamond and Sigmundson, 1999). Brenda insisted on urinating standing up, refused to undergo additional "feminizing" surgeries that had been planned, and, from age seven, daydreamed of her ideal future self "as a twenty-one-year-old male with a moustache, a sports car, and surrounded by admiring friends" (Colapinto, 2001: 93). She experienced academic failure and rejection and ridicule from her classmates, who dubbed her "Cavewoman." At age nine, Brenda had a nervous breakdown. At age 14, in a state of acute despair, she attempted suicide (Colapinto, 2001: 96, 262).

In 1980, when she was 14, Brenda learned the details of her sex reassignment from her father. At age 16, she decided to have her sex reassigned once more and to live as a man rather than as a woman. Advances in medical technology made it possible for Brenda, who

Intersexed infants are babies born with ambiguous genitals because of a hormone imbalance in the womb or some other cause.

David Reimer at about 30 years of age

CP PHOTO/Winnipeg Free Press

now adopted the name David, to have an artificial penis constructed. At age 25, David married a woman and adopted her three children, but that did not end his ordeal (Gorman, 1997). In May 2004, at the age of 38, David Reimer committed suicide.

Gender Identity and Gender Role

The story of Bruce/Brenda/David introduces the first big question of this chapter. What makes us male or female? Of course, part of the answer is biological. Your **sex** depends on whether you were born with distinct male or female genitals and a genetic program that released male or female hormones to stimulate the development of your reproductive system.

However, the case of Bruce/Brenda/David also shows that more is involved in becoming male or female than biological sex differences. Recalling his life as Brenda, David said, "[E]veryone is telling you that you're a girl. But you say to yourself, 'I don't *feel* like a girl.' You think girls are supposed to be delicate and *like* girl things—tea parties, things like that. But I like to *do* guy stuff. It doesn't match" (quoted in Colapinto, 1997: 66; our emphasis). As this quotation suggests, being male or female involves not just biology but also certain "masculine" and "feminine" feelings, attitudes, desires, and behaviours. These characteristics—sociologists refer to them as features of a person's **gender**—may or may not align with a person's biological sex.

Gender has three components:

1. **Sexuality** refers to a person's capacity for erotic experiences and expressions.
2. **Gender identity** refers to a person's sense of belonging to a particular sexual category ("male," "female," "homosexual," "lesbian," "bisexual," and so on).
3. **Gender role** refers to behaviour that conforms to widely shared expectations about how members of a particular sexual category are supposed to act.

Contrary to first impressions, the case of Bruce/Brenda/David suggests that, unlike sex, gender is not determined just by biology. Research shows that babies first develop a vague sense of being a boy or a girl at about the age of one. They develop a full-blown sense of gender identity between the ages of two and three (Blum, 1997). We can therefore be confident that Bruce/Brenda/David already knew he was a boy when he was assigned a female gender identity at the age of 22 months. He had, after all, been raised as a boy by his parents and treated as a boy by his brother for almost two years. He had seen boys behaving differently from girls on TV and in storybooks. He had played with stereotypical boys' toys. After his gender reassignment, the constant presence of his twin brother reinforced those early lessons on how boys ought to behave. In short, baby Bruce's *social* learning of his gender identity was already far advanced by the time he had his sex-change operation. Many researchers believe that if gender reassignment occurs before the age of 18 months, it will usually be successful (Creighton and Mihto, 2001; Lightfoot-Klein, Chase, Hammond, and Goldman, 2000). However, once the social learning of gender takes hold, as with baby Bruce, it is apparently very difficult to undo, even by means of reconstructive surgery, hormones, and parental and professional pressure. The main lesson we draw from this story is not that biology is destiny but that the social learning of gender begins very early in life.

The first half of this chapter helps you understand what makes people conventionally male or female. We first outline two competing perspectives on gender differences. The first argues that gender is inherent in our biological makeup and that society must reinforce those tendencies if it is to operate smoothly. Functionalist theory is compatible with this argument. The second perspective argues that gender is constructed mainly by social influences and may be altered to benefit society's members. Conflict, feminist, and symbolic interactionist theories are compatible with the second perspective.

In our discussion, we examine how people learn conventional gender roles in the course of everyday interaction, during socialization in the family and at school, and through advertising. We show that most of this learning is "heteronormative." **Heteronormativity** is the belief that sex is binary (one ought to be either male or female as conventionally understood)

Your **sex** depends on whether you were born with distinct male or female genitals and a genetic program that released either male or female hormones to stimulate the development of your reproductive system.

Gender refers to the feelings, attitudes, desires, and behaviours that are associated with a particular sexual category.

Sexuality refers to a person's capacity for erotic experiences and expressions.

Gender identity refers to a person's sense of belonging to a particular sexual category.

Gender role refers to behaviour that conforms to widely shared expectations about how members of a particular sexual category are supposed to act.

Heteronormativity is the belief that sex is binary (one must be either male or female as conventionally understood) and that sex ought to be perfectly aligned with gender (one's sexuality, gender identity, and gender role ought to be either male or female as conventionally understood).

Heterosexuality is the preference for members of the "opposite" sex as sexual partners.

and that sex ought to be perfectly aligned with gender (one's sexuality, gender identity, and gender role ought to be either male or female as conventionally understood). Thus, most people regard **heterosexuality**—the preference for members of the "opposite" sex as sexual partners—as normal, and they seek to enforce it. Yet, for reasons that are still poorly understood, some people resist and even reject the gender that is assigned to them based on their biological sex. When this occurs, negative sanctions are often applied to get them to conform or to punish them for their deviance. People often use emotional and physical violence to enforce conventional gender roles.

The second half of the chapter examines one of the chief consequences of people learning conventional gender roles. Gender, as currently constructed, creates and maintains social inequality. We illustrate this point in two ways. We investigate why gender is associated with an earnings gap between women and men in the paid labour force. We also show how gender inequality encourages sexual harassment and rape. In concluding our discussion of sexuality and gender, we discuss social policies that sociologists have recommended to decrease gender inequality and thereby improve women's safety.

Summing Up

- One's *sex* depends on whether one is born with distinct male or female genitals and a genetic program that releases either male or female hormones to stimulate the development of the reproductive system.
- *Gender* refers to the feelings, attitudes, desires, and behaviours that are associated with a particular sexual category—specifically, the capacity for erotic experiences and expressions (sexuality); self-identification as male, female, homosexual, lesbian, bisexual, and so on (gender identity); and behaviour that conforms to widely shared expectations about how members of a particular sexual category are supposed to act (gender role).

THEORIES OF GENDER

Most arguments about the origins of gender differences in human behaviour adopt one of two perspectives. Some analysts see gender differences as a reflection of naturally evolved dispositions. Sociologists call this perspective **essentialism** because it views gender as part of the nature or "essence" of a person's biological makeup (Weeks, 2000). Other analysts see gender differences as a reflection of the different social positions occupied by women and men. Sociologists call this perspective *social constructionism* because it views gender as "constructed" by people living in historically specific social structures and cultures. Conflict, feminist, and symbolic interactionist theories focus on various aspects of the social construction of gender. We now summarize and criticize essentialism. We then turn to social constructionism.

Essentialism is a school of thought that views gender differences as a reflection of biological differences between women and men.

Modern Essentialism: Sociobiology and Evolutionary Psychology

Sigmund Freud (1977 [1905]) offered an early essentialist explanation of male–female differences. However, in recent decades, sociobiologists and evolutionary psychologists have offered the most influential variant of the theory. According to sociobiologists and evolutionary psychologists, all humans instinctively try to ensure that their genes are passed on to future generations. However, men and women develop different strategies to achieve this goal. A woman has a bigger investment than a man does in ensuring the survival of any offspring because she produces only a small number of eggs during her reproductive life and, at most, can give birth to about 20 children. It is therefore in a woman's best interest to maintain primary responsibility for her genetic children and to find the best mate with whom to fertilize her eggs. He is the man who can best help support the children after birth. In contrast, most men can produce hundreds of millions of sperm in a single ejaculation, and this feat can be repeated often (Saxton, 1990: 94–5). Thus, a man increases the chance his and only his genes will be passed on to future generations if he is promiscuous yet jealously possessive of his partners. Moreover, since men compete with other men for sexual access to women, men evolve competitive and aggressive dispositions that include physical violence (DeSteno and Salovey, 2001). Women, says one evolutionary psychologist, are greedy for money, while men want casual sex with women, treat women's bodies as their property, and react violently to women who incite male sexual jealousy. These are "universal features of our evolved selves" that presumably contribute to the survival of the human species (Buss, 2000). From the point of view of sociobiology and evolutionary psychology, then, gender differences in behaviour are based in biological differences between women and men.

Functionalism and Essentialism

Functionalists reinforce the essentialist viewpoint when they claim that traditional gender roles help to integrate society (Parsons, 1942). In the family, wrote Talcott Parsons, women traditionally specialize in raising children and managing the household. Men traditionally work in the paid labour force. Each generation learns to perform these complementary roles by means of gender role socialization.

For boys, noted Parsons, the essence of masculinity is a series of "instrumental" traits, such as rationality, self-assuredness, and competitiveness. For girls, the essence of femininity is a series of "expressive" traits, such as nurturance and sensitivity to others. Boys and girls first learn their respective gender traits in the family as they see their parents going about their daily routines. The larger society also promotes gender role conformity. It instils in men the fear that they won't be attractive to women if they are too feminine, and it instils in women the fear that they won't be attractive to men if they are too masculine. In the functionalist view, then, learning the essential features of femininity and masculinity integrates society and allows it to function properly.

A Critique of Essentialism from the Conflict and Feminist Perspectives

Conflict and feminist theorists disagree sharply with the essentialist account. They lodge four main criticisms against it.

First, *essentialists ignore the historical and cultural variability of gender and sexuality.* Wide variations exist in what constitutes masculinity and femininity. Moreover, the level of gender inequality, the rate of male violence against women, the criteria used for mate selection, and other gender differences that appear universal to the essentialists vary widely too. This variation deflates the idea that there are essential and universal behavioural differences between women and men. Three examples help illustrate the point:

1. In societies with low levels of gender inequality, the tendency decreases for women to stress the good provider role in selecting male partners, as does the tendency for men to stress women's domestic skills (Eagley and Wood, 1999).
2. When women become corporate lawyers or police officers or take other jobs that involve competition or threat, their production of the hormone testosterone is stimulated, causing them to act more aggressively. Aggressiveness is partly role-related (Blum, 1997: 158–88).
3. Literally hundreds of studies conducted mainly in North America show that women are developing traits that were traditionally considered masculine. Women have become considerably more assertive, competitive, independent, and analytical in the past few decades (Biegler, 1999; Duffy, Gunther, and Walters, 1997; Nowell and Hedges, 1998; Twenge, 1997).

Definitions of *male* and *female* traits vary across societies. For example, the ceremonial dress of male Wodaabe nomads in Niger may appear "feminine" by conventional North American standards.

M. ou Me. Desjeux, Bernard/CORBIS

As these examples show, gender differences are not constants and they are not inherent in men and women. They vary with social conditions.

The second problem with essentialism is that *it tends to generalize from the average, ignoring variations within gender groups*. On average, women and men do differ in some respects. For example, one of the best-documented gender differences is that men are, on average, more verbally and physically aggressive than women are. However, when essentialists say men are inherently more aggressive than women are, they make it seem as if that is true of all men and all women. As Figure 11.1 illustrates, it is not. When trained researchers measure verbal or physical aggressiveness, scores vary widely within gender groups. There is considerable overlap in aggressiveness between women and men. Many women are more aggressive than the average man and many men are less aggressive than the average woman.

Third, *little or no evidence directly supports the essentialists' major claims*. Sociobiologists and evolutionary psychologists have not identified any of the genes that,

FIGURE 11.1

The Distribution of Aggressiveness among Men and Women

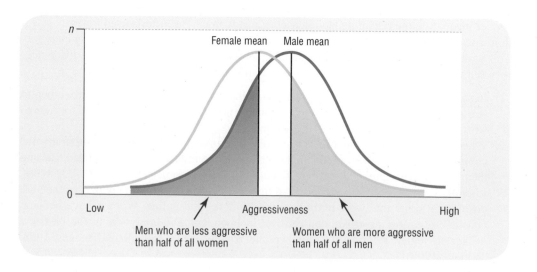

they claim, cause male jealousy, female nurturance, the unequal division of labour between men and women, and so forth.

Finally, *essentialists' explanations for gender differences ignore the role of power.* Essentialists assume that existing behaviour patterns help to ensure the survival of the species and the smooth functioning of society. However, as conflict and feminist theorists argue, essentialists generally ignore the fact that men are usually in a position of greater power and authority than women are.

Conflict theorists dating back to Marx's collaborator, Friedrich Engels, have located the root of male domination in class inequality (Engels, 1970 [1884]). According to Engels, men gained substantial power over women when preliterate societies were first able to produce more than the amount needed for their own subsistence. At that point, some men gained control over the economic surplus. They soon devised two means of ensuring that their offspring would inherit the surplus. First, they imposed the rule that only men could own property. Second, by means of socialization and force, they ensured that women remained sexually faithful to their husbands. As industrial capitalism developed, Engels wrote, male domination increased because industrial capitalism made men still wealthier and more powerful while it relegated women to subordinate, domestic roles.

Feminist theorists doubt that male domination is so closely linked to the development of industrial capitalism. For one thing, they note that gender inequality is greater in precapitalist, agrarian societies than in industrial capitalist societies. For another, male domination is evident in societies that call themselves socialist or communist. These observations lead many feminists to conclude that male domination is rooted less in industrial capitalism than in the patriarchal authority relations, family structures, and patterns of socialization and culture that exist in most societies (Lapidus, 1978: 7).

Despite this disagreement, conflict and feminist theorists concur that behavioural differences between women and men result less from any essential differences between them than from men being in a position to impose their interests on women. From the conflict and feminist viewpoints, functionalism, sociobiology, and evolutionary psychology can themselves be seen as examples of the exercise of male power, that is, as rationalizations for male domination and sexual aggression.

Social Constructionism and Symbolic Interactionism

Essentialism is the view that masculinity and femininity are inherent and universal traits of men and women, whether because of biological or social necessity or some combination of the two. In contrast, social constructionism is the view that *apparently* natural or innate features of life, such as gender, are actually sustained by *social* processes that vary historically and culturally. As such, conflict and feminist theories may be regarded as types of social constructionism. So may symbolic interactionism. Symbolic interactionists, you will recall, focus on the way people attach meaning to things in the course of their everyday communication. One of the things to which people attach meaning is what it means to be a man or a woman. We illustrate the symbolic interactionist approach by first considering how boys and girls learn masculine and feminine roles in the family and at school. We then show how gender roles are maintained in the course of everyday social interaction and through advertising in the mass media.

Gender Socialization

Barbie dolls have been around since 1959. Based on the creation of a German cartoonist, Barbie is the first modern doll modelled after an adult. Some industry experts predicted mothers would never buy dolls with breasts for their little girls. Were *they* wrong! Mattel sells about 10 million Barbies and 20 million accompanying outfits annually. The Barbie trademark is worth $1 billion.

What do girls learn when they play with Barbie? The author of a website devoted to Barbie undoubtedly speaks for millions when she writes, "Barbie was more than a doll to me. She was a way of living: the Ideal Woman. When I played with her, I could make her do

"Barbie was more than a doll to me. She was a way of living: the Ideal Woman."

and be ANYTHING I wanted. Never before or since have I found such an ideal method of living vicariously through anyone or anything. And I don't believe I am alone. I am certain that most people have, in fact, lived their dreams with Barbie as the role player" (Elliott, 1995; Nicolaiedis, 1998; Turkel, 1998).

One dream that Barbie stimulates among many girls concerns body image. After all, Barbie is a scale model of a woman with a 40-18-32 figure (Hamilton, 1996: 197). Researchers who compared Barbie's gravity-defying proportions with the actual proportions of several representative groups of adult women concluded that the probability of this body shape is less than 1 in 100 000 (Norton, Olds, Olive, and Dank, 1996). (Ken's body shape is far more realistic at 1 in 50.)

Nevertheless, since the 1960s, Barbie has served as an identifiable symbol of stereotypical female beauty (Magro, 1997). Her pre-set Barbie Workout Scale registers a lithe 110 pounds (50 kilograms). The closets of her pink house are jammed with outfits. Bathrooms, gyms, and beauty parlours feature prominently among the Barbie sets available. Her quest for physical perfection seems largely geared to the benefit of Ken, her boyfriend (Nelson and Robinson, 2002: 131). When girls play with Barbie, they learn to want to be slim, blonde, shapely, and, implicitly, pleasing to men.

A comparable story, with competition and aggression as its theme, could be told about how boys' toys, such as Transformers, teach stereotypical male roles. True, a movement to market more gender-neutral toys arose in the 1960s and 1970s. However, it has now been overtaken by the resumption of a strong tendency to market toys based on gender. As *The Wall Street Journal* pointed out, "gender-neutral is out, as more kids' marketers push single-sex products" (Bannon, 2000: B1).

Toys are only part of the story of gender socialization and hardly its first or final chapter. Research shows that, from birth, infant boys and girls who are matched in length, weight, and general health are treated differently by parents—and by fathers in particular. Girls tend to be identified as delicate, weak, beautiful, and cute, boys as strong, alert, and well coordinated (Rubin, Provenzano, and Lurra, 1974). Recent attempts to update and extend this investigation found that although parents' gender-stereotyped perceptions of newborns have declined, especially among fathers, they have not disappeared entirely (Fagot, Rodgers, and Leinbach, 2000; Gauvain, Fagot, Leve, and Kavanagh, 2002; Karraker, Vogel, and Lake, 1995). When viewing videotape of a nine-month-old infant, adult experimental subjects tend to label its startled reaction to a stimulus as "anger" if the child has earlier been identified by the experimenters as a boy and as "fear" if it has earlier been identified as a girl, *whatever the infant's actual sex* (Condry and Condry, 1976; Martin, 1999).

Parents, and especially fathers, are more likely to encourage their sons to engage in boisterous and competitive play and discourage their daughters from doing likewise. In general, parents tend to encourage girls to engage in cooperative, role-playing games (Fagot, Rodgers, and Leinbach, 2000; Gauvain et al., 2002; Parke, 2001, 2002). These different play patterns lead to the heightened development of verbal and emotional skills among girls and to more concern with winning and the establishment of hierarchy among boys (Tannen, 1990). Boys are more likely than girls are to receive praise for assertiveness, and girls are more likely than boys are to receive rewards for compliance (Kerig, Cowan, and Cowan, 1993). Given this early socialization, it seems perfectly "natural" that boys' toys stress aggression, competition, spatial manipulation, and outdoor activities, while girls' toys stress nurturing, physical attractiveness, and indoor activities (Hughes, 1995). Still, what seems natural must be continuously socially reinforced. Presented with a choice between playing with a tool set and a dish set, preschool boys are about as likely to choose one as the other—unless the dish set is presented as a girl's toy and they think their fathers would view playing with it as "bad." Then, they tend to pick the tool set (Raag and Rackliff, 1998).

A movement to market more gender-neutral toys emerged in the 1960s and 1970s. However, it has now been overtaken by the resumption of a strong tendency to market toys based on gender.

It would take someone who has spent very little time in the company of children to think they are passive objects of socialization. They are not. Parents, teachers, and other authority figures typically try to impose their ideas of appropriate gender behaviour on children, but children creatively interpret, negotiate, resist, and self-impose these ideas all the time. Gender, we might say, is something that is done, not just given (Messner, 2000; West and Zimmerman, 1987). This fact is nowhere more evident than in the way children play.

Gender Segregation and Interaction

Consider the grade 4 and 5 classroom that sociologist Barrie Thorne (1993) observed. The teacher periodically asked the children to choose their own desks. With the exception of one girl, they always segregated *themselves* by gender. The teacher then drew on this self-segregation in pitting the boys against the girls in spelling and math contests. Cross-gender antagonism and expression of within-gender solidarity characterized these contests. Similarly, when children played chasing games in the schoolyard, groups often *spontaneously* crystallized along gender lines. These games had special names, some of which, such as "chase and kiss," had clear sexual meanings. Provocation, physical contact, and avoidance were all sexually charged parts of the game.

Although Thorne found that contests, chasing games, and other activities often involved self-segregation by gender, she observed many cases of boys and girls playing together. She also noticed quite a lot of boundary crossing involving boys playing stereotypically girls' games and girls playing stereotypically boys' games. The most common form of boundary crossing involved girls who were skilled at sports that were central to the boys' world: soccer, baseball, and basketball. If girls demonstrated skill at these activities, boys often accepted them as participants. Finally, Thorne noticed occasions in which boys and girls interacted without strain and without strong gender identities. For instance, activities requiring cooperation, such as a group radio show or art project, lessened attention to gender. Another situation that lessened strain between boys and girls, causing gender to recede in importance, occurred when adults organized mixed-gender encounters in the classroom and in physical education periods. On such occasions, adults legitimized cross-gender contact. Mixed-gender interaction was also more common in less public and crowded settings. Thus, boys and girls were more likely to play together in a relaxed way in the relative privacy of their neighbourhoods. In contrast, in the schoolyard, where their peers could scrutinize them, gender segregation and antagonism were more evident.

In sum, Thorne's research makes two important contributions to our understanding of gender socialization. First, children are actively engaged in the process of constructing gender roles. They are not merely passive recipients of adult demands. Second, although schoolchildren tend to segregate themselves by gender, boundaries between boys and girls are sometimes fluid and sometimes rigid, depending on social circumstances. In other words, the content of children's gendered activities is by no means fixed.

Myrleen Cate/Index Stock

In her research on schoolchildren, sociologist Barrie Thorne noticed quite a lot of "boundary crossing" between boys and girls. Most commonly, boys accepted girls as participants in soccer, baseball, and basketball games if the girls demonstrated skill at these sports.

This is not to suggest that adults have no gender demands and expectations. They do, and their demands and expectations contribute importantly to gender socialization. For instance, many schoolteachers and guidance counsellors still expect boys to do better in the sciences and math and girls to achieve higher marks in English (Lips, 1999). Parents often reinforce these stereotypes in their evaluation of different activities (Eccles, Jacobs, and Harold, 1990). Although not all studies comparing mixed and single-sex schools suggest that girls do much better in the latter, most do (Bornholt, 2001; Jackson and Smith, 2000). In single-sex schools, girls typically experience faster cognitive development; higher occupational aspirations and attainment; greater self-esteem and self-confidence; and more teacher attention, respect, and encouragement in the classroom. They also develop more egalitarian attitudes toward the role of women in society. Why? Because such schools place more emphasis on academic excellence and less on physical attractiveness and heterosexual popularity. They provide more successful same-sex role models. And they eliminate sex bias in teacher–student and student–student interaction since there are no boys around (Hesse-Biber and Carter, 2000: 99–100).

> A **gender ideology** is a set of interrelated ideas about what constitutes appropriate masculine and feminine roles and behaviour.

Adolescents must usually start choosing courses in school by the age of 14 or 15. By then, they have well-formed **gender ideologies**, or sets of interrelated ideas about what constitutes appropriate masculine and feminine roles and behaviour. One aspect of gender ideology becomes especially important around grades 9 and 10: adolescents' ideas about whether, as adults, they will focus mainly on the home, paid work, or a combination of the two. Adolescents usually make course choices with gender ideologies in mind. Boys are strongly inclined to consider only their careers in making course choices. Most girls are inclined to consider both home responsibilities and careers, although a minority considers only home responsibilities and another minority considers only careers. Consequently, boys tend to choose career-oriented courses, particularly in math and science, more often than girls do. College and university accentuate the pattern (see Chapter 17, Education).

Young women tend to choose courses that lead to lower-paying jobs because they expect to devote a large part of their lives to child rearing and housework (Eccles, Roeser, Wigfield, and Freedman-Doen, 1999). When Canadian undergraduates were asked to identify their preference, 53 percent of the women but only 6 percent of the men selected "graduation, full-time work, marriage, children, stop working at least until youngest child is in school, then pursue a full-time job" as their preferred lifestyle sequence (Schroeder, Blood, and Maluso, 1993).

These choices sharply restrict women's career opportunities and earnings in science and business. More than three-quarters of the people working full-year, full-time in the 10 lowest-paid occupations in Canada are women (Department of Justice Canada, 2004). We examine the wage gap between women and men in depth in the second half of this chapter.

The Mass Media and Body Image

The social construction of gender does not stop at the school steps. Outside school, children, adolescents, and adults continue to negotiate gender roles as they interact with the mass media. If you systematically observe the roles played by women and men in television, movies, magazines, music videos, TV commercials, and print media advertisements, you will discover a pattern noted by sociologists since the 1970s. Women will more frequently be seen cleaning house, taking care of children, modelling clothes, and acting as objects of male desire (Signorielli, 1998). Men will more frequently be seen in aggressive, action-oriented, and authoritative roles. The effect of these messages on viewers is much the same as that of the Disney movies and Harlequin romances we discussed in Chapter 4, Socialization: They reinforce the normality of traditional gender roles.

People even try to shape their bodies after the images portrayed in the mass media. The human body has always served as a sort of personal billboard that advertises gender. However, the importance of body image to our self-definition has grown over the past century (Brumberg, 1997). As body image became more important for self-definition, the ideal body image became thinner, especially for women. For example, although Miss America beauty pageant winners became only a little taller between 1922 and 1999, they became much thinner (Curran, 2000). As one eating disorders expert observed, "Beauty pageants, like the rest of our media-driven culture, give young women in particular a message, over and over again, that it's exceedingly important to be thin to be considered successful and attractive" (quoted in Curran, 2000).

Why did body image become more important to people's self-definition during the twentieth century? Why was slimness stressed? Part of the answer to both questions is that more North Americans grew overweight as their lifestyles became more sedentary. As they

Marilyn Monroe was widely considered the most attractive woman in the world in the 1950s. Katy Perry was ranked #1 on *Maxim's* "Hot 100" list in 2010.

became better educated, they also grew increasingly aware of the health problems associated with being overweight. The desire to slim down was, then, partly a reaction to bulking up.

But that is not the whole story. The rake-thin models who populate modern ads are not promoting good health. They are promoting an extreme body shape that is unattainable for most people (Tovee, Mason, Emery, McClusky, and Cohen-Tovee, 1997). They do so because it is good business. The fitness, diet, low-calorie food, and cosmetic surgery industries do billions of dollars of business a year in North America (Hesse-Biber, 1996). Bankrolled by these industries, advertising in the mass media blankets us with images of slim bodies and makes these body types appealing. Once people become convinced that they need to develop bodies like the ones they see in ads, many of them are really in trouble because these body images are impossible for most people to attain.

Research shows just how widespread dissatisfaction with our bodies is and how important a role the mass media play in generating our discomfort. One survey of North American university graduates showed that 56 percent of women and 43 percent of men were dissatisfied with their overall appearance (Garner, 1997). Only 3 percent of the dissatisfied women, but 22 percent of the dissatisfied men, wanted to gain weight. This difference reflects the greater desire of men for muscular, stereotypically male physiques. Most of the dissatisfied men, and even more of the dissatisfied women (89 percent), wanted to lose weight. This finding reflects the general societal push toward slimness and its greater effect on women. According to the National Population Health Survey, even though Canadian women are almost five times as likely as Canadian men are to be *underweight* (14 percent vs. 3 percent), they are more likely to report recent attempts to lose weight, even if they are already within the healthy weight range (Health Canada, 1999a: 118).

A recent 26-country study analyzed women's body dissatisfaction worldwide (Swami et al., 2010). Researchers presented

The low-calorie and diet food industry promotes an ideal of slimness that is often impossible to attain and that generates widespread body dissatisfaction.

samples of men and women with a chart showing a series of female figures. They then asked respondents to indicate which figure they preferred and which figure most closely resembled their own (see Figure 11.2). The average age of respondents was 24.7 years. Even though the sample was young (and therefore relatively slim), the overwhelming majority of women wanted to be slimmer than they were. Their body ideal varied from one region to the next, but their actual self-reported body image was heavier than their body ideal in every world region. North and South American women were more dissatisfied with their bodies than were women from other regions, and North and South American men viewed heavier women more unfavourably than did men from other regions. Still, men everywhere preferred heavier women than women thought men preferred. Significantly, women's level of body dissatisfaction did not vary greatly from one region to the next, probably because more exposure to Western and Western-style mass media was associated with greater preference for thin women, and respondents tended to be highly exposed to such mass media, with its strong emphasis on female thinness.

Body dissatisfaction motivates many people—more than 80 percent of women and more than 50 percent of men in North America—diet (Garner, 1997). Some are willing to live dangerously. About a quarter of women and a sixth of men in North America say they would willingly trade more than three years of their life to achieve their weight goals. Half of female smokers and 30 percent of male smokers say they smoke to control their weight. Surveys suggest that between 1 percent and 5 percent of North American women suffer from anorexia nervosa (characterized by weight loss, excessive exercise, food aversion, distorted body image, and an intense and irrational fear of body fat and weight gain). About the same percentage of North American female college and university students suffer from bulimia, characterized by cycles of binge eating and purging (through self-induced vomiting or the use of laxatives, purgatives, or diuretics). For college and university men, the prevalence of bulimia is between 0.2 percent and 1.5 percent (Averett and Korenman, 1996: 305–6).

Male–Female Interaction

The gender roles children learn in their families, at school, and through the mass media form the basis of their social interaction as adults. For instance, by playing team sports, boys tend to learn that social interaction is most often about competition, conflict, self-sufficiency, and hierarchical relationships (leaders versus the led). They understand the importance of taking centre stage and boasting about their talents (Messner, 1995). Because

FIGURE 11.2

Female Figure Rating across World Regions

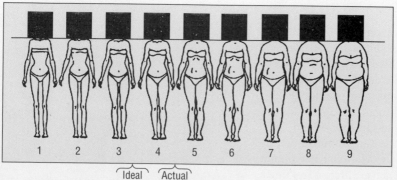

Women's Dissatisfaction Score*	
North America	1.4
South America	1.4
Africa	1.3
Scandinavia	1.1
East Asia	1.1
Western Europe	1.0
Southeast Asia	0.9
Eastern Europe	0.8
Oceania	0.8
South & West Asia	0.5

*Actual self-reported regional average minus ideal regional average

1   2   3   4   5   6   7   8   9

Ideal regional averages: 3.0–3.7

Actual self-reported regional averages: 4.0–4.7

Source: Swami, Viren et al. 2010. "The Attractive Female Body Weight and Female Body Dissatisfaction in 26 Countries across 10 World Regions: Results of the International Body Project I." *Personality and Social Psychology Bulletin* 36, 3: 309–25.

many of the most popular video games for boys exclude female characters (Game Boy wasn't named Game Boy for nothing!), use women as sex objects, or involve violence against women, they reinforce some of the most unsavoury lessons of traditional gender socialization (Dietz, 1998). In contrast, by playing with dolls and baking sets, girls tend to learn that social interaction is most often about maintaining cordial relationships, avoiding conflict, and resolving differences of opinion through negotiation (Subrahmanyam and Greenfield, 1998). They learn the importance of giving advice and not promoting themselves or being bossy.

Because of these early socialization patterns, misunderstandings between men and women are common. A stereotypical example: Harold is driving around lost. However, he refuses to ask for directions because doing so would amount to an admission of inadequacy and therefore a loss of status. Meanwhile, it seems perfectly natural to Sybil to want to share information, so she urges Harold to ask for directions. The result: conflict between Harold and Sybil (Tannen, 1990: 62).

Gender-specific interaction styles also have serious implications for who is heard and who gets credit at work. Here are two cases uncovered by Deborah Tannen's research (1994a: 132–59):

- A female office manager doesn't want to seem bossy or arrogant. She is eager to preserve consensus among her co-workers. Therefore, she spends a good deal of time soliciting their opinions before making an important decision. She asks questions, listens attentively, and offers suggestions. She then decides. However, her male boss sees her approach as indecisive and incompetent. He wants to recruit leaders for upper-management positions, so he overlooks the woman and selects an assertive man for a senior job that just opened up.
- Male managers are inclined to say "I" in many situations, as in "I'm hiring a new manager and I'm going to put him in charge of my marketing division" or "This is what I've come up with on the Lakehill deal." This sort of phrasing draws attention to personal accomplishments. In contrast, Tannen heard a female manager talking about what "we" had done, when in fact she had done all the work alone. This sort of phrasing camouflages women's accomplishments.

The contrasting interaction styles illustrated above can result in female managers not getting credit for competent performance. That may be part of the reason why women sometimes complain about a **glass ceiling**, a social barrier that makes it difficult for them to rise to the top level of management. As we will soon see, factors other than interaction styles, such as outright discrimination and women's generally greater commitment to family responsibilities, also support the glass ceiling. Yet gender differences in interaction styles seem to play an independent role in constraining women's career progress.

The **glass ceiling** is a social barrier that makes it difficult for women to rise to the top level of management.

Summing Up

- By holding that traditional gender roles help to integrate society, functionalists support the essentialist view that gender differences reflect innate biological differences between women and men.
- In contrast, social constructionists (including conflict theorists, symbolic interactionists, and feminists) hold that gender is largely learned through socialization processes and patterns of gender inequality that vary across societies.

HOMOSEXUALITY

Sexuality and Resistance to Conventional Gender Roles

The preceding discussion outlines some powerful social forces that push us to define ourselves as conventionally masculine or feminine in behaviour and appearance. For most people, gender socialization by the family, the school, and the mass media is compelling and sustained by daily interactions. However, a minority of people resists conventional gender roles, suggesting that there are varying degrees of "maleness" and "femaleness."

Transgendered people defy society's gender norms and blur widely accepted gender roles (Cole, Denny, Eyler, and Samons, 2000: 151). For example, some transgendered people are cross-dressers—people who gender-identify with one sex and sometimes or dress in clothing generally considered appropriate to the "opposite" sex. About 1 in 5000 to 10 000 people in North America is transgendered. Some transgendered people are **transsexuals**. They identify with a gender that is culturally inconsistent with their biological sex to the extent that they want to alter their gender entirely by changing their appearance or resorting to medical intervention. Transsexuals believe they were born with the "wrong" body. They identify with, and want to live fully as, members of the "opposite" sex. They often take the lengthy and painful path to a sex change operation. About 1 in 30 000 people in North America is a transsexual (Nolen, 1999). **Homosexuals** are people who prefer sexual partners of the same sex, and **bisexuals** are people who enjoy sexual partners of either sex. People usually call homosexual men *gay* and homosexual women *lesbians*.

Fewer than 2 percent of Canadians describe themselves as homosexual or bisexual (Statistics Canada, 2004a). However, many people who have had same-sex sexual experiences or desires consider themselves heterosexual. They may resist other labels because they experience homosexual urges only intermittently or rarely, and also because they face widespread animosity against non-heterosexuals (Flowers and Buston, 2001; Herdt, 2001; Laumann, Gagnon, Michael, and Michaels, 1994: 299).

A 2004 survey of North American university students showed that homosexual experiences and desires are far more frequent than homosexual identification. Men were 3.5 times as likely to say they had homosexual experiences and desires as they were to identify as gay. Women were 5.6 times as likely to say they had same-sex sexual experiences or desires as to identify as lesbians (see Figure 11.3).

Transgendered people break society's gender norms by defying the rigid distinction between male and female.

Transsexuals believe they were born with the "wrong" body. They identify with, and want to live fully as, members of the "opposite" sex.

Homosexuals are people who prefer sexual partners of the same sex. People usually call homosexual men *gay* and homosexual women *lesbians*.

Bisexuals are people who enjoy sexual partners of both sexes.

FIGURE 11.3

Homosexuality Indicators, North American University Students, 2004, and University of Toronto SOC101 Students, 2010 (in percent).

Sources: Brym (2010); Ellis, Robb, and Burke (2005: 572–73).

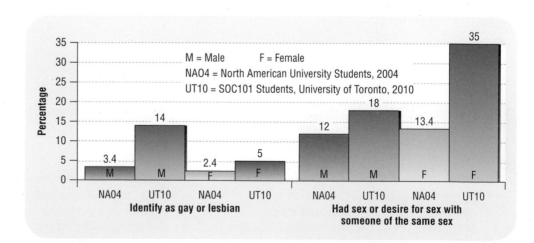

One of this book's authors (Brym) surveyed members of his large introductory sociology class at the University of Toronto on their sexual orientation in 2010. He also found big differences between sexual identity, on the one hand, and sexual desire and behaviour, on the other. Interestingly, he also found a considerably higher percentage of homosexual identifiers than the 2004 North American university survey found. Probable reasons for the difference include the following: (1) Toronto is a large urban centre where liberal attitudes, including attitudes toward sexuality, are more widespread than they are in North America as a whole; (2) six years of liberalizing attitudes had passed between the two surveys; and (3) Toronto contains one of the three biggest homosexual communities in North America (the others are New York and San Francisco) and is therefore especially attractive to homosexuals.

More remarkably, fully 35 percent of women in the U of T survey said they had some same-sex experience or desire, twice as many as the corresponding percentage for men. What might account for this difference? One plausible explanation is that many heterosexual men find sex between women titillating, so a considerable number of young women engage in sexual acts with other women for the benefit of men—a growing phenomenon according to analysts who have observed the party, bar, and club scenes in recent years (Rupp and Taylor, 2010).

Enforcing Heteronormativity

Transgendered people, transsexuals, bisexuals, and homosexuals have lived in every society. Some societies have held such people in high regard. Ancient Greece encouraged homosexuality. Many Aboriginal North American nations celebrate what the Ojibwa call "two-spirited" people, who are said to incorporate both masculine and feminine attributes. Traditionally, two-spirited people were given high-prestige roles, such as healer or fortune-teller. Some tribes recognized as many as six genders (Cameron, 2005; Lang, 1996).

More frequently, societies have forbidden non-heteronormative behaviour (see Box 11.1 on page 280). For example, many countries have laws targeting homosexuality on the books (see Figure 11.4) Only 10 countries (Argentina, Belgium, Canada, Iceland, the Netherlands, Norway, Portugal, South Africa, Spain, and Sweden) allow same-sex marriage and recognize it countrywide.

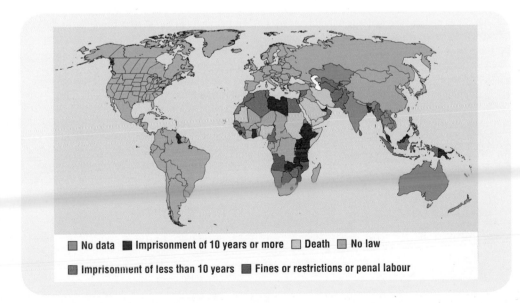

No data ■ **Imprisonment of 10 years or more** ■ **Death** ■ **No law**

■ **Imprisonment of less than 10 years** ■ **Fines or restrictions or penal labour**

FIGURE 11.4

Punishment for Male–Male Sexual Relations, 2010

Source: International Gay, Lesbian, Bisexual, Trans and Intersex Association, 2010.

BOX 11.1

Sociology at the Movies

BROKEBACK MOUNTAIN

It would not be an exaggeration to say that Westerns—often called "Cowboy and Indian" movies—shaped a generation of North Americans' expectations about gender and sexuality. John Wayne, Gary Cooper, Jimmy Stewart, and many others became role models for North American men and their idea of masculinity: silent but strong, gentle toward the weak (women and children) but ferocious toward the evil (often Aboriginals), community-minded but ultimately lone, rugged individualists. Even today, it's hard not to be stirred and engrossed by such classic Westerns as *The Man Who Shot Liberty Valance* and *High Noon*.

Westerns, however, have not been a popular genre since the 1970s. The Civil Rights movement questioned the racial ideology of many Westerns, which presumed the superiority of the white race against the native populations. The movement against the war in Vietnam challenged the vision of the world as a place that ought to be pacified and ruled by whites. The feminist movement criticized the patriarchal masculine viewpoint of Westerns. The few Westerns since the 1970s have therefore deviated from classical Westerns, often parodying them.

© Focus Films/Everett Collection/CP Picture Archives

Jack (Jake Gyllenhaal; left) and Ennis (Heath Ledger) in *Brokeback Mountain*

Brokeback Mountain, nominated for the best picture Oscar, traces the romantic love between two cowboys. They fall in love in the early 1960s, when both are 19 years old, long before they had heard of gay culture or even the notion of homosexual identity. They lead seemingly conventional married lives. Yet they continue to love each other and carry on their affair for two decades, periodically telling their wives that they are going on fishing trips together but raising suspicions when they fail to bring any fish home. More than the passion, however, what the movie depicts is the high emotional cost of keeping one's sexual orientation and one's love a secret. Eventually, their marriages crumble, their social relationships suffer, and happiness and fulfillment prove elusive.

One of the reasons that Ennis (the late Heath Ledger, nominated for the best actor Oscar) cannot imagine the possibility of settling down with Jack (Jake Gyllenhaal, nominated for the best supporting actor Oscar) is a childhood experience. His father took him to see two men who were beaten to death, two "tough old birds" who happened to be "shacked up together." Fear of expressing his homosexuality was thus instilled early on. (In fact, both men deny their homosexuality. After their first night together, Ennis says to Jack, "You know I ain't queer." To which Jack replies, "Me neither.") Jack and Ennis's affair ends when Jack is beaten to death by homophobic men. Three grisly murders of gay men, then, provide the tragic backdrop to *Brokeback Mountain*. How much have things changed since the 1960s, '70s, and '80s? Could *Brokeback Mountain* be set in today's society?

We do not yet well understand why some individuals develop homosexual orientations. Some scientists believe that the cause of homosexuality is mainly genetic, others
think it is chiefly hormonal, while still others point to life experiences during early childhood as the most important factor (Jannini, Blanchard, Camperio-Cianai, and Bancroft,
2010). The scientific consensus is that homosexuality "emerges for most people in early
adolescence without any prior sexual experience.... [It] is not changeable" (American
Psychological Association, 1998). A study of homosexual men in the United States found
that 90 percent believed they were born with their homosexual orientation and only 4 percent felt that environmental factors were the sole cause (Lever, 1994). Polls suggest that
the general public increasingly believes that homosexuality is not so much a preference
as an innate orientation. People who believe that homosexuality is a preference tend to be
less tolerant of gays and lesbians than are those who think homosexuality is innate (Rosin
and Morin, 1999: 8).

In general, sociologists are less interested in the origins of homosexuality than in
the way it is socially constructed, that is, in the wide variety of ways it is expressed and
repressed (Plummer, 1995). It is important to note in this connection that homosexuality
has become less of a stigma over the past century. Two factors are chiefly responsible for this, one scientific, the other political. In the twentieth century, sexologists—
psychologists and physicians who study sexual practices scientifically—first recognized
and stressed the wide diversity of existing sexual practices. Alfred Kinsey was among
the pioneers in this field. He and his colleagues interviewed thousands of men and
women. In the 1940s, they concluded that homosexual practices were so widespread that
homosexuality could hardly be considered an illness affecting a tiny minority (Kinsey,
Pomeroy, and Martin, 1948; Kinsey et al., 1953; see also Box 2.2 in Chapter 2, How
Sociologists Do Research).

If sexologists provided a scientific rationale for belief in the normality of sexual
diversity, sexual minorities themselves provided the social and political energy needed to
legitimize sexual diversity among an increasingly large section of the public. Especially
since the 1970s, gays and lesbians have built large communities and subcultures, particularly in major urban areas (Greenhill, 2001; Ingram, 2001). They have gone public
with their lifestyles (Owen, 2001). They have organized demonstrations, parades, and
political pressure groups to express their self-confidence and demand equal rights with

CP Picture Archive/David _ucas

Especially since the 1970s,
gays and lesbians have gone
public with their lifestyles,
thus helping to legitimize
homosexuality and sexual
diversity in general.

the heterosexual majority (Goldie, 2001). This has done much to legitimize homosexuality and sexual diversity in general.

Yet opposition to people who don't conform to conventional gender roles remains strong at all stages of the life cycle. When you were a child, did you ever poke fun at a sturdily built girl who was good at sports by referring to her as a "dyke"? As an adolescent or a young adult, have you ever insulted a man by calling him a "fag?" If so, your behaviour was not unusual. Many children and adults believe that heterosexuality is superior to homosexuality, and they are not embarrassed to say so. "That's so gay!" is commonly used as an expression of disapproval among teenagers.

Among adults, such opposition is just as strong. What is your attitude today toward transgendered people, transsexuals, and homosexuals? Do you, for example, think relations between adults of the same sex are always, or almost always, wrong? If so, you are again not that unusual. A national survey of Canadians found that almost one in three Canadians believes same-sex relations are "always wrong." Although discouraging to some people, this figure represents an increase in Canada's acceptance of homosexuality over the past three decades. In 1975, 63 percent of Canadians thought that homosexuality is always wrong (*Maclean's*, 2002: 12). Canada became the world's fourth country to legalize same-sex marriage in 2005 (the Netherlands was first in 2001), but a survey conducted that year showed that only 48 percent of Canadians favoured same-sex marriage (CBC News, 2005). Tolerance is advancing and is most widespread among young Canadians, but substantial hostility remains.

Antipathy to homosexuals is so strong among some people that they are prepared to back up their beliefs with force. A study of about 500 young adults in the San Francisco Bay Area, perhaps the most sexually tolerant area in the world, found that 1 in 10 admitted physically attacking or threatening people he or she believed were homosexuals. Twenty-four percent reported engaging in anti-gay name-calling. Among male respondents, 18 percent reported acting in a violent or threatening way and 32 percent reported name-calling. In addition, a third of those who had *not* engaged in anti-gay aggression said they would do so if a homosexual flirted with, or propositioned, them (Franklin, 1998; see also Bush and Sainz, 2001; Faulkner and Cranston, 1998).

The consequences of such attitudes can be devastating. For example, 14-year-old Christian Hernandez of Niagara Falls, Ontario, told his best friend that he was gay. "He told me he couldn't accept it," recalls Hernandez. "And he began to spread it around." For two years, Hernandez was teased and harassed almost daily. After school one day, a group of boys waited for him. Their leader told Hernandez that "he didn't accept faggots, that we brought AIDS into the world" and stabbed him in the neck with a knife. Hernandez required a week's hospitalization. When he told his parents what had happened, his father replied that he'd "rather have a dead son than a queer son" (Fisher, 1999).

Homophobic people are afraid of homosexuals.

Research suggests that some anti-gay crimes may result from repressed homosexual urges on the part of the aggressor (Adams, Wright, and Lohr, 1998). From this point of view, aggressors are **homophobic** or afraid of homosexuals because they cannot cope with their own, possibly subconscious, homosexual impulses. Their aggression is a way of acting out a denial of these impulses. Although this psychological explanation may account for some anti-gay violence, it seems inadequate when set alongside the finding that fully half of all young male adults admitted to some form of anti-gay aggression in the San Francisco study cited above. An analysis of the motivations of these San Franciscans showed that some of them did commit assaults to prove their toughness and heterosexuality. Others committed assaults just to alleviate boredom and have fun. Still others believed they were defending themselves from aggressive sexual propositions. A fourth group acted violently because they wanted to punish homosexuals for what they perceived as moral transgressions (Franklin, 1998). It seems clear, then, that anti-gay violence is not just a question of abnormal psychology but a broad cultural problem with several sources (see Box 11.2).

It's Your Choice

HATE CRIME LAW AND HOMOPHOBIA

On November 17, 2001, Aaron Webster, a 42-year-old gay man, was beaten to death in Vancouver with either a baseball bat or a pool cue by a group of three to four men. Tim Chisholm, Aaron's friend for 15 years, discovered Aaron's bloodied body, naked except for his hiking boots, in a parking lot in Stanley Park. After phoning 911, Chisholm attempted CPR on his unconscious friend. It was no use. Aaron died in Chisholm's arms before help could arrive.

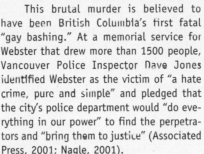

This brutal murder is believed to have been British Columbia's first fatal "gay bashing." At a memorial service for Webster that drew more than 1500 people, Vancouver Police Inspector Dave Jones identified Webster as the victim of "a hate crime, pure and simple" and pledged that the city's police department would "do everything in our power" to find the perpetrators and "bring them to justice" (Associated Press, 2001; Nagle, 2001).

One issue raised by Webster's death concerns the definition of hate crime (Wetzel, 2001). Hate crimes are criminal acts motivated by a victim's race, religion, or ethnicity. Under section 319 of the Canadian Criminal Code, the willful promotion of hatred against any identifiable group (that is, "any section of the public distinguished by colour, race, religion, or ethnic group") and the advocacy of genocide are crimes punishable by up to two years' imprisonment. In 1999, following the gay bashing of a student in Fredericton, New Brunswick, then Justice Minister Anne McLellan announced that she would introduce amendments to protect lesbians and gays from hate crimes. She did not do so. Following Webster's murder, MP Svend Robinson introduced a Private Member's Bill that sought to include sexual orientation among the grounds protected by hate crimes legislation.

If hate motivates a crime, Canadian law now requires that the perpetrator be punished more severely than otherwise. Under section 718.2 of the Criminal Code of Canada, "evidence that the offence was motivated by bias, prejudice or hate based on race, national or ethnic origin, language, colour, religion, sex, age, mental or physical disability, sexual orientation or any other similar factor" is to be considered an aggravating circumstance in sentencing convicted offenders. For example, assaulting a person during an argument generally carries a lighter punishment than assaulting a person because he or she is gay or Jewish or black. However, despite this provision in law, "gay-bashers are often able to rely on the discredited 'homosexual panic' defence, claiming they were justified in committing murder because the victim 'came on' to them" (EGALE, 2001).

Do you think crimes motivated by the victim's sexual orientation are the same as crimes motivated by the victim's race, religion, or ethnicity? If so, why? If not, why not? Do you think crimes motivated by the perceived sexual orientation of the victim should be included in the legal definition of a hate crime? Why or why not?

Summing Up

- "Male" and "female" are not binary opposites. Varying degrees of maleness and femaleness exist.
- There are three dimensions of sexuality—identity, desire, and behaviour—and the correlation among them is far from perfect.
- Most people use positive and negative sanctions to ensure that others conform to conventional heterosexual gender roles. Some people resort to violence to enforce conformity and punish deviance.

GENDER INEQUALITY

The Origins of Gender Inequality

Earlier we learned that gender inequality varies across societies. We now turn to the question of how gender inequality originated.

Contrary to what essentialists say, men have not always enjoyed much more power and authority than women have. Substantial inequality between women and men has existed for only about 6000 years. It was socially constructed. Three major socio-historical processes account for the growth of gender inequality.

Long-Distance Warfare and Conquest

The anthropological record suggests that women and men were about equal in status in nomadic, foraging societies, the dominant form of society for 90 percent of human history. Rough gender equality was based on women producing a substantial amount of the band's food, up to 80 percent in some cases (see Chapter 15, Families).

The archaeological record from "Old Europe" tells a similar story. Old Europe is a region stretching roughly from Poland in the north to the Mediterranean island of Crete in the south, and from Switzerland in the west to Bulgaria in the east (see Figure 11.5). Between 7000 and 3500 BCE, men and women enjoyed approximately equal status throughout the region. In fact, the religions of the region gave primacy to fertility and creator goddesses. Kinship was traced through the mother's side of the family. Then, sometime between 4300 and 4200 BCE, all this began to change. Old Europe was invaded by successive waves of warring peoples from the Asiatic and European northeast (the Kurgans) and the deserts to the south (the Semites). Both the Kurgan and Semitic civilizations were based on a steeply

FIGURE 11.5
Old Europe

Source: Gimbutas, 1982: 16.

hierarchical social structure in which men were dominant. Their religions gave primacy to male warrior gods. They acquired property and slaves by conquering other peoples and imposed their religions on the vanquished. They eliminated, or at least downgraded, goddesses as divine powers. God became a male who willed that men should rule women. Laws reinforced women's sexual, economic, and political subjugation to men. Traditional Judaism, Christianity, and Islam all embody ideas of male dominance, and they all derive from the tribes that conquered Old Europe in the fifth millennium BCE (Eisler, 1987; Lerner, 1986).

Plow Agriculture

Long-distance warfare and conquest catered to men's strengths, greatly enhancing male power and authority. Large-scale farming using plows harnessed to animals had a similar effect. Plow agriculture originated in the Middle East around 5000 years ago. It required that strong adults remain in the fields all day for much of the year. It also reinforced the principle of private ownership of land. Since men were on average stronger than women were, and since women were restricted in their activities by pregnancy, childbirth, and nursing, plow agriculture made men more powerful socially. Thus, men owned land, and ownership was passed from the father to the eldest son (Coontz and Henderson, 1986).

The Separation of Public and Private Spheres

In the agricultural era, economic production was organized around the household. Men may have worked apart from women in the fields but the fields were still part of the *family* farm. In contrast, during the early phase of industrialization, men's work moved out of the household and into the factory and the office. Most men became wage or salary workers. Some men assumed decision-making roles in economic and political institutions. Yet while men went public, women who could afford to do so remained in the domestic or private sphere. The idea soon developed that this was a natural division of labour. This idea persisted until the second half of the twentieth century, when a variety of social circumstances, ranging from the introduction of the birth control pill to women's demands for entry into higher education, finally allowed women to enter the public sphere in large numbers.

We thus see that, according to social constructionists, gender inequality derives not from any inherent biological features of men and women but from three main socio-historical circumstances: the arrival of long-distance warfare and conquest, the development of plow agriculture, and the assignment of women to the domestic sphere and men to the public sphere during the early industrial era.

The Earnings Gap Today

After reading this brief historical overview, you might be inclined to dismiss gender inequality as ancient history. If so, your decision would be hasty. Gender inequality is evident if we focus on the earnings gap between men and women, one of the most important expressions of gender inequality today.

Canadian data on the earnings of women and men were first reported in 1967. At that time, the ratio of female to male earnings stood at around 58 percent. In 1992, it passed 70 percent and has fluctuated near that level since then (see the green line in Figure 11.6 on page 286). Table 11.1 on page 286 shows that women earn less than men do in every major occupational category.

Reasons for the Gender Gap in Earnings

Four main factors contribute to the gender gap in earnings (Bianchi and Spain, 1996; England, 1992):

1. *Gender discrimination.* In February 1985, when Microsoft already employed about 1000 people, it hired its first two female executives. According to a well-placed source involved in the hiring, both women got their jobs because Microsoft was trying to win a U.S. Air Force contract. Under the government's guidelines, it didn't have enough women in top management positions to qualify. The source quotes then 29-year-old

FIGURE 11.6

Ratio of Female to Male Earnings, by Marital Status, Canada, 1976–2008

Source: Ratio of Female to Male Earnings, by Marital Status, Canada, 1976–2008, adapted from Statistics Canada CANSIM Database http:// www5.statcan.gc.ca/cansim/ home-accueil?lang=eng, Table 202-0104 (accessed 19 November 2010).

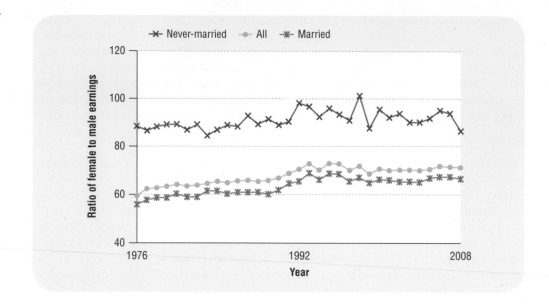

Gender discrimination involves rewarding men and women differently for the same work.

Bill Gates, president of Microsoft, as saying, "Well, let's hire two women because we can pay them half as much as we will have to pay a man, and we can give them all this other 'crap' work to do because they are women" (quoted in Wallace and Erickson, 1992: 291). This incident is a clear illustration of **gender discrimination**, rewarding women and men differently for the same work. Discrimination on the basis of sex is against the law in Canada. Yet progress is slow; as noted earlier, the female–male earnings ratio has not improved since 1992. If the rate of improvement between 1976 and 2008 were to persist, women would not earn as much as men do until 2085.

TABLE 11.1

Women in Broad Occupational Categories, Canada, 1989, 1999, and 2009

Source: Adapted from the Statistics Canada, 2008, CANSIM Table 282-0010 and Table 202-0106. http://dc1.chass.utoronto .ca.myaccess.library.utoronto.ca/ cgi-bin/cansimdim/c2_getArrayDim .pl (accessed 20 November 2010).

	Percentage Females in Occupation			Women's Earnings as a Percentage of Men's Earnings, 2008
	1989	**1999**	**2009**	
Management	32.0	35.1	37.0	66.3
Business, finance, and administrative	71.5	71.2	71.0	61.5
Natural and applied science	19.5	20.7	22.3	82.5
Health	78.2	78.5	80.5	52.1
Social science, education, government service, and religion	59.2	64.8	69.6	63.4
Art, culture, recreation, and sport	50.1	54.1	54.4	84.4
Sales and service	55.4	5673	56.9	54.1
Trade, transport, equipment operators	5.4	6.0	6.4	61.0
Primary industry	20.2	21.6	19.5	45.4
Processing, manufacturing, utilities	31.4	32.2	30.1	54.9

2. *Women tend to be concentrated in low-wage occupations and industries.* The second factor leading to lower earnings for women is that the programs they select in high school and afterward tend to limit them to jobs in low-wage occupations and industries. The concentration of women in certain occupations and men in others is referred to as *occupational sex segregation.* Although women have made big strides since the 1970s, they are still concentrated in lower-paying clerical and service occupations and under-represented in higher-paying occupations (see Table 11.1). This is particularly true for women of colour, Aboriginal women, and women with disabilities (Chard, 2000: 229; Shain, 1995).

3. *Heavy domestic responsibilities reduce women's earnings.* In 2008, Canadian women who had never been married earned 86.4 cents for every dollar earned by men. The comparable figure for married women was 66.5 cents (compare the top and bottom lines in Figure 11.6). This 20-cent gap represents the economic cost to women of getting married and assuming disproportionately heavy domestic responsibilities. Of course, raising children can be one of the most emotionally satisfying experiences. However, that should not blind us to the fact it is also unpaid work that decreases the time available for education, training, and paid work. Because women are disproportionately involved in child rearing, they suffer the brunt of this economic reality. They devote fewer hours to paid work than men do, experience more labour-force interruptions, and are more likely than men are to take part-time jobs, which pay less per hour and offer fewer benefits than full-time work does (Waldfogel, 1997). Globally, women do between two-thirds and three-quarters of all unpaid child care, housework, and care for aging parents (Boyd, 1997: 55). Even when they work full-time in the paid labour force, women continue to shoulder a disproportionate share of domestic responsibilities (see Chapter 15, Families).

4. *Finally, people commonly consider work done by women less valuable than work done by men because they view it as involving fewer skills.* Women tend to earn less than men do because the skills involved in their work are often undervalued (Figart and Lapidus, 1996; Sorenson, 1994). For example, kindergarten teachers (nearly all of whom are women) earn significantly less than office machine repair technicians (nearly all of whom are men). It is, however, questionable whether it takes less training and skill to teach a young child the basics of counting and cooperation than it takes to get a photocopier to collate paper. As this example suggests, we apply somewhat arbitrary standards to reward different occupational roles. In our society, these standards systematically undervalue the kind of skills needed for jobs where women are concentrated.

We thus see that the gender gap in earnings is based on several *social* circumstances rather than on any inherent difference between women and men. This fact means that we can reduce the gender gap if we want to. Below, we discuss social policies that could create more equality between women and men. First, to stress the urgency of such policies, we explain how the persistence of gender inequality encourages violence against women.

Male Aggression against Women

Serious acts of aggression between men and women are common. Most are committed by men against women. Six percent of Canadian women under the age of 25 report being sexually assaulted and 9 percent report being stalked (Johnson, 2006: 36).

One study found that more than 20 percent of female Canadian postsecondary students said they gave in to unwanted sexual intercourse because a man's continued arguments and pressure overwhelmed them. Nearly 7 percent reported they had unwanted sexual intercourse because a man threatened or used some degree of physical force. Nearly 14 percent claimed that, while they were either intoxicated or under the influence of drugs, a man had attempted unwanted sexual intercourse (DeKeseredy and Kelly, 1993).

Another study found that half of first- and second-year university women reported unwanted attempts at intercourse by males of their acquaintance. "Strong" physical force accompanied one-third of these attempts and "mild" physical force another third. The women seemed constrained by traditional roles in their responses, which were largely passive and accepting; 37 percent did nothing. Only a minority gave a strong verbal response (26 percent) or a physical response (14 percent). The stronger the victim's response, the less likely it was that the attempted rape was completed, but half the attacks succeeded. None of the women reported the attack to the authorities and half talked to no one about it. The remainder told friends. Only 11 percent ended the relationship, whereas almost three-quarters either accepted or ignored the attack. Half continued to be friends (25 percent) or dating or sex partners (25 percent). Most blamed themselves at least partially (Murnen, Perot, and Byrne, 1989; Figure 11.7).

Why do men commit more frequent (and more harmful) acts of aggression against women than women commit against men? It is not because men on average are physically more powerful than women are. Greater physical power is more likely to be used to commit acts of aggression when norms justify male domination and men have much more *social* power than women do. When women and men are more equal socially, and norms justify gender equality, the rate of male aggression against women is lower. This is evident if we consider various types of aggressive interaction, including sexual assault and sexual harassment (see also the discussion of wife abuse in Chapter 15, Families).

Sexual Assault

Some people think rapists are men who suffer a psychological disorder that compels them to achieve immediate sexual gratification even if violence is required. Others think rape occurs because of flawed communication. They believe some victims give mixed signals to their assailants by, for example, drinking too much and flirting with them.

Such explanations are not completely invalid. Interviews with victims and perpetrators show that some offenders do suffer from psychological disorders. Others misinterpret

FIGURE 11.7

Percentage of University Students Who Severely Assaulted a Dating Partner in the Past Year, by Country (*n* = 6700)

Note: Data collected from 2001 to 2005, except for the U.S. data, which were collected in 1998.

Source: From *International Dating Violence Study*, tabulation courtesy of Murray A. Straus based on Emily M. Douglas and Murray A. Straus, (2006) "Assault and injury of dating partners by university students in 19 nations and its relation to corporal punishment experienced as a child," *European Journal of Criminology* 3: 293–318. Reprinted with permission.

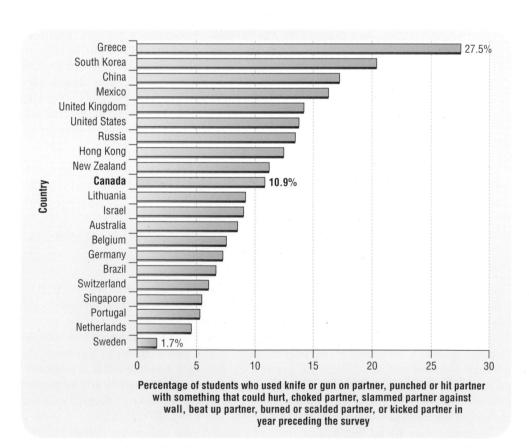

Percentage of students who used knife or gun on partner, punched or hit partner with something that could hurt, choked partner, slammed partner against wall, beat up partner, burned or scalded partner, or kicked partner in year preceding the survey

signals in what they regard as sexually ambiguous situations (Hannon, Hall, Kuntz, Laar, and Williams, 1995). But such cases account for only a small proportion of the total. Men who commit sexual assault are rarely mentally disturbed, and it is abundantly clear to most assailants that they are doing something their victims strongly oppose (Meyer, 1984; Senn, Desmarais, Veryberg, and Wood, 2000).

What then accounts for sexual assault being as common as it is? The fact that sexual assault is sometimes not about sexual gratification at all—some offenders cannot ejaculate or even achieve an erection—suggests a sociological answer. All forms of sexual assault involve domination and humiliation as principal motives. It is not surprising, therefore, that some offenders were physically or sexually abused in their youth. They develop a deep need to feel powerful as psychological compensation for their early powerlessness. Others are men who, as children, saw their fathers treat their mothers as potentially hostile figures who needed to be controlled or as mere objects available for male gratification. They saw their fathers as emotionally cold and distant. Raised in such an atmosphere, rapists learn not to empathize with women. Instead, they learn to want to dominate them (Lisak, 1992).

Other social situations also increase the rate of sexual aggression. One such situation is war. In war, conquering male soldiers often feel justified in wanting to humiliate the vanquished, who are powerless to stop them. Rape is often used for this purpose, as was especially well documented in the ethnic wars that accompanied the breakup of Yugoslavia in the 1990s and in the civil war in the Democratic Republic of Congo from 1998 until the present (Human Rights Watch, 1995; International Rescue Committee, 2010).

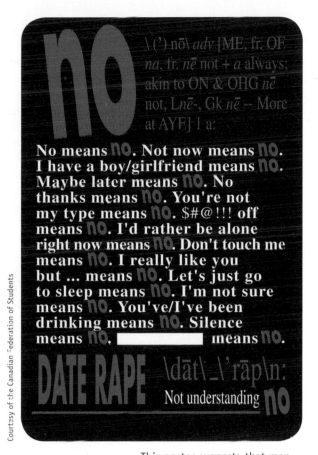

Courtesy of the Canadian Federation of Students

This poster suggests that men still need to be reminded that no means no.

The relationship between male dominance and sexual aggression is also evident in research on American fraternities. Many fraternities in the United States tend to emphasize male dominance and aggression as a central part of their culture. Sociologists who have interviewed fraternity members have shown that most fraternities try to recruit members who can reinforce a macho image and avoid any suggestion of effeminacy and homosexuality. Research also shows that fraternity houses that are especially prone to sexual assault tend to sponsor parties that treat women in a particularly degrading way. By emphasizing a very narrow and aggressive form of masculinity, some fraternities tend to facilitate sexual assault on campuses (Boswell and Spade, 1996).

Another social circumstance that increases the likelihood of sexual assault is participation in athletics. Of course, the overwhelming majority of athletes are not rapists. However, there are proportionately more rapists among men who participate in athletics than among non-athletes. That is because many sports embody a particular vision of masculinity in North American culture: competitive, aggressive, and domineering. By recruiting men who display these characteristics and by encouraging the development of these traits in athletes, sports can contribute to off-field aggression, including sexual aggression. Furthermore, among male athletes, there is a distinct hierarchy of sexual aggression. Male athletes who engage in contact sports are more prone to be rapists than are other athletes. There are proportionately even more rapists among athletes involved in collision and combative sports, notably football (Welch, 1997).

Sexual assault, we conclude, involves using sex to establish dominance. Its incidence is highest in situations where early socialization experiences predispose men to want to control women, where norms justify the domination of women, and where a big power imbalance between men and women exists. Studies of sexual harassment lead to similar conclusions.

Sexual Harassment

Quid pro quo sexual harassment takes place when sexual threats or bribery are made a condition of employment decisions.

Hostile environment sexual harassment involves sexual jokes, comments, and touching that interferes with work or creates an unfriendly work environment.

There are two types of sexual harassment. **Quid pro quo sexual harassment** takes place when sexual threats or bribery are made a condition of employment decisions—the exchange of a promotion for sexual favours, for example. (The Latin phrase *quid pro quo* means "something for something.") **Hostile environment sexual harassment** involves sexual jokes, comments, and touching that interferes with work or creates a hostile work environment. Research suggests that relatively powerless women are the most likely to be sexually harassed. Specifically, women who are young, unmarried, and employed in non-professional jobs are most likely to become objects of sexual harassment, particularly if they are temporary workers, if the ratio of women to men in the workplace is low, and if the organizational culture of the workplace tolerates sexual harassment (Rogers and Henson, 1997; Welsh, 1999).

Ultimately, male aggression against women, including sexual harassment and sexual assault, is encouraged by a lesson most of us still learn at home, in school, at work, through much of organized religion, and in the mass media—that it is natural and right for men to dominate women. Despite change, it is still more common for men to hold positions of power and authority than for women to hold such positions. Daily patterns of gender domination, viewed as legitimate by most people, are built into our courtship, sexual, family, and work norms.

This does not mean that all men endorse the principle of male dominance, much less that all men are inclined to engage in sexual assault or other acts of aggression against women. Many men favour gender equality, and most men never abuse a woman (Messerschmidt, 1993). Yet the fact remains that many aspects of our culture legitimize male dominance, making it seem valid or proper. For example, pornography, jokes about "dumb blondes," and leering might seem harmless. At a subtler, sociological level, however, they are assertions of the appropriateness of women's submission to men. Such frequent and routine reinforcements of male superiority increase the likelihood that some men will consider it their right to assault women physically or sexually if the opportunity to do so exists or can be created. "Just kidding" has a cost. For instance, researchers have found that university men who enjoy sexist jokes are more likely than other university men to report engaging in acts of sexual aggression against women (Ryan and Kanjorski, 1998).

We conclude that male aggression against women and gender inequality are not separate issues. Gender inequality is the foundation of aggression against women. In concluding this chapter, we consider how gender inequality can be decreased in the coming decades. As we proceed, you should bear in mind that gender equality is not just a matter of justice. It is also a question of safety.

Summing Up

- The advent of long-distance warfare, the development of plow agriculture, and the separation of public and private spheres were the three most important forces that led to the widening of gender inequality.
- Gender discrimination, occupational sex segregation, disproportionate domestic responsibilities, and the undervaluation of work done by women are the main pillars of the gender gap in earnings today.
- Gender inequality supports violence against women. Thus, violence against women is more frequent where the power imbalance between men and women is greatest and where socialization patterns support this imbalance.

TOWARD 2085

The twentieth century witnessed growing equality between women and men in many countries. In Canada, the decline of the family farm made children less economically useful and more costly to raise. As a result, women started having fewer children. The industrialization of Canada, and then the growth of the economy's service sector, increased demand for women in the paid labour force (Figure 11.8). This change gave them substantially more economic power and also encouraged them to have fewer children. The legalization and availability of contraception made it possible for women to exercise unprecedented control over their own bodies. The women's movement fought for, and won, increased rights for women on a number of economic, political, and legal fronts. All these forces brought about a massive cultural shift, a fundamental reorientation of thinking on the part of many Canadians about what women could and should do in society.

One indicator of the progress of women worldwide is the Gender Inequality Index (GII), computed annually by the United Nations. It takes into account inequality between men and women in terms of health, participation in the paid labour force, and political influence. A score of zero indicates equality with men on these three dimensions, while a score of 1 indicates maximum inequality.

As Figure 11.9 shows, the most gender-egalitarian countries in the world in 2008 were in northern Europe. Canada ranked sixteenth. In general, there is more gender equality in rich than in poor countries. Gender equality is partly a function of economic development. However, gender equality is also a function of government policy. Thus, in some former Eastern European and Central Asian communist countries, the GII is lower than we would expect given their level of economic development. Meanwhile, in some Islamic countries, gender inequality is higher than we would expect given their level of economic development. These anomalies exist because the former communist countries made gender equality a matter of public policy while many Islamic-majority countries have done just the opposite (Brym et al., 2005).

The GII figures suggest that Canadian women still have a considerable way to go before they achieve equality with men. For example, we saw that the gender gap in earnings is shrinking but will disappear only in 2085—and then only if it continues to diminish at the same rate as it did between 1976 and 2008. That is a big "if," because progress is never automatic.

Socializing children at home and in school to understand that women and men are equally adept at nearly all jobs is important for motivating women to excel in non-traditional fields. Hiring more women to compensate for past discrimination in hiring, firing, promotion, and training is also important. However, without in any way minimizing the need for such

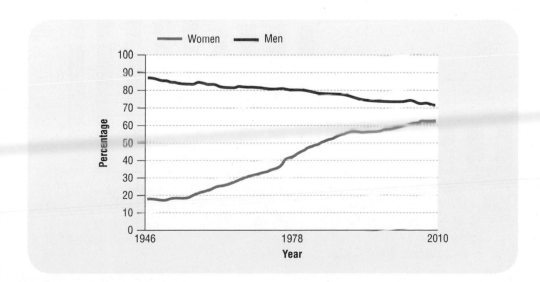

FIGURE 11.8

Percentage of Men and Women in Paid Labour Force, Canada, 1946–2010

Sources: Adapted from Statistics Canada, 2008, "Historical Statistics of Canada," http://www.statcan .ca/english/freepub/11-516-XIE/ sectiond/sectiond.htm (accessed May 2, 2008) and Statistics Canada. 2010, CANSIM Table 2820001. http://dc1.chass.utoronto. ca.myaccess.library.utoronto.ca/ cgi-bin/cansimdim/c2_getArrayDim .pl (accessed 20 November 2010).

initiatives, we should recognize that their impact will be muted if women continue to undertake disproportionate domestic responsibilities and if occupations containing a high concentration of women continue to be undervalued in monetary terms.

Two main policy initiatives will probably be required in the coming decades to bridge the gender gap in earnings. One is the development of a better child-care system. The other is the development of a policy of "equal pay for work of equal value." Let us consider each of these issues in turn.

Child Care

High-quality, government-subsidized, affordable child care is widely available in most Western European countries but not yet in Canada outside Quebec (Chapter 15, Families). Sixty percent of children in the United Kingdom are in regulated child care as are 69 percent of children in France and 78 percent in Denmark. In contrast, Canada's child-care efforts are a patchwork that has been chronically underfunded. Only 20 percent of Canadian children under the age of seven are in regulated child care (OECD, 2004: 7). As a result, many Canadian women with small children are either unable to work outside the home or able to work outside the home only on a part-time basis.

A universal system of daycare was proposed in Canada as early as 1970, but little was done at the federal level or in most provinces and territories. Quebec is an exception. In 1997, that province introduced a comprehensive family policy that attempts to integrate family benefits, paid parental leave, child care, and kindergarten. Its child-care component heralded universally available, affordable child care. A rapid expansion in the number of spaces occurred, although waiting lists grew as well. By 2004, 40 percent of the regulated daycare spaces available in Canada were in Quebec. Unfortunately, that was in part because no new spaces had been added outside Quebec in the preceding decade.

The need for child care exists. In 2001, 52 percent of Canadian preschoolers received some kind of care outside of the home, up from 42 percent just seven years earlier. However,

FIGURE 11.9

Gender Inequality Index, Top 10 and Bottom 10 Countries plus Canada, 2008

Source: United Nations. 2010. "Gender Inequality Index." http:// hdr.undp.org/en/media/HDR_2010_ EN_Table4_reprint.pdf (accessed 22 November 2010).

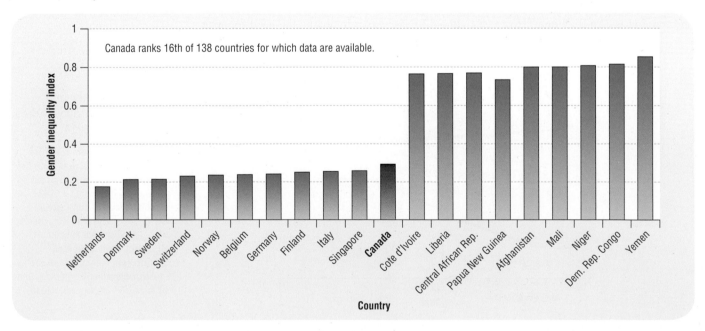

just 25 percent of these children were enrolled in daycare programs; a growing number were cared for by relatives: 14 percent, up from 8 percent in 1994 (Statistics Canada, 2005a).

In 2004, affordable, high-quality, regulated daycare was a central electoral promise of the victorious Liberal Party. By mid-2005, the beginnings of a national system began to take shape when the federal government reached child-care agreements with Saskatchewan, Manitoba, Ontario, and Newfoundland and Labrador. The system, had it taken root across the country, would potentially have paid for itself. One study estimated that a high-quality, affordable, universal system of child care and early child-care education would cost $7.9 billion, while the increased employment of mothers would be worth $6.2 billion and the improvement in child development would be worth $4.3 billion (Cleveland and Krashinsky, 1998). However, after he became prime minister in 2006, Stephen Harper scrapped the agreements in favour of taxable benefits of $1200 paid to parents for each child under age six. The amount and the targeting were widely criticized as failing to address what women who work for pay needed to support their families. In 2007–8, government child-care funding ranged from $195 per child in Alberta to $1694 per child in Quebec, with 7 of Canada's 10 provinces contributing less than $400 per child. Nationwide, there were enough regulated daycare spaces for just under 20 percent of children up to age 12 (Beach, Friendly, Ferns, Prabhu, and Forer, 2009: 183, 186).

Equal Pay for Work of Equal Value

On paper, Canadian women have had the right to equal pay for the same jobs done by men since the 1950s. Unfortunately, although early laws proclaimed lofty goals, they failed to result in fair wages.

In the 1980s, researchers found that women earn less than men partly because jobs in which women are concentrated are valued less than jobs in which men are concentrated. They therefore tried to establish gender-neutral standards by which they could judge the dollar value of work. These standards include such factors as the education and experience required to do a particular job and the level of responsibility, amount of stress, and working conditions associated with it. Researchers felt that, by using these criteria to compare jobs in which women and men are concentrated, they could identify pay inequities. The underpaid could then be compensated accordingly. In other words, women and men would receive **equal pay for work of equal value**, even if they did different jobs. During the mid-1980s, some governments amended the law to state that women should be paid equally for work of equal value. This amendment required employers to compare the rates of pay for women and men in dissimilar jobs that nevertheless involved the same level of skill, effort, and responsibility, and the same working conditions. In 1985, Manitoba became the first Canadian province to demand that its public sector be proactive and implement plans for equal pay for work of equal value—or pay equity, as it is often called. Pay equity is now official policy in 10 of 13 Canadian jurisdictions (Alberta, Saskatchewan, and the Northwest Territories are the exceptions). However, provisions vary widely. Enforcement mechanisms are meagre and employers have found various ways to argue that unequal wages do not signify discrimination based on sex. Thus, although pay equity is undoubtedly a significant step toward achieving gender equality, inequity remains, as evidenced by the persistence of the wage gap between working men and women.

Equal pay for work of equal value refers to the equal dollar value of different jobs. It is established in gender-neutral terms by comparing jobs in terms of the education and experience needed to do them and the stress, responsibility, and working conditions associated with them.

The Women's Movement

Improvements in the social standing of women do not depend just on the sympathy of government and business leaders. Progress on this front has always depended in part on the strength of the organized women's movement. That is likely to be true in the future, too. In concluding this chapter, it is therefore fitting to consider the state of the women's movement and its prospects.

The first wave of the women's movement emerged during the late nineteenth century and lasted into the early 1920s. Its most important public achievements in Canada were the

CP Picture Archive/Jonathan Hayward

The second wave of the women's movement started to grow in the mid-1960s. Members of the movement advocated equal rights with men in education and employment, the elimination of sexual violence, and control over their own reproduction.

right to vote and the right to be considered persons, and not personal property, under Canadian law. In 1916, women in Alberta, Manitoba, and Saskatchewan were granted the right to vote in provincial elections. All the other provinces followed suit by 1925 except Quebec, which granted women the right to vote only in 1940. These rights were first granted to white women. Women from certain ethnic and racial groups did not receive the franchise until later (Nelson and Robinson, 2002).

In the mid-1960s, the second wave of the women's movement emerged. Second-wave feminists were inspired in part by the successes of the civil rights movement in the United States. They felt that women's concerns were largely ignored despite persistent and pervasive gender inequality. Like their counterparts more than half a century earlier, they held demonstrations, lobbied politicians, and formed women's organizations to further their cause. They demanded equal rights with men in education and employment, the elimination of sexual violence, and control over their own reproduction. However, the second wave of the women's movement did not always or consistently recognize, include, or champion the needs of all Canadian women equally. It was not until the 1980s that the second wave of the women's movement began to respond positively to the claim that white, middle-class feminists have "denied, dismissed, and denigrated" the experiences of women of different races, abilities, and classes (Cassidy, Lord, and Mandell, 1998: 26).

There is considerable diversity in the modern feminist movement concerning ultimate goals. Three main streams can be distinguished (Tong, 1989):

1. *Liberal feminism* is the most popular current in the women's movement today. Its advocates believe that the main sources of women's subordination are learned gender roles and the denial of opportunities to women. Liberal feminists advocate nonsexist methods of socialization and education, more sharing of domestic tasks between women and men, and the extension to women of all the educational, employment, and political rights and privileges men enjoy.

2. *Socialist feminists* regard women's relationship to the economy as the main source of women's disadvantages. They believe that the traditional nuclear family emerged along with inequalities of wealth and that the economic and sexual oppression of women has its roots in capitalism. Socialist feminists also assert that the reforms proposed by liberal feminists are inadequate, because they can do little to help working-class women, who are too poor to take advantage of equal educational and work opportunities. Socialist feminists conclude that only the elimination of private property and the creation of economic equality can bring about an end to the oppression of all women.

3. *Radical feminists*, in turn, find the reforms proposed by liberals and the revolution proposed by socialists inadequate. Patriarchy—male domination and norms justifying that domination—is more deeply rooted than capitalism, say the radical feminists. After all, patriarchy predates capitalism. Moreover, it is just as evident in self-proclaimed communist societies as it is in capitalist societies. Radical feminists conclude that the very idea of gender must be changed to bring an end to male domination. Some radical feminists argue that new reproductive technologies, such as in vitro fertilization, are bound to be helpful in this regard because they can break the link between women's bodies and child bearing (see Chapter 15, Families). However, the revolution envisaged by radical feminists goes beyond the realm of reproduction to include all aspects of male sexual dominance. From their point of view, pornography, sexual harassment, restrictive contraception, sexual assault, incest, sterilization, and physical assault must be eliminated for women to reconstruct their sexuality on their own terms.

This thumbnail sketch by no means exhausts the variety of streams of contemporary feminist thought. For example, since the mid-1980s, *anti-racist* and *postmodernist* feminists have criticized liberal, socialist, and radical feminists for generalizing from the experience of white women and failing to understand how women's lives are rooted in particular historical and racial experiences (hooks, 1984). These new currents have done much to extend the relevance of feminism to previously marginalized groups.

Partly because of the political and intellectual vigour of the women's movement, some feminist ideas have gained widespread acceptance in Canadian society over the past three decades. Most Canadians, men and women, agree or strongly agree that being able to have a paying job is either important or very important for women's personal happiness. About 7 of 10 Canadian men and women agree or strongly agree that both spouses should contribute to household income. However, these values appear to conflict with other attitudes and beliefs. For example, more than half of Canadians agree or strongly agree that preschool-age children are likely to suffer if both parents are employed. And around 45 percent of Canadians agree or strongly agree that a "job is alright, but what most women really want is a home and children" (Ghalam, 1997: 16).

Our own experience suggests that traditional patterns of gender socialization weigh heavily on many men. For example, John Lie grew up in a patriarchal household. His father worked outside the home, and his mother stayed home to do nearly all the housework and child care. "I remember my grandfather telling me that a man should never be seen in the kitchen," recalls John, "and it is a lesson I learned well. In fact, everything about my upbringing—the division of labour in my family, the games I played, the TV programs I watched—prepared me for the life of a patriarch. I vaguely remember seeing members of the 'women's liberation movement' staging demonstrations on the TV news in the early 1970s. Although I was only about 11 or 12 years old, I recall dismissing them as slightly crazed, bra-burning man haters. Because of the way I grew up and what I read, heard, and saw, I assumed the existing gender division of labour was natural. Doctors, pilots, and professors should be men, I thought, and people in the 'caring' professions, such as nurses and teachers, should be women.

"But socialization is not destiny," John insists. "Entirely by chance, when I got to college I took some courses taught by female professors. It is embarrassing to say so now, but I was surprised that they seemed so much brighter, more animated, and more enlightening than my male high school teachers had been. In fact, I soon realized that many of my best professors were women. I think this is one reason why I decided to take the first general course in women's studies offered at my university. It was an eye opener. I soon became convinced that gender inequalities are about as natural and inevitable as racial inequalities. I also came to believe that gender equality could be as enriching for men as for women. Sociological reflection overturned what my socialization had taught me. Sociology promised—and delivered. I think many college-educated men have similar experiences today, and I hope I now contribute to their enlightenment."

Summing Up

- Economic development lowers gender inequality, and government policy can have similar effects.
- In Canada, the policies that could do most to lower the level of gender inequality involve the establishment of a universally accessible system of high-quality child care and the implementation of a universal system of equal pay for work of equal value.
- The main achievement of the first wave of the women's movement (late nineteenth century to early 1920s) was winning women's right to vote and their right to be considered persons under Canadian law. The second wave of the movement's movement (originating in the mid-1960s) demanded equal rights for women in education and employment, the elimination of sexual violence, and women's control over their own reproduction.

SUMMARY

1. **Are sex and gender rooted in nature?**
   Sex refers to certain anatomical and hormonal features of a person, while gender refers to the culturally appropriate expression of masculinity and femininity. Sex is largely rooted in nature, although people can change their sex by undergoing a sex-change operation and hormone therapy. In contrast, social and biological forces strongly influence gender. Sociologists study the way social conditions affect the expression of masculinity and femininity.

2. **What are some of the major social forces that channel people into performing culturally appropriate gender roles?**
   Various agents of socialization channel people into performing culturally approved gender roles. The family, the school, and the mass media are among the most important of these agents of socialization. Once the sex of children is known (or assumed), parents and teachers tend to treat boys and girls differently in terms of the kind of play, dress, and learning they encourage. The mass media reinforce the learning of masculine and feminine roles by making different characteristics seem desirable in boys and girls, men and women.

3. **What is homosexuality and why does it exist?**
   Homosexuals are people who prefer sexual partners of the same sex. We do not yet well understand the causes of homosexuality—whether it is genetic, hormonal, psychological, or some combination of the three. We do know that homosexuality does not appear to be a choice and that it emerges for most people without prior sexual experience in early adolescence. Sociologists are, in any case, more interested in the way homosexuality is expressed and repressed. For example, they have studied how, in the twentieth century, scientific research and political movements made the open expression of homosexuality more acceptable. Sociologists have also studied the ways in which various aspects of society reinforce heterosexuality and treat homosexuality as a form of deviance subject to tight social control.

4. **Aside from agents of socialization, are there other social forces that influence the expression of masculinity and femininity?**
   Yes. One of the most important non-socialization forces that influences the expression of masculinity and femininity is the level of social inequality between men and women. High levels of gender inequality encourage more traditional or conventional gender roles. There are fewer differences in gender roles where low levels of gender inequality prevail. Historically, high levels of gender inequality have been encouraged by far-ranging warfare and conquest, plow agriculture, and the separation of public and private spheres. Each of these changes enhanced male power and added a layer of what we now consider tradition to gender roles.

5. **How does the existence of sharply defined gender roles influence men's and women's income?**
   The gender gap in earnings derives from outright discrimination against women, women's disproportionate domestic responsibilities, women's concentration in low-wage occupations and industries, and the undervaluation of work typically done by women.

6. **What helps explain male aggression against women?**
   Male aggression against women is rooted in gender inequality. Thus, where women and men are more equal socially, and norms justify gender equality, the rate of male aggression against women is lower.

7. **How might the gender gap in earnings be reduced or eliminated?**
   Among the major reforms that could help eliminate the gender gap in earnings and reduce the level and expression of gender inequality are (1) the development of an affordable, accessible system of high-quality daycare and (2) the remuneration of men and women on the basis of their work's actual worth.

KEY TERMS

bisexuals (p. 278)

equal pay for work of equal value (p. 293)

essentialism (p. 268)

gender (p. 267)

gender discrimination (p. 286)

gender identity (p. 267)

gender ideology (p. 274)

gender role (p. 267)

glass ceiling (p. 277)

heteronormativity (p. 267)

heterosexuality (p. 268)

homophobic (p. 282)

homosexuals (p. 278)

hostile environment sexual harassment (p. 290)

intersexed (p. 266)

quid pro quo sexual harassment (p. 290)

sex (p. 267)

sexuality (p. 267)

transgendered (p. 278)

transsexuals (p. 278)

WEB RESOURCES

Companion Website for This Book

http://www.compass4e.nelson.com

Begin by clicking on the Student Resources section of the website. Next, select the chapter you are studying from the pull-down menu. From the Student Resources page you have easy access to additional Weblinks and other resources. The website also has many useful tips to aid you in your study of sociology, including practice tests for each chapter.

InfoTrac® Search Terms

These search terms are provided to assist you in beginning to conduct research on this topic by visiting http://www.infotrac-college.com:

gender

glass ceiling

gender discrimination

sexual harassment

gender role

12

Sociology of the Body: Disability, Aging, and Death

IN THIS CHAPTER, YOU WILL LEARN THAT

- Seemingly natural features of the human body, such as height and weight, have social causes and consequences of far-reaching importance.

- Enhancing body image to conform to prevailing norms became especially important in urban, industrial societies.

- In different times and places, people have defined and dealt with disability in different ways.

- Age is an important basis of social stratification. However, the correlation between age and the command of resources is far from perfect, and political conflicts shape the degree to which any given age cohort exercises resource control.

- Although prejudice and discrimination against older people are common in Canada, older people have wielded increasing political power in recent decades.

NIP/TUCK

"Tell me what you don't like about yourself." With these simple words, plastic surgeons Christian Troy and Sean McNamara begin each consultation in the TV series *Nip/Tuck*. At first, the words seem unremarkable. Why *wouldn't* we assume that prospective cosmetic surgery patients are dissatisfied with their appearance? Yet once the words sink in, they shock us. They shock us, first, when we remember how widespread the incidence of body dissatisfaction is. About four million North Americans underwent cosmetic surgery, including minimally invasive cosmetic procedures such as Botox injections, in 2008, up nearly tenfold since 1992 (American Society of Plastic Surgeons, 2009). Add to this number the many people who want cosmetic surgery but cannot afford it, and we can reasonably conclude that body dissatisfaction is not an individual idiosyncrasy but a mass social phenomenon. The plastic surgeons' words are shocking, too, because they point to dissatisfaction that is more than skin deep. Troy and McNamara don't ask prospective patients what they dislike about their

© FXNetworks/Courtesy Everett Collection/CP Picture Archive

bodies. They ask them what they dislike about their *selves*. Implicit in their question is the assumption that our bodies faithfully represent our selves—that weight, proportions, hairiness, and so forth, say something fundamentally important about a person's character. It is an assumption that most people share.

Embedded in the idea that our bodies reflect our selves is a sociological principle that is the main lesson of this chapter. The human body is not just a wonder of biology; it is also a sociological wonder (Turner, 1996). Its parts, its disabilities, its aging, and its death mean different things and have different consequences for different cultures, historical periods, and categories of people. For example, a person's height, weight, and attractiveness may seem to be facts of nature. Closer inspection reveals, however, that the standards by which we define a "normal" or "desirable" body vary historically. Moreover, a person's height, weight, and perceived attractiveness influence his or her annual income, health, likelihood of getting married, and much else. We explore the relationship between body characteristics and social status in the next section.

The relationship between the body and society is especially clear in the case of disability. The very definition of what constitutes a disability has varied over time and place. So have strategies for dealing with disabilities. In the following pages, we illustrate these variations. Among other things, we show that the dominant treatment tendency since the nineteenth century has involved the rehabilitation and integration of people with disabilities into "normal" society. Then, in the early twentieth century, some governments tried to eliminate people with disabilities altogether. Finally, in the late twentieth century, people with disabilities began to assert their dignity and normality. One consequence of this new attitude is a vigorous move toward self-help and the establishment of independent communities of people with disabilities.

In this chapter's final section, we turn to the problems of aging and death. We show that aging is not just a natural process of growth and decline. Age is one basis of social inequality. Thanks to improved social policy and medical advances, the social condition of the aged is much better than it was just half a century ago. However, older people face prejudice and discrimination. The systems for providing personal care and adequate pensions are in trouble. Poverty is a looming possibility for some and a bitter reality for others. We survey each of these issues and conclude by training our sociological eye on the ultimate social problems: dying and death.

Summing Up

- Various aspects of the human body mean different things and have different consequences for different cultures, historical periods, and categories of people.
- For example, the definition of what constitutes a disability has varied over time and place, as have strategies for dealing with disabilities.
- Similarly, aging is not just a natural process of growth and decline, and age is one basis of social inequality.

SOCIETY AND THE HUMAN BODY

The Body and Social Status

Height

In an experiment, four people of the same height and roughly similar appearance were introduced to a group of students. The first person was introduced as a fellow undergraduate, the second as a graduate student, the third as an assistant professor, and the fourth as a professor. Members of the group were asked to rank the four people in terms of their height. Despite the fact that all four were of equal stature, the students estimated that the professor was the tallest, the assistant professor next tallest, then the graduate student, and finally the undergraduate. Apparently believing that physical stature reflects social stature, the students correlated social status with height ("Short Guys Finish Last," 1995–96).

Is this perception accurate? Do tall people really tend to enjoy high social status? And why are some people tall in the first place? We can begin to answer these questions by first acknowledging that genes are an important determinant of any particular individual's height. However, the great majority of human *populations* are approximately the same genetically. A complex series of *social* factors determines the average height of most populations, whether the population consists of members of a country, a class, a racial or an ethnic group, and so on. Moreover, a complex series of social consequences flow from differences in height.

Figure 12.1 shows some of the main social causes and consequences of height. For purposes of illustration, consider the impact of family income on stature. Average family income is the single most important determinant of the quality of a person's diet, especially protein consumption. Higher family income translates into a higher-quality diet. In turn, the quality of diet during childhood strongly influences a person's stature. Thus, Japanese men were on average five centimetres (two inches) taller at the end of the twentieth century than they were at mid-century (French, 2001). Norwegian men were on average nearly eight centimetres (three inches) taller in 1984 than in 1761 (Floud, Wachter, and Gregory, 1990). North American–born children of immigrants are taller on average than their parents who

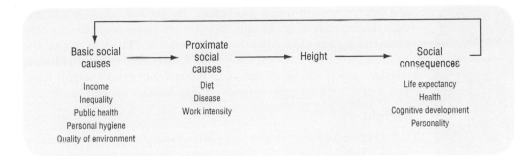

FIGURE 12.1

Selected Social Causes and Consequences of Height in Human Populations

Source: Adapted from Steckel, 1995: 1908.

were born abroad (Roberts, 1995). In all these cases, the main cause of growing stature is the same: A higher standard of living led to an improved diet that allowed the human body to come closer to realizing its full growth potential. The correlation between per capita family income and average height across many countries is very strong ($r = 0.82$ or higher; Steckel, 1995: 1912).

As we might expect, within countries there is also a correlation between stature and class position. Class differences in height are smaller than they were centuries ago. Even today, however, members of upper classes are on average taller than members of middle classes, who are in turn taller than members of working classes are. The Scandinavian countries are the exceptions that prove the rule. There are no differences in stature between classes in Scandinavia. That is because class inequality is less pronounced in Sweden, Norway, and the rest of Scandinavia than elsewhere (Floud, Wachter, and Gregory, 1990; Kingston, 1997).

The *consequences* of stature are important too. Scrutiny of many sources, ranging from U.S. Army records since the Civil War to all Norwegian X-ray records from the 1950s, reveals that, on average, tall people live longer than others do. In only three of the United States presidential elections held over the past century did the shorter candidate win ("Short Guys Finish Last," 1995–96). Tall people also earn more than others do and tend to reach the top of their profession more quickly (Kingston, 1997; McCulloch, 2003). One of the most thorough studies of the effect of height on income was recently conducted in Canada. Tom Perks (2005) found that an additional centimetre in height is associated with an additional $222 in annual income for men and an additional $57 for women. This means that over 10 years, a man who is 10 centimetres taller than another man but like him in all other relevant respects will earn $22 200 more on average. Remarkably, Perks also found that, in Canada, height has a bigger effect on income than whether one is an immigrant or a member of a visible minority group.

At least part of the reason that short people tend to be less successful in some ways than tall people are is that they experience subtle discrimination based on height. This argument may seem far-fetched. However, your own attitudes may help drive the point home. Is it important that you choose a spouse who is taller than you are? If you are a woman, there is a very good chance you will answer yes. Is it important that you choose a spouse who is shorter than you are? If you are a man, there is a very good chance you will answer yes. Why is this so? Practically speaking, it is unimportant whether the husband or the wife is taller. Yet the overwhelming majority of people believe that husbands should be taller than wives. They find it odd when a husband is shorter than his wife is or even when they are the same height. This attitude is widespread because, for most people, height is an indicator of status and most people believe that men should enjoy higher status than women do. You can extend this example to other kinds of relationships. Think about the leaders of your sports teams, friendship circles, college or university tutorials, families,

Rubens's *The Toilette of Venus* (1613). Venus, the Roman goddess of beauty, as depicted by Peter Paul Rubens four centuries ago. Would Venus need a tummy tuck and a membership in a diet club to be considered beautiful today?

and other groups to which you belong. Height will surely not be the only determinant of leadership, but you are likely to observe a tendency for leaders to be taller than followers are. This is so despite the fact that there is no practical reason that leaders need to be tall. Finally, consider where you sit in the status hierarchy based on height. Have you ever felt advantaged or disadvantaged because of your height?

Weight

What is true for height is also true for body weight. Body weight influences status because of the cultural expectations we associate with it. Thus, one study of more than 10 000 young adults found that overweight women tend to complete four fewer months of school than do women who are not overweight. They are also 20 percent less likely to be married. An overweight woman's household is likely to earn nearly $8500 less per year than the household of a woman who is not overweight does. Overweight women are 10 percent more likely to live in poverty. The consequences of being overweight are less serious for men. Still, overweight men are 11 percent less likely to be married than men who are not overweight (Gortmaker et al., 1993; Averett and Korenman, 1996).

Interestingly, the negative effects of being overweight are evident even for women matched in terms of their social and economic backgrounds. This fact suggests the need to revise the simple, conventional view that poverty encourages obesity. It is certainly true that poor women have fewer opportunities and resources that would allow them to eat healthier diets, get more exercise, and bring down their weight. For example, if you live in a poor, high-crime neighbourhood, it is dangerous to go out for a speed walk and you may not be able to afford anything more nutritious than high-calorie fast food when you go out for a meal. However, the reverse is also true: Obesity in and of itself tends to make women poorer. This conclusion seems reasonable because, as noted, for women matched in terms of their social and economic backgrounds, being overweight still has negative effects on income. There is apparently a "reciprocal relationship" between obesity and social class, with each variable affecting the other (Gortmaker et al., 1993).

In preindustrial societies, people generally favoured well-rounded physiques because they signified wealth and prestige. Not surprisingly, beautiful women as depicted by the great artists of the past tend to be on the heavy side from our contemporary perspective.

In contrast, in our society, being well rounded usually signifies undesirability. Being overweight in Canada has become a source of negative stereotyping and even outright discrimination. Many of us think of overweight people as less attractive, industrious, and disciplined than thin people.

Yet the percentage of overweight people is big and growing in Canada, with men accounting for about two-thirds of the recent increase. The likelihood of being overweight increases with age and decreases with class and education (Godley and McLaren, 2010; Statistics Canada, 2002a, 2002b; see Figure 12.2 and Figure 12.3). Thus, a large and expanding number of Canadians live with a stigma that affects their life chances.

Sociology of the Body

The Body and Society

Our discussion of height and weight should make it clear that our bodies are not just biologically but also socially defined. Let us develop this point by considering how social forces influence the way we manipulate our body image. We then turn to an

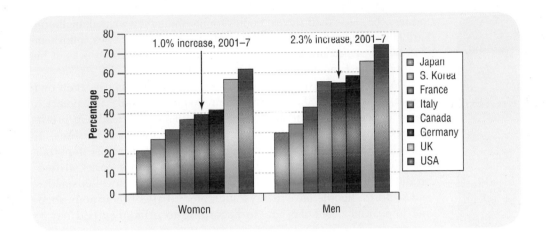

FIGURE 12.2

Percentage of Adults Who Are Overweight, Selected Countries, 2007

Note: Overweight adults have a BMI of 25 or higher (BMI = weight in kilograms divided by the square of height in metres).

Source: OECD. "Health: Key Tables from OECD." http://www.oecd-ilibrary.org/social-issues-migration-health/health-key-tables-from-oecd_20758480;jsessionid=1uk47wcovz5qu.delta (accessed 26 October 2010).

analysis of disability—how we define it and how people with and without disabilities deal with it.

In Canada and other highly developed countries, people tend to think they have rights over their own bodies. For instance, the feminist movement asserts the right of every woman to control her own reproductive functions through birth control (Gordon, 1990). Yet people have not always endorsed this view, and some Canadians still contest it. For instance, slaves' bodies were the property of their owners. In most slave societies,

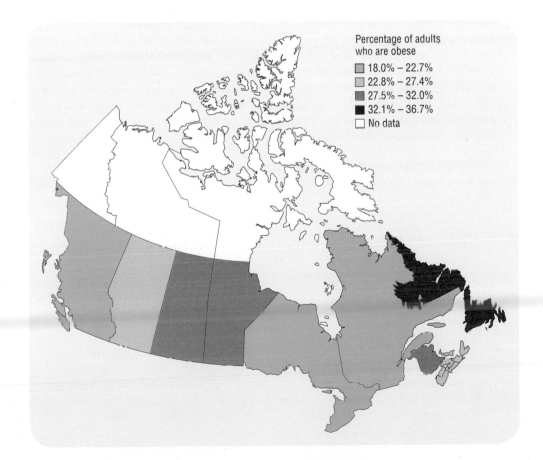

FIGURE 12.3

The Regional Distribution of Obesity in Canada, 2004

Note: Obese adults have a BMI of 30 or higher (BMI = weight in kilograms divided by the square of height in metres.)

Source: Body Mass Index (BMI). Health Canada, 2004. Reproduced with the permission of the Minister of Health, 2011.

Sinibaldi/Corbis

Many of the most important social distinctions—gender, race, age, tribe, and so forth—are "written" on the body by different styles of dress, jewellery, tattoos, cosmetics, and so on. People have always attempted to affect their body shape and appearance, but they do so according to principles laid out by society.

masters could use their slaves' bodies for anything they wanted, including hard labour and sex. Similarly, in deeply patriarchal societies, a husband effectively owned his wife's body. Because his wife's body was at his disposal, a husband could rape his wife with impunity.

Despite the widespread view that people have rights over their own bodies, most people do not treat their bodies in wildly idiosyncratic ways. Instead, norms of body practice influence us. Catholic priests are defined partly by sexual abstinence. Male Jews and Muslims are typically defined partly by circumcision. Many of the most important social distinctions—gender, race, age, tribe, and so on—are "written" on the body by different styles of dress, jewellery, tattoos, cosmetics, and so forth. People have always attempted to affect their body shape and appearance, but they do so according to principles laid out by society.

For social, economic, and technological reasons, enhancing body image to conform to prevailing norms became especially important in urban, industrial societies.

- *Socially*, urbanized societies present people with many more opportunities to meet and interact with strangers. This increases the need for the kinds of status cues and impression management techniques that can make social interaction easier (see Chapter 5, Social Interaction). Manipulating body image helps grease the wheels of social interaction in complex societies by making it clear to strangers exactly who you are.
- *Economically*, industrialized societies enable people to afford body enhancement. For example, peasants in preindustrial societies had no access to relatively inexpensive, mass-produced clothing and jewellery, something we take for granted.
- *Technologically*, we have created many new techniques for transfiguring the body (see Box 12.1). Consider something as basic as your teeth and gums. Until recently, the daily practice of brushing, much less of flossing, was uncommon. Two hundred years ago, a 40-year-old might boast a nice set of wooden dentures; poor people were often toothless and lacked false teeth. Today, dental hygiene, dentistry, and orthodontics allow many people to enjoy a set of straight, white teeth for a lifetime, with bridges, crowns, and implants indistinguishable from the real thing.

Thus, social, economic, and technological forces have transformed the way we manipulate our body image. As you will now see, they have also radically altered the way we deal with disability.

Summing Up

- Many features of the human body, including height and weight, have social causes and consequences.
- Enhancing body image to conform to prevailing norms is especially important in urbanized, industrialized societies because it helps to grease the wheels of social interaction, it is affordable, and it is technologically feasible.

BOX 12.1

Sociology at the Movies

NEVER LET ME GO

Anxiety about the relationship between technology and the human body has been growing at least since Mary Shelley published *Frankenstein* in 1818. Today, we face a new class of misgivings—and accompanying controversy—because it has become possible to grow human body parts from general-purpose stem cells. Almost all research in this area requires the removal of stem cells from an embryo, a procedure that destroys the embryo. Hence the controversy: Should we kill to prolong life?

On the horizon is an even more controversial procedure, first anticipated in Aldous Huxley's *Brave New World* (1932). In the novel, artificially cloned humans are given different aptitudes and then allocated to different social classes. Recently, some scientists, including Princeton University biologist Lee Silver and Nobel Prize–winning physicist Freeman Dyson, have applauded the idea of such genetically engineered social stratification (Brave, 2003).

Never Let Me Go is a masterfully directed and well acted movie that underscores some of genetic engineering's likely dangers.

Scene from *Never Let Me Go*

Kathy, Tommy, and Ruth are 11-year-old students at Hailsham Boarding School. They are nurtured to the very pinnacle of good health and meticulously socialized to take pride in their exalted life's purpose: donating their vital organs to grievously ill people. They undergo a series of operations beginning around the age of 28 and expect to "complete"—that is, die—shortly afterward. They are clones raised specifically for that end.

The problem is that they are also people. Kathy and Tommy fall in love as children, but Ruth intervenes to steal Tommy away from Ruth. As an adult who has already undergone two donor operations, Ruth (played by Keira Knightley) finally grows remorseful. She enables Kathy (Carey Mulligan) and Tommy (Andrew Garfield) to request a "deferral," a rumoured program that gives couples who are truly in love an opportunity to live together for a few years before they complete. However, in the end, we discover that the deferral program does not exist and, indeed, never existed; that Hailsham was a special school set up to discover whether clones have souls; and that Hailsham has now been shut down because the question of whether clones have souls has become irrelevant in a world where demand for healthy body parts far outstrips moral qualms. This is the cowardly new world toward which professors Silver and Dyson want to drive us.

DISABILITY

The Social Construction of Disability

Pity the poor lefty, for centuries considered inferior. About 400 years ago, the Catholic Church declared left-handed people servants of the Devil and burned some of them at the stake. Then it forced lefties to become right-handed in school. In Japan as recently as the early twentieth century, left-handedness in a wife was grounds for divorce. Natives in Papua New Guinea don't let their left thumbs touch their beer mugs because they believe that would poison the beer. Maori women in New Zealand weave ceremonial cloth with the right hand because they believe that using the left desecrates the cloth. Some African tribes along the Niger River do not allow women to prepare food with the left hand for fear of being poisoned. Almost universally, people have considered left-handedness a disability, so much so that the sentiment has been embedded in many languages. In Russian, to do something *na levo* means to do it under the table or illegally, but literally it means "on the left." In English, the word *left* derives from an Old English word that means "weak" or "worthless." Also in English, *gauche* means "ill-mannered"—but the French from which it is derived means "left." (In contrast, *adroit* means "proper" in English—but the French from which it is derived means "to the right.") In Latin, "right" is *dexter* (as in the English *dextrous*, a desirable attribute) while "left" is *sinister*, which of course means "evil" in English. *Linkisch* is German for "leftish"—and "awkward."

To us, negative attitudes toward left-handedness seem nonsensical. We don't think of left-handed people—roughly 10 percent of the population—as **impaired** or deficient in physical or mental capacity. Nor do we think of them as having a **disability** or being incapable of performing within the range of "normal" human activity. The fact that so many people once thought otherwise suggests that definitions of disability are not based on self-evident biological realities. Instead, they vary socially and historically. Note also that some people, but not others, consider a 1.5-metre-tall (4-foot-tall) person to have a disability, and that most people must be convinced by advertising that erectile dysfunction in a 75-year-old man is a disability. These examples suggest that definitions of disability differ across societies and historical periods, and that in any one time and place, people may disagree over these definitions.

Rehabilitation and Elimination

Modern Western approaches to disability emerged in the nineteenth century. All scientists and reformers of the time viewed disability as a self-evident biological reality. Some scientists and reformers sought the **rehabilitation** of those with disabilities. Rehabilitation involves curing disabilities to the extent possible through medical and technological intervention. It also entails trying to improve the lives of people with disabilities by means of care, training, and education. Finally, it seeks to integrate people with disabilities into "normal" society (Stiker, 1999 [1982]; Terry and Urla, 1995). The desire for rehabilitation motivated the establishment of schools for the blind, the widespread use of prosthetics, the construction of wheelchair-accessible buildings, and so forth. It also prompted the passage of laws that benefit those with disabilities by mandating accessibility to buildings, public transportation, and jobs. These laws have done much to help integrate people with disabilities into "normal" society.

Other scientists and reformers took a different tack. They sought to eliminate disability altogether by killing people who had a disability or sterilizing them and preventing them from having children. The Nazis adopted this approach in Germany beginning in 1933. They engineered the sterilization and killing of the mentally "deficient" and the physically "deviant," including the blind and the deaf (Proctor, 1988).

One of the ugliest chapters in our history involves the government-funded, forced sterilization of Aboriginal North American women from the 1920s to the 1970s. The "disability" these women were alleged to have was that they were Aboriginal and were deemed by physicians to be having too many babies. Tubal ligations and hysterectomies were performed as a form of birth control on many thousands of Aboriginal North Americans, some of them minors, without their informed consent. In two cases, doctors told 15-year-old girls they were having their tonsils out and then proceeded to remove their ovaries. Tremendous damage had been inflicted on the Aboriginal North American population by the time such practices were outlawed. According to one estimate, in 1982, when 15 percent of white North American women of childbearing age had been sterilized for various reasons, the figure for Aboriginal North American women was about 40 percent (DeFine, 1997; England, n.d.; Johansen, 1998; *The Sterilization*, 1996).

Impaired people are considered deficient in physical or mental capacity.

A **disability** is a physical or mental problem that keeps people from performing within the range of "normal" human activity.

Rehabilitation involves curing disabilities to the extent possible through medical and technological intervention; trying to improve the lives of people with disabilities by means of care, training, and education; and integrating people with disabilities into society.

Ableism

Perhaps a tenth of the world's people identify themselves as having a disability or are characterized as such by others (Priestly, 2001). Because the human environment is structured largely around the norms of those without disabilities, people with disabilities suffer many disadvantages. Their deprivations are still greater if they are seniors, women, or members of a lower class or a disadvantaged racial or ethnic group.

Specifically, people routinely stigmatize people with disabilities, negatively evaluating them because of a characteristic that supposedly sets them apart from others. People also routinely employ stereotypes when dealing with people with disabilities, expecting them to behave according to a rigid and often inaccurate view of how everyone with that disability acts. The resulting prejudice and discrimination against people with disabilities is called **ableism**. An historical example of ableism is the widespread belief among nineteenth-century Western educators that blind people are incapable of high-level or abstract thought. Because of this prejudice, the blind were systematically discouraged from pursuing intellectually challenging tasks and occupations. Similarly, an 1858 article in the *American Annals of the Deaf and Dumb* held that "the deaf and dumb are guided almost wholly by instinct and their animal passions. They have no more opportunity of cultivating the intellect and reasoning facilities than the savages of Patagonia or the North American Indians" (quoted in Groce, 1985: 102). Racists think of members of racial minorities as naturally and incurably inferior. Ableists think of people with disabilities in the same way. As the preceding quotation suggests, racists and ableists were often the same people.

Ableism involves more than active prejudice and discrimination. It also involves the largely unintended *neglect* of the conditions of people with disabilities. This point should be clear to anyone who has to get around in a wheelchair. Many buildings were constructed without the intention of discriminating against people in wheelchairs, yet they are extremely inhospitable to them. Impairment becomes disability when the human environment is constructed largely on the basis of ableism. Ableism exists through both intention and neglect.

> **Ableism** is prejudice and discrimination against people who have disabilities.

Challenging Ableism: The Normality of Disability

In 1927 science fiction writer H. G. Wells published a short story called "The Country of the Blind" (Wells, 1927). It provocatively reversed the old saying that "in the country of the blind, the one-eyed man is king." In the story, the protagonist, Nuñez, survives an avalanche high in the Andes. When he revives in a mountain valley, he discovers he is on the outskirts of an isolated village whose members are all blind because of a disease that struck 14 generations earlier. For them, words like *see*, *look*, and *blind* have no meaning.

Because he can see, Nuñez feels vastly superior to the villagers; he thinks he is their "Heaven-sent King and master." Over time, however, he realizes that his sight places him at a disadvantage vis-à-vis the villagers. Their senses of hearing and touch are more highly developed than his are, and they have designed their entire community for the benefit of people who cannot see. Nuñez stumbles where his hosts move gracefully and he constantly rants about seeing—which only proves to his hosts that he is out of touch with reality. The head of the village concludes that Nuñez is "an idiot. He has delusions; he can't do anything right." In this way, Nuñez's vision becomes a disability. He visits a doctor who concludes there is only one thing to do. Nuñez must be cured of his ailment. As the doctor says,

> Those queer things that are called eyes … are diseased … in such a way as to affect his brain. They are greatly distended, he has eyelashes, and his eyelids move, and consequently his brain is in a state of constant irritation and distraction.… I think I may say with reasonable

Lightscapes Photography, Inc./Corbis

The social environment turns an impairment into a disability. Architecture and urban planning that neglect some modes of mobility make life difficult for people who depend on wheelchairs.

certainty that, in order to cure him complete, all that we need to do is a simple and easy surgical operation—namely, to remove these irritant bodies.

Thus, Wells suggests that in the country of the blind, the man who sees must lose his vision or be regarded as a raving idiot.

Wells's tale is noteworthy because it makes blindness seem normal. Its depiction of the normality of blindness comes close to the way many people with disabilities today think of their disabilities—not as a form of deviance but as a different form of normality. As one blind woman wrote, "If I were to list adjectives to describe myself, blind would be only one of many, and not necessarily the first in significance. My blindness is as intrinsically a part of me as the shape of my hands or my predilection for salty snacks.... The most valuable insight I can offer is this: blindness is normal to me" (Kleege, 1999: 4).

The idea of the normality of disability has partly supplanted the rehabilitation ideal, which, as we saw, originated in the nineteenth century. Reformers without disabilities led the rehabilitation movement. They represented and assisted people with disabilities, who participated little in efforts to improve the conditions of their existence. This situation began to change in the 1960s. Inspired by other social movements of the era, people with disabilities began to organize themselves (Campbell and Oliver, 1996; Shapiro, 1993). The founding of the Disabled Peoples International in 1981 and inclusion of the rights of those with disabilities in the United Nations Universal Declaration of Human Rights in 1985 signified the growth—and growing legitimacy—of the new movement globally. Since the 1980s, people with disabilities have begun to assert their autonomy and the "dignity of difference" (Charlton, 1998; Oliver, 1996). Rather than requesting help from others, they insist on self-help. Rather than seeing disability as a personal tragedy, they see it as a social problem. Rather than regarding themselves as deviant, they think of themselves as inhabiting a different but quite normal world.

The deaf community typifies the new challenge to ableism. Increasingly, deaf people share a collective identity with other deaf people (Becker, 1980: 107). Members of the deaf community have a common language and culture, and they tend to marry other deaf people (Davis, 1995: 38). Rather than feeling humiliated by the seeming disadvantage of deafness, they take pride in their condition. Indeed, many people in the deaf community are eager to remain deaf even if medical treatment can "cure" them (Lane, 1992). As one deaf activist put it, "I'm happy with who I am ... I don't want to be 'fixed.' ... In our society everyone agrees that whites have an easier time than blacks. But do you think a black person would undergo operations to become white?" (quoted in Dolnick, 1993: 38).

Summing Up

- Since the nineteenth century, movements to rehabilitate, eliminate, and normalize people with disabilities have emerged.
- Ableism—prejudice and discrimination against people who have disabilities—exists because of intention and neglect.

AGING

Sociology of Aging

Disability affects some people. Aging affects us all. Many people think of aging as a natural process that inevitably thwarts our best attempts to delay death. Sociologists, however, see aging in a more complex light. For them, aging is also a process of socialization or learning new roles appropriate to different stages of life (see Chapter 4, Socialization). The sociological nature of aging is also evident in the fact that its significance varies from one society to the next. That is, different societies attach different meanings to the progression of life through its various stages. Menopause, for example, occurs in all mature women. In Canada, we often see it as a major life event. Thus, the old euphemism for menopause was the rather dramatic expression "change of life." In contrast, menopause is a relatively minor matter in Japan. Moreover, while menopausal Canadian women frequently suffer hot flashes, menopausal Japanese women tend to complain mainly about stiff shoulders (Lock, 1993). In many Western countries, complaining about stiff shoulders is a classic symptom of having just given birth. As this example shows, the stages of life are not just natural processes but events deeply rooted in society and culture. As we will see, the same holds for death.

Aging and the Life Course

All individuals pass through distinct stages of life, which, taken together, sociologists call the **life course**. These stages are often marked by **rites of passage**, or rituals signifying the transition from one life stage to another (Fried and Fried, 1980). Baptism, confirmation, the bar mitzvah and bat mitzvah, high school graduation, college or university convocation, the wedding ceremony, and the funeral are among the best-known rites of passage in Canada. Rituals do not mark all transitions in the life course, however. For example, in Canada people often complain about the "terrible twos," when toddlers defy parental demands in their attempt to gain autonomy. Similarly, when some Canadian men reach the age of about 40, they experience a "midlife crisis," in which they attempt to defy the passage of time and regain their youth. (It never works.)

Some stages of the life course are established not just by norms but also by law. For example, most societies have laws that stipulate the minimum age for smoking tobacco, drinking alcohol, driving a vehicle, and voting. Most societies have a legal retirement age. Moreover, the duration of each stage of life differs from one society and historical period to the next. For example, there are no universal rules about when a person becomes an adult. In preindustrial societies, adulthood arrived soon after puberty. In Japan, a person becomes an adult at 20. In Canada, adulthood arrives at 18 (the legal voting age and the legal drinking age in some provinces) or 19 (the legal drinking age in other provinces). Until the 1970s, the legal voting age was 21 and the legal drinking age ranged between 18 and 21.

Even the number of life stages varies historically and across societies. For instance, childhood was a brief stage of development in medieval Europe (Ariès, 1962 [1960]). In contrast, childhood is a prolonged stage of development in rich societies today, and adolescence is a new phase of development that was virtually unknown just a few hundred years ago (Gillis, 1981). Increased life expectancy and the need for a highly educated labour force made childhood and adolescence possible and necessary. (**Life expectancy** is the average age at death of the members of a population.)

Finally, although some life-course events are universal—birth, puberty, marriage, and death—not all cultures attach the same significance to them. Thus, ritual practices marking these events vary. For example, formal puberty rituals in many preindustrial societies are extremely important because they mark the transition to adult responsibilities. However, adult responsibilities do not immediately follow puberty in industrial and postindustrial societies because of the introduction of a prolonged period of childhood and adolescence. Therefore, formal puberty rituals are less important in such societies.

Age Cohort

As you pass through the life course, you learn new patterns of behaviour that are common to people about the same age as you are. Sociologically speaking, a category of people born in the same range of years is called an **age cohort**. For example, all Canadians born between 1980 and 1989 form an age cohort. **Age roles** are patterns of behaviour that we expect of people in different age cohorts. Age roles form an important part of our sense of self and

The **life course** refers to the distinct phases of life through which people pass. These stages vary from one society and historical period to another.

Rites of passage are cultural ceremonies that mark the transition from one stage of life to another (e.g., baptisms, confirmations, weddings) or from life to death (funerals).

Life expectancy is the average age at death of the members of a population.

An **age cohort** is a category of people born in the same range of years.

Age roles are norms and expectations about the behaviour of people in different age cohorts.

others (Riley, Foner, and Waring, 1988). As we pass through the stages of the life course, we assume different age roles. To put it simply, a child is supposed to act like a child, an older person like an older person. We may find a 5-year-old dressed in a suit cute but look askance at a lone 50-year-old on a merry-go-round. "Act your age" is an expression that can be applied to people of all ages who do not conform to their age roles. Many age roles are informally known by character types, such as the "rebellious teenager" and "wise old woman." We formalize some age roles by law. For instance, the establishment of minimum ages for smoking, drinking, driving, and voting formalizes certain aspects of the adolescent and adult roles.

We find it natural that children in the same age cohort, such as preschoolers in a park, should play together or that people of similar age cluster together at parties. Conversely, many people find romance and marriage between people widely separated by age problematic and even repulsive.

Differences between age cohorts are sufficiently large in Canada that some sociologists regard youth culture as a distinct subculture. Adolescents and teenagers—divided though they may be by gender, class, race, and ethnicity—frequently share common interests in music, movies, and so forth (Allahar and Côté, 1994).

Generation

A **generation** is an age group that has unique and formative historical experiences.

A **generation** is a special type of age cohort. Many people think of a generation as people born within a 15- to 30-year span. Sociologists, however, usually define generation more narrowly. From a sociological point of view, a generation comprises members of an age cohort who have unique and formative experiences during youth. Age cohorts are statistically convenient categories, but most members of a generation are conscious of belonging to a distinct age group. For example, "baby boomers" are North Americans who were born in the prosperous years from 1946 to 1964. Most of them came of age between the mid-1960s and the early 1970s. Common experiences that bind them include major historical events (the war in Vietnam, Trudeaumania, Canada's centenary, Expo '67) and popular music (the songs of the Beatles, the Rolling Stones, and the Guess Who). "Generation X" followed the baby boomers. Members of Generation X faced a period of slower economic growth and a job market glutted by the baby boomers. Consequently, many of them resented having to take so-called McJobs when they entered the labour force. Vancouver's Douglas Coupland, the novelist who invented the term Generation X, cuttingly defined a McJob as a "low pay, low-prestige, low-dignity, low-benefit, no-future job in the service sector. Frequently considered a satisfying career choice by people who have never held one" (Coupland, 1991: 5).

Tragedies can help to crystallize the feeling of being a member of a particular generation. For instance, when you are much older you will probably remember where you were when you heard about the attacks of September 11, 2001. Such memories may someday distinguish you from those who are too young to remember these tragic events. The outbreak of World War II may play a similar role in the memory of your grandparents.

The crystallization of a generational "we-feeling" among youth is a quite recent phenomenon. The very ideas of youth and adolescence gained currency only in the nineteenth century because of increased life expectancy, extended schooling, and other factors. Middle-class youth culture often challenged tradition and convention (Gillis, 1981). It was marked by a sense of adventure and rebellion, especially against parents, that manifested itself in political liberalism and cultural radicalism.

Finally, we note that generations sometimes play a major role in history. Revolutionary movements, whether in politics or the arts, are sometimes led by members of a young generation who aggressively displace members of an older generation (Eisenstadt, 1956; Mannheim, 1952).

Erica Lansner/Getty Images

Woodstock. A generation comprises members of an age cohort who have unique and formative experiences during their youth.

Aging and Inequality

Age Stratification

Age stratification refers to social inequality between age cohorts. It exists in all societies and we can observe it in everyday social interaction. For example, there is a clear status hierarchy in most high schools. On average, students in grade 12 enjoy higher status than those in grade 10 do, while students in grade 10 enjoy higher status than those in grade 9 do.

The very young are often at the bottom of the stratification system. Such age stratification is evident in rich countries today, where poverty is more widespread among children than among adults, and it was even more evident in preindustrial and early industrial societies. In some preindustrial societies, people occasionally killed infants so populations would not grow beyond the ability of the environment to support them. Facing poverty and famine, parents sometimes abandoned children. Many developing countries today are overflowing with orphans and street children. During the early stages of Western industrialization, adults brutally exploited children. The young chimney sweeps in *Mary Poppins* may look cute, but during the Industrial Revolution skinny "climbing boys" as young as four were valued in Britain because they could squeeze up crooked chimney flues no more than half a metre in diameter 12 hours a day. Space was tight, so they worked naked, and they rubbed their elbows, knees, noses, and other protrusions raw against the soot, which was often hot. The first description of job-related cancer appeared in an article published in 1775. "Soot-wart," as it was then known, killed chimney sweeps as young as eight (Nuland, 1993: 202–5).

Gerontocracy

Some people believe that ancient China and other preindustrial societies were **gerontocracies**, or societies in which the oldest men ruled, earned the highest income, and enjoyed the most prestige. Even today, people in some industrialized countries pay more attention to age than North Americans do. In South Korean corporations, for instance, when a new manager starts work, everyone in the department who is older than the new manager may resign or be reassigned. Given the importance of age seniority in South Korea, it is considered difficult for a manager to hold authority over older employees. Older employees in turn find it demeaning to be managed by a younger boss (Lie, 1998).

Although some societies may approximate the gerontocratic model, its extent has been exaggerated. Powerful, wealthy, and prestigious leaders are often mature, but not the oldest, people in a society. Canada today is typical of most societies, past and present, in this regard. For example, total income rises with age, reaching its peak in the 45–54 age cohort, and then declines through later life (Statistics Canada, 2010k).

In general, true gerontocracy is rare. Like King Lear, seniors often give up power and become marginalized. Even in traditional societies that held seniors in high esteem, aging was not usually seen as an unambiguous good. After all, aging denotes physical and mental decline and the nearness of death. Ambivalence about aging—especially as people reach the oldest age cohorts—is a cultural universal. As one historian writes, "Youth has always and everywhere been preferred to old age. Since the dawn of history, old people have regretted [the loss of] their youth and young people have feared the onset of old age" (Minois, 1989 [1987]).

Just as true gerontocracy is uncommon, so is rule by youth. True, as noted previously, relatively young age cohorts sometimes supply most of a country's political leadership. This happened in revolutionary France in the late eighteenth century, revolutionary Russia in the early twentieth century, and revolutionary China in the mid-twentieth century. However, youthful ruling cadres may become gerontocracies in their own right, especially in non-democratic societies. This was the case with the Russian communist leadership in the 1980s and the Chinese communist leadership in the 1990s; the young generation that grabbed power half a century earlier still clung on as senility approached.

Age stratification is social inequality between age cohorts.

A **gerontocracy** is a society ruled by older people.

Theories of Age Stratification

The Functionalist View

How can we explain age stratification? *Functionalists* observe that in preindustrial societies, family, work, and community were tightly integrated (Parsons, 1942). People worked in and with their family, and the family was the lifeblood of the community. However, industrialization separated work from family. It also created distinct functions for different age cohorts. Thus, while traditional farming families lived and worked together on the farm, the heads of urban families work outside the home. Children worked for their parents in traditional farming families but in urban settings they attend schools. At the same time, industrialization raised the standard of living and created other conditions that led to increased life expectancy. The cohort of retired people thus grew. And so it came about that various age cohorts were differentiated in the course of industrialization.

At least in principle, social differentiation can exist without social stratification. But, according to the functionalists, age stratification did develop in this case because different age cohorts performed functions of differing value to society. For example, in preindustrial societies, older people were important as a storehouse of knowledge and wisdom. With industrialization, their function became less important and so their status declined. Age stratification, in the functionalist view, reflects the importance of each age cohort's current contribution to society, with children and seniors distinctly less important than adults employed in the paid labour force. Moreover, all societies follow much the same pattern. Their systems of age stratification "converge" under the force of industrialization.

Conflict Theory

Conflict theorists agree with the functionalists that the needs of industrialization generated distinct categories of youth and seniors. They disagree, however, on two points. First, they dispute that age stratification reflects the functional importance of different age cohorts (Gillis, 1981). Instead, they say, age stratification stems from competition and conflict. Young people may participate in a revolutionary overthrow and seize power. Seniors may organize politically to decrease their disadvantages and increase their advantages in life.

The second criticism lodged by conflict theorists concerns the problem of convergence. Conflict theorists suggest political struggles can make a big difference in how much age stratification exists in a society. We saw, for example, that child poverty is higher in the United States than in other rich countries. That is because in other rich countries, particularly in Continental Western Europe, successful working-class political parties have struggled to implement more generous child welfare measures and employment policies that lower the poverty level. This suggests that the fortunes of age cohorts are shaped by other forms of inequality, such as class stratification (Gillis, 1981; Graff, 1995). Power and wealth do not necessarily correlate perfectly with the roles the functionalists regard as more or less important. Competition and conflict may redistribute power and wealth between age cohorts.

Symbolic Interactionist Theory

Symbolic interactionists focus on the meanings people attach to age-based groups and age stratification. They stress that the way in which people understand aging is nearly always a matter of interpretation. Symbolic interactionists have done especially important research in community studies of seniors. They have also helped us to understand better the degree and nature of prejudice and discrimination against seniors. For example, one study examined how movies from the 1940s to the 1980s contributed to the negative stereotyping of older people, particularly women. Among other things, it found that young people were overrepresented numerically in the movies (as compared with their representation in the general population) and tended to be portrayed as leading active, vital lives. Older women were underrepresented numerically and tended to be portrayed as unattractive, unfriendly, and unintelligent (Brazzini, McIntosh, Smith, Cook, and Harris, 1997).

Seniors

Canada's population, along with that of many other rich countries around the world, is greying. In 1901, only 5 percent of Canada's population was 65 or older and the median age of Canadians was just 22.7 years (Novak, 1997). In contrast, according to the 2006 census, the median age was 39.5 years, and 13.7 percent of the population was 65 or older (Statistics Canada, 2007a).

Another way of considering the greying of Canada is to examine **population pyramids**, graphs that show the percentage of the population in various age/sex cohorts (Figure 12.4 and Figure 12.5 on page 314). In 1901, Canada's population pyramid looked very much like a true pyramid. The base of the pyramid was wide, indicating that most people were younger, and the top was small, suggesting a small senior population. By 2050, however, Canada's population pyramid will look more like a T, indicating roughly the same percentage of people in all age cohorts except the oldest, which will be much more numerous. This change in population composition has wide-ranging implications for our social security system, housing, education, employment, and health care.

The number of seniors in Canada has increased for three main reasons. First, nearly a third of Canada's citizens (approximately 10 million people) were born during the 20-year "baby boom" after World War II. During that period, Canadian families averaged four children, resulting in more baby boomers per capita than in the United States, Australia, and New Zealand (Nikiforuk, 1999). Second, life expectancy has increased because of improvements in medical care, sanitation, nutrition, and housing. Third, Canada's current low birth rate contributes to a higher percentage of older people.

Population pyramids are graphs that show the percentage of the population in various age and sex cohorts.

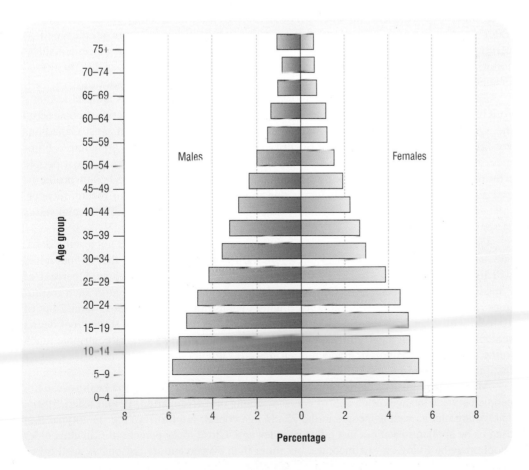

FIGURE 12.4
Population Pyramid, Canada, 1901

Source: McVey and Kalbach, 1995.

FIGURE 12.5

Population Pyramid, Canada, 2050 (projected)

Source: U.S. Census Bureau, International Database.

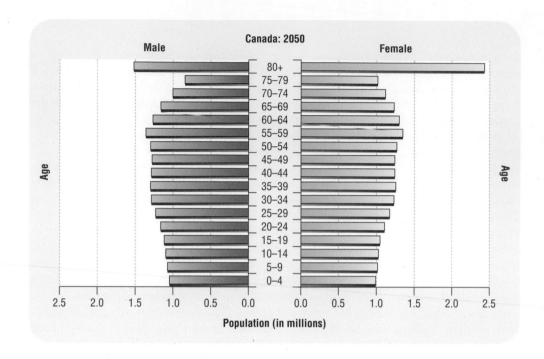

Ageism and the Decline of Old Stereotypes

Ageism is prejudice and discrimination against older people.

Especially in a society that puts a premium on vitality and youth, such as Canada's, being older is still a social stigma. **Ageism** is prejudice about, and discrimination against, older people. Ageism is evident, for example, when older men are stereotyped as "grumpy." Ageism affects women more than men. Thus, the same person who considers some older men "distinguished-looking" may disparage older women as "haggard" (Banner, 1992).

Often, however, seniors do not conform to the negative stereotypes applied to them, which is why the old stereotypes are in decline. In Canada, 65 is sometimes considered the age at which people become seniors since 65 is the age at which most Canadians become eligible to receive Old Age Security benefits. But just because someone is 65 or older does not mean he or she is decrepit and dependent. On the contrary, most people who retire from an active working life are far from being a tangle of health problems and a burden on society. This change is due to the medical advances of recent decades, the healthier lifestyles followed by many older people, and the improved financial status of seniors.

Contrary to stereotypes, the housing arrangements of older people are not usually desolate and depressing (Hochschild, 1973; Myerhoff, 1978). The likelihood that an individual will live in a special-care home increases with age, but in 2001 only about 5 percent of Canadian men and 9 percent of Canadian women over the age of 65 lived in such institutions. More than 7 out of 10 seniors lived with a spouse or alone, and fewer than 2 out of 10 lived with other relatives (Statistics Canada, n.d.). Moreover, although stereotypes depict seniors as burdens on their families, evidence shows that Canada's seniors contribute much to the lives of their children, grandchildren, friends, neighbours, and communities (Vanier Institute of the Family, 2000: 172).

Many sociologists of aging refer to seniors who enjoy relatively good health—usually people between the ages of 65 and 74—as the "young old" (Neugarten, 1974; Laslett, 1991). The young old, as well as people in the 75–84 age cohort, are far from the stereotypes that used to be applied to seniors just a few decades ago. Close to 20 percent of Canada's older people may be living on low incomes, but more than 80 percent are reasonably well off or even well-to-do.

Consider these profiles of older Toronto-area women: Ruth Goldsmith, 76, enjoys financial stability. She exercises every morning (Aquafit, the treadmill, or yoga), meets friends for lunch, goes to the theatre and the symphony, travels to music festivals in Quebec, belongs to a book club, volunteers at the Older Women's Network, visits her sister in England annually, and is planning a trip to Israel. At 72, she learned how to use a computer. She dotes on her daughter and three grandchildren. Her friend, Margaret Hawthorn, 69, has a good pension from her years as a university librarian. She owns a car and a house and enjoys babysitting her grandson once a week. She also enjoys lawn bowling, swimming, and cycling, and has become fluent in Spanish. She travels extensively, sometimes off the beaten path; once she visited Baffin Island. She works for the NDP and is involved in a big garden res-

The active life of many seniors today is a far cry from traditional stereotypes.

toration project. "I have to say that this is the best time—and I've had a reasonably good life," Hawthorn remarks. Nan Cooper, 67, has taken up painting in retirement and has rented an apartment in Italy so she can spend time visiting art galleries. Rosalie Brown, 73, loves dancing—square, ballroom, and line—and complains that she and her friend Margaret Hawthorn are so busy, they have to make appointments to see each other. "I feel I'm into maybe a bit too much," she says. She dates regularly and says it is as pleasurable as when she was younger. In a survey of 5000 older Canadians, two-thirds of respondents said they view retirement as an opportunity to start a new business and the same number said retirement freed them up to pursue a "dream job." Noticeably absent from this vibrant group are old people in rocking chairs eating cat food for supper (Galt, 2006; Kopun, 2006).

The "Old Old"

The situation is different for people 85 and older, whom sociologists refer to as the "old old." The rising number of old old concerns many people because the old old are most likely to suffer general physical decline and life threatening diseases. Among seniors, the old old are also the most likely to face social isolation and poverty.

Significantly, the sex ratio (the number of men compared with the number of women) falls with age. In other words, because women live longer than men do on average, there are more women than men among seniors. This imbalance is most marked in the oldest age cohorts. Therefore, poverty and related problems among the oldest Canadians are in part a gender issue.

Economic inequality between older women and men is largely the result of women's lower earning power when they are younger. Women are entering the paid workforce in increasing numbers, but there are still more women than men who are homemakers and do not work for a wage. Therefore, fewer women than men receive employer pensions when they retire (Nelson and Robinson, 2002). Moreover, women who are in the paid labour force tend to earn less than men do. As a result, when they retire, their employer pensions are generally inferior. Consequently, the people most in need—older women—receive the fewest retirement benefits.

The Power and Wealth of Seniors

Since the 1960s, Canadian seniors have benefited from rising incomes. In 1951 seniors earned on average about half that of Canadians of working age, but now the annual income of these two categories is close to the same (Statistics Canada, 1998b). Because of income security programs, such as the Guaranteed Income Supplement, the Old Age Security pension, and the Spouse's Allowance, Canadian seniors do not have to rely on welfare any more frequently than people in the general population do. The poverty rate for seniors is about the same as the poverty rate for non-seniors (National Council of Welfare, 1998a).

One reason for the improved economic security of seniors is that they are well organized politically. Their voter participation rate is above average, and they are overrepresented among those who hold positions of political, economic, and religious power. Many groups seek to improve the status of seniors. One of the earliest and most radical groups in North America was the Gray Panthers, founded in 1970, with 50 000 to 70 000 members. Much larger is CARP, Canada's Association for the Fifty-Plus, with about 370 000 members. CARP is a nonprofit association that does not accept funding from any government body. It speaks out on a wide range of issues important to those over 50.

Seniors' activism may have led to a redistribution of resources away from young people. For example, while educational funding has declined, funding has increased for medical research related to diseases that disproportionately affect older people. This redistribution of resources has led to the growth of the belief in some rich countries that seniors are a burden on the economy and especially on the nation's youth. Increasingly, young people in communities with a high proportion of wealthy retired people are expressing resentment (Peritz, 1999). In anticipation of government shortfalls, South Korea requires workers to save 35 percent of their income for retirement. In Japan, government benefits can be cancelled if redistribution of tax money is needed to ensure "equity between the generations" (Peterson, 1997). Whether Canadians are prepared to tolerate such tax burdens and cutbacks is questionable (see Box 12.2).

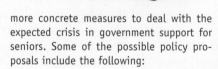

BOX 12.2
It's Your Choice

A SOCIAL SECURITY CRISIS?

One of the greatest triumphs of public policy has been the development of the public health system, which has led to a substantial increase in life expectancy. Another major public policy achievement is social welfare, especially as it applies to seniors. The combination of social security, medicare, and other government programs goes a long way toward ensuring that seniors are not doomed to poverty and illness.

A longer and more secure lifespan is a wonderful thing. However, some scholars and policymakers worry that a major crisis is looming. Canada may not be able to afford government programs for seniors in the future because of the expected retirement of baby boomers, those born in the 20-year period after World War II. Many Canadians born in that period contribute to social security and other measures to support older people. As the baby boomers begin to retire from the active labour force, however, fewer Canadians will be contributing to government coffers.

Some scholars argue that economic growth and higher immigration could offset the expected decline in the active labour force. However, others argue that we need more concrete measures to deal with the expected crisis in government support for seniors. Some of the possible policy proposals include the following:

- increase national savings
- lower health care costs, especially the disproportionately higher burden of medical costs for seniors
- provide government support only to the truly needy, thereby eliminating or lowering social security and other federal benefits for the well-off

What do you think? Should Canadians worry about the expected crisis in social security and other government programs that support seniors? If you expect the potential crisis to erupt in your lifetime, what should you be doing now to avert the crisis? What are the advantages and disadvantages of each of the policy proposals listed above? What kind of lifestyle do you expect to lead when you are in your 60s, 70s, and 80s? Do you think you will be working full time, or will you be fully or partly retired?

Summing Up

- The duration and number of life stages varies across societies and historical periods.
- The most powerful people in most societies are middle-aged, while the least powerful are children.
- Discrimination against seniors is a common problem.
- While functionalists hold that age stratification is based on the functional importance of different age groups, conflict theorists note that political struggles can substantially change the distribution of rewards among different age cohorts.
- The rapid aging of Canadian society has profound implications for Canada's health and social security systems.

DEATH AND DYING

It may seem odd to say so, but the ultimate social problem everyone must face is his or her own demise. Why are death and dying *social* problems and not just religious, philosophical, and medical issues?

For one thing, attitudes toward death vary widely across time and place. So do the settings within which death typically takes place. Although individuals have always dreaded death, in most traditional societies, such as Europe until early modern times, most people accepted it (Ariès, 1982). That is partly because most people apparently believed in life after death, whether in the form of a continuation of life in Heaven or in cyclical rebirth. What also made death easier to accept is that the dying were not isolated from other people. They continued to interact with household members and neighbours, who offered them continuous emotional support. Finally, because the dying had previous experience giving emotional support to other dying people, they could more easily accept death as part of everyday life.

In contrast, we tend to separate dying and death from everyday life. Most terminally ill patients want to die peacefully and with dignity at home, surrounded by their loved ones. Yet about 80 percent of Canadians die in hospitals. Often, hospital deaths are sterile, noiseless, and lonely. Dying used to be public. It is now private. The frequent lack of social support makes dying a more frightening experience for many people (Elias, 1985 [1982]). In addition, our culture celebrates youth and denies death (Becker, 1973). We use diet, fashion, exercise, makeup, and surgery to prolong youth or at least the appearance of youth. This makes us less prepared for death than our ancestors were.

Our reluctance to accept death is evident from the many euphemisms we use as a means of distancing ourselves from it. People used to say that the dead had "entered the Pearly Gates" or had gone to "sing in God's heavenly choir." We are now more likely to say that the dead have "passed away" or "gone to meet their maker" in "a better place" or that they lie in "their final resting place." Sometimes we use humorous expressions as a distancing mechanism. We say that people have "croaked" or "kicked the bucket" or "cashed in their chips" or that they are now "pushing up daisies." These and other similar expressions allow us to separate ourselves symbolically from the horror of death.

Psychiatrist Elisabeth Kübler-Ross's analysis of the stages of dying also suggests how reluctant we are to accept death (Kübler-Ross, 1969). She based her analysis on interviews with patients who were told they have an incurable disease. At first, the patients went into *denial*, refusing to believe their death was imminent. Then they expressed *anger*, seeing their demise as unjust. *Negotiation* followed; they pled with God or with fate to delay their death. Then came *depression*, when they resigned themselves to their fate but became deeply despondent. Only then did the patients reach the stage of *acceptance*, when they put their affairs in order, expressed regret over not having done certain things when they had the chance, and perhaps spoke about going to Heaven.

Euthanasia

The reluctance of many Canadians to accept death is evident in the debate over euthanasia, also known as mercy killing or assisted suicide (Rothman, 1991). Various medical technologies, including machines that are able to replace the functions of the heart and lungs, can prolong life beyond the point that was possible in the past. This raises the question of how to deal with people who are near death. In brief, is it humane or immoral to hasten the death of terminally ill patients?

Euthanasia is any "deliberate act undertaken by one person with the intention of ending the life of another person to relieve that person's suffering, where that act is the cause of death" (McTeer, 1999: 117). A narrower definition of euthanasia involves a doctor prescribing or administering medication or treatment that is *intended* to end a terminally ill patient's life. This form of euthanasia is sometimes referred to as *active euthanasia* inasmuch as it involves the commission of an act. So-called *passive euthanasia* involves intentionally withholding a life-saving medical procedure.

In Canada, assisting suicide or intentional killing, even in an attempt to end suffering, is a crime. In addition, doctors are legally prevented from withholding or withdrawing life-sustaining procedures. They are also legally obliged to ensure that patients whom they believe to be suicidal are prevented from harming themselves. Nevertheless, the reality of modern medicine is that doctors do practise passive euthanasia; not all of them, but rare is the doctor that has not, at the request of the patient, the patient's family, or on his or her own accord, decided to discontinue life-support. Studies also show that many doctors have acquiesced to life-ending drug dosages in cases of advanced terminal illness (Duhaime, 1997).

Many Canadians support a terminally ill person's right to die and believe that doctor-assisted suicide for terminally ill people should be legal. Just over three-quarters of Canadians believe that an individual who helps end the life of a loved one suffering from an incurable and extremely painful illness should not be prosecuted. However, almost 60 percent of Canadians oppose "mercy killing" by a parent of a child who has severe disabilities. Although 42 percent believe that access to euthanasia is necessary for those who are critically ill or have severe disabilities because current nursing-home and end-of-life care is inadequate, almost three-quarters agree that "if people with disabilities or those with chronic or terminal disease had access to adequate pain management and social services, there would be less demand for euthanasia" (Canada NewsWire, 2001).

Montreal physician Balfour Mount, who has been called Canada's father of palliative care, expressed a similar viewpoint when he noted that "our courts voted against euthanasia by the narrowest of margins, while … our governments have failed to give adequate support to palliative care" ("Poor Palliative Care," 2001). Mount warns that unless more palliative care is provided, the "appeal of [euthanasia and assisted suicide] as a 'compassionate' alternative to overcrowded clinical services, inadequate fiscal resources, and increasing family caregiver burden is unlikely to lessen."

Euthanasia is bound to become a major political issue in coming decades as medical technologies for prolonging life improve, the number of older people increases, and the cost of medical care skyrockets. Some people will uphold extending the lives of terminally ill patients by all means possible as an ethical imperative. Others will regard it as immoral because it increases suffering and siphons scarce resources from other pressing medical needs.

Euthanasia (also known as mercy killing and assisted suicide) involves a doctor prescribing or administering medication or treatment that is intended to end a terminally ill patient's life.

CP Photo Archive/Chuck Stoody

Sue Rodriguez, who suffered from amyotrophic lateral sclerosis (ALS; also known as Lou Gehrig's disease), launched a legal battle for the right to have a doctor help her die. She argued that the section of the *Criminal Code* that makes assisted suicide a criminal offence violates three rights guaranteed to all Canadians under the *Canadian Charter of Rights and Freedoms*: the right to life, liberty, and security of the person; the right not to be discriminated against on the basis of disability; and the right not to be subjected to cruel and unusual punishment. The Supreme Court of British Columbia dismissed her application. In 1993, the Supreme Court of Canada, in a 5–4 decision, dismissed her appeal.

Summing Up

- Canadians tend to separate dying and death from everyday life, partly because they are reluctant to accept death as a natural part of life.
- Canadians' attitudes toward death are reflected in the debate over euthanasia, which is bound to become more heated as technology for prolonging life improves and becomes more expensive while the number of older adults soars.

SUMMARY

1. The human body is a biological wonder. In what sense is it a sociological wonder too? The body's parts, its disabilities, its aging, and its death mean different things and have different consequences for different cultures, historical periods, and categories of people. The human body cannot be fully understood without appreciating its sociological dimension.

2. What is the connection between body type and social status?
Because low status influences diet and other factors, it is associated with people of short stature and people who are overweight. In turn, people of short stature and people who are overweight tend to receive fewer social rewards because of their body type.

3. In what sense do people have rights over their own body?
Most people believe they should and do have rights over their own body. Advances in medical technology and changing social norms encourage us to transform our bodies through surgery, prosthesis, and other means. However, we do not treat our bodies in idiosyncratic ways. Norms of body practice influence us.

4. Are disabilities defined similarly everywhere and at all times? Have disabilities always been handled in the same way?
No. The definition of disability varies over time and place. For example, some people used to consider left-handedness and being Aboriginal as disabilities, but we do not share that view. As far as treatment is concerned, we also see much variation. People with disabilities have traditionally suffered much prejudice and discrimination, but attempts were made from the nineteenth century on to integrate and rehabilitate them. Some governments sought to eliminate people with disabilities from society in the twentieth century. Recently, people with disabilities have begun to organize themselves, assert the normality of disability, and form communities of those with disabilities.

5. What is sociological about the aging process?
People attach different meanings to aging in different societies and historical periods. Thus, the stages of life vary in number and significance across societies.

6. Is there a positive correlation between age and status?
Although it is true that the young have been, and still are, disadvantaged in many ways, it is rarely true that the eldest people in society are the best off. In most societies, including Canada, people of middle age have the most power and economic clout.

7. **What are the main approaches to age stratification?**
Functionalist theory emphasizes that industrialization led to the differentiation of age cohorts and the receipt of varying levels of reward by each age cohort based on its functional importance to society. This supposedly results in the convergence of age stratification systems in all industrialized societies. Conflict theory stresses the way competition and conflict can result in the redistribution of rewards between age cohorts and the divergence of age stratification systems. Symbolic interactionists focus not on these macrosociological issues but on the meanings people attach to different age cohorts.

8. **How is Canada aging?**
Canada's population is aging rapidly. Between 1901 and 2006 the median age of Canadians increased from 22.7 to 39.5 years, while the proportion of Canadians 65 or older increased from 5 percent to 13.7 percent. The age–sex distribution looked like a pyramid in 1901, but by 2050 all age–sex cohorts but one will be about the same size; only people 80 and over will form a disproportionately large part of the population. As the population ages, the ratio of men to women falls.

9. **How are seniors faring economically in Canada?**
Economically speaking, senior Canadians are faring reasonably well, partly because they have considerable political power. However, economic inequality exists between older women and men, largely because of women's lower earning power when they are younger; they have smaller pensions and fewer assets once they retire.

10. **If seniors in Canada are doing reasonably well economically and politically, then does this mean that they don't face significant problems in our society?**
Older Canadians face much prejudice and discrimination based on age because our society values youth and vitality and because some people think that seniors command a disproportionately large share of societal resources at the expense of young people.

11. **What is sociological about death and dying?**
Attitudes toward death vary widely across time and place, as do the settings within which death typically takes place. For example, many Canadians are reluctant to accept death, as is evident in the debate over euthanasia.

KEY TERMS

ableism (p. 307)

age cohort (p. 309)

age roles (p. 309)

age stratification (p. 311)

ageism (p. 314)

disability (p. 306)

euthanasia (p. 318)

generation (p. 310)

gerontocracy (p. 311)

impaired (p. 306)

life course (p. 309)

life expectancy (p. 309)

population pyramids (p. 313)

rehabilitation (p. 306)

rite of passage (p. 309)

WEB RESOURCES

Companion Website for This Book

http://www.compass4e.nelson.com

Begin by clicking on the Student Resources section of the website. Next, select the chapter you are studying from the pull-down menu. From the Student Resources page you have easy access to additional Weblinks and other resources. The website also has many useful tips to aid you in your study of sociology, including practice tests for each chapter.

InfoTrac® Search Terms

These search terms are provided to assist you in beginning to conduct research on this topic by visiting http://www.infotrac-college.com:

age discrimination
disability
euthanasia

4

Institutions

13

Work and the Economy

IN THIS CHAPTER, YOU WILL LEARN THAT

- Three work-related revolutions—in agriculture, manufacturing, and the provision of services—have profoundly altered the ways in which people earn a living and how societies are organized.

- The drive for profits has led to the "deskilling" of many jobs and the spread of part-time employment, but work has not degraded overall because more than three-quarters of employment is in the service sector, where there are relatively many good jobs.

- With varying degrees of success, people seek to control work through unions, professional organizations, corporations, and markets.

- The growth of large corporations and global markets has shaped the transformation of work in recent decades and will shape the choices you face as a member of the labour force and as a citizen.

Rey Kamensky/Shutterstock

THE PROMISE AND HISTORY OF WORK

Salvation or Curse?

The computerization of the office began in earnest in the early 1980s. Soon, the image of the new office emerged. It was a checkerboard of three-metre-by-three-metre cubicles. Three padded walls, two metres high, framed each cubicle. Inside, a computer terminal sat on a desk. A worker quietly tapped away at a keyboard, seemingly entranced by the glow of a video screen.

Sociologist Shoshana Zuboff visited many such offices soon after they were computerized. She sometimes asked the office workers to draw pictures capturing their job experience before and after computerization. The pictures were strikingly similar. Smiles changed to frowns, mobility became immobility, sociability was transformed into isolation, freedom turned to regimentation. Two of the workers' pictures are shown in Figure 13.1 below. Work automation and standardization emerge from these drawings as profoundly degrading and inhuman processes (Zuboff, 1988).

The image conveyed by these drawings is only one view of the transformation of work in the Information Age. There is another, and it is vastly different. Bill Gates argues that computers reduce our work hours. They make goods and services cheaper by removing many distribution costs of capitalism (think of online sites reducing the need for bookstores). Computers also allow us to enjoy our leisure time more (Gates with Myhrvold and Rinearson, 1996). This vision is well captured by the arresting cover of *Wired* magazine

Before

Before

After

After

"Before I was able to get up and hand things to people without having someone say, what are you doing? Now, I feel like I am with my head down, doing my work."

"My supervisor is frowning because we shouldn't be talking. I have on the stripes of a convict. It's all true. It feels like a prison in here."

FIGURE 13.1

One View of the Effects of Computers on Work

Shoshana Zuboff asked office workers to draw pictures representing how they felt about their jobs before and after a new computer system was introduced. Here are before and after pictures drawn by two office workers. Notice how even the flower on one worker's desk wilted after the new computer system was introduced.

Source: From Shoshana Zuboff, *In the Age of the Smart Machine: The Future of Work and Power* (Basic Books: New York), 1988, p. 146–47. Copyright © 1988 Basic Books, Inc. Reprinted by permission of Basic Books, a member of Perseus Books, L.L.C.

FIGURE 13.2

Another View of the Effect of Computers on Work

Wired magazine is always on high about the benefits of computer technology.

reprinted as Figure 13.2. According to *Wired*, computers liberate us. They allow us to become more mobile and more creative. Computerized work allows our imaginations to leap and our spirits to soar.

These strikingly different images form the core questions of the sociology of work, our focus in this chapter. Is work a salvation or a curse? Or is it perhaps both at once? Is it more accurate to say that work has become more of a salvation or a curse over time? Or is work a salvation for some and a curse for others?

To answer these questions, we first sketch the three work-related revolutions of the past 10 000 years. Each revolution has profoundly altered the way we sustain ourselves and the way we live. Next, we examine how job skills have changed over the past century. We also trace changes in the number and distribution of "good" and "bad" jobs over time and project these changes into the near future. We then analyze how people have sought to control work through unions, professional organizations, corporations, and markets. Finally, we place our discussion in a broader context. The growth of large corporations and markets on a global scale has shaped the transformation of work over the past quarter century. Analyzing these transformations will help you appreciate the work-related choices you face both as a member of the labour force and as a citizen.

Economic Sectors and Revolutions

The **economy** is the institution that organizes the production, distribution, and exchange of goods and services.

The **economy** is the social institution that organizes the production, distribution, and exchange of goods and services. Conventionally, analysts divide the economy into three sectors. The *primary* sector includes farming, fishing, logging, and mining. In the *secondary* sector, raw materials are turned into finished goods; manufacturing takes place. Finally, in the *tertiary* sector, services are bought and sold. These services include the work of nurses, teachers, lawyers, hairdressers, computer programmers, and so on. Often, the three sectors of the economy are called the agricultural, manufacturing, and service sectors.

Each economic sector rose to dominance through a revolution in the way people work, and each revolution sharply restructured social inequality (Gellner, 1988; Lenski, 1966):

- *The Agricultural Revolution.* Ten thousand years ago, nearly all humans lived in nomadic tribes. Then, people in the fertile valleys of the Middle East, Southeast Asia, and South America began to herd cattle and grow plants by using simple hand tools. Stable human settlements spread. About 5000 years ago, farmers invented the plow. By attaching plows to large animals, they substantially increased the land under cultivation. **Productivity**—the amount produced for every hour worked—soared.

- *The Industrial Revolution.* International exploration, trade, and commerce helped stimulate the growth of markets from the fifteenth century on. **Markets** are social relations that regulate the exchange of goods and services. In a market, prices are established by how plentiful goods and services are (supply) and how much they are wanted (demand). In the late 1700s, the steam engine, railroads, and other technological innovations greatly increased the ability of producers to supply markets. This was the era of the Industrial Revolution. Beginning in England, the Industrial Revolution spread to Western Europe, North America, Russia, and Japan within a century, making manufacturing the dominant economic sector.

- *The Postindustrial Revolution.* Service jobs were rare in pre-agricultural societies because nearly everyone had to do physical work for the tribe to survive. As productivity increased, however, service-sector jobs became numerous. By automating much factory and office work, the computer accelerated this shift in the last third of the twentieth century. In Canada today, more than three-quarters of the labour force is employed in the service sector (see Figure 13.3).

The Division and Hierarchy of Labour

Besides increasing productivity and causing shifts between sectors in employment, the Agricultural, Industrial, and Postindustrial Revolutions altered the way work was socially organized. For one thing, the **division of labour** increased. That is, work tasks became more specialized with each successive revolution. In pre-agrarian societies there were four main jobs: hunting wild animals, gathering edible wild plants, raising children, and tending to the tribe's spiritual needs. In contrast, a postindustrial society, such as Canada's, boasts tens of thousands of different kinds of jobs.

Productivity refers to the amount of goods or services produced for every hour worked.

Markets are social relations that regulate the exchange of goods and services. In a market, the prices of goods and services are established by how plentiful they are (supply) and how much they are wanted (demand).

The **division of labour** refers to the specialization of work tasks. The more specialized the work tasks in a society, the greater the division of labour.

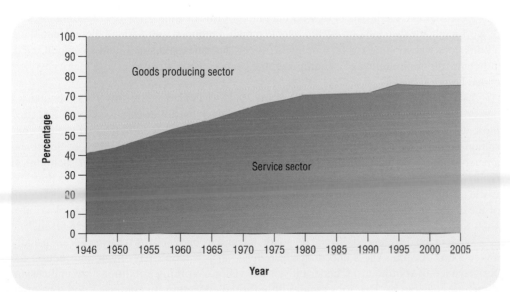

FIGURE 13.3

Estimated Distribution of Canadian Labour Force in Goods Production and Services, 1946–2005

Source: Adapted from Crompton and Vickers, 2000; Statistics Canada, 2005h.

In some cases, increasing the division of labour involves creating new skills (e.g., website design, laser eye surgery). Some new jobs require long periods of study. Foremost among these are the professions, such as medicine, law, and engineering. In other cases, increasing the division of labour involves breaking a complex range of skills into a series of simple routines.

If the division of labour increased as one work revolution gave way to the next, then social relations among workers also changed. In particular, work relations became more hierarchical, with superordinates exercising authority and subordinates following commands.

Summing Up

- The agricultural, industrial, and postindustrial revolutions moved the focus of the economy from primary production to manufacturing to the provision of services.
- The three work-related revolutions increased the productivity of labour, the division of labour, and the hierarchical nature of work.

"GOOD" VERSUS "BAD" JOBS

John Lie once had a job as a factory worker in Honolulu, where he grew up. "The summer after my second year in high school," John recalls, "I decided it was time to earn some money. I had expenses, after all, but only an occasionally successful means of earning money: begging my parents. Scouring the help wanted ads in the local newspaper, I soon realized I wasn't really qualified to do anything in particular. Some friends at school suggested I apply for work at a pineapple-canning factory. So I did.

"At the factory, an elderly man asked me a few questions and hired me. I was elated—but only for a moment. A tour of the factory floor ruined my mood. Row upon row of conveyor belts carried pineapples in various states of disintegration. Supervisors chastened the employees to work faster yet make fewer mistakes. The smell, the noise, and the heat were unbearable. After the tour, the interviewer announced I would get the graveyard shift (11 p.m. to 7 a.m.) at minimum wage.

"The tour and the prospect of working all night finished me off. Now dreading the idea of working in the factory, I wandered over to a mall. I bumped into a friend there. He told me a bookstore was looking for an employee (9 to 5, no pineapple smell, and air conditioned, although still minimum wage). I jumped at the chance. Thus, my career as a factory worker ended before it began.

"A dozen years later, just after I got my Ph.D., I landed one of my best jobs ever. I taught for a year in South Korea. However, my salary hardly covered my rent. I needed more work desperately. Through a friend of a friend, I found a second job as a business consultant in a major corporation. I was given a big office with a panoramic view of Seoul and a personal secretary who was both charming and efficient. I wrote a handful of sociological reports that year on how bureaucracies work, how state policies affect workers, how the world economy had changed in the past two decades, and so on. I accompanied the president of the company on trips to the United States. I spent most of my days reading books. I also went for long lunches with colleagues and took off several afternoons a week to teach."

What is the difference between a "good" job and a "bad" job, as these terms are usually understood? As John Lie's anecdote illustrates, bad jobs don't pay much and require the performance of routine tasks under close supervision. Working conditions are unpleasant, sometimes dangerous. Bad jobs require little formal education. In contrast, good jobs often require higher education. They pay well. They are not closely supervised and they encourage workers to be creative in pleasant surroundings. Other distinguishing features of good and bad jobs are not apparent from the anecdote. Good jobs offer secure employment, opportunities for promotion, and other significant benefits. In a bad job, you can easily be fired, you receive few if any fringe benefits, and the prospects for promotion are few (Adams, Betcherman, and Bilson, 1995; Lowe, 2000). Bad jobs are often called "dead-end" jobs.

Most social scientists who discuss today's service revolution tend to have both good and bad jobs in mind. Yet most jobs fall between the two extremes sketched above. They have some mix of good and bad features. What can we say about the overall mix of jobs in Canada? Are there more good jobs than bad jobs? And what does the future hold? Are good jobs or bad jobs likely to become more plentiful? What are your job prospects? These are tough questions, not least because some conditions that influence the mix of good and bad jobs are unpredictable. Nonetheless, social research sheds some light on these issues (Beaudry and Green, 1998; Krahn and Lowe, 1998).

The Deskilling Thesis

Harry Braverman (1974) proposed one view of the future of work. He argued that owners (capitalists) organize work to maximize profits. One way to increase profits is to break complex tasks into simple routines. This increased division of labour in the workforce has three important consequences. First, employers can replace workers with machinery. Second, given the simplification of work, employers can replace skilled workers with less expensive, unskilled workers. Third, employers can control workers more directly since less worker discretion and skill is needed to complete each task. As a result, the future of work, as Braverman saw it, involves a **deskilling** trend.

We can best understand deskilling as the separation of conception from execution in work. For example, in the 1910s, Henry Ford introduced the assembly line. It enabled him to produce affordable cars for a mass market. Workers executed highly specialized, repetitive tasks requiring little skill at a pace set by their supervisors. Automotive designers and managers conceived of the end-product and the machinery necessary to build it. The workers merely executed the instructions of their superiors. The term **Fordism** is now often used to refer to mass-production, assembly-line work.

Around the same time, Frederick W. Taylor developed the principles of **scientific management**. After analyzing the movements of workers as they did their jobs, Taylor

Deskilling refers to the process by which work tasks are broken into simple routines requiring little training to perform. Deskilling is usually accompanied by the use of machinery to replace labour wherever possible and increase management control over workers.

Fordism is a method of industrial management based on assembly-line methods of producing inexpensive, uniform commodities in high volume.

Scientific management, developed in the 1910s by Frederick W. Taylor, is a system for improving productivity. After analyzing the movements of workers as they did their jobs, Taylor trained them to eliminate unnecessary actions. This technique is also known as Taylorism.

Charlie Chaplin's 1929 movie *Modern Times* was a humorous critique of the factory of his day. In the movie, Chaplin gets a tic and moves like a machine on the assembly line. He then gets stuck on a conveyor belt and run through a machine. Finally, he is used as a test dummy for a feeding machine. The film thus suggests that workers were being used for the benefit of the machines rather than the machines being used for the benefit of the workers.

trained them to eliminate unnecessary actions and greatly improve their efficiency. Workers became cogs in a giant machine known as the modern factory.

Sociologists lodged several criticisms against Braverman's deskilling thesis, perhaps the most serious of which was that he was not so much wrong as irrelevant. That is, even if his characterization of factory work was accurate, factory workers represent only a small proportion of the labour force—and a smaller proportion every year, as the manufacturing sector shrinks and the service sector expands. According to some of Braverman's critics, the vital question is not whether jobs are becoming worse in manufacturing but whether good jobs or bad jobs are growing in services, the sector that accounts for about three-quarters of Canadian jobs today. Put another way, does the deskilling thesis apply to both industrial labour and service work?

Shoshana Zuboff's analysis of office workers, mentioned at the beginning of this chapter, suggested that Braverman's insights apply beyond the factory walls (Zuboff, 1988; see Lowe, 1987, on the evolution of office work in Canada). Zuboff argues that the computerization of the office in the 1980s involved increased supervision of deskilled work. And she is right, at least in part. The computer did eliminate many jobs and routinize others. It allowed supervisors to monitor every keystroke, thus taking worker control to a new level. Today, employees who consistently fall behind a prescribed work pace or use their computers for personal purposes can easily be identified and then retrained, disciplined, or fired.

Part-Time Work

The growth of part-time work in Canada has added to concern about the erosion of meaningful, dignified employment. The proportion of part-time workers in the Canadian labour force more than doubled between 1976 and 2000. In 2010, 19.4 percent of people in the Canadian labour force were part-timers, working fewer than 30 hours a week. Among men, the figure was 12.1 percent, among women, 27.3 percent (Statistics Canada, 2011c).

For two reasons, the expansion of part-time work is not a serious problem in itself. First, some part-time jobs are good jobs in the sense we defined above. Second, some people want to work part time and can afford to do so (Marshall, 2001). For example, some people who want a job also want to devote a large part of their time to family responsibilities. Part-time work affords them that flexibility. Similarly, many high school and university students who work part time are happy to do so.

Although the growth of part-time jobs is not problematic for voluntary part-time workers or people who have good part-time jobs, an increasingly large number of people depend on part-time work for the necessities of full-time living. And the plain fact is that most part-time jobs are bad jobs. Thus, part-time workers make up about two-thirds of the people working at or below minimum wage. Moreover, the fastest-growing category of part-time workers comprises *involuntary* part-timers. According to official statistics, one-third of part-time workers want to be working more hours. Moreover, official statistics underestimate the scope of the problem. Surveys show that about one-third of women officially classified as voluntary part-time workers would work more hours if good child care or elder care were available (Duffy, Glenday, and Pupo, 1997).

The downside of part-time work is not only economic, however. Nor is it just a matter of coping with dull routine. If you've ever had a bad part-time job, you know that one of its most difficult aspects involves maintaining your self-respect in the face of low pay, benefits, security, status, and creativity. In the words of Dennis, a McDonald's employee interviewed by one sociologist, "This isn't really a job. … It's about as low as you can get. Everybody knows it" (quoted in Leidner, 1993: 182).

And, Dennis might have added, nearly everybody lets you know he or she knows it. Ester Reiter (1991) studied fast-food workers in Toronto, many of whom are teenagers working part time. These workers are trained, Reiter noted, to keep smiling no matter how demanding or rude their customers may be. The trouble is you can only count backward from 100 so many times before feeling utterly humiliated. Anger often boils over.

The difficulty of maintaining your dignity as a fast-food worker is compounded by the high premium most young people place on independence, autonomy, and respect. The problem this creates for teenagers who take jobs in fast-food restaurants is that their constant deference to customers violates the norms of youth culture. Therefore, fast-food workers are typically stigmatized by their peers. They are frequently the brunt of insults and ridicule (Newman, 1999: 97).

Fast-food workers undoubtedly represent an extreme case of the indignity endured by part-timers. However, the problem exists in various guises in many part-time jobs. For instance, if you work as a "temp" in an office, you are more likely than are other office workers to be the victim of sexual harassment (Welsh, 1999). You are especially vulnerable to unwanted advances because you lack power in the office and are considered "fair game." Similar challenges to status legitimacy and personal integrity are found among "substitute teachers" (Clifton and Roberts, 1993). Thus, the form and depth of degradation may vary from one part-time job to another but, as your own work experience may show, degradation seems to be a universal feature of this type of deskilled work.

A Critique of the Deskilling Thesis

The deskilling thesis captures the trend toward the simplification of previously complex jobs, but it paints an incomplete picture insofar it focuses on the bottom of the occupational hierarchy. Taking a broader perspective and examining the entire occupational structure, we find that not all jobs are being deskilled. Deskilling seems to be occurring mainly in jobs that are characteristic of the "old" economy, such as assembly-line manufacturing, rather than the "new" economy, such as biotechnology and informatics. In fact, even on Ford's assembly line, not all jobs were deskilled. A new group of workers was required to design the assembly line and the new production machinery. New jobs higher up the skill hierarchy were therefore necessary.

In general, if deskilling has occurred for some jobs, has "reskilling" or "upskilling" of other jobs offset this trend? Evidence suggests that although much of the growing service sector is associated with the growth of "dead-end" jobs, more of it is associated with an enlargement of skilled employment. Table 13.1 uses national survey evidence from five countries to examine the skill levels of workers in the goods-producing and the service sectors. Skilled jobs were identified as those requiring high levels of conceptual autonomy and complexity. The results show that, in all countries, jobs in the service sector require higher levels of skill than do jobs in the goods-producing sector. They undermine the notion that the overall workforce is becoming deskilled because higher skill requirements are reported in the service economy, which is the fastest-growing sector.

Braverman and Zuboff underestimated the continuing importance of skilled labour in the economy. Assembly lines and computers may deskill many factory and office jobs, but if deskilling is to take place, then some members of the labour force must invent, design, advertise, market, install, repair, and maintain complex machines, including computerized and robotic systems. Most of these people have better jobs than the factory and office workers analyzed by Braverman and Zuboff. Moreover, although technological innovations kill off entire job categories, they also create entire new industries with many good jobs.

Economic Sector	Country					
	Canada	United States	Norway	Sweden	Finland
Goods-producing sector	26	25	31	23	25
Service sector	42	38	47	43	46
Difference between sectors	16	13	16	20	21

TABLE 13.1

Percentage of Employees in Skilled Jobs by Sector and Country

Source: Clement and Myles, 1994: 7.

The growing service sector includes routine jobs requiring little training and creative jobs requiring a higher education.

Lanny Ziering/Jupiter Images

LWA-JDC/CORBIS

The rapid growth of digital research and development communities in Silicon Valley, Waterloo, and Kanata (outside Ottawa) illustrates the trend.

Our analysis of good and bad jobs raises another question: How has the introduction of information technology affected workers' skills and income? Research suggests that computers magnify pay differences among skill levels. They augment high skill levels but replace low skill levels. People in high-skill occupations, like design or editing, earn higher wages if they use computers at work. In contrast, people who use, say, a computerized cash register require little new training. Their hourly wage is unaffected by the introduction of the new technology—but their work hours are often reduced. These findings suggest that the introduction of computers tends to enlarge the number and quality of good jobs and reduce the number of bad jobs. However, it does not improve the quality of bad jobs (Pabilonia and Zoghi, 2005a, 2005b).

In sum, the information technology revolution has transformed work, but little evidence suggests that it has degraded work overall. On the other hand, it is causing the income gap to grow between skilled workers who use information technology and those who do not, and between skilled and less skilled workers.

The Social Relations of Work

The rise of a more knowledge-intensive economy has had a big impact on the *social relations* of work. The Industrial Revolution began an era of work that required brute force and obedience to authority. With the spinning jenny, the assembly line, and the increasing use of machinery in production, more and more work became industrialized. Workers were closely supervised in factory settings, and an increasing division of labour meant that the skill content of certain jobs eroded.

It is misleading, however, to think that it takes less skill now to produce the goods and services we use than it did in previous centuries. We reach this conclusion if we focus on the skills associated with specific jobs or job tasks, but not if we focus on the skills associated with the entire process of providing goods and services. If anything, this process requires more skill because of the complexity of goods and services we now produce.

As Clement and Myles (1994) argue, the skill content of the entire labour process has risen, although much of that skill content now resides in managerial and administrative spheres. After the Industrial Revolution, a managerial revolution took place. It involved the separation of conception and execution. More of the job of conception shifted to the managerial and administrative realm. Before the mass-produced sweater, individual artisans determined the patterns and colours they would use. Now, workers in most textile sweatshops have no discretion over what they produce. Managers choose patterns and colours and they pass along orders to supervisors who direct shop floor production.

The rise of a managerial class that began with the advent of the manufacturing era has intensified in the postindustrial service revolution. Many service sector jobs are knowledge intensive, and "postindustrial services employ more skilled managers than firms in goods and distribution" (Clement and Myles, 1994: 80). As well, these managers tend less often to have surveillance and supervision roles, and more often to have real decision-making power. The net result is the rise of a new middle class with greater power to make decisions about what is to be done and how to do it.

The newer social relations of work are starkly illustrated in Silicon Valley. Some top executives there earn many millions of dollars annually. Even at less lofty levels, there are many thousands of high-paying, creative jobs in the Valley (Bjorhus, 2000). Amid all this wealth, however, the electronics assembly factories in Silicon Valley are little better than high-tech sweatshops. Most workers in the electronics factories earn less than 60 percent of the Valley's average wage, work long hours, are frequently exposed to toxic substances, and suffer industrial illnesses at three times the average rate for other manufacturing jobs. Although the opulent lifestyles of Silicon Valley's millionaires are often featured in the mass media, a more accurate picture of the Valley also incorporates those who execute the demands of the knowledge workers and executives. It is not just single jobs that are changing but the full spectrum of jobs that is being transformed.

Figure 13.4 illustrates the changing nature of the Canadian occupational structure. Based on projections by Human Resources Development Canada, the chart shows the areas of the economy, across a set of skill dimensions, that are expected to grow in the next decade. This pattern is consistent with the pattern of growing income inequality discussed in Chapter 8, Social Stratification. There, you will recall, we noted growing inequality between the top 40 percent of income earners and the remaining 60 percent.

FIGURE 13.4

Sample Occupations in Emerging Sectors

Source: Adapted from Human Resources Development Canada, 2000.

Emerging (Growth) Sector	University	College/Technical	High School or Less Than High School
Environment	Biophysicist, agrologist, forest management, environmental engineer	Air quality specialist, environmental technologist, pollution prevention officer, regulations officer	Landfill equipment operator, sylviculture and forestry worker, aquaculture and marine harvest labourer
Biotechnology	Biologist, biophysics, engineering, food science and technology, pharmacy, bioethics	Chemical technician, biological technician, water supply manager, inspector in public and environmental health	Information clerk; reporting, scheduling, and distribution occupations; labourer
Multimedia	Lawyer specializing in protecting intellectual property rights, translator, network architect, information librarian	Animation designer, Web designer, production designer, ideas manager, videographer	Product tester, librarian and information clerk
Aerospace	Aeronautics specialist, aerospace engineer, software engineering, astrophysicist, sales and marketing specialist	Mechanic, aircraft inspector, machinist, tool and die maker, industrial design technologist	Assembler, machining, aircraft electronic assembler

Labour Market Segmentation

The processes described above are taking place in the last of the three stages of labour market development identified by David Gordon and his colleagues (Gordon, Edwards, and Reich, 1982). The period from about 1820 to 1890 was one of *initial proletarianization* in North America. During this period, a large industrial working class replaced craft workers in small workshops. Then, from the end of the nineteenth century until the start of World War II, the labour market entered the phase of *labour homogenization*. Extensive mechanization and deskilling took place during this stage. Finally, the third phase of labour market development is that of **labour market segmentation**. During this stage, which began after World War II and continues to the present, large business organizations emerged. Thousands of small businesses continue to exist at this stage. However, different kinds of jobs are associated with small businesses than with large business organizations. Good jobs with security and relatively high wages tend to be concentrated in large firms, while smaller businesses cannot afford the same wages and job security provisions. The result is a *segmented* labour market. In these two different settings, workers, and the work they do, have different characteristics:

- The **primary labour market** is made up disproportionately of highly skilled, well-educated workers. They are employed in large corporations that enjoy high levels of capital investment. In the primary labour market, employment is relatively secure, earnings are high, fringe benefits are generous, and opportunities for advancement within the firm are good. Often the work is unionized because workers have the collective ability to exert pressure on their large employer.

- The **secondary labour market** contains a disproportionately large number of women and members of ethnic minority groups, especially recent immigrants. Employees in the secondary labour market tend to be unskilled and lack higher education. They work in small firms with low levels of capital investment. Employment is insecure, earnings are low, fringe benefits are meagre, and mobility prospects are limited. These firms are often subcontracted by large corporations that minimize their risk by off-loading seasonal work (for example, in logging and oil exploration) and work for which demand is volatile (for example, in auto parts supply and house construction).

This characterization may seem to advance us only a little beyond our earlier distinction between good jobs and bad jobs. However, proponents of labour market segmentation theory offer fresh insights into two important issues. First, they argue that people find work in different ways in the two labour markets. Second, they point out that social barriers make it difficult for individuals to move from one labour market to the other. To appreciate these points, it is vital to note that workers do more than just work. They also seek to control their work and prevent outsiders from gaining access to it. Some workers are more successful in this regard than others. Understanding the social roots of their success or failure permits us to see why the primary and secondary labour markets remain distinct. Therefore, we now turn to a discussion of forms of worker control.

Worker Resistance and Management Response

One of the criticisms lodged against Braverman's analysis of factory work is that he inaccurately portrays workers as passive victims of management control. In reality, workers often resist the imposition of task specialization and mechanization by managers. They go on strike, change jobs, fail to show up for work, sabotage production lines, and so forth (Burawoy, 1979; Clawson, 1980; Dunk, 1991). In these ways, worker resistance caused management to modify its organizational plans.

In the 1930s, the **human relations school of management** emerged as a challenge to Frederick W. Taylor's scientific management approach. It advocated less authoritarian

Labour market segmentation is the division of the market for labour into distinct settings. In these settings, work is found in different ways and workers have different characteristics. There is only a slim chance of moving from one setting to another.

The **primary labour market** comprises mainly highly skilled, well-educated workers. They are employed in large corporations that enjoy high levels of capital investment. In the primary labour market, employment is secure, earnings are high, and fringe benefits are generous.

The **secondary labour market** contains a disproportionately large number of women and members of ethnic minorities, particularly recent immigrants. Employees in the secondary labour market tend to be unskilled and lack higher education. They work in small firms that have low levels of capital investment. Employment is insecure, earnings are low, and fringe benefits are meagre.

The **human relations school of management** emerged in the 1930s as a challenge to Taylor's scientific management approach. It advocated less authoritarian leadership on the shop floor, careful selection and training of personnel, and greater attention to human needs and employee job satisfaction.

leadership on the shop floor and encouraged careful selection and training of personnel and greater attention to human needs and employee job satisfaction.

In the following decades, owners and managers of big companies in all the rich industrialized countries realized they had to make still more concessions to labour if they wanted a loyal and productive workforce. These concessions included not just higher wages but also more decision-making authority about product quality, promotion policies, job design, product innovation, company investments, and so forth. The biggest concessions to labour were made in countries with the most powerful trade union movements, such as Sweden, which has a unionization rate of more than 70 percent. In these countries, unions are organized in nationwide umbrella organizations that negotiate directly with centralized business organizations and governments over wages and labour policy. At the other extreme is the United States, where less than 12 percent of the non-agricultural work force is in a union (Olsen, 2002: 134).

Canada is located between these two extremes, although closer to the American than the Swedish model. In Canada in 2008, 4.59 million employees were union members (30.4 percent of the non-agricultural workforce; see Human Resources and Social Development Canada, 2008). Here, there is no centralized, nationwide bargaining among unions, businesses, and governments. Two indicators of the relative inability of Canadian workers to wrest concessions from their employers are given in Figure 13.5 and Figure 13.6 on page 336. Canadians work more hours per week than people in many other rich industrialized countries do. They also have fewer paid vacation days per year. However, Canadian workers are better off than their American counterparts are on these two measures.

In the realm of industry-level decision making, too, Canadian workers lag behind workers in Western Europe and Japan. We can see this if we briefly consider the two main

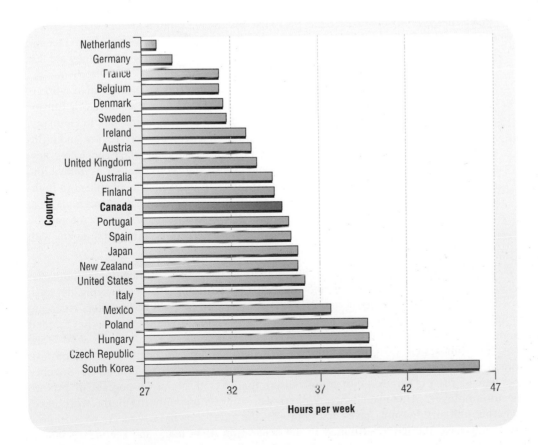

Hours per week

FIGURE 13.5
Average Hours Worked per Week, Selected Countries, 2006

Source: OECD, 2008.

FIGURE 13.6

Average Paid Vacation
Days per Year, Selected
Countries, 2004

Source: InfoPlease, 2005, "Average
Number of Vacation Days Around
the World per Year." Retrieved
November 21, 2005 (http://www
.infoplease.com/ipa/A0922052.html).
Reprinted with permission.

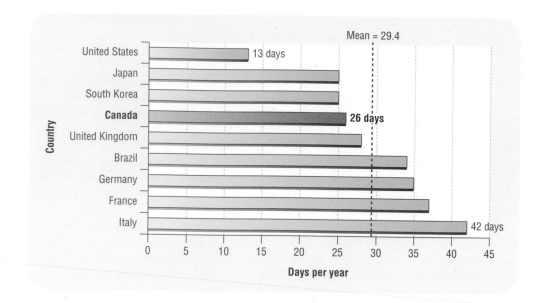

The **quality of work life**
movement originated in Sweden
and Japan. It involves small groups
of a dozen or so workers and managers collaborating to improve both
the quality of goods produced and
communication between workers
and managers.

Codetermination is a German
system of worker participation that
allows workers to help formulate
overall business strategy. German
workers' councils review and
influence management policies on
a wide range of issues, including
when and where new plants should
be built and how capital should
be invested in technological
innovation.

types of decision-making innovations that have been introduced in the factories of the rich industrialized countries since the early 1970s:

1. *Reforms that give workers more authority on the shop floor* include those advanced by the **quality of work life** movement. *Quality circles* originated in Sweden and Japan. They involve small groups of a dozen or so workers and managers collaborating to improve both the quality of goods produced and the communication between workers and managers. In some cases, this approach has evolved into a system that results in high productivity gains and worker satisfaction. Quality circles have been introduced in some Canadian industries, including automotive and aerospace. However, they are less widespread here than in Western Europe and Japan.

2. *Reforms that allow workers to help formulate overall business strategy* give workers more authority than do quality circles. For example, in much of Western Europe workers are consulted not just on the shop floor but also in the boardroom. In Germany, this system is known as **codetermination**. German workers' councils review and influ- ence management policies on a wide range of issues, including when and where new plants should be built and how capital should be invested in technological innovation. There are a few North American examples of this sort of worker involvement in high- level decision making, mostly in the auto industry. Worker participation programs were widely credited with improving the quality of North American cars and increasing the auto sector's productivity in the 1980s and 1990s, making it competitive again with Japanese carmakers.

Unions have clearly played a key role in increasing worker participation in industrial decision making since the 1920s and especially since the 1970s. To varying degrees, owners and managers of big corporations have conceded authority to workers to create a more stable, loyal, and productive workforce. In Canada, governments too have ceded some workplace authority to unionized workers. Public sector employees who work for government, Crown corporations, public schools, and the health care system are much more likely than their private sector counterparts are to be unionized. Seventy percent of the public sector is unionized compared with about 20 percent of private sector employees. Understandably, workers who enjoy more authority in the workplace, whether unionized or not, have tried to protect the gains they have won. As we will now see, they have thereby contributed to the separation of primary and secondary labour markets.

Unions and Professional Organizations

Unions are organizations of workers that seek to defend and promote their members' interests. By bargaining with employers, unions have succeeded in winning improved working conditions, higher wages, and more worker participation in industrial decision making for their members. One indicator of the power of unions is that the hourly wage gap between unionized and nonunionized full-time workers is about $3, and the hourly wage gap between unionized and nonunionized part-time workers is about $7 (Alberta Federation of Labour, 2005).

In conjunction with employers, unions have also helped develop systems of labour recruitment, training, and promotion. These systems are sometimes called **internal labour markets** because they control pay rates, hiring, and promotions within corporations (Creese, 1999). At the same time, they reduce competition between a firm's workers and external labour supplies.

In an internal labour market, training programs that specify the credentials required for promotion govern advancement through the ranks. Seniority rules specify the length of time a person must serve in a given position before being allowed to move up. These rules also protect senior personnel from layoffs according to the principle of "last hired, first fired." Finally, in internal labour markets, recruitment of new workers is usually limited to entry-level positions. In this way, the intake of new workers is controlled. Senior personnel are assured of promotion and protection from outside competition. For this reason, internal labour markets are sometimes called "labour market shelters."

Labour market shelters operate not only among unionized factory workers but also among professionals, such as doctors, lawyers, and engineers. **Professionals** are people with specialized knowledge acquired through extensive higher education. They enjoy a high degree of work autonomy and usually regulate themselves and enforce standards through professional associations. The Canadian Medical Association is probably the best-known and one of the most powerful professional associations in the country. Professionals exercise authority over clients and subordinates. They operate according to a code of ethics that emphasizes the altruistic nature of their work. Finally, they specify the credentials needed to enter their professions and thus maintain a cap on the supply of new professionals. This practice reduces competition, ensures high demand for their services, and keeps their earnings high. In this way, the professions act as labour market shelters, much like unions. (For further discussion of professionalization, see Chapter 17, Education.)

Unions are organizations of workers that seek to defend and promote their members' interests.

Internal labour markets are social mechanisms for controlling pay rates, hiring, and promotions within corporations while reducing competition between a firm's workers and external labour supplies.

Professionals are people with specialized knowledge acquired through extensive higher education.

Barriers between the Primary and Secondary Labour Markets

We saw above that many workers in the secondary labour market do not enjoy the high pay, job security, and benefit packages shared by workers in the primary labour market, many of whom are members of unions and professional associations. We can now add that these workers find it difficult to exit the "job ghettos" of the secondary labour market, because three social barriers make the primary labour market difficult to penetrate:

1. *Often, there are few entry-level positions in the primary labour market.* One set of circumstances that contributes to the lack of entry-level positions in the primary labour market is corporate "downsizing" and plant shutdowns. These took place on a wide scale in Canada and the United States throughout the 1980s and early 1990s, as well as during the recession of 2007–9. The lack of entry-level positions is especially acute during periods of economic recession. Big economic forces, such as plant shutdowns and recessions, prevent upward mobility and often result in downward mobility.

2. *Workers often lack informal networks linking them to good job openings.* People frequently find out about job availability through informal networks of friends and acquaintances (Granovetter, 1995). These networks often consist of people with the

same ethnic and racial backgrounds. Recent immigrants, and especially refugees, who compose a disproportionately large share of workers in the secondary labour market and tend not to be white, are less likely than others are to find out about job openings in the primary labour market, where the labour force is disproportionately white. Even within ethnic groups, the difference between getting good work and having none is sometimes a question of having the right connections.

3. *Workers usually lack the required training and certification for jobs in the primary labour market.* What is more, because of their low wages and scarce leisure time, they usually cannot afford to upgrade either their skills or their credentials. Impersonal economic forces, a lack of network ties, and insufficient education often cause people to get stuck, usually permanently, in the secondary labour market.

The Time Crunch and Its Effects

Although the quality of working life is higher in the primary labour market than in the secondary labour market, we must be careful not to exaggerate the differences. Overwork and lack of leisure have become central features of our culture, and this is true in both labour markets. We are experiencing a growing time crunch. All the adults in most Canadian households work full time in the paid labour force and many adolescents work part time. Some people work two jobs to make ends meet. Many managers, truck drivers, and professionals work 10 or more hours a day because of tight deadlines, demands for high productivity, and a trimmed-down workforce.

Over the past 50 years, the average number of hours that people spend working at their primary job has remained stable at between 35 and 40 per week. However, given the growth of part-time labour discussed earlier, the average work week has remained stable over the last half century only because a growing number of Canadians are working longer hours (Shields, 1999). In 1976, 31 percent of employed Canadian men and 10 percent of employed Canadian women worked more than 40 hours a week. In 2004, 35 percent of men and 16 percent of women worked more than 40 hours a week. Twenty-one percent of men and 8 percent of women worked more than 50 hours a week (Statistics Canada, 2005b). Add to this the heavy demands of family life, especially for women, and you can readily understand why stress, depression, aggression, and substance abuse are on the rise in both the secondary and the primary labour markets.

Stress is the feeling of being unable to cope with life's demands given one's resources. Work is the leading source of stress throughout the world. Connected to rising stress is the rate of severe depression. In some countries, including Canada, people born after 1955 are three times more likely to experience serious depression than their grandparents were (Weissman, 1992). According to a World Health Organization study, severe depression is the second leading contributor to "disease burden" (years lived with a disability) in the rich postindustrial countries. It is predicted to rise to the number-one position by 2020 (Vernarec, 2000).

There are three main reasons that leisure is on the decline and the pace of work is becoming more frantic for many people in the paid labour force (Schor, 1992). First, effective corporate advertising is pushing Canadians to consume goods and services at higher and higher levels all the time. To satisfy these advertising-induced "needs," people must work longer. Second, most corporate executives apparently think it is more profitable to push employees to work more hours than to hire new employees and pay expensive benefits for them. Third, most Canadian workers in the private sector are not in a position to demand reduced working

Bedtime at Yahoo! Inc. In high-tech industries, working on very little sleep is common. Here, David Filo, co-founder of Yahoo!, takes a nap under his desk.

Meri Simon. From "Getting a Life Offline," Jeff Bliss. *Financial Post.* June 29, 2000. C3. © San Jose Mercury News.

hours and more vacation time because few of them are unionized. They lack clout and suffer the consequences in terms of stress, depression, and other work-related ailments.

Summing Up

- The drive for profits has led to the deskilling of many jobs and the spread of part-time employment, but work has not degraded overall because more than three-quarters of employment is in the service sector, there are more good jobs than bad jobs.
- The income gap is growing between skilled workers who use information technology and those who do not, between skilled and less skilled workers, and between the primary and secondary labour markets.
- Workers seek to control work and establish internal labour markets through unions and professional organizations, but their success varies, depending on how powerful they are.

THE PROBLEM OF MARKETS

One conclusion we can draw from the preceding discussion is that the secondary labour market is a relatively **free market**. That is, the supply and demand for labour regulate wage levels and other benefits. If supply is high and demand is low, wages fall. If demand is high and supply is low, wages rise. Workers in the secondary labour market lack much power to interfere in the operation of the forces of supply and demand.

In contrast, the primary labour market is a more **regulated market**. Wage levels and other benefits are not established by the forces of supply and demand alone; workers and professionals are in a position to influence the operation of the primary labour market to their advantage.

Our analysis suggests that the freer the market, the higher the resulting level of social inequality. In the freest markets, many of the least powerful people are unable to earn enough to subsist, while a few of the most powerful people can amass huge fortunes. Because of this propensity to growing inequality, the secondary labour market cannot be entirely free. Canadian governments have had to establish a legal minimum wage to prevent the price of unskilled labour from dropping below the point at which people are literally unable to make a living (see Box 13.1 on page 340).

The question of whether free or regulated markets are better for society lies at the centre of much debate in economics and politics, but the dichotomy is too simplistic. First, no markets are completely unregulated. Regulation is always a matter of degree, as the varied structure of markets across cultures and historical periods demonstrates (Lie 1992). Second, the degree and type of market regulation depends on how power, norms, and values are distributed among various social groups. Consequently, the costs and benefits of regulation may be socially distributed in many different ways.

The "neoclassical" school of contemporary economics challenges this understanding of the social dimension of markets (Becker, 1976; Mankiw, 1998). Instead of focusing on how power, norms, and values shape markets, neoclassical economists argue that free markets maximize economic growth. We can use the minimum wage to illustrate their point. According to neoclassical economists, if the minimum wage is eliminated entirely, everyone will be better off. For example, in a situation where labour is in low demand and high supply, wages will fall, increasing profits. Higher profits will in turn allow employers to invest more in expanding their businesses. The new investment will

In a **free market**, prices are determined only by supply and demand.

In a **regulated market**, various social forces limit the capacity of supply and demand to determine prices.

BOX 13.1

Social Policy: What Do You Think?

SHOULD WE ABOLISH THE MINIMUM WAGE?

"Flipping burgers at Mickey D's is no way to make a living," a young man once told John Lie. Having tried his hand at several minimum-wage jobs as a teenager, John knew the young man was right.

In Canada, the provinces and territories set the minimum wage. In 2011 it ranged from $8.75 in British Columbia to $10.25 in Ontario, with most provinces and territories around the $9 range. At about $9 an hour, a minimum-wage job may be fine for teenagers, many of whom are supported by their parents. However, it is difficult to live on your own, much less to support a family, on a minimum-wage job, even if you work full time. This is the problem with the minimum wage: It does not amount to a living wage for many people.

In the 2000s, about half of the Canadians who received minimum wage for their work were adults over the age of 20. Women were overrepresented in this category, and many of them were single mothers. Use $9 per hour as the base and calculate the annual income of someone working 52 weeks per year at 40 hours per week. The result: $18 720. This falls below the low-income cutoff for single people living in communities with 30 000 or more people. Welcome to the world of the "working poor." Could you live on $18 720 a year, especially if you had to support a child?

Given the thousands of Canadians who cannot lift themselves and their children out of poverty even if they work full time, many scholars and policymakers suggest raising the minimum wage (Goldberg and Green, 1999). Others disagree (Law, 1999). They fear that raising the minimum wage would decrease the number of available jobs. Others disagree in principle with government interference in the economy. Some scholars and policymakers even advocate the abolition of the minimum wage.

What do you think? Should the minimum wage be raised? Should someone working full time be entitled to live above the low-income cutoff? Or should businesses be entitled to hire workers at whatever price the market will bear?

create new jobs, and rising demand for labour will drive wages up. Social inequality may increase but eventually *everyone* will be better off thanks to the operation of the free market.

One real-world difficulty with neoclassical theory is that resistance to the operation of free markets increases as you move down the social hierarchy. People at the low end of the social hierarchy usually fight falling wages. A social environment full of strikes, riots, and industrial sabotage is unfavourable to high productivity and new capital investment. That is why the economic system of a society at a given time is a more or less stable set of compromises between advocates and opponents of free markets. Markets are only as free as people are prepared to tolerate, and their degree of tolerance varies historically and among cultures (Berger and Dore, 1996; Doremus, Keller, Pauly, and Reich, 1998).

In the rest of this chapter, we offer several illustrations of how sociologists analyze markets. First, we compare capitalism, communism, and democratic socialism, the main types of economic system in the world today. Second, we examine the ability of big corporations to shape Canadian markets. Finally, we extend our analysis of corporate and free market growth to the global level. We identify advocates and opponents of these developments and sketch the main work-related decisions that face us in the twenty-first century.

ACCOUNT OF THE

SALE of a WIFE, by J. NASH,

IN THOMAS-STREET MARKET,

On the 29th of May, 1823.

This day another of those disgraceful scenes which of late have so frequently annoyed the public markets in this country took place in St. Thomas's Market, in this city; a man (if he deserves the name) of the name of John Nash, a drover, residing in Rosemary-street, appeared there leading his wife in a halter, followed by a great concourse of spectators; when arrived opposite the Bell-yard, he publicly announced his intention of disposing of his better half by Public Auction, and stated that the biddings were then open; it was a long while before any one ventured to speak, at length a young man who thought it a pity to let her remain in the hands of her present owner, generously bid 6d.! In vain did the anxious seller look around for another bidding, no one could be found to advance one penny, and after extolling her qualities, and warranting her sound, and free from vice, he was obliged, rather than keep her, to let her go at that price. The lady appeared quite satisfied, but not so the purchaser, he soon repented of his bargain, and again offered her to sale, when being bid nine-pence, he readily accepted it, and handed the lady to her new purchaser, who, not liking the transfer, made off with her mother, but was soon taken by her purchaser, and claimed as his property, to this she would not consent but by order of a magistrate, who dismissed the case. Nash, the husband, was obliged to make a precipitate retreat from the enraged populace.

Copy of Verses written on the Occasion :

COME all you kind husbands who have scolding
wives,
Who thro' living together are tired of your lives,
If you cannot persuade her nor good natur'd make her
Place a rope round her neck & to market pray take her

Should any one bid, when she's offer'd for sale,
Let her go for a trifle lest she should get stale,
If six-pence be offer'd, & that's all can be had,
Let her go for the same rather than keep a lot bad.

Come all jolly neighbours, come dance sing & play,
Away to the wedding where we intend to drink tea ;
All the world assembles, the young and the old,
For to see this fair beauty, as we have been told.

Here's success to this couple to keep up the fun,
May bumpers go round at the birth of a son ;
Long life to them both, and in peace & content
May their days and their nights for ever be spent.

Shepherd, Printer, No. 6, on the Broad Weir, Bristol.

Capitalism, Communism, and Democratic Socialism

Capitalism

The world's dominant economic system today is **capitalism**. Capitalist economies have two distinctive features.

1. *Private ownership of property.* In capitalist economies, individuals and corporations own almost all the means of producing goods and services. Individuals and corporations are therefore free to buy and sell just about anything. Like individuals, **corporations** are legal entities. They can enter contracts and own property. However, corporations are taxed at a lower rate than individuals are. Moreover, the corporation's owners typically

Capitalism is the dominant economic system in the world. Private ownership of property and competition in the pursuit of profit characterize capitalist economies.

Corporations are legal entities that can enter into contracts and own property. They are taxed at a lower rate than individuals are and their owners are normally not liable for the corporation's debt or any harm it may cause the public.

are not liable if the corporation harms consumers or goes bankrupt. Instead, the corporation is legally responsible for damage and debt.

2. *Competition in the pursuit of profit.* The second hallmark of capitalism is that producers compete to offer consumers desired goods and services at the lowest possible price. In a purely capitalist economy the government does not interfere in the operation of the economy. Presumably, everyone benefits; the most efficient producers make profits while consumers can buy at low prices.

In reality no economy is perfectly free. The state had to intervene heavily to create markets in the first place. For example, 500 years ago the idea that land was a commodity that could be bought, sold, and rented on the free market was utterly foreign to Aboriginal North Americans. To turn the land into a marketable commodity, European armies had to force Aboriginal North Americans off the land and eventually onto reserves. Governments had to pass laws regulating the ownership, sale, and rent of land. Without the military and legal intervention of government, no market for land would exist.

Today, governments must also intervene in the economy to keep the market working effectively. For instance, governments create and maintain roads and ports to make commerce possible. They pass laws governing the minimum wage, occupational health and safety, child labour, and industrial pollution to protect workers and consumers from the excesses of corporations. If very large corporations get into financial trouble, they can expect the government to bail them out, rationalizing the policy by claiming that their bankruptcy would be devastating to the economy. This happened most recently during the recession of 2007–9, when the government gave GM Canada and Chrysler Canada low-interest loans to prevent their bankruptcy. The government also plays an influential role in supporting some leading companies, such as Bombardier Inc. in Montreal, manufacturer of aerospace and rail equipment.

Which capitalist economies are the most free and which are the least free? The International Institute for Management Development (IMD International) in Switzerland publishes a widely respected annual index of competitiveness. The index is based on the amount of state ownership of industry and other indicators of market freedom. Figure 13.7 gives the scores for the 10 most and 10 least competitive countries in 2010. The most competitive countries are

FIGURE 13.7

The World Competitiveness Scoreboard, 2010

Source: IMD International, 2010, "The World Competitiveness Yearbook 2010." Retrieved March 1, 2011 (http://www.imd.org/research/publications/wcy/upload/PressRelease.pdf).

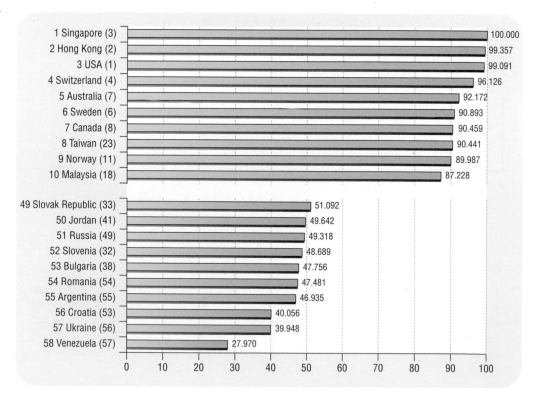

Singapore (scoring 100), Hong Kong (99.36) and the United States (99.09). Venezuela ranks fifty-eighth, with a score of 27.97. Canada ranks seventh, with a score of 90.46.

Communism

Communism is the name Karl Marx gave to the classless society that, he said, is bound to develop out of capitalism. Socialism is the name usually given to the transitional phase between capitalism and communism. No country in the world is or ever has been communist in the pure sense of the term. About two dozen countries in Asia, South America, and Africa consider themselves socialist. These include China, North Korea, Vietnam, and Cuba. As an ideal, however, communism is an economic system with two distinct features:

1. *Public ownership of property.* Under communism, the state owns almost all the means of producing goods and services. Private corporations do not exist. Individuals are not free to buy and sell goods and services. The stated aim of public ownership is to ensure that all individuals have equal wealth and equal access to goods and services.
2. *Government planning.* Five-year state plans establish production quotas, prices, and most other aspects of economic activity. The political officials who design the state plans, not the forces of supply and demand, determine what is produced, in what quantities, and at what prices. A high level of control is required to implement these rigid state plans. As a result, democratic politics is not allowed to interfere with state activities. Only one political party exists—the Communist party. Elections are held regularly, but only members of the Communist party are allowed to run for office (Zaslavsky and Brym, 1978).

Until recently, the countries of central and eastern Europe and central Asia were single-party, socialist societies. The most powerful of these countries was the Soviet Union, which was composed of Russia and 14 other socialist republics. In perhaps the most surprising and sudden change in modern history, the countries of the region began introducing capitalism and holding multiparty elections in the late 1980s and early 1990s.

The collapse of socialism in central and eastern Europe and central Asia is attributable to several factors. For one thing, the citizens of the region enjoyed few civil rights. For another, their standard of living was only about half as high as that of people in the rich industrialized countries of the West. The gap between East and West grew as the arms race between the Soviet Union and the United States intensified in the 1980s. The standard of living fell as the Soviet Union mobilized its economic resources to try to match the quantity and quality of military goods produced by the United States. Dissatisfaction was widespread and expressed itself in many ways, including strikes and political demonstrations. It grew as television and radio signals beamed from the West made the gap between socialism and capitalism more apparent to the citizenry. Eventually, the Communist parties of the region felt they could no longer govern effectively and so began to introduce reforms.

Democratic Socialism

Several prosperous and highly industrialized countries in northwestern Europe, such as Sweden, Denmark, and Norway, are democratic socialist societies. So are France and Germany, albeit to a lesser degree. Such societies have two distinctive features (Olsen, 2002):

1. *Public ownership of certain basic industries.* In democratic socialist countries, the government owns certain basic industries entirely or in part. Still, as a proportion of the entire economy, the level of public ownership is not high—far lower than the level of public ownership in socialist societies. The great bulk of property is privately owned, and competition in the pursuit of profit is the main motive for business activity, just as in capitalist societies.
2. *Substantial government intervention in the market.* Democratic socialist countries enjoy regular, free, multiparty elections. However, unlike in Canada, political parties backed by a strong trade union movement have formed governments in democratic socialist countries for much of the post–World War II period. The governments that these unions back intervene strongly in the operation of markets for the benefit of ordinary workers. Taxes are considerably higher than they are in capitalist countries. Consequently, social services are more generous, and workers earn more, work fewer hours, and enjoy more

Communism is a social and an economic system in which property is owned by public bodies; government planning, not the market, determines production and distribution.

paid vacation days. Since the 1980s, the democratic socialist countries have moved in a somewhat more capitalist direction. In particular, they have privatized some previously government-owned industries and services. Still, these countries retain their distinct approach to governments and markets, which is why democratic socialism is sometimes called a "third way" between capitalism and socialism.

The Corporation

Oligopolies are giant corporations that control part of an economy. They are few in number and tend not to compete against one another. Instead, they can set prices at levels that are most profitable for them.

In an **oligopoly**, a small number of giant corporations control part of an economy. When just a few corporations dominate an economic sector, they can influence prices, thus forcing consumers to pay more for goods and services. They can also exercise excessive influence on governments to deregulate their operations or help them in other ways (see Box 13.2). However, in Canada and other Western countries, so-called antitrust laws limit their growth. In 1889, Canada first introduced legislation restricting businesses from combining or colluding to control markets. Replaced in 1923 by the Combines Investigation Act, the law allows government to review corporate mergers and acquisitions.

BOX 13.2

Sociology at the Movies

INSIDE JOB

Inside Job, the 2010 Oscar winner for best documentary, stars the titans of the American financial industry and the government officials who should have been in charge of regulating them. It shows in detail how they colluded to operate a financial scheme that shook the U.S. and worldwide financial markets. The scheme lured millions of ordinary Americans into home ownership at apparently little cost, but when it collapsed, it cost the world $30 trillion, threw 30 million people out of work, and doubled the U.S. national debt.

Beginning in the 1980s, Republican and Democratic presidents appointed men who held senior jobs in the financial sector, or who were sympathetic to its interests, to key economic policy positions. These

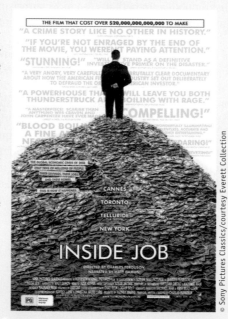

THE FILM THAT COST OVER $20,000,000,000,000 TO MAKE
"A CRIME STORY LIKE NO OTHER IN HISTORY."
"IF YOU'RE NOT ENRAGED BY THE END OF THE MOVIE, YOU WEREN'T PAYING ATTENTION."
"STUNNING!"
"A VERY ANGRY, VERY CAREFULLY... BRUTALLY CLEAR DOCUMENTARY ABOUT HOW THE AMERICAN FINANCIAL INDUSTRY SET OUT DELIBERATELY TO DEFRAUD THE ORDINARY AMERICAN INVESTOR."
"A POWERHOUSE THAT WILL LEAVE YOU BOTH THUNDERSTRUCK AND BOILING WITH RAGE."
"COMPELLING!"
"BLOOD BOILING... A FINE..."
"DARING!"
CANNES
TORONTO
TELLURIDE
NEW YORK
INSIDE JOB
DIRECTED BY CHARLES FERGUSON · NARRATED BY MATT DAMON

© Sony Pictures Classics/courtesy Everett Collection

men engineered the deregulation of the financial sector, which involved scrapping laws that prevented banks from making high-risk investments with depositors' money.

The financial sector profited handsomely from deregulation. For example, starting in the 1990s, when people bought mortgages from financial companies, the lenders would sell the mortgages to investment banks for a fee. These banks would then bundle thousands of mortgages with thousands of commercial loans, car loans, student loans, credit card debt, and so on. These packages were known as "collateralized debt obligations," or CDOs. Investment banks paid rating agencies a fee to evaluate the CDOs. Because they were not liable for inaccurate ratings, the agencies gave many of the CDOs the highest possible rating, which is what the investment banks wanted so the CDOs would be attractive to big investors. Big investors then bought the CDOs and received loan payments directly from borrowers (see Figure 13.8).

For a while, the system worked like a charm. The more loans that were made, the more cheap money borrowers received; the bigger the fees

However, the law has been only partly effective in stabilizing the growth of oligopolies. You need look no further than your local gas station to find an example that continues to suggest price competition is not as vigorous as the idea of "antitrust" implies. Canadian banking provides another illustration of corporate concentration. There are just 11 domestic banks. Several of them are so small you have likely never heard of them. The top four banks, as ranked by the value of their assets, control about 85 percent of all banking assets in the country. Such concentration is a world apart from the early nineteenth century, when most businesses, including banks, were family owned and served only local markets (National Council of Welfare, 1998b; Whittington, 1999).

An important effect of Canadian competition law is to encourage big companies to diversify. That is, rather than increasing their share of control in their own industry, corporations often move into new industries, the better to avoid antitrust laws. Big companies that operate in several industries at the same time are called **conglomerates**. Bell Canada Enterprises (BCE), which has telephone, television, newspaper, Internet, and other interests, is one example of the rapidly expanding conglomerates operating the world over. Big companies are swallowed up by still bigger ones in wave after wave of corporate mergers (Mizruchi, 1982, 1992).

Conglomerates are large corporations that operate in several industries at the same time.

FIGURE 13.8

How CDOs Work

1. Borrower takes out a mortgage. →
2. Lender (financial institution) sells mortgage to investment bank for a fee. →
3. Investment bank creates a package of many mortgages and other loans (called a "collateralized debt obligation," or CDO), pays rating agency to give the CDO a high rating, and sells the package to a big investor for a fee. →
4. Big investor buys CDO and receives loan payments from borrowers.

5. Borrowers make payments to investors—or not, in which case the system collapses.

received by lenders, investment banks, and rating agencies; and the greater the flow of loan payments to big investors. Everyone benefited—until the borrowers couldn't keep up with their loan payments. Then, the system fell apart. To sell more mortgages and other loans, many lenders required little or no collateral and had offered low "teaser rates" for a year or two to borrowers who lacked much income.

When the teaser rates expired, interest rates jumped to unaffordable levels. Soon, millions of American lost their homes, the home construction industry came to a virtual standstill, and the ripple effects ushered in the worst economic crisis since the Great Depression (1929–39). Because many of the big CDO investors were foreign pension funds, municipalities, and banks, the crisis spread worldwide.

Senior U.S. politicians in both parties and senior executives in the financial sector were responsible for deregulation, but were the financial titans *criminally* responsible for the economic crisis? Congressional hearings excerpted in *Inside Job* disclosed that investment bankers knew full well that the CDOs they were selling were, in the redolent phrases of two Goldman Sachs executives, a "shitty deal" and "a piece of crap." In fact, knowing that the CDOs were worthless and would eventually fail, major financial institutions bought many billions of dollars of special insurance against their failure. In other words, they were misleading big investors to buy CDOs that they knew were junk, raking in big fees for the service, and then buying insurance to make even more money when the CDOs failed. Some big investors are now suing American financial institutions for fraud.

None of the major players responsible for the financial crisis has gone to jail. Some have paid fines without admitting guilt. More accurately, their companies paid the fines using taxpayer money— cash received when the federal government bailed them out of the financial crisis.

Interlocking directorates are formed when an individual sits on the board of directors of two or more non-competing companies.

Outright ownership of a company by a second company in another industry is only one way corporations may be linked. **Interlocking directorates** are another. Interlocking directorates are formed when an individual sits on the board of directors of two or more non-competing companies. (Antitrust laws prevent an individual from sitting on the board of directors of a competitor.) For instance, the board of directors of BCE includes, among others, the president of Petro-Canada, the chair of the Royal Bank, and a former president of Canadian National Railway and Bombardier. Such interlocks enable corporations to exchange valuable information and form alliances for mutual benefit. They also create useful channels of communication to, and influence over, government since some board members of major corporations are likely to be former senior politicians (Carroll, 1986; Marchak, 1991).

Of course, small businesses continue to exist. In Canada, 78 percent of all businesses have fewer than five employees, and 97 percent have fewer than 50 employees (see Table 13.2). Small firms, which are a critical feature of the Canadian economy, are particularly important in the service sector. However, compared with large firms, profits in small firms are typically low, and bankruptcies are common. Small firms often use outdated production and marketing techniques. Jobs in small firms frequently have low wages and meagre benefits.

A sizable portion of the Canadian labour force works in large corporations. Specifically, about 4 in 10 workers are employed in firms with more than 500 employees, even though the percentage of such firms is very small (0.2 percent). Among Canada's largest private sector employers is the Loblaw food chain, owned by George Weston Ltd., with more than 138 000 employees. Onex Corporation, a conglomerate, employs more than 90 000 Canadians in diverse firms that include interests in health care, hotels, gas stations, and insurance.

Globalization

As noted earlier, since the early 1980s, Canada has been hit by wave after wave of corporate "downsizing." Especially in the older manufacturing industries, thousands of blue-collar workers and middle managers have been fired. Periodically, unemployment has soared and social problems, such as alcoholism and domestic violence, have become acute. Some people blame government for the plant shutdowns. They say taxes were so high, big corporations could no longer make decent profits. Others blame the unemployed themselves. They say powerful unions drove up the hourly wage to the point where companies lost money.

Beginning in the 1980s, workers, governments, and corporations got involved as unequal players in the globalization of the world economy. Japan and Germany had fully recovered from the devastation of World War II. With these large and robust industrial economies now firing on all cylinders, American and Canadian-based multinationals were forced to cut costs and become more efficient to remain competitive. On a scale far larger than ever before, they began to build branch plants in low-wage countries, such as Mexico

TABLE 13.2

Percentage of Employees and Percentage of Firms by Size of Firm, 2003

Source: Adapted from Sri Kanagarajah, 2006, *Business Dynamics in Canada*, 2003. Ottawa: Ministry of Industry, Statistics Canada. Catalogue No. 61-534-XIE. Retrieved February 5, 2011 (http://www.statcan.gc.ca/pub/61-534-x/61-534-x2006001-eng.pdf).

Size of Firm	Percentage of All Employees	Percentage of All Firms
0–19 Employees	21.45	92.0
20–99 Employees	19.68	6.6
100–499 Employees	15.68	1.1
500+ Employees	43.19	0.2
Total	100.00	100.0

and China, to take advantage of cheap labour and low taxes. Multinational corporations based in Japan and other highly industrialized countries followed suit.

Although multinational corporations could easily move investment capital from one country to the next, workers were rooted in their communities and governments were rooted in their nation-states. Multinationals thus had a big advantage over the other players in the globalization game. They could threaten to move plants unless governments and workers made concessions. They could play one government off against another in the bidding war for new plants. And they could pick up and leave when it became clear that relocation would do wonders for their bottom line.

Today, more than three decades after the globalization game began in earnest, it is easier to identify the winners than the losers. The clear winners are the stockholders of multinational corporations whose profits have soared. The losers, at least initially, were blue-collar workers. To cite just one example, in the past two decades General Motors has cut its workforce in Canada and the United States by about one-half in the face of stiff competition from automotive giants in Japan and Germany in particular.

Even while these cuts were being made, however, some large manufacturers were hiring. For instance, employment at Bombardier grew dramatically, and this Canadian-owned rail and aerospace firm is now a world leader. In the service sector, employment soared, as we have seen.

Globalization in the Less Developed Countries

It is still too soon to tell whether the governments and citizens of the less developed countries will be losers or winners in the globalization game. On the one hand, it is hard to argue with the assessment of the rural Indonesian woman interviewed by Diane Wolf. She prefers the regime of the factory to the tedium of village life. In the village, the woman worked from dawn till dusk doing household chores, taking care of siblings, and feeding the family goat. In the factory, she earns less than $1 a day sewing pockets on men's shirts in a hot factory. Yet because work in the factory is less arduous, pays something, and holds out the hope of even better work for future generations, the woman views it as nothing less than liberating (Wolf, 1992). Many workers in other regions of the world where branch plants of multinationals have sprung up in recent decades feel much the same way. A wage of $3 an hour is excellent pay in Mexico, and workers rush to fill jobs along Mexico's northern border with the United States.

Yet the picture is not all bright. The governments of developing countries attract branch plants by imposing few if any pollution controls on their operations, with dangerous consequences for the environment. Typically, fewer jobs are available than the number of workers who are drawn from the countryside to find work in the branch plants. This results in the growth of urban slums that suffer from high unemployment and unsanitary conditions. High-value components are often imported. Therefore, the branch plants create few good jobs involving design and technical expertise. Finally, some branch plants—particularly clothing and shoe factories in Asia—exploit children and women, requiring them to work long workdays at paltry wages and in unsafe conditions.

Companies such as Nike and the Gap have been widely criticized for conditions in their overseas sweatshops. Nike is the market leader in sports footwear. It has been at the forefront of moving production jobs overseas to such places as Indonesia. There, Nike factory workers make about 10 cents an hour. That is why labour costs account for only about 4 percent of the price of a pair of Nike shoes. Workdays in the factories stretch as long as 16 hours. Substandard air quality and excessive exposure to toxic chemicals are normal. An international campaign aimed at curbing Nike's labour practices has had only a modest impact. For example, in 1999 wages in the Indonesian factories were raised about a penny an hour ("The Nike Campaign," 2000).

The Future of Work and the Economy

Although work and the economy have changed enormously over the years, one thing has remained constant for centuries. Businesses have always looked for ways to cut costs and boost profits. Two of the most effective means they have adopted for accomplishing these goals involve introducing new technologies and organizing the workplace in more efficient ways. Much is uncertain about the future of work and the economy. However, it is a pretty safe bet that businesses will continue to follow these established practices.

Just how these practices will be implemented is less predictable. For example, it is possible to use technology and improved work organization to increase productivity by complementing the abilities of skilled workers. Worldwide, the automotive, aerospace, and computer industries have tended to adopt this approach. They have introduced automation and robots on a wide scale. They constantly upgrade the skills of their workers. And they have proven the benefits of small autonomous work groups for product quality, worker satisfaction, and therefore the bottom line. Conversely, new technology and more efficient work organization can be used to replace workers, deskill jobs, and employ low-cost labour—mainly women and minority group members—on a large scale. Women are entering the labour force at a faster rate than men are. Competition from low-wage industries abroad remains intense. Therefore, the second option is especially tempting in some industries.

Our analysis suggests that each of the scenarios described above will tend to predominate in different industries and labour markets. The pressure of competition will continue to prompt innovation and restructuring. However, we have also suggested that workplace struggles have no small bearing on how technologies are implemented and work is organized. To a degree, therefore, the future of work and the economy is up for grabs.

AP Photo/Pat Roque

Some people in the rich, industrialized countries oppose the globalization of commerce. Shown here are demonstrators marching in the streets of Toronto in 2010 as part of a protest against the G20 economic summit.

Summing Up

- The degree to which markets are free or regulated depends on how power is distributed in them and the nature of the norms and values that govern them.
- The three main economic systems are capitalism, communism, and democratic socialism. Capitalism is the dominant economic system in the world.
- Corporations disproportionately influence the economy and politics through oligopolies, conglomerates, and interlocking directorates.
- Multinational corporations maximize shareholder profits by outsourcing work to low-wage, low-tax countries.

SUMMARY

1. **How and when has work been subject to revolutionary transformations?**
   The first work-related revolution began about 10 000 years ago when people established permanent settlements and started herding and farming. The second work-related revolution began about 230 years ago when various mechanical devices, such as the steam engine, greatly increased the ability of producers to supply markets. The third revolution in work is marked by growth in the provision of various services. It accelerated in the final decades of the twentieth century with the widespread use of the computer.

2. **How did the revolutions affect work?**
   Each revolution in work increased productivity and the division of labour, caused a sectoral shift in employment, and made work relations more hierarchical. However, for the past three decades the degree of hierarchy has been lowered in some industries, resulting in productivity gains and more worker satisfaction.

3. **What trends changed work in the twentieth century?**
   Deskilling and the growth of part-time jobs were two of the main trends in the workplace in the twentieth century. However, skilled labour has remained important in the economy.

4. **How has the growth in the number of good jobs and bad jobs influenced the structure of labour markets?**
   Good jobs have become more plentiful but the number of bad jobs is also growing rapidly. The result is a segmentation of the labour force into primary and secondary labour markets. Various social barriers limit mobility from the secondary to the primary labour market.

5. **How have workers responded to deskilling and efforts to increase control over jobs?**
   Workers have resisted attempts to deskill and control jobs. As a result, business has had to make concessions by giving workers more authority on the shop floor and in formulating overall business strategy. Such concessions have been biggest in countries where workers are more organized and powerful.

6. **What groups have fostered internal labour markets and why have they done so?**
   Unions and professional organizations have established internal labour markets to control pay rates, hiring, and promotions in organizations and reduce competition with external labour supplies.

7. **Can markets be classified as free versus regulated?**
   No. Markets are free or regulated to *varying degrees*. No market that is purely free or completely regulated could function for long. A purely free market would create unbearable inequalities and a completely regulated market would stagnate.

8. **What kinds of institutions dominate today's economy?**
   Corporations are the dominant economic players in the world today. They exercise disproportionate economic and political influence by forming oligopolies, conglomerates, and interlocking directorates.

9. **What strategies have corporations followed and how have their strategies affected different groups?**
   Growing competition among multinational corporations has led big corporations to cut costs by building more branch plants in low-wage, low-tax countries. Stockholders have profited from this strategy. However, the benefits for workers in both the industrialized and the less developed countries have been mixed.

KEY TERMS

capitalism (p. 341)

codetermination (p. 336)

communism (p. 343)

conglomerates (p. 345)

corporations (p. 341)

deskilling (p. 329)

division of labour (p. 327)

economy (p. 326)

Fordism (p. 329)

free market (p. 339)

human relations school of
management (p. 334)

interlocking directorates (p. 346)

internal labour markets (p. 337)

labour market segmentation
(p. 334)

markets (p. 327)

oligopolies (p. 344)

primary labour market (p. 334)

productivity (p. 327)

professionals (p. 337)

quality of work life (p. 336)

regulated market (p. 339)

scientific management (p. 329)

secondary labour market (p. 334)

unions (p. 337)

WEB RESOURCES

Companion Website for This Book

http://www.compass4e.nelson.com

Begin by clicking on the Student Resources section of the website. Next, select the chapter you are studying from the pull-down menu. From the Student Resources page you have easy access to additional Weblinks and other resources. The website also has many useful tips to aid you in your study of sociology, including practice tests for each chapter.

InfoTrac® Search Terms

These search terms are provided to assist you in beginning to conduct research on this topic by visiting http://www.infotrac-college.com:

capitalism

deskilling

corporation

free market

communism

CHAPTER

14

Politics

IN THIS CHAPTER, YOU WILL LEARN THAT

- Political sociologists analyze the distribution of power in society and its consequences for political behaviour and public policy.

- Sociological disputes about the distribution of power often focus on how social structures, especially class structures, influence political life.

- Some political sociologists analyze how state institutions and laws affect political behaviour and public policy.

- Three waves of democratization have swept the world in the past 180 years.

- Societies become highly democratic only when their citizens win legal protections of their rights and freedoms. This typically occurs when their middle and working classes become large, organized, and prosperous.

- Enduring social inequalities limit democracy even in the richest countries.

- Sometimes people reject the rules that govern normal politics, resulting in war. As state structures have changed, so have patterns of warfare.

Airedale Brothers/Stone+/Getty Images

INTRODUCTION

Free Trade and Democracy

Just four days before what some people call the most important Canadian election of the twentieth century—the "free trade election" of 1988—the outcome seemed clear. A Gallup poll published on November 17 showed the Liberals with a commanding 43 percent of the popular vote. The Progressive Conservatives (PCs) trailed far behind at 31 percent. The New Democratic Party (NDP) stood at 22 percent.

However, just 100 hours before the first votes were cast, a little-known organization, the Canadian Alliance for Trade and Job Opportunities (CATJO), swung into high gear. With a campaign budget larger than that of the two opposition parties combined, CATJO funded a media blitz promoting the PCs and their free trade policies. A barrage of brochures, newspaper ads, and radio and television commercials supported the idea that Canadian prosperity depended on the removal of all taxes and impediments to trade between Canada and the United States. CATJO argued that if goods and services could be bought and sold across the border without hindrance, and capital invested without restraint, good jobs would proliferate and Canada's future would be assured.

Before the media blitz, an Angus Reid poll disclosed that most Canadians disagreed with CATJO's rosy assessment: 54 percent opposed free trade and 35 percent supported it. A majority of Canadians sensed that free trade might open Canada to harmful competition with giant American companies, leading to job losses and deteriorating living standards. Yet the CATJO onslaught succeeded in overcoming some of these fears. Its media campaign hammered the pro-free-trade message into the minds of the Canadian public and drew attention away from the opposition. Then, on election day, the unexpected happened. The PCs won with 43 percent of the popular vote. A mere six weeks later, on January 1, 1989, the Canada–U.S. Free Trade Agreement was implemented. In October 1992, as shown in the photo on this page, officials initialled the North American Free Trade Agreement, bringing Mexico into the free trade zone established in 1989 by Canada and the United States. The agreement went into effect January 1, 1994.

Who backed CATJO? Its sole sponsor was the Business Council on National Issues (BCNI), an organization comprising the chief executive officers of 150 of Canada's leading corporations. These were people with a clear stake in free trade. Their companies stood to benefit from increased business activity between Canada and the United States and unrestricted freedom to invest wherever profits promised to be higher (Richardson, 1996). The degree to which the Canadian people as a whole have benefited from free trade is a matter of ongoing debate.

The 1988 free trade election raises important political questions. Does the victory of the PCs illustrate the operation of government "of the people, by the people, for the people," as Abraham Lincoln defined democracy in his famous speech at Gettysburg in 1863? The election certainly allowed a diverse range of Canadians to express conflicting views. In the end, the people got the government they elected. This fact suggests that Lincoln's characterization of politics applied as well to Canada in 1988 as it did to the United States in 1863.

However, big business's access to a bulging war chest might lead us to doubt that Lincoln's definition applies. Few groups can act like CATJO and put together $18 million for a media campaign aimed at swaying the opinions of Canadians. Should we therefore conclude that (in the words of one wit) Canada is a case of government "of the people, by the lawyers, for the businessmen"?[1]

Mexican, American, and Canadian ministers initial NAFTA in October 1992.

George Bush Presidential Library

The free trade election of 1988 raises questions that lie at the heart of political sociology. What accounts for the degree to which a political system responds to the demands of all its citizens? As you will see, political sociologists have often answered this question by examining the effects of social structures, especially class structures, on politics. Although this approach contributes much to our understanding of political life, it is insufficient by itself. A fully adequate theory of democracy requires that we also examine how state institutions and laws affect political processes. We elaborate these points in the second section of this chapter.

From the mid-1970s until the early 1990s, a wave of competitive elections swept across many formerly non-democratic countries. Most dramatically, elections were held in the former Soviet Union at the end of this period. Western analysts were ecstatic. By the mid-1990s, however, it became clear that their optimism was naive. Often, the new regimes turned out to be feeble and limited democracies. As a result, political sociologists began to reconsider the social preconditions of democracy. We review of some of their work in this chapter's third section. We conclude that genuine democracy is not based just on elections. In addition, large classes of people must win legal protection of their rights and freedoms for democracy to take root and grow. This has not yet happened in most of the world. Finally, in this chapter's fourth section, we discuss some of the ways in which people step outside the rules of normal electoral politics to change society. We focus on two types of "politics by other means": war and terrorism.

Some analysts believe that politics in the rich industrialized countries is less likely to be shaped by class inequality in the future. Our reading of the evidence is different. In concluding this chapter, we argue that persistent class inequality is the major barrier to the progress of democracy in such countries as Canada.

Before developing these themes, we define some key terms.

What Is Politics? Key Terms

Politics is a machine that helps to determine "who gets what, when, and how" (Lasswell, 1936). Power fuels the machine. **Power** is the ability to control others, even against their will (Weber, 1947: 152). Having more power than others do gives you the ability to get more valued things sooner. Having less power than others do means you get fewer valued things later. Political sociology's chief task is figuring out how power drives different types of political machines.

The use of power sometimes involves force. For example, one way of operating a system for distributing jobs, money, education, and other valued things is by throwing people who do not agree with the system in jail. In this case, people obey political rules because they are afraid to disobey. More often, people agree with the distribution system or at least accept it grudgingly. For instance, most people pay their taxes without much pressure from the Canada Revenue Agency. They pay their parking tickets without serving jail time. They recognize the right of their rulers to control the political machine. When most people basically agree with how the political machine is run, raw power becomes **authority**. Authority is legitimate, institutionalized power. Power is *legitimate* when people regard its use as morally correct or justified. Power is *institutionalized* when the norms and statuses of social organizations govern its use. These norms and statuses define how authority should be used, how individuals can achieve authority, and how much authority is attached to each status in the organization (see Box 14.1 on page 354).

Max Weber (1947) described three ideal bases on which authority can rest (while stressing that real-world cases often rest on varying mixes of the pure types):

1. **Traditional authority**. Particularly in tribal and feudal societies, rulers inherit authority through family or clan ties. The right of a family or a clan to monopolize leadership is widely believed to derive from the will of a god.
2. **Legal-rational authority.** In modern societies, authority derives from respect for the law. Laws specify how a person can achieve office. People generally believe these laws are rational. If someone achieves office by following these laws, his or her authority is respected.

Power is the ability to impose one's will on others.

Authority is legitimate, institutionalized power.

Traditional authority, the norm in tribal and feudal societies, involves rulers inheriting authority through family or clan ties. The right of a family or clan to monopolize leadership is widely believed to derive from the will of a god.

Legal-rational authority is typical of modern societies. It derives from respect for the law. Laws specify how a person can achieve office. People generally believe these laws are rational. If someone achieves office by following these laws, people respect his or her authority.

Sociology at the Movies

GANGS OF NEW YORK

Most nation-states may be imposing structures, but there was a time when little was solid, when every nation-state lacked legitimacy in the eyes of many of its citizens, contending groups vied for dominance, violence was widely used to secure power, all was in the balance, and it was uncertain how things would turn out. Martin Scorsese's *Gangs of New York* recounts such a time: New York between the 1840s and the American Civil War.

"The forge of hell" is the way one character describes the city. Elections are rigged, city officials sell their services to the highest bidder, fire fighters loot the buildings they "save," rival police forces brawl in the streets, the poor riot against the draft, Union soldiers force immigrants straight off the boat into uniform, and an audience greets an actor playing Abraham Lincoln with volleys of rotten fruit. At the centre of it all are the mobs of Irish immigrants who battle second- and third-generation "nativists" for political control—the Irish, led by Priest Vallon (Liam Neeson), the nativists led by the vicious William Cutting, widely known as Bill the Butcher (played by Daniel Day-Lewis, who was nominated for a Best Actor Oscar for his performance). With a ferocity unrivalled in the history of cinema,

Miramax/Courtesy Everett Collection/CP Picture Archive

Amsterdam (Leonardo DiCaprio) leads his men to battle in *Gangs of New York*.

the gangs attack each other on the Lower East Side of Manhattan. When the dust settles, Priest Vallon's young son, Amsterdam (Leonardo DiCaprio), swears to avenge his father's death.

At the level of its individual characters, the film is motivated by Amsterdam's quest. But because Scorsese is blessed with a deep sociological understanding of his subject matter, the individual characters become vehicles for a larger story, the chaotic origins of the American state. In the 1860s, New York was practically destroyed when the poor refused to be drafted to fight in the Civil War. They rioted and looted wealthy neighbourhoods

until government ships in the harbour fired their cannons on them and troops marched in to silence them once and for all. The American state was, in fact, weak well into the 1870s, when it was still common for independent militias funded by wealthy local capitalists to counter labour unrest and riots by the poor (Isaacs, 2002).

In the final scene of *Gangs of New York*, an adult Amsterdam stands in a graveyard with his girlfriend, Jenny Everdeane (Cameron Diaz), remembering the victims of the Draft Riots. The scene fast forwards, and as it does, Amsterdam and Jenny disappear while the tombstones fade and vegetation grows over them. The camera pans up to focus on the familiar skyline of New York, solid and seemingly eternal. Thanks to *Gangs of New York*, however, we remember the frailty of all states and their conflict-ridden origins.

3. **Charismatic authority.** Sometimes, extraordinary, charismatic individuals challenge traditional or legal-rational authority. They claim to be inspired by a god or some higher principle that transcends other forms of authority. One such principle is the idea that all people are created equal. Charismatic figures sometimes emerge during a **political revolution**, an attempt by many people to overthrow existing political institutions and establish new ones. Political revolutions take place when widespread and successful movements of opposition clash with crumbling traditional or legal-rational authority.

Politics takes place in all social settings—intimate face-to-face relationships, families, universities, and so on. However, political sociology is concerned with institutions that specialize in the exercise of power and authority. Taken together, these institutions form the **state**. The state comprises institutions that formulate and carry out a country's laws and public policies. In performing these functions, the state regulates citizens in **civil society**. Civil society is "made up of areas of social life—the domestic world, the economic sphere, cultural activities and political interaction—which are organized by private or voluntary arrangements between individuals and groups outside the direct control of the state" (Held, 1987: 281; see Figure 14.1 on page 356).

In turn, citizens in civil society control the state to varying degrees. In an **authoritarian** state, citizen control is sharply restricted. In a **totalitarian** state, it is virtually nonexistent. In a **democracy**, citizens exert a relatively high degree of control over the state. They do this partly by choosing representatives in regular, competitive elections.

In modern democracies, citizens do not control the state directly. They do so through a variety of organizations. **Political parties** compete for control of government in regular

Charismatic authority is based on a belief in the claims of extraordinary individuals that they are inspired by a god or some higher principle.

A **political revolution** is the overthrow of political institutions by an opposition movement and its replacement by new institutions.

The **state** consists of the institutions responsible for formulating and carrying out a country's laws and public policies.

Civil society is the private sphere of social life.

The three faces of authority according to Weber: traditional authority (King Louis XIV of France, circa 1670), charismatic authority (Vladimir Lenin, Bolshevik leader of the Russian Revolution of 1917), and legal-rational authority (Stephen Harper in the 2008 Canadian federal election campaign).

Archive Iconografico, S.S./Corbis

SuperStock

THE CANADIAN PRESS/Tom Hanson

FIGURE 14.1

The Institutions of State and Civil Society

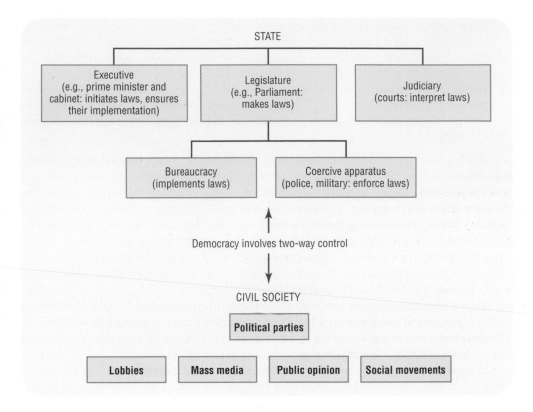

Authoritarian states sharply restrict citizen control of the state.

In a **totalitarian** state, citizens lack almost any control of the state.

In a **democracy**, citizens exercise a high degree of control over the state. They do this mainly by choosing representatives in regular, competitive elections.

Political parties are organizations that compete for control of government. In the process, they give voice to policy alternatives and rally adult citizens to vote.

Lobbies are organizations formed by special interest groups to advise and influence politicians.

The **mass media** are print, radio, television, and other communication technologies. In a democracy, the mass media help keep the public informed about the quality of government.

Public opinion refers to the values and attitudes of the adult population as a whole.

Social movements are collective attempts to change all or part of the political or social order by means of rioting, petitioning, striking, demonstrating, and establishing lobbies, unions, and political parties.

elections. They put forward policy alternatives and rally adult citizens to vote. Special interest groups, such as trade unions and business associations, form **lobbies**. They advise politicians about their members' desires. They also remind politicians how much their members' votes, organizing skills, and campaign contributions matter. The **mass media** keep a watchful and critical eye on the state. They keep the public informed about the quality of government. **Public opinion** refers to the values and attitudes of the adult population as a whole. It is expressed mainly in polls, emails, and letters to lawmakers, and it gives politicians a reading of citizen preferences. Finally, when dissatisfaction with normal politics is widespread, protest sometimes takes the form of **social movements**. A social movement is a collective attempt to change all or part of the political or social order. Social movements help to keep governments responsive to the wishes of the citizenry (see Chapter 21, Collective Action and Social Movements).

Bearing these definitions in mind, we now consider the merits and limitations of various sociological theories of democracy.

Summing Up

- The use of power may involve force, but it more frequently depends on people recognizing the legitimacy of its use, at which point raw power becomes legitimate authority.
- A political system may be characterized by the relationship between state (the institutions that formulate and carry out a country's laws and public policies) and civil society (the institutions outside of the state's direct control).
- The greater the degree to which civil society influences the operation of the state, the more democratic the political system.

THEORIES OF DEMOCRACY

A Functionalist Account: Pluralist Theory

In the early 1950s, New Haven, Connecticut, was a city of about 150 000 people. It had seen better times. As in many other American cities, post–World War II prosperity and new roads had allowed much of the white middle class to resettle in the suburbs, eroding the city's tax base. It also left much of the downtown to poor residents and members of minority groups. Some parts of New Haven became slums.

Beginning in 1954, Mayor Richard Lee decided to do something about the city's decline. He planned to attract new investment, eliminate downtown slums, and stem the outflow of the white middle class. Urban renewal was a potentially divisive issue. However, according to research conducted at the time, key decisions were made in a highly democratic manner. The city government listened closely to all major groups. It adopted policies that reflected the diverse wants and interests of city residents.

The social scientists who studied New Haven politics in the 1950s followed **pluralist theory** (Dahl, 1961; Polsby, 1959). They argued that the city was highly democratic because power was widely dispersed. They showed that few of the most prestigious families in New Haven were economic leaders in the community. Moreover, neither economic leaders nor the social elite monopolized political decision making. Different groups of people decided various political issues. Some of these people had low status in the community. Moreover, power was more widely distributed than in earlier decades. The pluralists concluded that no single group exercised disproportionate power in New Haven.

The pluralists believed that politics worked much the same way in the United States as a whole and in other democracies, such as Canada. Democracies, they said, are heterogeneous societies with many competing interests and centres of power. No single power centre can dominate consistently. Sometimes one category of voters or one set of interest groups wins a political battle, sometimes another. Most often, however, politics involves negotiation and compromise between competing groups. Because no one group is always able to control the political agenda or the outcome of political conflicts, democracy is guaranteed, argued the pluralists.

Pluralists closely followed the functionalist script. They viewed the political system as an institution that helps society achieve its collective goals and interests, in the process integrating its members and keeping it in equilibrium (Parsons, 1963). The notion that different segments of society might have fundamentally opposed goals and interests, that some groups are consistently more powerful than others are, and that politics could be a disruptive endeavour that sometimes promotes disequilibrium and on occasion even tears a society apart was foreign to the pluralist mindset.

Pluralist theory holds that power is widely dispersed. As a result, no group enjoys disproportionate influence, and decisions are usually reached through negotiation and compromise.

Conflict Approaches I: Elite Theory

Elite theorists sharply disagreed with the pluralist account. They argued that groups with opposing goals and interests confront each other in the political arena, and that while conflict is not always overt, it is never far below the surface of political affairs. Moreover, powerful groups exercise far more control over political life than less powerful groups do.

Foremost among early elite theorists was C. Wright Mills (1956). Mills defined **elites** as small groups that occupy the command posts of a society's most influential institutions. In the United States, the country Mills analyzed, these institutions include the 200 to 300 biggest corporations, the executive branch of government, and the military. Mills wrote that the people (nearly all men) who control these institutions make important decisions that profoundly affect all members of society. Moreover, they do so without much regard for elections or public opinion.

Mills showed how the corporate, state, and military elites are connected. People move from one elite group to another during their careers. Their children intermarry. They maintain

Elite theory holds that small groups occupying the command posts of most influential institutions make important decisions that profoundly affect all members of society. Moreover, they do so without much regard for elections or public opinion.

Elites are small groups that control the command posts of institutions.

close social contacts. They tend to be recruited from upper-middle and upper classes. Yet Mills denied that these connections turn the three elites into what Marx called a **ruling class,** a self-conscious and cohesive group of people, led by big corporate shareholders, who act to shore up capitalism. Mills insisted that the three elites are relatively independent of one another. They may see eye to eye on many issues, but each has its own sphere of influence; Conflict among elite groups is frequent (Alford and Friedland, 1985: 199; Mills, 1956: 277).

A **ruling class** is a self-conscious, cohesive group of people in elite positions. They act to advance their common interests, and corporate executives lead them.

The Elitist Critique of Pluralism

Most political sociologists today question the pluralist account of democratic politics. That is because research has established the existence of large, persistent, wealth-based inequalities in political influence and political participation.

John Porter's *The Vertical Mosaic* (1965) was the first in a series of Canadian studies that demonstrate the weaknesses of pluralism and corroborate aspects of elite theory (Brym, 1989; Clement, 1975; Olsen, 1980). These studies show that a disproportionately large number of people in Canada's political and other elites come from upper-class and upper-middle-class families. For example, about 40 percent of Canadian prime ministers, premiers, and cabinet ministers were born into the richest 10 percent of families in the country (Olsen, 1980: 129). In their youth, members of Canada's elite are likely to have attended expensive private schools. As adults, they tend to marry the offspring of other elite members and belong to exclusive private clubs. In the course of their careers, they often move from one elite group to another. Arguably, people with this sort of background cannot act dispassionately on behalf of all Canadians, rich and poor. Controversy persists over whether Canada's elites form a ruling class. Porter (1965), noting frequent conflict among elites, argued against the view that a ruling class controls Canada. Some of his students disagreed. They argued that the interests of large corporations dominate Canadian political life (Clement, 1975; Olsen, 1980). However, both Porter and his students did agree on one point: Contrary to pluralist claims, Canada's well-to-do consistently exercise disproportionate influence over political life in this country.

Studies of political participation in Canada add weight to the elitist view (Blais, Gidengil, Nadeau, and Nevitte, 1997; Frank, 1992; Mishler, 1979: 88–97). Many surveys show that political involvement decreases with social class (see Figure 14.2 and Box 14.2). For example, the likelihood of voting falls with a person's class position. The likelihood of phoning or writing a member of Parliament, helping a candidate in an election campaign, contributing money to a political party, and running for office declines even more steeply as we move down the class hierarchy. As intensity of political participation declines, so does political influence (Eagles, 1993). Consequently, although political apathy and cynicism are high among Canadians, the

FIGURE 14.2

Political Donations and Cynicism by Income, Canada, 2008

Source: "Canadian Election Panel Study, 2004-2006-2008." 2010. http://sda.chass.utoronto.ca/cgi-bin/sdapub/hsda?harcsda+ces040608 (accessed 27 November 2010).

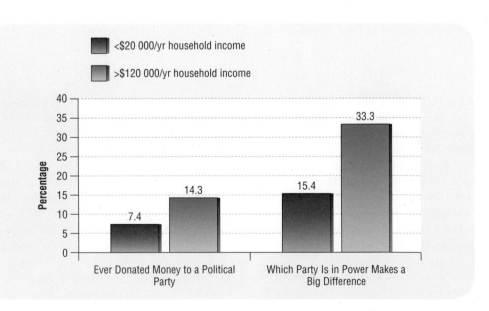

BOX 14.2

It's Your Choice

INCREASING THE PARTICIPATION OF WOMEN IN CANADIAN POLITICS

Just as political participation decreases with social class, so it varies by gender. On the whole, women are less politically active than men are. The gender gap in political participation is due to sociological and historical factors. It has been reduced by political pressure and resulting public policy innovations. It can be further reduced by the same means.

By demonstrating, petitioning, and gaining the support of influential liberal-minded men, Canadian women won the right to vote federally in 1917 and in Yukon and all provinces except Quebec by 1925. Quebec fell into line in 1940 and the Northwest Territories in 1951. Some women have since been elected to Parliament and to provincial and territorial legislatures. As of 2011, 24.6 percent of federal members of Parliament and provincial or territorial members

of legislative assemblies were women. However, critics emphasize that this level was reached in the late 1990s and then more or less stabilized. Over that same period, fewer women than men were put forward as candidates by their parties. Many fewer women were appointed to cabinet positions. And only once, between June and October 1993 did Canada have a female prime minister (Kim Campbell). As these facts suggest, the more influential the type of political activity, the fewer women we find (Bashevkin, 1993; Equal Voice, 2005).

Active involvement in political life, especially running for office, requires time and money. Women are disadvantaged in this regard. As you saw in Chapter 11 (Sexualities and Gender Stratification), women have lower socioeconomic status than men do on average. Women are also saddled with more domestic responsibilities than men are. These factors prevent many women from running for office. In addition, political parties influence the nomination of candidates for elected office and thus help determine where women run. Most parties tend to assign female candidates to ridings where chances of winning are low (Brodie, 1991).

Public policy analysts note that female political participation can increase if these barriers are removed (Boyd, 2001; Brodie, 1991). For example, laws could be passed that would allow candidates to take unpaid leave from their jobs to contest nominations and elections, set spending limits for nomination and election campaigns, make contributions for nomination campaigns tax-deductible, treat child-care and housekeeping costs

CP Picture Archive/Tom Hanson

Kim Campbell, Canada's only female prime minister, June to October 1993

as reimbursable campaign expenses, and so on. Additionally, laws could be enacted that make government subsidies to political party campaigns dependent on the proportion of their elected candidates that are women. In such a system, party subsidies would increase with the proportion of women elected, thus creating a powerful disincentive for parties to place most female candidates in ridings where they are likely to lose. The means to increase the participation of women in politics are available. Whether these means are implemented is your choice.

poorest Canadians are the most politically apathetic and cynical. They have less interest in politics than do the well-to-do, and they are more likely to think that government does not care what they think. As one of the world's leading political sociologists wrote, "The combination of a low vote and a relative lack of organization among the lower-status groups means that they will suffer from neglect by the politicians who will be receptive to the wishes of the more privileged, participating, and organized strata" (Lipset, 1981: 226–27).

Conflict Approaches II: Marxist Rejoinders to Elite Theory

Although compelling in some respects, elite theory has its critics, Marxists foremost among them. One group of Marxists, known as "instrumentalists," denies that elites enjoy more or less equal power. Actually, they say, elites form a ruling class dominated by big business. From their point of view, the state is an arm (or "instrument") of the business elite. Big business gains control of the state in three main ways. First, members of wealthy families occupy important state positions in highly disproportionate numbers. Second, government officials rely mainly on the representatives of big business for advice. Third, political parties rely mainly on big business for financial support. According to some Marxists, members of different elites may disagree about specific issues. However, because of the three control mechanisms just listed, they always agree about one issue: the need to maintain the health of the capitalist system (Miliband, 1973 [1969]).

A second group of Marxists, known as "structuralists," offers a somewhat different interpretation of why the state in capitalist society is necessarily biased in favour of big business. For structuralists, it is not so much the *social origins* of high government officials or the *social ties* linking them with big business that encourages the state to act with a pro-capitalist bias. Rather, the capitalist state acts as an arm of big business because it is constrained to do so by *the nature of the capitalist system itself*. For example, if Canadian government officials take actions that deeply damage capitalist interests, investment would be redirected to countries with regimes that are kinder to company profits. Such a move would cost Canada jobs and prosperity. It would be highly unpopular. The government could easily fall. Fearing this outcome, governments in capitalist societies find their field of action restricted to policies that ensure the well-being of big business. According to structuralists, it is the very fact that the state is embedded in a capitalist system that forces it to act in this way (Poulantzas, 1975 [1968]).

It follows from both the instrumentalist and the structuralist positions that ordinary citizens, especially members of the working class, rarely have much influence over state policy. According to Marxists, true democracy can emerge only if members of the working class and their supporters overthrow capitalism and establish a socialist system (see Chapter 13, Work and the Economy).

Conflict Approaches III: Power Resource Theory

Both Marxist and elite theories leave big questions unanswered. For one thing, they pay little attention to how political parties lose office while other political parties get elected. Nor are they much concerned with the effect of one party or another on public policy. In fact, for Marxist and elite theorists, elections are little more than sideshows. They believe that elites or a ruling class always control society, regardless of election outcomes. Therefore, they contend, the victory of one party over another does not deserve much sociological attention because it does not substantially affect the lives of ordinary men and women.

In contrast, many political sociologists today think it matters a great deal which party is in office. After all, the lives of ordinary men and women are hugely affected by whether the governing party supports or opposes free trade, weaker environmental standards, less publicly funded medical care, bigger government subsidies for child care, abortion on demand, and so forth. Elite theorists are correct to claim that power is concentrated disproportionately in the hands of the well-to-do, but we still need a theory that accounts for the successes and failures of different parties and policies in different times and places. That is where **power resource theory** is helpful. It focuses on how *variations* in the distribution of power affect the fortunes of parties and policies over the long term.

To understand power resource theory, first consider your own party preference. For many reasons, you may support one political party over another. Your family may have a long tradition of voting for one party. You may have never really questioned this support.

Power resource theory holds that the distribution of power among major classes partly accounts for the successes and failures of different political parties over the long term.

Maybe you support a party because you admire the energy, integrity, or track record of its leader. Or you might support a party because you agree with its policies on a range of issues. What factors lead *you* to prefer one party over another?

If a party's policies influence your vote, you are like many Canadians. In fact, Canadian voters cluster in two main policy groups. Voters on the *left* promote extensive government involvement in the economy. Among other things, this means they favour a strong "social safety net" of health and welfare benefits to help the less fortunate members of society. As a result, left-wing policies often lead to less economic inequality. In contrast, voters on the *right* favour a reduced role for government in the economy. They want to see a smaller welfare state and emphasize the importance of individual initiative in promoting economic growth. Economic issues aside, leftists and rightists also tend to differ on social or moral issues. Leftists tend to support equal rights for women and racial and sexual minorities. Rightists tend to support more traditional social and moral values.

Figure 14.3 shows one indicator of how left and right sentiments translated into support for Canada's five political parties in 2008. Using data from the 2008 Canadian Election Survey, we first found, for supporters of each political party, the percentage of people who favour more federal spending on welfare. This is one indicator of the percentage of people on the left. We then found the percentage of people who support corporate tax cuts. This is one indicator of the percentage of people on the right. Finally, we subtracted the percentage on the right from the percentage on the left. This difference is what we call the "left-right index." The higher the value of the left-right index, the more left-wing a party is. Clearly, there are big differences between parties. Supporters of the Conservatives are farthest to the right. Supporters of the Liberals are close to the middle of the Canadian political spectrum. The New Democrats are furthest to the left. Do you think of yourself as a supporter of one of these parties? Is your choice related to its policies?

The policies favoured by different parties have different effects on different categories of people. Therefore, different parties tend to be supported by different classes, regions, religious groups, races, and other groups. Do you think the policies of your preferred party favour the class, region, religious group, or race to which you belong? If so, how? If not, why not?

In most Western democracies, one of the main factors that distinguishes political parties is differences in *class* support (Korpi, 1983: 35; Lipset and Rokkan, 1967; Manza, Hout, and Brooks, 1995). However, the tendency for people in different classes to vote for different parties varies from one country to the next. In Canada, the tendency is relatively weak.

The strength of the tendency for people in different classes to vote for different parties depends on many factors. One of the most important is how socially organized or cohesive classes are (Brym with Fox, 1989: 57–91; Brym, Gillespie, and Lenton, 1989). For example, an upper class that can create such organizations as the Business Council on National Issues and CATJO, which supported the PCs so effectively in the 1988 free trade election, is more powerful than an upper class that cannot take such action. If an upper class makes such efforts, while a working class fails to organize itself, right-wing candidates have a better

FIGURE 14.3

Left versus Right, Canadian Federal Parties, 2008

Note: The left versus right index is the percentage of each party's supporters who favoured more federal spending on welfare minus the percentage who favoured lower corporate taxes.

Source: "Canadian Election Panel Study, 2004-2006-2008." 2010. http://sda.chass.utoronto.ca/cgi-bin/sdapub/hsda?harcsda+ces040608 (accessed 27 November 2010).

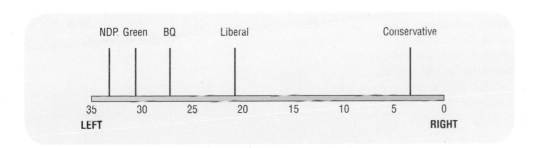

chance of winning office. Conservative policies are more likely to become law. Similarly, a working class that can unionize many workers is more powerful than one with few unionized workers. That is because unions often collect money for the party that is more sympathetic to union interests. They also lobby on behalf of their members and try to convince members to vote for the pro-union party. If workers become more unionized, while an upper class fails to organize itself, then left-wing candidates have an improved chance of winning office. Policies that favour lower classes are more likely to become law. This is the main insight of power resource theory. *Organization is a source of power. Change in the distribution of power between major classes partly accounts for the fortunes of different political parties and different laws and policies* (Esping-Andersen, 1990; Korpi, 1983; O'Connor and Olsen, 1998; Shalev, 1983).

You can see how power resource theory works by looking at Table 14.1, which divides 18 industrialized democracies in the three decades after World War II into three groups. In group one are countries like Sweden, where democratic socialist parties usually controlled government. (Democratic socialist parties are at least as left wing as the NDP in Canada.) In group two are countries like Australia, where democratic socialist parties sometimes controlled, or shared in control of, government. In group three are countries like Canada, where democratic socialist parties rarely or never shared in control of government. The group averages in column one show that democratic socialist parties are generally more successful in countries where workers are more unionized. The group averages in columns two and three show more economic inequality exists in countries that are weakly unionized and have no democratic socialist governments. In other words, by means of taxes and social policies, democratic socialist governments ensure that the rich earn a smaller percentage of national income and the poor form a smaller percentage of the population. Studies of pensions, medical care, and other state benefits in the rich industrialized democracies reach similar conclusions. In general, where working classes are more organized and powerful, disadvantaged people are economically better off (Lindert, 2004; Myles 1989; O'Connor and Brym, 1988; Olsen and Brym, 1996).

TABLE 14.1

Some Consequences of Working-Class Power in 18 Rich Industrialized Countries, 1946–1976

Note: "Percentage Poor" is the average percentage of the population living in relative poverty according to OECD standards, with the poverty line standardized according to household size.

Source: Korpi, 1983: 40, 196.

	Percentage of Non-agricultural Workforce Unionized	Percentage of Total National Income to Top 10% of Earners	Percentage Poor
Mainly democratic socialist countries (Sweden, Norway)	68.5	21.8	4.3
Partly democratic socialist countries (Austria, Australia, Denmark, Belgium, UK, New Zealand, Finland)	46.6	23.6	7.8
Mainly non-democratic-socialist countries (Ireland, West Germany, Netherlands, USA, Japan, Canada, France, Italy, Switzerland)	28.0	28.3	10.8

Class is not the only factor that distinguishes political parties. Historically, *religion* has also been an important basis of party differences. For example, in Western European countries with large Catholic populations, such as Switzerland and Belgium, parties differ partly on the basis of the religious affiliation of their supporters. In recent decades, *ethnicity and race* have become cleavage factors of major and growing importance in some countries. For example, in the United States, African Americans have overwhelmingly supported the Democratic Party since the 1960s (Brooks and Manza, 1997). Ethnicity has become an increasingly important division in French politics because of heavy Arab immigration from Algeria, Morocco, and Tunisia since the 1950s and growing anti-immigration sentiment among a substantial minority of whites (Veugelers, 1997). *Regional* groups distinguish parties in other countries, such as Canada, where some parties have been particularly attractive to Westerners, others to Québécois. Power resource theory focuses mainly on how the shifting distribution of power between working and upper classes affects electoral success. However, we can also use the theory to analyze the electoral fortunes of parties that attract different religious groups, races, regional groups, and so on.

In the 2002 election for the French presidency, right-wing candidate Jean-Marie Le Pen placed second. Le Pen's anti-immigrant campaign highlighted the degree to which political cleavages in France are based not just on class but also on race.

Conflict Approaches IV: State-Centred Theory

Democratic politics is a contest among various class, racial, ethnic, religious, and regional groups to control the state for their own advantage. When power is substantially redistributed because of such factors as change in the cohesiveness of these social groups, old ruling parties usually fall and new ones take office.

Note, however, that a winner-take-all strategy would be nothing short of foolish. If winning parties passed laws that benefited only their supporters, they might cause mass outrage and even violent opposition. Yet it would be bad politics to allow opponents to become angry, organized, and resolute. After all, winners want more than just a moment of glory. They want to be able to enjoy the spoils of office over the long haul. To achieve stability, they must give people who lose elections a voice in government. That way, even determined opponents are likely to recognize the government's legitimacy. Pluralists thus make a good point when they say that democratic politics is about accommodation and compromise. They lose sight only of how accommodation and compromise typically give more advantages to some rather than others, as both elite theorists and power resource theorists stress.

There is, however, more to the story of politics than conflict between classes, religious groups, regions, and so forth. Theda Skocpol and others who follow **state-centred theory** show how the state itself can structure political life (Block, 1979; Evans, Rueschemeyer, and Skocpol, 1985; Skocpol, 1979). They regard senior elected officials and state bureaucrats not as agents of economic elites but as major political players in their own right. Moreover, they hold that major political struggles become embodied in the very structure of states. That is, historically important political battles typically end with the passage of new laws and the creation of new political institutions. These laws and institutions go on to influence political life until political conflict becomes serious enough to alter them once again. Until then, the state influences political life *to some degree independently of day-to-day political conflict and the distribution of power at a given time*. This argument is a valuable supplement to power resource theory (see Table 14.2 on page 364).

To illustrate state-centred theory, recall first that all societies are divided into different classes, religious groups, regions, and so on. In principle, any one or a combination of these social divisions may be reflected in the policies of different political parties and the social characteristics of party supporters. For example, in some societies, politics is mostly about the attempts of different *classes* to control the state for their own

State-centred theory holds that the state itself can structure political life, to some degree, independently of the way power is distributed between classes and other groups at a given time.

TABLE 14.2

Five Sociological Theories
of Capitalist Democracy
Compared

	Pluralist	Elite	Marxist	Power-Resource	State-Centred
How is power distributed?	Dispersed	Concentrated	Concentrated	Concentrated	Concentrated
Who are the main power holders?	Various groups	Elites	Ruling class	Upper class	State officials
On what is their power based?	Holding political office	Controlling major institutions	Owning substantial capital	Owning substantial capital	Holding political office
What is the main basis of public policy?	The will of all citizens	The interests of major elites	Capitalist interests	The balance of power among classes, etc.	The influence of state structures
Do lower classes have much influence on politics?	Yes	No	Rarely	Sometimes	Sometimes

advantage; in other societies, politics is more about the attempts of different *regions* to control the state for their own advantage; and so forth. What then determines which social division—class, region, or another factor—will predominate in political life? State-centred theory provides useful insights into this issue. According to state-centred theory, the state may be organized in such a way as to bias politics toward one social division or another.

Consider Canada. We saw above that different Canadian political parties tend to attract people from different social classes. However, that tendency is weak. Compared with most other democracies, class differences among parties are small in Canada. In contrast, regional differences are comparatively large (Butovsky, 2001; Gidengil, 1992). These large regional differences are evident, for example, in the results of the 2011 federal election (see Figure 14.4).

In Quebec, the Bloc Québécois was the most popular federal political party from the time it first ran federally (1993) until 2011. Although Quebec voters have twice rejected referenda calling for sovereignty, most Bloc supporters favour holding a third referendum in the hope of achieving the separation of Quebec from Canada. In the 2011 federal election, the province swung wildly toward the NDP. Although not in favour of sovereignty for Quebec, the NDP supports more autonomy for Quebec than the Conservatives and the Liberals do.

The Conservative Party grew from a merger between the Conservative Alliance, which was almost entirely limited to the West, and the remnants of the Progressive Conservatives, mainly from Ontario eastward, excluding Quebec. The former Conservative Alliance members retain a strong belief that the central government neglects Western interests and include those who have advocated separation from Canada as the ultimate remedy. In the 2011 election, the Conservatives made big gains in Ontario, but they are still strongest in the Prairies.

What produces such a strong regional bias (and a correspondingly weak class bias) in Canadian political life? The answer lies in the history of Canadian politics and, in particular,

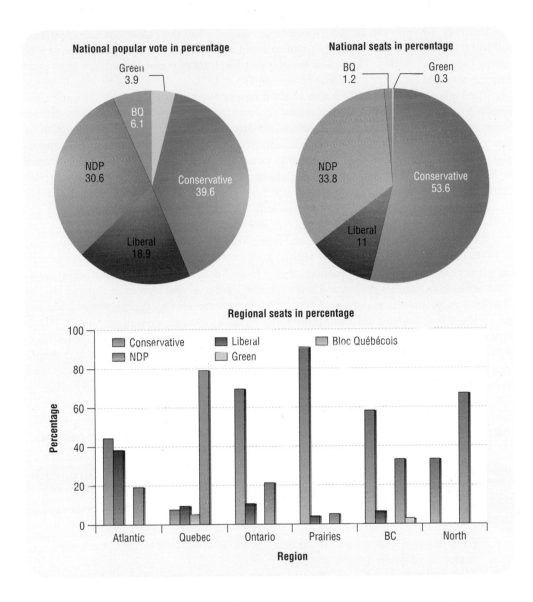

FIGURE 14.4
Results of 2011 Canadian Federal Election

Source: Elections Canada. 2011. "Official Voting Results: Forty-First General Election 2011." http:// www.elections.ca/scripts/ovr2011/ default.html (retrieved 6 September 2011).

in the way that history has structured the laws and policies of the Canadian state. In other words, the explanation for the regional bias of Canadian politics is state-centred.

Before Confederation in 1867, the British North American colonies enjoyed few unifying ties. Vast geographical barriers separated them. No railway or telegraph line linked them. Lower Canada (now Quebec) had become part of British North America by military conquest just a century earlier. It was divided from the other colonies by religion (Catholic versus Protestant), ethnicity (French versus English), and lingering resentment.

Despite these divisions, British North American businessmen tried to forge a union among the colonies in the mid-1860s. They did so because they faced a big problem that only unification could solve: the loss of their export markets. The British were dismantling the protected market known as the British Empire. The Americans had turned against free trade. To make matters worse, the British North American colonies had accumulated a crippling debt load by borrowing to help finance railroad construction, while certain elements in the United States were threatening to expand the border of their country northward. In this context, the business and political leaders of British North America regarded Confederation as a means of creating a new market and an expanded tax base by encouraging mass immigration and promoting economic growth.

However, to unify the British North American colonies, the Fathers of Confederation had to be careful. For one thing, they had to avoid consulting ordinary citizens for fear of having their plan rejected. They knew the colonies had little in common and that most ordinary citizens had no interest in union (Ryerson, 1973: 355).

The Fathers of Confederation also found it necessary to draft a founding document, the British North America (BNA) Act, that played down the deep divisions between the British North American colonies. Most important, the BNA Act left ambiguous the question of how power would be distributed between federal and provincial governments. This vagueness enabled the Fathers of Confederation to form their union, but it also left the door open to the bickering and bargaining that has characterized federal–provincial/territorial relations ever since 1867. Especially after World War II, the BNA Act (and later the Canadian Constitution) allowed power to continue to drift from the federal to the provincial and territorial governments and thus entrenched regionalism in Canadian political life.

A landmark in the decentralization and regionalization of Canadian politics was reached in 1959. In that year, Quebec and the federal government agreed that a provincial or territorial government not wanting to participate in a federal program could receive federal funds to set up its own parallel program. Thereafter, the provincial and territorial right to opt out of federal programs was widely used not just by Quebec but also by the other provinces and territories, which insisted on having the same rights as Quebec (Bélanger, 2000). Power continued to decentralize and regionalize as the provinces gained more control over taxation, resource revenues, immigration policy, language use, and so on. Canada was a deeply regionally divided society from the start, and the state—through the country's basic laws and policies—entrenched regional divisions. The result was a country in which politics is defined less as a struggle between classes than as a struggle between regions (Brym, 1992). Said differently, from the perspective of state-centred theory, class conflict is given less voice than is regional conflict in Canada because of the way the state structures politics.

Summing Up

- Pluralists hold that democratic politics is about compromise and the accommodation of all group interests.
- Elite theorists argue that, despite accommodation and compromise, power is concentrated in the hands of high-status groups, whose interests the political system serves best.
- Marxists claim that elites form a ruling class led by large corporate shareholders.
- Power resource theorists contend that, despite the concentration of power in society, substantial shifts in the distribution of power do occur, and they have big effects on voting patterns and public policies in the long term.
- State-centred theorists posit that state structures also exert an important effect on politics.

THE FUTURE OF DEMOCRACY

Two Cheers for Russian Democracy

In the winter of 1989, the Institute of Sociology of the Russian Academy of Science invited Robert Brym and nine other Canadian sociologists to attend a series of seminars in Moscow. The seminars were designed to acquaint some leading sociologists in the Soviet Union with Western sociology. The weather was frigid, but the country was in the midst of a great thaw. Totalitarianism was melting, leaving democracy in its place. Soviet sociologists had never

Peter Turnley/CORBIS

Although luxury businesses like Versace do brisk business in Moscow, the streets are filled with homeless people. That is because the richest 10 percent of Russians earn 15 times as much as the poorest 10 percent, making Russia one of the most inegalitarian countries in the world.

been free to read and research what they wanted, and they were eager to learn from North American and European scholars (Brym, 1990).

"Or at least so it seemed," says Robert. "One evening about a dozen of us were sitting around comparing the merits of Canadian whisky and Russian vodka. Soon, conversation turned from Crown Royal versus Moskovskaya to Russian politics. 'You must be so excited about what's happening here,' I said to my Russian hosts. 'How long do you think it will be before Russia will have multi-party elections? Do you think Russia will become a liberal democracy like Canada, or a socialist democracy like Sweden?'

"One white-haired Russian sociologist slowly rose to his feet. His colleagues privately called him 'the dinosaur.' It soon became clear why. '*Nikogda*,' he said calmly and deliberately—'never.' '*Nikogda*,' he repeated, his voice rising sharply in pitch, volume, and emphasis. Then, for a full minute he explained that capitalism and democracy were never part of Russia's history, nor could they be expected to take root in Russian soil. 'The Russian people,' he proclaimed, 'do not want a free capitalist society. We know *freedom* means the powerful are free to compete unfairly against the powerless, exploit them, and create social inequality.'

"Everyone else in the room disagreed with the dinosaur's speech, in whole or in part. However, not wanting to cause any more upset, we turned the conversation back to lighter topics. After 15 minutes, someone reminded the others that we had to rise early for the next day's seminars. The evening ended, its great questions unanswered."

Today, more than two decades later, the great questions of Russian politics remain unanswered. And it now seems there was some truth in the dinosaur's speech after all. Russia first held multi-party elections in 1991. Surveys found that most Russians favoured democracy over other types of rule. However, support for democracy soon fell because the economy collapsed and the poverty rate jumped (Gerber and Hout, 1998; see Chapter 13, Work and the Economy).

Democratic sentiment weakened as economic conditions worsened (Whitefield and Evans, 1994). In elections held in the mid-1990s, support for democratic parties plunged as support for communist and extreme right-wing nationalist parties surged (Brym, 1995, 1996d). National surveys find that as many as 97 percent of the citizens of some countries view democracy as the ideal form of government. In Russia, the figure is just 51 percent (Klingemann, 1999). Democracy allowed a few Russians to enrich themselves at the expense of most others. Therefore, many citizens equated democracy not with freedom but with distress.

Russia's political institutions reflect the weakness of Russian democracy. Power is concentrated in the presidency to a much greater degree than in the United States. The Parliament and the judiciary do not act as checks on executive power. Only a small number of Russians belong to political parties. Voting levels are low. National television stations are tightly state-controlled. Minority ethnic groups (especially Muslims from the Caucasus) are sometimes treated arbitrarily and cruelly. Clearly, Russian democracy has a long way to go before it can be considered on par with democracy in the West.

The limited success of Russian democracy raises an important question. What social conditions must exist for a country to become fully democratic? We turn to this question next. To gain perspective, we first consider the three waves of democratization that have swept the world since 1828 (Huntington, 1991: 13–26; see Figure 14.5).

The Three Waves of Democracy

The first wave of democratization began when more than half the white adult males in the United States became eligible to vote in the 1828 presidential election. By 1926, 33 countries enjoyed at least minimally democratic institutions: the United States, most countries in Western Europe, the British dominions (Australia, Canada, and New Zealand), Japan, and four Latin American countries (Argentina, Colombia, Chile, and Uruguay). However, a democratic reversal occurred between 1922 and 1942. During that period, fascist, communist, and militaristic movements caused two-thirds of the world's democracies to fall under authoritarian or totalitarian rule.

The second wave of democratization swept across a large part of the world between 1943 and 1962. The Allied victory in World War II returned democracy to many of the defeated powers, including West Germany and Japan. The end of colonial rule brought democracy to some states in Africa and elsewhere. Some Latin American countries formed limited democracies. However, even by the late 1950s, the second wave was beginning to exhaust itself. Soon, the world was in the midst of a second democratic reversal. Military dictatorships replaced many democracies in Latin America, Asia, and Africa. One-third of the democracies that existed in 1958 were authoritarian regimes by the mid-1970s.

The third and biggest wave of democratization began in 1974 with the overthrow of military dictatorships in Portugal and Greece. It crested in the early 1990s. In Southern and Eastern Europe, Latin America, Asia, and Africa, a whole series of authoritarian regimes fell. In 1991, Soviet communism collapsed. By 1995, 117 of the world's 191 countries were democratic in the sense that their citizens could choose representatives in regular, competitive elections. That amounts to 61 percent of the world's countries containing nearly 55 percent of the world's population (Diamond, 1996: 26).

FIGURE 14.5

The Three Waves of Democratization, 1828–1995

Sources: Diamond, 1996: 28; Huntington, 1991: 26.

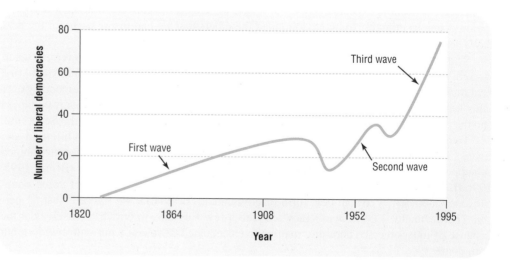

William Vanderson/Hulton Archive/Getty Images

Nigeria celebrates independence from Britain in 1960. In 1993, General Sani Abacha annulled the presidential election, became head of state, and began a reign of brutal civil rights violations. The world's third wave of democratization was drawing to a close.

The third wave seems less dramatic, however, if we bear in mind that these figures refer to **formal democracies**—countries that hold regular, competitive elections. Many of these countries are not **liberal democracies**. That is, like Russia, they lack the freedoms and constitutional protections that make political participation and competition meaningful. In formal but non-liberal democracies, substantial political power may reside with a military that is largely unaffected by the party in office. Certain cultural, ethnic, religious, or regional groups may not be allowed to take part in elections. The legislative and judicial branches of government may not constrain the power of the executive branch. Citizens may not enjoy freedom of expression, assembly, and organization. Instead, they may suffer from unjustified detention, exile, terror, and torture. At the end of 1995, 40 percent of the world's countries were liberal democracies, 21 percent were non-liberal democracies, and 39 percent were non-democracies, but the percentage of liberal democracies was already falling (Diamond, 1996: 28; U.S. Information Agency, 1998–99). The third wave was subsiding.

Formal democracy involves regular, competitive elections.

A **liberal democracy** is a country whose citizens enjoy regular, competitive elections *and* the freedoms and constitutional protections that make political participation and competition meaningful.

The Social Preconditions of Democracy

Liberal democracies emerge and endure when countries enjoy considerable economic growth, industrialization, urbanization, the spread of literacy, and a gradual decrease in economic inequality (Huntington, 1991: 39–108; Lipset, 1981: 27–63, 469–76, 1994; Moore, 1967; Rueschemeyer, Stephens, and Stephens, 1992; Zakaria, 1997). Economic development creates middle and working classes that are large, well organized, literate, and well off. When these classes become sufficiently powerful, their demands for civil liberties and the right to vote and run for office have to be recognized. If powerful middle and working classes are not guaranteed political rights, they sweep away kings, queens, landed aristocracies, generals, and authoritarian politicians in revolutionary upsurges. In contrast, democracies do not emerge where middle and working classes are too weak to wrest big political concessions from pre-democratic authorities. In intermediate cases—where, say, a country's military is about as powerful a political force as its middle and working classes— democracy is precarious and often merely formal. The history of unstable democracies is largely a history of internal military takeovers (Germani and Silvert, 1961).

Apart from the socioeconomic conditions noted above, favourable external political and military circumstances help liberal democracy endure. Liberal democracies, even strong ones such as France, collapse when fascist, communist, and military regimes and empires defeat them. They revive when democratic alliances win world wars and authoritarian empires break up. Less coercive forms of outside political intervention are sometimes effective, too. For example, in the 1970s and 1980s, the European Union helped liberal democracy in Spain, Portugal, and Greece by integrating these countries in the Western European economy and giving them massive economic aid.

In sum, powerful, pro-democratic foreign states and strong, prosperous middle and working classes are liberal democracy's best guarantees. It follows that liberal democracy will spread in the less economically developed countries only if they prosper and enjoy support from the United States and the European Union, the world centres of liberal democracy.

Recognizing the importance of the United States and the European Union in promoting democracy in many parts of the world should not obscure two important facts. First, the United States is not always a friend of democracy. For example, between the end of World War II and the collapse of the Soviet Union in 1991, democratic regimes that were sympathetic to the Soviet Union were often destabilized by the United States and replaced by anti-democratic governments. American leaders were willing to export arms and offer other forms of support to anti-democratic forces in Iran, Indonesia, Chile, Nicaragua, Guatemala, and other countries because they believed it was in the United States' political and economic interest to do so (see Chapter 9, Globalization, Inequality, and Development). For similar reasons, the United States supports non-democratic regimes in Saudi Arabia, Kuwait, and elsewhere today. Desire for access to oil, copper, and even bananas (among other commodities), combined with fear of communist influence, have often outweighed democratic ideals in the United States. Anti-American attitudes in many parts of the world are based on American *opposition* to popular rule.

Second, just because the United States promotes democracy in many parts of the world, we should not assume that liberal democracy has reached its full potential in that country or, for that matter, in any of the other rich postindustrial countries that promote democracy internationally, including Canada. We saw otherwise in our discussion of the limited participation and influence of disadvantaged groups in Canadian politics. It seems fitting, therefore, to conclude this chapter by briefly assessing the future of liberal democracy in Canada.

Postmaterialism and the Dilemma of Canadian Politics

Postmaterialism claims that growing equality and prosperity in the rich industrialized countries have resulted in a shift from class-based to value-based politics.

A recent school of thought, **postmaterialism**, holds that economic or material issues are becoming less important in Canadian politics. Specifically, postmaterialists argue as follows: Liberal democracies are less stratified than both non-liberal democracies and non-democracies are. That is, in liberal democracies, the gap between rich and poor is less extreme and society as a whole is more prosperous. In fact, say the postmaterialists, prosperity and the moderation of stratification have reached a point where they have fundamentally changed political life in Canada. They claim that, as recently as half a century ago, most people were politically motivated mainly by their economic or material concerns. As a result, parties were distinguished from one another chiefly by the way they attracted voters from different classes. Now, however, many—if not most—Canadians have supposedly had their basic material wants satisfied. Young people in particular, who grew up in relatively prosperous times, are less concerned with material issues, such as whether their next paycheque can feed and house their family. They are more concerned with postmaterialist issues, such as women's rights, civil rights, and the environment. The postmaterialists conclude that the old left–right political division, based on class differences and material issues, is being replaced. The new left–right political division, they say, is based on age differences and postmaterialist issues (Clark and Lipset, 1991; Clark, Lipset, and Rempel, 1993; Inglehart, 1997).

Although Canada is certainly more prosperous and less stratified than are the less developed countries of the world, it seems to us that postmaterialists are wrong to think that affluence is universal in this country or that inequality is decreasing. Chapter 8, Social Stratification, documents these facts at length. Canada has a comparatively high poverty rate among rich industrialized countries, and income inequality has been increasing for decades. Unemployment and poverty are particularly widespread among youth—the people who, in the postmaterialist view, are the most affluent and least concerned with material issues. About two-thirds of single Canadians under the age of 25 live below the low-income cutoff. This suggests that, today, more new voters are poor than at any time since at least 1980, when data on youth poverty were first collected. Under these circumstances, we should not be surprised. Canadian public opinion polls repeatedly show that the leading concerns of Canadians are unemployment and related material issues.

We thus arrive at the key dilemma of Canadian politics. Material issues—essentially problems of class inequality—continue to loom large in the minds of most Canadians. However, as we have seen, Canadian politics focuses on regional, not class issues. In other words, a disconnect exists between Canadian priorities and Canadian politics. This probably accounts in part for the declining rate of political participation and the high rates of political cynicism and apathy we have observed, particularly among lower classes (refer back to Figure 14.2 and see Figure 14.6). It probably also accounts in large measure for the fact that

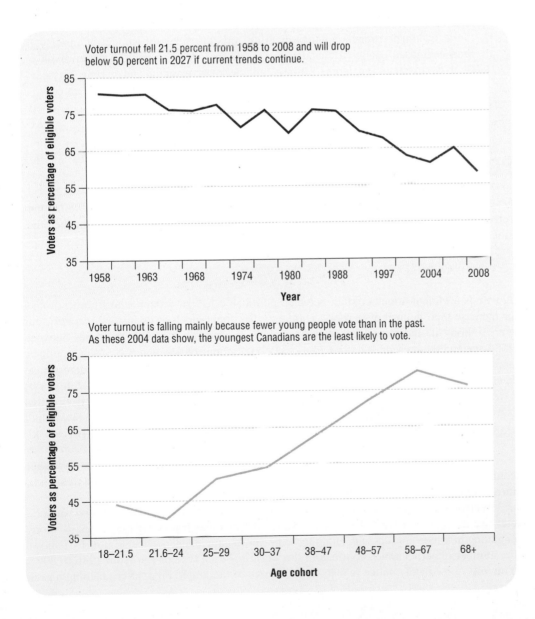

FIGURE 14.6

Voter Turnout, Canadian Federal Elections, 1958–2008

Source: Elections Canada, 2006, "Report of the Chief Electoral Officer of Canada on the 39th General Election of January 23, 2006"; 2004, "Estimation of Voter Turnout by Age Group at the 38th General Election"; and 2008, "40th General Election." Retrieved October 16, 2008 (http://enr.elections.ca).

Canadians are increasingly turning to unconventional means of influencing public policy. In 1980, 24 percent of Canadians said they had joined a boycott, attended an unlawful demonstration, joined an unofficial strike, or occupied a building or a factory at least once. Ten years later, that figure stood at 33 percent. Participation in such unconventional political activities is most common among young, highly educated people (Nevitte, 1996: 75–109). This suggests that the future of Canadian politics may lie in part outside "normal" politics. We take up the theme of challenges to established power in Chapter 21, Collective Action and Social Movements.

Participating in social movements is not the only way people step outside the rules of normal electoral politics to change society. We conclude our discussion by considering two other types of "politics by other means": war and terrorism.

Summing Up

- Three waves of democracy have swept the world since the nineteenth century. Each was followed by an undertow that eroded some of its advances.
- Solid economic growth, industrialization, urbanization, the spread of literacy, and decreased economic inequality typically precede the crystallization of liberal democracy. The large, literate, and well-off working and middle classes that emerge from such conditions typically demand and achieve a loud voice in political affairs.

POLITICS BY OTHER MEANS

Much political conflict is constrained by rules that all sides accept. Yet people sometimes reject the rules. In extreme cases, each side in a conflict denies the legitimacy of the other sides and uses force to disempower the others. The result is war.

War

A **war** is a violent armed conflict between politically distinct groups who fight to protect or increase their control of territory. Humanity has spent much of its history preparing for war, fighting it, and recovering from it; war has broken out some 14 000 times between 3600 BCE and the present. It has killed roughly one billion soldiers and two billion civilians, approximately 3 percent of the people born in the last 5600 years. (This is an underestimate because it necessarily ignores armed conflict among people without a recorded history.) Overall, however, and taking a long historical view, wars have become more destructive over time with "improvements" in the technology of human destruction. The twentieth century was history's deadliest, with about 100 million war deaths (Beer, 1974; Brzezinski, 1993; Haub, 2000).

War is an expensive business, and the United States spends far more than any other country financing it. The United States accounts for about a third of world military expenditures and nearly 30 percent of world arms export agreements (Grimmett, 2006).

Wars take place between countries (interstate wars) and within countries (civil or societal wars). A special type of interstate war is the colonial war, which involves a colony engaging in armed conflict with an imperial power to gain independence. Figure 14.7 shows the number of active armed conflicts in the world for each type of war from 1946 to 2007. You will immediately notice two striking features of the graph. First, after reaching a peak

A **war** is a violent armed conflict between politically distinct groups who fight to protect or increase their control of territory.

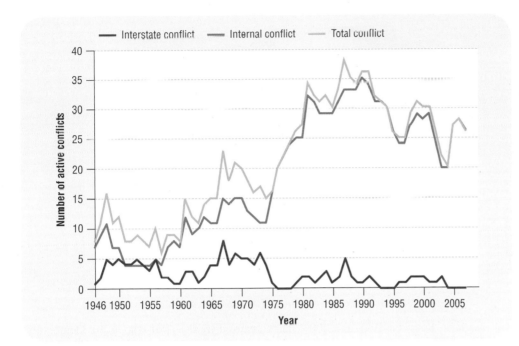

FIGURE 14.7

Global Trends in Violent
Conflict, 1946–2007

Source: Hewitt, J. Joseph (2010).
"Trends in Global Conflict,
1946–2007", in J. Joseph Hewitt,
Jonathan Wikenfeld, and Ted
Robert Gurr (eds.). *Peace and
Conflict 2010: Executive Summary*.
College Park (Md.) Center for
International Development and
Conflict Management, University of
Maryland, p. 19.

between the mid- to late 1980s, the number of armed conflicts dropped sharply. Second, since the mid-1950s, most armed conflict in the world has been societal rather than interstate. Today, countries rarely go to war against each other. They often go to war with themselves as contending political groups fight for state control or seek to break away and form independent states. Don't let the mass media distort your perception of global war. Wars like the recent U.S.–Iraq war account for little of the total magnitude of armed conflict, although they loom large in the media. Wars like the recent conflict in the Democratic Republic of Congo account for most of the total magnitude of armed conflict yet are rarely mentioned in the media. From 2003 to 2007, the U.S.–Iraq war killed roughly 170 000 combatants

The civil war in the Democratic
Republic of Congo (1994–2003)
caused millions of deaths.

FIGURE 14.8

The Risk of Future
Instability, 2008–10

Source: Hewitt, J. Joseph
(2010). "The Peace and Conflict
Instability Ledger: Ranking States
on Future Risks", in J. Joseph
Hewitt, Jonathan Wikenfeld, and
Ted Robert Gurr (eds.). *Peace
and Conflict 2010: Executive
Summary*. College Park (Md.) Center
for International Development and
Conflict Management, University of
Maryland, p. 6.

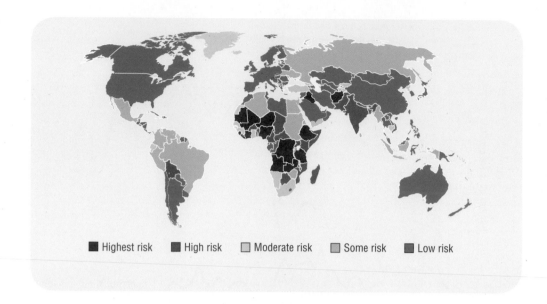

■ Highest risk   ■ High risk   □ Moderate risk   □ Some risk   ■ Low risk

and civilians. Between 1998 and 2003, deaths caused by the civil war in the Democratic Republic of Congo numbered in the millions (CBC News, 2007; Coghlan et al., 2006; "Iraq Body Count," 2008; "Iraq Coalition Casualty Count," 2008).

War risk varies from one country to the next (Figure 14.8), but what factors determine the risk of war on the territory of a given country? Figure 14.9 helps us answer that question by classifying the countries of the world by type of government and level of prosperity. Government types include democracy, autocracy (absolute rule by a single person or party), and "intermediate" forms. Intermediate types of government include some elements of democracy (e.g., regular elections) and some elements of autocracy (e.g., no institutional checks on presidential power). In this graph, a country's gross domestic product per capita (GDPpc) indicates its level of prosperity. The graph divides the world's countries into quarters by GDPpc.

FIGURE 14.9

Type of Government by
Income Category

Source: Marshall and Gurr, 2003: 11.

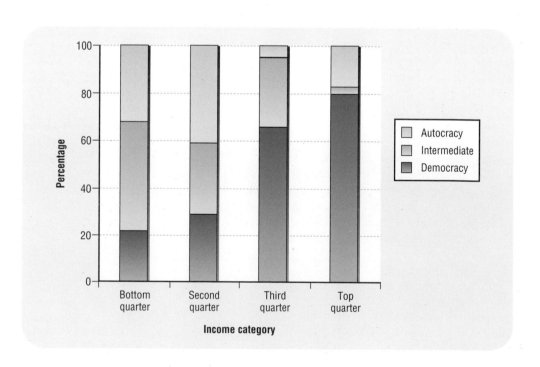

Given our earlier discussion of the social preconditions of democracy, it should ne no surprise that democracy is more common and autocracy less common in prosperous countries. What is particularly interesting about Figure 14.9 is the distribution of countries with *intermediate* types of government. Countries with intermediate types of government are at the highest risk of war, especially societal or civil war. A democratic government tends to be stable because it enjoys legitimacy in the eyes of its citizens. An autocratic government tends to be stable because it rules with an iron fist. In contrast, an intermediate type of government is characterized neither by high legitimacy nor by iron rule. It is therefore most prone to collapsing into societal war, with armed political groups fighting each other for state control. We conclude that economic development and democratization are the two main factors leading to less war. (Of course, countries that avoid war on their own territory may nonetheless engage in war elsewhere, the United States being the prime example. Since 1850, the United States has intervened militarily in other countries more than once a year on average; see Kohn, 1988).

Terrorism and Related Forms of Political Violence

We can learn much about the predicament of the world today by lingering a moment on the question of why societal warfare has largely replaced interstate warfare since World War II. As usual, historical perspective is useful (Tilly, 2002).

From the rise of the modern state in the seventeenth century until World War II, states increasingly monopolized the means of coercion in society. This had three important consequences. First, as various regional, ethnic, and religious groups came under the control of powerful central states, the number of regional, ethnic, and religious wars declined and interstate warfare became the norm. Second, because states were powerful and monopolized the means of coercion, conflict became more deadly. Third, civilian life was pacified because the job of killing for political reasons was largely restricted to state-controlled armed forces. Thus, even as the death toll from war rose, civilians were largely segregated from large-scale killing. As late as World War I (1914–18), civilians composed only 5 percent of war deaths.

All this changed after World War II (1939–45). Since then, there have been fewer interstate wars and more civil wars, guerrilla wars, massacres, terrorist attacks, and instances of attempted ethnic cleansing and genocide perpetrated by militias, mercenaries, paramilitaries, suicide bombers, and the like. Moreover, large-scale violence has increasingly been visited on civilian rather than on military populations. By the 1990s, civilians composed fully 90 percent of war deaths. The mounting toll of civilian casualties is evident from data on terrorist attacks (Figure 14.10 on page 376).

The change in the form of collective violence came about for three main reasons (Tilly, 2002). First, decolonization and separatist movements roughly doubled the number of independent states in the world, and many of these new states, especially in Africa and Asia, were too weak to control their territories effectively. Second, especially during the Cold War (1946–91), the United States, the Soviet Union, Cuba, and China often subsidized and sent arms to domestic opponents of regimes that were aligned against them. Third, the expansion of international trade in contraband provided rebels with new means of support. They took advantage of inexpensive international communication and travel to establish support communities abroad and export heroin, cocaine, diamonds, dirty money, and so forth. In sum, the structure of opportunities for engaging in collective violence shifted radically after World War II. As a result, the dominant form of collective violence changed from interstate to societal warfare.

Al-Qaeda

From this perspective, and whatever its individual peculiarities, al-Qaeda is a typical creature of contemporary warfare. It originated in Afghanistan, a notoriously weak and dependent state. The United States supported al-Qaeda's founders militarily in their struggle against the Soviet occupation of Afghanistan in the 1980s. Al-Qaeda organized international heroin, diamond, and money-laundering operations. It established a network of operatives

FIGURE 14.10

Total and Fatal Tourist
Attacks, 1970–2007

Source: LaFree, Gary, Laura
Dugan, and R. Kim Cragin (2010).
"Trends in Global Terrorism",
in J. Joseph Hewitt, Jonathan
Wikenfeld, and Ted Robert Gurr
(eds.). *Peace and Conflict 2010:
Executive Summary*. College Park
(Md.) Center for International
Development and Conflict
Management, University of
Maryland, p. 22.

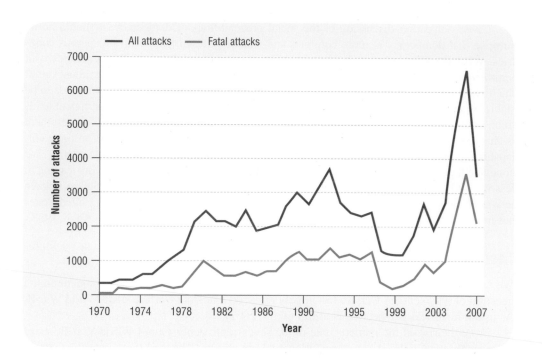

around the world. All of this was made possible by changes in the structure of opportunities for collective violence after World War II.

International terrorists often demand autonomy or independence for some country, population, or region (Pape, 2003). For example, among Al-Qaeda's chief demands are Palestinian statehood and the end of American support for the wealthy regimes in Saudi Arabia, Kuwait, and the Gulf states. Al-Qaeda has turned to terror as a means of achieving these goals because other ways of achieving them are largely closed off. The United States considers support for the oil-rich Arab countries to be in the national interest. It has so far done little to further the cause of Palestinian statehood. Staunch opponents of American policy cannot engage in interstate warfare with the United States because they lack states of their own. At most, they are supported by states that lack the resources to engage in sustained warfare with the United States, including Iran. Because the existing structure of world power closes off other possibilities for achieving political goals, terror emerges as a viable alternative for some people.

Summing Up

- As the modern state started monopolizing the means of coercion in society beginning in the seventeenth century, interstate warfare became the norm, warfare became more deadly, and relatively few civilians died in war. When many weak states emerged after World War II, civil wars became the norm and civilian deaths accounted for most war deaths.
- Civil wars proliferate when outside powers get involved in them and rebels take advantage of increased opportunities to engage in illegal trade and establish support communities abroad. Similarly, international terrorism benefits from the combination of weak states, outside support, and new ways of mobilizing resources.

NOTE

1. We say "businessmen" advisedly. Very few women are among Canada's richest people.

SUMMARY

1. What accounts for the level of democracy in a society?
The level of democracy in a society depends on the distribution of power. When power is concentrated in the hands of few people, society is less democratic than it is when it is distributed among many people.

2. What are the major sociological theories of democratic politics?
Pluralists correctly note that democratic politics is about negotiation and compromise. However, they fail to appreciate that economically advantaged groups have more power than disadvantaged groups. *Elite theorists* correctly note that power is concentrated in the hands of advantaged groups. However, they fail to appreciate how variations in the distribution of power influence political behaviour and public policy. *Marxists* correctly argue that the interests of large business are generally off-limits to challenges. However, they understate the degree to which ordinary citizens, including members of the working class, sometimes influence state policy. *Power resource theorists* usefully focus on changes in the distribution of power in society and their effects. However, they fail to appreciate what *state-centred theorists* emphasize—that state institutions and laws also independently affect political behaviour and public policy.

3. What are the social preconditions of democracy?
Citizens win legal protection of rights and freedoms when their middle and working classes become large, organized, and prosperous; and when powerful, friendly, pro-democratic foreign states support them.

4. What does it mean to say that democracy has developed in waves?
During three periods, democracy spread rapidly in the world. Then the spurt of democratization slowed or reversed. The first wave began when more than half the white adult males in the United States became eligible to vote in the 1828 presidential election. By 1926, 33 countries enjoyed at least minimally democratic institutions. However, between 1922 and 1942, fascist, communist, and militaristic movements caused two-thirds of the world's democracies to fall under authoritarian or totalitarian rule. The second wave of democracy began after World War II, when Allied victory returned democracy to many fascist states, and wars of colonial independence led to the formation of a series of new democracies. Military dictatorships then replaced many of the new democracies; a third of the democracies in 1958 were authoritarian regimes by the mid-1970s. The third wave of democracy began in Portugal in 1974. It had slowed and in some cases reversed by the end of the twentieth century.

5. What is the difference between formal and liberal democracy and why is the distinction important for understanding the third wave of democratization?
Many new democracies that emerged from the most recent wave of democratization are formal, not liberal democracies. Their citizens enjoy regular, competitive elections (the formal side of democracy) but lack legal protection of rights and freedoms (the liberal side).

6. Does postmaterialist theory require a major rethinking of the way Canadian democracy works?
Postmaterialists think Canada has reached a new and higher stage of democratic development. However, enduring social inequalities prevent even the most advanced democracies from being fully democratic.

7. What are the main causes of war?
The risk of war declines with a country's level of prosperity and its level of democratization.

8. How has the nature of the state affected patterns of warfare?

The rise of the modern state in the seventeenth century led to the monopolization of the means of coercion in society. Once centralized state armies became the major military force in society, interstate warfare became the norm, warfare became more deadly, and relatively few civilians died in war. However, the emergence of many weak states after World War II encouraged the outbreak of societal or civil wars, which are now the norm. Civilian deaths now account for most war deaths. Societal wars gain impetus when hostile outside powers get involved in them and rebels take advantage of increased opportunities to engage in illegal trade and establish support communities abroad. International terrorism has benefited greatly from the combination of weak states, outside support, and new ways of mobilizing resources.

KEY TERMS

authoritarian (p. 356)	**political parties (p. 356)**
authority (p. 353)	**political revolution (p. 355)**
charismatic authority (p. 355)	**postmaterialism (p. 370)**
civil society (p. 355)	**power (p. 353)**
democracy (p. 356)	**power resource theory (p. 360)**
elite theory (p. 357)	**public opinion (p. 356)**
elites (p. 357)	**ruling class (p. 358)**
formal democracy (p. 369)	**social movements (p. 356)**
legal-rational authority (p. 353)	**state (p. 355)**
liberal democracy (p. 369)	**state-centred theory (p. 363)**
lobbies (p. 356)	**totalitarian (p. 356)**
mass media (p. 356)	**traditional authority (p. 353)**
pluralist theory (p. 357)	**war (p. 372)**

WEB RESOURCES

Companion Website for This Book

http://www.compass4e.nelson.com

Begin by clicking on the Student Resources section of the website. Next, select the chapter you are studying from the pull-down menu. From the Student Resources page you have easy access to additional Weblinks and other resources. The website also has many useful tips to aid you in your study of sociology, including practice tests for each chapter.

InfoTrac® Search Terms

These search terms are provided to assist you in beginning to conduct research on this topic by visiting http://www.infotrac-college.com:

civil society
legitimacy
political party
ruling class
voting

CHAPTER 15

Families

IN THIS CHAPTER, YOU WILL LEARN THAT

- The traditional "nuclear" family is less common than it used to be. Several new family forms are becoming more prevalent. The frequency of one family form or another varies by class, ethnicity, sexual orientation, and region of the country.

- One of the most important forces underlying the change from the traditional nuclear family is the entry of most women into the paid labour force. Doing paid work increases women's ability to leave unhappy marriages and control whether and when they will have children.

- Marital satisfaction increases as we move up the class structure, in places where divorce laws are liberal, when teenage children leave the home, in families where partners share housework equally, and among spouses who enjoy a satisfying sex life.

- The worst effects of divorce on children can be eliminated if there is no parental conflict and the children's standard of living does not fall after divorce.

- The decline of the traditional nuclear family is sometimes associated with a host of social problems, such as poverty, welfare dependency, and crime. However, some countries have adopted policies that reduce these problems.

IS "THE FAMILY" IN DECLINE?

Social-structural arrangements are "tight" to the degree they demand conformity to norms. Lance Roberts grew up in a structurally tight, middle-class, suburban family and neighbourhood in Edmonton in the 1950s that bears little resemblance to most families today.

"By the standards of the time, everything in my neighbourhood appeared normal. The streets were filled with new thousand-square-foot bungalows. All the houses were built by a single developer, following one of six standardized floor plans. When you entered a friend's house you could tell it was a replica of yours, or some other friend's. Every yard was fenced, almost all in one of three conventional styles. Building variation was evident only in the garages. Most were the single-car variety, built of second-hand materials by neighbourhood fathers. Their varying degrees of design knowledge and construction technique mostly accounted for differential results. The one major exception was 'the Doctor' (whose title was always expressed with deference, and who was actually a veterinarian). His double-car garage was built, as my father pointed out, 'by professionals.'

ShutterStock/Losevsky Pavel

"Many of the fathers in the neighbourhood, including my father, worked at the nearby Imperial Oil refinery. The only exceptions were 'the Doctor' and an immigrant from Holland—'the Dutchman.' He delivered bread in a van and always honked his horn three times when he finished his deliveries mid-afternoon. That was the full extent of deviance I can recall.

"Almost every family had two children. The exception was the Dutchman, who had five children. Every student in the neighbourhood attended the same local public schools, where, for as many years as anyone could remember, the same teachers taught the same subjects to the same grades. My parents never missed a parent–teacher interview, and it seemed nobody else's did either.

"Not surprisingly, I took the conformity pervading my childhood for granted. However, in my final year of elementary school, two cracks appeared in my social life. First, during a Christmas holiday a new kid who had moved into the neighbourhood disappeared with his family. When he returned in January, he told stories of his holiday in an exotic place called Hawaii. I repeated his stories about this tropical paradise at dinner and asked why our family didn't go there. I was told that our family couldn't afford such luxury and, then, with a dismissive tone, my father added that my friend's father 'let the mother work.' As I lay in bed that evening I remember thinking, 'Mothers can work? And this leads to Hawaii?'

"The second crack in the facade of normality opened up during a school civics project on the importance of voting. While having an after-school snack I asked my mother if she voted in the last election. She replied, 'Yes, of course; it's our civic responsibility.' I then inquired how she voted. She replied, 'The same as your father.' 'Why the same as dad?' I asked. The logic of my mother's reply astounded me: 'Because if I voted any differently, I would cancel out his vote.' Try as I might I could not rationalize that ballots should be cast to avoid 'cancelling out' a spouse's vote.

"These childhood revelations about the possibility of mothers working and spousal voting independence were the thin edge of a wedge that eventually shattered my structurally tight understanding of families. In the course of a generation, the world of Canadian families changed from structurally tight to structurally loose. Social expectations about family life shifted from impositions that required conformity to suggestions that required interpretation. Recent changes in Canadian families have been so extensive that my adult children find reports of my childhood family's rigid structure as remote from their experience as I found my friend's report on Hawaii."

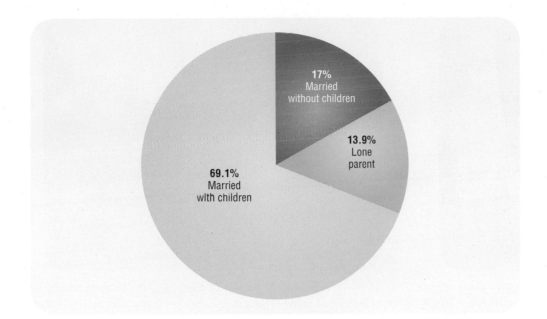

FIGURE 15.1
Family Types, 1901

Source: Canadian Families Project, 1999.

17%
Married without children

13.9%
Lone parent

69.1%
Married with children

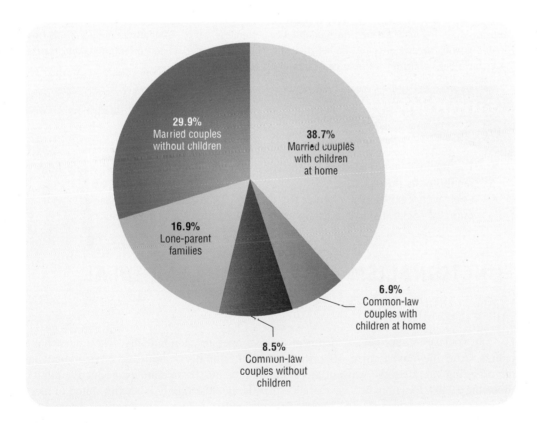

FIGURE 15.2
Family Types, 2006

Source: Statistics Canada, 2007, "Number of Children at Home (8) and Census Family Structure (7) for the Census Families in Private Households of Canada, Provinces, Territories, Census Metropolitan Areas and Census Agglomerations, 2001 and 2006 Censuses—20% Sample Data." Retrieved February 10, 2011 (http://www12.statcan.ca/english/census06/data/topics/RetrieveProductTable.cfm?ALEVEL=3&APATH=3&CATNO=&DETAIL=1&DIM=&DS=99&FL=0&FREE=0&GAL=0&GC=99&GK=NA&GRP=1&IPS=&METH=0&ORDER=1&PID=89016&PTYPF=88971&RL=0&S=1&ShowAll=No&StartRow=1&SUB=683&Temporal=2006&Theme=68&VID=0&VNAMFE=&VNAMCE=).

29.9%
Married couples without children

38.7%
Married couples with children at home

16.9%
Lone-parent families

6.9%
Common-law couples with children at home

8.5%
Common-law couples without children

Once these conditions changed, the nuclear family became less prevalent and a variety of new family forms spread. We discuss how these new family forms are structured and how their frequency varies by class, ethnicity, sexual orientation, and region. Although new family forms solve some problems, they are hardly an unqualified blessing. The chapter's concluding section therefore considers the kinds of policies that might help alleviate some of the most serious concerns faced by families today.

Father Knows Best was one of the most popular TV sitcoms of the 1950s. It portrayed a smoothly functioning, happy, white, middle-class, mother-homemaker, father-breadwinner family. *Modern Family* reached the TV screen in 2009. Jay, a white Anglo-Saxon man in his 60s, is divorced and married to Gloria, who is Colombian, divorced, in her 30s, and has a young son from her first marriage (Manny). Jay has two adult children—Claire (married with three children) and Mitchell (who, together his male partner, have adopted a Vietnamese baby). Comparing family sitcoms from the 1950s with today's sitcoms, we see that age, ethnicity, race, sexual orientation, and marital status have been transformed from constants into variables.

Summing Up

- The nuclear family used to be the most prevalent family form, but many new family forms now exist.
- Controversy exists over whether the decline of the nuclear family causes a wide range of social ills or is a useful adaptation to new social pressures.

FUNCTIONALISM AND THE NUCLEAR IDEAL

Functional Theory

For any society to survive, its members must cooperate economically. They must have babies. And they must raise offspring in an emotionally supportive environment so the offspring can learn the ways of the group and eventually operate as productive adults. Since the 1940s, functionalists have argued that the nuclear family is ideally suited to meet these challenges. In their view, the nuclear family performs five main functions: it provides a basis for regulated sexual activity, economic cooperation, reproduction, socialization, and emotional support (Murdock, 1949: 1–22; Parsons, 1955).

Functionalists cite the pervasiveness of the nuclear family as evidence of its ability to perform these functions. They acknowledge that other family forms exist. **Polygamy** expands the nuclear unit "horizontally" by adding one or more spouses (almost always wives) to the household. Polygamy is still legally permitted in many less industrialized countries of Africa and Asia. However, the overwhelming majority of families are monogamous, because they cannot afford to support several wives and many children. The **extended family** expands the nuclear family "vertically" by adding another generation—one or more of the spouses' parents—to the household. Extended families used to be common throughout the world.

Polygamy expands the nuclear family "horizontally" by adding one or more spouses (usually women) to the household.

The **extended family** expands the nuclear family "vertically" by adding another generation—one or more of the spouses' parents—to the household.

They still are in some places. However, according to the functionalists, the basic building block of the extended family (and of the polygamous family) is the nuclear unit.

George Murdock was a functionalist who conducted a famous study of 250 mainly preliterate, foraging societies (sometimes called "hunting-and-gathering societies") in the 1940s. Murdock wrote, "Either as the sole prevailing form of the family or as the basic unit from which more complex familial forms are compounded, [the nuclear family] exists as a distinct and strongly functional group in every known society" (Murdock, 1949: 2). Moreover, the nuclear family, Murdock continued, is everywhere based on **marriage**. He defined marriage as a socially approved, presumably long-term, sexual and economic union between a man and a woman. It involves rights and obligations between spouses and between spouses and their children.

Does this functionalist account provide an accurate picture of family relations across history? To assess its adequacy, we discuss families in the two settings on which functionalists focused their attention: (1) foraging societies, and (2) middle-class North American families in the 1950s.

Marriage is a socially approved, presumably long-term sexual and economic union between a man and a woman. It involves reciprocal rights and obligations between spouses and between parents and children.

Foraging Societies

Foraging societies are nomadic groups of 100 or fewer people. A gendered division of labour exists among foragers. Most men hunt and most women gather wild, edible plants. Women also do most of the child care. However, research on foragers shows that men often tend babies and children in such societies (Leacock, 1981; Lee, 1979; Turnbull, 1961). After an unsuccessful hunt, they often gather food. In some foraging societies, women hunt. Thus, the gender division of labour is less strict than functionalists assume. Moreover, the gender division of labour is not associated with large differences in power and authority because women produce up to 80 percent of the food. Overall, men have few privileges that women don't also enjoy.

Foragers travel in small camps or bands. The band decides by consensus when to send out groups of hunters. When they return from the hunt, they distribute game to all band members based on need. Hunters do not decide to go hunting based on their nuclear family's needs. Nor do hunters distribute game to only their nuclear family. Contrary to Murdock (1949), it is the band, not the nuclear family, that is the most efficient social organization for providing everyone with valuable food sources.

There is rough gender equality among the !Kung-San, a foraging society in the Kalahari Desert in Botswana. That is partly because women play such a key economic role in providing food.

PeterJohnson/Corbis

In foraging societies, parents consider children an investment in the future. However, foragers do not always want more children for purposes of economic security. In fact, they consider too many children a liability. Subsistence is uncertain in foraging societies, and when band members deplete an area of game and edible plants, they move elsewhere. As a result, band members try to keep the ratio of children to productive adults low.

Life in foraging societies is highly cooperative. Women and men often care for each other's children. In contrast to the functionalists' claim that socialization is the "basic and irreducible" function of the nuclear family, it is the band, not the nuclear family, that assumes responsibility for child socialization in foraging societies. Socialization is more a public than a private matter. As a seventeenth-century Innu man from northern Quebec said to a Jesuit priest who was trying to convince him to adopt European ways of raising children, "Thou hast no sense. You French people love only your own children; but we all love all the children of our tribe" (quoted in Leacock, 1981: 50).

In sum, research on foraging societies calls into question many of the functionalists' generalizations. In foraging societies, relations between the sexes are quite egalitarian. Parents do not view children just as an investment in the future. Each nuclear unit does not execute the important economic and socialization functions in isolation and in private. Cooperative band members execute most economic and socialization functions in public.

Let us now assess the functionalist theory of the family in the light of evidence concerning Canadian middle-class families in the years just after World War II.

The Canadian Middle Class in the 1950s

As a description of family patterns in the 15 years after World War II, functionalism has some merit. During the Great Depression (1929–39) and World War II (1939–45), Canadians were forced to postpone marriage (if they married at all) because of widespread poverty, government-imposed austerity, and physical separation. After this long and dreadful ordeal, many Canadians just wanted to settle down, have children, and enjoy the peace, pleasure, and security that family life seemed to offer. Conditions could not have been better for doing just that. The immediate postwar era was one of unparalleled optimism and prosperity. Real per capita income rose, as did the percentage of Canadians who owned their own homes. By the mid-1950s, employment and personal income reached all-time highs. Various services and legislative amendments created during World War II to encourage wives and mothers to join the labour force were rescinded. The expectation was that a return to "normal" meant the resumption of the men's provider and women's housewife roles (Kingsbury and Scanzoni, 1993).

Mimi Matte's *Family Outing* (1998): In the 1950s, married women often hid their frustrations with family life.

Courtesy of the artist and Bau-Xi Gallery, Toronto ON, Canada

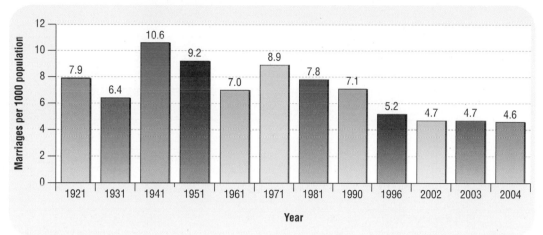

FIGURE 15.3

Marriage Rates,
1921–2004

Source: Adapted from Statistics
Canada, "Selected marriage
statistics, 1921–1990—Diskette,"
Catalogue 82-552, October 1,
1992, CANSIM, and *The Daily*,
Catalogue 11-001, Thursday,
January 29, 1998, available at
http://www.statcan.ca/Daily/
English/980129/d980129.
htm#ART1, and Tuesday,
December 21, 2004, available at
http://www.statcan.ca/Daily/
English/041221/d04122d.htm.

These conditions resulted in a "marriage boom" in Canada (see Figure 15.3). Increasingly, Canadians lived in married-couple families. The proportion of "never married" Canadians decreased and the average age at first marriage dropped between 1941 and 1956 from 24.4 to 23.4 years for brides, and from 27.6 to 26.1 years for bridegrooms (McVey and Kalbach, 1995: 225; see Figure 15.4). A second result was a baby boom. During this period, Canadian families averaged four children—resulting in proportionally more baby boomers than in the United States, Australia, and New Zealand (Nikiforuk, 1999). And unlike the situation today, married men were much more likely than married women were to be working for pay. For example, in 1951, 90 percent of married men but only 11.2 percent of married women were in the paid labour force.

Not all women, of course, could afford to stay out of the workforce. Poor women have often worked both inside and outside the home. However, middle-class women engaged in what has been called an "orgy of domesticity" in the postwar years, devoting increasing attention to child rearing and housework. They also became increasingly concerned with the emotional quality of family life as love and companionship became firmly established as the main motivation for marriage (Coontz, 1992: 23–41; Skolnick, 1991: 49–74).

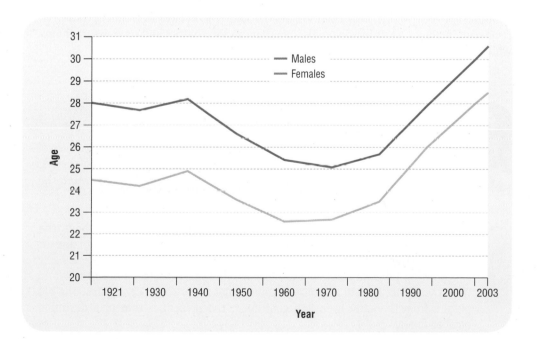

FIGURE 15.4

Average Age at First
Marriage

Sources: Adapted from Statistics
Canada, "Marriage and Conjugal
Life in Canada, 1991," Catalogue
91-534, April 23, 1992; and *The
Daily*, Catalogue 11-001, Monday,
June 2, 2003. Retrieved July 1,
2004 (http://www.statcan.ca/Daily/
English/030602/d030602a.htm).

FIGURE 15.5

Total Fertility Rate, Canada,
1950–2008

Source: United Nations Statistical
Division Common Database (http://
data.worldbank.org/indicator/
SP.DYN.TFRT.IN).

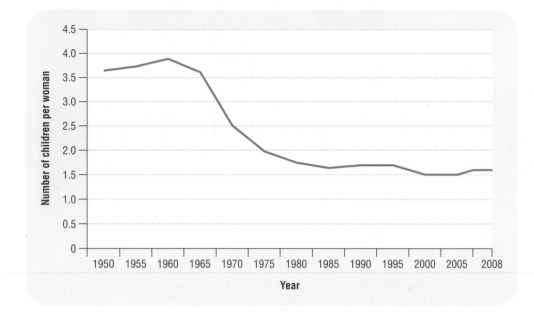

The **marriage rate** is the number
of marriages that occur in a year
for every 1000 people in the
population.

The **divorce rate** is the number
of divorces that occur in a year
for every 1000 people in the
population.

The postwar situation the functionalists described was in many respects a historical aberration (Cherlin, 1992: 6–30). Trends in divorce, marriage, and childbearing show a gradual *weakening* of the nuclear family from the early twentieth century until the end of World War II, and the resumption of a weakening trend beginning in the 1960s. The **marriage rate** (the number of marriages that occur in a year for every 1000 people in the population) peaked at 10.9 marriages in 1942 and 1946 and then started to fall. The **divorce rate** (the number of divorces that occur in a year for every 1000 people in the population) started to increase in the 1960s with the introduction of more liberal divorce laws. The average number of children per woman peaked in 1961 and then dropped (see Figure 15.5 above). The early functionalists, it seems, generalized too hastily from the families they knew best—their own. By the early 1960s, the earlier trends in Canada had reasserted themselves. The big picture from the beginning of the twentieth century until the present is that of a gradually weakening nuclear family.

Functionalists missed the big picture largely because they ignored the degree to which (1) the traditional nuclear family is based on gender inequality and (2) changes in power relations between women and men have altered family structures in recent decades. These issues are the chief focus of sociologists working in the conflict and feminist traditions, to which we now turn.

Summing Up

- Functionalists believe that the nuclear family is ideally suited to promoting the necessary social functions of sexual regulation, economic cooperation, reproduction, socialization, and emotional support.
- Evidence from foraging societies questions functionalist beliefs about the importance of gender inequality, investment in children, and the private pursuit of socialization and economic functions.
- The growing predominance of the nuclear family in the immediate post–World War II years occurred in response to an unusual set of social conditions. The big picture from the early twentieth century to the present is that of a declining nuclear family.

CONFLICT AND FEMINIST THEORIES

The idea that power relations between women and men explain the prevalence of different family forms was first suggested by Marx's close friend and coauthor, Friedrich Engels. Engels argued that the traditional nuclear family emerged along with inequalities of wealth. For once wealth was concentrated in the hands of a man, wrote Engels, he became concerned about how to transmit it to his children, particularly his sons. Engels asked, How could a man safely pass on an inheritance? Only by controlling his wife sexually and economically. Economic control ensured that the man's property would not be squandered and would remain his and his alone. Sexual control, in the form of enforced female monogamy, ensured that his property would be transmitted only to *his* offspring. Engels concluded that only the elimination of private property and the creation of economic equality—in a word, communism—could bring an end to gender inequality and the traditional nuclear family (Engels, 1970 [1884]: 138–9).

Engels was right to note the long history of male economic and sexual domination in the traditional nuclear family. Early Canadian law was informed by a vision of the family in which the wife's labour belonged to her husband. Although a series of legal reforms have altered the situation, as recently as the mid-twentieth century, a wife could not rent a car, take a loan, or sign a contract without her husband's permission.

However, Engels was wrong to think that communism would eliminate gender inequality in the family. Gender inequality has been as common in societies that call themselves communist as in those that call themselves capitalist. For example, the Soviet Union left "intact the fundamental family structures, authority relations, and socialization patterns crucial to personality formation and sex-role differentiation. Only a genuine sexual revolution [or, as we prefer to call it, a *gender revolution*] could have shattered these patterns and made possible the real emancipation of women" (Lapidus, 1978: 7).

Because gender inequality exists in non-capitalist (including pre-capitalist) societies, most feminists believe something other than, or in addition to, capitalism accounts for gender inequality and the persistence of the traditional nuclear family. In their view, *patriarchy*—male dominance and norms justifying that dominance—is more deeply rooted in the economic, military, and cultural history of humankind than the classical Marxist account allows. For them, only a genuine gender revolution can alter this state of affairs.

Just such a revolution in family structures, authority relations, and socialization patterns gained force in Canada and other rich industrialized countries about 60 years ago, although its roots extend back to the eighteenth century. As you will now see, the revolution is evident in the rise of romantic love and happiness as bases for marriage, the rising divorce rate, women's increasing control over reproduction through their use of contraceptives, and women's increasing participation in the system of higher education and the paid labour force, among other factors. We begin by considering the sociology of mate selection.

Summing Up

- Conflict theorists see the proliferation of non-nuclear families as a response to changes in power relations between women and men.

POWER AND FAMILIES

Love and Mate Selection

The first line of the theme song of the TV sitcom *Love and Marriage* repeats a line that most North Americans take for granted: "Love and marriage go together like a horse and carriage" (see Figure 15.6 on page 390). In contrast, most of us view marriage devoid of

FIGURE 15.6

The Components of Love

According to psychologist Robert Sternberg, love can be built from three components: passion (erotic attraction), intimacy (confiding in others and shared feelings), and commitment (intention to remain in the relationship). In actual relationships, these components may be combined in various ways to produce different kinds of love. The fullest love requires all three components. Research shows that, in long-term relationships, passion peaks fairly quickly and then tapers off. Intimacy rises more gradually but remains at a higher plateau. Commitment develops most gradually but also plateaus at a high level.

Source: Sternberg, 1986.

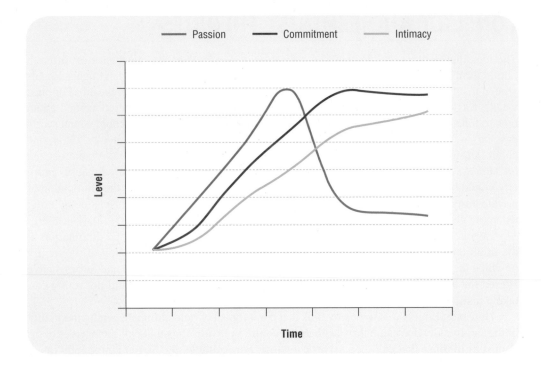

love as tragic. Yet in most societies throughout human history, love had little to do with marriage. Third parties, not brides and grooms, typically arranged marriages. The selection of marriage partners was based mainly on calculations intended to maximize their families' prestige, economic benefits, and political advantages.

The idea that love should be important in the choice of a marriage partner first gained currency in eighteenth-century England with the rise of liberalism and individualism, philosophies that stressed freedom of the individual over community welfare (Stone, 1977). However, the intimate linkage between love and marriage that we know today emerged only in the early twentieth century, when Hollywood and the advertising industry began to promote self-gratification on a grand scale. For these new spinners of fantasy and desire, an important aspect of self-gratification was heterosexual romance leading to marriage (Rapp and Ross, 1986).

Clark Gable and Vivien Leigh in *Gone with the Wind* (1939): Hollywood glamorized heterosexual, romantic love and solidified the intimate linkage between love and marriage that we know today.

The Everett Collection/CP Picture Archive

Consider, for example, the results of a study that asked 497 male and 673 female university undergraduates in 10 countries and Hong Kong the following question: "If a man (woman) had all the qualities you desired, would you marry this person if you were not in love with him (her)?" The results (presented in Figure 15.7) suggest that in free-choice cultures, where the value of individualism is highly prized, love has come to be defined as *the* essential basis for marriage. In the United States, a country often considered to be the most individualistic society in the world, only 4 percent of the students said they would marry someone whom they were not in love with—even if that person possessed all the qualities they were looking for in a partner (Levine, Sato, Hashimoto, and Verma, 1995).

Social Influences on Mate Selection

The big change in mate selection in the twenty-first century is taking place online. The first online dating service started up around 1996. According to a survey of 24 000 people in 18 countries, just 7 percent of Internet users visited online dating sites in 1997. By 2009, that figure rose to 30 percent. Amazingly, 15 percent of Internet users in 2009 reported that they had found their current partner on the Web. Social networking sites, such as Facebook, are gaining in popularity over dedicated online dating sites as places to meet partners (Brym and Lenton, 2001; "More People," 2011).

Although online dating increases the number and range of potential mates to which people have access, social forces continue to influence mate selection. Some dating sites cater to Christians. Others cater to Muslims, Jews, Blacks, Hispanics, Asians, Russians, gays, white women and black men, vegetarians, environmentalists, students, and even animal lovers, country music enthusiasts, and female prison inmates ("100 Best," 2011). People fall in love, but they still tend to do so within clearly defined social boundaries.

Specifically, three sets of social forces influence whom you are likely to fall in love with and marry (Kalmijn, 1998: 398–404).

First, potential spouses bring *resources* to the "marriage market" that they use to attract mates and compete against rivals. These resources include financial assets, status, values, tastes, and knowledge. Most people want to maximize the financial assets and status they gain from marriage, and they want a mate who has similar values, tastes, and knowledge. Consequently, the assets you bring to the marriage market influence whom you marry.

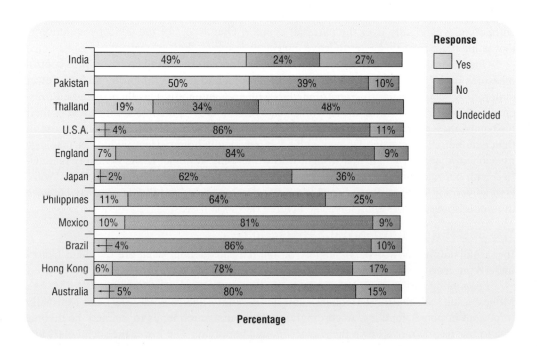

Percentage

FIGURE 15.7

Responses to Question: "If a man (woman) had all the other quantities you desired, would you marry this person if you were not in love with him (her)?"

Note: Some percentages do not add to 100 percent because of rounding.

Source: From Robert Levine, Suguru Sato, Tsukasa Hashimoto, and Jyoti Verma, "Love and Marriage in Eleven Cultures," *Journal of Cross-Cultural Psychology* 26, 5(1995): 554–71. Reprinted by permission of Sage Publications.

Second, because marriage between people from different groups may threaten the cohesion of one or both groups, *third parties* often intervene to prevent marriages outside the group. Families, neighbourhoods, communities, and religious institutions raise young people to identify with the groups they are members of and think of themselves as different from members of other groups. They also apply sanctions to young people who threaten to marry outside the group. Ethnic intermarriage is becoming increasingly common in Canada, but especially among recent immigrants it is comparatively rare (Dugger, 1996; Kalbach, 2000; Kitano and Daniels, 1995).

The third set of sociological factors that influence whom you are likely to fall in love with and marry has to with *demographic* variables. The chance of marrying inside your group increases with the group's size and geographical concentration. If you are a member of a small group or a group that is dispersed geographically, you stand a greater chance of having to choose an appropriate mate from outside your group. There may simply be too few "prospects" in your group from which to choose (Brym, Gillespie, and Gillis, 1985). In addition, the ratio of men to women in a group influences the degree to which members of each sex marry inside or outside the group. For instance, war and imprisonment may eliminate many male group members as potential marriage partners. This may encourage female group members to marry outside the group or forgo marriage altogether. Finally, because people usually meet potential spouses in "local marriage markets"—schools, universities and colleges, places of work, neighbourhoods, bars, and clubs—the degree to which these settings are socially segregated influences mate selection. You are more likely to marry outside your group if local marriage markets are socially heterogeneous.

As a result of the operation of these three sets of social forces, the process of falling in love and choosing a mate is far from random. People tend to marry within racial, ethnic, religious, and educational categories (Kalmijn, 1998: 406–8). We are freer than ever before to fall in love with and marry anyone we want, and the Internet increases our freedom in that regard. As in all things, however, social forces still constrain our choices to varying degrees.

Marital Satisfaction

Just as mate selection came to depend more on romantic love over the years, so marital stability came to depend more on having a happy rather than merely a useful marriage. This change has occurred because women in Canada and many other societies have become more autonomous, especially over the past half century. One aspect of the gender revolution is that women are freer than ever to leave marriages in which they are unhappy.

One factor that contributed to women's autonomy was the legalization of birth control measures in the 1960s, which made it easier for women to delay childbirth and have fewer children. A second factor that contributed to women's autonomy was their increased presence in the paid labour force. Once women enjoyed a source of income independent of their husbands, they gained the means to decide the course of their own lives to a greater extent than ever before. A married woman with a job outside the home is less tied to her marriage by economic necessity than is a woman who works only at home. If she is deeply dissatisfied with her marriage, she can more easily leave. In addition, beginning in the late 1960s, laws governing divorce were changed to make divorce easier and divide property between divorcing spouses more equitably. The divorce rate soon rose.

The Social Roots of Marital Satisfaction

If marital stability now depends largely on marital satisfaction, what are the main factors underlying marital satisfaction?

Economic factors certainly loom large (Collins and Coltrane, 1991: 394–406; 454–64). Money issues are the most frequent subjects of family quarrels, and they are especially important in poorer families. Accordingly, marital satisfaction tends to fall and the divorce rate to rise as you move down the socioeconomic hierarchy. The lower the social class and the lower the educational level of the spouses, the more likely it is that financial pressures will make them unhappy and the marriage unstable. In contrast, the marital satisfaction of both husbands and wives generally increases when wives enter the paid labour force, mainly because of the beneficial financial effects. However, if either spouse spends so much time on the job that he or she neglects the family, marital satisfaction falls.

Divorce laws also influence marital satisfaction. On average, married people are happier than unmarried people are. Moreover, when people are free to end unhappy marriages and remarry, the average level of happiness increases among married people. Thus, the level of marital happiness has increased in Canada over the past few decades, especially for wives, partly because it has become easier to get a divorce. For the same reason, in countries where getting a divorce is more difficult (e.g., Italy and Spain), husbands and wives tend to be less happy than in countries where getting a divorce is easier (e.g., the United States and Canada; Stack and Eshleman, 1998).

Another influence on marital satisfaction is *the family life cycle*. In Canada, the divorce rate peaks at year five of marriage and then falls (Ambert, 1998: 5). For marriages that last longer, marital satisfaction reaches a low point after about 15 to 20 years. Marital satisfaction generally starts high, falls when children are born, reaches a low point when children are in their teenage years, and rises again when children reach adulthood (Glenn, 1990; Rollins and Cannon, 1974). Nonparents and parents whose children have left home ("empty nesters") enjoy the highest level of marital satisfaction. Parents who are just starting families or who have adult children living at home enjoy intermediate levels of marital satisfaction. Marital satisfaction is lowest during the "establishment" years, when children are attending school (Keller, 2000). Although most people get married at least partly to have children, it turns out that children, and especially teenagers, usually put big emotional and financial strains on families. Such strain results in relatively low marital satisfaction.

Marital happiness depends on the *division of labour in the household* too. Couples who share housework and child care equally are happier than those who don't. The less equally couples share domestic responsibilities, the more tension there is among all family members (Hochschild with Machung, 1989; Risman and Johnson-Sumerford, 1998). Equitable sharing tends to increase with education (Greenstein, 1996).

Finally, couples who enjoy good *sexual relations* are happier than those who don't. Some experts argue that general marital happiness leads to sexual compatibility, but the reverse may also be true. Good sex may lead to a good marriage. After all, sexual preferences are deeply rooted in our psyches and our earliest experiences. They can't easily be changed to suit the wishes of our partners. If spouses are sexually incompatible, they may find it hard to change, even if they communicate well, argue little, and are generally happy on other grounds. On the other hand, if a husband and wife are sexually compatible, they may work hard to resolve other problems in the marriage for the sake of preserving their good sex life. Thus, the relationship between marital satisfaction and sexual compatibility is probably reciprocal. Each factor influences the other.

Religion has little effect on level of marital satisfaction. However, religion does influence the divorce rate. Thus, American states with a high percentage of regular churchgoers and a high percentage of fundamentalists have lower divorce rates than other states do (Sweezy and Tiefenthaler, 1996).

Let us now see what happens when low marital satisfaction leads to divorce.

Divorce

Before 1968, divorce was a complex legal process, and it was rare. Adultery was the only grounds for divorce in Canada, except in Nova Scotia, where cruelty was sufficient grounds even before Confederation (Morrison, 1987). The Divorce Act of 1968 expanded the grounds for granting a divorce to include mental or physical cruelty, rape, gross addiction to alcohol or other drugs, sodomy, bestiality, and homosexual acts. The dissolution of a marriage was also permitted on grounds of unspecified "marital breakdown" if couples lived apart for a number of years. The 1985 amendment of Canada's Divorce Act specified only one ground for divorce—marital breakdown, defined in three ways: (1) the spouses lived apart for one year, (2) one of the spouses committed adultery, or (3) one spouse treated the other with mental or physical cruelty. Today, a spouse seeking divorce no longer has to prove grounds. Instead, a marriage is legally dissolved if the relationship is "irretrievably broken." Following these amendments, the divorce rate reached a historic high in 1987 and has since declined. About 38 percent of Canadian marriages now end in divorce.

Economic Effects

Women's income usually declines after divorce, while men's generally rises (Finnie, 1993). This result occurs because husbands tend to earn more than wives do, children typically live with their mothers after divorce, and child-support payments are often inadequate. Although child poverty in Canada is not restricted to single-parent families, a far higher proportion of children of single parents and, in particular, lone-parent mothers live in low-income circumstances (see Figure 15.8).

In the past, Canadian laws regarding the division of marital assets on divorce and the awarding of alimony contributed to women's declining living standards post-divorce. For example, in the early 1970s, Irene Murdock, a farm wife, claimed that her labours over the course of 15 years had earned her a share in the family farm. However, the Supreme Court of Canada ruled that her work was simply that of an "ordinary farm wife" and did not entitle her to share in the property that she and her husband had accumulated during their marriage (Steel, 1987: 159).

Although all Canadian provinces and territories have laws requiring spouses to share assets in the event of marital breakdown, the precise definition of what constitutes a "family asset" varies and creates inconsistencies across jurisdictions (Dranoff, 2001: 257). In addition, although the monetary value of tangible "family assets," such as money in the bank or a house, can be calculated and shared, the valuable "new property" in today's society is the earning power of a professional degree, highly paid employment, work experience, a skilled trade, or other human capital (Glendon, 1981). On divorce, the wife *may* get an equal share

---

FIGURE 15.8

Incidence (Percentage) Living with Low Income among Canadian Families, 1994–2008

Note: Elderly families are those with heads 65 years of age or older. Couples without children, two-parent, and lone-parent families are under age 65.

Source: Adapted from Statistics Canada, "Income in Canada," 2003, Catalogue 75-202. Retrieved May 12, 2005 (http://www.statcan.ca/english/freepub/75-202-XIE/75-202-XIE2003000.pdf). and CANSIM Table 202-0802.

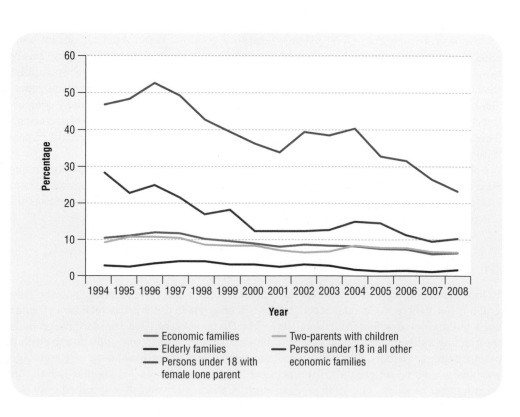

of tangible property, but that does not usually result in her beginning post-divorce life on an equal footing with her former husband—especially if she retains physical custody of the couple's children and if she sacrificed her education and career so he could earn a college or university degree.

Child support is money paid by the non-custodial parent to the custodial parent for the purpose of supporting the children of a separated marital, cohabiting, or sexual relationship. Under the Divorce Act, either parent may be ordered to pay child support. However, because mothers retain custody in most cases—and because women are more likely to be economically disadvantaged in employment—the vast majority of those ordered to pay child support are fathers.

Every jurisdiction in Canada requires parents to support their children following separation or divorce. However, court orders do not guarantee that child support will be paid. In practice, default rates have been high, and orders for child and spousal support have often been difficult to enforce. All Canadian provinces and territories now have programs to protect against non-payment of child support. Nonetheless, the problem of "deadbeat parents" remains significant (Families against Deadbeats, 2000).

Some analysts argue that the principal reason for nonpayment of child support is the unemployment or underemployment of the non-custodial parent. From this point of view, creating jobs, not withholding wages, is the solution to insufficient child support (Braver, Fitzpatrick, and Bay, 1991: 184–85; Meyer and Bartfield, 1996). Others recommend that Canada adopt the model of guaranteed child support used in France and Sweden. In these countries, the government gives the custodial parent the full amount awarded in child support, and assumes responsibility for collecting the money from the assigned parent (Salt, 1991).

> **Child support** involves money paid by the non-custodial parent to the custodial parent for the purpose of supporting the children of a separated marital, cohabiting, or sexual relationship.

Emotional Effects

Although divorce enables spouses to leave unhappy marriages, serious questions have been raised about the emotional consequences of divorce for children, particularly in the long term. Some scholars claim that divorcing parents are trading the well-being of their children for their own happiness. What does research say about this issue?

Some research shows that divorce tends to have long-term, negative behavioural consequences for children, including juvenile delinquency and drug and alcohol abuse (Wallerstein and Blakeslee, 1989; Wallerstein, Lewis, and Blakeslee, 2000). However, most of this research is based on families who seek psychological counselling. Such families are a small and unrepresentative minority of the population. By definition, they have more serious emotional problems than the large majority, which does not need psychological counselling after divorce. One must be careful not to generalize from such studies. Another problem with much of this research is that some analysts fail to ask whether factors other than divorce might be responsible for the long-term distress experienced by many children of divorced parents.

Researchers who rely on representative samples and examine the separate effects of many factors on children's well-being show that on average the overall effect of divorce on children's well-being is not strong and is declining over time (Amato and Keith, 1991). Much of the distress that children of divorce experience is caused by parental conflict. Divorce without parental conflict does children much less harm. In fact, children in divorced families have a higher level of well-being on average than do children in high-conflict intact families.

Most children in divorced families experience a decline in living standards, and that also affects their well-being negatively. So does losing contact with one parent as a role model, source of emotional support, practical help, and supervision. Note, however, that many of the behavioural and adjustment problems experienced by children of divorce existed before the divorce took place. We cannot therefore attribute them to the divorce itself (Cherlin et al., 1991; Furstenberg and Cherlin, 1991; Stewart et al., 1997). Thus, claiming that divorcing parents trade the well-being of their children for their own happiness is an exaggeration.

SuperStock

A high level of parental conflict creates long-term distress among children. Divorce without parental conflict does children much less harm. Children in divorced families have a higher level of well-being on average than do children in high-conflict, intact families.

Reproductive Choice

We have seen that the power women gained from working in the paid labour force put them in a position to leave a marriage if it made them deeply unhappy. Another aspect of the gender revolution women are experiencing is that they are increasingly able to decide what happens in the marriage if they stay. For example, women now have more say over whether they will have children and, if so, when they will have them and how many they will have.

Children are increasingly expensive to raise. They no longer give the family economic benefits, as they did, say, on the family farm. Most women want to work in the paid labour force, many of them to pursue a career. Consequently, most women decide to have fewer children, to have them further apart, and to have them starting at an older age. Some decide to have none at all (Dalphonse, 1997).

A woman's decision not to have children may be carried out by means of contraception or abortion. Abortion was declared a criminal offence in Canada in 1892. In the 1960s, an abortion reform movement spearheaded by Dr. Henry Morgentaler urged the repeal of abortion laws that, in his words, "compelled the unwilling to bear the unwanted" (in Dranoff, 2001: 16). In 1969 the law was changed to permit "therapeutic abortion" if performed by a physician in an accredited hospital and if a three-member committee certified that the continuation of the pregnancy would likely endanger the health of the mother. In 1988, the Supreme Court of Canada struck down the law on abortion on the grounds that it contravened a woman's right to control her own reproductive life and, as such, contravened her constitutionally protected guarantee to security of her person. In 1989, the Supreme Court unanimously determined that the civil law in Quebec, the Quebec Charter, and the common law do not protect fetal life or interests. In 1993, the Supreme Court of Canada struck down legislation that banned abortion clinics. By 1995, abortion clinics outside hospitals operated throughout Canada, with the exception of Prince Edward Island and the territories.

In 2006, 91 377 Canadian women obtained abortions (Statistics Canada, 2010j). On a global scale, the abortion rate in Canada is low at about 15 per thousand women between ages 15 and 44. The comparable rate is 21 in the United States and 54 in Russia (United Nations, 2008).

Attitudes toward abortion are mixed. A 2006 survey showed that 31 percent of Canadians believe that the life of a fetus should be protected at conception, 33 percent believe it should be protected at some point during pregnancy, and 30 percent believe that legal protection should start at birth. Since 2002, the proportion of Canadians believing that legal protection of the fetus should start at conception fell by 6 percent (Robinson, 2006). Abortion attitudes vary by age, with teens more likely than adults to approve of the availability of legal abortion for any reason (55 versus 43 percent, respectively; Bibby, 2001: 250–51). Ninety percent of adults and 84 percent of teens support the availability of legal abortion when rape is involved.

Right-to-life versus pro-choice activists have been clashing since the 1970s. Right-to-life activists object to the decriminalization of abortion; pro-choice activists want the current situation preserved. Both groups have tried to influence public opinion and lawmakers to achieve their aims. A few extreme right-to-life activists (almost all men) have resorted to violence (Gegax and Clemetson, 1998).

What are your views on abortion? Do you think your opinions are influenced by your social characteristics (income, education, occupation, religiosity, etc.)? In thinking about this issue, you will find it useful to know that right-to-life activists tend to be homemakers living in religious, middle-income families. They argue that life begins at conception. Therefore, they say, abortion destroys human life and is morally indefensible. They advocate adoption instead of abortion. In their opinion, the pro-choice option is selfish, expressing greater concern for career advancement and sexual pleasure than for moral responsibility (Erwin, 1988).

In contrast, pro-choice activists tend to be women pursuing their own careers. They are more highly educated, less religious, and better off financially than right-to-life activists are.

They argue that every woman has the right to choose what happens to her own body and that bearing an unwanted child can harm not only a woman's career but the child, too. For example, unwanted children are more likely to be neglected or abused. They are also more likely to get in trouble with the law because of inadequate adult supervision and discipline. Furthermore, according to pro-choice activists, religious doctrines claiming that life begins at conception are arbitrary. So, what is your view? And to what degree is it influenced by your social characteristics?

Sociologists Randall Collins and Scott Coltrane (1991) argue that a repeal of abortion laws would likely return us to the situation that existed in the 1960s. Many abortions took place then, but because they were illegal, they were expensive, hard to obtain, and posed more dangers to women's health. If abortion laws were repealed, they predict that poor women and their unwanted children would suffer most. Taxpayers would wind up paying bigger bills for welfare and medical care.

Reproductive Technologies

For most women, exercising reproductive choice means being able to prevent pregnancy and birth by means of contraception and abortion. For some women, however, it means *facilitating* pregnancy and birth by means of reproductive technologies. Some couples are infertile. With a declining number of desirable children available for adoption, and a persistent and strong desire by most people to have children, demand is strong for techniques to help infertile couples, some homosexual couples, and some single women have babies.

Reproductive technologies are used in four main ways. In *artificial insemination*, a donor's sperm is inserted in a woman's vaginal canal or uterus during ovulation. In *surrogate motherhood*, a donor's sperm is used to artificially inseminate a woman who has signed a contract to surrender the child at birth in exchange for a fee. In *in vitro fertilization*, eggs are surgically removed from a woman and joined with sperm in a culture dish, and an embryo is then transferred back to the woman's uterus. Finally, various *screening techniques* are used on sperm and fetuses to increase the chance of giving birth to a baby of the desired sex and to end pregnancies deemed medically problematic.

Social, Ethical, and Legal Issues

Reproductive technologies raise several sociological and ethical issues (Achilles, 1993). One is discrimination. Most reproductive technologies are expensive. Surrogate mothers can charge $20 000 or more to carry a child. In vitro fertilization can cost $100 000 or more. Poor and middle-income earners who happen to be infertile cannot afford these procedures. In addition, there is a strong tendency for members of the medical profession to deny single women and homosexual couples access to reproductive technologies; the medical community discriminates not just against those of modest means but against non-nuclear families.

A second problem introduced by reproductive technologies is that they render the terms *mother* and *father* obsolete, or at least vague. Is the mother the person who donates the egg, carries the child in her uterus, or raises the child? Is the father the person who donates the sperm or raises the child? As these questions suggest, a child conceived through a combination of reproductive technologies and raised by a heterosexual couple could have as many as three mothers and two fathers! This is not just a problem of terminology. If it were, we could just introduce new distinctions like "egg mother," "uterine mother," and "social mother" to reflect the new reality. The real problem is social and legal. It is unclear who has what rights and obligations to the child, and what rights and obligations the child has vis-à-vis each parent. This lack of clarity has already caused anguished court battles over child custody. In 2011, a British court may have set a precedent by letting a surrogate mother keep her baby despite having signed a contract to hand it over to a couple for £4500 ($7400; Allen, Ellicott, and Eccles, 2011). Reproductive technologies, in short, have caused people to rethink the very nature of the family.

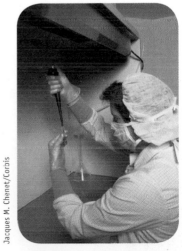

Jacques M. Chenet/Corbis

Fertilizing an egg in vitro

Public debate on a wide scale is needed to decide who will control reproductive technologies and to what ends. Reproductive technologies may bring the greatest joy to infertile people. They may also prevent the birth of children with diseases such as muscular dystrophy and multiple sclerosis. However, reproductive technologies may continue to benefit mainly the well-to-do, reinforce traditional family forms that are no longer appropriate for many people, and cause endless legal wrangling and heartache.

Housework, Child Care, and Senior Care

As we have seen, women's increased paid-labour-force participation, their increased participation in the system of higher education, and their increased control over reproduction transformed several areas of family life. It has also affected the division of housework, child care, and senior care, although not dramatically. Women still do a disproportionate amount of unpaid domestic work (Hochschild with Machung, 1989). A recent study of household labour in 10 rich countries found that women are responsible for 70 percent to 88 percent of unpaid work hours (Bittman and Wajcman, 2000:173). In Canada, 20 percent of women—but only 8 percent of men—devote 30 hours or more to unpaid household work. Men are almost twice as likely as women are to claim they do not devote any time to unpaid household work (Statistics Canada, 2010f).

Even these figures do not reveal the whole picture. Men tend to do low-stress chores that can often wait a day or a week. These jobs include mowing the lawn, maintaining the car, and painting the fence. Although fathers are often happy to play with young children, they spend less time than mothers do providing the more intensive forms of child care, such as feeding, washing, dressing, and medical care. In general, women tend to do the repetitive, higher stress chores that cannot wait. In short, the picture falls short of a revolution (Harvey, Marshall, and Frederick, 1991).

Two main factors shrink the gender gap in housework, child care, and senior care. First, the smaller the gap between the husband's and the wife's earnings, the more equal the division of household labour. Apparently, women are routinely able to translate earning power into domestic influence. Their increased status enables them to get their husbands to do more around the house. In addition, women who earn relatively high incomes are also able to use some of their money to pay outsiders to do domestic work.

Attitude is the second factor that shrinks the gender gap in domestic labour. The more a husband and wife agree that there *should* be equality in the household division of labor, the more equality there is. Seeing eye-to-eye on this issue is often linked to both spouses having a postsecondary education (Greenstein, 1996). Thus, if there is going to be greater equality between men and women in doing household chores, two things have to happen. There must be greater equality between men and women in the paid labour force and broader cultural acceptance of the need for gender equality.

Equality and Spouse Abuse

About 12 percent of police-reported violent crime in Canada involves spousal violence, and 83 percent of victims of spousal violence are women. Women are three times as likely as men are to suffer an injury, five times as likely to require medical attention, and five times as likely to report that the violence they experienced caused them to fear for their lives. Compared with men, women are more likely to report being beaten, choked, or threatened with a gun or knife, or having these weapons used against them. Compared with women, men are more likely to report being slapped, having something thrown at them, or being kicked, bitten, or hit (Bunge, 2000; Statistics Canada, 2009d).

Three main types of spousal violence exist (Johnson and Ferraro, 2000):

- *Common couple violence* occurs when partners have an argument and one partner lashes out physically at the other. For a couple that engages in this type of violence, violent acts are unlikely to occur often, escalate over time, or be severe. Both partners are about equally likely to engage in common couple violence, regardless of their gender.

- *Intimate terrorism* is part of a general desire of one partner to control the other. Where one partner engages in intimate terrorism, violent acts are likely to occur often, escalate over time, and be severe. Among heterosexual couples, the aggressor is usually the man.
- *Violent resistance* is the third main type of domestic violence. Among heterosexual couples, it typically involves a woman violently defending herself against a man who has engaged in intimate terrorism.

For heterosexual couples, spousal violence is associated with the level of gender equality in the family and in the larger society. The higher the level of gender inequality, the greater the frequency of spousal violence. Thus, severe wife assault is more common in lower-class, less highly educated families in which gender inequality tends to be high and men are likely to believe that male domination is justified. Severe wife abuse is also more common among couples who witnessed their mothers being abused and who were themselves abused when they were children, although research suggests that these socialization factors are considerably less influential than was once believed (Gelles, 1997; Simons, Wu, Johnson, and Conger, 1995; Smith, 1990). Still, male domination in both childhood socialization and current family organization increases the likelihood of severe wife assault.

In addition, Straus (1994) demonstrates that wife assault is associated with gender inequality in the larger society. Comparing measures of wife assault and gender inequality in each U.S. state, he found that as gender equality increases—as women and men become more equal in the larger society—wife assault declines. We conclude that for heterosexual couples, the incidence of domestic violence is highest where a big power imbalance between men and women exists, where norms justify the male domination of women, and, to a lesser extent, where early socialization experiences predispose men to behave aggressively toward women.

Summing up, we can say that conflict theorists and feminists have performed a valuable sociological service by emphasizing the importance of power relations in structuring family life. A substantial body of research shows that the gender revolution that has been taking place for half a century has influenced the way we select mates, our reasons for being satisfied or dissatisfied with marriage, our propensity to divorce, the reproductive choices women make, the distribution of housework and child care (see Box 15.2 on page 400), variations in the rate of severe domestic violence—in short, all aspects of family life. As you will now learn, the gender revolution has also created a much greater diversity of family forms.

Summing Up

- Access to marriage resources, the influence of third parties, and demographic variables shape the circumstances in which romantic love emerges.
- Marital dissatisfaction is enhanced by limited financial resources, restrictive divorce laws, child-rearing challenges, inequitable domestic responsibilities, and a poor sex life.
- The economic effects of divorce fall disproportionately on women and children.
- Despite recent improvements, most women continue to perform the high-stress family responsibilities.
- The incidence of family violence increases under conditions of gender inequality.

It's Your Choice

IS SPANKING EVER APPROPRIATE?

On July 4, 2001, child welfare workers took seven children, aged 6 to 14, from their home in southern Ontario amid concern they were being spanked with paddles by their fundamentalist Christian parents. The children's parents, members of the Church of God, admitted they used paddles to discipline their children. However, they noted that doing so was consistent with the teachings of their religion. A media statement released by the Church of God noted the group's belief that "the Word of God advocates corporal punishment under certain circumstances" (Church of God, 2001). According to the group's spiritual adviser, Daniel Layne, "The whole issue is spanking and discipline, and how we see in modern times that when parents don't discipline their children it leads to all kinds of social problems. . . . Switching is used as a last resort, but the Scriptures clearly call for it and we won't give it up" (quoted in Clairborne, 2001).

The children were returned to their home on July 26, after their parents agreed to abstain from the use of corporal punishment while the case was before the courts. Children's Aid Society (CAS) workers were given unannounced access to the children in their homes and at school and allowed to discuss alternative methods of child discipline with the parents. However, more than 100 members of the Church of God fled Canada over fears that authorities would attempt to seize their children. In January 2002, the Ontario Court of Appeal found in favour of the children's parents and upheld the right of parents, teachers, and persons standing in place of parents to physically discipline their young charges (McCarten, 2002).

In contrast to such countries as Austria, Cyprus, Denmark, Finland, Italy, Norway, and Sweden, where the use of corporal punishment against children is prohibited by law, Canadian law has, since 1892, allowed parents to use corporal punishment as a form of child discipline. However, not all Canadians agree with the decision of the Ontario Court of Appeal in the Church of God case—or with the decisions rendered in other Canadian courtrooms. For example, one of the leading decisions used by our courts to interpret this section of the Criminal Code specifies that "the mere fact that the children disciplined suffered contusions and bruises is not in itself proof of exercise of undue force."

Is spanking ever appropriate? Experts themselves have conflicting opinions about this issue. Sociologist Murray Straus (1994) advises parents never to hit children of any age under any circumstances. Considerable evidence suggests that children who are spanked by their parents (including those who are otherwise loving) are more likely to cheat, lie, bully, be intention-

ally cruel to others, disobey in school, and misbehave in various ways (Stormshak, Bierman, McMahon, and Lengua, 2000; Straus, 1996; Straus and Mouradian, 1998; Straus and Stewart, 1999; Straus, Sugerman, and Giles-Sims, 1997). Research also links being spanked to depression and suicide in childhood, alcohol and/or drug abuse in adolescence, and, during adulthood, a heightened likelihood of abusing one's own children and/or engaging in spousal violence (Garvey, 1999; Straus and Kantor, 1994; Turner and Finkelhor, 1996). Spanking apparently teaches children that it is acceptable to hit someone and that those who love you may hit you with impunity. This message confuses love and violence— and sets the stage for subsequent abusive acts directed against intimate partners (Straus and Yodanis, 1996).

In contrast, other researchers contend that Straus and others may be overstating and oversimplifying the situation (Gilbert, 1997). One review of the literature on non-abusive and customary physical punishment by parents reports that the observed consequences of such punishment vary by method employed, the child's personality, subcultural factors, and other factors (Larzelere, 2000). Some studies find that non-abusive spanking as an occasional backup form of child discipline had such beneficial outcomes as reduced noncompliance and fighting among two- to six-year-olds.

What do you think? Do you agree with the decision of the Ontario Court of Appeal in the Church of God case? Is corporal punishment an appropriate form of child discipline? Is corporal punishment child abuse? Should parents spank their children? Should Canada repeal the law that allows corporal punishment? Is spanking a training ground for violence against intimate partners later in life?

FAMILY DIVERSITY

Heterosexual Cohabitation

About 90 percent of Canadians marry at least once, but marriage is becoming less important for some Canadians. As early as 1995, when asked, "In order for you to be happy in life, is it very important, important, not very important, or not at all important to be married?" just two thirds of Canadian women rated marriage as important or very important. Younger Canadians were less likely than older Canadians to consider marriage important or very important. Those living in Quebec were markedly less likely to do so: 53 percent of women and 59 percent of men in Quebec considered marriage important or very important (Wu, 2000: 65–66). Although living in a common-law relationship may be a prelude to marriage for some people, for others it has become an alternative to legal marriage.

Since the Canadian census first started collecting information on cohabitation in 1981, the number of cohabiting people 15 years of age and older has nearly tripled—from 5.6 percent to 15.4 percent of all families. In Quebec, the 2006 figure was fully 35 percent (Statistics Canada, 2009b). Most Canadian women ages 18 to 49 approve of premarital sex and non-marital cohabitation when couples intend to marry at some point in the future. Some 55 percent of women outside Quebec and 73 percent of women in Quebec believe it is acceptable for couples to live together when they have no intention of making a long-term commitment and are simply sexually attracted to each other. In both cases, younger women and women in Quebec are particularly likely to voice such approval (Wu, 2000: 59).

Same-Sex Marriage and Civil Unions

In 2001, the Netherlands became the first country in the world to legalize same-sex marriage. Belgium, Spain, Canada, South Africa, Norway, Iceland, Sweden, and Argentina followed suit over the remainder of the decade. Many other West European countries allow homosexuals to register their partnerships under the law in so-called civil unions. Civil unions recognize the partnerships as having some or all of the legal rights of marriage.

Overall, the direction of change is clear. Amid sharp controversy, the legal and social definition of "family" is being broadened to include cohabiting, same-sex partners in long-term relationships. This change reflects the fact that most homosexuals, like most heterosexuals, want a long-term, intimate relationship with one other adult (Chauncey, 2005). In fact, in Denmark, where homosexual couples can register partnerships under the law, the divorce rate for registered homosexual couples is lower than for heterosexual married couples (Religious Tolerance.org, 2011).

Raising Children in Homosexual Families

Some same-sex couples are raising children who (1) were the offspring of previous, heterosexual marriages, (2) were adopted, or (3) resulted from artificial insemination. Many people believe that children brought up in homosexual families will develop a confused sexual identity, exhibit a tendency to become homosexuals themselves, and suffer discrimination from children and adults in the "straight" community. Unfortunately, there is little research in this area and much of it is based on small, unrepresentative samples. Nevertheless, the research findings are consistent. They suggest that children who grow up in homosexual families are much like children who grow up in heterosexual families. For example, a 14-year study assessed 25 young adults who were the offspring of lesbian families and 21 young adults who were the offspring of heterosexual families (Tasker and Golombok, 1997). The researchers found that the two groups were equally well adjusted and displayed little difference in sexual orientation. Two respondents from the lesbian families

In 2002, in a precedent-setting move hailed by gay-rights activists as the first of its kind in the world, full parental rights were extended to homosexual couples in Quebec. In addition, same-sex couples were granted the same status and obligations as heterosexual married couples when they entered into a civil union. Here, lesbians react as the Quebec legislature passes the law.

CP Picture Archive/Clement Allard

considered themselves lesbians, whereas all of the respondents from the heterosexual families considered themselves heterosexual. Even violence between same-sex partners occurs at approximately the same rate as it does in heterosexual relationships (Chesley, MacAulay, and Ristock, 1991).

Homosexual and heterosexual families do differ in some respects. Lesbian couples with children record higher satisfaction with their partnerships than do lesbian couples are without children. In contrast, among heterosexual couples, it is the childless who record higher marital satisfaction (Koepke, Hare, and Moran, 1992). On average, the partners of lesbian mothers spend more time caring for children than do the husbands of heterosexual mothers. Because children usually benefit from adult attention, this must be considered a plus. Homosexual couples also tend to be more egalitarian than heterosexual couples are, sharing most decision making and household duties equally (Rosenbluth, 1997). That is because they tend to reject traditional marriage patterns. The fact that they tend to experience similar gender socialization and earn about the same income also encourages equality (Kurdek, 1996; Reimann, 1997). In sum, available research suggests that raising children in lesbian families has no apparent negative consequences for the children. Indeed, there may be some benefits for all family members above the benefits offered by families in which the spouses are heterosexual.

Lone-Parent Families

During the first half of the twentieth century, lone-parent families were generally the result of the death of one parent (Oderkirk and Lochhead, 1992). Today, solo parenting is usually the product of separation or divorce, after which child custody is typically granted to mothers. In 2006, 16 percent of Canadian families were headed by a lone parent and 81 percent of those families were headed by women. Poverty is far more prevalent among female-headed single parent families than among any other type of family. The poverty rate in female-headed single-parent families is more than double the rate in male-headed single parent families.

Low levels of social support, family dysfunction, and parental depression all have significant negative effects on children and are more common in low-income households (National Council of Welfare, 1999). Child poverty is related to school failure, negative

Divorce is responsible for the majority of lone-parent families in Canada today. Female-headed lone-parent families are far more common than male-headed lone-parent families.

involvement with parents, stunted growth, reduced cognitive abilities, limited emotional development, and a high likelihood of dropping out of school (Duncan, Yeung, Brooks-Gunn, and Smith, 1998; Fields and Smith, 1998).

Zero-Child Families

In Canada, what we prefer to call "zero-child families" are increasingly common. Our admittedly clumsy term seems necessary because the alternatives are so value laden: a "childless family" implies that a family without children lacks something it should have, while the more recent "child-free family" suggests that a family without a child is unencumbered and that a child is therefore a burden. To maintain neutrality, we resort to clumsiness.

Roughly a fifth of North American women between the ages of 40 and 44 have never given birth (Lamanna and Riedmann, 2003: 369). To explain this fact we must first recognize that not having a child may be the result of circumstances beyond a couple's control. For example, one or both partners may be infertile, and some evidence suggests that infertility is a growing issue, perhaps because of chemical pollutants in the air and water. It seems that not having a child is more often a matter of choice, however, and the main reasons for the increasing prevalence of zero-child families are the rising cost of raising a child and the growth of attractive alternatives.

Just how expensive are children? In 2004, the cost of raising a child in Manitoba to the age of 18 was about $167 000 (Canadian Council on Social Development, 2007). College or university is extra. That amounts to a lot of money that could be spent on investments, the couple's own education, and other desirable things. Mothers bear most of the cost of lost economic opportunities. Usually, they are the ones whose careers are disrupted when they decide to stay home to raise children and who lose income, benefits, and pension payments in the process.

Couples also incur non-economic costs when they have a child, the most important of which is stress. The birth of a child requires that couples do more work in the home, give up free time and time together, develop an efficient daily routine, and divide responsibilities. All this adds sources of disagreement and tension to daily life, so it is little wonder that marital satisfaction declines with a child in the house.

Alternative attractions decrease the desire of some couples to have a child. People with high income, high education, and professional and managerial occupations are most likely to have zero-child families. Such people tend to place an especially high value on mobility, careers, and leisure-time pursuits. Usually, they are neither frustrated nor unhappy that they do not have a child. Despite their tendency to feel negatively stereotyped as "selfish," they tend to be more satisfied with their marriage than are couples with a child (Lamanna and Riedmann, 2003: 380).

Summing Up

- Marriage is becoming less common as cohabitation rates increase.
- The growing prevalence of same-sex unions and solo-parenting and zero-child families illustrates the diversity of legitimate family forms in Canada today.

FAMILY POLICY

Having discussed several aspects of the decline of the traditional nuclear family and the proliferation of diverse family forms, we can now return to the big question posed at the beginning of this chapter: Is the decline of the nuclear family a bad thing for society? Said differently, do two-parent families—particularly those with stay-at-home moms—provide the kind of discipline, role models, help, and middle-class lifestyle that children need to stay out of trouble with the law and grow up to become well-adjusted, productive members of society? Conversely, are family forms other than the traditional nuclear family the main source of teenage crime, poverty, welfare dependency, and other social ills?

The answer suggested by research is clear: yes and no (Houseknecht and Sastry, 1996; Popenoe, 1996; Sandqvist and Andersson, 1992). Yes, the decline of the traditional nuclear family can be a source of many social problems. No, it doesn't have to be that way.

The United States is a good example of how social problems can emerge from nuclear family decline. Sweden is a good example of how such problems can be averted. These two cases represent two models that Canadians should consider when thinking about our own family policies. The top panel of Table 15.1 shows that *on most indicators of nuclear family decline, Sweden leads the United States*. In Sweden, a smaller percentage of people get married. People usually get married at a later age than in the United States. The proportion of births outside of marriage is twice as high as in the United States. A much larger proportion of Swedish than of American women with children under the age of three work in the paid labour force.

The bottom panel of Table 15.1 shows that *on most measures of children's well-being, Sweden also leads the United States*. Thus, in Sweden, children enjoy higher average reading test scores than children do in the United States. The poverty rate in two-parent families is only one-fifth the American rate, while the poverty rate in single-parent families is only one-eleventh as high. The rate of infant abuse is one-eleventh the American rate. The rate of juvenile drug offences is less than half as high. Sweden does have a higher rate of juvenile delinquency than the United States. However, the lead is slight and concerns only minor offences. Overall, then, the decline of the traditional nuclear family has gone further in Sweden than in the United States, but children are much better off on average. How is this possible?

One explanation is that Sweden has something the United States lacks: a substantial family-support policy. When a child is born in Sweden, a parent is entitled to a year of parental leave at 80 percent of his or her salary and an additional 90 days at a flat rate. Fathers can take 10 days of leave when the baby is born. Parents are entitled to free consultations at "well-baby clinics." Like all citizens of Sweden, they receive free health care from the

Indicators of Nuclear Family "Decline"	United States	Sweden	#1 "Decline"
Median age at first marriage			
Men	26.5	29.4	Sweden
Women	24.4	27.1	Sweden
Percentage of 45–49 population never married			
Men	5.7	15.4	Sweden
Women	5.1	9.1	Sweden
Non-marital birth rate	25.7	50.9	Sweden
One-parent households with children <15 as % of all households with children <15	25.0	18.0	U.S.A
Percentage of mothers in labour force with children <3	51.0	84.0	Sweden
Total fertility rate	2.0	2.0	Tie
Average household size	2.7	2.2	Sweden

Indicators of Child Well-Being	United States	Sweden	#1 "Well Being"
Mean reading performance score at 14	5.14	5.29	Sweden
Percentage of children in poverty			
Single-mother households	59.5	5.2	Sweden
Two-parent households	11.1	2.2	Sweden
Death rate of infants from abuse	9.8	0.9	Sweden
Suicide rate for children 15–19 (per 100 000)	11.1	6.2	Sweden
Juvenile delinquency rate (per 100 000)	11.6	12.0	U.S.A
Juvenile drug offence rate (per 100 000)	558.0	241.0	Sweden

TABLE 15.1

The "Decline" of the Nuclear Family and the Well-Being of Children: The United States and Sweden Compared

Source: Adapted from Houseknecht and Sastry, 1996.

state-run system. Temporary parental benefits are available for parents with a sick child under the age of 12. One parent can take up to 60 days off work per sick child per year at 80 percent of his or her salary. All parents can send their children to heavily government-subsidized, high-quality daycare. Finally, Sweden offers its citizens generous direct cash payments based on the number of children in each family.[1]

Among industrialized countries, the United States stands at the other extreme. Since 1993, a parent is entitled to 12 weeks of *unpaid* parental leave. About 40 million citizens have no health care coverage, although coverage is scheduled to become compulsory in 2016. Health care is at a low standard for many millions more. There is no system of state daycare and no direct cash payments to families based on the number of children they have. The value of the dependant deduction on income tax has fallen by nearly 50 percent in current dollars since the 1940s. Thus, when an unwed Swedish woman has a baby, she knows she can rely on state institutions to maintain her standard of living and help give her child an enriching social and educational environment. When an unwed American woman has a baby, she is pretty much on her own. She stands a good chance of sinking into poverty, with all the negative consequences that has for her and her child.

Canada stands midway between these two extremes. In a study of 33 countries, Canada tied for fifth place on the number of weeks it allows new parents to take off work, but it stood fifteenth in terms of generosity of maternity leave payments (Smyth, 2003). There are enough regulated daycare spaces for only a fifth of Canadian children up to age 12, and the

Painting class in a state-subsidized daycare facility in Stockholm, Sweden

Jonathan Blair/Corbis

average annual government allocation for child care is under $500 per child. These averages are far below comparable figures for Western European countries. Much of the debate surrounding family policy in Canada concerns whether we should move in the direction of the American or Swedish model.

In Canada, people commonly raise three criticisms against generous family-support policies. First, some people say such policies encourage illegitimate births, long-term dependence on welfare, and the breakup of two-parent families. However, research shows that neither the divorce rate nor the rate of births to unmarried mothers is higher when welfare payments are more generous (Albelda and Tilly, 1997; Ruggles, 1997; Sweezy and Tiefenthaler, 1996).

A second criticism of generous family-support policies focuses on child care. Some critics say that non-family child care is bad for children under the age of three. In their view, only parents can provide the love, interaction, and intellectual stimulation infants and toddlers need for proper social, cognitive, and moral development. However, when studies compare family care and daycare involving a strong curriculum, a stimulating environment, plenty of caregiver warmth, low turnover of well-trained staff, and a low ratio of caregivers to children, they find that daycare has no negative consequences for children over the age of one (Clarke-Stewart, Gruber, and Fitzgerald, 1994; Harvey, 1999). Research also shows that daycare has some benefits, notably enhancing a child's ability to make friends. The benefits of high-quality daycare are even more evident in low-income families, which often cannot provide the kind of stimulating environment offered by high-quality daycare.

The third criticism lodged against generous family-support policies is that they are expensive and have to be paid for by high taxes. This is true. Swedes, for example, pay higher taxes than just about anyone else in the world. They have made the political decision to pay high taxes, partly to avoid the social problems and associated costs that sometimes emerge when the traditional nuclear family is replaced with other family forms and no institutions are available to help family members in need. The Swedish experience teaches us, then, that there is a clear trade-off between expensive family-support policies and low taxes. It is impossible to have both, and the degree to which any country favours one or the other is a political choice.

Summing Up

- Social policies that support families can mitigate many of the adverse consequences that emerge as the nuclear family is replaced with more diverse family forms.

NOTE

1. We are grateful to Gregg Olsen, Department of Sociology, University of Manitoba, for this information.

SUMMARY

1. What is the traditional nuclear family, and how prevalent is it compared with other family forms?

   The traditional nuclear family consists of a father-provider, mother-homemaker, and at least one child. Today, only slightly more than one in eight Canadian households are traditional nuclear families. Many different family forms have proliferated in recent decades, including cohabiting couples (with or without children), same-sex couples (with or without children), and single-parent families. The frequency of these forms varies by class, sexual orientation, and other factors.

2. What is the functionalist theory of the family, and how accurate is it?

   The functionalist theory holds that the nuclear family is a distinct and universal family form because it performs five important functions in society: sexual regulation, economic cooperation, reproduction, socialization, and emotional support. The theory is most accurate in depicting families in Canada and other Western societies in the two decades after World War II. Families today and in other historical periods depart from the functional model in important respects.

3. What are the emphases of Marxist and feminist theories of families?

   Marxists stress how families are tied to the system of capitalist ownership. They argue that only the elimination of capitalism can end gender inequality in families. Feminists note that gender inequality existed before capitalism and in communist societies. They stress how the patriarchal division of power and patriarchal norms reproduce gender inequality.

4. What consequences does the entry of women into the paid labour force have?

   Among other changes, the entry of women into the paid labour force increases their power to leave unhappy marriages and control whether and when to have children.

5. What accounts for variations in marital satisfaction?

   Marital satisfaction is lower at the bottom of the class structure, in places where divorce laws are strict, when children reach their teenage years, in families where housework is not shared equally, and among couples who do not have a good sexual relationship.

6. Under what circumstances are the effects of divorce on children worst?

   The effects of divorce on children are worst if there is a high level of parental conflict and the children's standard of living drops.

7. Does growing up in a homosexual household have any known negative effects on children?
   Children who grow up in homosexual families are much like children who grow up in heterosexual families.

8. Are various social problems a result of the decline of the traditional nuclear family?
   People sometimes blame the decline of the traditional nuclear family for increasing poverty, welfare dependence, and crime. However, some countries have adopted policies that largely prevent these problems. Therefore, the social problems are in a sense a political choice.

KEY TERMS

child support (p. 395)

divorce rate (p. 388)

extended family (p. 384)

marriage (p. 385)

marriage rate (p. 388)

nuclear family (p. 381)

polygamy (p. 384)

traditional nuclear family (p. 381)

WEB RESOURCES

Companion Website for This Book

http://www.compass4e.nelson.com

Begin by clicking on the Student Resources section of the website. Next, select the chapter you are studying from the pull-down menu. From the Student Resources page you have easy access to additional Weblinks and other resources. The website also has many useful tips to aid you in your study of sociology, including practice tests for each chapter.

InfoTrac® Search Terms

These search terms are provided to assist you in beginning to conduct research on this topic by visiting http://www.infotrac-college.com:

divorce
extended family
family values
marriage
nuclear family

CHAPTER 16

Religion

IN THIS CHAPTER, YOU WILL LEARN THAT

- The structure of society and a person's place in it influence his or her religious beliefs and practices.

- Under some circumstances, religion creates societal cohesion, while under other circumstances it promotes social conflict and social change. When religion creates societal cohesion, it also reinforces social inequality.

- Religion governs fewer aspects of most people's lives today than in the past. However, a religious revival has taken place in various parts of the world in recent decades, and many people still adhere strongly to religious beliefs and practices.

- Diverse possibilities for religious participation compete in modern societies. For example, although most people are becoming more secularized, many people are becoming more religious.

- History suggests that the major world religions were movements of moral and social improvement that arose in times of great adversity and were led by charismatic figures. As they consolidated, they became more conservative.

- People are more religious when they are brought up in a religious family, reside in regions where religion is highly authoritative, and are very young or very old.

© Miroslaw Oslizlo/Vetta Collection/ iStockphoto

NFI

RELIGION AND SOCIETY

Robert Brym started writing the first draft of this chapter just after returning from a funeral. "Roy was a fitness nut," says Robert, "and cycling was his sport. One perfect summer day, he was out training with his team. I wouldn't be surprised if the sunshine and vigorous exercise turned his thoughts to his good fortune. At 41, he was a senior executive in a medium-sized mutual funds firm. His boss, who treated him like a son, was grooming him for the presidency of the company. Roy had three vivacious children, ranging in age from 1 to 10, and a beautiful, generous, and highly intelligent wife. He was active in community volunteer work and everyone who knew him admired him. But on this particular summer day, he suddenly didn't feel well. He dropped back from the pack and then suffered a massive heart attack. Within minutes, he was dead.

"During *shiva*, the ritual week of mourning following the death of a Jew, hundreds of people gathered in the family's home and on their front lawn. I had never felt such anguish before. When we heard the steady, slow, clear voice of Roy's 10-year-old son solemnly intoning the mourner's prayer, we all wept. And we asked ourselves and one another the inevitable question: Why?"

In 1902, the great psychologist William James observed that this question lies at the root of all religious belief. Religion is the common human response to the fact that we all stand at the edge of an abyss. It helps us cope with the terrifying fact that we must die (James, 1976 [1902]: 116). It offers us immortality, the promise of better times to come, and the security of benevolent spirits who look over us. It provides meaning and purpose in a world that might otherwise seem cruel and senseless.

The motivation for religion may be psychological, as James argued. However, the content and intensity of our religious beliefs, and the form and frequency of our religious practices, are influenced by the structure of society and our place in it. In other words, the religious impulse takes literally thousands of forms. It is the task of the sociologist of religion to account for this variation. Why does one religion predominate here, another there? Why is religious belief more fervent at one time than at another? Under what circumstances does religion act as a source of social stability and under what circumstances does it act as a force for social change? Are we becoming more or less religious? These are all questions that have occupied the sociologist of religion, and we touch on all of them here. Note that we will not have anything to say about the truth of religion in general or the value of any religious belief or practice in particular. These are questions of faith, not science. They lie outside the province of sociology.

The cover of *Time* magazine once asked, "Is God Dead?" As a sociological observation, there can be little doubt about the answer. In Canada, more than 80 percent of adults

Stockbyte/Getty

and more than 70 percent of teenagers agree with the statement "God or a higher power cares about you" (Bibby, 2001: 252). By these measures (and by other measures we will examine below), God is still very much alive. Nonetheless, as we will show, the scope of religious authority has declined in Canada and many other parts of the world. That is, religion governs fewer aspects of life than it used to. Some Canadians still look to religion to deal with all of life's problems. But increasingly more Canadians expect that religion can help them deal with only a restricted range of spiritual issues. Other institutions—medicine, psychiatry, criminal justice, education, and so forth—have grown in importance as the scope of religious authority has declined.

Although a smaller proportion of the public is active in organized religions now than in the past, many people remain involved. Among the latter, growing evidence suggests that the level of participation in religious services and practices is on the rise. Relatively intense, demanding fundamentalist and conservative religious traditions are gaining strength as more liberal traditions become less appealing. Is this a sign of an overall revival of religion? It is too early to tell. But you will see that viewing the field of religion as a kind of market comprising "sellers" and "buyers" of religious services allows us to understand how and why an overall pattern of decline can be observed alongside growing religious intensity among a large minority of Canadians.

Before we address the issues noted above, let us see how the founding fathers of sociology and some important contemporary innovators in the field have treated the problem of religion in society.

THEORETICAL APPROACHES TO THE SOCIOLOGY OF RELIGION

Durkheim's Functionalist Approach

More than one person has said that hockey is Canada's "national religion." Do you agree with that opinion? Before making up your mind, consider that 80 percent of Canadians tuned in to at least part of the gold medal men's hockey game between Canada and the United States at the 2010 Vancouver Winter Olympics, making them the largest TV audience in Canadian history. As when Canada's men's hockey team came from behind to defeat the Soviets in 1972, the nation virtually came to a standstill ("Gold Medal," 2010).

Apart from drawing a huge audience, the Stanley Cup playoffs generate a sense of what Durkheim would have called "collective effervescence." That is, the Stanley Cup excites us by making us feel part of something larger than we are: the Montreal Canadiens, the Edmonton Oilers, the Toronto Maple Leafs, the Vancouver Canucks, the Calgary Flames, the Ottawa Senators, the institution of Canadian hockey, the spirit of Canada itself. As celebrated Canadian writer Roch Carrier (1979: 77) wrote in his famous short story, "The Hockey Sweater": "School was ... a quiet place where we could prepare for the next hockey game, lay out our next strategies. As for church, ... there we forgot school and dreamed about the next hockey game. Through our daydreams it might happen that we would recite a prayer: we would ask God to help us play as well as Maurice Richard." For many hours each year, hockey enthusiasts transcend their everyday lives and experience intense enjoyment by sharing the sentiments and values of a larger collective. In their fervour, they banish thoughts of their own mortality. They gain a glimpse of eternity as they immerse themselves in institutions that will outlast them and athletic feats that people will remember for generations to come.

So do you think the Stanley Cup playoffs are a religious event? There is no god of the Stanley Cup (although the nickname of Canadian hockey legend Wayne Gretzky—The Great One—suggests that he transcended the status of a mere mortal). Nonetheless, the Stanley Cup playoffs meet Durkheim's definition of a religious experience. Durkheim said that when people live together, they come to share common sentiments and values. These common sentiments and values form a **collective conscience** that is larger than any individual's. On occasion, we experience the collective conscience directly. This causes us to distinguish the secular, everyday world of the **profane** from the religious, transcendent world of the **sacred**. We designate certain objects as symbolizing the sacred. Durkheim called these objects **totems**. We invent certain public practices to connect us with the sacred. Durkheim referred to these practices as **rituals**. The effect (or function) of rituals and of religion as a whole is to reinforce social solidarity, said Durkheim.

Durkheim would have found support for his theory in research showing that, in Quebec from 1951 to 1992, the early ousting of the Montreal Canadiens from the Stanley Cup playoffs was associated with an increased tendency for young men to commit suicide during the hockey series (Trovato, 1998). Similarly, in the United States, the suicide rate dips during the two days preceding football's Super Bowl Sunday and on Super Bowl Sunday itself, as well as on the final day of the baseball World Series (Curtis, Loy, and Karnilowicz, 1986).

The **collective conscience** comprises the common sentiments and values that people share as a result of living together.

The **profane** refers to the secular, everyday world.

The **sacred** refers to the religious, transcendent world.

Totems are objects that symbolize the sacred.

Rituals in Durkheim's usage are public practices designed to connect people to the sacred.

From a Durkheimian point of view, the Stanley Cup playoffs can be considered a religious ritual.

CP Photo/Jeff McIntosh

These patterns are consistent with Durkheim's theory of suicide, which predicts a lower suicide rate when social solidarity increases and a higher suicide rate when social solidarity decreases (see Chapter 1, A Sociological Compass).

Durkheim would consider the Stanley Cup and the team insignia to be totems. The insignia represent groups we identify with. The trophy signifies the qualities that professional hockey stands for: competitiveness, sportsmanship, excellence, and the value of teamwork. The hockey games themselves are public rituals enacted according to strict rules and conventions. We suspend our everyday lives as we watch the enactment of the ritual. The ritual heightens our experience of belonging to certain groups, increases our respect for certain institutions, and strengthens our belief in certain ideas. These groups, institutions, and ideas all transcend us. Thus, the Stanley Cup playoffs may fairly be regarded as a sacred event in Durkheim's terms. They cement society in the way Durkheim said all religions do (Durkheim, 1976 [1915]). Do you agree with this Durkheimian interpretation of the Stanley Cup playoffs? Why or why not? Do you see any parallels between the Durkheimian analysis of the Stanley Cup playoffs and sports in your community or university?

Religion, Feminist Theory, and Conflict Theory

Durkheim's theory of religion is a functionalist account. It offers useful insights into the role of religion in society. Yet conflict and feminist theorists lodge two main criticisms against it. First, it overemphasizes religion's role in maintaining social cohesion. In reality, religion often incites social conflict. Second, it ignores the fact that when religion does increase social cohesion, it often reinforces social inequality.

Religion and Social Inequality

Consider first the role of major world religions and social inequality (see Figure 16.1 and Table 16.1 on pages 414 and 415). Little historical evidence helps us understand the social conditions that gave rise to the first world religions, Judaism and Hinduism, 3800

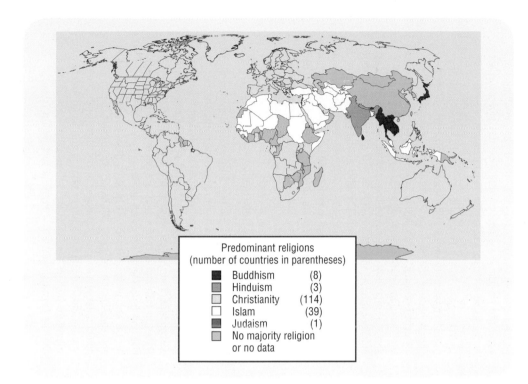

FIGURE 16.1
The World's Predominant Religions

This map shows the predominant religion in each of the world's countries, defined as the religion to which more than 50 percent of a country's population adheres.

Source: Adherents.com (2001).

to 4000 years ago. But we know enough about the rise of Buddhism, Christianity, and Islam between 2700 and 1500 years ago to say that the impulse to find a better world is often encouraged by adversity in this one. We also know that Moses, Jesus, Muhammad, and Buddha all promoted a message of equality and freedom. Finally, we know that over generations, the charismatic leadership of the world religions became "routinized." The **routinization of charisma** is Weber's term for the transformation of divine enlightenment into a permanent feature of everyday life. It involves turning religious inspiration into a stable social institution—a church—with defined roles, such as interpreters of the divine message, teachers, dues-paying laypeople, and so forth. The routinization of charisma typically makes religion less responsive to the needs of ordinary people, and it often supports social inequalities and injustices, as you will now see.

The **routinization of charisma** is Weber's term for the transformation of divine enlightenment into a permanent feature of everyday life.

Religion and the Subordination of Women

It was Marx who first stressed how religion often tranquillizes the underprivileged into accepting their lot in life. He called religion "the opium of the people" (Marx, 1970 [1843]: 131).

We can draw evidence for Marx's interpretation from many times, places, and institutions. For example, as feminists note, the major world religions have traditionally placed women in a subordinate position, reinforcing patriarchy. Consider the following scriptural examples of the subordination of women:

- Corinthians in the *New Testament* emphasizes that "women should keep silence in the churches. For they are not permitted to speak, but should be subordinate, as even the law says. If there is anything they desire to know, let them ask their husbands at home. For it is shameful for a woman to speak in church."
- The *Sidur*, the Jewish prayer book, includes this morning prayer, which is recited by Orthodox and ultra-Orthodox men: "Blessed are you, Lord our God, King of the Universe, who did not make me a woman."
- The *Koran*, the holy book of Islam, contains a Book of Women in which it is written that "righteous women are devoutly obedient.... As to those women on whose part you fear disloyalty and ill-conduct, admonish them, refuse to share their beds, beat them."

TABLE 16.1
The Five World Religions: Origins, Beliefs, and Divisions

	Origins	Beliefs	Divisions
Judaism	Judaism originated about 4000 years ago in what is now Iraq, when Abraham first asserted the existence of just one God. About 800 years later, Moses led the Jews out of Egyptian bondage. The emancipation of the Jews from slavery was a defining moment in the history of Judaism.	The central teachings rest on belief in one God (*Yahweh*) and on the idea that God sanctions freedom and equality. The 613 divine commandments (*mitzvot*) mentioned in the Five Books of Moses (*Torah*) form the core of orthodox Jewish practice The *mitzvot* include prescriptions for justice, righteousness, and observance: rest and pray on the Sabbath, honour the old and the wise, do not wrong a stranger in buying or selling, do not seek revenge or hold a grudge, etc. The *Torah* forms part of the Old Testament.	In seventeenth-century Eastern Europe, ecstatic *Chasidic* sects broke away from the bookish Judaism of the time. In nineteenth-century Germany, the Reform movement allowed prayer in German, the integration of women in worship, etc. Orthodox Judaism was a reaction against the liberalizing tendencies of Reform and involved a return to traditional observance. Conservative Judaism crystallized in Britain and the United States in the nineteenth century to reconcile what its practitioners regarded as the positive elements in Orthodoxy with the dynamism of Reform. Reconstructionism is a liberal twentieth-century movement known for its social activism and gender egalitarianism.
Christianity	Christianity originated about 35 CE in what is now Israel. Jesus, a poor Jew, criticized the Judaism of his time for its external conformity to tradition and ritual at the expense of developing a true relationship to God as demanded by the prophets.	Believe in God and love him; love your neighbour—these are the two main lessons of Jesus. These teachings were novel because they demanded that people match outward performance with inner conviction. It was not enough not to murder. Nor was it enough not to commit adultery. One could not even lust after a neighbour's wife (Matthew V, 21–30). These teachings made Jesus anti-authoritarian and even revolutionary. Admonishing people to love their neighbours impressed upon them the need to emancipate slaves and women. Christians retained the Jewish Bible as the Old Testament, adding the gospels and letters of the apostles as the New Testament.	In 312 CE, the Roman Emperor converted to Christianity and turned Christianity into a state religion, after which the Church became the dominant institution in Europe. In the sixteenth century, Martin Luther, a German priest, challenged the Christian establishment by seeking to establish a more personal relationship between the faithful and God. His ideas quickly captured the imagination of half of Europe and led to the split of Christianity into Catholicism and Protestantism. In the Middle Ages, Christianity had split into Western and Eastern halves, the former centred in Rome, the latter in Constantinople (now Istanbul, Turkey). Various Orthodox churches today derive from the Eastern tradition. Protestantism has been especially prone to splintering because it emphasizes the individual's relationship to God rather than a central authority. Today, there are hundreds of different Protestant churches.
Islam	Islam originated about 600 CE in what is now Saudi Arabia. The powerful merchants of Mecca had become greedy and corrupt, impoverishing and enslaving many people. Also, fear grew that the Persian and Roman Empires might soon fall, bringing the end of the world. Into this crisis stepped Muhammad, who claimed to have visions from God.	People who profess Islam have five duties. At least once in their life they must recite the Muslim creed aloud, correctly, with full understanding, and with heartfelt belief. (The creed is "There is no god but Allah and Muhammad is his prophet.") Five times a day they must worship in a religious service. They must fast from sunrise to sunset every day during the ninth month of the lunar calendar (Ramadan). They must give charity to the poor. And at least once in their life they must make a pilgrimage to the holy city of Mecca. Muhammad's teachings were written down in the Koran.	A dispute broke out over how the followers of Muhammad could identify his successor. The Sunni argued that the successor should be an elected member of a certain Meccan tribe. The Shia claimed that the successor should be Muhammad's direct descendant. Today, most Muslims are Sunni. The Shia, concentrated in Iran and southern Iraq, are generally more conservative and fundamentalist. Islam spread rapidly in the Middle East, Africa, and parts of Europe. It began a great cultural flowering and considerable religious tolerance. Wahabbism, a Sunni fundamentalist movement, originated in the eighteenth century and became the state religion of what is now Saudi Arabia. Shia subgroups include the "Twelvers" (about 80 percent of the Shia) and the Ismailis. Sufism is a mystical sect within Islam.

Hinduism

Hinduism originated about 2000 BCE in India in unknown circumstances. It had no single founder.

Hinduism has many gods, all of them thought to be aspects of the one true God. The major texts are epic poems such as the *Bhagavad Gita*. Only the body dies in Hindu belief. The soul returns in a new form after death. The form in which it returns depends on how one lives one's life. Hindus believe that people who live in a way that is appropriate to their position in society will live better future lives. One may reach a state of spiritual perfection (*nirvana*) that allows the soul to escape the cycle of birth and rebirth, and reunite with God. But people who do not live in a way that is appropriate to their position in society supposedly live an inferior life when they are reincarnated. These ideas made upward social mobility nearly impossible because, according to Hindu belief, striving to move out of one's station in life ensures reincarnation in a lower form.

Unlike the Western religions, Hinduism assimilates rather than excludes other religious beliefs and practices. Traditionally, Western religions rejected non-believers unless they converted. God tells Moses on Mount Sinai, "You shall have no other gods before me." In contrast, in the *Bhagavad Gita*, Krishna says that "whatever god a man worships, it is I who answer the prayer." This attitude of acceptance helped Hinduism absorb many of the ancient religions of the peoples on the Indian subcontinent. It also explains why there are such wide regional and class variations in Hindu beliefs and practices. Hinduism as it is practised bears the stamp of many other religions.

Buddhism

About 600 BCE, Gautama Buddha objected to the state ritualism of Hinduism and sought to achieve a direct relationship with God. He rejected Hindu ideas of caste and reincarnation, and offered a new way for everyone to achieve spiritual enlightenment, promising salvation to everyone.

Buddha promoted the "Four Noble Truths": (1) Life is suffering. Moments of joy are overshadowed by sorrow. (2) All suffering derives from desire. We suffer when we fail to achieve what we want. (3) Suffering ceases by training ourselves to eliminate desire. (4) We can eliminate desire by behaving morally, focusing intently on our feelings and thoughts, meditating, and achieving wisdom. Buddhism does not presume the existence of one true God. Rather, it holds out the possibility of everyone becoming a god of sorts. Similarly, it does not have a central church or text, such as the Bible.

Buddhism is notable for the diversity of its beliefs and practices. Buddhism spread rapidly across Asia after India's ruler adopted it as his own religion in the third century BCE. He sent missionaries to convert people in Tibet, Cambodia (Kampuchea), Nepal, Sri Lanka (formerly Ceylon), Myanmar (formerly Burma), China, Korea, and Japan. The influence of Buddhism in the land of its birth started to die out after the fifth century CE and is negligible in India today. One of the reasons for the popularity of Buddhism in East and Southeast Asia is that Buddhism is able to co-exist with local religious practices. Unlike Western religions, Buddhism does not insist on holding a monopoly on religious truth.

Sources: Brown (1996); Flood (1996); Gombrich (1996); Gottwald (1979); Hodgson (1974); Lapidus (2002 [1988]); Lopez (2001); McManners (1990); Robinson and Johnson (1997 [1982]); Rodinson (1996); Roth (1961); Schwartz (2003).

It is also significant that Catholic priests and Muslim mullahs must be men, as must Jewish rabbis in the Conservative and Orthodox denominations. However, the major world religions are becoming less patriarchal in many parts of the world. Vibrant feminist movements exist among Muslims, Catholics, Orthodox Jews, and so on. Women have been allowed to serve as Protestant ministers since the mid-nineteenth century and as rabbis in the more liberal branches of Judaism since the 1970s. In the United Church of Canada, more than two-thirds of seminarians are now women (Kaasa, 2002). In the meantime, there is a serious shortage of male candidates for the priesthood among Roman Catholics, perhaps portending change in that church as well.

Religion and Class Inequality

If, after becoming routinized, religion has often supported gender inequality, it has also often supported class inequality. In medieval and early modern Europe, Christianity promoted the view that the Almighty ordains class inequality, promising rewards to the lowly in the afterlife ("the meek shall inherit the earth"). The Hindu scriptures say that the highest caste sprang from the lips of the supreme creator, the next highest caste from his shoulders, the next highest from his thighs, and the lowest, "polluted" caste from his feet. They warn that if people attempt to achieve upward mobility, they will be reincarnated as animals. And the Koran says that social inequality is due to the will of Allah (Ossowski, 1963: 19–20).

Religion and Social Conflict

A **church** is a bureaucratic religious organization that has accommodated itself to mainstream society and culture.

In the sociological sense of the term, a **church** is any bureaucratic religious organization that has accommodated itself to mainstream society and culture. As we have seen, church authorities often support gender and class inequality. However, religiously inspired protest against inequality often erupts from below.

A famous example of such protest involves the role of black churches in spearheading the American civil rights movement during the 1950s and 1960s (Morris, 1984). Their impact was both organizational and inspirational. Organizationally, black churches supplied the ministers who formed the civil rights movement's leadership and the congregations whose members marched, boycotted, and engaged in other forms of protest. Additionally, Christian doctrine inspired the protesters. Perhaps their most powerful religious idea was that blacks, like the Jews in Egypt, were slaves who would be freed. (It was, after all, Michael—regarded by Christians as the patron saint of the Jews—who rowed the boat ashore.) Some white segregationists reacted strongly against efforts at integration, often meeting the peaceful protesters with deadly violence. But the American South was never the same again. Religion had helped promote the conflict needed to make the South a more egalitarian and racially integrated place.

Closer to home, it is worth remembering the important role played in the creation of our medicare system and our social welfare network by the radical Christianity of the early twentieth-century Social Gospel movement. The Social Gospel movement took on force in the depths of the Great Depression (1929–39). It emphasized that Christians should be as concerned with improving the here and now as with life in the hereafter. The efforts of Tommy Douglas, a Baptist minister with an M.A. in sociology, the leader of the Co-operative Commonwealth Federation (precursor of the New Democratic Party), and the father of medicare in Canada, exemplify the Social Gospel concern with social justice. In Canada too, then, religion has sometimes promoted conflict and change.

In sum, religion can maintain social order under some circumstances, as Durkheim said. When it does so, however, it often reinforces social inequality. Moreover, under other circumstances religion can promote social conflict.

Weber and the Problem of Social Change: A Symbolic Interactionist Interpretation

If Durkheim highlighted the way religion contributes to social order, Max Weber stressed the way religion can contribute to social change. Weber captured the core of his argument in a memorable image: If history is like a train, pushed along its tracks by economic and political interests, then religious ideas are like railroad switches, determining exactly which tracks the train will follow (Weber, 1946: 280).

Weber's most famous illustration of his thesis is his short book *The Protestant Ethic and Spirit of Capitalism*. Like Marx, Weber was interested in explaining the rise of modern capitalism. Again like Marx, he was prepared to recognize the "fundamental importance of the economic factor" in his explanation (Weber, 1958 [1904–05]: 26). But Weber was also bent on proving the one-sidedness of any exclusively economic interpretation. He did so by offering what we would today call a symbolic interactionist interpretation of religion. True, the term "symbolic interactionism" was not introduced into sociology until more than half a century after Weber wrote *The Protestant Ethic*. Yet Weber's focus on the worldly significance of the meanings people attach to religious ideas makes him a forerunner of the symbolic interactionist tradition.

For specifically religious reasons, wrote Weber, followers of the Protestant theologian John Calvin stressed the need to engage in intense worldly activity and to display industry, punctuality, and frugality in their everyday life. In the view of men like John Wesley and Benjamin Franklin, people could reduce their religious doubts and ensure a state of grace by working diligently and living simply. Many Protestants took up this idea. Weber called it the Protestant ethic (Weber, 1958 [1904–5]: 183). According to Weber, the Protestant ethic had wholly unexpected economic consequences. Where it took root, and where economic conditions were favourable, early capitalist enterprise grew most robustly.

Subsequent research showed that the correlation between the Protestant ethic and the strength of capitalist development is weaker than Weber thought. In some places, Catholicism has coexisted with vigorous capitalist growth and Protestantism with relative economic stagnation (Samuelsson, 1961 [1957]). Nonetheless, Weber's treatment of the religious factor underlying social change is a useful corrective to Durkheim's emphasis on religion as a source of social stability. Along with Durkheim's work, Weber's contribution stands as one of the most important insights into the influence of religion on society.

Summing Up

- Durkheim and other functionalists have argued that the main function of religion is to increase social cohesion by providing ritualized opportunities for people to experience the collective conscience.
- Marx and other conflict theorists have argued that religion usually reinforces social inequality, although it sometimes incites social conflict.
- Feminists emphasize the traditionally patriarchal nature of the major world religions in both doctrinal matters and leadership roles.
- Max Weber inspired the symbolic interactionist interpretation of religion, which emphasizes the sacred meanings that people attach to various objects and practices, and the consequences of those meanings for everyday life.

THE RISE, DECLINE, AND PARTIAL REVIVAL OF RELIGION

Secularization

In 1651, British political philosopher Thomas Hobbes described life as "poore, nasty, brutish, and short" (Hobbes, 1968 [1651]: 150). His description fit the recent past. The standard of living in medieval and early modern Europe was abysmally low. On average, a

The persecution of witches in the early modern era was partly an effort to eliminate competition and establish a Christian monopoly over spiritual life. *Burning of Witches by Inquisition in a German Marketplace*. After a drawing by H. Grobert.

©Bettmann/Corbis/Magma

Robert Brym

Secularization

The **secularization thesis** says that religious institutions, actions, and consciousness are on the decline worldwide.

person lived only about 35 years. The forces of nature and human affairs seemed entirely unpredictable. In this context, magic was popular. It offered easy answers to mysterious, painful, and capricious events.

As material conditions improved, popular belief in magic, astrology, and witchcraft gradually lost ground (Thomas, 1971). Christianity substantially replaced them. The better and more predictable times made Europeans more open to the teachings of organized religion. In addition, the Church campaigned vigorously to stamp out opposing belief systems and practices. The persecution of witches in this era was partly an effort to eliminate competition and establish a Christian monopoly over spiritual life.

The Church succeeded in its efforts. In medieval and early modern Europe, Christianity became a powerful presence in religious affairs, music, art, architecture, literature, and philosophy. Popes and saints were the rock musicians and movie stars of their day. The Church was the centre of life in both its spiritual and its worldly dimensions. Church authority was supreme in marriage, education, morality, economic affairs, politics, and so forth. European countries proclaimed official state religions. They persecuted members of religious minorities.

In contrast, a few hundred years later, Max Weber remarked on how the world had become thoroughly "disenchanted." By the turn of the twentieth century, he said, scientific and other forms of rationalism were replacing religious authority. His observations formed the basis of what came to be known as the **secularization thesis**, undoubtedly the most widely accepted argument in the sociology of religion until the 1990s. According to the secularization thesis, religious institutions, actions, and consciousness are unlikely to disappear, but they are certainly on the decline worldwide (Tschannen, 1991).

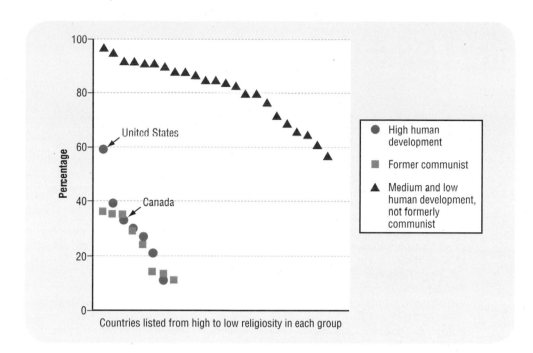

FIGURE 16.2

Percentage of People Who Think Religion Is Very Important, 44 Countries

This figure is derived from a survey of 38 000 people in 44 countries. (Poland is a former communist country and the UN ranks it 37th in its list of 53 countries in the "high human development" group. It is classified here as a former communist country.)

Sources: Pew Research Center, 2002; United Nations, 2002.

Religious Revival and Religious Fundamentalism

Despite the consensus about secularization that was evident in the 1980s, many sociologists modified their judgments in the 1990s. One reason for the change was that survey evidence showed that religion was not in an advanced state of decay. In many places, it was in robust health (see Figure 16.2 above). In Canada, 45 percent of Canadians said they attended religious services about once a week or more often in 2005. True, that figure was down by more than 20 percent from the 1940s. Yet in 2005, 82 percent of Canadians still said they believed in God—49 percent definitely and 33 percent with occasional doubt (Clark, 2003: 2; Bibby, 2011: 316; see Table 16.2).

The second reason many sociologists have modified their views about secularization is that an intensification of religious belief and practice has taken place among some people in recent decades. For example, since the 1960s, fundamentalist religious organizations have increased their membership. In North America, this tendency has been especially pronounced among Protestants (Finke and Starke, 1992). **Fundamentalists** interpret their scriptures literally, seek to establish a direct, personal relationship with the higher being(s) they worship, and are relatively intolerant of non-fundamentalists (Hunter, 1991). Fundamentalists often support conservative social and political issues (Bruce, 1988; see Box 16.1 on page 420).

Fundamentalists interpret their scriptures literally, seek to establish a direct, personal relationship with the higher being(s) they worship, are relatively intolerant of non-fundamentalists, and often support conservative social and political issues.

	1975	2005
Pray privately weekly or more often	37	45
Believe in God or a higher power	86	82
Identify with a religion	96	84
Attend monthly services	41	34
Attend weekly services	31	25

TABLE 16.2

Religious Involvement in Canada (in percent)

Source: Bibby, 2006: 205.

Sociology at the Movies

HARRY POTTER AND THE DEATHLY HALLOWS: PART I AND PART II

Harry Potter and the Deathly Hallows: Part I and *Part II* are the seventh and eighth movies in the highly popular series about a magical world of witches and wizards. In the first movie of the series, we learned that the hero, Harry Potter (played by Daniel Radcliffe) was orphaned at the age of one when the most evil wizard of all, Lord Voldemort, murdered Harry's parents and tried to kill Harry. Harry went to live with his unwelcoming relatives, the Dursleys, who housed him in a closet under their stairs. Shortly before his eleventh birthday, Harry's life is turned upside down. He learns that his dead parents were wizards, and so is he. He is summoned by a blizzard of letters to Hogwarts School of Witchcraft and Wizardry. The school, housed in a thousand-year-old castle and headed by the renowned Professor Dumbledore, provides select students with a seven-year program of instruction.

Harry Potter and the Deathly Hallows: Part I follows the story of Harry (Daniel Radcliffe) and his friends Hermione Granger (Emma Watson) and Ron Weasley (Rupert Grint) into maturity. The movie opens with the horrifying Lord Voldemort (Ralph Fiennes) and his Death Eaters plotting the destruction of Harry and his friends. When Harry and his friends get wind of the plot, they fly off to mysterious and remote locations so they can hide from Lord Voldemort while simultaneously searching out clues to the whereabouts of missing bits of his soul. Presumably, if they can make his soul whole again, he will end his evil and destructive ways. The final showdown between Harry and Lord Voldemort takes place in the final movie of the series. Voldemort succeeds in destroying Hogwarts, and the students who survive must choose between the hero and the villain.

All entries in the Harry Potter series have been enormously successful at the box office. Children are prominent in the lineups, many of them outfitted as if for Halloween. Some of them come to the movies on organized school field trips after studying the Harry Potter books at school.

Although most people view the Harry Potter series as harmless, others see things differently. They denounce both the films and the books on which they are based as "demonic." Many of the detractors are conservative Protestants who claim that the books glorify witchcraft, make "evil look innocent," and subtly draw "children into an unhealthy interest in a darker world that is occultic and dangerous to physical, psychological

During the same period, religious movements became dominant forces in many other countries. Hindu nationalists formed the government in India from 1998 to 2004. Jewish fundamentalists were always important players in Israeli political life, often holding the balance of power in Israeli governments, but they have become even more influential in recent years (Kimmerling, 2001: 173–207). A revival of Muslim fundamentalism began in Iran in the 1970s. Muslim fundamentalism then swept much of the Middle East, Africa, and parts of Asia. In Iran, Afghanistan, and Sudan, Muslim fundamentalists took power. Other predominantly Muslim countries' governments introduced elements of Islamic religious law (*shari'a*), either from conviction or as a precaution against restive populations (Lewis, 2002: 106). Religious fundamentalism has thus become a worldwide political phenomenon. In not a few cases it has taken extreme forms and involved violence as a means of establishing fundamentalist ideas and institutions (Juergensmeyer, 2000). At the same time, the Catholic Church played a critically important role in undermining communism in Poland, and Catholic "liberation theology" animated the successful fight against right-wing governments in Latin America (Kepel, 1994 [1991]; Smith, 1991). All these developments amount to a religious revival that was quite unexpected in, say, 1970.

Scene from *Harry Potter and the Deathly Hallows: Part I*

and spiritual well-being" (Shaw, 2001). Two years before he became Pope Benedict XVI, Cardinal Ratzinger wrote a letter of support to a Bavarian sociologist who had written a book critical of the Potter phenomenon. The future pope told her, "It is good that you are throwing light on Harry Potter, because these are subtle seductions that work imperceptibly, and because of that deeply, and erode Christianity in the soul before it can even grow properly"

(Associated Press, 2005). The controversy about the Potter series eased somewhat as some conservative Christian commentators claimed to find Christian themes in the movies and the books ("Finding God," 2005). But the controversy had been great enough to place J. K. Rowling, author of the Harry Potter books, fourth on the American Library Association's list of Top Ten Challenged Authors 1990–2004 (American Library Association, 2005).

Do you agree with efforts to ban the Harry Potter books and condemn the movies? In general, do you think that religious organizations should be able to get schools to ban books and movies? If so, do you draw the line at some types of influence? Would it be acceptable if a white religious organization got a predominantly white school to ban the works of Toni Morrison and Maya Angelou because they say derogatory things about whites? Would it be acceptable if a Jewish religious organization got a predominantly Jewish school to ban Shakespeare's *The Merchant of Venice* because it portrays Jews in an unflattering way? Would it be acceptable if a religious organization strongly influenced by feminism convinced students in an all-girls school to ban the works of Ernest Hemingway ("too sexist") or if an anti-feminist religious organization convinced students in an all-boys school to ban the writings of Margaret Atwood ("too anti-male")? In general, should religious organizations be allowed to influence schools to censor, or should censoring by religious organizations be banned?

The Revised Secularization Thesis

The spread of fundamentalist religion and the resilience and relative importance of religion in some highly developed countries, especially the United States, led some sociologists to revise the secularization thesis in the 1990s. The revisionists acknowledge that religion has become increasingly influential in the lives of some individuals and groups over the past 30 years. They insist, however, that the scope of religious authority has continued to decline in most people's lives. That is, for most people, religion has less and less to say about education, family issues, politics, and economic affairs, even though it may continue to be an important source of spiritual belief and practice. In this sense, secularization continues (Chaves, 1994; Yamane, 1997).

According to the **revised secularization thesis**, in most countries, worldly institutions have broken off (or differentiated) from the institution of religion over time. One such worldly institution is the education system. Religious bodies used to run schools and institutions of higher learning that are now run almost exclusively by non-religious authorities. Moreover, like other specialized institutions that separated from the institution of religion, the educational system is generally concerned with worldly affairs rather than with spiritual matters. Similarly, laws are enacted that confine religious standards to issues that are private and personal (see Box 16.2 on page 422).

The **revised secularization thesis** holds that worldly institutions break off from the institution of religion over time. As a result, religion governs an ever-smaller part of most people's lives and becomes largely a matter of personal choice.

BOX 16.2

It's Your Choice

SHOULD FAMILY LAW ALLOW FOR ARBITRATION BASED ON DIFFERENT RELIGIOUS TRADITIONS?

In Ontario, a 1991 law authorized the use of religious rules to govern legal decisions. Members of various religious groups were allowed to settle disputes by agreeing to binding arbitration that would conform to religious precepts. Issues that could be settled included divorce, child custody, and matters of inheritance. Under this allowance, disputes were settled by appeals to diverse legal traditions, including those of Aboriginals, Catholics, Mennonites, Jehovah's Witnesses, and Jews.

Controversy erupted over whether Islamic law, or *shari'a*, should be similarly treated. Some within the Islamic community were strongly opposed. Homa Arjomand, a refugee immigrant to Canada from Iran, organized an international campaign against the creation of *shari'a* courts in Canada (International Campaign, 2005). However, proponents pointed to a clear issue of equity—if Christians and Jews were allowed to practise their traditions, why could Muslims not do so as well?

A former Ontario attorney general and feminist activist, Marion Boyd, was commissioned to report on the matter. In the balance were conflicting ideals of multiculturalism and women's rights. Boyd's report of December 20, 2004, attempted to strike a balance. She supported the principle of extending family arbitration rights to Muslims but within strict limits defined by a list of 46 safeguards. Supporters included the rabbi who headed the Toronto *beth din* (court). But with headlines like "Will Canada introduce *shari'a* law?" echoing worldwide, critics continued to raise alarms about Canada becoming the first Western nation to formally recognize legal standards widely regarded as unjust to women (Trevelyan, 2004).

Ontario Premier Dalton McGuinty took a decisive stand on the symbolic date of September 11, 2005. He announced his intention to introduce legislation to abolish all family law arbitration based on religious traditions. "There will be one law for all Ontarians," he said (Freeze and Howlett, 2005).

What do you think? Should a society committed to multiculturalism allow people to practise their own traditions in resolving family disputes? Should individuals who assent of their own free will not be permitted to use such means? Or should the government use the power of law only when the rules apply to all citizens without exceptions?

The overall effect of the differentiation of secular institutions has been to make religion applicable only to the spiritual part of most people's lives. Because the scope of religious authority has been restricted, people look to religion for moral guidance in everyday life less often than they used to. Moreover, most people have turned religion into a personal and private matter rather than one imposed by a powerful, authoritative institution. Said differently, people feel increasingly free to combine beliefs and practices from various sources and traditions to suit their own tastes.

The Market Model

Another way to understand how a religious revival can take place in the midst of an overall decline in religious participation is to think of religion as a market. In this view, religious organizations are suppliers of services such as counselling, pastoral care, youth activities, men's and women's groups, performance groups, lectures, and discussions. These services are demanded by people who desire religious activities. Religious denominations are similar to product brands offering different "flavours" of religious experience (Barna, 2002; Bibby, 2002, 2004).

The market model raises the question of what motivates people to participate in religion. Some sociologists highlight the role of otherworldly or supernatural rewards

(Stark and Bainbridge, 1987, 1997). They argue that religion promises such rewards in exchange for particular types of behaviour. It follows that religion is particularly appealing to poor people because the wealthy enjoy material benefits and therefore have less need and desire for supernatural promises.

However, some sociologists question whether supernatural rewards interest only the poor, noting the many historical examples of people who gave up their wealth to live a simple, spiritual life. They also argue that religions offer worldly benefits that attract the well-to-do (Collins 1993). For instance, religious organizations regularly bestow public recognition on the wealthiest and most powerful people in society, as Toronto's Timothy Eaton Memorial Church, among others, testifies. For such reasons, religion may appeal to the rich just as much as it appeals to the poor.

The market model usefully clarifies the social bases of heterogeneity and change in religious life by emphasizing that religious observance in North America is a highly decentralized, largely unregulated, "industry" in which innovation and competition flourish. The market model also draws attention to the potential advantages of diversification. People often assume that an official or state religion, such as Christianity in the Roman Empire or Islam in contemporary Iran, is the best guarantee of religiosity. However, the market model emphasizes that religious diversity can also be a source of strength because it allows individuals to shop around for a religious organization that corresponds to their particular tastes. This may help explain why the United States, which has long banned state support for religion, has an exceptionally high rate of religious participation for a highly industrialized country (refer back to Figure 16.2). In contrast, some regions in which state and religion remained entwined until quite recently, such as Quebec, have experienced some of the sharpest dropoffs in participation in religious organizations.

Summing Up

- The secularization thesis—the view that religious institutions, actions, and consciousness are on the decline worldwide—is confounded by the resilience of religion in many countries and a religious revival that has taken place in many areas of the world over the past few decades.
- The revised secularization thesis maintains that despite the resilience and revival of religion for some people, religion is increasingly a private matter that affects fewer areas of life than was the case in the past.
- The market model views religious organizations as suppliers of religious services that people who desire religious activities demand. From this standpoint, religious denominations are like product brands offering different "flavours" of religious experience, and the popularity of different denominations is the result of innovation and competition in the religious marketplace.

RELIGION IN CANADA AND THE WORLD

Church, Sect, and Cult

Sociologists generally divide religious groups into just three types: churches, sects, and cults (Stark and Bainbridge, 1979; Troeltsch, 1931 [1923]; see Table 16.3 on page 424). As noted earlier, a *church* is any bureaucratic religious organization that has accommodated itself to mainstream society and culture. As a result, it may endure for many hundreds, if

TABLE 16.3

Church, Sect, and Cult Compared

Source: Statistics Canada, 2005, "Overview: Canada Still Predominantly Roman Catholic and Protestant." Retrieved November 28, 2005 (http://www12.statcan. ca/english/census01/Products/ Analytic/companion/rel/canada. cfm#growth).

	Church	Sect	Cult
Integration into society	High	Medium	low
Bureaucratization	High	Low	Low
Longevity	High	Low	Low
Leaders	Formally trained	Charismatic	Charismatic
Class base	Mixed	Low	Various but segregated

Ecclesia are state-supported churches.

Denominations are the various streams of belief and practice that some churches allow to coexist under their overarching authority.

Sects usually form by breaking away from churches because of disagreement about church doctrine. Sects are less integrated into society and less bureaucratized than churches are.

Charismatic authority is based on a belief in the claims of extraordinary individuals that they are inspired by a god or some higher principle.

Cults are small groups of people deeply committed to a religious vision that rejects mainstream culture and society.

not thousands, of years. The bureaucratic nature of a church is evident in the formal training of its leaders, its strict hierarchy of roles, and its clearly drawn rules and regulations. Its integration into mainstream society is evident in its teachings, which are generally abstract and do not challenge worldly authority. In addition, churches integrate themselves into the mainstream by recruiting members from all classes of society.

Churches take two main forms. First are **ecclesia** or state-supported churches. For example, Christianity became the state religion in the Roman Empire in 392 CE, and Islam is the state religion in Iran and Sudan today. State religions impose advantages on members and disadvantages on non-members. Tolerance of other religions is low in societies with ecclesia.

Alternatively, churches may be pluralistic, allowing diversity within the church and expressing tolerance of non-members. Pluralism allows churches to increase their appeal by allowing various streams of belief and practice to coexist under their overarching authority. These subgroups are called **denominations**. For example, United Church, Anglican, Baptist, Lutheran, and Presbyterian are the major Protestant denominations in Canada today.

Table 16.4 shows the percentage of Canadians who belonged to the major religions and denominations in Canada in 2001, the latest year for which census data on the subject are available. Roman Catholics remained the largest religious group at 43 percent of the population. Protestants were the second-largest group at 29 percent, down from 36 percent in 1991.

Sects typically form by breaking away from churches because of disagreement about church doctrine. Sometimes, sect members choose to separate themselves geographically, as the Hutterites do in their some 200 colonies, mostly in the Western provinces. However, even in urban settings, strictly enforced rules concerning dress, diet, prayer, and intimate contact with outsiders can separate sect members from the larger society. Hasidic Jews in Toronto and Montreal prove the viability of this isolation strategy. Sects are less integrated into society and less bureaucratized than churches. They are often led by **charismatic** leaders, men and women who claim to be inspired by supernatural powers and whose followers believe them to be so inspired. These leaders tend to be relatively intolerant of religious opinions other than their own. They tend to recruit like-minded members mainly from lower classes and marginal groups. Worship in sects tends to be highly emotional and based less on abstract principles than immediate personal experience (Stark, 1985: 314). Usually, sect-like groups appeal to the less affluent and churchlike groups to the more affluent. Many sects are short-lived, but those that do persist tend to bureaucratize and turn into churches. If religious organizations are to enjoy a long life, they require rules, regulations, and a clearly defined hierarchy of roles.

Although major Muslim subgroups are sometimes called denominations by non-Muslims, they are in some respects more appropriately seen as sects. That is because they often do not recognize one another as Muslim and sometimes come into violent conflict with one another, like the Sunni and Shi'a in Iraq today.

Cults are small groups of people deeply committed to a religious vision that rejects mainstream culture and society. Typically, charismatic individuals lead cults. They tend to

	Number	Percentage
Catholic	12 936 910	43.65
Roman Catholic	12 793 125	43.16
Ukrainian Catholic	126 200	0.43
Other Catholic	17 585	0.06
Protestant	8 654 850	29.20
United Church	2 839 125	9.58
Anglican	2 035 500	6.87
Baptist	729 475	2.46
Lutheran	606 590	2.05
Presbyterian	409 830	1.38
Pentecostal	369 480	1.24
Other Protestant	1 664 850	5.62
Christian Orthodox	479 620	1.62
Christian, not included elsewhere	780 450	2.63
Muslim	579 640	1.96
Jewish	329 995	1.11
Buddhist	300 345	1.01
Hindu	297 200	1.00
Sikh	278 410	0.94
Eastern religions	37 545	0.13
Other, para religious	63 975	0.22
No religious affiliation	4 900 095	16.53
Total	29 639 035	100.00

TABLE 16.4

Religious Adherence, Canada, 2001 (in percent)

Source: Statistics Canada, 2005, "Overview: Canada Still Predominantly Roman Catholic and Protestant." Retrieved November 28, 2005 (http://www.12statca.ca/english/census01/Products/Analytic/companion/rel/Canada.cfm#growth).

be class-segregated groups, recruiting members from only one segment of the stratification system: high, middle, or low. For example, many North American cults today recruit nearly all their members from among the university educated. Some of these cults seek converts almost exclusively on university and college campuses (Kosmin, 1991). Because they propose a radically new way of life, cults tend to recruit few members and soon disappear. There are, however, exceptions—and some extremely important ones at that. Jesus and Muhammad were both charismatic leaders of cults. They were so compelling that they and their teachings were able to inspire a large number of followers, including rulers of states. Their cults were thus transformed into churches.

Canada's changing immigration patterns have resulted in large gains for some religious groups. Notably, the number of Muslims more than doubled between 1991 and 2001 and reached an estimated 884 000 or 2.7 percent of the population in 2006. Hindus, Sikhs, Buddhists, and Jews each represented about 1 percent of the population in that year. Still, about two-thirds of recent immigrants are Christian while in 2006 about a fifth of Canadians said they had no religious affiliation (Statistics Canada, 2010h).

Religiosity

It is now time to conclude our discussion by considering some social factors that determine how important religion is to people; that is, their **religiosity**.

Religiosity refers to how important religion is to people.

We can measure religiosity in various ways. Strength of belief, emotional attachment to a religion, knowledge about a religion, frequency of performing rituals, and frequency of applying religious principles in daily life all indicate how religious a person is (Glock, 1962). Ideally, we ought to examine many measures to get a fully rounded and reliable picture of the social distribution of religiosity. For simplicity's sake, however, we focus on just two measures here: whether people attend religious services at least weekly and whether they regard their level of involvement in religious activities at various points in their life as having been high, moderate, low, or none.

Figure 16.3 focuses on the second measure for Canada. A fascinating pattern emerges from data. The Canadians most heavily involved in religious activities are preteens and seniors. As a result, involvement forms a U-shaped curve, falling among teenagers and young adults and then beginning to rise steadily after the age of 24. How can we explain this pattern? Preteens have little say over whether they attend classes in religious instruction. Their parents may take them to children's religious services. For many preteens, religious involvement is high because it is something that is required of them, even if their parents do not always follow suit. Meanwhile, elderly people have more time and need for religion. Because they are not usually in school, employed in the paid labour force, or busy raising a family, they have more opportunity than younger people do to go to church, synagogue, mosque, or temple. Moreover, because seniors are generally closer to illness and death than are younger people, they are more likely to require the solace of religion. To a degree, then, involvement in religious activities is a life-cycle issue. Children are relatively actively involved in religious activities because they are required to be, and seniors are relatively actively involved because they feel greater need for religious involvement and are in a position to act on that need.

Another issue is at stake here, too. Different age groups live through different times, and today's older people reached maturity when religion was a more authoritative force in society. A person's current religious involvement depends partly on whether he or she grew up in more religious times. Thus, although young people are likely to become more religiously involved as they age, they are unlikely ever to become as involved as seniors are today.

FIGURE 16.3

Religious Involvement over Time by Group

Source: Bibby, 2001: 275.

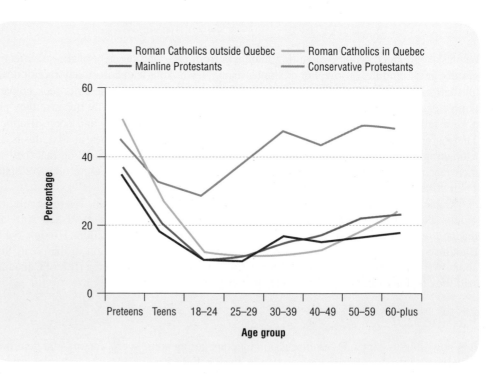

Omni Photo Communications Inc./Index Stock

Religiosity is partly a learned behaviour. Whether parents give a child a religious upbringing is likely to have a lasting impact on the child.

Adding weight to our historical argument is research showing that the likelihood of attending religious services at least weekly (our second measure of religiosity) depends on the region of the country in which a person lives. In particular, Canadians who live in the Atlantic provinces are more likely than other Canadians are to attend church weekly (Bibby, 1995: 126). New Brunswick, Nova Scotia, Prince Edward Island, and Newfoundland and Labrador are Canada's poorest and least industrialized provinces, and traditional religion is still quite deeply entrenched there. Religion is a more authoritative force in Atlantic Canada than elsewhere in the country because the region is less modernized than the other provinces.

Finally, we note that people whose parents attended religious services frequently are more likely to do so themselves (Jones, 2000). That is because religiosity is partly a *learned* behaviour. Whether parents give a child a religious upbringing is likely to have a lasting impact on the child.

We have not supplied an exhaustive list of the factors that determine religiosity. Even our brief overview, however, suggests that religiosity depends in part on obligation, opportunity, need, and learning. The people who are most religiously involved and attend religious services most frequently are those who must, those who were taught to be religious as children, those who were brought up in religiously authoritative environments, those who need organized religion most because of their advanced age, and those who have the most time to go to services.

The Future of Religion

A significant religious revival is taking place among some segments of the population in Canada and other countries today. At the same time, secularization seems to be a long-term, overall trend. In pre-1971 censuses, fewer than 1 percent of Canadians said they had no religious affiliation, but a 2009 poll placed the figure at 23 percent. In that same year, more than half of Canadians between the ages of 15 and 29 said they either have no religious affiliation or never attend a worship service (Valpy, 2010; Valpy and Friesen, 2010).

In the twenty-first century, gradual secularization will likely continue, but strong contrary trends are likely to crop up in various times and places. A substantial minority of people will undoubtedly continue to desire deep involvement with religious organizations, practices, and beliefs. This involvement will allow them to add meaning to their lives, and especially to important events associated with celebration and mourning throughout the life cycle. The fact that today's religious revival was quite unexpected just a few decades ago should warn us against being overly bold in our forecasts. It seems to us, however, that the two contradictory social processes of secularization and revival are likely to persist for some time to come, resulting in a more religiously polarized world.

Summing Up

- Religious organizations include churches, sects and cults, which vary in terms of their integration into society, degree of bureaucratization, longevity, leadership, and class base.
- Although Canada remains an overwhelmingly Christian country, partly because most immigrants are Christian, the Muslim community in particular has grown quickly in the last few decades.
- Attendance of religious services in Canada is most widespread among the very young and the elderly, among Atlantic Canadians, and among people whose parents attended religious services frequently.
- The twin phenomena of growing overall secularization and increased religiosity among some segments of the population are likely to lead to a world that is more polarized along religious lines.

SUMMARY

1. **What was Durkheim's theory of religion and what are the main criticisms that have been lodged against it?**
   Durkheim argued that the main function of religion is to increase social cohesion by providing ritualized opportunities for people to experience the collective conscience. Critics note that Durkheim ignored the ways religion can incite social conflict and reinforce social inequality.

2. **What was Weber's theory of religion and what is the main criticism that has been lodged against it?**
   Weber argued that religion acts like a railroad switch, determining the tracks along which history will be pushed by the force of political and economic interest. Protestantism, for example, invigorated capitalist development. Critics note that the correlation between economic development and the predominance of Protestantism is not as strong as Weber thought.

3. **How has feminism contributed to the debate about the role of religion in society?**
   Feminists have emphasized the patriarchal nature of all major world religions and promoted gender equality in doctrinal matters and the recruitment of personnel to priestly positions. Although some religions and denominations have resisted gender equality, others have embraced it.

4. What is the secularization thesis and what are the main criticisms that have been lodged against it?

The secularization thesis holds that religious institutions, actions, and consciousness are on the decline worldwide. Critics of the secularization thesis point out that there has been a religious revival in North America and elsewhere. They also note that survey and other evidence shows that religion in North America and elsewhere is resilient.

5. What is the revised secularization thesis?

The revised secularization thesis recognizes the religious revival and the resilience of religion but still maintains that the scope of religious authority has declined over time. The revisionists say that religion is increasingly restricted to the realm of the spiritual; it governs fewer aspects of people's lives and is more a matter of personal choice than it used to be.

6. What is the market model of religious life?

The market model of religious life characterizes religious organizations as suppliers of services that are in demand by people who desire religious activities. Accordingly, denominations compete in religious markets to establish congregations while congregations compete to attract local followings. As a result of this competition, religious choices are diverse and changing, and an overall tendency toward secularization may coexist with an intensification of religious practice on the part of a substantial minority of people.

7. What do the main world religions have in common?

The main world religions are founded by charismatic personalities in times of great trouble. The founding of new religions is typically animated by the desire for freedom and equality, always in the afterlife, and often in this one. The routinization of charisma typically makes religion less responsive to the needs of ordinary people and it often supports injustices.

8. What determines an individual's religiosity?

An individual's religiosity is determined by such factors as socialization (whether he or she was brought up in a religious family), the authoritativeness of religion in his or her area of residence (residing in a region where religion is authoritative increases the individual's religiosity), and the individual's age (high religiosity is associated with the very young and the elderly).

KEY TERMS

charismatic authority (p. 424)

church (p. 416)

collective conscience (p. 411)

cults (p. 424)

denominations (p. 424)

ecclesia (p. 424)

fundamentalists (p. 419)

profane (p. 411)

religiosity (p. 425)

revised secularization thesis (p. 421)

rituals (p. 411)

routinization of charisma (p. 413)

sacred (p. 411)

sects (p. 424)

secularization thesis (p. 418)

totems (p. 411)

WEB RESOURCES

Companion Website for This Book

http://www.compass4e.nelson.com

Begin by clicking on the Student Resources section of the website. Next, select the chapter you are studying from the pull-down menu. From the Student Resources page you have easy access to additional Weblinks and other resources. The website also has many useful tips to aid you in your study of sociology, including practice tests for each chapter.

InfoTrac® Search Terms

These search terms are provided to assist you in beginning to conduct research on this topic by visiting http://www.infotrac-college.com:

cult
secularization
fundamentalism

CHAPTER
17

Education

IN THIS CHAPTER, YOU WILL LEARN THAT

- A complete system of schools, from elementary to post-graduate, is the prerequisite of industrial society and is found in all rich societies. Consequently, national wealth and national education levels are strongly related.

- School systems carry out two tasks: homogenizing and sorting. Students are made similar by indoctrination into a common cultural system but are also steered into different social classes.

- Mass education, once established, brings about nearly universal literacy and numeracy. Mass education makes large populations linguistically and culturally uniform, providing the basis for nationalism.

- Functionalists believe that education fosters meritocracy. Conflict theorists argue that the high cost of education favours the wealthy and that schools inevitably favour students whose parents are highly educated.

- Inside schools, inequalities are reproduced by a hidden curriculum that values middle-class manners and attitudes, testing and tracking that segregate students by class background, and self-fulfilling prophecies of poor performance by lower-class students.

- Women now exceed men in years of completed schooling. However, men remain more likely to complete programs that lead to high pay.

Janaka Dharmasena/Shutterstock

THE RIOT IN ST. LÉONARD

On the night of September 10, 1969, a confrontation that had long been brewing in the Montreal suburb of St. Léonard boiled over. A march organized by the French unilinguist *Ligue pour l'intégration scolaire* paraded through a predominantly Italian neighbourhood. Despite pleas for calm from leaders on both sides, many people turned out to march while others, hostile to the marchers' cause, showed up to line the route. Scuffles broke out and a full-scale brawl ensued. Roughly a thousand people participated. Police read the Riot Act and made about 50 arrests.

Commentators of all political persuasions deplored the violence, but today the St. Léonard riot is recognized as a turning point in Quebec history. It culminated in Bill 101, the law making French the language of public administration, imposing French language tests for admission to the professions, requiring most businesses with more than 50 employees to operate mainly in French, and requiring collective agreements to be drafted in French. Bill 101 also ensured that in Quebec children of immigrants are required to receive primary and secondary schooling in French.

A year before the street violence erupted, the language of instruction in public schools emerged as a hotly contested issue. Political commentators raised concerns that French was in demographic decline and that francophones were at risk of becoming a minority in the province's biggest city, Montreal. They noted that in 1963, the St. Léonard school board had responded to an influx of new residents of Italian descent by establishing the option of bilingual education. Soon, more than 90 percent of children with neither English nor French background ("allophones") were enrolling in the bilingual track and, of those, 85 percent continued to English secondary schools. The public school system was contributing heavily to the Anglicization of Montreal.

Brian Summers/First Light

In 1968, the St. Léonard school board eliminated bilingual programs, setting off a cycle of protests and counter-protests. Allophone parents, mainly of Italian descent and forming 30 percent of the community, withdrew children from the public schools and organized their own "basement schools" in English. Meanwhile, francophone unilinguists mobilized and were able to dominate school board elections and win a referendum requiring a unilingual school system. Elites tried but failed to find a middle ground. Ultimately, in 1976, the Parti Québécois won their first election, Bill 101 was enacted, and immigrants' children were restricted to French schools by law.

It is hardly surprising that schooling in Quebec has evoked sharp controversy. Schools are hugely important institutions. They teach students a common culture that forms a framework for social life. They shape work, politics, and much else. Moreover, which children have access to which schools is the starting point for sorting children into adult jobs and social classes. Not surprisingly, therefore, fierce conflicts often arise around such educational issues as who can or must go to what kinds of schools and what will be taught.

Schools are important and sometimes controversial because they endow young people with the key capacities of communication, coordination, and economic productivity. Schools accomplish two main tasks: homogenizing and sorting. They create homogeneity out of diversity by instructing all students in uniform curriculum, and they sort students into paths that terminate in different social classes. Homogeneity is achieved by enforcing common standards that serve as a cultural common denominator. Sorting favours students who develop the greatest facility in the common culture while confining those of lesser skills to subordinate work roles and lower ranks in the class structure.

Homogenizing and sorting are organized at primary, secondary, and postsecondary levels, and, within those levels, in public and private institutions. Individuals typically move in a regulated way from one educational site to the next. Curricula are adapted to what has been taught earlier, often in other places, and to prepare students for subsequent studies.

To fully understand education, we must grasp its broader implications. For example, mass schooling is a relatively recent development that is closely tied to industrialism and to maintaining a modern, productive economy. However, industrialism needs interchangeable workers who can move among ever-changing, technically sophisticated production facilities. Potential workers have to be culturally homogenized so they have similar outlooks and a common language, but some of them have to be identified as able and willing to receive specialized training to carry out technically demanding tasks.

Although the number of years people devote to education has steadily risen, more education is easier to obtain if you are born in a rich country and into a prosperous family. In turn, more education ensures better treatment in labour markets, such as lower rates of unemployment and higher earnings. Thus, education turns students into citizens by giving them a common outlook but it also reproduces the class structure and the structure of global inequality.

Summing Up

- Schools perform two main functions: they homogenize young people by socializing them into a shared culture and they sort young people into different levels of certification and, ultimately, different social classes.

MASS EDUCATION: AN OVERVIEW

The education system has displaced organized religion as the main purveyor of formal knowledge, and it is second in importance only to the family as an agent of socialization (see Chapter 4, Socialization). By the time you finished high school, you had spent nearly 13 000 hours in a classroom.

Three hundred years ago, only a small minority of people learned to read and write. A century ago most people in the world never attended school. As late as 1950, only about 10 percent of the world's countries boasted systems of compulsory mass education (Meyer, Ramirez, and Soysal, 1992). Even today, many countries in Africa have literacy rates below 50 percent, while in nations like India and Egypt a third of the population is illiterate.

In contrast, Canada has just over 16 000 elementary and secondary schools employing nearly 276 000 teachers, who educate 5.3 million children. (Elementary schools are primary schools, high schools are secondary schools, and colleges and universities are postsecondary institutions.) In 2008–9, university enrolment stood at 1.11 million (Human Resources and Skills Development Canada [HRSDC], 2011b). The proportion of people between the ages of 25 and 64 with a college or university degree is higher in Canada than in any other country at 49 percent (Japan is in second place at 43 percent, the United States third at 41 percent; HRSDC, 2011b). Enrolment rates are more than 95 percent for five-year-olds and remain at about that level through the mandatory schooling age of 16–18 years. Since 1990, the proportion of Canadians over the age of 14 with trade or college certification or a university degree has increased from about 30 percent to over 50 percent (HRSDC, 2011b). Clearly, in Canada education is a way of life.

Universal mass education is a recent phenomenon and is limited to relatively wealthy countries (see Figure 17.1 on page 434). Around 1900, Canada and the United States were the first countries to approach universal educational participation by young people. Societies that today are highly advanced in terms of economy and technology, such as Japan, Italy, and England, lagged far behind.

FIGURE 17.1

Elementary School
Enrolments per 1000
Children Aged 5–14 for
Various Countries,
1870–1930

Source: Peter H. Lindert, *Growing
Public: Social Spending and Economic
Growth since the Eighteenth Century*
(Cambridge, UK, New York: 2004),
pp. 91–93. Reprinted with the
permission of Cambridge University
Press.

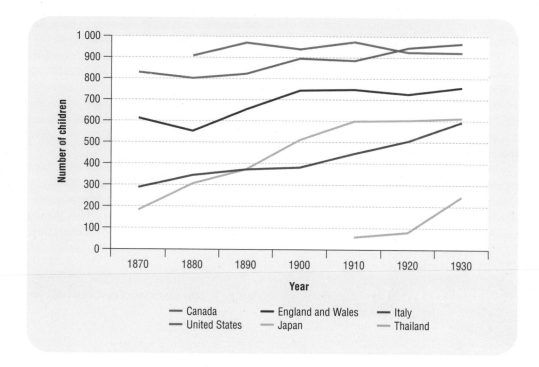

For most of history, families were chiefly responsible for socializing the young and training them to perform adult roles. Thus, in preindustrial Europe, the vast majority of children learned to work as adults by observing and helping their elders in the largely agricultural economy. Only a small urban minority had much use for skills like reading and arithmetic. The literate and numerate few were typically trained in religious institutions. In fact, before the rise of Protestantism, priests held a virtual monopoly on literacy. The Catholic Church's authority depended on the *in*ability of ordinary people to read the Bible. It even went so far as to persecute people who made the Bible available in local languages. William Tyndale, whose English translation became the standard King James Bible, was burned at the stake for his efforts in 1536.

Uniform Socialization

Creating systems of education with sufficient resources to include all children was a social change of breathtaking scope. Training in families had been decentralized, unorganized, and uneven in quality. Religious training was never widely available and tended to set people apart from the surrounding community. Replacing these forms of instruction with a centralized and rationalized system created strong pressures toward uniformity and standardization. Diversity among families, regions, and religious traditions gradually gave way to homogenized indoctrination into a common culture.

Canada was something of an exception because, in the nineteenth century, the provinces recognized separate school systems for Catholics and Protestants. However, lack of recognition of distinct religious tracks by postsecondary institutions pressured secondary schools to cover the same topics in the same fashion in preparing their students for more advanced training. As a result, students today can travel thousands of kilometres for higher education and experience no more discontinuity than do those who attend the nearest school.

Surrendering children to state control was not universally popular, especially at first. Some students preferred skipping class to sitting in school, and special police (truant officers) were charged with tracking down absentees, who were then punished. Effective mass education was achieved only through laws that made attendance compulsory. All Canadian provinces and territories now require parents to ensure their children are educated up to a certain age. Although more than 5 percent of families send children to private schools, and about 80 000 children are home-schooled (Fraser Institute, 2007), some 94 percent of families surrender their children to public schooling (Statistics Canada, 2001a). Although some children resist schooling's forced drill toward cultural ideals that are at odds with their other experiences, they are in a small minority.

Rising Levels of Education

Making education available to everyone, whether they liked it or not, was only a starting point. The amount of education that people receive has risen steadily, and this trend shows no sign of abating. In 1951, fewer than 1 in 50 Canadians had completed a university degree. Completing university allowed a person entry into a narrow elite. Today, nearly 1 in 5 Canadians over age 14 has a university degree, and over half have postsecondary education. In 50 years, a rarity became common (Table 17.1).

Canadians' growing commitment to higher education is illustrated by Table 17.1. Since 1990, the percentage of those without a high school diploma almost halved (from 38 to 20 percent), while those with a university degree nearly doubled (from 11 to 21 percent). Widespread growth in postsecondary education reflects the recognition that education is the most viable option for improving employment opportunities.

Sociologists distinguish *educational attainment* from *educational achievement*. **Educational achievement** is the knowledge or skills that an individual acquires. Achievement refers to mastery of educational content and, in principle, is reflected in grades. We say "in principle" because the validity of grades is a matter of debate (see Box 17.1 on page 436) **Educational attainment** reflects participation in educational programs and is measured by the number of years of schooling completed or, for higher levels, certificates and degrees earned. In theory, educational attainment and achievement are directly related. More time in educational institutions leads to more knowledge and skills. In practice, the connection is looser, since educational exposure affects students differently. Nonetheless, educational exposure is necessary, so who continues schooling and who does not raises important issues that we address below. In principle, selection might depend only on individual educational achievements. In practice, non-academic factors, including family background, play a large role in determining who completes an advanced education.

Educational achievement is the learning of valuable skills and knowledge.

Educational attainment is the number of years of schooling successfully completed or, for higher learning, the degrees or certificates earned.

Individual Advantages and Disadvantages

Higher educational attainment helps people get jobs and earn more. Figure 17.2 on page 437 illustrates how education level influenced rates of unemployment in Canada in 2009. Lower rates of unemployment were associated with more education. People who did not finish high school had an unemployment rate three times as high as did people with a university degree.

Education also increases earnings. As Figure 17.3 on page 437 shows, the odds of earning high pay steadily improve as educational attainment increases. In 2009, people with a certificate less than a bachelor's degree earned $30 116, those with a university degree averaged $58 767, while those with more than a bachelor's degree earned $69 230 (Statistics Canada, 2009c). The pattern is far from rigid—people with every level of education are found at each level of earnings. However, more education and better earnings tend to go together.

Without high school diploma	20
High school diploma	20
Some postsecondary	8
College or trade certification	31
University degree	21

TABLE 17.1

Population Ages 14 and over, by Highest Level of Educational Attainment, Canada, 2010 (in percent)

Source: HRSDC calculations based on Statistics Canada. Labour force survey estimates (LFS), by educational attainment, sex and age group, annual (CANSIM Table 282-0004). Ottawa: Statistics Canada, 2011. Retrieved April 29, 2011 (http://www4.hrsdc.gc.ca/.3ndic.1t.4r@-eng.jsp?iid=29).

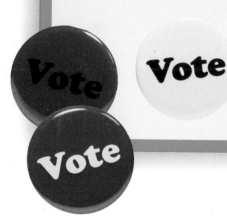

Social Policy: What Do You Think?

IS GRADE INFLATION HARMFUL?

In schools and universities, grades are the principal indicator of educational achievement. Grades are supposed to reflect what students know. But do they? We can test the validity of school grades by comparing the grades teachers assign to standardized examination results. When this comparison was completed in New Brunswick and Newfoundland and Labrador, the results revealed substantial grade inflation (Laurie, 2007). In math, for example, the average standardized exam score was 60 percent,

while school grades in math averaged 74 percent.

Two sociologists (Côté and Allahar, 2007) report that grade inflation is a clear trend in Canadian universities. By their estimate, under half of undergraduate students received grades of A or B in the 1970s. Today, comparable figures range between 60 and 80 percent, depending on the institution and course. In the early 1980s, about 40 percent of students applying to Ontario's universities had A averages; now over 60 percent do.

Some commentators attribute grade inflation to an attitude of entitlement among the current generation of students (Laurie, 2007; Tylee, 2005). Many in this generation attended elementary schools with "no-fail" policies and now consider high grades a right. Failure is not considered a possible outcome, and Cs are no longer considered average. In a recent survey of first-year university students, 70 percent rated themselves as above average (a statistical impossibility; Côté and Allahar, 2007). Students now come

to university with the orientation of consumers who expect to receive good grades in exchange for paying tuition.

Educational institutions are agents of socialization. Setting expectations is an important part of this process. Grade inflation promotes lowered expectations. If high grades are easily awarded, good students are not challenged to strive for excellence. Likewise, grade inflation gives weaker students a false sense of their competence, which does little to encourage them to improve. Schools and universities that participate in grade inflation are shifting their mandate from the promotion of excellence to keeping more students in the education system for a longer time.

What do you think? Did you have to work hard in school to get good grades? Do your university courses challenge you to achieve excellence? Does paying tuition give students a right to high grades or even passing grades? What consequences does grade inflation in the educational system have for the economy? Why do you think grade inflation has taken place?

In the next section, we examine how mass education arose. We then examine theories that connect the rise of mass education to industrialization, arguing that education provides a basis for collective and individual wealth and motivates widespread loyalty to culture and society. We will see how education reproduces class inequality. We conclude by reviewing a series of recent developments and future challenges for Canada's system of mass schooling.

The Rise of Mass Schooling

What accounts for the spread of mass schooling? Sociologists usually highlight four factors: the development of the printing press that led to inexpensive book production, the Protestant Reformation, the spread of democracy, and industrialism. Let us consider each of these factors in turn.

First, the printing press: In 1436, Johannes Gutenberg introduced the printing press with movable type in Europe. The effect was revolutionary. Books were expensive when scribes were the only source of new copies. The printing press led to a dramatic fall in book prices and an explosion of supply. Many of the new printed books were in the vernacular—languages used every day by common folk—and not in the Latin that only scholars understood. Literacy spread beyond elite circles, first in cities and eventually into rural areas, as inexpensive books fostered demand for schools to teach children the useful art of reading (Eisenstein, 1983).

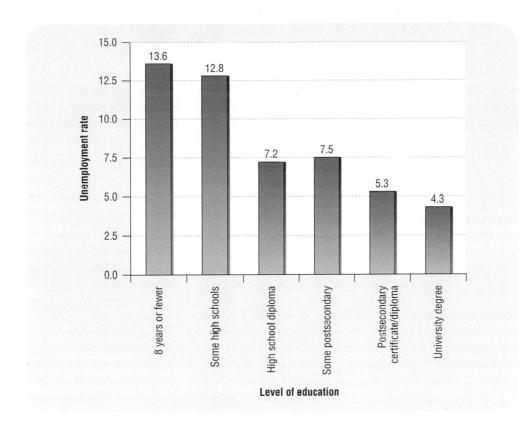

FIGURE 17.2

Unemployment Rate by
Highest Level of Education
Completed, Canada, 2008–9
(in percent)

Source: Statistics Canada,
2008–09, Labour Force Survey.
"Unemployment Rate and
Employment Rate, by Education
Level". Retrieved March 20, 2011
(http://www.rhdcc-hrsdc.qc.ca/eng/
employment/ei/reports/eimar_2009/
annex/ann ex1_5.shtml).

Second, Protestantism: The Catholic Church relied on priests to convey dogma to believers. The education of priests was a primary motivation for the foundation of European universities in the Middles Ages. However, in the early sixteenth century, Martin Luther, a German monk, began to criticize the Catholic Church. Protestantism grew out of his criticisms. The Protestants believed that the Bible alone, and not Church doctrine, should guide Christians. They expected Christians to have more direct contact with the word of God than was allowed by the Catholic Church. Accordingly, Protestants needed to be able to read the scriptures for themselves. The rise of Protestantism was thus a spur to popular literacy.

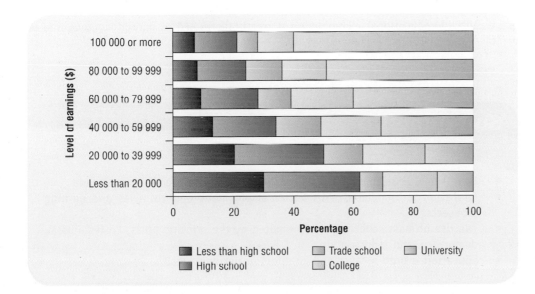

FIGURE 17.3

Earnings by Amount of
Education, Canada, 2006

Source: Created from analysis of
Statistics Canada 2006 Census,
public use microdata files, May 3,
2011.

Third, democracy: The rise of political democracy led to free education for all children. Where local populations acquired the democratic means to tax themselves, tax-supported schools arose. France, which gave all men voting rights in 1848, expanded education before England, where the right to vote was not widespread until a few decades later. This side of the Atlantic followed a similar pattern (Lindert, 2004: 107). The earliest school systems were established in Upper Canada and the northern United States about 1870. By 1900, Canada and the United States were the first countries in the world in which enrolment rates for all children ages 5 to 14 exceeded 90 percent. Another first: at least in elementary education, girls were enrolled at almost the same rate as boys were.

Mass Schooling and National Wealth

The fourth and most important reason for the rise of mass schooling was industrialization. Mass education was widely recognized as an absolute necessity for creating an industrial economy.

The Industrial Revolution began in England in the 1780s. Germany and the United States soon sought to catch up to England, and by the turn of the twentieth century, they had surpassed it. Observers noted that both Germany and the United States had school systems that offered places to nearly all young people. Literacy and numeracy were widespread, although what counted as literacy in those days would not impress us today. Historians assess literacy of that period by counting the rate at which people signed marriage registers or similar documents with a name and not merely an X or another mark. However, as the number of people achieving such minimal performance rose, so did the number of people with much higher levels of literacy. Eventually, it was evident that a highly productive economy requires an education system large enough to create a mass labour force, and rich enough to train and employ researchers able to work at the cutting edge of modern science. Democratic countries led the way, but communist countries, like the former Soviet Union, also invested heavily in education to foster economic development.

Today, investment in education is acknowledged as an important step in achieving great national wealth. However, the connection between education and wealth is by no means automatic. Some countries educate a relatively small proportion or a relatively large proportion of their population given their level of wealth (United Nations, 2005).

Education is not only a *source* of wealth; it is also a *product* of wealth. After all, education is expensive. Raising education levels for entire populations requires overcoming a vicious cycle: A significant fraction of a country's population must invest a great deal of time and money to become educated before there are enough teachers to instruct nearly everyone. This time and money must somehow be saved from the pressures of producing enough to supply necessities, like food and shelter. What is true for individuals is also true for societies: Education enhances the ability to generate earnings and wealth, but educational accumulation is greatly facilitated by earlier accumulation of wealth (see Box 17.2).

Summing Up

- Educational achievement and educational attainment are rising in Canada.
- Education is associated with better employment opportunities and earning prospects.
- The rise of mass schooling was promoted by the printing press, Protestantism, democracy, and industrialism.
- Education is both a cause and an effect of national wealth.

Social Policy: What Do You Think?

ARE VIRTUAL CLASSROOMS NEXT?

Because education is so expensive, governments, universities, and public school boards are always looking for ways to cut costs. In recent years, online courses have become increasingly popular in Canada and elsewhere. They maximize revenue by accommodating more students than can be fit into a classroom and they minimize the cost of overhead (building construction and maintenance) and labour (instructors' salaries). Are virtual classrooms—online courses without instructors—next?

You can imagine Naomi Baptiste's surprise when she arrived at her pre-calculus class at North Miami Beach Senior High School in September 2010 and found a bank of computers instead of a teacher (Herrera, 2011). Naomi is one of 7000 students in Miami-Dade public schools who were enrolled in classes without teachers in the academic year 2010–11. Only a classroom "facilitator" was available to make sure students progressed and to deal with technical issues.

While virtual classrooms save money, quality of learning is a separate issue. Alix Braun, a sophomore at Miami Beach High taking Advanced Placement macroeconomics in a virtual classroom, said, "none of [my classmates] want to be there." According to Chris Kirchner, an English teacher at Coral Reef Senior High School in Miami, "the way our state is dealing with class size is nearly criminal" (quoted in Herrera, 2011).

Virtual classrooms (sometimes blended with intermittent, real classroom instruction) are spreading to K–8 public schools in Florida and to public schools in other states, such as Illinois and Nebraska. Can Canada be far behind? What kinds of students are most likely to be required to take classes in virtual classrooms? How will the spread of virtual classrooms likely affect social stratification?

THE FUNCTIONS OF EDUCATION

Latent Functions

Schools do not merely carry out training; they also concentrate young people for extended periods in common locations. In children's early years, the law requires attendance. In more advanced programs, economic incentives and family pressures encourage student attendance. Certain latent or unintended consequences arise from segregating people by age and forcing them to spend much of their time together.

One result is that schools encourage the development of a separate youth culture that can conflict with parents' values (Coleman, 1961). When students are asked to rank the popularity of fellow students, rankings don't centre on academic achievement. Instead, they signify athletic and social success. Many students who are low on such peer rankings find the youth culture of school alienating.

Role conflict occurs when a person's situation presents incompatible demands. One result of role conflict is alienation or disconnection from others, as Lance Roberts recalls from his own high school experience. "I attended high school in the 1960s and, besides girls, had two major interests—grades and basketball. These interests were connected since, if your grades were poor, you were ineligible to play on the varsity basketball team. In my school, unacceptable grades were below 45 percent. For students on athletic teams, unacceptable grades were circled in red on your report card. Three red circles and you were off the team.

CP Picture Archive/Jacques Boissinot

Schools concentrate young people into a small number of places for extended periods of time. This has unintended consequences, such as encouraging the growth of a separate youth culture.

"During basketball season, our team practised three times a day. Report cards were distributed just before lunch, so at the noon practice, the locker room was full of inquiries and boasts about red circles. Statements like 'How many did you get?' and 'I was damn lucky, I thought Mr. Charles would give me a third one for sure' filled the room. Since our top three players were routinely in danger of ineligibility, their opinions set the standard. The norm was clear: Getting red circles was acceptable (even preferable), as long as you remained eligible to play.

"In my first year on the team, a teammate asked, 'Hey, how many red circles?' My report of 'none' was greeted with mean-spirited laughter from several players and endless chiding, bordering on harassment. As an impressionable adolescent who desperately wanted my teammates to accept me, the chastisement hurt.

"When I mentioned this situation at dinner that evening, my parents gave a united, emphatic reply: 'Anything less than your best school performance is unacceptable.' This external demand reinforced the lesson I took away from my just-completed summer job as a labourer. Educational achievement was important to my family and me.

"Nonetheless, I found the conflicting expectations of parents and teammates stressful. In class and out, I was awash with anxiety. I obsessed over the red-circle issue. I withdrew and felt lonely, isolated, and powerless. I dreaded going to practice for fear of hearing my new nickname, 'Egghead.' My performance both on the court and in class suffered. The coach inquired about what was troubling me, but I was too embarrassed to tell my story.

"On the next round of report cards, my grades dropped—but not nearly enough to qualify for membership in the red-circle club. Lower grades produced a predictable response from my parents, and I was still stuck with an outsider stigma by key teammates. I was irritable and felt overwhelmed and sad. Role conflict generated debilitating stress.

"The conclusion of the basketball season brought relief. However, my experience was so stressful I decided not to play basketball the following year. I matured during my season off and returned to the courts in my final year of high school, but not without lasting memories of what role conflict can do."

Encouraging the development of a separate youth culture is only one of the latent functions performed by schools. At higher levels, educational institutions also serve as a "marriage market" that brings potential mates together. Students in educational institutions often share common social class and related background characteristics. Moreover, since many students postpone mate selection until they complete their education, potential mates often share similar educational qualifications. In these ways, educational settings encourage the choice of partners who share social origins and destinations (Rytina, Blau, Blum, and Schwartz, 1988). The result is **assortative mating**—choosing a mate who is similar to oneself on various ranking criteria.

Assortative mating occurs when marriage partners are selected so that spouses are similar on various criteria of social rank.

Schools also perform other unintended functions. For example, in the early years they provide the custodial service of keeping children under close surveillance for much of the day and freeing parents to work. University and college attendance postpones full-time labour force participation, which helps restrict job competition and support wage levels (Bowles and Gintis, 1976). Through their encouragement of critical, independent thinking, educational institutions can also become "schools of dissent" that challenge authoritarian regimes and promote social change (Brower, 1975; Freire, 1972).

Manifest Functions: The Logic of Industrialism

The characteristics of institutions in preindustrial societies vary widely. Functionalists argue that industrialism causes convergence among societies, dictating that social institutions develop according to a common pattern. Said differently, social institutions must perform certain common, manifest (or intended) functions to make industrialism possible. In particular, industrialism requires the widespread application of science and technology in the economy, making work more specialized and technical, and changing working conditions (Kerr, Dunlop, Harbison, and Myers, 1960: 36). The education system mirrors these trends.

Cultural Homogeneity and Solidarity

Durkheim saw people as continuously torn between egoistic needs and moral impulses, with schools enhancing the moral side by working to create cultural uniformity and social solidarity. By instilling a sense of authority, discipline, and morality in children, schools make society cohesive (Durkheim, 1956, 1961 [1925]).

Contemporary sociologists acknowledge Durkheim's argument and broaden it. They point to a variety of manifest functions schools perform that are aimed at creating solidarity through cultural homogeneity. For example, Canadian schools teach students civic responsibility, pride in their nation, respect for the law, and to think of democracy as the best form of government and capitalism as the best type of economic system (Callahan, 1962). Schools also transmit shared knowledge and culture between generations, thereby fostering a common cultural identity.

Common School Standards

The uniformity of much industrial work requires an education system that teaches workers common standards. Staffing schools to meet this goal was a huge challenge. A large number of student teachers had to be taught the same outlook and skills. Language was a problem too because, until recently, substantial variations in language and dialect existed within small areas. Creating cultural conformity required designating certain conventions of grammar, spelling, and pronunciation as correct and imposing these conventions on teacher-candidates and certification centres. A demanding and expensive system had to be created in which a privileged few were recruited to elite institutions, socialized to the new standards, and then sent back to peripheral regions to impose the uniform standards on students. By this means, the language conventions at such university centres as Oxford and the Sorbonne were established as the cultural ideal against which student performances were judged.

National Solidarity

Before the rise of public education, an individual identified with the idiosyncratic worldview of his or her local community. As public education grew, mass socialization shifted to a common set of cultural beliefs, norms, and values directed by a central state. In this way, public education promoted membership in a national community composed of individuals who were mostly strangers but who felt connected because of a shared culture. They became part of an "imagined community" known as the nation.

The loyalties of imagined communities were centred on states because only states could afford the enormous expense of mass education. States provided classrooms with flags, rituals, patriotic songs, and historical myths, along with adults who supplied enthusiastic leadership. Legal requirements meant participation was not a matter of choice. Upper Canada led the world in not only providing universal education but requiring it. In 1871, Ontario pioneered compulsory education by fining parents whose children ages 7 to 12 did not attend school for at least four months each year. Since then, all provinces and territories have gradually tightened such requirements; most now require that students stay in school until they turn 16. Tightening requirements had the desired effect of increasing the number of years children spent in school and, subsequently, reducing unemployment rates (Oreopoulos, 2005). Such benefits soften the harsh realities of required participation imposed on those who unwillingly participate in state-sponsored public schooling.

Functionalists are correct in saying that mass education offers many people a ticket to economic, social, and cultural success. They also have a point when they argue that mass education socializes students into a common culture that enhances economic development.

Nonetheless, the functionalist view of education is one-sided. While education can produce these positive individual and social outcomes, it does not do so for everyone. Institutionalized education also produces division and disadvantage, as you will now learn.

Summing Up

- Education performs latent functions, including the creation of a separate youth culture and a marriage market.
- The manifest functions of mass education include promoting cultural uniformity and national solidarity. Common school standards also prepare students for participation in an industrial economy.

SORTING INTO CLASSES AND HIERARCHIES: CONFLICT PERSPECTIVES

Functionalists argue that modern educational institutions provide all students with equal opportunity to excel. In this view, differences in ability, motivation, and effort allow some students to perform better than others do. Those who learn poorly get inferior jobs, but that's the nature of a **meritocracy**—a social hierarchy in which rank is allocated by tests of individual merit. In a meritocracy, some children are born to lower-ranked families but if they perform well in school they can expect upward mobility. Likewise, some children are born to higher-ranked families but if they perform poorly in school they can expect downward mobility (Bell, 1973).

Conflict theorists challenge the functionalist assumption that educational attainment and subsequent social ranking are regulated by performance based on individual merit. They identify other factors that contribute to educational and economic success, and we survey several of them here. We also examine several prominent features of primary and secondary schooling that tend to preserve the stratification system. We begin by first examining how higher education and advanced degrees are forms of privilege that are less accessible to those with lower-class backgrounds.

A **meritocracy** is a social hierarchy in which rank corresponds to individual capacities fairly tested against a common standard.

Economic Barriers to Higher Education

It might be possible to create an education system in which academic performance is the sole criterion for allocating people to the stratification system. However, few academic programs admit only qualified people and supply all who do qualify with funding to meet all expenses. In most cases, higher education in Canada and elsewhere requires students and their families to shoulder significant financial burdens. Tuition fees are rising. On average, Canadian full-time undergraduates paid $5138 in tuition fees in 2010–11, up from $1185 in 1988–89. Taking inflation into account, this represents a 164 percent increase. During the 1990s, undergraduate tuition increased at an annual average rate of nearly 10 percent, and since 2000 it has increased at an annual average rate of nearly 4 percent (Statistics Canada, 2009k). Moreover, tuition is only part of the cost of a year at school, particularly for those who leave home to pursue their studies.

Social class origin strongly affects how much formal education people attain (Goldthorpe and Breen, 1997). Many countries, Canada among them, have greatly expanded postsecondary education in the past 50 or 60 years. Expansion has lessened class effects, but it has not eliminated them.

How exactly does family income affect postsecondary participation rates? The evidence shows a clear social gradient in which postsecondary education increases at every step of the family income ladder. While access to postsecondary education is much less restricted by family income in Canada than it is in the United States, substantial social inequality remains. About a third of students from families in the bottom quarter of the income distribution attend postsecondary institutions, while about half from families in the top quarter do (Belley, Frenette, and Lochner, 2010; Statistics Canada, 2007). In addition, while the average student loan on completion of university was $16 341 in 2008–9 ($10 085 on completion of college), students from less affluent families have to borrow more money to complete their education, so they face a significantly weightier economic burden when they graduate (HRSDC, 2011a).

Credentialism and Professionalization

Because postsecondary education is a valuable asset that children from richer families are more likely to obtain, education becomes a tool for **social exclusion**—setting up boundaries so that certain social opportunities and positions are not open to all (Parkin, 1979). Exclusion occurs when some groups have more resources than others do, allowing them to obtain educational credentials that allow them to amass still more privileges. Note that social exclusion takes place even if advanced education does not lead to useful knowledge or genuine skills; esoteric skills, such as knowledge of classical music or fine art, may still be used to distinguish insiders from outsiders.

Social exclusion is achieved by creating barriers that restrict certain opportunities or positions to members of one group.

Credential inflation takes place when qualifying for specific jobs requires more and more certificates and degrees over time. Because certificates and degrees are expensive, credential inflation contributes to social exclusion. Credential inflation occurs in part because the technical knowledge required for jobs has increased. For example, because aircraft engines and avionics systems are more complex than they were, say, 75 years ago, working as an airplane mechanic today requires more expertise. Certification ensures that the airplane mechanic can meet the high technical demands of the job. However, in many jobs there is a poor fit between credentials and responsibilities. On-the-job training, not a diploma or a degree, often gives people the skills they need to get the job done. Nonetheless, credential inflation takes place partly because employers find it a convenient sorting mechanism. For example, an employer may assume that a university graduate has certain manners, attitudes, and tastes that will be useful in a high-profile managerial position. The effect is to exclude people from less advantaged families from such positions, while favouring individuals from families and groups with the advantages that facilitate education (Collins, 1979).

Credential inflation occurs when it takes ever more certificates or degrees to qualify for a particular job.

Credential inflation is fuelled by **professionalization**, which occurs when members of an occupation insist that people earn certain credentials to enter the occupation. Professionalization ensures the maintenance of standards. It also keeps earnings high. After all, if "too many" people enter a given profession, the cost of services offered by that profession is bound to fall. This helps explain why, on average, physicians earn more than university professors who have Ph.D.s. The Canadian Medical Association is a powerful organization that regulates and effectively limits entry into the medical professions (see Chapter 19, Health and Medicine). Canadian professors have never been in a position to form such a powerful organization. Because professionalism promotes high standards and high earnings, it has spread widely.

Professionalization occurs to the degree that certain levels and types of schooling are established as criteria for gaining access to an occupation.

Cultural Capital

French sociologist Pierre Bourdieu wrote extensively about the role of education in maintaining social inequality. His central theme grew out of an analogy with the theories of Karl Marx. Marx had emphasized the role of economic capital—ownership of the physical means of producing wealth—in sustaining inequality. Bourdieu argued that education was central to the creation and transmission of **cultural capital**—learning and skills that ensured superior positions in productive activity (Bourdieu, 1998b; Bourdieu and Passeron, 1979).

Cultural capital is the stock of learning and skills that increases the chance of securing a superior job.

TABLE 17.2

Rates of Participation in
Postsecondary Education by
Highest Level of Parental
Education for Canadians
Ages 24–26, 2007

Source: Adapted from Statistics
Canada PISA Data, "Participation in
Post-Secondary Education." Retrieved
March 17, 2011 (http://www.pisa
.gc.ca/eng/participation.shtml).

Pedagogic violence is Bourdieu's
term for the application by teachers
of punishments intended to
discourage deviation from the
dominant culture.

Parental Education	Participation rate in . . .	
	College	University
Less than high school	43	32
High school	40	37
Some postsecondary	35	43
Postsecondary graduate	28	60

Cultural capital is expensive and difficult to acquire. Bourdieu emphasized that learning in school involves **pedagogic violence**, the application by teachers of punishments intended to discourage deviation from the dominant culture. Teachers routinely insist that there is one "correct" way to speak, spell, or do arithmetic. They lay down intricate rules, and individuals must learn to follow them with little pause for reflection or judgment. Such learning involves long periods of disciplinary pressure.

For Bourdieu, much of what schools teach is how to evaluate people. Tastes in books, music, food, and clothing come to reflect level of schooling. The books or music that people discuss signals their place in the class structure.

Although schools pressure all students to internalize shared cultural standards, students are not equally receptive. The cultural standard designated as correct or proper in schools matches what families practise at home *to varying degrees*. If your parents are university professors, from your earliest babbling you will be imitating the speech patterns of the dominant cultural group. Families from less advantaged countries or regions enjoy the least overlap with the ideal. If your parents come from rural Newfoundland or Bangladesh, and especially if they lack a higher education, teachers are likely to spend a lot of time correcting your English. Children from such families often struggle to meet teachers' standards.

When teachers evaluate performance, they inevitably reward students who are close to the standards of the dominant culture. Although some students from all backgrounds succeed, a student's stock of cultural capital—of disciplined familiarity with the dominant culture—will influence how hard or easy success is. Advantaged children will find rewards easier to achieve. Children from families with less cultural capital will be punished more and will tend to experience school as less pleasant.

A key part of Bourdieu's argument is readily confirmed. Table 17.2 above shows how much growing up with parents who are highly educated enhances one's educational attainment. University attendance is nearly twice as common among students whose parents have a postsecondary degree as among those whose parents did not graduate from high school.

Summing Up

- Families with few financial resources experience restricted access to higher education.
- Through credentialism and professionalism, education acts as a mechanism of social exclusion.
- Limited cultural capital restricts higher educational achievement.

REPRODUCING INEQUALITY: THE CONTRIBUTION OF SYMBOLIC INTERACTIONISM

Most sociologists find the conflict perspective on education more credible than the functionalist view. Based on the evidence, they believe that the benefits of education are unequally distributed and tend to **reproduce the existing stratification system** (Jencks et al., 1972).

Factors other than class matter too. Students with higher grades are more likely to advance to higher education. Parental encouragement plays a role, as does support from peers and teachers. However, research consistently finds that such social supports are part of how class advantage is transmitted; it is the wealthier students with more highly educated parents who are likely to enjoy more parental, peer, and teacher support. Furthermore, family income and parental education contribute to educational attainment over and above any influence they exert on academic performance and social support, insofar as they provide students with cultural capital that assists their advancement (Lambert, Zeman, Allen, and Bussière, 2004).

Why do schools fail to overcome class differences? Symbolic interactionists emphasize three social mechanisms that operate to reproduce inequality: the hidden curriculum, testing and tracking, and self-fulfilling prophecies.

> The **reproduction of the existing stratification system** refers to social processes that ensure that offspring enter a rank or class similar or identical to that of their parents.

The Hidden Curriculum

Apart from academic and vocational subjects, students learn a **hidden curriculum** in school (Snyder, 1971; see Chapter 4, Socialization). Teachers and school administrators never state that understanding it contributes powerfully to educational achievement, and they never teach it formally, but "getting it" is central to success.

The content of the hidden curriculum centres on obedience to authority and conformity to cultural norms. Teachers expect students to accept the curriculum, institutional routines, and grading system without question. Students who comply do well; those who do not are headed for trouble. Success stories are most common among middle- and upper-class children who are well-endowed with cultural capital and whose socialization at home has cultivated the hidden curriculum's standards of dress, speech, motivation, and deferred gratification.

Staying in school requires accepting the terms of the hidden curriculum and feeling positively involved. Researchers at Statistics Canada explored this phenomenon by developing measures of academic and social involvement. Social involvement included not feeling like an outsider and believing that people cared what a student said. Academic involvement consisted of liking teachers, not skipping classes, and regarding class content as "not useless." Chances of continuing to higher education were twice as high for students who reported social acceptance or positive attitudes toward the formal organization, authority, and procedures of the school (Shaienks and Gluszynski, 2007).

> The **hidden curriculum** in school teaches obedience to authority and conformity to cultural norms.

Testing and Tracking

Most schools in Canada are composed of children from various socioeconomic, racial, and ethnic backgrounds. Apart from the hidden curriculum, testing and tracking maintain these social inequalities in schools. IQ tests sort students, who are then channelled into high-ability (enriched), middle-ability, and low-ability (special needs) classrooms based on test scores. Often, the results are classrooms that are stratified by socioeconomic status, race, and ethnicity, much like the larger society. For example, Toronto Board of Education research showed that while 20 percent of black students were enrolled in low-level academic programming, only 10 percent of white students and 3 percent of Asian students were similarly streamed (Henry, Tator, Mattis, and Rees, 2000: 239).

Nobody denies that students vary in their abilities and that high-ability students require special challenges to reach their full potential. Nor does anyone deny that underprivileged students tend to score low on IQ tests. The controversial question is whether IQ is mainly genetic or social in origin. If IQ is genetic in origin, then it cannot be changed, so improving the quality of schooling for the underprivileged is arguably a waste of money (Herrnstein and Murray, 1994). If IQ is social in origin, IQ tests and tracking only reinforce social differences that could otherwise be reduced by changing the social circumstances of students.

Most sociologists believe that IQ reflects social standing in great part. That is because all that IQ tests can ever measure is acquired proficiency with a cultural system. How much exposure a person has had to whatever examiners count as correct will play a large role in testing. Even the most able Canadian children would perform abysmally if tested in Mongolian. IQ test results turn on a combination of two factors: (1) how effectively an individual absorbs what his or her environment offers, and (2) how closely his or her environment reflects what the test includes.

Most sociologists believe that members of underprivileged groups tend to score low on IQ tests because they do not have the training and the cultural background needed to score high (Fischer et al., 1996). To support their argument, they point to cases in which changing social circumstances result in changes in IQ scores. For instance, in the first decades of the twentieth century, most Jewish immigrants to North America tested well below average on IQ tests. This was sometimes used as an argument against Jewish immigration (Gould, 1996; Steinberg, 1989). Today, most North American Jews test above average in IQ. Since the genetic makeup of Jews has not changed in the past century, why the change in IQ scores? Sociologists point to upward mobility. During the twentieth century, most Jewish immigrants worked hard and moved up the stratification system. As their fortunes improved, they made sure their children had the skills and the cultural resources needed to do well in school. Average IQ scores rose as the social standing of Jews improved.

Consider also the "Flynn effect," named after political scientist James R. Flynn, who first pointed it out (Flynn, 1987). Flynn showed that average IQ scores increase over time on every major test, in every age range, and in every industrialized country (Neisser, 1997: 2). He observed increases of as much as 21 points in only 30 years. Typical improvements in test performance were large. For example, differences between children and their grandparents were far greater than differences observed across race and class divides in contemporary societies. This evidence suggests that IQ tests do not provide a fixed measuring rod that captures innate abilities or, for that matter, any sort of trait fixed by genetic endowment. It therefore makes sense to invest a lot in the early education of the underprivileged (see Box 17.3).

Self-Fulfilling Prophecies

A third social mechanism that operates in schools to reproduce inequality is the self-fulfilling prophecy. A self-fulfilling prophecy is an expectation that helps to cause what it predicts. In a classic study, Ray Rist (1970) revealed how a self-fulfilling prophecy can influence a person's life chances. He found that after just eight days of observing students in a kindergarten classroom, and without giving a formal intelligence test, the teacher felt she could confidently assign the children to one of three tables. She assigned "fast learners" to Table 1, closest to her own desk and "slow learners" to Table 3, at the back of the class. Students she judged to be "average" were seated at Table 2, in the middle of the classroom. On what basis did she make these distinctions? Probing the issue, Rist found that the key variable distinguishing the students was social class. Children at

PhotoDisk/Getty Images

Canada was one of the first countries in the world to link its student body to the Internet. By 1997, almost all Canadian schools had Internet access through the SchoolNet electronic network.

BOX 17.3

It's Your Choice

IS SCHOOL ENOUGH?

Sociologists began to understand how little schools could do on their own to encourage upward mobility and end poverty in the 1960s, when sociologist James Coleman and his colleagues conducted a monumental study of academic performance (Coleman et al., 1966). What they found was that differences in the quality of schools—measured by assessment of such factors as school facilities and curriculum—accounted at most for about a third of the variation in students' academic performance. At least two-thirds of the variation in academic performance was due to inequalities imposed on children by their homes, neighbourhoods, and peers. Forty years later, little research contradicts Coleman's finding.

Various social commentators have argued that if we are to improve the success of disadvantaged students, we must develop policies aimed at improving the social environment of young, disadvantaged children *before* they enter the formal education system (Hertzman, 2000). Compensatory education programs for preschool children were largely developed in the United States and attempt to meet the needs of children who are socially and economically disadvantaged. In Canada, such programs have also been aimed at "children with special needs" and "at-risk children"—those who, because of one or more factors in their background, are believed to face a heightened risk of poor academic

performance or social adjustment. Although the traditional focus of early childhood education has been on children's social and emotional development, at least some of these compensatory education programs focus on children's intellectual development.

Survey research shows that household income is associated with developmental maturity and future success at school (Doherty, 1997). In addition, as family income decreases, the likelihood that children will experience a host of other problems that will negatively influence their school performance increases. For example, poor health, hyperactivity, and delayed vocabulary development are all higher among children in low-income families than among children in middle- and high-income families (Ross, 1998). Children who score low on school readiness are also more likely to have mothers with low levels of education and to be living in neighbourhoods that their mothers characterize as unsafe or as lacking in social cohesiveness (Health Canada, 1999b: 79).

Some observers believe that early developmental programs can decrease the chances of developmental problems in children and enhance their school performance. For example, Head Start programs are based on the belief that to assist children, the entire family must be helped. They provide access to food

banks, nutrition programs, literacy programs, parental support groups, and parenting courses. Promoting child readiness for school is also a key element of Head Start. Evaluations of Head Start programs in Canada report such benefits as more students completing school with better grades, requiring fewer medical and mental health services, and being less exposed to violent and alcoholic parents (Government of Canada, 2001). Head Start programs have been identified as particularly important in increasing the educational success of Aboriginal students.

While the cost of providing early childhood intervention programs is substantial, investments made in the critical early years of a child's life benefit not only Canada's children but the economy as well. One study reports that "every dollar spent in early intervention can save seven dollars in future expenditures in health and social spending" (Health Canada, 1999b: 88).

Do you believe that early childhood intervention programs are useful in improving the educational success of children? If not, why not? If so, do you feel that attendance in these programs should be compulsory? Should parents who refuse to send their children to such programs be penalized? What background factors should be used to select children and their families for inclusion in such programs?

Native Child and Family Services

BOX 17.4

Sociology at the Movies

THE GREAT DEBATERS

The Civil War (1861–65) outlawed slavery in the United States, but legal and violent resistance against black rights persisted for more than a century. For example, in 1866 an amendment to the Texas Constitution stipulated that all taxes paid by blacks had to be used to maintain black schools, and that it was the duty of the legislature to "encourage colored schools" ("Jim Crow Laws: Texas," 2008). In this segregationist atmosphere, the Methodist Church founded Wiley College in the northeast corner of Texas in 1873 "for the purpose of allowing Negro youth the opportunity to pursue higher learning in the arts, sciences and other professions" (Wiley College, 2007).

In 1923, Wiley hired Melvin Tolson to teach speech and English. He proceeded to build up the college debating team to the point where they challenged and beat the mighty University of Southern California for the 1935 national debating championship. The victory shocked and scandalized much of the country's white population even as it instilled pride in African Americans, provided them with a shining model of academic achievement, and motivated black youth to strive for new heights. No self-fulfilling prophecy condemning black students to academic mediocrity operated at Wiley. To the contrary, Tolson worked his students hard, demanded excellence, and expected the best from them. Supported by the black community, they rose to his challenge.

The Great Debaters shows why the 1935 victory was so difficult.

Everett Collection/CP Picture Archive

English professor Melvin B. Tolson led the Wiley College debate team to a national championship against the University of Southern California (portrayed as Harvard in *The Great Debaters*) in 1935.

Tolson (played by Denzel Washington) is harassed by the local sheriff, who brands him a troublemaker for trying to unionize local black and white sharecroppers. On one out-of-town road trip, Tolson and his debating team come across a white mob that has just lynched a black man and set his body on fire. They barely escape with their lives. The pervasive racism of the times might discourage and immobilize lesser people, but it steels Tolson and his debaters, who feel compelled to show the world what blacks are capable of achieving even in the most inhospitable circumstances.

The successes of historically black colleges raise an important policy issue that is being debated in Canada's big cities today. Can segregated black public schools benefit black youth and should they be funded out of general tax revenue? Critics of separate black public schools argue that Canadian multiculturalism seeks to teach tolerance and respect for all cultures, and that separate public schools for any minority group would therefore be a step backward. Arguably, however, integrated public schools are still the home of self-fulfilling prophecies that make it difficult for black students to excel. Their curricula do little if anything to instil pride in the achievements of the black community. As a result, some black public school students dangerously identify academic excellence with "acting white," thus helping to condemn themselves to mediocre academic achievement and restricted social mobility. From this point of view, the achievements of historically black colleges like Wiley should be taken as a model of what is possible when black students are academically challenged and nourished in a non-threatening environment.

Table 1 were overwhelmingly middle class, while those assigned to Tables 2 and 3 were more likely to come from poorer homes. The assignment of these children was consequential because the children at Table 1 received more attention, were treated better, and, as the year progressed, came to see themselves as superior to the other children. In contrast, the other students tended to be ignored by the teacher and were referred to by the Table 1 children as "dumb." Unsurprisingly, they did not fare well. The following year, the grade 1 teacher took note of what the children had accomplished in kindergarten. The Table 1 children once again assigned to places in the classroom that marked them as superior.

Rist's findings suggest that, rather than valuing all students equally and treating them as if they have equally good prospects, teachers may suspect that disadvantaged students and students who are members of some minority groups are intellectually inferior. In turn, these students may come to feel rejected by teachers, other classmates, and the curriculum. Students from minority groups may also be disadvantaged by overt racism and discrimination. In response, students presumed to be inferior and marginalized in the classroom often cluster together out of resentment and in defiance of authority. Some of them eventually reject academic achievement as a goal. Discipline problems, ranging from apathy to disruptive and illegal behaviour, can result. Consistent with this argument, the dropout rate for Aboriginals (22.6 percent) is about three times as high as it is for non-Aboriginals (HRSDC, 2011b). In contrast, research shows that challenging lower-class students and those from minority groups, giving them emotional support and encouragement, giving greater recognition in the curriculum to the accomplishments of the groups from which they originate, creating an environment in which they can relax and achieve—all these strategies explode the self-fulfilling prophecy and improve academic performance (see Box 17.4).

In sum, schools reproduce the stratification system because of the hidden curriculum, IQ testing and tracking, and the self-fulfilling prophecy that disadvantaged and minority students are bound to do poorly. These social mechanisms increase the chance that students who are socially marginal and already disadvantaged will earn low grades and wind up with jobs near the bottom of the occupational structure.

Summing Up

- The hidden curriculum operates to restrict the educational success of less advantaged students.
- The cultural bias in IQ testing and associated tracking disadvantages underprivileged students.
- Self-fulfilling prophecies contribute to academic success and failure.

PROSPECTS AND CHALLENGES FOR EDUCATION IN CANADA

Gender Differences: A Feminist Perspective

With every passing decade, Canadians spend more time in school, and with every passing decade, women's level of education increases relative to men's. Women currently receive more than 60 percent of university degrees awarded annually (Statistics Canada, 2010l). There are about 20 percent more Canadian women than men over the age of 14 with at least a bachelor's degree. Women still lag behind men in medicine and dentistry, and among people with master's degrees and Ph.D.s, but they are catching up (Table 17.3 on page 450). With women obtaining more degrees annually, it will not be long before university-educated women will be more numerous than university-educated men.

TABLE 17.3

Highest University Degree Obtained, for Population Age 15+, by Sex, Canada, 2006

Source: Statistics Canada, 2007, "Highest Certificate, Diploma or Degree (14), Age Groups (10A) and Sex (3) for the Population 15 Years and Over of Canada, Provinces, Territories, Census Metropolitan Areas and Census Agglomerations, 2006 Census—20% Sample Data." Retrieved March 5, 2011 (http://www12.statcan.ca/ english/census06/data/topics/ RetrieveProductTable.cfm? Temporal=2006&PID=93609&GID= 837928&METH=1&APATH=3&PTYPE= 88971&THEME=75&AID=&FREE= 0&FOCUS=&VID=0&GC=99&GK= NA&RL=0&d1=1).

	Women	Men	Ratio of Women to Men
Bachelor's degree	1 603 040	1 378 425	1.2
University certificate or diploma above bachelor level	269 480	224 060	1.2
Degree in medicine, dentistry, etc.	54 705	82 145	0.7
Master's degree	402 910	464 065	0.9
Ph.D.	55 850	121 090	0.5

However, as feminists note, these figures mask the ways in which greater female participation in postsecondary education still conforms to traditional gender divisions. Figure 17.4 shows the distribution of university degrees by gender and academic field in Canada. Women outnumber men overall, but men predominate in business and management, architecture and engineering, physical and life sciences, math, computer and life sciences, and agricultural and related sciences. Differences between women and men are narrowing, but a strong tendency still exists for women to be concentrated in less scientifically oriented fields that pay less, notably the field of education.

Participation and Aboriginal Background

Barriers to education other than gender are also substantial. For example, Canadians with Aboriginal backgrounds lag behind other Canadians. Thus, 34 percent of Aboriginal people do not have a high school diploma, compared with 15 percent of non-Aboriginals. Only 8 percent of Aboriginal people receive university degrees, while 23 percent of non-Aboriginals do (Statistics Canada, 2008d). Despite gains in recent years, equal educational achievement among Aboriginal people is a long way off.

International Competition

Although access to higher education in Canada remains uneven, the Canadian accomplishment in higher education is impressive when compared with that of other countries. Figure 17.5 shows rankings of countries in the rate of education for working-age

FIGURE 17.4

University Degrees by Field of Study and Gender, Canada, 2006 (in '000s)

Source: Statistics Canada, 2007, "Major Field of Study—Classification of Instructional Programs, 2000 (13), Highest Postsecondary Certificate, Diploma or Degree (12), Age Groups (10A) and Sex (3) for the Population 15 Years and Over with Postsecondary Studies." Retrieved March 15, 2011 (http:// www12.statcan.ca/english/ census06/data/topics/ListProducts .cfm?Temporal=2006&APATH= 3&THEME=75&FREE=0&GRP=1).

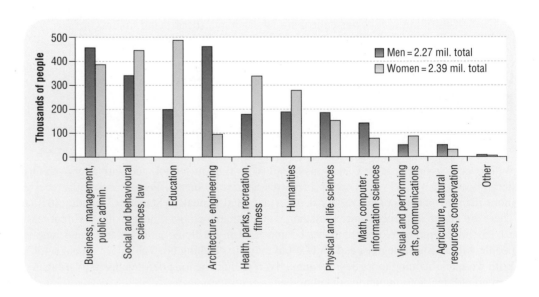

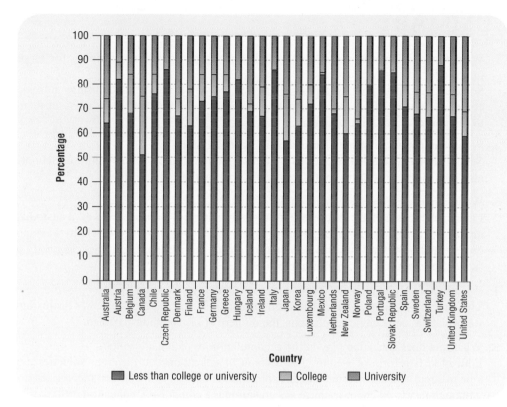

FIGURE 17.5

Educational Attainment of Adult Population (25–64), Selected Countries, in Percent, 2008

Source: Measured by the OECD, Various Countries, 2008; OECD, 2010

adults in 2008. Canada had the highest percentage of adults with postsecondary education. Still, several other countries have a higher rate of *university* graduation. Some relative latecomers, like South Korea, are making up ground by providing today's youth with many more years in school than earlier generations received. Canada's century-long place at the head of the class may give way before too long to such a newcomer.

In the 1990s, some observers raised doubts about the quality of Canada's education system. Suspicions grew that students were not applying themselves and learning enough, and that curricula and requirements had become lax. Critics were in for a surprise. The Organisation for Economic Co-operation and Development (OECD) organized a Programme for International Student Assessment (PISA) to assess the academic performance of 15-year-olds. Thirty-one countries were included and great care was taken to ensure that comparisons would be valid. When the first results came in, in 2001, Canadian students placed second in reading, sixth in mathematics, and fifth in science. These results placed Canada among a select group of countries that performed well on all three measures. The 2009 PISA results included 65 countries. These were the top five overall: (1) South Korea, (2) Finland, (3) Japan, (4) Canada, (5) New Zealand (Fleischman, Hopstock, Pelczar, and Shelley, 2010: 8–9, 18, 24). This ranking is a remarkable showing of which all Canadians should be proud.

Summing Up

- Women perform better than men do in higher education, even though they are underrepresented in higher paying professions.
- Limited Aboriginal educational achievement continues to contribute significantly to social inequality in Canada.
- Canada is among the top performers in international achievement assessments.

SUMMARY

1. What kind of societies provide education for all and specialized training for large minorities?

   Societies that have achieved industrialism, and the wealth industrialism brings, provide complete systems of schooling that take in nearly all children and allow many of them to remain in school for many years.

2. What manifest functions are performed by school systems?

   Schools homogenize future citizens by indoctrination into a common culture. Schools also sort and steer students to different class positions as adults.

3. What latent functions are carried out by schools?

   Latent functions include the creation of a youth culture, a marriage market, a custodial and surveillance system for children, a means of maintaining wage levels by keeping college and university students temporarily out of the job market, and occasionally a "school of dissent" that opposes authorities.

4. What factors account for the rise of mass, compulsory education?

   The spread of mass, compulsory education was encouraged by the Protestant Reformation, democratic revolutions, the modern state, and industrialization.

5. What role does education play in the accumulation of national wealth?

   Education is a form of wealth. The amount of education that different societies are able to supply for their future citizens corresponds closely with national income levels. Although nearly all countries have systems of mass, compulsory education, illiteracy is still widespread in poor countries.

6. What are the results of education according to functionalists?

   Functionalists argue that education is critically important for industrialization. They also argue that education ensures meritocracy.

7. What consequences of education do conflict theorists identify?

   Conflict theorists argue that education intensifies nationalism. They also argue that success at school is easier for privileged people, so education perpetuates privilege.

8. What is credential inflation and how does it relate to professionalization?

   Credential inflation (the need for more certification and diplomas to qualify for a given job) has been fuelled by the increasing technical requirements of many jobs. It has also been encouraged by the ability of people in certain occupations to exercise control over their occupations (professionalization). Credential inflation is thus a means of excluding people from the professions to maintain high standards and income levels.

9. What is cultural capital and how does it influence schooling?

   Parents who are advantaged are more likely to have acquired larger stocks of scarce, valued skills—that is, cultural capital. In turn, their children find it easier to win rewards at school by repeating what is familiar from their home life. Children from less advantaged families may have to unlearn family practices, such as vocabulary, grammar, or pronunciation, that are stigmatized as culturally inferior. This makes schooling less pleasant, which in turn is a major factor in the decision to forgo further education.

10. What are some interaction processes in school that tend to reinforce class differences among students?

    Positive and negative expectations by teachers result in self-fulfilling prophecies that favour students from privileged backgrounds and discourage students from less privileged origins. A hidden curriculum encourages teachers to reward conformity to middle-class values and standards.

11. What do feminists say about the fact that women are more numerous than men among university graduates?

Feminist scholars point out that the rising levels of female participation in postsecondary and graduate training are largely confined to a narrow range of academic fields and thereby tend to perpetuate occupational segregation by gender.

12. What do standardized tests measure and what are their effects?

Standardized tests are supposed to measure innate ability (IQ tests) or mathematical and reasoning abilities related to performance in college or university. To some extent, they do. Thus, to a degree, they help to sort students by ability and aid in the creation of a meritocracy. However, they also measure students' preparedness to learn and thrive in school, and preparedness is strongly related to background factors, such as a family's class position. Therefore, standardized tests also help to reproduce existing social inequalities.

KEY TERMS

assortative mating (p. 440)

credential inflation (p. 443)

cultural capital (p. 443)

educational achievement (p. 435)

educational attainment (p. 435)

hidden curriculum (p. 445)

meritocracy (p. 442)

pedagogic violence (p. 444)

professionalization (p. 443)

reproduction of the existing stratification system (p. 445)

social exclusion (p. 443)

WEB RESOURCES

Companion Website for This Book

http://www.compass4e.nelson.com

Begin by clicking on the Student Resources section of the website. Next, select the chapter you are studying from the pull-down menu. From the Student Resources page you have easy access to additional Weblinks and other resources. The website also has many useful tips to aid you in your study of sociology, including practice tests for each chapter.

InfoTrac® Search Terms

These search terms are provided to assist you in beginning to conduct research on this topic by visiting http://www.infotrac-college.com:

educational achievement

educational attainment

globalization

multiculturalism

CHAPTER

18

The Mass Media

IN THIS CHAPTER, YOU WILL LEARN THAT

- Movies, television, and other mass media sometimes blur the distinction between reality and fantasy.

- The mass media are products of the nineteenth and especially the twentieth centuries.

- Historically, the growth of the mass media is rooted in the rise of Protestantism, democracy, and capitalism.

- The mass media make society more cohesive.

- The mass media foster social inequality.

- Although the mass media are influential, audiences filter, interpret, resist, and even reject media messages if they are inconsistent with their beliefs and experiences.

- The mass media misrepresent women and members of racial minorities in important ways.

- The interaction between producers and consumers of media messages is most evident on the Internet.

THE SIGNIFICANCE OF THE MASS MEDIA

Illusion Becomes Reality

The turn of the twenty-first century was thick with movies about the blurred line separating reality from fantasy. *The Truman Show* (1998) gave us Jim Carrey as an insurance agent who discovers that everyone in his life is an actor. He is the unwitting subject of a television program that airs 24 hours a day. In *The Matrix* (1999), Keanu Reeves plays Neo, who finds that his identity and his life are illusions. Like everyone else in the world, Neo is hardwired to a giant computer that uses humans as an energy source. The computer supplies people with nutrients to keep them alive and simulated realities to keep them happy.

The most disturbing movie in this genre, however, is *American Psycho* (2000), directed by Canadian Mary Harron. Based on a novel that was banned in some parts of North America when it was first published in 1991, the movie is the story of Patrick Bateman, Wall Street yuppie by day, cold and meticulous serial killer by night. Unfortunately, the public outcry over the horrifying murder scenes virtually drowned out the book's important sociological point. *American Psycho* is really about how people become victims of the mass media and consumerism. Bateman, the serial murderer, says he is "used to imagining everything happening the way it occurs in movies." When he kisses his lover, he experiences "the 70 mm image of her lips parting and the subsequent murmur of 'I want you' in Dolby sound" (Ellis, 1991: 265). In Bateman's mind, his 14 murder victims are mere props in a movie in which he is the star. He feels no more empathy for them than an actor would for any other stage object. The mass media have so completely emptied him of genuine emotion he even has trouble remembering his victims' names. At the same time, however, the mass media have so successfully infused him with consumer values he can describe his victims' apparel in great detail—styles, brand names, stores where they bought their clothes, even prices. Thus, in *American Psycho*, killer and killed are both victims of consumerism and the mass media.

In different ways, these movies suggest that the fantasy worlds created by the mass media are increasingly the only realities we know, and they are every bit as pervasive and influential as religion was 500 or 600 years ago. Do you think this is an exaggeration dreamed up by filmmakers and novelists? If so, consider that the average Canadian spends more than three hours a day watching television, over 2.5 hours listening to the radio, and just under an hour reading magazines, newspapers, and books (Moscovitch, 1998, Statistics Canada, 2008j, 2009c). Add to this the number of hours Canadians spend going to the movies, using the Internet, listening to CDs, and playing video games, and it is clear that we spend close to 40 percent of our time interacting with the mass media—more than we do sleeping, working, or going to school. You might want to keep a tally of your activities for a couple of days to find out how you fit into this pattern of activity. Ask yourself, too, what you get out of your interactions with the mass media. Where do you get your ideas about how to dress, how to style your hair, and what music to listen to? Where do your hopes, aspirations, and dreams come from? If you're like most people, much of your reality is media generated. Canadian media guru Marshall McLuhan, who coined the term *global village* in the early 1960s, said the media are extensions of the human body and mind (McLuhan, 1964). More than four decades later, it is perhaps equally valid to claim that the human body and mind are extensions of the mass media (Baudrillard, 1983, 1988; Bourdieu, 1998a).

What Are the Mass Media?

The term **mass media** refers to print, radio, television, and other communication technologies. Often, *mass media* and *mass communication* are used interchangeably to refer to the transmission of information from one person or group to another. The word *mass* implies

Canadian media guru Marshall McLuhan said the media are extensions of the human body and mind.

The **mass media** are print, radio, television, and other communication technologies. The word *mass* implies that the media reach many people. The word *media* signifies that communication does not take place directly through face-to-face interaction.

that the media reach many people. The word *media* signifies that communication does not take place directly through face-to-face interaction. Instead, technology intervenes or mediates in transmitting messages from senders to receivers. Furthermore, communication via the mass media is usually one-way, or at least one-sided. There are few senders (or producers) and many receivers (or audience members). Thus, most newspapers print a few readers' letters in each edition, but journalists and advertisers write virtually everything else. Ordinary people may appear on the *Dr. Phil* show or even delight in a slice of fame on *Survivor*. However, producers choose the guests and create the program content. Similarly, a handful of people may visit your personal website, but popular websites, such as Google, Facebook, and YouTube, get hundreds of millions of hits a day.

Usually, then, members of the audience cannot exert much influence on the mass media. They can choose only to tune in or tune out. And even tuning out is difficult because it excludes us from the styles, news, gossip, and entertainment most people depend on to grease the wheels of social interaction. Few people want to be cultural misfits. However, this does not mean that people are always passive consumers of the mass media. As noted below, we filter, interpret, and resist what we see and hear if it contradicts our experiences and beliefs. Even so, in the interaction between audiences and media sources, the media sources usually dominate.

To appreciate fully the impact of the mass media on life today, we need to trace their historical development. That is the first task we set ourselves in the following discussion. We then critically review theories of the mass media's effects on social life. As you will see, each of these theories contributes to our appreciation of media effects. Finally, we assess developments on the media frontier formed by the Internet, television, and other mass media. We show that, to a degree, the new media frontier blurs the distinction between producer and consumer and has the potential to make the mass media somewhat more democratic, at least for those who can afford access.

The Rise of the Mass Media

It may be difficult for you to imagine a world without the mass media. Yet, as Table 18.1 shows, most of the mass media are recent inventions. The first developed systems of

One of the most famous photographs in Canadian history is the driving of the last spike of the Canadian Pacific Railway (CPR) on November 7, 1885, at Craigellachie, British Columbia. The man holding the hammer is Donald Smith, who financed much of the construction of the CPR. The taller man standing behind him to his right in the stovepipe hat is Sir Sandford Fleming, the mastermind behind standard time. The railroads spearheaded the introduction of standard time, which could be coordinated thanks to the introduction of the telegraph.

Year (CE)	Media Development
1450	Movable metal type used in Germany, leading to the Gutenberg Bible
1702	First daily newspaper, London's *Daily Courant*
1833	First mass-circulation newspaper, *New York Sun*
1837	Louis Daguerre invents a practical method of photography in France
1844	Samuel Morse sends the first telegraph message between Washington and Baltimore
1875	Alexander Graham Bell sends the first telephone message
1877	Thomas Edison develops the first phonograph
1895	Motion pictures are invented
1901	Italian inventor Guglielmo Marconi transmits the first transatlantic wireless message from England to St. John's, Newfoundland
1906	First radio voice transmission
1920	First regularly scheduled radio broadcast, Pittsburgh
1925	78 rpm record chosen as a standard
1928	First commercial TV broadcast in United States; Canada follows in 1931
1949	Network TV begins in the United States
1952	VCR invented
1961	First cable television, San Diego
1969	First four nodes of the United States Department of Defense's ARPANET (precursor of the Internet) set up at Stanford University; University of California, Los Angeles; University of California, Santa Barbara; and the University of Utah
1975	First microcomputer marketed
1976	Satellite TV first broadcast
1983	Cellphone invented
1989	World Wide Web conceived by Tim Berners-Lee at the European Laboratory for Particle Physics in Switzerland
1990	Windows 3.0 released (first mass-marketed graphical operating system)
1995	Internet Explorer 1.0 first released with Windows
1999	Wi-Fi (wireless Internet) becomes publicly available
2001	First-generation iPod released Digital satellite radio introduced
2003	iTunes Music Store opens online Camera phones invented First BlackBerry smart phone released
2005	Facebook.com becomes public YouTube founded
2007	iPhone first released
2010	E Ink (Pearl display) invented, making e-readers like Kindle widely available

TABLE 18.1

The Development of the Mass Media

Sources: Berners-Lee, 1999; Croteau and Hoynes, 1997: 9–10; "The Silent Boom," 1998.

The newspaper was the dominant mass medium even as late as 1950.

Vintage Images/Jupiter Images

writing appeared only about 5500 years ago in Egypt and Mesopotamia (now southern Iraq). The print media became truly a mass phenomenon only in the nineteenth century. The inexpensive daily newspaper, costing a penny, first appeared in the United States in the 1830s. At that time, long-distance communication required physical transportation. To spread the news, you needed a horse, a railroad, or a ship. The slow speed of communication was costly. For instance, the last military engagement between Britain and the United States in the War of 1812–14 was the Battle of New Orleans. It took place 15 days *after* a peace treaty was signed. The good news did not reach the troops near the mouth of the Mississippi until they had suffered 2100 casualties, including 320 dead.

The newspaper was the dominant mass medium even as late as 1950 (Schudson, 1991; Smith, 1980). However, change was in the air in 1844, when Samuel Morse sent the first telegraphic signal (Pred, 1973). From that time on, long-distance communication no longer required physical transportation. The transformative power of the new medium was soon evident. For example, until 1883, hundreds of local time zones existed in North America. The correct time was determined by local solar time and was typically maintained by a clock in a church steeple or a respected jeweller's shop window. Virtually instant communication by telegraph made it possible to coordinate time and establish just six time zones in Canada. Railroad companies spearheaded the move to standardize time. A Canadian civil and railway engineer, Sir Sandford Fleming, was the driving force behind the worldwide adoption of standard time (Blaise, 2001).

Most of the electronic media are creatures of the twentieth century. The first commercial television broadcasts date from the 1920s. The U.S. Department of Defense established ARPANET in 1969. It was designed as a system of communication between computers that would automatically find alternative transmission routes if one or more nodes in the network broke down because of, say, nuclear attack. ARPANET begat the

Internet, which in turn begat the hyperlinked system of texts, images, and sounds known as the World Wide Web around 1991. Today, about two billion people worldwide use the Web. It was a quick trip—a mere 140 years separate the Pony Express from the home videoconference.

Causes of Media Growth

The rise of the mass media can be explained by three main factors—one religious, one political, and one economic:

1. *The Protestant Reformation.* In the sixteenth century, Catholics relied on priests to tell them what was in the Bible. In 1517, however, Martin Luther protested certain practices of the Church. Among other things, he wanted people to develop a more personal relationship with the Bible. Within 40 years, Luther's new form of Christianity—Protestantism—was established in half of Europe. Suddenly, millions of people were being encouraged to read. The Bible became the first mass media product in the West and by far the best-selling book.

   Technological improvements in papermaking and printing made the diffusion of the Bible and other books possible (Febvre and Martin, 1976 [1958]). The most significant landmark was Johannes Gutenberg's invention of the printing press. In the 50 years after Gutenberg produced his monumental Bible in 1455, more books were produced than in the previous 1000 years. The printed book enabled the widespread diffusion and exchange of ideas. It contributed to the Renaissance (a scholarly and artistic revival that began in Italy around 1300 and spread to all of Europe by 1600) and to the rise of modern science (Johns, 1998).

   A remarkable feature of the book is its durability. Many electronic storage media became obsolete just a few years after being introduced. For instance, eight-track tapes are icons of the 1970s and 5.25-inch floppy disks are icons of the early 1980s. They are barely remembered today. In contrast, books are still being published today, more than 550 years after Gutenberg published his Bible. More than 23 000 books are published in Canada each year (UNESCO, 2008).

2. *Democratic movements.* A second force that promoted the growth of the mass media was political democracy. From the eighteenth century on, the citizens of France, the

The Gutenberg Bible

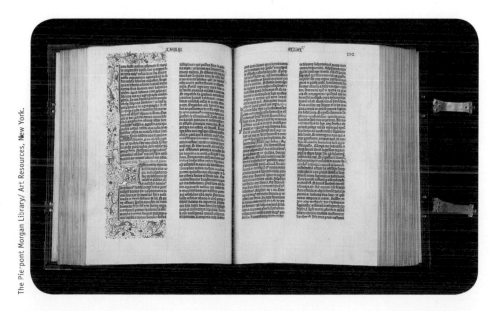

The Pierpont Morgan Library/ Art Resources, New York.

United States, and other countries demanded and achieved representation in government. At the same time, they wanted to become literate and gain access to previously restricted centres of learning. Democratic governments, in turn, depended on an informed citizenry and therefore encouraged popular literacy and the growth of a free press (Habermas, 1989).

Today, the mass media, and especially TV, mould our entire outlook on politics. TV's influence first became evident in the 1960 U.S. presidential election. That was the year of the first televised presidential debate—between John F. Kennedy and Richard Nixon. One of the four reporters who asked questions during the debate later recalled: "The people who watched the debate on their television sets apparently thought Kennedy came off better than Nixon. Those who heard the debate on radio thought Nixon was superior to Kennedy" (quoted in "The Candidates Debate," 1998). Kennedy smiled. Nixon perspired. Kennedy relaxed. Nixon fidgeted. The election was close, and most analysts believe that Kennedy got the edge simply because 70 million viewers thought he looked better on TV. Television was thus beginning to redefine the very nature of politics.

Soon, Canadian politicians were hiring "image consultants." Often, image manipulation used techniques honed in the United States. Usually the media consultants' advice led to the desired results. This included the much maligned "negative advertising" techniques. While voters claim they do not approve of negative advertising, the fact is that it is effective (Kinsella, 2007). The Conservative Party's use of negative advertising branding Liberal Party leader Michael Ignatieff as a disloyal, power-hungry Canadian is widely believed to have been an important factor enabling the Conservatives to win a majority government in 2011.

It is commonly claimed that television and other mass media have over-simplified politics. Some analysts say that politics has been reduced to a series of more or less well-managed images, catchy slogans, and ever-shorter uninterrupted comments or "sound bites." From this point of view, candidates are marketed for high office like Kellogg's sells breakfast cereal, and a politician's stage presence is more important than his or her policies in determining success at the polls.

3. *Capitalist industrialization.* The third major force stimulating the growth of the mass media was capitalist industrialization. Modern industries required a literate and numerate workforce. They also needed rapid means of communication to do business efficiently. Moreover, the mass media turned out to be a major source of profit in their own right.

The sources of the mass media are deeply embedded in the religious, political, and economic needs of our society. Moreover, the mass media are among the most important institutions in our society today. How, then, do sociologists explain the effects of the mass media on society? To answer this question, we now summarize the relevant sociological theories.

Summing Up

- The mass media shape perceptions of reality.
- Print media dominated until the mid-twentieth century. Since then, electronic media have dominated.
- The Protestant Reformation and the growth of democracy and capitalism were the major factors underlying the growth of the mass media.

THEORIES OF MEDIA EFFECTS

Functionalism

As societies develop, they become larger and more complex. The number of institutions and roles proliferates. Because of the sheer scale of society, face-to-face interaction becomes less viable as a means of communication. As a result, the need increases for new means of coordinating the operation of the various parts of society. For example, people in New Brunswick must have at least a general sense of what is happening in Alberta, and they need to share certain basic values with Albertans if they are going to feel they are citizens of the same country. The mass media do an important job in this regard. The nineteenth-century German philosopher Georg Hegel once said that the daily ritual of reading the newspaper unites the secular world, just as the ritual of daily prayer once united the Christian world. Stated more generally, his point is valid. The nationwide distribution of newspapers, magazines, movies, television, and Internet cements the large, socially diverse, and geographically far-flung population of Canada. In a fundamental sense, the nation is an imagined community, and the mass media make it possible for us to imagine it (Anderson, 1991).

Thus, the mass media perform an important function by *coordinating* the operation of industrial and postindustrial societies. But, according to functionalist theorists, their significance does not stop there (Wright, 1975). In addition, the mass media are also important agents of *socialization*. Families have relinquished their former nearly exclusive right to transmit norms, values, and culture. The mass media have stepped into the breach. They reinforce shared ideals of democracy, competition, justice, and so forth (see Chapter 4, Socialization).

A third function of the mass media involves *social control*; the mass media help ensure conformity. For example, news broadcasts, TV dramas, and "reality TV" programs pay much attention to crime, and they regularly sing the praises of heroes who apprehend and convict criminals. By exposing deviants and showcasing law enforcement officials and model citizens, the mass media reinforce ideas about what kinds of people deserve punishment and what kinds of people deserve rewards. In this way, they reproduce the moral order. Some people think the *Jerry Springer* show is outlandish, and in a way it is. From a sociological point of view, however, it is also a deeply conservative program, for when television audiences become upset about marital infidelities and other outrages, they are reinforcing some of the most traditional norms and thus serving as agents of social control.

Canadians now spend nearly 40 percent of their time interacting with the mass media.

Reed Kaestner/Corbis/Magma

As Nobel Prize–winning author Saul Bellow wrote, "a scandal [is] after all a sort of service to the community" (Bellow, 1964: 18).

The mass media's fourth and final function is to provide *entertainment*. Television, movies, magazines, and so on give us pleasure, relaxation, and momentary escape from the tension and tedium of everyday life. How often have you come home after a long and frustrating day at college, university, or work, picked up the remote control, channel surfed, concluded that there's nothing really worth watching, but settled for a sitcom or some other form of easily digestible entertainment? How about checking out some YouTube videos? It is precisely because some products of the mass media require little effort on the part of the audience that they are important. They relieve stress. Moreover, they do so in a way that doesn't threaten the social order. Without such escapes, who knows how our daily tensions and frustrations might express themselves?

Conflict Theory

Clearly, functionalism offers valuable insights into the operation of the mass media. However, conflict theorists have criticized the functional approach for paying insufficient attention to the social inequality fostered by the mass media. Specifically, conflict theorists say functionalism exaggerates the degree to which the mass media serve the interests of the entire society. They contend that some people benefit from the mass media more than others do. In particular, the mass media favour the interests of dominant classes and political groups (Gitlin, 1983; Herman and Chomsky, 1988; Horkheimer and Adorno, 1986 [1944]; Iyengar, 1991).

Conflict theorists maintain that there are two ways in which dominant classes and political groups benefit disproportionately from the mass media. First, the mass media broadcast beliefs, values, and ideas that create widespread acceptance of the basic structure of society, including its injustices and inequalities. Second, ownership of the mass media is highly concentrated in the hands of a small number of people and is highly profitable for them. Thus, the mass media are a source of economic inequality. Let us consider these issues in more detail.

Media Ownership

For decades, most of the Canadian mass media have been owned by fewer than a dozen families: the Siftons, the Thomsons, the Bassetts, the Southams, the Irvings, the Honderiches, the Blacks, and, more recently, the Shaws, the Rogerses, and the Péladeaus. There are just five multimedia giants in the country. In order of size (as measured by annual revenue), they are as follows:

1. *CTVglobemedia Inc.* Owned by Bell Canada (BCE), CTVglobemedia controls the CTV television network, *The Globe and Mail*, CFCF (the biggest English-language television station in Montreal), CKY (Manitoba's biggest TV station), *Report on Business* TV, TSN (The Sports Network), national CHUM radio, and so on. Approximate revenue: $4.3 billion.

2. *Rogers Communications Inc.* Controlled by the Rogers family and based in Toronto, Rogers is one of the country's largest cable TV and broadband Internet service providers. It controls the Shopping Channel, CFMT (a multicultural television station in Toronto), Sportsnet, the Toronto Blue Jays, dozens of radio stations, scores of consumer and business magazines (including *Maclean's*, *Flare*, and *Canadian Business*), and so on. Approximate revenue: $3.9 billion.

3. *Shaw Communications Inc.* Controlled by the Shaw family of Calgary, Shaw Communications is another of the country's largest cable TV and broadband Internet service providers. It also owns 49 radio stations, Global Television, and television specialty stations, including the Food Network, History Television, and Showcase. Approximate revenue: $3.1 billion.

4. *CBC/Radio Canada.* The fourth-largest multimedia giant in Canada is the only one that is publicly owned. Its most important assets are an English-language television network, a French-language television network, and four commercial-free radio networks.

Approximate revenue: $1.6 billion, 56 percent of which is a federal government grant and the balance of which comes from advertising, program sales, and so on (see Box 18.1).

5. *Quebecor Inc.* Controlled by the Péladeau family of Montreal, Quebecor publishes 28 daily newspapers including *Le journal de Montréal, Le journal de Québec, the Ottawa Sun, the Toronto Sun, the London Free Press, the Winnipeg Sun, the Edmonton Sun, the Calgary Sun,* and the *Kingston Whig-Standard.* It also owns the largest cable TV provider in Quebec, Quebec's largest private TV network (TVA), Canoe.ca, and so on. Approximate revenue: $1 billion.

BOX 18.1

Social Policy: What Do You Think?

SHOULD CANADA'S BROADCASTERS BE SUBJECT TO MORE GOVERNMENT REGULATION?

The use of the air ... that lies over the ... land of Canada is a natural resource over which we have complete jurisdiction.... I cannot think that any government would be warranted in leaving the air to private exploitation and not reserving it for . . . the use of the people. Without [complete government control of broadcasting from Canadian sources, radio] can never become the agency by which national consciousness may be fostered and national unity ... strengthened.

—Prime Minister R. B. Bennett, House of Commons, May 18, 1932 (quoted in Competition Bureau, 2002)

What was self-evident to Prime Minister Bennett 80 years ago is a matter of controversy today. Some Canadians, like Bennett, still argue for strict government control of the mass media. Like Bennett, they believe that the mass media should be used to strengthen Canadian culture. Others want a more or less free market in which the great bulk of programming is American in origin or, failing that, American in style. Here we review the state of government regulation of Canadian broadcasting and ask you to decide whether you approve of the status quo or think that more or less government regulation is needed.

The Canadian Radio-television and Telecommunications Commission (CRTC) was established by an act of Parliament in 1968 as an independent agency responsible for regulating Canada's broadcasting and telecommunications systems. Its self-described mandate is to promote Canadian culture and economic competitiveness:

Our mandate is to ensure that programming in the Canadian broadcasting system reflects Canadian creativity and talent, our linguistic duality, our multicultural diversity, the special place of aboriginal people within our society and our social values. At the same time, we must ensure that Canadians have access to reasonably priced, high-quality, varied and innovative communications services that are competitive nationally as well as internationally. ("The CRTC's Mandate," 2002)

In practice, promoting Canadian culture means ensuring that 35 percent of the popular music played on English-language commercial radio stations between 6 a.m. and 6 p.m., Monday through Friday, is Canadian. Regulations for "ethnic" and French-language stations are somewhat different. Privately owned television stations must achieve a yearly Canadian content level of 60 percent between 6 a.m. and midnight and 50 percent between 6 p.m. and midnight. Canadian content rules for the CBC are slightly more demanding. "Canadian" means that the producer of the program is Canadian, key creative personnel are Canadian, and 75 percent of service costs and postproduction lab costs are paid to Canadians.

As a result of these regulations, about half of TV broadcasts in English Canada and 65 percent of popular music broadcasts are American. Moreover, many American TV and radio stations are widely available in Canada via cable, satellite, or the airwaves. (Over 90 percent of Canadian households subscribe to cable or use satellite services; Canadian Media Research, 2006). It seems reasonable to conclude that at least three-quarters of the TV and popular music to which Canadians have access is American.

Bearing the above facts in mind, do you think the Canadian government does enough or too much to ensure the preservation and enrichment of Canadian culture through the broadcast industry? Should the government be in the business of protecting Canadian culture at all? Should it allow free-market forces to shape the structure and content of Canadian broadcasting? Would a free-market approach to broadcasting enable Canadians to get what they really want, or would it allow powerful American broadcasters to completely dominate the marketplace and virtually eliminate Canadian content?

About 90 percent of the mass media in Canada are privately owned. Over time, concentration of the privately owned media has increased. That is, fewer and fewer people control Canada's mass media with every passing decade. Moreover, it is not just the *degree* of media concentration that has changed. The *form* of media concentration began to shift in the 1990s, too. Until the 1990s, media concentration involved mainly "horizontal integration." A small number of firms tried to control as much production as possible in their particular fields (newspapers, radio, television, etc.). In the 1990s, however, "vertical integration" became much more widespread. Media firms sought to control production and distribution in *many* fields. They became media "conglomerates." Today, a media conglomerate may own any combination of television networks, stations, and production facilities; magazines, newspapers, and book publishers; cable channels and cable systems; video store chains; sports teams; Web portals; and software companies. A media conglomerate can create content and deliver it in a variety of forms. For instance, Rogers Communications Inc. owns the Toronto Blue Jays, creates sports entertainment, broadcasts it on its television stations, carries the signal to viewers' homes via its cable system, and spins off Blue Jays merchandise that it can sell at Rogers Video stores.

Media Bias

Does the concentration of the mass media in fewer and fewer hands deprive the public of independent sources of information, limit the diversity of opinion, and encourage the public to accept their society as it is? Conflict theorists think so. They argue that when a few conglomerates dominate the production of news in particular, they squeeze out alternative points of view.

Quebecor Media's recent launch of Sun News Network illustrates the conflict theorists' view. As noted above, Quebecor is one of the largest media conglomerates in Canada. In 2011 it launched the 24-hour television news network with an unapologetically right-wing, conservative slant. Kory Teneycke, Conservative Prime Minister Harper's former press secretary, holds a key post in the organization, while Ezra Levant and other well-known conservative commentators regularly contribute their observations. The new network has been labelled "Fox News North" by its detractors, since it is modelled on the popular American right-wing programming of Fox News.

Sun News Network is a blatant example of corporate-controlled media using its power to promote its ideological interests. However, according to Edward Herman and Noam Chomsky (1988), several other, more subtle mechanisms help to bias the news in a way that supports powerful corporate interests and political groups. These biasing mechanisms include advertising, sourcing, and flak:

- *Advertising.* Most of the revenue earned by television stations, radio stations, newspapers, and magazines comes from advertising by large corporations. According to Herman and Chomsky, these corporations routinely seek to influence the news so it will reflect well on them. In one American survey, 93 percent of newspaper editors said advertisers have tried to influence their news reports. Thirty-seven percent of newspaper editors admitted to being influenced by advertisers (Bagdikian, 1997). In addition, big advertisers may influence the news even without overtly trying to influence news carriers. For fear of losing business, news carriers may soften stories that big advertisers might find offensive.
- *Sourcing.* Studies of news-gathering show that most news agencies rely heavily for information on press releases, news conferences, and interviews organized by large corporations and government agencies. These sources routinely slant information to reflect favourably on their policies and preferences. Unofficial news sources are consulted less often. Moreover, unofficial sources tend to be used only to provide reactions and minority viewpoints that are secondary to the official story.
- *Flak.* Governments and big corporations routinely attack journalists who depart from official and corporate points of view. For example, Brian Ross, the leading investigative reporter for *20/20*, prepared a segment about Disney World in 1998. Ross claimed

that Disney was so lax in doing background checks on employees that it had hired pedophiles. ABC killed the story before airtime. ABC is owned by Disney (McChesney, 1999). Similarly, tobacco companies have systematically tried to discredit media reports that cigarettes cause cancer. In a notorious case, the respected public affairs show *60 Minutes* refused to broadcast a damaging interview with a former Philip Morris executive because CBS was threatened with legal action by the tobacco company. (This incident is the subject of the Oscar-nominated movie *The Insider*, starring Russell Crowe.)

On the whole, the conflict theorists' arguments are compelling. We do not, however, find them completely convincing (Gans, 1979). After all, if 37 percent of newspaper editors have been influenced by advertisers, 63 percent have not. News agencies may rely heavily on government and corporate sources, but this does not stop them from routinely biting the hand that offers to feed them and evading flak shot their way. The daily newspaper is full of examples of mainstream journalistic opposition to government and corporate viewpoints. Even mainstream news sources, although owned by media conglomerates, do not always act like the lap dogs of the powerful (Hall, 1980).

Still, conflict theorists make a valid point if they restrict their argument to how the mass media support core societal values. In their defence of core values, the mass media *are* virtually unanimous (see Box 18.2 on page 466). For example, the mass media enthusiastically support democracy and capitalism. We cannot think of a single instance of a major Canadian news outlet advocating a fascist government or a socialist economy in Canada. Moreover, when conservative media critics complain of liberal bias in the media, they routinely use the CBC as their example. If the CBC is the best example of left-wing bias, the range of mass media opinion is narrow indeed.

Similarly, the mass media virtually unanimously endorse consumerism as a way of life. As discussed in Chapter 3, Culture, consumerism is the tendency to define ourselves in terms of the goods and services we purchase. Endorsement of consumerism is evident in the fact that advertising fills the mass media and is its lifeblood. Estimated advertising expenditures in Canada are now about $23 billion a year, compared with expenditures of about $28 billion a year for universities and colleges (Canadian Marketing Association, 2007; Statistics Canada, 2010m). We are exposed to a staggering number of ads each day; in fact, some estimates place the number in the thousands. Companies pay filmmakers to use their brand-name products conspicuously in their movies. In some magazines, ads figure so prominently a reader must search for the articles.

It is only when the mass media deal with news stories that touch on less central values that we can witness a diversity of media opinion. *Specific* government and corporate policies are often the subject of heated debate in the mass media. Thus, despite the indisputable concentration of media ownership, the mass media are diverse and often contentious on specific issues that do not touch on core values.

Interpretive Approaches

The view that the mass media powerfully influence a passive public is common among both functionalists and conflict theorists. Many people believe that violence on TV causes violence in real life, pornography on the magazine stands or online leads to immoral sexual behaviour, and adolescents are more likely to start smoking cigarettes when they see popular movie stars lighting up.

Functionalists and conflict theorists share this top-down, deterministic view; members of both schools of thought stress how the mass media bridge social differences and reinforce society's core values. True, the two schools of thought differ in that functionalists regard core values as serving everyone's interests while conflict theorists regard them as favouring the interests of the rich and powerful. By focusing so tightly on core values, however, both approaches understate the degree to which audience members interpret media messages in different ways. The signal contribution of symbolic interactionist and related approaches is that they highlight the importance of such interpretive acts.

BOX 18.2

Sociology at the Movies

REDACTED

War is an ugly business, creating a big problem for elected governments who decide to wage war. If the electorate is fully informed about the facts of war, they are less likely to support it. To manage this issue, governments use the mass media to provide the public with a selective view of a war's causes, conditions, and consequences.

The invasion of Iraq in 2003 by the United States was initiated for questionable motives. Declarations that Iraq was non-compliant with United Nations resolutions were unsubstantiated assertions that the regime had weapons of mass destruction were never demonstrated; Iraq's al Qaeda connections to the 9/11 tragedy were nonexistent. President Bush's administration had good reason to think that public support of "Operation Iraqi Freedom" was soft. Accordingly, they launched an expensive mass media campaign to "sell the war" through advertising.

To express his opposition to the Iraq War, director Brian De Palma produced *Redacted*, a fictional film based on real events. The main characters are a group of U.S. soldiers who control a surveillance checkpoint. The central event is the rape of a teenage girl who ends up murdered, along with the rest of her family.

In the film, the director shows that the realities of war are often brutal and always multisided. In one scene, for instance, a car speeds through a U.S.-controlled checkpoint. From the soldiers' viewpoint, the driver received clear warnings to stop for inspection. Because they were ignored, the soldiers fire repeatedly and kill a

© Magnolia Pictures/Courtesy Everett Collection

Scene from *Redacted*

woman in the passenger seat. It turns out, however, that the driver was a young Iraqi man hurriedly driving his pregnant sister to the hospital to deliver her baby. He entered the checkpoint and saw the U.S. soldiers waving him through. He couldn't understand why they began firing. The two different versions of these events were reported to the American and Iraqi publics.

This movie's principal point is that the mass media inevitably present a selective version of events. Their version of "truth" aims at shaping the views of their audience toward particular goals. This use of the mass media becomes especially evident when reporting events like wars that are full of ambiguity, contradiction, and harshness. Redaction, the deliberate censoring and obscuring of actual events, is central to the power of all mass media.

Like De Palma's earlier film about the Vietnam War (*Casualties of War*, 1989), *Redacted* sensitizes viewers to how mass media presentations bias their understanding of events. The fact that De Palma is making the same point about American foreign wars two decades after his first attempt is disheartening. Nonetheless, during those two decades the mass media experienced encouraging democratization. Digitization allows a wide range of audiences to record and broadcast alternative views of reality. New social media have changed the mass media. De Palma exploits this change by blending all manner of social media accounts into *Redacted*. The multidimensional portrait of Iraqi reality includes a collage of cellphone photos, surveillance camera footage, video segments, and documentary excerpts. Effective war propaganda relies on audiences receiving a uniform message. De Palma's film suggests that social media may provide an effective challenge to such a monopoly of interpretation and encourage independent assessments about the worthiness of war.

Just how much influence do the mass media actually exert over audiences? The question is mired in controversy, but it seems that the top-down, deterministic view is one-sided. You may recall our discussion of media violence in Chapter 2, How Sociologists Do Research. There we found that most experimental research on the subject is plagued by a validity problem. Simply stated, experiments on media violence may not be measuring what they say they are measuring. The sociological consensus seems to be that TV violence influences only a small percentage of viewers to commit acts of violence in the real world.

There are other reasons for questioning the strength of media effects. For instance, researchers have known for half a century that people do not change their attitudes and behaviours just because the media tell them to do so. That is because the link between persuasive media messages and actual behaviour is indirect. A **two-step flow of communication** takes place (Katz, 1957; Schiller, 1989; Schudson, 1995). In step 1, respected people of high status evaluate media messages. They are the opinion leaders of a neighbourhood or a community, people who are usually more highly educated, well-to-do, or politically powerful than others in their circle are. Because of their high status, they exercise considerable independence of judgment. In step 2, opinion leaders *may* influence the attitudes and behaviours of others. In this way, opinion leaders filter media messages. The two-step flow of communication limits media effects. If people are influenced to vote for certain candidates, buy certain products, or smoke cigarettes, it is less because the media tell them to and more because opinion leaders suggest they should.

Yet another persuasive argument that leads us to question the effects of the mass media comes from interpretive sociologists, such as symbolic interactionists and interdisciplinary "cultural studies" experts. They use in-depth interviewing and participant observation to study how people actually interpret media messages.

British sociologist Stuart Hall (1980), one of the foremost proponents of this approach, emphasizes that people are not empty vessels into which the mass media pour a defined assortment of beliefs, values, and ideas. Rather, audience members take an active role in consuming the products of the mass media. They filter and interpret mass media messages in the context of their own interests, experiences, and values. Thus, in Hall's view, any adequate analysis of the mass media needs to take into account both the production and the consumption of media products. First, he says, we need to study the meanings intended by the producers. Then we need to study how audiences consume or evaluate media products. Intended and received meanings may diverge; audience members may interpret media messages in ways other than those intended by the producers (Hall, 1980; Seiter, 1999).

Here is a personal example of the way audiences may interpret media messages in unexpected ways: When John Lie's parents were preparing to emigrate to the United States in the late 1960s, his mother watched many American movies and television shows. One of her favourite TV programs was *My Three Sons*, a sitcom about three boys living with their father and grandfather. From the show she learned that boys wash dishes and vacuum the house in the United States. When the Lie family emigrated to Hawaii, John and his brother—but not his sister—had to wash dishes every night. When John complained, his mother reassured him that "in America, only boys wash dishes."

Even children's television viewing turns out to be complex when viewed through an interpretive lens. Research shows that young children distinguish "make-believe" media violence from real-life violence (Hodge and Tripp, 1986). That is one reason watching *South Park* has not produced a nation of *South Park* clones. Similarly, research shows differences in the way working-class and middle-class women relate to TV. Working-class women tend to evaluate TV programs in terms of how realistic they are more than middle-class women do. This critical attitude reduces their ability to identify strongly with many characters, personalities, and storylines. For instance, working-class women know from their own experience that families often don't work the way they are shown on TV. They view the idealized, middle-class nuclear family depicted in many television shows with a mixture of nostalgia and skepticism (Press, 1991). Age also affects how we relate to television. Senior viewers tend to be selective and focused in their television viewing. In

The **two-step flow of communication** between mass media and audience members involves (1) respected people of high status and independent judgment evaluating media messages, and (2) other members of the community being influenced to varying degrees by these opinion leaders. Because of the two-step flow of communication, opinion leaders filter media messages.

contrast, people who grew up with cable TV and a remote control often engage in channel surfing, conversation, eating, and housework, zoning in and out of programs in anything but an absorbed fashion (Press, 1991). The idea that such viewers are sponges, passively soaking up the values embedded in TV programs and then mechanically acting on them, is inaccurate.

Feminist Approaches

Finally, let us consider feminist approaches to the study of mass media effects. In the 1970s, feminist researchers focused on the representation—more accurately, the misrepresentation—of women in the mass media. They found that in TV dramas, women tended to be cast as homemakers, as secretaries, and in other subordinate roles, while men tended to be cast as professionals and authority figures. Women usually appeared in domestic settings, men in public settings. Advertising targeted women only as purchasers of household products and appliances. Furthermore, researchers discovered that the news rarely mentioned issues of importance for many women, such as wage discrimination in the paid labour force, sexual harassment and abuse, child-care problems, and so on. News reports sometimes trivialized or denounced the women's movement. Newsworthy issues (the economy, party politics, international affairs, and crime) were associated with men, and men were much more likely than women were to be used as news sources and to deliver the news (Watkins and Emerson, 2000: 152–53).

Most of this early feminist research assumed that audiences are passive. Analysts argued that the mass media portray women in stereotypical fashion; audience members recognize and accept the stereotypes as normal and even natural; and the mass media thereby reinforce existing gender inequalities. However, in the 1980s and 1990s, feminist researchers criticized this simple formula. They realized that audience members selectively interpret media messages and sometimes even contest them.

A good example of this subtler and less deterministic approach is a study by Andrea Press and Elizabeth Cole (1999) of audience reaction to abortion as portrayed on TV shows. Over a four-year period, Press and Cole conducted 34 discussion groups involving 108 women. The women watched three TV programs focusing on abortion and then discussed their attitudes and their reactions to the shows. The programs were pro-choice and dealt with women who chose abortion to avoid poverty.

Press and Cole found complex, ambivalent, and sometimes contradictory attitudes toward abortion among audience members. However, four distinct clusters of opinion emerged:

1. *Pro-life women from all social classes* formed the most homogeneous group. They thought abortion is never justified. On principle, they rejected the mass media's justifications for abortion.
2. *Pro-choice working-class women who thought of themselves as members of the working class* adopted a pro-choice stand as a survival strategy, not on principle. They did not condone abortion, but they feared that laws restricting abortion would be applied prejudicially against women of their class. Therefore, they opposed any such restrictions. At the same time, they rejected the TV message that financial hardship justifies abortion.
3. *Pro-choice working-class women who aspired to middle-class status* distanced themselves from the "reckless" members of their own class who sought abortions on the TV shows. They tolerated abortion for such people but they rejected it for themselves and for other "responsible" women.
4. *Pro-choice middle-class women* believe that only an individual woman's feelings can determine whether abortion is right or wrong in her own case. Many of them had deep reservations about abortion, and many of them rejected it as an option for themselves. However, they staunchly defend the right of all women, especially the kind of women portrayed in the TV shows they watched, to choose abortion.

One of the most striking aspects of Press and Cole's findings is that, for different reasons, three of the four categories of audience members (categories 1, 2, and 3) were highly skeptical of TV portrayals of the abortion issue. Their class position and attitudes acted as filters influencing how they reacted to TV shows and how they viewed the abortion issue. Moreover, three of the four categories of audience members (categories 2, 3, and 4) rejected the simple pro-choice versus pro-life dichotomy often portrayed by the mass media. Many pro-choice women expressed ambivalence about abortion and even rejected it as an option for themselves. We must conclude that real women are typically more complicated than the stereotypes promoted in the mass media, and that women in the audience typically know that.

In recent years, some feminists have focused on the capacity of the mass media to reproduce and change the system of racial inequality in North American society. In the work of these scholars, the twin issues of female misrepresentation and active audience interpretation reappear, this time with a racial twist. On the one hand, they find that certain stereotypical images of women of colour recur in the mass media. Women of African heritage, for example, often appear in the role of the welfare mother, the highly sexualized Jezebel, and the mammy. On the other hand, they recognize that some mass media, especially independent filmmaking and popular music, have enabled women of colour to challenge these stereotypes. The music and videos of Erykah Badu, Missy Elliott, Lauryn Hill, Beyoncé Knowles, and Alicia Keys are especially noteworthy in this regard. These artists write and produce their own music. They often direct their own videos. Their work is a running critical commentary on real-world issues confronting young black women. Thus, in terms of both production and content, their work breaks down the established roles and images of black women in North America (Watkins and Emerson, 2000: 159–56).

Still, stereotypes persist. A 2009 study of North American primetime TV found men predominating in law enforcement, professional, and criminal roles. The shows portrayed men working in the paid labour force twice as often as women (Signorielli, 2009). Women's prime-time TV characters played "non-prestigious" roles 21 percent of the time, while only 13 percent of male characters were of this type (Figure 18.1).

Apart from her outstanding recording career, Beyoncé Knowles's songs encourage empowerment for young black women. She typifies confidence, style, motivation, and success in music, the movies, and product marketing.

FIGURE 18.1

Gender Differences in Prime-Time TV Characters (percentages)

Note: Category selection results in percentages under 100.

Adapted from Signorielli, 2009.

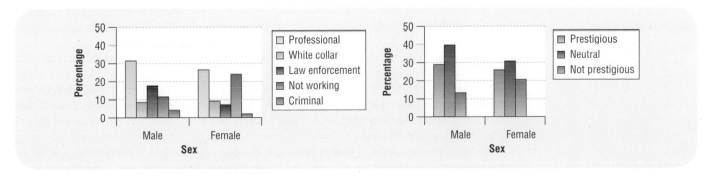

The way in which the mass media treat women and members of various minority groups has for the most part improved over time. We have come a long way since the 1950s, when virtually the only blacks on TV were men who played butlers and buffoons. Research suggests that the mass media still have a long way to go before they cease reinforcing traditional stereotypes in North America (Signorielli, 2009). But research also suggests that audiences and artists are hardly passive vehicles of these stereotypes, instead struggling to diversify the way the mass media characterize them.

Summing Up

- Functionalism identifies the main social effects of mass media as coordination, socialization, social control, and entertainment. By performing these functions, the mass media help make social order possible.
- Conflict theory qualifies the functionalist perspective by noting that media concentration and control by a privileged minority contribute to economic inequality and maintain the core values of a stratified social order.
- Interpretive approaches remind us that audience members are people, not programmable robots. We filter, interpret, resist, and sometimes reject media messages according to our own interests and values.
- Feminist approaches highlight the misrepresentation of women and members of racial minorities in the mass media. They also emphasize the ways in which women and members of racial minorities have successfully challenged these misrepresentations and sought to diversify the characterization of race and gender by the mass media.

DOMINATION AND RESISTANCE ON THE INTERNET

We have emphasized the interaction that normally takes place between the mass media and its audiences. To drive the point home, we now offer an in-depth analysis of domination and resistance on the Internet. As you will see, the Internet provides fresh opportunities for media conglomerates to restrict access to paying customers and accumulate vast wealth. Simultaneously, however, the Internet gives consumers new creative capabilities, partially blurring the distinction between producer and consumer. The Internet, we conclude, has the potential to make the mass media more democratic—at least for those who can afford access.

To develop this idea, let us first consider the forces that restrict Internet access and augment the power of media conglomerates. We then discuss some countertrends.

Access

The Internet requires an expensive infrastructure of personal computers, servers, and routers; an elaborate network of fibre-optic, copper-twist, and coaxial cables; and many other components. This infrastructure has to be paid for, primarily by individual users. As a result, access is not open to everyone—far from it. In Canada, for example, households that are richer, better educated, urban, and younger are most likely to enjoy Internet access (Statistics Canada, 2010c).

Nor is Internet access evenly distributed globally. In Sweden, more than 90 percent of the population is connected. Canada, the United States, Singapore, and South Korea have penetration rates of around 80 percent. By contrast, many underdeveloped regions have rates in the single digits. Globally, the rate of Internet connectivity is much higher in rich countries than in poor countries.

Content

American domination remains a striking feature of Internet content. The world's top search engine is Google, with YouTube, Facebook, Yahoo rounding out the most visited sites. Some analysts say that American domination of the web is an example of **media imperialism**. Media imperialism is the control of a mass medium by a single national culture and the undermining of other national cultures. France and Canada are perhaps the countries that have spoken out most strongly against the perceived American threat to their national culture and identity. Some French and Canadian media analysts deeply resent the fact that the United States is the world's biggest exporter and smallest importer of mass media products, including web content. Like much in the world, this profile is changing with the growing influence of Asia. In 2010, Sina.com (approximating Yahoo), QQ.com (approximating MSN messenger), and Baidu.com (a search engine)—all originating in China—were among the world's most visited websites.

The problem of media imperialism is particularly acute in Canadian broadcasting because the country has a small population (smaller than California's), is close to the United States, and is about 75 percent English speaking. Private broadcasters dominate the Canadian market and rely mainly on American entertainment programming. Moreover, the widespread use of cable and satellite dishes permits most Canadians to receive American programming directly from source.

According to some media analysts, the Internet not only restricts access and promotes American content but also increases the power of media conglomerates. That is evident, for example, in the realm of **media convergence**. Media convergence is the blending of the World Wide Web, television, telephone, and other communications media into new, hybrid media forms.

Television access and cellphone expansion are recent illustrations of media convergence. Not long ago, popular television programs were available only when they were initially broadcast or later through reruns. Now television programs are continuously available through the Internet. Anyone with access can log on to CBC.ca, NBC.com, or

Media imperialism is the domination of a mass medium by a single national culture and the undermining of other national cultures.

Media convergence is the blending of the World Wide Web, television, and other communications media as new, hybrid media forms.

Media imperialism: watching *Grease* on Enaotai Island in West Papua, New Guinea

Associated Press, Melbourne Age/AP/Wide World Photos

thecomedynetwork.ca and watch full episodes of recently aired shows. This transformation is possible because Internet connections can now transfer at speeds 10 times as fast as a few years ago.

Major media convergence is also happening with cellphones, especially iPhones and the BlackBerry. People can now surf the Internet, send email, watch videos, listen to music, as well as download "apps" and games on one portable device sold as a "phone." The fierce competition related to upgrading from 3G to 4G networks (and beyond) foretells that media convergence will continue, as download speeds, reliability, and efficiency increase.

Media convergence, like all significant change, comes with struggle and debate. A recent illustration is the contest over whether Internet customers should be charged a flat fee or whether user-based billing should apply. Major service providers like Bell Canada and Shaw argue that Internet usage should be like any other service—the more you use, the more you pay. Opponents argue that technological improvements have more than compensated for usage increases and that user-based billing is merely a marketing gimmick to inflate customer costs and corporate profits unfairly.

Efforts by huge media conglomerates to shape media convergence and control access may seem like an old story. In some respects it is. Ownership of every mass medium has become more concentrated over time. Because entry costs are so high, only media giants can participate and, following conflict theorists expectations, concentrated corporate powers pursue their vested interests.

However, the Internet story comes with a twist. The big media conglomerates may be able to carve out new and lucrative niches for themselves through media convergence. However, they can never fully dominate the Internet because this is the first mass medium that makes it relatively easy for consumers to become producers.

People are not just passive users of the Internet. Instead, they help to create it. A quick review of current facts regarding YouTube, massively multiplayer online games (MMOGs) and virtual worlds, Facebook, and Twitter illustrates how important user contributions are to the social construction of Internet reality.

Internet users watch over two billion YouTube videos per day. Interested viewers have plenty of choice since, on average, 24 hours of digital footage is uploaded to YouTube servers every minute. Emerging from all this user-generated content are explosively successful "viral videos." Viral videos typically have short but impressive lifespans, and gain fame (or infamy) from showing something funny, touching, or extremely unusual. Often viral videos command tens of millions of viewers. Among music videos, hundreds of millions of views is not uncommon.

Large audiences are also found for MMOGs. World of Warcraft has more than 11 million registered users. Aion has more than 3 million. Second Life is marketed as a user-created virtual world with millions of registered accounts. The entire Second Life world is created by premium users who can buy virtual land and establish their preferred realities.

For audience generation, nothing currently trumps Facebook, which claims to have more than 750 million active users who use the site 15.5 hours a month on average. The average Facebook user has 130 "friends" and creates an average of 90 pieces of content a month (Facebook, 2011).

Twitter is another fast-growing phenomenon. Since its inception in 2006, large audiences have taken to receiving and producing text messaging "tweets." Some celebrities have millions of followers.

Add to this roster the millions of personal websites, the tens of thousands of public-access cameras, the huge array of discussion groups and discussion forums devoted to every imaginable topic, and we must temper the image of the Internet as a medium that is subject to increasing domination by large conglomerates. In many respects, the trend is the contrary. Individual users are making independent, creative contributions to Internet growth (see Box 18.3). Similarly, the view that the growth of the Web is an example of American media imperialism has not gone unchallenged. Where some media analysts see American media imperialism, others see globalization and postmodernization, social processes we introduced in Chapter 3, Culture. From the latter point of view, all

It's Your Choice

MUSICAL ATTENTION DEFICIT DISORDER (MADD)

Young people's culture has always been faster than the culture of older people. Older people process information more slowly than young people do because, as we age, we have fewer and less efficient neurons. However, in recent years, technological innovation has encouraged young people's attention spans to shorten and the generational gap in processing speed to grow (Fox and Brym, 2009).

In particular, electronic media make it possible to cater to the neurological advantages that young people have over older people. When *Sesame Street* became a huge TV hit in 1969, part of its appeal was that its story segments were shorter than those on other children's programs. Decades of research by the Children's Television Workshop suggests that shows like *Sesame Street*

© Kevin Dodge/Corbis

condition children to regard brevity as normal. The widespread adoption of the personal computer and the Internet in the 1980s and 1990s reinforced the need for speed. Quick information gathering, instant communication, and rapid-fire gaming, once considered spectacular, are now routine.

The speed with which teenagers check Facebook, channel surf, listen to music, and engage in instant messaging often bewilders parents, who are unable to process what appear to them to be lightning-fast events. Many teenagers seem unable to listen to an entire song without becoming distracted. They often use MP3 players to skim songs, listening to each for less than a minute. A fast-paced media- and technology-rich environment affords plenty of opportunities to multitask. At clubs, DJs

playing for a young crowd find it necessary to mix songs quickly to maintain a tight dance floor and excite people. In contrast, quick mixing represents information overload for an older crowd, which quickly becomes irritated unless the DJ plays songs in their entirety. Thus, although built on neurological foundations that have always separated younger from older generations, shortening attention spans have been nurtured by technological change in the electronic media.

Does this description of MADD fit your observations of differences between generations? How would you rate your level of MADD? To what extent did your childhood experience encourage MADD development? Do nightclubs enhance your level of MADD?

cultures, including that of the United States, are becoming less homogeneous and more fragmented as they borrow elements from one another. Thus, if you look carefully at the Web, you will see that even U.S. sites adopt content liberally from Latin America, Asia, and elsewhere. Just as international influences are evident in today's hairstyles, clothing fashions, foods, and popular music, so we can see the Internet as a site of globalization (Widyastuti, 2010).

Of course, nobody knows exactly how the social forces we have outlined will play themselves out. A phenomenon like Napster emerges, enabling millions of people to share recorded music freely on the Web using a central server. Some analysts point to Napster as evidence of Internet democratization. Then the media conglomerates take Napster to court, forcing it to stop the giveaway on the grounds it is effectively stealing royalties from musicians and profits from music companies. Then new Napster-like programs, such as Kazaa, Limewire, Gnutella, and BitTorrent emerge. These programs allow people to share recorded music and videos on the Web *without* a central server, making them virtually impossible to shut down. Despite repeated legal actions to try to curb organizations like Kazaa and the Pirate Bay, the dispersed locations of management, servers, developers, coding, and users make litigation and enforcement extremely problematic. And so the tug of war between conglomeration and democratization continues, with no end in sight. One thing is clear, however. The speed of technological innovation and the many possibilities for individual creativity on the Internet make this an exciting era to be involved in the mass media and to study it sociologically.

Summing Up

- Internet access is unequally distributed. Richer categories of people enjoy more access.
- Internet content is dominated by Western, and particularly American, perspectives and interests.
- Media convergence is creating new forms of mass media.
- Corporate domination of Internet-based mass media is continuously challenged by the creative contributions individuals and groups of content producers.

SUMMARY

1. What are the mass media?

   The mass media are means of transmitting information and entertainment from one person or group to another. The communication is typically from a few senders to many receivers. The mass media sometimes blur the line between reality and fantasy.

2. Which historical forces stimulated the growth of the mass media?

   Three main historical forces stimulated the growth of the mass media. The Protestant Reformation of the sixteenth century encouraged people to read the Bible themselves. The democratic movements that began in the late eighteenth century encouraged people to demand literacy. Beginning in the late nineteenth century, capitalist industrialization required rapid means of communication and fostered the mass media as important sources of profit.

3. What are the main theories of mass media effects?

   Functionalism stresses that the mass media act to coordinate society, exercise social control, and socialize and entertain people. Conflict theory stresses that the mass media reinforce social inequality. They do this both by acting as sources of profit for the few people who control media conglomerates and by promoting core values that help legitimize the existing social order. Interpretive approaches to studying the mass media stress that audiences actively filter, interpret, and sometimes even resist and reject media messages according to their interests and values. Feminist approaches concur and also emphasize the degree to which the mass media perpetuate gender and racial stereotypes.

KEY TERMS

mass media (p. 455)

media convergence (p. 471)

media imperialism (p. 471)

two-step flow of communication
(p. 467)

WEB RESOURCES

Companion Website for This Book

http://www.compass4e.nelson.com

Begin by clicking on the Student Resources section of the website. Next, select the chapter you are studying from the pull-down menu. From the Student Resources page you have easy access to additional Weblinks and other resources. The website also has many useful tips to aid you in your study of sociology, including practice tests for each chapter.

InfoTrac® Search Terms

These search terms are provided to assist you in beginning to conduct research on this topic by visiting http://www.infotrac-college.com:

cultural studies
media bias
media concentration
media convergence
media imperialism

19

Health and Medicine

IN THIS CHAPTER, YOU WILL LEARN THAT

- Health risks are unevenly distributed in human populations. Men and women, upper and lower classes, rich and poor countries, and privileged and disadvantaged members of racial and ethnic groups are exposed to various health risks to varying degrees.

- On several measures of health, Canada ranks among the top countries in the world. Still, many low-income and moderate-income Canadians have limited or no access to many health services.

- The average health status of Americans is lower than the average health status of people in other rich postindustrial countries. That is partly because the level of social inequality is higher in the United States and partly because the health care system makes it difficult for many people to receive adequate care.

- The dominance of medical science is due to its successful treatments and the way in which doctors excluded competitors and established control over their profession and their clients.

- In some respects, modern medicine is a victim of its own success. For example, the wide availability of antibiotics has led to lax hygiene in hospitals, the spread of drug-resistant germs, and an epidemic of hospital infections leading to death.

- Along with standard medicine, patient activism, alternative medicine, and holistic medicine promise to improve the quality of health care in Canada and globally.

NOAH SEELAM/AFP/Getty Images

THE BLACK DEATH

In 1346, rumours reached Europe of a plague sweeping the East. Originating in Asia, the epidemic spread along trade routes to China and Russia. A year later, 12 galleys sailed from southern Russia to Italy. Diseased sailors were aboard. Their lymph nodes were swollen and eventually burst, causing a painful death. Anyone who came in contact with the sailors was soon infected. As a result, their ships were driven out of several Italian and French ports in succession. Yet the disease spread relentlessly, again moving along trade routes to Spain, Portugal, and England. Within two years, the Black Death, as it came to be known, had killed a third of Europe's population. Six hundred and fifty years later, the plague still ranks as the most devastating catastrophe in human history (Herlihy, 1998; McNeill, 1976; Zinsser, 1935).

Museo del Prado, Madrid, Spain/Giraudon. Paris/SuperStock

Today we know that the cause of the plague was a bacillus that spread from fleas to rats to people. It spread so efficiently because many people lived close together in unsanitary conditions. In the middle of the fourteenth century, however, nobody knew anything about germs. Therefore, Pope Clement VI sent a delegation to Europe's leading medical school in Paris to discover the cause of the plague. The learned professors studied the problem. They reported that a particularly unfortunate conjunction of Saturn, Jupiter, and Mars in the sign of Aquarius had occurred in 1345. The resulting hot, humid conditions caused the earth to emit poisonous vapours. To prevent the plague, they said, people should refrain from eating poultry, waterfowl, pork, beef, fish, and olive oil. They should not sleep during the daytime or engage in excessive exercise. Nothing should be cooked in rainwater. Bathing should be avoided at all costs.

We do not know whether the pope followed the professors' advice. We do know he made a practice of sitting between two large fires to breathe pure air. Because heat destroys the plague bacillus, this practice may have saved his life. Other people were less fortunate. Some rang church bells and fired cannons to drive the plague away. Others burned incense, wore charms, and cast spells. However, other than the pope, the only people to have much luck in avoiding the plague were the well-to-do (who could afford to flee the densely populated cities for the countryside) and the Jews (whose religion required that they wash their hands before meals, bathe once a week, and conduct burials soon after death).

Some of the main themes of the sociology of health and medicine are embedded in the story of the Black Death, or at least implied by it. First, recall that some groups were more likely to die of the plague than others were. This is a common pattern. Health risks are almost always unevenly distributed. Women and men, upper and lower classes, rich and poor countries, and privileged and disadvantaged members of racial and ethnic groups are exposed to health risks to varying degrees. This suggests that health is not just a medical issue but also a sociological one. The first task we set ourselves below is to examine the sociological factors that account for the uneven distribution of health in society.

Second, the story of the Black Death suggests that health problems change over time. Epidemics of various types still break out, but there can be no Black Death where sanitation and hygiene prevent the spread of disease. Today we are also able to treat many infectious diseases, such as tuberculosis and pneumonia, with antibiotics. Twentieth-century medical

Life expectancy is the average age at death of the members of a population.

science developed these wonder drugs and many other life-saving therapies. Medical successes allow people to live longer than they used to. **Life expectancy** is the average age at death of the members of a population. Life expectancy in Canada in 1831 was approximately 40 years for men and 42 years for women (Lavoie and Oderkirk, 2000: 3). In contrast, life expectancy in 2009 was 81 years. Yet, because of increased life expectancy, degenerative conditions such as cancer and heart disease have an opportunity to develop in a way that was not possible a century ago (see Table 19.1).

The story of the Black Death raises a third issue, too. We cannot help being struck by the superstition and ignorance surrounding the treatment of the ill in medieval times. Remedies were often herbal but also included earthworms, urine, and animal excrement. People believed it was possible to maintain good health by keeping body fluids in balance. Therefore, cures that released body fluids were common. These included hot baths, laxatives, and diuretics, which increase the amount of urine. If these treatments didn't work, bloodletting was often prescribed. No special qualifications were required to administer medical treatment. Barbers doubled as doctors.

TABLE 19.1

Leading Causes of Death, Canada, 1901 and 2007

Sources: Dawson, 1906; Statistics Canada, 2011d.

1901	Percentage of Deaths
1. Tuberculosis	12.0
2. Bronchitis and pneumonia	10.0
3. Affections of the intestines	9.1
4. Senile debility	7.4
5. Congenital debility	7.0
6. Diseases of the heart	5.6
7. Apoplexy and paralysis	4.4
8. Diphtheria and croup	3.9
9. Accidents	3.4
10. Cancer	2.8
Other	34.4
Total	100.0

2007	
1. Cancer	29.6
2. Major heart disease	21.5
3. Stroke	5.9
4. Chronic lower respiratory diseases	4.5
5. Accidents	4.2
6. Diabetes	3.1
7. Alzheimer's disease	2.5
8. Influenza and pneumonia	2.3
9. Kidney disease	1.6
10. Suicide	1.5
Other	23.3
Total	100.0

However, the backwardness of medieval medical practice, and the advantages of modern scientific medicine, can easily be exaggerated. For example, medieval doctors stressed the importance of prevention, exercise, a balanced diet, and a congenial environment in maintaining good health. We now know this is sound advice. Conversely, one of the great shortcomings of modern medicine is its emphasis on high-tech cures rather than on preventive and environmental measures. Therefore, in the final section of this chapter, we investigate how the medical professions gained substantial control over health issues and promoted their own approach to well-being, and how those professions have been challenged in recent years.

HEALTH AND INEQUALITY

Defining and Measuring Health

To measure the health of a population, sociologists typically examine the negative: rates of illness and death. They reason that healthy populations experience less illness and longer life than unhealthy populations. We follow this approach here.

Assuming ideal conditions, how long can a person live? To date, the record is held by Jeanne Louise Calment, a French woman who died in 1997 at the age of 122. (Other people claim to be older, but they lack authenticated birth certificates.)

Calment was an extraordinary individual. She took up fencing at age 85, rode a bicycle until she was 100, gave up smoking at 120, and released a rap CD at 121 (Matalon, 1997). In contrast, only 1 in 100 people in the world's rich countries now lives to be 100. Since 1840, life expectancy in the world's rich countries has increased at a steady rate of 2.5 years per decade. Further increases seem likely. By 2009, the world's highest life expectancy was 83 years in Japan, Hong Kong, and San Marino (Population Reference Bureau, 2010). By 2050, the upper limit is projected to reach 92 years (Oeppen and Vaupel, 2002).

Unfortunately, conditions are nowhere near ideal. Life expectancy throughout the world is generally less than the 83 years in Japan today. Figure 19.1 shows life expectancy in selected countries. Life expectancy was one to four years shorter in Canada and the other rich postindustrial countries than it was in Japan. But in India, life expectancy was only 64 years. People in the impoverished African country of Lesotho have the world's shortest life expectancy at 41 years.

Accounting for the difference between the highest average human lifespan in the world and life expectancy in a given country is one of the main tasks of the sociologist of health. For example, although the current highest average human lifespan is 83 years, life expectancy

C3 Picture Archive/Associated Press AP

In the twenty-first century, the maximum lifespan may increase because of medical advances. So far, the record for longevity is held by Jeanne Louise Calment, a French woman who died in 1997 at the age of 122.

FIGURE 19.1
Life Expectancy, Selected Countries and Years

Sources: Population Reference Bureau, 2010; Tuljapurkar, Li, and Boe, 2000.

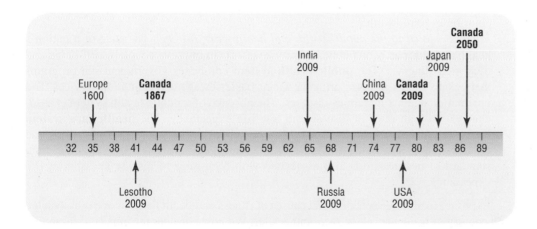

in Canada is 81 years. This implies that, on average, Canadians are being deprived of about two years of life because of avoidable *social* causes ($83 - 81 = 2$). Avoidable social causes deprive the average citizen of Lesotho of 49 years of life ($83 - 41 = 42$). Clearly, social causes have a big—and variable—impact on illness and death. We must therefore discuss them in detail.

The Social Causes of Illness and Death

People get sick and die because of natural causes in many cases. One person may have a genetic predisposition to cancer. Another may come in contact with a deadly Ebola virus in the environment. However, over and above such natural causes of illness and death, we can single out three types of *social* causes:

1. *Human-environmental factors.* Major health risks arise from how human activity shapes environments. Divisions like social class, occupation, and nationality often correspond to sharp differences in the surroundings in which people work and live. Some environments foster good health, while others impose added risks for poor health. For example, the introduction of sour gas wells and logging operations around the reserves of the Lubicon First Nation in Alberta resulted in a dramatic increase in illness. More than one in three members of the Lubicon population suffers from such health problems as tuberculosis, respiratory difficulties, and cancer at rates far above the national average (Barlow and May, 2000: 183). In general, hazardous waste sites and polluting industries tend to be located near First Nations communities or areas populated by the poor, the politically marginalized, or certain visible minority groups, thus contributing to lower levels of health (Brym et al., 2011; see also Chapter 22, Technology and the Global Environment, at http://www.compass4e.nelson.com).

2. *Lifestyle factors.* Smoking, excessive use of alcohol and drugs, poor diet, lack of exercise, and social isolation are among the chief lifestyle factors associated with poor health and premature death. For example, smoking is associated with lung cancer, cardiovascular disease, strokes, emphysema, spontaneous abortion, premature birth, and neonatal death. In Canada, about 50 000 deaths a year are caused by smoking and other use of tobacco products. Tobacco use accounts for about a fifth of all deaths, far outweighing the combined impact of suicide, homicide, and accidents (Makomaski, Illing and Kaiserman, 2004). Social isolation, too, affects a person's chance of becoming ill and dying prematurely. Thus, unmarried people have a greater chance of dying prematurely than do married people. At any age, the death of a spouse increases a person's chance of dying, while remarrying decreases the chance of dying (Helsing, Szklo, and Comstock, 1981). Social isolation is a particularly big problem among older people who retire, lose a spouse and friends, and cannot rely on family members or state institutions for social support. Such people are prone to fall into a state of depression, which contributes to ill health.

3. *Factors related to the public health and health care systems.* The state of a nation's health depends partly on public and private efforts to improve people's well-being and treat their illnesses. The **public health system** comprises government-run programs that ensure access to clean drinking water, basic sewage and sanitation services, and inoculation against infectious diseases. The absence of a public health system is associated with high rates of disease and low life expectancy. The **health care system** comprises a nation's clinics, hospitals, and other facilities for ensuring health and treating illness. The absence of a system that ensures its citizens access to a minimum standard of health care is also associated with high rates of disease and shorter life expectancy.

Exposure to all three sets of social causes of illness and death listed above is associated with country of residence, class, race, and gender. We now consider the impact of these factors, beginning with country of residence.

The **public health system** comprises government-run programs that ensure access to clean drinking water, basic sewage and sanitation services, and inoculation against infectious diseases.

The **health care system** is composed of a nation's clinics, hospitals, and other facilities for ensuring health and treating illness.

Country of Residence

HIV/AIDS is the leading cause of death in the poverty-stricken part of Africa south of the Sahara desert. Figure 19.2 shows that in 2009, 22.5 million sub-Saharan Africans—5 percent of the adult population—were living with HIV/AIDS. In contrast, 0.5 percent of North American adults and 0.2 percent of Western European adults were living with HIV/AIDS. This means that HIV/AIDS is 10 times more common in sub-Saharan Africa than in North America and nearly 17 times more common than in Western Europe (UNAIDS, 2010). Yet spending on research and treatment is concentrated overwhelmingly in the rich countries of North America and Western Europe. As the case of HIV/AIDS illustrates, global inequality influences the exposure of people to different health risks.

Prosperity increases health through biomedical advances, such as new medicines and diagnostic tools. In particular, vaccines against infectious diseases have done much to improve health and ensure longer life. However, the creation of a sound public health system was even more important in this regard. If a country can provide its citizens with clean water and a sewage system, epidemics decline in frequency and severity while life expectancy soars.

The industrialized countries started to develop their public health systems in the mid-nineteenth century. Social reformers, concerned citizens, scientists, and doctors joined industrialists and politicians in urging governments to develop health policies that would help create a healthier labour force and citizenry (Bricker and Greenspon, 2001: 178–83; Goubert, 1989 [1986]; McNeill, 1976). But what was possible in North America and Western Europe 150 years ago is not possible in many developing countries today. Most of us take clean water for granted, but more than a sixth of the world's people do not have access to a sanitary water supply (de Villiers, 1999).

Other indicators of health inequality for selected countries are given in Table 19.2 on page 482. We see that, in general, there is a positive association between national wealth and good health. Canada, the United States, and Japan are rich countries. They spend a substantial part of their wealth on health care. Many physicians and nurses service the populations. As a result, **infant mortality** (the annual number of deaths before the age of one for every 1000 live births) is low. India, which is poorer than Canada, the United States, and Japan, spends a smaller proportion of its wealth on health care. Accordingly, its population is less healthy in a number of respects. The sub-Saharan country of Lesotho is one of the poorest countries in the world. It spends little on health care, has few medical personnel, and suffers from high rates of infant mortality.

A health worker at Nazareth House in Cape Town, South Africa, lavishes care and attention on some of the 41 infected children in her care. Nearly one-fifth of South Africa's adult population is infected with HIV/AIDS.

Infant mortality is the number of deaths before the age of one for every 1000 live births in a population in one year.

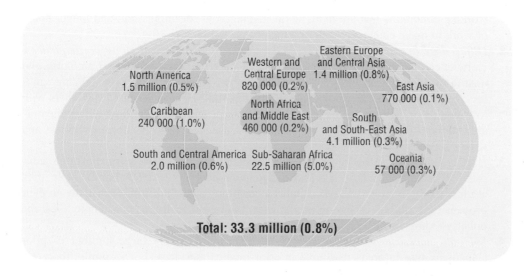

South and Central America
2.0 million (0.6%)

North America
1.5 million (0.5%)

Caribbean
240 000 (1.0%)

Western and
Central Europe
820 000 (0.2%)

Eastern Europe
and Central Asia
1.4 million (0.8%)

North Africa
and Middle East
460 000 (0.2%)

East Asia
770 000 (0.1%)

South
and South-East Asia
4.1 million (0.3%)

Sub-Saharan Africa
22.5 million (5.0%)

Oceania
57 000 (0.3%)

Total: 33.3 million (0.8%)

FIGURE 19.2

People with HIV/AIDS, 2009 (adult prevalence in parentheses)

Source: UNAIDS. 2010. "Global Report." http://www.unaids.org/documents/20101123_GlobalReport_em.pdf (accessed 7 December 2010) page 20-21.

TABLE 19.2
Health Indicators, Selected Countries, 2009

Source: World Health Organization. 2010. "WHO Statistical Information System (WHOSIS)" http://www.who.int/whosis/en/index.html (accessed 1 April 2010).

Country	Expenditure on Health as Percentage of Gross Domestic Product (2006)	Nurses and Midwives per 10 000 Population	Physicians per 10 000 Population	Infant mortality per 1000 Live Births	Percentage of Population with Access to Improved Drinking Water Source
Japan	7.7	95	21	1	100
Canada	8.8	101	19	3	100
United States	13.2	94	26	4	99
India	4.3	13	6	39	89
Lesotho	6.2	6	1	52	78

Class Inequalities and Health Care

In Canada, despite our system of universal health care, socioeconomic status is correlated with numerous aspects of health and illness (Raphael, 2004). On average, people with low income die at a younger age than do people with high income. Canadians experience lower rates of sickness, improved health, and longer life expectancies at each step up the income ladder (Health Canada, 1999a, 1999b). A broad range of psychiatric conditions is associated with low socioeconomic status (Williams and Collins, 1999). Poverty is also associated with high rates of tobacco and alcohol consumption, obesity, physical inactivity, and violence (Health Canada, 1999a).

Why does health deteriorate as we move down the class hierarchy? Sociologists have proposed several explanations:

1. *High stress and the inability to cope with it.* People in lower classes experience relatively high stress levels because of their deprived and difficult living conditions (Kessler et al., 1994). Stress is linked to a variety of physical and mental health problems, including high blood pressure, cancer, chronic fatigue, violence, and substance abuse. Moreover, people higher in the class structure are often able to turn stress off by, say, taking a day off work or going on vacation. Many problems are more burdensome when resources like money and influence are unavailable. Upper-class people can pay others to fix their cars or their offspring's legal mishaps or whatever else may arise. Lower-class families may have to go into debt or simply accept some bad outcomes as unavoidable (Cockerham, 1998; Epstein, 1998; Evans, 1999, Wilkinson and Marmot, 2003). Mishaps aside, lower-class families endure greater crowding; poorer dwelling quality; working conditions that are more noxious, dangerous, or unpleasant; and longer hours of work to make ends meet—all of which cause stress.

2. *Differences in the earliest stages of development that have lifelong consequences.* Deficiencies in nutrition during pregnancy, maternal stress, maternal smoking and misuse of drugs and alcohol, insufficient exercise, and inadequate prenatal care cause less than optimal fetal development (Wilkinson and Marmot, 2003: 14). Mothers with low income or little education are more likely to provide their children with unfavourable starts to life, and this has strong health consequences for a lifetime (Forrest and Riley, 2004).

3. *Lack of knowledge.* People who are less educated and who have less exposure to educated advisers tend to have less knowledge about healthy lifestyles. For example, they are less likely to know what constitutes a nutritious diet. This, too, contributes to their propensity to illness. Illness, in turn, makes it more difficult for poor people to escape poverty (Abraham, 1993).

4. *Unequal access to health resources.* A disproportionately large number of poor Canadians live in areas that have inferior medical services. For example, there are

fewer hospitals, physicians, and nurses per capita in rural areas than in urban areas. As well, the quality of preventive, diagnostic, and treatment facilities is generally superior in urban areas. Moreover, although access to health care remains largely unrelated to income because of Canada's medicare system, many low- and moderate-income Canadians have limited or no access to eye care, dentistry, mental health counselling, and prescription drugs (Boychuk, 2002; Health Canada, 1999b).

5. *Environmental exposure.* As noted earlier, poor people are more likely to be exposed to environmental risks that have a negative impact on their health. There is a striking lack of incinerators, pulp and paper mills, oil refineries, dumpsites, factories, and mines in Westmount (Montreal), Tuxedo (Winnipeg), Rosedale (Toronto), and other wealthy Canadian neighbourhoods (see Chapter 22, Technology and the Global Environment).

Biomedical advances increase life expectancy, but the creation of a sound public health system has even more dramatic effects.

Racial Inequalities in Health Care

Racial disparities in health status are also large. For example, the life expectancy of Status Indians[1] is seven to eight years shorter than that of non-Aboriginal Canadians, and illegal drug use is high among Aboriginal peoples (Canadian Aboriginal News, 2001; Canadian Institute for Health Information, 2004; Scott, 1997). Despite the health risks posed to both the mother and the developing fetus, a national survey found that 76 percent of Inuit women and 54 percent of Indian women smoke during pregnancy, about triple the national average (Canadian Centre on Substance Abuse, 1999).

Such health disparities are partly due to economic differences among racial groups. In addition, researchers have emphasized how racially marginalized groups are subject to negative health outcomes because of the cumulative effects of social exclusion based on race. Researchers have observed these effects for African Americans in the United States, Aboriginal Canadians, and other groups (Galabuzi, 2004; Wilkinson and Marmot, 2003).

How does social exclusion influence health apart from the fact that excluded groups experience higher rates of poverty? In brief, labour market segregation, high unemployment, low occupation status, substandard housing, dangerous or distressed neighbourhoods, homelessness, dangerous worksites, extended hours, multiple jobs, and experience with everyday forms of racism lead to unequal health service utilization and differential health status (Galabuzi, 2004: 3). Even when members of socially excluded groups are employed, they are more likely to continue to live in inferior areas because of racial discrimination in housing, and such areas typically suffer from reduced access to medical services. Those who nevertheless seek medical services often encounter racially based misunderstanding or even hostility. The cumulative result of these factors is considerable. For example, 27 percent of First Nations members living on reserves report fair or poor health, compared with only 12 percent of other Canadians (Canadian Institute for Health Information, 2004: 81).

Gender Inequalities in Health Care: The Feminist Contribution

Feminist scholars have brought health inequalities based on gender to the attention of the sociological community. In a review of the relevant literature, one researcher concluded that such gender inequalities are substantial (Haas, 1998):

- Gender bias exists in medical research. Public health systems have been slow to address and more likely to neglect women's health issues than men's health issues. Thus, until recently, more research has focused on "men's diseases," such as cardiac arrest, than on "women's diseases," such as breast cancer. Similarly, women have been excluded from participating in major health research studies that have examined the relationship between Aspirin use and heart disease; and how cholesterol levels, blood pressure, and smoking affect heart disease (Johnson and Fee, 1997). Medical research is only beginning to explore the fact that women may react differently from men to some illnesses and may require different treatment regimes.

- Gender bias also exists in medical treatment. For example, women undergo fewer kidney transplants, cardiac procedures, and other treatments than men do.
- Because, on average, women live longer than men do, they experience greater lifetime risk of functional disability and chronic illness, and greater need for long-term care. The low status of women in many less developed countries results in their being nutritionally deprived and having less access to medical care than do men. As a result, women in less developed countries suffer high rates of mortality and **morbidity** (acute and chronic illness) because of high rates of complication associated with pregnancy and childbirth. About one-quarter to one-half of deaths among women in less developed countries are attributed to pregnancy-related complications ("Maternal Mortality," 1998).
- Canadian women face a higher risk than men do of poverty after divorce and of widowhood. Because, as we have seen, poverty contributes to ill health, we could expect improvements in women's economic standing to be reflected in improved health status for women.

Morbidity refers to acute and chronic illness.

In sum, although on average women live longer than men do, gender inequalities have a negative impact on women's health. Women's health is negatively affected by differences between women and men in access to gender-appropriate medical research and treatment, as well as the economic resources needed to secure adequate health care.

Comparative Health Care from a Conflict Perspective

We noted earlier that rich countries spend more on health care than poor countries do. Consequently, their populations enjoy longer life expectancy. We should not infer from this generalization that money always buys good health, however. The United States spends nearly twice as much per person on health care as Japan does and nearly 60 percent more than Canada does. The United States has about a third more doctors per 10 000 people than Canada does and about a quarter more than Japan does. Yet the United States has a higher rate of infant mortality and shorter life expectancy than Canada and Japan do. The American case shows that spending more money on health care does not always improve the health of a nation.

What accounts for the American anomaly? Why do Americans spend far more on health care than any other country in the world yet wind up with a population that, on average, is less healthy than the populations of other rich countries?

One reason for the anomaly is that the gap between rich and poor is greater in the United States than in Canada, Japan, and other rich countries. In general, the higher the level of inequality in a country, the more unhealthy its population is (Wilkinson, 1996). Because, as we saw in Chapter 8, Social Stratification, the United States contains a higher percentage of poor people than do other rich countries, its average level of health is lower. Moreover, because income inequality has widened in the United States since the early 1970s, health disparities among income groups have grown (Williams and Collins, 1995).

A second reason for the American anomaly is that the cost of health care is unusually high in the United States (Anderson, Reinhardt, Hussey, and Petrosyan, 2003: 89). Physicians, hospitals, pharmaceutical companies, and other providers of health care goods and services are able to charge substantially higher prices in the United States than elsewhere (see Box 19.1). To understand why they are able to do so, we must examine the American health care system in comparative perspective.

You will recall from our discussion in Chapter 1, A Sociological Compass, and elsewhere that conflict theory is concerned mainly with the question of how privileged groups seek to maintain their advantages and subordinate groups seek to increase theirs. As such, it is an illuminating approach to analyzing the American health care system. We can usefully see health care in the United States as a system of privilege for some and disadvantage for others that contributes to the poor health of less well-to-do Americans.

Consider, for example, that the United States lacks a public health care system that covers the entire population. In the U.K., Sweden, and Denmark, public spending on health

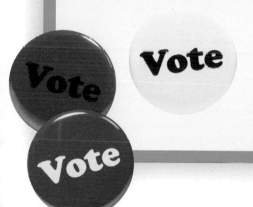

BOX 19.1
Social Policy: What Do You Think?

THE HIGH COST OF PRESCRIPTION DRUGS

Americans pay more for prescription drugs than anyone else in the world does—in 2009, 58 percent more the Canadians did (Patent Medicine Prices Review Board, 2009). Between 1998 and 2002, the price of prescription drugs in the United States increased three times as fast as the rate of inflation and as faster as any other item in the nation's health care budget. Seniors and people with chronic medical conditions, such as diabetes, feel the burden most acutely because they are the biggest prescription drug users.

Other rich countries keep prescription drug prices down through some form of government regulation. For example, since 1987, Canadian drug companies have not been able to increase prices of brand-name drugs above the inflation rate. New brand-name drugs cannot exceed the highest Canadian price of comparable drugs used to treat the same disease. For new brand-name drugs that are unique and have no competitors, the price must be no higher than the median price for that drug in the United Kingdom, France, Italy, Germany, Sweden, Switzerland, and the United States. If a company breaks the rules, the government requires a price adjustment. If the government deems that a company has deliberately flouted the law, it imposes a fine (Patent Medicine Prices Review Board, 2002). Not surprisingly, more than a million Americans now regularly buy their brand-name prescription drugs directly from Canadian pharmacies.

American drug manufacturers justify their high prices by claiming they need the money for research and development (R&D). The American public benefits from R&D, they say, while lower drug prices impair R&D in other countries.

Their argument would be more convincing if evidence showed that price curbs actually hurt R&D. However, in the U.K., where the government regulates prescription drug costs, drug companies spend 20 percent of their sales revenue on R&D. In the United States, the figure is just 12.5 percent. In Canada, expenditure on R&D increased 1500 percent in the 15 years following the beginning of government regulation in 1987. This hardly suggests that price regulation hurts R&D (Barry, 2002c; Patent Medicine Prices Review Board, 2002: 49).

What we can say with confidence is that the pharmaceutical industry is the most profitable industry in the United States by far. We also know that drug companies spend about half as much on advertising and promotions as they do on R&D. This drives up drug prices. Finally, we know that the pharmaceutical industry spends more on lobbying and political campaign contributions than any other U.S. industry. Most of the lobbying effort is aimed at influencing members of Congress to maintain a free market in drug prices (Barry, 2002a, 2002b, 2002c).

Why do you think the United States is at the forefront of attempts to maintain a free market in prescription drugs? In countries that regulate prescription drugs, like Canada, are there negative consequences to extending regulation? If so, what are they? If not, then how might prescription drugs be further regulated to benefit the population?

care is about 85 percent of the total; in Japan and Germany it is around 80 percent; and in France, Canada, Italy, and Australia it is around 70 percent. The governments of Germany, Italy, Belgium, Denmark, Finland, Greece, Iceland, Luxembourg, Norway, and Spain cover almost all health care costs, including drugs, glasses, dental care, and prostheses. In the United States, only seniors, the poor, and veterans receive medical benefits from the government under the Medicare, Medicaid, and military health care programs. The American government pays only about 45 percent of all medical costs out of taxes.

In 2010, the United States became the last of the world's rich countries to ensure that its population (or at least 95 percent of it) would at least be covered by private health insurance. Before the new law was passed, about 15 percent of Americans lacked health insurance and another 15 percent lacked adequate coverage (Anderson et al., 2003; "Health Care Systems," 2001; Schoen, Doty, Collins, and Holmgren, 2005; Starr, 1994). However, even after the new law is fully implemented in 2016, the distinctive feature of the American health care system—substantial private provision—will persist. It is an expensive mechanism that leaves many people poorly served (see Box 19.2 on page 486).

Sociology at the Movies

SICKO

As late as January 2010, about 15 percent of Americans had no access to health care and another 15 percent lacked adequate coverage. It would be too easy to tell horror stories about the former, so Michael Moore's *Sicko* does not dwell on them. Instead, his widely acclaimed documentary tells viewers how ordinary Americans who had health care were routinely shocked to discover just how inadequate their coverage was. Here are three cases in point:

- A woman faints on a sidewalk and is taken to the hospital by ambulance, but her insurer bills her for the trip because she didn't have it pre-authorized. "How could I have it pre-authorized when I was unconscious?" she asks.
- When the World Trade Center was attacked in 2001, some brave souls volunteered to help rescue people. Many of them later developed respiratory and other problems but their insurers refused to cover their medical and drug expenses because they voluntarily put themselves at risk.
- A life of hard work enabled Larry and Donna to own their own house and put all six of their children through college. Now retired, and with Larry

© Lions Gate/Courtesy Everett Collection/CP Picture Archive

In *Sicko*, an astonished Michael Moore learns that in Britain, doctors are paid more if their patients become healthier.

in poor health, they must sell their house to pay for medical fees not covered by their insurer. They are forced to move into a small room in the home of one of their adult children.

The lack of a public health care system and relatively little government regulation of the private system have made such occurrences common in the United States. Privately owned Health Maintenance Organizations (HMOs) administer medical treatment in return for a fee paid by individuals, unions, and employers. As profit-seeking companies, HMOs have routinely sought to deny claims and avoid expensive procedures. Some of the worst excesses of HMOs will be curbed by new American laws that started to come into effect in 2010, but they have until now acted in a way that lowers life expectancy in the United States below the level of life expectancy in other rich countries.

Moore visits Canada, France, the U.K., and Cuba, and makes the health care systems of these countries seem perfect. They are not. For example, Canadians know all too well that governments and the medical community are working hard to shorten waiting times for elective surgery and diagnostic procedures, increase the availability of expensive imagining equipment, and deal with overcrowded hospital emergency rooms. But whatever the shortcomings of universal medical care, *Sicko* serves as a cautionary tale for those who sing the praises of privatization. As Moore says, "If you want to stay healthy in America, don't get sick."

The Canadian Health Care System

Canada has a national health insurance system that is sometimes loosely described as **socialized medicine**. Despite differences in how socialized medicine works in such countries as the U.K., Sweden, Germany, and Italy, common to all such systems is the fact that the government (1) directly controls the financing and organization of health services, (2) directly pays providers, (3) guarantees equal access to health care, and (4) allows some private care for individuals who are willing to pay for their medical expenses (Cockerham, 1998). Canada does not have a true system of socialized medicine, however, in that the government does not employ Canadian physicians. Most of Canada's physicians are independent practitioners who are paid on a fee-for-service basis and submit claims directly to the provincial or territorial health insurance plan for payment.

Tommy Douglas is often called Canada's "father of medicare." Douglas began his career as a Baptist minister and was strongly influenced by the Christian social gospel, which called for progressive social reform. In 1933, he earned an M.A. in sociology from McMaster University. He led the Co-operative Commonwealth Federation (CCF) to victory in Saskatchewan in 1944, making it the first democratic socialist party to win a North American election. (Subsequently, Douglas helped turn the CCF into the New Democratic Party.) He served as premier of Saskatchewan from 1944 to 1961, introducing many social reforms, including universal medical care. This stirred up sharp opposition, including a province-wide physicians' strike, but Saskatchewan's medicare system ultimately succeeded and in 1968 it became a model for the whole country (CBC News, 2004a).

Although Canada's health care system is often lauded as among the best in the world, big problems exist. One source of concern is waiting times for services. Although our health care system is based on the premise that "all citizens will have access to the care they need within a reasonable time period" (Health Canada, 1999b), many people agree that some waits are too long. In 2007, 46.2 percent of Canadians who sought specialist consultation for a new condition were successful in receiving an appointment in one month or less, while nearly one in seven had to wait three months or more. Waiting periods were slightly longer for non-emergency surgery and somewhat shorter for diagnostic tests (see Figure 19.3). Such waits are typically stressful and often painful.

The future of health care was a central issue in the 2004 federal election. The Liberals under Paul Martin won a narrow victory on a pledge to shore up the existing system. Two months after the election, $41 billion was added to the health care budget over the next 10 years.

In countries with **socialized medicine**, the government (1) directly controls the financing and organization of health services, (2) directly pays providers, (3) guarantees equal access to health care, and (4) allows some private care for individuals who are willing to pay for their medical expenses.

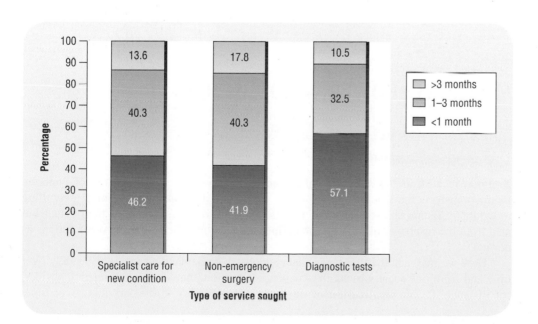

FIGURE 19.3

Waiting Times for Canadians Seeking Health Care Services, 2007

Source: *A Federal Report on Comparable Health Indicators 2008.* Health Canada, 2008. Minister of Public Works and Government Services Canada, 2011.

In 2005, the Supreme Court ruled in favour of a man who had sued the province of Quebec after he was told that the wait for a hip replacement would be more than a year and that he was forbidden from purchasing such service. The Supreme Court ruled that such delays in access amounted to denial of access. Many commentators believe that the ruling opens the door to a two-tier system in which private insurance and provision operate alongside the public system. Implicit in such a system is preferred treatment for the well-to-do. Some individuals and organizations, such as the Canadian Medical Association and elements in the Conservative Party, welcomed the Supreme Court decision, but supporters of equal access feared its consequences. However, the Supreme Court decision could spur the federal government to reorganize and inject still more money into the system, thereby cutting wait times and minimizing the perceived need for private provision. It thus remains to be seen how this controversy will play out.

Summing Up

- The social causes of death and illness include human-environmental factors, lifestyle factors, and factors related to the quality of public health and the health care system.
- Exposure to all three sets of social causes of illness and death is associated with country of residence, class, race, and gender.
- Class and ill health are negatively correlated because people lower in the class hierarchy experience more stress and are less able to cope with it, expose unborn children to more health risks, have less knowledge about how to maintain a healthy lifestyle, have less access to health resources, and are more exposed to environmental health risks at work and in their neighbourhoods than are people higher in the class hierarchy.
- Good-quality health care is unavailable to many Americans because of the high level of social inequality and the dominance of privatized health care in that country. A lower level of social inequality and more government regulation in Canada's health care system has resulted in universal access. However, Canadians still face lengthy waiting times for elective surgery and diagnostic procedures, inadequate access to expensive imaging equipment, and overcrowding in hospital emergency rooms.

MEDICINE, POWER, AND CULTURE

Symbolic Interaction, Labelling, and the Medicalization of Deviance

You may recall from our discussion of deviance that one of the preoccupations of symbolic interactionism is the labelling process (see Chapter 7, Deviance and Crime). According to symbolic interactionists, deviance results not just from the actions of the deviant but also from the responses of others, who define some actions as deviant and other actions as normal.

Here we may add that the *type* of label applied to a deviant act may vary widely over time and from one society to another, depending on how that act is interpreted. Consider, for instance, the **medicalization of deviance**, which refers to the fact that, over time,

The **medicalization of deviance** is the tendency for medical definitions of deviant behaviour to become more prevalent over time.

"medical definitions of deviant behaviour are becoming more prevalent in … societies like our own" (Conrad and Schneider, 1992: 28–29). In an earlier era, much deviant behaviour was labelled "evil." Deviants tended to be chastised, punished, and otherwise socially controlled by members of the clergy, neighbours, family members, and the criminal justice system. Today, however, a person prone to drinking sprees is more likely to be declared an alcoholic and treated in a detoxification centre. A person predisposed to violent rages is more likely to be medicated. A person inclined to overeating is more likely to seek therapy and, in extreme cases, surgery. A heroin addict is more likely to seek the help of a methadone program. As these examples illustrate, what used to be regarded as willful deviance is now often regarded as involuntary deviance. More and more, what people used to define as "badness" they now define as "sickness." As our definitions of deviance change, deviance is increasingly coming under the sway of the medical and psychiatric establishments (see Figure 19.4).

How did the medicalization of deviance come about? What social forces are responsible for the growing capacity of medical and psychiatric establishments to control our lives? To answer these questions, we examine changing definitions of mental illness because they show especially clearly how a thin line can separate science from politics in the field of health care.

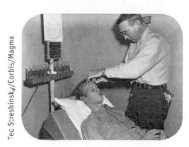

An example of the medicalization of deviance: A lobotomy is performed in a prison in the 1960s to "cure" the inmate of criminality.

The Political Sociology of Mental Illness

In 1974, a condition that had been considered a psychiatric disorder for more than a century ceased to be labelled as such by the American Psychiatric Association (APA). Did the condition disappear because it had become rare to the point of extinction? No. Did the discovery of a new wonder drug eradicate the condition virtually overnight? Again, no. In fact, in 1974 the condition was perhaps more widespread and certainly more public than ever before. Paradoxically, just as the extent of the condition was becoming more widely appreciated, the APA's "bible," the *Diagnostic and Statistical Manual of Mental Disorders (DSM)*, ceased to define it as a psychiatric disorder.

The "condition" we are referring to is homosexuality. In preparing the third edition of the *DSM* for publication, a squabble broke out among psychiatrists over whether homosexuality is in fact a psychiatric disorder. Gay and lesbian activists, who sought to destigmatize homosexuality, were partly responsible for a shift in the views of many psychiatrists on this subject. In the end, the APA decided that homosexuality is not a psychiatric disorder and deleted the entry in the *DSM*. The APA's membership confirmed the decision in 1974.

FIGURE 19.4

An Example of the Medicalization of Deviance

Five American surveys conducted in the 1950s and 1960s presented respondents with the boxed anecdote. The graph shows the percentage of respondents who considered the behaviour described in the anecdote evidence of mental illness. Notice the difference between the 1950s and the 1960s. (Nearly 100 percent of the psychiatrists who evaluated the anecdote thought it illustrated "simple schizophrenia.")

Source: Material adapted from table "Results of Studies Using Vignettes in Defining Problem Behavior" from *Deviance and Medicalization: From Badness to Sickness*, Expanded Edition by Peter Conrad and Joseph W. Schneider. Used by permission of Temple University Press. © 1992 by Temple University. All rights reserved.

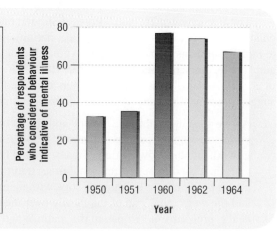

"Now here's a young woman in her twenties, let's call her Betty Smith … she has never had a job, and she doesn't seem to want to go out and look for one. She is a very quiet girl, she doesn't talk much to anyone—even her own family, and she acts like she is afraid of people, especially young men her own age. She won't go out with anyone, and whenever someone comes to visit her family, she stays in her own room until they leave. She just stays by herself and daydreams all the time and shows no interest in anything or anybody."

The controversy over homosexuality was only one of several *political* debates that erupted among psychiatrists in the 1970s and 1980s (Shorter, 1997: 288–327):

- The *DSM* task force initially decided to eliminate the term "neurosis" on the grounds that its role as a cause of mental disorder had never been proven experimentally. The decision outraged the psychoanalytic community because "neurosis" is a keystone of its Freudian theories. As a result, psychoanalysts threatened to block publication of the third edition of the *DSM*. In 1979, the APA's board backed down, placing "neurosis" in parentheses after "disorder." The compromise had nothing to do with science.

- When veterans of the Vietnam War began returning to the United States after 1971, they faced great difficulty re-entering American society. The war was unpopular, so veterans were not widely greeted as heroes. The U.S. economy went into a tailspin in 1973, making jobs difficult to find. Finally, the veterans had suffered high levels of stress during the war itself. Many of them believed their troubles were psychiatric in nature, and soon a nationwide campaign was underway, urging the APA to recognize posttraumatic stress disorder (PTSD) in its manual. Many psychiatrists were reluctant to do so. Nonetheless, the third edition of the *DSM* listed the disorder. To be sure, the campaign succeeded partly on the strength of evidence that extreme trauma has psychological (and at times physiological) effects. However, in addition, as one activist later explained, the PTSD campaign succeeded because "[we] were better organized, more politically active, and enjoyed more lucky breaks than [our] opposition" did (Chaim Shatan, quoted in Scott, 1990: 308). Again, politics and not just science helped shape the definition of a mental disorder.

- Feminists were unhappy that the 1987 edition of *DSM* contained such listings as self-defeating personality disorder. The *DSM* claimed that this disorder is twice as common among women as it is among men. Feminists countered that the definition is an example of blaming the victim. Under pressure from feminists, the 1994 edition of *DSM* dropped the concept.

Some mental disorders have obvious organic causes, such as chemical imbalances in the brain. These organic causes can often be identified. Often they can be treated with drugs or other therapies. Moreover, experiments can be conducted to establish the effectiveness of one treatment or another. However, the examples listed above show that the definitions of many other mental disorders depend not just on scientific evidence but also on social values and political compromise.

At the beginning of the twentieth century, the federal government recognized just one mental disorder: imbecility/insanity. By 1975, the *DSM* recognized 106 mental disorders. The 1994 edition of the *DSM* lists 297 mental disorders, a remarkable increase of 9.5 percent *per year* over 19 years. As the number of mental disorders grew, so did the proportion of people presumably affected by them. The Canadian Mental Health Association (2001) estimates that one in five Canadians will be affected by a mental illness at some time in their lives. The most common mental disorder, depression, is estimated to affect one in four Canadian women and one in ten Canadian men at some point in their lives (Canadian Psychiatric Association, 2002).

The University of Toronto's Edward Shorter, one of the world's leading historians of psychiatry, notes that in psychiatric practice, definitions of mental disorders are often expanded to include ailments with dubious or unknown biological foundations (e.g., "minor depression" and "borderline schizophrenia"; Shorter, 1997: 228). In addition, as we have seen, the number of conditions labelled as mental disorders increased rapidly during the twentieth century. We suggest four main reasons for expansion in the number and scope of such labels:

1. As we saw in Chapter 13, Work and the Economy, Canadians are now experiencing more stress and depression than ever before, mainly because of the increased demands of work and the growing time crunch. Mental health problems are thus more widespread than they used to be. At the same time, traditional institutions for dealing with mental health problems are less able to cope with them. The weakening authority of the church and the weakening grip of the family over the individual leave the treatment of mental health problems more open to the medical and psychiatric establishments.

2. The number of mental disorders has inflated also because powerful organizations demand it. Because public and private organizations find the classification of mental disorders useful, the number of disorders has proliferated. On occasion, the profit motive may be starkly apparent as pharmaceutical companies rush to patent products they claim will cure these conditions. Consider the repackaging of Prozac, the world's most widely prescribed antidepressant, as Serafem, a treatment for women suffering from the newly named premenstrual dysphoric disorder. Prozac represented a pharmaceutical goldmine for Eli Lilly, its manufacturer, accounting for a third of the company's US$6.5 billion in annual revenues. However, in 2001, Eli Lilly's patent on Prozac ended, allowing other manufacturers to sell generic versions of this drug at a fraction of the cost. In response, Prozac was quickly renamed and repatented as a treatment for another group of consumers (Bell, 2002: 34).

3. The cultural context stimulates inflation also in the number and scope of mental disorders. Assailed by the latest bestsellers in the self-help section of our bookstores and lectured by radio "therapists," we may be encouraged to turn our problems into medical and psychological conditions, sometimes without inquiring deeply into the disadvantages of doing so. For example, in 1980 the term *attention deficit disorder* (ADD) was coined to label hyperactive and inattentive schoolchildren, mainly boys. By the mid-1990s, North American doctors were writing more than six million prescriptions a year for Ritalin, an amphetamine-like compound that controls ADD.

   Evidence shows that some children diagnosed with ADD have problems absorbing glucose in the brain or suffer from imbalances in chemicals that help the brain regulate behaviour (Optometrists Network, 2000). Yet the diagnosis of ADD is typically conducted *clinically*, that is, by interviewing and observing children to see whether they exhibit signs of serious inattention, hyperactivity, and impulsivity. This means that many children diagnosed with ADD may have no organic disorder at all. Some cases of ADD may be due to the school system failing to capture children's imagination. Some may involve children acting out because they are deprived of attention at home. Some may involve plain old-fashioned high-spiritedness. A plausible case could be made that Winnie the Pooh suffers from ADD. In fact, this case *was* made by psychiatrists at the Dalhousie University Medical School in Halifax (Shea, Gordon, Hawkins, Kawchuk, and Smith, 2000). However, once hyperactivity and inattentiveness in school are defined as a medical and psychiatric condition, officials routinely prescribe drugs to control the problem and tend to ignore possible *social* causes.

4. The fourth main reason for inflation in the number and scope of mental disorders is that various professional organizations have promoted them. Consider posttraumatic stress disorder. There is no doubt that PTSD is a real condition and that many veterans suffer from it. However, once the disorder was officially recognized in the 1970s, some therapists trivialized the term, for example, talking about PTSD "in children exposed to movies like *Batman*" (Shorter, 1997: 290). Some psychiatric social workers, psychologists, and psychiatrists may magnify the incidence of such mental disorders because doing so increases their stature and their patient load. Others may do so simply because the condition becomes "trendy." Whatever the motive, overdiagnosis is the result.

The Professionalization of Medicine

The preceding discussion shows that the diagnosis and treatment of some mental disorders is not a completely scientific enterprise. Social and political processes are sometimes as important as scientific principles in determining how we treat mental disorders. Various mental health professions compete for patients, as do different schools of thought within professions. Practitioners offer a wide and sometimes confusing array of treatments and therapies. In some cases their effectiveness is debatable, and there is at least some reason to remain skeptical of their ultimate worth.

In the early nineteenth century, the practice of medicine was in an even more chaotic state. Herbalists, faith healers, midwives, druggists, and medical doctors vied to meet the health needs of the public. A century later, the dust had settled. Medical science was victorious. Its first series of breakthroughs involved identifying the bacteria and viruses responsible for various diseases and then developing effective procedures and vaccines to combat them. These and subsequent triumphs in diagnosis and treatment convinced most people of the superiority of medical science over other approaches to health. Medical science worked, or at least it seemed to work more effectively and more often than other therapies did.

It would be wrong, however, to think that scientific medicine came to dominate health care only because it produced results. A second, sociological reason for the rise to dominance of scientific medicine is that doctors were able to professionalize. As noted in Chapter 13, Work and the Economy, a profession is an occupation that requires extensive formal education. Professionals regulate their own training and practice. They restrict competition within the profession, mainly by limiting the recruitment of practitioners. They minimize competition with other professions, partly by laying exclusive claim to a field of expertise. Professionals are usually self-employed. They exercise considerable authority over their clients. And they profess to be motivated mainly by the desire to serve their community even though they earn a lot of money in the process. Professionalization, then, is the process by which people gain control and authority over their occupation and their clients. It results in professionals enjoying high occupational prestige and income, and considerable social and political power (Freidson, 1986; Johnson, 1972; Starr, 1982).

The professional organization of Canadian doctors is the Canadian Medical Association (CMA), founded in 1867 by 167 doctors in Quebec City. It quickly set about broadcasting the successes of medical science and criticizing alternative approaches to health as quackery and charlatanism. The CMA was able to have laws passed to restrict medical licences to graduates of approved schools and to ensure that only graduates of those schools could train the next generation of doctors. By restricting entry into the profession, and by specifying what "paramedical" practitioners could and could not do, members of the medical establishment ensured their own status, prestige, and high incomes. For example, midwifery was originally included in the work of the Victorian Order of Nurses, founded in 1897 by the National Council of Women to assist rural women who otherwise lacked access to health care. However, "opposition of the medical establishment in Canada was so great to what it saw as an infringement of its prerogatives that the idea was allowed to die" (Mitchinson, 1993: 396). In short, when medicine became a profession, it also became a monopoly.

The modern hospital is the institutional manifestation of the medical doctors' professional dominance. Until the twentieth century, most doctors operated small clinics and visited patients in their homes. However, the rise of the modern hospital was guaranteed by medicine's scientific turn in the mid-nineteenth century. Expensive equipment for diagnosis and treatment had to be shared by many physicians. This required the centralization of medical facilities in large, bureaucratically run institutions that strongly resist deviations from professional conduct. Practically nonexistent in 1850, hospitals are now widespread. Yet despite their undoubted benefits, economic as well as health related, hospitals and the medicine practised in them are not an unqualified blessing, as you are about to learn.

The Social Limits of Modern Medicine

In early February 2003, a 64-year-old professor of medicine from Guangzhou, the capital of Guangdong Province in southern China, came down with an unidentified respiratory ailment. It did not bother him enough to cancel a planned trip to Hong Kong, so on February 12 he checked into that city's Metropole Hotel. Ironically, as it turned out, the desk clerk assigned him room 911. Other ninth-floor guests included an elderly couple from Toronto and three young women from Singapore. All these people, along with a local resident who visited the hotel during this period, fell ill between February 15 and 27 with the same respiratory ailment as the professor. The professor died on March 4. The Canadian couple returned to Toronto on February 23 and the wife died at her home on March 5. The eventual diagnosis: severe acute respiratory syndrome, or SARS, a new (and in 9 percent of cases, deadly) pneumonia-like illness for which there is no vaccine and no cure.

SARS originated in Guangdong Province. By June 12, 8445 cases of SARS had been identified in 29 countries, and 790 people had died of the disease. Quickly and efficiently, global travel had spread HIV/AIDS, West Nile virus, and now SARS from remote and isolated locales to the world's capitals. The United Nations has labelled Toronto the world's most multicultural city. It has a large Chinese population, mainly from Hong Kong. It is therefore not surprising that, outside of China, Hong Kong, and Taiwan, Toronto became the world's number one SARS hot spot (Abraham, 2003; World Health Organization, 2003).

Once identified as a potential SARS case, a person is quarantined at home for 10 days. However, if people exhibit symptoms of the disease, they go to a poorly ventilated institution where the air is maintained at a constant warm temperature that is ideal for the multiplication of germs. In this institution, many young and older people with weakened immune systems congregate. A steady stream of germs pours in around the clock. Staff members too often fail to follow elementary principles of good hygiene. That institution is a hospital. There, germs spread. Most of the 238 people in Toronto who had SARS as of June 12, 2003, caught it while in the hospital, before stringent isolation and disinfection procedures were imposed.

Our characterization of hospitals as ideal environments for the spread of germs may seem harsh. It is not. Hospitals have become dangerous places in North America. In Canada, about 80 percent of hospitals fall seriously short in preventing patients from getting hospital infections. Some 250 000 patients experience hospital infections every year. If the government classified hospital infections as a cause of death, it would be the fourth-leading cause of death in the country (Zoutman et al., 2003).

The situation has deteriorated largely because we invest disproportionately in expensive, high-tech diagnostic equipment and treatment while we skimp on simple, labour-intensive, time-consuming hygiene. Cleaning staffs are too small and insufficiently trained. Nurses are too few. According to research by the Harvard School of Public Health, these are the kinds of factors correlated with hospital-acquired infections. As one registered nurse says, "When you have less time to save lives, do you take 30 seconds to wash your hands? When you're speeding up you have to cut corners. We don't always wash our hands. I'm not saying it's right, but you've got to deal with reality" (quoted in Berens, 2002a).

It was not always the reality. Until the 1940s, North American hospital workers were obsessed with cleanliness. They had to be. In the era before the widespread use of antibiotics, infection often meant death. In the 1950s, however, the prevention of infections in hospitals became less of a priority because antibiotics became widely available. It was less expensive to wait until a patient got sick and then respond to symptoms by prescribing drugs than to prevent the sickness in the first place. Doctors and nurses have grown lax about hygiene over the past half-century. One American report cites a dozen health care studies showing that about half of doctors and nurses do not disinfect their hands between patients (Berens, 2002a). One small hospital north of Montreal cut serious infections by 80 percent simply by improving hygiene (CBC News, 2004b).

Using antibiotics indiscriminately has its own costs. When living organisms encounter a deadly threat, only the few mutations that are strong enough to resist the threat survive and go on to reproduce. Accordingly, if you use a lot of antibiotics, "super germs" that are resistant to these drugs multiply. This is just what has happened.[2] Penicillin could kill nearly all *Staphylococcus* germs in the 1940s, but by 1982 it was effective in fewer than 10 percent of cases. In the 1970s, doctors turned to the more powerful methicillin, which in 1974 could kill 98 percent of *Staphylococcus* germs. By the mid-1990s, it could kill only about 50 percent. It has thus come about that various strains of drug-resistant germs now cause pneumonia, blood poisoning, tuberculosis, and other infectious diseases. Drug-resistant germs that could formerly survive only in the friendly hospital environment have now adapted to the harsher environment outside the hospital walls. Pharmaceutical companies are racing to create new antibiotics to fight drug-resistant bugs, but germs mutate so quickly that our arsenal is shrinking (Berens, 2002b).

The epidemic of infectious diseases caused by slack hospital hygiene and the overuse of antibiotics suggests that social circumstances can constrain the success of modern medicine.

High-tech solutions to medical problems sometimes collide with social realities, failing to produce envisaged outcomes.

Meanwhile, many people are growing skeptical of the claims of modern medicine. They are beginning to challenge traditional medicine and explore alternatives that rely less on high technology and drugs and are more sensitive to the need for maintaining balance between humans and their environment in the pursuit of good health. In concluding this chapter, we explore some of these challenges and alternatives.

Recent Challenges to Traditional Medical Science

Patient Activism

By the mid-twentieth century, the dominance of medical science in Canada was virtually complete. Any departure from the dictates of scientific medicine was considered deviant. Thus, when sociologist Talcott Parsons defined the **sick role** in 1951, he first pointed out that illness suspends routine responsibilities and is not deliberate. Then he stressed that people playing the sick role must want to be well and must seek competent help, cooperating with health care practitioners at all times (Parsons, 1951: 428 ff.). Must they? According to Parsons's definition, a competent person suffering from a terminal illness cannot reasonably demand that doctors refrain from using heroic measures to prolong his or her life. And by his definition, a patient cannot reasonably question doctors' orders, no matter how well educated the patient and how debatable the effect of the prescribed treatment. Although Parsons's definition of the sick role may sound plausible to many people born before World War II, it probably sounds authoritarian and utterly foreign to most younger people.

That is because things have changed. The public is more highly educated now than it was in 1951. Many people now have the knowledge, vocabulary, self-confidence, and political organization to participate in their own health care rather than passively accepting whatever experts tell them. Research shows that this trend is evident even among older Canadians and lower-income earners. Canadian baby boomers and younger generations are even less likely to follow a doctor's advice uncritically; in fact, only one-third do so (Bricker and Greenspon, 2001: 221). Increasingly, patients are taught to perform simple, routine medical procedures themselves. Many people now use the Internet to seek information about various illnesses and treatments.[3] Increasingly, they are uncomfortable with doctors acting as authoritarian parents and patients acting as dutiful children. Surveys show that 90 percent of Canadians now prefer that their doctor offer many treatment options rather than a single course of action. Eighty-six percent say they usually ask their doctor many questions about procedures, 76 percent say they are more likely to question their doctor now than they were in the past, and about 70 percent claim to always ask their doctor about prescribed medicines (Bricker and Greenspon, 2001: 119–220). Doctors now routinely seek patients' informed consent for some procedures rather than deciding what to do on their own. Similarly, most hospitals have established ethics committees, which were unheard of only four decades ago (Rothman, 1991). These are responses to patients demanding a more active role in their own care.

Some recent challenges to the authority of medical science are organized and political. For example, when AIDS activists challenged the stereotype of AIDS as a "gay disease" and demanded more research funding to help find a cure, they changed research and treatment priorities in a way that could never have happened in, say, the 1950s or 1960s (Epstein, 1996). Similarly, when feminists supported the reintroduction of midwifery and argued against medical intervention in routine childbirths, they challenged the wisdom of established medical practice. The previously male-dominated profession of medicine considered the male body the norm and paid relatively little attention to "women's diseases," such as breast cancer, and "women's issues," such as reproduction. This, too, is now changing thanks to feminist intervention (Boston Women's Health Book Collective, 1998; Rothman, 1982, 1989; Schiebinger, 1993). And although doctors and the larger society traditionally

Playing the **sick role**, according to Talcott Parsons, involves the non-deliberate suspension of routine responsibilities, wanting to be well, seeking competent help, and cooperating with health care practitioners at all times.

treated people with disabilities as incompetent children, various movements now seek to empower them (Charlton, 1998; Zola, 1982). As a result, attitudes toward people with disabilities are changing (see Chapter 12, Sociology of the Body: Disability, Aging, and Death).

Alternative Medicine

Other challenges to the authority of medical science are less organized and less political than those just mentioned. Consider, for example, alternative medicine. In 1994–95, only 15 percent of Canadians used such services (Park, 2005). In 2005, more than 13 percent of Canadians had used some form of alternative medicine in the past year (see Figure 19.5). The most widely used health alternative is chiropractic.

Women are nearly twice as likely as men to use alternative health care. Most users are between the ages of 25 and 65. Use is greatest in British Columbia, Alberta, and Saskatchewan, and lowest in Atlantic Canada and Nunavut. Those with chronic disorders, including back problems and multiple chemical sensitivities, are more likely to consult an alternative health service provider. Income and education are positively correlated with use of alternative medicine (Park, 2005).

Despite the growing popularity of alternative medicine, many medical doctors were hostile to it until recently. They lumped all alternative therapies together and dismissed them as unscientific (Campion, 1993). By the late 1990s, however, a more tolerant attitude was evident in many quarters. For some kinds of ailments, physicians began to recognize the benefits of at least the most popular forms of alternative medicine. For example, a 1998 editorial in the respected *New England Journal of Medicine* admitted that the beneficial effect of chiropractic on low back pain is "no longer in dispute" (Shekelle, 1998). This change in attitude was due in part to new scientific evidence from Canadian research showing that spinal manipulation can be a relatively effective and inexpensive treatment for low back pain (Manga, Angus, and Swan, 1993). At the same time, however, alternative forms of medicine should not be assumed to be entirely risk-free. For example, to date, the majority of Canadian lawsuits against chiropractors have involved claims of muscular skeletal dysfunction, strains and sprains, and rib fractures. In a few cases, more serious injury has occurred, including ruptured vertebral arteries and death (Cohen, 1999. 50).

Nevertheless, the medical profession's grudging acceptance of chiropractic in the treatment of low back pain indicates what we can expect in the uneasy relationship between scientific and alternative medicine in coming decades. Although many, if not most, alternative therapies (such as aromatherapy and foot reflexology) are non-invasive and relatively harmless, doctors and most of the public will, for the most part, remain skeptical of alternative therapies unless properly conducted experiments demonstrate their beneficial effects.

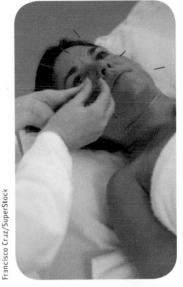

Acupuncture is one of the most widely accepted forms of alternative medicine.

Francisco Cruz/SuperStock

FIGURE 19.5

Percentage of Canadians Who Contacted an Alternative Health Care Provider in the Past Year, by Sex and Province, 2007

Source: Percent of Canadians Who Contacted an Alternative Health Care Provider in Past Year, by Sex and Province, 2010. Contact with Alternative Health Care Providers in the Past 12 Months by Age Group and Sex, Household Population Aged 12 and over, Canada, Provinces, Territories. Health Regions (June 2005 Boundaries) and Peer Groups, every 2 years, adapted from Statistics Canada CANSIM Database http://www5.statcan.gc.ca/cansim/home-accueil?lang=eng, Table 105-0462 (accessed 2 April 2010).

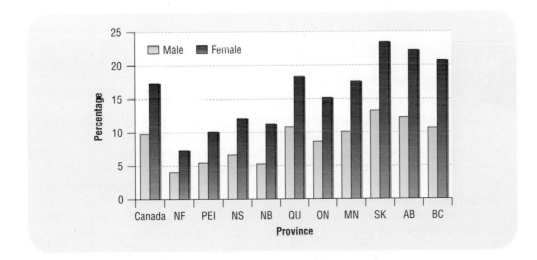

Holistic Medicine

Medical doctors understand that a positive frame of mind often helps in the treatment of disease. For example, research shows that strong belief in the effectiveness of a cure can by itself improve the condition of about one-third of people suffering from chronic pain or fatigue (Campion, 1993). This is known as the **placebo effect**. Doctors also understand that conditions in the human environment affect people's health. However, despite their appreciation of the effect of mind and environment on the human body, traditional scientific medicine tends to respond to illness by treating disease symptoms as a largely physical and individual problem. Moreover, scientific medicine continues to subdivide into more specialized areas of practice that rely more and more heavily on drugs and high-tech machinery. Most doctors are less concerned with maintaining and improving health by understanding the larger mental and social context within which people become ill.

Traditional Indian and Chinese medicine takes a different approach. India's Ayurvedic medical tradition views individuals in terms of the flow of vital fluids or "humours" and their health in the context of their environment. In this view, maintaining good health requires not only balancing fluids in individuals but also balancing the relationship between individuals and the world around them (Zimmermann, 1987 [1982]). In spite of significant differences, the fundamental outlook is similar in traditional Chinese medicine. Chinese medicine and its remedies, ranging from acupuncture to herbs, seek to restore individuals' internal balance, as well as their relationship to the outside world (Unschuld, 1985). Contemporary **holistic medicine**, the third and final challenge to traditional scientific medicine we will consider, takes an approach similar to these "ethnomedical" traditions. Practitioners of holistic medicine argue that good health requires maintaining a balance between mind and body, and between the individual and the environment.

Most holistic practitioners do not reject scientific medicine. However, they emphasize disease *prevention*. When they treat patients, they take into account the relationship between mind and body and between the individual and his or her social and physical environment. Holistic practitioners thus seek to establish close ties with their patients and treat them in their homes or other relaxed settings. Rather than expecting patients to react to illness by passively allowing a doctor to treat them, they expect patients to take an active role in maintaining their good health. And, recognizing that industrial pollution, work-related stress, poverty, racial and gender inequality, and other social factors contribute heavily to disease, holistic practitioners often become political activists (Hastings, Fadiman, and Gordon, 1980).

In sum, patient activism, alternative medicine, and holistic medicine represent the three biggest challenges to traditional scientific medicine today. Few people think of these challenges as potential replacements for scientific medicine. However, many people believe that, together with traditional scientific approaches, these challenges will help improve the health status of people in Canada and throughout the world in the twenty-first century.

The **placebo effect** is the positive influence on healing of a strong belief in the effectiveness of a cure.

Holistic medicine emphasizes disease prevention. Holistic practitioners treat disease by taking into account the relationship between mind and body and between the individual and his or her social and physical environment.

Summing Up

- Deviance is becoming increasingly medicalized—that is, defined as involuntary actions that should be dealt with by physicians and psychiatrists.
- Scientific medicine came to dominate health because it produced favourable results and because physicians professionalized.
- Scientific medicine sometimes creates serious problems, as is evident in the spread of hospital infections.
- Patient activism, alternative medicine, and holistic medicine may, in conjunction with scientific medicine, help improve the health of Canadians.

NOTES

1. Status Indians are people whose names appear on the Indian Register maintained by the Department of Indian and Northern Affairs.

2. It surely has not helped that antibiotics are routinely added to cattle feed to prevent disease and thereby lower beef production costs. This practice only builds up resistance to antibiotics in humans.

3. There are at least two health-related dangers to using the Internet, however. First, some people may misinterpret information or assume that unreliable sources are reliable. Second, sexual courtship on the Internet may lead to real-world meetings and therefore contribute to the spread of HIV/AIDS and other sexually transmitted diseases.

SUMMARY

1. Are all causes of illness and death biological?
   Ultimately, yes. However, *variations* in illness and death rates are often due to social causes. The social causes of illness and death include human-environmental factors, lifestyle factors, and factors related to the public health and health care systems. All three factors are related to country of residence, class, race, and gender. Specifically, health risks are lower among upper classes, rich countries, and members of privileged racial and ethnic groups than among lower classes, poor countries, and members of disadvantaged racial and ethnic groups. In some respects related to health, men are in a more advantageous position than women are.

2. Does Canada have one of the world's best health systems?
   Canada ranks high on most indicators of population health, but room for improvement remains. There are disparities in health status associated with socioeconomic status, gender, and age. Some racial minority groups, Aboriginal Canadians in particular, remain especially vulnerable to threats in the physical environment, including the dangers of damaging toxins and environmental pollutants.

3. Does the United States have one of the world's best health systems?
   As a rich country, the United States has far better health outcomes than poorer countries. It has outstanding technology and affords some of the best care anywhere to those who can afford it. However, the prices paid for medical services in the United States are considerably higher than elsewhere, and substantial numbers of citizens lack adequate insurance yet have no access to public provision. As a result, overall health outcomes are inferior to those achieved elsewhere for considerably less expenditure.

4. How has medicine interacted with conceptions of deviant behaviour?
   Over time, medical definitions of deviance have become more common. The recent history of psychiatry shows that social values and political compromise can be as important as science in determining the classification of some mental disorders.

5. What are the "social limits of medicine"?
   High-tech solutions to medical problems sometimes collide with social realities, failing to produce envisaged outcomes. For instance, shortsighted cost cutting has encouraged the overuse of antibiotics and the neglect of basic hygiene in hospitals, resulting in more hospital-caused infections and the spread of drug-resistant germs.

6. What are the main challenges and alternatives to traditional medicine?
   Several challenges to traditional scientific medicine promise to improve the quality of health care in Canada and worldwide. These include patient activism, alternative medicine, and holistic medicine.

KEY TERMS

health care system (p. 480)

holistic medicine (p. 496)

infant mortality (p. 481)

life expectancy (p. 478)

medicalization of deviance (p. 488)

morbidity (p. 484)

placebo effect (p. 496)

public health system (p. 480)

sick role (p. 494)

socialized medicine (p. 487)

WEB RESOURCES

Companion Website for This Book

http://www.compass4e.nelson.com

Begin by clicking on the Student Resources section of the website. Next, select the chapter you are studying from the pull-down menu. From the Student Resources page you have easy access to additional Weblinks and other resources. The website also has many useful tips to aid you in your study of sociology, including practice tests for each chapter.

InfoTrac® Search Terms

These search terms are provided to assist you in beginning to conduct research on this topic by visiting http://www.infotrac-college.com:

age discrimination

health maintenance organizations

life expectancy

public health

5

Social Change

CHAPTER

20

Population and Urbanization

IN THIS CHAPTER, YOU WILL LEARN THAT

- Many people think that only natural conditions influence human population growth. However, social forces are important influences too.

- In particular, sociologists have focused on two major social determinants of population growth: industrialization and social inequality.

- Industrialization also plays a major role in causing the movement of people from countryside to city.

- Cities are not as anonymous and alienating as many sociologists once believed them to be.

- The spatial and cultural forms of cities depend largely on the level of development of the societies in which they are found.

POPULATION

The City of God

Rio de Janeiro, Brazil, site of the 2016 summer Olympics, is one of the world's most beautiful cities. Along the warm, blue waters of its bays lie flawless beaches, guarded by four- and five-star hotels and pricey shops. Rising abruptly behind them is a mountain range, partly populated, partly covered by luxuriant tropical forest. The climate seems perpetually balanced between spring and summer. The inner city of Rio is a place of great wealth and beauty, devoted to commerce and the pursuit of leisure.

Rio is also a large city. With a metropolitan population of more than 12.5 million people in 2011, it is the twenty-third biggest metropolitan area in the world, larger than Chicago, Paris, and London. Not all of its inhabitants are well off, how-

Donald Kelin/SuperStock

ever. Brazil is characterized by more inequality of wealth than most other countries in the world. Slums started climbing up the hillsides of Rio about a century ago. Fed by a high birth rate and people migrating from the surrounding countryside in search of a better life, slums, such as the one shown in the photo, are now home to about 20 percent of the city's residents (Unger and Riley, 2007).

Some of Rio's slums began as government housing projects designed to segregate the poor. One such slum, as famous in its own way as the beaches of Copacabana and Ipanema, is *Cidade de Deus* (the "City of God"). Founded in the 1960s, it had become one of the most lawless and dangerous parts of Rio by the 1980s. It is a place where some families of four live on $50 a month in houses made of cardboard and discarded scraps of tin, a place where roofs leak and rats run freely. For many inhabitants, crime is survival. Drug traffickers wage a daily battle for control of territory, and children as young as six perch in key locations with walkie-talkies to feed information to their bosses on the comings and goings of passersby.

Cidade de Deus is also the name of a brilliant movie released in 2002. Based in part on the true-life story of Paulo Lins, who grew up in a slum and became a novelist, *Cidade de Deus* chronicles the gang wars of the 1970s and 1980s. It leaves us with the nearly hopeless message that, in a war without end, each generation of drug traffickers starts younger and is more ruthless than its predecessor.

Paulo Lins escaped Brazil's grinding poverty. So did Luiz Inácio Lula da Silva, Brazil's president from 2003 to 2010. They are inspiring models of what is possible. They are also reminders that the closely related problems of population growth and urbanization are more serious now than ever. Brazil's 41 million people in 1940 multiplied to about 194 million in 2010. The country is now as urbanized as Canada, with more than three-quarters of its population living in urban areas (estimated from Bernardes, 2011).

This chapter tackles the closely connected problems of population growth and urbanization. We first show that population growth is a process governed less by natural laws than by social forces. We argue that these social forces are not related exclusively to industrialization, as social scientists commonly believed just a few decades ago. Instead, social inequality also plays a major role in shaping population growth.

We next turn to the problem of urbanization. Today, population growth is typically accompanied by the increasing concentration of the world's people in urban centres. As recently as 40 years ago, sociologists typically believed that cities were alienating and anomic (or normless). We argue that this view is an oversimplification. We also outline the social roots of the city's physical and cultural evolution from preindustrial to postindustrial times.

A "population explosion"? Hong Kong is one of the most densely populated places on earth.

Demographers are social-scientific analysts of human population.

The Population "Explosion"

Twelve thousand years ago there were only about 6 million people in the world. Ten thousand years later, world population had risen to 250 million, and it increased to some 760 million by 1750. After that, world population skyrocketed. The number of humans reached one billion in 1804 and six billion in 1999. In 2011, the world population reached 7 billion (Figure 20.1). Where 1 person stood 12 000 years ago, there are now 1050 people; statistical projections suggest that, by 2100, there will be about 1700 people. Of those 1700, fewer than 250 will be standing in the rich countries of the world. More than 1450 of them will be in the developing countries of South America, Asia, and Africa.

Many analysts project that, after passing the 9.4 billion mark around 2150, world population will level off. But given the numbers cited previously, is it any wonder that some population analysts say we're now in the midst of a population "explosion"? Explosions are horrifying events. They cause widespread and severe damage. They are fast and unstoppable. And that is exactly the imagery some population analysts, or **demographers**, want to convey (e.g., Ehrlich and Ornstein, 2010; Figure 20.2). Many books, articles, and television programs deal with the population explosion. Images of an overflowing multitude in, say, Bangladesh, Nigeria, or Brazil remain fixed in our minds. Some people are frightened enough to refer to overpopulation as catastrophic. They link it to recurrent famine, brutal ethnic warfare, and other massive and seemingly intractable problems.

If this imagery makes you feel that the world's rich countries must do something about overpopulation, you're not alone. In fact, concern about the population "bomb" is as old as the social sciences. In 1798, Thomas Robert Malthus, a British clergyman of the Anglican faith, proposed a highly influential theory of human population (Malthus, 1966 [1798]). As you will soon see, contemporary sociologists have criticized, qualified, and in part rejected his theory. But because much of the sociological study of population is, in effect, a debate with Malthus's ghost, we must confront the man's ideas squarely.

The Malthusian Trap

Malthus's theory rests on two undeniable facts and a questionable assumption. The facts: People must eat, and they are driven by a strong sexual urge. The assumption: Although

FIGURE 20.1

World Population, 1750–2150 (in billions, projected)

Sources: Livi-Bacci, 1992: 31; Population Reference Bureau, 2003.

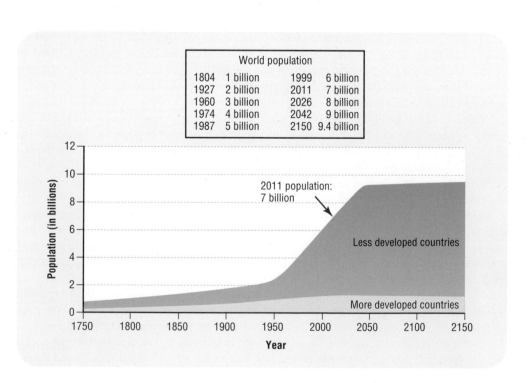

World population			
1804	1 billion	1999	6 billion
1927	2 billion	2011	7 billion
1960	3 billion	2026	8 billion
1974	4 billion	2042	9 billion
1987	5 billion	2150	9.4 billion

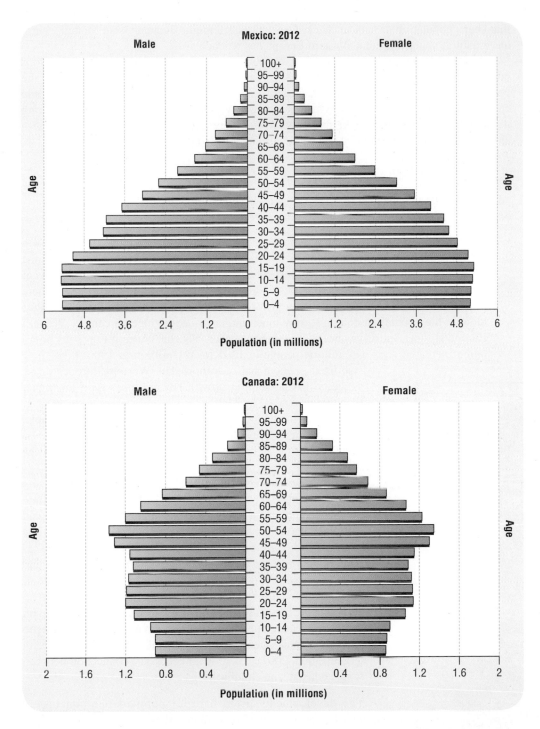

Mexico: 2012

Male · Female

Age · Age

Population (in millions)

Canada: 2012

Male · Female

Age · Age

Population (in millions)

FIGURE 20.2

How Demographers Analyze Population Composition and Change

The main purpose of demography is to figure out why the size, geographical distribution, and social composition of human populations change over time. The basic equation of population change is $P2 = P1 + B - D + I - E$, where $P2$ is population size at a given time, $P1$ is population size at an earlier time, B is the number of births in the interval, D is the number of deaths in the interval, I is the number of immigrants arriving in the interval, and E is the number of emigrants leaving in the interval. A basic tool for analyzing the composition of a population is the "age–sex pyramid," which shows the number of males and females in each age cohort of the population at a given point in time. Age–sex pyramids for Canada and Mexico are shown here for 2012. Why do you think they look so different? Compare your answer to that of the theory of the demographic transition, discussed in this section.

Source: U.S. Census Bureau, 2011.

the food supply increases slowly and arithmetically (1, 2, 3, 4, etc.), population size grows quickly and geometrically (1, 2, 4, 8, etc.). Based on these ideas, Malthus concluded that "the superior power of population cannot be checked without producing misery or vice" (Malthus, 1966 [1798]): 217–18). Specifically, only two forces can hold population growth in check. First are "preventive" measures, such as abortion, infanticide, and prostitution. Malthus called these "vices" because he morally opposed them and thought everyone else ought to also. Second are "positive checks," such as war, pestilence, and famine. Malthus recognized that positive checks create much suffering. Yet he felt they are the only forces that can be allowed to control population growth. Here, then, is the so-called **Malthusian trap**: a cycle of population growth followed by an outbreak of war, pestilence, or famine

The **Malthusian trap** refers to a cycle of population growth followed by an outbreak of war, pestilence, or famine that keeps population, growth in check.

that keeps population growth in check. Population size might fluctuate, said Malthus, but it has a natural upper limit that Western Europe has reached.

Although many people supported Malthus's theory, others reviled him as a misguided prophet of doom and gloom (Winch, 1987). For example, people who wanted to help the poor disagreed with Malthus. He felt such aid was counterproductive. Welfare, he said, would enable the poor to buy more food. With more food, they would have more children. And having more children would only make them poorer than they already were. Better to leave them alone, said Malthus, and thereby reduce the sum of human suffering in the world.

A Critique of Malthus

Although Malthus's ideas are in some respects compelling, events have cast doubt on several of them. Specifically:

- Since Malthus proposed his theory, technological advances have allowed rapid growth in how much food is produced for each person on the planet. This is the opposite of the slow growth Malthus predicted. For instance, in the last decade, the world production of cereals has increased 19 percent (United Nations, 2010a). If, as Malthus claimed, there is a natural upper limit to population growth, it is unclear what that limit is. Malthus thought the population couldn't grow much larger in late-eighteenth-century Western Europe without "positive checks" coming into play. Yet the Western European population increased from 187 million people in 1801 to 321 million in 1900. It has now stabilized at about half a billion. The Western European case suggests that population growth has an upper limit far higher than that envisaged by Malthus.

- Population growth does not always produce misery. For example, despite its rapid population increase over the past 200 years, Western Europe is one of the most prosperous regions in the world.

- Helping the poor does not generally result in the poor having more children. For example, in Western Europe, social welfare policies (employment insurance, state-funded medical care, paid maternity leave, pensions, etc.) are the most generous on the planet. Yet the size of the population is quite stable. In fact, as you will learn, some forms of social welfare produce rapid and large *decreases* in population growth, especially in the poor, developing countries.

- Although the human sexual urge is as strong as Malthus thought, people have developed contraceptive devices and techniques to control the consequences of their sexual activity (World Health Organization, 2007). There is no necessary connection between sexual activity and childbirth.

The developments listed here all point to one conclusion. Malthus's pessimism was overstated. Human ingenuity seems to have enabled us to wriggle free of the Malthusian trap, at least for the time being.

We are not, however, home free. Today there are renewed fears that industrialization and population growth are putting severe strains on the planet's resources. As established by the online chapter that accompanies this book, Chapter 22, Technology and the Global Environment, we must take these fears seriously. It is encouraging to learn that the limits to growth are as much social as they are natural and therefore avoidable rather than inevitable. However, we will see that our ability to avoid the Malthusian trap in the twenty-first century requires all the ingenuity and self-sacrifice we can muster. For the time being, however, let us consider the second main theory of population growth, the theory of the demographic transition.

Albrecht Dürer's *The Four Horsemen of the Apocalypse* (woodcut, 1498). According to Malthus, only war, pestilence, and famine could keep population growth in check.

Scala/Art Resource, NY

Demographic Transition Theory

According to **demographic transition theory**, the main factors underlying population dynamics are industrialization and the growth of modern cultural values (Chesnais, 1992 [1986]; Coale, 1974; Notestein, 1945; see Figure 20.3). The theory is based on the observation that the European population developed in four distinct stages.

The Preindustrial Period

In the first, preindustrial stage of growth, a large proportion of the population died every year from inadequate nutrition, poor hygiene, and uncontrollable disease. In other words, the **crude death rate** was high. The crude death rate is the annual number of deaths (or "mortality") per 1000 people in a population. During this period, the **crude birth rate** was high too. The crude birth rate is the annual number of live births per 1000 people in a population. In the preindustrial era, most people wanted to have as many children as possible. That was partly because relatively few children survived till adulthood. In addition, children were considered a valuable source of agricultural labour and a form of old age security in a society consisting largely of peasants and lacking anything resembling a modern welfare state.

The Early Industrial Period

The second stage of European population growth was the early industrial, or transition, period. At this stage, the crude death rate dropped. People's life expectancy, or average lifespan, increased because economic growth led to improved nutrition and hygiene. However, the crude birth rate remained high. With people living longer and women having nearly as many babies as in the preindustrial era, the population grew rapidly. Malthus lived during this period of rapid population growth, and that accounts in part for his alarm.

The Mature Industrial Period

The third stage of European population growth was the mature industrial period. At this stage, the crude death rate continued to fall. The crude birth rate fell even more dramatically. The crude birth rate fell because economic growth eventually changed people's traditional beliefs about the value of having many children. Having many children made sense in an agricultural society, where children were a valuable economic resource. In contrast, children were more of an economic burden in an industrial society, since breadwinners were employed outside the home and children contributed little, if anything, to the economic

Demographic transition theory explains how changes in fertility and mortality affected population growth from preindustrial to postindustrial times.

The **crude death rate** is the annual number of deaths per 1000 people in a population.

The **crude birth rate** is the annual number of live births per 1000 people in a population.

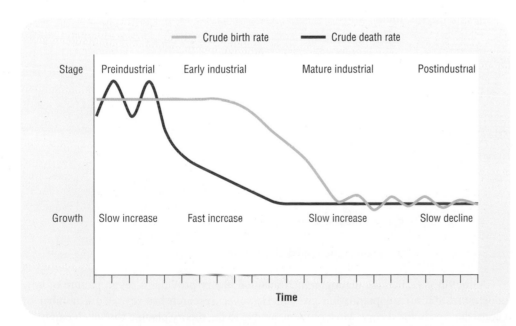

FIGURE 20.3
Democratic Transition Theory

Cultural lag refers to the gap that occurs between rapidly techno-logical change and slower changes in norms and values.

The **replacement level** is the number of children that each woman must have on average for population size to remain stable, ignoring migration. The replacement level is 2.1.

Immigration, or **in-migration**, is the inflow of people into one country from one or more other countries and their settlement in the destination country.

Emigration, or **out-migration**, is the outflow of people from one country and their settlement in one or more other countries.

welfare of the family. Note, however, that the crude birth rate took longer to decline than the crude death rate did. This phenomenon is called **cultural lag** and refers to conditions in which people's values change more slowly than their technologies do. People can put in a sewer system or a water purification plant to lower the crude death rate faster than they can change their minds about something as fundamental as how many children to have. Eventually, however, the technologies and outlooks that accompanied modernity led people to postpone getting married and to use contraceptives and other birth-control methods. As a result, population stabilized during the mature industrial period. This demonstrates the validity of one of the demographer's favourite sayings: "Economic development is the best contraceptive."

The Postindustrial Period

In the last two decades, the total fertility rate has continued to fall. (We defined the total fertility rate in Chapter 15, Families, as the average number of children that would be born to a woman over her lifetime if she had the same number of children as women in each age cohort in a given year.) In fact, it fell below the **replacement level** in some countries. The replacement level is the number of children each woman must have on average for popula-tion size to remain stable. Ignoring any inflow of settlers from other countries (**immigration, or in-migration**) and any outflow to other countries (**emigration, or out-migration**), the replacement level is 2.1. This means that, on average, each woman must give birth to slightly more than the two children needed to replace her and her mate. Slightly more than two chil-dren are required because some children die before they reach reproductive age.

By the 1990s, some Europeans were worrying about declining fertility and its possible effects on population size. As you can see in Table 20.1, Europe as a whole has a fertility rate below the replacement level. In fact, about a third of the world's countries, including Canada, China, and Japan, now have a fertility level below the replacement level, and the number of such countries is growing. Because of the proliferation of low-fertility societies, some scholars suggest that we have now entered a fourth, postindustrial stage of population development. In this fourth stage of the demographic transition, the number of deaths per year exceeds the number of births (Powell and Leedham, 2009).

TABLE 20.1

Total Fertility Rate by Region and Selected Countries, 2010

Source: Population Reference Bureau, 2010 Retrieved March 12, 2011 (http://www.prb.org/Datafinder/Topic/Bar.aspx?sort=v&order=d&variable=93).

Niger	7.4
Uganda	6.5
Ethiopia	5.4
Africa	4.7
India	2.6
South America	2.2
Asia	2.2
North America*	2.0
United States	2.0
Sweden	1.9
Canada	1.7
China	1.5
Europe	1.6
Japan	1.3
South Korea	1.2

*Canada and the United States only

As outlined earlier, the demographic transition theory provides a rough picture of how industrialization affects population growth. However, research has revealed a number of inconsistencies in the theory. Most of them are due to the theory placing too much emphasis on industrialization as the main force underlying population growth (Coale and Watkins, 1986). For example, demographers have found that reductions in fertility sometimes occur when standards of living stagnate or decline, not just when they improve through industrialization. Thus, in Russia and some developing countries today, declining living standards have led to a deterioration in general health and a subsequent decline in fertility. Because of such findings, many scholars have concluded that an adequate theory of population growth must pay more attention to social factors other than industrialization and, in particular, to the role of social inequality.

Population and Social Inequality

Karl Marx

One of Malthus's staunchest intellectual opponents was Karl Marx. Marx argued that the problem of overpopulation is specific to capitalism (Meek, 1971). In his view, overpopulation is not a problem of too many people. Rather, it is a problem of too much poverty. Do away with the exploitation of workers by their employers, said Marx, and poverty will disappear. If a society is rich enough to eliminate poverty, then by definition its population is not too large. By eliminating poverty, we also solve the problem of overpopulation in Marx's view.

Marx's analysis makes it seem that capitalism can never generate enough prosperity to solve the overpopulation problem. He was evidently wrong. Overpopulation is not a serious problem in Canada or the United States or Japan or Germany today.[1] It *is* a problem in most of Africa, where capitalism is weakly developed and the level of social inequality is much higher than in the postindustrial societies. Still, a core idea in Marx's analysis of the overpopulation problem rings true. As some contemporary demographers argue, social inequality is an important cause of overpopulation. In the following, we illustrate this argument by first considering how gender inequality influences population growth. Then we discuss the effects of class inequality on population growth.

Gender Inequality and Overpopulation

The effect of gender inequality on population growth is well illustrated by the case of Kerala, a state in India with more than 30 million people. The most recent census shows Kerala's total fertility rate at 1.7, about two-thirds of India's national rate and below the replacement level of 2.1. How did Kerala achieve this remarkable feat? Is it a highly industrialized oasis in the midst of a semi-industrialized country, as we might expect given the arguments of demographic transition theory? To the contrary, Kerala is not highly industrialized. In fact, it is among the poorer Indian states, with a per capita income less than the national average. Then has the government of Kerala strictly enforced a state childbirth policy similar to China's? The Chinese government strongly penalizes families that have more than one child and it allows abortion at 8.5 months. As a result, China had a total fertility rate of 1.5 in 2010. In Kerala, however, the government keeps out of its citizens' bedrooms. The decision to have children remains a strictly private affair.

The women of Kerala achieved a low total fertility rate because their government systematically raised their status over a period of decades (Franke and Chasin, 1992; Sen, 1994). The government helped to create a realistic alternative to a life of continuous childbearing and child rearing. It helped women understand that they could achieve that alternative if they wanted to. In particular, the government organized successful campaigns and programs to educate women, increase their participation in the paid labour force, and make family planning widely available. These government campaigns and programs resulted in Keralan women enjoying the highest literacy rate, the highest labour force participation rate, and the highest rate of political participation in India. Given their desire for education, work, and political involvement, most Keralan women want small families, so they use contraception to prevent unwanted births. Thus, by lowering the level of gender inequality, the government of Kerala solved its overpopulation problem. In general, where

women tend to have more power [the society has] low rather than high mortality and fertility. Education and employment, for example, often accord women wider power and

The **sex ratio** is the ratio of women to men in a geographical area.

influence, which enhance their status. But attending school and working often compete with childbearing and child rearing. Women may choose to have fewer children in order to hold a job or increase their education. (Riley, 1997; Box 20.1)

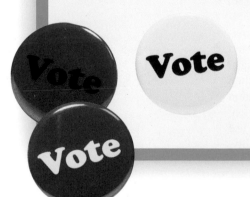

BOX 20.1

Social Policy: What Do You Think?

HOW CAN WE FIND 100 MILLION MISSING WOMEN?

World population is expected to grow to about 9.4 billion by 2050 and then level off.

Two main factors are causing the rate of world population growth to fall: economic development and the emancipation of women. Agricultural societies need many children to help with farming, but industrial societies require fewer children. Because many countries in the developing world are industrializing, the rate of world population growth is falling apace. The second main factor responsible for the declining growth rate is the improving economic status and education of women. Once women become literate and enter the non-agricultural paid labour force, they quickly recognize the advantages of having few children. The birth rate plummets. In many developing countries, that is just what is happening.

In other developing countries, the position of women is less satisfactory. We can see this by examining the ratio of women to men, or the **sex ratio** (United Nations, 2009).

In Canada in 2011, the sex ratio was about 1.05. That is, there were 105 women for every 100 men. This is about average for a highly developed country. The surplus of women reflects the fact that men are more likely than women are to be employed in health-threatening occupations, consume a lot of cigarettes and alcohol, and engage in riskier and more violent behaviour, while women are the hardier sex, biologically speaking.

In the world as a whole, the picture is reversed. There were just 98 women for every 100 men in 2000. In India and China, there were only 94 women for every 100 men. Apart from Asia, North Africa is the region that suffers most from a deficit of women.

What accounts for variation in the sex ratio? The sex ratio is low where women have less access to health services, medicine, and adequate nutrition than do men (Borooah and Dubey, 2009; Sen, 2001). These factors are associated with high female mortality. Another factor is significant in China, India, and some other Asian countries. In those countries, some parents so strongly prefer sons over daughters that sex-selective abortions contribute to the low sex ratio. Parents who strongly prefer sons over daughters are inclined to abort female fetuses. In contrast, in highly developed countries, women and men have approximately equal access to health services, medicine, and adequate nutrition while sex-selective abortions are rare. Therefore, there are more women than men. By this standard, the world as a whole is "missing" about 5 women for every 100 men (because 103 − 98 = 5). This works out to about 100 million women missing in 2000 because of sex-selective abortions and unequal access to resources of the most basic sort.

We can "find" many of the missing 100 million women partly by eliminating gender inequalities in access to health services, medicine, and adequate nutrition. Increased female literacy and employment in the paid labour force are the most effective paths to eliminating such gender inequalities. That is because literate women who work in the paid labour force are in a stronger position to demand equal rights and are more likely to be married to men with similar sympathies.

The question of how to eliminate sex-selective abortions is more difficult. Economic factors do not account for variation in the use of sex-selective abortions. In some affluent parts of Asia with high levels of female education and economic participation, sex-selective abortions are common; India's lowest sex ratio—at 79, it is, in fact, the lowest sex ratio in the world—can be found in the wealthy northern states of Punjab and Haryana (Rahman, 2004).[2] In some other parts of Asia with low levels of female education and economic participation, sex-selective abortions are relatively rare. The best explanation for variations in sex-selective abortions seems to be that preference for sons is a strong *cultural* tradition in some parts of Asia. In India, for example, it may not be coincidental that sex-selective abortions are most widespread in the North and the West, where the nationalist and fundamentalist Hindu party, BJP, is most popular. Hindu nationalism and religious fundamentalism may feed into a strong preference for sons over daughters.

This leaves open the question of how, if at all, reformers inside and outside the region might rectify the situation. Cultural and religious traditions do not easily give way to economic forces (Brym et al., 2005). Meanwhile, a strong preference for sons over daughters adds millions to the number of missing women every year.

Class Inequality and Overpopulation

Unravelling the Keralan mystery is an instructive exercise. It establishes that population growth depends not just on a society's level of industrialization but also on its level of gender inequality. *Class* inequality influences population growth too. We turn to the South Korean case to illustrate this point.

In 1960, South Korea had a total fertility rate of 6.0. This prompted one American official to remark that "if these Koreans don't stop overbreeding, we may have the choice of supporting them forever, watching them starve to death, or washing our hands of the problem" (quoted in Lie, 1998: 21). Yet by 1989, South Korea's total fertility rate had dropped to a mere 1.6. By 2010 it fell to 1.2. Why? The first chapter in this story involves land reform, not industrialization. The government took land from big landowners and gave it to small farmers. Consequently, small farmers' standard of living improved. This eliminated a major reason for high fertility. Once economic uncertainty decreased, so did the need for child labour and support of elderly parents by adult offspring. Soon, the total fertility rate began to fall. Subsequent declines in the South Korean total fertility rate were due to industrialization, urbanization, and the higher educational attainment of the population. But a decline in class inequality in the countryside first set the process in motion.

The reverse is also true. Increasing social inequality can lead to overpopulation, war, and famine. For example, in the 1960s the governments of El Salvador and Honduras encouraged the expansion of commercial agriculture and the acquisition of large farms by wealthy landowners. The landowners drove peasants off the land. The peasants migrated to the cities, where they hoped to find employment and a better life. Instead, they often found squalor, unemployment, and disease. Suddenly, two countries with a combined population of fewer than five million people had a big "overpopulation" problem. Competition for land increased and contributed to rising tensions. This eventually led to the outbreak of war between El Salvador and Honduras in 1969 (Durham, 1979).

Similarly, economic inequality helps to create famines. As Nobel Prize–winning economist Amartya Sen notes, "Famine is the characteristic of some people not *having* enough food to eat. It is not the characteristic of there not *being* enough food to eat" (Sen, 1981: 1; our emphasis). Sen's distinction is crucial, as his analysis of several famines shows. Sen found that, in some cases, although food supplies did decline, enough food was available to keep the stricken population fed. However, suppliers and speculators took advantage of the short supply. They hoarded grain and increased prices beyond the means of most people. In other cases, there was no decline in food supply at all. Food was simply withheld for political reasons—that is, to subdue a population, or because many people were not considered entitled to receive it by the authorities. For example, in 1932–33, Stalin instigated a famine in Ukraine that killed millions. His purpose: to bring the Ukrainian people to their knees and force them to give up their privately owned farms and join state-owned, collective farms. The source of famine, Sen concludes, is not underproduction or overpopulation but inequality of access to food (Drèze and Sen, 1989).

Summing Up

- Malthus predicted that dramatic population expansion is curtailed by outbreaks of war, pestilence, and famine.
- Improvements in technology and social programs have moderated Malthus's predictions.
- Demographic transition theory holds that the trend toward low birth and death rates is driven by industrialization and modernization.
- Class and gender inequalities are major barriers to lower population growth.

Mexico City during one of its frequent smog alerts. Of the world's 10 biggest cities in 2015, only one—Tokyo—will be in a highly industrialized country. All the others, including Mexico City, will be in developing countries.

Murry Sill/Index Stock Imagery

URBANIZATION

We have seen that overpopulation remains a troubling problem because of lack of industrialization and too much gender and class inequality in much of the world. We may now add that overpopulation is in substantial measure an *urban* problem. Driven by lack of economic opportunity in the countryside, political unrest, and other factors, many millions of people flock to big cities in the world's poor countries every year. Thus, most of the fastest-growing cities in the world today are in semi-industrialized countries. As Table 20.2 shows, in 1900, 9 of the 10 biggest cities in the world were in industrialized Europe and the United States. By 2015, in contrast, 6 of the world's 10 biggest cities will be in Asia, 2 will be in Africa, and 2 will be in Latin America. Only 1 of the 10 biggest cities—Tokyo—will be in a highly industrialized country. Urbanization is, of course, taking place in the world's rich countries too. According to the 2006 census, more than 8 in 10 Canadians now reside in cities, with about 53 percent living in Canada's 10 largest metropolitan areas: Toronto, Montreal, Vancouver, Ottawa-Gatineau, Calgary, Edmonton, Quebec City, Winnipeg, Hamilton, and London (Statistics Canada, 2007f). In North America as a whole, the urban population is expected to increase to 84 percent of the total population by 2030. In Africa and Asia, however, the urban population is expected to increase much faster to 62 percent by 2050 (United Nations, 2011).

TABLE 20.2

World's 10 Largest Metropolitan Areas, 1900 and 2015, Projected (in Millions)

Sources: Department of Geography, Slippery Rock University, 1997, 2003.

1900		2015	
London, England	6.5	Tokyo, Japan	28.7
New York, United States	4.2	Mumbai (Bombay), India	27.4
Paris, France	3.3	Lagos, Nigeria	24.4
Berlin, Germany	2.4	Shanghai, China	23.4
Chicago, United States	1.7	Jakarta, Indonesia	21.2
Vienna, Austria	1.6	São Paulo, Brazil	20.8
Tokyo, Japan	1.5	Karachi, Pakistan	20.6
Saint Petersburg, Russia	1.4	Beijing, China	19.4
Philadelphia, United States	1.4	Dhaka, Bangladesh	19.0
Manchester, England	1.3	Mexico City, Mexico	18.8

From the Preindustrial to the Industrial City

To a degree, urbanization results from industrialization. Many great cities of the world grew up along with the modern factory, which drew hundreds of millions of people out of the countryside and transformed them into urban, industrial workers. Industrialization is not, however, the whole story behind the growth of cities. As we have just seen, the connection between industrialization and urbanization is weak in the world's less developed countries today. Moreover, cities first emerged in Syria, Mesopotamia, and Egypt 5000 or 6000 years ago, long before the growth of the modern factory. These early cities served as centres of religious worship and political administration. Similarly, it was not industry but international trade in spices, gold, cloth, and other precious goods that stimulated the growth of cities in preindustrial Europe and the Middle East. Thus, the correlation between urbanization and industrialization is far from perfect (Bairoch, 1988 [1985]; Jacobs, 1969; Mumford, 1961; Sjöberg, 1960).

Preindustrial cities differed from those that developed in the industrial era in several ways. Preindustrial cities were typically smaller, less densely populated, built within protective walls, and organized around a central square and places of worship. The industrial cities that began to emerge at the end of the eighteenth century were more dynamic and complex social systems. A host of social problems, including poverty, pollution, and crime, accompanied their growth. The complexity, dynamism, and social problems of the industrial city were all evident in Chicago at the turn of the twentieth century. Not surprisingly, therefore, it was at the University of Chicago that modern urban sociology was born.

The Chicago School and the Industrial City

From the 1910s to the 1930s, the members of the **Chicago school** of sociology distinguished themselves by their vividly detailed descriptions and analyses of urban life, backed up by careful in-depth interviews, surveys, and maps showing the distribution of various features of the social landscape, all expressed in plain yet evocative language (Lindner, 1996 [1990]). Three of its leading members, Robert Park, Ernest Burgess, and Roderick McKenzie, proposed a theory of **human ecology** to illuminate the process of urbanization (Park, Burgess, and McKenzie, 1967 [1925]). Borrowing from biology and ecology, the theory highlights the links between the physical and social dimensions of cities and identifies the dynamics and patterns of urban growth.

The theory of human ecology, as applied to urban settings, holds that cities grow in ever-expanding concentric circles. It is sometimes called the "concentric zone model" of the city. Three social processes animate this growth (Hawley, 1950). **Differentiation** refers to the process by which urban populations and their activities become more complex and heterogeneous over time. For instance, a small town may have a diner, a pizza parlour, and a Chinese restaurant. But if that small town grows into a city, it will likely boast a variety of ethnic restaurants reflecting its more heterogeneous population. Moreover, in a city, members of different ethnic and racial groups and socioeconomic classes may vie with one another for dominance in particular areas. Businesses may also try to push residents out of certain areas to establish commercial zones. When this happens, people are engaging in **competition**, an ongoing struggle by different groups to inhabit optimal locations. Finally, **ecological succession** takes place when a distinct group of people moves from one area to another, and a second group moves into the old area to replace the first group. For example, a recurrent pattern of ecological succession involves members of the middle class moving to the suburbs, with

The **Chicago school** founded urban sociology in the United States in the first decades of the twentieth century.

Human ecology is a theoretical approach to urban sociology that borrows ideas from biology and ecology to highlight the links between the physical and social dimensions of cities and identify the dynamics and patterns of urban growth.

Differentiation in the theory of human ecology refers to the process by which urban populations and their activities become more complex and heterogeneous over time.

In the theory of human ecology, **competition** refers to the struggle by different groups for optimal locations in which to reside and set up their businesses.

Ecological succession in the theory of human ecology refers to the process by which a distinct urban group moves from one area to another and a second group comes in to replace the group that has moved out.

Carcassone, France, a medieval walled city

working class and poor immigrants moving into the inner city. In Chicago in the 1920s, differentiation, competition, and ecological succession resulted in the zonal pattern illustrated by Figure 20.4.

For members of the Chicago school, the city was more than just a collection of socially segregated buildings, places, and people. It also involved a way of life they called **urbanism**. They defined urbanism as "a state of mind, a body of customs[,] ... traditions, ... attitudes and sentiments" specifically linked to city dwelling (Park, Burgess, and McKenzie, 1967 [1925]: 1). Louis Wirth (1938) developed this theme. According to Wirth, rural life involves frequent face-to-face interaction among a few people. Most of these people are familiar with one another, share common values and a collective identity, and strongly respect traditional ways of doing things. Urban life, in contrast, involves the absence of community and of close personal relationships. Extensive exposure to many socially different people leads city dwellers to become more tolerant than rural folk are. However, urban dwellers also withdraw emotionally and reduce the intensity of their social interaction with others. In Wirth's view, interaction in cities is therefore superficial, impersonal, and focused on specific goals. People become more individualistic. Weak social control leads to a high incidence of deviance and crime.

After Chicago: A Critique

The Chicago school dominated North American urban sociology for decades and still inspires much interesting research (E. Anderson, 1990; Balakrishnan and Selvanathan, 1990). However, three major criticisms of this approach to understanding city growth have gained credibility over the years.

> **Urbanism** is a way of life that, according to Louis Wirth, involves increased tolerance but also emotional withdrawal and specialized, impersonal, and self-interested interaction.

FIGURE 20.4

The Concentric Zone Model of Chicago, about 1920

Source: From "The Growth of the City: An Introduction to a Research Project" Ernest W. Burgess, pp. 47–62 in *The City* by Robert E. Park et al. Copyright © 1967 University of Chicago Press. Used with permission.

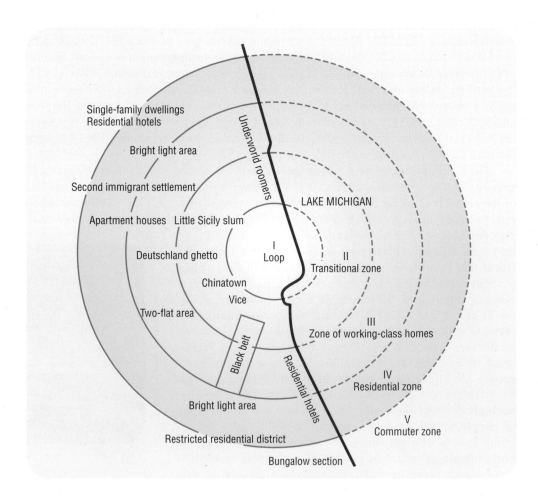

One criticism focuses on Wirth's characterization of the "urban way of life." Research shows that social isolation, emotional withdrawal, stress, and other problems may be just as common in rural as in urban areas (Crothers, 1979; Webb and Collette, 1977, 1979). After all, in a small community a person may not be able to find anyone with whom to share a particular interest or passion. Moreover, farm work can be every bit as stressful as work on an assembly line.

Research conducted in Toronto and other North American cities also shows that urban life is less impersonal, anomic, and devoid of community than the Chicago sociologists made it appear. True, newcomers (of whom there were admittedly many in Chicago in the 1920s) may find city life bewildering if not frightening. Neighbourliness and friendliness to strangers are less common in cities than in small communities (Fischer, 1981). However, even in the largest cities, most residents create social networks and subcultures that serve functions similar to those performed by the small community. Friendship, kinship, ethnic and racial ties, as well as work and leisure relations, form the bases of these urban networks and subcultures (Fischer, 1984 [1976]; Jacobs, 1961; Wellman, 1979). Consider in this context that the United Nations identifies Toronto as the most multicultural city in the world, with more foreign-born than Canadian-born residents. Boasting more than 60 ethnic communities and 100 spoken languages, "Toronto's multicultural population is a source of community support for people in everyday life" (Geddes, 1997: 91; see also Bricker and Greenspon, 2001). Cities, it turns out, are clusters of many different communities, prompting one sociologist to refer to city dwellers as "urban villagers" (Gans, 1962).

A second problem with the Chicago school's approach concerns the applicability of the concentric zone model to other times and places. Canada, for example, has managed to avoid the American "ghetto" syndrome. In this country we do not find the deep and enduring poverty that characterizes so many central-city neighbourhoods in the United States (Janigan, 2002: 26). True, the urban population is growing more slowly than the poor urban population, and it contains a large number of unemployed immigrants who know little English or French, Aboriginal peoples lacking much formal education, and single parents on social assistance (Canadian Council on Social Development, 2008). Research also shows that in the last few decades, socioeconomic and ethnic residential segregation has increased in Canada's large cities, leading one urban sociologist to conclude that "[t]he socioeconomic status of urbanites increases directly with the distance of their residence from the city centre" (Gillis, 1995: 13.17; see also Kazemipur and Halli, 2000). Still, the core areas of most Canadian cities remain economically vibrant and socially viable, and they boast desirable and expensive housing. We conclude that the concentric zone theory has limited applicability to Canada.

Evidence from preindustrial cities supports the view that the concentric zone model was most applicable to American industrial cities in the first quarter of the twentieth century. In preindustrial cities, slums were more likely to be found on the outskirts. Wealthy districts were more likely to be found in the city core. Commercial and residential buildings were often not segregated (Sjöberg, 1960).

Finally, we note that after the automobile became a major means of transportation, some cities expanded not in concentric circles but in wedge-shaped sectors along natural boundaries and transportation routes (Hoyt, 1939). Others grew up around not one but many nuclei, each attracting similar kinds of activities and groups (Harris and Ullman, 1945; Figure 20.5 on page 514). All of this serves to cast doubt on the universality of the concentric zone theory.

The third main criticism of the human ecology approach is that it presents urban growth as an almost natural process, slighting its historical, political, and economic foundations in capitalist industrialization. The Chicago sociologists' analysis of competition in the transitional zone came closest to avoiding this problem. However, their discussions of differentiation and ecological succession made the growth of cities seem more like a force of nature than a process rooted in power relations and the urge to profit.

FIGURE 20.5

The Peripheral Model of Cities: An Alternative to the Concentric Zone Model

Source: Harris (1997).

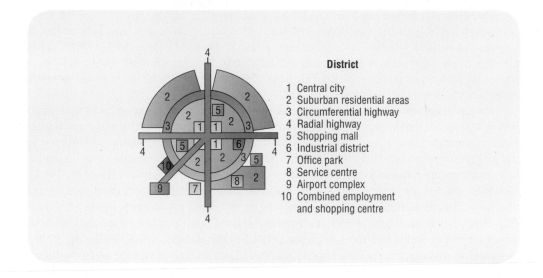

District

1 Central city
2 Suburban residential areas
3 Circumferential highway
4 Radial highway
5 Shopping mall
6 Industrial district
7 Office park
8 Service centre
9 Airport complex
10 Combined employment and shopping centre

The **new urban sociology** emerged in the 1970s and stressed that city growth is a process rooted in power relations and the urge to profit.

The so-called **new urban sociology**, heavily influenced by conflict theory, sought to correct this problem (Gottdiener, 2010). For new urban sociologists, urban space is not just an arena for the unfolding of social processes like differentiation, competition, and ecological succession. Instead, they see urban space as a set of *commodified* social relations. That is, urban space, like all commodities, can be bought and sold for profit. As a result, political interests and conflicts shape the growth pattern of cities. John Logan and Harvey Molotch (1987), for example, portray cities as machines fuelled by a "growth coalition." This growth coalition comprises investors, politicians, businesses, property owners, real estate developers, urban planners, the mass media, professional sports teams, cultural institutions, labour unions, and universities. All these partners try to get government subsidies and tax breaks to attract investment dollars. Reversing the pattern identified by the Chicago sociologists, this investment has been used to redevelop decaying downtown areas in many North American cities since the 1950s. In Canada, this approach is evident

Africville relocation meeting, Seaview Baptist Church, circa 1962. Halifax's Africville relocation project illustrates how poor urban residents typically have little say over redevelopment plans (Clairmont and Magill, 1999). Africville was settled around 1850 by blacks fleeing slavery in the United States, but it suffered drastic decline after World War I. The Halifax municipal government began to phase Africville out of existence in 1963 against the wishes of its residents. The city promised generous financial compensation and alternative housing, but some residents still refused to move. They were threatened with the expropriation of their property and eventually the community was bulldozed.

in the development of Harbourfront, a 28-hectare (70-acre) property along Toronto's Lake Ontario that mixes recreational, cultural, residential, and commercial elements (Church, Greenberg, and McPhedran, 1997). It is also notable in the re-invigoration of Gastown and the former Expo '86 lands in Vancouver, Quebec City's thriving Lower Town, and the restoration and revitalization of Calgary's and Winnipeg's downtown areas (Janigan, 2002: 25).

According to Logan and Molotch (1987), members of the growth coalition present redevelopment as a public good that benefits everyone. This ideology tends to silence critics, prevent discussion of alternative ideas and plans, and veil the question of who benefits and who does not. In reality, the benefits of redevelopment are often unevenly distributed. Most redevelopments are "pockets of revitalization surrounded by areas of extreme poverty" (Hannigan, 1998a: 53). That is, local residents often enjoy few if any direct benefits from redevelopment. Indirectly, they may suffer when budgets for public schooling, public transportation, and other amenities are cut to help pay for development subsidies and tax breaks. The growth coalition is not, however, all-powerful. Community activism often targets local governments and corporations that seek unrestricted growth. Sometimes activists meet with success (Castells, 1983). Yet for the past 50 years, the growth coalition has managed to reshape the face of North American cities, more or less in its own image (see Box 20.2 on page 516).

The Corporate City

Through the efforts of the growth coalition, the North American industrial city, typified by Chicago in the 1920s, gave way after World War II to the **corporate city**. University of Toronto sociologist John Hannigan defines the corporate city as "a vehicle for capital accumulation—that is, ... a money-making machine" (Hannigan, 1998b: 345).

In the suburbs, urbanized areas outside the political boundaries of cities, developers built millions of single-family detached homes for the corporate middle class. These homes boasted large backyards and a car or two in every garage. A new way of life developed, which sociologists dubbed **suburbanism**. Every bit as distinctive as urbanism, suburbanism organized life mainly around the needs of children. It also involved higher levels of conformity and sociability than did life in the central city (Fava, 1956). Suburbanism became fully entrenched as developers built shopping malls to serve the needs of suburbanites. This construction reduced the need to travel to the central city for consumer goods.

The suburbs were at first restricted to the well-to-do. However, following World War II, brisk economic growth and government assistance to veterans put the suburban lifestyle within the reach of middle-class Canadians. Extensive road-building programs, the falling price of automobiles, and the baby boom that began in 1946 also stimulated mushroom-like suburban growth.

Because of the expansion of the suburbs, urban sociologists today often focus their attention not on cities but on **census metropolitan areas (CMAs)**, a term coined by Statistics Canada (Table 20.3 on page 517). Each CMA includes a large urban area (known as the urban core) along with adjacent urban and rural areas (urban and rural "fringes") that are highly integrated into the urban core. The Statistics Canada definition of a CMA also specifies that it has an urban core population of at least 100 000 at the time of the most recent census.

CMAs also include two recent developments that indicate the continuing decentralization of urban Canada: the growth of rural residential areas within commuting distance of a city (Figure 20.6 on page 517) and the emergence of **edge cities** where clusters of malls, offices, and entertainment complexes arise, often beside major highways (Garrau, 1991). Edge cities are the "sprawling outer suburbs" of major metropolitan areas (Janigan, 2002: 25). The growth of edge cities in Canada, though less pronounced than in the United States, has been stimulated by many factors. Among the most important are the mounting costs of operating businesses in city cores and the growth of new telecommunication technologies

The **corporate city** refers to the growing post–World War II perception and organization of the North American city as a vehicle for capital accumulation.

Suburbanism is a way of life outside city centres that is organized mainly around the needs of children and involves higher levels of conformity and sociability than life in the central city.

A **census metropolitan area (CMA)** includes a large urban area (known as the urban core) along with adjacent urban and rural areas (urban and rural "fringes") that are highly integrated into the urban core.

Edge cities are clusters of malls, offices, and entertainment complexes that arise at the convergence point of major highways.

BOX 20.2

Sociology at the Movies

THE GARDEN

On April 29, 1992, Los Angeles erupted in three days of civil disorder, violence, and looting. The Los Angeles riots led to dozens of deaths and thousands of injuries. Property damage topped a billion dollars. The rioters were protesting the widely publicized acquittal of police officers involved in the arrest and beating of unarmed black motorist Rodney King. This series of events, fuelled by media coverage, caused racial tensions in the city to boil over. In 1994, a 46-hectare (114-acre) community garden was established in downtown South Central Los Angeles as an effort to heal the wounds of the social conflict. The amazing story of this urban green space and its people is captured in Scott Hamilton Kennedy's Oscar-nominated documentary, *The Garden*.

The people who worked the community garden were fully invested in the project. Their mentality is captured in their political slogan: ¡*Tierra y libertad*! (Land and liberty!). As one of the garden's Mexican immigrant farmers exclaims, "*Sin tierra no somos nada*" ("Without land, we are nothing"). For the underclass of South Central Los Angeles, the garden represented subsistence, renewal, and community in the midst of lives dominated by deprivation, stagnation, and alienation.

The urban garden flourished and so did the local community—until property speculator Ralph Horowitz revived a

© Oscilloscope Pictures/Courtesy Everett Collection

Scene from *The Garden*

decades-old lawsuit claiming lawful ownership of the city-owned land. The lawsuit sparked a bitter court battle lasting several years and involving the garden farmers, the surrounding Latino and black communities, city politicians, citizen groups, and an army of lawyers. In a real-life drama of shady backroom political deals, interpersonal strife, and racial conflict, the courts eventually awarded the land to Mr. Horowitz. In one of the film's heartbreaking scenes, the city permits the demolition of the garden by bulldozers in 2006 to make way for a proposed warehouse and a soccer field. To date, the lot remains vacant.

The Garden illustrates the commodification process through which

urban space is bought and sold. In the first instance the land is used to effect a reduction in racial tensions in the wake of the riots. Then the land is sold to a self-interested developer who brashly states, "I don't feel any compunction about putting the land to the use for which it is intended." Of course, Mr. Horowitz's intentions for the land express only his interest. Multiple interests compete for urban spaces. Urban planners and interested others must continuously struggle with resolving the conflicting interests of developers and less powerful groups. *The Garden* illustrates an important sociological principle: the pursuit of self-interest can never optimize collective interests. There is no invisible hand guiding the construction of urban realities. Although all citizens are responsible for doing what they can to create environments they consider productive, beautiful, and just, *The Garden* shows that the success of their efforts is determined by their power.

1901		2006	
CMA	Population	CMA	Population
Montreal	266 826	Toronto	5 113 149
Toronto	207 971	Montreal	3 635 571
Quebec City	68 834	Vancouver	2 116 581
Ottawa	59 902	Ottawa-Gatineau	1 130 761
Hamilton	52 550	Calgary	1 079 310
Winnipeg	42 336	Edmonton	1 034 945
Halifax	40 787	Quebec City	715 515
Saint John	40 711	Winnipeg	694 668
London	37 983	Hamilton	692 911
Vancouver	26 196	London	457 720

TABLE 20.3

The 10 Largest Census Metropolitan Areas in Canada, 1901 and 2006

Sources: Adapted from Kearney and Ray, 1999: 147; Statistics Canada, 2007d.

Gentrification is the process of middle-class people moving into rundown areas of the inner city and restoring them.

that are changing the location of work. Home offices, mobile employees, and decentralized business locations are all made possible by these technologies.

In the early 1960s, Toronto urban critic Jane Jacobs (1961) warned of the dangers of sprawling suburbs and decaying downtowns in *The Death and Life of Great American Cities*. Her forecasts, it seems, proved to be less valid for Canada than for the United States. The municipal governments of Vancouver, Quebec City, Calgary, and other Canadian cities decided to reinvigorate their downtowns. In addition, deteriorating conditions in many of Canada's central cities were reduced by **gentrification**—a process whereby portions of the inner city are taken over by middle-class or higher-income groups and renovated and upgraded to desirable residential areas (Ley, 1996). Still, some Canadian cities, such as Winnipeg, followed a more American pattern. The downtown core underwent a process of

FIGURE 20.6

Rural Population, Canada, 2006

Canada's rural population fell below half the total population in 1931. In 2006, it composed just 20 percent of the total population. As the accompanying graph indicates, however, there are wide variations in rurality among provinces and territories. The least populous parts of Canada (the north and the Atlantic provinces) are the most rural parts of the country, while the most populous parts (Ontario, Quebec, British Columbia, and Alberta) are the least rural.

In absolute terms, the rural population is decreasing in some parts of Canada but increasing in others. Rural population increase is occurring where individuals can easily commute to cities, where people want to retire, and in the north, where Aboriginal Canadians form a large percentage of the population and their birth rate is high. Rural areas experiencing population decrease are witnessing substantial out-migration of people under the age of 30 and a low birth rate (Bollman, 2000).

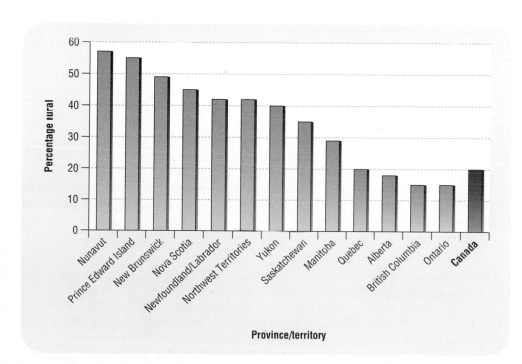

Source: HRSDC, 2006. Retrieved March 17, 2011 (http://www4.hrsdc.gc.ca/.3ndic.1t.4r@-eng.jsp?iid=34).

decline as the middle class fled, pulled by the promise of a suburban lifestyle and pushed by such factors as racial animosity and fear of crime. Recent trends in Winnipeg indicate, however, that successful initiatives to reinvigorate the urban core are leading to gentrification (Plooy, 2009).

Some analysts suggest that many of the problems confronting cities are best resolved by amalgamation. They view the creation of "megacities," such as Toronto, now the fifth-largest city in North America, with considerable optimism. They argue that when it comes to responding to many urban problems—building adequate roads and public transit systems, improving the environment, providing efficient and cost-effective services, and negotiating with provincial or territorial and federal governments—bigger is better.

Although Winnipeg, Halifax, Saint John, Hamilton, and Fort McMurray are among the Canadian cities that have opted for amalgamation, some analysts maintain that "smaller is smarter." Critics argue that amalgamation often *increases* costs (Istar, 2001). They also contend that, when compared with larger governmental units, smaller units are more democratic, accountable, and responsive to their citizens; sensitive to local, community, and neighbourhood issues; and capable of responding to local opinion on the types and levels of services desired. Large governments, they claim, are difficult to control, show greater resistance to innovation and government reform, and are more likely to be influenced by special interests and professional advocates, such as lobbyists (Cox, 1997).

The Postmodern City

Many of the conditions that plagued the industrial city—poverty, inadequate housing, structural employment—are evident in Canadian cities today. However, since about 1970, a new urban phenomenon has emerged alongside the legacy of old urban forms. This is the **postmodern city** (Hannigan, 1995a). The postmodern city has three main features.

The **postmodern city** is a new urban form that is more privatized and socially and culturally fragmented and globalized than the corporate city.

1. The postmodern city is more *privatized* than is the corporate city because access to formerly public spaces is increasingly limited to those who can afford to pay. Privatization is evident in closed-off "gated communities" that boast controlled-access front gates and foot patrols on the lookout for intruders. Privatization is also apparent in the construction of gleaming office towers and shopping areas that sometimes replace public urban green spaces. It is evident in pay-for-use public toilets and "patrons-only" washrooms. In the United States, the tendency is even more notable. For example, the private areas of downtown Los Angeles are increasingly intended for exclusive use by middle-class visitors and professionals who work in the information sector, including financial services, the computer industry, telecommunications, entertainment, and so on.

2. The postmodern city is also more *fragmented* than the corporate city is. That is, it lacks a single way of life, such as urbanism or suburbanism. Instead, a variety of lifestyles and subcultures proliferate in the postmodern city. They are based on race, ethnicity, immigrant status, class, and sexual orientation.

3. The postmodern city is more *globalized* than is the corporate city. New York, London, and Tokyo epitomize the global city (Sassen, 1991). They are centres of economic and financial decision making. They are also sites of innovation, where new products and fashions originate. They have become the command posts of the globalized economy and its culture.

The processes of privatization, fragmentation, and globalization are evident in the way the postmodern city has come to reflect the priorities of the global entertainment industry. Especially in the 1990s, the city and its outlying districts came to resemble so many Disneyfied "Magic Kingdoms" based on capital and technologies from the United States, Japan, Britain, Canada, and elsewhere. There we find the latest entertainment technologies and spectacular thrills to suit nearly every taste. The postmodern city gets its distinctive flavour from its theme parks, restaurants and nightclubs, waterfront developments, refurbished casinos, giant malls, megaplex cinemas, IMAX theatres, virtual-reality arcades, ride simulators, sports complexes, book and CD megastores, aquariums, and hands-on science "museums." In the postmodern city, nearly everything becomes entertainment or, more accurately, combines entertainment with standard consumer activities. This produces hybrid activities, such as "shoppertainment," "eatertainment," and "edutainment."

John Hannigan has shown how the new venues of high-tech urban entertainment manage to provide excitement—but all within a thoroughly clean, controlled, predictable, and safe environment (Hannigan, 1998a). The new Magic Kingdoms are kept spotless, in excellent repair, and fully temperature- and humidity-controlled. They also provide a sense of security by touting familiar name brands and rigorously excluding anything and anybody that might disrupt the fun. For example, entertainment developments often enforce dress codes, teenager curfews, and rules that ban striking workers and groups espousing social or political causes from their premises. The most effective barriers to potentially disruptive elements, however, are affordability and access. User surveys show that the new forms of urban entertainment tend to attract middle-class and upper-middle-class patrons, especially whites. That is because they are pricey and some are inaccessible by public transit and too expensive for most people to reach by taxi.

Referring to the major role played by the Disney Corporation in developing the new urban entertainment complexes, an architect once said that North American downtowns would be "saved by a mouse" (quoted in Hannigan, 1998a: 193). But do the new forms of entertainment that dot the urban landscape increase the economic well-being of the communities in which they are established? Not much, beyond creating some low-level, dead-end jobs, such as security guard, wait staff, and janitor. Do they provide ways of meeting new people, seeing old friends and neighbours, and in general improving urban sociability? Not really. You visit a theme park with family or friends, but you generally stick close to your group and rarely have chance encounters with other patrons or bump into acquaintances. Does the high-tech world of globalized urban entertainment enable cities and neighbourhoods to retain and enhance their distinct traditions, architectural styles, and ambience? It would be hard to destroy the distinctiveness of such cities as New York, Montreal, or Vancouver, but many large North American cities are becoming homogenized as they provide the same entertainment services—and the same global brands—as Tokyo, Paris, and Sydney. If the mouse is saving our cities, perhaps he is also gnawing away at something valuable in the process.

Summing Up

- Industrialization contributes to urbanization, but the two processes are not highly correlated.
- The Chicago school asserts that differentiation, competition, and ecological succession create urban environments organized into concentric zones.
- New urban sociologists emphasize how power and profit motives drive social forces shaping urban renewal.
- After World War II, large corporate cities emerged with gentrification at their core and suburbanism at their periphery.
- Postmodern cities are characterized by privatization, fragmentation, and globalization.

NOTES

1. However, because people in the world's rich countries consume so much energy and other resources, they have a substantial negative impact on the global environment. See the online chapter that accompanies this book, Chapter 22, Technology and the Global Environment.

2. This is true not just in some of the more affluent states of India. Sex-selective abortions are also relatively common in well-to-do Singapore, Taiwan, and South Korea. However, the female-to-male sex ratio is rising in South Korea as the preference for boys recedes (Sang-Hun, 2007).

SUMMARY

1. What is the Malthusian theory of population growth? Does it apply today?
   Robert Malthus argued that although food supplies increase slowly, populations grow quickly. Because of these presumed natural laws, only war, pestilence, and famine can keep human population growth in check. Several developments cast doubt on Malthus's theory. Food production has increased rapidly. The limits to population size are higher than Malthus expected. Some populations are large yet prosperous. Some countries provide generous social welfare and still maintain low population growth rates. The use of contraception is widespread.

2. What is demographic transition theory?
   Demographic transition theory holds that the main factors underlying population dynamics are industrialization and the growth of modern cultural values. In the preindustrial era, both crude birth rates and crude death rates were high and population growth was therefore slow. In the first stage of industrialization, crude death rates fell, so population growth was rapid. As industrialization progressed and people's values about having children changed, the crude birth rate fell, resulting in slow growth again. Finally, in the postindustrial era, the crude death rate has risen above the crude birth rate in many societies. As a result, their populations shrink unless in-migration augments their numbers.

3. What factors aside from the level of industrialization affect population dynamics?
   The level of social inequality between women and men, and between classes, affects population dynamics, with lower levels of social inequality typically resulting in lower crude birth rates and less competition for scarce resources.

4. Is urbanization a function of industrialization?
   Much urbanization is associated with the growth of factories. However, religious, political, and commercial needs gave rise to cities in the preindustrial era. Moreover, the fastest-growing cities in the world today are in semi-industrialized countries.

5. What did members of the Chicago school contribute to our understanding of the growth of cities?
   The members of the Chicago school famously described and explained the spatial and social dimensions of the industrial city. They developed a theory of human ecology that explained urban growth as the outcome of differentiation, competition, and ecological succession. They described the spatial arrangement of the industrial city as a series of expanding concentric circles. The main business, entertainment, and shopping area stood in the centre, with the class position of residents increasing as they moved from inner to outer rings.

6. What are the main weaknesses of the Chicago school's analysis of cities?
   Subsequent research showed that the city is not as anomic as the Chicago sociologists made it appear. Moreover, the concentric zone pattern applies best to the American

industrial city in the first quarter of the twentieth century. Preindustrial cities, non-American cities, and contemporary cities do not fit the concentric zone pattern as well. Moreover, the new urban sociology criticized the Chicago school for making city growth seem like an almost natural process, playing down the power conflicts and profit motives that prompt the development of cities.

7. **What are the corporate and postmodern cities?**
The corporate city that emerged after World War II was a vehicle for capital accumulation that stimulated the growth of the suburbs and resulted in the decline of inner cities. The postmodern city that took shape in the last decades of the twentieth century is characterized by the increased globalization of culture, fragmentation of lifestyles, and privatization of space.

KEY TERMS

census metropolitan area (CMA) (p. 515)

Chicago school (p. 511)

competition (p. 511)

corporate city (p. 515)

crude birth rate (p. 505)

crude death rate (p. 505)

cultural lag (p. 506)

demographers (p. 502)

demographic transition theory (p. 505)

differentiation (p. 511)

ecological succession (p. 511)

edge cities (p. 515)

emigration (p. 506)

gentrification (p. 517)

human ecology (p. 511)

immigration (p. 506)

in-migration (p. 506)

Malthusian trap (p. 503)

new urban sociology (p. 514)

out-migration (p. 506)

postmodern city (p. 518)

replacement level (p. 506)

sex ratio (p. 508)

suburbanism (p. 515)

urbanism (p. 512)

WEB RESOURCES

Companion Website for This Book

http://www.compass4e.nelson.com

Begin by clicking on the Student Resources section of the website. Next, select the chapter you are studying from the pull-down menu. From the Student Resources page you have easy access to additional Weblinks and other resources. The website also has many useful tips to aid you in your study of sociology, including practice tests for each chapter.

InfoTrac® Search Terms

These search terms are provided to assist you in beginning to conduct research on this topic by visiting http://www.infotrac-college.com:

immigration
urbanization
migration
poverty

21

Collective Action and Social Movements

IN THIS CHAPTER, YOU WILL LEARN THAT

- People sometimes lynch, riot, and engage in other forms of non-routine group action to correct perceived injustices. Such events are rare, short-lived, spontaneous, and often violent. They subvert established institutions and practices. Nevertheless, most non-routine collective action requires social organization, and people who take part in collective action often act in a calculated way.

- Collective action can result in the creation of one or more formal organizations or bureaucracies to direct and further the aims of its members. The institutionaliza-tion of protest signifies the establishment of a social movement.

- People are more inclined to rebel against existing conditions when strong social ties bind them to many other people who feel similarly wronged; when they have the time, money, and other resources needed to protest; and when political structures and processes give them opportunities to express discontent.

- For social movements to grow, members must make the activities, goals, and ideology of the movement consistent with the interests, beliefs, and values of potential recruits.

- The history of social movements is a struggle for the acquisition of constantly broadening citizenship rights and opposition to those struggles.

HOW TO SPARK A RIOT

Robert Brym almost sparked a small riot once. "It happened in grade 11," says Robert, "shortly after I learned that water combined with sulphur dioxide produces sulphurous acid. The news shocked me. To understand why, you have to know that I lived in Saint John, New Brunswick, about 100 metres downwind of one of the largest pulp-and-paper mills in Canada. Waves of sulphur dioxide billowed from the mill's smokestacks day and night. The town's pervasive rotten-egg smell was a long-standing complaint in the area. But, for me, disgust turned to upset when I realized the fumes were toxic. Suddenly it was clear why many people I knew—especially people living near the mill—woke up in the morning with a kind of 'smoker's cough.' Through the simple act of breathing we were causing the gas to mix with the mois-ture in our bodies and form an acid that our lungs tried to expunge, with only partial success.

Jacob Yuri Wackerhausen/Shutterstock

"Twenty years later, I read the results of a medical research report showing that area residents suffered from rates of lung disease, including emphysema and lung cancer, significantly above the North American average. But even in 1968 it was evident my hometown had a serious problem. I therefore hatched a plan. Our high school was about to hold its annual model parliament. The event was notoriously boring, partly because, year in year out, virtually everyone voted for the same party, the Conservatives. But here was an issue, I thought, that could turn things around. A local man, K. C. Irving, owned the pulp and paper mill. *Forbes* magazine ranked him as one of the richest men in the world. I figured that when I told my fellow students what I had discovered, they would quickly demand the closure of the mill until Irving guaranteed a clean operation.

"Was *I* naive. As head of the tiny Liberal Party, I had to address the entire student body during assembly on election day to outline the party platform and rally votes. When I got to the part of my speech that explained why Irving was our enemy, the murmuring in the audience, which had been growing like the sound of a hungry animal about to pounce on its prey, erupted into loud boos. A couple of students rushed the stage. The principal sud-denly appeared from the wings and commanded the student body to settle down. He then took me by the arm and informed me that, for my own safety, my speech was finished. So, I discovered on election day, was our high school's Liberal Party. And so, it emerged, was my high-school political career.

"This incident troubled me for many years, partly because of the embarrassment it caused, partly because of the puzzles it presented. Why did I almost spark a small riot? Why didn't my fellow students rebel in the way I thought they would? Why did they continue to support an arrangement that was enriching one man at the cost of a community's health? Couldn't they see the injustice? Other people did. Nineteen sixty-eight was not just the year of my political failure in high school; it was also the year that student riots in France nearly toppled that country's government. In Mexico, the suppression of student strikes by the government left dozens of students dead. In the United States, students at Berkeley, Michigan, and other colleges demonstrated and staged sit-ins with unprecedented vigour. They supported free speech on their campuses, an end to American involvement in the war in Vietnam, increased civil rights for African Americans, and an expanded role for women in public affairs. It was, after all, the 1960s."

The Study of Collective Action and Social Movements

Robert didn't know it at the time, but by asking why students in Paris, Mexico City, and Berkeley rebelled while his fellow high-school students did not, he was raising the main question that animates the study of collective action and social movements. Under what social conditions do people act in unison to change, or resist change to, society? That is the main issue we address in this chapter.

We have divided the chapter into three sections:

Collective action occurs when people act in unison to bring about or resist social, political, and economic change.

1. We first discuss the social conditions leading to the formation of lynch mobs, riots, and other types of non-routine **collective action**. When people engage in collective action, they act in unison to bring about or resist social, political, and economic change (Schweingruber and McPhail, 1999: 453). Some collective actions are "routine" and others are "non-routine" (Useem, 1998: 219). Routine collective actions tend to be non-violent and follow established patterns of behaviour in bureaucratic social structures. For instance, when Mothers Against Drunk Driving (MADD) lobbies for tougher laws against driving under the influence of alcohol, when members of a community organize a campaign against abortion or for freedom of reproductive choice, and when workers form a union, they are typically engaging in routine collective action. Sometimes, however, "usual conventions cease to guide social action and people transcend, bypass, or subvert established institutional patterns and structures" (Turner and Killian, 1987: 3). On such occasions, people engage in non-routine collective action, which tends to be short-lived and sometimes violent. They may, for example, form mobs and engage in riots. Until the early 1970s, it was widely believed that people who engage in non-routine collective action lose their individuality and capacity for reason. Mobs and riots were often seen as wild and uncoordinated affairs, more like stampedes of frightened cattle than structured social processes. As you will see, however, sociologists later showed that this portrayal is an exaggeration. It deflects attention from the social organization and inner logic of extraordinary sociological events.

Social movements are collective attempts to change all or part of the political or social order by means of rioting, petitioning, striking, demonstrating, and establishing pressure groups, unions, and political parties.

2. We next outline the conditions underlying the formation of **social movements**. To varying degrees, social movements are enduring and bureaucratically organized collective attempts to change (or resist change to) part or all of the social order by petitioning, striking, demonstrating, and establishing lobbies, unions, and political parties. We will see that an adequate explanation of institutionalized protest also requires the introduction of a set of distinctively sociological issues. These concern the distribution of power in society and the framing of political issues in ways that appeal to many people.

3. Finally, we make some observations about the changing character of social movements. We argue that much of the history of social movements is the history of attempts by underprivileged groups to broaden their members' citizenship rights and increase the scope of protest from the local to the national to the global level.

We begin by considering the riot, a well-studied form of non-routine collective action.

NON-ROUTINE COLLECTIVE ACTION

The Vancouver Riot of 1907

Just after 9 p.m. on September 7, 1907, following a rousing chorus of "Rule Britannia," A. E. Fowler rose to address a crowd of several thousand people outside Vancouver City Hall. Fowler was secretary of the Seattle branch of the Asiatic Exclusion League, an organization of white trade unionists who were trying to convince the American and Canadian governments to keep Chinese, Japanese, Hindus, and Sikhs out of North America. Fowler was a fanatic. He was discharged from the U.S. Army for "unfitness by character and temperament" (quoted in Wynne, 1996). According to rumour, he spent time in the Washington State Asylum at Steilacoom. He certainly knew how to whip up a crowd's emotions. Just two days earlier, he had participated in an anti-Asian riot in Bellingham, Washington, 80 kilometres southeast of Vancouver. He described how 500 white men had invaded the lodgings of more than 1100 Sikh and Hindu mill workers under cover of night, dragged them half-naked from their beds, and beat them. Six of the victims were in hospital. Four hundred were in jail, guarded by police. Seven hundred and fifty had been driven across the U.S.–Canada border.

The Vancouver crowd liked what it heard. They cheered Fowler's impassioned description of the Bellingham violence as they waved little flags inscribed "A white Canada for us." According to one source, Fowler "whipped the crowd into a frenzy" by calling for a "straight-from-the-shoulder blow" against Asian immigration ("Chinese Community," 2001). Suddenly, someone threw a stone. It shattered a window in a nearby Chinese-owned shop. The crowd, its prejudices having been reinforced and inflamed by Fowler, took this as a cue. Its members surged uncontrollably into Vancouver's Chinatown, hurling insults, throwing rocks through windows, and beating and occasionally stabbing any Chinese people who were unable to flee or hide. With Chinatown reduced to a mass of broken glass, the crowd then moved on to the Japanese quarter, a few blocks away. The rioting continued for about three hours.

The next morning's papers in Toronto, Manchester, and London agreed on the main reason for the riot. The Toronto *Globe* said the riot was caused by "a gang of men from Bellingham." The *Manchester Guardian* said it had "proof of the correctness of the theory . . . that the anti-Japanese rioting in Vancouver was due to American agitators" (quoted in Wynne, 1996). In short, according to the papers, the riot resulted less from local social conditions than from the incitement of foreign hoodlums, the half-crazed Fowler foremost among them. Surely, the newspapers suggested, good white Canadian citizens could not be responsible for such an outrage.

Rare Books and Special Collections, University of British Columbia Library, Photo XXXVI-17

Aftermath of the Vancouver riot, 1907

Breakdown Theory: A Functionalist Approach to Collective Action

Until about 1970, most sociologists believed at least one of three conditions must be met for non-routine collective action, such as the 1907 Vancouver riot, to emerge. First, a group of people—leaders, led, or both—must be socially marginal or poorly integrated in society. Second, their norms must be strained or disrupted. Third, they must lose their capacity to act rationally by getting caught up in the supposedly inherent madness of crowds. Following Charles Tilly and his associates, we may group these three factors together as the **breakdown theory** of collective action. That is because all three factors assume collective action results from the disruption or breakdown of traditional norms, expectations, and patterns of behaviour (Tilly, Tilly, and Tilly, 1975: 4–6). At a more abstract level, breakdown theory may be seen as a variant of functionalism, for it regards collective action as a form of social imbalance that results from various institutions functioning improperly (see Chapter 1, A Sociological Compass). Specifically, most pre-1970 sociologists would have said that the Vancouver riot was caused by one or more of the following factors:

Breakdown theory suggests that social movements emerge when traditional norms and patterns of social organization are disrupted.

1. *The discontent of socially marginal people.* This was the factor Ontario and British newspapers emphasized when they singled out "foreign agitators" as the main cause of the disturbance. According to the papers, the Vancouver rioters were galvanized by people from outside the community; people who had little in common with the solid citizens of Vancouver; people who were skilled in whipping crowds into a frenzy and getting them to act in extraordinary and violent ways. Breakdown theorists often single out such socially marginal, outside agitators as a principal cause of riots and other forms of collective action.

Sometimes, however, breakdown theorists focus on the social marginality of the led. Often, they say, a large number of the ordinary people who participate in riots, mobs, lynchings, and the like are poorly integrated in society. For example, they may be recent migrants to the area, that is, people who are unsettled and unfamiliar with the peaceable norms and conventions of the community. Pre-1970 sociologists could have made a case for the presence of many such people in Vancouver. The completion of the Canadian Pacific Railway more than two decades earlier and the ongoing construction of other railways had stimulated rapid economic growth and urbanization in British Columbia. Construction, mining, and lumbering were all boom industries. It is at least possible (although it has not been demonstrated empirically) that a large proportion of the rioters in 1907 were poorly integrated newcomers.

2. *The violation of norms* (sometimes called **strain**) is the second factor that pre-1970 sociologists would have stressed in trying to account for the 1907 Vancouver riot (Smelser, 1963: 47–48, 75). Arguably, two norms were violated in Vancouver in 1907, one cultural, the other economic. With rapid economic growth stimulating demand for labour, the number of Asian immigrants in British Columbia grew quickly in the early part of the twentieth century. By 1907, one-quarter of male workers in the province were of Asian origin. Their languages, styles of dress, religions, foods—in short, their entire way of life—offended many residents, who were of British origin. They regarded the Asian immigrants as "a threat to their cultural integrity" (Citizenship and Immigration Canada, 2000). From their point of view, Asian-Canadian cultural practices were violations of fundamental Anglo-Canadian norms.

> **Strain** refers to breakdowns in traditional norms that precede collective action.

A second source of strain may have been the result of rapid economic growth causing British Columbians' material expectations to grow out of line with reality. According to proponents of breakdown theory, it is not grinding poverty, or **absolute deprivation**, that generates riots and other forms of collective action so much as **relative deprivation**. Relative deprivation refers to the growth of an intolerable gap between the social rewards people expect to receive and those they actually receive. Social rewards are widely valued goods, such as money, education, security, prestige, and so forth. Accordingly, people are most likely to engage in collective action when rising expectations (brought on by, say, rapid economic growth and migration) exceed social rewards (sometimes brought on by economic recession or war; Davies, 1969; Gurr, 1970). Neither recession nor war affected Vancouver in 1907. But in that era of heady economic expansion, economic expectations may have risen beyond what society was able to provide. Hence the mounting frustration of Vancouver's workers that left them open to the influence of men like Fowler.

> **Absolute deprivation** is a condition of extreme poverty.

> **Relative deprivation** is an intolerable gap between the social rewards people feel they deserve and the social rewards they expect to receive.

3. *The inherent irrationality of crowd behaviour* is the third factor likely to be stressed in any pre-1970 explanation of the Vancouver riot. Gustave Le Bon, an early French interpreter of crowd behaviour, wrote that an isolated person might be a cultivated individual. In a crowd, however, the individual is transformed into a "barbarian," a "creature acting by instinct" possessing the "spontaneity, violence," and "ferocity" of "primitive beings" (Le Bon, 1969 [1895]: 28). Le Bon argued that this transformation occurs because people lose their individuality and willpower when they join a crowd. Simultaneously, they gain a sense of invincible group power that derives from the crowd's sheer size. Their feeling of invincibility allows them to yield to instincts they would normally hold in check. Moreover, if people remain in a crowd long enough, they enter something like a hypnotic state. This leaves them open to the suggestions of manipulative leaders and ensures that extreme passions spread through the crowd like a contagious disease. (Sociologists call Le Bon's argument the **contagion** theory of crowd behaviour.) For all these reasons, Le Bon held, people in crowds are often able to perform extraordinary and sometimes outrageous acts. "Extraordinary" and "outrageous" certainly describe the actions of the citizens of Vancouver in 1907.

> **Contagion** is the process by which extreme passions supposedly spread rapidly through a crowd like a contagious disease.

Assessing Breakdown Theory

Can social marginality, contagion, and strain fully explain what happened in Vancouver in 1907? Can breakdown theory adequately account for collective action in general? The short answer is no. Increasingly since 1970, sociologists have uncovered flaws in all three elements of breakdown theory and proposed alternative frameworks for understanding collective action. To help you appreciate the need for these alternative frameworks, let us reconsider the three elements of breakdown theory in the context of the Vancouver riot.

Social Marginality

Although it is true that Fowler and some of his associates were "outside agitators," the plain fact is that "if there had not been many local people who were deeply concerned about Oriental immigration, no amount of propaganda from the outside would have aroused the crowds" (Wynne, 1996). Moreover, the parade of 7000 to 9000 people who marched to city hall to hear Fowler's incendiary speech was organized locally by Vancouver trade unionists, ex-servicemen, and clergymen: pillars of the community. This fits a general pattern. In most cases of collective action, leaders and early joiners tend to be well-integrated members of their communities, not socially marginal outsiders (Brym, 2010a [1980]; Brym and Economakis, 1994; Economakis and Brym, 1995; Lipset, 1971 [1951]).

Contagion

No evidence suggests that the violence of September 7, 1907, was premeditated. But neither were the day's events spontaneous and unorganized acts of "contagion." A Vancouver branch of the Asiatic Exclusion League had been formed more than a month earlier and held three meetings before September 7. Two hundred people attended its third meeting on August 23. They carefully mapped out the route for the parade, ending at city hall. They decided to hire a brass band. They arranged for the manufacture of flags emblazoned with racist slogans. They arranged to mobilize various local organizations to participate in the parade. They decided who would be invited to speak at city hall and what demands would be made of the government. Sophisticated planning went into organizing the day's events.

As the Vancouver example shows, and as much research on riots, crowds, and demonstrations has confirmed, non-routine collective action may be wild and violent, but it is usually socially structured. In the first place, non-routine collective action is socially structured by the predispositions that unite crowd members and predate their collective action. Thus, if the Vancouver rioters had not shared racist attitudes, they never would have organized and assembled for the parade and engaged in the riot in the first place (Berk, 1974; Couch, 1968; McPhail, 1991). Second, non-routine collective action is socially structured by ideas and norms that emerge in the crowd itself, such as the idea to throw rocks through the windows of Chinese- and Japanese-owned shops in Vancouver (Turner and Killian, 1987). Third, non-routine collective action is structured by the degree to which different types of participants adhere to emergent and preexisting norms. Leaders, rank-and-file participants, and bystanders adhere to such norms to varying degrees (Zurcher and Snow, 1981). Fourth, preexisting social relationships among participants structure non-routine collective action. For instance, relatives, friends, and acquaintances are more likely than strangers are to cluster together and interact in riots, crowds, demonstrations, and lynchings (McPhail, 1991; McPhail and Wohlstein, 1983; Weller and Quarantelli, 1973). Thus, non-routine collective action is socially organized in a number of ways, none of which is highlighted by focusing on contagion.

Strain

Contrary to the argument of many breakdown theorists, a large body of post-1970 research shows that, in general, levels of deprivation, whether absolute or relative, are not commonly associated with the frequency or intensity of outbursts of collective action, either in Canada or elsewhere (McPhail, 1994; Torrance, 1986: 115–45). In other words, although feelings of deprivation are undoubtedly common among people who engage in collective action, they are also common among people who do not engage in collective action. Deprivation may therefore be viewed as a necessary, but not a sufficient, condition for collective action. For example, although Asian immigration upset many Anglo-Canadians in Vancouver, the roots of the 1907 riot ran deeper than the violation of their cultural norms. They were embedded in the way the local labour market was organized. Typically, where low-wage workers of one race and high-wage workers of another race compete for the same jobs, racist attitudes develop or are reinforced because high-wage workers resent the presence of low-wage competitors (see Chapter 10, Race and Ethnicity). Conflict almost inevitably results. This happened when African Americans first migrated from the South to northern and western American cities in the early twentieth century. In Chicago, New York, and Los Angeles, the split labour market fuelled deep resentment, animosity, and even anti-black riots on the part of working-class whites (Bonacich, 1972). Similarly, the 1907 Vancouver riot was ultimately the result of the way social life and, in particular, the labour market were organized in the city.

We conclude that non-routine collective action is a two-sided phenomenon. Breakdown theory alerts us to one side. Collective action is partly a reaction to the violation of norms that threatened to *disorganize* traditional social life. But breakdown theory diverts attention from the other side of the phenomenon. Collective action is also a response to the *organization* of social life. And so we arrive at the starting point of post-1970 theories of collective action and social movements. For the past four decades, most students of the subject have recognized that collective action is often not a short-term reaction to disorganization and deprivation. Instead, it is a long-term attempt to correct perceived injustice that requires a sound social-organizational basis.

Summing Up

- Breakdown theory attributes non-routine collective action to the discontent of socially marginal people, the violation of core norms ("strain"), and the inherent rationality of crowds. However, research shows that none of these factors is correlated with non-routine collective action.

SOCIAL MOVEMENTS

According to breakdown theory, people typically engage in non-routine collective action soon after social breakdown occurs. In this view, rapid urbanization, industrialization, mass migration, unemployment, and war often lead to a buildup of deprivations or the violation of important norms. Under these conditions, people soon take to the streets.

In reality, however, people often find it difficult to turn their discontent into an enduring social movement. Social movements emerge from collective action only when the discontented succeed in building up a more or less stable membership and organizational base. Once this is accomplished, they typically move from an exclusive focus on short-lived actions, such as demonstrations and riots, to more enduring and routine activities. Such activities include establishing a publicity bureau, founding a newspaper, and running for public office. These and similar endeavours require hiring personnel to work full-time on various movement activities. Thus, the creation of a movement bureaucracy takes time, energy, and money. On these grounds alone, we should not expect social breakdown to result quickly in the formation of a social movement.

Solidarity Theory: A Conflict Approach

Research conducted since 1970 shows that, in fact, social breakdown often does not have the expected short-term effect. That is because several social-structural factors modify the effects of social breakdown on collective action. For example, Charles Tilly and his associates studied collective action in France, Italy, and Germany in the nineteenth and twentieth centuries (Lodhi and Tilly, 1973; Snyder and Tilly, 1972; Tilly, 1979a; Tilly, Tilly, and Tilly, 1975). They systematically read newspapers, government reports, and other sources so they could analyze a representative sample of strikes, demonstrations, and acts of collective violence. (They defined acts of collective violence as events in which groups of people seized or damaged other people or property.) They measured social breakdown by collecting data on rates of urban growth, suicide, major crime, prices, wages, and the value of industrial production. Breakdown theory would be supported if they found that levels of social breakdown rose and fell with rates of collective action. They did not.

As the top panel of Table 21.1 shows for France, nearly all the correlations between collective violence and indicators of breakdown are close to zero. This means that acts of collective violence did not increase in the wake of mounting social breakdown, nor did they decrease in periods marked by less breakdown.

Significantly, however, Tilly and his associates found stronger correlations between collective violence and some other variables. You will find them in the bottom panel of Table 21.1. These correlations hint at the three fundamental lessons of the **solidarity theory** of social movements, a variant of conflict theory (see Chapter 1, A Sociological Compass) and the most influential approach to the subject since the 1970s:

1. Inspecting Table 21.1, we first observe that collective violence in France increased when the number of union members rose. It decreased when the number of union members fell. Why? Because union organization gave workers more power, and that increased their capacity to pursue their aims—if necessary, by demonstrating, striking, and engaging in collective violence. We can generalize from the French case as follows: Most collective action is part of a power struggle. The struggle usually

Solidarity theory suggests that social movements are social organizations that emerge when potential members can mobilize resources, take advantage of new political opportunities, and avoid high levels of social control by authorities.

	Correlation with Frequency of Collective Violence
Breakdown variables	
Number of suicides	.00
Number of major crimes	−.16
Deprivation variables	
Manufactured goods prices	.05
Food prices	.08
Value of industrial production	.10
Real wages	.03
Organizational variable	
Number of union members	.40
Political process variable	
National elections	.17
State repression variable	
Days in jail	−.22

TABLE 21.1

Correlates of Collective Violence, France, 1830–1960

Notes: Correlations can range from −1.0 (indicating a perfect, inversely proportional relationship) to 1.0 (indicating a perfect, directly proportional relationship). A correlation of zero indicates no relationship. The correlation between the major crime and the rate of collective violence is negative, but it should be positive according to breakdown theory. The exact years covered by each correlation vary.

Source: Adapted from Tilly, Tilly, and Tilly, 1975: 81–82.

Resource mobilization refers to the process by which social movements crystallize because of the increasing organizational, material, and other resources of movement members.

intensifies as groups whose members feel disadvantaged become more powerful relative to other groups. How do disadvantaged groups become more powerful? By gaining new members, becoming better organized, and increasing their access to scarce resources, such as money, jobs, and means of communication (Bierstedt, 1974). French unionization is thus only one example of **resource mobilization**, a process by which groups engage in more collective action as their power increases because of their growing size and increasing organizational, material, and other resources (Gamson, 1975; Jenkins, 1983; McCarthy and Zald, 1977; Oberschall, 1973; Tilly, 1978; Zald and McCarthy, 1979).

2. Table 21.1 also shows that there was somewhat more collective violence in France when national elections were held. Again, why? Because elections gave people new political opportunities to protest. By providing a focus for discontent and a chance to put new representatives with new policies in positions of authority, election campaigns often serve as invitations to engage in collective action. Chances for protest also emerge when influential allies offer support, when ruling political alignments become unstable, and when elite groups are divided and come into conflict with one another (Tarrow, 1994: 86–9; Useem, 1998). Said differently, collective action takes place and social movements crystallize not just when disadvantaged groups become more powerful but also when privileged groups and the institutions they control are divided and therefore become weaker. As economist John Kenneth Galbraith once said about the weakness of the Russian ruling class at the time of the 1917 revolution, if someone kicks in a rotten door, some credit has to be given to the door. In short, this second important insight of solidarity theory links the timing of collective action and social movement formation to the emergence of new **political opportunities** (McAdam, 1982; Piven and Cloward, 1977; Tarrow, 1994).

Political opportunities for collective action and social movement growth occur during election campaigns, when influential allies offer insurgents support, when ruling political alignments become unstable, and when elite groups become divided and conflict with one another.

3. The third main lesson of solidarity theory is that government reactions to protest influence subsequent protest (see Box 21.1). Specifically, governments can try to lower the frequency and intensity of protest by taking various **social control** measures (Oberschall, 1973: 242–83). These measures include making concessions to protesters, co-opting the most troublesome leaders (for example, by appointing them advisers), and violently repressing collective action. The last point explains the modest correlation in Table 21.1 between frequency of collective violence and governments throwing more people into jail for longer periods. In France, more violent protest often resulted in more state repression. However, the correlation is modest because social control measures do not always have the desired effect. For instance, if grievances are very deeply felt, and yielding to protesters' demands greatly increases their hopes, resources, and political opportunities, government concessions may encourage protesters to press their claims further. And although the firm and decisive use of force usually stops protest, using force moderately or inconsistently often backfires. That is because unrest typically intensifies when protesters are led to believe that the government is weak or indecisive (Piven and Cloward, 1977: 27–36; Tilly, Tilly, and Tilly, 1975: 244).

Social control refers to methods of ensuring conformity, for example, the means by which authorities seek to contain collective action through co-optation, concessions, and coercion.

Discussions of strain, deprivation, and contagion dominated analyses of collective action and social movements before 1970. Afterward, analyses of resource mobilization, political opportunities, and social control dominated the field. Let us now make the new ideas more concrete. We do so by analyzing the ups and downs of one of the most important social movements in twentieth-century Canada, the union movement, and its major weapon, the strike.

Strikes and the Union Movement in Canada

You can appreciate the significance of solidarity theory by considering patterns of strike activity in Canada. When blue-collar and white-collar workers go out on strike, they withhold their labour to extract concessions from employers or governments in the form of

BOX 21.1

It's Your Choice

STATE SURVEILLANCE OF DEMONSTRATIONS

On June 15, 2000, members of the Ontario Coalition Against Poverty (OCAP) organized a demonstration of about 1000 people in front of the provincial legislature at Queen's Park to protest the policies of Mike Harris's Progressive Conservative government toward the poor and homeless. It didn't take long before a violent confrontation developed between protesters and the police. Gary Morton, one of the demonstrators, described the events as follows:

OCAP versus then Ontario Premier Mike Harris, Toronto, June 15, 2000

CP Picture Archive/Maclean's Photo/Phill Snel

An angry crowd of protesters ... marches across the city to the legislature at Queen's Park. They make noise, bang drums and chant. When they arrive, huge numbers of riot police meet them.... [T]he protesters send a delegation to the barricades at the front. Their demand—that they be allowed to address the legislature on homeless issues. The response is that no such thing will be allowed and no representative of the Harris Government will be speaking to them. The delegation informs the crowd of this and they surge forward to [the] barricades.... The people at the front grab the barricades and walk backward with them, opening a hole for the crowd to get through. Then all hell breaks loose. Gas smoke rolls and police charge out swinging batons. Some protesters struggle with them and others throw a few things like small water bottles. Horseback cops follow up, riding in from the north to force the crowd back and then swinging back in from the south. Between the horse sweeps the riot cops charge out and then get pushed back in. The police slowly gain ground. People are being picked off and beaten and cops begin to charge viciously into the larger body of peaceful protesters. At this point many people, myself included, begin to throw anything they can at the police. Bottles of water, mud and stones from the garden, picket signs. Brutality increases; anarchists tear apart a sidewalk and throw the chunks of stone at police. Horse charges swing in through the grassy area of the park and as the fight continues for some time we get forced out on the road, which we block. . . . The police are now saying that they are going to review their videos frame by frame. (Morton, 2000)

The videos to which Morton refers came from seven cameras police set up to record the demonstration. In addition, police had a still photographer and several plainclothes officers with disposable cameras on duty. Two cameras belonging to Queen's Park security officers were also rolling during the melee. Finally, after the demonstration, the police seized film and videotape of the demonstration from television networks and newspapers.

What effect might police surveillance of demonstrations have on collective action? In the first place, if journalists fear their film and videos might be seized, they may be less likely to produce objective news reports. For example, a journalist might be disinclined to film a demonstrator being beaten by the police knowing that the film could be edited and used to identify and prosecute the demonstrator (Canadian Journalists for Free Expression, 2000). Moreover, according to sociologist Gary Marx, surveillance systems can be "used against those with the 'wrong' political beliefs; against racial, ethnic, or religious minorities; and against those with lifestyles that offend the majority" (quoted in Boal, 1998). One journalist comments: "Social psychologists say that taping political events can affect a participant's self-image, since being surveilled is unconsciously associated with criminality. Ordinary citizens shy away from politics when they see activists subjected to scrutiny. As this footage is splayed across the nightly news, everyone gets the meta-message: hang with dissenters and you'll end up in a police video" (Boal, 1998). In short, police surveillance of demonstrations may limit dissent and the free expression of political opinion.

What do you think? In the interest of maintaining law and order, should the police be entirely free to record demonstrations by using cameras? Should they be allowed to seize film and videos from journalists? Or do such actions infringe the fundamental democratic rights of both the media and the citizenry?

higher wages and improved social welfare benefits. How do resource mobilization, political opportunity, and social control influence the willingness of workers to challenge the authority of employers and governments in this way?

Resource Mobilization

Consider first the effect of resource mobilization on the frequency of strikes. Research shows that in Canada between the mid-1940s and the mid-1970s, strike activity was high when (1) unemployment was low, (2) union membership was high, and (3) governments were generous in their provision of social welfare benefits. Low unemployment indicates a strong economy. Workers are inclined to strike when business activity is robust because they know employers and governments can afford to make concessions. (Employers make bigger profits and governments collect more taxes during economic booms.) A high level of unionization is also conducive to more strike activity because unions provide workers with leadership, strike funds, and coordination. Thus, as resource mobilization principles suggest, strong social ties among workers (as indicated by a high level of unionization) and access to jobs and money (as indicated by a booming economy) increase challenges to authority (as indicated by strikes).[1]

Figure 21.1 shows the pattern of strike activity in Canada between the end of World War II and 2008. It adds substance to the resource mobilization approach. Until 1974, the trend in strike activity was upward. In fact, in the 1970s, Canada was the most strike-prone country in the world. This was a period of growing prosperity, low unemployment, expanding state benefits, and increasing unionization. With access to more organizational and material resources, workers challenged authority increasingly more often in the three decades after World War II.

In 1973, however, economic crisis struck. As a result of war and revolution in the Middle East, oil prices tripled, and then tripled again at the end of the decade. Inflation increased and unemployment rose. Soon, the government was strapped for funds and had to borrow heavily to maintain social welfare programs. Eventually, the debt burden was so heavy the government felt obliged to cut various social welfare programs. At the same time, federal and provincial and territorial governments introduced laws and regulations limiting the right of some workers to strike and putting a cap on the wage gains that workers could demand. Unionization reached a peak in 1978, stabilized, and then began to decline (see Figure 21.2).

FIGURE 21.1

Weighted Frequency of Strikes, Canada, 1946–2008

Sources: International Labour Organization (2010); *Labour Organizations in Canada* (1973: xxii-xxiii); *1994–1995 Directory of Labour Organizations in Canada* (1995: xiii); *1998 Directory of Labour Organizations in Canada* (1998: 15); "Chronological Perspective on Work Stoppage in Canada" (1999, 2001a, 2001b); *Strikes and Lockouts in Canada 1968* (1970: 12–13); *Strikes and Lockouts in Canada 1985* (1985: 9); *Workplace Information Directorate* (1996).

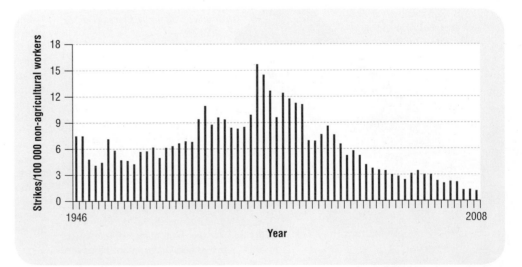

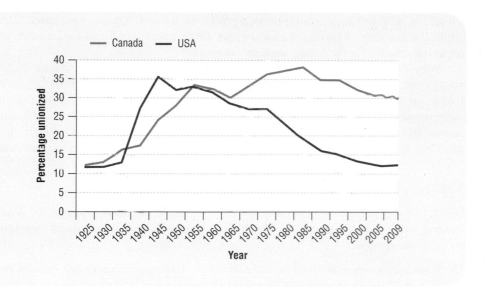

FIGURE 21.2

Percentage of
Non-agricultural Workers
Unionized, Canada and
United States, 1925–2009

Sources: Human Resources and Skills
Development Canada (2010); *Labour
Organizations in Canada 1972*, 1973:
xxii–xxiii; *1994–1995 Directory of
Labour Organizations in Canada*,
1995: xiii; *1998 Directory of Labour
Organizations* in Canada, 1998: 15;
U.S. Bureau of Labor Statistics,
1998, 1999, 2001.

Strike action was made even more difficult when Canada signed the free trade deal with the United States and Mexico in 1994. It was now possible for some employers to threaten to relocate to the United States or Mexico in the face of protracted strikes. Thus, in the post-1973 climate, the organizational and material resources of workers fell. As a result, strike activity plummeted. In 1974, nearly 16 strikes took place for every 100 000 Canadian non-agricultural workers. By 2008, that number had fallen to just over 1 (Brym, 2008).

Political Opportunities

Comparing Canada with the United States allows us to highlight the effect of *political opportunities* on the health of the union movement. These two cases illustrate that opportunities for union growth are greater when privileged groups and the institutions they control are divided and therefore become weaker. Opportunities for union growth are fewer when privileged groups are socially cohesive and are backed by strong institutions.

The United States and Canada have similar industrial and occupational structures. As the world's two largest trading partners, and linked by a free trade agreement, they are subject to most of the same economic forces. Yet, as Figure 21.2 shows, trends in **union density** (the percentage of the non-agricultural labour force that is unionized) started to diverge in the mid-1960s. In 2009, 12.3 percent of non-agricultural employees in the United States were members of a union. In Canada, the figure was 29.9 percent. Why?

John F. Kennedy won the closely contested American presidential election of 1960 partly because of the union movement's support. Because of his victory, government employees were awarded the right to unionize in 1961. Their rights were sharply restricted, however. Striking, bargaining collectively over wages and benefits, and compulsory membership were not allowed. Therefore, public-sector unions did not become a very effective or popular means for furthering employee interests.

The situation in Canada in the early 1960s was different. A new pro-labour political party, the New Democratic Party (NDP), was established in Canada in 1961 with the support of the union movement. The NDP gained enough popularity among voters to be able to exert considerable influence over government policy. In fact, in the mid-1960s, the ruling Liberal Party would have lost office without NDP support. The NDP used its political leverage to convince the government to extend full union rights to public-sector workers, including the right to strike and bargain collectively. Government employees soon joined unions in droves—and to a considerably greater extent than in the United States. Moreover, partly as

Union density is the number of union members in a given location as a percentage of non-agricultural workers. It measures the organizational power of unions.

a result of NDP influence, restrictions on private-sector unionization were eased. Thus, in Canada, union density increased after the mid-1960s because political forces made unions attractive vehicles for furthering workers' interests.

Why, then, has the union movement been more successful in Canada than in the United States since the 1960s? Because in the United States a unified political establishment was able to prevent the union movement from gaining rights that would make it attractive to more workers. Meanwhile, in Canada, a more divided political establishment could not prevent the creation of a legal environment that was favourable to union growth. In both cases, we see how political opportunities affect the growth or decline of social movements.

Social Control

Finally, we turn to the most disruptive and violent strike in Canadian history—the Winnipeg General Strike of 1919—because it illustrates well three features of the use of *social control* on social movements:

1. *If authorities show indecision or weakness, movement partisans often become bolder.* In April 1918, three unions of Winnipeg city employees walked off the job, demanding higher wages. A month later, the strikers and their employers had nearly hammered out a settlement. Just before signing off on the deal, however, the Winnipeg city council added a clause demanding that city workers pledge never to go on strike again. In angry reaction, nearly all city employees walked off the job. The same day, the city council capitulated. The striking workers got almost everything they demanded. After many bitter defeats, this victory convinced Winnipeg's workers they could get what they wanted by participating in a general strike, that is, a strike in which all employees walk off the job. The city council's capitulation emboldened the workers (Bercuson, 1974: 7).

2. The second thing the Winnipeg strike teaches us about the use of social control on social movements is that *violence, especially the most extreme forms of violence, is most often initiated by authorities, not movement partisans.* On May 15, 1919, negotiations broke down over building and metalworkers' demands for union recognition and higher wages. They called a general strike. The next morning, the city was paralyzed. Nearly all workers

The Winnipeg General Strike of 1919 was the most disruptive and violent strike in Canadian history.

National Archives of Canada/PA163001

walked off the job. The strike leaders made every effort to keep the streets peaceful. The police, who supported the strike, even agreed to continue working to help maintain law and order. The city council, however, was opposed to having pro-strike police officers on duty. So they fired the entire police force, replacing them with a large group of untrained "special police" who were hostile to the strike. The special police celebrated their first day of service by riding their horses and swinging their batons into a crowd listening to a speech downtown. That was the first act of violence during the Winnipeg General Strike, but it was by no means the last. In addition to the special police, a mobile military force of 800 men armed with rifles and machine guns was recruited and trained to deal with the strikers. On the afternoon of Saturday, June 21, that is just what they did. Striking workers had been gathering downtown to hold a parade in defiance of a ban issued by the mayor. They spotted a streetcar driven by a scab (replacement worker), cut the electricity powering it, smashed its windows, slashed its seats, and set the interior on fire. Fifty-four Royal North-West Mounted Police on horses and 36 in trucks were dispatched to break up the crowd. They charged twice. The crowd responded by throwing rocks and bottles. The Mounties then opened fire on the crowd and continued firing for several minutes. One worker was killed and many more were wounded. There is no evidence that workers fired any shots (Bercuson, 1974: 27). As is usually the case when we compare the violence exercised by authorities with the violence exercised by movement partisans, the authorities came out on top (Tilly, Tilly, and Tilly, 1975).

3. Finally, the Winnipeg strike teaches us that *violent repression can still discontent, at least for a time*. That was certainly the case in Winnipeg. Four days after "Bloody Saturday," as June 21 came to be known, the Strike Committee called off the walkout, the strikers having failed to achieve any of their objectives. It took another quarter-century of strikes, many of them bitterly fought, before a larger and more powerful Canadian working class achieved the main demand of the Winnipeg General Strike and won the legal right to form unions.

Summing Up

- Solidarity theory focuses on how shifts in the balance of power between disadvantaged and privileged groups, the opening and closing of political opportunities, and the exercise of social control by authorities influence social movement formation.

FRAMING DISCONTENT: A SYMBOLIC INTERACTIONIST APPROACH

As we have seen, solidarity theory helps to explain the emergence of many social movements. Still, the rise of a social movement sometimes takes solidarity theorists by surprise. So does the failure of an aggrieved group to press its claims by means of collective action. It seems, therefore, that something lies between (1) the capacity of disadvantaged people to mobilize resources for collective action and (2) the recruitment of a substantial number of movement members. That "something" is **frame alignment** (Benford, 1997; Carroll and Ratner, 1996a, 1996b; Goffman, 1974; Snow, Rochford Jr., Worden, and Benford, 1986; Valocchi, 1996). Frame alignment is the process by which social movement leaders make their activities, ideas, and goals congruent with the interests, beliefs, and values of potential new recruits to their movement—or fail to do so. Thanks to the efforts of scholars operating mainly in the symbolic interactionist tradition (see Chapter 1, A Sociological Compass), frame alignment has recently become the subject of sustained sociological investigation (see Box 21.2 on page 536).

Frame alignment is the process by which individual interests, beliefs, and values become congruent and complementary with the activities, goals, and ideology of a social movement.

BOX 21.2

Sociology at the Movies

THE DAY AFTER TOMORROW

Most summers, Hollywood releases a disaster movie in which a highly implausible catastrophe serves as the backdrop for heroism and hope. Audiences return home momentarily frightened but ultimately safe in the knowledge that the chance of any such cataclysm is vanishingly remote.

The Day after Tomorrow follows the usual script. The movie opens with a sequence of bizarre meteorological events. A section of ice nearly the size of Prince Edward Island breaks off the Antarctic ice cap. Snow falls in New Delhi. Hail the size of grapefruits pounds Tokyo. Enter Jack Hall (Dennis Quaid), a scientist whose research suggests an explanation: Sudden climate change is a very real possibility. The idea becomes a political football when the vice-president of the United States ridicules it, but once torrential rains and a tidal wave flood New York City, Hall's theories are vindicated. In a matter of days, temperatures plummet—at one point falling 10 degrees Fahrenheit a minute to 150 degrees Fahrenheit below the freezing point. The entire Northern Hemisphere is plunged into a new ice age. Almost everyone freezes to death in the northern United States, while millions of desperate southerners flee into Mexico.

The Day after Tomorrow is based on the hypothesis that the melting of the polar ice caps because of global warming may be adding enough fresh water to the oceans to disrupt the flow of the Gulf Stream, the ocean current that carries warm water

20th Century Fox/Courtesy Everett Collection/CP Picture Archive

Scene from *The Day after Tomorrow*

up the east coast of North America and the west coast of Europe. Computer simulations suggest that decreased salinity could push the Gulf Stream southward, causing average winter temperatures to drop by 5.6 degrees Celsius in northeastern Canada, the United States, and other parts of the Northern Hemisphere.

A recent Pentagon study suggests that such climate change could cause droughts, storms, flooding, border raids, large-scale illegal migration from poor regions, and even war between nuclear powers over scarce food, drinking water, and energy (Joyce and Keigwin, 2004; Stipp, 2003). *The Day after Tomorrow* greatly exaggerates the suddenness and magnitude of what scientists mean by abrupt climate change. "Abrupt" can mean centuries to climatologists, and temperature drops of 10 degrees Fahrenheit a minute are

pure fantasy. Still, at the movie's core lies an ominous possibility.

The Day after Tomorrow also teaches us an important sociological lesson about the framing of issues by social movements and their opponents. Environmental problems do not become social issues spontaneously. They are socially constructed in what might be called a "framing war." Just as Jack Hall and the vice-president spar over the credibility of Hall's prediction of sudden climate change, so do groups with different interests dispute environmental problems, framing them in different ways so as to win over public opinion.

The Day after Tomorrow became involved in the framing war because in the months leading up to the release of the movie, environmentalists started piggybacking their message on it. They bombarded journalists with emails explaining global warming and offering interviews with leading scientists on the subject. Newspapers and magazines around the world subsequently carried stories on the issue. Environmentalists then distributed flyers to moviegoers as they left theatres (Houpt, 2004). In this way, *The Day after Tomorrow* became not just another disaster movie but also part of the framing war around one of the major environmental issues of the day.

Examples of Frame Alignment

Frame alignment can be encouraged in several ways. For example:

1. Social movement leaders can reach out to other organizations that, they believe, contain people who may be sympathetic to their movement's cause. Thus, leaders of an anti-nuclear movement may use the mass media, telephone campaigns, and direct mail to appeal to feminist, anti-racist, and environmental organizations. In doing so, they assume these organizations are likely to have members who would agree at least in general terms with the anti-nuclear platform.

2. Movement activists can stress popular values that have so far not featured prominently in the thinking of potential recruits. They can also elevate the importance of positive beliefs about the movement and what it stands for. For instance, in trying to win new recruits, movement members might emphasize the seriousness of the social movement's purpose. They might analyze the causes of the problem the movement is trying to solve in a clear and convincing way. Or they might stress the likelihood of the movement's success. By doing so, they can increase the movement's appeal to potential recruits and perhaps win them over to the cause.

3. Social movements can stretch their objectives and activities to win recruits who are not initially sympathetic to the movement's original aims. This may involve a "watering down" of the movement's ideals. Alternatively, movement leaders may decide to take action calculated to appeal to non-sympathizers on grounds that have little or nothing to do with the movement's purpose. When rock, punk, or reggae bands play at nuclear disarmament rallies or gay liberation festivals, it is not necessarily because the music is relevant to the movement's goals. Nor do bands play just because movement members want to be entertained. The purpose is also to attract non-members. Once attracted by the music, however, non-members may make friends and acquaintances in the movement and then be encouraged to attend a more serious-minded meeting.

As we see, then, there are many ways in which social movements can make their ideas more appealing to a larger number of people. However, movements must also confront the fact that their opponents routinely seek to do just the opposite. That is, although movements seek to align their goals, ideas, and activities with the way potential recruits

The Live 8 concert to fight global poverty in Barrie, Ontario, July 2005, featured Bruce Cockburn, Kevin Hearn of the Barenaked Ladies, Neil Young, Gordon Lightfoot, and many other Canadian music stars. When bands play at protest rallies or festivals, it is not just for entertainment and not just because the music is relevant to a social movement's goals. The bands also attract non-members to the movement. This is one way of framing a social movement's goals to make them appealing to non-members.

CP Photo/Acrian Wyld

frame issues, their adversaries seek to *disalign* the way issues are framed by movements and potential recruits.

The B.C. Forest Alliance provides a good illustration of this process (Doyle, Elliott, and Tindall, 1997). Launched in British Columbia in 1991, the B.C. Forest Alliance was created and bankrolled by a group of senior forest industry executives and guided by the world's largest public relations firm. Its goal was to counter the province's environmental movement. It did so in two main ways. First, in its TV and print ads, the alliance claimed it represented the "middle ground" in the debate between forest companies and environmentalists. In practice, the alliance rarely criticized forest companies while it routinely characterized environmentalists as dope-smoking hippies with untenable ideas, such as shutting down the entire forest industry. Actually, very few environmentalists hold such extreme opinions, and research shows that the middle class in British Columbia broadly supports environmental groups. The second way the alliance sought to counter the environmental movement was by arguing more environmentalism means fewer jobs. This was a huge oversimplification. Job losses in the forest industry were also caused by the introduction of new technologies in some areas, aging equipment in others, First Nations land claims, and resource depletion through overharvesting and inadequate reforestation.

Muddying the waters in this way is typical of social movement opponents. Frame alignment should therefore be viewed as a conflict-ridden process in which social movement partisans and their opponents use the resources at their disposal to compete for the way in which potential recruits and sympathizers view movement issues.

An Application of Frame Alignment Theory: Back to 1968

Frame alignment theory stresses the strategies employed by movement members to recruit non-members who are like-minded, apathetic, or even initially opposed to the movement's goals. Resource mobilization theory focuses on the broad social-structural conditions that facilitate the emergence of social movements. One theory usefully supplements the other.

The two theories certainly help clarify the 1968 high-school incident described at the beginning of this chapter. In light of our discussion, it seems evident that two main factors prevented Robert Brym from influencing his classmates when he spoke to them about the dangers of industrial pollution from the local pulp-and-paper mill.

First, he lived in a poor and relatively unindustrialized region of Canada where people had few resources they could mobilize on their own behalf. Per capita income and the level of unionization were among the lowest of any state, province, or territory in North America. The unemployment rate was among the highest. In contrast, K. C. Irving, who owned the pulp-and-paper mill, was so powerful that most people in the region could not even conceive of the need to rebel against the conditions of life he created for them. He owned most of the industrial establishments in the province. Every daily newspaper, most of the weeklies, all of the TV stations, and most of the radio stations were his, too. Little wonder people rarely heard a critical word about his operations. Many people believed that Irving could make or break local governments single-handedly. Should we therefore be surprised that mere high-school students refused to take him on? In their reluctance, Robert's fellow students were only mimicking their parents, who, on the whole, were as powerless as Irving was mighty (Brym, 1979).

Second, many of Robert's classmates did not share his sense of injustice. Most of them regarded Irving as the great provider. They thought his pulp-and-paper mill, as well as his myriad other industrial establishments, gave many people jobs. They regarded that fact as more important for their lives and the lives of their families than the pollution problem Robert raised. Frame alignment theory suggests Robert needed to figure out ways to build bridges between their understanding and his. He did not. Therefore, he received an unsympathetic hearing.

We can briefly summarize what we have learned about the causes of collective action and social movement formation with the aid of Figure 21.3.

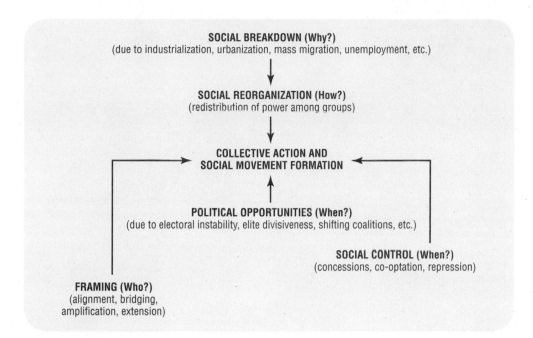

FIGURE 21.3
Determinants of Collective
Action and Social Movement
Formation

Summing Up

- Frame alignment theory analyzes the process by which individual interests, beliefs, and values become congruent and complementary with the activities, goals, and ideology of a social movement or fail to do so, thereby facilitating or preventing the formation of social movements.

THE HISTORY AND FUTURE OF SOCIAL MOVEMENTS

The Past 300 Years

In 1700, social movements were typically small, localized, and violent. In Europe, poor residents of a city might riot against public officials in reaction to a rise in bread prices or taxes. Peasants on an estate might burn their landowner's barns (or their landowner) in response to his demand for a larger share of the crop. However, as the state grew, the form of protest changed. The state started taxing nearly all its citizens at higher and higher rates as government services expanded. It imposed a uniform language and often a common curriculum in a compulsory education system. It drafted most young men for army service. It instilled in its citizens all the ideological trappings of modern nationalism, from anthems to flags to historical myths.

As the state came to encompass most aspects of life, social movements changed in three ways. First, they became national in scope. That is, they typically directed themselves against central governments rather than against local targets. Second, their membership grew. This was partly because potential recruits were now literate and could communicate by using the printed word. In addition, big new social settings—factories,

In medieval Europe, social movements were small, localized, and violent. For example, a medieval French historian reported that in 1358, "there were very strange and terrible happenings in several parts of the kingdom.... They began when some of the men from the country towns came together in the Beauvais region. They had no leaders and at first they numbered scarcely a hundred. One of them got up and said that the nobility of France ... were disgracing and betraying the realm, and that it would be a good thing if they were all destroyed. At this they all shouted: 'He's right! He's right! Shame on any man who saves the gentry from being wiped out!' They banded together and went off, without further deliberation and unarmed except for pikes and knives, to the house of a knight who lived near by. They broke in and killed the knight, with his lady and children, big and small, and set fire to the house" (Froissart, 1968 [c. 1365]: 151).

Civil citizenship recognizes the right to free speech, freedom of religion, and justice before the law.

Political citizenship recognizes the right to run for office and vote.

Social citizenship recognizes the right to a certain level of economic security and full participation in the social life of the country.

Bibliotheque Nationale de France

offices, densely populated urban neighbourhoods—could serve as recruitment bases. Third, social movements became less violent. That is, their size and organization often allowed them to bureaucratize, stabilize, and become sufficiently powerful to get their way without frequently resorting to extreme measures (Tilly, 1978, 1979a, 1979b; Tilly, Tilly, and Tilly, 1975).

Social movements often used their power to expand the rights of citizens. We may identify four stages in this process, focusing on Britain and the United States. In Britain, rich property owners fought against the king in the eighteenth century for **civil citizenship**. Civil citizenship is the right to free speech, freedom of religion, and justice before the law. The male middle class and the more prosperous strata of the working class fought against rich property owners in the nineteenth century for **political citizenship**. Political citizenship is the right to vote and run for office. In early twentieth-century Britain, women and poorer workers succeeded in achieving these same rights despite the opposition of many well-to-do men in particular. During the remainder of the century, blue-collar and white-collar workers fought against the well-to-do for **social citizenship**. Social citizenship is the right to a certain level of economic security and full participation in social life with the help of the modern welfare state (Marshall, 1965).

The timing of the struggle for citizenship rights was different in the United States. Universal suffrage for white males was won earlier in the nineteenth century than in Europe. This accounts in part for the greater radicalism of the European working class. It had to engage in a long and bitter struggle for the right to vote, while its American counterpart was already incorporated into the political system (Lipset, 1977). Another important distinguishing feature of the United States concerns African Americans. The 15th Amendment to the Constitution gave them the right to vote in 1870. However, most of them were unable to exercise that right, at least in the South, from the late nineteenth century until the 1960s. That was because of various restrictions on voter registration, including poll taxes and literacy tests. The civil rights movement of the 1960s was in part a struggle over this issue. It helped to create a community that is more politically radical than its white counterpart is.

New Social Movements

So-called **new social movements** emerged in the 1970s (Melucci, 1980, 1995). What is new about new social movements is the breadth of their goals, the kinds of people they attract, and their potential for globalization. Let us consider each of these issues in turn.

Goals

Some new social movements promote the rights not of specific groups but of humanity as a whole to peace, security, and a clean environment. Such movements include the peace movement, the environmental movement, and the human rights movement. Other new social movements, such as the women's movement and the gay rights movement, promote the rights of particular groups that have been excluded from full social participation. Accordingly, gay rights groups have fought for laws that eliminate all forms of discrimination based on sexual orientation. They have also fought for the repeal of laws that discriminate on the basis of sexual orientation, such as anti-sodomy laws and laws that negatively affect parental custody of children (Adam, Duyvendak, and Krouwel, 1999). Since the 1960s, the women's movement has succeeded in getting admission practices altered in professional schools, winning more freedom of reproductive choice for women, and opening up opportunities for women in the political, religious, military, educational, medical, and business systems (Adamson, Briskin, and McPhail, 1988). The emergence of the peace, environmental, human rights, gay rights, and women's movements marked the beginning of a fourth stage in the history of social movements. This fourth stage involves the promotion of **universal citizenship**, or the extension of citizenship rights to all adult members of society and to society as a whole (Roche, 1995; Turner, 1986: 85–105).

Membership

New social movements are also novel in that they attract a disproportionately large number of highly educated, relatively well-to-do people from the social, educational, and cultural fields. Such people include teachers, professors, journalists, social workers, artists, actors, writers, and student apprentices to these occupations. For several reasons, people in these occupations are more likely to participate in new social movements than are people in other occupations. Their higher education exposes them to radical ideas and makes those ideas appealing. They tend to hold jobs outside the business community, which often opposes their values. And they often become personally involved in the problems of their clients and audiences, sometimes even becoming their advocates (Brint, 1984; Rootes, 1995).

Globalization Potential

Finally, new social movements are new in that they have more potential for globalization than did old social movements.

Until the 1960s, social movements were typically *national* in scope. That is why, for example, the intensity and frequency of urban race riots in the United States in the 1960s did not depend on such local conditions as the degree of black–white inequality in a given city (Spilerman, 1970, 1976). Instead, African Americans came to believe that racial problems were nationwide and capable of solution only by the federal government. Congressional and presidential action (and inaction) on civil rights issues, national TV coverage of race issues, and growing black consciousness and solidarity helped shape this belief (Myers, 1997; Olzak and Shanahan, 1996; Olzak, Shanahan, and McEneaney, 1996).

Many new social movements that gained force in the 1970s increased the scope of protest beyond the national level. For example, members of the peace movement viewed federal laws banning nuclear weapons as necessary. Environmentalists felt the same way about federal laws protecting the environment. However, environmentalists also recognized that the condition of the Brazilian rain forest affects climactic conditions worldwide. Similarly, peace activists understood that the spread of weapons of mass destruction could destroy all of humanity. Therefore, members of the peace and environmental movements pressed for *international* agreements binding all countries to protect the environment and stop the spread of nuclear weapons. Social movements went global (Smith, 1998).

New social movements became prominent in the 1970s. They attract a disproportionately large number of highly educated people in the social, educational, and cultural fields, and universalize the struggle for citizenship.

Universal citizenship recognizes the right of marginal groups to full citizenship and the rights of humanity as a whole.

A protester in Tahrir Square, Cairo, Egypt, 2011, helping to overthrow the authoritarian regime of President Hosni Mubarak. In late 2010, Mohamed Bouazizi, a 27-year-old Tunisian street vendor, set himself on fire to protest harassment and humiliation by local officials. His action catalyzed an uprising that overthrew the Tunisian government and then spread to Egypt, Yemen, Bahrain, Libya, Syria, and elsewhere in the Middle East and North Africa. By the end of 2011, the "Arab Spring" had stimulated the growth of the "Occupy" movement in North America and Western Europe. Although global communication networks helped these movements spread, we must be careful not to exaggerate their causal importance, as the text explains.

AFP/Getty Images

Inexpensive international travel and communication facilitate the globalization of social movements. New technologies make it easier for people in various national movements to work with like-minded activists in other countries. In the age of CNN, inexpensive jet transportation, fax machines, websites, email, Facebook, and Twitter, it is easier than ever to see the connection between apparently local problems and their global sources and to act both locally and globally.

Some observers claim that Facebook and Twitter make otherwise unthinkable protests possible because they allow the powerless to express their grievances and coordinate their actions with ease. However, such claims overstate the beneficial effects of new technology on global social movements. Most Facebook friends are really acquaintances, and most Twitter followers don't know the people they are following personally. It is relatively easy to get such socially distant people on networking sites to participate in certain actions—but only if participation requires little sacrifice. Thus, the Facebook page of the Save Darfur Coalition has nearly 1.3 million members, but they have donated an average of just nine cents each to the organization (Gladwell, 2010). Big sacrifices in the name of political principles require strong social ties, not the weak ties offered by Twitter accounts and Facebook pages. Typically, individuals join a movement, and they attract clusters of friends, relatives, and members of the same unions, cooperatives, fraternities, college dorms, churches, mosques, and neighbourhoods. This pattern occurs because involvement in a social movement is likely to require big sacrifices, and you need to be close to others before you can reasonably expect them to share your ideas and willingness to sacrifice for a cause (McAdam, 1982).

The case of Greenpeace, one of the largest and most visible global social movements, illustrates the continuing importance of sacrifice based on strong ties. Originating in Vancouver in the mid-1970s, Greenpeace now has 57 branches in 47 countries (Greenpeace, 2010). It certainly uses Facebook, Twitter, RSS feeds, and YouTube videos to communicate its message, raise money, and attract new recruits. However, its campaigns require the investment of enormous amounts of time and energy by highly dedicated activists. For instance, when Greenpeace mounts a campaign to eliminate the international transportation and dumping of toxic wastes in less developed countries, its representatives had to visit local environmental groups in Africa, supply them with organizing kits to help them tie their local concerns to global political efforts, publish a newsletter to keep them up to date on legal issues, and so on. Greenpeace frequently coordinates such global campaigns, enabling weak environmental organizations in developing countries to act more effectively. However, it cannot do so by relying mainly on weakly tied members of a Twitter group. Its successes depend on the sacrifices of dedicated activists bound together by strong social ties.

We conclude by coming full circle and returning to the anecdote with which we began this chapter. In 1991, Robert Brym visited his hometown. He hadn't been back in years. As he entered the city, he vaguely sensed that something was different. "I wasn't able to identify the change until I reached the pulp-and-paper mill," says Robert. "Suddenly, it was obvious. The rotten-egg smell was virtually gone. I discovered that in the 1970s a local woman whose son developed a serious case of asthma took legal action against the mill and eventually won. The mill owner was forced by law to install a 'scrubber' in the main smokestack to remove most of the sulphur dioxide emissions. Soon, the federal government was putting pressure on the mill owner to purify the polluted water that poured out of the plant and into the local river system." Apparently, local citizens and the environmental movement had caused a deep change in the climate of opinion. This change influenced the government to force the mill owner to spend millions of dollars to clean up his operation. It took decades, but what was political heresy in 1968 became established practice by 1991. That is because environmental concerns had been amplified by the voice of a movement that had grown to global proportions. In general, as this case illustrates, globalization helps ensure that many new social movements transcend local and national boundaries and promote universalistic goals.

CF PHOTO/Frank Gunn

Greenpeace is a highly successful environmental movement that originated in Vancouver in the mid-1970s. It now has offices in 40 counties.

Summing Up

- Over the past 300 years, the scope of social movements has grown from local to national to international dimensions.
- As the scope of social movements grew, so did demands for civil, political, social, and universal citizenship.

NOTE

1. Some of these generalizations do not apply to countries with a long tradition of labour government. For example, since World War II Sweden has experienced high levels of unionization and low strike rates. That is because Swedish workers and their representatives are involved in government policymaking. Decisions about wages and benefits tend to be made in negotiations among unions, employer associations, and governments rather than on the picket line.

SUMMARY

1. Common sense and some sociological theory suggest that riots and other forms of collective action are irrational and unstructured actions that take place when people are angry and deprived. Is this view accurate?

   In the short term, deprivation and strain from rapid social change are generally *not* associated with increased collective action and social movement formation. Mobs, riots, and other forms of collective action may be wild and violent, but social organization and rationality underlie much crowd behaviour.

2. Which aspects of social organization facilitate rebellion against the status quo?

   People are more inclined to rebel against the status quo when social ties bind them to many other people who feel similarly wronged and when they have the time, money, organization, and other resources needed to protest. In addition, collective action and social movement formation are more likely to occur when political opportunities allow them. Political opportunities emerge through elections, increased support by influential allies, the instability of ruling political alignments, and divisions among elite groups.

3. How do the attempts of authorities to control unrest affect collective action?

   Authorities' attempts to control unrest mainly influence the timing of collective action. They may offer concessions to insurgents, co-opt leaders, and employ coercion.

4. What is "framing"?

   For social movements to grow, members must make the activities, goals, and ideology of the movement congruent with the interests, beliefs, and values of potential new recruits. Doing so is known as *framing*.

5. How have social movements changed in the past three centuries?

   In 1700, social movements were typically small, localized, and violent. By mid-twentieth century, social movements were typically large, national, and less violent. In the late twentieth century, new social movements developed broader goals, recruited more highly educated people, and developed global potential for growth.

6. How is the history of social movements tied to the struggle for the acquisition of citizenship rights?

   The history of social movements is a struggle for the acquisition of constantly broadening citizenship rights. These rights include (1) the right to free speech, religion, and justice before the law (civil citizenship), (2) the right to vote and run for office (political citizenship), (3) the right to a certain level of economic security and full participation in the life of society (social citizenship), and (4) the right of marginal groups to full citizenship and the right of humanity as a whole to peace and security (universal citizenship).

KEY TERMS

absolute deprivation (p. 526)	**relative deprivation (p. 526)**
breakdown theory (p. 525)	**resource mobilization (p. 530)**
civil citizenship (p. 540)	**social citizenship (p. 540)**
collective action (p. 524)	**social control (p. 530)**
contagion (p. 526)	**social movements (p. 524)**
frame alignment (p. 535)	**solidarity theory (p. 529)**
new social movements (p. 541)	**strain (p. 526)**
political citizenship (p. 540)	**union density (p. 533)**
political opportunities (p. 530)	**universal citizenship (p. 541)**

WEB RESOURCES

Companion Website for This Book

http://www.compass4e.nelson.com

Begin by clicking on the Student Resources section of the website. Next, select the chapter you are studying from the pull-down menu. From the Student Resources page you have easy access to additional Weblinks and other resources. The website also has many useful tips to aid you in your study of sociology, including practice tests for each chapter.

InfoTrac® Search Terms

These search terms are provided to assist you in beginning to conduct research on this topic by visiting http://www.infotrac-college.com:

collective action
frame alignment
relative deprivation
resource mobilization
unions

Abraham, Carolyn. 2003. "Hong Kong Hotel Is Focus of Pneumonia Investigation." *globeandmail.com*, March 20. Retrieved June 16, 2003 (http://globeandmail.workopolis.com/servlet/Content/fasttrack/20030320/UBUGGN?section=Healthcare).

Abraham, Laurie Kaye. 1993. *Mama Might Be Better Off Dead: The Failure of Health Care in Urban America*. Chicago: University of Chicago Press.

Achilles, Rhona. 1993. "Desperately Seeking Babies: New Technologies of Hope and Despair." Pp. 214–29 in Bonnie J. Fox, ed. *Family Patterns, Gender Relations*. Toronto: Oxford University Press.

Adam, Barry, Jan Willem Duyvendak, and Andre Krouwel. 1999. *The Global Emergence of Gay and Lesbian Politics*. Philadelphia: Temple University Press.

Adams, Henry E., Lester W. Wright, Jr., and Bethany A. Lohr. 1996. "Is Homophobia Associated with Homosexual Arousal?" *Journal of Abnormal Psychology* 105: 440–45.

Adams, Michael. 1997. *Sex in the Snow: Canadian Social Values at the End of the Millennium*. Toronto: Penguin.

Adams, R. J., G. Betcherman, and B. Bilson. 1995. *Good Job, Bad Jobs, No Jobs: Tough Choices for Canadian Labor Law*. Toronto: C.D. Howe Institute.

"Adams Mine." 2000. Retrieved October 8, 2000 (http://server1.nt.net/customers/13/tpc/www/togarbag.htm#Anchor-First-14210).

Adamson, Nancy, Linda Briskin, and Margaret McPhail. 1988. *Feminist Organizing for Change: The Contemporary Women's Movement in Canada*. Toronto: Oxford University Press.

Adherents.com. 2001. "Religion Statistics: Predominant Religions." Retrieved November 30, 2001 (http://www.adherents.com/adh_predom.html).

Adler, Patricia A., and Peter Adler. 1998. *Peer Power: Preadolescent Culture and Identity*. New Brunswick, NJ: Rutgers University Press.

Akwagyiram, Alexis. 2009. "Hip-Hop Comes of Age." *BBCNews* October 12. Retrieved January 11, 2011 (http://news.bbc.co.uk/2/hi/8286310.stm).

Albas, Daniel, and Cheryl Albas. 1989. "Modern Magic: The Case of Examinations." *The Sociological Quarterly* 30: 603–13.

Albelda, Randy, and Chris Tilly. 1997. *Glass Ceilings and Bottomless Pits: Women's Work, Women's Poverty*. Boston, MA: South End Press.

Alberta Federation of Labour. 2005. "Why Join a Union?" Retrieved November 21, 2005 (http://www.afl.org/need-a-union/why-join.cfm).

Albrow, Martin. 1997. *The Global Age: State and Society Beyond Modernity*. Stanford, CA: Stanford University Press.

Aldrich, Howard E. 1979. *Organizations and Environments*. Englewood Cliffs, NJ: Prentice-Hall.

Alford, Robert R., and Roger Friedland. 1985. *Powers of Theory: Capitalism, the State, and Democracy*. Cambridge, UK: Cambridge University Press.

Allahar, Anton, and James E. Côté. 1994. *Generation on Hold: Coming of Age in the Late Twentieth Century*. Toronto: Stoddart.

Allen, Robert C. 1999. *Education and Technological Revolutions: The Role of the Social Sciences and the Humanities in the Knowledge Based Economy*. Ottawa: Social Sciences and Humanities Research Council of Canada. Retrieved May 8, 2001 (http://www.sshrc.ca/english/resnews/researchresults/allen99.pdf).

Allen, Vanessa, Claire Ellicott, and Louise Eccles. 2011. "'I Couldn't Give My Baby Away . . . They Only Wanted a Toy': Surrogate Mother Fought Legal Battle after Learning That Would-Be Parents Were Violent." *MailOnline*. Retrieved July 13, 2011 (http://www.dailymail.co.uk/news/article-1356176/Surrogate-mother-wins-case-baby-giving-birth.html).

Amato, Paul R., and Bruce Keith. 1991. "Parental Divorce and the Well-Being of Children: A Meta-Analysis." *Psychological Bulletin* 110: 26–46.

Ambert, Anne-Marie. 1998. "Divorce: Facts, Figures and Consequences." Vanier Institute of the Family. Retrieved March 27, 2001 (http://www.vifamily.ca/cft/divorce/divorce.htm).

American Library Association. 2005. "Top Ten Challenged Authors 1990–2004." Retrieved December 14, 2005 (http://childrensbooks.about.com/gi/dynamic/offsite.htm?zi=1/XJ&sdn=childrensbooks&zu=http%3A%2F%2Fwww.ala.org%2Fbbooks%2Ftop100bannedbooks.html).

American Psychological Association. 1998. "Answers to Your Questions About Sexual Orientation and Homosexuality." Retrieved June 14, 2000 (http://www.apa.org/pubinfo/orient.html).

American Society of Plastic Surgeons. 2009. "2008 Cosmetic Surgery Trends." Retrieved November 26, 2010 (http://www.plasticsurgery.org/Media/stats/2008-ASPS-member-surgeon-cosmetic-trends-statistics.pdf).

American Sociological Association. 1999. *Code of Ethics and Policies and Procedures of the ASA Committee on Professional Ethics*. Washington, DC.

Anderson, Benedict R. O'G. 1991. *Imagined Communities: Reflections on the Origin and Spread of Nationalism*. London, UK: Verso.

Anderson, Craig, and Brad J. Bushman. 2002. "The Effects of Media Violence on Society." *Science* 295, 5564: 2377–79.

Anderson, Elijah. 1990. *Streetwise: Race, Class, and Change in an Urban Community*. Chicago: University of Chicago Press.

Anderson, Gerald F., Uwe E. Reinhardt, Peter S. Hussey, and Varduhi Petrosyan. 2003. "It's the Prices, Stupid: Why the United States Is So Different from Other Countries." *Health Affairs* 22, 3: 89–105.

Anderson, Michael. 2003. "Reading Violence in Boys' Writing." *Language Arts* 80, 3: 223–30.

Ariès, Phillipe. 1962 [1960]. *Centuries of Childhood: A Social History of Family Life*, Robert Baldick, trans. New York: Knopf.

———. 1982. *The Hour of Our Death*. New York: Knopf.

Arnett, Jeffrey Jensen. 1995. "Adolescents' Uses of Media for Self-Socialization." *Journal of Youth and Adolescence* 24: 519–33.

Asch, Solomon. 1955. "Opinion and Social Pressure." *Scientific American* July: 31–35.

Asia Pacific Foundation of Canada. 2002. "Generous at Heart, Prudent at Pocket. Foreign Aid and Trade: What Do Canadians Think?" Retrieved May 13, 2006 (http://www.asiapacific.ca/analysis/pubs/listing.cfm?ID_Publication=222).

Associated Press. 2001. "Vancouver Gay Man Beaten to Death: Police Suspect Hate Crime." Retrieved May 12, 2002 (http://www.planetqnews.com/0812/11.shtml).

———. 2005. "Writer: Pope Expressed Concern over Harry Potter Books." *USA Today* July 14. Retrieved December 13, 2006 (http://www.usatoday.com/news/world/2005-07-14-pope-potter_x.htm).

Averett, Susan, and Sanders Korenman. 1996. "The Economic Reality of the Beauty Myth." *Journal of Human Resources* 31: 304–30.

Babbie, Earl. 2000. *The Practice of Social Research*, rev. 9th ed. Belmont, CA: Wadsworth.

Baer, Doug. 1999. "Educational Credentials and the Changing Occupational Structure." Pp. 92–106 in J. Curtis, E. Grabb, and N. Guppy, eds. *Social Inequality in Canada: Patterns, Problems, Policies*, 3rd ed. Scarborough, ON: Prentice Hall Allyn and Bacon Canada.

Bagdikian, Ben H. 1997. *The Media Monopoly*, 5th ed. Boston: Beacon.

Bairoch, Paul. 1988 [1985]. *Cities and Economic Development: From the Dawn of History to the Present*, Christopher Braider, trans. Chicago: University of Chicago Press.

Balakrishnan, T. R., and K. Selvanathan. 1990. "Residential Segregation in Metropolitan Canada." In S. Halli, F. Travato, and L. Driedger, eds. *Ethnic Demography*. Ottawa: Carleton University Press.

Banner, Lois W. 1992. *In Full Flower: Aging Women, Power, and Sexuality*. New York: Knopf.

Bannon, Lisa. 2000. "Why Girls and Boys Get Different Toys." *The Wall Street Journal* February 14: B1, B4.

Baran, Paul A. 1957. *The Political Economy of Growth*. New York: Monthly Review Press.

Barber, Benjamin. 1996. *Jihad vs. McWorld: How Globalism and Tribalism Are Reshaping the World*. New York: Ballantine Books.

Barlow, Maude, and Elizabeth May. 2000. *Frederick Street: Life and Death on Canada's Love Canal*. Toronto: HarperCollins.

Barna, G. 2002. *Grow Your Church from the Outside In: Understanding the Unchurched and How to Reach Them*. Ventura, California: Regal Books.

Barnard, Chester, I. 1938. *The Functions of the Executive*. Cambridge, MA: Harvard University Press.

Barnet, Richard J., and John Cavanagh. 1994. *Global Dreams: Imperial Corporations and the New World Order*. New York: Simon & Schuster.

Bar-On, D. 1999. *The Indescribable and the Undiscussable: Reconstructing Human Discourse after Trauma*. Ithaca, NY: Cornell University Press.

Barry, Patricia. 2002a. "Ads, Promotions Drive up Drug Costs." *AARP*. Retrieved June 17, 2003 (http://www.aarp.org/bulletin/departments/2002/medicare/0310_medicare_1.html).

———. 2002b. "Drug Industry Spends Huge Sums Guarding Prices." *AARP*. Retrieved June 17, 2003 (http://www.aarp.org/bulletin/departments/2002/medicare/0510_medicare_1.html).

———. 2002c. "Drug Profits vs. Research." *AARP*. Retrieved June 17, 2003 (http://www.aarp.org/bulletin/departments/2002/medicare/0605_medicare_1.html).

Barth, Fredrik, ed. 1969. *Ethnic Groups and Boundaries: The Social Organization of Cultural Difference*. Boston: Little, Brown.

Bashevkin, Sylvia. 1993. *Toeing the Line: Women and Party Politics in English Canada*, 2nd ed. Toronto: Oxford University Press.

Baudrillard, Jean. 1983. *Simulations*. New York: Semiotext(e).

———. 1988. *America*. Chris Turner, trans. London: Verso.

Bauman, Zygmunt. 1991. *Modernity and the Holocaust*. Ithaca, NY: Cornell University Press.

Beach, Jane, Martha Friendly, Carolyn Ferns, Nina Prabhu, and Barry Forer. 2009. *Early Childhood Education and Care in Canada 2008*, 8th ed. Retrieved March 21, 2010 (http://www.childcarecanada.org/ECEC2008/#toc).

Beaudry, P., and D. Green. 1998. *Individual Responses to Changes in the Canadian Labour Market*, Paper Number 9. Ottawa: Industry Canada.

Beck, Ulrich. 1992 [1986]. *Risk Society: Towards a New Modernity*, Mark Ritter, trans. London, UK: Sage.

Becker, Ernest. 1973. *The Denial of Death*. New York: Free Press.

Becker, Gary. 1976. *The Economic Approach to Human Behavior*. Chicago: University of Chicago Press.

Becker, Gaylene. 1980. *Growing Old in Silence*. Berkeley: University of California Press.

Becker, Howard S. 1963. *Outsiders: Studies in the Sociology of Deviance*. New York: Free Press.

Beer, Frances A. 1974. *How Much War in History: Definitions, Estimates, Extrapolations and Trends*. Beverly Hills, CA: Sage.

Bélanger, Claude. 2000. "Readings in Quebec History: Opting Out." Retrieved February 18, 2001 (http://members.nbci.com/history_1/his951/readings/opting.htm).

Bell, Daniel. 1973. *The Coming of Post-Industrial Society: A Venture in Social Forecasting*. New York: Basic Books.

Bell, Gregory Boyd. 2002. "No Straightjacket Required." *This* 35, 4: 29–34.

Bellow, Saul. 1964. *Herzog*. New York: Fawcett World Library.

Benford, Robert D. 1997. "An Insider's Critique of the Social Movement Framing Perspective." *Sociological Inquiry* 67: 409–39.

Bercuson, David. 1974. "The Winnipeg General Strike." Pp. 1–32 in Irving Abella, ed. *On Strike: Six Key Labour Struggles in Canada, 1919–1949*. Toronto: James Lewis & Samuel.

Berens, Michael J. 2002a. "Infection Epidemic Carves Deadly Path." *Chicago Tribune* July 21. Retrieved June 16, 2003 (http://www.chicagotribune.com/news/specials/chi-0207210272jul21.story).

———. 2002b. "Drug-Resistant Germs Adapt, Thrive Beyond Hospital Walls." *Chicago Tribune* June 23. Retrieved June 16, 2003 (http://www.chicagotribune.com/news/specials/chi-0207230231jul23.story).

Berger, Peter L., and Thomas Luckmann. 1966. *The Social Construction of Reality: A Treatise in the Sociology of Knowledge*. Garden City, NY: Doubleday.

Berger, S., and R. Dore, eds. 1996. *National Diversity and Capitalism*. Ithaca, NY: Cornell University Press.

Berk, Richard A. 1974. *Collective Behavior*. Dubuque, IO: Brown.

Berkowitz, S. D. 1982. *An Introduction to Structural Analysis: The Network Approach to Social Research*. Toronto: Butterworths.

Bernardes, A. 2011. *Urbanização Brasileira*. Retrieved January 15, 2011 (http://www.mre.gov.br/cdbrasil/itamaraty/web/port/band.htm).

Berners-Lee, Tim. 1999. "Tim Berners-Lee." Retrieved May 2, 2000 (http://www.w3.org/People/Berners-Lee/Overview.html).

Besserer, Sandra. 2002. "Criminal Victimization: An International Perspective: Results of the 2000 International Crime Victimization Survey." *Juristat* 22, 4 (May). Catalogue no. 85-002-XPE.

Betcherman, G., and G. Lowe. 1997. *The Future of Work in Canada: A Synthesis Report*. Ottawa: Canadian Policy Research Networks.

Bianchi, Suzanne M., and Daphne Spain. 1996. "Women, Work, and Family in America." *Population Bulletin* 51, 3: 2–48.

Bibby, Reginald W. 1987. *Fragmented Gods: The Poverty and Potential of Religion in Canada*. Toronto: Irwin.

———. 1995. *The Bibby Report: Social Trends Canadian Style*. Toronto: Stoddart.

———. 2001. *Canada's Teens: Today, Yesterday, and Tomorrow*. Toronto: Stoddart.

———. 2002. *Restless God: The Renaissance of Religion in Canada*. Toronto: Stoddart.

———. 2004. *Restless Churches: How Canada's Churches Can Contribute to the Emerging Religious Renaissance*. Ottawa: Novalis.

Bibby, Reginald W. 2011. "Religion." Pp. 309–34 in Robert J. Brym, ed. *New Society*. Toronto: Nelson.

Biegler, Rebecca S. 1999. "Psychological Interventions Designed to Counter Sexism in Children: Empirical Limitations and Theoretical Foundations." Pp. 129–52 in W. B. Swann, Jr., J. H. Langlois, and L. A. Gilbert, eds. *Sexism and Stereotypes in Modern Society: The Gender Science of Janet Taylor Spence*. Washington, DC: American Psychological Association.

Bierstedt, Robert. 1963. *The Social Order*. New York: McGraw-Hill.

———. 1974. "An Analysis of Social Power." Pp. 220–41 in *Power and Progress: Essays in Sociological Theory*. New York: McGraw-Hill.

Bissoondath, Neil. 2002. *Selling Illusions: The Cult of Multiculturalism in Canada*, rev. ed. Toronto: Penguin.

Bittman, Michael, and Judy Wajcman. 2000. "The Rush Hour: The Character of Leisure Time and Gender Equity." *Social Forces* 79: 165–89.

Bjorhus, J. 2000. "Gap Between Execs, Rank and File Grows Wider." *San Jose Mercury News* June 18. Retrieved June 20, 2000 (http://www.mercurycenter.com/premium/business/docs/disparity18.htm).

Black, Donald. 1989. *Sociological Justice*. New York: Oxford University Press.

Blais, André, Elisabeth Gidengil, Richard Nadeau, and Neil Nevitte. 1997. "1997 Canadian Election Survey." Retrieved December 1, 1998 (http://prod.library.utoronto.ca/datalib/codebooks/utm/elections/1997).

Blaise, Clark. 2001. *Time Lord: The Remarkable Canadian Who Missed His Train and Changed the World*. Toronto: Knopf Canada.

Blau, Peter M. 1963. *The Dynamics of Bureaucracy: A Study of Interpersonal Relationships in Two Government Agencies*, rev. ed. Chicago: University of Chicago Press.

———. 1964. *Exchange and Power in Social Life*. New York: Wiley.

Blauner, R. 1972. *Racial Oppression in America*. New York: Harper & Row.

Block, Fred. 1979. "The Ruling Class Does Not Rule." Pp. 128–40 in R. Quinney, ed. *Capitalist Society*. Homewood, IL: Dorsey Press.

"Bloomberg Game Changers: Mark Zuckerberg." 2010. [Video]. Retrieved October 9, 2010 (http://www.bloomberg.com/video/63583008/).

Blossfeld, H., and Y. Shavit, eds. 1993. *Persistent Inequality: Changing Educational Attainment in Thirteen Countries*. Boulder, CO: Westview Press.

Blum, Deborah. 1997. *Sex on the Brain: The Biological Differences between Men and Women*. New York: Penguin.

Blumberg, Paul. 1989. *The Predatory Society: Deception in the American Marketplace*. New York: Oxford University Press.

Blumer, Herbert. 1969. *Symbolic Interactionism: Perspective and Method*. Englewood Cliffs, NJ: Prentice-Hall.

Boal, Mark. 1998. "Spycam City." *The Village Voice* (September 30–October 6). Retrieved March 26, 2001 (http://www.villagevoice.com/issues/9840/boal.shtml).

Bollman, Ray D. 2000. "Rural and Small Town Canada: An Overview." Statistics Canada and Rural Secretariat, Agriculture and Agri-Food Canada. Retrieved May 11, 2005 (http://www.statcan.ca/english/freepub/21F0018XIE/21F0018XIE2001001.htm).

Bonacich, Edna. 1972. "A Theory of Ethnic Antagonism: The Split Labor Market." *American Sociological Review* 37: 547–59.

———. 1973. "A Theory of Middleman Minorities." *American Sociological Review* 38: 583–94.

Bornholt, Laurel. 2001. "Self-Concepts, Usefulness and Behavioural Intentions in the Social Context of Schooling." *Educational Psychology* 21, 1 (March): 67–78.

Bornschier, Volker, and Christopher Chase-Dunn. 1985. *Transnational Corporations and Underdevelopment.* New York: Praeger.

Boroditsky, Lera. 2010. "Lost in Translation." *The Wall Street Journal* July 23. Retrieved June 7, 2011 (http://online.wsj.com/article/SB10001424052748703467304575383131592767868.html).

Borooah, Vani K., and Amaresh Dubey. 2009 "Measuring Regional Backwardness: Poverty, Gender, and Children in the Districts of India." *Margin—The Journal of Applied Economic Research* 1, 4: 403–40.

Boston Women's Health Book Collective, ed. 1998. *Our Bodies, Our Selves for the New Century: A Book by and for Women.* New York: Simon & Schuster.

Boswell, A. Ayres, and Joan Z. Spade. 1996. "Fraternities and Collegiate Rape Culture: Why Are Some Fraternities More Dangerous Places for Women?" *Gender and Society* 10: 133–47.

Bouchard, Thomas J., Jr., David T. Lykken, Matthew McGue, Nancy L. Segal, and Auke Tellegen. 1990. "Sources of Human Psychological Differences: The Minnesota Study of Twins Reared Apart." *Science* 250, 4978: 223–26.

Boulding, Elise. 1976. *The Underside of History.* Boulder, CO: Westview.

Bourdieu, Pierre. 1977 [1972]. *Outline of a Theory of Practice*, Richard Nice, trans. Cambridge, UK: Cambridge University Press.

———. 1984 [1979]. *Distinction: A Social Critique of the Judgment of Taste*, R. Nice, trans. Cambridge, MA: Harvard University Press.

———. 1998a. *On Television.* New York: New Press.

———. 1998b. *Practical Reason: On the Theory of Action.* Stanford, CA.: Stanford University Press.

Bourdieu, Pierre, and Jean Claude Passeron. 1979. *The Inheritors: French Students and Their Relation to Culture.* Chicago: University of Chicago Press.

———. 1990. *Reproduction in Education, Society and Culture*, 2nd ed. R. Nice, trans. London: Sage.

Bowles, Samuel, and Herbert Gintis. 1976. *Schooling in Capitalist America: Educational Reform and the Contradictions of Economic Life.* New York: Basic Books.

Boychuk, Gerard W. 2002. "Federal Spending in Health: Why Here? Why Now?" Pp. 121–36 in G. Bruce Doern, ed. *How Ottawa Spends 2002–2003: The Security Aftermath and National Priorities.* Toronto: Oxford University Press.

Boyd, Monica. 1997. "Feminizing Paid Work." *Current Sociology* 45, 2 (April): 49–73.

———. 1999. "Canadian, eh? Ethnic Origin Shifts in the Canadian Census." *Canadian Ethnic Studies* 31, 3: 1–19.

———. 2001. "Gender Inequality." Pp. 178–207 in Robert J. Brym, ed. *New Society: Sociology for the 21st Century*, 3rd ed. Toronto: Harcourt Canada.

———. 2002. "Educational Attainments of Immigrant Offspring: Success or Segmented Assimilation?" *International Migration Review* 36, 4: 1037–60.

Boyd, Monica, John Goyder, Frank E. Jones, Hugh A. McRoberts, Peter C. Pineo, and John Porter. 1985. *Ascription and Achievement: Studies on Mobility and Status Attainment in Canada.* Ottawa: Carleton University Press.

Boyd, Monica, and Doug Norris. 2001. "Who Are the 'Canadians'? Changing Census Responses, 1986–1996." *Canadian Ethnic Studies* 33, 1: 1–25.

Braithwaite, John. 1981. "The Myth of Social Class and Criminality Revisited." *American Sociological Review* 46: 36–57.

———. 1989. *Crime, Shame and Reintegration.* New York: Cambridge University Press.

Brave, Ralph. 2003. "James Watson Wants to Build a Better Human." *AlterNet* May 29. Retrieved January 19, 2005 (http://www.alternet.org/story/16026).

Braver, Sanford L., Pamela J. Fitzpatrick, and R. Curtis Bay. 1991. "Noncustodial Parent's Report of Child Support Payments." *Family Relations* 40, 2 (April): 180–85.

Braverman, H. 1974. *Labour and Monopoly Capital: The Degradation of Work in the Twentieth Century.* New York: Monthly Review Press.

Brazzini, D. G., W. D. McIntosh, S. M. Smith, S. Cook, and C. Harris. 1997. "The Aging Woman in Popular Film: Underrepresented, Unattractive, Unfriendly, and Unintelligent." *Sex Roles* 36: 531–43.

Brechin, Steven R., and Willett Kempton. 1994. "Global Environmentalism: A Challenge to the Postmaterialism Thesis." *Social Science Quarterly* 75: 245–69.

Breen, Richard, and John Goldthorpe. 1997. "Explaining Educational Differentials." *Rationality and Society* 9: 275–305.

Brennan, Teresa. 2003. *Globalization and Its Terrors: Daily Life in the West.* London: Routledge.

Bricker, Darrell, and Edward Greenspon. 2001. *Searching for Certainty: Inside the New Canadian Mindset.* Toronto: Doubleday Canada.

Brimelow, Peter. "The Silent Boom." *Forbes*, July 7, 1998.

Brint, Stephen. 1984. "New Class and Cumulative Trend Explanations of the Liberal Political Attitudes of Professionals." *American Journal of Sociology* 90: 30–71.

Brodie, Janine. 1991. "Women and the Electoral Process in Canada." Pp. 3–59 in Kathy Megyery, ed. *Women in Canadian Politics: Toward Equity in Representation.* Toronto: Dundurn Press.

Bronowski, J. 1965. *Science and Human Values*, revised ed. New York: Harper & Row.

Brooks, Clem, and Jeff Manza. 1997. "Social Cleavages and Political Alignments: U.S. Presidential Elections, 1960 to 1992." *American Sociological Review* 62: 937–46.

Brower, David. 1975. *Training the Nihilists: Education and Radicalism in Tsarist Russia.* Ithaca, NY: Cornell University Press.

Brown, Lyn Mikel, and Carol Gilligan. 1992. *Meeting at the Crossroads: Women's Psychology and Girls' Development.* Cambridge, MA: Harvard University Press.

Brown, Peter. 1996. *The Rise of Western Christendom: Triumph and Diversity, A.D. 200–1000.* Oxford: Blackwell.

Browne, Kevin D., and Catherine Hamilton-Giachritsis. 2005. "The Influence of Violent Media on Children and Adolescents: A Public-Health Approach." *The Lancet* 365, 9460: 702–10.

Browning, Christopher R. 1992. *Ordinary Men: Reserve Police Battalion 101 and the Final Solution in Poland.* New York: HarperCollins.

Bruce, Steve. 1988. *The Rise and Fall of the New Christian Right: Conservative Protestant Politics in America 1978–1988.* Oxford, UK: Clarendon Press.

Brumberg, Joan Jacobs. 1997. *The Body Project: An Intimate History of American Girls.* New York: Random House.

Bumiller, Elisabeth. 2010, "We Have Met the Enemy and He Is PowerPoint." *The New York Times* 26 April. Retrieved October 23, 2010 (http://www.nytimes.com).

Brym, Robert J. 1979. "Political Conservatism in Atlantic Canada." Pp. 59–79 in Robert J. Brym and R. James Sacouman, eds. *Underdevelopment and Social Movements in Atlantic Canada.* Toronto: New Hogtown Press.

———. 1989. "Canada." Pp. 177–206 in Tom Bottomore and Robert J. Brym, eds. *The Capitalist Class: An International Study.* New York: New York University Press.

———. 1990. "Sociology, *Perestroika*, and Soviet Society." *Canadian Journal of Sociology* 15: 207–15.

———. 1992. "Some Advantages of Canadian Disunity: How Quebec Sovereignty Might Aid Economic Development in English-speaking Canada." *Canadian Review of Sociology and Anthropology* 29: 210–26.

———. 1995. "Voters Quietly Reveal Greater Communist Leanings." *Transition: Events and Issues in the Former Soviet Union and East-Central and Southeastern Europe* 1, 16: 32–35.

———. 1996a. "The Ethic of Self-Reliance and the Spirit of Capitalism in Russia." *International Sociology* 11: 409–26.

———. 1996b. "Reevaluating Mass Support for Political and Economic Change in Russia." *Europe-Asia Studies* 48: 751–66.

———. 1996c. "'The Third Rome' and 'The End of History': Notes on Russia's Second Communist Revolution." *Canadian Review of Sociology and Anthropology* 33: 391–406.

———. 1996d. "The Turning Point in the Presidential Campaign." Pp. 44–49 in *The 1996 Presidential Election and Public Opinion.* Moscow: VTsIOM. [In Russian.]

———. 2001. "Jewish Immigrants from the Former Soviet Union in Canada, 1996." *East European Jewish Affairs* 31: 36–43.

———. 2007. "Six Lessons of Suicide Bombers." *Contexts* 6, 4: 40–5.

———. 2008. "Affluence, Power and Strikes in Canada, 1973–2000." Pp. 55–68 in Edward Grabb and Neil Guppy, eds. *Social Inequality in Canada: Patterns, Problems, Policies*, 6th ed. Scarborough, ON: Prentice-Hall Canada.

———. 2009. *Canadian Society and the 2006 Census*. Toronto: Nelson.

———. 2010a [1980]. *Intellectuals and Politics*, facsimile ed. London, UK: Routledge.

———. 2010b. "Survey of SOC01 Students." University of Toronto.

Brym, Robert J., and Bader Araj. 2006. "Suicide Bombing as Strategy and Interaction: The Case of the Second *Intifada*," *Social Forces* 84: 1965–82.

Brym, Robert J., et al. 2011. "The Social Bases of Cancer." Pp. 80–102 in *Sociology as a Life or Death Issue*, 2nd. Canadian ed. Toronto: Nelson.

Brym, Robert, et al. 2005. "In Faint Praise of the World Bank's Gender Development Policy," *Canadian Journal of Sociology* 30: 95–111.

Brym, Robert J., and Evel Economakis. 1994. "Peasant or Proletarian? Blacklisted Pskov Workers in St. Petersburg, 1913." *Slavic Review* 53: 120–39.

Brym, Robert J., and Rhonda Lenton. 2001. "Love Online: A Report on Digital Dating in Canada." Toronto: MSN.CA. Retrieved December 20, 2001 (http://www.nelson.com/nelson/harcourt/sociology/newsociety3e/loveonline.pdf).

Brym, Robert J., Michael Gillespie, and A. Ron Gillis. 1985. "Anomie, Opportunity, and the Density of Ethnic Ties: Another View of Jewish Outmarriage in Canada." *Canadian Review of Sociology and Anthropology* 22: 102–12.

Brym, Robert J., Michael Gillespie, and Rhonda L. Lenton. 1989. "Class Power, Class Mobilization, and Class Voting: The Canadian Case." *Canadian Journal of Sociology* 14: 25–44.

Brym, Robert J., with Bonnie J. Fox. 1989. *From Culture to Power: The Sociology of English Canada*. Toronto: Oxford University Press.

Brym, Robert J., with the assistance of Rozalina Ryvkina. 1994. *The Jews of Moscow, Kiev and Minsk: Identity, Antisemitism, Emigration*. New York: New York University Press.

Brym, Robert J., William Shaffir, and Morton Weinfeld, eds. 1993. *The Jews in Canada*. Toronto: Oxford University Press.

Brzezinski, Zbigniew. 1993. *Out of Control: Global Turmoil on the Eve of the Twenty-First Century*. New York: Scribner.

Bullard, Robert D. 1994. *Dumping in Dixie: Race, Class and Environmental Quality*, 2nd ed. Boulder, CO: Westview Press.

Bumiller, Elisabeth. 2010. "We Have Met the Enemy and He Is PowerPoint." *The New York Times* 26 April.Retrieved October 23, 2010 (http://www.nytimes.com).

Bunge, Valerie Pottie. 2000. "Spousal Violence." Pp. 11–21 in Statistics Canada. *Family Violence in Canada: A Statistical Profile 2000*. Catalogue no. 85-224-XIE. Ottawa: Minister of Industry.

Burawoy, Michael. 1979. *Manufacturing Consent: Changes in the Labor Process Under Monopoly Capitalism*. Chicago: University of Chicago Press.

Burgess, Ernest. W. 1967 [1925]. "The Growth of the City: An Introduction to a Research Project." Pp. 47–62 in Robert E. Park, Ernest W. Burgess, and Roderick D. McKenzie. *The City*. Chicago: University of Chicago Press.

Burleigh, Michael. 2000. *The Third Reich: A New History*. New York: Hill & Wang.

Burns, Tom, and G. M. Stalker. 1961. *The Management of Innovation*. London, UK: Tavistock.

Bush, Irene R., and Anthony Sainz. 2001. "Competencies at the Intersection of Difference, Tolerance, and Prevention of Hate Crimes." Pp. 205–24 in Mary E. Swigonski and Robin S. Mama, eds. *From Hate Crimes to Human Rights: A Tribute to Matthew Shepard*. New York: Haworth Press.

"The Business of Touch." 2006. Retrieved April 7, 2006 (http://www.businessoftouch.com/index2.html).

Buss, David M. 2000. *Dangerous Passion: Why Jealousy Is as Necessary as Love and Sex*. New York: Free Press.

Butovsky, Jonah. 2001. *The Decline of the New Democrats: The Politics of Postmaterialism or Neoliberalism?* Ph.D. dissertation, Department of Sociology, University of Toronto.

Buxton, L. H. D. 1963. "Races of Mankind." Pp. 864–66 in *Encyclopedia Britannica*, vol. 18. Chicago: Encyclopedia Britannica, Inc.

Callahan, Raymond E. 1962. *Education and the Cult of Efficiency: A Study of the Social Forces That Have Shaped the Administration of the Public Schools*. Chicago: University of Chicago Press.

Calverley, Donna. 2010. "Adult Correctional Services in Canada, 2008/2009." Statistics Canada. Retrieved November 11, 2010 (http://www.statcan.gc.ca/pub/85-002-x/2010003/article/11353-eng.htm).

Calverley, Donna, Adam Cotter, and Ed Halla. 2010. "Youth Custody and Community Services in Canada, 2008/2009." *Juristat*. Retrieved November 11, 2010 (http://www.statcan.gc.ca/pub/85-002-x/2010001/article/11147-eng.htm).

Cameron, Michelle. 2005. "Two-Spirited Aboriginal People." *Canadian Woman Studies* 24, 2/3: 123–27.

"Campaign for Labor Rights." 2004. Retrieved February 8, 2011 (http://www.clrlabor.org/alerts/1997/nikey001.html).

Campbell, D., and J. Stanley. 1963. *Experimental and Quasi-experimental Designs for Research*. Chicago: Rand McNally.

Campbell, F. A., and C. T. Ramey. 1994. "Effects of Early Intervention on Intellectual and Academic Achievement: A Follow-up Study of Children from Low-income Families." *Child Development* 65: 684–99.

Campbell, Jane, and Mike Oliver. 1996. *Disability Politics: Understanding Our Past, Changing Our Future*. London: Routledge.

Campion, Edward W. 1993. "Why Unconventional Medicine?" *New England Journal of Medicine* 328: 282.

Canada NewsWire. 2001. "Euthanasia Prevention Coalition Responds to Leger Marketing Poll." Retrieved June 15, 2003 (http://www.newswire.ca/releases/July2001/03/c9446.html).

Canadian Aboriginal News. 2001. "Innu, Health Officials Settle Differences over Treatment for Gas Sniffers." Retrieved June 16, 2006 (http://www.candianaboriginal.com/health/health26b.htm).

Canadian Centre on Substance Abuse. 1999. *Canadian Profile 1999: Alcohol, Tobacco and Other Drugs*. Ottawa: Centre on Substance Abuse and Centre for Addiction and Mental Health.

Canadian Coalition for Nuclear Responsibility. 2000. Retrieved October 8, 2000 (http://www.ccnr.org/#topics).

Canadian Council on Social Development. 2007. "Families: A Canadian Profile." Retrieved November 15, 2008 (http://www.ccsd.ca/factsheets/family).

———. 2008. *The Economic Well-Being of Children in Canada*. Retrieved March 15, 2011 (http://www.ccsd.ca/research.htm).

"Canadian Election Panel Study, 2004–2006–2008." 2010. Retrieved November 27 2010 (http://sda.chass.utoronto.ca/cgi-bin/sdapub/hsda?harcsda+ces040608).

Canadian Families Project. 1999. *Profiling Canada's Families in 1901*. Victoria: University of Victoria.

Canadian Institute for Health Information. 2004. *Improving the Health of Canadians*. Ottawa: Canadian Institute for Health Information.

Canadian Journalists for Free Expression. 2000. "CJFE Disappointed at Ontario Superior Court Ruling Against Media Freedom." Retrieved March 22, 2001 (http://www.cjfe.org/releases/2000/seizures.html).

Canadian Marketing Association. 2007. "Canadian Ad Spend across All Media Signals Strong Growth to 2011: CMA." Retrieved September 20, 2011 (http://www.the-cma.org/?wce=c=47lk=227708).

Canadian Media Research. 2006. "How Many Canadians Subscribe to Cable TV or Satellite TV?" Canadian Radio-television and Telecommunications Commission. Retrieved October 20, 2011 (http://www.crtc.gc.ca/eng/publications/reports/radio/cmri.htm).

Canadian Mental Health Association. 2001. "Depression and Manic Depression." Retrieved June 16, 2006 (http://www.cmha.ca/english/store/mh_pamphlets/mh).

Canadian Psychiatric Association. 2002. "Anxiety, Depression and Manic Depression." Retrieved June 16, 2006 (http://www.cpa-apc.org/MIAW/pamphlets/Anxiety.arp).

Cancer Care Nova Scotia. n.d. "Cancer Statistics in Nova Scotia: An Overview, 1995–1999." Retrieved January 12, 2008 (http://cancercare.ns.ca/media/documents/CancerinNS_Overview.pdf).

Cancio, A. S., T. D. Evans, and D. J. Maume. 1996. "Reconsidering the Declining Significance of Race: Racial Differences in Early Career Wages." *American Sociological Review* 61: 541–56.

"The Candidates Debate." 1998. MSNBC News. Retrieved May 2, 2000 (http://msnbc.com/onair/msnbc/TimeAndAgain/archive/ken-nix/Default.asp?cp1=1).

Cardinal, H. 1977. *The Rebirth of Canada's Indians*. Edmonton: Hurtig Publishers.

Cardoso, Fernando Henrique, and Enzo Faletto. 1979. *Dependency and Development in Latin America*, Marjory Mattingly Urquidi, trans. Berkeley: University of California Press.

Caron, Roger. 1979. *Go-Boy! The True Story of a Life Behind Bars*. London, UK: Arrow Books.

Carpenter, Dave. 2003. "McDonald's High-Tech with Kitchen, Kiosks." Kiosk.com. Retrieved October 23, 2003 (http://www.kiosk.com/articles_detail.php?ident=1856).

Carrier, Roch. 1979. *The Hockey Sweater and Other Stories*, Sheila Fischman, trans. Toronto: Anansi.

Carroll, William. 1986. *Corporate Power and Canadian Capitalism*. Vancouver: University of British Columbia Press.

Carroll, William, and Robert S. Ratner. 1996a. "Master Frames and Counter-Hegemony: Political Sensibilities in Contemporary Social Movements." *Canadian Review of Sociology and Anthropology* 33: 407–35.

———. 1996b. "Master Framing and Cross-Movement Networking in Contemporary Social Movements." *The Sociological Quarterly* 37, 4: 601–25.

Cassidy, B., R. Lord, and N. Mandell. 1998. "Silenced and Forgotten Women: Race, Poverty and Disability." Pp. 26–54 in Nancy Mandell, ed. *Race, Class and Sexuality*, 2nd ed. Scarborough: Prentice-Hall Allyn and Bacon.

Castells, Manuel. 1983. *The City and the Grassroots: A Cross-Cultural Theory of Urban Social Movements*. Berkeley, CA: University of California Press.

Cavalli-Sforza, L. L., P. Menozzi, and A. Piazza. 1994. *The History and Geography of Human Genes*. Princeton, NJ: Princeton University Press.

CBC News. 2004a. "The Greatest Canadian." Retrieved April 6, 2006 (http://www.cbc.ca/greatest).

———. 2004b. "Hospital Hygiene Cuts Severe Infections by 80 Per Cent." Retrieved July 27, 2005 (http://www.cbc.ca/story/science/national/2004/01/15/hand_washque04015.html?print).

———. 2005. "Canadians Deeply Split on Same-Sex Marriage, Poll Suggests." Retrieved May 2, 2008 (http://www.cbc.ca/story/canada/national/2005/04/10/gay-marriage-050410.html).

———. 2007. "Casualties in the IRAQ War." Retrieved January 13, 2008 (http://www.cbc.ca/news/background/iraq/casualties.html).

———. 2010a. "Canadians Split on Pot, Death Penalty." 18 March. Retrieved November 11, 2010 (http://www.cbc.ca/canada/story/2010/03/18/ekos-poll018.html).

———. 2010b. "Cheese Recall Affects Sandwich Businesses." December 6. Retrieved December 7, 20110 (http://www.cbc.ca/consumer/story/2010/12/06/con-saputo-cheese-sandwich.html).

Central Intelligence Agency. 2001. *The World Factbook 2001*. Retrieved June 25, 2002 (http://www.cia.gov/cia/publications/factbook).

———. 2002. *The World Factbook 2002*. Retrieved October 6, 2008 (http://www.faqs.org/docs/factbook/index.html).

Centre for Economic Policy Research. 2002. *Making Sense of Globalization: A Guide to the Economic Issues*. London.

Chagnon, Napoleon. 1992. *Yanomamö: The Last Days of Eden*. New York: Harcourt, Brace Yovanovich.

Chang, Ha-Joon. 2002. *Kicking Away the Ladder: Development Strategy in Historical Perspective*. London: Anthem Press.

Chard, Jennifer. 2000. "Women in a Visible Minority." Pp. 219–44 in *Women in Canada, 2000: A Gender-Based Statistical Report*. Ottawa: Statistics Canada.

Charlton, James I. 1998. *Nothing about Us without Us: Disability Oppression and Empowerment*. Berkeley, CA: University of California Press.

Chauncey, George. 2005. *Why Marriage? The History Shaping Today's Debate over Gay Equality*. New York: Basic Books.

Chaves, Mark. 1994. "Secularization as Declining Religious Authority." *Social Forces* 72: 749–74.

Cherlin, Andrew J. 1992. *Marriage, Divorce, Remarriage*, rev. ed. Cambridge, MA: Harvard University Press.

Cherlin, Andrew J., Frank F. Furstenberg, Jr., P. Lindsay Chase-Lansdale, Kathleen E. Kiernan, Philip K. Robins, Donna Ruane Morrison, and Julien O. Teitler. 1991. "Longitudinal Studies of Effects of Divorce on Children in Great Britain and the United States." *Science* 252: 1386–89.

Chesley, L., D. MacAulay, and J. L. Ristock. 1991. *Abuse in Lesbian Relationships: A Handbook of Information and Resources*. Toronto: Counselling Centre for Lesbians and Gays.

Chesnais, Jean-Claude. 1992 [1986]. *The Demographic Transition: Stages, Patterns, and Economic Implications*, Elizabeth Kreager and Philip Kreager, trans. Oxford, UK: Clarendon Press.

"Chinese Community." 2001. Retrieved March 15, 2001 (http://www.direct.ca/news/cchi/chin02.shtml).

Chomsky, Noam. 1991. *Deterring Democracy*. London: Verso.

"Chronological Perspective on Work Stoppages in Canada." 1999. Retrieved June 30, 2001 (http://labour.hrdc-drhc.gc.ca/doc/wid-dimt/eng/ws-at/table.cfm).

"Chronological Perspective on Work Stoppages in Canada." 2001a. Retrieved March 22, 2001 (http://labour.hrdc-drhc.gc.ca/doc/wid-dimt/eng/ws-at/table.cfm).

"Chronological Perspective on Work Stoppages in Canada (Work Stoppages Involving One or More Workers), 1976–2000." 2001b. Retrieved March 27, 2001 (http://labour-travail.hrdc-drhc.gc.ca/doc/wid-dimt/eng/ws_at/table.cfm).

Church of God. 2001. Retrieved March 27, 2001 (http://www.childrentaken.com/mediastatement.html).

Church, Gardner, Kenneth Greenberg, and Marilou McPhedran. 1997. "Toronto: An Urban Alternative." Pp. 93–112 in Robert Geddes, ed. *Cities in Our Future: Growth and Form, Environmental Health and Social Equity*. Washington, DC: Island Press.

CIA. 2011. *World Factbook*. Retrieved October 29, 2011 (https://www.cia.gov/library/publications/the-world-factbook/).

Cicourel, Aaron. 1968. *The Social Organization of Juvenile Justice*. New York: Wiley.

Citizenship and Immigration Canada. 2000. "The Vancouver Riot of 1907." Retrieved March 16, 2001.

———. 2004. *Facts and Figures: Immigration Overview, Permanent and Temporary Residents*. Ottawa: Citizenship and Immigration Canada. Retrieved November 30, 2005 (http://www.cic.gc.ca/english/pdf/pub/facts2004.pdf).

———. 2009. "Canada Facts and Figures: Immigrant Overview Permanent and Temporary Residents." Retrieved April 25, 2011 (http://www.cic.gc.ca/english/resources/statistics/menu-fact.asp).

Clairborne, William. 2001. "Canadians from Sect Flee to U.S. over Right to Spank." Retrieved November 30, 2005 (http://www.nospank.net/n-127.htm).

Clairmont, Donald H., and Dennis W. Magill. 1999. *Africville: The Life and Death of a Canadian Black Community*, 3rd ed. Toronto: Canadian Scholars' Press.

Clapp, Jennifer. 1998. "Foreign Direct Investment in Hazardous Industries in Developing Countries: Rethinking the Debate." *Environmental Politics* 7, 4: 92–113.

Clark, S. D. 1968. *The Developing Canadian Community*, 2nd ed. Toronto: University of Toronto Press.

Clark, Terry Nichols, and Seymour Martin Lipset. 1991. "Are Social Classes Dying?" *International Sociology* 6: 397–410.

Clark, Terry Nichols, Seymour Martin Lipset, and Michael Rempel. 1993. "The Declining Political Significance of Class." *International Sociology* 8: 293–316.

Clark, W. 2003. "Pockets of Belief: Religious Attendance Patterns in Canada." *Canadian Social Trends* 68 (Spring): 2–5.

Clark, Warren. 2000. "Religious Observance, Marriage and Family." Pp. 109–14 in *Canadian Social Trends: Volume 3*. Toronto: Thompson Educational Publishing.

Clarke, Harold D., Jane Jenson, Lawrence LeDuc, and Jon H. Pammett. 1996. *Absent Mandate: Canadian Electoral Politics in an Era of Restructuring*, 3rd ed. Toronto: Gage.

Clarke-Stewart, K. Alison, Christian P. Gruber, and Linda May Fitzgerald. 1994. *Children at Home and in Day Care*. Hillsdale, NJ: Lawrence Erlbaum.

Clawson, D. 1980. *Bureaucracy and the Labor Process: The Transformation of U.S. Industry, 1860–1920*. New York: Monthly Review Press.

Clement, W. 1975. *The Canadian Corporate Elite: An Analysis of Economic Power*. Toronto: McClelland & Stewart.

Clement, W., and J. Myles. 1994. *Relations of Ruling: Class and Gender in Postindustrial Societies*. Montreal and Kingston: McGill-Queen's University Press.

Clement, W. H. P. 1897. *The History of the Dominion of Canada*. Toronto: William Briggs.

Cleveland, Gordon, and Michael Krashinsky. 1998. *The Benefits and Costs of Good Child Care: The Economic Rationale for Public Investment in Young Children*. Toronto: University of Toronto.

Clifton, Rodney, and Lance Roberts. 1993. *Authority in Schools*. Toronto: Prentice-Hall.

Clinard, Marshall B., and Peter C. Yeager. 1980. *Corporate Crime*. New York: Free Press.

Cloward, Richard A., and Lloyd E. Ohlin. 1960. *Delinquency and Opportunity: A Theory of Delinquent Gangs*. New York: Free Press.

Coale, Ansley J. 1974. "The History of Human Population." *Scientific American* 23, 3: 41–51.

Coale, Ansley J., and Susan C. Watkins, eds. 1986. *The Decline of Fertility in Europe*. Princeton, NJ: Princeton University Press.

Cockerham, William C. 1998. *Medical Sociology*, 7th ed. Upper Saddle River, NJ: Prentice-Hall.

Coghlan, Banjamin, Richard J. Brennan, Pascal Ngoy, David Dofara, Brad Otto, Mark Clements, and Tony Stewart. 2006. "Mortality in the Democratic Republic of Congo: A Nationwide Survey." *The Lancet* 367: 44–51.

Cohen, Albert. 1955. *Delinquent Boys: The Subculture of a Gang*. New York: Free Press.

Cohen, Lynne. 1999. "Suing the Alternative Health-Care Provider." *Canadian Lawyer* November/December: 47–51.

Cohen, Stanley. 1972. *Folk Devils and Moral Panics: The Creation of the Mods and Rockers*. London: MacGibbon and Kee.

Colapinto, John. 1997. "The True Story of John/Joan." *Rolling Stone* December 11: 54–73, 92–97.

———. 2001. *As Nature Made Him: The Boy Who Was Raised as a Girl*. Toronto: HarperCollins.

Cole, Michael. 1995. *Cultural Psychology*. Cambridge, MA: Harvard University Press.

Cole, S., D. Denny, A. E. Eyler, and S. L. Samons. 2000. "Issues of Transgender." Pp. 149–95 in L. T. Szuchman and F. Mascarella, eds. *Psychological Perspectives on Human Sexuality*. New York: Wiley.

Coleman, James S. 1961. *The Adolescent Society*. New York: Free Press.

———. 1988. "Social Capital in the Creation of Human Capital." *American Journal of Sociology* 94: 95–120.

———. 1990. *Foundations of Social Theory*. Cambridge, MA: Harvard University Press.

Coleman, James, Ernest Campbell, Carol Hobson, James McPartland, Alexander Mood, Frederic Weinfeld, and Robert York. 1966. *Equality of Educational Opportunity*. Washington, DC: United States Department of Health, Education, and Welfare, Office of Education.

Collins, Randall. 1979. *The Credential Society: An Historical Sociology of Education*. New York: Academic Press.

———. 1982. *Sociological Insight: An Introduction to Non-obvious Sociology*. New York: Oxford University Press.

———. 1993. "Review of *A Theory of Religion* by Rodney Stark and William S. Bainbridge." *Journal for the Scientific Study of Religion* 32, 4: 402–4, 406.

Collins, Randall, and Scott Coltrane. 1991. *Sociology of Marriage and the Family*, 3rd ed. Chicago: Nelson-Hall.

Competition Bureau. 2002. "Comments of the Commissioner of Competition to the Standing Committee on Canadian Heritage on the Study of the State of the Canadian Broadcasting System." Ottawa: Government of Canada. Retrieved May 19, 2002 (http://strategis.ic.gc.ca/pics/ct/writtensubmission.pdf).

Condry, J., and S. Condry. 1976. "Sex Differences: The Eye of the Beholder." *Child Development* 47: 812–19.

Conley, Dalton. 1999. *Being Black, Living in the Red: Race, Wealth, and Social Policy in America*. Berkeley: University of California Press.

Conrad, Peter, and Joseph W. Schneider. 1992. *Deviance and Medicalization: From Badness to Sickness*, expanded ed. Philadelphia: Temple University Press.

Converse, J. M., and S. Presser. 1986. *Survey Questions: Handcrafting the Standardized Questionnaire*. Newbury Park, CA: Sage.

Cooley, Charles Horton. 1902. *Human Nature and the Social Order*. New York: Scribner's.

Coontz, Stephanie. 1992. *The Way We Never Were: American Families and the Nostalgia Trap*. New York: Basic Books.

Coontz, Stephanie, and Peta Henderson. 1986. *Women's Work, Men's Property: The Origins of Gender and Class*. London, UK: Verso.

Coser, Rose Laub. 1960. "Laughter among Colleagues: A Study of the Functions of Humor among the Staff of a Mental Hospital." *Psychiatry* 23: 81–95.

Côté, James, and Anton L. Allahar. 2007. *Ivory Tower Blues: A University System in Crisis*. Toronto: University of Toronto Press.

Couch, Carl J. 1968. "Collective Behavior: An Examination of Some Stereotypes." *Social Problems* 15: 310–22.

Coupland, Douglas. 1991. *Generation X: Tales for an Accelerated Culture*. New York: St. Martin's Press.

Cox, Wendell. 1997. "Local and Regional Governance in the Greater Toronto Area: A Review of Alternatives." Retrieved March 27, 2001 (http://www.publicpurpose.com/tor-demo.htm).

Creese, G. 1999. *Contracting Masculinity: Gender, Class, and Race in a White-Collar Union, 1944–1994*. Don Mills, ON: Oxford University Press Canada.

Creighton, Sarah, and Catherine Mihto. 2001. "Managing Intersex." *BMJ: British Medical Journal* 323, 7324 (December): 1264–65.

Crompton, Susan, and Michael Vickers. 2000. "One Hundred Years of Labour Force." *Canadian Social Trends* Summer: 2–5.

Croteau, David, and William Hoynes. 1997. *Media/Society: Industries, Images, and Audiences*. Thousand Oaks, CA: Pine Forge Press.

Crothers, Charles. 1979. "On the Myth of Rural Tranquility: Comment on Webb and Collette." *American Journal of Sociology* 84: 429–37.

Crozier, Michel. 1964 [1963]. *The Bureaucratic Phenomenon*. Chicago: University of Chicago Press.

"The CRTC's Mandate." 2002. Retrieved May 15, 2003 (http://www.crtc.gc.ca/eng/BACKGRND/Brochures/B29903.htm).

Curran, John. 2000. "Thinner Miss Americas: Study: Some Contestants Undernourished." ABCNEWS.com. Retrieved February 15, 2001 (wysiwyg://7/http://abcnews.go.com/sections/living/DailyNews/missamerica000322.htmk).

Curtis, James, John Loy, and Wally Karnilowicz. 1986. "A Comparison of Suicide-Dip Effects of Major Sport Events and Civil Holidays." *Sociology of Sport Journal* 3: 1–14.

CyberPress. 2001. "The Recidivist Roger Caron Stopped Once Again" (translated from the French), October 14. Retrieved October 10, 2002 (http://216.239.37.120/transl).

Dahl, Robert A. 1961. *Who Governs?* New Haven, CT: Yale University Press.

Dalphonse, Sherri. 1997. "Childfree by Choice." *The Washingtonian* 32, 5: 48–57.

Darwin, Charles. 1859. *On the Origin of Species by Means of Natural Selection*. London: John Murray.

———. 1871. *The Descent of Man*. London: JohnMurray.

Davies, J. B. 1999. "Distribution of Wealth and Economic Inequality." Pp. 138–50 in J. Curtis, E. Grabb, and N. Guppy, eds. *Social Inequality in Canada: Patterns, Problems, Policies*, 3rd ed. Scarborough, ON: Prentice Hall Allyn and Bacon Canada.

Davies, James C. 1969. "Toward a Theory of Revolution." Pp. 85–108 in Barry McLaughlin, ed. *Studies in Social Movements: A Social Psychological Perspective*. New York: Free Press.

Davis, Fred. 1992. *Fashion, Culture, and Identity*. Chicago: University of Chicago Press.

Davis, Kingsley, and Wilbert. E. Moore. 1944. "Some Principles of Stratification." *American Sociological Review* 10: 242–49.

Davis, Lennard J. 1995. *Enforcing Normalcy: Disability, Deafness, and the Body*. London: Verso.

Davis, Mike. 1990. *City of Quartz: Excavating the Future in Los Angeles*. New York: Verso.

Dawson, S. E. 1906. "Principal Causes of Death." Table IV. *Fourth Census of Canada, 1901, Volume IV*. Ottawa: Library and Archives Canada.

Dee, Thomas S., and Brian A. Jacob. 2010. *Rational Ignorance in Education: A Field Experiment in Student Plagiarism*. Cambridge, MA: National Bureau of Economic Research. Retrieved January 15, 2011 (http://www.nber.org/papers/w15672).

DeFine, Michael Sullivan. 1997. "A History of Governmentally Coerced Sterilization: The Plight of the Native American Woman." Retrieved April 24, 2003 (http://www.geocities.com/CapitolHill/9118/mike2.html).

DeKeseredy, Walter S., and Katherine Kelly. 1993. "The Incidence and Prevalence of Woman Abuse in Canadian University and College Dating Relationships." *Canadian Journal of Sociology* 18: 137–59.

Department of Geography, Slippery Rock University. 1997. "World's Largest Cities, 1900." Retrieved May 2, 2000 (http://www.sru.edu/depts/artsci/ges/discover/d-6-8.htm).

———. 2003. "World's Largest Urban Agglomerations, 2015." Retrieved August 2, 2006 (http://www1.sru.edu/gge/faculty/hughes/100/100-6/d-6-9b.htm).

Department of Justice, Canada. 2004. "Pay Equity: A New Approach to a Fundamental Right." Retrieved May 14, 2006 (http://canada.justice.gc.ca/en/payeqsal/index.html).

Derber, Charles. 1979. *The Pursuit of Attention: Power and Individualism in Everyday Life.* New York: Oxford University Press.

DeSoya, Indra, and John Oneal. 1999. "Boon or Bane? Reassessing the Productivity of Foreign Direct Investment with New Data." *American Sociological Review* 64: 766–782.

DeSteno, David, and Peter Salovey. 2001. "Evolutionary Origins of Sex Differences in Jealousy: Questioning the 'Fitness' of the Model." Pp. 150–56 in W. Gerrod Parrott, ed. *Emotions in Social Psychology: Essential Readings.* Philadelphia: Psychology Press.

Deutscher, Guy. 2010. "Does Your Language Shape How You Think?" *The New York Times* August 26. Retrieved June 7, 2011 (http://www.nytimes.com).

de Villiers, Marq. 1999. *Water.* Toronto: Stoddart.

Diamond, Larry. 1996. "Is the Third Wave Over?" *Journal of Democracy* 7, 3: 20–37. Retrieved May 1, 2000 (http://muse.jhu.edu/demo/jod/7.3diamond.html).

Diamond, Milton, and H. Keith Sigmundson. 1999. "Sex Reassignment at Birth." Pp. 55–75 in Stephen J. Ceci and Wendy W. Williams, eds. *The Nature–Nurture Debate: The Essential Readings.* Maldan, MA: Blackwell.

Dietz, Tracy L. 1998. "An Examination of Violence and Gender Role Portrayals in Video Games: Implications for Gender Socialization and Aggressive Behavior." *Sex Roles* 38: 425–42.

DiMaggio, Paul, and Walter Powell. 1983. "The Iron Cage Revisited: Institutional Isomorphism and Collective Rationality in Organizational Fields." *American Sociological Review* 48: 147–60.

Doberman, J. 1997. *Darwin's Athletes: How Sport Has Damaged Black America and Preserved the Myth of Race.* Boston: Houghton Mifflin.

Doherty, G. 1997. *Zero to Six: The Basis for School Readiness.* Ottawa: Applied Research Branch, Human Resources Development Canada (#R-97-8E).

Dolnick, Edward. 1993. "Deafness as Culture." *The Atlantic Monthly* 272, 3: 37–48.

Donahue, John J., III, and Steven D. Levitt. 2001. "The Impact of Legalized Abortion on Crime." *Quarterly Journal of Economics* 116: 379–420.

Dore, Ronald. 1983. "Goodwill and the Spirit of Market Capitalism." *British Journal of Sociology* 34: 459–82.

Doremus, P. N., W. W. Keller, L. W. Pauly, and S. Reich. 1998. *The Myth of the Global Corporation.* Princeton, NJ: Princeton University Press.

Douglas, Jack D. 1967. *The Social Meanings of Suicide.* Princeton, NJ: Princeton University Press.

Douglas, Emily M., and Murray A. Straus. (2006) "Assault and Injury of Dating Partners by University Students in 19 Nations and Its Relation to Corporal Punishment Experienced as a Child." *European Journal of Criminology* 3: 293–318.

Doyle, Aaron, Brian Elliott, and David Tindall. 1997. "Framing the Forests: Corporations, the B.C. Forest Alliance, and the Media." Pp. 240–68 in William Carroll, ed. *Organizing Dissent: Contemporary Social Movements in Theory and Practice,* 2nd ed. Toronto: Garamond Press.

Dranoff, Linda Silver. 2001. *Everyone's Guide to the Law.* Toronto: HarperCollins.

Drèze, Jean, and Amartya Sen. 1989. *Hunger and Public Action.* Oxford, UK: Clarendon Press.

Duffy, A., D. Glenday, and N. Pupo, eds. 1997. *Good Jobs, Bad Jobs, No Jobs: The Transformation of Work in the 21st Century.* Toronto: Harcourt Brace.

Duffy, Jim, Georg Gunther, and Lloyd Wulters. 1997. "Gender and Mathematical Problem Solving." *Sex Roles* 37: 477–94.

Dugger, Karen. 1996. "Social Location and Gender-Role Attitudes: A Comparison of Black and White Women." Pp. 32–51 in Esther Ngan-Ling Chow, Doris Wilkinson, and Maxine Baca Zinn, eds. *Race, Class, and Gender.* Newbury Park, CA: Sage.

Duhaime, Lloyd. 1997. "Euthanasia in Canada." Retrieved August 9, 2000 (wysiwyg://17/http://www.duhaime.org/ca-euth.htm).

Duncan, Greg, W. Jean Yeung, Jeanne Brooks-Gunn, and Judith Smith. 1998. "How Much Does Childhood Poverty Affect the Life Chance of Children?" *American Sociological Review* 63: 402–23.

Dunk, T. 1991. *It's a Working Man's Town: Male Working Class Culture in Northwestern Ontario.* Montreal: McGill-Queen's University Press.

Durham, William H. 1979. *Scarcity and Survival in Central America: Ecological Origins of the Soccer War.* Stanford, CA: Stanford University Press.

Durkheim, Émile. 1938. *The Rules of Sociological Method,* trans. S. Solovay and J. Mueller; ed. G. E. G. Catlin. Chicago: University of Chicago Press.

———. 1951 [1897]. *Suicide: A Study in Sociology,* G. Simpson, ed., J. Spaulding and G. Simpson, trans. New York: Free Press.

———. 1956. *Education and Sociology,* Sherwood D. Fox, trans. New York: Free Press.

———. 1961 [1925]. *Moral Education: A Study in the Theory and Application of the Sociology of Education,* Everett K. Wilson and Herman Schnurer, trans. New York: Free Press.

———. 1973 [1899–1900]. "Two Laws of Penal Evolution." *Economy and Society* 2: 285–308.

———. 1976 [1915]. *The Elementary Forms of the Religious Life,* Joseph Ward Swain, trans. New York: Free Press.

Dutton, Judy. 2000. "Detect His Lies Every Time." *Cosmopolitan* April: 126.

Dyson, Freeman. 1999. *The Sun, the Genome, and the Internet.* New York: Oxford University Press.

Eagles, Munroe. 1993. "Money and Votes in Canada: Campaign Spending and Parliamentary Election Outcomes, 1984 and 1988." *Canadian Public Policy* 19: 432–49.

Eagley, Alice H., and Wendy Wood. 1999. "The Origins of Sex Differences in Human Behaviour: Evolved Dispositions versus Social Roles." *American Psychologist* 54: 408–23.

Eccles, Jacquelynne S., Robert Roeser, Allan Wigfield, and Carol Freedman-Doen. 1999. "Academic and Motivational Pathways through Middle Childhood." Pp. 287–377 in Lawrence Balter, ed. *Child Psychology.* Philadelphia: Psychology Press.

Eccles, J. S., J. F. Jacobs, and R. D. Harold. 1990. "Gender Role Stereotypes, Expectancy Effects and Parents' Socialization of Gender Differences." *Journal of Social Issues* 46: 183–201.

Economakis, Evel, and Robert J. Brym. 1995. "Marriage and Militance in a Working Class District of St. Petersburg, 1896–1913." *Journal of Family History* 20: 23–43.

Edel, Abraham. 1965. "Social Science and Value: A Study in Interrelations." Pp. 218–38 in Irving Louis Horowitz, ed. *The New Sociology: Essays in Social Science and Social Theory in Honor of C. Wright Mills.* New York: Oxford University Press.

EGALE. 2001. "Svend Robinson Introduces Bill, EGALE Renews Call for Hate Crimes Protection in Wake of Murder of Gay Man in Vancouver." Press release, November 22. Retrieved February 10, 2002 (http://www.egale.ca/pressrel/011122.htm).

eHarlequin.com. 2000. "About eHarlequin.com." Retrieved May 17, 2000 (http://eharlequin.women.com/harl/globals/about/00bkrd11.htm).

Ehrlich, Paul R., Gretchen C. Daily, Scott C. Daily, Norman Myers, and James Salzman. 1997. "No Middle Way on the Environment." *Atlantic Monthly* 280, 6: 98–104. Retrieved October 8, 2000 (http://www.theatlantic.com/issues/97dec/enviro.htm).

Ehrlich, Paul, and Robert Ornstein. 2010. *Humanity on a Tightrope: Thoughts on Empathy, Family, and Big Changes for a Viable Future.* Lanham, MD: Rowman & Littlefield.

Eichler, Margrit. 1987. *Nonsexist Research Methods,* Boston: Allen & Unwin.

———. 1988a. *Families in Canada Today,* 2nd ed. Toronto: Gage.

———. 1988b. *Nonsexist Research Methods: A Practical Guide.* Boston: Unwin Hyman.

Einstein, Albert. 1954. *Ideas and Opinions,* Carl Seelig, ed., Sonja Bargmann, trans. New York: Crown.

Eisenstadt, S. N. 1956. *From Generation to Generation.* New York: Free Press.

Eisenstein, Elizabeth L. 1983. *The Printing Revolution in Early Modern Europe.* Cambridge/New York: Cambridge University Press.

Eisler, Riane. 1987. *The Chalice and the Blade: Our History, Our Future.* New York: HarperCollins.

Ekman, Paul. 1978. *Facial Action Coding System*. New York: Consulting Psychologists Press.

Elections Canada. 2005. "Estimation of Voter Turnout by Age Group at the 38th General Election." Retrieved June 28, 2006 (http://www.elections.ca/loi/report_e.pdf).

———. 2006. "Report of the Chief Electoral Officer of Canada on the 39th General Election of January 23, 2006." Retrieved October 16, 2008 (http://enr.elections.ca).

———. 2008, "40th General Election." Retrieved October 16, 2008 (http://enr. elections ca).

———. 2011. "Official Voting Results: Forty-First General Election 2011." Retrieved September 6, 2011 (http://www.elections.ca/scripts/ovr2011/default.html).

Elias, Norbert. 1985 [1982]. *The Loneliness of the Dying*, Edmund Jephcott, trans. Oxford, UK: Blackwell.

———. 1994 [1939]. *The Civilizing Process*, Edmund Jephcott, trans. Cambridge, MA: Blackwell.

Elliott, H. L. 1995. "Living Vicariously through Barbie." Retrieved November 19, 1998 (http://ziris.syr.edu/path/public_html/barbie/main.html).

Ellis, Brett Easton. 1991. *American Psycho*. New York: Vintage.

Ellis, Lee, Brian Robb, and Donald Burke. 2005. "Sexual Orientation in United States and Canadian College Students." *Archives of Sexual Behavior* 34: 569–81.

Ellul, Jacques. 1964 [1954]. *The Technological Society*, John Wilkinson, trans. New York: Vintage.

Engels, Frederick. 1970 [1884]. *The Origins of the Family, Private Property and the State*, Eleanor Burke Leacock, ed., Alec West, trans. New York: International Publishers.

England, Charles R. n.d. "A Look at the Indian Health Service Policy of Sterilization, 1972–1976." Retrieved April 23, 2003 (http://www.dickshovel.com/IHSSterPol.html).

England, Paula. 1992. *Comparable Worth: Theories and Evidence*. Hawthorne, NY: Aldine de Gruyter.

Entine, J. 2000. *Taboo: Why Black Athletes Dominate Sports and Why We Are Afraid to Talk about It*. New York: Public Affairs.

Epstein, Helen. 1998. "Life and Death on the Social Ladder." *New York Review of Books* 45, 12 (16 July): 26–30.

Epstein, Steven. 1996. *Impure Science: AIDS, Activism, and the Politics of Knowledge*. Berkeley, CA: University of California Press.

Equal Voice. 2005. "The Facts, Ma'am." Retrieved June 12, 2006 (http://www.equalvoice.ca/research.html).

Erwin, J. 1988. "R.E.A.L. Women, Anti-Feminism, and the Welfare State." *Resources for Feminist Research* 17, 3 (September): 147–49.

Esping-Andersen, Gøsta. 1990. *The Three Worlds of Welfare Capitalism*. Princeton, NJ: Princeton University Press.

Estrich, Susan. 1987. *Real Rape*. Cambridge, MA: Harvard University Press.

"Ethnic Groups in the World." 2001. *Scientific American*. Retrieved December 4, 2001 (http://www.sciam.com/1998/0998issue/0998numbers.html).

Evans, Peter B., Dietrich Rueschemeyer, and Theda Skocpol. 1985. *Bringing the State Back In*. Cambridge, UK: Cambridge University Press.

Evans, Robert G. 1999. "Social Inequalities in Health." *Horizons* (Policy Research Secretariat, Government of Canada) 2, 3: 6–7.

Facebook. 2010. "Timeline." Retrieved October 9, 2010 (https://www.facebook.com/press/info.php?timeline).

———. 2011. "Statistics." Retrieved September 20, 2011 (http://www.facebook.com/press/info.php?statistics).

"Face of the Web Study Pegs Global Internet Population at More Than 300 Million." 2000. Retrieved October 2, 2000 (http://www.angusreid.com/media/content/displaypr.cfm?idto_view5100).

Fagot, Berly I., Caire S. Rodgers, and Mary D. Leinbach. 2000. "Theories of Gender Socialization." Pp. 65–89 in Thomas Eckes, ed. *The Developmental Social Psychology of Gender*. Mahwah, NJ: Lawrence Erlbaum Associates.

Families Against Deadbeats. 2000. Retrieved June 14, 2003 (http://www.wantedposters.com).

Farrell, Colin. n.d. "The Canadian Prison Strap." Retrieved May 12, 2006 (http://www.corpun.com/canada2.html).

Fattah, Ezzat A. 1991. *Understanding Criminal Victimization: An Introduction to Theoretical Victimology*. Scarborough, ON: Prentice Hall.

Faulkner, Anne H., and Kevin Cranston. 1998. "Correlates of Same-Sex Sexual Behavior in a Random Sample of Massachusetts High School Students." *Journal of Public Health* 88, February: 262–66.

Fava, Sylvia Fleis. 1956. "Suburbanism as a Way of Life." *American Sociological Review* 21: 34–37.

Febvre, Lucien, and Henri-Jean Martin. 1976 [1958]. *The Coming of the Book: The Impact of Printing 1450–1800*, David Gerard, trans. London: NLB.

Feeley, Malcolm M., and Jonathan Simon. 1992. "The New Penology: Notes on the Emerging Strategy of Corrections and its Implications." *Criminology* 30: 449–74.

Fekete, John. 1994. *Moral Panics: Biopolitics Rising*. Toronto: Robert Davies.

Felson, Richard B. 1996. "Mass Media Effects on Violent Behavior." *Annual Review of Sociology* 22: 103–28.

Fernandez-Dols, Jose-Miguel, Flor Sanchez, Pilar Carrera, and Maria-Angeles Ruiz-Belda. 1997. "Are Spontaneous Expressions and Emotions Linked? An Experimental Test of Coherence." *Journal of Nonverbal Behavior* 21: 163–77.

Fields, Jason, and Kristin Smith. 1998. "Poverty, Family Structure, and Child Well-Being." Population Division. Washington, DC: U.S. Bureau of Census.

Figart, Deborah M., and June Lapidus. 1996. "The Impact of Comparable Worth on Earnings Inequality." *Work and Occupations* 23: 297–318.

"Finding God in Harry Potter." 2005. *The Christian Post* 16 July. Retrieved December 14, 2005 (http://www.christianpost.com/article/education/895/section/finding.god.in.harry.potter/1.htm).

Finke, Roger, and Rodney Starke. 1992. *The Churching of America, 1776–1990: Winners and Losers in Our Religious Economy*. New Brunswick, NJ: Rutgers University Press.

Finnie, Ross. 1993. "Women, Men and the Economic Consequences of Divorce: Evidence from Canadian Longitudinal Data." *Canadian Review of Sociology and Anthropology* 30, 2: 205–41.

Firebaugh, Glenn, and Frank D. Beck. 1994. "Does Economic Growth Benefit the Masses? Growth, Dependence and Welfare in the Third World." *American Journal of Sociology* 59: 631–53.

Fischer, Claude S. 1981. "The Public and Private Worlds of City Life." *American Sociological Review* 46: 306–16.

———. 1984 [1976]. *The Urban Experience*, 2nd ed. New York: Harcourt Brace Jovanovich.

Fischer, Claude S., Michael Hout, Martín Sánchez Jankowski, Samuel R. Lucas, Ann Swidler, and Kim Voss. 1996. *Inequality by Design: Cracking the Bell Curve Myth*. Princeton, NJ: Princeton University Press.

Fisher, John. 1999. *A Report on Lesbian, Gay and Bisexual Youth*. Ottawa: EGALE.

Fleischman, Howard L., Paul J. Hopstock, Marisa P. Pelczar, and Brooke E. Shelley. 2010. "Highlights from PISA 2009." Washington, DC: U.S. Department of Education. Retrieved May 24, 2011 (http://nces.ed.gov/pubs2011/2011004.pdf).

Flood, Gavin D. 1996. *An Introduction to Hinduism*. Cambridge: Cambridge University Press.

Floud, Roderick, Kenneth Wachter, and Annabel Gregory. 1990. *Height, Health and History: Nutritional Status in the United Kingdom, 1750–1980*. Cambridge: Cambridge University Press.

Flowers, Paul, and Katie Buston. 2001. "'I Was Terrified of Being Different': Exploring Gay Men's Accounts of Growing-Up in a Heterosexist Society." *Journal of Adolescence, Special Issue: Gay, Lesbian, and Bisexual Youth* 24, 1 (February): 51–65.

Flynn, James R. 1987. "Massive IQ Gains in 14 Nations: What IQ Tests Really Measure." *Psychological Bulletin* 101: 171–91.

Fong, Eric, and Elic Chan. 2008. "An Account of Immigration Studies in the United States and Canada, 1990–2004." *Sociological Quarterly*, 49: 483–502.

"Foreign Direct Investment in 2007." 2008. *EconomyWatch*. Retrieved November 16, 2010 (http://www.economywatch.com/foreign-direct-investment/2007.html).

Forrest, C. B., and A. W. Riley. 2004. "Childhood Origins of Adult Health: A Basis for Life-Course Health Policy." *Health Affairs* 23, 5: 155–64.

Förster, M., and M. Pellizzari. 2000. *Trends and Driving Factors in Income Distribution and Poverty in the OECD Area*. Labour Market and Social Policy Occasional Papers No. 42. Paris: OECD.

Forman, Murray. 2001. "It Ain't All about the Benjamins: Summit on Social Responsibility in the Hip-Hop Industry." *Journal of Popular Music Studies* 13: 117–23.

Foucault, Michel. 1977. *Discipline and Punish: The Birth of the Prison*, Alan Sheridan, trans. New York: Pantheon.

Fox, Yale, and Robert J. Brym. 2009. "Musical Attention Deficit Disorder." Darwin vs. The Machine. Retrieved May 30, 2010 (http://www.darwinversusthemachine.com/2009/10/musical-attention-deficit-disorder).

Francis, D. 1992. *The Imaginary Indian: The Image of the Indian in Canadian Culture*. Vancouver, BC: Arsenal Pulp Press.

Franco, Zeno, and Philip Zimbardo. 2006–07. "The Banality of Heroism." *Greater Good* 3, 2: 33–4. Retrieved January 3, 2008 (http://greatergood.berkeley.edu/greatergood/archive/2006fallwinter/francozimbardo.html).

Frank, Jeffrey. 1992. "Voting and Contributing: Political Participation in Canada." *Canadian Social Trends* 27:2–6.

Frank Porter Graham Child Development Center. 1999. "Early Learning, Later Success: The Abecedarian Study." Retrieved August 10, 2000 (http://www.fpg.unc.edu/~abc/abcedarianWeb/index.htm).

Frank, Thomas, and Matt Weiland, eds. 1997. *Commodify Your Dissent: Salvos from the Baffler*. New York: Norton.

Franke, Richard W., and Barbara H. Chasin. 1992. *Kerala: Development through Radical Reform*. San Francisco: Institute for Food and Development Policy.

Frankel, Glenn. 1996. "U.S. Aided Cigarette Firms in Conquests Across Asia." *Washington Post* November 17: A01. Retrieved February 8, 2003 (http://www.washingtonpost.com/wp-srv/national/longterm/tobacco/stories/asia.htm).

Franklin, Karen. 1998. "Psychosocial Motivations of Hate Crime Perpetrators." Paper presented at the annual meetings of the American Psychological Association (San Francisco: 16 August).

Fraser Institute. 2007 *Home Schooling: From the Extreme to the Mainstream*. Studies in Educational Policy. Retrieved March 10, 2011 (http://www.fraserinstitute.org/research-news/display.aspx?id=13089).

Freedman, Jonathan L. 2002. *Media Violence and Its Effect on Aggression: Assessing the Scientific Evidence*. Toronto: University of Toronto Press.

Freedom House. 2010. "Freedom in the World 2010 Population Statistics." Retrieved February 12, 2011 (http://freedomhouse.org/template.cfm?page=544).

Freeze, Colin, and Karen Howlett. 2005. "McGuinty Government Rules out Use of Sharia Law." *The Globe and Mail*. Retrieved December 8, 2005 (http://www.theglobeandmail.com/servlet/story/RTGAM.20050912.wxsharia12/BNStory/National).

Freidson, Eliot. 1986. *Professional Powers: A Study of the Institutionalization of Formal Knowledge*. Chicago: University of Chicago Press.

Freire, Paolo. 1972. *The Pedagogy of the Oppressed*. New York: Herder and Herder.

French, Howard W. 2001. "The Japanese, It Seems, Are Outgrowing Japan." *The New York Times* February 1: 4A.

Freud, Sigmund. 1962 [1930]. *Civilization and Its Discontents*, James Strachey, trans. New York: Norton.

———. 1973 [1915–17]. *Introductory Lectures on Psychoanalysis*, James Strachey, trans., James Strachey and Angela Richards, eds. Harmondsworth, UK: Penguin.

———. 1977 [1905]. *On Sexuality*, James Strachey, trans., Angela Richards, comp., and ed. Harmondsworth, UK: Penguin.

Freudenburg, William R. 1997. "Contamination, Corrosion and the Social Order: An Overview." *Current Sociology* 45, 3: 19–39.

Fried, Martha Nemes, and Morton H. Fried. 1980. *Transitions: Four Rituals in Eight Cultures*. New York: Norton.

Friedenberg, Edgar Z. 1959. *The Vanishing Adolescent*. Boston: Beacon Press.

Fröbel, Folker, Jürgen Heinrichs, and Otto Kreyre. 1980. *The New International Division of Labour: Structural Unemployment in Industrialised Countries and Industrialisation in Developing Countries*. Pete Burgess, trans. Cambridge: Cambridge University Press.

Froissart, Jean. 1968 [c. 1365]. *Chronicles*, selected and translated by Geoffrey Brereton. Harmondsworth, UK: Penguin.

Furstenberg, Frank F., Jr., and Andrew Cherlin. 1991. *Divided Families: What Happens to Children When Parents Part*. Cambridge, MA: Harvard University Press.

Galabuzi, G.-E. 2004. *Social Inclusion as a Determinant of Health*. Ottawa: Public Health Agency of Canada. Retrieved July 2, 2005 (http://www.phac-aspc.gc.ca/ph-sp/phdd/overview_implications/03_inclusion.html).

Gallup Organization. 2000. "Gallup Poll Topics: A-Z." Retrieved July 25, 2002 (http://www.gallup.com/poll/indicators/indhomosexual.asp).

Galper, Joseph. 1998. "Schooling for Society." *American Demographics* 20, 3: 33–34.

Galt, Virginia. 2006. "'Working Retired' in Demand as Work Force Ages." *The Globe and Mail* February 4: B11.

Gambetta, Diego, ed. 1988. *Trust: Making and Breaking Cooperative Relations*. Oxford, UK: Blackwell.

Gamson, William A. 1975. *The Strategy of Social Protest*. Homewood, IL: Dorsey Press.

Gamson, William A., Bruce Fireman, and Steven Rytina. 1982. *Encounters with Unjust Authority*. Homewood, IL: Dorsey Press.

Gans, Herbert. 1962. *The Urban Villagers: Group and Class in the Life of Italian-Americans*. New York: Free Press.

———. 1979. *Deciding What's News: A Study of CBS Evening News, NBC Nightly News, Newsweek and Time*. New York: Pantheon.

———. 1991. "Symbolic Ethnicity: The Future of Ethnic Groups and Cultures in America." Pp. 430–43 in Norman R. Yetman, ed. *Majority and Minority: The Dynamics of Race and Ethnicity in American Life*, 5th ed. Boston, MA: Allyn and Bacon.

Garfinkel, Harold. 1967. *Studies in Ethnomethodology*. Englewood Cliffs, NJ: Prentice-Hall.

Garfinkel, Simson. 2000. *Database Nation: The Death of Privacy in the 21st Century*. Cambridge, MA: O'Reilly.

Garland, David. 1990. *Punishment and Modern Society: A Study in Social Theory*. Chicago: University of Chicago Press.

Garner, David M. 1997. "The 1997 Body Image Survey Results." *Psychology Today* 30, 1: 30–44.

Garrau, Joel. 1991. *Edge City: Life on the New Frontier*. New York: Doubleday.

Garvey, Christine Ann. 1999. "The Intergenerational Transmission of Discipline." *Dissertation Abstracts International, Section A: The Sciences and Engineering* 60, 3-B (September): 1027.

Gaskell, Jane, Arlene McLaren, and Myra Novogrodsky. 1995. "What's Worth Knowing? Defining the Feminist Curriculum." Pp. 100–18 in E. D. Nelson and B. W. Robinson, eds. *Gender in the 1990s: Images, Realities, and Issues*. Scarborough: Nelson Canada.

Gates, W., with N. Myhrvold and P. Rinearson. 1996. *The Road Ahead*. New York: Penguin.

Gauvain, Mary, Beverly I. Fagot, Craig Leve, and Kate Kavanagh. 2002. "Instruction by Mothers and Fathers During Problem Solving with Their Young Children." *Journal of Family Psychology* 6, 1 (March): 81–90.

Geddes, Robert, ed. 1997. *Cities in Our Future: Growth and Form, Environmental Health and Social Equity*. Washington, DC: Island Press.

Gegax, T. Trent, and Lynette Clemetson. 1998. "The Abortion Wars Come Home." *Newsweek* November 9: 34–35.

Gelbspan, Ross. 1999. "Trading Away Our Chances to End Global Warming." *Boston Globe* May 16: E2.

Gelles, Richard J. 1997. *Intimate Violence in Families*, 3rd ed. Thousand Oaks, CA: Sage.

Gellner, E. 1988. *Plough, Sword and Book: The Structure of Human History*. Chicago: University of Chicago Press.

Gerber, Theodore P., and Michael Hout. 1998. "More Shock than Therapy: Market Transition, Employment, and Income in Russia, 1991–1995." *American Journal of Sociology* 104. 1–50.

Germani, Gino, and Kalman Silvert. 1961. "Politics, Social Structure and Military Intervention in Latin America." *European Journal of Sociology* 11: 62–81.

Gerschenkron, Alexander. 1962. *Economic Backwardness in Historical Perspective: A Book of Essays*. Cambridge, MA: Harvard University Press.

Ghalam, Nancy Z. 1997. "Attitudes Towards Women, Work and Family." *Canadian Social Trends* 46: 13–17.

Ghosh, Bobby. 2011. "Rage, Rap and Revolution: Inside the Arab Youth Quake." *Time.com* February 17. Retrieved February 17, 2011 (http://www.time.com/time/world/article/0,8599,2049808,00.html).

Giddens, Anthony. 1990. *Sociology: A Brief But Critical Introduction*, 3rd ed. New York: Harcourt Brace Jovanovich.

Gidengil, Elisabeth. 1992. "Canada Votes: A Quarter Century of Canadian National Election Studies." *Canadian Journal of Political Science* 25: 219–48.

Gilbert, Susan. 1997. "2 Spanking Studies Indicate Parents Should Be Cautious." *The New York Times* August 20.

Gill, Richard T. 1997. *Posterity Lost: Progress, Ideology, and the Decline of the American Family*. London, UK: Rowman & Littlefield.

Gilligan, Carol. 1982. *In a Different Voice: Psychological Theory and Women's Development*. Cambridge, MA: Harvard University Press.

Gillis, A. R. 1995. "Urbanization." Pp. 13.1–13.35 in Robert J. Brym, ed. *New Society Brief Edition: Sociology for the 21st Century*. Toronto: Harcourt Brace.

Gillis, John R. 1981. *Youth and History: Tradition and Change in European Age Relations, 1770–Present*, expanded student ed. New York: Academic Press.

Gilman, S. L. 1991. *The Jew's Body*. New York: Routledge.

Gilpin, Robert. 2001. *Global Political Economy: Understanding the International Economic Order*. Princeton, NJ: Princeton University Press.

Gimbutas, Marija. 1982. *Goddesses and Gods of Old Europe*. Berkeley and Los Angeles: University of California Press.

Gitlin, Todd. 1983. *Inside Prime Time*. New York: Pantheon.

Gladwell, Malcolm. 2010. "Small Change: Why the Revolution Will Not Be Tweeted." *The New Yorker* 4 October. Retrieved November 27, 2010 (http://www.newyorker.com/reporting/2010/10/04/101004fa_fact_gladwell).

Glazer, Nathan. 1997. *We Are All Multiculturalists Now*. Cambridge, MA: Harvard University Press.

Gleick, James. 2000. *Faster: The Acceleration of Just about Everything*. New York: Vintage.

Glendon, Mary Ann. 1981. *The New Family and the New Property*. Toronto: Butterworths.

Glenn, Norval D. 1990. "Quantitative Research on Marital Quality in the 1980s: A Critical Review." *Journal of Marriage and the Family* 52 (November): 818–31.

Global Reach. 2001. "Global Internet Statistics (by Language)." Retrieved September 23, 2001 (http://www. glreach.com/globstats/index.php3).

———. 2004. "Global Internet Statistics (by Language)." Retrieved January 27, 2005 (http://www.glreach.com/globstats).

Glock, Charles Y. 1962. "On the Study of Religious Commitment." *Religious Education* 62, 4: 98–110.

Goddard Institute for Space Studies. 2010. "Global Temperature Anomalies in 0.01 Degrees Celsius." Retrieved December 1, 2010 (http://data.giss.nasa.gov/gistemp/tabledata/GLB.Ts.txt).

Godley, Jenny, and Lindsay McLaren. 2010. "Socioeconomic Status and Body Mass Index in Canada: Exploring Measures and Mechanisms." *Canadian Review of Sociology* 47: 381–403.

Goffman, Erving. 1959. *The Presentation of Self in Everyday Life*. Garden City, NY: Anchor.

———. 1961. *Asylums: Essays on the Social Situation of Mental Patients and Other Inmates*. Garden City, NY: Anchor Books.

———. 1963. *Stigma: Notes on the Management of Spoiled Identity*. Englewood Cliffs, NJ: Prentice-Hall.

———. 1971. *Relations in Public: Microstudies of the Public Order*. New York: Basic Books.

———. 1974. *Frame Analysis*. Cambridge, MA: Harvard University Press.

Goldberg, M., and D. Green. 1999. *Raising the Floor: The Social and Economic Benefits of Minimum Wages in Canada*. Vancouver: Canadian Center for Policy Alternatives.

Goldie, Terry. 2001. *In a Queer Country: Gay & Lesbian Studies in the Canadian Context*. Vancouver: Arsenal Pulp Press.

"Gold Medal Men's Hockey Game Gets Record Canadian TV Audience." *The Province* 1 March. Retrieved March 28, 2010 (http://www.theprovince.com/entertainment/Gold+medal+hockey+game+gets+record+Canadian+audience/2628644/story.html).

Goldstein, Jay E. 1978. "The Prestige of Canadian Ethnic Groups: Some New Evidence." *Canadian Ethnic Studies* 10: 84–95.

Goldthorpe, J. H., and Richard Breen. 1997. "The Integration of Sociological Research and Theory." *Rationality and Society* 9: 405–26.

Goll, David. 2002. "True Priority of Office Ethics Clouded by Scandals." *East Bay Business Times* August 19. Retrieved January 13, 2003 (http://eastbay.bizjournals.com/eastbay/stories/2002/08/19/smallb3.html).

Gombrich, Richard Francis. 1996. *How Buddhism Began: The Conditioned Genesis of the Early Teachings*. London: Athlone.

Goode, Erich, and Nachman Ben-Yehuda. 1994. *Moral Panics: The Social Construction of Deviance*. Cambridge, MA: Blackwell.

Gordon, D. M., R. Edwards, and M. Reich. 1982. *Segmented Work, Divided Workers: The Historical Transformation of Labor in the United States*. New York: Cambridge University Press.

Gordon, Linda. 1990. *Woman's Body, Woman's Right: Birth Control in America*, rev. ed. Harmondsworth, UK: Penguin.

Gordon, Sarah. 1984. *Hitler, Germans, and the Jewish Question*. Princeton, NJ: Princeton University Press.

Gorman, Christine. 1997. "A Boy without a Penis." *Time* March 24: 83.

Gortmaker, S. L., A. Must, J. M. Perrin, A. M. Sobol, and W. H. Dietz. 1993. "Social and Economic Consequence of Overweight in Adolescence and Young Adulthood." *New England Journal of Medicine* 329, 14: September 30: 1008–12.

Gottdiener, Mark. 2010. *The New Urban Sociology*. Boulder, CO: Westview Press.

Gottfredson, Michael, and Travis Hirschi. 1990. *A General Theory of Crime*. Stanford, CA: Stanford University Press.

Gottwald, Norman K. 1979. *The Tribes of Yahweh: A Sociology of the Religion of Liberated Israel, 1250–1050 B.C.E.* Maryknoll, NY: Orbis.

Goubert, Jean-Pierre. 1989 [1986]. *The Conquest of Water*, Andrew Wilson, trans. Princeton, NJ: Princeton University Press.

Gould, Stephen Jay. 1988. "Kropotkin Was No Crackpot." *Natural History* 97, 7: 12–18.

———. 1996. *The Mismeasure of Man*, rev. ed. New York: Norton.

Government of Canada. 2001. "Early Intervention Programs." Retrieved February 14, 2003 (http://www.crime-prevention.org/english/publications/youth/mobilize/early_e.html).

———. 2002. "Study Released on Firearms in Canada." Retrieved December 29, 2005 (http://www.cfc-ccaf.gc.ca/media/news_releases/2002/survey-08202002_e.asp).

Graff, Harvey J. 1995. *Conflicting Paths: Growing Up in America*. Cambridge, MA: Harvard University Press.

Granovetter, Mark. 1973. "The Strength of Weak Ties." *American Sociological Review* 78: 1360–80.

———. 1995. *Getting a Job: A Study of Contacts and Careers*. Chicago: University of Chicago Press.

Green, Adam Isaiah. 2007. "Queer Theory and Sociology: Locating the Subject and the Self in Sexuality Studies." *Sociological Theory* 25: 26–45.

Greenhill, Pauline. 2001. "Can You See the Difference: Queerying the Nation, Ethnicity, Festival, and Culture in Winnipeg." Pp. 103–21 in Terry Goldie, ed. *In a Queer Country: Gay & Lesbian Studies in the Canadian Context*. Vancouver: Arsenal Pulp Press.

Greenpeace. 2010. "Greenpeace Worldwide." Retrieved November 30, 2010 (http://www.greenpeace.org/international/en/about/worldwide).

Greenstein, Theodore N. 1996. "Husbands' Participation in Domestic Labor: Interactive Effects of Wives' and Husbands' Gender Ideologies." *Journal of Marriage and the Family* 58: 585–95.

Grescoe, P. 1996. *The Merchants of Venus: Inside Harlequin and the Empire of Romance*. Vancouver: Raincoast.

Grimmett, Richard F. 2006. "Conventional Arms Transfers to Developing Nations, 1998–2005." Congressional Research Service. Retrieved January 12, 2008 (http://www.fas.org/sgp/crs/weapons/RL33696.pdf).

Groce, Nora Ellen. 1985. *Everyone Here Spoke Sign Language: Hereditary Deafness on Martha's Vineyard*. Cambridge, MA: Harvard University Press.

Guillén, Mauro F. 2001. "Is Globalization Civilizing, Destructive or Feeble? A Critique of Five Key Debates in the Social-Science Literature." *Annual Review of Sociology* 27: 235–60. Retrieved February 6, 2003 (http://knowledge.wharton.upenn.edu/PDFs/938.pdf).

Guppy, N., and S. Davies. 1998. *Education in Canada: Recent Trends and Future Challenges*. Ottawa: Ministry of Industry.

Guppy, Neil, and R. Alan Hedley. 1993. *Opportunities in Sociology*. Montreal: Canadian Sociology and Anthropology Association.

Gurr, Ted Robert. 1970. *Why Men Rebel*. Princeton, NJ: Princeton University Press.

Haas, Jack, and William Shaffir. 1987. *Becoming Doctors: The Adoption of a Cloak of Competence*. Greenwich, CT: JAI Press.

Haas, Jennifer. 1998. "The Cost of Being a Woman." *New England Journal of Medicine* 338: 1694–95.

Habermas, Jürgen. 1989. *The Structural Transformation of the Public Sphere*, Thomas Burger, trans. Cambridge, MA: MIT Press.

Hacker, Andrew. 1997. *Money: Who Has How Much and Why*. New York: Scribner.

Hagan, John. 1989. *Structuralist Criminology*. New Brunswick, NJ: Rutgers University Press.

———. 1994. *Crime and Disrepute*. Thousand Oaks, CA: Pine Forge Press.

Hagan, John, John Simpson, and A. R. Gillis. 1987. "Class in the Household: A Power-Control Theory of Gender and Delinquency." *American Journal of Sociology* 92: 788–816.

Haines, Herbert H. 1996. *Against Capital Punishment: The Anti–Death Penalty Movement in America, 1972–1994*. New York: Oxford University Press.

Hall, Edward. 1959. *The Silent Language*. New York: Doubleday.

———. 1966. *The Hidden Dimension*. New York: Doubleday.

Hall, Stuart. 1980. "Encoding/Decoding." Pp. 128–38 in Stuart Hall, Dorothy Hobson, Andrew Lowe, and Paul Willis, eds. *Culture, Media, Language: Working Papers in Cultural Studies, 1972–79*. London: Hutchinson.

Hamilton, Roberta. 1996. *Gendering the Vertical Mosaic: Feminist Perspectives on Canadian Society*. Toronto: Copp-Clark.

Hancock, Graham. 1989. *Lords of Poverty: The Power, Prestige, and Corruption of the International Aid Business*. New York: Atlantic Monthly Press.

Hancock, Lynnell. 1994. "In Defiance of Darwin: How a Public School in the Bronx Turns Dropouts into Scholars." *Newsweek* October 24: 61.

Haney, Craig, W. Curtis Banks, and Philip G. Zimbardo. 1973. "Interpersonal Dynamics in a Simulated Prison." *International Journal of Criminology and Penology* 1: 69–97.

Hannigan, John. 1995a. "The Postmodern City: A New Urbanization?" *Current Sociology* 43, 1: 151–217.

———. 1995b. *Environmental Sociology: A Social Constructionist Perspective*. London: Routledge.

———. 1998a. *Fantasy City: Pleasure and Profit in the Postmodern Metropolis*. New York: Routledge.

———. 1998b. "Urbanization." Pp. 337–59 in Robert J. Brym, ed. *New Society: Sociology for the 21st Century*, 2nd ed. Toronto: Harcourt Brace Canada.

Hannon, Roseann, David S. Hall, Todd Kuntz, Van Laar, and Jennifer Williams. 1995. "Dating Characteristics Leading to Unwanted vs. Wanted Sexual Behavior." *Sex Roles* 33: 767–83.

Harding, David J., Cybelle Fox, and Jal D. Mehta. 2002. "Studying Rare Events through Qualitative Case Studies: Lessons from a Study of Rampage School Shootings." *Sociological Methods and Research* 31, 2: 174–217.

Harris, Chauncy D., and Edward L. Ullman. 1945. "The Nature of Cities." *Annals of the American Academy of Political and Social Science* 242: 7–17.

Harris, Marvin. 1974. *Cows, Pigs, Wars and Witches: The Riddles of Culture*. New York: Random House.

Harrison, Bennett. 1994. *Lean and Mean: The Changing Landscape of Corporate Power in the Age of Flexibility*. New York: Basic Books.

Hartnagel, Timothy F. 2000. "Correlates of Criminal Behaviour." Pp. 94–136 in Rick Linden, ed. *Criminology: A Canadian Perspective*, 4th ed. Toronto: Harcourt Canada.

Harvey, Andrew S., Katherine Marshall, and Judith A. Frederick. 1991. *Where Does the Time Go?* Ottawa: Statistics Canada.

Harvey, Elizabeth. 1999. "Short-Term and Long-Term Effects of Early Parental Employment on Children of the National Longitudinal Survey of Youth." *Developmental Psychology* 35: 445–49.

Hastings, Arthur C., James Fadiman, and James C. Gordon, eds. 1980. *Health for the Whole Person: The Complete Guide to Holistic Medicine*. Boulder, CO: Westview Press.

Haub, Carl. 2000. "How Many People Have Ever Lived on Earth?" Retrieved June 5, 2003 (http://www.discover.com/ask/main57.html).

Hawley, Amos. 1950. *Human Ecology: A Theory of Community Structure*. New York: Ronald Press.

Häyry, Matti, and Tuija Lehto. 1998. "Genetic Engineering and the Risk of Harm." Paper presented at the 20th World Congress of Philosophy. Boston, Retrieved January 17, 2005 (http://www.bu.edu/wcp/Papers/Bioe/BioeHay2.htm).

Haythornthwaite, Caroline, and Barry Wellman. 2002. "The Internet in Everyday Life: An Introduction." Pp. 3–41 in B. Wellman and C. Haythornthwaite, eds. *The Internet in Everyday Life*. Oxford: Blackwell.

Health Canada. n.d. "Canadian Cancer Statistics, 2003." Retrieved January 12, 2008 (http://www.cancer.ca/vgn/images/portal/cit_776/61/38/56158640niw_stats_en.pdf).

———. 1999a. "Toward a Healthy Future: Second Report on the Health of Canadians." Prepared by the Federal, Provincial, and Territorial Advisory Committee on Population Health for the Meeting of Ministers of Health, Charlottetown, PEI. September. Retrieved December 25, 1999 (http://www.hc-sc.gc.ca).

———. 1999b. "Statistical Report on the Health of Canadians." Retrieved December 25, 1999 (http://www.hc-sc.gc.ca/hppb/phdd/report/state/englover.html).

———. 2004. "Aboriginal Health: The Government of Canada's Role in Aboriginal Health Care." Retrieved May 17, 2006 (http://www.hc-sc.gc.ca/hcs-sss/delivery-prestation/fptcollab/2004-fmm-rpm/fs-if_02_e.html).

———. 2008. "Map of Obesity According to Measured Body Mass Index (BMI) in Adults in Canada (Both Males and Females)." Retrieved November 24, 2010 (http://www.hc-sc.gc.ca/fn-an/surveill/atlas/map-carte/mass_adult_obes_mf-hf-eng.php).

———. 2009. "Healthy Canadians: A Federal Report on Comparable Health Indicators 2008." Retrieved April 2, 2010 (http://www.hc-sc.gc.ca/hcs-sss/pubs/system-regime/2008-fed-comp-indicat/index-eng.php).

"Health Care Systems: An International Comparison." 2001. Ottawa: Strategic Policy and Research, Intergovernmental Affairs. Retrieved June 13, 2003 (http://www.pnrec.org/2001papers/DaigneaultLajoie.pdf).

Hechter, M. 1974. *Internal Colonialism: The Celtic Fringe in British National Development, 1536–1966*. Berkeley, CA: University of California Press.

Hechter, Michael. 1987. *Principles of Group Solidarity*. Berkeley, CA: University of California Press.

Held, David. 1987. *Models of Democracy*. Stanford, CA: Stanford University Press.

Helsing, Knud J., Moyses Szklo, and George W. Comstock. 1981. "Factors Associated with Mortality after Widowhood." *American Journal of Public Health* 71: 802–9.

Henry, Frances, Carol Tator, Winston Mattis, and Tim Rees. 2000. *The Colour of Democracy: Racism in Canadian Society*, 2nd ed. Toronto: Harcourt Brace Canada.

Henry, Frances, et al. 2001. "The Victimization of Racial Minorities in Canada." Pp. 145–60 in Robert J. Brym, ed. *Society in Question: Sociological Readings for the 21st Century*. Toronto: Harcourt Canada.

Herdt, Gilbert. 2001. "Social Change, Sexual Diversity, and Tolerance for Bisexuality in the United States." Pp. 267–83 in Anthony R. D'Augelli and Charlotte J. Patterson, eds. *Lesbian, Gay, and Bisexual Identities and Youth: Psychological Perspectives*. New York: Oxford University Press.

Herlihy, David. 1998. *The Black Death and the Transformation of the West*. Cambridge, MA: Harvard University Press.

Herman, Edward S., and Noam Chomsky. 1988. *Manufacturing Consent: The Political Economy of the Mass Media*. New York: Pantheon.

Herrera, Laura. 2011. "In Florida, Virtual Classrooms with No Teachers." *The New York Times* January 17. Retrieved May 24, 2011 (http://www.nytimes.com).

Herrnstein, Richard J., and Charles Murray. 1994. *The Bell Curve: Intelligence and Class Structure in American Life*. New York: Free Press.

Hersch, Patricia. 1998. *A Tribe Apart: A Journey into the Heart of American Adolescence*. New York: Ballantine Books.

Hertzman, Clyde. 2000. "The Case for Early Childhood Development Strategy." *Isuma: Canadian Journal of Policy Research* 1, 2: 11–18.

Hesse-Biber, Sharlene. 1996. *Am I Thin Enough Yet? The Cult of Thinness and the Commercialization of Identity*. New York: Oxford University Press.

Hesse-Biber, Sharlene, and Gregg Lee Carter. 2000. *Working Women in America: Split Dreams*. New York: Oxford University Press.

Hewitt, J. Joseph, Jonathan Wilkenfeld, and Ted Robert Gurr. 2010. "Peace and Conflict 2010: Executive Summary." Retrieved November 27, 2010 (http://www.cidcm.umd.edu/pc/executive_summary/exec_sum_2010.pdf).

Hirschi, Travis. 1969. *Causes of Delinquency*. Berkeley, CA: University of California Press.

Hirschman, Albert O. 1970. *Exit, Voice, and Loyalty: Responses to Decline in Firms, Organizations, and States*. Cambridge, MA: Harvard University Press.

Hirst, Paul, and Grahame Thompson. 1999. *Globalization in Question: The International Economy and the Possibilities of Governance*, 2nd ed. London: Polity.

Hobbes, Thomas. 1968 [1651]). *Leviathan*. Middlesex, UK: Penguin.

Hobsbawm, Eric. 1994. *Age of Extremes: The Short Twentieth Century, 1914–1991*. London: Abacus.

Hochberg, Fred P. 2002. "American Capitalism's Other Side." *The New York Times* July 25. Retrieved July 25, 2002 (http://www.nytimes. com).

Hochschild, Arlie Russell. 1973. *The Unexpected Community: Portrait of an Old Age Subculture*. Berkeley, CA: University of California Press.

———. 1979. "Emotion Work, Feeling Rules, and Social Structure." *American Journal of Sociology* 85: 551–75.

———. 1983. *The Managed Heart: Commercialization of Human Feeling*. Berkeley: University of California Press.

Hochschild, Arlie Russell, with Anne Machung. 1989. *The Second Shift: Working Parents and the Revolution at Home*. New York: Viking.

Hodge, Robert, and David Tripp. 1986. *Children and Television: A Semiotic Approach*. Cambridge, UK: Polity.

Hodgson, Marshall G. S. 1974. *The Venture of Islam: Conscience and History in a World Civilization*, 3 vols. Chicago: University of Chicago Press.

Hodson, R., and T. Sullivan. 1995. *The Social Organization of Work*, 2nd ed. Belmont CA: Wadsworth.

Homans, George Caspar. 1961. *Social Behavior: Its Elementary Forms*. New York: Harcourt, Brace and World.

hooks, bell. 1984. *Feminist Theory: From Margin to Center*. Boston: South End Press.

Hopkins, Terence K., and Immanuel Wallerstein. 1986. "Commodity Chains in the World Economy Prior to 1800." *Review* 10: 157–70.

Horkheimer, Max, and Theodor W. Adorno. 1986 [1944]. *Dialectic of Enlightenment*, John Cumming, trans. London: Verso.

Houpt, Simon. 2004. "Pass the Popcorn, Save the World." *The Globe and Mail* May 29: R1, R13.

Houseknecht, Sharon K., and Jaya Sastry. 1996. "Family 'Decline' and Child Well-Being: A Comparative Assessment." *Journal of Marriage and the Family* 58: 726–39.

Hoyt, Homer. 1939. *The Structure and Growth of Residential Neighborhoods in American Cities*. Washington, DC: Federal Housing Authority.

Huesmann, L. Rowell, Jessica Moise-Titus, Cheryl-Lynn Podolski, and Leonard D. Eron. 2003. "Longitudinal Relations between Children's Exposure to TV Violence and their Aggressive and Violent Behavior in Young Adulthood: 1977–1992." *Developmental Psychology* 39, 2: 201–21.

Hughes, Fergus P. 1995. *Children, Play and Development*, 2nd ed. Boston: Allyn and Bacon.

Hughes, H. Stuart. 1967. *Consciousness and Society: The Reorientation of European Social Thought, 1890–1930*. London: Macgibbon and Kee.

Human Resources Development Canada. 2000. "Job Futures 2000." Retrieved June 2001 (http://jobfutures.ca/doc/jf/emerging/emerging .shtml#sample).

Human Resources and Skills Development Canada. 2006. "Canadians in Context—Geographic Distribution." *Indicators of Well-Being in Canada*. Retrieved March 17, 2011 (http://www4.hrsdc .gc.ca/.3ndic.1t.4r@-eng.jsp?iid=34).

———. 2010. "Union Membership in Canada—2009." Retrieved November 27, 2010 (http://www.hrsdc.gc.ca/eng/labour/labour_ relations/info_analysis/union_membership/index2009.shtml).

———. 2011a. "Average Student Loan Balance at Completion of Studies." Retrieved May 23, 2011 (http://www.hrsdc.gc.ca/eng/learning/canada_ student_loan/Publications/annual_report/2008-2009/tables/ loan_balances.shtml).

———. 2011b. "Learning—Educational Attainment." *Indicators of Well-Being in Canada*. Retrieved April 29, 2011 (http://www4.hrsdc .gc.ca/.3ndic.1t.4r@-eng.jsp?iid=29).

———. 2011c. "Annex 1.5—Unemployment Rate and Employment, by Education Level." *Employment Programs: Employment Insurance*.

Retrieved March 20, 2011 (http://www.rhdcc-hrsdc.gc.ca/eng/ employment/ei/reports/eimar_2009/annex/annex1_5.shtml).

Human Resources and Social Development Canada. 2008. "Union Membership in Canada—2007." Retrieved May 2, 2008 (http://www .hrsdc.gc.ca/en/lp/wid/union_membership.shtml).

Human Rights Watch. 1995. *The Human Rights Watch Global Report on Women's Human Rights*. New York: Human Rights Watch.

Hunter, James Davison. 1991. *Culture Wars: The Struggle to Define America*. New York: Basic Books.

Huntington, Samuel. 1991. *The Third Wave: Democratization in the Late Twentieth Century*. Norman, OK: University of Oklahoma Press.

Ignatieff, Michael. 2000. *The Rights Revolution*. Toronto: Anansi.

Ignatiev, N. 1995. *How the Irish Became White*. New York: Routledge.

IMD International. 2007. "The World Competitiveness Scoreboard 2007." Retrieved May 1, 2008 (http://www.imd.ch/research/publications/wcy/ upload/scoreboard.pdf).

———. 2010. "The World Competitiveness Yearbook 2010." Retrieved March 1, 2011 (http://www.imd.org/research/publications/wcy/upload/ PressRelease.pdf).

InfoPlease. 2005. "Average Number of Vacation Days Around the World Per Year." Retrieved November 21, 2005 (http://www.infoplease.com/ ipa/A0922052.html).

Inglehart, Ronald. 1997. *Modernization and Postmodernization: Cultural, Economic, and Political Change in 43 Societies*. Princeton, NJ: Princeton University Press.

Ingram, Gordon Brent. 2001. "Redesigning Wreck: Beach Meets Forest as Location of Male Homoerotic Culture in Placemaking in Pacific Canada." Pp. 188–208 in Terry Goldie, ed. *In a Queer Country: Gay & Lesbian Studies in the Canadian Context*. Vancouver: Arsenal Pulp Press.

Inkeles, Alex, and David H. Smith. 1976. *Becoming Modern: Individual Change in Six Developing Countries*. Cambridge, MA: Harvard University Press.

Intergovernmental Panel on Climate Change. 2007. "Climate Change 2007." Retrieved May 2, 2007 (http://www.ipcc.ch).

International Campaign against Shari'a Court in Canada. 2005. "Homepage." Retrieved December 8, 2005 (http://www.nosharia.com).

International Gay, Lesbian, Bisexual, Trans and Intersex Association. "Punishment for Male–Male Sexual Relations. Retrieved November 21, 2010 (http://ilga.org).

International Labour Organization. 2010. "LABORSTA Internet." Retrieved November 27, 2010 (http://laborsta.ilo.org).

International Monetary Fund. 2009. "World Economic and Financial Surveys: World Economic Outlook Database. Retrieved January 2, 2010 (http://www.imf.org/external/pubs/ft/weo/2009/02/weodata/ index.aspx).

International Rescue Committee. 2010. "Rape in Congo." Retrieved November 23, 2010 (http://www.theirc.org/special-reports/rape- congo).

"International Tourism Challenged by Deteriorating Global Economy." 2009. *UNWTO World Tourist Barometer* 7, 1. Retrieved November 16, 2010 (http://www.unwto.org/facts/eng/pdf/barometer/UNWTO_ Barom09_1_en_excerpt.pdf).

Internet Systems Consortium. 2010. "Internet host count history: Number of Internet hosts." Retrieved November 16, 2010 (http://www.isc.org/ solutions/survey/history).

"Internet Usage Statistics." Retrieved January 4, 2008 (http://www .internetworldstats.com/stats.htm).

Internet World Statistics. 2007. "Internet World Users by Language." Retrieved December 17, 2007 (http://www.internetworldstats.com/ stats7.htm).

Internet World Statistics. 2010a. "Internet World Users by Language." Retrieved December 17, 2010 (http://www.internetworldstats.com/ stats7.htm).

———. 2010b. "World Internet Usage and Population Statistics." Retrieved December 26, 2010 (http://www.internetworldstats.com/stats.htm).

"Iraq Body Count." 2008. Retrieved January 12, 2008 (http://www .iraqbodycount.org).

"Iraq Coalition Casualty Count." 2008. Retrieved January 12, 2008 (http:// icasualties.org/oif).

Isaacs, Larry. 2002. "To Counter 'The Very Devil' and More: The Making of Independent Capitalist Militias in the Gilded Age." *American Journal of Sociology* 108: 353–405.

Isajiw, W. W. 1978. "Olga in Wonderland: Ethnicity in a Technological Society." Pp. 29–39 in L. Driedger, ed. *The Canadian Ethnic Mosaic: A Quest for Identity* Toronto: McClelland & Stewart.

istar. 2001. "Why Small Is Smarter." Retrieved June 12, 2004 (http://home. istar.ca/~gskarzn/go/SMALL.IITM).

Iyengar, Shanto. 1991. *Is Anyone Responsible? How Television Frames Political Issues.* Chicago: University of Chicago Press.

Jackson, Carolyn, and Ian David Smith. 2000. "Poles Apart? An Exploration of Single-Sex and Mixed-Sex Educational Environments in Australia and England." *Educational Studies* 26, 4 (December): 409–22.

Jacobs, Jane. 1961. *The Death and Life of Great American Cities.* New York: Random House.

———. 1969. *The Economy of Cities.* New York: Random House.

James, Harold. 2001. *The End of Globalization: Lessons from the Great Depression.* Cambridge, MA: Harvard University Press.

James, William. 1976 [1902]. *The Varieties of Religious Experience: A Study in Human Nature.* New York: Collier Books.

Janigan, Mary. 2002. "Saving Our Cities." *Maclean's* 3 June: 22–27.

Janis, Irving. 1972. *Victims of Groupthink.* Boston: Houghton Mifflin.

Jannini, Emmanuelle A., Ray Blanchard, Andrea Camperio-Cianai, and John Bancroft. 2010. "Male Homosexuality: Nature or Culture?" *Controversies in Sexual Medicine* 7: 3245–53.

Jencks, Christopher, Marshall Smith, Henry Acland, Mary Jo Bane, David Cohen, Herbert Gintis, Barbara Heyns, and Stephan Michelson. 1972. *Inequality: A Reassessment of the Effect of Family and Schooling in America.* New York: Basic Books.

Jenkins, J. Craig. 1983. "Resource Mobilization Theory and the Study of Social Movements." *Annual Review of Sociology* 9: 527–53.

Jensen, Margaret Ann. 1984. *Love's Sweet Return. The Harlequin Story.* Toronto: Women's Press.

"Jim Crow Laws: Texas." 2008. Retrieved March 7, 2008 (http://www .jimcrowhistory.org/scripts/jimcrow/insidesouth.cgi?state=Texas).

Johansen, Bruce E. 1998. "Sterilization of Native American Women." Retrieved April 24, 2003 (http://www.ratical.org/ratville/sterilize .html).

John Howard Society. 1999. *Fact Sheet: Population Trends and Crime* Toronto: John Howard Society of Ontario.

Johns, Adrian. 1998. *The Nature of the Book: Print and Knowledge in the Making.* Chicago: University of Chicago Press.

Johnson, Chalmers. 2000. *Blowback: The Costs and Consequences of American Empire.* New York: Metropolitan Books.

Johnson, Holly. 2006. "Measuring Violence against Women: Statistical Trends, 2006." Ottawa: Statistics Canada. Retrieved May 2, 2008 (http://www.statcan.ca/english/research/85-570-XIE/ 85-570-XIE2006001.pdf).

Johnson, Jeffrey G., Patricia Cohen, Elizabeth M. Smailes, Stephanie Kasen, and Judith S. Brook. 2002. "Television Viewing and Aggressive Behavior during Adolescence and dulthood." *Science* 295, 5564: 2468–71.

Johnson, Michael P., and Kathleeen J. Ferraro. 2000. "Research on Domestic Violence in the 1990s: Making Distinctions." *Journal of Marriage and the Family* 62: 948–63.

Johnson, S. 2004. "Adult Correctional Services in Canada, 2002/03." *Juristat: Canadian Centre for Justice Statistics* 24, 10: 16. Retrieved May 8, 2005 (http://www.statcan.ca/bsolc/english/bsolc?catno= 85-002-X20040108409).

Johnson, Terence J. 1972. *Professions and Power.* London: Macmillan.

Johnson, Tracy L., and Elizabeth Fee. 1997. "Women's Health Research: An Introduction." Pp. 3–26 in Florence P. Haseltine and Beverly Greenberg Jacobson, eds. *Women's Health Research: A Medical and Policy Primer.* Washington, DC: Health Press International.

Jones, Frank. 2000. "Are Children Going to Religious Services?" Pp. 202–05 in *Canadian Social Trends* 3. Toronto: Thompson Educational Publishing.

Jones, Laura. 1997. "Global Warming Is All the Rage These Days ... Which Enrages Many Doubting Scientists." The Fraser Institute. Retrieved May 5, 2002 (http://oldfraser.lexi.net/media/media releases/1997/19971201a.html).

Joyce, Terrence, and Lloyd Keigwin, 2004. "Abrupt Climate Change: Are We on the Brink of a New Little Ice Age?" Ocean and Climate Change Institute, Woods Hole Oceanographic Institution. Retrieved

(http://www.whoi.edu/institutes/occi/currenttopics/abruptclimate joyce_keigwin.html).

Jubilee Debt Campaign. 2010. "Getting into Debt." Retrieved February 12, 2011 (http://www.jubileedebtcampaign.org.uk/Getting%20into% 20Debt+6281.twl).

Juergensmeyer, Mark. 2000 *Terror in the Mind of God: The Global Rise of Religious Violence.* Berkeley, CA: University of California Press.

Kaasa, Kristin. 2002. "This Is Women's Work, and It's About Time." *United Church Observer* (July–August). Retrieved November 12, 2005 (http://www.ucobserver.org/archives/julyaug02_ministry.htm).

Kalbach, Madeline. A., and Warren. E. Kalbach. 1998. "Becoming Canadian: Problems of an Emerging Identity." *Canadian Ethnic Studies* 31, 2: 1–17.

Kalbach, Madeline A. 2000. "Ethnicity and the Altar." Pp. 111–21 in Madeline A. Kalbach and Warren E. Kalbach, eds. *Perspectives on Ethnicity in Canada: A Reader.* Toronto: Harcourt Canada.

Kalmijn, Matthijs. 1998. "Intermarriage and Homogamy: Causes, Patterns, Trends." *Annual Review of Sociology* 24: 395–421.

Kanagarajah, Sri. 2006. *Business Dynamics in Canada, 2003.* Statistics Canada Catalogue No. 61-534-XIE. Ottawa: Ministry of Industry.

Kanter, Rosabeth Moss. 1977. *Men and Women of the Corporation.* New York: Basic Books.

———. 1989. *When Giants Learn to Dance: Mastering the Challenges of Strategy, Management, and Careers in the 1990s.* New York: Simon and Schuster.

Karl, Thomas R., and Kevin E. Trenberth. 1999. "The Human Impact on Climate." *Scientific American* 281, 6 (September): 100–105.

Karraker, Katherine Hildebrandt, Dena Ann Vogel, and Margaret Ann Lake. 1995. "Parents' Gender-Stereotyped Perceptions of Newborns: The Eye of the Beholder Revisited." *Sex Roles* 33, 9–10 (November): 687–701.

Katz, Elihu. 1957. "The Two-Step Flow of Communication: An Up-to-Date Report on an Hypothesis." *Public Opinion Quarterly* 21: 61–78.

Kay, Fiona, and John Hagan. 1998. "Raising the Bar: The Gender Stratification of Law Firm Capitalization." *American Sociological Review* 63: 728–43.

Kazemipur, Abdolmohammad, and Shiva S. Halli. 2000. *The New Poverty: Ethnic Groups and Ghetto Neighbourhoods.* Toronto: Thompson Educational Publishing, Inc.

———. 2001. "The Changing Colour of Poverty in Canada." *Canadian Review of Sociology and Anthropology* 38, 2: 217–38.

Kearney, Mark, and Randy Ray. 1999. *The Great Canadian Book of Lists.* Toronto: Dundurn Group.

Keister, Lisa A. 2000. *Wealth in America: Trends in Wealth Inequality.* Cambridge: Cambridge University Press.

Keister, Lisa A., and Stephanie Moller. 2000. "Wealth Inequality in the United States." *Annual Review of Sociology* 26: 63–81.

Keller, Larry. 2000. "Double Earners: Double Trouble." CNN.com November 13. Retrieved May 10, 2011 (http://edition.cnn.com/2000/ CAREER/trends/11/13/dual.earners).

Kemper, T. D. 1978. *A Social Interactional Theory of Emotion.* New York: Wiley.

———. 1987. "How Many Emotions Are There? Wedding the Social and Autonomic Components." *American Journal of Sociology* 93: 263–89.

Kennedy, Paul. 1993. *Preparing for the Twenty-First Century.* New York: HarperCollins.

Kepel, Gilles. 1994 [1991]. *The Revenge of God: The Resurgence of Islam, Christianity and Judaism in the Modern World,* Alan Braley, trans. University Park, PA: Pennsylvania State University Press.

Kerig, Patricia K., Philip A. Cowan, and Carolyn Pape Cowan. 1993. "Marital Quality and Gender Differences in Parent–Child Interaction." *Developmental Psychology* 29: 931–39.

Kerr, Clark, John T. Dunlop, Frederick H. Harbison, and Charles A. Myers. 1960. *Industrialism and Industrial Man: The Problems of Labor and Management in Economic Growth.* New York: Oxford University Press.

Kessler, Ronald C., Katherine A. McGonagle, Shanyang Zhao, Christopher B. Nelson, Michael Hughes, Suzann Eshleman, Hans Ulrich Wittchen, and Kenneth S. Kendler. 1994. "Life-time and 12-Month Prevalence of DSM-III-R Psychiatric Disorders in the United States." *Archives of General Psychiatry* 51: 8–19.

Kimmerling, Baruch. 2003. *Politicide: Ariel Sharon's War against the Palestinians.* London: Verso.

Kingsbury, Nancy, and John Scanzoni. 1993. "Structural-Functionalism." Pp. 195–217 in Pauline G. Boss, William J. Doherty, Ralph LaRossa, Walter R. Schumm, and Suzanne K. Steinmetz, eds. *Sourcebook of Family Theories and Methods: A Contextual Approach*. New York: Plenum.

Kingston, Peter. 1997. "Top of the Class." *The Guardian* October 21: 2.

Kinsella, Warren. 2007. *The War Room: Political Strategies for Business, NGOs, and Anyone Who Wants to Win*. Toronto: Dundurn.

Kinsey, Alfred C., Wardell B. Pomeroy, and Clyde E. Martin. 1948. *Sexual Behavior in the Human Male*. Philadelphia: W. B. Saunders.

Kinsey, Alfred C., Wardell B. Pomeroy, Clyde E. Martin, and Paul H. Gebhard. 1953. *Sexual Behavior in the Human Female*. Philadelphia: W. B. Saunders.

Kitano, Harry, and Roger Daniels. 1995. *Asian Americans: Emerging Minorities*, 2nd ed. Englewood Cliffs, NJ: Prentice-Hall.

Kleege, Georgina. 1999. *Sight Unseen*. New Haven, CT: Yale University Press.

Klein, Naomi. 2000. *No Logo: Taking Aim at the Brand Bullies*. New York: HarperCollins.

Kling, Kristen C., Janet Shibley Hyde, Carolin J. Showers, and Brenda N. Buswell. 1999. "Gender Differences in Self-Esteem: A Meta-Analysis." *Psychological Bulletin* 125, 4: 470–500.

Klingemann, Hans-Dieter. 1999. "Mapping Political Support in the 1990s: A Global Analysis." In Pippa Norris, ed. *Critical Citizens: Global Support for Democratic Governance*. Oxford, UK: Oxford University Press. Retrieved October 20, 2001 (http://ksgwww.harvard.edu/people/pnorris/Chapter_1.htm).

"Kobe Bryant Resumes Endorsement Career." 2005. *USA Today* July 10. Retrieved February 8, 2011 (http://www.usatoday.com/life/people/2005-07-10-kobe-bryant_x.htm).

Koepke, Leslie, Jan Hare, and Patricia B. Moran. 1992. "Relationship Quality in a Sample of Lesbian Couples with Children and Child-Free Lesbian Couples." *Family Relations* 41: 224–29.

Kohlberg, Lawrence. 1981. *The Psychology of Moral Development: The Nature and Validity of Moral Stages*. New York: Harper and Row.

Kohn, Alfie. 1988. "Make Love, Not War." *Psychology Today* 22, 6: 35–38.

Kolko, Gabriel. 2002. *Another Century of War?* New York: New Press.

Konrath, Sara. 2010. "Changes in Dispositional Empathy in American College Students Over Time: A Meta-Analysis." *Personality and Social Psychology Review* 15 (May): 180–98.

Kopun, Francine. 2006. "Older, Single Women Cast off Cat-Food Cliché." *Toronto Star* March 11: A01.

Korpi, Walter. 1983. *The Democratic Class Struggle*. London: Routledge and Kegan Paul.

Kosmin, Barry A. 1991. *Research Report of the National Survey of Religious Identification*. New York: CUNY Graduate Center.

Krahn, Harvey, and Graham S. Lowe, eds. 1998. *Work, Industry, and Canadian Society*, 3rd ed. Scarborough: Nelson.

Kropotkin, Petr. 1908. *Mutual Aid: A Factor of Evolution*, revised ed. London: W. Heinemann.

Kübler-Ross, Elisabeth. 1969. *On Death and Dying*. New York: Macmillan.

Kuhn, Thomas. 1970 [1962]. *The Structure of Scientific Revolutions*, 2nd ed. Chicago: University of Chicago Press.

Kurdek, Lawrence A. 1998. "Relationship Outcomes and Their Predictors: Longitudinal Evidence from Heterosexual Married, Gay Cohabiting and Lesbian Cohabiting Couples." *Journal of Marriage and the Family* 60, 3: 553–68.

Kurtz, Howard. 1997. "U.S. Television News Distorts Reality of Homicide Rates." *Edmonton Journal* August 13: A5.

Kurzweil, Ray. 1999. *The Age of Spiritual Machines: When Computers Exceed Human Intelligence*. New York: Viking Penguin.

La Prairie, Carol. 1996. *Examining Aboriginal Corrections in Canada*. Ottawa: Supply and Services Canada.

Labour Organizations in Canada 1972. 1973. Ottawa: Economics and Research Branch, Canada Department of Labour. Cat. No. L2-2-1972.

LaFeber, Walter. 1993. *Inevitable Revolutions: The United States in Central America*, 2nd ed. New York: Norton.

———. 1999. *Michael Jordan and the New Global Capitalism*. New York: Norton.

Lamanna, Mary Ann and Agnes Riedmann. 2003. *Marriages and Families: Making Choices in a Diverse Society*, 8th ed. Belmont CA: Wadsworth.

Lambert, M., Klarka Zeman, Mary Allen, and Patrick Bussière. 2004. "Who Pursues Postsecondary Education, Who Leaves and Why: Results from the Youth in Transition Survey." Ottawa, Statistics Canada.

Retrieved May 27, 2006 (http://www.statcan.ca/cgi-bin/downpub/listpub.cgi?catno=81-595-MIE2004026).

Lane, Harlan. 1992. *The Mask of Benevolence: Disabling the Deaf Community*. New York: Alfred A. Knopf.

Lang, Sabine. 1998. *Men as Women, Women as Men: Changing Gender in Native American Cultures*. Austin TX: University of Texas Press.

Lapidus, Gail Warshofsky. 1978. *Women in Soviet Society: Equality, Development, and Social Change*. Berkeley, CA: University of California Press.

Lapidus, Ira M. 2002. *A History of Islamic Societies*, 2nd ed. Cambridge: Cambridge University Press.

Larzelere, Robert E. 2000. "Child Outcomes of Nonabusive and Customary Physical Punishment by Parents: An Updated Literature Review." *Clinical Child & Family Psychology Review* 3, 4 (December): 199–221.

Laslett, Peter. 1991. *A Fresh Map of Life: The Emergence of the Third Age*, reprinted ed. Cambridge, MA: Harvard University Press.

Lasswell, Harold. 1936. *Politics: Who Gets What, When and How*. New York: McGraw-Hill.

Laumann, Edward O., John H. Gagnon, Robert T. Michael, and Stuart Michaels. 1994. *The Social Organization of Sexuality: Sexual Practices in the United States*. Chicago: University of Chicago Press.

Laurie, Robert. 2007. "Are We Setting Up Students to Fail?" *Atlantic Institute for Market Studies* June 5. Retrieved May 24, 2011 (http://www.macleans.ca/article.jsp?content=20070605_153207_13228).

Lavoie, Yolande, and Jillian Oderkirk. 2000. "Social Consequences of Demographic Change." Pp. 2–5 in *Canadian Social Trends*, Volume 3. Toronto: Thompson Educational Publishing.

Law, M. T. 1999. "The Economics of Minimum Wage Laws." *Public Policy Sources* 14. Retrieved May 29, 2000 (http://www.fraserinstitute.ca/publications/pps/14).

Laxer, Gordon. 1989. *Open for Business: The Roots of Foreign Ownership in Canada*. Toronto: Oxford University Press.

Leacock, Eleanor Burke. 1981. *Myths of Male Dominance: Collected Articles on Women Cross-Culturally*. New York: Monthly Review Press.

Le Bon, Gustave. 1969 [1895]. *The Crowd: A Study of the Popular Mind*. New York: Ballantine Books.

Lee, Richard B. 1979. *The !Kung San: Men, Women and Work in a Foraging Society*. Cambridge, UK: Cambridge University Press.

Lefkowitz, Bernard. 1997a. *Our Guys: The Glen Ridge Rape and the Secret Life of the Perfect Suburb*. Berkeley, CA: University of California Press.

———. 1997b. "Boys Town: Did Glen Ridge Raise Its Sons to Be Rapists?" *Salon* August 13. Retrieved March 20, 2003 (http://www.salon.com/aug97/mothers/guys970813.html).

Leidner, Robin. 1993. *Fast Food, Fast Talk: Service Work and the Routinization of Everyday Life*. Berkeley, CA: University of California Press.

Lenski, G. 1966. *Power and Privilege: A Theory of Social Stratification*. New York: McGraw Hill.

Lenski, G., P. Nolan, and J. Lenski. 1995. *Human Societies: An Introduction to Macrosociology*, 7th ed. New York: McGraw-Hill.

Lenton, Rhonda L. 1989. "Homicide in Canada and the U.S.A." *Canadian Journal of Sociology* 14: 163–78.

Lerner, Gerda. 1986. *The Creation of Patriarchy*. New York: Oxford University Press.

Levine, R. A., and D. T. Campbell. 1972. *Ethnocentrism: Theories of Conflict, Ethnic Attitudes, and Group Behavior*. New York: Wiley.

Levine, Robert, Suguru Sato, Tsukasa Hashimoto, and Jyoti Verma. 1995. "Love and Marriage in Eleven Cultures." *Journal of Cross-Cultural Psychology* 26, 5: 554–71.

Levy, Frank. 1998. *The New Dollars and Dreams: American Incomes and Economic Change*. New York: Russell Sage Foundation.

Lewis, Bernard. 2002. *What Went Wrong? Western Impact and Middle Eastern Response*. New York: Oxford University Press.

Lewontin, R. C. 1991. *Biology as Ideology: The Doctrine of DNA*. New York: HarperCollins.

Ley, David. 1996. *The New Middle Class and the Remaking of the Central City*. Oxford, UK: Oxford University Press.

Li, Peter. 1995. "Racial Supremacism under Social Democracy." *Canadian Ethnic Studies* 27, 1: 1–17.

———. 1998. *The Chinese in Canada*, 2nd ed. Toronto: Oxford University Press.

———. 2000. "Earning Disparities between Immigrants and Native-Born Canadians." *Canadian Review of Sociology and Anthropology* 37, 3: 289–311.

Lian, J. Z., and D. R. Matthews. 1998. "Does the Vertical Mosaic Still Exist? Ethnicity and Income in Canada, 1991." *Canadian Review of Sociology and Anthropology* 35: 461–81.

Lie, John. 1992. "The Concept of Mode of Exchange." *American Sociological Review* 57: 508–23.

———. 1998. *Han Unbound: The Political Economy of South Korea.* Stanford, CA: Stanford University Press.

———. 2001. *Multiethnic Japan.* Cambridge, MA: Harvard University Press.

Light, I. 1991. "Immigrant and Ethnic Enterprise in North America." Pp. 307–18 in N. R. Yetman, ed. *Majority and Minority: The Dynamics of Race and Ethnicity in American Life,* 5th ed. Boston: Allyn and Bacon.

Lightfoot-Klein, Hanny, Cheryl Chase, Tim Hammond, and Ronald Goldman. 2000. "Genital Surgery on Children Below the Age of Consent." Pp. 440–79 in Lenore T. Szuchman and Frank Muscarella, eds. *Psychological Perspectives on Human Sexuality.* New York: Wiley.

Lindert, Peter H. 2004. *Growing Public: Social Spending and Economic Growth Since the Eighteenth Century.* New York: Cambridge.

Lindner, Rolf. 1996 [1990]. *The Reportage of Urban Culture: Robert Park and the Chicago School,* Adrian Morris, trans. Cambridge, UK: Cambridge University Press.

Lips, Hilary M. 1999. *A New Psychology of Women: Gender, Culture and Ethnicity.* Mountain View, CA: Mayfield Publishing.

Lipset, Seymour Martin. 1963. "Value Differences, Absolute or Relative: The English-Speaking Democracies." Pp. 248–73 in *The First New Nation: The United States in Historical Perspective.* New York: Basic Books.

——— 1971. *Agrarian Socialism: The Cooperative Commonwealth Federation in Saskatchewan,* revised ed. Berkeley, CA: University of California Press.

———. 1977. "Why No Socialism in the United States?" Pp. 31–363 in Seweryn Bialer and Sophia Sluzar, eds. *Sources of Contemporary Radicalism.* Boulder, CO: Westview Press.

———. 1981. *Political Man: The Social Bases of Politics,* 2nd ed. Baltimore: Johns Hopkins University Press.

———. 1994. "The Social Requisites of Democracy Revisited." *American Sociological Review* 59: 1–22.

Lipset, Seymour Martin, and Stein Rokkan. 1967. "Cleavage Structures, Party Systems, and Voter Alignments: An Introduction." Pp. 1–64 in Seymour Martin Lipset and Stein Rokkan, eds. *Party Systems and Voter Alignments: Cross-National Perspectives.* New York: Free Press.

Lipset, Seymour Martin, Martin A. Trow, and James S. Coleman. 1956. *Union Democracy: The Internal Politics of the International Typographical Union.* Glencoe, IL: Free Press.

Lisak, David. 1992. "Sexual Aggression, Masculinity, and Fathers." *Signs* 16: 238–62.

Livernash, Robert, and Eric Rodenburg. 1998. "Population Change, Resources, and the Environment." *Population Bulletin* 53, 1. Retrieved October 8, 2000 (http://www.prb.org/pubs/population_bulletin/bu53-1.htm).

Livi-Bacci, Massimo. 1992. *A Concise History of World Population.* Cambridge, MA: Blackwell.

Lock, Margaret. 1993. *Encounters with Aging: Mythologies of Menopause in Japan and North America.* Berkeley, CA: University of California Press.

Lodhi, Abdul Qaiyum, and Charles Tilly. 1973. "Urbanization, Crime, and Collective Violence in 19th Century France." *American Journal of Sociology* 79: 296–318.

Lofland, John, and Lyn H. Lofland. 1995. *Analyzing Social Settings: A Guide to Qualitative Observation and Analysis,* 3rd ed. Belmont, CA: Wadsworth.

Lofland, L. H. 1985. "The Social Shaping of Emotion: Grief in Historical Perspective." *Symbolic Interaction* 8: 171–90.

Logan, John R., and Harvey L. Molotch. 1987. *Urban Fortunes: The Political Economy of Place.* Berkeley, CA: University of California Press.

Logan, Ron. 2001. "Crime Statistics in Canada, 2000." *Juristat* 21, 8 (July). Catalogue no. 85-002-XPE.

Lonmo, Charlene. 2001. "Adult Correctional Services in Canada, 1999–2000." *Juristat* 21, 5 (July). Catalogue no. 85-002-XPE.

Lopez, Donald S. 2001. *The Story of Buddhism: A Concise Guide to Its History and Teachings.* San Francisco: Harper.

Lowe, G. S. 1987. *Women in the Administrative Revolution: The Feminization of Clerical Work.* Toronto: University of Toronto Press.

———. 2000. *The Quality of Work: A People-Centred Agenda.* Don Mills, ON: Oxford University Press.

Lowman, John, Robert T. Menzies, and Ted S. Palys. 1987. *Transcarceration: Essays in the Sociology of Social Control.* Aldershot, ON: Gower.

Lyon, David, and Elia Zureik, eds. 1996. *Computers, Surveillance, and Privacy.* Minneapolis: University of Minnesota Press.

MacKinnon, Catharine A. 1979. *Sexual Harassment of Working Women.* New Haven, CT: Yale University Press.

Maclean's. 2002. "Acceptable but Not Equal." 3 June: 12.

MacLennan, Hugh. 1945. *Two Solitudes.* Toronto: Collins.

Magro, Albert M. 1997. "Why Barbie Is Perceived as Beautiful." *Perceptual & Motor Skills* 85, 1 (August): 363–74.

Makomaski Illing, E. M., and M. J. Kaiserman. 2004. "Mortality Attributable to Tobacco Use in Canada and Its Regions, 1998." *Canadian Journal of Public Health* 95: 38–44.

Malthus, Thomas Robert. 1966 [1798]. *An Essay on the Principle of Population,* J. R. Bodnar, ed. London: Macmillan.

Manga, Pran, Douglas E. Angus, and William R. Swan. 1993. "Effective Management of Low Back Pain: It's Time to Accept the Evidence." *Journal of the Canadian Chiropractic Association* 37: 221–29.

Mankiw, N. G. 1998. *Principles of Macroeconomics.* Fort Worth, TX: Dryden Press.

Mann, Susan A., Michael D. Grimes, Alice Abel Kemp, and Pamela J. Jenkins. 1997. "Paradigm Shifts in Family Sociology? Evidence from Three Decades of Family Textbooks." *Journal of Family Issues* 18: 315–49.

Mannheim, Karl. 1952. "The Problem of Generations." Pp. 276–320 in *Essays on the Sociology of Knowledge,* Paul Kecskemeti, ed. New York: Oxford University Press.

Manza, Jeff, Michael Hout, and Clem Brooks. 1995. "Class Voting in Capitalist Democracies since World War II: Dealignment, Realignment, or Trendless Fluctuation?" *Annual Review of Sociology* 21: 137–62.

Marchak, M. P. 1991. *The Integrated Circus: The New Right and the Restructuring of Global Markets.* Montreal: McGill-Queen's University Press.

Markowitz, Fran. 1993. *A Community in Spite of Itself: Soviet Jewish Émigrés in New York.* Washington, DC: Smithsonian Institute Press.

Marshall, Katherine. 2001. "Part-Time by Choice." *Perspectives on Labour and Income* 13, 1: 20–27. Retrieved June 3, 2009 (http://dsp-psd.pwgsc.gc.ca/dsp-psd/Pilot/Statcan/75-001-XIE/75-001-XIE.html).

Marshall, Monty G., and Ted Robert Gurr. 2003. "Peace and Conflict 2003." College Park: Department of Government and Politics, University of Maryland. Retrieved June 3, 2003 (http://www.cidcm.umd.edu/inscr/PC03print.pdf).

Marshall, S. L. A. 1947. *Men Against Fire: The Problem of Battle Command in Future War.* New York: Morrow.

Marshall, T. H. 1965. "Citizenship and Social Class." Pp. 71–134 in T. H. Marshall, ed. *Class, Citizenship, and Social Development: Essays by T. H. Marshall.* Garden City, NY: Anchor.

Marth, Michael. 2009. "Adult Criminal Court Statistics, 2006/2007." Statistics Canada. Retrieved November 10, 2010 (http://www.statcan.gc.ca/pub/85-002-x/2008005/article/10567-eng.htm).

Martin, Carol Lynn. 1999. "A Developmental Perspective on Gender Effects and Gender Concepts." Pp. 45–74 in William B. Swann, Jr., Judith H. Langlois, and Lucia Albino Gilbert, eds. *Sexism and Stereotypes in Modern Science: The Gender Science of Janet Taylor Spence.* Washington, DC: American Psychological Association.

Marx, Karl. 1904 [1859]. *A Contribution to the Critique of Political Economy,* N. Stone, trans. Chicago: Charles H. Kerr.

———. 1970 [1843]. *Critique of Hegel's "Philosophy of Right,"* Annette Jolin and Joseph O'Malley, trans. Cambridge, MA: Harvard University Press.

Marx, Karl, and Friedrich Engels. 1972 [1848]. "Manifesto of the Communist Party." Pp. 331–62 in R. Tucker, ed. *The Marx-Engels Reader.* New York: Norton.

Matalon, Jean-Marc. 1997. "Jeanne Calment, World's Oldest Person, Dead at 122." *The Shawnee News-Star* August 5. Retrieved May 2, 2000 (http://www.news-star.com/stories/080597/life1.html).

"Maternal Mortality: A Preventable Tragedy." 1998. *Popline* 20: 4.

Matsueda, Ross L. 1988. "The Current State of Differential Association Theory." *Crime and Delinquency* 34: 277–306.

———. 1992. "Reflected Appraisals, Parental Labeling, and Delinquency: Specifying a Symbolic Interactionist Theory." *American Journal of Sociology* 97: 1577–611.

McAdam, Doug. 1982. *Political Process and the Development of Black Insurgency, 1930–1970.* Chicago: University of Chicago Press.

McCarten, James. 2002. "Child Spanking Law Upheld by Ontario Court: Child's Rights Group Ponders Taking Case to Supreme Court." Retrieved July 15, 2003 (http://www.oacas.org/Whatsnew/newsstories/jan02news/spankinglawupheld.pdf).

McCarthy, John D., and Mayer N. Zald. 1977. "Resource Mobilization and Social Movements: A Partial Theory." *American Journal of Sociology* 82: 1212–41.

McChesney, Robert W. 1999. "Oligopoly: The Big Media Game Has Fewer and Fewer Players." *The Progressive* November: 20–24. Retrieved August 7, 2000 (http://www.progressive.org/mcc1199.htm).

McClelland, W. R. 1931. "Precautions for Workers in the Treating of Radium Ores." *Investigations in Ore Dressing and Metallurgy.* Ottawa: Bureau of Mines. Retrieved October 8, 2000 (http://www.ccnr.org/radium_warning.html).

McConaghy, Nathaniel. 1999. "Unresolved Issues in Scientific Sexology." *Archives of Sexual Behavior* 28, 4: 285–318.

McCormick, Chris, ed. 1999. *The Westray Chronicles: A Case Study in Corporate Crime.* Halifax: Fernwood.

McCulloch, Robert. 2003. "Height and Income." Retrieved April 22, 2003 (http://www.wired.com/news/print/0.1294.41658.00.html1).

McDonald's Corporation. 2005. "Poutine-large." Retrieved December 1, 2005 (http://www.mcdonalds.ca/en/food/ingredient.aspx?menuid=262).

McGinn, Anne Platt. 1998. "Promoting Sustainable Fisheries." Pp. 59–78 in Lester R. Brown, Christopher Flavin, Hilary French et al. *State of the World 1998.* New York: Norton.

McKeon, Matt. n.d. "The Evolution of Privacy on Facebook." Retrieved October 9, 2010 (http://www.mattmckeon.com/facebook-privacy).

McLaren, A. 1990. *Our Own Master Race: Eugenics in Canada, 1885–1945.* Toronto: McClelland & Stewart.

McLuhan, Marshall. 1964. *Understanding Media: The Extensions of Man.* New York: McGraw-Hill.

McMahon, Maeve W. 1992. *The Persistent Prison? Rethinking Decarceration and Penal Reform.* Toronto: University of Toronto Press.

McManners, John, ed. 1990. *Oxford Illustrated History of Christianity.* Oxford: Oxford University Press.

McNeill, William H. 1976. *Plagues and Peoples.* Garden City, NY: Anchor Press.

McPhail, Clark. 1991. *The Myth of the Madding Crowd.* New York: Aldine de Gruyter.

———. 1994. "The Dark Side of Purpose: Individual and Collective Violence in Riots." *The Sociological Quarterly* 35: 1–32.

McPhail, Clark, and Ronald T. Wohlstein. 1983. "Individual and Collective Behaviors within Gatherings, Demonstrations, and Riots." *Annual Review of Sociology* 9: 579–600.

McRoberts, Kenneth. 1988. *Quebec: Social Change and Political Crisis,* 3rd ed. Toronto: McClelland & Stewart.

McTeer, Maureen A. 1999. *Tough Choices: Living and Dying in the 21st Century.* Toronto: Irwin Law.

McVey, Wayne W., Jr., and Warren E. Kalbach. 1995. *Canadian Population.* Scarborough, ON: Nelson.

Mead, G. H. 1934. *Mind, Self and Society.* Chicago: University of Chicago Press.

Meek, Ronald L., ed. 1971. *Marx and Engels on the Population Bomb: Selections from the Writings of Marx and Engels Dealing with the Theories of Thomas Robert Malthus.* Dorothea L. Meek and Ronald L. Meek, trans. Berkeley, CA: Ramparts Press.

Melucci, Alberto. 1980. "The New Social Movements: A Theoretical Approach." *Social Science Information* 19: 199–226.

———. 1995. "The New Social Movements Revisited: Reflections on a Sociological Misunderstanding." Pp. 107–19 in Louis Maheu, ed. *Social Classes and Social Movements: The Future of Collective Action.* London, UK: Sage.

Menzies, C. R. 1999. "First Nations, Inequality and the Legacy of Colonialism." Pp. 236–44 in J. Curtis, E. Grabb, and N. Guppy, eds. *Social Inequality in Canada,* 3rd ed. Scarborough, ON: Prentice Hall Allyn and Bacon Canada Inc.

Merton, Robert K. 1938. "Social Structure and Anomie." *American Sociological Review* 3: 672–82.

———. 1968 [1949]. *Social Theory and Social Structure.* New York: Free Press.

Messerschmidt, J. W. 1993. *Masculinities and Crime: Critique and Reconceptualization of Theory.* Lanham, MD: Roman and Littlefield.

Messner, Michael. 1995. "Boyhood, Organized Sports, and the Construction of Masculinities." Pp. 102–14 in Michael S. Kimmel and Michael A. Messner. *Men's Lives,* 3rd ed. Boston: Allyn and Bacon.

———. 2000. "Barbie Girls versus Sea Monsters: Children Constructing Gender." *Gender & Society, Special Issue* 14, 6 (December): 765–84.

Meyer, David R., and Judi Bartfield. 1996. "Compliance with Child Support Orders in Divorce Cases." *Journal of Marriage and the Family* 58, 1: 201–12.

Meyer, John W., Francisco O. Ramirez, and Yasemin Nuhoglu Soysal. 1992. "World Expansion of Mass Education, 1870–1980." *Sociology of Education* 65: 128–49.

Meyer, John W., and W. Richard Scott. 1983. *Organizational Environments: Ritual and Rationality.* Beverly Hills, CA: Sage.

Meyer, Thomas. 1984. "'Date Rape': A Serious Campus Problem that Few Talk About." *Chronicle of Higher Education* 5 December: 1, 12.

Michels, Robert. 1949 [1911]. *Political Parties: A Sociological Study of the Oligarchical Tendencies of Modern Democracy,* E., and C. Paul, trans. New York: Free Press.

Milanovic, Branko. 2010. "The Consequences of Inequality and Wealth Distribution." Retrieved February 16, 2010 (http://ineteconomics.org/people/participants/branko-milanovic)

Miles, R. 1989. *Racism.* London: Routledge.

Milgram, Stanley. 1974. *Obedience to Authority: An Experimental View.* New York: Harper.

Miliband, Ralph. 1973 [1969]. *The State in Capitalist Society.* London: Fontana.

Milligan, Shelly. 2010. "Youth Court Statistics, 2008/09." Statistics Canada. Retrieved November 10, 2010 (http://www.statcan.gc.ca/pub/85-002-x/2010002/article/11294-eng.htm#a5).

Milloy, John S. 1999. *A National Crime: The Canadian Government and the Residential School System, 1879 to 1986.* Winnipeg: University of Manitoba Press.

Mills, C. Wright. 1956. *The Power Elite.* New York: Oxford University Press.

———. 1959. *The Sociological Imagination.* New York: Oxford University Press.

Minois, George. 1989 [1987]. *History of Old Age: From Antiquity to the Renaissance,* Sarah Hanbury Tenison, trans. Chicago: University of Chicago Press.

Mishler, William. 1979. *Political Participation in Canada.* Toronto: Macmillan of Canada.

Mitchinson, Wendy. 1993. "The Medical Treatment of Women." Pp. 391–421 in Sandra Burt, Lorraine Code, and Lindsay Dorney, eds. *Changing Patterns: Women in Canada,* 2nd ed. Toronto: McClelland & Stewart.

Mittelman, James H. 2000. *The Globalization Syndrome: Transformation and Resistance.* Princeton, NJ: Princeton University Press.

Mizruchi, M. S. 1982. *The American Corporate Network, 1904–1974.* Beverly Hills, CA: Sage.

———. 1992. *The Structure of Corporate Political Action: Interfirm Relations and Their Consequences.* Cambridge, MA: Harvard University Press.

Mohr, Johann W., and Keith Spencer. 1999. "Crime." Pp. 587–89 in James H. Marsh, editor in chief. *The Canadian Encyclopedia,* Year 2000 Edition. Toronto: McClelland & Stewart.

Molm, Linda D. 1997. *Coercive Power in Social Exchange.* Cambridge, UK: Cambridge University Press.

Money, John, and Anke Ehrhardt. 1972. *Man and Woman, Boy and Girl.* Boston: Little Brown.

Montgomery, M. 1965. "The Six Nations and the Macdonald Franchise." *Ontario History* 57: 13.

Mooney, Linda A., David Knox, Caroline Schacht, and Adie Nelson. 2001. *Understanding Social Problems*. Toronto: Nelson Thomson Learning.

Moore, Barrington, Jr. 1967. *Social Origins of Dictatorship and Democracy: Lord and Peasant in the Making of the Modern World*. Boston: Beacon.

Moore, Oliver. 2010. "Smuggled alcohol recalls tragedy of Davis Inlet." *The Globe and Mail* 2 October: A6.

"More People Using Dating Sites to Find Love." 2011. IndianExpress.com February 17. Retrieved May 10, 2011 (http://www.indianexpress.com/news/more-people-using-dating-sites-to-find-love/751342/0).

Morissette, René, and Xuelin Zhang. 2006. "Revisiting Wealth Inequality," *Pespectives* (Statistics Canada). Retrieved May 1, 2008 (http://www.statcan.ca/english/freepub/75-001-XIE/11206/art-1.pdf).

Morris, Aldon D. 1984. *The Origins of the Civil Rights Movement: Black Communities Organizing for Change*. New York: Free Press.

Morris, Norval, and David J. Rothman, eds. 1995. *The Oxford History of the Prison: The Practice of Punishment in Western Society*. New York: Oxford University Press.

Morrison, Nancy. 1987. "Separation and Divorce." Pp. 125–43 in M. J. Dymond, ed. *The Canadian Woman's Legal Guide*. Toronto: Doubleday.

Morton, Gary. 2000. "Showdown at Queen's Park." Retrieved March 22, 2001 (http://www.tao.ca/earth/toronto/archive/1999/toronto01278.html).

Moscovitch, Arlene. 1998. "Electronic Media and the Family." Vanier Institute of the Family. Retrieved May 14, 2003 (http://www.vifamily.ca/cft/media/media.htm).

Mumford, Lewis. 1961. *The City in History: Its Origins, Its Transformations, and Its Prospects*. New York: Harcourt, Brace, and World.

Mundell, Helen. 1993. "How the Color Mafia Chooses Your Clothes." *American Demographics* November. Retrieved May 2, 2000 (http://www.demographics.com/publications/ad/93 ad/9311 ad/ad281.htm).

Murdock, George Peter. 1937. "Comparative Data on the Division of Labor by Sex." *Social Forces* 15: 551–53.

———. 1949. *Social Structure*. New York: Macmillan.

Murnen, Sarah K., Annette Perot, and Don Byrne. 1989. "Coping with Unwanted Sexual Activity: Normative Responses, Situational Determinants and Individual Differences." *Journal of Sex Research* 26: 85–106.

Murphy, Brian, Paul Roberts, and Michael Wolfson. 2007. "A Profile of High-Income Canadians, 1982–2004." Ottawa: Statistics Canada. Retrieved May 1, 2008 (http://www.statcan.ca/english/research/75F0002MIE/75F0002MIE2007006.pdf).

Myerhoff, Barbara. 1978. *Number Our Days*. New York: Dutton.

Myers, Daniel J. 1997. "Racial Rioting in the 1960s: An Event History Analysis of Local Conditions." *American Sociological Review* 62: 94–112.

Myles, John. 1989. *Old Age in the Welfare State: The Political Economy of Public Pensions*, 2nd ed. Lawrence, KA: University Press of Kansas.

Nagle, Matt. 2001. "Gay Man Murdered in Vancouver's Stanley Park." *Seattle Gay News* November 23. Retrieved May 10, 2003 (http://www.sgn.org/2001/11/23).

Nakhaie, M. R. 1997. "Vertical Mosaic among the Elites: The New Imagery Revisited." *Canadian Review of Sociology and Anthropology* 34, 1: 1–24.

National Basketball Association. 2000. "New York Knicks History." Retrieved May 29, 2000 (http://nba.com/knicks/00400499.html#2).

National Council of Welfare. 1998a. "Profiles of Welfare: Myths and Realities: A Report by the National Council of Welfare." Retrieved March 13, 2000 (http://www.ncwnbes.net/htmdocument/reportprowelfare.repprowelfare.htm).

———. 1998b. *Banking and Poor People: Talk Is Cheap*. Ottawa: The Council.

———. 1999. "Children First: A Pre-Budget Report by the National Council of Welfare." Retrieved March 13, 2000 (http://www.ncwnbes.net.htmdocument/reportchildfirst.htm).

———. 2004. *Poverty Profile 2001*. Ottawa: Ministry of Public Works.

National Media Archive. 1998. "A Computerized Database of Canadian National Television News." Retrieved January 16, 2001 http://oldfraser.lexi.net/national media archive/onbalnce.html).

National Opinion Research Center. 2004. *General Social Survey, 1972–2002*. Chicago: University of Chicago. Machine readable file.

———. 2006. *General Social Survey 1972-2004*. Chicago: University of Chicago. Machine readable file.

National Rifle Association. 2005. "Guns, Gun Ownership, & RTC at All-Time Highs, Less 'Gun Control,' and Violent Crime at 30-Year Low." Retrieved December 29, 2005 (http://www.nraila.org/Issues/FactSheets/Read.aspx?ID5126).

Neal, Mark Anthony. 1999. *What the Music Said: Black Popular Music and Black Public Culture*. New York: Routledge.

Neisser, Ulric. 1997. "Rising Scores on Intelligence Tests." *American Scientist* 85, 5: 440–47.

Nelson, Adie, and Barrie W. Robinson. 2002. *Gender in Canada*, 2nd ed. Toronto: Prentice Hall.

Nelson, Dean, and Barney Henderson. 2009. "Slumdog Child Stars Miss Out on the Movie Millions." *Telegraph.co.uk* 26 January. Retrieved January 2, 2010 (http://www.telegraph.co.uk/news/worldnews/asia/4347472/Poor-parents-of-Slumdog-millionaire-stars-say-children-were-exploited.html).

Neugarten, Bernice. 1974. "Age Groups in American Society and the Rise of the Young Old." *Annals of the American Academy of Political and Social Science* 415: 187–98.

Nevitte, Neil. 1996. *The Decline of Deference*. Peterborough, ON: Broadview Press.

Newman, K. 1999. *No Shame in My Game: The Working Poor in the Inner City*. New York: Knopf and the Russell Sage Foundation.

Nicolaiedis, Nicos. 1998. "Pierre Marty's 'Doll' and Today's Barbies." *Revue française de psychanalyse, Special Issue: Psychosomatique et pulsionnalité* 62, 5 (Nov–Dec): 1579–81.

"The Nike Campaign." 2000. Retrieved June 23, 2000 (http://www.web.net/~msn/3nike.htm).

Nikiforuk, Andrew. 1998. "Echoes of the Atomic Age: Cancer Kills Fourteen Aboriginal Uranium Workers." *Calgary Herald* March 14: A1, A4. Retrieved October 8, 2000 (http://www.ccnr.org/deline deaths.html).

———. 1999. "A Question of Style." *Time* 31 May: 58–59.

1994–1995 Directory of Labour Organizations in Canada. 1995. Ottawa: Minister of Supply and Services Canada. Cat. No. L2-2-1995.

1998 Directory of Labour Organizations in Canada. 1998. Ottawa: Workplace Information Directorate.

Nisbett, Richard E., Kaiping Peng, Incheol Choi, and Ara Norenzayan. 2001. "Culture and Systems of Thought: Holistic versus Analytic Cognition." *Psychological Review* 108: 291–310.

Nolen, Stephanie. 1999. "Gender: The Third Way." *The Globe and Mail* September 25: D1, D4.

Norton, Kevin I., Timothy S. Olds, Scott Olive, and Stephen Dank. 1996. "Ken and Barbie at Life Size." *Sex Roles* 34, 3–4 (February): 287–94.

Notestein, F. W. 1945. "Population—The Long View." Pp. 36–57 in T. W. Schultz, ed. *Food for the World*. Chicago: University of Chicago Press.

Novak, Mark. 1997. *Aging and Society: A Canadian Perspective*, 3rd ed. Scarborough, ON: Nelson.

Nowak, Martin A., Robert M. May, and Karl Sigmund. 1995. "The Arithmetics of Mutual Help." *Scientific American* 272, 6: 76–81.

Nowell, Amy, and Larry V. Hedges. 1998. "Trends in Gender Differences in Academic Achievement from 1960 to 1994: An Analysis of Differences in Mean, Variance, and Extreme Scores." *Sex Roles* 39: 21–43.

Nuland, Sherwin B. 1993. *How We Die: Reflections on Life's Final Chapter*. New York: Vintage.

O'Connor, Julia S., and Robert J. Brym. 1988. "Public Welfare Expenditure in OECD Countries: Towards a Reconciliation of Inconsistent Findings." *British Journal of Sociology* 39: 47–68.

O'Connor, Julia S., and Gregg M. Olsen, eds. 1998. *Power Resources Theory and the Welfare State: A Critical Approach*. Toronto: University of Toronto Press.

O'Malley, Martin, and Amina Ali. 2001. "Sticks, Stones and Bullies." CBC.ca. Retrieved June 23, 2002 (http://cbc.ca/national/news/bully).

O'Neil, Dennis. 2004. "Patterns of Subsistence: Classification of Cultures Based on the Sources and Techniques of Acquiring Food and other Necessities." Retrieved January 12, 2005 (http://anthro.palomar.edu/subsistence).

Oberschall, Anthony. 1973. *Social Conflict and Social Movements*. Englewood Cliffs, NJ: Prentice-Hall.

Oderkirk, Jillian, and Clarence Lochhead. 1992. "Lone Parenthood: Gender Differences." *Canadian Social Trends* 27, Spring: 16–19.

OECD (Organisation for Economic Co-operation and Development). 2001. "Knowledge and Skills for Life: First Results from PISA 2000." Retrieved December 5, 2001 (http://www.pisa.oecd.org/knowledge/summary/g.htm).

———. 2004. "Early Childhood Education and Care Policy: Canada Country Note." Retrieved May 14, 2009 (http://www.oecd.org/dataoecd/42/34/33850725.pdf).

———. 2007. "Aid Statistics, Donor Aid Charts." Retrieved December 20, 2007 (http://www.oecd.org/countrylist/0,3349,en_2649_34447_1783495_1_1_1_1,00.html).

———. 2008a. "Aid Targets Slipping Out of Reach?" Retrieved February 12, 2011 (http://www.oecd.org/dataoecd/47/25/41724314.pdf).

———. 2008b. "Average Annual Hours Actually Worked per Worker." Retrieved May 1, 2008 (http://stats.oecd.org/wbos/Index.aspx?DatasetCode=ANHRS).

———. 2010a. "Education at a Glance 2010: OECD Indicators." Retrieved April 12, 2011 (http://www.oecd.org/document/52/0,3746,en_2649_39263238_45897844_1_1_1_1,00.html).

———. 2010b. "Health: Key Tables from OECD." Retrieved October 26, 2010 (http://www.oecd-ilibrary.org/social-issues-migration-health/health-key-tables-from-oecd_20758480;jsessionid=1uk47wcovz5qu.delta).

Oeppen, Jim, and James W. Vaupel. 2002. "Demography: Enhanced: Broken Limits to Life Expectancy." *Science* 296: 1029–31.

Ogmundson, R., and J. McLaughlin. 1992. "Trends in the Ethnic Origins of Canadian Elites: The Decline of the BRITS?" *The Canadian Review of Sociology and Anthropology* 29: 227–42.

Oliver, Melvin L., and Thomas M. Shapiro. 1995. *Black Wealth/White Wealth: A New Perspective on Racial Inequality.* New York: Routledge.

Oliver, Mike. 1996. *Understanding Disability: From Theory to Practice.* Basingstoke, UK: Macmillan.

Olsen, Dennis. 1980. *The State Elite.* Toronto: McClelland & Stewart.

Olsen, Gregg M. 2002. *The Politics of the Welfare State: Canada, Sweden, and the United States.* Don Mills, ON: Oxford University Press Canada.

Olsen, Gregg, and Robert J. Brym. 1996. "Between American Exceptionalism and Swedish Social Democracy: Public and Private Pensions in Canada." Pp. 261–79 in Michael Shalev, ed. *The Privatization of Social Policy? Occupational Welfare and the Welfare State in America, Scandinavia and Japan.* London: Macmillan.

Olzak, Susan, and Suzanne Shanahan. 1996. "Deprivation and Race Riots: An Extension of Spilerman's Analysis." *Social Forces* 74: 931–62.

Olzak, Susan, Suzanne Shanahan, and Elizabeth H. McEneaney. 1996. "Poverty, Segregation, and Race Riots: 1960 to 1993." *American Sociological Review* 61: 590–614.

Omega Foundation. 1998. "An Appraisal of the Technologies of Political Control: Summary and Options Report for the European Parliament." Retrieved April 29, 2000 (http://home.icdc.com/~paulwolf/eu_stoa_2.htm).

Omi, M., and H. Winant. 1986. *Racial Formation in the United States.* New York: Routledge.

"100 Best Dating Sites." 2011. Retrieved May 10, 2011 (http://www.100bestdatingsites.com).

Optometrists Network. 2000. "Attention Deficit Disorder." Retrieved August 14, 2000 (http://www.add-adhd.org/ADHD_attention-deficit.html).

Oreopoulos, Philip. 2005. "Canadian Compulsory School Laws and Their Impact on Educational Attainment and Future Earnings." Ottawa: Statistics Canada. Retrieved May 27, 2006 (http://www.statcan.ca/english/research/11F0019MIE/11F0019MIE2005251.pdf).

Organization of African Unity. 2000. *Rwanda: The Preventable Genocide.* Retrieved January 15, 2005 (http://www.visiontv.ca/RememberRwanda/Report.pdf).

Ornstein, Michael D. 1998. "Survey Research." *Current Sociology* 46, 4: 1–87.

Ossowski, Stanislaw. 1963. *Class Structure in the Social Consciousness*, S. Patterson, trans. London: Routledge and Kegan Paul.

Ouimet, M. 2002. "Explaining the American and Canadian Crime 'Drop' in the 1990s." *Canadian Journal of Criminology* 44, 1: 33–50.

Owen, Michelle K. 2001. "'Family' as a Site of Contestation: Queering the Normal or Normalizing the Queer?" Pp. 86–102 in Terry Goldie, ed. *In a Queer Country: Gay and Lesbian Studies in the Canadian Context.* Vancouver: Arsenal Pulp Press.

Pabilonia, Sabrina Wulff, and Cindy Zoghi. 2005a. "Returning to the Returns to Computer Use." BLS Working Paper 377. Washington DC: U.S. Department of Labor, Bureau of Labor Statistics.

———. 2005b. "Who Gains from Computer Use?" *Perspectives on Labor and Income* 6, 7: 5–11.

Pacey, Arnold. 1983. *The Culture of Technology.* Cambridge, MA: MIT Press.

Pammett, Jon H. 1997. "Getting Ahead Around the World." Pp. 67–86 in Alan Frizzell and Jon H. Pammett, eds. *Social Inequality in Canada.* Ottawa: Carleton University Press.

Pape, Robert A. 2003 "The Strategic Logic of Suicide Terrorism." *American Political Science Review* 97: 343–61.

———. 2005. *Dying to Win: The Strategic Logic of Suicide Terrorism.* New York: Random House.

Paperny, Anna Mehler. 2011. "Antibullying Movement Is in the Pink." *The Globe and Mail*, March 14. Retrieved April 24, 2011 (http://www.globeandmail.com).

Park, Jungwee. 2005. "Use of Alternative Health Care." *Health Reports* 16, 2: 39–43.

Park, Robert Ezra, Ernest W. Burgess, and Roderick D. McKenzie. 1967 [1925]. *The City.* Chicago: University of Chicago Press.

Parke, Ross D. 2001. "Paternal Involvement in Infancy: The Role of Maternal and Paternal Attitudes." *Journal of Family Psychology* 15, 4 (December): 555–58.

———. 2002. "Parenting in the New Millennium: Prospects, Promises and Pitfalls." Pp. 65–93 in James P. McHale and Wendy S. Grolnick, eds. *Retrospect and Prospect in the Psychological Study of Families.* Mahwah, NJ: Lawrence Erlbaum Associates, Inc.

Parkin, F. 1979. *Marxism and Class Theory.* New York: Columbia University Press.

Parshall, Gerald. 1998. "Brotherhood of the Bomb." *US News and World Report* 125, 7 (17–24 August): 64–68.

Parsons, Talcott. 1942. "Age and Sex in the Social Structure of the United States." *American Sociological Review* 7: 604–16.

———. 1951. *The Social System.* New York: Free Press.

———. 1955. "The American Family: Its Relation to Personality and to the Social Structure." Pp. 3–33 in Talcott Parsons and Robert F. Bales, eds. *Family, Socialization and Interaction Process.* New York: Free Press.

———. 1963. "On the Concept of Political Power." *Proceedings of the American Philosophical Society* 107, 3: 232–62.

Pascual, Brian. 2002. "Avril Lavigne Hates Britney Spears." *ChartAttack* April 19. Retrieved January 15, 2003 (http://teenmusic.about.com/gi/dynamic/offsite.htm?site=http%3A%2F%2Fwww.chartattack.com%2Fdamn%2F2002%2F04%2F1901.cfm).

Patent Medicine Prices Review Board. 2002. "Annual Report." Retrieved June 17, 2003 (http://www.pmprb-cepmb.gc.ca/CMFiles/ar-2002e21IRA-6162003-196.pdf).

Patent Medicine Prices Review Board. "Annual Report 2009." Retrieved December 8, 2010 (http://www.pmprb-cepmb.gc.ca/english/view.asp?x=1340&mid=1193).

Pence, Leah, and Monique Jacobs. 2001. "Tracking the Elusive Traditional Family." *UVic KnowlEDGE* 2, 9. Retrieved June 12, 2006 (http://communications.uvic.ca/edge/v2n09_17sep01.pdf).

Pendakur, K., and R. Pendakur. 1998. "The Colour of Money: Earnings Differentials among Ethnic Groups in Canada." *Canadian Journal of Economics* 31: 518–48.

Pendakur, R. 2000. *Immigrants and the Labour Force: Policy, Regulation and Impact.* Montreal: McGill-Queen's University Press.

Peritz, Ingrid. 1999. "Birth Rate in Quebec Lowest Since 1908." *The Globe and Mail* October 4: A1.

Perks, Thomas A. 2005. *Height as a Factor in Social Inequality: Analyses Based on Five Canadian National Surveys.* Ph.D. dissertation, Department of Sociology, University of Waterloo.

Perreault, Samuel. 2009. "The Incarceration of Aboriginal people in Adult Correctional Services." Statistics Canada. Retrieved November 10, 2010 (http://www.statcan.gc.ca/pub/85-002-x/2009003/article/10903-eng.htm).

Perrow, Charles B. 1984. *Normal Accidents.* New York: Basic Books.

Peters, John F. 1994. "Gender Socialization of Adolescents in the Home: Research and Discussion." *Adolescence* 29: 913–34.

Peterson, Peter. 1997. "Will America Grow Up Before It Grows Old?" P. 70 in Harold A. Widdison, ed. *Social Problems: Annual Editions.* Guilford, CN: Dushkin.

Pettersson, Jan. 2003. "Democracy, Regime Stability, and Growth." *Scandinavian Working Papers in Economics.* Retrieved February 13, 2003 (http://swopec.hhs.se/sunrpe/abs/sunrpe2002_0016.htm).

Pew Research Center for the People and the Press. 2002. "Among Wealthy Nations U.S. Stands Alone in its Embrace of Religion." Retrieved May 3, 2003 (http://people-press.org/reports/display.php3?ReportID_167).

Piaget, Jean, and Bärbel Inhelder. 1969. *The Psychology of the Child,* Helen Weaver, trans. New York: Basic Books.

Pineo, P. C., and J. Porter. 1985. "Ethnic Origin and Occupational Attainment." In M. Boyd, J. Goyder, F. E. Jones, H. A. McRoberts, P. C. Pineo, and J. Porter, eds. *Ascription and Achievement: Studies in Mobility and Status Attainment.* Ottawa: Carleton University Press.

Pinker, Steven. 2002. *The Blank Slate: The Modern Denial of Human Nature.* New York: Viking.

PISA Canada. 2007. *Measuring Up: Canadian Results of the OECD PISA Study: The Performance of Canada's Youth in Science, Reading and Mathematics.* Statistics Canada Catalogue no. 81-590-XIE.

Piven, Frances Fox, and Richard A. Cloward. 1977. *Poor People's Movements: Why They Succeed, How They Fail.* New York: Vintage.
———. 1993 [1971]. *Regulating the Poor: The Functions of Public Welfare,* updated ed. New York: Vintage.

Plooy, Gareth. 2009. "Crying Wolf over Gentrification." *The Uniter* July 17. Retrieved April 6, 2011 (http://uniter.ca/view/961).

Plummer, Kenneth. 1995. *Telling Sexual Stories: Power, Change and Social Worlds.* London, UK: Routledge.

Podolny, Joel M., and Karen L. Page. 1998. "Network Forms of Organization." *Annual Review of Sociology* 24: 57–76.

Pollution Watch. 2008. "An examination of pollution and poverty in the City of Toronto." Retrieved December 7, 2010 (http://www.toronto.ca/demographics/pdf/pollutionwatch_toronto_fact_sheet.pdf).

Polsby, Nelson W. 1959. "Three Problems in the Analysis of Community Power." *American Sociological Review* 24: 796–803.

Pool, Robert. 1997. *Beyond Engineering: How Society Shapes Technology.* New York: Oxford University Press.

"Poor Palliative Care Encourages Euthanasia." 2001. March 19. Retrieved June 15, 2003 (http://www.savemedicare.com/n19ma01a.htm).

Popenoe, David. 1996. *Life without Father: Compelling New Evidence that Fatherhood and Marriage Are Indispensable for the Good of Children and Society.* New York: Martin Kessler Books.
———. 1998. "The Decline of Marriage and Fatherhood." Pp. 312–19 in John J. Macionis and Nicole V. Benokraitis, eds. *Seeing Ourselves: Classic, Contemporary and Cross-Cultural Readings in Sociology,* 4th ed. Upper Saddle River, NJ: Prentice Hall.

Population Reference Bureau. 2003. "Human Population: Fundamentals of Growth." Retrieved August 2, 2003 (http://www.prb.org/Content/NavigationMenu/PRB/Educators/Human_Population/Population_Growth/Population_Growth.htm).

Population Reference Bureau. 2010. "2010 World Population Data Sheet." Retrieved March 12, 2011 (http://www.prb.org/pdf10/10wpds_eng.pdf).

Porter, John. 1965. *The Vertical Mosaic: An Analysis of Social Class and Power in Canada.* Toronto: University of Toronto Press.
———. 1979. *The Measure of Canadian Society: Education, Equality, and Opportunity.* Toronto: Gage.

Portes, Alejandro. 1996. "Global Villagers: The Rise of Transnational Communities." *The American Prospect* 25: 74–77. Retrieved April 29, 2000 (http://www.prospect.org/archives/25/25port.html).

Portes, A., and R. D. Manning. 1991. "The Immigrant Enclave: Theory and Empirical Examples." Pp. 319–32 in N. R. Yetman, ed. *Majority and Minority: The Dynamics of Race and Ethnicity in American Life,* 5th ed. Boston: Allyn and Bacon.

Postel, Sandra. 1994. "Carrying Capacity: Earth's Bottom Line." Pp. 3–21 in Linda Starke, ed. *State of the World 1994.* New York: Norton.

Postman, Neil. 1982. *The Disappearance of Childhood.* New York: Delacorte.

Poulantzas, Nicos, 1975 [1968]. *Political Power and Social Classes,* T. O'Hagan, trans. London: New Left Books.

Powell, J., and C. Leedham. 2009. "Comparative Aging in Post-Industrial Society." Pp. 141–60 in J. Powell and J. Hendricks, eds., *The Welfare State in Postindustrial Society: A Global Analysis.* New York: Springer.

Pred, Allan R. 1973. *Urban Growth and the Circulation of Information.* Cambridge, MA: Harvard University Press.

Press, Andrea. 1991. *Women Watching Television: Gender, Class and Generation in the American Television Experience.* Philadelphia: University of Pennsylvania Press.

Press, Andrea L., and Elizabeth R. Cole. 1999. *Speaking of Abortion: Television and Authority in the Lives of Women.* Chicago: University of Chicago Press.

Priestly, Mark. 2001. "Introduction: The Global Context of Disability." Pp. 3–25 in Mark Priestly, ed. *Disability and the Life Course: Global Perspectives,* Cambridge: Cambridge University Press.

Proctor, Robert N. 1988. *Racial Hygiene: Medicine under the Nazis.* Cambridge, MA: Harvard University Press.

Province of Nova Scotia. 2008. "Counties of Nova Scotia." Retrieved January 12, 2008 (http://www.gov.ns.ca/snsmr/muns/info/mapping/counties.asp).

Provine, Robert R. 2000. *Laughter: A Scientific Investigation.* New York: Penguin.

Quaschning, Volker. 2003. "Development of Global Carbon Dioxide Emissions and Concentration in Atmosphere." Retrieved March 2, 2005 (http://www.volker-quaschning.de/datserv/CO2/index_e.html).

Raag, Tarja, and Christine L. Rackliff. 1998. "Preschoolers' Awareness of Social Expectations of Gender: Relationships to Toy Choices." *Sex Roles* 38: 685–700.

Rahman, Shaikh Azizur. 2004. "Where the Girls Aren't." *The Globe and Mail* October 16: F2.

Raphael, D. 2004. *Social Determinants of Health: Canadian Perspectives.* Toronto: Canadian Scholars' Press.

Rapp, R., and E. Ross. 1986. "The 1920s: Feminism, Consumerism and Political Backlash in the U.S." Pp. 52–62 in J. Friedlander, B. Cook, A. Kessler-Harris, and C. Smith-Rosenberg, eds. *Women in Culture and Politics.* Bloomington, IN: Indiana University Press.

Reiman, Jeffrey H. 2003. *The Rich Get Richer and the Poor Get Prison: Ideology, Class, and Criminal Justice,* 7th ed. Boston: Allyn & Bacon.

Reimann, Renate. 1997. "Does Biology Matter? Lesbian Couples' Transition to Parenthood and Their Division of Labor." *Qualitative Sociology* 20, 2: 153–85.

Reiter, Ester. 1991. *Making Fast Food: From the Frying Pan into the Fryer.* Montreal: McGill-Queen's University Press.

Reitz, Jeffrey. 2007. "Tapping Immigrants' Skills." Pp. 130–40 in Robert J. Brym, ed. *Society in Question: Sociological Readings for the 21st Century,* 5th ed. Toronto: Nelson.

Reitz, Jeffrey G., and Raymond Breton. 1994. *The Illusion of Difference: Realities of Ethnicity in Canada and the United States.* Toronto: C.D. Howe Institute.

Religious Tolerance.org. 2011. "Same-Sex Marriages (SSM), Civil Unions & Domestic Partnerships." Retrieved August 7, 2011 (http://www.religioustolerance.org/hom_marr.htm).

Remennick, Larissa I. 1998. "The Cancer Problem in the Context of Modernity: Sociology, Demography, Politics." *Current Sociology* 46, 1: 1–150.

"Rich 100." 2011. *Canadian Business.* Retrieved September 6, 2011 (http://list.canadianbusiness.com/rankings/rich100/2010/ranking/Default.aspx?sp2=1&d1=a&sc1=0).

Richardson, J. 1832, *Wacousta; Or the Prophecy: A Tale of the Canadas.* London, UK: Cadell.

Richardson, R. Jack. 1996. "Canada and Free Trade: Why Did It Happen?" Pp. 200–09 in Robert J. Brym, ed. *Society in Question.* Toronto: Harcourt Brace Canada.

Richler, Mordecai. 1959. *The Apprenticeship of Duddy Kravitz.* Don Mills ON: A. Deutsch.

Ridgeway, Cecilia L. 1983. *The Dynamics of Small Groups.* New York: St. Martin's Press.

Rifkin, Jeremy. 1998. *The Biotech Century: Harnessing the Gene and Remaking the World.* New York: Jeremy P. Tarcher/Putnam.

Riley, Matilda White, Anne Foner, and Joan Waring. 1988. "Sociology of Age." Pp. 243–90 in Neil Smelser, ed. *Handbook of Sociology.* Newbury Park, CA: Sage.

Riley, Nancy. 1997. "Gender, Power, and Population Change." *Population Bulletin* 52, 1. Retrieved August 25, 2000 (http://www.prb.org/pubs/population_bulletin/bu52-1.htm).

The Ring (University of Victoria's community newspaper). 2000. "Comment." February 4. Retrieved March 15, 2001 (http://www.communications.uvic.ca/Ring/00feb04/cover.html).

Risman, B. J., and D. Johnson-Sumerford. 1998. "Doing It Fairly: A Study of Postgender Marriages." *Journal of Marriage and the Family* 60: 23–40.

Rist, Ray. 1970. "Student Social Class and Teacher Expectations: The Self-Fulfilling Prophecy in Ghetto Education." *Harvard Educational Review* 40, 3 (August): 411–51.

Ritzer, George. 1996. "The McDonalidzation Thesis: Is Expansion Inevitable?" *International Sociology* 11: 291–307.

Robbins, Liz. 2005. "Nash Displays Polished Look: On the Court, of Course." *The New York Times* January 19. Retrieved January 19, 2005 (http://www.nytimes.com).

Roberts, C. G. D. 1915. *A History of Canada for High Schools and Academics*. Toronto: Macmillan.

Roberts, D. F. 1995. "The Pervasiveness of Plasticity." Pp.1–17 in *Human Variability and Plasticity*, C. G. N. Mascie-Taylor and Barry Bogin, eds. Cambridge: Cambridge University Press.

Roberts, Julian, and Thomas Gabor. 1990. "Race and Crime: A Critique." *Canadian Journal of Criminology* 92, 2 (April): 291–313.

Robertson, Ian. 1987. *Sociology*, 3rd ed. New York: Worth Publishing.

Robertson, Roland. 1992. *Globalization: Social Theory and Global Culture*. Newbury Park, CA: Sage.

Robinson, B. A. 2006."Abortion Access: Two Canadian, and One British, Public Opinion Polls on Abortion." Religious Tolerance.org. Retrieved September 7, 2011 (http://www.religioustolerance.org/abopollca.htm).

Robinson, Richard H., and Willard L. Johnson. 1997. *The Buddhist Religion: A Historical Introduction*, 4th ed. Belmont, CA: Wadsworth.

Roche, Maurice. 1995. "Rethinking Citizenship and Social Movements: Themes in Contemporary Sociology and Neoconservative Ideology." Pp. 186–219 in Louis Maheu, ed. *Social Classes and Social Movements: The Future of Collective Action*. London, UK: Sage.

Rodinson, Maxime. 1996. *Muhammad*, 2nd ed. Anne Carter, trans. London: Penguin.

Roediger, D. R. 1991. *The Wages of Whiteness: Race and the Making of the American Working Class*. London: Verso.

Roethlisberger, Fritz J., and William J. Dickson. 1939. *Management and the Worker*. Cambridge, MA: Harvard University Press.

Rogan, Mary. 2001. "An Epidemic of Gas Sniffing Decimates Arctic Indian Tribe." *The New York Times on the Web*. Retrieved March 4 (http://www.uwec.edu/Academic/Curric/majstos/p390/Articles/030301gas-sniffing-Indians.htm).

Rogers, Jackie Krasas, and Kevin D. Henson. 1997. " 'Hey, Why Don't You Wear a Shorter Skirt?' Structural Vulnerability and the Organization of Sexual Harassment in Temporary Clerical Employment." *Gender and Society* 11: 215–37.

Rollins, Boyd C., and Kenneth L. Cannon. 1974. "Marital Satisfaction over the Family Life Cycle." *Journal of Marriage and the Family* 36: 271–84.

Romaniuc, A. 1984. "Fertility in Canada: From Baby-boom to Baby-bust." *Current Demographic Analysis*. Ottawa: Statistics Canada.

Ron, James. 2007. Personal communication. Norman Paterson School of International Affairs, Carleton University, Ottawa. December 20.

Rootes, Chris. 1995. "A New Class? The Higher Educated and the New Politics." Pp. 220–35 in Louis Maheu, ed. *Social Classes and Social Movements: The Future of Collective Action*. London, UK: Sage.

Rose, Michael S. 2001. "The Facts Behind the Massacre." Catholic World News 17 October. Retrieved January 15, 2005 (http:///www.cwnews.com/news/viewstory.cfm?recnum=20654).

Rosenbloom, Stephanie. 2007. "On Facebook, Scholars Link up with Data." *The New York Times* 17 December. Retrieved October 9, 2010 (http://www.nytimes.com).

Rosenbluth, Susan C. 1997. "Is Sexual Orientation a Matter of Choice?" *Psychology of Women Quarterly* 21: 595–610.

Rosenthal, Robert, and Lenore Jacobson. 1968. *Pygmalion in the Classroom: Teacher Expectation and Pupils' Intellectual Development*. New York: Holt, Rinehart, and Winston.

Rosin, Hanna, and Richard Morin. 1999. "In One Area, Americans Still Draw a Line on Acceptability." *Washington Post*, National Weekly Edition, 16, 11 (11 January): 8.

Ross, D., P. Roberts, and K. Scott. 2000. "Family Income and Child Well-Being." *Isuma, Canadian Journal of Policy Research* 1, 2 (Autumn): 51–56.

Ross, David. 1998. "Rethinking Child Poverty." *Insight, Perception* 22, 1: 9–11.

Rostow, W. W. 1960. *The Stages of Economic Growth: A Non-Communist Manifesto*. New York: Cambridge University Press.

Roth, Cecil. 1961. *A History of the Jews*. New York: Schocken.

Rothman, Barbara Katz. 1982. *In Labor: Women and Power in the Birthplace*. New York: Norton.

———. 1989. *Recreating Motherhood: Ideology and Technology in a Patriarchal Society*. New York: Norton.

Rothman, David J. 1991. *Strangers at the Bedside: A History of How Law and Bioethics Transformed Medical Decision Making*. New York: Basic Books.

———. 1998. "The International Organ Traffic." *New York Review of Books* 45, 5: 14–17.

Rubin, J. Z., F. J. Provenzano, and Z. Lurra. 1974. "The Eye of the Beholder." *American Journal of Orthopsychiatry* 44: 512–19.

Rueschemeyer, Dietrich, Evelyne Huber Stephens, and John Stephens. 1992. *Capitalist Development and Democracy*. Chicago: University of Chicago Press.

Ruggles, Steven. 1997. *Prolonged Connections: The Rise of the Extended Family in 19th-Century England and America*. Madison, WI: University of Wisconsin Press.

Rupp, Leila J., and Verta Taylor. 2010. "Straight Girls Kissing." *Contexts* 9, 4: 28–32.

Rural Advancement Foundation International. 1999. "The Gene Giants." Retrieved May 2, 2000 (http://www.rafi.org/web/allpub-one.shtml?dfl=allpub.db&tfl=allpub-one-frag.ptml&operation=display&ro1=recNo&rf1=34&rt1=34&usebrs=true).

Rushton, J. P. 1995. *Race, Evolution and Behaviour: A Life History Perspective*. New Brunswick, NJ: Transaction Publishers.

Russett, Cynthia Eagle. 1966. *The Concept of Equilibrium in American Social Thought*. New Haven, CT: Yale University Press.

Ryan, Kathryn M., and Jeanne Kanjorski. 1998. "The Enjoyment of Sexist Humor, Rape Attitudes, and Relationship Aggression in College Students." *Sex Roles* 38: 743–56.

Ryerson, Stanley. 1973. *Unequal Union: Roots of Crisis in the Canadas, 1815–1873*, 2nd ed. Toronto: Progress.

Rytina, Steven, Peter M. Blau, Terry Blum, and Joseph Schwartz. 1988. "Inequality and Intermarriage: A Paradox of Motive and Constraint." *Social Forces* 66: 645–75.

Sahlins, Marshall D. 1972. *Stone Age Economics*. Chicago: Aldine.

Salt, Robert. 1991. "Child Support in Context: Comments on Rettig, Christensen, and Dahl." *Family Relations* 40, 2 (April): 175–78.

Sampson, Robert, and John H. Laub. 1993. *Crime in the Making: Pathways and Turning Points through Life*. Cambridge, MA: Harvard University Press.

Samson, Colin, James Wilson, and Jonathan Mazower. 1999. *Canada's Tibet: The Killing of the Innu*. London UK: Survival. Retrieved May 1, 2001 (http://www.survival.org.uk/pdf/Innu%20report.pdf).

Samuelsson, Kurt. 1961 [1957]. *Religion and Economic Action*, E. French, trans. Stockholm: Scandinavian University Books.

Sanchez, F. J. P., and Roda, M. D. S. 2003. "Relationships between Self-Concept and Academic Achievement in Primary Students." *Electronic Journal of Research in Educational Psychology and Psychpedagogy* 1, 1: 95–120.

Sandqvist, Karin, and Bengt-Erik Andersson. 1992. "Thriving Families in the Swedish Welfare State." *Public Interest* 109: 114–16.

Sang-Hun, Choe. 2007. "Where Boys Were Kings, a Shift Towards Baby Girls." *The New York Times* December 23. Retrieved December 23, 2007 (http://www.nytimes.com).

Sarlo, C. 2001. *Measuring Poverty in Canada*. Vancouver: Fraser Institute.

Sartre, J. 1965 [1948]. *Anti-Semite and Jew*, G. J. Becker, trans. New York: Schocken.

Sassen, Saskia. 1991. *The Global City: New York, London, Tokyo*. Princeton, NJ: Princeton University Press.

Saxton, Lloyd. 1990. *The Individual, Marriage, and the Family*, 9th ed. Belmont, CA: Wadsworth.

Scarr, Sandra, and Richard A. Weinberg. 1978. "The Influence of 'Family Background' on Intellectual Attainment." *American Sociological Review* 43: 674–92.

Schiebinger, Londa L. 1993. *Nature's Body: Gender in the Making of Modern Science*. Boston: Beacon Press.

Schiff, Michel, and Richard Lewontin. 1986. *Education and Class: The Irrelevance of IQ Genetic Studies*. Oxford, UK: Clarendon Press.

Schiller, Herbert I. 1989. *Culture Inc.: The Corporate Takeover of Public Expression*. New York: Oxford University Press.

Schlesinger, Arthur. 1991. *The Disuniting of America: Reflections on a Multicultural Society*. New York: Norton.

Schoen, Cathy, Michelle M. Doty, Sara R. Collins, Alyssa L. Holmgren. 2005. "Insured But Not Protected: How Many Adults Are Underinsured?" *Health Affairs Web Supplement* W5. 289, 1. Retrieved July 2, 2005 (http://content.healthaffairs.org/cgi/reprint/hlthaff.w5 .289v1).

Schor, Juliet B. 1992. *The Overworked American: The Unexpected Decline of Leisure*. New York: Basic Books.

———. 1999. *The Overspent American: Why We Want What We Don't Need*. New York: Harper.

Schroeder, K. A., L. L. Blood, and D. Maluso. 1993. "Gender Differences and Similarities between Male and Female Undergraduate Students Regarding Expectations for Career and Family Roles." *College Student Journal* 27: 237–49.

Schudson, Michael. 1991. "National News Culture and the Rise of the Informational Citizen." Pp. 265–82 in Alan Wolfe, ed. *America at Century's End*. Berkeley, CA: University of California Press.

———. 1995. *The Power of News*. Cambridge, MA: Harvard University Press.

Schuettler, Darren. 2002. "Earth Summit Bogs Down in Bitter Trade Debate." *Yahoo! Canada News* 28 August. Retrieved February 12, 2002 (http://ca.news.yahoo.com/020828/5/olia.html).

Schwartz, Stephen. 2003. *The Two Faces of Islam: The House of Sa'ud from Tradition to Terror*. New York: Doubleday.

Schweingruber, David, and Clark McPhail. 1999. "A Method for Systematically Observing and Recording Collective Action." *Sociological Methods and Research* 27: 451–98.

Scott, Janny. 1998. "Manners and Civil Society." *Journal* 2, 3. Retrieved April 12, 2003 (http://www.civnet.org/journal/issue7/ftjscott.htm).

Scott, K. 1997. "Indigenous Canadians." Pp. 133–64 in D. McKenzie, R. Williams, and E. Single, eds. *Canadian Profile: Alcohol, Tobacco and Other Drugs, 1997*. Ottawa: Canadian Centre on Substance Abuse.

Scott, Shirley Lynn. 2003. "The Death of James Bulger." *Court TV's Crime Library*. Retrieved July 23, 2003 (http://www.crimelibrary.com/notorious_murders/young/bulger/1.html?sect=10).

Scott, Wilbur J. 1990. "PTSD in DSM-III: A Case in the Politics of Diagnosis and Disease." *Social Problems* 37: 294–310.

Seiter, Ellen. 1999. *Television and New Media Audiences*. Oxford, UK: Clarendon Press.

Sen, Amartya. 1981. *Poverty and Famines: An Essay on Entitlement and Deprivation*. Oxford, UK: Clarendon Press.

———. 1994. "Population: Delusion and Reality." *New York Review of Books* 41, 15: 62–71.

———. 2001. "Many Faces of Gender Inequality." *The Frontline* 9 November. Retrieved August 5, 2003 3 (http://www.ksg.harvard.edu/gei/Text/Sen-Pubs/Sen_many_faces_of_gender_inequality.pdf).

Senn, Charlene Y., Serge Desmarais, Norine Veryberg, and Eileen Wood. 2000. "Predicting Coercive Sexual Behavior across the Lifespan in a Random Sample of Canadian Men." *Journal of Social and Personal Relationships* 17, 1 (February): 95–113.

Shaienks, Danielle, and Tomasz Gluszynski. 2007. "Participation in Postsecondary Education: Graduates, Continuers and Drop Outs, Results from YITS Cycle 4. Programme for International Student Assessment, Government of Canada." Retrieved March 17, 2011 (http://www.pisa.gc.ca/eng/participation.shtml).

Shain, A. 1995. "Employment of People with Disabilities." *Canadian Social Trends* 38: 8–13.

Shakur, Sanyika (a.k.a. Monster Kody Scott). 1993. *Monster: The Autobiography of an L.A. Gang Member*. New York: Penguin.

Shalev, Michael. 1983. "Class Politics and the Western Welfare State." Pp. 27–50 in S. E. Spiro and E. Yuchtman-Yaar, eds. *Evaluating the Welfare State: Social and Political Perspectives*. New York: Academic Press.

Shapiro, Joseph P. 1993. *No Pity: People with Disabilities Forging a New Civil Rights Movement*. New York: Times Books.

Shattuck, Roger. 1980. *The Forbidden Experiment: The Story of the Wild Boy of Aveyron*. New York: Farrar, Straus, and Giroux.

Shaw, Karen. 2001. "Harry Potter Books: My Concerns." Retrieved June 15, 2003 (http://www.reachouttrust.org/regulars/articles/occult/hpotter2.htm).

Shaw, Martin. 2000. *Theory of the Global State: Globality as Unfinished Revolution*. Cambridge: Cambridge University Press.

Shea, Sarah E., Kevin Gordon, Ann Hawkins, Janet Kawchuk, and Donna Smith. 2000. "Pathology in the Hundred Acre Wood: A Neurodevelopmental Perspective on A. A. Milne." *Canadian Medical Association Journal* 163, 12: 1557–59. Retrieved December 12, 2000 (http://www.cma.ca/cmaj/vol-163/issue-12/1557.htm).

Shekelle, Paul G. 1998. "What Role for Chiropractic in Health Care?" *New England Journal of Medicine* 339: 1074–5.

Sherif, M., L. J. Harvey, B. J. White, W. R. Hood, and C. W. Sherif. 1988 [1961]. *The Robber's Cave Experiment: Intergroup Conflict and Cooperation*. Middletown, CT: Wesleyan University Press.

Sherrill, Robert. 1997. "A Year in Corporate Crime." *The Nation* 7 April: 11–20.

Shields, M. 1999. "Long Working Hours and Health." *Health Reports* 11, 2: 33–48.

Shkilnyk, Anastasia. 1985. *A Poison Stronger Than Love: The Destruction of an Ojibway Community*. New Haven, CT: Yale University Press.

"Short Guys Finish Last." 1995–96. *The Economist* December 23–January 5: 19–22.

Short, James F., Jr., and Fred L. Strodtbeck. 1965. *Group Process and Gang Delinquency*. Chicago: University of Chicago Press.

Shorter, Edward. 1997. *A History of Psychiatry: From the Era of the Asylum to the Age of Prozac*. New York: Wiley.

Signorielli, Nancy. 1998. "Reflections of Girls in the Media: A Content Analysis Across Six Media: Overview." Retrieved July 15, 2000 (http://childrennow.org/media/mc97/ReflectSummary.html).

———. 2009. "Race and Sex in Prime Time: A Look at Occupations and Occupational Prestige." *Mass Communication and Society*, 12:. 332–52.

Silberman, Steve. 2000. "Talking to Strangers." *Wired* 8, 5: 225–33, 288–96. Retrieved May 23, 2002 (http://www.wired.com/wired/archive/8.05/translation.html).

"The Silent Boom." 1998. *Fortune* 7 July: 170–71.

Simmel, Georg. 1950. *The Sociology of Georg Simmel*, Kurt H. Wolff, trans. and ed. New York: Free Press.

Simon, Jonathan. 1993. *Poor Discipline: Parole and the Social Control of the Underclass, 1890–1990*. Chicago: University of Chicago Press.

Simons, Ronald L., Chyi-In Wu, Christine Johnson, and Rand D. Conger. 1995. "A Test of Various Perspectives on the Intergenerational Transmission of Domestic Violence." *Criminology* 33: 141–60.

Simons-Morton, B., and R. Chen. 2009. "Peer and Parent Influences on School Engagement among Early Adolescents." *Youth & Society*, 41: 3–25.

Sissing, T. W. 1996. "The Black Community in the History of Québec and Canada." Retrieved June 14, 2003 (http://www.qesnrecit.qc.ca/mpages/title.htm).

Sjöberg, Gideon. 1960. *The Preindustrial City: Past and Present*. New York: Free Press.

Skinner, B. F. 1953. *Science and Human Behavior*. New York: Macmillan.

Skocpol, Theda. 1979. *States and Revolutions: A Comparative Analysis of France, Russia, and China*. Cambridge, UK: Cambridge University Press.

Skolnick, Arlene. 1991. *Embattled Paradise: The American Family in an Age of Uncertainty*. New York: Basic Books.

Smeeding, Timothy M. 2004. "Public Policy and Economic Inequality: The United States in Comparative Perspective." Working Paper No. 367. Syracuse NY: Maxwell School of Citizenship and Public Affairs, Syracuse University. Retrieved January 30, 2005 (http://www.lisproject.org/publictions/LISwps/367.pdf).

Smelser, Neil. 1963. *Theory of Collective Behavior*. New York: Free Press.

Smith, Adam. 1981 [1776]. *An Inquiry into the Nature and Causes of the Wealth of Nations*, vols. 1 and 2. Indianapolis, IN: Liberty Press.

Smith, Anthony. 1980. *Goodbye Gutenberg: The Newspaper Revolution of the 1980s*. New York: Oxford University Press.

Smith, Christian. 1991. *The Emergence of Liberation Theology: Radical Religion and Social Movement Theory*. Chicago: University of Chicago Press.

Smith, Jackie. 1998. "Global Civil Society? Transnational Social Movement Organizations and Social Capital." *American Behavioral Scientist* 42: 93–107.

Smith, Michael. 1990. "Patriarchal Ideology and Wife Beating: A Test of a Feminist Hypothesis." *Violence and Victims* 5: 257–73.

Smyth, Julie. 2003. "Sweden Ranked as Best Place to Have a Baby: Canada Places Fifth on Maternity Leave, 15th for Benefits." *National Post* 17 January. Retrieved June 27, 2004 (http://www.childcarecanada.org/ccin1/2003/ccin1_17_03.html).

Snider, Laureen. 1999. "White-Collar Crime." Pp. 2504 in James H. Marsh, editor in chief. *The Canadian Encyclopedia, Year 2000 Edition*. Toronto: McClelland & Stewart Inc.

Snow, David A., E. Burke Rochford Jr., Steven K. Worden, and Robert D. Benford. 1986. "Frame Alignment Processes, Micromobilization, and Movement Participation." *American Sociological Review* 51: 464–81.

Snyder, Benson R. 1971. *The Hidden Curriculum*. New York: Alfred A. Knopf.

Snyder, David, and Charles Tilly. 1972. "Hardship and Collective Violence in France, 1830–1960." *American Sociological Review* 37: 520–32.

Sofsky, Wolfgang. 1997 [1993]. *The Order of Terror: The Concentration Camp*, William Templer, trans. Princeton, NJ: Princeton University Press.

Sorenson, Elaine. 1994. *Comparable Worth: Is It a Worthy Policy?* Princeton, NJ: Princeton University Press.

Spencer, Herbert. 1975 [1897–1906]. *The Principles of Sociology*, 3rd ed. Westport, CT: Greenwood Press.

Spilerman, Seymour. 1970. "The Causes of Racial Disturbances: A Comparison of Alternative Explanations." *American Sociological Review* 35: 627–49.

———. 1976. "Structural Characteristics of Cities and the Severity of Racial Disorders." *American Sociological Review* 41: 771–93.

———. 2000. "Wealth and Stratification Processes." *Annual Review of Sociology* 26: 497–524.

Spitz, René A. 1945. "Hospitalism: An Inquiry into the Genesis of Psychiatric Conditions in Early Childhood." Pp. 53–74 in *The Psychoanalytic Study of the Child*, vol. 1. New York: International Universities Press.

———. 1962. "Autoerotism Re-examined: The Role of Early Sexual Behavior Patterns in Personality Formation." Pp. 283–315 in *The Psychoanalytic Study of the Child*, vol. 17. New York: International Universities Press.

Spitzer, Steven. 1980. "Toward a Marxian Theory of Deviance." Pp. 175–91 in Delos H. Kelly, ed. *Criminal Behavior: Readings in Criminology*. New York: St. Martin's Press.

Stacey, Judith. 1996. *Brave New Families: Stories of Domestic Upheaval in Late Twentieth Century America*. New York: Basic Books.

Stack, Stephen, and J. Ross Eshleman. 1998. "Marital Status and Happiness: A 17-Nation Study." *Journal of Marriage and the Family* 60: 527–36.

Stark, Rodney. 1985. *Sociology*. Belmont, CA: Wadsworth.

Stark, Rodney, and William Sims Bainbridge. 1979. "Of Churches, Sects, and Cults: Preliminary Concepts for a Theory of Religious Movements." *Journal for the Scientific Study of Religion* 18: 117–31.

———. 1987. *A Theory of Religion*. New York: Lang.

———. 1997. *Religion, Deviance, and Social Control*. New York: Routledge.

Starr, Paul. 1982. *The Social Transformation of American Medicine*. New York: Basic Books.

———. 1994. *The Logic of Health Care Reform: Why and How the President's Plan Will Work*, rev. ed. New York: Penguin.

Statistics Canada. 1992a. *Marriage and Conjugal Life in Canada* (Catalogue No. 91-534). Ottawa: Statistics Canada.

———. 1992b. *Selected Marriage Statistics, 1921–1990* [Diskette] (Catalogue No. 82-552). Ottawa: Statistics Canada.

———. 1998a. "Marriages and Divorces." *The Daily* January 29. Retrieved March 27, 2001 (http://www.statcan.gc.ca/daily-quotidien/980129/dq980129-eng.htm#ART1).

———. 1998b. "1996 Census: Labour Force Activity, Occupation and Industry, Place of Work, Mode of Transportation to Work, Unpaid Work." *The Daily* March 17. Retrieved May 26, 2006 (http://www.statcan.ca/Daily/English/980317/d980317.htm).

———. 1999. "Low-Income Measures, Low Income After Tax Cut-offs and Low Income After Tax Measure." Retrieved November 14, 2008 (http://www.statcan.ca/english/freepub/13F0019X1B/13F0019X1B1997000.pdf).

———. 2000a. "Household Environmental Practices." Retrieved October 7, 2000 (http://www.statcan.ca/english/Pgdb/Land/Environment/envir01a.htm).

———. 2000b. "Population." Retrieved October 7, 2000 (http://www.statcan.ca/english/Pgdb/People/Population/demo02.htm).

———. 2000c. "Population by Aboriginal Group, 1996 Census." Retrieved October 7, 2000 (http://www.statcan.ca/english/Pgdb/People/Population/demo39a.htm).

———. 2001a. "Trends in the Use of Private Education." *The Daily* July 4. Retrieved May 26, 2006 (http://www.statcan.ca/Daily/English/010704/d010704b.htm).

———. 2001b. "Television Viewing: Fall 1999." *The Daily* January 25. Retrieved July 23, 2002 (http://www.statcan.ca/Daily/English/010125/d010125a.htm).

———. 2002a. "Canadian Community Health Survey: A First Look." Retrieved May 16, 2005 (http://www.statcan.ca/Daily/English/020508/d020508a.htm).

———. 2002b. "National Longitudinal Survey of Children and Youth: Childhood Obesity." Retrieved May 16, 2005 (http://www.statcan.ca/Daily/English/021018/d021018b.htm).

Statistics Canada. 2003a. "Canada's Ethnocultural Portrait: The Changing Mosaic." *2001 Census Analysis Series* (Catalogue 96F0030), January. Retrieved April 13, 2007 (http://www.statcan.ca/english/IPS/Data/96F003XIE2001008.htm).

Statistics Canada. 2003b. "Income in Canada." Catalogue 75-202. Retrieved May 12, 2005 (http://www.statcan.ca/english/freepub/75-202-XIE/75-202-XIE2003000.pdf).

Statistics Canada. 2003c. "Marriages, 2000." *The Daily* June 2. Retrieved May 12, 2005 (http://www.statcan.gc.ca/daily-quotidien/030602/dq030602a-eng.htm).

———. 2003d. "Religions in Canada." *2001 Census Analysis Series*. Retrieved November 28, 2005 (http://www12.statcan.ca/english/census01/Products/Analytic/companion/rel/canada.cfm).

———. 2004a. "Marriages, 2002." *The Daily* December 21. Retrieved May 26, 2006 (http://www.statcan.ca/Daily/English/041221/d041221d.htm).

———. 2004b. "University Finances." *The Daily* August 19. Retrieved December 9, 2005 (http://www4.statcan.ca/survey/2005WES_InviteE/proceed.cgi?loc=http://www.statcan.ca/english/dai-quo).

———. 2005a. "Child Care, 1994/95 and 2000/01." *The Daily* February 7. Retrieved March 11, 2006 (http://www.statcan.ca/Daily/English/050207/d050207b.htm).

———. 2005b. "Labour Force Survey Estimates by Actual Hours Worked, Main or All Jobs, Sex and Age Group, Annual." Table 282-0018. Retrieved May 26, 2006 (http://cansim2.statcan.ca/cgi-win/CNSMCGI.EXE?LANG=E&SDDSLOC=//www.statcan.ca/english/sdds/*.htm&ROOTDIR=CII/&RESULTTEMPLATE=CII/CII_PICK&ARRAY_PICK=1&ARRAYID=2820018).

———. 2005c. "Latest Release from the Labour Force Survey." Retrieved November 21, 2005 (http://www.statcan.ca/english/Subjects/Labour/LFS/lfs-en.htm).

———. 2005d. "Overview: Canada Still Predominantly Roman Catholic and Protestant." Retrieved November 28, 2005 (http://www12.statcan.ca/english/census01/Products/Analytic/companion/rel/canada.cfm#growth).

———. 2007a. "Age and Sex Highlight Tables, 2006 Census." Retrieved January 11, 2008 (http://www12.statcan.ca/english/census06/data/highlights/agesex/Index.cfm).

———. 2007b. "Highest Certificate, Diploma or Degree (14), Age Groups (10A) and Sex (3) for the Population 15 Years and Over of Canada, Provinces, Territories, Census Metropolitan Areas and Census Agglomerations, 2006 Census—20% Sample Data." Retrieved March 5, 2011 (http://www12.statcan.ca/english/census06/data/topics/RetrieveProductTable.cfm?Temporal=2006&PID=93609&GID=837928&METH=1&APATH=3&PTYPE=88971&THEME=75&AID=&FREE=0&FOCUS=&VID=0&GC=99&GK=NA&RL=0&d1=1).

———. 2007c. "Immigration in Canada: A Portrait of the Foreign-born Population, 2006 Census: Immigration: Driver of Population Growth." Retrieved January 3, 2008 (http://www12.statcan.ca/english/census06/analysis/immcit/foreign_born.cfm).

———. 2007d. "Major Field of Study—Classification of Instructional Programs, 2000 (13), Highest Postsecondary Certificate, Diploma or Degree (12), Age Groups (10A) and Sex (3) for the Population 15 Years and Over with Postsecondary Studies." Retrieved March 15, 2011 (http://www12.statcan.ca/english/census06/data/topics/ListProducts.cfm?Temporal=2006&APATH=3&THEME=75&FREE=0&GRP=1).

———. 2007e. "Number of Children at Home (8) and Census Family Structure (7) for the Census Families in Private Households of Canada, Provinces, Territories, Census Metropolitan Areas and Census Agglomerations, 2001 and 2006 Censuses—20% Sample Data." Retrieved February 10, 2011 (http://www.statcan.ca/english/census06/data/topics/RetrieveProductTable.cfm?ALEVEL=3&APATH=3&CATNO=&DETAIL=1&DIM=&DS=99&FL=0&FREE=0&GAL=0&GC=99&GK=NA&GRP=1&IPS=&METH=0&ORDER=1&PID=89016&PTYPE=88971&RL=0&S=1&ShowAll=No&StartRow=1&SUB=683&Temporal=2006&Theme=68&VID=0&VNAMEE=&VNAMEF=).

———. 2007f. "Population and Dwelling Count Highlight Tables, 2006 Census." Retrieved January 13, 2008 (http://www12.statcan.ca/english/census06/data/popdwell/Tables.cfm).

———. 2007g. "Population by Immigrant Status and Period of Immigration, 2006 Counts, for Canada, Provinces and Territories—20% Sample Data." Retrieved January 21, 2011 (http://www12.statcan.ca/english/census06/data/highlights/Immigration/Table403.cfm?Lang=E&T=403&GH=4&SC=1&S=99&O=A).

———. 2008a. "Distribution of Total Income, by Economic Family Type, 2005 Constant Dollars, Annual." CANSIM, Table 202-0401. Retrieved January 12, 2008 (http://cansim2.statcan.ca/cgi-win/cnsmcgi.exe?Lang=E&RootDir=CII/&ResultTemplate=CII/CII__&Array_Pick=1&ArrayId=2020401).

———. 2008b. *Earnings and Incomes of Canadian over the Past Quarter Century, 2006 Census.* Retrieved January 20, 2011 (http://www12.statcan.ca/english/census06/analysis/income/pdf/97-563-XIE2006001.pdf).

———. 2008c. "Earnings of Individuals, by Selected Characteristics and National Occupational Classification (NOC-S)" (CANSIM Table 202-0106). Retrieved November 20, 1010 (http://dc1.chass.utoronto.ca.myaccess.library.utoronto.ca/cgi-bin/cansimdim/c2_getArrayDim.pl).

———. 2008d. "Educational Portrait of Canada, 2006 Census" (Cat. No. 97-560-X2006001). Retrieved March 6, 2008 (http://www12.statcan.ca/english/census06/analysis/education/pdf/97-560-XIE2006001.pdf).

———. 2008e. "Ethnic Origins, 2006 Counts, for Canada, Provinces and Territories—20% Sample Data." Retrieved April 5, 2008 (http://www12.statcan.ca/english/census06/data/highlights/ethnic/pages/Page.cfm?Lang=E&Geo=PR&Code=01&Data=Count&Table=2&StartRec=1&Sort=3&Display=All&CSDFilter=5000).

———. 2008f. "Historical Statistics of Canada." Retrieved May 2, 2008 (http://www.statcan.ca/english/freepub/11-516-XIE/sectiond/sectiond.htm).

———. 2008g. "Labour Force Survey Estimates (LFS), by National Occupational Classification for Statistics (NOC-S) and Sex" (CANSIM Table 282-0010). Retrieved November 20, 2010 (http://dc1.chass.utoronto.ca.myaccess.library.utoronto.ca/cgi-bin/cansimdim/c2_getArrayDim.pl).

———. 2008h. "Market, Total and After-Tax Income, by Economic Family Type and Income Quintiles (CANSIM Table 2020701). Retrieved January 17, 2011 (http:www.statcan.gc.ca/pub/75-202-x/2007000/t195-eng.htm).

———. 2008i. "Median Earnings and Employment for Full-Year, Full-Time Earners, All Occupations, Both Sexes, for Canada, Provinces and Territories—20% Sample Data." Retrieved January 20, 2011 (http://www12.statcan.ca/english/census06/data/highlights/earnings/Table801.cfm?Lang=E&T=801&GH=4&SC=1&SO=99&O=A).

———. 2008j. "Screen Time among Canadian Adults: A Profile." *Health Reports* 19, 2: June. Retrieved February 22, 2010 (http://www.statcan.gc.ca/pub/82-003-x/2008002/article/10600-eng.pdf).

———. 2008k. "Visible Minority Groups, Percentage Distribution (2006), for Canada, Provinces and Territories—20% Sample Data." Retrieved April 5, 2008 (http://www12.statcan.ca/english/census06/data/highlights/ethnic/pages/Page.cfm?Lang=E&Geo=PR&Code=01&Table=1&Data=Dist&StartRec=1&Sort=2&Display=Page).

———. 2009a. "Aboriginal People as a Proportion of Admissions to Remand, Provincial and Territorial Sentenced Custody, Probation and Conditional Sentence, by Jurisdiction, 2007/2008" (Table 4).

Retrieved November 10, 2010 (http://www.statcan.gc.ca/pub/85-002-x/2009003/article/10903/tbl/t4-eng.htm).

———. 2009b. "Couple Families by Presence of Children of all Ages in Private Households, 2006 Counts, for Canada, Provinces and Territories—20% Sample Data." Retrieved March 25, 2010 (http://www12.statcan.ca/census-recensement/2006/dp-pd/hlt/97-553/pages/page.cfm?Lang=E&Geo=PR&Code=01&Table=1&Data=Count&Age=1&StartRec=1&Sort=2&Display=Page).

———. 2009c. "Family Income and Participation in Post-secondary Education." Retrieved February 10, 2011 (http://www.statcan.gc.ca/pub/81-599-x/81-599-x2009004-eng.htm).

———. 2009d. *Family Violence in Canada: A Statistical Profile.* Retrieved March 25, 2010 (http://www.phac-aspc.gc.ca/ncfv-cnivf/pdfs/fv-85-224-XWE-eng.pdf).

———. 2009e. "Low Income Cut-Offs Before and After Tax by Community and Family Size, 2009 Constant Dollars, Annual (Table 202-0801)." Retrieved April 25, 2011 (http://estat.statcan.gc.ca/cgi-win/cnsmcgi.exe?Lang=E&EST-Fi=EStat/English/CII_1-eng.htm).

———. 2009f. "Market, Total and After-Tax Income, by Economic Family Type and Income Quintiles, 2009 (CANSIM Table 2020701). Retrieved January 17, 2011 (http://www.statcan.gc.ca/pub/75-202-x/2009000/t/701.ivt).

———. 2009g. "Number and Proportion of Persons Aged 25 to 64 by Level of Educational Attainment and Age Groups, Canada, 2006" (Table 4). *2006 Census Analysis Series.* Retrieved February 10, 2011 (http://www12.statcan.ca/census-recensement/2006/as-sa/97-560/table/t2-eng.cfm).

———. 2009h. "Persistence of Low Income, by Selected Characteristics, Every 3 Years" (CANSIM Table 202-0807). Retrieved January 20, 2011 (http://www4.hrsdc.gc.ca/.3ndic.1t.4r@-eng.jsp?iid=83#M_1).

———. 2009i. "Persons in Low Income before Tax" (CANSIM Table 202-0802). Retrieved January 20, 2011 (http://www40.statcan.ca/l01/cst01/famil41a-eng.htm).

———. 2009j. Uniform Crime Report Survey, 1998-2009. File #ucr2520051. Machine readable file. Retrieved November 10, 2010 (http://datalib.chass.utoronto.ca/inventory/3000/3575.htm).

———. 2009k. "University Tuition Fees," *The Daily* October 20. Retrieved April 11, 2011 (http://www.statcan.gc.ca/daily-quotidien/091020/dq091020b-eng.htm).

———. 2010a. "Adult Criminal Court Survey, Number of Cases, by Sex of Accused, Annually (Table 2520044)." CANSIM Database. Retrieved March 7, 2010 (http://www.chass.utoronto.ca).

———. 2010b. "Age Groups (13) and Sex (3) for the Population of Canada, Provinces and Territories, 1921 to 2006 Censuses - 100% Data." Retrieved November 10, 2010 (http://www12.statcan.ca/census-recensement/2006/dp-pd/tbt/Rp-eng.cfm?LANG=E&APATH=3&DETAIL=0&DIM=0&FL=A&FREE=0&GC=0&GID=0&GK=0&GRP=1&PID=88977&PRID=0&PTYPE=88971,97154&S=0&SHOWALL=0&SUB=0&Temporal=2006&THEME=66&VID=0&VNAMEE=&VNAMEF=).

———. 2010c. "Canadian Internet Use Survey." Retrieved September 20, 2011 (http://www.statcan.gc.ca/daily-quotidien/110525/dq110525b-eng.htm).

———. 2010d. "Contact with Alternative Health Care Providers in the Past 12 Months, by Age Group and Sex, Household Populations Aged 12 and Over, Canada, Provinces, Territories, Health Regions (June 2005 Boundaries) and Peer Groups, every 2 Years." CANSIM Table 1050462. Retrieved Retrieved May 2, 2011 (http://dc2.chass.utoronto.ca.myaccess.library.utoronto.ca/ggi-bin/cansimdim/c2_get-ArrayDim.pl).

———. 2010e. "Female-to-Male Earnings Ratios, by Selected Characteristics, 2009 Constant Dollars, Annual (Percent)." CANSIM, Table 202-0104. Retrieved November 19, 2010 (http://dc1.chass.utoronto.ca.myaccess.library.utoronto.ca/cgi-bin/cansimdim/c2_seriesCart.pl).

———. 2010f. "General Social Survey: Time Use." Retrieved May 2, 2011 (http://www.statcan.gc.ca/daily-quotidien/110712/dq110712b-eng.htm).

———. 2010g. "Labour Force Survey Estimates (LFS), by Sex and Detailed Age Group, Unadjusted for Seasonality." CANSIM Table 282-0001. Retrieved November 20, 2010 (http://dc1.chass.utoronto.ca.myaccess.library.utoronto.ca/cgi-bin/cansimdim/c2_getArrayDim.pl).

———. 2010h. "Projections of the Diversity of the Canadian Population." Retrieved March 13, 2010 (http://www.statcan.gc.ca/pub/91-551-x/91-551-x2010001-eng.pdf).

———. 2010i. "Suicide and Suicide Rate, by Sex and Age Group." Retrieved October 4, 2010 (http://www40.statcan.ca/l01/cst01/hlth66a-eng.htm).

———. 2010j. "Therapeutic Abortion Survey." Retrieved March 22, 2011 (http://www.statcan.gc.ca/cgi-in/imdb/p2SV.pl?Function=getSurvey&SDDS=3209&lang=en&db=imdb&adm=8&dis=2).

———. 2010k. "Total Income, by Economic Family Type, Age Group and Income Source" (CANSIM Table 202-0404). Retrieved November 26, 2010 (http://dc1.chass.utoronto.ca.myaccess.library.utoronto.ca/cgi-bin/cansimdim/c2_getArrayDim.pl).

———. 2010l. "University Enrolment." The Daily July 14, 2010. Retrieved April 11, 2011 (http://www.statcan.gc.ca/daily-quotidien/100714/dq100714a-eng.htm).

———. 2010m. "University Expenditures, by Type of Expenditure, Canada and Provinces, 1999/2000 and 2004/2005 to 2008/2009" (Table B.2.13). Retrieved September 20, 2011 (http://www.statcan.gc.ca/pub/81-582-x/2010004/tbl/tblb2.13-eng.htm).

———. 2010n. "Youth court Survey, Number of Cases, by Sex of Accused, Annually." CANSIM Table 2520048. Retrieved March 7, 2010 (http://www.chass.utoronto.ca).

———. 2011a. "Current And Forthcoming Minimum Hourly Wage Rates For Experienced Adult Workers in Canada." Retrieved September 6, 2010 (http://srv116.services.gc.ca/dimt-wid/sm-mw/rpt1.aspx?lang=eng).

———. 2011b. "Homicide Survey, Number of Solved Homicides, by Type of Accused-Victim Relationship, Canada, Annual." CANSIM Table 253-0006. Retrieved May 10, 20100 (http://dc2.chass.utoronto.ca.myaccess.library.utoronto.ca/cgi-bin/cansimdim/c2_getArrayDim.pl).

———. 2011c. "Inside the Labour Market Downturn." The Daily February 23. Retrieved April 2, 2011 (http://www.statcan.gc.ca/daily-quotidien/110223/dq110223b-eng.htm).

———. 2011d. "Leading Causes of Death, Total Population, by Age Group and Sex, Canada, Annually" CANSIM Table 1020561. Retrieved September 20, 2011 (http://dc2.chass.utoronto.ca.myaccess.library.utoronto.ca/cgi-bin/cansimdim/c2_getArrayDim.pl).

———. n.d.. "More Seniors Living with a Spouse, More Living Alone and Fewer Living in Health Care Institutions." Retrieved January 11, 2008 (http://www12.statcan.ca/english/census01/products/analytic/companion/fam/canada.cfm#seniors).

Stearns, Carol Zisowitz, and Peter N. Stearns. 1985. "Emotionology: Clarifying the History of Emotions and Emotional Standards." American Historical Review 90: 813–36.

———. 1986. Anger: The Struggle for Emotional Control in America's History. Chicago: University of Chicago Press.

Steckel, Richard H. 1995. "Stature and the Standard of Living." Journal of Economic Literature 33: 1903–1940.

Steel, Freda M. 1987. "Alimony and Maintenance Orders." Pp. 155–67 in Sheilah L. Martin and Kathleen E. Mahoney, eds. Equality and Judicial Neutrality. Toronto: Carswell.

Steinberg, Stephen. 1989. The Ethnic Myth: Race, Ethnicity, and Class in America, updated ed. Boston: Beacon Press.

The Sterilization of Leilani Muir. 1996. Montreal: National Film Board. (video).

Sternberg, Robert J. 1986. "A Triangular Theory of Love." Psychological Review 93: 119–35.

———. 1998. In Search of the Human Mind, 2nd ed. Fort Worth, TX: Harcourt Brace.

Sternheimer, K. E. 2007. "Do Video Games Kill?" Contexts 6, 1: 13–17.

Stewart, Abigail, Anne P. Copeland, Nia Lane Chester, Janet E. Malley, and Nicole B. Barenbaum. 1997. Separating Together: How Divorce Transforms Families. New York: Guilford Press.

Stiglitz, Joseph E. 2002. Globalization and Its Discontents. New York: Norton.

Stiker, Henri-Jacques. 1999 [1982]. A History of Disability, William Sayers, trans. Ann Arbor: University of Michigan Press.

Stipp, David. 2003. "The Pentagon's Weather Nightmare." Fortune 26 January. Retrieved May 29, 2004 (http://paxhumana.info/article.php3?id_article=400).

Stone, Lawrence. 1977. The Family, Sex and Marriage in England, 1500–1800. New York: Harper and Row.

Stopford, John M., and Susan Strange. 1991. Rival States, Rival Firms: Competition for World Market Shares. Cambridge: Cambridge University Press.

Stormshak, Elizabeth A., Karen L. Bierman, Robert J. McMahon, and Liliana J. Lengua. 2000. "Parenting Practices and Child Disruptive Behavior Problems in Early Elementary School." Journal of Clinical Child Psychology 29, 1 (March): 17–29.

Stotsky, Sandra. 1999. Losing Our Language: How Multicultural Classroom Instruction Is Undermining Our Children's Ability to Read, Write, and Reason. New York: Free Press.

Stouffer, Samuel A., Edward A. Suchman, Leland C. De Vinney, Shirley A. Star, and Robin M. Williams, Jr. 1949. The American Soldier, 4 vols. Princeton, NJ: Princeton University Press.

Straus, Murray A. 1994. Beating the Devil Out of Them: Corporal Punishment in American Families. New York: Lexington Books.

———. 1996. "Presentation: Spanking and the Making of a Violent Society." Pediatrics 98: 837–49.

Straus, Murray A., and Glenda Kaufman Kantor. 1994. "Corporal Punishment of Adolescents by Parents: A Risk Factor in the Epidemiology of Depression, Suicide, Alcohol Abuse, Child Abuse, and Wife Beating." Adolescence 29, 115: 543–56.

Straus, Murray A., and Vera E. Mouradian. 1998. "Impulsive Corporal Punishment by Mothers and Antisocial Behavior and Impulsiveness of Children." Behavioral Science & the Law 16, 3: 353–62.

Straus, Murray A., and Julie H. Stewart. 1999. "Corporal Punishment by American Parents: National Data on Prevalence, Chronicity, Severity, and Duration in Relation to Child and Family Characteristics." Clinical Child & Family Psychology Review 2, 2 (June): 55–70.

Straus, Murray A., David B. Sugerman, and Jean Giles-Sims. 1997. "Spanking by Parents and Subsequent Antisocial Behavior of Children." Archives of Pediatrics & Adolescent Medicine 151, 8: 761–73.

Straus, Murray A., and Carrie L. Yodanis. 1996. "Corporal Punishment in Adolescence and Physical Assaults on Spouses Later in Life: What Accounts for the Link?" Journal of Marriage and the Family 58, 4: 825–924.

Strauss, Anselm L. 1993. Continual Permutations of Action. New York: Aldine de Gruyter.

Stretesky, Paul, and Michael J. Hogan. 1998. Environmental Justice: An Analysis of Superfund Sites in Florida." Social Problems 45: 268–87.

Strikes and Lockouts in Canada 1968. 1970. Cat. No. L2-1/1968. Ottawa: Economic and Research Branch, Canada Department of Labour.

Strikes and Lockouts in Canada 1985. 1985. Cat. No. L160-2999/85B. Ottawa: Minister of Supply and Services Canada.

Subrahmanyam, Kaveri, and Patricia M. Greenfield. 1998. "Computer Games for Girls: What Makes Them Play?" Pp. 46–71 in Justine Cassell and Henry Jenkins, eds. From Barbie to Mortal Kombat: Gender and Computer Games. Cambridge, MA: MIT Press.

Sullivan, Mercer L. 2002. "Exploring Layers: Extended Case Method as a Tool for Multilevel Analysis of School Violence." Sociological Methods and Research 31, 2: 255–85.

Sumner, William Graham. 1940 [1907]. Folkways. Boston: Ginn.

Sutherland, Edwin H. 1939. Principles of Criminology. Philadelphia: Lippincott.

———. 1949. White Collar Crime. New York: Dryden.

Suttles, G. D. 1968. The Social Order of the Slum: Ethnicity and Territory in the Inner City. Chicago: University of Chicago Press.

Swami, Viren, et al. 2010. "The Attractive Female Body Weight and Female Body Dissatisfaction in 26 Countries across 10 World Regions: Results of the International Body Project I." Personality and Social Psychology Bulletin 36, 3: 309–25.

Sweezy, Kate, and Jill Tiefenthaler. 1996. "Do State-Level Variables Affect Divorce Rates?" Review of Social Economy 54: 47–65.

Swiss Re. 2005 "Sigma Natural Catastrophes and Man-Made Disasters in 2004." Retrieved March 2, 2005 (http://www.swissre.com).

———. 2007. "Natural Catastrophes and Man-Made Disasters in 2006." Retrieved April 30, 2007

———. 2009. "Natural Catastrophes and Man-Made Disasters in 2008." Sigma 2. Retrieved December 2, 2010 (http://media.swissre.com/documents/sigma2_2009_en.pdf).

———. 2010. "Natural Catastrophes and Man-Made Disasters in 2009." Sigma 1. Retrieved December 2, 2010 (http://media.swissre.com/documents/sigma2_2009_en.pdf).

Sykes, Gresham, and David Matza. 1957. "Techniques of Neutralization: A Theory of Delinquency." American Sociological Review 22: 664–70.

Sylwester, Kevin. 2002. "Democracy and Changes in Income Inequality." *International Journal of Business and Economics* 1: 167–78.

Szasz, Andrew, and Michael Meuser. 1997. "Environmental Inequalities: Literature Review and Proposals for New Directions in Research and Theory." *Current Sociology* 45, 3: 99–120.

Tajfel, Henri. 1981. *Human Groups and Social Categories: Studies in Social Psychology*. Cambridge, UK: Cambridge University Press.

Tannen, Deborah. 1990. *You Just Don't Understand Me: Women and Men in Conversation*. New York: William Morrow.

———. 1994a. *Talking from 9 to 5: How Women's and Men's Conversational Styles Affect Who Gets Heard, Who Gets Credit, and What Gets Done at Work*. New York: William Morrow.

———. 1994b. *Gender and Discourse*. New York: Oxford University Press.

Tarrow, Sidney. 1994. *Power in Movement: Social Movements, Collective Action and Politics*. Cambridge, UK: Cambridge University Press.

Tasker, Fiona L., and Susan Golombok. 1997. *Growing Up in a Lesbian Family: Effects on Child Development*. New York: Guilford Press.

Tavris, C. 1992. *The Mismeasure of Woman*. New York: Simon & Schuster.

Tec, Nechama. 1986. *When Light Pierced the Darkness: Christian Rescue of Jews in Nazi-Occupied Poland*. New York: Oxford University Press.

Terry, Jennifer, and Jacqueline Urla, eds. 1995. *Deviant Bodies: Critical Perspectives on Difference in Science and Popular Culture*. Bloomington: Indiana University Press.

Thoits, Peggy A. 1989. "The Sociology of Emotions." *Annual Review of Sociology* 15: 317–42.

Thomas, Jennifer. 2009. "Youth Court Statistics, 2006/2007." Statistics Canada. Retrieved November 10, 2010 (http://www.statcan.gc.ca/pub/85-002-x/2008004/article/10568-eng.htm).

———. 2010. "Adult Criminal Court Statistics, 2008/09." Statistics Canada. Retrieved November 10, 2010 (http://www.statcan.gc.ca/pub/85-002-x/2008004/article/10568-eng.htm).

Thomas, Keith. 1971. *Religion and the Decline of Magic*. London: Weidenfeld and Nicholson.

Thomas, Mikhail. 2002. "Adult Criminal Court Statistics, 2000–01." *Juristat* 22, 2. Statistics Canada Catalogue no. 85-002-XPE.

Thomas, W. I., and F. Znaniecki. 1958 [1918–20]. *The Polish Peasant in Europe and America: Monograph of an Immigrant Group*, 2nd ed. (2 vols.). New York: Dover Publications.

Thomas, William Isaac. 1966 [1931]. "The Relation of Research to the Social Process." Pp. 289–305 in Morris Janowitz, ed. *W.I. Thomas on Social Organization and Social Personality*. Chicago: University of Chicago Press.

Thompson, E. P. 1967. "Time, Work Discipline, and Industrial Capitalism." *Past and Present* 38: 59–67.

Thompson, Kenneth, ed. 1975. *Auguste Comte: The Foundation of Sociology*. New York: Wiley.

Thorne, Barrie. 1993. *Gender Play: Girls and Boys in School*. New Brunswick, NJ: Rutgers University Press.

Tilly, Charles. 1978. *From Mobilization to Revolution*. Reading, MA: Addison-Wesley.

———. 1979a. "Collective Violence in European Perspective." Pp. 83–118 in H. Graham and T. Gurr, eds. *Violence in America: Historical and Comparative Perspective*, 2nd ed. Beverly Hills: Sage.

———. 1979b. "Repertoires of Contention in America and Britain, 1750–1830." Pp. 126–55 in Mayer N. Zald and John D. McCarthy, eds. *The Dynamics of Social Movements: Resource Mobilization, Social Control, and Tactics*. Cambridge, MA: Winthrop Publishers.

———. 2002. "Violence, Terror, and Politics as Usual." Unpublished paper, Department of Sociology, Columbia University.

Tilly, Charles, Louise Tilly, and Richard Tilly. 1975. *The Rebellious Century, 1830–1930*. Cambridge, MA: Harvard University Press.

Tkacik, Maureen. 2002. "The Return of Grunge." *The Wall Street Journal* December 11: B1, B10.

Toffler, Alvin. 1990. *Powershift: Knowledge, Wealth, and Violence at the Edge of the 21st Century*. New York: Bantam.

Tong, Rosemarie. 1989. *Feminist Thought: A Comprehensive Introduction*. Boulder, CO: Westview.

Tönnies, Ferdinand. 1988 [1887]. *Community and Society (Gemeinschaft und Gesellschaft)*. New Brunswick, NJ: Transaction.

Tonry, Michael. 1995. *Malign Neglect: Race, Crime, and Punishment in America*. New York: Oxford University Press.

Tooby, John, and Leda Cosmides. 1992. "The Psychological Foundations of Culture." Pp. 19–136 in Jerome Barkow, Lea Cosmides, and John Tooby, eds. *The Adapted Mind: Evolutionary Psychology and the Generation of Culture*. New York: Oxford University Press.

Torpey, J. 2001. "Making Whole What Has Been Smashed: Reflections on Reparations." *The Journal of Modern History* 73: 333–58.

Torrance, Judy M. 1986. *Public Violence in Canada*. Toronto: University of Toronto Press.

Tovee, M. J., S. M. Mason, J. L. Emery, S. E. McClusky, and E. M. Cohen-Tovee. 1997. "Supermodels: Stick Insects or Hourglasses?" *Lancet* 350: 1474–75.

Trading Economics. 2010. "Canada GDP Growth Rate." Retrieved November 10, 2010 (http://www.tradingeconomics.com/Economics/GDP-Growth.aspx?Symbol=CAD).

Travers, Jeffrey, and Stanley Milgram. 1969. "An Experimental Study of the Small World Problem." *Sociometry* 32: 425–43.

Trevelyan, Laura. 2004. "Will Canada Introduce Sharia Law?" BBC News. Retrieved December 8, 2005 (http://news.bbc.co.uk/2/hi/programmes/fromour_own_correspondent/3599264.stm).

Troeltsch, Ernst. 1931 [1923]. *The Social Teaching of the Christian Churches*, Olive Wyon, trans. 2 vols. London, UK: Allen and Unwin.

Trovato, Frank. 1998. "The Stanley Cup of Hockey and Suicide in Quebec, 1951–1992." *Social Forces* 77, 1 (September): 105–27.

Tschannen, Olivier. 1991. "The Secularization Paradigm: A Systematization." *Journal for the Scientific Study of Religion* 30: 395–415.

Tschoegl, Adrian E. 2007. "McDonald's—Much Maligned, but an Engine of Economic Development." *Global Economy Journal* 7, 4: 1–16.

Tsutsui, William M. 1998. *Manufacturing Ideology: Scientific Management in Twentieth-Century Japan*. Princeton, NJ: Princeton University Press.

Tufts, Jennifer. 2000. "Public Attitudes Toward the Criminal Justice System." *Juristat* 20, 12 (December). Catalogue no. 85-002-XPE.

Tuljapurkar, Shripad, Nan Li, and Carl Boe. 2000. "A Universal Pattern of Mortality Decline in the G7 Countries." *Nature* 405: 789–92.

Tumin, M. 1953. "Some Principles of Stratification: A Critical Analysis." *American Sociological Review* 18: 387–94.

Turkel, Ann Ruth. 1998. "All About Barbie: Distortions of a Transitional Object." *Journal of the American Academy of Psychoanalysis* 26, 1: 165–77.

Turkle, Sherry. 1995. *Life on the Screen: Identity in the Age of the Internet*. New York: Simon & Schuster.

Turnbull, Colin M. 1961. *The Forest People*. New York: Doubleday.

Turner, Bryan S. 1986. *Citizenship and Capitalism: The Debate over Reformism*. London, UK: Allen and Unwin.

———. 1996. *The Body and Society: Explorations in Social Theory*, 2nd ed. London: Sage.

Turner, Heather A., and David Finkelhor. 1996. "Corporal Punishment as a Stressor among Youth." *Journal of Marriage and the Family* 58, 1: 155–66.

Turner, Ralph H., and Lewis M. Killian. 1987. *Collective Behavior*, 3rd ed. Englewood Cliffs, NJ: Prentice-Hall.

Twenge, Jean M. 1997. "Changes in Masculine and Feminine Traits over Time: A Meta-analysis." *Sex Roles* 36: 305–25.

———. 2006. *Generation Me: Why Today's Young Americans Are More Confident, Assertive, Entitled—and More Miserable Than Ever Before*. New York: Random House.

Tylee, Catherine. 2005. "Grade Expectations: When Is an 'A' Not Quite an 'A'?" *New Media Journalism*. Retrieved April 11, 2011 (http://www.fims.uwo.ca/newmedia2006/default.asp?id=424).

"U.K. Panel Calls Climate Data Valid." 2010. *The New York Times* 30 March. Retrieved April 1, 2010 (http://www.nytimes.com).

Union of International Associations. 2001. "International Organizations by Year and Type, 1909–1999 (Table 2)." *Yearbook of International Organizations*. Retrieved February 14, 2006 (http://www.uia.org/statistics/organizations/ytb299.php).

———. 2010. "Yearbook of International Organizations." Retrieved November 16, 2010 (http://www.uia.be/yearbook).

U.S. Bureau of Labor Statistics. 1998. "Union Members Summary." Retrieved January 2, 2001 (http://stats.bls.gov/news.release/union2.nws.htm).

———. 1999. "Union Members Summary." Retrieved March 17, 2001 (http://stats.bls.gov/news.release/union2.nws.htm).

———. 2001. "Union Members Summary." Retrieved March 21, 2001 (http://www.bls.gov/news.release/union2.nws.htm).

———. 2008. "Access to Historical Data for Union Membership." Retrieved January 9, 2008 (http://www.bls.gov/webapps/legacy/cpslutab1.htm).

U.S. Bureau of the Census. 2008. "International Data Base." Retrieved January 14, 2008 (http://www.census.gov/ipc/www/idb/pyramids.html).

———. 2011. "Total Midyear Population for the World: 1950–2050." Retrieved November 6, 2011 (http://www.census.gov/population/international/data/idb/worldpoptotal.php).

U.S. Department of Commerce. 1998. "Statistical Abstract of the United States: 1998." Retrieved October 8, 2000 (http://www.census.gov/prod/3/98pubs/98statab/sasec1.pdf).

U.S. Department of Commerce, National Oceanic and Atmospheric Administration. 2008. "Trends in Atmospheric Carbon Dioxide—Mauna Loa." Retrieved January 12, 2008 (http://www.esrl.noaa.gov/gmd/ccgg/trends).

U.S. Department of Labor. 2010. "CPI Inflation Calculator." Retrieved December 2, 2010 (http://www.bls.gov/data/inflation_calculator.htm).

U.S. Environmental Protection Agency, Office of Air Quality Planning and Standards. 2000. "National Air Pollutant Emission Trends, 1900–1998." Retrieved August 3, 2000 (http://www.epa.gov/ttn/chief/trends98/emtrnd.html).

U.S. Information Agency. 1998–99. *The People Have Spoken: Global Views of Democracy*, 2 vols. Washington, DC: Office of Research and Media Reaction.

UNAIDS. 2010. "Global Report." Retrieved December 7, 2010 (http://www.unaids.org/documents/20101123_GlobalReport_em.pdf).

Ungar, Sheldon. 1992. "The Rise and (Relative) Decline of Global Warming as a Social Problem." *Sociological Quarterly* 33: 483–501.

———. 1995. "Social Scares and Global Warming: Beyond the Rio Convention." *Society and Natural Resources* 8: 443–56.

———. 1998. "Bringing the Issue Back In: Comparing the Marketability of the Ozone Hole and Global Warming." *Social Problems* 45: 510–27.

———. 1999. "Is Strange Weather in the Air? A Study of U.S. National Network News Coverage of Extreme Weather Events." *Climatic Change* 41: 133–50.

Unger, Alon, and Lee W. Riley. 2007. "Slum Health: From Understanding to Action." *PLOS Medicine* 4, 10: e295. Retrieved October 20, 2010 (http://www.plosmedicine.org/article/info:doi/10.1371/journal.pmed.0040295).

United Nations. 1997. "Percentage of Population Living in Urban Areas in 1996 and 2030." Retrieved May 2, 2000 (http://www.undp.org/popin/wdtrends/ura/uracht1.htm).

———. 1998a. "Universal Declaration of Human Rights." Retrieved January 25, 2003 (http://www.un.org/Overview/rights.html).

———. 1998b. "World Population Growth from Year 0 to 2050." Retrieved July 3, 1999 (http://www.popin.org/pop1998/4.htm).

———. 2002. "Human Development Report 2002." New York: Oxford University Press. Retrieved April 16, 2003 (http://hdr.undp.org/reports/global/2002/en).

———. 2004. "UNAIDS 2004 Report on the Global AIDS Epidemic 2004 (PDF version)." Retrieved June 26, 2005 (http://www.unaids.org/bangkok2004/report_pdf.html).

———. 2005. "Human Development Indicators." Retrieved April 25, 2005 (http://hdr.undp.org/reports/global/2005/pdf/HDR05_HDI.pdf).

———. 2007. "AIDS Epidemic Update 07." Geneva. Retrieved January 16, 2008 (http://data.unaids.org/pub/EPISlides/2007/2007_epiupdate_en.pdf).

———. 2008. "UN Data Abortion Rate." Retrieved March 23, 2011 (http://data.un.org/Data.aspx?d=GenderStat&f=inID%3A12).

———. 2009. "Gender Empowerment Measure and Its Components." *Human Development Report 2009*. Retrieved March 19, 2010 (http://hdrstats.undp.org/en/indicators/126.html).

———. "FAO Cereal Supply and Demand." Retrieved June 10, 2011 (http://www.fao.org/worldfoodsituation/wfs-home/csdb/en).

———. 2010b. "Gender Inequality Index." Retrieved November 22, 2010 (http://hdr.undp.org/en/media/HDR_2010_EN_Table4_reprint.pdf).

———. 2010c. "Human Development Statistical Tables." *Human Development Report 2010*. Retrieved November 16, 2010 (http://hdr.undp.org/en/media/HDR_2010_EN_Tables.pdf).

———. 2011. "World Population to Reach 10 Billion by 2100 if Fertility in All Countries Converges to Replacement Level." May 3. Retrieved September 6, 2011 (http://esa.un.org/unpd/wpp/other-information/Press_Release_WPP2010.pdf).

United Nations Conference on Trade and Development. 2007. *World Investment Report 2007*. Geneva. Retrieved December 19, 2007 (http://www.unctad.org/en/docs/wir2007p1_en.pdf).

United Nations Educational, Scientific and Cultural Organization (UNESCO). 2001. "World Culture Report 2000—Cultural Trade and Communications Trends: International Tourism." Retrieved February 6, 2003 (http://www.unesco.org/culture/worldreport/html_eng/stat2/table18.pdf).

———. 2008. "International Literacy Statistics: A Review of Concepts, Methodology and Current Data." Retrieved March 27, 2010 (http://www.uis.unesco.org/template/pdf/Literacy/LiteracyReport2008.pdf).

United Nations World Tourism Organization. 2007. "International Tourist Arrivals." Retrieved December 19, 2007 (http://unwto.org/facts/eng/pdf/historical/ITA_1950_2005.pdf).

Unschuld, Paul. 1985. *Medicine in China*. Berkeley, CA: University of California Press.

Useem, Bert. 1998. "Breakdown Theories of Collective Action." *Annual Review of Sociology* 24: 215–38.

Valocchi, Steve. 1996. "The Emergence of the Integrationist Ideology in the Civil Rights Movement." *Social Problems* 43: 116–30.

Valpy, Michael. 2010. "Young Increasingly Shun Religious Institutions." *The Globe and Mail* 14 December. Retrieved December 20, 2010 (http://www.theglobeandmail.com/news/national/young-increasingly-shun-religious-institutions/article1837678).

Valpy, Michael, and Joe Friesen. 2010. "Canada Marching from Religion to Secularization." *The Globe and Mail* 10 December. Retrieved December 20, 2010 (http://www.theglobeandmail.com/news/national/canada-marching-from-religion-to-secularization/article1833451).

Vanier Institute of the Family. 2000. *Profiling Canada's Families II*. Nepean, ON: Vanier Institute of the Family.

Vernarec, E. 2000. "Depression in the Work Force: Seeing the Cost in a Fuller Light." *Business and Health* 18, 4: 48–55.

Veugelers, John. 1997. "Social Cleavage and the Revival of Far Right Parties: The Case of France's National Front." *Acta Sociologica* 40: 31–49.

Vygotsky, Lev S. 1987. *The Collected Works of L. S. Vygotsky*, vol. 1, N. Minick, trans. New York: Plenum.

Wade, Robert, and Martin Wolf. 2002. "Are Global Poverty and Inequality Getting Worse?" *Prospect* March: 16–21.

Wald, Matthew L., and John Schwartz. 2003. "Alerts Were Lacking, NASA Shuttle Manager Says." *The New York Times* July 23. Retrieved July 23, 2003 (http://www.nytimes.com).

Waldfogel, Jane. 1997. "The Effect of Children on Women's Wages." *American Sociological Review* 62: 209–17.

Walker, John. 2010. "Student Plagiarism in Universities: What Are We Doing about It?" *Higher Education Research and Development* 17, 1: 89–106. Retrieved January 17, 2011 (http://dx.doi.org/10.1080/0729436980170105).

Wallace, James, and Jim Erickson. 1992. *Hard Drive: Bill Gates and the Making of the Microsoft Empire*. New York: Wiley.

Wallerstein, Immanuel. 1974–89. *The Modern World-System*, 3 vols. New York: Academic Press.

Wallerstein, Judith S., and Sandra Blakeslee. 1989. *Second Chances: Men, Women, and Children a Decade after Divorce*. New York: Ticknor & Fields.

Wallerstein, Judith S., Julia Lewis, and Sandra Blakeslee. 2000. *The Unexpected Legacy of Divorce: A 25 Year Landmark Study*. New York: Hyperion.

Wallich, P., and M. Mukerjee. 1996. "Regulating the Body Business." *Scientific American* 274, 3 (March): 12–13.

Walmsley, Roy. 2009. "World Prison Population List (eighth edition)." Retrieved March 7, 2010 (http://www.kcl.ac.uk/depsta/law/research/icps/downloads/wppl-8th_41.pdf).

Wanner, Richard. 1999. "Expansion and Ascription: Trends in Educational Opportunity in Canada, 1920–1994." *Canadian Review of Sociology and Anthropology* 36 (August): 409–42.

Wasserman, Stanley, and Katherine Faust. 1994. *Social Network Analysis: Methods and Applications*. Cambridge: Cambridge University Press.

Watkins, S. Craig, and Rana A. Emerson. 2000. "Feminist Media Criticism and Feminist Media Practices." *Annals of the American Academy of Political and Social Science* 571: 151–66.

Watson, James D. 1968. *The Double Helix: A Personal Account of the Discovery of the Structure of DNA*. New York: Atheneum.

———. 2000. *A Passion for DNA: Genes, Genomes, and Society*. Cold Spring Harbor, NY: Cold Spring Harbor Laboratory Press.

Watson, James L., ed. 1997. *Golden Arches East: McDonald's in East Asia*. Stanford, CA: Stanford University Press.

Webb, Eugene J., Donald T. Campbell, Richard D. Schwartz, and Lee Sechrest. 1966. *Unobtrusive Measures: Nonreactive Research in the Social Sciences*. Chicago: Rand McNally.

Webb, Stephen D., and John Collette. 1977. "Rural–Urban Differences in the Use of Stress-Alleviating Drugs." *American Journal of Sociology* 83: 700–707.

———. 1979. "Reply to Comment on Rural–Urban Differences in the Use of Stress-Alleviating Drugs." *American Journal of Sociology* 84: 1446–52.

Weber, Max. 1946. *From Max Weber: Essays in Sociology*, rev. ed., H. Gerth and C. W. Mills, eds., and trans. New York: Oxford University Press.

———. 1947. *The Theory of Social and Economic Organization*, T. Parsons, ed., A. M. Henderson and T. Parsons, trans. New York: Free Press.

———. 1958 [1904–5]. *The Protestant Ethic and the Spirit of Capitalism*. New York: Scribner.

———. 1963 [1922]. *The Sociology of Religion*, Ephraim Fischoff, trans. Boston: Beacon Press.

———. 1964 [1949]. "'Objectivity' in Social Science and Social Policy." Pp. 49–112 in Edward A. Shils and Henry A. Finch, trans., and eds. *The Methodology of the Social Sciences*. New York: Free Press of Glencoe.

———. 1978. *Economy and Society*, Guenther Roth and Claus Wittich, eds. Berkeley, CA: University of California Press.

Weeks, Carly. 2009. "The Dark Side of 'Free-Range' Chickens." *The Globe and Mail* January 15. Retrieved December 7, 2010 (http://www .theglobeandmail.com/life/article966564.ece).

Weeks, Jeffrey. 2000. *Making Sexual History*. Cambridge, UK: Polity Press.

Weis, Joseph G. 1987. "Class and Crime." Pp. 71–90 in Michael Gottfredson and Travis Hirschi, eds. *Positive Criminology*. Beverly Hills, CA: Sage.

Weisbrot, Mark, and Dean Baker. 2002. "The Relative Impact of Trade Liberalization on Developing Countries." Center for Economic and Policy Research, 11 June. Washington, DC. Retrieved February 10, 2003 (http://www.cepr.net/relative_impact_of_trade_liberal.htm).

Weisbrot, Mark, Dean Baker, Egor Kraev, and Judy Chen. 2001. "The Scorecard on Globalization, 1980–2000." Center for Economic and Policy Research. Washington, DC. Retrieved February 10, 2003 (http://www.cepr.net/globalization/scorecard_on_globalization.htm).

Weissman, M. 1992. "The Changing Rate of Major Depression: Cross-National Comparisons." *Journal of the American Medical Association* 268, 21: 3098–105.

Welch, Michael. 1997. "Violence Against Women by Professional Football Players: A Gender Analysis of Hypermasculinity, Positional Status, Narcissism, and Entitlement." *Journal of Sport and Social Issues* 21: 392–411.

Weller, Jack M., and E. L. Quarantelli. 1973. "Neglected Characteristics of Collective Behavior." *American Journal of Sociology* 79: 665–85.

Wellman, Barry. 1979. "The Community Question: The Intimate Networks of East Yorkers." *American Journal of Sociology* 84: 201–31.

Wellman, Barry, and Stephen Berkowitz, eds. 1997. *Social Structures: A Network Approach*, updated ed. Greenwich, CT: JAI Press.

Wellman, Barry, Peter J. Carrington, and Alan Hall. 1997. "Networks as Personal Communities." Pp.130–184 in Barry Wellman and S. D. Berkowitz, eds. *Social Structures: A Network Approach*, updated ed. Greenwich, CT: JAI Press.

Wells, H. G. 1927. "The Country of the Blind." Pp. 123–46 in *Selected Short Stories*. Harmondsworth, UK: Penguin. Retrieved April 24, 2003 (http://www.fantasticfiction.co.uk/etexts/y3800.htm).

Welsh, Sandy. 1999. "Gender and Sexual Harassment." *Annual Review of Sociology* 25: 169–90.

West, Candace, and Don Zimmerman. 1987. "Doing Gender." *Gender and Society* 1: 125–51.

Wetzel, Janice Wood. 2001. "Human Rights in the 20th Century: Weren't Gays and Lesbians Human?" Pp. 15–31 in Mary E. Swigonski and Robin S. Mama, eds. *From Hate Crimes to Human Rights: A Tribute to Matthew Shepard*. New York: Haworth Press.

Wheeler, Stanton. 1961. "Socialization in Correctional Communities." *American Sociological Review* 26: 697–712.

Whitaker, Reg. 1987. *Double Standard*. Toronto: Lester and Orpen Dennys.

Whitefield, S., and G. Evans. 1994. "The Russian Election of 1993: Public Opinion and the Transition Experience." *Post-Soviet Affairs* 10: 38–60.

Whittington, L. 1999. *The Banks: The Ongoing Battle for Control of Canada's Richest Business*. Toronto: Stoddart.

Whorf, Benjamin Lee. 1956. *Language, Thought, and Reality*, John B. Carroll, ed. Cambridge, MA: MIT Press.

"Why Britney Spears Matters." 2001. *The Laughing Medusa*. Retrieved April 18, 2006 (http://www.gwu.edu/~medusa/2001/britney.html).

Widyastuti, Adeline. 2010. *The Globalization of New Media Exposure: The Dependency on the Internet*. Saarbrücken, Germany: Lambert.

Wilensky, Harold L. 1967. *Organizational Intelligence: Knowledge and Policy in Government and Industry*. New York: Basic Books.

———. 1997. "Social Science and the Public Agenda: Reflections on the Relation of Knowledge to Policy in the United States and Abroad." *Journal of Health Politics, Policy and Law* 22: 1241–65.

Wiley College. 2007 "History of Wiley College." Retrieved March 7, 2008 (http://www.wileyc.edu/wly_content/departments/administrative/ history.php).

Wilkinson, Richard G. 1996. *Unhealthy Societies: The Afflictions of Inequality*. London: Routledge.

Wilkinson, Richard, and Michael Marmot, eds. 2003. *Social Determinants of Health: The Solid Facts*. Copenhagen: World Health Organization Regional Office for Europe.

Willardt, Kenneth. 2000. "The Gaze He'll Go Gaga For." *Cosmopolitan* April: 232–37.

Williams, David R., and Chiquita Collins. 1995. "U.S. Socioeconomic and Racial Differences in Health: Patterns and Explanations." *Annual Review of Sociology* 21: 349–86.

———. 1999. "U.S. Socioeconomic and Racial Differences in Health: Patterns, and Explanations." Pp. 349–76 in Kathy Charmaz and Debora A. Paterniti, eds. *Health, Illness, and Healing: Society, Social Context, and Self*. Los Angeles: Roxbury.

Willis, Paul. 1984 [1977]. *Learning to Labour: How Working-Class Kids Get Working-Class Jobs*. New York: Columbia University Press.

Wilson, William Julius. 1987. *The Truly Disadvantaged: The Inner City, the Underclass, and Public Policy*. Chicago: University of Chicago Press.

Wilson, Edward O. 1975. *Sociobiology: The New Synthesis*. Cambridge, MA: Belknap Press of the Harvard University Press.

Winch, Donald. 1987. *Malthus*. Oxford, UK: Oxford University Press.

Winton, R. 2005. "L.A. Home Turf for Hundreds of Neighborhood Criminal Groups. Los Angeles Community Policing." Retrieved May 13, 2005 (http://www.lacp.org/2005-Articles-Main/ LAGangsInNeighborhoods.html).

Wired. 1999. December.

Wirth, Louis. 1938. "Urbanism as a Way of Life." *American Journal of Sociology* 44: 1–24.

Wolf, D. L. 1992. *Factory Daughters: Gender, Household Dynamics, and Rural Industrialization in Java*. Berkeley, CA: University of California Press.

Wolf, Naomi. 1997. *Promiscuities: The Secret Struggle for Womanhood*. New York: Vintage.

Wolff, Edward N. 1996. *Top Heavy: The Increasing Inequality of Wealth in America and What Can Be Done About It*, expanded ed. New York: New Press.

"Woman Soldier in Abuse Spotlight." 2004. *BBC News World Edition* May 7. Retrieved March 3, 2005 (http://news.bbc.co.uk/2/hi/ americas/3691753.stm).

Wong, L., and M. Ng. 1998. "Chinese Immigrant Entrepreneurs in Vancouver: A Case Study of Ethnic Business Development." *Canadian Ethnic Studies* 30: 64–85.

Wood, Julia. 1999. *Everyday Encounters: An Introduction to Interpersonal Communication*, 2nd ed. Belmont, CA: Wadsworth.

Woodbury, Anthony. 2003. "Endangered Languages." Linguistic Society of America. Retrieved July 19, 2003 (http://www.lsadc.org/web2/ endangeredlgs.htm).

Woodrow Federal Reserve Bank of Minneapolis. 2000. "What's a Dollar Worth?" Retrieved October 8, 2000 (http://woodrow.mpls.frb.fed.us/ economy/calc/cpihome.html).

Workplace Information Directorate. 1996. *Special Tabulation of Strikes Statistics for 1986–95*. Ottawa: Human Resources Development Canada.

World Bank. 2011a. "GDP Per Capita (current US$)." Retrieved November 3, 2011 (http://data.worldbank.org/indicator/NY.GDP .PCAP.CD).

———. 2011b. "Fertility Rate, Total (Births per Woman). Retrieved March 23, 2011 (http://data.worldbank.org/indicator/SP.DYN.TFRT.IN).

World Conservation Union. 2004. "Species Extinction." Retrieved January 12, 2008 (http://www.iucn.org/themes/Ssc/red_list_2004/Extinction_media_brief_2004.pdf).

World Health Organization. 2001. "Female Genital Mutilation." Retrieved January 20, 2003 (http://www.who.int/frh-whd/FGM).

———. 2002. "World Report on Violence and Health." Geneva: 186–87. Retrieved April 22, 2005 (http://www.who.int/violence_injury_prevention/violence/world_report/en/full_en.pdf).

———. 2003. "Cumulative Number of Reported Probable Cases." Retrieved June 16, 2003 (http://www.who.int/csr/sars/country/2003_06_16/en).

———. 2007. "Core Health Indicators." Retrieved January 16, 2008 (http://www.who.int/whosis/database/core/core_select.cfm).

———. 2010a. "Female Genital Mutilation." Retrieved June 8, 2011 (http://www.who.int/mediacentre/factsheets/fs241/en).

———. 2010b. "Suicide Prevention (SUPRE)." Retrieved October 4, 2010 (http://www.who.int/mental_health/prevention/suicide/suicideprevent/en).

———. 2010c. "WHO Statistical Information System (WHOSIS." Retrieved April 1, 2010 (http://www.who.int/whosis/en/index.html).

Worldmapper. 2006. "Absolute Poverty." University of Sheffield. Retrieved 11 March 2010 (http://www.worldmapper.org/posters/worldmapper_map180_ver5.pdf).

World Tourism Organization. "International Tourist Arrivals by Country of Destination." *UNWTO World Tourism Barometer*. 2008. 6, 2. Retrieved November 16, 2010 (http://www.tourismroi.com/Content_Attachments/27670/File_633513750035785076.pdf).

World Values Survey. 2005. Machine readable data set. Ann Arbor, MI: Inter-University Consortium for Political and Social Research.

Worthington, Peter. 2002. "Aspers Get Press in U.S.: Washington Post Weighs in on 'Free-Speech' Debate." *Toronto Sun* January 28. Retrieved May 17, 2002

Wortley, Scot, and Julian Tanner. 2011. "The Racial Profiling Debate: Data, Denials, and Confusion." Pp. 295–302 in Robert J. Brym, ed. *Society in Question*. Toronto: Nelson.

Wright, Charles Robert. 1975. *Mass Communication: A Sociological Perspective*. New York: Random House.

Wright, Robert. 2010. "Zuckerberg: Non-Evil Non-Genius." *The New York Times* 5 October. Retrieved October 9, 2010 (http://www.nytimes.com).

Wu, Zheng. 2000. *Cohabitation: An Alternative Form of Family Living*. Don Mills, ON: Oxford University Press.

Wynne, Robert E. 1996. "American Labor Leaders and the Vancouver Anti-Oriental Riot." *Pacific Northwest Quarterly* 86: 172–79. Retrieved March 15, 2001 (http://www.vcn.bc.ca/acww/html/body_riot.html).

Yamane, David. 1997. "Secularization on Trial: In Defense of a Neosecularization Paradigm." *Journal for the Scientific Study of Religion* 36: 109–22.

Yancey, W. L, E. P. Ericksen, and G. H. Leon. 1979. "Emergent Ethnicity: A Review and Reformulation." *American Sociological Review* 41: 391–403.

Yates, Gayle Graham, ed. 1985. *Harriet Martineau on Women*. New Brunswick, NJ: Rutgers University Press.

Zakaria, Fareed. 1997. "The Rise of Illiberal Democracy." *Foreign Affairs* 76, 6: 22–43.

Zald, Meyer N., and John D. McCarthy. 1979. *The Dynamics of Social Movements*. Cambridge, MA: Winthrop.

Zaslavsky, Victor, and Robert J. Brym. 1978. "The Functions of Elections in the USSR." *Soviet Studies* 30: 62–71.

Zimbardo, Philip G. 1972. "Pathology of Imprisonment." *Society* 9, 6: 4–8.

Zimbardo, Philip. 2008. *The Lucifer Effect: Understanding How Good People Turn Evil*. New York: Random House.

Zimmermann, Francis. 1987 [1982]. *The Jungle and the Aroma of Meats: An Ecological Theme in Hindu Medicine*, Janet Lloyd, trans. Berkeley, CA: University of California Press.

Zimring, Franklin E., and Gordon Hawkins. 1995. *Incapacitation: Penal Confinement and the Restraint of Crime*. New York: Oxford University Press.

Zinsser, Hans. 1935. *Rats, Lice and History*. Boston: Little, Brown.

Zola, Irving Kenneth. 1982. *Missing Pieces: A Chronicle of Living with a Disability*. Philadelphia: Temple University Press.

Zoutman, D. E., B. D. Ford, E. Bryce, M. Gourdeau, G. Hebert, E. Henderson, S. Paton, Canadian Hospital Epidemiology Committee, Canadian Nosocomial Infection Surveillance Program, Health Canada. 2003. "The State of Infection Surveillance and Control in Canadian Acute Care Hospitals." *American Journal of Infection Control* 31, 5: 266–73.

Zuboff, S. 1988. *In the Age of the Smart Machine: The Future of Work and Power*. New York: Basic Books.

Zurcher, Louis A., and David A. Snow. 1981. "Collective Behavior and Social Movements." Pp. 447–82 in Morris Rosenberg and Ralph Turner, eds. *Social Psychology: Sociological Perspectives*. New York: Basic Books.

Index

Notes: Entries and page numbers in bold refer to key terms and the pages in the text on which they are defined. Page numbers that begin with "22" (e.g., 22-11, 22-14–22-15) refer to Chapter 22, the online chapter.